WORLD WEEDS

WORLD WEEDS

Natural Histories and Distribution

LeRoy Holm

Jerry Doll

Eric Holm

Juan Pancho

James Herberger

John Wiley & Sons, Inc.
New York · Chichester · Weinheim · Brisbane · Singapore · Toronto

Library of Congress Cataloging in Publication Data:

World Weeds: Natural Histories and Distribution / LeRoy Holm . . . [et al.].
  p. cm.
  Includes bibliographical references (p.) and indexes.
  ISBN 0-471-04701-5 (cloth : alk. paper)
  1. Weeds—Identification. 2. Weeds—Geographical distribution.
  I. Holm, LeRoy G.
  SB611.W39 1996
  632′.58—dc20   96-4670

Printed in the United States of America

10 9 8 7 6 5 4 3 2 1

Dedication

To our families, and to hundreds of persons across the earth who held the ladder for nearly four decades, as we reached ever upward to heights we could never fully grasp in our search for a better understanding of the biology of the plants that cause one of the greatest losses of food production to all of the world's agriculture.

Contents

Preface

As Samuel Johnson (1709–1784), the Englishman, completed the first "Dictionary of the English Language, 1755," he observed in his Preface: "I saw that one enquiry only gave occasion to another, that book referred to book, that to search was not always to find, and to find was not always to be informed, and that thus to pursue perfection was, like the first inhabitants of Arcadia, to chase the sun which when they had reached the hill where he seemed to rest, was still beheld at the same distance from them."

As we conclude, with this book, our search of almost four decades for the names of the plants that cause 90 percent of the losses of food due to weeds in agriculture across the world, we can appreciate, perhaps more than most, the mystery of Samuel Johnson's observation. And we would add that, with all of our books and resources, and our travel across the very large landscape of agriculture, at times we seemed as dwarfs as we worked among 500 people from many countries who possessed great knowledge of the biology of the weeds around them. Often their education was limited, few books were available to them, but they were keen observers and they reasoned adroitly and skillfully about the biology that unfolded before them. They were *our* teachers.

As we began there were guesses that there were 50 to 5000 weedy species in man's crops. With this volume and our companion books, "The World's Worst Weeds" (Holm et al. 1977) and "A Geographical Atlas of World Weeds" (Holm et al. 1979), you may see that the number is about 200 species—and we now know their names, biology, and distribution. Two hundred species is a manageable problem, especially when compared with the possibility that there might have been several thousand species. Yet, in early 1995, Dr. Keith Moody of the International Rice Research Institute (Philippines), in an address to the Weed Science of America, reminded us that ninety percent of man's principal food crop, rice, is grown in Asia where most of it is still weeded by hand! Much remains to be done.

We have presented here most of the known biology of each species, maps of their distribution in more than 100 countries, illustrations designed to help with identification, an index of common names, and a bibliography of 3300 references to lead students and researchers to further details that are contained in the principal papers. Is there some practical use for so much information? The answer is that each day begins at breakfast for those who are fortunate. Weeds, through competition in our fields, take away the food that the world badly needs. They continue to enter into the daily affairs of human beings on land and water by reducing the quality of what we may already have harvested and they frequently create problems for human and animal health. They decrease the quantity and quality of vegetable fibers, wool, hides, and many meat and milk products, and interfere with fishing, irrigation, hydroelectric power production, and the movement of large and small vessels. To recognize the true breadth of the problem, to know the names of the most dangerous species, and to have access to what man already knows about their biology can only help us as we go about our work.

The book is timely in terms of the recent interest in biology, as we endeavor to provide more holistic weed management systems and to cope with the appearance of herbicide-resistant biotypes on a scale we can hardly imagine.

Finally, it is to the individuals whose names appear below that we are indebted for so much of our Good Fortune. They were at times both architects and builders, for their suggestions often changed the course of our work. We wish to offer our warmest thanks:

To Dr. Charles Gunn, Carole Ritchie, and Anita Speight of the United States Department of Agriculture for their special care in providing us with references difficult to obtain.

To the Department of Agronomy, University of Wisconsin (USA) for encouragement and time to devote to the book.

To Jim Holman, Director, Statistical Laboratory, Ohio Agricultural Research and Development Center, Wooster, Ohio (USA) for help in maintaining our data base over the years.

To Marian Holm who performed a thousand tasks with grace and ease and a wonderful good cheer that surely must be reflected in the pages of this book.

To John Fryer of England, Werner Koch of Germany, Keith Moody of the Philippines, and Larry Burrill of the United States for their inspiration and encouragement during these long years.

To the late Emmanuel Rochecouste, Australia, a mentor and a source of inspiration, who supported us and gave us heart every step of the way.

To Professor Yang-Han Li, who alone made it possible to have excellent weed maps of China.

To the gifted Ernesto S. Calara, University of the Philippines, who was our Master Illustrator until his untimely death at 25 years of age.

To the United States National Herbarium for the loan of herbarium sheets of *Matricaria*, *Papaver*, *Raphanus*, and *Tagetes* species as we prepared our illustrations.

To the late Regina Hughes, Botanist, the Smithsonian Institute, Washington, D.C. (USA), who gave permission for the use of several of her illustrations of weed plants.

To the USDA scientists at state experiment stations for helping us to obtain references that were difficult to locate.

And finally to John Wiley and Sons, Inc., Publishers, and especially to Dr. Philip Manor, for their seemingly eternal patience, and for the time that allowed us to do this book as well as we possibly could.

In the book, "The Last Nomad," you may read the memoirs of Wilfred Thesiger (1980), an Englishman who traversed, *on foot*, more of the world's vast burning deserts, high mountains, and limitless great swamps and marshes than any other single human being. In the southern deserts of Arabia there is an "Empty Quarter," a region so vast and dangerous that in an earlier time aircraft were not permitted to fly over it. In the dedication of his book following an *1100 mile* trek, *on foot*, across the "Empty Quarter," Thesiger paid this tribute to his fellow trekkers: "Without you I could not have gone five miles."

Much of the credit for the successful completion of the volume before you rests on the shoulders of hundreds of weed scientists, men and women who accompanied us on our strange and tiring journey in search of the world's worst weeds. We thank you for your help, your encouragement, the information you provided, and your companionship along the way. To you, and to all of those above, we pay tribute as we say, "Without you we could not have gone five miles"! We are truly grateful!

Introduction

W E WISH TO PROVIDE further information about the nature and depth of our probing to obtain data on weed biology, the system for procuring data on weed distribution and the preparation of the maps, and the significance of the ranking data used in the agricultural importance section at the end of each chapter.

THE SOURCE OF THE INFORMATION ON BIOLOGY

Please be aware that we have made an effort to use the approved scientific names as given in the International Rules of Botanical Nomenclature. The information was gathered in a systematic literature search for the period from 1955 to late 1992. Our bibliography goes well beyond computer data bases, for our searches often turned up material published from 1750 onward. For some species the most skillful and meticulous work on anatomy and morphology was done in centuries past. This book was 13 years in the writing. For species that were written about early we systematically procured all new research information, and all species were updated with such information from 1992 to the present.

There was no effort to review every paper ever published on a species, for many were repetitious and some not worthwhile for our purposes. For example, *Elodea canadensis* has been used as a laboratory plant for physiology instruction, has also been widely used for photosynthesis studies, and is a major aquatic weed. After an initial sort of hundreds of references and papers, 1300 remained. From these we were able to select, read, and finally bring forth a story that seems to tell us all that man knows about the biology of *Elodea* that may serve in a study of its weediness. We could not include the details and photographs of careful anatomical and cytological studies, the chemical procedures for isolation of secondary metabolites, or the clinical studies on weed toxicity to humans and animals. We hope that our extensive references to such research will lead the reader into the literature pertinent to his or her research interest.

There were no suitable computer data bases with biological information before 1970. For the period 1955 to 1970 we therefore searched the "Bibliography of Agriculture" *by hand* for all of our species. About this time Dr. Charles Gunn, Botanist, United States Department of Agriculture (USDA), Beltsville, Maryland (USA); Carole Ritchie, Botanist (USDA), Laurel, Maryland (USA); and Anita Speight, USDA and National Agricultural Library, Current Awareness Literature Service, Beltsville, Maryland (USA), began the search of several data bases for biological data needed to keep abreast of weed species listed in the new United States Federal Noxious Weed Law. Many of their species were candidates for or had already been included in this book. As we shared mutual tasks with them, they included all our species in their searches and we received biweekly printouts covering about 1500 biological journals for ten years.

It is likely that these books include in one place more biological data on the world's principal weeds than has been gathered to this time. We urge that students and researchers examine this body of knowledge before starting another search of all the world's journals. To provide a comprehensive resource was one of our purposes for writing this book.

THE PREPARATION OF THE WEED DISTRIBUTION MAPS

We gathered most of our records while standing in crop fields and mud with farmers and experiment station workers. Much was obtained from documents written by workers about their own country's weed flora. Some was obtained by taking living plant material back to herbaria or experts at the headquarters where we worked.

We have covered more than 100 countries. The aggregate space occupied on earth by China, the former Soviet Union, Canada, and the United States would be roughly equal to all other agricultural countries combined. We found it necessary to recognize the topographic and climatic diversity of the nine largest countries and to work with the weed floras independently by regions—usually three to five. For example, the tremendous heat of the desert areas of the former Soviet Union in Central Asia supports a different weed flora than can be seen in the eastern Maritime Provinces of that country. We placed our species' symbols accordingly.

Our aim was not to produce detailed weed surveys for particular territories or countries, but to provide a pattern of distribution for the world. The reader should also be aware that our maps do not depict the total world distribution of a species we have worked with—only the area in which it behaves as a weed.

The reader may truly come upon a blank space on one of our maps where he or she knows a species to be present. Or, on the contrary, the reader may be sure that we have erroneously placed a weed species symbol in a place where such a plant cannot survive. The world is a very large place and we hoped for 90 percent accuracy in our work. We hope that, even with small adjustments of two or three symbols, our maps may still present the larger world distribution pattern for that species, and that we may all go forward with our work.

Finally, with this knowledge, we hope that weed scientists and helpers may now take courage in seeking help from nearby neighbors who have similar weed problems, or perhaps communicate with persons at a distance who have already worked out a solution for a weed problem. We need not all initiate a new research project at the appearance of a different weed. Someone may already have the answer.

THE SIGNIFICANCE OF THE RANKS
OF WEED IMPORTANCE

Every ranking was provided by a weed scientist for his own country. We have not made up estimates or provided ratings of importance from the work or documents of other people.

As our experience grew, we perceived that we were being taught by those with whom we visited, worked, or corresponded that, although it goes unrecorded, there seems to be some common understanding about Serious, Principal, and Common weeds. When you are standing in a field with a farmer, he may often point to two or three weeds in his field that cause the most trouble. There is no question about his meaning—these are the Serious weeds. When asked for the weeds of next importance, he may point to two or three more— rarely does he name ten more. We have thus referred to these half-dozen weeds as Principal for his field. A Common weed is one that is very widespread in many or all crops and regions of a country. It may require constant effort and expense to hold it at bay, but it never seriously threatens a crop.

The countries or societies that have tried to work out a "numbers" system that is reliable for ratings of importance, workable in all crops, applicable to large areas, and can be standardized as a universal system have met with disappointment. For our work we had to ask a question: "How would a rating of 6 differ from 4 or 8 in expressions from dozens of workers, concerning hundreds of weed species, in 50 to 100 countries with many different languages across the world?"

Where a species is said to be a Serious or a Principal weed, you may know that a weed scientist of the country has given such a ranking for that weed species in a given crop in some area of his country. This does not imply that a total evaluation of every weed species for every crop has been completed in his area on a country-wide scale. There are few countries in the world that may even make estimates at such a high level.

One

Acanthospermum hispidum DC.

Asteraceae (Compositae), Aster Family

ACANTHOSPERMUM HISPIDUM is native to tropical America but is now widely distributed in tropical and subtropical areas of the world, occurring in nearly 40 countries and causing serious control problems in many crops. The species is a member of the **Heliantheae** tribe of the **Asteraceae** family and is one of three species in the *Acanthospermum* genus. The binomial is descriptive of this herbaceous annual plant. *Akanthos* is Greek for spine, thorn, or prickle and *sperma* means seed; *hispidum* is the Latin term for bristly or rough.

FIGURE 1-1   The distribution of *Acanthospermum hispidum* DC. across the world where it has been reported as a weed.

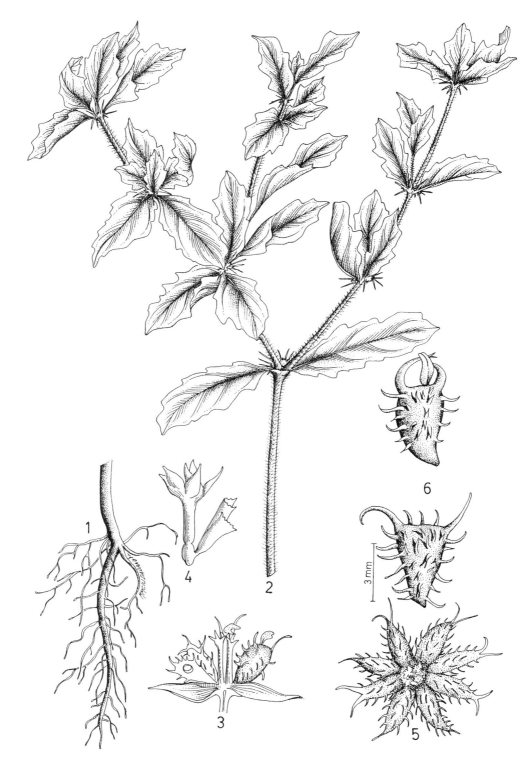

FIGURE 1-2 *Acanthospermum hispidum* DC.: 1. taproot; 2. flowering branch; 3. cross-section of inflorescence; 4. floret; 5. fruit; 6. achene, two views.

DESCRIPTION

A. hispidum (Figure 1-2) is an herbaceous or subherbaceous *annual* plant; *taproot* highly branched, relatively shallow; *stems* erect 20 to 60 cm tall, regularly branching into two, dull green, covered with coarse white hairs; *leaves* opposite, dull green, shortly hairy, simple, sessile, obovate to oblanceolate, blunt or rounded tips, 3 to 7 cm long, 1 to 3 cm wide, entire or irregularly toothed with three distinct veins; *inflorescence* star-shaped, small, solitary, terminal, and axillary, sessile to subsessile, about 6 mm in diameter; *flowers* unisexual, *ray flowers* pistillate, female, yellowish-green, 7 to 8, uniseriate, the corolla strap-shaped and 3-toothed; *disk flowers* male, corolla regular, tubular and 5-toothed; *fruit* a star-shaped cluster of 5 to 10 (usually 8), flat, thick, triangular, achenes about 6 mm long, 3 mm wide at apex, covered with numerous stiff, short, hooked spines, with 2 much longer, horn-like, straight or curved spines at apex, straw colored to yellowish-brown.

The hairy stem, yellow-green florets, opposite leaves and fruits with hooked spines (two longer than the rest arising from the apex) and arranged in the form of flat stars are the distinguishing characteristics of this species.

HABITAT AND DISTRIBUTION

A. hispidum (Figure 1-1) is adapted to a wide range of soil and climatic conditions. It is particularly adapted to light textured soils but also grows well in heavy textured soils. It is commonly found in cultivated upland crops, roadsides, pastures, waste areas, around corrals, and along railroads and cattle trails. The bristly seeds cling to animals, clothing, and other objects and are readily transported to other areas. Once introduced, it can rapidly become a serious crop menace. In less than 20 years after its introduction into India in 1945, it became a widespread and serious weed (Chakravarti 1963). It is very competitive and widespread in Brazil, its region of origin, and is one of the most aggressive annual weeds in Zimbabwe (Rhodesia) (Thomas 1970). It is found from sea level to 1300 m in the Dominican Republic (Jurgens 1977) and would be able to live well outside the currently infested areas of the United States (Carter 1950). Plants grew well in a soil of *pH* 8.2 in India (Murthy and Rao 1978) and were found to accumulate zinc, especially in the leaves, when grown on zinc deposit areas (Tiagi and Aery 1981).

BIOLOGY AND ECOLOGY

A. hispidum has been closely studied in Zimbabwe and India. Schwerzel (1970a,b) in Zimbabwe found that pure stands could produce over 10,000 kg/ha of seed that contained nearly one billion seeds. More seeds were produced by plants that emerged early in the growing season than by those emerging later; however, viability of the seeds increased from 63 to 88% and the germination of fresh seed from 36 to 84% as emergence date was delayed from December 1 to January 20. The plant flowers sooner in dry seasons than in wet ones and ripe seed forms 30 to 50 days after flowering. Pure stands of *A. hispidum* had 310,000 plants/ha and nearly all produced seed. Hosamani et al. (1971) counted 455 seeds/plant and plants only 7 to 8 cm tall produced seed in Brazil (Lloyd 1956).

In Zimbabwe (1975–82), Thomas has also done extensive work on *A. hispidum*. Many more seedlings are found in the summer season than in the winter. Eighty percent of the seed retains viability after burial for 1 yr and some viability is maintained after 3 yr at 24 cm. In irrigated fields, seed viability drops to 1% after 7 yr. Freshly harvested seed has 36% germination; in dry storage, this may drop to 15% after 1 yr and seeds lost their viability after 7 yr in dry storage. Similar germination trends occurred with seed buried in the field.

Most seeds of *A. hispidum* emerge within 3 yr after production and all seeds die within 8 yr whether the field is cultivated or not (Schwerzel and Thomas 1979). Percent emergence is also similar with or without cultivation. While freshly harvested seed is not completely dormant, germination can reach 80% by storing for 2 mo at 4°C and presoaking with KNO_3 when ready to germinate. Sandpaper and acid scarification reduce germination by 50 and 80%, respectively (Pate 1979). Freezing the seeds for 2 mo also reduced viability. Seven-month-old seed treated with KNO_3 had 60% germination regardless of the pretreatment conditions and under both light and dark regimes. Seedlings emerge in the field for extended periods if soil moisture is adequate.

In India, Shetty et al. (1982) observed that *A. hispidum* is sensitive to shade and that it is less competitive in mixed cropping systems than in mono-cultured crops. With 90% shade, dry matter production was reduced 80% and low shade levels reduced seed production by 50%. Murthy and Rao (1978) noted that plant height was not appreciably changed by shade but that leaf area increased 34% in shade while leaf thickness was reduced 15%. Shoot and root dry weights were reduced 35 and 25%, respectively, in the shade. The weed is sensitive to crop competition and disappears from nongrazed pastures after a few years (Wild 1946).

Das et al. (1981) thoroughly studied the photosynthetic efficiency of this C_3 plant. Among the crop and weed species studied, *A. hispidum* had the lowest rate of biomass accumulation (2.43 g/m^2/day) and the lowest concentration of chlorophyll (33 $\mu g/cm^2$). This suggests that it may not be highly competitive with crops. The wavy, branched taproot is more or less evenly distributed in the surface soil level (Shetty and Maiti 1978). The lateral roots absorb most of the water and nutrients. A detailed description of the root, cotyledon, stem and leaf anatomy was published by Mirashi and Bhogaonkar (1974). The roots and stems have resin ducts and the stem and leaves have both nonglandular hairs and capitate, shortly stalked glandular trichomes. Leaves have twice as many stomata on the adaxial (546/mm^2) than the abaxial (272/mm^2) side (Veeranjaneyulu and Das 1984). Leaf resistance measurements show that *A. hispidum* stomata remain open at mid-day, while those of most species tend to close. This species contains nearly equal quantities of chlorophyll a and b and has a CO_2 compensation point of 78 ppm and a specific leaf weight of 275 mg/dm^2.

Both seeds and leaves contain phenolic acids that are allelopathic to other plants. Leachates from intact seeds and leaves inhibit germination and root and shoot growth of several crops (Leela 1985).

A. hispidum is a monoecious composite plant with male flowers in the center and female flowers at the margins of flower heads. Pollination occurs primarily by wind and self-pollination is common. Santos and Stubblebine (1987) determined that the ratio of male to female flowers varies with the environment. The ratio tends to 1:1 when the population density of *A. hispidum* is low, the system of land use is varied, and cropping conditions are unfavorable for the weed. Under inverse conditions, the ratio tends to change toward more female flowers.

In Australia *A. hispidum* may have over 2% KNO_3 but no cases of nitrate poisoning have been reported (Everist 1974). Miller et al. (1963) noted that cattle in Nigeria will not touch the plant when spines are present but that the leaves are rich in protein. They ensiled

A. hispidum and found that the protein content was 9.2%, with 36% crude fiber and a low level of digestible organic matter. Even after the spines were softened by silage fermentation, cattle consumed very little and the authors conclude that it is not a suitable forage species.

A. hispidum is toxic to animals when consumed on a daily basis (Ali and Adam 1978a, b). Over 50% of the mice given as little as 1% *A. hispidum* in their diet died before the completion of the 6-mo feeding study. Mice consuming up to 50% dried, ground stems and leaves developed symptoms sooner than those fed less concentrated diets and ground seeds killed mice more rapidly than shoots. Plants collected at the flowering stage were ground and administered to goats in a drench at 5 or 10 g fresh weight/kg of body weight. Some goats died within 6 to 9 days at both levels of consumption. Damage in both mice and goats occurred in the intestines, lungs, liver, and kidneys. Symptoms included anorexia, diarrhea, weakness, and accelerated respiration. Effects were found on the goat testes that suggest male fertility problems could arise in animals consuming *A. hispidum*. Perhaps the hairy stems and resins in the plant deter animals from consuming this species. Regardless of the reason, it is fortunate that animals appear to avoid feeding on a potentially harmful plant, especially since it can be an important weed of overgrazed pastures (Wild 1946).

AGRICULTURAL IMPORTANCE

Nearly 40 countries (Figure 1-1) report *A. hispidum* as a weed problem in 25 crops. It is one of the three principal species in Zimbabwe and parts of Brazil, and ranks among the ten most serious weeds in peanuts in the United States. Hawaii and Australia have declared it a noxious weed. It cannot be present in hay sold within Australia and imported products contaminated with *A. hispidum* must be quarantined (Anon. [Australia] 1982). Both South Africa and Zimbabwe report that the bristly seeds reduce the quality of wool and the spines cause lesions that may take up to 6 wk to heal.

A. hispidum is an important weed of maize, cotton, soybeans, and peanuts. It is a serious or principal weed of edible beans in Brazil; dryland crops, pineapple, sugarcane, sunflowers, and vegetables in India; dryland and irrigated vegetable crops in Australia; cotton in Brazil, Mozambique, South Africa, Tanzania, and Zimbabwe; maize in Bolivia, Brazil, Sri Lanka, and southern United States; orchards in the western United States, pastures in Australia, Botswana, Brazil, Gambia, Nigeria, South Africa, and Zimbabwe; peanuts in India, South Africa, and southern United States; rice in Ivory Coast; upland rice in India; soybeans in Brazil, India, and the United States; and sugarcane in Brazil.

It is a common weed of barley and wheat in Peru; edible beans in Honduras; cassava in Ghana; citrus in Mozambique; cotton in Mozambique, Paraguay and South Africa; cowpeas, millet and upland rice in Senegal; horticultural crops in South Africa; maize in Ghana, Honduras, Peru, Senegal, South Africa and Zimbabwe; orchards in Honduras; pastures in Tanzania; peas in India; peanuts in Ghana, Senegal and Zimbabwe; rubber in Thailand; sorghum in Senegal and South Africa; soybeans in Zimbabwe; sugarcane in Peru and South Africa; sunflower in South Africa; tobacco in Argentina, South Africa and Zimbabwe; tomatoes in Nicaragua; and vegetables in Ghana and South Africa.

In addition *A. hispidum* is an unranked weed of edible beans, millet, potatoes and tomatoes in India; citrus in Brazil; cotton in Bolivia and Nigeria; cowpeas and upland rice in Nigeria; dryland crops in Ivory Coast; maize in Mozambique, Nigeria and Tanzania; peanuts in Gambia, Nigeria and Zimbabwe; sorghum in Australia and India; soybean in

Bolivia and Nigeria; sugarcane in Argentina, Australia, Mozambique and Nigeria; tobacco and wastelands in Australia; and wheat in Argentina and the United States.

While this species is a serious weed in numerous crops, few competition studies have been done. Davis et al. (1977) found that most of the losses in soybeans in Brazil resulted from interference at harvest time. When early emerging weeds decline, *A. hispidum* emerges and forms a canopy over the crop during the pod-filling period. Researchers in India also observed large increases in dry matter production late in the season (Shetty et al. 1982).

Peanut seed yields decrease linearly as the time of *A. hispidum* interference increases (Walker et al. 1989). Even 2 wk of interference can reduce yields, while 8 wk without interference gives maximum production. With peanuts in rows 91 cm wide, full season interference from 1, 2, 4, and 8 plants/m of row reduced peanut yields 14, 26, 43 and 50%, respectively. *A. hispidum* interference for 13 wk reduced peanut forage biomass 54%; in contrast the weed's biomass in this period was reduced only 32% by peanut interference.

An excellent account of the aggressiveness of the weed in Brazil is given by Lloyd (1956). He searched for native pests to consider in potential biological control programs for *A. hispidum* in Nigeria and after extensive travels in Brazil (and a brief amount of time in Venezuela and Colombia) concluded that there was little hope of finding effective bio-control pests. Some aphids (*Macrosiphum* species) and leafhoppers (*Agallia* species) were encountered in Brazil, but no leaf or seed feeders were found nor were any significant injury effects noted on plants. This is not surprising since the weed is a serious competitor even in its center of origin, reflecting the lack of important pests or predators.

While few insects are associated with *A. hispidum*, it serves as a host of several important diseases. Examples include *Verticillium albo-atrum* (Silva and Tokeshi 1979) and tomato leaf curl that is transmitted by white flies (Mariappan and Narayanasamy 1972). Lloyd (1956) noted that it hosts at least two viruses that attack tobacco, sugar beets, tomatoes and flax. An unidentified fungus was observed attacking the leaves of *A. hispidum* in Brazil (Hoffman 1980) and it hosts the cotton insect *Calidea dregii* in Tanzania (Reed and Kayumbo 1965).

A. hispidum is used in several home remedies in Brazil (Lorenzi 1982). The root is used to cure coughing and bronchitis and a boiled tea of the leaves reduces fever, promotes sweating, and cures diarrhea.

COMMON NAMES

Acanthospermum hispidum

ARGENTINA	cuajrilla, torito
AUSTRALIA	star burr
BOLIVIA	espinoso, estrella, torito
BRAZIL	amor de negro, carrapicho de carneiro, espinho de carneiro, federacao, retirante
COLUMBIA	carrapichno, cuajrilla, espinho de cigano
DOMINICAN REPUBLIC	mala mujer
EAST AFRICA	jina la kawaida
HAWAII	star burr

INDIA	kattu nerinji, saroto
MAURITIUS	herbe tricorne
NIGERIA	kasinyawo
PARAGUAY	toro rati
SOUTH AFRICA	regop sterklits, upright starbur
UNITED STATES	bristly starbur, goathead, Texas cockspur
ZAMBIA	kanjata, nchesa, nseeto, upright starbur
ZIMBABWE	upright starbur, sibama yauli

Two

Achyranthes aspera L.

Amaranthaceae, Amaranth Family

A<small>CHYRANTHES ASPERA</small> is an herbaceous to semi-woody plant widely disbursed in tropical and subtropical regions of the world. It has been most intensely studied in India. While often found in non-agricultural habitats, it infests a diversity of crops. The genus name is from the Greek *achyr* for chaff or bran, while the species name refers to the rough texture of the spikes.

FIGURE 2-1   The distribution of *Achyranthes aspera* L. across the world where it has been reported as a weed.

FIGURE 2-2 *Achyranthes aspera* L.: 1. flowering branch; 2. portion of spike; 3. flower; 4. seed; 5. seedling.

DESCRIPTION

A. aspera (Figure 2-2) is a coarse, rambling or erect widely branched *annual* or short-lived *perennial* with a semi-woody base; *taproot* long with lateral branches throughout; *stem* 0.5 to 2 m tall, angularly-ribbed, generally square, more or less densely hairy and thickened above the nodes; *leaves* opposite, oblong-obovate to elliptic or obovate from an acute or obtuse base; tip acuminate, acute, obtuse or rounded; *blade* entire, flat or somewhat wavy, more or less pubescent, 2 to 10 cm long, 0.7 to 5 cm wide; *petiole* 0.5 to 1.5 cm long; *inflorescence* terminal spikes, rigid, 10 to 50 cm long excluding the peduncle, with paired branches below; *rachis* robust, angularly-ribbed, more or less hairy; *flowers* small, green, perfect, densely arranged at top of spike, less clustered in the center, scattered and often in pairs near the base; subtended by long-acuminate *bracts* or *bracteoles*, 2 to 3.5 mm long, stiff and spiny, erect before anthesis reflexed later, persistent; *sepals* 5, green with pale margins, ovate-lanceolate, acuminate, 3.5 to 5.5 mm long during anthesis, five *filaments* 2.2 to 3.5 mm long; *pseudo-staminodia* with or without dorsal, truncate, long-fringed scales; *ovary* top-shaped with 1- to 2-mm *style*; *fruit* an *utricle* (a small prickly bur), 2.5 to 2.8 mm long, rounded at the base; enclosed by persistent perianth and bracts, 4 to 5 mm long, detaching easily from rachis; *seed* 2 to 3 mm long, 1 to 1.5 mm wide, truncate above, reddish to dark brown and shiny, enclosed in chaffy calyx parts that remain attached.

This species is readily distinguished by the opposite leaves, branched stem and spiny bracts that are erect before flowering but then become reflexed and readily adhere to animals and clothing.

DISTRIBUTION AND HABITAT

A. aspera (Figure 2-1) is indigenous to Africa and Asia but is now found in nearly 60 countries with tropical and subtropical environments. It frequently occurs in waste areas, and along roadsides, foot paths, railroads and sand dunes. *A. aspera* can be a serious weed in pastures, plantation crops, and occasionally in irrigated and cultivated crops. It often infests fence rows, open woodland, and the borders of forests and coffee fields.

It has adapted to a wide range of environments. In Zambia it is found on heavy soils, often near ant hills and rivers (Vernon 1983), while in most countries it is common on light textured soils. It tolerates soil *pH* to 8 and grows from sea level in Hawaii and Colombia to 2500 m in Uganda (Masefield 1939). *A. aspera* seems to have reached a stable population as a weed of nurseries, orchards, and gardens in northern Israel (Dafni and Heller 1980) but may be evolving from a mesophyte to a xerophyte in India (Shrivastava 1960). Other references to environmental adaptations include a preference for shady, moist areas in Cuba, open woodland and arable crops in Zimbabwe, pastures in Colombia, and orchards and sand dunes in Malaysia. In India, it is often associated with *Cassia tora*, is most frequent in coarse textured soils (Mall and Sharma 1967), and was the most frequent of 41 species in a fallowed field during the rainy season but was not found during the dry season (Sharma 1981).

BIOLOGY

The taproot of *A. aspera* is laterally branched throughout and the branches point obliquely downward. This is atypical of other **Amaranthaceae** species that do not form lateral branches on the lower section of the taproot (Shetty and Maiti 1978). In the preflower stage, *A. aspera* contained 2.2% N, 2.1% CaO, 1.3% K_2O, and 1.6% P_2O_5 (Singh and Singh 1939). The shoot contained more K than the root and this element was present in higher concentrations in the winter than in the summer in India (Ratra and Misra 1970). N, P, and Ca were also more concentrated in the shoots but were most abundant in plants during the summer.

The lower leaf surface has more than twice as many stomata as the upper surface (186 vs. 80 stomata/mm^2). *A. aspera* had a transpiration rate of 37.2 mg/cm^2/hr, a transpiration ratio of 707 g water/g dry matter produced, and had the highest ratio of all species tested (Das and Santakumari 1977). It is a C_3 plant with a dark respiration rate of 2885 µl O_2/g dry weight/hr in young, fully expanded leaves. Compared to *Amaranthus spinosus*, a C_4 plant of the same family, *A. aspera* had 44% less dark respiration, 12% less protein, an equal starch content, and 38% more total sugar content (Naidu et al. 1980).

Allelopathy studies by Rao et al. (1979) in India tested the effects of macerated shoot and root tissue of fruiting *A. aspera* plants and seeds in water extracts on the germination of millet (*Pennisetum typhoideum*) seeds. Extracts of 2 and 4% (w/v) were added to petri dishes that contained the millet seeds on filter paper. Seed, root, and shoot sources of the extract greatly inhibited millet germination after 90 hr, with little difference between the 2 and 4% extracts. Averaged across concentrations, the percentages of germination inhibition were 70, 63 and 64% for seeds, roots, and shoots, respectively. Leaf sheath elongation and root growth were totally stopped by seed and root extracts while some growth occurred in the presence of shoot extracts.

A. aspera has been described as a variable plant. For example, it flowers from August to September in India (Kanodia and Gupta 1972) and throughout the year in the Philippines. It has no photoperiodic requirement for flowering. On arable land it grows as an annual, while in shaded and protected areas it is often a perennial (Sen 1981). Townsend (1973, 1974) has described the varietal differences of *A. aspera* as well as those of closely related species. Its basic chromosome number is 21.

Shrivastava (1960) gives a detailed anatomical analysis of *A. aspera* var. *prophyristachya.* It flowers from September to March in India and has two free medullary vascular bundles in the region of the upper four to five internodes. They then fuse to form a single vascular bundle in the rest of the plant. He uses additional internal and morphological characteristics to separate this variety from *A. aspera* var. *aspera.* Lower flowers on the spike develop first and mature fruits are formed 1 to 2 mo after pollination. Pollen grains are spherical with a wrinkled surface due to large granules and short protuberances around the pores (Zandonella and Lecocq 1977). Nectaries appear as large rings at the base of the stamens.

A single *A. aspera* plant produces from 2970 seeds/plant in Cuba (Rodriguez and Cepero 1984), 3600 in India (Hosamani et al. 1971), to 9450 in the Philippines. One thousand seeds weigh 2.6 g in the Philippines (Pancho 1964) and 1.3 g in Sri Lanka (Pemadasa and Wickramasinghe 1979). Seeds germinate equally well under light, shade and dark conditions (Fenner 1980). Fresh untreated seeds germinate readily and completely at temperatures of 20 to 35°C. However, root and shoot length decrease at temperatures of 30°C or higher (Khan et al. 1984). A cycle of hydration-dehydration (24 hr) has no effect on germination.

Reports of seed requiring an after-ripening period to germinate were clarified by Pandya and Pathak (1980). The fruit (utricle) of *A. aspera* is enclosed by a hardened perianth and persistent bracts and bracteoles collectively called the husk. Germination of freshly harvested utricles was nil for over 30 days. After 6 mo in storage, half of the seed germinated. However, washing fresh utricles in water for 24 hr gave 100% germination. Husks were removed from seeds and soaked in water for 24 hr. When this extract was used to germinate *A. aspera* seeds on filter paper, no germination occurred. Thus time or mechanical removal of the husk are required for fresh seeds to germinate.

Most seeds emerge from 2 to 5 cm deep. Nearly 40% of the seeds planted at 8 cm or deeper germinated but failed to emerge (Fenner 1985). Seed germination and seedling emergence are greater in sandy textured than in silty soils and both germination and emergence decline as soil moisture decrease (Pemadasa and Wickramasinghe 1979). As soil surface roughness increases, the rate of and final germination increase with more of the seeds in the hollows germinating.

Seeds of *A. aspera* contaminated the seeds of the forage grass *Setaria sphacelata* in Kenya. They were not removed from this species by mechanical cleaners, but these machines easily separated these weed seeds from clover and lucerne seed (Bogdan 1966).

The spiny fruits adhere readily to clothing and animal fur. Bullock and Primack (1977) did an interesting study in natural stands of *A. aspera* in Costa Rica. A cotton cloth was placed on a wooden board and they walked with the board held vertically through pure or mixed stands of *A. aspera*. Seeds were found on the cloth from 10 to 90 cm above the ground, with the peak between 50 and 70 cm. Once the fruit became attached to the cloth it adhered tightly. The authors calculated that most seeds would be dispersed 2.5 km on articles of clothing worn on an open trail. However, "walking" the board through a stand of high grass gave a mean dispersal distance of only 34 m, because many seeds were brushed off by the grass.

Rabbits in three regions of Kenya were examined monthly for one year for seeds of *A. aspera* in their fur (Agnew and Flux 1970). Seeds were present in rabbits at 600 and 1200 m above sea level but not at 1800 m. Since rabbits clean their coats daily, encountering even a few seeds in their fur suggests they are very instrumental in spreading the propagules of *A. aspera*. Seeds may move in animals as well as on them. Carlquist (1967) speculates that *A. aspera* was introduced into the Hawaiian Islands by birds, and the same has occurred among islands in the Indian Ocean (Ridley 1930).

AGRICULTURAL IMPORTANCE AND UTILITY

A. aspera is found in 23 crops in nearly 60 countries (Figure 2-1) and is frequently reported as a weed of sugarcane, pasture, and rice culture. It is a serious or principal weed of cassava, cotton, maize, lowland rice, sugarcane, tea, and wastelands in India; cassava, maize and upland rice in Indonesia; and pastures in Central America, Colombia, Ecuador, India, and West Africa.

It is a common weed of bananas in Honduras; edible beans in Bangladesh and Cuba; bananas, sorghum and tobacco in Nicaragua; cassava in the Philippines; cacao in Indonesia; cotton in Thailand; irrigated crops in Australia; pastures in Australia, Hawaii and South Africa; potatoes in India; sorghum and tobacco in Nicaragua; and sugarcane in Bangladesh and Thailand.

A. aspera also infests bananas, edible beans, sorghum and tobacco in Honduras; cereals in Kenya; coconuts in Cambodia and Vietnam; cacao in Dominican Republic and

Honduras; coffee in Dominican Republic, East Africa, Nicaragua and Saudi Arabia; cotton in Honduras and Thailand; dryland crops, sorghum, jute, and soybeans in India; maize in Honduras, Thailand and Zambia; nurseries in Israel; oil palm in Indonesia; orchards in Honduras, Israel, and Saudi Arabia; pastures in New Caledonia and New Guinea; rice in Honduras; Nicaragua and Thailand; lowland rice in the Philippines and upland rice in India; rubber and tea in Indonesia; tomatoes in Nicaragua; vegetables in Israel and New Caledonia; and wastelands in Australia and South Africa.

Even though *A. aspera* is a weed in 23 crops, no data on losses due to competition were found. The presence of *A. aspera* in pastures reduces their productivity, especially when flowering and fruiting occur, because the spiny bracts are painful for livestock to graze. The fruits become lodged in wool, reducing its market value.

Most reported uses of *A. aspera* for medicinal purposes are from India. Seeds have been used to treat cardiac and renal dropsy, as an emetic, and in hydrophobia cases (Batta and Rangaswami 1973). Powders from the plant are used to treat boils and piles, and for diuresis, and liquid preparations are applied to skin eruptions and warts (Anandalwar and Venkateswara 1981). Several saponins in the seeds have been identified and examined for medical effects. They increase the force of heart contractions and have a diuretic effect that would be beneficial in treating cardiac failures (Gupta et al. 1972). In China *A. aspera* seeds are used as an antispasmodic, diuretic, decoction for bleeding and both as an antifertility treatment and to induce labor (Duke and Ayensu 1985).

A. aspera also contains ecdysterone, a potential insect chemosterilant (Banerji et al. 1971). Seeds contain considerably more ecdysterone (on a weight basis) than stems, leaves, and roots. Alkaloids are nearly three times more abundant in the shoots than in the roots (0.74 vs. 0.27%, w/w).

A. aspera has been used by some African groups to make salt, to relieve the pain of scorpion stings in India, as a vegetable leaf in Java, and in dye making (Uphof 1968). Plants are high in protein (>20%), fiber (20%), total carbohydrate (20%), and Ca (1.8%), making *A. aspera* a good pot-herb.

A. aspera is infested with the thrip *Caliothrips indicus* most of the year (Daniel et al. 1984). As the density of the weed declines, thrip infestation levels rise. After peanut planting, the thrips migrate from the weed to the crop during the rainy season but not to irrigated peanuts in the dry season, because the weed density is very high during this period. In India, *A. aspera* can host the leaf spot *Cercospora achyranthus* (Kulkarni et al. 1973) and a mosaic virus that can infect ten other plant species (Mariappan et al. 1973). It is an alternate host of the root-knot nematode under natural Philippine conditions (Valdez 1968).

COMMON NAMES

Achyranthes aspera

AUSTRALIA	chaff-flow
CHINA	pinyin, dao koa cao
COLOMBIA	cadillo chichoborugo, cadillo de mazorca, mazotillo, rabo de chancho, rabo de raton
CUBA	rabo de gato
HAWAII	achyranthes

INDIA	andhajhara, apamaranga, apang, champang michel, chirchra, kadaladi, latjira, nayuruvi, sohbyrthit, undakanta
KENYA	devil's horsewhip
MADAGASCAR	vatofotsy
MAURITIUS	herbe sergen
MICRONESIA	kikitoun, chichitoun
PHILIPPINES	angud, dokot-dokot, bagat-bagat guela, hangod, lopo-lopo, niknikitan, ragradi, saramo
PUERTO RICO	rabo de raton
SAUDI ARABIA	na'eem, no'oeim
SOUTH AFRICA	langklits-kafblom, rough-chaff flower
THAILAND	phan nguu
UGANDA	devil's horsewhip
VENEZUELA	lengua de vaca
ZIMBABWE	devil's horsewhip, dombo

Three

Aeschynomene indica L.

Papilionaceae (Leguminosae), Pea Family

ESCHYNOMENE INDICA is found throughout the tropics and subtropics of the world and is particularly abundant in Asia. While a member of the legume group, it is seldom used for livestock feed. It is somewhat unique in having both root and stem nodules inhabited by nitrogen-fixing bacteria. The plant is found frequently in wet soils, near canals and rivers, along roadsides and in waste areas. The genus name is from the Greek *aischynomenes*, meaning modest or ashamed in reference to the leaves of many species that close when touched. The species name suggests the plant is of Indian origin.

FIGURE 3-1   The distribution of *Aeschynomene indica* L. across the world where it has been reported as a weed.

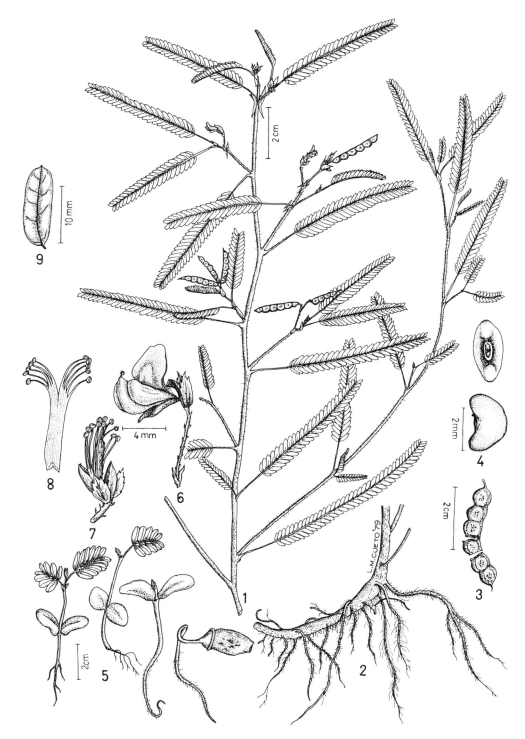

FIGURE 3-2   *Aeschynomene indica* L.: 1. fruiting branch; 2. root system; 3. pod; 4. seed two views; 5. seedlings; 6. flower; 7. same, petals removed to show stamens; 8. stamens; 9. leaflet, enlarged.

DESCRIPTION

A. indica (Figure 3-2) is an erect, glabrous, widely branched, suffrutescent *annual* herb, 0.3 to 1.2 m tall; *root* a slightly branched taproot; *stems* slender, fistular, often woody at the base, warty, sometimes hairy when young with many cylindrical branches; *leaves* alternate, even-pinnate with rachis 3 to 5 cm or longer; *leaflets* linear-oblong, obtuse, 4 to 5 mm long, 1-nerved, numerous and close together; *stipules* lanceolate, 1 cm long, membranous and deciduous; *inflorescence* composed of short, hairy, axillary racemes, 1- to 4-flowered; *wings* obliquely obovate or oblong, equal to or slightly shorter than glabrous *keel*; *flowers* perfect, small; *stamens* in two bundles of 5 each; *standard* 2 to 9 mm long, yellow or yellowish white, often suffused with purple; upper lip of *calyx* shortly 2-dentate, lower lip very shortly 3-dentate; *petals* drop as flower opens; *fruit* a dry, dehiscent, simple *legume* or pod, linear-oblong, straight or curved, 1 to 5 cm long and 4 mm wide, glabrous; composed of 4 to 10 joints with a group of confluent ridge-like tubercles, finally breaking into 1-seeded segments; *seeds* kidney shaped, 3 to 3.5 mm long, shiny black.

This species is distinguished by the fistular stem, nodules on the roots and lower stem, the yellow flowers, and pods that are shallowly incised along the lower suture.

DISTRIBUTION AND HABITAT

A. indica (Figure 3-1) is most frequently found in poorly drained areas, wet pastures, along rivers and canals, and in or around paddy fields. It is widely distributed in Asia and is found to 1500 m in the Himalayas (Biswas and Calder 1936) and from subtropical to cool temperate regions of Japan (Numata and Yoshizawa 1975). It is relatively prevalent in western Africa and Australia but occurs in just two South American countries and only in the southern region of the United States. Sen (1981) surveyed fields in India and 10 to 20% of the paddy rice fields had *A. indica* during September through November, but it was present in less than 10% of uncultivated fields.

ECOLOGY AND BIOLOGY

While usually associated with wet soils, marshy areas and paddy fields, it is a principal weed in the Senegal River Valley, where the annual precipitation is only 300 to 500 mm (Hernandez 1978). In the southern United States, *A. indica* can grow in water with *pH* 8.5 and 2.9 ppm of Cl (Beal 1977). The plant accumulates heavy metals when growing in regions of industrial pollution. *A. indica* roots and stems contained 8.9 and 7 ppm Cd, respectively, when growing in a soil with 7 ppm Cd in the upper 10 cm. In a soil with 410 ppm Zn, root and stem tissue had 510 and 328 ppm Zn, respectively. Thus plants reflect the relative concentration of these elements in the soil. Unpolluted soil had 0.5 ppm Cd and 91 ppm Zn (Tazaki and Ushijima 1977).

A. indica formed adventitious shoots when decapitated 1 cm below the cotyledonary node in both the cotyledon and 4-leaf stages (Langston et al. 1984). The shoots appeared within 5 days after excision and arose not from callus tissue but from the hypocotyl itself.

A. indica is a C_3 plant, is a tetraploid with a 2n chromosome number of 40 and has stomata on both leaf surfaces. An anatomical examination of *A. indica* leaves found 206 and 250 stomata/mm^2 on the adaxial and abaxial surfaces, respectively (Kothari and Shar

1975). They prepared detailed drawings of the stomata of this and several related genera and developed an identification key based on differences in stomata and leaf surface characteristics. *A. indica* flowers at various times and durations in different regions. It flowers all year in the Philippines, from August to October in Japan, and from August to November in India, with peak flowering in the first 2 mo in that area. Anthers are about 1 mm long and contain over 5000 pollen grains each (Mondal and Roy 1984). Flowers are highly self-pollinated.

The most frequently studied feature of *A. indica* is the stem nodules. Root nodules are widely reported on this species and the occurrence of nodules at the base of the stem is also frequent, especially if plants have been partially flooded for a period. Aerial stem nodules have been reported more recently. Yatazawa and Yoshida (1979) noted 5 to 10 nodules/10 cm of stem up to 50 cm above the soil. Nodules contain *Rhizobium* that fix N and can be easily removed mechanically from stems. Stem nodule development is thought to be an ecological adaptation to allow plants to produce available N when soil moisture conditions were unfavorable for rhizobium activity in root nodules. However, nodules also form on non-submerged plants. When N was supplied to plants under controlled conditions, no stem nodules developed but root nodules were formed (Yatazawa and Susilo 1980).

Similar results were found by Eaglesham and Szalay (1983), who also discovered that seven of nine *Aeschynomene* species formed stem nodules and several of them did so even with N present in the root zone. They measured 2.3 stem nodules per *A. indica* plant with a total weight of 2.3 mg. The origins of root and stem nodules differ in that root nodules arise from the pericycle and stem nodules originate in the cortex (Allen and Allen 1981). Otherwise, root and stem nodules are similar in size, shape, internal structure, and the presence of hemoglobin. Both root and stem rhizobia can induce stem nodules (Sasakawa et al. 1986). Infection occurs through lenticles on the stem. Eighteen days after inoculation, stem nodules fix N at the same rate as root nodules. In the field, only about 10% of the *A. indica* plants have stem nodules, thus relatively little N is fixed in this manner. However, if stem nodules could be induced on leguminous crops, a significant benefit would result.

The plant reproduces only by seed, yet few reports on germination were found. Stem cuttings often have been used to propagate plants for N fixation studies. Chaghtai et al. (1983) noted higher germination in green (42%) and yellow light (23%) than in normal light (5%). Red light prevented germination. Eaglesham and Szalay (1983) improved germination by acid scarification. Individual seeds weigh about 11 mg. Seed pods are buoyant and dispersal is facilitated by moving water and possibly birds (Ridley 1930).

AGRICULTURAL IMPORTANCE

A. indica is reported to infest 10 crops in 35 countries (Figure 3-1), yet no data on competition losses in crops were found. It most frequently infests rice and is a serious or principal weed of rice in Cambodia, Ecuador, Korea, Madagascar, Sri Lanka and Thailand; is a common rice weed in Bangladesh, India, the Philippines, Senegal, and the southern United States; and infests rice in China, Colombia, Indonesia, Laos, Vietnam, and west Africa. It is a serious or principal weed of sorghum in India; maize in Thailand; pastures in Ecuador, Ghana, New Guinea and the Philippines; and soybeans in India.

It is a common weed of irrigated crops in Australia; soybeans and vegetables in the southern United States; and tobacco in the Philippines.

In addition, *A. indica* is a reported unranked weed of cassava and peanuts in Indonesia; coconut in Vietnam; legumes in the Philippines; maize in India, the Philippines and Thailand; millet in India; pastures in Australia, Guatemala and the United States; soybean in the southern United States; vegetables in Australia and the United States and wheat in Nepal.

It is not reported to host any economic insect or diseases, but a fungus, *Colletotrichum gloeosporioides*, virulently attacks a related species (*A. virginica*) in the southern United States. This phenomenon has been exploited commercially and a bioherbicide is available to selectively control *A. virginica* in rice and soybeans (Daniel et al. 1973). The researchers applied the fungus to *A. indica*. It infected and stunted plants, but the infection was not sufficient to kill plants.

The plant has value as a forage and green manure crop. It is a source of fodder for livestock in sandy, infertile soils and river edges of western Zambia (Allen and Allen 1981). It is particularly nutritious for browsing before the stems become woody. The seeds have 7% oil, which was relatively low among the 43 leguminous species tested (Gunstone et al. 1972). The oil composition is similar to that of cotton seed. In South Korea, two cuttings/yr of *A. indica* yielded 62 ton/ha fresh weight. This species fixed 2.8 to 5.6 times more N than soybean and total N content reached 4.7% in the stems and leaves at flowering (Jung et al. 1987).

In India the plant is used as fuel for firing pottery, to make floats, rafts and baskets for the fishing industry, and the charcoal is used for gunpowder and fireworks (Uphof 1968).

COMMON NAMES

Aeschynomene indica

FIJI	sensitive vetch
INDIA	bendukasa, kathshola, kottiram, nellittali, shola takkai, tiga jiluga
INDONESIA	katisan, peupeuteyan
JAPAN	kusanemu
PHILIPPINES	makahiyang lalaki, tagalog
THAILAND	sano haag kai
UNITED STATES	Indian jointvetch

Four

Alopecurus aequalis Sobol.

Poaceae (Gramineae), Grass Family

ALOPECURUS AEQUALIS is an annual grassy weed found in lowland areas of several temperate regions. In comparison to *A. myosuroides*, our knowledge of this species is quite limited. The genus name is derived from the Greek words *alopec* meaning fox, and *ouros* signifying tail and the species name suggests a symmetrical shape.

FIGURE 4-1　The distribution of *Alopecurus aequalis* Sobol. across the world where it has been reported as a weed.

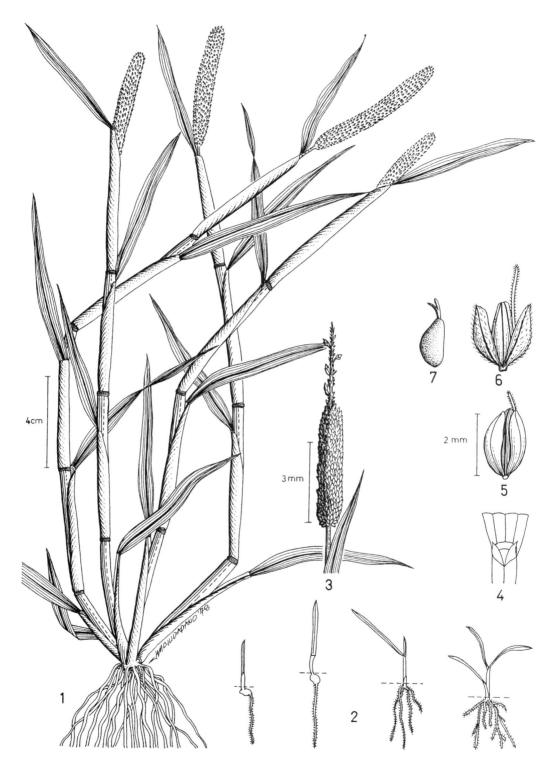

FIGURE 4-2 *Alopecurus aequalis* Sobol.: 1. habit; 2. seedling; 3. inflorescence; 4. upper portion of leaf sheath with ligule; 5. spikelet, 6. same, opened; 7. grain.

DESCRIPTION

A. aequalis (Figure 4-2) is an *annual* or *winter annual* grass; *roots* fibrous; *stems* tufted, 20 to 60 cm in height, smooth, erect or bent below and occasionally rooting from the nodes; *leaves* 5 to 12 cm long, shorter near plant base, 2 to 5 mm wide, smooth, sheaths somewhat inflated, blades flat; *ligule* membranous with margin entire, 2 to 5 mm long; *inflorescence* dense spike-like panicles, cylindrical, 3 to 8 cm long, 3 to 6 mm wide, yellowish green; *glumes* 3-veined, outer one covered with appressed hairs, obtuse, awnless, 2 to 2.5 mm long, united at base; *lemma* equal to glume in length, membranous, glabrous except for 5 nerves covered with hairs; *awn* attached just below lemma middle, short, almost hidden, extending 1 mm or less beyond the glumes, straight or slightly bent; *anthers* 1 mm long, bright orange to golden yellow when dry; *fruit* a 1-seeded, dry, indehiscent *caryopsis* or grain, 2.3 to 2.9 mm long, no prominent callus at base; glumes, lemma, and awn persistent.

The distinguishing characteristics of this plant are the bright orange anthers, the short awn arising from the lower part of the lemma, long hairs on the glume nerves, and seed without callus at the base.

HABITAT AND BIOLOGY

This species is common in shallow lakes, marshes, swamps, and bogs as well as the banks of streams and rivers, poorly drained sites and roadsides. It is abundant before plowing in land to be planted to rice in Japan, where it is one of the most serious winter annual weeds of both lowland and upland crops. It is a major rice weed in Nepal to 1900 m. Noda et al. (1965) found 474 seedlings/m^2 in well-drained soils and 36,800 seedlings/m^2 in very poorly drained soils.

A. aequalis has been most thoroughly studied in Japan, where it is one of the most abundant weeds in lowland fields after rice harvest. It behaves as a winter annual and flowers from March to May. Two ecotypes exist in Japan (Matumura 1967). Seeds of the lowland type are 2.9 mm long and weight 45 mg/100 seeds, while those of the upland type are 2.3 mm in length and weigh only 18 mg/100 seeds. The lowland type flowers earlier (April 12) than the upland type (April 21) and is a long-day to day-neutral plant, while the upland type is only a long-day plant. Since these differences were consistent between biotypes collected at 15 upland and lowland locations, they are probably genetically controlled. Matumura proposes that *A. aequalis* var. *amurensis* be used to designate the lowland type (predominant in East Asia) and *A. aequalis* be applied to the upland biotype that is also found in other temperate regions of the world.

The most extensive studies on *A. aequalis* var. *amurensis* have been done by Arai and co-workers (1956a,b; 1958, 1959, 1960, 1961a,b). A comprehensive summary of their work on the life cycle, ecology, seed biology, and competition was published by Arai (1961). Viable seeds occur within 15 to 20 days after heading. Freshly harvested seed is dormant for 3 to 4 mo after harvest. The seed coat neither causes dormancy nor prevents imbibition. Freezing does not break dormancy, but 40% of the seeds in a moist environment at 1 to 5°C for 1 to 2 wk germinated at 20°C. Seeds germinate between 5 and 30°C with an optimum germination temperature of 20°C. Seeds can germinate in media with *pH*s from 4.5 to 7.5. Nearly 40% of the seed collected in the northern United States in July germinated by fall (Hoffman et al. 1980). Seed overwintered outdoors germinated up to 62% if kept moist during the winter and 82% if kept dry. Germination is higher in the light than in darkness.

Matumura (1967) noted variation in germination behavior between upland and lowland biotypes. The lowland type has more pronounced dormancy and higher germination percentages after storage. Low oxygen levels and temperatures of 30 to 35°C in wet soil break seed dormancy. Arai (1961) speculates that these conditions present during paddy rice production break *A. aequalis* dormancy and account for its subsequent abundance in winter crops or fallowed paddy fields.

Seeds are killed in compost (Arai et al. 1958) but can be disseminated in irrigation water. Kelley and Bruns (1975) collected 8.8 seeds/254 kl of water flowing in irrigation canals in the western United States. Seventy nine percent of the seeds germinated.

Seeds can germinate under flooded conditions but the optimum soil moisture for germination is about 80% (Arai 1961). Coarse seedbeds reduce the number of *A. aequalis* seedlings by 60% as compared to a fine seedbed. Seedlings emerge from greater depths in moist than in dry soils. Peak emergence in Japan occurs around mid-December (Noda et al. 1965). Seedlings emerge over a 40-day period, most coming from 0 to 0.7 cm. Most of the roots develop in the upper 10 cm of soil.

In a 10-yr study, Millar (1973) found soil disturbance essential to *A. aequalis* appearance in Canadian wetlands. Disturbance could be due to animal burrowing activity, die-off of other species, cultivation, or livestock trampling. Two years of continuous flooding caused the species to disappear. Disturbance must be regular for this plant to persist in nature. Reducing the light 50% 2 wk before heading had little effect on the weed's development. At 80% shade, the number of seed heads and viable seeds were reduced and maturity was delayed (Aria 1961).

There is a close correlation between low soil P levels and the absence of *A. aequalis* in rice fields of Korea (Shin 1963). No plants were found in fields with an average of 20 ppm available P_2O_5 but they were abundant when the levels were 78 ppm. Soil *pH* and level of K, Ca and Na did not affect the weed's distribution. Morishima and Oka (1980) used the lowland biotype to study *A. aequalis* tolerance to soil copper levels near copper mines. The weed was found in soils with *pH*s of 5.3 and copper levels up to 122 ppm. Plants growing in fields with high copper levels had high survival rates over the winter. At 50 ppm Cu and higher, *A. aequalis* became the dominant species. Copper tolerant types were found among populations growing in nonpolluted fields, suggesting that shifts to tolerant biotypes would be rapid if contamination occurred. Typhoons occasionally flood rice fields with salt water. Seeds of some weeds common in rice fields are not injured by flooding with salt water for 30 to 50 days. When the soil chloride level dropped to 0.2 to 0.3%, *A. aequalis* germinated and it was then safe to plant rice (Kurauchi 1956).

This species has a *2n* chromosome count of 14 and the lowest pollen-to-ovule ratios of the six *Alopecurus* species studied (Sieber and Murray 1979). They call the weed a "facultative outbreeder," meaning that cross-pollination occurs but that plants can self-pollinate for several generations before deleterious inbreeding effects are apparent.

AGRICULTURAL IMPORTANCE

A. aequalis is reported as a weed of 10 crops in 27 countries (Figure 4-1) and is most serious in rice and cereals. Nearly all references to it as a weed come from Asia, but it is also found in Europe, North America, and the former Soviet Union. In Japan it is the most serious weed of barley, rape, rye, winter wheat, and other winter season crops. It is a principal weed of rice in Japan, Nepal, and the Philippines; and is reported to infest rice in China, Hungary, and Taiwan. It is a serious or principal weed of barley in Korea; potatoes, rape, vegetables, and wheat in Taiwan; and wheat in China. It is a common weed of barley, oats and wheat in Canada; and vineyards in Turkey. It infests cereals in Finland and Turkey; winter season crops, flax, and tobacco in Taiwan; and vegetables in China. It also infests aquatic habitats in Bulgaria, New Zealand, and the United States.

The competitive effects of *A. aequalis* with barley and wheat are most serious during the jointing stage (Arai 1961). There is a nearly perfect negative correlation between weed biomass and wheat and barley production. The weed can host the southern root-knot nematode (*Meloidogyne incognita*) and the rice leafhopper (*Nephotettix cinticeps*) (Bendixen et al. 1979, 1981).

COMMON NAMES

Alopecurus aequalis

CANADA	short-awned foxtail, vulpin a courtes aretes
ENGLAND	orange foxtail, short awn foxtail
FRANCE	vulpin fauve
GERMANY	Rotgelber Fuchschwanz
JAPAN	suzumeno-teppo
NEW ZEALAND	orange foxtail
UNITED STATES	short awn foxtail

Five

Alopecurus myosuroides Huds.

Poaceae (Gramineae), Grass Family

A LOPECURUS MYOSUROIDES is one of the most serious grass weeds in cereal fields of western Europe. Its winter annual growth habit is ideally adapted to winter cereal production; recent crop management changes to earlier fall planting and continuous cereal production have led to rapid increases in *A. myosuroides* populations. It is native to Europe and the Mediterranean region and, interestingly, is most abundant and serious in its center of origin.

FIGURE 5-1 The distribution of *Alopecurus myosuroides* Huds. across the world where it has been reported as a weed.

FIGURE 5-2 *Alopecurus myosuroides* Huds.: 1. habit; 2. lemma; 3. glumes; 4. pistil; 5. floret.

DESCRIPTION

A. myosuroides (Figure 5-2) is an *annual* or *winter annual* tufted grass with shallow fibrous *roots*; *stems* slender, erect to decumbent at the base, 20 to 75 cm tall and sometimes purplish; *leaves* linear-lanceolate, smooth, flat, and pointed, 5 to 15 cm long, 2 to 8 mm wide; *ligule* obtuse, membranous, 2 to 4 mm long, fringed with hairs; *inflorescence* a spike-like panicle somewhat tapering at each end, 4 to 10 cm in length, 3 to 5 mm wide; *spikelets* 4 to 7 mm long, strongly compressed laterally; *glumes* pointed, 4 to 5 mm long, white with 3 green nerves, ciliated on keel and united at base; *lemma* 4- or 5-nerved, equal in size to glumes with a twisted *awn* 5 to 8 mm long from its base; *palea* absent; *fruit* a 1-seeded, dry, indehiscent *caryopsis*, ovoid, yellowish, 1 mm wide, 2 to 3 mm long, callus at base large, thick and conspicuous; glumes, awn, and lemma remain attached to caryopsis.

The distinguishing characteristics of *A. myosuroides* are its membranous ligule fringed with hairs, the "fox tail" style of inflorescence and the twisted awn arising from the base of the lemma.

HABITAT AND DISTRIBUTION

A. myosuroides (Figure 5-1) is abundant in the cereal fields of England, France, Germany, and many other European countries. Its history as a weed dates to the Neolithic times of 5000 to 1800 B.C. when it was a weed in emmer and one-grained wheat (Moss 1980c). It appears to be most serious in oceanic and suboceanic climates where the mean July temperatures are above 15°C and annual rainfall is below 1020 mm. In England, it is not found over 300 m above sea level (Salisbury 1964) and was originally found in poorly drained, heavy textured soils. Changes in cropping practices and the elimination of broadleaf weed competition in cereals with herbicides have allowed this weed to invade well-drained and lighter soils as well. Barralis (1968) observed that *A. myosuroides'* presence is linked to human activities and it is never far from cultivated land. Interestingly, while found in most regions of the United States, it is not an important weed, even in areas of intensive winter cereal production.

BIOLOGY

A. myosuroides has been investigated by many researchers and its biology is well understood. Since it is most serious in winter cereal production, most of the growth and development studies have been done in the temperate-climate cereal regions of Europe.

Seeds germinate in the late summer and early fall, although some may germinate in the spring as well. When wet fall weather occurs, germination is prolific; in relatively dry fall seasons, fall and spring germination levels are similar (Stryckers and Delputte 1965). Ninety percent of the seeds germinate in the upper 2.5 to 5 cm of soil (Naylor 1970, Moss 1981a) and seedling emergence is best in soil temperatures of 13 to 24°C (Barralis 1968). Seedlings are killed by soil disturbance. While over 3000 seedlings/m² have been observed (Wellington and Hitchings 1965), the most productive plant population is 400 plants/m² and dense seedling populations will naturally adjust to about this level through intraspecific competition (Moss 1980b). If the fall population is 100 plants/m² or more, it remains constant until spring; fall populations higher than this level are usually lower by spring (Moss 1981a, 1987a).

Time of germination significantly affects early plant development. Seeds germinated without competition on August 20 in England formed plants with 98 tillers each by December and 85 in February. Seeds germinated on October 16, December 12, and February 5 formed plants with 50 tillers when mature, and spring-germinated plants had 60 to 85 tillers each at maturity. Plants initiated in August flowered from mid-April to late May. All others flowered during May and June. Only plants started in August produced tillers that fall (Wellington and Hitchings 1966). When competing with cereals, plants that emerge in the fall vary in their stage of development. Most have one to two tillers by winter; others may have four or five tillers or only one to three leaves (Wellington and Hitchings 1965). In France, plants with fewer than three leaves are killed by temperatures of −10°C or less. Fully tillered plants can survive temperatures of −25°C (Barralis 1968).

A. myosuroides that germinates in the spring in fall sown wheat, does not flower (Stryckers and van Himme 1972). However, in the absence of competition, spring plants catch up to fall germinated plants. Plants growing between rows produce more tillers than those growing in the row.

Tillering begins when plants are in the 3- to 4-leaf stage. The number of tillers per plant varies according to the crop and weed density. When grown alone, plants can produce 150 seed heads; in a dense crop, perhaps only a single head/plant is formed (Moss 1980c). Usually 2 to 12 heads/plant are formed. Both spring and fall tillers may form on the same plant.

Anthesis begins at the apex of the seed head and proceeds downward over a 7- to 10-day period. *A. myosuroides* is self-incompatible and is wind pollinated, with a 2*n* chromosome count of 14. Sieber and Murray (1979) consider it an obligate outbreeder. Of the six *Alopecurus* species they studied, this one had the highest pollen to ovule ratio, assuring ample pollen for cross-pollination.

Seeds (caryopsis plus the attached glumes and lemma) are shed 13 to 30 days after flowering. Secondary shoots may arise on some tillers, but 80 to 90% of the seed is produced by primary tillers (Wellington and Hitchings 1966). Plants that germinate in August, October, December, and March produce about the same number of seeds. There are fewer heads formed in the later germinating plants, but each one is denser and longer than those in plants that germinate in August.

Moss (1981b) studied *A. myosuroides* populations at 14 sites in England and found that head length varied from 69.6 to 89.4 mm, seed number from 80 to 124/head, seeds/mm of head from 1.09 to 1.43 and viability from 49 to 77%. Seed production ranged from 31,500 to 77,000/m². In winter wheat in England, over 95% of the weed's seed is shed before harvest; barley is harvested earlier and thus only 50% of the seed had dropped when harvested. Since 70% of the seeds drop from mid-July to mid-August, Moss (1983) estimated that 180 to 300 million seeds/ha would be harvested in barley and many fewer in wheat. In Germany, cutting wheat with a binder before threshing resulted in 75% of the *A. myosuroides* seed being harvested with the crop. If left to dry in the field and then combine harvested, 68% of the weed seed had dropped (Petzold 1959).

Naylor (1972c) and Thurston (1972a) also report considerable variation in tillering and seed production. Seeds produced may be as few as 100 to over 7500/plant. Plants present at harvest may range from 10- to 30-wk old. As many as 50% of the spikelets lack viable seed. This could be caused by poor pollination, damage from the insect *Contarinia mereci*, or ergot (*Claviceps purpurea*). Seed weight is 1.3 mg/caryopsis, but it may vary 2.5-fold between the lightest and heaviest. Naylor (1972c) found 23,000 seeds/m² in the soil.

Fresh seed has a 4- to 6-wk after-ripening period giving the plant its winter annual habit. Germination of fresh seed is enhanced by removing the glumes and lemma and treating with gibberellic acid (Koch 1968). Seeds that remain dormant beyond the after-ripening period, germinate if the glumes are removed (Wellington and Hitchings 1966). Less primary dormancy occurs in seeds harvested later in the season. Ten to 20% of the seeds have a long primary dormancy. Alternating temperatures help break this dormancy (Wellington and Hitchings 1965). High temperatures during the ripening period result in seeds with shorter dormancy periods, while seeds formed during moist conditions have a longer dormancy than seeds produced under dry conditions (Thurston 1972a). The optimum temperature for germination is 15 to 20°C, the minimum is 2 to 5°C and the maximum is 30°C (Koch 1970). *A. myosuroides* requires 4.5 to 8% oxygen to reach 75% germination (Mullverstedt 1963a).

Germination can vary greatly between populations and seasons, assuring the presence of some *A. myosuroides* each year. Moss (1983) reported fewer viable seeds produced early in the season than later in the season, and Wellington and Hitchings (1966) obtained 32 to 67% germination from three populations collected within 10 km. The variation in the amount of dormant seed from plants may be genetically controlled (Thurston 1972b). Light usually stimulates germination but seeds can germinate in the dark as well. Red light enhances seed germination (Froud-Williams 1981). Seeds exhibit a cyclic germination pattern with high germination in autumn and spring and low germination in summer even in favorable conditions (Froud-Williams et al. 1984b).

Maximum germination occurs in soils at field capacity (Barralis 1968) and seed survival is greater at 10 to 18 cm than at 2.5 cm, in sand than in peat or loam soils, and in flooded than in non-flooded soils (Lewis 1961). Seeds in saturated soil become dormant and do not immediately germinate when removed from saturated soil. Dormancy was not induced in seeds when the water table was 7.5 cm below the seeds (Rothamsted Experiment Station 1963). Lewis (1973) buried *A. myosuroides* seeds at three depths in a loam and peat soil. Few seeds survived even 1 yr in peat, but survival was 22, 10, and 53% after 4 yr in a mineral soil at 13, 26, and 39 cm, respectively. Some seeds survived for 10 yr after burial. Plant populations in the field are not always correlated with seed reservoirs in the soil.

Seed survival in the soil is greater in no-tillage than tillage systems. Seed populations decline rapidly in tilled fields, with less than 5% of the original population remaining after 3 yr. Most seed loss occurred in the summer and early fall months in England (Moss 1985, 1987a). However, because some seeds live up to 10 yr, attempts to eradicate *A. myosuroides* are unlikely to succeed.

Thurston (1964) studied the effect of mineral nutrition of the plant on its growth, seed production, and seed germination. Fertilized plants produced three times as much biomass as plants in unfertilized soil. Seed from unfertilized plants, however, had a 70% germination rate and those from fertilized plants a 50% rate. Wellington and Hitchings (1966) monitored the development of viable seed after flowering. Seven percent of the seeds harvested in the milk stage and with the glumes removed germinated after 6 wk. Thus even apparently immature seed heads may contain viable seed. Four percent of the seed collected in the dough stage germinated with the glumes removed when fresh and 13% after 6 wk. Once the seeds were past the dough stage, they matured normally. A comprehensive review of the biology of this species was prepared by Thurston (1972a).

COMPETITION AND CONTROL

Competitive losses in cereal yield often occur in the fall season. Fall removal of *A. myosuroides* increases wheat yields more than spring removal (North and Livingston 1970, Wilson 1979). Spring herbicide applications gave only 63% of the yield increase of fall treatments and partial *A. myosuroides* control early was more beneficial than higher levels of control later in the season.

Naylor (1970) in England attempted to devise a method to predict the densities of *A. myosuroides*. Soil samples were brought into the greenhouse and the emergence of the weed in the sampled fields and greenhouse was monitored. The correlations were sufficient so that the "predictive index" could be used to predict when control would be necessary. However, Moss (1979) found that the April plant population of *A. myosuroides* could not be predicted from the November seed population in the soil.

Because several effective postemergence herbicides control *A. myosuroides*, it is feasible to use thresholds to determine if treatment is necessary. However, results vary considerably between researchers and more than just weed density must be considered to arrive at an economic threshold. *A. myosuroides* densities less than 20 to 30 plants/m^2 generally do not reduce cereal yields (Guillement 1972; Naylor 1972a,b; Nieman 1979; Moss 1980c). Moss (1980c) suggests 50 plants/m^2 justify spraying, but also acknowledges that crop vigor affects the tillering capacity of *A. myosuroides*, which makes thresholds difficult to use reliably. For example, he found that 200 plants/m^2 can reduce yields by 20%, while Naylor (1972b) observed a 32% yield loss with 100 plants/m^2. Thresholds in areas of continuous cereal production may be of little value because infested fields have an abundance of *A. myosuroides*. Widdowson et al. (1980) were forced to abandon agronomic studies in continuous wheat due to interference from this species. Yield losses became significant after the tenth year even though herbicides were used.

Nitrogen appears to be the primary element involved in competition between *A. myosuroides* and cereals. The weed absorbs nearly the same levels of N, P, and K as wheat and barley when grown separately in nutrient solutions, and reduces the N level in rye, wheat and maize leaves when grown together in the field (Koch and Kocher 1968). While *A. myosuroides* responds to N fertilization, the competitive ability of cereals is greatest at optimum N levels (Welbank 1963, Naylor 1972a, Thurston 1972b). The number of cereal heads per unit area is reduced more than other parameters. The moisture content of the harvested grain increases as the density of *A. myosuroides* increases (Nieman 1979).

The weed emerges one to four weeks after the fall cereal is seeded. Studies in Germany have shown that in the early stages of crop growth, wheat is taller than *A. myosuroides*. Thus competition for light is not an important factor in yield loss. After tillering, the weed's development equals and may exceed that of wheat and at flowering it is taller than wheat (Koch and Rademacher 1966). This plant is less competitive on light textured and well-drained soils (Nieman 1979, Moss 1980c). *A. myosuroides* may emerge in spring sown cereals but yield losses seldom occur.

Cultural practices affect the competitiveness of *A. myosuroides*. Spring cereal seeding has been cited as one means to avoid yield losses. Fall seeding dates also influence this weed's competitive ability. Later fall plantings allow additional soil tillage to destroy emerged plants and delay planting until after the optimum time of *A. myosuroides* germination (Naylor 1972c). However, the current trend in England and other European countries is to plant cereals from late-September to mid-October rather than late-October to mid-November (Moss 1980c). The near elimination of broadleaf weed competition can allow *A. myosuroides* to become the dominant species (Koch 1964).

Straw management and tillage greatly influence the seedbank population of *A. myosuroides* and these factors have been thoroughly studied by researchers in England (Pollard and Cussans 1976, Pollard et al. l982, Moss 1979, 1980a,b,c; 1981a, 1987a). Plowing reduces the *A. myosuroides* population more than tine cultivation or zero tillage systems. Moss (1981a) planted 1500 *A. myosuroides* seeds/m^2 in a non-infested field in 1975. Tine cultivation allowed a 26-fold increase in seed population from 1976 to 1978. As many as 100 seed heads/m^2 with 150,000 seeds were produced under tine cultivation. Pollard and Cussans (1976) also found that tine cultivation gave more *A. myosuroides* plants than plowing or no tillage.

In a simulated field study, Mullverstedt (1963b) placed seeds 5 cm deep in a sieved (2.5 mm) soil and cultivated to 10 cm with tines spaced 3 cm apart. Eighteen percent of the seeds moved upward, 10% downward and the rest remained at 5 cm. A second harrowing moved seeds even further from the original depth.

Seeds can remain dormant for more than one year. When seeds were buried by fall plowing and no new seeds were produced the following season, summer plowing the following year caused many *A. myosuroides* seedlings to emerge. Without tillage, most seedlings emerge the season the seeds are produced. Plants in tilled areas form more tillers than plants in non-tilled fields. Two seasons of fallowing the land can reduce the seed population by 95% of the original level, but if cereals are planted, a rapid buildup of the seed reservoir occurs.

Burning cereal straw destroys many more *A. myosuroides* seeds than baling, but the seed population increases even with annual burning (Moss 1981a). Burning increases *A. myosuroides* germination at 2 mm below the surface but not at greater depths, perhaps by breaking dormancy. In a detailed burning study, Moss (1980b) found that the peak temperature was achieved 20 to 30 sec after the initial temperature increase. Temperatures in the burning swath reach 700 to 800°C while, at 2 to 3 mm below the soil surface, temperatures never exceed 60°C. Seeds on the surface are destroyed, but minimal soil cover is sufficient to give protection. Imbibed seeds are less affected by burning than dry seeds. In the fall, the number of seeds in areas where the straw was baled can be 16 times higher than in areas where burning was done. Seeds added to burned sites had higher germination percentages than seeds placed in baled areas. Burning and then plowing mask the effect of burning since more seeds are brought to the soil surface, but the seed reservoir is reduced, and straw burning should be integrated into control programs when feasible.

In a long-term control study, *A. myosuroides* populations increased from 172 plants/m^2 to over 1000 in five seasons of winter wheat (Roebuck 1972). Yield in the uncontrolled areas declined three-fold, while annual applications of effective herbicides increased yield 39% compared to non-treated plots. Wheat treated with herbicides every other year was highly infested with the weed in the years without treatment, but even in these years it yielded 20% more than plots that were never treated. Biological control of *A. myosuroides* is unlikely to succeed since it is most serious in its center of origin and no indigenous pests have reduced its competitiveness or spread. For an excellent review on *A. myosuroides* control, see Moss (1980c).

Biotypes of *A. myosuroides* resistant to methibenzuron in the Netherlands, to chlorotoluron and isoproturon in the United Kingdom, and to triazines in Czechoslovakia and Israel have been reported. Thirty-eight seed lots of *A. myosuroides* were collected in fields that had received repeated applications of chlorotoluron or isoproturon. Testing for resistance to chlorotoluron found that six lots were resistant, nine were intermediate (25 to 75% control at normal rates), and 23 were susceptible (Moss 1987b).

AGRICULTURAL IMPORTANCE

A. myosuroides is a reported weed of 23 crops in 37 countries (Figure 5-1) and is most important in European cereals, where it is as serious as *Avena fatua*. In England, for example, 19% of the winter cereal fields were infested with this weed (Froud-Williams and Chancellor 1982). Interestingly, it is not an important weed in other temperate regions of the world.

It is a serious or principal weed of barley in France and Iran; cereals in Belgium, Bulgaria, Denmark, England, Germany, Hungary, Italy, the Netherlands, Sweden, and Turkey; wheat in Iran and Turkey; and winter wheat in Belgium, England, France, and Italy. It is a serious or principal weed of field beets in Belgium; edible beans and carrots in England; citrus in Lebanon; peas and rape in France; potatoes in Belgium; sugar beets in Belgium, France, Germany, and the Netherlands; and vegetables in England.

It is a common weed of barley in England; beets in Germany; cereals in Austria and the former Yugoslavia; peas in the Netherlands; rape in Germany; rice in Turkey; and wheat in Greece and Israel.

Also *A. myosuroides* is reported as an unranked weed of barley in Belgium, Bulgaria, Germany, the Netherlands, Saudi Arabia, and Spain; edible beans in Germany; beets and carrots in Belgium; cereals in France, Greece, Poland, the former Soviet Union, and Switzerland; clover, pasture and sugar beets in England; cotton in Iraq; flax in Belgium and France; lucerne in Italy, Spain, and the United States; legumes and oats in Belgium; maize in France and Germany; onions in Jordan and the Netherlands; orchards in Italy; peas in Belgium and Germany; oil seed rape in England, the Netherlands, and Sweden; rye in Germany and Sweden; rice in China and the southern United States; vegetables in France; wheat in Iraq, Jordan, Saudi Arabia, and Spain; and winter wheat in Germany, the Netherlands, and Sweden.

A. myosuroides infests over 66% of the fields in some regions of England and, in the entire country, 650,000 ha of cereals are infested. Over half the fields have more than 625 seeds/m^2 to a 15-cm depth and over 20% have more than 5000 seeds/m^2 (Roberts and Chancellor 1986).

Seeds of *A. myosuroides* often occur as a contaminant of harvested forage seeds and grains. Surveys in England have found 2 to 3% of the legume seeds and 4 to 14% of the pasture grass seeds to be contaminated. In 1969, over 2400 ha of seed crops were rejected at harvest due to the abundance of this weed. This represented 65% of all the rejections that year. Tonkin (1968b) surveyed four cereals for 7 yr in England and found 2.2% of the harvested barley and 2.8% of the wheat contained *A. myosuroides* seed. There were no trends toward less contamination over the period. The number of seeds/225 g of cereal varied from 1 to 402 for wheat and 1 to 569 for barley. From 6 to 19% of the forage grass seed samples were contaminated in 1960–61, but this declined to 3 to 10% 7 yr later. Wellington (1957) calculated that the legal limit of 0.5% contamination in orchardgrass seed, if sown at 8 kg/ha, gives 50,000 *A. myosuroides* seeds/ha. In cereals, a 1% level of contamination would result in 17 seeds/m^2 of this weed (Sagar and Mortimer 1976). If consumed by cattle, viable seeds are excreted in the droppings (Salisbury 1964).

A. myosuroides is an excellent host for ergot, a potentially serious wheat disease. Mantle and Shaw (1977) took isolates of *Claviceps purpurea* from *A. myosuroides* and found an alkaloid spectrum very similar to the ergot in wheat and the isolates belong to the highly infective group of ergots. Cross-pollinated grasses like *A. myosuroides* are more susceptible to ergot as their stigmas are more exposed than those of self-pollinated species. Because the grass weed matures earlier than wheat, the sclerotia from ergot exude honey-dew that can be easily spread to flowering wheat by rain splashes, especially since both plants are at the same height and because its flowering time is ideally suited to the spread of ergot to wheat. Therefore, *A. myosuroides* is considered the most important alternate host of ergot in wheat. Effective control of this weed would reduce the reservoir of ergot inoculum in the soil and would limit ergot epidemics in wheat.

This grass can also host diseases such as *Gaeumannomyces graminus*, *Puccinia graminis*, *P. coronata*, and *Cercosperella herpotrichoides*; and the aphids *Macrosiphon granarum* and *Aphis avenae* (Thurston 1972a).

COMMON NAMES

Alopecurus myosuroides

AUSTRALIA	slender foxtail
BELGIUM	duist, vulpin des champs
CHINA	kan-mai-nion
DENMARK	ager-raevehale
ENGLAND	blackgrass, slender foxtail
FINLAND	rikkapuntarpaa
FRANCE	vulpin des champs
GERMANY	Acker-Fuchsschwanzgras
GREECE	aleponoura
ITALY	amaranto, erba codina
LEBANON	mousetail grass, slender foxtail
NETHERLANDS	duist
NEW ZEALAND	blackgrass
NORWAY	akerreverumpe
POLAND	wyczyniec polny
PORTUGAL	rabo de raposa
SPAIN	alopecuro, cola de zorra, cola de rata
SWEDEN	renkavle
SWITZERLAND	fuchsschwanz, mauseschwanz-ahnlicher, vupin des champs
TAIWAN	ta-suei-khan-mai-tsao
TURKEY	tilki kuyrugu
UNITED STATES	pacific meadow foxtail, slender foxtail
YUGOSLAVIA	misji repak, njivni lisicjirep

Six

Alternanthera philoxeroides (Mart.) Griseb.

Amaranthaceae, Amaranth Family

ALTERNANTHERA PHILOXEROIDES (alligatorweed) is a much-feared weed of waterways across the world. It can quickly send floating stems more than 15 m across the water from an anchored shore infestation. It is generally found within the thermal tropics or the mild regions of the temperate zones. It is best known as an aquatic weed but it is also found in several of man's cultivated crops and in pastures. It is a problem weed of 10 crops in 30 countries.

FIGURE 6-1   The distribution of *Alternanthera philoxeroides* (Mart.) Griseb. across the world where it has been reported as a weed.

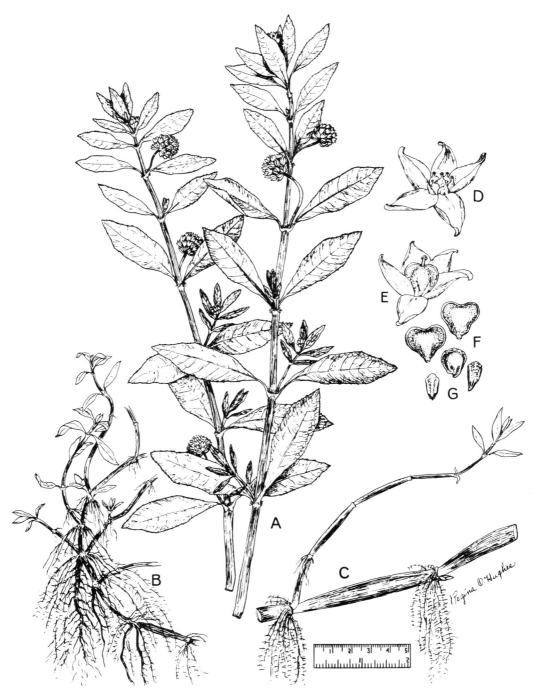

FIGURE 6-2 *Alternanthera philoxeroides* (Mart.) Griseb.: A. habit; B. roots and seedling; C. part of aquatic growth, new shoot from rooting node; D. flower; E. persistent chaffy flower with the single mature achene; F. achenes; G. seeds.

DESCRIPTION

A. philoxeroides (Figure 6-2) is a *perennial* aquatic or semi-terrestrial marshy herb, decumbent, stoloniferous, or ascending from a creeping or floating rooted base, mat-forming *adventitious roots* develop at most nodes; *stems* much branched, forming dense masses in water or occasionally on shore, hollow, longitudinally striate, with a longitudinal hairy groove on two opposite sides of internodes, otherwise glabrous; *leaves* opposite, glabrous, entire, thin, lanceolate, oblong to narrowly obovate, rounded or acute, latter may be tipped with tiny spine, base cuneate, distinct midrib below, 9 cm long x 1.5 cm wide; *petioles* 1 to 6 mm; *inflorescence* a several flowered whitish head, axillary or terminal on branches, their stalks to at least 5.5 cm, 1.5 mm thick; *perianth* almost sessile above, *bracteoles* dorsally compressed, shining white, glabrous, 4.5 to 8 mm long; *stamens* 5, united into a tube that bears *stamens* and *staminodia* alternately on upper rim; one *style*, one *stigma* capitate, papillate, cylindrical, globose, glandular; *fruit* a 1-seeded *utricle* falling off with perianth, often before maturity.

The two grooves of hairs on the internodes and the hollow stems are characteristics that aid in the recognition of this species.

DISTRIBUTION AND HABITAT

A. philoxeroides (Figure 6-1) is a troublesome weed in eastern Australia and New Zealand, is widespread in south and east Asia, is in southern Europe and east and west Africa, and inhabits many regions of the Americas between latitude 35° North and South.

About 50 years ago we became aware that it was traveling widely in Asia and had moved south to Australia. The plant grows best in aquatic sites but may establish as a terrestrial species in wet and poor pastures and in irrigated lands. Julien and Bourne (1988) reported that *A. philoxeroides* is rapidly invading pastures and waterways in 15 coastal areas of New South Wales.

The weed prefers level areas of shore or shallow water where it is protected from wave erosion. As with many weeds, it thrives in eutrophic conditions and thus often increases where urban and industrial development have polluted and degraded water quality. Severe storms may strip the leaves from anchored mats or tear the tangled vegetation loose and move it to a new location.

In the United States, Australia, India, and South America the plant is most troublesome in warm regions but it can adapt to a variety of microclimates and may therefore appear in colder regions where its growth is slowed, the leaves are killed by frost, but with winter survival of roots and some stems. In severe winters there is perennation by the underground roots and stems.

This plant requires a moist habitat. In terrestrial sites rainfall is important for flooding and keeping groundwater levels high. Terrestrial plants of this species may remain under water for several days without ill effects. When the plant has become established in areas at maximum water levels, it creeps over debris toward open water, out onto the water, and forms mats with its prostrate stems. In a set of measurements made by Penfound (1940) in the central United States, new shoots appeared in mid-March, were 40 cm long 6 wk later and 63 cm long at 8 wk. The stems were 150 cm long at 11 wk (anthesis) and at 22 wk, the plant had formed a mat that was 5 m^2.

In Australia the weed grows mainly on red podzolic soils and in sand and silt deposits in river systems. As elsewhere, the plant prefers fresh water but is found along the inland tidal reaches of rivers that run to the sea. Permanent stands may be found in the upper tidal areas with semi-permanent stands at intermediate distances from the sea. Plants surviving at higher salt concentrations are usually on mats that had broken loose and were pushed toward the sea. Burkhalter et al. (1972) and Hockley (1974) found that *A. philoxeroides* tolerates salt water of about 10% sea strength in quiet areas, but 30% in areas that are flowing. The plant is more tolerant of saline conditions than water hyacinth (*Eichhornia crassipes*).

In summary, alligatorweed probably grows in a wider range of water and soil conditions than any other major aquatic weed, and therein lies its danger for man's activities. Its growth is equally startling whether free floating, loosely attached and forming a mat, or as an emersed plant in a wet or relatively dry field. It loves fresh water of high fertility but can tolerate saline soils and waters.

PROPAGATION

A. philoxeroides flowers profusely in several areas of the world. In the temperate zones, flowers are produced from mid-summer to late fall. They are polygamous for male, female, and perfect flowers can be found on the same spike. Inflorescences can be found on horizontal floating stems as well as on vertical shoots. Many tiny white flowers arise on heads that are at the tips of terminal shoots or are on long, straight peduncles in the axils of the uppermost leaves. Gangstad and Solymosy (1973) suggest that pollination occurs only at night, or on cloudy days, by night-flying or heliophobic pollinators.

Most students and observers of alligatorweed do not believe, however, that viable seed is produced in the field. In Australia, Java, and the United States, areas long troubled by the weed, no seedlings have ever been reported (Mitchell 1978, Penfound 1940). Penfound reported finding ovaries with immature seeds in the field. Gangstad and Solymosy (1973) collected field seed and obtained germination by extracting the utricle, a small, bladdery, 1-seeded, indehiscent fruit found in some amaranths. It is often reported that the pistil does not produce fruit and simply falls with the flower before plant maturity. Aranha et al. (1980), in the São Paulo region of Brazil, reported that this weed reproduces by seeds and stolons on lowland soils.

Julien and Broadbent (1980) have recently reviewed the vegetative propagation of this species. Perhaps the one most important advantage it has is the rapid growth of the hollow stems to form mats that can be torn loose by storms, or lifted and dislodged by high water levels, to free them for movement to new sites where they colonize new areas. Or the mats may be torn into many fragments, each capable of securing a new area. The mats are quite self-sufficient and can overcome most competitors. Stem fragments with one node can begin a new plant system.

The biomass of the plant in Florida, in the United States, doubled (in the field) in about 50 days in summer (Brown 1973). In excess of 1000 stems/m^2 may develop in the field but not all develop into long stems. At all stem nodes there are two viable axillary buds. The following types of plant material produced roots and shoots when wholly or partially inserted into wet sand: mat stems, emergent leaf-bearing stems, buried stems with thickened nodes, new shoots developing from underground stems, and root material from the soil (unpublished data of Julien and Broadbent).

Quimby (1974) studied the influence of environmental factors on bud break by exposing emersed and submerged nodes to light or darkness, aeration, a nitrogen atmosphere, and the addition of sucrose. The emersed nodes were not affected by light, darkness, or a cold treatment of 17 days at 2 to 4°C. An atmosphere of 100% nitrogen completely inhibited bud break in darkness. Submerged nodes responded only in light, cold treatments had no effect, and a 5% sucrose solution inhibited shoot growth 65% in the light. The dark suppression of bud break was not relieved by aeration or sucrose. The author believes all this confirms and helps to explain why inundation by turbid waters greatly inhibits shoot initiation and growth of rooted alligatorweed along the margins of water bodies.

A. philoxeroides is a decussate plant in which the opposite bud primordia in the leaf axils are of unequal size from the time of inception. The larger buds are arranged on one helix and the smaller on another in the helicoidal system. They do not grow out with equal vigor, even after decapitation of the supporting stem growth. If the stem is slit vertically the bud growth is equal (Cutter 1972). The author suggests the regulation of the bud break is due to the normal apical dominance as well as the dominance in size by the larger bud over the smaller.

Quimby and Kay 1977 also found that if mats become too thick all growth below will stop. Growth resumes if top mat layers are disturbed to allow light to enter.

To provide material for experimental work, Hardcastle (1958) cut terminals of alligatorweed under water in the field, and placed them in jars of soil and water without exposing the vascular system to air. The basal ends of the cuttings, surrounded by mud, were rooted in 2 wk.

MORPHOLOGY AND PHYSIOLOGY

The normal growth cycle for *A. philoxeroides* begins with a parental rootstock on a mudflat, sloping river bank or drainage canal. The much branched plant spreads over the water, supporting vertical growth as it goes. Matthews (1975) and Mitchell (1978) report stem extensions of 17 m from the place of origin. Stems may lose their connection to their soil-rooted origins if a mat becomes very large. Mitchell (1978) in Australia states that alligatorweed may find it difficult to survive in water deeper than 1.5 to 2.5 m. There is speculation that mats can float without attachment to the substrate for only a limited time, perhaps a year and a half.

As the weather cools growth slows, then ceases, but the mats continue to float. In spring new growth develops from axillary and terminal buds on matted stems of several ages. Julien and Broadbent (1980) prepared a good summary of growth patterns of alligatorweed in various environments.

Because of dependence on a good moisture supply this plant is most familiar in aquatic sites. There its leaves are larger, darker green, stems are taller and thicker, with large internal air spaces. The stem, which is small at the junction with the root, increases threefold in diameter before it reaches the water surface. The cortex now has some aerenchyma, but much of the increase in size is due to the large internal cavity.

The filamentous roots of terrestrial plants become interwoven with old prostrate stems and may form a dense mat of 10 cm thickness. Larger roots descend to 0.5 m. Penfound (1940) discovered that the roots of plants standing in water do not enter the soil even if they are in contact with substrate. Should the water begin to recede the roots enter the soil immediately. New shoots can arise from larger roots and stolons even if they are buried in considerable mud. In a favorable circumstance, Penfound reported four root masses in plots 30 cm^2 in size. Such plants have relatively large roots at the plant base. The cortex does not have aerenchyma.

Kay and Haller (1984) demonstrated that a broad-stemmed type of *A. philoxeroides* and a narrow-stemmed form may represent two distinct biotypes. The former produces significantly greater dry weights when grown in (1) a root-emersed sand culture or (2) as a root-emersed terrestrial plant in top soil. The stems of the second biotype were significantly longer in these and other treatments. Wain et al. (1984) further confirmed the differences in these biotypes with an examination of eight different protein/enzyme systems in electrophoretic studies. Okade et al. (1985) reported an aggressive weedy biotype (hexaploid) of alligatorweed in many cultivated fields near Balcarce, Buenos Aires province, Argentina. The hexaploid plants were very vigorous. Ordinary tillage did not control this weedy type and may have contributed to its spread. It has a high competitive and colonizing ability.

In a study of the production of biomass, uptake of mineral nutrients and biochemical assimilates, Boyd (1969b) and Boyd and Blackburn (1970) found that the net dry matter production was already complete by mid-July. The net production of several biochemical constituents was completed by mid-June. The maximum rate of productivity was late May and early June. The percentage composition of most chemical constituents then declined steadily as the season progressed. Most mobile mineral nutrients were absorbed before the time of maximum growth and were then used for subsequent growth. Lawrence and Mixon (1970) determined that alligatorweed was capable of absorbing nutrients far in excess of what could be utilized physiologically.

Longstreth et al. (1984) grew alligatorweed at five NaCl concentrations and found the net rate of CO_2 uptake declined 50% over a range of 0 to 400 millimoles of NaCl. Dry weight production and net CO_2 uptake were closely correlated at the different salinities. On a mesophyll cell area basis, soluble protein levels were quite constant in leaves developed at the above salt concentrations while total chlorophyll decreased at all salinities.

Alligatorweed is found in many habitats and therefore receives different quantities of light. The dry matter allocation patterns in low light (LL) to high light (HL) were studied by Longstreth and Mason (1984) at four photosynthetic photon flux densities (PPFD) (with light energy at wavelengths of 400 to 700 nm), to determine the effect on productivity and partitioning of the biomass.

At 56 days the average dry weight of plants grown at HL, 40 mol/m^2/day (1 mole of photons/sec/m^2 = 1 Einstein/sec/m^2 or 6.02 x 10^{17} photons/sec/m^2) was more than 9-fold greater than in the LL. The ratio of leaf area to plant dry weight tended to increase as the PPFD treatment decreased. The relationship between PPFD treatment and dry weight was linear at 56 days.

The minimum PPFD necessary for growth was estimated to be 5 mol/m^2/day. They estimated that dry matter production on a per plant basis could continue to increase up to the maximum PPFD received in unshaded habitats in the southeastern United States. Longstreth and coworkers also studied the photosynthesis rate and mesophyll surface area in expanding leaves when grown at two light levels (Longstreth et al. 1985).

A. philoxeroides undergoes a hypoxic quiescence during dark submergence. Quimby and Kay (1977) and Quimby et al. (1978) found that white or red light stimulated growth from submerged cuttings but far red light did not. Further, the growth that normally occurs in these cuttings under white light was completely inhibited by photosystem II inhibitors DCMU and simazine. They concluded that sprouting and early season growth of submerged, illuminated alligatorweed is dependent upon the O_2 produced by photosystem II to support respiration and to overcome hypoxic quiescence.

Datta and Chatterjee (1969) completed cytological studies of three species of *Alternanthera*.

ECONOMIC IMPORTANCE

A. philoxeroides, when present, interferes with many of the activities for which we use water. It alters the ecology of the area both above and below its heavy vegetation. The mats restrict light penetration, interfere with the growth of submerged floras and faunas, and may produce anoxic conditions. It mixes with and replaces the flora of ditches, banks, and shallow waters. Water flow is restricted and sedimentation increases. Flooding conditions are aggravated because the weed prevents the flushing of debris out of streams, drains, and canals. During storms the mats tear loose and pile up against poles, fences, and bridges. The plants create a favorable environment for breeding and harboring disease vectors and mosquitoes. Alligatorweed threatens navigation, irrigation systems, intakes of electric power plants, and the use of water for recreational purposes.

Alligatorweed is a serious or principal aquatic weed in Australia, Indonesia, New Zealand, Thailand, and the west, south, and east coasts of the United States; of pastures in India, of lowland rice in Taiwan and the United States, and of vegetables in Indonesia. It once was a serious weed in lowland rice in the southern United States, and though it persists it can be brought under control with herbicides. It is a major weed of irrigation systems in the United States. Following a survey of weeds in rice across the world, Noda (1977) reported that *A. philoxeroides* is a major weed of transplanted rice wherever it is grown.

Also, *A. philoxeroides* is a weed of unknown rank of the following: aquatic weed of waterways in Argentina and Brazil, irrigation systems in Brazil and Indonesia; maize, pastures, and sweet potatoes in New Zealand; potatoes in India, rice in Brazil, China, India, Indonesia, Paraguay, and Thailand; sugar cane in Brazil; and vegetables in China.

Two species of insects have been released in several places in the world in the last decade for the biological control of this species. The adults and larvae of a flea beetle (*Agasicles hygrophila*) feed on leaves and stems, allowing rot organisms to also enter the tissues, with the combined result that stems collapse, the mats rot and finally break up and sink. The larvae of a moth (*Vogtia malloi*) tunnel inside the stems and damage vascular tissues. It has not been successful against terrestrial stands and it sometimes suffers from winter kill.

When the two insects are released together, *Vogtia* is often overshadowed by the very effective destruction of vegetation by *Agasicles*. The latter is also subject to winter kill. It does not diapause in winter and thus needs some of the weed to live on. Both the larvae and adult beetles also prefer floating vegetation. These insects are very promising for the control of this weed. In Florida in the United States, for example, *A. philoxeroides* still must be controlled with chemicals or other methods in special areas such as ornamental ponds and agricultural areas of the south where populations of the insect do not build to effective levels. In more northerly locations the beetle does not tolerate low temperatures and is not effective against terrestrial forms of the weed. For the extended aquatic systems of Florida, however, it is generally agreed that alligatorweed is no longer a major problem—the beetle introductions have been successful!

Mechanical harvesting has not been successful for this species because the rapid regrowth from root and stem fragments provides new infestations immediately. Newton et al. (1979) found that alligatorweed survived even high stocking rates of grass carp (*Ctenopharyngodon idella*) in their experiments.

Birds, especially waterfowl, and small animals seek shelter in adult stands of alligatorweed. Tender shoots from new growth are sold at vegetable markets in south Asia.

Zhou et al. (1988) recently determined the structure of alternanthin, a C-flavone glycoside isolated from *A. philoxeroides*. The compound has been used in China for treatment of virus diseases such as hepatitis, epidemic parotitis (mumps), hemorrhagic fevers, and influenza.

COMMON NAMES

Alternanthera philoxeroides

ARGENTINA	camalote, gamba rusa, lagunilla, raiz colorada
AUSTRALIA	alligatorweed
BRAZIL	carrapicho de brejo, erva de jacare, tripa de sapa
INDIA	chanchi
MEXICO	lagarto
NEW ZEALAND	alligatorweed
PARAGUAY	gamba rusa, hierba alligator, raiz colorada
THAILAND	pak ped nam
UNITED STATES	alligator grass, alligatorweed
URUGUAY	gambarrosa, lagunilla, raiz colorada

Seven

Alternanthera sessilis (L.) DC.

Amaranthaceae, Amaranth Family

THE HABITATS OF *ALTERNANTHERA PHILOXEROIDES*, often called alligatorweed, and *A. sessilis* tend to overlap in transition zones between wet and dry lands. The latter, which appears in more than 30 crops across the world, is more terrestrial than aquatic and the reverse is true of alligatorweed. The two species have a general resemblance in the vegetative stages, with a decumbent habit early then becoming erect. The stems of *A. philoxeroides*, however, are taller, thicker and more robust than those of *A. sessilis* and the white flowers of the former, axillary or terminal, are borne on peduncles 5 to 7 cm long, while

FIGURE 7-1   The distribution of *Alternanthera sessilis* (L.) DC. across the world where it has been reported as a weed.

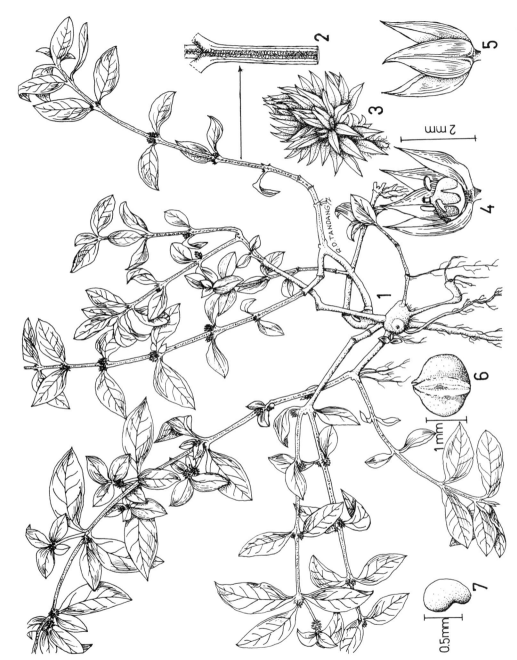

FIGURE 7-2 *Alternanthera sessilis* (L.) DC.: 1. habit; 2. portion of stem, enlarged; 3. head; 4. flower partly excised; 5. perianth; 6. utricle; 7. seeds.

those of the latter are commonly nested in leaf axils. *A. sessilis* is reported as a weed in more than 65 countries.

DESCRIPTION

A. sessilis (Figure 7-2) is a creeping *perennial* or under favorable circumstances a short-lived *annual*; *stems* weakly erect, or more commonly with lower stems prostrate with *adventitious roots* at nodes, with many weakly erect branches, when inundated stems float lower stems may become partly hollow, may sometimes be tinged with purple longitudinal rows of hairs on opposite sides of the stems, pubescent at nodes; *leaves* opposite, sessile, variable in size and shape, glabrous or nearly so, varying from linear-lanceolate to elliptic-lanceolate, 1.25 to 5 to 7 cm long, to 3 cm wide, acute or obtuse, entire or obscurely toothed; *inflorescence* a head, sessile in leaf axils, or may be spike-like, becoming a short cylinder as it develops, solitary or clustered, globose to oblong, white with pinkish tint in some areas, 5 to 7 mm long; *sepals* lanceolate, acute or acuminate, 2 to 2.5 mm long; *stamens* 2 or 3; *fruit* a *utricle*, falling with perianth, broadly obcordate, deeply notched but not lobed at apex (emarginate), smooth, dark brown (at some sites clearly exposed), 2 to 3 mm long.

According to Datta and Biswas (1979) there were important differences in the gross morphology of aquatic and terrestrial forms in the biotypes they worked with in India. The aquatic forms had large numbers of adventitious roots, 1 to 10 cm in length, developing from each node. They did not resemble tap roots but were fibrous, while the terrestrial forms had few nodal roots, averaging 50 cm in length, with the thick stout nature of tap roots. The stems of aquatic forms were floating or erect, with swollen hollow internodes near basal plant regions; some stems were very long. In terrestrial forms the stems were prostrate, decumbent or climbing to hanging if supported. They were short, had limited growth, and the mid portion of internodes had a small lumen. Leaves of terrestrial forms may have 2 to 3 times more branches than aquatic forms. Finally, the aquatic leaves were longer (7 cm average), elliptical, mostly obtuse, and entire. Terrestrial forms were more linear, highly serrated, and averaged about 1 cm in length.

DISTRIBUTION AND HABITAT

A. sessilis (Figure 7-1) is widely distributed as a weed in Central America, reaches north to the southern United States and southward beyond the equator to southern Brazil. It is very widely distributed around most of the perimeter of Africa, with the exception that it is not troublesome in all areas of the north. It extends from the eastern Mediterranean to India, where it is widely distributed, thence to the Far East, where there are many locations in Asia. It is in a cluster of islands of the South Pacific, in central China, and in Japan and Hawaii.

In India this plant is sometimes included in the "aquatic floras" of Madhya Pradesh and other areas because it is so often found in and near ponds, canals and reservoirs. It prefers places with constant or periodically high humidity and so may be found in swamps, shallow ditches, and fallow rice fields. R. Singh et al. (1983) reported that *A. sessilis* was unaffected by flood-water 90 cm deep for 4 days.

The species may, however, tolerate extremely dry conditions on ditch banks, along roadsides, and in gardens, plantations, and cultivated crops. It is in wet places in low and mid-country in Sri Lanka and invades from the banks of canals and reservoirs of the Gezira cotton scheme in Sudan. As water levels begin to move upward in June and July in Lake Volta in Ghana, *A. sessilis* grows quickly and profusely and is then able to keep ahead of the rising water. It often grows in a mixed association of several other aquatic species.

BIOLOGY

There has been little research on the biology of this weed species. Datta and Biswas (1979), in an autecological study of the plant in Bengal, recorded marked morphological variation within the species. It is adapted to both xerophytic and hydrophytic locations, but the range of tolerance to these changing habitats is not reflected in corresponding anatomical changes. In Bengal the plant preferred loamy, alkaline soils low in exchangeable Ca and high in N. Naidu et al. (1980) reported that its photosynthetic system is that of a C_3 plant.

The species reproduces by seed and vegetatively by stems that run along the soil surface and root at the nodes. When grown in pots in pond-bed soil Datta and Biswas (1979) found no germination of seeds buried deeper than 1 cm. Growth is quite vigorous at the end of the growing season. The plant flowers and fruits all year in some areas, although in Mysore, India, for example, flowering occurs from early August through December. The flowers are self-pollinated. The fruits and/or bladdery seeds are dispersed by wind and water. The study in Bengal found an average production of 2000 seeds/plant (Datta and Biswas 1979). These authors also reported on the anatomy and morphology of *A. sessilis*.

Earlier Datta and Biswas (1968) made a study of seed germination and seedling growth. When seeds were held at 10 to 40°C in the dark, germination was 5% from 20 to 40°C. When seeds from these treatments were transferred to room temperature and diffuse light (presumably at natural daylength) seeds previously kept in darkness at 10 and 20°C now germinated at the level of 24 and 21% respectively. Seeds held 6 days at 10°C and 1 day at 30°C gave more than 20% germination. There was thus some stimulation from the cold temperatures.

Light, whether continuous or intermittent, has a pronounced effect on seed germination in this species. In general, over many types of experiments, germination was about 40% in light but only 2 to 5% in darkness. Light thus overrides the need for the variations in temperature often required by dormant seeds. Seed lots that exhibited about 40% germination when held in light, gave 28% germination when held in darkness and treated with 0.125% KNO_3 (that can partially substitute for light). In another similar experiment in which 0.25% thiourea was substituted for the KNO_3, germination was 75% in darkness, thus it served as a very good substitute for light.

White light from fluorescent tubes prompted better germination than red light or darkness, while red light or darkness were better than far-red light. Germination was enhanced under all types of radiation and in darkness by a mixture of KNO_3 and thiourea.

Kaul (1972) later confirmed the need for light in germination, the inhibition by far-red light and the improvement in germination with various nitrate salts. He found that a 16-hour photoperiod was most favorable for this process and in contrast to the above research that red light was better than white light. Germination under blue and orange light also exceeded that in white light. He studied a water soluble extract of the perianth and pericarp of *A. sessilis* that inhibited seed germination.

AGRICULTURAL IMPORTANCE

A. sessilis is a weed of both paddy and upland rice. It is a serious weed of rice in Gambia, Mozambique, Nigeria, and one of the most widespread and serious weeds of rice in Thailand. It is a principal weed of lowland rice in Bangladesh, India, the Philippines, and Taiwan; of upland rice in Dominican Republic and India; and of rice in Ivory Coast. Also it is reported to infest rice in Burma, Cambodia, China, Egypt, Indonesia, Laos, Madagascar, Malaysia, Nigeria, Surinam, and Vietnam. Noda (1977), after completing a survey of rice weeds for the world, reported *A. sessilis* as a principal weed in transplanted rice. It is also a principal weed of maize in Nigeria, mangoes in the Philippines, tropical pastures in Ghana, India and Taiwan; and of sorghum in the Philippines. It is reported to be a principal weed of various aquatic systems in Australia, Ghana, and the United States; and of several upland crops in Brazil.

It is a common weed of cotton in Colombia; cowpeas, maize, millet, peanuts and soybeans in the Philippines; jute and maize in India, maize in Indonesia, roselle in Indonesia, sugarcane in India and Trinidad, taro in Samoa, tea in Indonesia, and vegetables in Ghana.

In addition, *A. sessilis* is a weed of unknown rank in many other crops and places in the world, some of which are mentioned below. For example, as herbicides were used to remove annuals in crops in Taiwan, *A. sessilis* was among the perennials that came in, with the result that this and other species have now had to be placed on their noxious weed list. It infests banana, flax, jute, maize, rape, sorghum, soybean, sugar cane, and sweet potato in Taiwan; cassava, potato, tea, and various aquatic systems in India; cassava, sweet potatoes, and tropical pastures in Nigeria; oil palm, peanuts, sugarcane, and soybeans in Indonesia; soybeans and aquatic systems in Thailand; cowpeas, jute, and vegetables in Bangladesh; and abaca, legumes, tobacco, and tropical pastures in the Philippines.

It is present in many irrigation and aquatic systems in Malaysia, Sudan, Surinam, and Zimbabwe; coffee in New Guinea, maize in some areas of the United States, sugarcane in Hawaii and Mauritius, and upland crops of several kinds in Ivory Coast and the Philippines. In Upper Volta it is considered one of the most noxious of the semi-aquatic weeds.

On rice fields of Taiwan, into which soybeans are drilled directly into stubble, burning rice straw has resulted in significant control of this species.

In the southern United States this plant is sometimes browsed by cattle and deer. In Sri Lanka, the Philippines and elsewhere the fresh, young shoots are sometimes for sale in the vegetable markets.

COMMON NAMES

Alternanthera sessilis

BURMA	pazun-sa
CAMBODIA	choeug bangkong
DOMINICAN REPUBLIC	sanguinaria, santoma cimarrona

EGYPT	hamel, hamool, luqmet el-hamal, sessile-flowered globe amaranth
HAWAII	sessile joyweed
INDIA	bhaji, chanchi, marhi-ki-bam, mitikanduri
INDONESIA	bagem kremah, daon tolod, krema
JAPAN	tsuru-nogeito
LAOS	nea kan to sarng
MALAYSIA	keremak
MAURITIUS	brede emballages, serenti
NIGERIA	enigi
PHILIPPINES	bilanamanut, bonga-bonga, gogoat, sakit, tagtago
PUERTO RICO	sanguinaria
SRI LANKA	mukunu-venna, pannankani
THAILAND	pak ped dam, phak-pet-thai
TURKEY	gazel lokmasi
UNITED STATES	sessile joyweed
VIETNAM	rau deu

Eight

Amaranthus retroflexus L. and Amaranthus viridis L.

Amaranthaceae, Amaranth Family

A MARANTHUS RETROFLEXUS and *Amaranthus viridis* are representatives of a very large family of 65 genera and about 900 species. Closely related plants within the genus are among the few dicots with the potential of becoming grain crops. In the time of the Aztec Empire in Mexico they were the equal of maize in the food supply of that civilization. The leaves of many amaranths appear in the regular diets of several cultures (Sauer 1950, 1967).

These species rank with *Cyperus rotundus* and *Cynodon dactylon* as the most widely distributed weed species in the arable crops of the world. *A. retroflexus* is in 60 crops in 70 countries while *A. viridis* is in 50 crops in more than 80 countries. They are often called "pigweeds."

The literature on the biology of *A. retroflexus* has increased at an astonishing rate in the past two decades because it was one of the two species to first exhibit resistance to the widely used herbicides, the triazines. This discovery has proven to be one of the most important events since the inception of weed science.

DESCRIPTIONS

Amaranthus retroflexus

A. retroflexus (Figure 8-1) is a monoecious, erect, finely hairy, freely-branching, herbaceous *annual* growing to 2 m tall; *taproot* pink or red, depth varies with soil profile; *leaves* alternate, egg-shaped or rhombic-ovate, cuneate at base, up to 10 cm long, margins somewhat wavy, veins prominent on underside, apex may be sharp, petiole shorter or longer than leaf; *flowers* numerous, small, borne in dense blunt spikes 1 to 5 cm long, densely crowded onto terminal panicle 5 to 20 cm long but may be smaller on upper axils; 3 spiny-tipped, rigid, awl-shaped bracts surround the flower, exceeding calyx, length 4 to 8 mm, persistent; *tepals* 5, much longer than fruit, usually definitely recurved at tips, obovate or highly spatulate, 1 *pistil* and 5 stamens; *style* branches erect or a bit recurved; *fruit* a *utricle*, membra-

FIGURE 8-1 *Amaranthus retroflexus* L.: A. habit; B. pistillate spikelet; C. utricle; D. seeds.

nous, flattened, 1.5 to 2 mm long, dehiscing by a transverse line at the middle, wrinkled upper part falling away; *seed* oval to egg-shaped, somewhat flattened, notched at the narrow end, 1 to 1.2 mm long, shiny black or dark red-brown.

Sauer (1950, 1967) feels this species is quite stable and uniform; within races the variation between individuals may not exceed the variability observed within a single inflorescence. The amaranths are, however, notorious for the ability to hybridize. In a highly artificial habitat *A. retroflexus* forms many sterile hybrids.

There is a special need to comment on the care needed in defining this species. *A. retroflexus* was one of the first weeds with biotypes resistant to herbicides and in the ensuing scramble for information it was realized that in several places the amaranth population was made up of several look-alike species. Those who attempted to separate *A. retroflexus* from the associated *A. hybridus* and *A. powellii* with taxonomic keys found it difficult and the confusion of separation led to some errors and loss of time in early herbicide resistance research. Sauer (1967) has pointed out that the trouble arises from attempts to separate them by color and growth form; he believes it must be done with the use of morphological features of the inflorescence, bracts and tepals. Because these weeds are cited so frequently, and sometimes incorrectly, in research on herbicide use, Ahrens et al. (1981) constructed an orderly key based on floral characteristics to distinguish between them.

The inflorescence branches of *A. retroflexus* and *A. hybridus* are numerous, short, 1 to 1.5 cm in diameter, and crowded on the panicle while those of *A. powellii* are few but long, 5 to 25 cm, and widely spread in the inflorescence. These branches are rounded at the apex in *A. retroflexus* but taper to a point in *A. hybridus*. In *A. retroflexus* and *A. powellii* the floral bracts are 4 to 8 mm long; 2 or 3 times longer than the tepals, and those of *A. hybridus* are one-half as long and 1 to 2 times longer than the tepals.

The tepals of *A. retroflexus* and *A. hybridus* are 5 in number (and this does not vary), 3 to 4 mm long in *A. retroflexus* and about one-half of that in *A. hybridus*; they are recurved, obtuse, rounded truncate and sometimes notched at the apex in *A. retroflexus* and straight and acute in *A. hybridus*. The tepals of *A. powellii* are 3 to 5 in number, 2 to 4 mm in length, straight and acute.

In sum, *A. retroflexus* can be initially identified by the rounded (not pointed) shape of its recurved tepals and the shorter, more crowded branches of its inflorescence, and if need be by a more detailed examination of the floral structures. This species has the familiar name "redroot pigweed" in many places in the world.

Amaranthus viridis

A. viridis (Figure 8-2) is a monoecious, prostrate to erect, sparsely hairy, branched herbaceous *annual* 30 to 80 cm tall; *stems* freely branching, stout, round, grooved lengthwise, green to somewhat reddish; *taproot* long; *leaves* alternate, long-petioled, smooth, darker green above, margins entire, 2 to 6 cm wide, triangular-ovate 3 to 9 cm long, apex may be obtuse but more often is acute and sometimes notched; *inflorescence* numerous florets borne on slender, dense, axillary and leafless terminal spikes, 5 to 15 cm long, greenish to purplish; *flowers* small about 1 mm long, subtended by small *bracts* or *bracteoles*, shorter than perianth, membranous, narrowly ovate, apex with awn; *perianth* 3-lobed, acute at apex, lower surface with green midrib; *sepals* 3, shorter than fruit, sometimes with transparent white margins, 1 mm long, lanceolate; *pistillate flowers* one *pistil*, style 3-branched, single chamber ovary; *staminate flowers* with 5 *stamens*, opposite sepals; *fruit* indehiscent

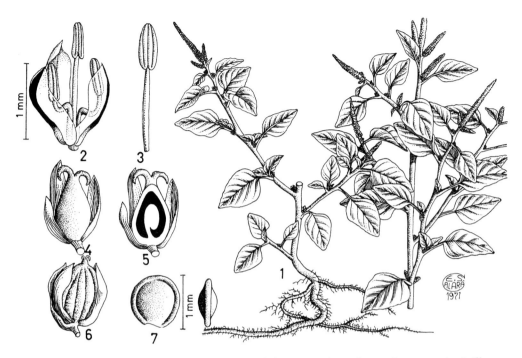

FIGURE 8-2   *Amaranthus viridis* L.: 1. habit; 2. staminate flower; 3. stamen; 4. pistillate flower 5. same, vertical section; 6. utricle; 7. seed, two views.

utricle, globose, surface wrinkled, 1.5 mm long, longer than the persistent floral envelope; *seed* disk-shaped, with blunt margin, or almost globular, 1 to 1.25 mm in diameter, shiny brown or black.

DISTRIBUTION AND HABITAT

Although *A. retroflexus* and *A. viridis* are very widespread weeds throughout the world their distribution patterns are not the same (Figures 8-3 and 8-4). Overall, *A. viridis* tends to avoid the cool regions of the north temperate zone. In Asia it is much more prevalent than *A. retroflexus* from south India to the east and down through the islands of the Pacific. Both species are well established in Australia. In Africa, as in Asia, *A. retroflexus* is not troublesome as a weed in the hot, warm regions south of the Sahara, with the exception of countries on the lower eastern coast.

In Europe both species are in England (Salisbury 1964, Roberts 1986) but only red-root pigweed ventures northward to the Scandinavian countries. The patterns of distribution for the two species are similar in the Americas, with the exception that *A. viridis* is not a worrisome weed in the Plains and western regions of Canada and the United States.

A. retroflexus, *A. hybridus*, and *A. powellii*, which have been so much involved in herbicide resistance studies, and *A. quitensis*, are frequently misidentified (Michael 1977). The

FIGURE 8-3 The distribution of *Amaranthus retroflexus* L. across the world where it has been reported as a weed.

FIGURE 8-4 The distribution of *Amaranthus viridis* L. across the world where it has been reported as a weed.

first three species are important weeds in parts of Canada, the United States and Central America (see also Ahrens et al. 1981). He believes that *A. quitensis* may be the most important of this group in South America.

In Norway redroot pigweed is found in the southwest regions near grain elevators and it is believed the seed came in from the Americas with seedstocks and grain. In the former Soviet Union, Gusev (1972) found 14 species of monoecious, weedy amaranths across the country, with redroot pigweed being most widely distributed, and believes most of them are recent introductions from America.

In a Canadian study of north-south segments of agricultural land across the breadth of the continent, Alex (1982) found *A. retroflexus* to be one of the most widely distributed of all weeds. As in the United States, it is now recognized that in many areas the populations of *A. hybridus* and *A. powellii* were often unwittingly included in studies of *A. retroflexus*.

In Mongolia, redroot pigweed is thus far one of the few weeds introduced from the New World. It has become a major problem for irrigated areas in the south and west. At 1800 m in the mountainous areas of India, on stony, infertile soils, redroot pigweed is a cultivated crop used as a staple food in place of wheat (Hilbig 1982).

This weed thrives in cultivated fields, home gardens, waste places and on ditch banks. It prefers open, sunny areas and appears quickly when soil is disturbed. In southwest Ontario, Canada, Weaver and McWilliams (1980) found *A. retroflexus*, *A. hybridus* and *A. powellii* on soils ranging from sandy loam to clay to muck, with no correlation between soil type and species distribution. McWilliams (1966) found *A. retroflexus* was rare on highly acid soils in the United States. Also in the United States, Buchanan et al. (1975) grew several weeds in plots ranging in *pH* from 4.7 to 6.3 on sandy loam. The growth of redroot pigweed was severely reduced below *pH* 5.2. In Canada, Joel (1929) made a study of weedy vegetation on different soils and different climatic zones of Saskatchewan and found that *A. retroflexus* favored moist areas, and in low places with alkaline soils it tended to be the dominant weed. Hoveland et al. (1976) found *A. retroflexus* to be extremely responsive to levels of K and P in soils of the southern United States.

Archibold and Hume (1983) used seed traps and soil cores to study the annual seed rain on soils at ten stations over an area of 1300 km^2 in Canada. Seeds of redroot pigweed were far more abundant than those of any other species in soil cores at normal tillage depths. These seeds, and those of *Thlaspi arvense*, were more numerous in the surface seed traps than those of any others of the 40 species examined. A survey of the source of weed seeds entering agricultural fields in Iran revealed that 10 million/ha came from sheep manure, 180,000/ha from farmer-saved seed and 120/ha from irrigation water. *A. retroflexus* is one of the major weeds of summer crops (Dastgheib 1989).

In irrigation canals in the central United States, redroot pigweed was present in greater quantity than any other species of the 30 species recorded. They entered sugar beet and maize fields via irrigation water in larger numbers than any species except *Echinochloa crus-galli* (Wilson 1980).

In Poland, tree sparrows (*Passer montanus*) may reach populations of 500/km^2 and feed on plant seed most of the year. *A. retroflexus* is one of the five most common weeds in the area and produces 600 to 1200 kg/ha, dry weight, of seed annually. The birds consumed 50% of all *A. retroflexus* seeds produced in one season (Pinowski and Wojcik 1968).

In cultural sites in the western United States, Agogino and Feinhandler (1957) found *A. retroflexus* seeds 2500 to 4500 years old. In the Tehuacan Valley in southern Mexico they found seed of cultivated amaranths from 5000 to 6700 B.C. This suggests these plants are among the oldest food crops in the New World.

PROPAGATION

All reproduction of *A. retroflexus* and *A. viridis* is by seed. In the light of new information of the past two decades, we can no longer assume "the seed" of a species to be constant in morphology and physiology with reliable standard germination temperatures, light requirements, dormancy characteristics, and more. In addition, the quest for pigweed plants resistant (R) and susceptible (S) to the triazine herbicides has revealed some inconsistencies in previous interpretations of germination experiments because some populations may have contained two or more species.

In a plant that ranges so widely over the world, it is to be expected that there will be no general dormancy pattern or standard germination requirements, but instead a polymorphism borne of adaptations needed to live in so many places and in such different ecological situations. For example, McWilliams et al. (1968) have shown that the genetic-based differences in germination of *A. retroflexus* may be correlated with different climates and that this may explain some of the variation in germination results reported in the literature. Cavers and Steel (1984) have shown that the largest seeds of this weed are produced first, with progressively smaller seeds being produced as the season progresses. They learned as well that variations in size, weight, and dormancy between different populations could well be due to differences in maturity of sampled plants and that this aging process is governed by site, soil, and climate. General comparisons should only be made with large numbers of seeds henceforth, for the variation in seed weight within some populations is sufficient to obscure comparisons of seed size between plants or between populations. Germination experiments with *A. retroflexus* and other species must be interpreted with these variables of response and behavior in mind.

Seed quantities of 230,000 and 500,000 by single large plants of pigweed have been reported by Stevens (1957) and Priszter (1950). Seed is dispersed by wind, water, and birds, with manure, with movement of farm machines, and as a contaminant in crop seed.

In experiments on pigweed by Chadoeuf-Hannel and Barralis (1983) temporary or permanent water deficits resulted in greater seed weight and less dormancy. Schimpf (1977) found greater seed weight in drier circumstances and suggests this may be explained by emergence of seedlings from deeper soil horizons having greater soil moisture. Overall, he feels there is better correlation of seed weight with long-term moisture availability than with short-term climatic fluctuations. Increased seed weight is also reported to follow seed maturation at low temperatures. The production of progressively smaller seeds by *A. retroflexus* as the season advances, as referred to above in the work of Cavers and Steel, sometimes resulted in a 25% difference in seed weight. There were large differences in the seed weight patterns of individuals of the same species. McWilliams (1966) and McWilliams et al. (1968) found that seed weight is positively correlated with latitude. Baker (1972) found that seeds of *A. retroflexus* become lighter in weight at higher elevations in the western United States.

The duration of seed viability varies with site, soil, conditions of the storage place, seed fitness at the outset, and other factors. Barton (1945) and others have found dormancy in freshly harvested seed of *A. retroflexus* but research workers have also reported populations in which, at some seasons, almost all seeds are viable at harvest (Egley and

Chandler 1978, Weaver and McWilliams 1980). The former found a 90% decrease in seed viability after 18 mo of burial but almost no decrease after 30 mo in dry storage. Burnside et al. (1981) in the central United States buried pigweed seeds and found little loss of viability in 10 yr. In the 100-year Beal buried seed experiment in the north-central United States, some *A. retroflexus* seeds were still viable after 40 yr (Darlington and Steinbauer 1961).

Germination of *A. viridis* seeds remained constant for 1 yr while buried at several depths from 2.5 to 25 cm. The quantity of seeds germinating was not significantly different from any soil depth (Horng and Leu 1978).

Pigweed seeds can survive only a few weeks in silage and manure (Zahnley and Fitch 1941, Schokker 1988, Blackshaw and Rode 1991). Seeds fed to lambs, upon excretion, gave good initial germination, but there was decreasing viability as time spent in the digestive tract increased (Ozer 1982). Ridley (1930) observed seedlings of *A. viridis* growing from horse dung on Christmas Island in the Pacific. High survival of *A. viridis* in the digestive tract of chickens was reported by Rodriguez et al. (1983) in Cuba. When held in flowing fresh water, 12 to 28% of *A. retroflexus* seeds germinated at 27 mo and 9% at 33 mo (Bruns and Rasmussen 1958).

Several studies of seed germination from different soil depths have been carried out under diverse circumstances but, in general, emergence from about 1 cm seems to be optimum (Wiese and Davis 1967, Siriwardana and Zimdahl 1983). In the former Soviet Union, *A. retroflexus* germinated well at a soil density of 0.9 g/cm^3 whereas higher densities were favorable for several companion annual weeds. Germination of the weed seeds proceeded at all depths to 27 cm but was best at shallow depths. There was no germination at a soil density of 1.3 g/cm^3 (Averkin 1978b).

As with most world weeds, seed germination experiments are numerous with the seed sources obscure and the methods so variable that a listing of all results would serve no purpose here. Following a literature survey of seed germination requirements for many major weeds, Koch (1970) concluded that the optimum temperature for seeds of *A. retroflexus* was 35 to 40°C. Freshly harvested seed reacted strongly to temperature changes, while older seeds exhibited little or no response.

The germination of *A. retroflexus* is controlled by phytochrome and is often stimulated by light and temperature levels (Kadman-Zahavi 1960, Maguire and Overland 1959, Taylorson and Hendricks 1971, 1972). Imbibed seeds show a more rapid uptake of water and rehydration, processes that are quickened by higher temperatures (Taylorson and Hendricks 1969, 1972; Weaver and McWilliams 1980).

A. retroflexus seeds sometimes seem quite insensitive to light, for at their best germination temperature (35 to 40°C) they often germinate without regard for their usual light requirement. Optimum germination temperatures of 25 to 28°C and of 21°C have been reported from Bulgaria and northern Novosibirsk in Siberia, respectively. McWilliams et al. (1966, 1968) also reported a lower temperature for germination for this weed in northern populations of Canada. This gives northern plants an adaptive advantage because of their location in sites with short growing seasons.

An example of the effect of temperature on the early life of plants is given in the study of population of pigweed in the southern United States in which germination was found to have an optimum of 18°C for the night period (N) and 26°C in the daytime (D). The time for 50% germination for the seeds of these plants at D-10°C and N-3°C was 24 days, whereas at D-35°C and N-26°C it was 3 days (Wiese and Davis 1967, Wiese and Binning 1984).

Stewart (1926) found that seeds were not affected by heating to 90°C. Klein (1956) in Germany worked with a population of *A. retroflexus* that had minimum germination temperature of 7°C. Jordan (1981) found an increased germination rate of pigweed seeds after freezing them in liquid N (−196°C) and the rate improved with each of eight freeze-thaw cycles.

Axyris amaranthoides, in the **Chenopodiaceae**, similar in specific name to the genus we are discussing and called Russian pigweed in Canada, is reported to germinate on ice and frozen soil (Aamodt 1935).

Yamamoto and Ohba (1977) found that *A. viridis* was little affected in its emergence at different controlled soil moisture levels in irrigated fields but found a tendency for seed germination to be more responsive at high moisture.

There was a significant increase in germination of *A. retroflexus* and other annual weeds following the treatment of a clay loam soil in early May with 67 kg of ammonium nitrate or 9 to 18 kg/ha of sodium azide. Plants responded to the latter chemical at 4.5 kg/ha in autumn as well (Hurtt and Taylorson 1979).

It has been known for decades that ethylene stimulates seed germination and there has been renewed interest in this response since it proved to be useful in the field for the germination of parasitic witchweed, *Striga* spp. (Eplee 1975). Taylorson (1979) tested the effect of ethylene on seeds of more than 40 species of weeds, including pigweed, and found them to respond very favorably. He also demonstrated that phytochrome was involved in the reaction. Schonbeck and Egley (1979, 1981a,b) have provided further information on the effect of light, temperature, moisture and CO_2 when ethylene is used on pigweed seeds.

In the southern United States, Egley (1984) buried *A. retroflexus* seeds and exhumed them in the dark during the next 2 yr to test responses to germination stimuli such as ethylene, CO_2, light and temperature. In the first winter, dormancy decreased gradually until germination was 90% at 35°C without added stimulation. In the second winter, most of the remaining seeds responded weakly to the above stimuli, but 1 to 2% of the original seeds remained dormant and were highly insensitive to any stimulus presented to them.

When the seeds of *A. retroflexus* are imbibed, germination is largely governed by phytochrome activity. Taylorson (1972) gave pigweed seeds light treatments before and after burial, followed by periodic retrieval in darkness. The seeds were dormant and insensitive to light prior to burial but after retrieval they showed periods of phytochrome control. In soil disturbance studies to explore the effect on subsequent germination behavior of seeds of *A. retroflexus*, 50% germination of dormant seeds was obtained in the dark. A strong light break of 2 seconds caused complete germination (Kadman-Zahavi 1957, Sauer and Struik 1964). Maguire and Overland (1959) reported optimum germination of pigweed seeds in darkness with an alternating temperature of 20 to 30°C.

Pre-chilling of *A. retroflexus* seeds for several days at 20°C or less results in dark germination of seeds at 35°C. Taylorson and Hendricks (1969) believe this is due to the presence of a stable fraction of the far red absorbing form of phytochrome P_{FR} and as it is rehydrated upon imbibition it calls forth the germination response. Inactivation of P_{FR} proceeds four times more rapidly at 25°C or higher than at 20°C. The failure to germinate in the dark at 25°C or higher may be due to the rapid thermal shift of pre-existing P_{FR} to P_R.

In the past two decades, from the work of Gutterman (1972), Kigel et al. (1977, 1979) and Koller et al. (1977a), we have become aware that the photoperiodic regime of the seed-producing parents influences subsequent seed germination. Plants grown in a short 8-hr day (SD) produced seeds with higher germinability than those growing in a long 16-hr day (LD). If plants growing in LD were induced to flower earlier than they normally would by interposing 3 SD in the series, then the seeds of these parents were less germinable than those from non-induced plants growing in LD. Kigel et al. (1979) also demonstrated that this lower germinability decreased further when flower induction was applied in LD-plants, at a more advanced age of the plants.

Oladiran and Mumford (1985), in a study of germination at different temperatures and light and dark cycles, found that seeds of *A. viridis* were most sensitive to light stimulation 4 to 6 days after imbibition. Continuous white light at 25°C completely inhibited germination. Germination was largely under phytochrome control and it was effective in stimulating germination at suboptimal temperatures. In India, where *A. viridis* is a major weed problem, 55% germination was obtained in complete darkness and 64% in a regime of alternation of 24-hr periods of light and darkness at 25°C (Chavan and Trivedi 1962).

By shedding time at the end of the season (November), seeds produced in the northern hemisphere were less dormant than those produced in early August. Likewise, seed produced under the less favorable conditions of late June and July germinated more quickly than those on plants whose seedlings emerged in the more favorable time of March and April (Chadoeuf-Hannel and Barralis 1982). Seeds from plants grown in long-days were more dormant than those in an 8-hr day at 20°C or 16-hr day at 25°C. All of these seeds retain the dormancy characteristics acquired during their formation and maturation so that after dry storage for 6 mo, or in soil over winter, their variability in germination is less but is never totally suppressed.

Koblova (1962) demonstrated that *A. retroflexus* plants grown in the Caucasus mountain area of the former Soviet Union in years of low rainfall, high temperatures and abundant sun tended to have short seed dormancy periods. In general, seeds in dry habits had shorter dormancy periods than those formed in wet areas.

A multiyear Canadian weed seed dormancy study of 60 species in a large area of arable agricultural land revealed that in many species, including pigweed, dormancy varies with the year of seed origin, soil type, and the climatic conditions prevailing in the year of germination. Germination was generally high in the first year and declined thereafter, but germination continued until the seed supply was exhausted (Chepil 1946a,b). Baskin and Baskin (1977) studied the role of dormancy in the germination ecology of three summer annual weeds in the central United States and found that pigweed germinated in late spring and early summer whereas *Ambrosia artemisiifolia* and *Chenopodium album* germinated early to mid-spring. Following one year of after-ripening, the seeds of *Ambrosia* that did not germinate in spring acquired secondary dormancy. In the other species, seeds that did not germinate in favorable spring periods had no secondary dormancy and proceeded to germinate later in the growing season.

Germination polymorphism, the variable germination requirements of individuals in a population, was studied in *A. retroflexus* and other weeds in the western United States by Palmblad (1969). Several populations of *A. retroflexus* were found in different regions and states; at times they were only 9 km apart. The author reminds us that such a trait gives a species an obvious advantage in maintaining the population over a long period. It may allow a part of a population on arable land, arid land, or alpine locations to avoid such events as prolonged drought, frost, or continued soil disturbance.

PHYSIOLOGY AND MORPHOLOGY

Because *A. retroflexus* seems to have no general dormancy, photoperiodic, or germination requirement over its whole range, it has sometimes been difficult to decide whether populations of the species are intimately adapted to different environments or whether there is a general-purpose genotype with a wide range of environmental tolerance as discussed by Baker (1965). The weed is partially or highly self-fertilized with occasional outcrossing. It is mainly wind pollinated but occasionally receives help from insects. From the work of Allard (1965) and Heiner (1970), it seems these traits tend to maintain a homozygous genotype for a given population of *A. retroflexus*. Weedy species can adapt to slowly changing conditions and over many generations stabilize the gene pool. Should the environment be greatly altered, with the small amount of outcrossing, it is assumed that rapid changes in the gene pool can be made through natural selection.

With the advent of resistance to herbicides by *A. retroflexus* in the late 1960s we have seen that the plant designated by this epithet may actually be a group of similar species, some with their own biotypes. Murray (1940) reported a half-century ago that *A. retroflexus*, *A. hybridus*, and *A. powellii* hybridize readily, with the F_1 generation highly sterile and with few F_2 plants. Many hybrids that are fertile were later reported from the central and western United States (Sauer 1950, Tucker and Sauer 1958). Frost (1971) listed the records of the hybrids of the above three species and others in the genus. In India, within both wild and cultivated types of *Amaranthus*, Mohinder and Khoshoo (1974) reported genetic barriers between species and believe the intercrossing referred to above is much less common than has been assumed.

In the United States and Europe, pigweed emergence peaks in late spring and early summer, then continues steadily into August (Ogg and Dawson 1984, Roberts 1986). Slack (1981) in the western United States made weekly plantings of pigweed seed throughout the season and found that plant harvest weights declined with each successive planting, with the exception that seedlings emerging mid-season showed moderate weight increases. In the eastern United States, Vengris (1963) found that the earliest emerging *A. retroflexus* seedlings produced the tallest plants and the highest weed yields. There was less time to maturity for later emerging seedlings and these plants were progressively less competitive.

In one of the finest phenological studies on *A. retroflexus*, Heiner (1970) gathered populations from Manitoba, Canada, and North Dakota, Iowa, and Kansas in the United States, a span of 7° North latitude. The plants were grown in controlled chambers in North and South Environments established in Iowa. The regimes for these Environments were based on the photoperiod and day and night temperature regimes of Manitoba, 48° North, and Kansas, 41° South, with similar soils and fertilizer treatments in all chambers. Records were kept on major events in life cycles such as responses to photoperiod, temperature, fertilizer and competition between intraspecific populations. When growing without competition in the South Environment these populations produced twice as much seed and more total dry weight/plant than those in the North. This dominance was expressed in a self-thinning of plant numbers, enabling some plants to become very large with many seeds. In the competition studies in the North Environment, the Manitoba plants were the best competitors of all the populations. Heiner suggests that populations that started to flower and mature early were able to use soil moisture and nutrients before other populations could make critical demands on such resources at the time they began to flower.

A. retroflexus and *A. viridis* are C_4 plants using the C_4 dicarboxylic acid photosynthetic pathway that is generally characterized by a low CO_2 compensation point, high temperature optimum of net photosynthesis, high light saturation, an apparent lack of photorespiration, and greater efficiency of net photosynthesis as compared with C_3 plants (Welkie and Caldwell 1970, Oliver and Schreiber 1974, Johnson and Hatch 1968). The chlorenchymatous bundle sheaths and radiate mesophyll tissues (Krantz anatomy) are present in these species. The optimum temperature for photosynthesis is 30 to 40°C (Patterson 1976,

Singh, M. et al. 1974). The maximum photosynthetic rate for *A. retroflexus* is about 60 mg $CO_2/dm^2/hr^{-1}$ at 1.0 x 10^5 lux.

Oliver and Schreiber (1974) found *A. retroflexus* competitively superior to *Sida spinosa* and birdsfoot trefoil *Lotus corniculatus* because of the rapid enlargement of the leaf area, the leaf display, and the high photosynthetic rate that make it an efficient user of CO_2. A study of biomass productivity of C_3 and C_4 plants, including *A. retroflexus*, under different soil moisture and light conditions found that length and dry weight of pigweed shoots were severely diminished only at higher moisture levels. The plant was most competitive when under high water stress in full light (Oeztuerk et al. 1981). In a 2-year experiment Hoveland et al. (1978) found that vegetative development of *A. retroflexus* is quite sensitive to shade.

The relative uptake of N, P, K, Ca, and Mg in field-grown maize and *A. retroflexus* was studied by Vengris et al. (1955). They learned that the weed and crop drew equally on the N supply but that pigweed acquired much more of the available K, Ca, and Mg while receiving less P. In a study of changes in the weed flora of southern Germany from 1959 to 1964 and again from 1979 to 1984, Hilbig (1987) found that *A. retroflexus* had increased in root crop fields. He believes this is largely due to increases in soil fertility.

In a study of the decomposition of residues of three weed species, to include *A. retroflexus*, in no-till agriculture, it was found that 35% of the weed biomass N (38 kg/ha) was mineralized during 5 mo, indicating that weed residues can act as N reservoirs in this agricultural system (Parmelee et al. 1989). Sage and Pearcy (1987) and Sage et al. (1987) published an extensive comparison of N use efficiency between the C_4 plant *A. retroflexus* and C_3 *Chenopodium album*.

Removing weeds from crop fields on the Canadian Plains, including *A. retroflexus*, increased the protein content of the crop (Friesen et al. 1960). The organic and inorganic constituents of *A. retroflexus* have been studied by Earle and Jones (1962), Etten, van et al. (1963), Stoller and Weber (1970), Schroeder et al. (1974), Marten and Andersen (1975), Harrold and Nalewaja (1977), Tkachuk and Mellish (1977), and Klingman et al. (1982). The family **Amaranthaceae** belongs to a group of plants that contain betalain pigment instead of the anthocyanins found in most angiosperms (Heywood 1978).

In glasshouse experiments, Bhowmik and Doll (1982, 1983, 1984) reported that water extracts of dry residues of *A. retroflexus* inhibited radical elongation in maize and hypocotyl elongation in soybeans. Residues of the weed reduced maize yields 15 to 20% in the field. From a study of various temperature and light density responses they suggest that the allelochemicals in the weed residues may interfere with photosynthesis, and the partitioning of biomass into leaf component relative to total biomass may have caused the inhibitory effects (see also Gressel and Holm 1964).

If other conditions for flowering are satisfactory, *A. retroflexus* behaves at times as a facultative short-day plant. McWilliams et al. (1966) studied the photoperiodic behavior at different latitudes and suggested that only northern populations are facultative short-day plants. Weaver and McWilliams (1980) found in southern Canada that *A. retroflexus* would flower quickly in an 8-hr day and more slowly at 16 hr. Koller et al. (1977a,b) had shown previously that initiation of flowering in *A. retroflexus* is considerably advanced by a single 8-hr photoperiod given as early as 3 days after seedling emergence.

In the western United States pigweed seedlings grown for 7 consecutive days in an 8-hr photoperiod produced inflorescences in 14 days and then continued to flower at each node. In a 16-hr day they did not have inflorescences until 6 wk later, when the plants were 40 to 50 cm tall. On a seedling population basis, the percent of plants with a flowering response was in direct proportion to the number of short-days they were exposed to. Pigweed seedlings given five 8-hr days in the cotyledon or first leaf stage did not flower in 50 days; when in the 2- or 3-leaf stage, 80% flowered in the same light regime. There thus seems to be a minimum age or leaf surface required before pigweeds respond to photoperiod. In late summer, however, the authors observed seedlings in flower when 1 cm in height. Several workers have reported that pigweeds seem to bloom when 45 to 60 cm tall regardless of previous light conditions (Andersen and Salisbury 1977).

Light intensity has little influence on the time of flowering. Far red promotes flowering. The date of flowering is correlated with latitude and in the north temperate zone the most northern plants flower first.

The small monoecious flowers of *A. retroflexus* have a symmetrical pattern of development along the branches of the inflorescence. Each new flower pair develops at the base of each preceding flower at right angles. As the first seeds begin to develop, the growth slows and the symmetry is upset (Murray 1940). Unpollinated inflorescences may develop up to 250 flowers. The first flower in a series is the only staminate flower and it abscisses at pollen shedding. The stigmas are receptive for varying periods of time before the pollen is shed.

Fisher (1982) reported detailed anatomical studies of the leaf of *A. retroflexus*.

A. retroflexus has a high transpiration rate as compared with maize and several other weeds (Dillman 1931, Plavsic-Gojkovic et al. 1988). It has a larger cross-sectional area of phloem than the C_3 soybean plants (*Glycine max*), and thus the former has greater translocation capacity. This is due to the greater phloem area per bundle and more vascular bundles per unit leaf area (Gallaher et al. 1975).

Injections of P^{32} were placed in specific locations in the root zone to study the pattern of P uptake by *A. retroflexus*, bean (*Phaseolus vulgaris*) and *Setaria viridis*. Pigweed roots had an extensive reach laterally, roots of *setaria* penetrated to a greater depth, and the bean drew nutrients from a limited area (Chambers and Holm 1965).

As in all species, the root development profiles reported for *A. retroflexus* are influenced by soil type, seasonal growing conditions, age of the plant and several other factors. One example of such experiments is that of Davis et al. (1967) in which seven plants, including pigweed and sorghum, were studied at season's end. *A. retroflexus* had the smallest profile of the group, reaching 1 to 1.8 m laterally and to 2.4 m depth, but all this was in place at 10 wk. The authors believe that the extensive root system of pigweed developed quickly and is an important contribution to its competitive ability (see also Cole and Holch 1941).

Sampath and Mishra (1971) reported the discovery of nodule-like structures in the roots and stems of *A. viridis* that contained colonies of an unknown microorganism. From simple experiments they believe this may be a symbiotic relationship for fixing nitrogen.

Madhusoodanun and Pal (1981), in a cytological study of the vegetable Amaranths, reported *A. viridis* to be monoecious, self-compatible, and that it may be cross-pollinated at times. Narwal (1972) in India reported two distinct forms of *A. viridis* in the Punjab: an erect form in sunny dry areas and a geniculately ascending form in shady moist areas. Gifford and Rondet (1965) and Nougarede et al. (1965) made cytohistological studies of the apical meristem of *A. retroflexus* under various photoperiodic regimes.

RESISTANCE TO HERBICIDES

A. retroflexus was one of the two species to first show resistance to herbicides. In the past two decades 15 countries have reported more than 100 weed biotypes resistant to the active ingredient of 15 herbicides (LeBaron and Gressel 1982, Benbrook 1991). Costa Rica is the only Latin America country to report a resistant weed species, while all other continents have one to several problems. The early pigweed-triazine resistance was detected in nurseries and maize fields after several consecutive years of chemical use in the northwestern United States. Resistant populations (R) have also been found in orchards, vineyards, and many agronomic and horticultural crops and fields where triazine herbicides are in constant use.

The biotypes that became troublesome were not recognized to be present or different in any way until repeated herbicide treatments were used. It is possible that they would never have been weed problems if this new, selective pressure had not been applied to the fields in consecutive seasons. The R-plants were first thought of as biotypes of *A. retroflexus*, but we soon learned that in most cases they were other species in the population resembling *A. retroflexus*: *A. hybridus* and *A. powellii* (Bandeen et al. 1982). We now know that all three species have their own S- and R-biotypes as well.

Pfister et al. (1981) found that resistance to triazines is maternally inherited and is conferred by a single recessive gene. This gene alters triazine binding sites on the chloroplast membrane. A consequence of this is that R-genotypes, which are at a very low level in a population, can build up a resistant field population very quickly (Scott and Putwain 1981).

First attempts to explain resistance centered on studies of alteration in the uptake, translocation, or metabolism of the herbicide but these proved to be inadequate. It was soon learned that the resistance of these biotypes is based on differences at the active site, where there is a change within the chloroplast thylakoid system that prevents the binding of triazine herbicides that is associated with inhibition of photosynthesis.

Studies have shown that S-species and S-biotypes are more competitive than the R-types and have greater dry matter production with and without competition in the absence of the triazines. These results have led to speculation that this may explain the dominance of the S-types before repeated use of herbicides. There is more to be learned about this, however, for Benyamini et al. (1989) have recently reported R- and S-biotypes of several grass weeds in Israel that showed similar growth with or without competition. The authors suggest that in high light conditions in different parts of the world, R- and S-biotypes may not respond in the same way as in cooler temperate areas. High light intensity is often associated with high temperature and it was shown that triazine resistance is accompanied by increased sensitivity to higher temperatures. This too may be a factor in the geographic distribution of R-weeds.

ECONOMIC IMPORTANCE

A. retroflexus is a serious weed of barley in Canada, Korea, and the United States; of citrus in Spain, of coffee in Brazil, of cotton in Brazil, Israel, Mozambique, and South Africa, of flax in Canada, of maize in the former Afghanistan, Brazil, Hungary, Israel, Italy, Spain, Turkey, and Yugoslavia; of oats in Canada, of orchards in Spain, of peanuts in Israel and Lebanon, of potatoes in Hungary and Poland, of rape in Canada, of soybeans in Brazil and Lebanon, of sugar beets in Hungary, Lebanon, and the United States; of sunflowers in Canada and Hungary, of vegetables in Afghanistan, Lebanon, the former Soviet Union, Spain, and Turkey; and of wheat in Afghanistan, Canada, India, Korea, the former Soviet Union, and Tanzania.

It is a principal weed of asparagus, beets, rye and strawberries in Canada; of edible beans in Canada and Colombia, of cabbage in the former Soviet Union, of carrots in

Canada, the former Soviet Union and the United States; of cereals in Canada, Lebanon, and the United States; of citrus in Cyprus and Lebanon, of cotton in Bolivia, Colombia, Guatemala, Iran, Spain, Turkey, and the United States; of flax and lucerne in the United States, of maize in Austria, Bolivia, Colombia, Czechoslovakia, Guatemala, Lebanon, Madagascar, New Zealand, Romania, the former Soviet Union, and the United States; of millet in the former Soviet Union and the United States, of onions in Bolivia, Canada, Spain, and the United States; of orchards in Switzerland and Tunisia, of peas in Bulgaria and Canada, of peppers in Italy, of peanuts in the United States, of potatoes in Bulgaria, Canada, Lebanon, the United States, and the former Yugoslavia; of upland rice in Colombia and Japan, of sugar beets in Albania, Australia, Austria, Canada, Czechoslovakia, France, Germany, Iran, Israel, Italy, Romania, the former Soviet Union, and the former Yugoslavia; of soybeans in Bolivia, Spain, and the United States, of sunflowers in Iran and Spain, of tobacco in Canada, the former Soviet Union, and the United States; of vegetables in Canada, Iran, Jordan, Portugal, Switzerland, and the United States; of vineyards in the former Soviet Union, Spain, and Switzerland; and of wheat in Mozambique, Tanzania, and the United States.

It is a common weed of arable land in Germany, of edible beans in Italy and the United States, of beets in the United States, of cereals in Hungary and Tunisia, of citrus in Tunisia, of cotton and hemp in the former Soviet Union, of cucumbers in the United States, of hops in the former Yugoslavia, of legumes in Tunisia, of nurseries in Israel, of orchards in Australia, Israel, and the former Yugoslavia; of ornamentals in the United States, of pastures in Brazil, of peppers in Hungary, of sorghum in the United States, of soybean in Canada, of sugarcane in Argentina, of sunflowers in the United States and the former Yugoslavia, of tomatoes in Arabia and the United States, of vegetables in Australia, Israel, South Africa and Tasmania; and of wheat in the former Yugoslavia.

In addition to the above we have gathered information on 40 countries in which *A. retroflexus* is present in specific crops but is of unknown rank of importance. In large countries such as the former Soviet Union and the United States, the weed is present in 10 to 15 crops, and in another ten countries across the globe it is a weed of five or more crops. Most of the crops already appear in the categories given above and a further extensive list by crop and country would serve little purpose here.

A. viridis is reported in an equal number of crops, including many of those above, with an important difference. It is found in abaca, banana, cacao, dates, jute, mango, papaya, and taro—most of which are normally grown in plantation agriculture in warm regions of the tropics and subtropics, and often in humid areas. *A. retroflexus* is present but is not a problem in these crops.

The characteristic attraction for plantation fields by *A. viridis* is reflected in its distribution around the moist, warm belly of southeast Asia, into the Pacific Islands south of the Tropics of Cancer, as well as the humid coastal countries south and west of the African Sahara. The agriculture of these areas is seldom frequented by *A. retroflexus*.

By contrast, *A. retroflexus* is a weed of crops in ten or more European countries where *A. viridis* is not reported as a weed. Special mention should be made that *A. retroflexus* is a weed across the length and breadth of the former Soviet Union, the world's largest country, and although the presence of *A. viridis* is mentioned in some Soviet floras, as yet we have no reports that it has become a weed problem over this vast territory (Gusev 1972).

In spite of our efforts after several decades of using our best weed control tools, the persistent success of *A. retroflexus* as a competitor in our fields seems incomprehensible. Some examples: in a three-year weed management trial on 60 farms in wheat, oats, and barley in Canada, pigweed was still one of the principal weeds among 30 species studied (Friesen and Shebeski 1960); in Israel *A. retroflexus* is considered a very widespread common weed that in some localities becomes a major problem (Dafni and Heller 1980); in the south-central United States pigweed still infests more than 2 million ha of cotton, while north of this area in the Great Plains the farmers of western Nebraska report that widespread dissemination of *A. retroflexus* seed by surface irrigation water has made it their number one weed (Wilson 1980).

Hilbig (1987) reported that in southern Germany after 20 years of effort to control annual weeds in root crops, stands of *A. retroflexus* were increasing; and in Alberta and Saskatchewan, Canada, weed surveys in cultivated fields made in 1948 and again 30 years later confirmed that pigweed increased in frequency.

This species is regarded as increasingly hard to control in reduced and minimum tillage maize fields.

The number of studies on weed-crop competition with *A. retroflexus* is legion. In such research the experimental designs, climates, soils, and sites have varied greatly and it is impossible to generalize about the results. It is a destructive weed; on this there is full agreement. Henceforth we need only carefully designed experiments to seek out highly specialized information concerning the behavior of *A. retroflexus* in crop communities. Except for such studies, the use of our manpower and resources could be more wisely directed toward some of the unknowns in weed science. For those wishing to review information already available on the competitive ability of this species, the book of Zimdahl (1980) on weed competition is alone in its field and is excellent.

For our discussion, only three aspects of *A. retroflexus* competition will be given as illustrations. In the western United States, the soil seed reserves were studied in maize grown under furrow irrigation for 6 consecutive years. Herbicide combinations were used for weed control. At the outset 82% of the 1.3 billion weed seeds/ha in the upper 25 cm of soil were found to be from *A. retroflexus*. After the 6th cropping year the soil seed reserve of this species was reduced by 99%. The herbicide treatments were discontinued on one-half of some of the plots at the beginning of the 4th year and this increased the soil seed reserves as the weeds came back into the fields. In these plots, after 3 years without herbicide treatment, the soil seed bank reached 650 million seeds/ha or about 50% of the initial weed seed population and grain yields were reduced 39 and 14% in the 5th and 6th years, respectively (Schweizer and Zimdahl 1984).

In the central United States, during the year of establishment, lucerne planted alone, or with *Setaria faberii* or *A. retroflexus* yielded 5700, 1165 and 200 kg/ha, respectively, from two cuttings. From three cuttings in the following year, yields were 12,700, 10,400 and 3800 kg/ha, respectively (Schreiber and Oliver 1969). Competition and canopy architecture as affected by soybean row width and density of redroot pigweed were also studied by Legere and Schreiber (1989).

Working with the five different populations of *A. retroflexus* described earlier, gathered from Canada to Kansas in the United States, Heiner (1970) studied competition with soybeans in Iowa, in the United States. The most southerly population had a competitive advantage, for it could grow with increasing vigor as the crop canopy opened with the approach of maturity. The northerly population, which flowered and matured early, was very much suppressed by the soybeans and died after producing a few seeds.

In the weed competition book of Zimdahl (1980), almost 600 experiments are summarized, but only 7% of these were done outside Australia, Europe, and North America. Thus there are weed-crop communities in the tropics and subtropics about which we have no competition information. Further, as Harper (1964) and Zimdahl (1980) have reminded us, when weed competition studies are contemplated, it is well to remember that, studied in isolation, the performance of a species as a possible competitor may yield little information about its aggressiveness when grown in a field situation within a weed community with several other species that have tactics of their own for use in the search for water, nutrients, light, CO_2 and space.

In the central United States in a 10-year maize/soybean rotation trial, with various tillage systems, including no-till and limited tillage, Wrucke and Arnold (1982) found weed yields highest in no-till and lowest in conventional tillage. *A. retroflexus* was one of the major broadleaf weeds in the no-till plots.

Weed seed loss brought about by mice and insect vectors was studied in conventional and no-till soybean fields; *A. retroflexus* was among the seeds monitored. The amount of seed consumed was 2.3 times greater in no-till and the authors found selective and preferential feeding based on seed size and species. They suggest that in the long term, plant species and abundance could be changed by these practices (Brust and House 1988).

In a study of the effect of depth of plowing on pigweed seed germination in Hungary, fields were plowed to 20, 40, and 60 cm depths in autumn and to 20 cm in the subsequent 3 years. The total weight of new seeds was reduced in the first year by only 20% at 40 cm and 40% at 60 cm depth when compared with seeds at the normal plow depth of 20 cm. In the second year, the only effect was a 12% reduction in seed weight in the area plowed to 60 cm depth.

There are many reports of illness and death in domestic animals as a result of ingestion of pigweed. Sheep, hogs and young calves are more susceptible than adult cattle and horses. Oxalates, sometimes seen as crystals, in histologic sections of ailing animals, account for some of the nephrotoxic symptoms. Toxic levels of nitrates have also been responsible for sickness and some animal losses (Campbell 1924, Osweiler et al. 1969, McBarren 1983, Wohlgemuth et al. 1987, Spearman and Johnson 1989).

COMMON NAMES

Amaranthus retroflexus

ARGENTINA	yuyo colorado, atac, ataco, bledo, caa-ruru
AUSTRALIA	redroot
BOLIVIA	ataco coman, chiori
BRAZIL	bredo, carura aspero, caruru, caruru gigante
CANADA	amarante a racine rouge, redroot pigweed
CHILE	bledo
DENMARK	opret anarant, tilbagebjet anarant
ENGLAND	common amaranth
FINLAND	vihrea revonhanta
FRANCE	amarante recourbee, amarante reflechie
GERMANY	Fuchsschwanz, Rauhhaariger Amarant, Zuruckgekrummter

IRAN	taj khoroos
ITALY	amaranto, biedone
JAPAN	aogeito
LEBANON	redroot pigweed
MADAGASCAR	amatarika
MEXICO	quelite
NETHERLANDS	papegaaienkruid
NEW ZEALAND	redroot
NORWAY	duskamarant
PERU	yuyo
SPAIN	amaranto, atacu, bledo, marxant
SWEDEN	svinamarant
TANZANIA	amaranthe reflechie
TUNISIA	amaranthe reflechie
TURKEY	horoz kuyruga, kirmizi koklu tilki kuyrugu
UNITED STATES	redroot pigweed
VENEZUELA	bledo, pira
YUGOSLAVIA	hrapavi stir

Amaranthus viridis

ARGENTINA	citaco
AUSTRALIA	green amaranth, prince of wales feather
BANGLADESH	shaknatey
BRAZIL	bredo, caruru bredo verde, caruru comun, caruru verde
BURMA	hin-nu-nwe
CUBA	bledo manso
DOMINICAN REPUBLIC	bledo
EGYPT	kabshoo-lignah
FRANCE	amaranthe verte, fleur de jalousie
GERMANY	Gruner Fuchsschwanz, Noterheinich
HAWAII	slender amaranth
HONDURAS	bledo
INDIA	chaulai, chilaka, chnamat, dhimdo, jangli chaulai, khutora, kuppai keerai, tanduliya
INDONESIA	bajam, bajem ajam, bajem dempo
JAPAN	honaga-inubiyu, aobiyu
MAURITIUS	brede malabar
MEXICO	bredo blanco
NIGERIA	tete

PARAGUAY	ka'a ruru
SOUTH AFRICA	misbredie
SRI LANKA	green pigweed, kappai-kirai, sinna-kirai, siri-kirai-pillu, sulu-kura
SUDAN	lisan el tair
THAILAND	kalurai, kilitis, kilitis pak-kham-tia, phak-krom, siitan
TRINIDAD	bhaji, chow roi bhajee, garden calalu
TURKEY	horoz ibigi
UNITED STATES	slender amaranth
VENEZUELA	pira blanca

Nine

Artemisia vulgaris L.

Asteraceae (Compositae), Aster Family

MANY MEMBERS OF THE *ARTEMISIA* are aromatic, they vary from small herbs to giant shrubs, and we know them as weeds, ornamental plants, and cultivated crops harvested for their medicinal value. In ancient Greece, Diana, Goddess of the Moon, was also called *Artemis* and it is from this that we have *Artemisia*. *A. vulgaris* is of uncertain origin. It is found in almost all farming systems on all continents and most of the island chains. It is reported in 25 crops in 56 countries (Figure 9-1).

FIGURE 9-1 The distribution of *Artemisia vulgaris* L. across the world where it has been reported as a weed.

FIGURE 9-2 *Artemisia vulgaris* L.: A. habit; B. enlarged leaves; C. panicle; D. flower head;
E. flowers; F. achenes.

DESCRIPTION

A. vulgaris (Figure 9-2) is a rank-smelling, extremely variable, usually herbaceous, erect perennial 0.5 m to several meters in height; stems branched, rigid (but sometimes drooping if very tall), may be reddish in late-season, may be suffrutescent, may be grooved and angular, reproduces mainly by seeds but may regenerate from fragments of rhizomatous rootstocks; *leaves* spirally arranged with shapes varying greatly between plant types, simple to bipinnatifid with lanceolate, pointed lobes or segments, coarsely toothed, green, glabrous above, white woolly beneath, *basal leaves* short petioled, stem *leaves* sessile; *flower heads*, erect, ovoid, nearly sessile or peduncled, seriate or fascicled, arranged in dense spikes in open or dense terminal or axillary panicles, branches ascending, heads 3 mm across and 3 to 4 mm long, containing 15 to 30 florets, involucre bell-shaped, cottony, with several lanceolate *bracts* with thin, dry, membranous margins; receptacle naked, flat or convex, outer ring of female florets characterized by the very slender corolla tube from which a long two-branched *style* emerges, marginal flowers glandular, inner bisexual florets 3 to 4 mm long with *corolla* lobes brownish-yellow in upper half, lobes becoming much reflexed, *stamens* with sharply pointed, sometimes sterile tips, style branches truncate with papillose *stigmas*, sometimes both marginal and disc flowers are fertile, flowers strongly aromatic with bitter taste; *fruit* an *achene* without pappus, broadest above the middle, tapering toward scar, tips rounded, ending in a small collar; *seed* commonly a bit curved, round in cross-section, longitudinal, silvery shining stripes running along slightly shiny surface, color brown to yellow-brown, 1 to 5 mm long, 0.5 mm wide, 1000 seeds weighing 0.1 gm.

DISTRIBUTION AND HABITAT

Those who write about *A. vulgaris* repeatedly copy a phrase from one another which indicates that the species is almost exclusively found as a companion of man in the cool parts of the north temperate zone with rare extensions southward. This gives a false impression of the plant that exhibits extreme morphological and physiological variability in differing ecological habitats and of its wonderful adaptability in several regions of the world. A glance at Figure 9-1 will show that, as a weed, it is quite happy to be in many very warm places. Ohsawa (1982) has shown that in tea alone it is a weed from Soviet Georgia at lat 43° N to 27° S in Corrientes, Argentina.

In addition to seed production, many perennials send out perennating stems above or below ground that travel long distances, as in bracken fern (*Pteridium*) species. These are known as wanderers, while more stationary species such as *Artemisia* send out shorter perennating stem-rhizome materials and get annual regrowth of buds from them (Hakansson 1982). Upon cultivation the stem fragments may quickly regenerate. The seeds of *A. vulgaris* are spread by wind and water, with movement of dry hay and other forages, as contaminants in crop seed, or from seeds on plant material caught up in a ball of soil, such as nursery stocks.

The natural habitat of *A. vulgaris* is frequently reported to be the dry, open soils of roadside verges and waste places. Again, it is much more adaptable than this, for it prospers on many soil types and in many farming systems across the world. It is found in glacial areas at 3700 m in the northern Himalayas, in the extreme cold of Siberia, and along streams and ditches. In agriculture it is on sparse dry grassland, in maize grown on meadow bog soils in the moist subtropics of Soviet Georgia, and in crops intensively cultivated. It is in the disturbed soils of arable agriculture in humid and superhumid localities of Mauritius island. Because of its hardy vigorous growth it suffers little from competition by other weed species and may often be found in pure stands.

PROPAGATION, REPRODUCTIVE PHYSIOLOGY, AND MORPHOLOGY

The production of viable seed and the extension of the rhizomes in *A. vulgaris* varies considerably across the world. Pawlowski et al. (1967–68) studied seed production in more than 40 species of weeds in the former Soviet Union. They found that species with the small seeds generally produced the greatest number and that *A. vulgaris*, which may produce 200,000 seeds/plant in one season, was the most fertile of all. Dorph-Petersen (1925) in Denmark found 95% viable seed of the species in some fields and reported that most of it germinated in the spring following the season of production. By contrast, in the eastern United States, only a small amount of fertile seed is produced. Guncan (1982) reported that seed collected from tea and hazelnut plantations near the Black Sea in Turkey would not germinate. Flowering is profuse in summer, but with no viable seed formed in Mauritius. In this warm, humid area, if the aerial portion of the plant is broken by animals, hoes, or machines, the basal remnants of the stem produce new underground rhizomes, each of which gives rise to two or three erect new stems that also produce a rhizome crop. On the Black Sea coast, 75% of the buds on rhizome fragments 2 to 5 cm long produced shoots but no roots (Guncan 1982).

In Germany, Lauer (1953) found 25°C to be the optimum temperature for germination of the seed of *A. vulgaris*. The minimum temperature for germination was 7°C and the maximum something over 35°C. Regimes of temperature alternation did not improve germination. In Italy, Crescini and Spreafico (1953) and Crescini et al. (1956) found the seeds to be sensitive to light and temperature. A brief exposure to light of low intensity was sufficient to stimulate germination of the achenes. As the seeds aged they became less dependent on light and eventually could germinate in darkness. Germination was favored if seeds were held 1 to 40 days at 1°C before exposure to higher temperatures, thus the light and cold treatment together gave better germination than either treatment alone. For experimental purposes, 5 to 10 cm pieces of rhizome, taken in February in the northern United States, have been used to start new plants. Stem cuttings taken at several stages of maturity have also been successfully rooted to start new plants. In Turkey, Guncan found the range of temperatures for sprouting rhizome fragment buds was 10 to 35°C, the minimum was 2 to 5°C, and the maximum was 40 to 42°C.

In the central United States, Henderson and Weller (1985) found that *A. vulgaris* produces about 52% ray and 48% disc flowers, both of which produce seed. Twenty-five percent of the ray flower seeds germinated at maturity. One week of cold (4.5°C), moist stratification increased germination to 50%.

From the excellent work of Bostock and Benton (1979) we are well-informed about the reproductive strategy of *A. vulgaris*, as well as that of four other perennial Composites that are common and widespread weeds: *Achillea millefolium, Cirsium arvense, Taraxacum officinale,* and *Tussilago farfara*. A comparison of their production of seeds and vegetative propagules helps to inform us as we consider the aggressive potential of *A. vulgaris*. These species differ greatly in their morphology, life history patterns and breeding systems. Wild plants were studied in disturbed ground and pot experiments with serial harvests each six weeks.

The measurement of total dry weight and its allocation to plant parts in such species necessitates a consideration of (1) the support organs (root, stem, leaf), (2) the seed reproductive organs, and (3) the vegetative reproductive organs. The resources that go to the seed reproductive organs are used (1) for the embryo which represents the reserves for the next generation, (2) the pericarp, which is an investment in protection of the embryo, together with the plume which makes spatial dispersion possible, and (3) an investment in other organs such as peduncles, perianth and so on, for that may contribute to the success of pollination, dispersal by wind, and other necessary functions.

In *Artemisia*, plants of different sizes produce similar numbers of achenes per capitulum. In terms of sexual reproduction, *A. vulgaris* has quite a striking position among the five species. It ranks lowest in number of ovules per capitulum, the percent of ovules which develop successfully, and the number of achenes produced and dispersed per capitulum. It suffers only moderate loss of achenes through predation by insect larvae feeding, whereas *Taraxacum* and *Tussilago* may lose entire capitula to birds.

However, the average number of capitula produced per stem in *Artemisia* was 1900, with some of the largest stems producing 7400; *Achillea* was second with 150 and 300, respectively. This resulted in an average of 9300 achenes produced per stem for *Artemisia* with *Taraxacum* in second place at 2170.

Despite having one of the smallest embryos and the lowest ovule success rate, *Artemisia* had the highest embryo-production efficiency because it has no plume or heavy pericarps and has a low allocation to the third category mentioned above: peduncles, etc. Of the five species, *Artemisia* had the lowest total seed-reproductive allocation, the least extension of its vegetative (propagule) fragments, and therefore the lowest allocation of its resources to these organs.

In later work they attempted to relate their data on dry weight costs for the production of seeds and vegetative propagules to frequency of establishment on four substrates with propagules buried at several depths. In sum, there was no simple relationship between embryo weight and frequency of establishment. By contrast there was a strong positive correlation between dry weight of vegetative propagules and the percentage that become established. For details of the establishment of seeds and vegetative fragments in several environments see Bostock and Benton (1983).

Odum (1965) in Denmark found seeds of *A. vulgaris* germinating in soil moved from the foundations of the buildings of a monastery built in the 14th century and believed that the seed was several hundred years old.

SYSTEMATICS AND MORPHOLOGICAL DIVERSITY

Khoshoo and Sobti (1958) and later Koul (1964–65) studied the cytology of the Indian biotypes of *A. vulgaris* gathered from very high altitudes in the northwest Himalayan range down to the plains at lower elevations, as well as some of the types endemic to Europe. It is one of the striking contributions to the biology of this species and helps us appreciate the extreme polymorphism of this plant across the world. Its variation and diversity has made it a very successful plant with wide geographical distribution and ecologic amplitude. We are reminded that some types persist in mountainous areas at 3700 m, others maintain themselves in rosette form in winter in the cold of Siberia, and very tall woody shrubs with thick and linear branches with long, broad leaves may be found at lower elevations on the plains of India. Koul believes that the occurrence of the species in these diverse areas exhibits a correlation with ecological, cytogenetical and morphological variations that may be seen in the plants.

In his studies, and in most of the other literature of that area, the genotypes from Europe suggest that the species is dibasic: $n = 8$ and $2n = 16$. Only diploid material of $2n = 18$ was found in the high elevations in the innermost Himalayas that have undergone a period of glaciation. In the middle lower ranges similar diploids were taken from the tops of mountains and for some distance down the sides. At lower elevations, with extensions down into valleys, no diploids were found but tetraploid forms ($2n = 36$) were dominant. Hexaploids ($2n = 54$) appeared at still lower elevations and studies of herbarium specimens show that these are present also in Ceylon, Burma, and Siberia. Morphologically the diploids are small herbs, the tetraploids are shrubby below with an herbaceous apex, and the hexaploids are giant shrubs. As ploidy level increases, the pubescence increases and the hair becomes thick and coarse, the leaves become larger and thicker, and the degree of leaflobing and the fineness of serration decreases. Koul suggests, ". . . it seems clear that the higher polyploids of *A. vulgaris* enjoy a choice of ranges and habitats greater than those of the lower forms (diploids) on account of the lack of special physiological differentiation in the latter."

Koul was able to observe normal meiosis in most of the pollen mother cells of diploid forms but the seeds produced in all of the forms were nonviable. This failure to set seed could be due to unfavorable environmental conditions or to an incompatibility mechanism. Koul believes that single clones were transplanted from their localities so that the seed failure may be due to self-incompatibility. In this circumstance, it makes no difference whether the pollen comes from the same flower, from other flowers of the plant, or from different plants of the same clone, for the seed sterility will continue as long as the pollen has the same genetic constitution. For full details of meiotic studies see Koul (1964).

The gene exchange on which species normally depend for continuity and for variability does not function in this *Artemisia* complex in India, but it is not a danger in the short term, for it has a very viable system of vegetative reproduction. As a result of the study, the author suggests that the European *A. vulgaris* with $2n = 16$ should be separated from the Indian *A. vulgaris* ($2n = 18, 36, 54$) because the two have different basic numbers and also because they show geographical isolation and genetic sterility. The possible origins of these variants are discussed at length in his paper.

Martinoli and Ogliotti (1970) also studied the cytotaxonomy of *A. vulgaris*. In the early 19th century the genus *Artemisia* was divided into four sections based on fundamental differences in flower structure. Amel'chenko (1978) studied the achenes of *Artemisia* genus and found five categories of underdevelopment that revealed the close relations of the species from different subgenera.

Korsmo (1935) prepared illustrations in color of the floral spikes, flower heads, and achenes of this species. Aliev (1971) studied factors influencing the form and depth of the root system. He found that *A. vulgaris* and some other species follow the paths of old roots, worm holes, insect tunnels, and soil cracks.

PHYSIOLOGY AND ECOLOGY

In the eastern United States, *A. vulgaris* is considered one of the ten most serious weeds in many kinds of nursery fields. It also grows vigorously in fence rows, vineyards, and gardens. Its rhizome system, which spreads rapidly when the plants are not disturbed, crowds out other plants and in lawns and orchards it can offer severe competition. In fields that are maintained by frequent and continuous cultivation, the weed is kept under control. An occasional cultivation is not satisfactory, for the broken rhizome segments are distributed throughout a field, only to grow again. A field left undisturbed for two full seasons will become heavily infested. Long-distance dispersal occurs when rhizome pieces are caught up in balls or pots of soil during shipment of nursery stock. In the eastern United States, the shoots begin to appear in early March, several weeks before other weeds emerge. Some farmers find it is one of the most difficult nursery weeds to control and they often find that it cannot be contained with mechanical cultivation alone.

Because it is obvious that lasting control of this perennial can only be achieved by destroying the rhizome system, Rogerson and Bingham (1964) conducted detailed field experiments to better understand the vegetative organ and to record the complete cycle of growth of the plant for one season. Greenhouse containers of rhizomes were planted 4 wk prior to the preparation of the soil in experimental fields. When the plants were 10 cm high in mid-April, each was placed in a square-meter plot. Entire plants were harvested at 7, 9, 12, and 18 wk after field planting.

The first evidence of rhizome formation on young plants was at 4 wk; at 6 wk they were developing rapidly. At 7 wk the unbranched plants were 25 cm tall, there was an average of 12 rhizomes per plant, their total length was 262 cm, and all were in the top 10 cm of soil. In a few plots new secondary plants were beginning to appear from new rhizomes.

At 9 weeks, rhizomes were branching and more secondary plants were appearing. At 12 weeks, the original and secondary shoots averaged 74 and 48 cm/plant, respectively, the rhizomes were now very well branched with an average fresh weight of 100 gm/plant and a length of 700 cm. Many new plants had now been initiated just below the soil surface. Rhizomes surfaced and re-entered the soil.

The first flowers appeared four months after field planting and flowering was completed one month later or about 18 weeks after planting. Some seed was found but the viability was not reported.

During the final six weeks of growth there was a four-fold increase in weight of foliage and the meter-square plots were covered by growth of secondary plants numbering about 15/plot and ranging from 10 to 90 cm in height. In the same period the rhizomes increased four-fold to 442 g fresh weight with much secondary branching, and the rhizome systems averaged 2350 cm/plant. When these data were extrapolated to fit an area of one hectare the rhizome weight was 5275 kg/ha with a total length of 114 km/ha, and a foliage weight of 3535 kg/ha. The work was done in a very dry season (although plots were irrigated when needed) and the schedule might be altered in a year of normal rainfall with the pattern of growth remaining about the same.

A general summary of the growth pattern reveals that rhizomes began to form at a rapid rate in the upper 10 cm of soil six weeks after planting. All rhizomes were found in this same zone at harvest. Rhizome length increased 10 times in the final 11 weeks and weight increased 17 times.

These very informative experiments may serve to focus our knowledge of this plant on the time of rhizome initiation and the periods of greatest production, factors that are very important in decisions to be made about proper cultural, mechanical, and/or chemical control techniques.

Nagai et al. (1979) studied the relationship of weeds to the copper (Cu) content of soils in pear orchards in Japan. *A. vulgaris*, one of the dominant weeds, was usually found in areas where the Cu content was less than 50 ppm. It was one of the weeds most sensitive to soil Cu and sometimes showed leaf chlorosis at 15 to 20 ppm. The pears were less sensitive to the metal than *A. vulgaris.*

The *Artemisias* have a long and interesting history of usefulness for man. They are an important genus of aromatic and medicinal herbs that contain a group of terpenes and glucosides that include wormwood oil and santonin. The latter is a powerful and well-known anthelmintic (used to expel parasitic worms). It has also been used as an antispasmodic and for the treatment of colic and stomach ailments. It is still used as a diuretic (for the promotion of urination), for the treatment of skin diseases, open sores, and as a remedy for asthma.

Kaul et al. (1976) studied the antifungal and antibacterial properties of the essential oils of this species. Extracts of the plant have been reported to have good larvicidal properties and weak insecticidal activity. LeFevre and Chappell (1962) found that aqueous extracts of green or dry roots, stems, leaves, and flowers inhibited the growth of lucerne seedlings by 50%. Melkania et al. (1982) in India and Hale (1982) reported an allelopathic effect of plant and litter extracts of *A. vulgaris.*

Artemisia is known for its ability to accumulate lead. Duvigneaud et al. (1975) studied lead accumulations on *Artemisia* plant parts 150 m from a freeway in Belgium. They found 40 ppm on the inflorescences and 30 ppm on leaves. At a distance of 50 m there were also 30 ppm on leaves. Much of the lead remained on the plant surface, with little absorption to the interior and limited entry through roots. The authors estimated that the emission of lead from such plants can reach levels as high as 400 gm/ha/yr.

AGRICULTURAL IMPORTANCE

A. vulgaris is a serious weed of barley and wheat in Korea, cereals and horticultural crops in Italy, citrus in the former Soviet Union, nurseries in the United States, tea in Indonesia and Soviet Georgia. It is a principal weed of filberts (hazelnuts) in Turkey, lucerne in Japan, maize in the former Soviet Union; and vegetables in Indonesia.

It is a common weed of barley, cabbage, maize, oats, peas, potatoes, and soybeans in Soviet Far East (Uljanova 1985); cereals in England and Tunisia, orchards in Bolivia, Japan and Turkey; pastures and rangelands in Bulgaria and Hawaii; vegetables and several summer season crops in western and eastern parts of the former Soviet Union, and vineyards in Italy.

This weed is in barley and oats in Denmark, cereals in Germany, Japan and Turkey; lucerne, maize, and orchards in Italy; maize in Indonesia, orchards in France and the former Soviet Union, rangelands and pastures in Japan, Norway, and Sweden; potatoes in Germany and Poland, upland rice in Indonesia and Japan, sugarcane in Reunion, tobacco in the Philippines, turnips in the United States; vineyards in France, and the former Soviet Union; and wheat in Italy, Finland, and Spain.

In Indonesia, as some of the most serious annual weeds in tea are removed, *A. vulgaris* is one of the perennials to become an early invader to replace the annuals. The competition offered to newly planted tea cuttings in fields in Java was studied by Soedarsan et al. (1976). *A. vulgaris* and six other annual and perennial weeds were sown in the plots as seeds, stolons or shoots with rhizomes 4 wk after the cuttings of tea were transplanted. Three weed species reduced the height of the tea early in the experiment but *A. vulgaris* did not visibly harm the tea until 6 mo after the weed was introduced. At 10 mo, however, it competed with the tea more severely than any other weed except the perennial grass *Imperata cylindrica.*

Ohsawa (1982) offered some reasons for the heavy infestations of *A. vulgaris* in tea fields. In its natural habitat the tea plant is a small tree in the understory of broadleaved forests; as a crop it grows shrub-like (about 150 cm) in humid, warm areas also favorable to this weed. As tea is pruned each three to four years, the bush area is opened to light, causing the weed to become vigorous below the crop plant, where it is very difficult to control.

A. vulgaris is a major problem in maize grown on meadow bog soils in the moist subtropical areas of the former Soviet Union, and in Georgia near the Black Sea, where it is also a serious problem in tea and citrus, it is also troublesome in bay laurel, grape vineyards and orchards. At times it is a dominant weed in lucerne in the Milano region, where Moja (1958) found that cutting the second year crop at the appropriate times and at the proper height was very effective in reducing the competition offered by the weed. In Sweden, Hakansson (1982) reported that *A. vulgaris* becomes a troublesome weed in older leys and pastures grown for cutting.

Sown meadows in Japan, consisting of grasses and legumes, require constant maintenance to keep them in good condition for long periods. Optimum cutting frequency and proper fertilization are major tools in the care of such fields. If a no-cutting practice is followed, the pastures quickly revert to the vegetation of abandoned semi-natural grasslands. One of the first weeds to enter is *Erigeron annuus*, closely followed by *A. vulgaris*. The tall-growing *A. vulgaris* eventually occupies large areas of such meadows (Nemoto et al. 1977). At the National Grassland Research Institute of Japan, *A. vulgaris* is included as one of the native species in forage experiments. Relatives of this species, the sagebrushes, however, are the scourge of rangelands in many places in the world.

Schuman and Howard (1978) planted this species to reclaim disturbed soil sites in the western United States and found that it grew satisfactorily and maintained itself for several years. It also showed excellent growth and survival in reclamation experiments at the sites of mining operations. Experimental work has also been done with the species in Germany for the restoration of strip mining areas (Hundt 1978).

Barrett (1983) suggests that the changes in soil fertility, improved threshing and cleaning of crop seed, and the introduction of new crops have resulted in a decline of *A. vulgaris* in arable fields in Europe.

In a search for insecticidal properties of indigenous Indian plants, Deshmukh et al. (1982) discovered that *A. vulgaris* ranked among the top four of twenty plants tested for the control of mosquitoes and houseflies. In China the twigs are woven into ropes and burned near habitations to drive away mosquitoes.

Qinghaosu (QHS) (also known as artemisinin) from leafy parts of *A. annua* (a near relative of *A. vulgaris*) is a sesquiterpene lactone that has been used successfully on several thousands of malaria cases, and is used for studies of derivatives of QHS to find more potent antimalariates.

Nandi (1982) in India reported that bovine haematuria (blood in urine) causes serious losses in Himalayan foothills following ingestion of *A. vulgaris*, *Pteridium aquilinum* and other weeds. Animals fed on a mixture of Napier grass (*Pennisetum purpureum*) and straw were not injured. *A. vulgaris* is boiled and eaten when young in the spring in parts of Japan. In some parts of Europe the young shoots and leaves are used as a condiment in the preparation of goose and pork dishes, while elsewhere in the Far East it flavors festive cakes. It is one of the ingredients of joss sticks that are burned in Asian temples.

COMMON NAMES

Artemisia vulgaris

ARGENTINA	yuyo de san vicente
BELGIUM	bijvoet
CANADA	armoise vulgaire, mugwort
DENMARK	gra bynke
ENGLAND	motherwort, mugwort
FINLAND	maruna
FRANCE	armoise vulgaire, herbe de Saint Jean
GERMANY	Beifuss, Echter Beifuss, Gemeiner Beifuss, Gewohnlicher Beifuss, Jung Fernkraut Wider, Mugwurz Wermut
INDONESIA	baru china, genje jawa, suket ganjahan
ITALY	amarella, artemisia, artemisia vulgare, assenzio selvatico, erbe di San Giovanni
JAPAN	yomogi
MAURITIUS	brede chinois
NETHERLANDS	bijvoet
NORWAY	burot
PHILIPPINES	yerba de Santa Maria
POLAND	bylica pospolita
PORTUGAL	erva-de-fogo
REUNION	armoise, marie therese
SPAIN	artemisa, hierba de San Juan
SWEDEN	grobo
THAILAND	kotochu lalampah
TURKEY	koyun otu, misk otu
UNITED STATES	green ginger, motherwort, mugweed, mugwort, sailor's tobacco
VENEZUELA	ajenjo

Ten

Asclepias curassavica L.

Asclepiadaceae, Milkweed Family

ASCLEPIAS CURASSAVICA is a perennial herb found in many tropical and subtropical regions of the Americas, Australia and Asia but is much less frequent in Africa. While often a weed in roadsides, pastures and waste areas, it is cultivated in gardens in Israel and the Sudan. The plant contains many biologically active chemicals. Some are potential heart drugs, while others may cause sickness or death to livestock. These properties are reflected in the genus name, *Asclepias*, which is derived from the Greek word, *Asklepios*, the Greek god of medicine and healing. The species name also suggests this plant has curative properties.

FIGURE 10-1   The distribution of *Asclepias curassavica* L. across the world where it has been reported as a weed.

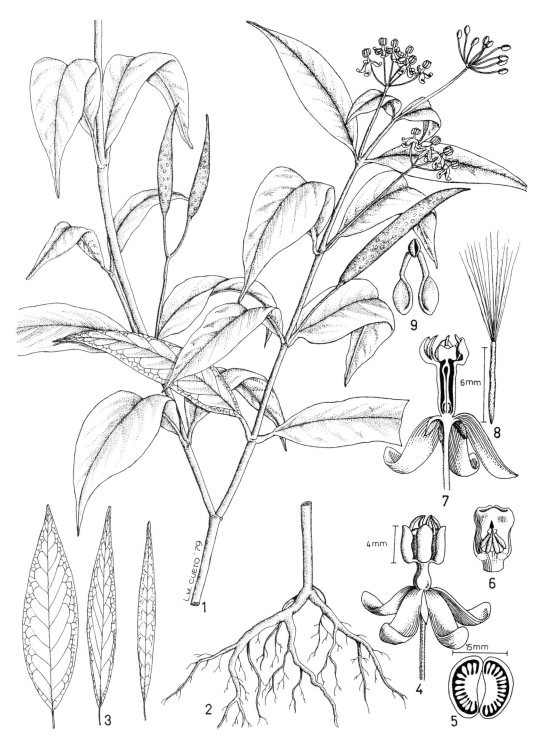

FIGURE 10-2 *Asclepias curassavica* L.: 1. flowering and fruiting branch; 2. root system; 3. leaves; 4. flower; 5. ovaries, cross section; 6. stigma and anthers; 7. flower, vertical section; 8. seed; 9. anther.

DESCRIPTION

A. curassavica (Figure 10-2) is an erect, glabrous, *perennial* sometimes *annual* herb; 30 to 120 cm tall, with a milky sap throughout; *stems* smooth, round, dull green or suffused with dull red; *leaves* simple, opposite, shortly petioled, lanceolate to oblong-lanceolate, acuminate; 7 to 13 cm long and 6 to 25 mm wide; the base narrowed; *inflorescence* an umbel with 6 to 15 flowers on terminal or axillary peduncles; *flowers* perfect, radial symmetry or irregularly shaped, bright red or orange with yellow centers; *sepals* 5, deeply divided, reflexed, green; *petals* 5, linear, base united into a fused corolla; *corolla lobes* red, reflexed, oblong, approximately 8 mm long; *corona scale* orange, 5-lobed, 3.5 to 4 mm long; *corona* hood shaped with inwardly curved horns; *stamens* 5, *anthers* with two pollen sacs; pollen aggregates into masses called *pollinia* or pollen sacs; *style filaments* united; *pistil* 2-carpelled; *fruit* a pair of dry, dehiscent, spindle-shaped *follicles*, 5 to 15 cm long, many-seeded, splitting lengthwise on one side at maturity; *seeds* ovate, flat, winged, 4 to 6 mm long, 2.2 to 4 mm wide, brown, minutely ridged, with a *pappus* of fine, white silky hairs at apex, 2 to 3 cm long.

This species is unique in having reflexed corolla lobes and the corona and style filaments united on top to form a broad stigma. The milky sap in all parts and the opposite leaves also help identify the plant.

HABITAT, ECOLOGY, AND BIOLOGY

A. curassavica is native to the tropical Americas and occurs most frequently in pastures, wastelands and along roadsides. It grows from sea level to over 1500 m in its region of origin when temperatures average 17°C or greater. While primarily found in tropical and subtropical climates, it can occur in temperate areas. It prefers open, sunny environments and is found on a wide range of soils. In lowland cultivated soils of Brazil, it behaves as an annual plant (Aranha et al. 1980). In heavily grazed pastures of Colombia, *A. curassavica* survives by growing near woody shrubs that protect it from trampling by cattle (Root and Chaplin 1976).

Flowering occurs all year in Central America and in April and May in Brazil. Flower color may vary from region to region. A yellow-flowered type in Japan is classified as *A. curassavica* forma *flaviflora* (Tawada 1972). In Puerto Rico, Velez and Overbeek (1950) reported plants with light green or white petals. Some taxonomists classify this one as *A. nivea,* while others consider it simply another variety of *A. curassavica*.

In Guyana South America, *A. curassavica* was sown at densities of 40 and 425 seeds/m^2. Viable colonies formed in 32 and 55% of the low and high density plantings, respectively (Thompson 1988). Heavy predation by monarch butterfly larva delayed plant development and maturity. Nevertheless, seed dispersal occurred 18 wk after colony establishment. Colonization by *A. curassavica* in cultivated land was considered unlikely in this coastal environment because young plants are affected by drought, predation and competition from other species.

Little is known of the biology of this plant. Stomata are present on both leaf surfaces (Mitra et al. 1974) and prominent plasmodesma are found between adjacent hair cells of the leaf epidermis (Inamdar et al. 1973). A detailed study of the morphology and anatomy of the plant's nectar system found that nectar accumulates in the corona and stigmatic chambers (Galil and Zeroni 1965). Butterflies are the most frequent flower visitors in Costa Rica (Bierzychudek 1981). The brightly colored flowers may enhance insect visits as plants

flower all year in Central America. It is not known whether insects are necessary for pollination. *A. curassavica* can be propagated via excised nodes supplied with appropriate hormones (Pramanik and Datta 1986). The chromosome number in regenerated plants varied from the normal $2n = 22$ to a high of 33 and a low of 18 in response to changes in auxin
and cytokinin levels.

The relationship between *A. curassavica* and leaf-feeding insects has been extensively
investigated. Euw et al. (1967) found the same cardiac glucosides (known as cardenolides)
in North African grasshoppers (*Poekilocerus bufonius*) feeding on *A. curassavica* as in the
plant itself. These substances can be ejected in solution through the insect's defensive
glands and each grasshopper contained sufficient cardenolides to kill a cat.

More thorough studies have been done with monarch and dandid butterflies on *A.
curassavica*. These insects acquire protection from predators after feeding on the plant. For
example, when bluejays eat butterflies that have fed on *A. curassavica*, the primary reaction
is vomiting due to the emetic properties of compounds in the plant (Everist 1974). After
two or three "emetic experiences" birds learn not to feed on these butterflies. Brower and
Glazier (1975) examined monarch butterflies and found the highest cardenolide concentrations in the insect's wings and this would give birds a bitter taste that would discourage
further feeding. The butterfly abdomen contained the greatest quantity of emetic substances and females had higher levels than males. The partitioning of cardenolides and
emetic poisons reflects a high state of evolutionary refinement in antipredator defenses.

Moisture content varies from 70 to over 90%, with the lower values common in more
mature plants and those sampled late in the day (van Emon and Seiber 1985). *A. curassavica* leaves contain 18% dry matter, 4.45% N and 4.56 calories/mg dry wt (Erickson 1973).
Monarch butterflies were more efficient in using the calories of *A. curassavica* than of three
other *Asclepias* species. Larva reared on *A. curassavica* had the highest daily biomass gain,
the shortest interval in the fourth instar, and converted the highest percentage of digested
matter into body weight. The monarch larva grew best on the most toxic species, *A. curassavica*. The dandid butterfly larva also grew best on this species (Smith 1978). The body
weight of adults fed *A. curassavica* was 1.6 times greater than that of butterfly larva feeding
on nontoxic species.

Milkweed bugs (*Oncopeltus* species) also feed on *A. curassavica*. Results of detailed
feeding studies and observations on these insects in Colombia and Costa Rica were reported
by Root and Chaplin (1976). The near elimination of *A. curassavica* by the monarch butterfly in Barbados has caused the milkweed bugs to disappear from that island (Blakley and
Dingle 1978).

AGRICULTURAL IMPORTANCE

A. curassavica is a reported weed of 21 crops in nearly 50 countries (Figure 10-1), principally in the Americas and Asia. Its economic importance is greatest in pastures where it is
reported as a serious or principal weed in Brazil, Central America, Ecuador, and Samoa; a
common pasture weed in Australia, Dominican Republic, Hawaii, Jamaica, Nicaragua, and
Surinam; and as an unranked weed of pastures in Colombia, Mexico, New Caledonia, New
Guinea, and the Solomon Islands.

It is a common weed of bananas, papaya, pineapple, sesame, sorghum, sugarcane,
sweet potatoes, and vegetables in Honduras; cereals and orchards in Turkey; coconut in
Trinidad; maize, rice, and sugarcane in Honduras and Mexico; and taro in Samoa.

In addition to the above it is an unranked weed of banana, coffee, cotton, mango, and sorghum in Mexico; edible beans, cassava, and sweet potato in Costa Rica; coconut in Cambodia; maize in Costa Rica and Nicaragua; sorghum and tobacco in Nicaragua; soybeans in Brazil; and sugarcane in Argentina and Costa Rica.

A. curassavica has been used as a home remedy for many health problems. The occasional common name of "ipecacuanha" is based on its emetic properties. In India it is used to treat warts, cancer, piles, and gonorrhea and as an emetic (Singh and Rastogi 1969). In chemical analyses on the plant, these investigators found 16 compounds and give detailed chemical characteristics of each. Smith (1978) measured 0.03% cardenolides in *A. curassavica* on a dry weight basis. Seiber et al. (1982) studied the cardenolide content in the leaves and latex of this and six other *Asclepias* species and gave structures of several cardenolides. These substances can be used to treat congestive heart failure since they increase the force of muscle contractions without a concomitant increase in oxygen consumption (Lewis and Lewis 1977). One of the cardenolides, asclepin, was isolated and studied by Arya (1979) in India. Plants yielded 0.011% asclepin. He gives the chemical structure and a full description of the compound. Kupchan et al. (1964) confirmed the plants' inhibitory activity against human carcinoma of the nasopharynx and identified the cytotoxic compound as calotropin. Alvarez and Del Pilar (1971) found *A. curassavica* among the three most active of 62 Mexican plants studied for stimulatory effects on the central nervous system of pigs, mice, rats, and cats.

While the cardenolides in this plant are harmless to insects, they cause serious reactions in vertebrate animals, and *A. curassavica* is often cited as a toxic species. When injected or force-fed, the plant can cause sickness or death. However, under natural conditions animals seldom consume the plant and hence it is not likely to affect livestock. In Australia, Everist (1974) noted that, during droughts, pigs, sheep, and cattle can be affected by consuming *A. curassavica*. A cow fed 1.4 kg over 2 days was somewhat affected; another cow given 0.7 kg in one meal was unaffected. A 300-kg steer developed heart problems and died within 15 min after drenching (administering the solution into the stomach by force) with a cold water extract of macerated plant material.

A thorough study on the toxicity of *A. curassavica* was done in Brazil by Tokarnia et al. (1972). Thirty-eight animals were fed various amounts of fresh plant material once or repeatedly over a 12-month period. No detectable effects were seen until at least 5 g/kg body weight were consumed. In some animals, 10 g/kg had no effect; however, one animal died when fed 10 g/kg. The maximum single dose eaten without causing death was 25 g/kg body weight. Symptoms included loss of appetite, diarrhea, irregular heartbeat, and bloat. Autopsies revealed hemorrhaging in the heart linings and deformed digestive tracts. If animals died of bloat this happened within 16 to 24 hr after ingestion. Plants harvested throughout the year caused diarrhea and loss of appetite, but bloat occurred only with plants harvested from October to April and heart disturbances with plants eaten in February through September. The toxic effects were not accumulative, but neither did the animals develop a tolerance to *A. curassavica* from repeated ingestion. Recovery from sickness caused by this species was rapid and complete once it was removed from the diet. As in Australia, the Brazilians note that the plant is usually not eaten. Symptoms of sickness have been reported but, under natural conditions, death from *A. curassavica* is rare.

A. curassavica and *A. speciosa* are potential alternative energy sources. Dried latex of *A. curassavica* gave 4660 cal/g, well below the 9000 cal/g of resin (van Emon and Seiber 1985). However, the heat content of dried stems is 4200 cal/g, close to that of hardwoods (4500 cal/g) and lignite coal (3900 cal/g). *A. curassavica* contained the highest (19.3%) protein content of 29 lactiferous species and was considered a promising source of hydrocarbon and other petrochemicals (Marimuthu et al. 1989).

This weed can host several important pests, such as cucumber mosaic virus (Silberschmidt 1955), powdery mildew (Sachan and Sharma 1980), aphids (Velez and Overbeek 1950), and the trypanosome *Phytomonas elmassiai*, a flagellate protozoa (Ayala et al. 1975). The plant hosts a trypetid fruit fly in the Sudan that forms galls and can kill young plants. In Brazil it hosts the root-knot nematode.

COMMON NAMES

Asclepias curassavica

ARGENTINA	bandera espanola, quiebra arado, yerba de la vibora
AUSTRALIA	red head cottonbush
BOLIVIA	flor de seda, mata caballo, platanillo lechoso, seda seda
BRAZIL	algodaozinho do campo, capitao de sala, erva de paina, oficial de sala
CHINA	lian sheng gui zi hua
COLOMBIA	algodoncillo, bencenuco, flor de muerte, mal cascada, oficial de sala, platanillo
CUBA	yerba de la calentura
DOMINICAN REPUBLIC	algodon de seda
EL SALVADOR	sangria, senorita
FIJI	false ipecacuanha
HAWAII	blood flower, butterfly weed
HONDURAS	viborano, vinorama
INDIA	kakatundi
JAMAICA	blood flower, redhead, wild ipecacuanha
MADAGASCAR	fanorimena
MEXICO	calerona, flor anaranjada, hierba de la vibora, lechosilla, marianilla, mata caballo
PANAMA	nino muerto
PERU	flor de muerte, flor de la reina, flor de seda, quita soliman
PUERTO RICO	algodoncillo, platanillo
TRINIDAD	false ipecacuanha, poison Joanna, redhead, red top
VENEZUELA	yuquillo

Eleven

Asphodelus tenuifolius Cav.

Liliaceae, Lily Family

IN EARLY GREECE THE ASPHODEL, with its pallid yellow flower and wan green leaves, was the peculiar flower of the dead. It was associated with tombs and arid places and was often planted near graves to provide food (seeds) for the soul of the dead during migration to heaven or hell. *A. tenuifolius* is a truly exceptional monocotyledonous plant in that it has what appears to be the taproot of a dicotyledonous plant. Actually the root is a peculiar bundle arrangement of fibrous roots, that at some soil depth penetrates the outer sheath to form a truly spreading, fibrous root system. The species is in a cosmopolitan fam-

FIGURE 11-1   The distribution of *Asphodelus tenuifolius* Cav. across the world where it has been reported as a weed.

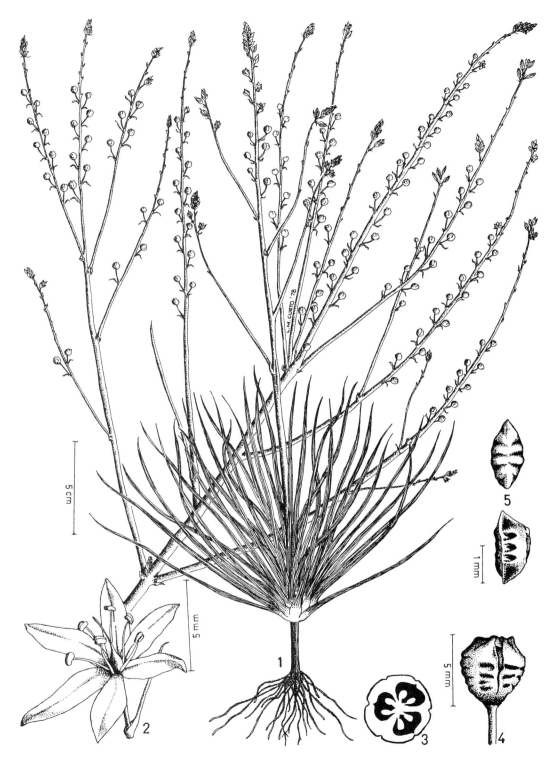

FIGURE 11-2 *Asphodelus tenuifolius* Cav.: 1. habit; 2. flower; 3. ovary, cross section; 4. fruit; 5. seed two views.

ily, most members of which are herbs, and a large portion of these have swollen storage organs, such as bulbs, rhizomes, and other fleshy root types. It is a serious weed in the India-Pakistan area and a close relative, *A. fistulosus*, is a serious weed in areas of Australia. Several transition forms between these two species may be seen in the eastern Mediterranean area.

DESCRIPTION

A. tenuifolius (Figure 11-2) is an erect *annual* herb; *root* (described later) yellowish in young plants and dark brown at maturity; *leaves* numerous, all basal, hollow, slender, gradually acuminate to a point, 10 to 40 cm long, the base sheathing, smooth to minutely hairy; seeming to arise as a "bunch" from the soil, *scapes* several, simple, sparse dichotomous branching in upper region, stout, 3 mm in diameter, up to 60 cm long; *flowers* campanulate, white with pink or purple stripe, in lax racemes; *bracteate*, pedicellate, short pedicel may be jointed; *petals* 1.5 cm long in 6 perianth segments; *stamens* 6; simple, superior, 3-carpelled, 3-loculed *ovary*; flowering progressing upward in the inflorescence over a period of weeks, normally flowers do not open until late afternoon and unless conditions are dull and cool will close and wither before the next day; *fruit* a 3-valved globular *capsule*, dehiscing at partitions into the cavity, transversely wrinkled, about 3 mm long; *seeds* 3-angled, 4 by 2.25 mm, blackish, finely pebbled texture, deep irregular dents on face and back.

DISTRIBUTION AND HABITAT

As seen in Figure 11-1, *A. tenuifolius* is generally present from the Canary Islands to the countries surrounding the Mediterranean Sea and across the Middle East to Afghanistan. To the south it is found from Sudan across the Arabian Peninsula to India and Malaysia. It is in Central America and northern South America. It surely causes the greatest difficulty in agricultural fields in the India-Pakistan area. It is found to 2200 m in the mountains of the India, Pakistan and Afghanistan borders. In agricultural lands, it prefers areas of temperature and rainfall that support wheat, peas, potatoes, mustard, and cotton.

In a region of heavy infestation in India, a series of experiments revealed that the weed is most competitive where the soil has a *pH* of 7, a water-holding capacity of 40%, an N level of 0.05%, and an organic matter content of 0.7 to 1.5% (Tripathi 1968).

PROPAGATION

A. tenuifolius reproduces by the seeds provided to cultivated fields in great quantity. The amount of weed seed in fields often continues to rise because the life cycle is generally completed and the seed is shed before the crop is harvested. The fruiting capsule breaks open into three parts, each of which contains two seeds. During this process, the seeds fall slightly away from the plant. Plants harvested with the crop will contain some seed that may thus be moved a long distance. Dirt on machines moves the seed from field to field. It is sometimes returned to fields with manure. Tripathi (1977) found the weed growing on 40% of the manure heaps observed. Tripathi (1968) collected seeds 8, 20, and 32 months before a germination trial and stored them in bottles. Germination was 22, 90, and 100%, respectively. Fresh and 6-month-old seed did not germinate. In other experiments, he demonstrated that seed giving low germination at harvest would provide 50 to 98% germination if cracked or scarified with acid. Seeds germinated at 33°C gave 2% emergence, but if held at 13°C for 17 hr and 24°C for 7 hr 36% emerged. Khan and Chaudhri (1957) obtained no germination at 0, 2, 7, 9, 30, or 40°C, but found favorable germination at alternating temperatures of 9 and 30°C. Stratification also broke dormancy and improved germination. They found an annual internal periodicity of germination. Seed harvested in May gave a maximum germination of 12% through September with their best treatments. Germination then increased gradually to 100% by December, after which it slowly decreased. They feel the internal capacity of the seed to germinate coincides exactly with the active phases of growth in the plant. Light had no effect on seed germination.

Seed dormancy in this species is thus shown to be due to both external and internal factors. The hard coat affects the exchange of gases and the uptake of water. In addition, the seed will only germinate at certain times of the year.

Tripathi (1968), at the end of the growing season, harvested seed that was (a) green and not fully developed, 2 wk after flowering; (b) green and fully developed, at 3 wk after flowering; and (c) fully ripe and dry. The seed was held in dry storage for 8 months; the green but fully developed seed showed 44% germination, while the seed that had ripened and dried in the field before harvest gave only 30% germination. After 20 months in dry storage, the latter seed gave 98%, the highest germination rate in the tests. Thus, the embryo slowly afterripens and scarification and/or other treatments are not required. Another very important finding came out of these tests. The seed harvested green and not fully developed gave 74% and the green but fully developed gave 90% germination at 20 months. This tells us that, whenever possible, the plants should be removed from the field before any seeds have progressed this far.

Seed output per plant ranged from 270 to 2300 on plants taken from five different wheat fields in India (Tripathi, 1968). The seed is found as a contaminant in wheat seed supplies in the Haryana area of India (Tripathi 1977).

MORPHOLOGY

The seedling exhibits an epigeal germination. The pointed, acute end of the seed breaks, the radicle grows out and down, while the plumule emerges and proceeds upward in a needle-like structure that bears the cotyledon and the seed coat at the tip. In about a week, the second leaf appears in the axil of the already developed plumule that functions as the first leaf, the stem being almost absent.

The vegetative stem, even in mature plants, is very much compressed, with a number of inflorescences arising in the axils of the half-sheathing leaves. The base of the compressed stem is continued downward into a taproot-like structure. The roots eventually reach to a depth of 12 to 20 cm, depending on soil type.

This weed, one of the most common in several of India's winter crops, has a peculiar root system that differs from ordinary monocotyledonous plants, and perhaps among the entire group of Angiosperms. This root system must be respected in the planning of control measures and in understanding the competition offered by the species.

Superficially, then, it has the appearance of the taproot system of the dicotyledons. Upon closer examination, the ridged and furrowed organ looks like a hard and compacted bundle of fibrous roots. The bundle sometimes twists and may have a rope-like appearance. Unlike the taproot, the vascular tissue here does not truly branch, but splits, and the ridges and furrows can be followed into thinner bundles from which different roots receive their vascular supplies. These in turn may show ridges and furrows that lead to further extensions of the root system. It is thus that a fibrous-type root system is later formed.

Internally it has been shown that the first roots are formed early in the hypocotyl of the seedling. The primary root persists and the intracortical roots that are formed travel downward in the cortex of the disc and the persistent primary root. They may even branch there. The branches ultimately come out singly or in groups of two or more. A periderm is developed around the cortex of the main root by a cambium, and where the intracortical roots are near this main periderm, partial periderms may be developed at their outer margins.

If these are compared to the adventitious roots of other monocotyledonous plants such as maize (*Zea mays*), it is seen that the roots of *A. tenuifolius*, instead of moving at right angles to the main root axis and coming out directly as in maize, first travel for some distance longitudinally through the main cortex, with some branching there before emergence.

Anatomical sections reveal that the branches move to the outside by rupturing the sheathing tissues, already bearing a well-developed root cap formed while inside the cortex. A cavity always precedes during this process, suggesting that the roots make their way by dissolution rather than tearing. Inspection of older, thicker branch roots, reveals that they are quite swollen in places before the branch roots break through.

The intracortical roots thus have a multiple vascular supply derived from a number of strands situated at widely different levels. The first roots are formed just below leaf traces and a part of their vascular supply is derived from them.

In sum, these roots seem to be unique among the Angiosperms in the following ways: (1) they have a multiple vascular supply derived from a number of strands situated at widely different levels, (2) the direct connection between each root and a leaf, and (3) the development of partial periderms only at points of contact with the main periderm (Mehta 1934, Pant 1943).

Sharma and Bhattacharyya (1957) have reported on cytological studies of the species in India.

PHYSIOLOGY

The seedlings of the weed begin to appear about 10 days after the crop planting. The morphology of early seedling development is outlined in the preceding section. From emergence in late October in India to the first weeks in December, the plant grows vegetatively. Then the first occasional flowers appear and flowering continues until the peak period in early January. Flowering is closely followed by fruiting and sometimes the number of fruits on a plant may equal the number of flowers at the end of the year. At the end of February, the leaves begin to dry and fall; near the end of March the capsules ripen and dehisce and a few green plants are to be seen in early April. In India Sant et al. (1979) made semi-monthly harvests of biomass of *A. tenuifolius* in wheat fields and found an initial slow increase in the aboveground parts, followed by a sudden increase between 60 and 100 days as vigorous flower and seed production began. The underground biomass increased to 105 days, then decreased as the plants repartitioned their resources. The total biomass increased to 120 days.

Tripathi (1968), in experiments in five wheat fields on as many different soil types, showed that the best performance in vegetative growth and seed production was on areas with abundant N and the highest levels of organic matter. He also carried out experiments with different densities of weeds and crops in a field. *Asphodelus* was found to be rather sensitive to the increased competition offered by high densities of crop plants.

Hand-pulling of this weed is common in India, but the unusual configuration of the sturdy root often results only in top removal with this method. To simulate this practice, clipping experiments were designed with the following treatments: (a) unclipped, (b) clipped during the vegetative growing period, (c) clipped during the flowering stage two months later, and (d) clipped at both b and c periods. The plants clipped during the vegetative period gave higher values for height, shoot spread, root length, number of capsules per plant, and dry weight of both shoots and roots when compared with unclipped plants. Clipping during the flowering stage, or at both the vegetative and flowering stage, was damaging to the plant. Thus we learn that top removal at one stage (are there others?) may be beneficial to weed growth, and it becomes obvious that if hand-weeding is the practice, it must be done repeatedly.

Khan and Chaudhri (1957) found that flowering is favored by long-days and that short-days promote vegetative growth. Experiments under continuous light revealed that the tendency to flower increased from October to December. An average of 22 nodes were formed before the plant flowered in October, but only 15 nodes in December. This internal rhythm of vegetative and flowering phases is thus consistent with the behavior in the field. In India it behaves as a winter annual, with emergence in October through November. It is vegetative during the short-days of winter and responds by flowering as the longer days of spring approach.

Sen and Harsha (1974) studied the stomata and guard cells of the attached and detached epidermis of onion *Allium cepa* and *Asphodelus* in India. As might be expected, the stomata were normally open during the day and closed at night. The aperture was wider before midday. Starch and chloroplasts were present in the guard cells of *Asphodelus*, but there were few chloroplasts and no starch was visible in their onion material. The study also reported treatments and responses of stomatal openings with changes in *pH* and sucrose and inorganic ion concentrations.

Saeed and Malik (1961) have reported on the amino acid composition of the proteins of *Asphodelus fistulosus*.

To investigate one factor in the competition of weeds with crops in India, Pandey et al. (1971) using P^{32} studied total P uptake for a 24-hr period in ten crops and weeds at 20-day intervals during the growing season. Purple Nutsedge (*Cyperus rotundus*), the world's worst weed, and wheat (*Triticum vulgare*), one of the world's major crops, were included in the study. *A. tenuifolius* exhibited a bimodal pattern of uptake, with peaks during the first 30 days and at 70 to 80 days at flowering and fruiting. By contrast, nutsedge had a very high rate of uptake during the first 2 weeks, followed by a gradual decline. Wheat showed a gradually rising uptake to 50 days and then a very vigorous increase to a very high level at flowering. On total P uptake for the season, wheat and nutsedge were among the most demanding, while *Asphodelus* was intermediate among the plants studied.

The study suggests that in India the rainy-season crops will have vigorous competition for P from a vigorous, vegetative perennial such as nutsedge, while winter-season crops will have early-season competition for P from several weeds, but must also face late-season high demands for P from plants such as *Asphodelus* growing in the same field.

From these studies, we learn that this weed completes its cycle with the crop and that a considerable portion of the weed seed is dispersed before the crop is harvested. If the weed can be disturbed or removed before seed set, the crop losses from this species can be minimized. The average seed output is very high and the plant is thus able to colonize new areas. Very high rates of increase in population may follow if the weed is unattended. We learn also that if hand-weeding cannot be done repeatedly, it may be best to use some other method.

AGRICULTURAL IMPORTANCE

A. tenuifolius is a weed of 15 crops in 17 countries (Figure 11-1) and is frequently reported a serious weed of wheat in India and Pakistan. It is a principal weed of chickpeas, lentils, linseed, peas, potatoes, tobacco, and many winter season crops in India. It is a weed of unknown rank in barley in India and Jordan; citrus, dates, lucerne, and vegetables in Arabia; maize in Malaysia; cotton, gram, mustard, sugar beets, and sugarcane in India; several winter crops in Pakistan; and wheat in Bangladesh, Jordan, and Nepal.

In all of agriculture, the heavy weed growth in late season following early treatments with short residual herbicides such as 2,4-D or low levels of triazine herbicides (to prevent crop injury in a subsequent year), may perpetuate the weed problem by allowing heavy seed production. In an effort to disrupt seed formation in several weeds, Singh and Saroha (1975) treated plants with 2,4-D at 1 kg/ha at several stages after anthesis. Later treatments allowed more and more viable seed production. Treatment at the time of 50% flowering prevented seed formation in *Asphodelus*. Treatment 5 weeks later reduced the number of viable seeds by 75%. The authors believe the male and female reproductive structures were severely injured prior to zygote formation. The zygote is usually complete within a week after flowering, and subsequently there is an increasing resistance to 2,4-D injury.

Sharma noticed that birds were feeding on *Asphodelus* seeds in the field and discovered that one gram of seed was fatal to some birds (Sharma, M. 1977).

COMMON NAMES

Asphodelus tenuifolius

INDIA	bhukat, bokat, pyazi
PAKISTAN	pyazi
SAUDI ARABIA	barok, basal-esh sheitan
UNITED STATES	asphodelus

Twelve

Azolla pinnata R.Br.

Salviniaceae, Salvinia Family

AZOLLA PINNATA is one of several water ferns. It has been intensively studied because it symbiotically hosts the nitrogen-fixing algae *Anabaena azollae* in its frond cavities. Several Asian countries use *Azolla* as a source of nitrogen for rice. However, this free-floating aquatic tropical is also a serious weed. It reproduces both vegetatively and sexually and can cover open bodies of water quickly. Its thick mats often eliminate mosquitoes and thus it is sometimes called "mosquito fern" (Svenson 1944).

FIGURE 12-1 The distribution of *Azolla pinnata* R.Br. across the world where it has been reported as a weed.

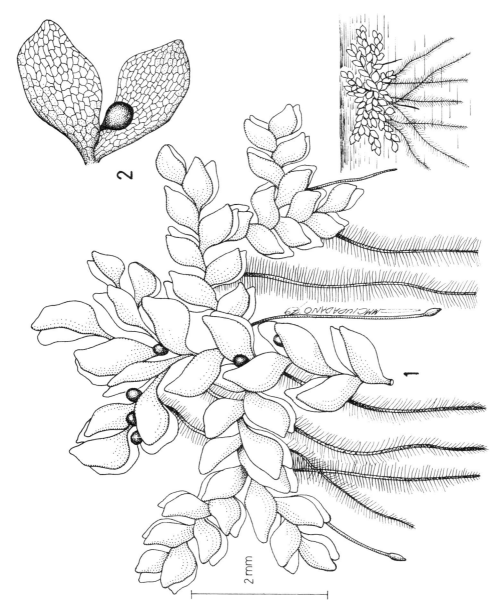

FIGURE 12-2 *Azolla pinnata* R.Br.: 1. whole plant, showing feathery roots and younger roots with root caps; 2. leaf with megasporocarp.

2 mm

DESCRIPTION

A. pinnata (Figure 12-2) is a free-floating *annual* plant; usually found in large clusters and may form mats several layers deep; usually green, occasionally orangish red to reddish purple; single plants are 1 to 2.5 cm in diameter, with triangular or polygonal shape, composed of a cluster of densely arranged fronds; *fronds* composed of two overlapping lobes arranged in two lateral rows; lobes 1 to 2 mm long with central cavity serving as a float; *lower lobes* submerged, lack chlorophyll; *upper lobes* thicker than lower lobes, do not touch water, have chlorophyll, and host bacterial symbiont in cavity connected to atmosphere by single pore at tip; fronds overlap to hide alternating branched, floating *rhizome*; branches of rhizome with abscission layer at point of attachment; *adventitious roots* arise at nodes on ventral side of rhizome, 1 to 4 cm long with numerous *root hairs* 1 to 2 mm long; a root cap covers root tip; *sporocarps* found where branching begins and they replace lower lobe of first frond on branch; short-stalked, enclosed by *involucre* on ventral side; *megasporocarps* 1 mm long, 0.5 mm wide with pointed ends, smaller than *microsporocarps*.

DISTRIBUTION AND HABITAT

A. pinnata is found in nearly all the Asian countries, in most of tropical Africa, New Zealand, and Australia (Figure 12-1). It is found in tropical regions and in lakes, marshes, ponds, paddy fields, ditches and rivers of warm temperature. Wave and wind action reduce *Azolla* growth and fragment the plants, thus it seldom occurs in large lakes or rapidly moving water. Because it is not dependent upon N in the water and is free-floating, it can inhabit areas other weeds cannot. The dissemination of *A. pinnata* in China, Vietnam, and Thailand has been promoted among rice growers for use as a N source, and similar practices are now encouraged in Indonesia, India, and other countries.

TAXONOMY AND MORPHOLOGY

Water ferns are not true ferns because they are free-floating aquatic plants and because they produce both male and female spores, whereas true ferns have only one type. The *Azolla* genus was described in 1785 (Svenson 1944). Six living species can be identified. *A. pinnata* is one of the oldest species in the genus, as fossil records date it to the Pleistocene era. The name is derived from the Greek *azo* to dry and *ollyo* to kill, suggesting the plant dies when not in water. Adventitious roots originate on the ventral side of the stem (Sud 1934) and hang freely in the water. The feathery appearance of the root hairs gave rise to the species name "*pinnata*" (Rao 1935).

A. pinnata is a member of the Salviniales, and the genus is divided into two sections based principally on the number of megaspore floats. Species in the Euazolla section have three floats while those, like *A. pinnata* in the Rhizosperma section, have nine floats (Svenson 1944). Because accurate identification of *Azolla* species is difficult, several synonyms have arisen, including *A. africana* and *A. imbricata* (Shen 1960, 1961; cited by Moore 1969). A thorough review of *Azolla* taxonomy was done by Tan et al. (1986).

Stomata occur in vertical rows on both surfaces of the upper lobe but only on the upper surface of the lower lobe. Stomata have one ring-like guard cell and may number 112 stomata/mm^2 (Inamdar et al. 1971). The guard cell is unique in that the mother-cell fails to form two distinct cells during cell division, thus it remains unicellular but is binucleate (Sen 1983).

REPRODUCTION

Azolla is capable of both vegetative and sexual reproduction. Its rapid expansion under proper environmental conditions is the result of vegetative reproduction that occurs when an abscission layer forms at the base of lateral rhizome, allowing it to separate from the main rhizome. A small root is present on the detached branch.

The sexual heterosporous (both male and female spores on the same plant) reproduction cycle often begins in the cooler months and starts when megasporocarps and microsporocarps form in the axils of older fronds (see Figure 12-3). Sporocarps occur in

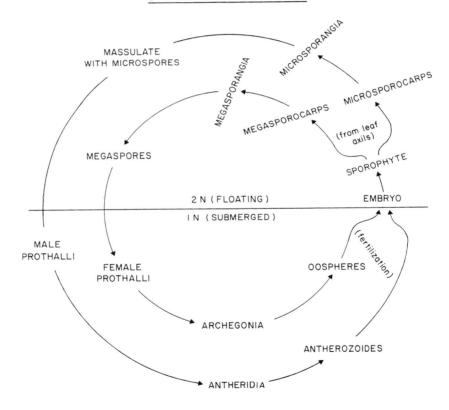

FIGURE 12-3   Life cycle of *Azolla*, illustrating the gametophyte and sporophyte generations.

pairs; normally a pair of either micro- or megasporocarps is formed, but occasionally one of each occurs. Each microsporocarp contains 7 to 100 stalked microsporangia, each producing 32 to 64 microspores. Microspores are not released individually but in complex structures of hardened mucilage known as "massulae." These hold clusters of microspores together and contain a hair-like appendage called "glochidium" on part of the microspore-massulae surface (microspores are about 1/20th the size of megaspores).

The megasporocarps develop the stalked megasporangia that produce one megaspore each. The megaspores have the characteristic nine floats of the Rhizosperma. The mega- and microspores dehisce from the mother plant at maturity and sink to the bottom (Sud 1934). Upon release from the microsporangia, the glochidia of the microspore-massulae become entangled with the megaspores.

A thorough description of *A. pinnata* embryology is given by Komar and Kapoor (1974). After a dormancy period of several months, megaspores (female) and microspores (male) germinate under water. Megaspores form a large prothallus that protrudes through the spore wall. Archegonia are formed on the upper surface of the prothallus and have a passageway leading to the egg. Microspores germinate inside the massulae. Motile sperms (antherzoides) develop that "escape" and swim toward the archegonium. When they reach the egg, fertilization occurs. The resulting embryo develops a root and foot as well as a shoot and cotyledons. As the cotyledon and first or second leaf emerge, the seedlings float to the water's surface (Campbell 1893).

Symbiosis with *Anabaena* is maintained throughout the sexual cycle (Peters et al. 1982). *Anabaena* spores or filaments are found within the megasporocarp, eliminating the need for the symbiont to live apart from its host. Spores germinate during or just after female gametophyte formation in the megasporocarp, producing additional filaments. The *Anabaena* begins to differentiate rapidly and then grows in harmony with the fern (Lumpkin and Plucknett 1980).

The life cycle of *A. pinnata* illustrates the retention of ancestral features in its ontogeny, i.e., the aquatic mode of fertilization with motile sperms (antherozoids) and the necessity of water for the sperms to achieve fertilization. In general appearance, method of reproduction, and internal structure, the species represents the progenitors of "modern plants" and gives us an idea of the nature of some of the earliest vascular plants on land.

GROWTH AND BIOLOGY

A. pinnata is found in many subtropical and tropical areas of the world but grows best in the less-severe seasons of the year and can completely cover the water's surface with one or more layers of plants. The ideal temperature for growth and N fixation is between 20 and 30°C, and if temperatures exceed 40°C *Azolla* may die (Lumpkin and Plucknett 1980). IRRI (1981) reported that the maximum growth of 27 strains occurred at 22°C and that growth was reduced by one-third at 33°C. Significant variation among strains was found and some thrive over a wide temperature range. A biotype in N. Australia gave a 14- to 16-fold fresh weight increase in 14 days at temperatures of 30/25, 38/30 and 40/32°C in 12 hr day/night periods (Chapman et al. 1981).

Azolla grows best in partial shade, and dry matter production is reduced at light intensities greater than 60,000 lux (Ashton and Walmsley 1976). A biotype from Sri Lanka survives and grows at light intensities of 75,000 lux and temperatures of 36°C (Kulasooriya et al. 1980). The Chinese hope to capitalize on this genetic variation and produce a hybrid

Azolla-Anabaena symbiont (Peters et al. 1981b). They would like to combine broad environmental tolerance, rapid sporulation, and high N fixation efficiency into the same strain. *Azolla* and *Anabaena* utilize most of the light in the 500 to 700 nm spectrum as the plant contains chlorophyll a and b and carotenoides, and the endophyte has chlorophyll a and other pigments (Peters et al. 1982).

Azolla has a high P requirement for optimum growth. If P is deficient, the normally green fronds become red or yellow. Subudhi and Singh (1979b) observed that P uptake by *Azolla* increased linearly as the applied P rate increased. The optimum level for growth and chlorophyll development was 1.2 mM of K_2HPO_4. Subudhi and Watanabe (1981) compared "batch culture", which has an initially high concentration in the growing medium, to a "continuous flow" method that maintains a constant P level. Maximum growth in batch culture occurred with 5 ppm P and at 0.13 to 0.43 ppm P with the continuous flow technique. *Azolla* growth slows if the P concentration in the plant tissue drops below 0.2 to 0.3 ppm. Great variation exists in the efficiency of P utilization among *Azolla* species and biotypes. At 0.03 ppm P, an *A. pinnata* biotype from Thailand doubled its biomass in 2.78 days; an Indonesian biotype took 4.38 days. These differences were attributed to the greater P removal efficiency of the Thailand *Azolla*.

Symptoms of P deficiency include reduced plant size, less chlorophyll, browning of the dorsal and ventral lobes and fewer *Anabaena* heterocysts in the frond cavity. The lack of P also induces longer roots that are easily broken. With P, roots were 1 to 1.5 cm long after 25 days; without P, they were 3 to 4 cm long (Kulasooriya et al. 1980).

Azolla also requires significant quantities of K, Ca, and Mg. The lack of P or Ca inhibits growth more than the absence of K or Mg (Subudhi and Singh 1979a). Iron, Mo, and Co are also essential for optimal growth. Saline conditions exceeding 1.3% salt reduce *Azolla* growth. Nutrient uptake is via the roots and not through the lower leaf lobe (Moore 1969).

There is an apparent interaction between *pH* of the water and light on *Azolla* growth. Highest growth rates occur with high light and high water *pH* or low light and low *pH* conditions (Ashton and Walmsley 1976). The optimum *pH* range is between 4.5 to 6.5. In some instances, *pH* indirectly affects *Azolla* growth by influencing microelement availability.

Azolla roots (Whatley and Gunning 1981) may contain chloroplasts. In older plants, chloroplasts are encountered near the root apex. Iswaran et al. (1980) detected a N-fixing bacterium in the phyllosphere of *A. pinnata* roots. The bacteria fixed 3.9 and 9.8 mg N/g sugar in 10 days under anaerobic and aerobic conditions, respectively.

Under favorable conditions, *Azolla* biomass doubles every 4 to 10 days. Such a fast growth rate results in rapid invasion of open waters. Biomass production from 24 (Lumpkin and Plucknett 1980) to 37 ton/ha fresh weight (Gopal 1967) have been reported. Subudhi and Singh (1979b) found that 0.5 g fresh weight of *Azolla* produced 32 g in 20 days under controlled conditions, and plants may completely cover the water's surface within 5 days after introduction in transplanted rice (Janiya and Moody 1981). Such an explosive reproduction potential underscores its threat as a weed.

As the bacteria in the fronds fix N, no external source of this element is necessary for near optimal *Azolla* growth and development. *Anabaena* is always present in *Azolla*, and the application of additional N into the growing medium often reduces *Azolla* growth except under cool temperatures when N fixation is reduced (Lumpkin and Plucknett 1980). *Anabaena* filaments without heterocysts inoculate each developing frond of the stem apex of *Azolla* (Peters et al. 1981a). Once the leaf matures, the algae cannot escape. The *Anabaena* filaments are always associated with the surface hairs of the frond cavity (Calvert and Peters 1981). No heterocysts are found in the growing tip region, but their frequency may reach 30% in mature fronds. Heterocyst development parallels nitrogenase activity.

A. pinnata is a C_3 plant and freshly harvested *Azolla* contains 93 to 94% water. On a dry weight basis, the plants contain 3 to 5% N, 1% P, 2 to 3% K, 6% fat, 60% carbohydrate, and 13 to 23% protein (Nat. Acad. Sci. 1976b). This composition makes *Azolla* useful either as a source of N or feed.

Anthocyanin production is induced when *Azolla* is exposed to unfavorable heat, moisture, or *pH*; nutrient deficiency; or insect damage. Kulasooriya et al. (1980) observed purpling of *A. pinnata* when P was limiting and under high light conditions; with no P and low light, no purpling occurred. Thus several factors may influence anthocyanin formation in *Azolla*.

NITROGEN FIXATION BY *Anabaena*

The intense interest in this small member of the plant world has focused primarily on its ability to host the N-fixing algae, *Anabaena azollae,* in the dorsal lobe cavities. The relationship is truly symbiotic. *Azolla* provides shelter, nutrients, and energy to the alga. *Anabaena* in turn fixes atmospheric N in excess of both its own and the fern's needs. Even with no N in the growing medium, *Azolla* grows normally (Cohn and Renlund 1953) unless cold temperatures greatly reduce N fixation (Lumpkin and Plucknett 1980).

Anabaena does not grow well outside *Azolla* fronds, and it fixes more N in the symbiotic environment than when isolated from *Azolla* (Becking 1976). Clark (1980) states that the rate of N fixation by *Anabaena* in *Azolla* fronds is 10 to 12 times more than that of free-living blue-green algae (Clark 1980). Its N-fixing efficiency is comparable to that of leguminous species.

Anabaena development parallels that of *A. pinnata*. Kaplan and Peters (1981) noted that *Anabaena* differentiates to form heterocysts as *Azolla* fronds begin to form a cavity. High light conditions produce more algae-free plants (Hill 1977). Algae-containing plants have a darker green center and fewer roots than algae-free plants. *Anabaena* filaments in young fronds divide rapidly and fix little N. Algae division stops long before the frond cavity fills, but the control mechanism for this is unknown. If fronds are numbered with the apex as zero, most fixation occurs between the 8th and 20th fronds.

Anabaena azollae is the only algae species found in *A. pinnata*. The alga consist of three types of cells linked together in filaments: vegetative cells for photosynthesis, heterocysts for N fixation, and akinetes or resting spores. Peters (1975) found the relative frequency of each cell type in mature fronds to be 61% vegetative, 23% heterocysts and 16% akinetes. Heterocysts develop at regular intervals on *Anabaena* filaments, lack photosystem II activity, and cannot fix CO_2. Even though the alga may contain 10 to 20% of the total chlorophyll of the association, they cannot produce sufficient carbohydrates by themselves to be efficient N fixers and must obtain supplemental energy from their host (Lumpkin and Plucknett 1980). Each cavity has 50,000 to 80,000 algal cells but they never exceed available space. Kaplan and Peters (1981) speculate that the 15 to 25 simple cavity hairs are involved with supplying fixed carbon to the alga, and the two branched hairs aid in the transfer of fixed N to the plant.

The alga fix N and excrete NH_3. A small amount of N is lost into the water, but most is retained in the *Azolla* plant as either extracellular NH_3 or intracellular organic nitrogen. Ammonia produced during fixation is released into the frond cavity and utilized by ammonia-assimilating enzymes (Lumpkin and Plucknett 1980). Nitrogen fixation is minimal in the apical region of the plant. Combined nitrogen is apparently transported to the apex, thus preventing heterocyst formation in the young fronds (Kaplan and Peters 1981).

Light and temperature affect N fixation. The fixation rate increases up to 40°C and continues for 5 hr after light has been reduced to 16% of full sunlight (Brotonegoro and Abdulkadir 1976). Nitrogen fixation by *Anabaena* has a Q_{10} of 2.2 in the 20 to 30°C range, but of only 1.3 between 30 and 40°C. Kulasooriya et al. (1980) obtained maximum N fixation at 30,000 lux, but the rate dropped at intensities above 50,000 lux, which parallels the response of *Azolla* in high light intensities. Fixation increased as P rate increased and N fixation ceased when P was absent.

The amount of N fixed by *Anabaena* has been calculated by many workers. Estimates vary from 62 to 125, 289, and 300 to 600 kg N/ha/year (Becking 1976, P. Singh 1981, and Roger and Reynaud 1979, respectively). On a dry weight basis, Brotonegoro and Abdulkadir (1976) observed the alga to fix 7.2 mg N/day/g dry weight of *Azolla*. Only 2% of the N is lost from growing plants (Moore 1969). Once a layer of *Azolla* forms on the water's surface, plants at the bottom of the layers begin to die, releasing their N. *A. pinnata* produces more biomass and is more completely mineralized than *A. filiculoides* and *A. mexicana* (Ito and Watanabe 1985). A Malaysian biotype fixed more N_2 than four biotypes from other countries.

The Vietnamese, Chinese, and Indonesians have utilized *Azolla* in rice culture for centuries. Legend holds that 300 years ago a peasant woman in Vietnam named Ba Heng discovered her rice grew better in the paddies if *Azolla* was present. Her keen observation evolved into a tradition of *Azolla* propagation. The Vietnamese still celebrate an annual fall festival in her honor. Some Vietnamese farmers in Thai Bing learned to keep *Azolla* alive during the hot period when it normally dies. Their technique apparently involves modifying the *pH* of the water so that it does not become too alkaline (Galston 1975). Farmers sell "starter stock" to other farmers in November. These plants are carefully propagated in nurseries and then moved into one corner of a flooded field. As the *Azolla* multiplies, the retaining dikes are moved until the entire paddy is covered. A 3-kg starter stock purchased in November could grow into 2500 kg of fresh *Azolla* by February. Similar propagation methods are employed in China (Clark 1980). A detailed description of many *Azolla* uses in North Vietnam is found in a report by Tuan and Thuyer (1967). A similar review of *Azolla* propagation and use in China is found in an FAO bulletin (Anon. [China] 1979), and a global assessment of *Azolla* use was published by IRRI (1987).

Vietnam had 400,000 ha of rice with *Azolla* in 1976 (Lumpkin and Plucknett 1980), and China uses *Azolla* on nearly 1.3 million hectares or approximately 10% of its rice area (Clark 1980). Both countries have "varieties" of *Azolla* that they recommend for N fixation. Careful synchronization of planting dates and water management are essential if rice and *Azolla* are grown simultaneously. Ideally *Azolla* should begin to die as rice starts tillering so that its N is released. If it lives longer, the N will not be available to the rice when needed, and *Azolla* is then considered a weed.

P. Singh (1977, 1981) found that incorporating 8 to 10 ton kg/ha fresh weight of *Azolla* into the soil before transplanting rice was equivalent to 30 to 40 kg/ha of N fertilizer. Srinivasan (1980) incorporated from 10,000 to 100,000 kg/ha of fresh *Azolla* 1 wk before transplanting and observed yields of 3900 kg/ha of rice for the control and 7300 kg/ha of rice with 60 ton/ha of *Azolla*. In general, *Azolla* provides rice the equivalent of 30 to 60 kg N/ha.

Field studies on the effect of fixed N on rice yields have lead to suggested management practices. Brotonegoro and Abdulkadir (1976) recommend (1) growing the fern prior to planting rice, (2) draining the field, (3) incorporating the *Azolla* into the soil, (4) waiting approximately 3 wk, (5) reflooding the field, and (6) transplanting rice. This procedure releases more fixed N to rice than if *Azolla* is left on the soil surface where N can be lost to the atmosphere as N_2 or leached as nitrate. *Azolla* decomposition is complete in approximately 3 wk, and reflooding the field at this time allows for maximum N utilization. Marx (1977) and Ito and Watanabe (1985) observed larger yield increases when *Azolla* was incorporated as compared to leaving the residues on the surface.

Successful use of *Azolla* requires supplemental P. One to 2 kg/ha of P_2O_5 should be added every 5 to 7 days. By making frequent applications, the total amount of P needed is less than when a large single application is made (Watanabe et al. 1980). Plants fix nearly 2 kg N/ha for each 1 kg P_2O_5 applied. Potassium and minor elements essential to N fixation may also be needed in some environments. Cow manure, rice hulls and rice chaff can also be used to promote *Azolla* growth. Insect damage must be monitored as *Azolla* is subject to attack by several foliage-feeding pests. Rice diseases or insects have not been found in *Azolla*; but when *Azolla* is transferred from one area to another, appropriate precautions to prevent inadvertent introduction of new rice pests should be taken.

In summary, there is great potential to utilize *Azolla* as a source of N in rice production. In 6 wk *Azolla* can fix as much N as a soybean crop and does not occupy extra land in the process. Careful management of soil and water nutrition, *pH*, water level, insects and rice planting dates and densities are essential to reap the benefits of this unique plant endophyte (plant within a plant) association.

AGRICULTURAL IMPORTANCE AND OTHER USES

A. pinnata occurs in much of Asia and Africa and has been reported as a weed in 30 countries, including Australia, Bangladesh, China, Indonesia, the Philippines, Thailand, and Vietnam. It is a serious or principal rice weed in India and Indonesia; a common rice weed in China; and an unranked weed of rice in Bangladesh, Cambodia, Sri Lanka, Laos, Madagascar, Nepal, the Philippines, Thailand, and Vietnam.

A. caroliniana and *A. mexicana* are widely distributed in warm-temperate and tropical regions of the Americas. *Azolla* species present the same problem as any other floating aquatic plant and can interfere with paddy rice production, because they can double their biomass in 2 to 4 days. Its dense mats can clog irrigation and drainage canals and interfere with fishing.

Azolla has been utilized for centuries as livestock feed in Indochina. It contains approximately 24% crude protein, 4.4% crude fat, 9.5% fiber, and 6.4% starch on a dry weight basis (Moore 1969). *Azolla* is high in K and its ashes can be mixed with fat to produce soap. It can be used to feed fish and to purify water of N, P, and heavy metal contaminants.

Chickens prefer eating fresh, green plants over dry or red plants (Subudhi and Singh 1978). No sickness or mortality was noted when chickens were fed *Azolla*, and a ration with up to 25% *Azolla* plants caused no loss in production. From 540 to 720 kg/ha/mo of plant protein could be provided by *Azolla* (Lumpkin and Plucknett 1980).

Azolla inhibits other weeds in paddy rice culture. Janiya and Moody (1981) introduced 0.5 kg *Azolla*/m² when rice was transplanted, and the surface was covered in as few as 5 days. *Azolla* reduced the growth of *Monochoria vaginalis* by 83 to 96%, *Echinochloa glabrescens* by 87 to 97%, and *Cyperus difformis* by 94 to 100%. *Scirpus maritimus* and *E. crusgalli* grew through the *Azolla* mat and were not controlled. Thus the usefulness of this weed management system varies with the weeds present. This method is also labor intensive, as the *Azolla* requires propagation in nurseries, frequent P and insecticide applications and careful water control. The system may require additional land to produce *Azolla*, and the plants need to be mechanically incorporated into the soil or killed with herbicide to release the N.

COMMON NAMES

Azolla pinnata

AUSTRALIA	ferny azolla
BANGLADESH	kutipana
CAMBODIA	chak krahan, chak pos kra bey
CHINA	hang ping, ho ping, lu ping, man chiang hung shu
GERMANY	Algen Farn
INDIA	pana
INDONESIA	kayu-apu dadak
JAPAN	a-aka-ukikusa, b-aka-ukikusa, o-aka-ukikusa
LAOS	nae harng hern
MADAGASCAR	ramilamina
PAKISTAN	kutipana
THAILAND	naedaeng
UNITED STATES	mosquito fern, water velvet
VIETNAM	beo-daw, beo-hoa dau, beo-giau

Thirteen

Boerhavia diffusa L.
and Boerhavia erecta L.

Nyctaginaceae, Four-O'Clock Family

BOERHAVIA DIFFUSA AND B. ERECTA are widely distributed weeds in tropical and sub-tropical regions of the world. Plants in the four-o' clock family are apetalous and have several features of the **Polygonaceae** family except that the *Boerhavia* species have opposite leaves. **Nyctaginaceae** members often have brightly colored petals or bracts. The *Bougainvillea* genus is one of the most attractive in the family and is a common ornamental. The family name is derived from the Greek *nyctos*, referring to night, because the flowers of several species close at dusk. This is why the family is referred to as the four-o'clocks. The *Boerhavia* genus is named after the Dutch naturalist, Hermann Boerhaave (thus the frequent but incorrect spelling as *Boerhaavia* in the literature). Taxonomists disagree on the number of species in this genus, citing three to forty valid members. The species names *diffusa* (meaning loose, open or widely spreading) and *erecta* are descriptive of the plant's growth habits.

DESCRIPTIONS

Boerhavia diffusa

B. diffusa (Figure 13-1) is a diffuse, spreading, laxly branched *annual* or *perennial* herb with a thick, fleshy *taproot*; *stems* prostrate initially, then upright from 40 to 150 cm in length, much branched, slender, often red-tinged to purplish, glabrous to slightly pubescent, swollen at the nodes; *leaves* simple, fleshy, scattered, opposite, pairs unequal in size, ovate, elliptic or oblong, 1 to 5 cm long, occasionally with wavy or lobed margins, base usually rounded, blunt at tip, dark green to purplish above and pale beneath; *petioles* 1 to 3 cm long, stipules lacking; *inflorescence* a lax cyme with slender branches, pink to red, fascicled or subumbellate flowers on terminal branchlets; *flowers* perfect, regular, about 1.5 to 2.5 mm long with a 5-lobed persistent *perianth*; 2 or 3 *stamens* just protruding beyond perianth; *pistil* 1-carpeled; *fruit* an *anthocarp* with *achene* enclosed in the hardened, persistent

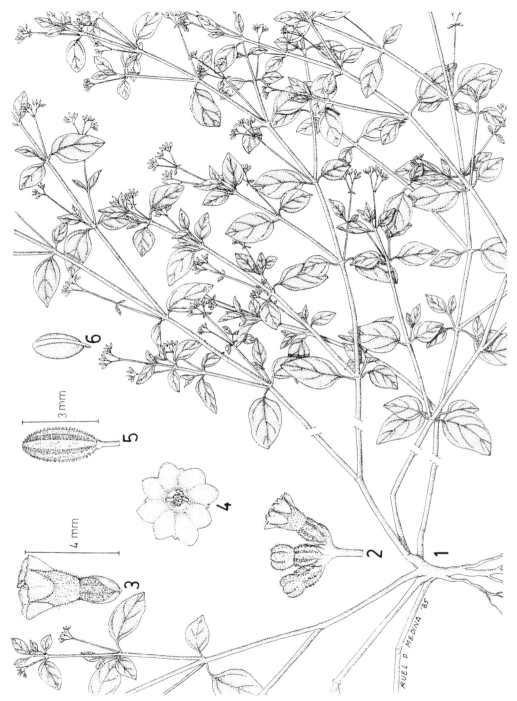

3 mm

4 mm

RUEL D. MEDINA '85

Figure 13-1   *Boerhavia diffusa* L.: 1. habit; 2. inflorescence; 3. single flower; 4. flower, front view; 5. fruit; 6. seed.

lower part of the calyx; densely viscid-glandular, 5-ribbed, obconical, 3 to 4.5 mm long, 1.75 mm wide; *seed* wrinkled, light brown, not separable from fruit.

  B. diffusa is distinguished by the branched, lax, cymose inflorescence with pink to red flowers, the 5-ribbed sticky fruits, the swollen nodes and pairs of unequal opposite leaves.

Boerhavia erecta

B. erecta (Figure 13-2) is a spreading or shortly decumbent herbaceous *annual* or *perennial* plant from a woody crown; *taproot* long, fleshy; *stem* smooth, reddish, semiwoody at base, up to 1 m in length; *leaves* opposite, ovate, variable in size and shape, one of each pair larger, 3 to 5.5 cm long, the other smaller, 1.5 to 2.5 cm long; green above and light green to whitish beneath; *petioles* about half the length of leaf blades; *inflorescence* an axillary or terminal, highly branched cyme, leafy only at the base; *flowers* occur as 2 or 3 together; *perianth* 2.75 to 3 mm high, constricted in midsection, the apical part widely campanulate; white or pale pink with 3 to 8 deeply notched lobes; *fruit* an *anthocarp*, obconical, 5-ribbed, 3 to 4 mm long, wedge-shaped and truncate at the apex, non-sticky; *seed* wrinkled, brown, 1.5 mm long, smooth, inseparable from fruit.

  This species is characterized by its opposite leaves, white to light pink flowers, and the five transverse ribs on the non-glandular fruits.

HABITAT AND ECOLOGY

Both species are widely distributed in Asia, Africa, the Pacific Islands, and South America (Figures 13-3 and 13-4). Only *B. diffusa* is reported in Australia, Brazil, and China. *B. diffusa* and *B. erecta* are common weeds in cultivated fields, perennial crops, roadsides, pastures and wastelands. They occur from sea level to 1500 m and behave as either annuals or perennials. *B. diffusa* can survive in very sandy soils, including sand dunes (Chakravarty and Bhati 1971). *B. diffusa* was the third most frequent species encountered in the rainy season of a semi-arid region of India (Sharma 1981). In the dry season it was the fourth most frequent weed. However, its relative density and cover values were lower than for several other species and consequently the importance index was lower in relative ranking both seasons. *B. diffusa*'s importance value was three times greater in the dry than the rainy season. This species often has a thickened, semi-tuberous root, which may account in part for its tolerance to dry conditions (Egunjobi 1969a).

  B. diffusa also thrives in well-fertilized and shady areas in Brazil (Lorenzi 1982) and is often found in association with *Portulaca oleracea* in Puerto Rico (Velez and Overbeek 1950). It can be found in Nigerian plantation crops throughout the year but is most abundant in the edges of fields (Komolafe 1976). Plants can flower throughout the year in India (Mudgal 1975) but seasonal cycles are common in cultivated fields. Pandya and Purohit (1976) observed that *B. diffusa* emerged 35 days after sorghum was planted. In the Philippines, *B. erecta* is common in continuous maize production systems but not when maize is grown in the dry season and rice in the wet season (Pamplona and Madrid 1979).

  Ecotypes of *B. diffusa* in India have adapted to specific soil conditions. Srivastava and Misra (1968) describe the "normal" ecotype as growing well on soils with low levels of exchangeable calcium (8.9 to 17.2 m.e./100 g soil). The "robust" type occurs on both low

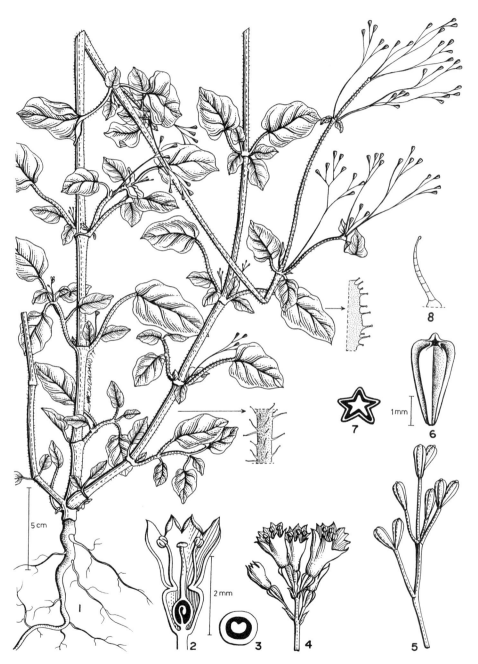

FIGURE 13-2   *Boerhavia erecta* L.: 1. habit; 2. flower, vertical section; 3. ovary cross-section; 4. flowering branch tip; 5. fruiting branch tip; 6. fruit; 7. cross section; 8. gland, enlarged.

FIGURE 13-3   The distribution of *Boerhavia diffusa* L. across the world where it has been reported as a weed.

FIGURE 13-4   The distribution of *Boerhavia erecta* L. across the world where it has been reported as a weed.

(9.8 m.e.) and high (64 m.e.) calcium soils. When the normal type is grown in high calcium soils, it appears stunted and shoot length is reduced nearly five-fold.

The viscous nature of *B. diffusa* seeds aids in their dispersal by people and animals. Carlquist (1967) found seeds on feathers near the eyes of sooty terns in Hawaii and believes that the species was introduced to the islands by birds. While *B. erecta* seeds are normally not sticky, when wetted while still attached to the plant, a slimy substance forms, allowing seeds to adhere to passing animals (Pijl, van der 1982). Thus both species have developed effective seed dispersal mechanisms.

BIOLOGY

While both species are widely distributed, more attention has been given to *B. diffusa* than to *B. erecta*. *B. diffusa* has abundant starch in the roots, while *B. erecta* roots are essentially starch-free (Surange and Pendse 1972). Both species have the C_4 pathway (Das and Santakumari 1978) giving them a high water use efficiency and explaining their adaptation to sandy soils and dry regions. *B. diffusa* has a photosynthetic rate of 65 mg CO_2/dm²/hr at the optimum temperature of 38°C, a chlorophyll a/b ratio of 4.5, and stomatal densities of 102 and 164/mm² for the upper and lower leaf surface, respectively (Das and Santakumari 1977). The transpiration rate of 12.4 mg H_2O/cm²/hr was the lowest of all the species tested. The transpiration ratio was 305 g of H_2O/g dry matter produced.

B. diffusa has a high level of nitrogen metabolizing enzymes and a high ratio of protein to chlorophyll (Raghavendra and Das 1976). Its $2n$ chromosome number is 26 (Srivastava and Misra 1968). Leaf cuttings either with or without an indolebutyric acid treatment formed roots first on the adaxial side of the cut petiole and later all around and along the petiole (Mitra and Bose 1957). *B. diffusa* root and shoot leachates reduced sorghum germination from 87% for the controls to 21 and 24%, respectively (Dharmaraj et al. 1988). The shoots of this species contain more phenolic compounds than roots.

Detailed anatomical studies of *B. diffusa* nodes in India found that the branches in the axils of the smaller leaf of each pair are always more developed than those in axils of the larger leaf (Pant and Mehra 1961). In addition to the primary branch, each leaf axil had one or two accessory branches. When flowering occurs, another axillary branch develops on the side of the small leaf. As the fruits mature, the extra branch drops from the plant. The unequal size of the opposite leaves at a node alternates from side to side in successive nodes. Nearly all leaves are asymmetric between the halves along the midrib. In reality, the leaves are not exactly opposite since the smaller leaf is somewhat below the larger one. The authors give detailed anatomical descriptions of the nodal and internodal regions. One unusual feature in *B. diffusa* is the variation from one to three vascular strands that supply each leaf. In most angiosperms this is a constant number. Adams and Baker (1962) observed that stems break readily at the lower nodes, reducing the effectiveness of hand and mechanical weeding.

Studies on the growth of these species are lacking. Hagerup (cited by Adams and Baker 1962) recorded fruits in *B. diffusa* within 8 to 10 days after germination. If true, this would be an example of extremely rapid reproduction. Germination of fresh seeds ranges from 2% (Noda et al. 1983) to 20% (Popay 1973). Neither seed scarification nor stratification enhance germination and temperatures of 40°C or greater reduce it (Popay 1973). Field studies by Popay and Ivens (1982) noted that most newly harvested seeds emerged within 5 to 8 days after a heavy rainfall. By the end of a long rainy season, 66% of the seeds had emerged, but some emergence occurred after four cropping cycles (2 yr). Similar studies with *B. erecta* found that the emergence of 6-month-old seed peaked between 20 and 45 days after planting but continued through 60 days. Under field conditions, this species behaved similarly to *B. diffusa*: 59% of the seeds emerged after one season and germination continued for more than 2 yr. Germination of *B. erecta* seeds improved as storage time increased to 12 mo but then declined (Popay 1973). Seed coat removal enhanced germination.

UTILITY

B. diffusa is eaten by chickens and pigs in Puerto Rico (Velez and Overbeek 1950). In the preflower stage, plants have 2% N, 1.9% CaO, 1.5% P_2O_5, 1.1% K_2O and 0.5% S (Singh and Singh 1939). The plant is a common ground cover species under trees planted on sand dunes in India and contains up to 17.3% crude protein. However, only 17% of the plant's biomass was consumed by heifers because it is apparently unpalatable to cattle. Sheep readily consume this species (Chakravarty et al. 1970, Chakravarty and Bhati 1971). Roots are used as human food in central Australia and leaves can be used in soups and as a potherb (Uphof 1968).

Medicinal uses of *B. diffusa* and *B. erecta* are widespread, especially in India. As a drug, it is called "punarnava" and has been used for nearly 2000 years. Most analyses of medicinal properties have been done with *B. diffusa*. *B. diffusa* has high levels of KNO_3 (0.33%) and contains the same alkaloid as *Trianthema portulacastrum*, which also has medicinal uses (Chopra and Chatterjee 1940). It is used as an emetic, laxative, and diuretic, and to treat asthma, anemia, oedema, jaundice, and dropsy. Boiled leaves are used as a snakebite remedy in Brazil (Lorenzi 1982).

Roots are preferred for medicinal uses and various formulations are prepared for specific treatments. For example, milk or water extracts are used as laxatives and diuretics, powders for anemia, and liquid preparations for jaundice (Anandalwar and Venkateswara 1981). Pharmaceutical companies in India used 20,000 kg as liquid, powder and pill formulations in 1981. Home uses would increase this amount considerably.

Mudgal (1975) tested the medicinal effects of different plant parts at various growth stages. Root and leaf extracts reduced blood pressure more than stem or whole plant extracts. The greatest diuretic and edemic effects occur with plants harvested in the rainy season and the least in the dry period. He proposes growing *B. diffusa* so that large amounts of biomass are available for harvest during the rainy season.

In Mexico *B. erecta* is used as a relaxant, and to treat spasms and epilepsy. The whole plant is sometimes used in cooking (Mendieta and Amo 1981). Calcium oxalate is present in all plant parts (Surange and Pendse 1972). *B. diffusa* contains an ecdysterone that affects insect molting (Suri et al. 1982). They believe the same compound induces the diuretic effect.

Researchers in India discovered that root extracts of *B. diffusa* can prevent viral infection in plants if applied 24 hr before inoculation (Verma et al. 1979a,b). The extract is only preventative and has no effect on the virus once infection occurs. Work with several crops and viruses demonstrated that the viral prevention ability is neither host nor virus specific. Some resistance is induced when plants are treated within 6 hr of infection and the effect is systemic. Treating lower leaves protects upper leaves as well. The effectiveness of the inhibitor is greatly reduced if actinomycin D is applied within 6 hr of the extract treatment.

Further tests showed that the inhibitor has properties of a glycoprotein that appears to stimulate production of substances that induce viral resistance.

AGRICULTURAL IMPORTANCE

B. diffusa is a reported weed of 27 crops in 61 countries (Figure 13-3) and is frequently reported in cotton and sugarcane. It is a serious or principal weed of bananas in Mozambique; beans in Jamaica; cotton in India, Mozambique, Peru, Tanzania, Trinidad, and Uganda; maize in Peru; peanuts in Tanzania; sugarcane in India, Indonesia, and Tanzania; and tobacco in the Philippines. It is a common weed of bananas, coffee, cotton, rice, tobacco, and wheat in Honduras; beans in Thailand; cassava in Ghana and India; cereals in India; cotton in Tanzania; cowpea and millet in Senegal; irrigated dryland crops in Australia; maize in Ghana, Guatemala, India, and Senegal; orchards in Thailand; pastures in Australia; peanuts in Bangladesh and Ghana; upland rice in Senegal; sugarcane in Bangladesh, Nigeria, and South Africa; sorghum in Honduras, Nicaragua, and Senegal; soybean in Thailand; and vegetables in Australia and Honduras.

B. diffusa is also an unranked weed of bananas in Nicaragua and Zambia; cacao, pastures, soybean, and sweet potato in Nigeria; cassava in Indonesia and Nigeria; cereals in Australia; citrus in Mozambique; coffee in the Congo and Nigeria; cotton in Kenya, Paraguay, Thailand, and Zambia; cowpea, nursery crops, pastures, soybeans, and sweet potatoes in Nigeria; dryland crops in Ivory Coast; jute in India; maize in Cambodia, Indonesia, Laos, Mexico, Nigeria, Paraguay, the Philippines, Thailand, and Vietnam; orchards in India and Saudi Arabia; pineapple and rubber in Thailand; rice in India, Indonesia, Ivory Coast, Nepal, Nicaragua, Nigeria, the Philippines, and Thailand; sorghum in India and Paraguay; and sugarcane in Mozambique, Peru, and Thailand.

B. erecta is a reported weed of 22 crops in 35 countries (Figure 13-4), especially in maize and cotton. It is a serious or principal weed of edible beans in Cuba; cotton in Kenya, Peru and Thailand; maize in Guatemala, Mexico, and Peru; and sugarcane in Indonesia and Peru.

It is a common weed of bananas, maize, peppers, and tomatoes in Costa Rica; edible beans in Bangladesh, Colombia, and Dominican Republic; cassava and coffee in Nicaragua; cotton in Colombia, Mexico, Nicaragua, and El Salvador; maize in Colombia, Dominican Republic, Nicaragua, the Philippines, El Salvador, and Venezuela; peanuts in Colombia and Dominican Republic; pineapple in Nicaragua; rice in Nicaragua and El Salvador; sorghum in Dominican Republic, Central America, and Mexico; soybeans in Colombia and Mexico; sugarcane in Bangladesh, Colombia, and Nicaragua; tobacco in the Philippines; and vegetables in Dominican Republic.

B. erecta is also an unranked weed of bananas in Honduras and Zambia; edible beans, pineapple, sorghum, and tobacco in Honduras; cassava in Ghana; citrus and coffee in El Salvador; cotton in Nicaragua and El Salvador; legumes and soybeans in the Philippines; mangos in Mexico; orchards in South Africa; plantation crops in Thailand; rice in India and Indonesia; sugarcane in Tanzania; taro in Samoa; vegetables in Nicaragua; and vineyards in Mexico.

In the Philippines uncontrolled populations of *B. diffusa* reduced maize yields by 70% (Pamplona et al. 1976) and uncontrolled *B. erecta* lowered soybean production 81% (Aquino and Pamplona 1981). Keeping soybeans weed-free of *B. erecta* for 40 days gave maximum yields. Increasing crop density to 200,000 plants/ha did not reduce the competitiveness of *B. erecta*. This suggests little sensitivity to shading and is consistent with both species occurring as weeds in coffee, bananas, orchards and sugarcane.

   B. diffusa hosts two leaf spot fungi (Kulkarni et al. 1973) and a strain of cucumber mosaic virus that infects eggplants in India (Khurana 1970). *B. erecta* hosts a leaf rust in Colombia (Perez 1956).

COMMON NAMES

Boerhavia diffusa

AUSTRALIA	tar-vine
BRAZIL	amarra-pinto, erva tosto, pega-pinto, tangara
COLOMBIA	rodilla de pollo
CUBA	mata pavo
DOMINICAN REPUBLIC	toston, yerba de puerco
EGYPT	at-hagg, ilimaaseeb, moddeid, sakomteet
EL SALVADOR	golandrina, iscorian
GHANA	hog weed
GUATEMALA	erispela, hierba de cabro, moradilla
HAWAII	alena, boerhavia
INDIA	atik, bishkhopra, mukkurattai, punarnava, rajasthan, rajkot, santh, santi, thikri
KENYA	tar vine
MALAYSIA	spreading hogweed
MAURITIUS	herbe pintade
MEXICO	hierba de puerco
NIGERIA	etupaela
PAKISTAN	it-sit
PARAGUARY	ka'a ruru pe
PHILIPPINES	katkatud, paanbalibis, tabtabokol
PUERTO RICO	toston, yerba de puerco
SAUDI ARABIA	moddeid
TANZANIA	boerhavia
THAILAND	khomhin pak, phak-khom-lin, spreading hog weed
TRINIDAD	hog weed, sow weed
UNITED STATES	creeping spiderling
VENEZUELA	toston
ZIMBABWE	tarweed

Boerhavia erecta

COLOMBIA	cadillo lagana, colombiana, golondrina, hierba blanca, iscorian
CUBA	toston
DOMINICAN REPUBLIC	toston, yerba de puerco
EL SALVADOR	iscorian, palo de leche
KENYA	spindlepod
MEXICO	hierba blanca, hoja morada
PHILIPPINES	paabilis
SOUTH AFRICA	erect boerhavia, regop boerhavia
UNITED STATES	erect spiderling
VENEZUELA	toston

Fourteen

Borreria alata (Aubl.) DC.

Rubiaceae, Madder or Bluet Family

BORRERIA ALATA is in the large family **Rubiaceae**, which is familiar to us because it supplies quinine, coffee, the lovely gardenia and bluet flowers, and the bedstraw weeds (Gallium) so common to Europe. *B. alata* has recently become very troublesome and is spreading rapidly. Initially it was a problem in plantation crops but it is now a major weed in many cultivated crops. It is a weed of 27 crops in 30 countries. Little is known of the biology of the *Borreria* weeds.

FIGURE 14-1   The distribution of *Borreria alata* (Aubl.) DC. across the world where it has been reported as a weed.

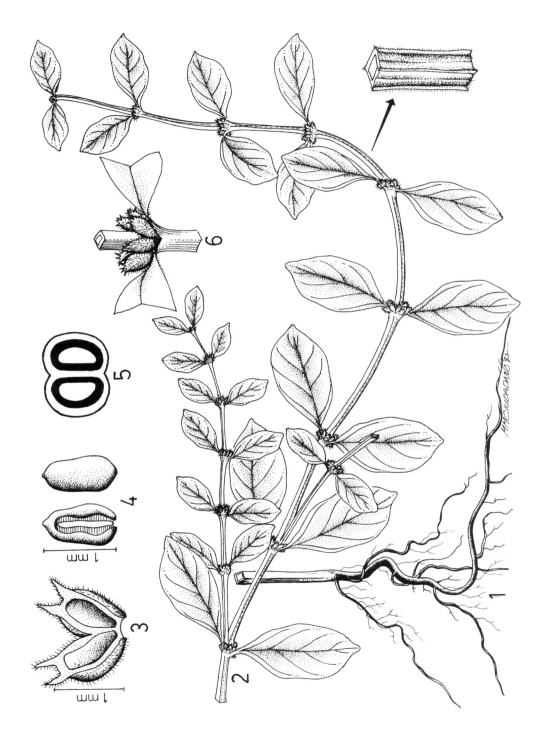

FIGURE 14-2 *Borreria alata* (Aubl.) DC.: 1. root system; 2. flowering and fruiting twig; 3. fruit valve opened; 4. seed, two views; 5. ovary, cross section; 6. node with fruit enlarged.

DESCRIPTION

B. alata (Figure 14-2) is a prostrate, ascending or erect *annual* herb, 5 to 100 cm, which may be yellowish, at times, in some areas it tends to be succulent; *stems* herbaceous, fleshy, quadrangular, slightly or distinctly 4-winged, glabrous or hairy, branched or unbranched; *leaves* opposite, variable in size and shape, oblong to ovate, 2 to 7 cm, yellowish-green, tip and base acute, margins entire, petiolate, generally hairy both surfaces but may be scabrous above and sparsely pubescent below with a greater concentration of long, stiff hairs along veins; veins 5 to 7 on each side of midrib, immersed above, and prominent below; paired leaf bases connected by stipular sheath, 1 mm high, bearing several pilose bristles, 2 to 8 mm long, toward upper margin; *flowers* sessile in dense axillary clusters; *ovary* inferior; *sepals* 4, ovate-lanceolate, acute 2 mm long, hairy, equal; *corolla* tubular, up to 1 cm long, 1.5 to 2.5 mm wide, 4 spreading lobes, light-purplish or bluish-white; *stamens* 4, inserted at throat of corolla; *stigma* with two linear lobes; *fruit* a capsule, ovoid, 2 to 4 mm long, hairy, one seed in each of 2 cells, splitting into basally connected halves when ripe; *seed* ovoid, 2 to 3 mm long, smooth or rough, brown with wide hilum.

Many *Borreria* species have quadrangular stems, some tend to be winged, and several are similar in appearance. Great care should be exercised in species identification because *B. articularis* (also called *B. hispida*) and *B. verticillata* are also weeds on several continents but *B. alata* is the most widespread and troublesome. Because some contemporary botanists remain loyal to the earlier *Spermacoce* genus designation for these plants, we have searched for information under that taxon as well.

DISTRIBUTION

Figure 14-1 shows that the weed exists in three clusters: around the Caribbean Sea, in northwest Africa, and in the South Pacific Islands and coastal countries of south Asia. Some believe the clusters were formed from local introductions that have subsequently migrated to adjacent areas. It occurs most frequently in a zone from the Equator to lat 25° N. It is frequently seen in roadside vegetation and quickly enters sites disturbed by man.

AGRICULTURAL IMPORTANCE

Because the spread of *B. alata* has accelerated in the past two decades it appears to some as a new problem, but it was a troublesome weed in tea and sugarcane in Indonesia more than fifty years ago. Today it is a serious weed in cassava, cocoa, rubber, and tea in Indonesia; maize, sweet potato, and vegetable crops in Malaysia; soybeans in Brazil; and tea in Bangladesh. It is a principal weed of cassava in Brazil; citrus in Malaysia; maize in Indonesia; oil palm in Malaysia and Sarawak; peanuts and several plantation crops in Indonesia; rubber in Thailand; soybeans in Sarawak; and tea in Burma, Thailand, and Sri Lanka.

It is a common weed in coffee and several cultivated crops in Brazil; cowpeas, maize, peanuts, upland rice, and sorghum in Senegal; jute and sugarcane in Bangladesh; oil palm and upland rice in Indonesia; pastures and taro in Sarawak; pineapple in Samoa; and rubber and sorghum in Malaysia. *B. alata* is a weed of unknown rank in edible beans, maize, and upland rice in Mexico; coffee in Cambodia, Indonesia, Sarawak, and Vietnam; cotton and several horticultural crops in Brazil; several dryland crops in Ivory Coast; maize in

Ghana and Laos; upland rice in Thailand; soybeans in Indonesia; sugarcane in Indonesia and Trinidad; taro and vegetable crops in Samoa; and tea in Burma.

This weed is in several crops in Taiwan and is ranked as a major problem in several crops in Bangladesh, Borneo, Indonesia, Malaysia, Sri Lanka, and Thailand. It is one of the main weeds in rubber in all of Southeast Asia (Hua et al. 1973). Amaratunga (1973), in Sri Lanka, reported that *B. alata* was first reported in a village near Colombo in 1963 and four years later, together with *Paspalum conjugatum*, it was a dominant weed in the low country tea estates. Riepma (1963, 1965) and Wong (1966) found in field trials in rubber plantations that after removal of several major grasses, such as *Axonopus compressus*, *Imperata*, *Ottochloa*, and *Paspalum*, *B. alata* quickly invades the sites.

OTHER *Borreria* SPECIES

B. articularis is also troublesome in man's fields and its biology has received more attention than *B. alata*; however, its distribution as a weed is less well known. *B. hispida* (meaning bristly) is synonymous with *B. articularis*, the two names being used randomly in the south Asia region. It is presently a weed of several crops in India, the Philippines, and Taiwan, but was a weed of sugarcane and tea in Indonesia more than a half century ago. In competition studies, Babu and Joshi (1970, 1974) and Babu (1975) found that yields of bajra and guar were reduced 50 and 60%, respectively, while mung beans were the most tolerant of the competition. Higher stand densities of bajra decreased the yield losses by *B. articularis*.

In the north of India, *B. articularis* is an ephemeral, emerging as the monsoons begin. It is a prolific seeder, the seed is shed as capsules dry, and the new seed will not germinate. The seed coat does not prevent imbibition of fluids. Germination is promoted by cold treatments and leaching with water. High temperatures promote germination but continuous light prevents it. Seeds in upper soil layers germinate readily when other conditions are satisfactory. It thus appears that a germination inhibitor is removed by washing with water or by the leaching action of rain in the field. When regional rainfall is patchy, seed germination is sporadic and emergence may continue over an extended period. This plant is well adapted for survival in a monsoon, semi-arid region.

Webb (1975) suggests that an important weed of sugarcane, as yet unnamed, in the Queensland region of Australia is similar to *B. hispida* and is of "land origin." A single plant produces thousands of seeds, with seeds of various ages emerging in the fields throughout the year. This weed may reproduce by means of vegetative fragments. It grows well on most soil types but is least vigorous on heavy, wet soils. A very extensive root system assists in the rapid recovery of injured plants. The tolerance of reduced light makes it a good competitor. In sugarcane the plant may reach 1 meter in height, creates machine harvesting problems, causes a poor burn, and competes for soil moisture when the crop is under stress in dry weather.

B. verticillata is a weed in the West Indies, northern South America, and along the Gulf Coast of Texas. It is a weed of beans in Brazil and pastures in Trinidad. On roadsides in the latter country, the weed tolerated 18 kg/ha of a triazine herbicide. It is a troublesome weed also in West Africa, where it is a weed of maize and peanuts in Ghana.

Fifteen

Brassica campestris L.

Brassicaceae (Cruciferae), Mustard Family

BRASSICA CAMPESTRIS is only one of nearly 3000 species in the **Cruciferae** family found across the world. Mustard family species are concentrated in the northern temperate zone and also in southwestern and central Asia, where there are more genera than elsewhere. Few species are found in the hot, humid tropics. The family name was derived from the Latin *cruci* for cross, and refers to the cross-like arrangement of the four flower petals.

FIGURE 15-1   The distribution of *Brassica campestris* L. across the world where it has been reported as a weed.

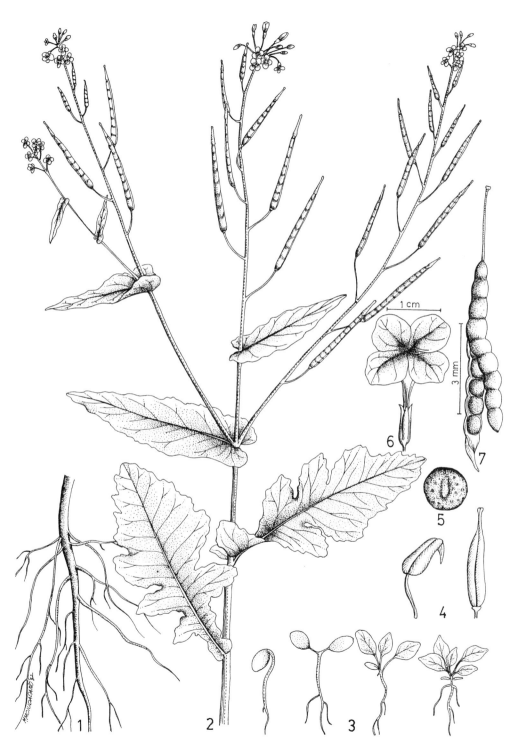

FIGURE 15-2 *Brassica campestris* L.: 1. root system; 2. flowering and fruiting branch; 3. seedling; 4. capsule, two views; 5. seed enlarged; 6. single flower; 7. dehiscing capsule.

The mustard family provides numerous vegetables, ornamentals, oil seeds and condiments for human use and feed for animals. Many species have been important food sources since ancient times. The ancestral cabbage, *Brassica oleraceae*, was grown in coastal areas of northern Europe for at least 8000 years. Other species are recorded in Sanskrit literature dating to 1500 B.C. The Romans and Greeks have described the medicinal uses of several *Brassica* and almost all plant parts are utilized in one species or another somewhere in the world. In some areas of Europe today, crucifers comprise 30% of the vegetable acreage, including radishes, cabbage, brussel sprouts, rape, mustard, turnips, and cauliflower. Even though a large number of species are cultivated, the mustard family does not provide a substantive part of our diet and thus ranks well below the grass and legume families in this respect.

Brassica is one of 380 genera in the **Cruciferae** family and contains over 30 species. *B. campestris* is one of six important crop species in the genus. *Brassica* is derived from the Celtic term "bresic" for cabbage and also means to "cut off the head." The species name, *campestris*, refers to plains or flat areas. This species includes oil, leaf, and root crops and is one of the three parents of other important crop species (Prakash and Hinata 1980). Nevertheless, wild types of *B. campestris* are weeds of many crops in both northern and southern temperate regions.

DESCRIPTION

B. campestris (Figure 15-2) is a smooth, bluish-green *annual* herb; *taproot* strong, stout; *stems* erect, 30 to 120 cm high, round and widely branching from below; *leaves* alternate, smooth, 15 to 20 cm long, 5 to 7 cm wide, irregularly pinnately lobed or dissected, lower leaves with large terminal lobe, petioled, stem leaves with ear-like projections that clasp the stem; *inflorescence* a long raceme; *flowers* perfect; *sepals* spreading, 4 to 6 mm long; *petals* 4, about 1 cm across, pale or bright yellow; *stamens* 6, 2 shorter than the rest; *fruit* a dry dehiscent 2-celled *silique*, a pod 3 to 8 cm long (exclusive of the 1 to 2.5 cm beak), pedicel 1 to 2.5 cm long, essentially divergent from the main stem, *valves* split from bottom up, leaving persistent central septum with a row of 6 to 12 seeds attached to each side; *seeds* black or dark brown to reddish brown, spherical, about 2 mm in diameter, with weak longitudinal rounded rib on one side, surface pitted and dull with more or less distinct reticulations.

The bluish-green leaves that clasp the stem by their ear-like lobes and the round, dark brown to black seeds borne in a beaked pod are the distinguishing characteristics of this species. Additionally, the seeds do not form mucilage when soaked in water and do not become glossy when rubbed between the fingers, as do those of *B. kaber*.

ECOLOGY AND BIOLOGY

B. campestris was domesticated as early as 2000 B.C. in Asia. McNaughton (1976) postulates that there were two centers of origin: one in Europe and another in present-day Afghanistan and Pakistan. It was used for oil by Asians who did not have access to olive oil and was used as lamp oil in Europe until petroleum became available. Wild relatives of *B. campestris* are prevalent in the high plateaus of the Irano-Turanian region (Tsunoda 1981) and this species forms part of the parentage of *B. napus* and *B. juncea*, other economically important species.

In Europe, seeds were found in the stomach of Tollund man and at sites domesticated during the late bronze age (Renfrew 1973). All plant parts were utilized as food and plants may also have been employed as a spice. Additional evolutionary information on *B. campestris* is found in the review by Prakash and Hinata (1980).

Weedy types of *B. campestris* originated in Europe and are now in most countries with temperate climates (Figure 15-1). It is most prevalent in cereal crops, old hayfields, and wastelands but has also been reported to infest soybeans, dry beans, maize, flax, peas, pastures, tea, and grapes. It occurs as a weed in nearly every country in the northern hemisphere with temperate climates, several Asian countries, through the Andean zone of South America and Argentina and Brazil, and in Australia and New Zealand.

At one time *B. campestris* may have been a winter annual or biennial plant (Prakash 1981). Varieties requiring vernalization are still grown in Sweden (McNaughton 1976). These plants need cold periods of 15 to 19 wk to induce flowering, while annual types flower without vernalization (Hodgson 1978).

The plant is found in regions with 350 to 1600 mm of annual precipitation, average temperatures from 5.6 to 25°C, and soil *pH* from 4.8 to 8.1 (Duke 1979). It grows well in many soil types. More *B. campestris* seedlings emerge at 1.5 than 3 cm and in soils at 100% than at 50% field capacity (Nuttall 1982). Optimum soil density for germination and emergence is 1 to 1.1 g/cm^3 and densities of 1.3 g/cm^3 inhibit emergence (Averkin 1978b).

B. campestris requires sulphur due to the S-containing compounds in the plant. Aulakh et al. (1980) measured 0.23 to 0.58% S in seeds and obtained the highest seed production by applying N and S to the soil. Grain protein increased from 14.6% in the controls to 28.1% at the high N and S rates and oil content rose from 40.9 to 47.1%. When grown in soils deficient in S, the alkaloid concentration in *B. campestris* leaves dropped (Singh 1979). Leaf alkaloid content increased until flowering and then decreased as seeds were formed. No alkaloids were found in the stems or roots.

B. campestris tolerates up to 0.5% Cl in the soil and can be used to predict when fields flooded with sea water can be safely planted to rice (Kurauchi 1956). However, salt can reduce *B. campestris* growth. Levels of 0.2 and 0.4% salt reduced straw weight by 16 and 52% and grain/plant ratio by 33 and 82%, respectively (Ansari 1972).

Drought stress during stem elongation and flowering reduces seed production (Richards and Thurling 1978a,b). Field studies in Australia revealed that drought stress increased as planting was delayed from June 21 to August 2. The number of branches dropped from 211 to 98/m^2, the number of seeds from 9.8 to 8.4/pod and the number of pods from 2488 to 1151/m^2, respectively, from the June 21 and August 2 planting dates. The most rapid plant growth occurred after flower initiation and delaying planting reduced the time between planting and flowering (79 days for June 21 seeding and 62 days for August 2). Drought affected plants from large seeds (0.63 g/100 seeds) and small seeds (0.46 g/100 seeds) similarly (Pandya et al. 1973).

B. campestris is a C_3 plant and stomata are found on many plant parts. The upper and lower leaf surfaces have 45 and 105 stomata/mm^2, respectively, and stems have 49, pods 85, and beaks 62/mm^2 (Major 1975). Thus several structures besides leaves can assimilate CO_2 in *B. campestris*.

This species is a major crop in several countries and researchers have studied the allelopathic effects of its straw on rotational crops. Kasting et al. (1974) planted barley, oats and wheat following a crop of *B. campestris* (rape seed) in Canada and observed reduced height, dry weight, root development, and yield of all crops. Additionally, toxins were readily leached from all plant parts. Subsequent studies by Waddington and Bowren (1978) attributed this effect to the N deficiency caused by changes in the C/N ratio upon mixing *B. campestris* straw into the soil.

B. campestris is a long-day plant. A single 16-hr day in the seedling stage triggered flowering in some biotypes (Friend 1968). The response was greatest (80%) at 25°C and less at either 17.5°C (50%) or 32.5°C (60%). Flowering occurred 4 wk after planting and ripe seeds formed between 8 and 12 wk (Friend 1969). No interactions between nutrient level and day length were noted. Six days after the long-day exposure, developing inflorescences were visible in dissected plants. More detailed morphological studies by Orr (1978) found that flora primordia were initiated 58 hr after the long-day exposure. Thus in only 2.5 days, *B. campestris* can shift from vegetative to reproductive growth.

Flowers of this plant are self-incompatible and require insects for cross-pollination. Kapil et al. (1971) observed bee activity started between 9:00 to 10:00 A.M., peaked from 12:30 to 2:00 P.M. and ceased by 5:00 P.M.

Seeds are relatively large as compared to many weeds and 1000 seeds weigh approximately 2 g (Korsmo 1935). Seeds have a three-week dormancy period and optimum germination takes place with alternating temperatures (Steinbauer and Frank 1954). In Argentina, day/night temperatures of 20/12°C gave 83% germination; at 30/20°C, only 16% of the seeds germinated, while at 7/4°C, 42% germinated (Soriano et al. 1963b). In Russia, *B. campestris* was the only weed of five species tested that germinated (24%) at a constant temperature of 8° C (Averkin 1978a). He found 18°C the optimum constant temperature for germination. Kondra et al. (1983) observed that germination occurred in 1, 1.7, 3.0, 6.0, and 12.7 days at constant temperatures of 21, 15, 9, 5, and 2°C, respectively, and germination was 34% at 2°C. Thus *B. campestris* is a well adapted, early emerging species in temperate climates.

Fully mature seeds have higher germination rates than less mature seeds (Gugnani et al. 1975). Planting larger seeds gives more vigorous seedlings, but there is no correlation between initial seed size and yield (Major 1977). Plants from small seed tend to flower later.

Seeds of *B. campestris* can survive incredibly long periods in the soil. An excavation at an old monastery site in Denmark founded around 1170 A.D. recovered seeds from 34 to 52 cm below the soil surface (Odum 1965). They were dated to be over 600 yr old, and 11 of them germinated! In a controlled experiment in Denmark, Madsen (1962) buried *B. campestris* seeds in 1934 at 20 cm in the soil and removed one set each spring for 25 yr. Seed germinated consistently for 18 yr and then failed to germinate until the 23rd yr. A 40-year-old grassland pasture in New Zealand was plowed and *B. campestris* emerged. While in pasture, no plants were present so the seedlings came from dormant seeds (Levy 1940). Thus seeds of this species persist for long periods in the soil.

Ambient temperature and seed moisture levels influence seed longevity. Takayanagi (1981) stored seeds at 30°C and those with 4.1% water retained 60% viability for 9 yr while those with 14.1% moisture died in 3 mo. If seeds were refrigerated at 9% moisture, 50% were viable after 15 yr and at 3.1% moisture, over 95% germinated.

UTILITY AND HERBICIDE RESISTANCE

In addition to the uses of *B. campestris* previously mentioned, the plant has also been analyzed for use as a forage (Ahuja et al. 1974). It contained 25.4, 21.5, and 15.6% protein at 24, 38, and 52 days after planting, respectively. Of the six crops tested, *B. campestris* had the lowest digestible dry matter and cellulose levels.

The plant has been used medicinally to treat skin and stomach diseases in India (Prakash 1981), root extracts are employed to treat tuberculosis and bladder infections, and seeds are used as mustard plasters in Brazil (Lorenzi 1982). Root extracts contain an antifungal substance called "rapine" that inhibits *Fusarium*, several yeasts and the animal parasite *Trichophyton rosaceum* (Gerretsen and Haagsma 1951). The oilseed meal is considered an excellent source of organic selenium. If the ration contains 15 to 20% *B. campestris* meal, no additional selenium is required in swine or poultry feed, and the meat and eggs then have a desirable level of selenium for human consumption (Arthur and Slinger 1979).

A strain of *B. campestris* resistant (R) to chloro-triazines was found in Quebec, Canada in 1977. Seeds of the atrazine susceptible (S) biotype germinated and emerged sooner and the seedlings grew faster than those of the R-biotype (Mapplebeck et al. 1982). The S-biotype also emerged from greater planting depths and produced more biomass than the R-biotype. Thus in nature the S-biotype is more competitive and dominates the R-biotype. The respiration rate of both biotypes is similar. However, the S-biotype incorporates 50% more CO_2 in photosynthesis than the R-biotype (Davis and Gressel 1981). The resistance is not due to differences in herbicide uptake, translocation or metabolism, but in binding differences between R- and S-biotypes within the chloroplasts (Ali and Souza Machado 1984).

Souza Machado and Bandeen (1982) crossed R- and S-biotypes of *B. campestris* and discovered that the cytoplasm of the maternal parent determines the response to atrazine. Resistance is controlled only by cytoplasmic DNA, which means it is not spread by pollen and that resistance could be introduced into crop varieties of this species. This was successfully done in Canada by Beversdorf et al. (1980), who released a commercial variety *B. campestris* tolerant to 3, 3, and 0.5 kg/ha of atrazine, cyanazine, and metribuzin, respectively. The new variety is also low (<1%) in erucic acid and no negative effects of the cytoplasm from the weedy biotype were noted.

AGRICULTURAL IMPORTANCE

B. campestris is a weed in more than 20 crops in over 50 countries (Figure 15-1). It is a serious or principal weed of cereals in Canada, Lebanon, New Zealand, and Tasmania; barley in Argentina, Bolivia, Colombia, Mexico, and Peru; oats in Argentina, Bolivia, and Mexico; and wheat in Argentina, Bolivia, Colombia, Guatemala, Italy, Mexico, Peru, and Uruguay. Also it is reported as a serious or principal weed of flax, linseed, and lucerne in Argentina; dry beans, maize, and sorghum in Honduras and Mexico; flax in Brazil; orchards in Honduras; pastures in Argentina, Bolivia, and the eastern United States; peas in Argentina and New Zealand; potatoes in Honduras and Venezuela; oilseed rape and safflowers in Mexico; sugar beets in France; and vegetables in Honduras and Tasmania.

It is a common weed of barley in Bolivia; cereals in Brazil, Bulgaria, Kenya, Tanzania, and Uganda; maize and potatoes in Colombia; vegetables in Madagascar and Mexico; and wheat in Brazil and Portugal.

B. campestris is a weed of unknown rank in edible beans in Brazil, Chile, and Costa Rica; cereals in Chile, Finland, Norway, Poland, Sweden; flax in Chile; maize in Chile and Peru; lucerne in the United States; orchards in Chile, Mexico, and Turkey; pastures in Chile, England, and the former Yugoslavia; potatoes in Chile, Costa Rica, Mexico, New Zealand, and the eastern United States; oilseed rape in Canada; sugar beets in New

Zealand; sugarcane in Argentina, Brazil, Costa Rica, and Peru; tea in Japan; vegetables in Chile and Turkey; vineyards in Chile and New Zealand; and wheat in India, Kenya, New Zealand, and Pakistan.

B. campestris was the principal weed in a competition study with barley done in Mexico and only 10 days of competition reduced yields as much as 25% (Mondragon et al. 1981). Some varieties required 40 to 50 weed-free days to obtain maximum yield, while others needed 60 days. *B. campestris* was the predominant weed when barley was planted in May but comprised only 37% of the weed complex if barley was planted in July.

This weed readily contaminates harvested grains. Twenty-one percent of the wheat samples tested in Kenya contained an average of 831 *B. campestris* seeds/kg of wheat. It was the third most abundant weed species observed and represented 11% of all the seeds found (Bogdan 1965). In Canada, fields infested with *B. campestris* are not suited for rape seed production since the seeds cannot be separated. In the 1800s, British growers often found weedy Brassicas contaminating seeds sold as crop Brassicas (Pieters and Charles 1901). In fact, factories were established to kill seeds of the weedy Brassicas by heat treatment, blend them with Brassica crop seed, and sell the mixture as pure crop seed. Because it is most difficult to distinguish between the seeds of weedy and crop Brassicas and because the weedy types did not germinate, the fraud often went unnoticed. The practice was stopped in 1869 when the British Parliament passed the "adulteration of seeds" bill.

The seeds of *B. campestris* may contain toxic levels of sulphur compounds such as glucosinolates. Van Etten and Tookey (1978) found these substances in 300 of the 1500 **Cruciferae** species tested. One to four compounds predominated in each species. Defatted oilseed meal of *B. campestris* contained 37,000 ppm of glucosinolates. This meal can be safely fed to livestock at levels up to 10% of the ration. Ruminants are affected less than monogastric animals because rumen microbes degrade the glucosinolates. *B. campestris* forage may have toxic levels of nitrate and give unpleasant flavors to milk (Muenscher 1955), and the erucic acid in its oil may increase heart lesions (Beare-Rogers et al. 1974). Canadian plant breeders have overcome one of these problems by producing commercial varieties of *B. campestris* (known as canola) essentially free of erucic acid (Beversdorf et al. 1980).

This weed can serve as a host to three races of the bacteria *Pseudomonas solanacearum* that attack potatoes, tobacco, and bananas (Belalcazar et al. 1968), to the parasitic plants *Orobanche aegyptiaca* and *O. cernua* (Singh and Singh 1971), to the fungus *Xanthomonas campestris* that causes black rot of crucifers (Schaad and Dianese 1981), and to tobacco streak virus (Cupertino et al. 1984).

COMMON NAMES

Brassica campestris

ARGENTINA	mostacilla, nabo, nabo blanco, nabo salvaje, nabo silvestre
AUSTRALIA	bird rape, wild turnip
BOLIVIA	nabo silvestre
BRAZIL	colza, mostarda, nabo, nabo branco
CANADA	bird rape, moutarde des oiseaux, wild turnip
CHILE	yuyo, mostaza
COLOMBIA	alpiste, mostaza silvestre, nabo, yuyo

DENMARK	agerkal
ENGLAND	wild turnip
FINLAND	peltokaali
FRANCE	navette sauvage
GERMANY	Rubsen
HAWAII	wild turnip
ITALY	rapa
KENYA	charlock
MADAGASCAR	anatsonga
MEXICO	colza, mostacilla, mostaza, nabo silvestre
NETHERLANDS	raapzaad
NEW ZEALAND	wild turnip
NORWAY	akerkal
PARAGUAY	mostaza, nabo, nabo salvaje, nabo silvestre
PORTUGAL	turnepo-amarelo
PUERTO RICO	nabo
SPAIN	nabo
SWEDEN	akerkal
URUGUAY	colza, nabo silvestre
UNITED STATES	wild turnip

Sixteen

Brassica kaber (DC.) L. C. Wheeler var. pinnatifida (Stokes), L. C. Wheeler (syn. Sinapis arvensis L.)

Brassicaceae (Cruciferae), Mustard Family

BRASSICA KABER is an annual species that originated in Eurasia but is now prevalent in temperate regions of Europe, North America, and the former Soviet Union. It belongs to the mustard family and the synonym, *Sinapis*, means mustard in Latin. The Greek term *sinapismo* refers to the use of this plant to prepare mustard plaster. *Kaber*

FIGURE 16-1   The distribution of *Brassica kaber* (DC.) L. C. Wheeler var. *pinnatifida* (Stokes) L. C. Wheeler across the world where it has been reported a weed.

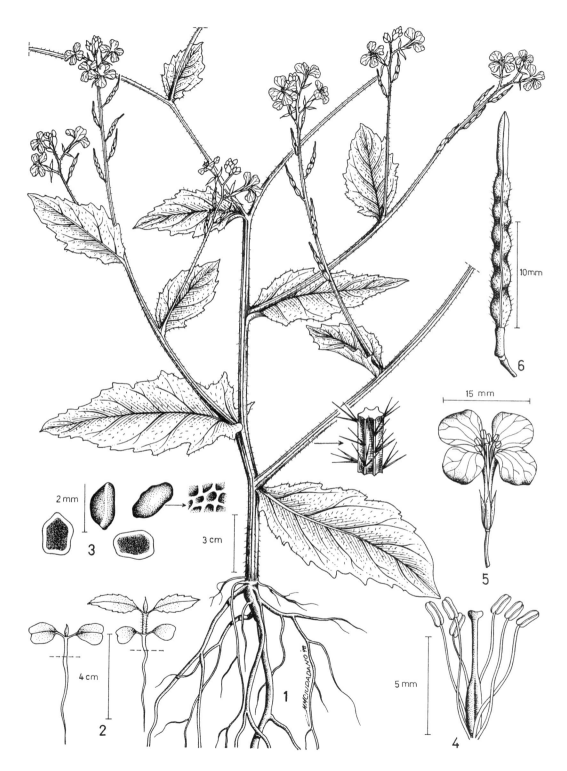

FIGURE 16-2 *Brassica kaber* (DC.) L. C. Wheeler var. *pinnatifida* (Stokes), L. C. Wheeler.:
1. habit; 2. seedling; 3. seed, four views; 4. flower, less perianth; 5. flower; 6. silique.

is Greek for pole or beam. Taxonomists have disagreed for over 200 years about whether the two genera should be combined. Most authorities currently recognize *Brassica* and *Sinapis* as separate genera. Takahata and Hinata (1980) consider *B. kaber* as the connecting species between these genera and this may explain the frequent use of both *B. kaber* and *S. arvensis* to identify this plant.

DESCRIPTION

B. kaber (Figure 16-2) is an erect *winter annual* or *annual* herb; *taproot* slender, highly branched; *stems* upright, 20 to 100 cm tall, branching above; branches purple at the base, usually with stiff hairs especially at the base; *leaves* alternate, sparsely hairy, particularly on the veins of the lower surface, obovate to deeply lobed or toothed; *lower leaves* long-petioled, deeply divided with large, terminal lobe and smaller lateral lobes; *upper leaves* smaller, without petioles, entire, coarsely toothed; *inflorescence* terminal and axillary racemes with bright yellow flowers; *flowers* perfect, 1.5 to 2.5 cm across; *sepals* 4, small, narrow and spreading from the base of the petals; *petals* 4, yellow, 8 to 12 mm long; *stamens* 4 long and 2 short; *pistil* 1; *fruit* a dry dehisent 2-celled *silique* (pod) 2.5 to 4 cm long on short, thick stalk, almost closely appressed to the stem, smooth and sometimes bristly hairy; somewhat flattened angular beak often prominently ribbed (3 to 5 ribs) lengthwise, one-third the length of pod with 1 seed in the base of beak; valves split from base upward releasing 6 to 16 seeds from each of 2 rows; *seeds* globular, 1 to 1.5 mm in diameter, dark brown to black or purplish, smooth or minutely reticulate, often with whitish scurfiness about the scar.

The variably lobed, petioled lower leaves; the entire, stalkless upper leaves and the ribbed pods are the key characteristics of this species. *B. kaber* seeds can be distinguished from those of *B. campestris* by the formation of mucilage after 5 min in water by *B. kaber* seeds, making them very slippery. Mucilage does not form on soaked *B. campestris* seeds.

ECOLOGY AND BIOLOGY

B. kaber grows in a wide range of soils and often appears unexpectedly in recently disturbed sites. Plants occur from sea level to 2300 m and in soils with *pH* as low as 5.5 (Fogg 1950). Growth was reduced 80% in soils of *pH* 4.6 to 4.8 as compared to *pH* 5.7 (Buchanan et al. 1975). No differences in growth were noted between soils of *pH* 5.7 and 6.5.

Most *B. kaber* seedlings appear in the spring and early summer, with a second flush in autumn (Edwards 1980). The later flush may arise from the non-dormant fraction of the seed formed in the spring. Nearly equal numbers of seedlings develop in the fall and spring on either tilled or undisturbed soil (Bibbey 1935). Plants emerge about 4 days after germination. Emergence varies with soil type (Chepil 1946a). Over 35% of the seeds 0 to 0.5 cm deep emerged, 2 to 6% emerged from 1 to 4 cm, and none emerged below 5 cm (Donald and Hoerauf 1985). *B. kaber* produces its maximum leaf area 45 to 50 days after emergence (Blackshaw et al. 1989). This is earlier than most crops, and gives the weed a competitive advantage in intercepting sunlight, especially in short-statured crops.

Flowering starts around 6 wk after emergence and peaks in June and July in northern latitudes but can continue until frost (Fogg 1950). *B. kaber* flowers earlier (34 days) in high light (13,000 lux) than in low light (48 days at 4000 lux) (Gustavsson 1989). This species grew more rapidly than barley in early season and produced the most biomass of nine species tested in a high fertility/low light environment. Plants are self-incompatible and are pollinated by many species of insects (Mulligan and Bailey 1975). Pollination of the same flower may occur for 2 to 3 wk, an unusually long period (Vigfusson 1970).

Detailed anatomical descriptions of the stem, petiole, leaf and root were done by Korsmo (1954). Stomata are present on both leaf surfaces. *B. kaber* has no consistent leaf movement patterns (Andersen and Koukkari 1979). Roots are much branched and can penetrate to 1.2 m (Kutschera 1960). This species has the C_3 pathway of carbon fixation.

Plants are high in sulphur (Tsenova 1975) and may respond to sulphur fertilization. Hoveland et al. (1976) obtained large growth responses by increasing the soil test phosphorous levels from 22 to 95 kg/ha and by raising the potassium levels from 70 to 165 kg/ha. Conklin and Biswas (1978) found that *B. kaber* was one of three weeds with a high asymbiotic nitrogen fixation rate. This indicates the rhizosphere of *B. kaber* has organisms capable of fixing atmospheric nitrogen. Drought stress reduced plant height from 87 to 8 cm, seeds/pod from 6 to 3, and seeds/plant from 610 to 16 (Fogg 1950). It is noteworthy that plants only 8 cm tall produced 16 seeds!

B. kaber contains growth-regulating substances. Germinating seeds of this weed inhibit the germination of wheat, fescue, ryegrass and red clover, but stimulate growth of lucerne and white clover (Stefureac and Fratilescu 1979). Decaying leaf and stem tissue contain compounds that reduce *Echinochloa crus-galli* growth (Erickson and Duke 1978). A volatile seed germination inhibitor in the valves and beaks of the fruit prevents seeds in the silique from germinating (Evenari 1949). Rademacher et al. (1961) used a connected pot technique and observed that root exudates from oats markedly reduce *B. kaber* growth, while extracts from the weed increase oat shoot weight. Water extracts from sunflower leaves reduce *B. kaber* germination by 75% but stem extracts have little effect. Diluting leaf and stem extracts increases seed germination up to 150% of the controls (Leather 1983).

SEED BIOLOGY

The population dynamics of *B. kaber* seeds have been researched for many years. Chepil (1946b) simulated cultural and mechanical farming practices in closely controlled outdoor areas. In the first year of several 5-year studies, 2000 seeds were placed on the soil surface or mixed 6 or 15 cm into the soil. After 5 yr, 49% of the seeds placed on the soil surface and not disturbed had germinated and only 1% of the original population was still viable. Only 14% of the seeds emerged if mixed to 15 cm and not tilled, but 16% were still viable after 5 yr. Forty-five percent of the seeds mixed to 6 cm and tilled germinated. *B. kaber* emergence was essentially complete before June 30, but was prolonged by monthly soil disturbance to 6 or 15 cm.

Similar experiments were done by Roberts and Boddrell (1983). Two thousand seeds were mixed with soil and "cultivated" three times annually for 5 yr. The trial was done over three 5-year periods. Maximum seedling emergence was usually in the first 2 yr, but sometimes it peaked in the third year. After 5 yr, 6% viable seed remained in the soil and they had accounted for 58% of the initial seed population.

Warnes and Andersen (1984) conducted long-term research in the north-central United States on the seed dynamics of *B. kaber* in a field that had a natural infestation of *B. kaber* for many years. Nine cultural and chemical practices were done for 7 yr. During the trial, no plants were allowed to set seed. Soil seed population was determined each fall. After seven seasons, non-disturbed sites (grass sod or chemical fallow) had approximately

50% of the original seed population. The lowest seed populations resulted by plowing three times annually and tilling as needed. This reduced the seed population by 97%, but 2.4 million seeds/ha remained in the upper 30 cm of soil. Systems with crops and tillage reduced the seed reservoir to 12 to 30% of the original level. The maize-soybean rotation depleted the seed population more rapidly than continuous wheat. In all treatments, the seed population of *B. kaber* dropped rapidly in the first 3 to 4 yr and then leveled off; the decline was hastened by tillage. All of these studies reflect the impracticality of eradicating *B. kaber*. For example, 12 yr of herbicide treatment in cereals reduced the seed population to less than 20% of the untreated areas (Hurle 1974). While this was more effective than mechanical measures alone (42% reduction), eradication was not achieved.

Edwards (1980) monitored the growth, development and seed population of *B. kaber* when started at populations of 2.8, 4.5, and 11.3 plants/m². In noninfested soils. The following year, plant densities had tripled. Intraspecific competition began at populations above 20 plants/m². If 200 seeds/m² were planted, within 1 yr the density reached nearly 5000/m² and was over 14,000/m² after 3 yr. Seeds matured 16 to 20 wk after germination and plant density and seed production were greatly reduced by drought. Seed reservoirs were lower if cereals were grown (6400/m²) than in fallowed areas plowed only once (32,500/m²). She also noted that populations fluctuated widely in the field. Densities of 65 to 264 plants/m² were common before phenoxy herbicides were introduced and now levels range from 3 to 36 plants/m² in cereals.

B. kaber seeds remain viable in the soil for extended periods. Estimates range from 69% after 10 yr (Kjaer 1948), 17% after 17 yr (Dorph-Petersen 1925), and 12% after 26 yr (Madsen 1962). Viability is usually lost within 10 yr if seeds are stored under dry conditions. Seed reservoirs range from a few million to over 35 million/ha (Kropac 1966). Seed production for plants grown without competition varied from 2000 to 3500/plant (Mulligan and Bailey 1975) to 4000 (Buckman 1855) and in dense plant populations, from 10 to 590 seeds/plant (Edwards 1980). Seed size and color are variable. Korsmo (1935) recorded an average of 1200 seeds/plant that weighed 1.25 mg each.

Dormancy is common in fresh seeds. Thorough studies by Edwards (1968a,b,c; 1969) found that the embryo is fully differentiated in mature seed and that dormancy is not due to mechanical inhibition of oxygen uptake, but rather to an inhibitor in both the seed coat and embryo. The formation of mucilage upon wetting seeds also reduces oxygen penetration to the embryo. Dormancy is broken by acid scarification and gibberellic acid treatment (Corns 1960b, Edwards 1968b, Hsiao 1980). Seed dormancy is also broken by a combination of changes in temperature, light and nitrate levels (Goudey et al. 1988). Exposure to red light following two days of incubation at 5°C and then raising the temperature to 20°C for 4 days resulted in more than 50% germination. Maximum germination occurred with 2.5 to 20 mol nitrate and these levels are common in many cultivated fields.

Seed dormancy is greatest in seeds in the lower pods on the raceme, but position within the pod does not affect dormancy. Seed dormancy is greater in *B. kaber* populations in Europe and the Middle East than in those from below the 45th parallel. Duran and Retamal (1985) planted seeds from several regions in one site. Seed size of the progeny was similar across all geographical origins of the parents. Germination varies from year to year (Roberts and Boddrell 1983) and between light and dark colored seeds (Fogg 1950, Witcombe and Whittington 1972). The latter researchers also discovered that selection techniques could be used to obtain relatively non-dormant seeds. They note that this process must have occurred during the evolution of wild species into crop plants, as our Brassica crops are generally non-dormant. Garbutt and Witcombe (1986) obtained 84 and 1% germination after

14 and seven generations of selection in non-dormant and dormant populations, respectively. Germination of the original non-selected population was 11%. Dormancy is inherited via the seed coat (maternally) and via the embryo genotype. Thus *B. kaber* has a genetic mechanism that builds ecological stability by imparting a range of dormancy types among seeds, as well as being controlled by more than a single factor.

B. kaber germination increases linearly as the red:far red light ratio (R:FR) increases (B. Frankland 1976). The color of the seed coat alters this response because pigments in dark-colored seeds strongly absorb the lower wavelengths, but allow some of the far red to pass though. This lowers the R:FR within the embryo, inhibiting germination of the darker seeds. Light does not affect germination of fresh seed (28%), but when buried in the soil over winter, light enhances sprouting (Holm 1972). Substituted phthalimides applied to the soil overcome the seed's light requirement and stimulate *B. kaber* germination to 3.8 cm below the soil surface. Seed treatments with these chemicals resulted in more than 80% emergence in the top 2.5 cm of soil.

Germination occurs between 30 to 80% soil moisture but not at 90%. Seeds begin to germinate when soils reach 4.4°C at 10 cm (Edwards 1980) and germination peaks with alternating temperatures of 19 to 26°C (Kolk 1962). Dormancy and seed viability are reduced by rubbing the seeds. Kolk dissected seeds and found the radicle lies unprotected against the seed coat and is thus easily damaged. Scarification with sulphuric acid (79%) or washing with potassium hydroxide (67%) increased germination more than mechanical scarification (30%) (Duran and Estrella 1985). Maximum germination occurred in 3 days for all seed treatment methods. Electron micrographs show that sulphuric acid rapidly dehydrates the seed coat and destroys the mucilage layer. Most seeds can be killed by 30 min of 50 to 60°C heat treatments in the soil and solar radiation under clear plastic may give practical control in small areas (Rubin and Benjamin 1984).

AGRICULTURAL IMPORTANCE

B. kaber is reported as a weed of 30 crops in 52 countries (Figure 16-1) and is frequently reported as a serious weed of cereals, sugar beets and maize. It is a serious or principal weed of cereals in Argentina, Australia, England, Germany, Hungary, Jordan, Norway, Poland, the former Soviet Union, Spain, Tasmania, Tunisia, Turkey, and the United States; barley in Canada, Greece, the former Soviet Union, Spain, and Sweden; oats in Canada, England, Greece, the former Soviet Union, and Sweden; and wheat in Afghanistan, Canada, Iran, Morocco, the former Soviet Union, Spain, Sweden, the United States, and the former Yugoslavia.

It is a serious or principal weed of beans in France and Greece; flax in Canada, France, and the United States; linseed in Argentina; lucerne and oilseed rape in Canada; maize in England, Germany, Hungary, Lebanon, Romania, the former Soviet Union, and the United States; onions in Lebanon; orchards, soybeans, tobacco, and vegetables in the former Soviet Union; peas in France and Greece; potatoes in Belgium and Turkey; rye in Sweden; sorghum in Bulgaria; sugar beets in Belgium, Canada, Czechoslovakia, France, Germany, Israel, the former Soviet Union, Spain, Sweden, Turkey, and the United States; sunflowers in Canada and the former Soviet Union,; vineyards in Spain; summer season crops in Sweden; and winter season crops in Israel.

It is a common weed of barley in France; cereals in Bulgaria, Italy, Scotland, and Switzerland; legumes in Tunisia; lucerne in Czechoslovakia; maize in the former Yugoslavia;

millet in the former Soviet Union; oats in Guatemala; orchards in Bulgaria and Turkey; potatoes, oilseed rape, and sunflowers in France; soybeans in the United States; sugar beets in Poland and the former Yugoslavia; vegetables in Scotland and Tasmania; vineyards in the former Soviet Union; and wheat in Guatemala, Mexico, the Netherlands, and Turkey.

Also *B. kaber* is a weed of unknown rank of these crops: barley, carrots, cereals, citrus, cotton, flax, hops, edible beans, lucerne, maize, millet, oats, oilseed rape, peas, potatoes, soybeans, sugarcane, sugar beets, sunflowers, tomatoes, vegetables, vineyards, and wheat, in one or more of these countries: Afghanistan, Albania, Argentina, Belgium, Bulgaria, Canada, Cyprus, Czechoslovakia, England, Germany, Greece, France, Hungary, Iraq, Italy, Lebanon, Ireland, New Caledonia, New Zealand, Poland, Portugal, Romania, Spain, Syria, Turkey, the United States, and the former Yugoslavia.

Chemical control of *B. kaber* with copper sulphate and sulphuric acid was attempted in the late 1800s (Fogg 1950). The advent of phenoxy and triazine herbicides provided effective control in many crops. Nevertheless, it has persisted after more than 30 yr of widespread herbicide use (Fryer and Chancellor 1970). In the mid-1930s, 10% of the oat samples tested in England were contaminated with *B. kaber* seed. Thirty years later, less than 2% of the samples were contaminated (Tonkin 1968a). Friesen and Shebeski (1960) surveyed numerous Canadian grain fields in the late 1950s and *B. kaber* was the most abundant weed. Surveys done in 1976 to 1979 found *B. kaber* throughout Saskatchewan, Canada (Thomas 1985). Average density for the weed was 3.3 plants/m^2 and 88% of the fields had 0.6 to 8 plants/m^2. Biotypes of *B. kaber* resistant to triazine herbicides are found in Ontario, Canada.

Numerous competition studies have been done in Europe and North America with *B. kaber* that document its economic importance. Welbank (1963) studied the competitiveness of *B. kaber* with wheat and kale in greenhouse trials and found it the most competitive weed of those tested. When grown alone, biomass production of this weed nearly tripled in response to N while *B. kaber* reduced the N content of wheat and kale leaves. He concludes that N uptake is the most important aspect of competition. Friesen et al. (1960) sampled 60 wheat and barley fields in Canada and found that grain produced without *B. kaber* competition was higher in nitrogen than grain growing with this weed. In Poland, *B. kaber* growth was 25% less than that of oats and barley one month after emergence, but the crops and weed contained equivalent quantities of phosphorous as the nutrient concentration in the crops was reduced (Gawlinski 1963). Fertilizing spring wheat in Canada reduced competition losses from *B. kaber* from 16 to 10% and also increased grain protein content (Nakoneshny and Friesen 1961).

Anderson (1956) summarized 9 yr of data in Canada for wheat, oats, and barley and found that when *B. kaber* comprised 1 to 20, 21 to 40, and 40 to 60% of the biomass, grain losses were 13, 43, and 62%, respectively. Wheat was the most and barley the least competitive crop with this weed. Low densities of *B. kaber* reduced maize yields 1.5- to 2-fold at low weed densities and 5- to 6-fold at high levels (Vorob'ev 1968). Both maize and *B. kaber* consumed the same quantities of water during July. Wheat production in Canada was reduced 36% by *B. kaber* in a drought year and 40% with rainfall the following year, suggesting that moisture competition is not an important factor for cereals (Pavlychenko and Harrington 1935).

High crop densities minimize the competitiveness of *B. kaber*. Populations of 200, 300, and 1000 plants/m^2 for peas, barley, and flax, respectively, nearly eliminated competition losses (Granstrom 1959). *B. kaber* competes with oilseed rape for water and densities of 20, 40, and 80 plants/m^2 reduced spring rape seed yields 28, 43, and 66%, respectively, in Ontario, Canada (Blackshaw et al. 1987). The weed's biomass was greater when grown with oilseed rape seed than as a monoculture (Blackshaw and Dekker 1988). *B. kaber* also produced more seeds per plant when grown in association with other species than when grown alone, demonstrating its competitiveness as a weed.

Yield losses were greater for peas and lower for barley and flax when crops and uncontrolled *B. kaber* were fertilized. This weed emerges sooner than peas and has a higher growth rate, maturing in 800 growing degree days as compared to 1000 for the crop (Nelson and Nylund 1962). In this crop, *B. kaber* competes primarily for water and light. Flax yields are reduced if more than 12 plants/m^2 of *B. kaber* are present in dry years and 30 plants/m^2 in wet years. Even if the weed is removed shortly after flax reaches the seedling stage, basal branching (and therefore crop yield) is reduced (Burrows and Olson 1955). *B. kaber* reached its maximum biomass in flax at 30 plants/m^2 in a dry year (3.1 t/ha dry weight) and 60 plants/m^2 in a wet year (1.5 t/ha).

When averaged over two locations in the north-central United States, densities of 3, 6, 13, and 26 *B. kaber* plants/m of soybean row reduced grain yield 46, 54, 61, and 70%, respectively (Berglund and Nalewaja 1969). The weed reduced crop height, dry matter production, pods/plant, seeds/pod, and thus seeds/plant. Each 100 kg/ha of *B. kaber* reduced soybean seed yield 41 kg/ha. Competition for 3 wk after emergence did not affect yields. Maximum yield loss occurred when *B. kaber* removal was delayed for 7 wk or more after emergence.

Detailed competition studies between barley and *B. kaber* have also been done. Idris and Milthorpe (1966) established specific ratios of weeds to crops in pots and placed them in a barley field to simulate natural conditions. *B. kaber* populations declined by 11% at 8 wk after emergence in pure stands and 28% in association with barley. Barley density was unaffected by weed density and barley seedlings were larger than those of *B. kaber*. The weed reached its maximum leaf area at 6 wk, after which it declined with leaf senescence. They noted reduced nitrogen content in barley when grown with *B. kaber*. The competitiveness of barley was attributed to its ability to intercept light. Barley competition reduced photosynthetic activity of *B. kaber* 35% at 6 wk and the number of racemes per mustard plant by over 50%. Richardson (1980) recorded barley yield losses of 48 to 71% at *B. kaber* densities of 70 to 390 plants/m^2. The weed reduced the number of heads per plant and grain weight per head, but some barley varieties were less affected than others.

Among the classical weed competition studies in history are those done by Pavlychenko and Harrington (1934, 1935) and Pavlychenko (1937). Their research documented that barley, oats, and wheat compete effectively with *B. kaber*. Without competition, *B. kaber* produced 228 g dry weight/plant, but, in competition with cereals, plants averaged only 1.5 g. Five days after emergence, *B. kaber* had less leaf area but more stomata/plant (79,800) than barley. At the flowering stage, the weed had 665 stomata/mm^2 and 490 million/plant.

The uniqueness of their research is seen in the studies of root development for *B. kaber* and cereals. Plants were grown singly or together in the field and large blocks of soil with the entire root system were removed. Soil was slowly washed away from the bottom of the block with a fine spray of water, and root distribution and size were recorded. When grown individually, *B. kaber* had 95 cm of roots 5 days after emergence and over 1200 cm at 21 days. Cereals had a greater total root length at 5 days after emergence, but at 21 days *B. kaber* root length exceeded those of all nine weeds and 11 cereal varieties studied.

They discovered that competition begins as soon as the root systems overlap and this transpires long before the aboveground plant parts interact. These pioneers also found that *B. kaber* affects wheat and barley root development differently. Barley root length was reduced 67, 19, and 14% at 5 and 40 days after emergence, and at maturity, respectively. In contrast, wheat root length was decreased 24, 30, and 33% at the same periods. Barley recovered from the initial detrimental effects of *B. kaber* to its root system while wheat did not. Pavlychenko (1937) found that *B. kaber* roots were twice as long as those of wheat at 22 and 40 days after emergence and that even in competition with wheat, each weed plant formed a root network totaling 165 m in length. Such detailed information is lacking for most of our important weed species.

In addition to the losses due to interference of *B. kaber* with crops, it can host *Aphis gossypii* (a serious cotton pest), red spider mites, cabbage root flies, and several nematode species (Bendixen et al. 1979, 1981).

Seeds are high in protein (30%) and lipids (25%), but are also high in erucic acid (6 to over 30%) and contain the glucosinolate, sinalbin (Daun 1983). Livestock poisoning following seed consumption has been reported in Canada and England (Kingsbury 1964). Hay infested with *B. kaber* can cause labor difficulties in pregnant ewes. Seeds in wheat reportedly affect flour taste and quantity. The amino acid balance in *B. kaber* compares favorably to that in the protein of hen's eggs and was the best of ten weed seeds tested for feed value in Canada (Tkachuk and Mellish 1977).

COMMON NAMES

Brassica kaber

ARGENTINA	hageng, sinapis
AUSTRALIA	charlock, wild mustard
BELGIUM	hederik, herik
BRAZIL	mostarda
CANADA	moutarde des champs, wild mustard
COLOMBIA	florcilla
DENMARK	agersennep
DOMINICAN REPUBLIC	mostaza
EGYPT	girilla, khardal
ENGLAND	charlock, wild mustard
FINLAND	rikkasinappi
FRANCE	moutarde des champs, moutarde sauvage, sanve, seneve
GERMANY	Acker-Senf, Wilder Ackersenf
GREECE	charlock
HUNGARY	vadrepce
IRAN	khardal barri
IRAW	charlock, field kale, khardal barri
ISRAEL	chardal hasadeh
ITALY	senape, senape selvatica, senape vera
LEBANON	charlock, hharsha, kabar afrit, khardal barri, lifaytah, wild mustard

MADAGASCAR	fantrotrar amleazaha
MEXICO	mostaza
MOROCCO	moutarde des champs
NETHERLANDS	herik, krodde
NEW ZEALAND	charlock
NORWAY	akersennep
POLAND	gorczyca polna, ognicha
PORTUGAL	mostarda dos campos
SAUDI ARABIA	kabar, khardal-barri, liftah, qirilla
SPAIN	jaramago, mostaza arvense, mostaza silvestre
SWEDEN	akersenap
TUNISIA	moutarde des champs
TURKEY	yabani hardal
UNITED STATES	wild mustard
URUGUAY	mostaza silvestre
YUGOSLAVIA	gorusica

Seventeen

Cardaria draba (L.) Desv.

Brassicaceae (Cruciferae), Mustard Family

CARDARIA DRABA (FORMERLY *LEPIDIUM*) is commonly known as hoary cress because of the hairy leaves and the close relation to the common upland-grown garden cress *Lepidium sativum*. It behaves as a troublesome perennial weed mainly in the temperate zones. The weed is dangerous because the roots penetrate very deeply, root fragments moved about during tillage regenerate quickly, and seed is produced in abundance. There is concern that recent limited-tillage systems may favor the spread of and competi-

FIGURE 17-1 The distribution of *Cardaria draba* (L.) Desv. across the world where it has been reported as a weed.

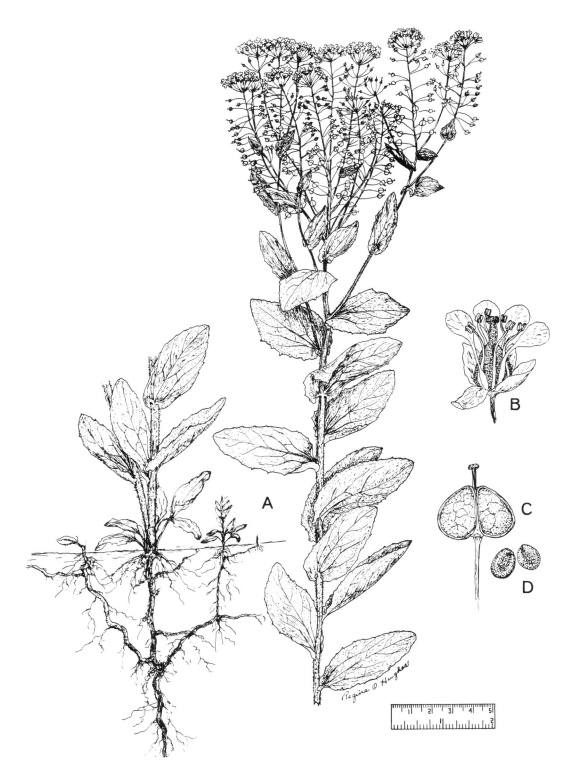

FIGURE 17-2   *Cardaria draba* (L.) Desv.: A. habit; B. flower; C. silicle; D. seeds.

tion from this weed. In an earlier period, *Cardaria* was once labeled the "most serious foreign weed menace in England."

DESCRIPTION

C. draba (Figure 17-2) is a *perennial herb* with rhizomes; *stems* erect, spreading sometimes sprawling, rigid flowering stems somewhat angular, 20 to 90 cm tall, branched above, sparsely hairy, grayish-green; *taproot* strong, deep with extensive horizontal food-storing branch system; *leaves* alternate, simple, 2 to 8 cm long, broad, oblong, almost entire to irregularly toothed, short hairs both surfaces, may be sinuate to cause rough surfaces; *upper leaves* elliptical to ovate, clasping stem with ear-like lobes at leaf base; *basal leaves* up to 7 cm, more slender, narrowing to a short *petiole*, sometimes withering before flowers open; *flowers* cruciform, numerous in corymb-like raceme, without bracts, up to 8 mm in diameter; *petals* 4, broad at apex, white or creamy, may be rose-colored in bud stage, about 3 to 5 mm long; *sepals* 4, 2.5 mm long, obtuse, glabrous, may be white-margined (Canada); *style* 0.8 to 1 mm; *stamens* 6; *fruit* with two seeds is a silicle or pod, heart-shaped, glabrous, about 4 mm long and somewhat broader, *pedicel* 6 to 15 mm, fruit two-valved, asymmetrical if only one seed develops, flattened laterally and tapering to prominent, persistent *style* above, indehiscent but often separates into one-seeded nutlets; *seed* about 2 mm long, 1.5 mm wide, slightly compressed, reddish brown, rounded at one end and narrowed to blunt point at other. Seeds weigh 1.5 to 2 gm per thousand.

This species may be recognized by its heart-shaped silicle topped by the short, persistent style, with body slightly inflated and becoming prominently veined at maturity.

We have here an instance that clearly demonstrates the necessity to distinguish between closely related species. Canada and the United States have *C. draba*, *C. chalapensis* (formerly *C. draba* var. *repens*), and *C. pubescens* (formerly *Hymenophysa pubescens*), known respectively by the common names heart-podded, lens-podded, and globe-podded hoary cress (Mulligan and Frankton 1962). Prior to Bellue's (1933) report of three distinct species of *Cardaria* in North America, all such plants were referred to *C. draba* (a practice sometimes followed today). These plants have different ecological tolerances, geographical distribution, and in addition they are weeds of arable land and differ markedly in their response to herbicides (Jenkins and Jackman 1938, Sexsmith 1964).

DISTRIBUTION AND HABITAT

C. draba is mainly a weed of temperate regions with sparse distribution in the warm regions of Central America, North Africa, the Arabian Peninsula, and central India (Figure 17-1). It covers North America, is in Europe, thence south-eastward through the Middle East to the western border of China. It is a weed of northern China and extends far to the east. In the former Soviet Union it is found in the maritimes in the Far East, around Irkutsk on Lake Baikal, and has wide distribution north, south and west of Novosibirsk. In the Southern Hemisphere it is found as a weed in southern Argentina, Natal in South Africa, and in Australia and New Zealand.

It is a strong, robust plant that thrives from the Arctic Circle in Finland to warm areas of seasonal aridity where it is a minor weed, as in Egypt, Morocco, Crete, and Corsica. It is seen up to 2100 m in altitude in the central and southern Alps and to 1600 m in southwest

Iran. It survives in areas of prolonged cold, to wit, on the Arctic Circle, where there are but 120 to 140 days above 4°C and the snow cover persists for 160 days on average.

There is a strong conviction that it has moved about the world with agricultural seed supplies: to North America with grass and lucerne seed 100 years ago and to Australia about the same time with lucerne seed and in ship's ballast, later to be distributed around the country with seed of clover, lucerne and oats moved from infested to clean areas. The weed was moved from continental Europe to the British Isles during a military expedition that originated in the Walcheren Islands of Holland. Carlquist (1967) believes the plant can be moved long distances by birds because a viscid, sticky coating allows the seed, when moist, to adhere to feathers and legs (also see Young and Evans 1973).

The weed is found where soil is disturbed on field margins, on fallow land in dry areas, on the banks of ditches and irrigation canals and in many waste places. It is moved along roads by transport of forage and root crops. It is mainly a weed of arable land and is encouraged in its movement from field to field by tillage that fragments rhizomes and roots. It is especially vigorous under irrigation. On occasion it is troublesome in poor pasture land.

The weed is found on a variety of loamy soils from light to heavy, and frequents gravelly places. It prefers neutral to alkaline soils.

PROPAGATION

Cardaria draba spreads by root and rhizome fragments that may give rise to new shoots throughout the season. It is a prolific seed producer, 2300/stem having been recorded by Stevens (1957). In the north temperate zone in Canada the flowering period is May to July, with mature seed produced one month later. In the United States the processes are about one month earlier.

In the studies of Brown and Porter (1942) in the central United States the minimum temperature for germination was 0.5°C (65%), the maximum was 40°C (5%), and the optimum was in the 20 to 30°C range, where germination was 75 to 80%. Light is not required but it does enhance germination. Oxygen levels below 10% and above 55% were unfavorable to germination. Viability decreased rapidly for seed buried at a 10 to 15 cm depth for 3 yr. Bellue (1946) found 93% germination at harvest, then 84, 31, and 0% after 1, 2, and 3 yr in storage, respectively. The germination of seed stored in fresh water dropped from 66 to 12% in 1 mo and to 2% after 2 mo (Bruns and Rasmussen 1953, 1957). Reports on the survival of seed in manure are conflicting (Anon. [USA] 1970).

Regeneration of root and rhizome sections of several dimensions have been studied and although 1 cm pieces may have 50% viability, larger pieces to 5 or 6 cm give better survival, produce more shoots and require less time before emergence. All of these activities are inhibited by burial at 7.5 cm. In general, such fragments produce shoots at one end and roots at the other (Henson 1969).

PHYSIOLOGY AND MORPHOLOGY

C. draba is a tough, vigorous perennial plant well able to adapt its growth habits to the place and season. It may be an early spring beginner and may finish its seed pods and dry up by mid-summer. Plants which emerge late may complete the cycle and remain green until frost. In some areas it may not flower until the second season. Its phenology is as varied as the places where it grows and a single example may suggest the basic pattern of the life cycle (Hodgson 1955, Scurfield 1962, Mulligan and Findlay 1974).

In the western United States, Hodgson recorded early spring growth when average temperature reached 2°C. Maximums at this time were 14°C and minimums −8°C. In one study in late March small rosettes were formed in 2 wk with at least one shoot on most rosettes in 4 wk. Flower buds formed at the end of April, 50% were in bloom 2 wk later, with 85% open in another week. Salisbury (1942) found the plants self-pollinated in England. Mulligan and Frankton (1962) reported self-incompatibility in the species, with out-crossing by insects. The flowers of *C. draba* are readily accessible to short-tongued insects (Knuth 1908). Hodgson found that 80% of the seed pods were formed by the end of May, with 50% of them mature 3 wk later, at which time they could contaminate first cuttings of legume and grass hay. The weed dried up after seed production. In these fields he found 3000 seeds on some plants and, if the weed stand was heavy, 450 kg/ha of weed seed was produced.

The horizontal vegetative extension of the plant and the development of the aerial portion varies with climatic conditions, soils, and competition. Kirk et al. (1943) and Selleck (1965) in Canada found several branch shoots on field plants at 25 days, with several horizontal roots in progress and the tap root down 25 cm. After 100 days the plants were 60 cm in diameter with 80 vegetative buds on the root system. Some plants were 3.7 m in diameter in one year and if growing without competition produced 450 shoots. In earlier experiments Selleck (1961) found an average perimeter extension of 60 cm/year, during which time the mean density of flowering and non-flowering shoots actually decreased 15 and 50%, respectively. The decrease in plant density, however, was accompanied by a 16-fold increase of plants under 75 cm as new seedlings emerged.

There are many reports of vertical extension of the taproot to 150 to 300 cm. Corns and Frankton (1952) reported a root 900 cm in length. The general pattern of branching is development of first roots from the radicle in the initial 2 to 3 wk of growth, first order lateral roots then grow out to later turn down and become vertical roots, which may grow deeper than the main taproot. Just below the point of turn-down, secondary laterals develop, and so on for several orders. Shoots (buds) can form anywhere on the system but usually arise just above the point where laterals turn down (Mulligan and Findlay 1974). Buds near the surface become rosettes, while those at greater depth may become rhizomes that are able to produce shoot buds later (Frazier 1943). From this it is easy to understand why dense colonies of such plants can exclude other vegetation. The plant is easily identified when in flower and this may prompt a decision about the need of control, but in areas where it does not flower until the second year it may have already established a sizeable rosette and a formidable root system before the problem seems serious.

If the crown or upper root system of this plant is injured, a new crown forms quickly from an adventitious bud on the upper root section.

The plant thus perennates by rootstocks that have abundant resources, can overwinter, and can put out vigorous new shoots in spring. Barr (1942) found the food reserves to be mostly sugars and starches which together may comprise 80% of the plant dry weight at times. For 24 days after a single cultivation, Barr surveyed the plant carbohydrates and found no change for 2 wk, after which there was an appreciable accumulation.

Simonds (1938) performed the most complete anatomical study of the embryo, root, stem, root-stem transition zone, and of the structure of specific major tissues. The anatomical work of Korsmo (1954) with its many illustrations is exceptional. Korsmo (1935) and Delorit (1970) have provided excellent color photographs and illustrations of the seed of this weed.

AGRICULTURAL IMPORTANCE

C. draba is a serious weed of maize and small grains in Hungary and the former Soviet Union; potatoes and sugar beets in Hungary; sunflowers, tobacco, vegetables, and vineyards in the former Soviet Union; and wheat in Iran and Italy. It is a principal weed of barley in the former Soviet Union; cereals in Australia and Jordan; maize in Czechoslovakia; horticultural crops, millet, and oats in the former Soviet Union; orchards in Spain and Switzerland; pastures and rangeland in South Africa and the United States; sugar beets in Iran; vineyards in France and Switzerland; and wheat in Australia. It is a common weed of barley in Canada and Greece; other small grains in Iran, Tunisia, and Turkey; citrus in Australia; hay fields in Canada and the United States; lucerne in Czechoslovakia and Argentina; oats in Canada and Greece; pastures in Argentina and Australia; rye in Greece; vineyards in Australia, Iran, Turkey, and the former Yugoslavia; and wheat in Canada, Greece, and Spain.

In addition, *C. draba* appears as a weed of unknown importance in the small grains of Bulgaria, France, Germany, Guatemala, Iraq, Lebanon, Netherlands, Portugal, Tasmania, and the United States; maize in Guatemala and the former Yugoslavia; lucerne in England and the Netherlands; pastures in Tasmania and hay fields of England. It is a weed of horticultural crops in Hungary; orchards and strawberries in England and France; potatoes in the Netherlands; vineyards in Germany; and cotton in Iran. It is found in the cultivated crops of Afghanistan, the Arabian Peninsula, Belgium, China, New Zealand, Rhodesia, and Syria.

In a survey of the weeds in 5000 ha of wheat in the area of Esfahan in Iran, Boluri (1977) found that weeds composed 15% of all vegetation in the field and *Cardaria* was one of the four most plentiful species. Because of its aggressive and competitive behavior, Meadly (1965) once ranked it as one of the worst weeds in Australia. In Victoria some of the wheat land lost one half its value because of yield reductions caused by *C. draba*, and was subsequently converted to grazing agriculture.

The species is regarded as a dangerous, rapidly spreading weed in the agriculture of the arid steppes of Russia and in the adjacent Siberian area. It is declared a noxious weed for Australia, Canada, Chile, Greece, the United States, and Tasmania, and the propagules are prohibited in the seed supplies for planting of pastures, forages and several arable, cultivated crops. Dispersal of the plant is encouraged when the abundant weed seed supplies are harvested with grain and hay.

Repeated mowing is of little use in infested fields. In experimental plots in the central plains of Canada, *C. draba* was eliminated in 3 yr following intensive tillage with disc or sub-surface blade cultivators. A total of 24 operations were required at 2-wk intervals in the first year, with a 3-wk interval in the two final years. The herbicide 2,4-D has been widely used for control but must be applied for 3 yr or more in the early bud stage before flowering or in the late fall rosette stage.

Perhaps the best management of this weed is a combination of competitive crops, tillage, and herbicides. Hodgson (1952) obtained a high level of control of an infestation in corn in the western United States in 3 yr by spraying the weed with 2,4-D at the flower bud stage, plowing 10 days later, then planting the corn and cultivating in a conventional manner. In wheat land he obtained control in 2 yr by spraying at the bud stage and again 6 wk later as new seedlings appeared, then working the field periodically until it was time for fall-seeding of the crop.

A disturbing report of a long-term experiment in Spain indicates that limited tillage systems encourage weed competition to the crop and the abundance of *C. draba* in cereals (Fernandez-Quintanilla et al. 1984). The role of this weed in the new systems of reduced tillage is as yet unknown.

In different times and places this weed has been routinely dried, ground and used as a pepper-like spice, hence the common name "peppergrass." Sheep will graze on young plants, but if cattle ingest sufficient amounts, the milk has an off-flavor.

After more than a century of causing trouble in man's crops, the chemistry of this plant is worthy of mention (Dornberger and Lich 1982). In a search for new chemical substances that may halt or delay the growth of cancer cells and other diseases, extracts of about 700 plant species, including *C. draba*, were screened to measure the growth of 23 different bacteria. The material from the aerial parts of this weed ranked among the three giving the most cytotoxic activity and the greatest interference with nucleic acid metabolism.

COMMON NAMES

Cardaria draba

ARGENTINA	cardo pendiente
AUSTRALIA	hoary cress
BELGIUM	pijlkruidkers
CANADA	cranson dravier, heart-podded hoary cress, perennial peppergrass, whitetop, whiteweed
CHILE	cardaria
DENMARK	hjerteskulpet karse
EGYPT	lislis, nafal
ENGLAND	hoary cress, hoary pepperwort, thanet cress
FINLAND	kynsimokrassi
FRANCE	cranson dravier, lepidier, pain blanc, passerage, passerage drave
GERMANY	Gemeine Pfeilkresse, Pfeilkresse, Stengelumfassende
GREECE	hoary cress
IRAN	ozmak
IRAQ	hoary cress, jinnaibrah
ITALY	cocola
LEBANON	hoary cress, kunaybrah, perennial peppergrass, whitetop, whiteweed
NETHERLANDS	pijlkruidkers
NEW ZEALAND	hoary cress
NORWAY	honningkarse
PORTUGAL	erva fome
SAUDI ARABIA	harf mashrigi, gana barri, lislis, nafal

SOUTH AFRICA	hoary cardaria, peperbos cardaria
SPAIN	babol, berro, capellanes, falsa coclearia, floreta, mastuerzo, mastuerzo oriental, papolas
SWEDEN	valsk krasse
TASMANIA	whiteweed
TURKEY	cok senelik yabani tere, kir teresi
UNITED STATES	hoary cress, lepidium, perennial peppergrass, whitetop

Eighteen

Carduus nutans L. and Carduus pycnocephalus L.

Asteraceae (Compositae), Aster Family

THERE ARE SEVERAL *CARDUUS* thistles that appear in the world's natural grasslands, improved pastures and arable crops. In an earlier time the names musk thistle and nodding thistle were used to designate the large-flowered species *Carduus nutans* as the most troublesome in agriculture. We know now that *C. thoermeri* and *C. macrocephalus* (also large-flowered species) are sometimes mixed with *C. nutans*, with the former also having wide distribution. They are often referred to as the large-flowered group. The life histories are similar and the biology which follows is essentially that of the group. It is in 18 crops in 32 countries.

C. pycnocephalus is one of the smaller-flowered, slender *Carduus* thistles. Although it is less robust, it is believed to be next in importance in agricultural fields, and the life history is similar to the above species. Notable exceptions or variations will be pointed out. It is in eight crops in 26 countries.

Carduus is an ancient Latin name for thistle; *nutans* is from *nuto*, to nod.

DESCRIPTIONS

Carduus nutans

C. nutans (Figure 18-1) is an erect, branched, winter *annual* or *biennial* herb from 35 cm to more than 2 m tall, partially winged as leaf bases continue as spiny ridges down the stem; *rosette*, tightly packed spreading or radiating basal leaves with little or no stem elongation, leaves not deeply lobed at first but later deeply cut, some leaves of older rosettes 30 to 50 cm long; upper *leaves* alternate, sessile, 10–20 cm, usually smooth, hairless both sides but some types slightly downy, dark green with some types gray-green, may have silvery leaf margins, veins may be in deep depressions on upper surface, prominent below, twice pinnately lobed, each deeply cut lobe with 3 to 5 points (spines), spines white to yellow; *root*, 1 or 2 roots appear early at hypocotyl-root junction, large fleshy taproot with many

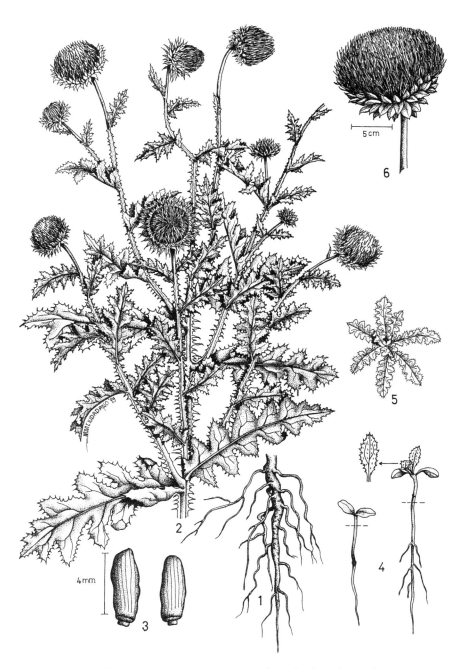

FIGURE 18-1   *Carduus nutans* L.: 1. root system; 2. flowering branch; 3. achene, two views; 4. seedlings 5. face view; 6. flower head.

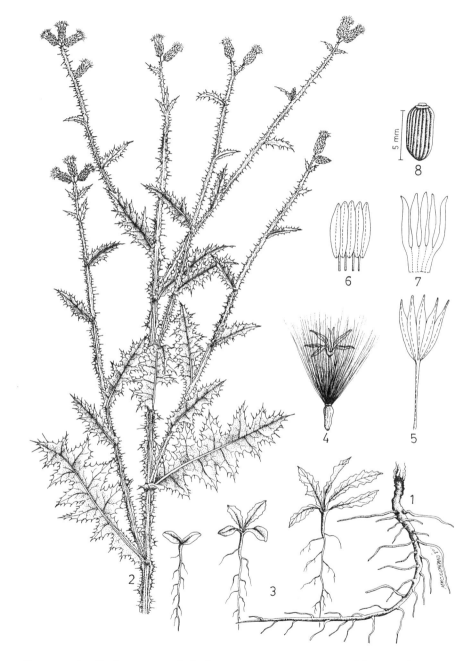

FIGURE 18-2 *Carduus pycnocephalus* L.: 1. root system; 2. portion of flowering branch; 3. seedling; 4. flower; 5. corolla and tube; 6. stamens; 7. corolla open; 8. achene

branches formed later, mature roots corky and hollow near soil surface; *flower heads* borne singly at ends of branches, 4 to 15 cm in diameter, head flat, inclined to droop (nod), individual florets open toward center from the rim, flowers deep rose, violet, reddish purple, attractive, fragrant, surrounded by many involucral bracts, each ending in a spine, outer bracts may turn backward, others turn forward; *seed*, an achene, 1.4 mm wide, 3.6 mm long, oblong, one edge curved, other straight, broadest toward tip, then seed tapers toward base which is rounded toward a small depressed scar, tip is truncate with terminal face depressed, leaving an encircling collar, below collar seed somewhat constricted, surface finely grooved, shiny, color is a brown shading of transverse, wavy ribbons on a yellowish brown base, lighter seeds straw colored, *pappus* consists of finely toothed unbranched bristles 2 to 3 cm long.

Carduus pycnocephalus

C. pycnocephalus (Figure 18-2) is a winter *annual* or *biennial* prickly *herb*, erect, to 1 or 2 m tall, stiff, branched, *stems* and *leaves* with loose cottony down, narrow wings on stem (see below) not present beneath flower head; stout tap *root*; *leaves*, alternate pinnatifid, with short, wavy, very prickly, deeply cut lobes, leaf base decurrent, prolonged down stem to form prickly narrow wings, basal leaves narrowed at base, stem leaves sessile, upper surface with indistinct white markings as in *Silybum marianum*; *flower heads*, small, oblong, in clusters of 2 to 5 at ends of spiny winged stems and branches, *florets* tubular, lobes of *corolla* purplish red to pink, may be white 3 times as long as throat; *involucral bracts* rather broad at base then narrowing to a prickle, margin and backs have small, rough, upwardly appressed trichomes especially on midvein, inner bracts about same length as florets; *achenes*, about 5 mm long, are of two types, a grayish green form with about 20 conspicuous longitudinal grooves, and a gray form, dull finish, just slightly rough, may be sticky; *pappus hairs*, light-colored, 1.5 to 2 cm long, minutely upwardly barbed, early deciduous.

The slender thistles, *C. pycnocephalus* and *tenuiflorus* occur together in Australia with identities confused. Parsons (1979) examined 1700 specimens and learned that one-half in major herbaria were unidentified or wrongly identified. He provided qualitative and quantitative comparisons and data for aid in separating them. Desrochers et al. (1988) have elaborated on the separation of subspecies of *C. nutans* by chemical means.

DISTRIBUTION AND HABITAT

A striking feature of the distribution of these species is their almost total absence from the tropics, with only occasional sightings at high elevations (Figures 18-3 and 18-4). The plants are quite unlikely to spread into warm regions because of the cold requirement in the rosette stage for the stimulation of flower initiation. As a weed, *C. nutans* is widespread in North America above Mexico, where it is found frequently in ranges and grasslands, is in the southern third of South America, extends from central and southern Europe southeastward through Eurasia to India, and has extensive distribution in New Zealand and Australia. The distribution of *C. pycnocephalus* is similar; in addition it is in Brazil and north and south Africa, but it is reluctant to colonize cool temperate areas.

As an example of the array of habitats that can be occupied by *C. nutans*, in the inter-mountain region of western North America it ranges from valleys of low altitude with

FIGURE 18-3   The distribution of *Carduus nutans* L. across the world where it has been reported as a weed.

FIGURE 18-4   The distribution of *Carduus pycnocephalus* L. across the world where it has been reported as a weed.

saline soils to acid soils at 2440 m. Plants can produce viable seeds in some areas that receive only 25 cm of annual rainfall. It grows vigorously and may produce 50 flower heads per plant in a spruce-fir zone at 2150 m. In Canadian prairies it is common in places covered (insulated?) by snow drifts such as gullies, fence lines, brush thickets, and the lee sides of stone piles. In Armenia and Pakistan it is found at 3000 and 1500 m, respectively. *C. pycnocephalus* grows at 2100 m in Morocco and 1800 m in Pakistan.

These thistles are generally adapted to sites of low fertility as well as to rich cropland. The major infestations are in Argentina, Australia, New Zealand, and much of North America. In Australia, with vast expanses of rangeland for cattle and sheep husbandry, these species, together with five other adventive thistles, have become prominent features of improved pastures on mainly basaltic soils in areas receiving 50 to 90 cm of evenly distributed annual rainfall. In an earlier time these plants were found around homesteads, stock camps, and rabbit warrens. They are now prospering on land that is above the natural fertility levels, with a frequent alternation of dry and wet summers, relatively cold winters (6 or more months with some freezing temperatures) and they have been favored by the introduction of clovers, superphosphate applications and irrigation. They seldom invade permanent pastures but readily enter fertile annual grass pastures if summer drought opens up bare patches (Michael 1968b, Matthews 1975, Parsons 1977). Using data from 300 climatic stations and information on the dispersal of *C. nutans* following its entrance into southeast Australia, Medd and Smith (1978) constructed a model for the prediction of the possible spread of the weed to other areas of the country.

C. nutans entered the eastern United States 100 years ago but became troublesome 40 years ago and spread very quickly. In Kentucky in the central United States 90 of 120 counties became infested in the 30 years after introduction (Lacefield and Gray 1970). In the west it began to spread into both native and sown pastures. In Canada it is reported to hybridize with *C. acanthoides*, a plumeless thistle, and the taxonomy is confused in some of the areas (Moore and Mulligan 1958, Mulligan and Moore 1961).

In Australia, England, and the eastern United States, *C. nutans* is fond of high-calcium soils and thrives in pastures on shallow soils in limestone and dolomite areas (Stuckey and Forsyth 1971). In Canada the weed frequents lands with a *pH* range of 6 to 9 that includes most soils in the southern part of the Canadian prairies.

The seeds of these two species are distributed by wind, surface water, machines, man, livestock, and wildlife. *Carduus* seeds have been found in the crop (an expanded esophagal section for food storage) of birds and also in their nests. Only a trace of *Carduus* seed was found in flowing irrigation water in a heavily infested area in the central United States. Delahunty (1962) in New Zealand found only a small amount of seed carried more than 125 cm from the parent plant. At high humidities the pappus adheres to the fruit more tenaciously and the moisture and fruit weight cause the fruit to be dropped near the mother plant if it is shed. Smith and Kok (1984) in the United States, in experimental studies of seed dispersal at controlled wind velocities, found less than 1% moved more than 100 m. Most were found within 50 m of the parent. Again it is clear, however, that even a very small percentage of seed moving out of the vicinity of a large population may still be a significant source of infestation for distant areas. See also Kelly et al. (1988).

The plumes seen blowing about in the wind are now known to be easily detached from the fruits. Ridley (1930) experimented with *C. pycnocephalus* in still air and found that even plumed seeds fell to the ground much more quickly than similar seeds of *Lactuca*, *Senecio*, and *Typha* species. This habit of seed deposition results in patches and clumps of thistles in pastures. In Australia entire heads with seeds sometimes fall to the ground.

REPRODUCTIVE PHYSIOLOGY AND MORPHOLOGY

Propagation of *C. nutans* and *C. pycnocephalus* is by seed. The preponderance of research on the biology of these species is focused on the reproductive structures and the physiological events that enable them to be very successful seed producers. For this reason the propagation and floral biology must all be brought together in this section.

In various parts of the world, the plants may be found as winter annuals, biennials, or, on occasion, annuals. Indeed, all of these patterns may be present in a given site at different times. As a biennial the plant emerges in autumn, remains vegetative as a rosette in the next season, and flowers in still a later season. Popay (1980) believes that most of the *C. nutans* in New Zealand behaves as a winter annual, emerging in autumn and flowering the next summer. On occasion, in New Zealand and elsewhere, in very favorable sites and seasons, the weather may stimulate emergence in very early spring, followed by summer rosette formation, with flower stalk elongation in autumn of the same season; in that case the plant behaves as an annual. This is unusual and such late plants are often damaged by frost. Groves and Kaye (1988) in Australia, in a comparison of seven introduced thistles, found that *C. pycnocephalus* germinates very well at low temperatures and thus may behave as a short season annual.

C. nutans is primarily an outcrossing species in the Northern Hemisphere but shows greater selfing rates in more northerly locations. As the corolla tube and style expand rapidly, flowers begin to open on the outer rim of the head. The elongation of the style ruptures some anthers and pollen grains may be seen on the stigma as it emerges from the tube-like corolla. Fertilization takes place as the style and stigma become fully elongated. Flowering proceeds inward on the capitula to full bloom within two days. Individual florets remain open about 24 hr. The florets within a head are compatible, but bees and other insects carry much pollen from other heads. Doing et al. (1969) in Australia found that the involucres of first flower heads are flatter and wider than those that follow, and do not produce viable seed. Flowering is determinate starting with the terminal heads (which may reach 10 cm in diameter) and progressing down the stem from branch to branch. The top two flower heads may be borne singly on tall stems, whereas lower branches may each have several flower heads (McCarty 1982). In the central United States bolting begins in overwintering plants in March, with first flowering in late May to early June and continuing for 8 to 10 weeks. It is not unusual to see pre-bud, flowering and mature seed development stages on the same plant. The plants die following seed maturation (McCarty 1982).

Henceforth, studies of the reproductive system of *C. pycnocephalus* must incorporate the results of Parsons (1977) and Olivieri et al. (1983) in their investigations of dimorphism in the achenes of the same capitulum. The inner and outer achenes differ in both morphology and physiology. The plant produces non-dormant, easily dispersed seeds at the center of the capitulum. The outer seeds have a variable dormancy, no special adaptation for dispersal, and some may germinate in 2 days, others in 3 yr.

In the south of France, Olivieri found the inner seeds to be cream colored, striated, sticky, and bear pappi that aid in wind dispersal. The outer seeds are not usually released from the capitulum and may germinate in the involucre after it falls. Seeds of both types collected in April showed 87 to 98% germination; for inner seeds this took 5 days, for outer seeds 3 wk.

As for other **Compositae** showing centripetal development of the capitulum, the outer florets of *C. pycnocephalus* develop first. In many capitula, following the staminate stage of the outer florets, the development of the pistillate stage coincides with anthesis of the inner florets. Thus, the outer florets may be selfed with pollen from within the same capitulum. The inner florets will now receive pollen largely from other capitula resulting in a higher probability of outcrossing. There is always the possibility that for these florets some selfing may exist as the style elongates through the tube formed by anthers and corolla. The capitula have the characteristics of entomophilous flowers (insect pollinated) and it is the main method for this species.

A study of seed maturation and quality at four stages (full bloom, 2 and 4 days after, and at full maturity of the head) revealed that the terminals that bloomed first produced many more seeds per head than those below that opened later. The harvest of seed from each head as the plant reached full bloom yielded only an average of 26 good-quality seeds per plant. When harvested in a similar fashion at 2 and 4 days after full bloom, and at full maturity, the production of good seeds was 72, 774, and 3580, respectively. Seed dissemination was initiated as early as 7 days after a head began to bloom (McCarty 1982). Doing et al. (1969) believes that seeds are normally shed 1 to 2 months after flowering.

Seed production by *C. nutans* may be very high in favorable sites but very low in poor sites, thus head and seed counts are of little use unless habitats are fully described. There are reports in the literature of 10 to several hundred heads per plant and a few thousand to more than 100,000 seeds per plant. McCarty (1982) established experimentally in central North America that only about one-third of the seed is viable in some years. McCarty (1964) established earlier that the weed may produce up to 11,000 seeds per plant in his area. The first flower heads to bloom (i.e., the terminal heads) may produce up to 1500 seeds per head, while the last to bloom may be limited to 25 or less. Canadian seed production is somewhat less.

It is generally believed that seed viability is low at or near harvest but the propagules that survive, if buried in the soil or placed in a circumstance unfavorable for germination, may survive up to 10 yr (Burnside et al. 1981). In the Hawke's Bay area on the North Island of New Zealand, Popay (1980) found that in winter, after the main flush of germination, there were still 5 million *C. nutans* seeds/ha on or near the soil surface. The smallest disturbance of the soil prompted germination.

In Australia also the initial seed viability is high at harvest, falls quickly, but with a small portion of seed surviving to reinfest fields annually. Popay and Thompson (1979) in New Zealand buried recoverable seed of *C. nutans* at three soil depths to 21 cm. After 3 yr very few seeds were left at 0 to 2 cm, 50% were left at 4 to 6 cm, and most seeds were still viable after 4 yr at 19 to 21 cm. Dry seed stored in a laboratory were less viable than those held at 4 to 6 cm in the soil. Bendall (1974, 1975) in Tasmania confirmed the high germination levels of *C. pycnocephalus* seeds at harvest, found good germination at a 1.5 cm soil depth, and no germination at all at 5 to 10 cm in the soil.

The findings of Burnside et al. (1981) in the United States that some seeds were still germinable after 19 yr of burial at 23 cm, and at two sites 700 km apart, suggests that as farms are shifted to reduced- or no-tillage systems, requiring nearly perfect weed control to prevent additional seed formation, all fields with *C. nutans* must be monitored for at least a decade to avoid continued deposits in the soil seed bank.

Most reports from around the world find little or no dormancy at harvest (Dorph-Peterson 1925, Doing et al. 1969, McCarty 1969, Evans et al. 1978) but there are exceptions (Lacefield and Gray 1970, Medd and Lovett 1978). The variations in the methods of testing for dormancy and/or germination as well as the existence of biotypes among the populations in different parts of the world surely contribute to the conflicting views about dormancy in the period immediately after seed formation. It is often not ascertained whether seeds that retain viability in the soil are dormant or simply resting in a microenvironment in which it is impossible to begin life. Bendall (1974, 1975) in Tasmania found that 85% of the seed of *C. pycnocephalus* contained an inhibitor that could easily be leached away to permit germination over a range of 10 to 30°C.

Doing et al. (1969) gathered seed from the Americas, Australia, and Europe, and found germination in greenhouses in 4 to 22 days. Seeds of the American *C. thoermeri* and the Australian *C. nutans* gave 100% germination within 2 wk. The seeds aged quickly, with the above Australian sample falling to 25% germination within two years. If conditions are favorable in the field, germination of *C. nutans* may occur at any time, usually within 2 to 3 wk of shedding seed, and viability may exceed 90% (McCarty 1964, Lee and Hamrick 1983, McCarty et al. 1984). The New Zealand musk thistle seeds exposed to light and moisture will germinate readily in the autumn following production (Popay 1980).

McCarty et al. (1969) found that scarification of the seed coat with sandpaper or removal of 1 mm of the radicular tip caused a slight increase in germination but also caused the resulting seedlings to be less vigorous. Medd and Lovett (1978) found that cutting, pricking, or removing the seed coat depressed germination in light but increased it significantly in the dark.

In a suitable medium for germination, temperature is of greatest influence on seed germination. Evans et al. (1978), with seeds of *C. pycnocephalus*, used 65 different germination treatments with temperatures varying from 2 to 40°C. There was some germination in 80% of the treatments and 100% was obtained in 32% of them. A stringy mucilage on seeds placed on the soil surface helped to promote germination.

Delahunty (1962) in New Zealand reported 65% germination of fresh seed of *C. nutans* at alternating temperatures of 18 and 30°C. In the central United States, McCarty et al. (1969) obtained some germination with seeds held at 5°C for 10 days. There was no germination at 35°C. Germination of fresh seeds began to decline if they were held in a moist, cold condition but remained viable if they were kept dry and cold.

Light has some effect on germination of these thistle seeds but is not a major influence. Doing et al. (1969) in Australia observed that germination was favored by light and reported that in the field new seedlings were found only on bare patches. Feldman et al. (1968) showed that germination and growth of seedlings was favored on sparsely vegetated areas. Medd and Lovett (1978) demonstrated that red light stimulated germination of the seeds of *C. nutans* ssp *nutans* and far-red light reversed the effect. Most seed germinated in dark or light between 15 and 30°C, with a higher average germination in the light.

These plants rarely complete a life cycle without low temperature vernalization in the rosette stage. Under high fertility and very favorable growing conditions, an occasional plant may emerge in early spring and flower and set seed in that season. Because of the difficulty of reproductive fertilization at low temperatures, seed viability may be poor in these instances. In the normal biennial pattern of behavior the rosettes enlarge in late summer and autumn (some reaching 1 m in diameter) and in mild climates grow slowly in winter. Temperatures near freezing are needed in the rosette stage to stimulate elongation of the flower stalk (bolting) in Australia (Doing et al. 1969). Using *C. nutans*, Medd and Lovett (1978) grew seedlings in short-days (8 hr) for periods up to 12 wk. Each lot was then divided and given vernalization treatments at 10/5°C day/night temperatures for periods up to 70 days. Short-days reduced the amount of cold needed to initiate bolting. For example, without any short-day treatment 56 days of cold were required to bring about 40% flowering. With a regime of 84 short-days prior to the cold treatment only 14 days were needed to bring 100% flowering.

In the United States, rosettes needed a minimum of 40 days at 10°C or less in both field and laboratory to initiate flowering. Additional low temperature periods speeded up elongation of flower stems. About 95% of the test plants required a cold period to promote flowering (Haderlie and McCarty 1980).

McCarty found that 50% of *C. nutans* seeds germinated in a *pH* range of 3 to 9 and tolerated 1000 ppm (by wt) of NaCl.

Hamrick and Lee (1987) found optimum levels of germination, survival, and early growth in soil areas with cracks, moderately irregular surface topographies, and micro-habitats that reduce evaporation. A light litter cover aided growth and establishment but heavy litter prevented seedlings from reaching the soil surface.

Parsons (1973) in Australia found seeds of *C. nutans* viable after passage through the digestive tracts of sheep, but Matthews (1975) in New Zealand reported the opposite.

PHYSIOLOGY AND MORPHOLOGY

C. nutans stands out as the species of this genus that has most interfered with man's activity across the world. In the European area, Kazmi (1964) studied the many forms of *Carduus* that are referred to as *C. nutans* and concluded that seven species were represented. These are sometimes referred to as the *C. nutans* "group" when an identification is difficult. His revision was based on only the European material and the distribution of each of the species elsewhere in the world has never been put in order. For 25 years McCarty (1985) maintained a nursery of the large-flowered species of *Carduus* in the Central Plains of the United States, with later collections from Canada and elsewhere in the United States. He concluded that there may be a total of seven *Carduus* thistles in the United States, with *C. nutans*, *C. macrocephalus*, and *C. thoermeri* (perhaps most widespread) representing the large flowered group.

The cycle of life usually begins with very early spring seedling emergence, with continuing germination through summer and early fall. Flowering of the plants may begin 4 to 22 months later. In Australia, when soil moisture becomes available, emergence normally proceeds as soon as seeds are shed in late summer or early autumn. Plants not emerging in this period do not find favorable conditions again until late spring of the next year. New fall seedlings grow slowly in winter and may form a 10 cm rosette by spring (Doing et al. 1969).

In the central United States, McCarty and Scifres (1969) planted seeds at weekly intervals from June 3 to September 3, found no winter-kill, and all plants flowered in June of the following year. Plants from the early sowings were larger than those emerging later. Thistles from the final three plantings had very small rosettes in winter. Experiments of Medd and Lovett (1978) showed that spacing of plants and fertilizer treatments had little effect on phenological development, but the need for a cold period made time of planting and emergence very important.

In general, mowing may be used to inhibit seed production but the practice must be timely and several cuttings are required. Severing stems stimulates growth of lateral branches, the plant spreads out and flowers develop at a lower level (Doing et al. 1969, Anon. [Australia] 1978).

Much has been recorded about population size and phenology for the early part of the life cycle, but very little has been reported on mortality rates and the effect of drought and cold on these plants. In field experiments in New Zealand, Popay, and Thompson (1979) made detailed measurements of populations and the fate of individual plants over a 3-yr period in a hill pasture subject to summer drought. The greatest thistle population was in late autumn and winter when most seedlings emerged. Many seedlings were lost and the population declined steadily in winter and spring, while the rosette plants of the first summer also showed a downward trend of survival. The remaining plants flowered in the second summer, the plants then died and there were no thistles in the pasture more than 2 yr old. Of more than 800 marked plants, only 20% survived to flower—15% in the first summer and the remainder in the second.

McCarty and Scifres (1969) in the United States marked 37 plants in June and recorded their development for 12 mo in a season that became very dry. Two plants perished in the heat of summer, seven died in autumn, four rosette plants were lost in winter and two plants died during flower stem elongation the next spring. The remaining 22 plants flowered 1 yr after emergence.

The same authors noticed considerable variation in size and general appearance of *C. nutans* plants across the state of Nebraska in the United States. They collected plants from 25 sites and placed them in one nursery for observation. Under these conditions all of the plants were quite alike in appearance and time of flowering, with the exception of one white flowered specimen taken from a pasture in eastern Nebraska.

The development of the embryo *Carduus natans* was studied by Mestre (1957).

AGRICULTURAL IMPORTANCE

C. nutans is a serious weed of lucerne, potatoes, rangeland, and pastures in Argentina and of pastures and rangelands in the United States. It is a principal weed of lucerne in New Zealand; pastures in Australia, Hungary, New Zealand, and Uruguay; and sorghum, sunflowers, and wheat in Argentina; and a common weed of barley, oats, and wheat in Canada, cereals in Turkey, flax in Argentina, orchards in Austria, Bolivia, Italy, and Uruguay; and of several crops unspecified in England, Germany, Poland, the former Soviet Union, and Turkey. It is a weed of unknown rank in cereals and forest plantations in New Zealand, irrigated lands in the United States, oats in Argentina, orchards and wheat in the former Soviet Union, pastures and rangelands in Bulgaria and Canada, sweet and red clover and timothy hay in the central United States, and a weed in one or more crops in France, Iran, Pakistan, Tasmania, and the former Yugoslavia.

C. pycnocephalus is a serious weed and has become dominant in the annual grass communities of rangelands in California in the United States. It is on the Australian Plant Quarantine list of prohibited seed imports because it is one of the most abundant and widespread pasture weeds in the areas of Mediterranean climate in southern Australia (Parsons 1977). It is a serious weed of grasslands and cereals in Afghanistan and wheat in Uruguay. It is a principal weed of cereals in Australia, pastures in Brazil, New Zealand, and Tasmania, and wheat in Iran.

It is a common weed of pastures in Argentina, Italy, and South Africa; vineyards in Turkey; and wheat in South Africa. It is found as a weed of unknown rank in clover in New Zealand, irrigation systems in Iraq, linseed in Argentina, orchards in Australia and Iraq, pastures in Iran, vegetables in Iraq, vineyards in France, Portugal, Spain, and the former Soviet Union; wastelands in Australia and Iraq; wheat in Argentina and Italy; and in one or more crops in Chile and Egypt.

C. pycnocephalus is in most parts of Europe, where it causes minor losses in several crops in the south. It is necessary to control infestations of the weed along the banks of the large Elbe River in northern Germany. It has been distributed with grass seed supplies in England, where the weed has been present since the interglacial periods.

In New Zealand there has been a rapid increase in the weed in the past three decades because of the increasing practice of top dressing with fertilizers and the use of more productive pasture species, with the result that increased stocking rates tend to open up the sod. Thistle seeds do not accumulate beneath a full sward. Overstocking in late summer and early autumn also tends to open the sward (Popay 1980). A spectacular spread of the weed prior to 1980 was due to a succession of dry summers that caused bare patches of ground. *C. nutans* and *C. pycnocephalus* are ranked among the six most troublesome nonpalatable herbaceous weeds in high-producing pastures (Bourdodot and Kelly 1986). In these areas thistle seeds may again contaminate grass seed supplies. The seeds of *Carduus* species become entangled in the wool of sheep and lambs and cause a devaluation of the wool at the slaughter houses.

C. nutans is the most troublesome of these thistles in the eastern United States, with 24,000 ha infested in the state of Virginia alone. It is spreading rapidly in Washington state at this time. In the western United States the species can be controlled in crop fields by tillage or mowing, but the weed moves along roads and fence lines to enter native and seeded ranges, irrigated pastures, wet meadows, and mixed native stands of rushes and sedges (Hull and Evans 1973). As infestations of *C. nutans* increase in size and severity, Dunn (1976) has reported that more than 1 county in 10 in the United States is troubled by the weed. Harris (1970) reported densities of 150,000 plants/ha in pastures in Saskatchewan, Canada.

C. nutans can grow as a winter annual in fall wheat plantings in Oklahoma in the central United States. Eighty-five percent of the seedlings that emerged in September produced seed before wheat harvest the following June. Only 5% of the plants emerging in October and November produced seed prior to wheat harvest (O'Bryan and Peeper 1986). In Ohio in the central United States, these weeds are found in pastures receiving moderate to heavy grazing by cows and sheep, in legume and grass hayfields and in abandoned fields. They are found in oat and wheat fields but not in maize or soybean fields. Beyond agricultural areas they are a nuisance on airports, railroads, and on the verges of highways and railroads. In Kentucky in the central United States, *C. nutans* ranks among the ten worst weeds in the state.

Because it is generally assumed that the path of spread for many weeds is along roadsides, Lane (1979) surveyed roadsides for the presence of 20 of the declared noxious weeds of Australia, and the extent of spread into adjacent farms. *Carduus* species and *Cirsium vulgare* were most widespread, but contrary to popular opinion roadside weeds do not usually spread into well-managed farmland. The author suggests there is an urgent need to reassess the general purposes for which money is spent on roadside weed control.

Everist (1974) in Australia reported field samples of *C. pycnocephalus* containing nitrate equivalent to 26% NO_3 (dry wt) during seasons favorable for nitrate accumulation. The species was suspected of causing serious cattle losses in New South Wales in one season and should therefore be regarded as potentially toxic.

COMPETITION AND ESTABLISHMENT OF *Carduus* SPECIES

The *Carduus* species are quite sensitive to competition. In New Zealand pastures, thistle seedlings emerge in autumn, but with moisture present can germinate any time the cover is disturbed. The young seedlings are very sensitive to the pasture competition and it has been estimated that 80% of all the seedlings die before flowering. Flushes of germination in autumn and spring can cause problems in lucerne. If a vigorous crop is allowed to grow for hay, the seedling thistles are smothered. In a crop that is grazed the seedlings become established and compete with the crop the following season (Delahunty 1962). In Tasmania the growth of *C. pycnocephalus* seedlings was studied on areas containing only thistles and it was found that they grew ten times faster than in adjacent pastures sown to annual grass mixtures that competed vigorously with the weeds (Harradine 1985).

McCarty and Scifres (1969) marked thistles in early spring in areas completely free of competing vegetation, as well as in pastures of natural vegetation. One year later the plants without competition had rosettes that were three times larger, had produced ten times as many flowers, and were twice as tall. Feldman et al. (1968), in the same area, studied establishment of *C. nutans* in 20-year-old pasture experimental areas with four types of pasture species and three levels of controlled grazing. In the first year more thistle seedlings became established in the non-grazed, early cool-season pastures than in non-grazed warm-season pastures of mixed species that developed later. In the former the reserve moisture and accumulated litter provided excellent germinating conditions. However, one year later only one thistle remained in non-grazed pastures, all others having succumbed to the heavy sward competition.

Medd (1979) in Australia experimented with several control measures for managing *C. nutans* in perennial pastures. Treatments included herbicides, continuous lax grazing, very heavy grazing for one week in early summer, and applications of N and P. Continuous lax grazing with an early season application of 2,4-D gave best control. If herbicides are used, Medd and Lovett (1978) suggest applications early enough to prevent flowering. Plants that emerge later will need winter vernalization and can be sprayed in the next spring.

In the rangelands of western North America, Reece and Wilson (1983) found that herbicide treatments must be repeated for several years to give herbage grasses time to renew the pasture and compete with the thistles. In a 3-year experiment, clopyralid and 2,4-D controlled thistles and increased grass production 220, 315, and 375% in 1st, 2nd, and 3rd yr, respectively. On the North Island of New Zealand the greenhouse experiments of Harrington et al. (1988) showed that *C. nutans* plants taken from two sites were 14 times more difficult to control with MCPA than plants from a third site. In field trials the weed was six times more resistant to MCPA at some sites. Matthews (1975) has cautioned that second-year rosettes should not be treated with herbicides until they are fully developed. Rosettes that are damaged before they are fully formed produce many new buds and extended growth from the swollen rootstock.

Bendall (1973, 1974) in Tasmania found that sheep tend to graze young *C. pycnocephalus* plants selectively and in some cases eliminate 90 to 95% of them. Experimental pastures were closed for about 6 to 10 wk and left untouched until thistle seedlings appeared and grasses were 10 to 15 cm tall. The pastures were then grazed at twice the normal stocking rate.

Research efforts for two decades have focused on two insects useful in bringing a slow decline in populations of musk and slender thistles. The weevil, *Rhinocyllus conicus*, was released in North America in 1968–1969 and another weevil, *Ceuthorynchidius horridus*, was released more recently. The adults of the former feed on leaves with little effect on the rest of the plant, but the larvae feed in the base of the flower head and interfere with seed production and viability. A high density prevents seed formation. The latter insect feeds on the growing point. It is estimated that 6 to 8 yr are required to build up sufficient insect populations for an area, with weed population decline beginning sometime later. Boldt and Kok (1982) and Kok et al. (1986) published a bibliography on the introduction and use of *R. conicus* for weed control.

Recent efforts to control these thistles with the pathogen *Puccinia* have been reported by Olivieri (1984) and Politis et al. (1984).

COMMON NAMES

Carduus nutans

ARGENTINA	cardo, cardo de banado, cardo del caballo, cardo negro, cardo pendiente
AUSTRALIA	nodding thistle
CANADA	chardon penche, nodding thistle
DENMARK	nikkende tidsel
ENGLAND	musk thistle
FINLAND	nuokkukarhiainen
FRANCE	chardon nu, chardon penche
GERMANY	Nikende Distel
ITALY	cardo rosso
NETHERLANDS	knikkende distel
NEW ZEALAND	nodding thistle
NORWAY	nikketistel
SPAIN	cardo almizclero, cardo rojo
SWEDEN	nicktistel
TASMANIA	nodding thistle
UNITED STATES	musk thistle, nodding thistle
URUGUAY	cardo ruso

Carduus pycnocephalus

ARGENTINA	cardito, cardo crespo
AUSTRALIA	shore thistle, slender thistle, slender-flowered thistle
CHILE	carcho, cardilla
EGYPT	libd, lisaan el kelb
ENGLAND	Corsican thistle
FRANCE	chardon a trochets
GERMANY	Knauelkopfige Distel
JAPAN	oni-hire-azami
LEBANON	firyas, Italian thistle, khudan, lisan-ul-kalb
MOROCCO	chardon a tetes denses

NEW ZEALAND	slender winged thistle
SOUTH AFRICA	Corsican thistle, korsikaanse dissel
SPAIN	cardo de clavero
UNITED STATES	Italian thistle
URUGUAY	cardo crespo

Nineteen

Cassia occidentalis L. and Cassia tora L. (syn. C. obtusifolia L.)

Caesalpiniaceae (Leguminosae), Pea Family

T HE *CASSIAS* ARE AMONG the 2500 species in 180 genera of **Caesalpiniaceae** subfamily of the **Leguminosae**. *Cassia* is an ancient Greek reference to several leguminous plants. *Cassia occidentalis* and *Cassia tora* are only two of the more than 600 members of the *Cassia* genus. They are annual herbaceous to semi-woody plants common throughout the tropical and subtropical regions of the world. Even though they are legumes, neither fixes nitrogen. Both species have medicinal value. *C. tora* can be used in the rations for some livestock species. However, *C. occidentalis* is often toxic if ingested by animals.

DESCRIPTIONS

Cassia occidentalis

C. occidentalis (Figure 19-1) is an erect *annual* somewhat branched, smooth, semi-woody, fetid herb or shrub, 0.8 to 1.5 m tall; *taproot* hard, stout, with a few lateral roots on midsection; *stems* reddish purple, the young ones 4-sided, becoming rounded with age; *leaves* alternate, even-pinnately compound, each one with 4 to 6 pair of nearly sessile opposite leaflets, fetid odor when crushed; each *leaflet* 4 to 6 cm long, 1.5 to 2.5 cm wide, ovate or oblong-lanceolate, with pointed tip and fine white hairs on margin; border often suffused with purple, terminal pair often the largest; *rachis* has large, ovoid, shining, dark purple gland at the base; *stipules* 5 to 10 mm long, often leaving an oblique scar; *inflorescence* composed of axillary and terminal racemes; *flowers* perfect, 2 cm long, with 5 yellowish green *sepals* with distinct red veins and 5 yellow *petals*; each flower with 6 fertile *stamens* and 4 *staminodia* that appear as small petals; *fruit* a dry, dehiscent, transversely partitioned, faintly recurved, laterally compressed, sickle-shaped *legume* (pod) 7 to 12 cm long, 8 to 10 mm wide, with rounded tip and containing 25 to 50 seeds; *seeds* oval-shaped, 3.5 to 4.5 mm wide, flattened, pale to dark brown, slightly shiny, smooth and with round-pointed tip.

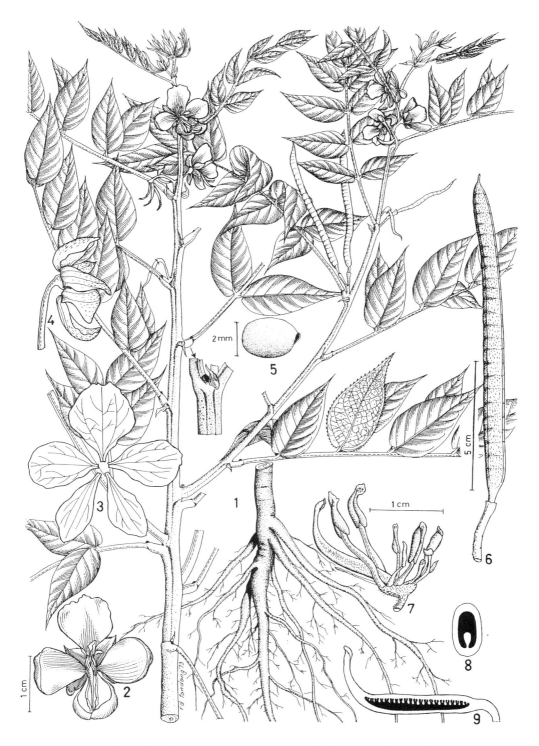

FIGURE 19-1 *Cassia occidentalis* L.: 1. habit; 2. flower; 3. perianth expanded; 4. sepals; 5. seed; 6. fruit; 7. flowers, petals and sepals excised to show stamens and pistil; 8. ovary, cross section, 9. vertical section.

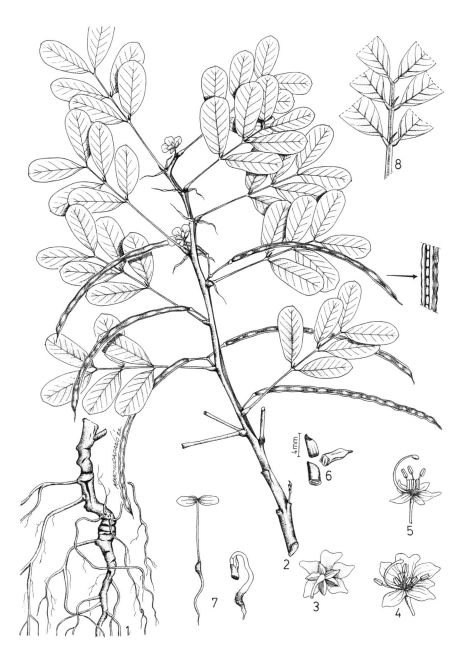

FIGURE 19-2 *Cassia tora* L.: 1. root system; 2. flowering and fruiting branch; 3. flower, dorsal view, 4. ventral view; 5. petals removed; 6. seed, three views; 7. seedlings; 8. biglandular leaf.

This species is characterized by the fetid odor of crushed leaves, reddish-purple stems, the ovoid gland immediately above the thickened petiole base, its bright yellow flowers and the sickle-shaped, laterally compressed pods.

Cassia tora

C. tora (Figure 19-2) is an erect, semi-woody *annual* herb 0.5 to 1.5 m tall with a stout *taproot*; *stem* smooth, often highly branched; *leaves* even-pinnately compound, 8 to 12 cm long, each with 3 pair of leaflets, rank-smelling when crushed; each *leaflet* 2 to 4 cm long, 1 to 2.5 cm wide, obovate to oblong-obovate, obtuse, tip with small sharp point, broadest in the middle; *rachis* with a gland between first and usually second pair of leaflets; *stipules* prominent, linear-lanceolate; *flowers* perfect, axillary as subsessile pairs on short peduncle; *pedicels* 6 to 10 mm long during flowering, 1 to 1.5 cm long when seed pod formed; *corolla* yellow 0.8 to 1.5 cm in diameter with 5 spreading *petals*, upper petal two-lobed; 7 fertile *stamens* and 3 *staminodia*; *fruit* a dry, dehiscent, somewhat curved, sickle-shaped, *legume* (pod) 15 to 25 cm long, 3 to 6 mm wide, with 25 to 30 seeds; *seeds* rhomboidal, 4 to 5 mm long, shiny, yellowish brown to tan.

The rank smell of crushed leaves, the presence of glands between the lowest pairs of leaflets and slender, rounded seed pods are the distinguishing characteristics of this species.

TAXONOMY

The classification of *C. occidentalis* is not a subject of debate among taxonomists. However, the classification of *C. tora* has been argued for many years. In 1753, Linnaeus described *C. tora* and *C. obtusifolia* as separate species (Singh 1968). They were combined into one species with the name *C. tora* in 1871. Several taxonomists have argued that they indeed represent two species and should be separated.

The characteristics proposed to separate *C. tora* and *C. obtusifolia* include biglandular or uniglandular leaf rachis, length of flower pedicel, length and width of petals, degree of fruit curvature (Mall 1957), aereole form (Brenan 1958), and seed coat and anther characteristics (Singh 1978). Singh and Brenan concluded that the number of glands is not sufficiently uniform to justify separation into two species. The chromosome numbers of uniglandular *C. obtusifolia* (n=14) and *C. tora* are the same, which suggests that *C. tora* arose from *C. obtusifolia* (Irwin and Turner 1960). Wilkinson (1970b) attempted to use the leaf cuticle alkane content of *C. tora* for chemotaxonomic purposes. He concluded that the variability in waxes between vegetative stages and the high proportion of alkane chains with less than 25 and more than 35 carbon atoms precluded the feasibility of this method.

Evolution may still be occurring among the *Cassias*. Sharma et al. (1974) reported a new species, *C. intermedia*, as the result of intraspecific hybridization between *C. occidentalis* and *C. hirsuta*. Such crossing among species and the fact that *C. tora* and *C. occidentalis* may be either self- or cross-pollinated (Delgado and Sousa 1977) may account for part of the morphological and ecological variation observed in these species.

Holm et al. (1979) listed *C. obtusifolia* as a synonym for *C. tora*. This classification is in agreement with taxonomists in the Botanical Laboratory of the United States Department of Agriculture and is the one used here. Readers should understand that we have included data on *C. tora* from papers which referred to the species as *C. obtusifolia*.

FIGURE 19-3   The distribution of *Cassia occidentalis* L. across the world where it has been reported as a weed.

FIGURE 19-4   The distribution of *Cassia tora* L. across the world where it has been reported as a weed.

This was especially true for studies done in the United States, since the Weed Science Society of America lists *C. obtusifolia* as the preferred taxon and *C. tora* as a synonym.

DISTRIBUTION AND HABITAT

C. occidentalis and *C. tora* are native to tropical South America but are now found throughout the tropical and subtropical regions of the world (Figures 19-3 and 19-4). They inhabit pastures, roadsides, and wastelands as well as cropland. Both are gregarious in nature and are found in clusters in noncultivated areas. Where humans aid in seed dispersal, they often appear uniformly distributed. They can grow in a wide range of soil types and have been reported in regions receiving as little as 640 mm annual precipitation and as much as 4290 mm, with an optimum of 1520 mm. Optimum temperatures are 25°C for *C. tora* and 23°C for *C. occidentalis* and the optimum soil *pH* is 6.25 (Duke 1979). *C. tora* can be found up to 1500 m above sea level in India (Misra 1969) and to 500 m in the Dominican Republic (Jurgens 1977). *C. occidentalis* is found from 0 to 1100 m in the latter country.

Soil *pH*s between 4.8 and 6.4 have little effect on *C. occidentalis* growth (Buchanan et al. 1975) and *C. tora* grows well in *pH*s from 4.6 to 7.9 (Murray et al. 1976). The primary root of *C. tora* was longer in a soil of *pH* 6.5 than in soils with lower *pH*s. Both species have a competitive advantage over crops with a narrower *pH* range for optimal growth. While both species grow best in moist conditions, they can tolerate dry soils. Hoveland and Buchanan (1973) reported *C. tora* germinated even at 10 bars osmotic pressure in a simulated drought experiment and concluded that it is well adapted to dry soils. *C. occidentalis* germination was reduced more than that of *C. tora* in dry soil (Daiya et al. 1980). Both species prefer heavy-textured soils over sandy soils, but are found over a wide range of soil types in either tilled or non-tilled fields.

BIOLOGY

C. occidentalis and *C. tora* have hard seeds and mechanical and acid scarification are equally effective in breaking dormancy. *C. occidentalis* seeds germinate over a wide range of temperatures with an optimum temperature range of 24 to 36°C (Teem et al. 1980). *C. tora* germinates in continuous light or darkness and under alternating light and dark conditions (Chavan and Trivedi 1962). Alternating day-night photoperiods cause low germination of *C. occidentalis*. Soaking seeds in absolute ethyl alcohol for 20 and 50 hr gave germination of 48 and 68%, respectively. One minute in 100 C water gave 30% germination and 40 min in sulfuric acid gave 98% (Kumari and Kohli 1984).

C. tora seeds germinate and survive under many conditions (Misra 1969). No germination occurs below 13 or above 40°C. Seeds stored at −15 to 50°C germinate when scarified and placed in a 30°C environment. Imbibed seeds frozen at −15°C for 6 days germinated normally when placed in a 30°C environment. Seed dry weight increases until the pods turn brown. The stage of maturity at harvest affects seed viability and germination. Misra (1969) found that if seeds are green at harvest they fail to germinate. Thirty-eight percent of the nonscarified seeds that were 10% yellow at harvest germinated, but scarified seeds at this stage did not. Scarification was beneficial only when 80% of the seeds in the pod were yellow, indicating that hard seed coats develop at this stage. Even though both species have hard seed coats, in dry storage they lose viability somewhat rapidly (Doll et al.

1976). Seeds stored for 3 yr had an overall germination of 22%, those stored at 0 and 10°C had lower viability (14%) than those stored at 20 and 30°C (30%). Nine-year-old seed had 9% germination (Ewart 1908) and 10% of the seed buried in the soil for 30 mo germinated (Egley and Chandler 1978).

C. tora germinates best when soil moisture is 75% of field capacity (Mall 1957). No seeds germinate when flooded, but they will germinate after being under water for 28 days. If soils are water-logged after emergence, little growth occurs. When an early rain triggers *C. tora* germination, it can tolerate up to 1 mo of subsequent dry weather (Misra 1969). *C. tora* is more drought tolerant than soybeans (Murray et al. 1976). *C. occidentalis* and *C. tora* seedling survival was reduced 40 and 10%, respectively, at 1/8 field capacity. At 1/16 field capacity, 8% of the *C. occidentalis* seedlings lived, but all *C. tora* seedlings died (Daiya et al. 1983). Maximum root and shoot growth was at field capacity for both species. Fresh weight of *C. tora* was reduced 34, 58, and 78% at ½, 1/4, and 1/16 field capacity, respectively. *C. occidentalis* fresh weight was reduced 12, 65, and 78% at these values.

Seeds of *C. tora* and *C. occidentalis* are relatively large, and seedlings can emerge from 12.7 cm but not from 15.2 cm (Teem et al. 1980). Nine days were required for emergence from the 12.7 cm depth. After 3 days, 22 and 63% of *C. occidentalis* and *C. tora* seed, respectively, emerged from 2.5 cm, indicating that the latter species would be the more competitive one. Seedling growth for both species is best between 30 to 36°C (Teem et al. 1980).

Seedbank populations of *C. tora* decline more with repeated disking than in nondisturbed soil (Bridges and Walker 1985). Nevertheless, plants growing in no-till environments produce more pods per plant than those growing with tillage. Weed densities below the competitive threshold allow seedbank populations to increase.

The root systems of both species consist of a stout, hard and curved taproot with relatively few secondary roots in the middle section of the taproot near the subsoil level (Shetty and Maiti 1978). Hand-pulling such a root system is difficult and plants can regrow from underground buds in the crown region. Both species are likely to remove soil moisture from deeper soil levels than other species. Optimum root growth occurs at 25°C, a normal soil temperature at planting time, indicating that the weed would compete immediately after emergence.

The response of *C. occidentalis* and *C. tora* to P and K is similar. Dry matter production was lower at 8 and 22 kg P/ha than at 90 kg/ha. Growth was normal at a medium level of K (164 kg/ha), indicating that growth of these species is more sensitive to P than K (Hoveland et al. 1976). The P uptake of several *C. tora* ecotypes in India varied from 0.14 to 0.95 ug P/seedling/day (Misra 1969). Mature plants absorbed very little P. *C. tora* grew well in soils low in N (Mall 1957), and yet neither *C. tora* nor *C. occidentalis* fix nitrogen (Allen and Allen 1981). Only 23% of the species in the **Caesalpiniaceae** subfamily have nodules (Rao and Rao 1974). Gaur (1980) tried unsuccessfully to inoculate both species with 17 strains of *Rhizobium* under sterile conditions. He grew the plants in soil from 13 locations in India and again failed to find nodulation. He concludes that the inability of these *Cassias* to fix nitrogen is due neither to antagonism from other soil microbes nor inhibitors in the plant, but to the absence of a specific *Rhizobium* to infect the root, or the morphological and physiological nature of the host plant prevents successful inoculation. *C. occidentalis* was the least effective wild legume tested as a green manure crop in India. It gave only 12.6 kg/ha/yr increase in soil N content and ranked last among the ten species evaluated (Sen and Paul 1959).

Intraspecific competition of *C. tora* increases plant height and branching decreases as plant density rises from 1 to 40 plants/m² (Singh 1969). Lateral spread of roots is less affected and root length is unchanged by plant density. Shoot and root dry matter production per plant decrease at populations above 20 plants/m². The number of flowers and fruits per plant drop at densities of 10 and 20 plants/m², respectively, indicating that crowding reduces the reproductive potential of each individual. The number of seeds/m² increases from 39 seeds with 1 plant/m² to a maximum of 571 seeds with 17 plants/m²; it drops to 144 seeds with 40 plants/m².

Bhatia and Chawan (1976) extracted a phenolic compound from *C. tora* seed coats that reduced the radicle length of itself, and the radicle and hypocotyl growth of sesame. Water extracts of ground seeds were more inhibitory than extracts with five organic solvents tested. *C. tora* germination and seedling growth were affected by leachates and extracts from *Polygonum orientale* (Datta and Chatterjee 1980). Soil collected from beneath *P. orientale* also inhibited *C. tora* germination and growth. Root extracts and exudates from *C. tora* stimulated fungal growth, especially of *Aspergillus* species (Sullia 1973).

Photoperiod dramatically affects *C. tora* growth and has been thoroughly studied by Misra (1969). As photoperiod increases from 6 to 15 hr, plants grow taller. Continuous light, however, gives short plants. The number of leaflets and dry matter production also increases up to 15 hr of light. However, pods are only produced when plants receive between 8 and 11 hr of light and thus *C. tora* is a short-day plant. Turner and Karlander (1975) found 6 to 12 hr of light induced 100% flowering, but no flowering occurred in 14 hr of light. Four or more cycles of 8 hr of light and 16 hr of dark caused all plants to flower regardless of subsequent photoperiod. One minute of red light at the 7th hour of darkness prevented flowering, but not when given at the 9th hour. Two minutes of far red light completely reversed the effect of red light, showing that phytochrome is the active photoreceptor pigment.

Wilkinson (1970a) obtained the highest fresh weight under 12 hr of light. Misra (1969) found maximum dry matter accumulation to occur at 70% of full sunlight. At 40% of sunlight, *C. tora* growth was significantly reduced. *C. tora* plants 22 to 29 days old transpired 27 g water/dm²/day and had a water use efficiency of 4 mg dry matter/g water (Patterson and Flint 1983). Its net photosynthetic rate of 47 mg CO_2/dm²/hr is typical of C_3 species and its stomata close gradually in response to decreased water availability.

Seeds of *C. tora* were collected from seven locations in India and grown under uniform conditions (Misra et al. 1968). In general, the greatest plant height, root penetration, lateral root development, shoot fresh weight, number of flowers, and number of seeds were with plants from lat 28° 38' N and the minimum values for these parameters were for plants from seeds collected near lat 25° N. These growth differences were found when seeds from plants grown in the first experiment were grown to maturity in a second experiment, indicating that biotypes of *C. tora* exist. Similar observations were made in the United States with seeds collected in nine southern states (Retzinger 1984). Differences in plant height (1 to 1.2 m), days to flowering (52 to 80), pods/plant (200 to 342), seeds/plant (5340 to 8520) were recorded (values are an average over 3 yr for plants grown at the same site). Year by seed source interactions occurred for several parameters measured but, in general, biotype traits were consistent from year to year.

C. tora and *C. occidentalis* exhibit cyclic leaf movements. This phenomenon has been studied in detail by Andersen and Koukkari (1979). Both species exhibited nearly identical movements and will be discussed together. Cotyledons moved rhythmically from an almost horizontal position during the day to an almost vertical one at night. Even when placed in continuous light, they moved rhythmically, but not to the same degree. If placed in different photoperiods, cotyledon movements adjusted to the new light and dark conditions. Leaf movement was also rhythmic. As it became dark, the petiole rose slightly and the upper pair of leaflets folded toward each other and finally touched. The leaflets also drooped downward, decreasing the angle between the petiole and leaflet. When light returned, movements reversed. Leaf movements are endogenously controlled. The principal difference between the two species was that *C. tora* petioles rose more in the dark than those of *C. occidentalis*. Leaf movements could significantly affect the results of a herbicide application if treated when leaf area changed in the evening or under heavy cloud cover.

Leaf area can vary 7-fold in a 24-hr period for *C. tora* (Kraatz and Andersen 1980). The greatest leaf area occurs 2.5 hr after sunrise, regardless of sky conditions. Shading leaves on sunny days increases their leaf area 48 to 68%. Thus in sunny conditions the leaves are partially folded. The authors speculate that this may be a mechanism to reduce leaf exposure during periods of very high light intensity and that there is a light threshold below which the leaf folds into the night position. Leaves also fold as soil moisture becomes limiting, which might enhance drought tolerance (Daiya et al. 1983).

Earlier work by Karve (1962) in India revealed circadian rhythm effects even on seed germination and the unfolding of cotyledons. When acid scarified seeds placed in the dark were given 30-min light exposures, germination fluctuated dramatically. Seeds receiving light at 3 and 27 hr germinated 35 to 40%, while those given light at 15, 18, and 21 hr, had 60 to 70% germination. When germinated seeds were kept in darkness, the cotyledons did not unfold. Exposing them to 15-min periods of light at 9 and 12 hr after being transferred from 28 to 18°C gave a 45 to 50% unfolding rate; when given light at 21, 24, and 27 hr, only 10% of the cotyledons unfolded. Thus many growth processes in these *Cassia* species are light influenced.

C. tora has stomata on both leaf surfaces, but the lower surface has proportionately more (Mall 1957). Chen et al. (1970) found the CO_2 compensation point to be 45 ppm, which is well above the 20 ppm level characteristic of competitive plants. Shades of 50% or more reduce the number of leaves and flowers, and shades above 67% prevent fruit set (Adhikary and Chatterjee 1972). The effects of photoperiod on fatty acid metabolism do not coincide with its effects on growth, suggesting independent photocontrol mechanisms (Wilkinson 1970a).

C. occidentalis anthers release their pollen through two angular pores at the apex and not by splitting open. The style is slightly recurved and self-pollination can occur. *C. tora* anthers have only one pore and the style is highly curved, placing the stigma very near the pores of the anthers. This species is both self- and cross-pollinated (Delgado and Sousa 1977).

Each *C. tora* seedpod contains 25 to 30 seeds. The number of seeds produced by isolated plants can reach 10,135 seeds (Pancho 1964), and heavy infestations in cotton produce over 900 kg/ha of seed (Creel et al. 1968). *C. occidentalis* pods have 25 to 35 seeds (Rochecouste 1959) and each plant has 30 to 40 pods, for a total of 750 to 1400 seeds per plant.

Seed composition of both species has been determined. *C. occidentalis* seeds contain 55% endosperm and the principal sugar is galactomannan (Gupta and Mukherjee 1973). Sotelo et al. (1980) analyzed seeds and found 22.5% protein, 14.2% crude fiber, and 55.6% carbohydrate. This species is rich in calcium (5.6%) and also contains 2.3% K_2O, 0.5% S and 1.6% P_2O_5 (Singh and Singh 1939). Massey and Sowell (1969) suggest that *C. occidentalis* be considered as a gum crop since the seeds contain 25% N-free gum. *C. tora* seeds contain 17.6% protein, 6.2% fiber, 0.33% P and 0.74% Ca (Patel et al. 1976). Alston and Irwin (1961) found 11 to 12 amino acids in *C. occidentalis* and *C. tora* and suggest that chromatography of secondary compounds would be useful to distinguish between *Cassia* species.

UTILITY

Both species have been utilized for various purposes for centuries. *C. tora* was used for medicinal purposes as early as 4000 B.C. (Nickell 1960). The seeds have glucosides that act as laxatives.

Decoctions of the leaves also serve as laxatives and are used to treat skin diseases. Plants have antibacterial activity and are used to treat ringworms (Gupta et al. 1966). The worm-killing compounds of *C. occidentalis* are less effective than drugs, as they require more time to kill worms (Budhiraja and Garg 1973). Roots of both species have been used as a snakebite remedy (Pandey 1971), and fruits of *C. tora* are used for several eye ailments, herpes, headaches, and arthritis in China (Duke and Ayensu 1985).

C. occidentalis seeds have frequently been used as a coffee substitute, hence the name "coffee senna." Research done in Egypt determined that *C. occidentalis* has no caffeine or tannin and could actually be a less harmful beverage than coffee (Hassan et al. 1974). They proposed a 1:1 mixture of coffee and *Cassia* seeds to reduce coffee imports. Seeds contain up to 25% N-free gum and have been considered as a source of gum for food products and paper sizing (White et al. 1971). The plant contains saponins that are used as soaps to wash clothes and remove head lice in Brazil (Torres et al. 1971).

C. occidentalis produces abundant seed but is susceptible to several diseases. Massey and Sowell (1969) observed seed yield variations of 0.1 to 5 ton/ha due to anthracnose (*Colletotrichum* sp.) infection. Treating seeds with hot water (55°C) killed the organism, but also reduced germination by 50%. High levels of anthracnose resistance were found in *C. occidentalis* collections from Mexico, the Virgin Islands, and Burma, so the potential to develop this species into a high yielding crop exists.

While *C. occidentalis* is toxic to many animals, *C. tora* has been tested as a livestock feed. Cold or hot water treatment reduces one or more potential toxins in the seed. Milking cows readily consumed boiled *C. tora* seeds and production was maintained when the ration contained 15% *C. tora* seeds, but dropped 13% when intake reached 30%. Bullocks fed 5 and 10% *C. tora* seed experienced no weight loss during an 8-wk feeding trial with significant savings in feed costs to the farmer (Patel and Patel 1972). Higher substitutions (20%) in the ration of buffalo calves were also economical and free of adverse effects. In fact, total digestible nutrients and feed consumption increased, giving higher weight gains when *C. tora* was included in the ration (Taparia et al. 1978). Broilers consumed rations with 15% *C. tora* seeds (Chand and Shukla 1973), but egg production of hens dropped dramatically when they were fed 5 and 10% *C. tora* seed (Page et al. 1977). Younger birds were more sensitive than older ones and the muscles of affected birds were pale, as if from vitamin E deficiency. Egg weight was not affected when laying hens consumed 1.5, 3, and 6% *C. tora* seed, but shell strength, egg production and feed consumption dropped (Charles and Muller 1975). *C. tora* leaves are high in protein (14.4%) and are highly palatable to poultry (Murty 1962). Birds actually consumed more feed with 5% *C. tora* leaves in the ration. Ten percent leaves caused detrimental results.

C. occidentalis and *C. tora* could be used as forage crops. They are highly digestible in the vegetative and flowering stages and contain adequate levels of crude protein (14 to 22%), Ca (1.12 to 1.35%), Mg (0.32 to 0.43%), and K (1.7 to 2.6%) in these stages to be fed to high-producing ruminants. Both are deficient in P if used as the sole source of feed and the Ca:P ratio of 8.4 to 15.3 is considerably above the ideal ratio of 1:1 to 2:1 (Bosworth et al. 1980). The strong odor of *C. tora* and *C. occidentalis* affects their palatability as a fresh forage, but cattle in India readily consumed silage of *C. tora* (Anon. [India] 1960). In the Sudan, *C. tora* leaves are fermented for 2 wk and then dried to yield a meat substitute for human use with 20% protein (Dirar 1984). The leaves are high in vitamins A, B_2, and C and are consumed in northern Senegal.

AGRICULTURAL IMPORTANCE

C. occidentalis is a weed of 23 crops in 66 countries (Figure 19-3) and frequents pastures and plantation crops. It is a serious or principal weed of edible beans and cotton in Colombia; cassava in Indonesia; coconuts in Samoa; maize in Brazil, Colombia, India, and Indonesia; pastures in Australia, Brazil, Colombia, Cuba, Hawaii, India, New Guinea, Samoa, and West Africa; rangeland in Korea; rice in Brazil; upland rice in Indonesia; sorghum in Brazil and Colombia; soybeans in Brazil; and sugarcane in India.

It is a common weed of edible beans and sunflowers in Cuba; citrus in Argentina; coconut in Cambodia; cotton in Bolivia and Honduras; jute in Bangladesh; maize in Honduras and the United States; orchards, sesame, and sorghum in Honduras; pastures in Dominican Republic; peanuts in the United States; sugarcane in Bangladesh and Hawaii; soybeans in Argentina and the United States; and wastelands in Australia.

Also *C. occidentalis* is a reported weed of unknown rank in edible beans, citrus, coffee, and cotton in Brazil; bananas in Samoa; cassava, cowpeas, rangeland, and sweet potatoes in Nigeria; coconut in the Philippines; cotton in the United States; dryland irrigated crops in Australia and India; jute and peanuts in India; orchards in Saudi Arabia; pastures in Mexico; pineapple in Hawaii; rice in the Philippines, Surinam and Vietnam; upland rice in India and Nigeria; rainy season crops in India; rubber in Malaysia; sugarcane in Brazil and Cuba; vegetables in Australia and the United States; and wastelands in Bolivia and Cuba.

C. tora is a reported weed of 26 crops in 67 countries (Figure 19-4) and is most prevalent in soybeans, pastures, peanuts, cotton, and sugarcane. It is a serious or principal weed of edible beans in Colombia; coconut in New Hebrides and Samoa; cotton in Bolivia, Colombia, and the United States; maize in Brazil, Colombia, and the United States; pastures in Australia, Brazil, Colombia, Gambia, India, New Hebrides Islands, Nigeria, Samoa, and Tonga Islands in Polynesia; peanuts in the United States; rice in Brazil; sorghum in Brazil, Colombia, and the United States; soybean in Bolivia, Brazil, and the United States; sugarcane in Fiji and India; summer season crops in India; taro in Samoa; and vegetables in Cuba.

It is a common weed of edible beans, orchards, sorghum, soybeans, and vegetables in Honduras; citrus in Argentina; coconut in Fiji, Laos, and the Philippines; cotton in Brazil; jute in Bangladesh and India; maize in Honduras and Madagascar; peanuts and upland rice in India; sugarcane in Bangladesh, Cambodia, Honduras, and the Philippines; and sunflowers in Cuba.

C. tora is a weed of unknown rank in abaca in the Philippines; bananas in Samoa; edible beans, citrus, and coffee in Brazil; cassava in Indonesia; cotton in Israel and Paraguay; cowpeas in Nigeria; maize in India, Indonesia, Nicaragua, and Paraguay; pastures in Cuba, Mexico, New Guinea, Nicaragua, and the Philippines; peanuts in Mexico; rice in Burma, Nepal, the Philippines, and Vietnam; upland rice in Fiji, Indonesia, and Taiwan; rainy season crops in India; rubber in Malaysia; sorghum in Nicaragua; sugarcane in Australia,

Brazil, Cuba, and Dominican Republic; sweet potatoes in Puerto Rico and Taiwan; and tobacco in the Philippines.

Many competition studies have been done in cotton, soybean, and peanut. While *C. tora* can tolerate up to 60 to 75% shade (Misra 1969, Hoveland et al. 1978), it is not a serious competitor after the crop shades the soil. In general, the critical period of competition from *C. tora* is 2 to 4 wk after planting. If uncontrolled, crop yields are dramatically reduced. Cotton yields were lowered 25% by 1.1 *C. tora* plants/m of row (Buchanan and Burns 1971). In subsequent studies, each *C. tora* plant/15 m of row reduced cottonseed yields 40 kg/ha (Buchanan et al. 1980). The response was linear for weed densities of 5 to 32 plants/15 m of row. Increasing cotton density from 47,000 to 187,000 plants/ha did not reduce the competitive losses due to *C. tora* (Street et al. 1981). Murray et al. (1976) concluded that 1, 2, and 3 *C. tora* plants/0.3 m of row reduced yields by 11, 23, and 46%, respectively. They also noted that *C. tora* is more competitive in wet than in dry years.

Thurlow and Buchanan (1972) determined that each *C. tora* plant/m of row reduced soybean yield by 92 kg/ha. Weeds in the row were less competitive than weeds 15 cm to the side. Each kg of *C. tora* dry weight equaled a loss of 0.27 to 0.38 kg of soybeans. In general, soybean is more competitive with *C. tora* than cotton. A single plant influences soybean plants up to 64 cm away, and the threshold for soybean in 90-cm-wide rows is 15.6 plants/10 m of row (Shurtleff and Coble 1985). Peanut can also compete effectively with *C. tora* if early-season control is effective (Buchanan et al. 1976). Competition for water is the principal effect of *C. tora* interference.

The competitive effects of *C. occidentalis* are less studied. Cotton yields were reduced 90 kg/ha for each increase of one *C. occidentalis* plant per 15 m of row between 1 and 32 plants (Higgins et al. 1985). Cotton stand and fiber quality were unaffected by the weed. Six weeks without competition gave maximum cotton yields and full-season competition reduced production 38%. However, yield losses vary with precipitation and disease on the weed (anthracnose) and are difficult to predict.

C. tora hosts several insects and diseases. The seed predator *Sennius instabilis* and the fungus *Alternaria cassiae* offer promise as biocontrol agents (Cock and Evans 1984). Both species can host economically important crop diseases, especially viruses. They also host nematodes that infect some crops.

If livestock feed is heavily contaminated with *C. occidentalis* seed, sickness and death may occur. Seeds of *C. occidentalis* may be toxic to rabbits, goats, sheep, cattle (Dollahite and Henson 1965) and chickens (Simpson et al. 1971). Muscle lesions that resemble vitamin E deficiency can develop in cattle and chickens. Stems and leaves may be toxic, but seeds are the most toxic plant part. Cattle may die if they consume only 0.5% of the seeds on a live weight basis (O'Hara et al. 1969). Early signs of poisoning include anorexia and diarrhea; more advanced signs are rapid breathing, progressive muscle incapacitation, stumbling gait, reluctance to move, and dark-colored urine 24 to 36 hr before death. Consumption of nonfatal levels of *C. occidentalis* may produce tougher beef meat (Mercer et al. 1967). Australian workers found the effects to be cumulative, at least on a short-term basis (Rogers et al. 1979). Low, repeated doses could cause poisoning provided doses were given not more than 10 days apart. They tested seeds that had been collected over a 64-day period and found the most mature seeds were the least toxic.

C. occidentalis plants and seeds contain emodin, oxymethyl anthraquinones, toxalbumin, tannic acid, and chrysarobin (Pandey 1971), but so far the causal agent of toxicity has not been determined. While the symptoms mimic vitamin E deficiency, administering vitamin E to animals that are consuming *C. occidentalis* actually hastens and intensifies the illness (O'Hara et al. 1970). Weight gain and feed intake of chickens was reduced when the ration had 2% *C. occidentalis* and 65% of the chickens that were eating 4% *C. occidentalis* seeds died (Simpson et al. 1971).

The toxicity of *C. tora* is little studied. Putnam et al. (1988) in the southern United States fed bull dairy caves weighing 135 to 160 kg 0, 12.5 or 50% of their ration as *C. tora* seeds for a 2-wk period. At both levels animals exhibited refusal to eat, diarrhea and decreased weight gain. Average daily weight gain dropped 30 and 60% for the low and high consumption levels, respectively. No toxicological symptoms were found and the loss in weight gain was attributed to the unpalatability of *C. tora* seeds rather than direct toxicity.

COMMON NAMES

Cassia occidentalis

ARGENTINA	cafecillo, cafe cimarron, cafe de bonpland, fedegoso, taperiba
AUSTRALIA	coffee senna
BOLIVIA	cafecillo
BRAZIL	cafe do Paraquay, cafe negro, fedegoso, fedegoso verdadeiro, lava-pratos, maioba, mamanga, mata-pasto, pajamarioba, tararues
CAMBODIA	khmuoch, sandk
COLOMBIA	aya-porotillo, aya-poroto, cafecillo, cafe de bonpland, hedionda
CUBA	guanina, hierba hedionda, platanillo
DOMINICAN REPUBLIC	brusca macho
FIJI	kavmoce
GUATEMALA	frijolillo, moquillo
HAWAII	coffee senna, miki palaoa
HONDURAS	frijolillo
INDIA	banar, kasandi, kasivinda, peyavarai, thagarai
INDONESIA	chinytngsat, kasingsat, menting, senting
JAMAICA	John crow pea, stinking weed, wild senna
MALAYSIA	hutan, kete pung, negro coffe
MAURITIUS	casse-puante
MEXICO	bataban, mezquitillo
NEW CALEDONIA	coffee senna
NIGERIA	rere
PANAMA	frijolillo
PARAGUAY	taperva, cafecillo
PHILIPPINES	andadasi, balatong-aso, duda, kabal-kabalan, sumting, tambal-isa
PUERTO RICO	hedionda
REUNION	indigo

THAILAND	chum het tet, khi-lekthet, ki ler pi
TRINIDAD	stinking weed, wild coffee
UNITED STATES	coffee senna
VENEZUELA	brusca

Cassia tora

AUSTRALIA	Java bean, foetid cassia
BANGLADESH	araich
BOLIVIA	aya-poroto, mamuri
BRAZIL	fedegoso, fedegoso-branco, mata pasto, matapasto liso
BURMA	dan-gywe
CAMBODIA	danghet, khmuoch
COLOMBIA	bicho, bichomacho, chilinchil
CUBA	guanina
DOMINICAN REPUBLIC	brusca cimarrona, brusca hembra
EL SALVADOR	comida de murcielago, frijolillo
FIJI	kaumoce
GUATEMALA	ejote de inviero, ejotil
INDIA	chakavat, chakramarda, chakunda panevartakla, kuvadio, senavu, takala, tantipu, turota
INDONESIA	ketepeng cilik, ketepeng kecil, ketepeng leutik
JAPAN	ebisugusa
MADAGASCAR	voamahatsara
MALAYSIA	foetid cassia, gelenggang ketchil, gelenggang padang
MAURITIUS	cassepuante, herhe pistache
PARAGUAY	taperva, taperva moroti, taperva sayju
PHILIPPINES	acacia-acasiahan, andadasi, baho-baho, balatong-aso, monggo-monggohan, tridax
PUERTO RICO	dormidera
TAIWAN	ebisu-gusa
THAILAND	chumhetthai
UNITED STATES	sicklepod
VENEZUELA	chiquichique
VIETNAM	muong hor

Twenty

Chenopodium ambrosioides L.

Chenopodiaceae, Goosefoot Family

CHENOPODIUM AMBROSIOIDES is a common annual (occasionally perennial) weed in numerous temperate and tropical areas. It originated in Central and South America and is now found in over 60 countries. The genus name is Greek for "goosefoot" in reference to the leaf shape of many species. The specific name, *ambros*, also from the Greek, was a fabled food of gods that conferred immortality. The plant is still widely used for insecticidal and medicinal purposes.

FIGURE 20-1   The distribution of *Chenopodium ambrosioides* L. across the world where it has been reported as a weed

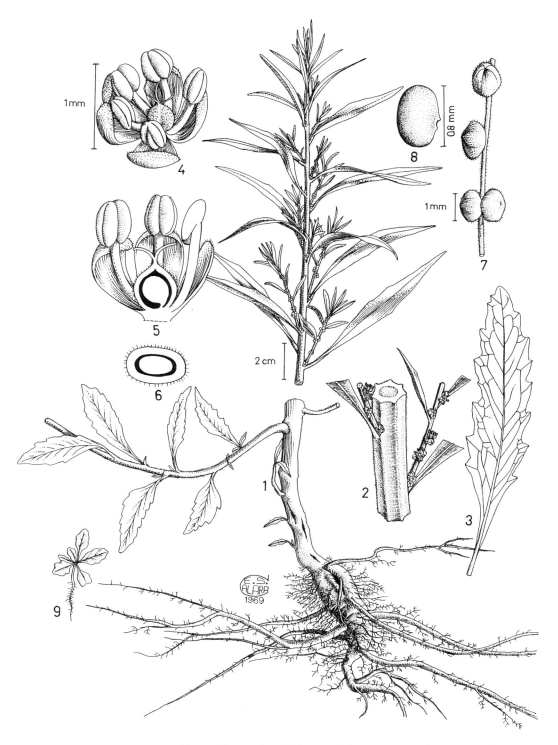

FIGURE 20-2 *Chenopodium ambrosioides* L.: 1. habit; 2. portion of stem; 3. leaf, enlarged; 4. flower; 5. ovary, vertical section 6. same, cross section; 7. fruits; 8. seed; 9. seedling.

DESCRIPTION

C. ambrosioides (Figure 20-2) is an erect *annual* (occasionally perennial) herbaceous plant 0.5 to 1.2 m tall; *root* a branched taproot; *stems* highly branched, angular, grooved, smooth or glandular pubescent; *leaves* alternate, ovate to oblong-lanceolate, 2 to 10 cm long, lower ones shortly to moderately petioled, margins with deep, wavy lobes; upper leaves narrower, entire and sessile or subsessile; both stem and leaves emit strong, rank aromatic smell when crushed; *inflorescence* terminal and axillary spikes 3 to 7 cm long with small bracts; *flowers* sessile, greenish, arranged in small dense or interrupted clusters; *stamens* 4 to 5; *stigmas* 2 to 4, long; *sepals* 3 to 5; *perianth* lobes ovate, upper half free, covering seed at maturity; *pericarp* rugose to smooth, thin, non-adherent to the seed; *fruit* an *utricle* surrounded by perianth, 0.6 to 0.7 mm in diameter and 0.5 mm thick; *seed* lens-shaped, reddish-brown to nearly black, smooth, polished.

The angular stem, aromatic stem and leaves, and small greenish flowers with two to four long stigmas arranged on an interrupted spike are the distinguishing characteristics of this species.

HABITAT AND BIOLOGY

C. ambrosioides is found on all continents (except the Arctic and Antarctic) and is obviously adapted to many environments (Figure 20-1). It is frequently found in disturbed sites, wastelands, along roadsides and ditches, and in annual and perennial crops. Plants occur from sea level to 1200 m on the Pacific islands of Hawaii and grow in annual precipitation ranges of 31 to 430 cm, in mean annual temperatures of 6.9 to 27.4°C and in soils with *pH* of 5.0 to 8.7 (Duke 1979). They grow as wetland hydrophytes in India, in coffee fields and in the shade of homes in Puerto Rico, and in heavily used soils in Bolivia. In Brazil, plants are most common in fertile, light-textured soils.

Kapoor et al. (1956) reported on its growth in India as they attempted to cultivate it as a crop. *C. ambrosioides* grew best between 270 and 900 m in sandy loam soils, had a high water requirement for maximum production and tolerated saline soils. Fruits matured 1 mo after flowering. Plants regrew readily when cut 10 cm above the soil surface and irrigated. New seedlings emerged after the first harvest was taken. Mathon (1980) observed that plants kept at 25°C with 16 hr or more of light died without flowering. In 10-hr days they flowered in 120 days, thus *C. ambrosioides* is a short-day plant.

Chloroplasts contain high levels of oxalic acid oxidase (Nagahisa and Hattori 1964). Levels were 50 times greater in this species than in four others tested, including *C. album*. The basic chromosome number is $2n = 32$ (Bassett and Crompton 1982) and plants have the C_3 carbon fixation pathway (Welkie and Caldwell 1970).

Fruits contain compounds that inhibit seed germination (Evenari 1949). In India, Datta and Ghosh (1987) studied the allelopathic effects of *C. ambrosioides* on five weed species. Leachates from decaying leaves and inflorescences inhibited germination and early growth of most species. The leguminous weeds *Cassia tora* and *C. sophera* were more tolerant of the allelochemicals than the other species. The inhibitor in the leaves may be a complex terpene.

Plants express notable morphological variation that is often due to phenotypic plasticity. Jorgensen (1970) recorded 28 species of *Chenopodium* in Norway and stated, "Some species show a bewildering variation, often parallel within different species." He found that sculpturing on the seed coat and perianth form were highly useful features to identify species.

In the Philippines, individual plants produced over 68,000 seeds and each weighed approximately .115 mg (Pancho 1964). In the central United States, Herron (1953) found seed production per plant ranged from 19,400 to 233,900/plant (average of 49,110) and seeds averaged .150 mg each. Seeds contain about 15% protein and 9% oil (Earle and Jones 1962) and fresh seed is highly dormant. Storage in moist peat at 3°C for 3 mo or longer increased germination, and dry storage at room temperature for 2 yr resulted in 93% germination (Herron 1953). Light and alternating temperatures enhance *C. ambrosioides* germination (Poggiali 1967). Pretreating seeds at 10°C for 14 days gave 84 and 22% germination at a constant temperature of 30°C and 20°C, respectively. This pretreatment, followed by alternating temperatures of 5 and 25°C with 8 hr of light and 16 hr of darkness, gave 98% germination.

Vernalization at 35°C for 5 days induces dormancy and no seeds germinate (Ohashi and Ichikawa 1960). Pretreatment at 5 and 15°C not only increases germination, but also affects flowering time and seed oil content.

UTILITY

This plant has been used for centuries to control insects, as a drug and in cooking. Its anthelmintic properties (to control internal worms) are reflected in one of its common names, "wormwood." *C. ambrosioides* fruits are rich in oil that contains the active component ascaridole. The stem and leaf glands also contain oil. The oil was previously registered as an official oil in the United States and Britain (Conway and Slocumb 1979) and the plant was grown commercially in the eastern United States (Kapoor et al. 1956) for its oil, which was sold for US$ 3.80/kg in the early 1900s (Pammel 1913). Oil was exported to Asia, which prompted Kapoor et al. (1956) in India to study *C. ambrosioides* culture as a commercial crop. They obtained 0.75 to 1.16% oil from the seed and the oil contained up to 70% ascaridole (as compared to 65% in the United States). The ascaridole content of the oil increased as plants matured (28, 47, 55, and 70% ascaridole for plants in the bud, first-flower, immature fruit, and ripe fruit stages, respectively). Plants contained approximately the same percentage of oil at each of these stages. High levels of potassium were necessary for optimum growth and high ascaridole content.

The oil from *C. ambrosioides* has been used to repel and kill insects, to treat internal worms and parasites, and as a diuretic and it also has fungicidal properties. At 1000 ppm the oil demonstrated strong antifungal activity against the damping off organism, *Rhizoctonia solani*, with no detrimental effects on the plant *Phaseolus aureus* (Dubey et al. 1983). The authors suggest that the oil would be an effective seed treatment. Plant extracts have nematicidal properties (Haseeb et al. 1978) and stem or leaf extracts have been used as abortifacients and occasionally to induce labor, to expel the placenta (Conway and Slocumb 1979), for toothaches and head colds, as a cathartic and antispasmodic remedy in Mexico (Mendieta and Amo 1981), and to stimulate milk flow and relieve postpartum pains in the United States (Krochmal et al. 1971). In Puerto Rico the leaves are described as edible (Martin and Ruberte 1978) and they are boiled in milk that is then given to children with worms (Velez and Overbeek 1950). In Colombia the oil is mixed with castor bean oil and administered to treat internal worms (Perez 1956). At times the leaves are used to spice beans or soups.

AGRICULTURAL IMPORTANCE

C. ambrosioides infests 25 crops in over 65 countries (Figure 20-1). It is a principal or serious weed of cereals in Italy; citrus in Argentina and the United States; horticultural crops in Italy; onions in Brazil; pastures in Australia and Bolivia; rice in Argentina; sweet potatoes in Taiwan; vegetables in Italy; and wheat in Mozambique and South Africa.

It is a common weed of edible beans in Honduras; cereals in South Africa; lucerne in Mexico; maize in Brazil, Honduras, Madagascar, and Zambia; onion and potatoes in Costa Rica; pastures in Hawaii; rice in Brazil; sugarcane in Bangladesh and South Africa; sesame and sorghum in Honduras; soybeans in Brazil; sweet potatoes in Costa Rica and Madagascar; vegetables and wheat in Honduras; and wastelands in Australia, Bolivia, and the United States.

C. ambrosioides is also reported as an unranked weed that infests barley in Colombia; edible beans and cotton in Brazil; beets in Costa Rica; cassava and tea in Taiwan; dryland crops and orchards in Australia; flax in Argentina and Taiwan; nursery crops and pastures in the southern United States; lucerne, pasture, and tobacco in Argentina; maize in Colombia, Egypt and India; peas in South Africa; peanuts in India; potatoes in Colombia; rice in Guatemala, India, Indonesia, the Philippines, Taiwan, and Vietnam; sugarcane in Brazil, India, Peru, and Taiwan; vegetables in Australia, Brazil, Ghana, New Caledonia, and Taiwan; vineyards in Australia; wheat in Argentina and Colombia; and wastelands in the former Yugoslavia.

C. ambrosioides has spread widely from its center of origin. It entered Ireland at the turn of the century as a contaminant of poultry feed (Johnson and Hensman 1910), probably in wheat imported from the Americas. It was introduced into Europe in the late 1500s. Plants were most likely taken from the Americas by early travelers for their medicinal value. However, as Lewis and Lewis (1977) state, the therapeutic levels of the oil are close to the minimum toxic levels and may cause death due to hyperemia of the central nervous system, convulsions, or cardiac and respiratory abnormalities. The oil is considered highly toxic in Brazil if excessive quantities are taken (Lorenzi 1982). This weed is a potentially poisonous plant to livestock with its ascaridole and sometimes high nitrate content (Everist 1974). It is generally avoided by animals since it has a strong foul odor. However, it occurs in lucerne in Argentina, where it is listed as a poisonous species. It hosts some isolates of the potato virus S in the Netherlands (Bokx 1970) and the nematode *Meloidogyne incognita* in the United States (Bendixen et al. 1979).

COMMON NAMES

Chenopodium ambrosioides

ARGENTINA	paico, paico macho
AUSTRALIA	Mexican tea
BRAZIL	ambrosia, erva pomba rola, erva de Santa Maria, mastruco, matacabra cha do Mexico
CHILE	paico
COLOMBIA	paico
DOMINICAN REPUBLIC	epasote

EGYPT	fihaniya, fiss el-kalb, nitna, mintina
ENGLAND	Indian goosefoot
FIJI	Mexican tea
FRANCE	cheopode ambroisine
GERMANY	Wohlriechender Gansefuss
HAWAII	Mexican tea
JAMAICA	bitter weed, Mexican tea, semi-contra, wormseed
JAPAN	ke-aritaso
MADAGASCAR	taimboritsiloz
MAURITIUS	botrice
MEXICO	epazote
NETHERLANDS	welriekende ganzevoet
NEW ZEALAND	Mexican tea
NORWAY	sitronmelde
PANAMA	paico
PARAGUAY	ka'are, paico
PERU	huacatay, paico
PHILIPPINES	alpasotis
PORTUGAL	erva formigueira
PUERTO RICO	pazote, pasote
RHODESIA	dungurachirombo, ibigicana, wormseed
SAUDI ARABIA	al-dhorbaih, al-zorbaih
SOUTH AFRICA	kruiehondebossie, wormseed goosefoot
SPAIN	paico, te espanol
UNITED STATES	Mexican tea
URUGUAY	paico macho, yerba de Santa Maria
VENEZUELA	paico, pasote
ZAMBIA	wormseed

Twenty-One

Chenopodium murale L.

Chenopodiaceae, Goosefoot Family

THIS PLANT IS A COMMON annual herbaceous weed in 57 countries (Figure 21-1). It originated in Eurasia and now occurs over a wide range of latitudes (New Zealand to Sweden) and altitudes (the coasts of Lebanon to the Bolivian Andes). It is found in cropland and wastelands, especially those with rich fertile soils. Its species name suggest the plant "grows on walls."

FIGURE 21-1   The distribution of *Chenopodium murale* L. across the world where it is has been reported as a weed.

178

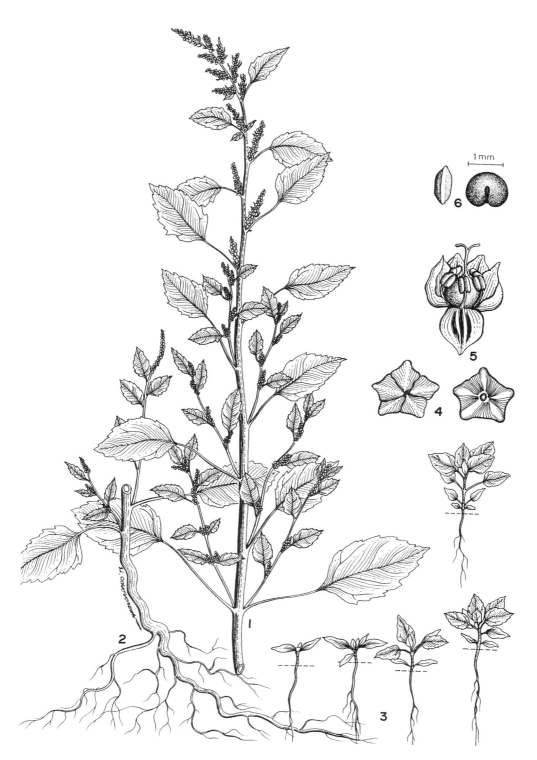

FIGURE 21-2 *Chenopodium murale* L.: 1. flowering branch; 2. root system; 3. seedlings; 4. flowers, face view, 5. partly open; 6. seed, two views.

DESCRIPTION

C. murale (Figure 21-2) is a stout, succulent somewhat aromatic *annual* herb; *root* a branched taproot; *stems* branched, erect except lower branches somewhat decumbent, slightly striated, smooth, 30 to 80 cm tall; *leaves* alternate, mealy when young, then dark green and shiny, ovate usually pointed at tip, 2 to 8 cm long, 1 to 6 cm wide, coarsely toothed with teeth directed forward, lower leaves on rather long petioles, upper ones shortly petioled, leafy almost to the top; *inflorescence* a cluster of flowers in loose cymose panicles, terminal and axillary; *flowers* perfect, small, greenish; *sepals* 5, conspicuously keeled, united below, not completely covering the fruit; *stamens* 5, *stigmas* 2; *fruit* an *utricle*; *seed* lens-shaped, 1.2 to 1.5 mm long, 1 to 1.3 mm wide, finely granular, yellowish-brown to dull black with distinctly keeled margin giving the appearance of a pie-plate rim.

The somewhat unpleasant odor, toothed leaves, conspicuously keeled sepals and pie-plate margins of the seeds are the distinguishing characteristics of this species.

ECOLOGY AND BIOLOGY

C. murale is adapted to many ecological conditions but grows most vigorously in soils rich in nitrogen. It grows from sea level to over 2000 m and in open and shaded sites. Sharma (1978) observed that it appears in wheat 4 wk after planting but ripens with the crop. Seeds are often harvested with the grain. In northern Europe, it flowers from July to September and is highly variable in morphological features (Engstrand and Gustafsson 1973). It is a long-day, C_3 plant with a $2n$ chromosome count of 18. Matthews (1975) noted that it germinates over a long period and, if under stress, plants set seed when only 10 to 15 cm tall. When growing under favorable conditions, plants are over 1 m tall before flowering.

While *C. ambrosioides* is rich in bioactivity for pest control and medicinal effects, *C. murale* is well documented for its allelochemical effect on other plants. Bhandari and Sen (1983) noted that leaf and inflorescence extracts of *C. murale* reduced the germination of *Brassica nigra* seeds, but that leaf and root extracts had no effect on wheat germination. Leaf extracts of *C. murale* reduced germination, weight and number of mustard seeds, while extracts from inflorescences increased mustard seed weight and number (Datta and Ghosh 1981). Leachates of fresh *C. murale* leaves and roots inhibited radicle growth of maize and beans (but not squash), while leachate from dried weed samples inhibited radicle growth of all crops and five of the six weed species tested (Anaya et al. 1987). *C. murale* extracts sprayed on dodder-infested (*Cuscuta* sp.) lucerne killed dodder but also seriously injured the crop (Habib and Rahan 1988). The toxins were principally phenolic compounds.

Single plants can produce over 24,000 seeds with an average weight of 0.68 mg each (Herron 1953). Seventeen percent of fresh seed germinated and, after only 4 to 5 mo storage at 3°C in moist sand or peat, nearly all seeds germinated. Dry storage at room temperature for 2 yr resulted in 92% germination. Germination varies between seed lots collected in different years and alternating temperatures enhance germination.

The longevity of *C. murale* seeds extracted from adobe bricks was studied by Spira and Wagner (1983). Earlier workers had removed and identified the seeds from wall bricks in the early 1930s, and they were kept in dry storage at room temperatures. Four of the 32 seeds that were 183 yr old were viable.

Singh and Saroha (1975) applied 2,4-D to plants at flowering and at weekly intervals thereafter. At maturity, 33% of the seeds from non-treated plants germinated. Treating at flowering or 1, 2, and 3 wk later reduced germination to 3, 7, 8, and 9%, respectively. Later treatments had less effect.

Seeds of *C. murale* are readily eaten by the common house sparrow in India. Adult males can consume 8.6 g of seed per day, thereby reducing the seed reservoir (Sharma 1977).

AGRICULTURAL IMPORTANCE

C. murale is a reported weed of 25 crops in 57 countries (Figure 21-1) and is frequently reported a principal weed in wheat. It is a serious or principal weed of carrots in Egypt; cereals and vegetables in Italy; cotton in Mexico and Peru; dates in Arabia; flax and safflower in Mexico; lucerne in Canada and the United States; millet in India; orchards in South Africa; potatoes in India; safflower in Mexico; sugar beets in Israel; sugarcane in Iran; vineyards in South Africa; and wheat in India, Mexico, Pakistan, and South Africa.

It is a common weed of barley in India; carrots, maize, and sorghum in Mexico; orchards Uruguay; sugarcane in Natal; vegetables in Arabia, India, South Africa, and the United States; winter season crops in India; and dryland crops in Australia.

C. murale is also reported as an unranked weed of edible beans in Mexico; cereals in Israel and New Zealand; citrus in Cyprus; coffee in Honduras; cotton in Greece, India, and the United States; flax in India and New Zealand; horticultural crops in Australia, Mexico, and South Africa; lucerne in Arabia and New Zealand; maize in Greece and India; orchards in Argentina, Congo, Iraq, and the United States; pastures in Australia and New Zealand; peas in New Zealand and South Africa; potatoes in Arabia, Argentina, and Nepal; rice in India and Nepal; sugar beets in Spain and the United States; sugarcane in Argentina, India, Peru, and South Africa; sunflower in Australia and Spain; tomatoes in Australia, Greece, and Tunisia; vegetables in Argentina, Australia, Greece, Iraq, and Lebanon; wheat in Arabia, Argentina, Honduras, and Nepal; and wastelands in Iraq and South Africa.

Densities of 248 plants/m^2 of *C. murale* and *C. album* reduced wheat yields by 16% in Pakistan (Saeed et al. 1977). *C. murale* is sometimes used to feed cattle in India but can have high nitrate levels and imparts an off-flavor to milk when consumed as young, succulent plants (Everist 1974). This species hosts the red spider mite (*Tetranychus urticae*) in India (Choudhury and Mukherjee 1971) and numerous viruses, including all six isolates of the potato virus S tested by Bokx (1970). Interestingly, *C. murale* extracts were the most effective of 29 species tested in inhibiting tobacco and cucumber mosaic viruses (Allan et al. 1978).

The plant has been used as a leafy vegetable in India and parts of Africa. While rich in minerals, the buildup of high oxalate levels as the plant develops limits its usefulness (Singh and Saxena 1972).

COMMON NAMES

Chenopodium murale

ARGENTINA	quinoa negra, yuyo negro
AUSTRALIA	nettleleaf goosefoot
BOLIVIA	yerba del susto
CHILE	quinguilla

DENMARK	mur-gasefod
DOMINICAN REPUBLIC	caledonia, corralera
EGYPT	abu efein, fisseih, fosseish
ENGLAND	nettle-leaved goosefoot
FRANCE	chenopode des murs
GERMANY	Mauer-Gansefuss
HAWAII	nettle goosefoot
INDIA	khar bathua
IRAW	wall goosefoot
ITALY	pie danserino
LEBANON	muntinab, nettle-leaved goosefoot
MEXICO	cardo russo, chual, quelite cenizo, quelito de coyote
MOROCCO	anserine murale
NETHERLANDS	muurganzevoet
NEW ZEALAND	nettle-leaved fathen
NORWAY	gatemelde
PERU	hierba del gallinazo
PORTUGAL	pe-de-ganso
SAUDI ARABIA	fiss-el-kilaab, khenza, lissan al teir, rain, rukd, sekran, thannoum
SOUTH AFRICA	muurhondebossie, nettle-leaved goosefoot
SPAIN	cenizo
SWEDEN	gatmalla
UNITED STATES	nettleleaf goosefoot
URUGUAY	quinoa negra, yuyo negro
VENEZUELA	cenizo
ZIMBABWE	nettleleaf goosefoot

Twenty-Two

Chondrilla juncea L.

Asteraceae (Compositae), Aster Family

CHONDRILLA JUNCEA is a perennial composite that is not an important weed in its region of origin of Eurasia. However, when introduced into Australia in the early 1900s, it quickly infested thousands of hectares of pastures, wheat fields, roadsides and waste areas. Its ability to reduce crop yield by competing for water and nitrogen, to regenerate rapidly from a deep branched taproot, and to seriously interfere with wheat harvest are reasons *C. juncea* is considered a noxious weed outside its center of origin. The

FIGURE 22-1   The distribution of *Chondrilla juncea* L. across the world where it has been reported as a weed.

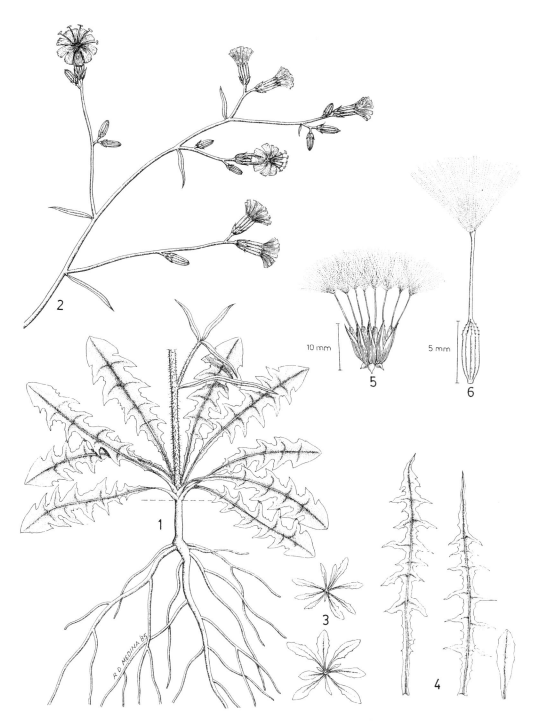

Figure 22-2 *Chondrilla juncea* L.: 1. basal leaves showing root system and lower part of stem with bristles; 2. tip portion of plant, showing narrow leaves and inflorescences; 3. seedling; 4. various leaf forms; 5. fully mature flower head; 6. seed with stalked parachute-like pappus.

genus name is from the Greek for chicory and the species refers to *Juncus* (rushes), which its leafless stems resemble.

DESCRIPTION

C. juncea (Figure 22-2) is a long-lived *perennial* herbaceous plant; *taproot* branched, up to 2 m deep, shoots from buds on taproot and lateral roots; *stems* 30 to 100 cm tall, nearly leafless, tough, stiff, greatly branched, and very slender, coarse downward-pointing hairs at base of stem, remainder smooth, bright green to yellow-green *rosettes* form after shoots emerge, up to 15 cm in diameter; *rosette leaves* glabrous, linear or lobed with lobes pointed toward base of plant; highly irregular; *stem leaves* few, alternate, linear, entire to toothed, up to 10 cm long; *inflorescence* an involucrate flower head that resembles a single flower, composed of 7 to 15 small strap-shaped ligulate florets; flower heads solitary or in groups of 2 to 5, sessile or on short peduncles, terminal and axillary; *involucre* cylindrical, pubescent, composed of several linear bracts 9 to 12 mm long; *flowers* of only ligulate florets, perfect, yellow; *fruit* a dry indehiscent *achene*, 3 to 4 mm long, dark olive to brown, cylindrical with five vertical ribs, barbed toward apex by small tooth-like projections; slender beak longer than achene; *pappus* of many white capillary bristles about 5 mm long, attached atop beak; all plant parts exude milky latex when cut or broken.

This species is a member of the **Lactucoideae** subfamily and the Euchondrilla section of the genus. It is closely related to *Cichorium intybus*, *Taraxacum officinale*, and *Sonchus asper* but is distinguished by its extensive branched root system, the leaf lobes that point toward the plant somewhat like a barbed spear, the nearly leafless highly branched and slender stems with basal hairs, the 5-ribbed achenes, and the milky latex in all plant parts.

DISTRIBUTION AND HABITAT

The plant has been in the eastern United States since 1870 but has not become a problem weed in that region. In 1938, *C. juncea* was introduced into the western United States, where it is now considered a noxious weed. This area has many similarities in soils, climate, and agricultural systems to southeastern Australia, where it is a principal weed. Subsequently *C. juncea* was found in Argentina, where it has already invaded over 100,000 hectares (Marsico 1978).

The spread and economic losses due to *C. juncea* have been greatest in Australia. After its introduction in 1914, it spread an average of 24 km/yr for 40 yr and is now found throughout the wheat-growing region of southeastern Australia. Its rapid dissemination is attributed to (1) large areas of very favorable climate, (2) the method of wheat production that includes a fallow period and shallow plowing, and (3) the absence of diseases and insects that attack *C. juncea* in Eurasia (Wapshere et al. 1974). Shallow repeated cultivation minimizes competition from other plants and breaks and spreads roots that form new colonies.

C. juncea survives in many climatic and soil conditions between lat 35° to 55° N in Eurasia, 38° to 48° N in the United States, and 26° to 38° S in Australia (Figure 22-1). It grows from sea level to 1800 m. The ideal climate for *C. juncea* is a cool winter, warm summer with no severe dry periods, and an increase in rainfall at the start of the cool season. It is found in areas with as little as 230 mm to over 1520 mm annual precipitation (McVean

1966) and, in areas of the northwestern United States, with less than 250 mm annual rainfall (Piper 1983).

C. juncea prefers sandy, well-drained, slightly acidic or alkaline soils. In Europe, it has been found on sand dunes containing 92% sand (Wapshere et al. 1974), but 80% sand in the soil gives the most growth. It is a plant of cultivated and undisturbed areas. Tillage stimulates new rosettes and broken root fragments give rise to new plants. The appearance of rosette leaves is perhaps why this species was sometimes misclassified as a biennial.

C. juncea inhabits light textured soils with a wide range of *pH* and fertility levels (Moore 1964). Hull and Groves (1973) found no relationship between the soil and microhabitat on the distribution of the A, B, and C biotypes of *C. juncea* in Australia. Infestations occur in soils with *pH* 5.3 to 8.9 (Panetta and Dodd 1987). Calcium and P are important for seedling establishment, and if deficiency symptoms appear, survival is doubtful (McVean 1966).

Wapshere et al. (1974) studied the abundance of *C. juncea* in the Mediterranean region. Few plants were found in well-managed vineyards and up to 10 plants/m^2 were found in poorly managed ones. Cereal crops of Spain and France were free of *C. juncea* due to their intensive crop rotation system. In southern Italy, cereals were infested to about the same degree as in Australia (4 to 53 plants/m^2), and both areas practice a wheat-fallow cropping system. The plant has spread in Australia because the wheat-fallow system removes natural vegetation, includes cultivation that propagates the species vegetatively and creates a favorable environment for seed germination, and adds fertilizer to which the weed favorably responds (Wells 1971b). The seeding rate of wheat in Australia is one third that of Europe, which means less crop competition with the weed (Wapshere 1970).

BIOLOGY

The biology of *C. juncea* has been intensively studied and excellent reviews of the species have been prepared by McVean 1966, Wells 1971b, Cullen and Groves 1977, and Panetta and Dodd 1987.

After seeds germinate, seedlings remain in the cotyledon stage for several weeks while the root develops (McVean 1966). The taproot penetrates rapidly, growing 1 to 2 cm/day; seedlings may have roots 18 cm long 36 days after planting (Moore 1964). Plants produce both thickened perennial roots with bud-generating potential and shorter feeding roots (Cuthbertson 1972). Lateral roots arise in acropetal succession behind the growing point of the taproot. Most lateral roots are short and live only one season. A few laterals near the soil surface thicken and grow 15 to 50 cm laterally before turning downward.

The taproot and lateral roots have a tremendous regeneration potential. Two- to four-week-old plants have a 40% chance of reproducing vegetatively; all five-week-old plants can be propagated by root cuttings. Taproot cuttings from 80 cm deep can produce shoots, but this capability varies with the plant's growth stage. Root segments taken during stem elongation and flowering have less regenerative ability than at other times (Rosenthal et al. 1968, Cuthbertson 1972). All shoots arise from the proximal end of root segments. Roots initially arise from the distal end of root segments and later at the shoot base. Root segments planted 1 m deep can emerge but emergence is greatest at 5 cm.

Root segments 13 weeks old or older have equal regenerative capacity, regardless of their position on the root. Regrowth can occur from roots cut to 120 cm deep, but most regeneration occurs in the upper 45 cm. Taproot cuttings as small as 1 cm long can form new plants under ideal conditions, but most sections this size would desiccate in the field. Regeneration generally increases as the segment length increases and burial depth decreases (Cuthbertson 1972). Root segments as short as 2 cm can have as many as three buds (Moore 1964). Latex exuded by injured roots dries, thereby protecting the root section (Wells 1971b). No new shoots arise from the broken root that is still attached to the parent plant.

Root buds sprout at (day/night) temperatures between 10/5°C and 30/25°C. The optimum temperature regime for sprouting is from 21/16 to 27/22°C and bud elongation is fastest at 27/22°C. Interestingly, the number of sprouted buds per shoot is similar (five to seven) for 5-, 10-, 15-, and 20-cm segments. This suggests that the process is auxin controlled and that the first buds determine the total number of sprouted buds for each root section. Thus the whole plant status and root segment position do not affect the number of buds that sprout (Kefford and Caso 1972).

In the field, Rosenthal et al. (1968) found more lateral root development in sparse stands of *Chondrilla* than in thick stands. Roots became thicker as distance from the taproot increased. Occasionally the root forms an abscission zone and new plants become independent from the parent plant. Plant populations also increase because several rosettes often form at the crown. In western Australia, plants with one rosette at the crown during the first year of growth had three crowns the next year. During the second year, plants form an average of six daughter rosettes. Biotype A plants form rosettes an average of 17 cm from the parent plant, while biotype B plants form rosettes an average of 24 cm away. (Biotypes are discussed in detail later in this section.)

Adventitious buds near the top of the taproots also form rosettes in the fall. Satellite rosettes are commonly formed on lateral branches of undisturbed plants. The next spring, stems emerge from the center of the rosette, elongate, branch, and produce many small flowers during the summer. By summer's end, the stems die back and new rosettes appear as autumn approaches. As photoperiod increases, time to bolting decreases, but time to flowering is unaffected (Ballard 1956). Ten long-days are sufficient to trigger early bolting. Plants receiving 8 hr of light never bolt and have narrower and more deeply lobed leaves than those growing under longer day lengths.

Both day length and temperature influence bolting (Cuthbertson 1965, 1966). Vernalization for 4 to 6 wk hastens bolting and flowering and reduces the number of rosette leaves. Non-vernalized plants flower when exposed to 14- to 16-hr photoperiods for more than 12 mo. Under shorter days, all vernalized plants eventually flower, but it takes twice as long under a 9-hr day length than under a 14-hr day length. The period of darkness, not the day length, controls elongation.

Temperature interacts with photoperiod and vernalization to control bolting in *C. juncea* (Caso and Kefford 1968). Vernalized plants grown at 15°C day and 10°C night temperatures bolted in all photoperiods, while non-vernalized plants required 12 hr of more light. Vernalized plants grown at 27°C day and 22°C night temperatures also needed 12 or more hours of light to bolt, and non-vernalized plants at this temperature needed a 14-hr photoperiod to induce bolting. Increasing the night temperature, but holding the day temperature constant, gave earlier bolting. The authors conclude that unlike most rosette-forming plants, *C. juncea* has no fixed cold requirement and that bolting is influenced by a complex set of interactions between vernalization, photoperiod, ambient day and night temperatures, and plant age. Thus plants behave as a weed under a wide range of climatic and latitudinal limits.

C. juncea is a prolific seed producer. Each plant may have 1500 capitula, each with 7 to 15 achenes (average 10) that are well-suited for dispersal by wind, water and animals.

Seeds are produced apomictically. Flowers open during the morning and close before sunset. On hot days, flowers are open only a few hours (McVean 1966). Seeds start shedding approximately 10 to 20 days after flowering and this continues for several months.

The quantity and quality of seed produced depends upon plant vigor before, during, and after flowering and up to seed maturity (Cullen and Groves 1977). With adequate soil moisture, only 3 to 4% of the achenes are sterile (Cuthbertson 1974). These can be identified by their smaller size, "pinched" appearance, and white or yellow color. Hot, dry summer weather increases the number of sterile achenes (Grant-Lipp 1966, McVean 1966). Viable seeds are produced soon after flowering. Within 3, 6, and 9 days of flowering, *C. juncea* produced 2, 25, and 84% viable seed, respectively (Cuthbertson 1970).

The seeds of biotype C of *C. juncea* have no dormancy and germinate whenever environmental conditions are favorable. Seeds seldom survive more than 1 yr in the soil and no seed reservoir accumulates (McVean 1966). Seeds in dry storage lose some viability after 1 yr and are nonviable after 3 or 4 yr. Germination rates above 90% have been reported for freshly harvested seed (Schirman and Robocker 1967, Cuthbertson 1974). Biotype A may have 40% dormant seed that requires a brief after-ripening period, but biotype C does not (Panetta and Dodd 1987). Fresh and 15-month-old seed germinated equally well between 15 and 30°C (Grant-Lipp 1966). Rapid water uptake occurs in the first 3 hr and germination is complete in 48 hr. Mature seeds contain 8 to 16% moisture and swell to 90 to 110% of their oven dry weight after imbibition. CO_2 levels up to 20% do not affect germination, but O_2 levels of 4% or less reduce germination.

C. juncea establishes rapidly by seed. Seedlings emerge in late summer or early fall and form a rosette during late fall and winter. Late summer showers followed by dry conditions can be detrimental to seedling establishment (Schirman and Robocker 1967) and deplete the soil seed supply (McVean 1966). Seeds germinate equally well in light and darkness and in all soil types, and the optimum germination temperature is 25°C (Cuthbertson 1970). Emergence, however, is generally related to soil type and planting depth. Few seeds germinate on the soil surface. Seedlings emerged from 13 mm in a clay soil and from 38 mm in clay loam, sandy loam and sandy soils. No seedling emerged from 51 mm in any soil, and maximum emergence in all soil types was from 6 mm. McVean (1966) observed emergence from as deep as 50 mm in sand, with shallower emergence depths in heavier soil. Seedling establishment occurs primarily in sites with a sandy topsoil (Groves and Hull 1970) that have an adequate moisture supply for 3 to 6 wk after germination (Cullen and Groves 1977).

Noticeable morphological variation occurs in *C. juncea*, and biotypes have been observed in most regions where the plant is found. Hull and Groves (1973) have thoroughly studied the three biotypes found in Australia. Biotype A is the most widespread and is easily distinguished by its narrow leaves. Its terminal apex remains dominant, and it usually has a tall single stem with regular 90-degree branching. Biotype C has the widest and least dissected leaves, and biotype B is intermediate in this characteristic. Both biotypes B and C have more tertiary branching than biotype A. These differences in morphological features were maintained through two generations. Just before bolting, rosettes of all biotypes produce five to nine leaves per week. Leaf emergence is equal for all biotypes, but flowering occurs in this order: B > A > C. Root segments of biotype C produce more buds than the A and B biotypes and therefore may require more intensive control measures. Biotype A is much more widespread than biotypes B and C, and biotype B is more prevalent than biotype C. All three biotypes can coexist, and the growth of one does not inhibit the development of the others. All biotypes are triploids and contain the same complement of chromosomes $2n = 15$ (Panetta and Dodd 1987). In the western United States, two biotypes have been encountered that differ in duration of flowering period, stem length and branching pattern, and root characteristics (Piper 1983).

The identification of biotypes is particularly critical in biological control programs, as the attacking organism is often very specific for the host it will feed on or infect. With this in mind, Greenham et al. (1972) developed electrical impedance parameters to separate biotypes. More recently, isozyme techniques have been developed for the same purpose. Burdon et al. (1980) found eight enzyme systems of the 14 studied to be sufficiently different between biotypes of *C. juncea* to allow positive identification. This process can be used on germinating seeds rather than larger plants and is a simple, clear-cut, and reproducible method of biotype separation. Further refinement in the electrophoresis technique allows biotype separation using roots, rosette leaves, or stem leaves so that seeds need not be collected to produce seedlings (Reinganum 1986). These methods can be used to monitor the development of new biotypes that might arise, especially in response to biocontrol measures. Even though *C. juncea* exhibits obligate apomixis, a new biotype could arise from autosegregation or mutation (Burdon et al. 1980).

COMPETITIVE EFFECTS AND CONTROL

The extensive and deep root system of *C. juncea* makes control extremely difficult and eradication nearly impossible. Nevertheless, much is known about the competitive capabilities of this species and how its impact can be reduced.

Cultural practices greatly influence the density of *C. juncea*. Kohn and Cuthbertson (1975) found that rotational grazing resulted in higher populations than continuous grazing (8.2 vs. 0.4 plants/m^2). When grazed rotationally, the weed built up root reserve and spread vegetatively, while continual grazing prevented the emergence of more rosettes. Sheep and cattle apparently find leaves and stems of this weed palatable (McVean 1966, Wells 1971b). Stems contain more N than lucerne but are much less digestible (Jones et al. 1971).

Applying 125 kg/ha/yr of superphosphate in pastures reduced the infestation from 7.3 to 1.4 plants/m^2. Phosphorous increased the competitive ability of the forage species, thereby reducing the *C. juncea* stand. Interestingly, weed populations were unaffected by stocking rates of 5 to 15 sheep per hectare.

Pasture grasses do not compete effectively with *C. juncea*, but leguminous species do. After 2 yr, lucerne reduced the infestation 92% on high-fertility soils and by 66% on poorer soils (Wells 1969). Lucerne densities of 54 plants/m^2 reduced the infestations by 75%. Subterranean clover and annual medic competed less effectively than lucerne. Pure swards of subterranean clover (*Trifolium subterranean* L.) reduced *C. juncea* stands more than pasture grasses or mixtures of legume and grass. After 4 yr, weed densities were reduced by 63% and dry weights by 80%. Clover often intercepted 95% of the light, thereby inhibiting *C. juncea* growth. A wheat crop grown the 5th year yielded well without herbicide treatment. The field was left undisturbed for 2 yr and *C. juncea* populations remained low, suggesting that a short-term legume in rotation with wheat may provide effective cultural control of this weed (Moore and Robertson 1964).

Competing crops need to provide high levels of shade to inhibit the spread of this weed. Shading initially results in fewer but larger rosette leaves (Hull and Groves 1973). To affect established rosettes, the light reaching the soil surface must be less than 1% of full sunlight, and clover 30 cm tall gives up to 99.5% shade (McVean 1966). Light reductions of 90% at the soil surface prevent seedling establishment.

Unfortunately, cultural control is less effective in wheat. *C. juncea* has been described as a weed of cultivation and can increase rapidly under low levels of tillage, especially in wheat-fallow production systems. In fact, the practice of pasturing with sheep during the fallow period increases the weed's densities by reducing competition from other species and burying seeds so that seed survival and germination are increased (Wapshere 1970). Intensive cultivation (Wapshere et al. 1974) and cultivation during the dry season (Wells 1970) reduce *Chondrilla* densities. Cultivations every 6 to 8 wk can eliminate the plant (Cullen and Groves 1977).

C. juncea is not known to be allelopathic but competes for soil moisture and N. Yield losses in wheat have a logarithmic relationship to *C. juncea* density. With 1 to 10 plants/m^2, yields were 1.4 t/ha; 11 to 100 plants/m^2, reduced yields 50% (to 0.7 ton/ha), and another ten-fold increase in plant density (>100/m^2) reduced yields to 0.3 t/ha (Wells 1971b). The weed is most serious in wheat grown on soils low in nitrogen where even low densities can reduce wheat yield (Myers and Lipsett 1958). Applying nitrogen increased the leaf number and size, but not the number of rosettes in wheat.

Yield losses to competition often occur before 2,4-D is normally applied; thus treatment may not increase yields but improves crop harvestability by preventing *Chondrilla* stem elongation. When herbicides were applied early or in the fallow period, wheat yields were increased by conserving moisture and up to 30 kg N/ha (Myers and Lipsett 1958, Cuthbertson 1969). Cultivation during the fallow period can also increase wheat yield, but may not reduce *Chondrilla* density in the wheat crop (Wells 1971a).

Caso and Kefford (1973) found 2,4-D kills only the foliage and a short section of the root, while foliarly applied picloram is translocated and kills buds up to 25 cm down the root and affects buds 40 cm deep. Temperatures above 25°C reduced the control with 2,4-D but not with picloram. Treatment after bolting is most effective because the regenerative ability of the roots is lowest at this part of its life cycle (Cuthbertson 1972).

Picloram acts through foliar and root absorption and generally controls *Chondrilla* longer than other herbicides. Treatments sometimes approach eradication (Schirman and Robocker 1967, Molnar 1971). Picloram used during the fallow period may persist until the wheat is planted, especially in dry years, and cultivation before or after picloram application reduces control. Treatment in the fall under cool, wet weather gives the best results (Molnar 1971). Clopyralid gives long-term selective control of *C. juncea* in wheat (Panetta and Dodd 1987).

Biocontrol research followed studies by Wapshere (1970) that revealed differences in *C. juncea* densities between the Mediterranean region and Australia. He recognized that several of the natural enemies of *C. juncea* in its center of origin were not in Australia. Some natural enemies were in Australia but were ineffective. For example, two species of powdery mildew present on *C. juncea* in Australia (*Leveillula taurica* and *Erysiphe cichoracearum*) did not reduce its spread or level of infestation. Among the differences in agronomic practices between the regions, he felt that the 2- to 3-yr wheat-fallow system did not allow natural predators sufficient time to build up damaging populations.

Wapshere et al. (1974) found the powdery mildews to be less damaging to the weed than *Puccinia*. They observed that two very devastating organisms in Europe, the fungal rust, *Puccinia chondrillina*, and the gall mite, *Aceria chondrillae*, were not found in Australia. Hasan (1972), Hasan and Wapshere (1973), and Wapshere et al. (1974) described the distribution, biology, host specificity, and potential of *P. chondrillina* for biological control of *Chondrilla*. The fungus is active throughout the year in most areas of the Eurasian region where *C. juncea* is found. It occurred on 91 and 72% of the sites sampled in France and Italy, respectively (Wapshere et al. 1974). It appears on new rosettes as they emerge in the fall and spreads rapidly until winter starts. Small seedlings and rosettes are usually killed within 3 to 4 wk. Growth of large rosettes is severely inhibited. Spread of the disease continues in the spring, and it attacks the flower stalk once elongation begins. *Puccinia* reduces root reserves and seed production of the weed and only attacks *Chondrilla* species.

The *Puccinia* spreads by urediospores. These germinate best at 16 to 18°C. Spore development is faster at 24°C (Blanchette and Lee 1981), but germination tube growth is highest at 10°C (Hasan and Wapshere 1973). Disease development is rapid between 5 and 25°C, but infection is best at cooler temperatures. Germination of the urediospores and penetration of the plant by the germination tube occurs within 16 hr and is more rapid in the dark than in light. Since rapid infection requires a moist environment (like dew on the leaf surface), cool temperatures and darkness, the fungus should be released at dusk in the spring when there will be a dew (Blanchette and Lee 1981). In the field, Hasan and Wapshere (1973) observed leaf kill within 25 to 35 days after releasing *Puccinia*. Root reserves were lower and the stand of *Chondrilla* was reduced 50% in one season.

Early attempts to infect Australian *C. juncea* with *P. chondrillina* from France, Italy and Spain failed (Hasan 1972). Then a strain of Puccinia from southeastern Italy was found that virulently attacks the narrow-leaf biotype (biotype A) of Australian *C. juncea*. After thorough testing to assure specificity, *P. chondrillina* was released in Australia in 1971.

The developments after its release have been summarized by Cullen (1973). *Puccinia* spores spread very rapidly in Australia, moving 1 m the first generation, 8 km by the fourth, and 320 km by the twelfth —and all within 7 months! The successful introduction was due to the high weed density, favorable weather and the release of a very effective strain. *Puccinia* has now spread throughout southeastern Australia (Groves and Williams 1975). However, the strain introduced in 1971 attacks only biotype A. This is the most widespread biotype, but such selectivity by the fungus has caused a shift in biotypes (Burdon et al. 1981). Biotype A has remained relatively static in distribution since 1968. Biotype B was the most limited in distribution initially, but from 1968 through 1980 moved southward while biotype C moved rapidly northward. Even at sites where all bio-types were present in 1968, their relative abundance has shifted. For example, at one site, biotype A declined from 67 to 3% of the population from 1968 to 1980; biotype B increased from 30 to 78%; and biotype C from 3 to 19% in the same period. These shifts are thought to be due primarily to the fact that *P. chondrillina* and the gall mite preferen-tially attack biotype A rather than biotypes B and C.

A nation-wide evaluation in Australia has documented the impact of biocontrol efforts on *C. juncea* (Cullen 1976). Significant reductions in plant density and recovery rate of root reserves have occurred. *P. chondrillina* not only attacked the weed in pastures but in crops as well. Once the fungus is established in a crop, it persists and not only reduces *Chondrilla* density but also results in weaker plants that cause less interference at harvest time. The effect of the disease on root reserves dramatically weakens the plant, rendering it less competitive. Cullen speculates that a 33% reduction in root growth is equal to at least a 25% reduction in competition.

Other organisms have been studied for their specificity for *Chondrilla* and possible release in Australia. These include the gall mite *Aceria* (Caresche and Wapshere 1974), and the gall midge *Cystiphora schmidti* (Caresche and Wapshere 1975). The gall mite was intro-duced in 1971 and attacks aerial buds, thereby preventing seed production. A strain of gall mite located in Greece proved to be the most efficient against the narrow-leaf biotype of *Chondrilla* common in Australia. Mite strains are also specific for each weed biotype. The mites live on the rosette leaves and "ride" the elongating *Chondrilla* stems in the spring and form galls in the vegetative and flower buds instead of branches or flowers. Seed production is stopped and the growth of the plant is stunted. As the stems die, the mites move back to the rosettes where they overwinter.

The gall midge was released in the early 1970s (Cullen 1973). It lays eggs in the leaves and stems that form galls, each with a larvae inside. The gall midge attacks all three biotypes of *Chondrilla* in Australia equally well. A root moth *Bradyrrhoa gilveolella* also attacks all biotypes of *C. juncea* in Australia, is specific for this species and *Taraxacum* and was successfully released in Australia (Cullen 1980).

The success of the biocontrol program in Australia has lessened the importance of *C. juncea*. The attacking organisms have been found to cohabitate in the weed and also interact with crops to suppress the weed. Groves and Williams (1975) studied the competitive ability of subterranean clovers with *Chondrilla* infested with or free of *Puccinia*. Clover alone reduced weed growth 70%; rust alone reduced it 49%; and when the clover competed with diseased *Chondrilla*, weed growth was reduced 96%. Cullen (1973) reported that even in the early years after release, when *Chondrilla* densities were not reduced by *Puccinia*, shoot dry weights were reduced by 90%, no seeds were produced and wheat was more competitive.

AGRICULTURAL IMPORTANCE

C. juncea is a reported weed of 17 crops in 24 countries (Figure 22-1) and is frequently reported as a weed of wheat. Besides reducing yield, the wiry stem can make cereal harvest nearly impossible. In less than 60 yr, it spread from southeast Australia to 1000 km north and 3000 km west. It is a noxious and prohibited weed in most states of Australia.

It is a serious or principal weed of horticultural crops in Italy and the former Soviet Union; millet, oats, and tobacco in the former Soviet Union; orchards and wheat in Australia; pastures in Australia and the western United States (over 2 million ha infested); sugar beets in Iran; and vineyards in Australia, the former Soviet Union, and the western United States.

It is a common weed of barley in the former Soviet Union; citrus in Australia; pastures in Bulgaria; winter wheat and vineyards in Spain; and wastelands in the former Yugoslavia.

C. juncea is a reported weed of unknown rank in barley, cotton, orchards, and sugar beets in Iran; cereals in Turkey; lucerne in Australia and the former Yugoslavia; maize, sunflowers, and vegetables in the former Soviet Union; pastures in Argentina; peas and oilseed rape in Australia; vineyards in France, Jordan, Lebanon, and Turkey; and wheat in Argentina, Iran, Portugal, and the western United States.

C. juncea provides a palatable and nutritious forage in the rosette stage through flowering until the stem becomes lignified. Continuous grazing by sheep keep plants in the rosette stage during the summer when other forages are scarce. Grazing prevents, or at least reduces, seed production (Cuthbertson 1966).

COMMON NAMES

Chondrilla juncea

ARGENTINA	chondrilla, yuyo esqueleto
AUSTRALIA	skeleton weed
FRANCE	chondrille effilee, chondrille a tige de Jone
GERMANY	Binsen Knorpelsata, Grunfeste
IRAN	qanderoonak
ITALY	lattugaccio
LEBANON	chondrilla, go'ded, gum succory, hindiba barri, maruriayh, ya'did
NETHERLANDS	knikbloem
PORTUGAL	leituga-branca
SPAIN	achicoria dulce, achicoria juncal, alotxa, mastec
TURKEY	ak hindiba
UNITED STATES	rush skeletonweed
YUGOSLAVIA	zutenica

Twenty-Three

Chrysanthemum leucanthemum L.

Asteraceae (Compositae), Aster Family

CHRYSANTHEMUM LEUCANTHEMUM is well known for both its beauty and noxiousness. The bright yellow and white flowers appear in ornamental gardens and it has served as one parent of the commercialized "shasta" chrysanthemum. The genus and species are derived from Greek words meaning gold and white flowering. Nevertheless, its spreading roots and prolific seed production give it the ability to invade pastures, roadsides, lawns, gardens, and waste areas. It has been declared a noxious weed in many areas.

FIGURE 23-1 The distribution of *Chrysanthemum leucanthemum* L. across the world where it has been reported as a weed.

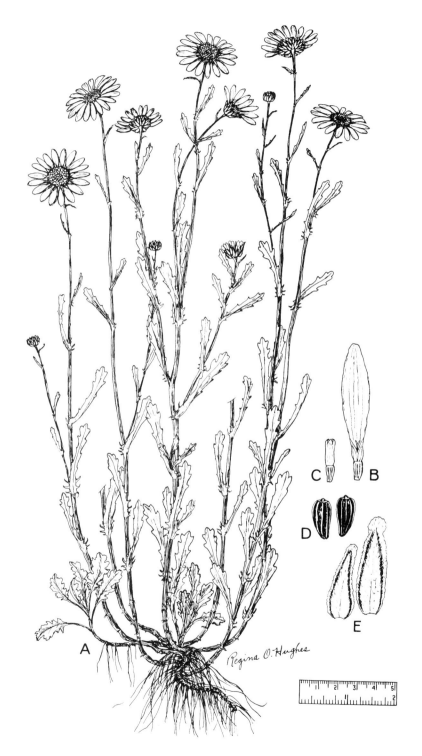

FIGURE 23-2 *Chrysanthemum leucanthemum* L.: A. habit; B. ray flower; C. disk flower; D. achenes; E. involucral bracts.

DESCRIPTION

C. leucanthemum (Figure 23-2) is a *perennial* plant 30 to 90 cm tall with shallow, branched *rhizomes* with strong fibrous *adventitious roots*; *stems* arise from upturned rhizomes or buds on root crown; smooth to sparsely pubescent; simple or branched above, upper stem 8- to 10-furrowed, lower stems round; *lower leaves* with winged petiole, spatulate, coarsely dissected or irregularly toothed, to 15 cm long; *upper leaves* alternate, sessile, semi-clasping the stem, lanceolate or oblanceolate, coarsely dentate, often with few lobes at base, up to 8 cm long; all leaves smooth, dark green, often glossy; *inflorescence* terminal, involucrate flower heads 2 to 6 cm in diameter, on solitary, naked stalks; *involucral bracts* at base of each head numerous, firm, overlapping, light green with brown margins; *ray flowers* 20 to 30, pistillate, ligulate, white, each 10 to 18 mm long, 3 to 7 mm wide; *disc flowers* numerous, perfect, tubular, bright yellow, 1.5 to 2.7 cm in diameter; *fruit* a dry, indehiscent *achene*, circular in outline, without a pappus, 10 silvery to gray elevated ridges that meet at each end, furrows dark brown to black, 1.5 to 2.5 mm long with *tubercle* at apex elongate-ovate, often slightly curved.

The key characteristics of *C. leucanthemum* are the spreading roots, dark green, glossy leaves and bright yellow and white daisy-like flowers. The entire plant emits a slightly disagreeable odor when crushed.

BIOLOGY AND HABITAT

A native of Europe, *C. leucanthemum* now occurs as a weed in 40 countries (Figure 23-1) and is especially abundant in Europe and North America. It is common in overgrazed pastures, waste areas and meadows and grows in a wide range of soils, especially those low in nutrients and *pH*. It can invade wet meadows as well as sandy hillsides. This species grows in high rainfall areas of Australia (over 900 mm/yr) and in Europe to lat 70° N and 1000 m elevation. Howarth and Williams (1968) grew plants in sand culture and found the optimum levels of N, P and Ca were 100, 10, and 100 ppm, respectively.

Most seeds germinate in the autumn, but growth is slow during the first winter and spring (Parsons 1973). Extensive rhizome and crown development take place during the first summer and the crown send up new shoots in autumn. Flowers appear in late spring and summer during the second year. Flowering may be delayed for more than 5 yr if plants are competing with forage species (Salisbury 1942). In Czechoslovakia, plants flower when soil temperatures are 16.3°C at 350 m and at 12.7°C at 1000 m (Habovstiak and Javorkova 1977). Plants require vernalization before flowering. Plants vernalized before October do not always flower, while those growing until October or later and vernalized at 10°C for 30 or more days flower normally. Older plants bolt and flower sooner than younger ones (Tsukamoto et al. 1971). Removing flower heads promotes development of many lateral shoots.

Plant genotype also influences flowering. The species is polymorphic; the basic $2n$ chromosome count is 18, but types with 36 and 54 chromosomes are known (Mulligan 1965). Diploids are shorter lived and flower the year they germinate (Bocher and Larsen 1957). They also flower abundantly the second year, but most diploids are weak and die the third year. Tetraploid plants do not flower until the second season and then live for many years. Hexaploids flower abundantly the first year and then live indefinitely. Diploid plants are the predominant type in North America and northwest Europe, while tetraploids are more prevalent in southern and northeastern Europe. Mulligan (1965) suggests that polyploids are better adapted to specialized environments. Tetraploids grown in low nutrient levels allocate more biomass to the roots, with less to the flower heads and similar quantities to the leaves as plants in higher nutrient levels. Low light levels cause relatively more biomass to be allocated to achenes compared to higher intensities (Boutin and Morisset 1988). Thus *C. leucanthemum* shows a plastic response with respect to environmental stress.

Each inflorescence has many flowers but not all produce seed. Salisbury (1942) found an average of 14 heads/plant, with an annual production of 2700 seeds/plant. A maximum of 26,000 seeds/plant was reported by Dorph-Petersen (1925). Individual achenes weigh .2 to .5 mg. Parsons (1973) calculated the number of seeds produced/unit area in an infested pasture and measured 10,710 seeds/m². Seed populations in soil can be as high as 6.6 million/ha in the top 18 cm (Milton 1943). One million seeds/ha were present in arable fields and up to 4.2 million in grasslands (Champness and Morris 1948). Seeds can live 20 yr in the soil in Australia and viability is not lost by passing through livestock (Parsons 1973). Seeds buried 20, 55, and 105 cm in the soil survived for 39 yr in England, but most had lost viability after 30 yr. Depth of burial had little effect on seed survival (Toole and Brown 1946).

Fresh seeds germinate readily (85%) in light at 20°C and in alternating temperatures of 20 and 30°C (Povilaitis 1956). All seeds kept moist at 20°C for 28 days germinated when exposed to light. Seeds that have overwintered outdoors germinate in light or dark conditions. Seeds produce some mucilage upon wetting and germinate on the soil surface (Oomes and Elberse 1976). Soil with 15% or greater moisture content is adequate for seed germination. Seeds on the soil surface imbibe 75% of their weight in 4 hr and the final level is 125% of the initial weight. Germination of *C. leucanthemum* was the least affected by soil moisture levels and surface conditions of six grassland plants studied.

Korsmo (1954) gives detailed descriptions and anatomical drawings of *C. leucanthemum*. Stomata are found on both leaf surfaces and in the furrows of the upper stems. The species is a long-day plant and flowers from June to August in the Northern Hemisphere. Seeds are shed in August and September (Howarth and Williams 1968). When seedlings have six leaves, the primary root is replaced by a well-developed system of lateral rhizomes. These are somewhat shallow and give rise to new shoots.

AGRICULTURAL IMPORTANCE

C. leucanthemum is a weed of 13 crops in 40 countries (Figure 23-1) and is frequently reported a principal weed of pastures. It is a serious or principal weed of barley, flax, oats, oilseed rape, sunflowers, and wheat in Canada; lucerne in Hungary; and pastures in Chile, Hawaii, Hungary, Sweden, and the United States.

It is a common weed of cereals in Austria, Canada, and Tunisia; legumes in Tunisia; maize in South Africa; pastures in Australia, Bulgaria, New Zealand, Norway, and the former Yugoslavia; and wastelands in the United States.

It is also an unranked weed of barley in Colombia and Finland; cereals in Poland; lucerne in Argentina and the United States; pastures in Belgium, Canada, Colombia, England, France, and Switzerland; potatoes in Colombia; rye in Ireland; and wheat in Argentina, Chile, Colombia, Finland, Portugal, and the United States.

C. leucanthemum is of greatest concern in grasslands, especially as grazing intensity increases. Controlled grazing and fertilization reduce its seriousness. The weed competes with cereals and in Canada oat yield was reduced 16% by uncontrolled *C. leucanthemum* (Anderson 1956).

Seeds were imported to Sweden with timber (Petterson 1940) and into Ireland as a contaminant of perennial and Italian ryegrass and timothy (Johnson and Hensman 1910). Australia has prohibited importing any commodity contaminated with *C. leucanthemum*. It is a noxious weed in several states of the United States. *C. leucanthemum* was introduced into the northwestern United States in the late 1800s. By 1937 it had spread to over half the counties in the region (Forcella 1985). Its dissemination was primarily as a contaminant of forage grass and legume seed.

Plants are not poisonous but impart an off-flavor to milk if consumed. Horses, sheep and goats will consume *C. leucanthemum*, while cows and pigs do not (Howarth and Williams 1968). Plants have only 8.4% protein and are high in fiber (29%) (Pammel 1913). Seeds, however, are rich in both protein (24%) and oil (23%) and are free of starch, alkaloids, and tannin (Earle and Jones 1962). Leaves are sometimes used in salads, and tea made from the whole plant has antispasmodic and diuretic properties and is used to treat whooping cough and asthma (Spencer 1940). Plants can host aster yellows (Anderson 1956) and several nematode species (Bendixen et al. 1979, 1981).

COMMON NAMES

Chrysanthemum leucanthemum

ARGENTINA	Margarita
AUSTRALIA	oxeye daisy
BELGIUM	Margriet
CANADA	Marguerite blanche, oxeye daisy
CHILE	Margarita
COLOMBIA	Margarita
DENMARK	hvid okseodje
ENGLAND	oxeye daisy
FINLAND	paivankakkara
FRANCE	chrysantheme des moissons, grande Marguerita, leuchantheme vulgaire, Marguerite
GERMANY	Gemeine Wucherblume, Orakelblume, Wiesen Wucherblume
HAWAII	oxeye daisy
INDONESIA	Margrit
ITALY	cota-buona, grande Margherita
JAPAN	furansugiku
NETHERLANDS	Margriet
NEW ZEALAND	oxeye daisy
NORWAY	prestekrage
SPAIN	Margarita mayor, Margariton
SWEDEN	prastkrage
UNITED STATES	oxeye daisy

Twenty-Four

Cichorium intybus L.

Asteraceae (Compositae), Aster Family

For CENTURIES, IN MANY summer fields and waysides of the world, the breathtaking beauty of a full stand of *Cichorium intybus* in the morning sun has quickened the spirits of folks who dwell or travel in pastoral communities. The flower petals surely favor us with one of the loveliest of all the blue colors. Each flower opens with the morning sun and closes at noon.

The plant bears the name chicory, or some derivative of it, across the world. The weedy biotypes are tall biennial or perennial herbs with a deep tap root and crown from

FIGURE 24-1   The distribution of *Cichorium intybus* L. across the world where it has been reported as a weed.

FIGURE 24-2 *Cichorium intybus* L.: A. habit; B. terminal portion of inflorescence;
C. flower; D. achenes.

which the shoots arise. It is a troublesome weed in more than 40 countries and sites on agricultural lands and is serious in many of them. It is found in 30 different crops. As a very old companion of man, it has supplied food for humans and livestock, been used for medical purposes, and is perhaps most widely known as a coffee additive that imparts an interesting bitter flavor admired by some.

C. *intybus* is a member of the largest plant family, **Asteraceae**, is most frequently found in the temperate zones and is not well adapted to the tropical rain forests where the competition is so intense.

DESCRIPTION

C. *intybus* (Figure 24-2) is a *biennial* or *perennial* herb with milky juice; *stems* erect, round, ribbed, hollow, 30 to 150 cm tall; branches stiff, spreading, usually rough-hairy; *taproot* fleshy, long, often contorted, with milky sap; *leaves* alternate, sessile, clasping, hairy, basal, and lower leaves irregularly deeply cut, sometimes resembling the dandelion *Taraxacum*, 8 to 12 or up to 40 cm long, 2 to 12 cm wide, upper stem leaves smaller, entire to dentate, oblong to lanceolate, may be auriculate, 3 to 7 cm long, gradually becoming reduced and bract-like on the upper parts of the stem; *flower* heads stalkless or at tips of short branches, distributed along the rigid, nearly glabrous, almost leafless stems and branches, some terminal, 1 to 3 in a cluster or solitary, several flowered; *flowers* perfect, bright blue and very showy, corolla spatulate, oblong, all ligulate, thinly long hairy on the back, 1.5 to 2 cm long; *involucral bracts* in 2 rows, the inner 8 to 10 in number, the outer 5 and only one-half as long, sometimes spiny or with gland-tipped hairs, and spreading, receptacle chaffy; *achenes* roughly peg-shaped, irregularly 3 to 5 angled or ribbed, beakless, widest at truncate apex and tapering to truncate base, apex tipped with *pappus* of short, minute scales, bristle-like, seed oval to 3- to 5-sided in cross-section, in lateral view some much curved, color gray, straw, or light or dark brown, with black or brown mottling on mature seeds, 2 to 3 mm long and 1 to 1.5 mm wide, *flower* heads in England normally produce 10 to 15 fruits, seed weight about 1.3 mg, cultivated races with larger seeds. Plants may have straggly appearance because of the leafless upper stems with dried fruits.

According to Salisbury (1964), the escapes from cultivated forms that are used for culinary purposes can be distinguished because the leaves are toothed, not lobed, and are devoid of coarse hairs. Canadian records show a type with purple flowers and India claims a yellow flower.

DISTRIBUTION AND HABITAT

C. *intybus* behaves as a weed in agriculture with greatest frequency in the two temperate zones (Figure 24-1). It is most frequent in western Asia, Australia, Europe, and North America with the exception of Mexico. It is less frequent along the equator, or in the Pacific Islands, or in Africa, with only a few scattered reports in north and south. There are no reports from Central America. The general choice of climate, soil, and environment resembles that for sugar beet culture, yet its tolerances are sufficiently broad that it is found in the extreme north of the former Soviet Union (Dorogostayskaya 1972), as well as in hot, arid and semi-arid regions of Arabia, North Africa and around the Mediterranean. In Great Britain, Canada, and the United States the weed favors high lime soils, but it is found

on very many soil types across the world. In the southeastern United States it is a weed of organic (peat) soils.

It is found in many types of pasture, nurseries, industrial sites, waste places and is in many arable crops. Hamel and Dansereau (1949) in Quebec, Canada, studied the distribution of 26 common weeds in six habitats: hoed or cultivated areas, cereal fields, young prairie, old prairie, pastures, and abandoned land. Chicory was confined to cereals and young and old prairie.

The weed is found over all of Europe, but it is troublesome only in Portugal and Spain. In Canada the weed is abundant in the east and is often found in southern British Columbia. There are very few records of the weed in the area from the Great Lakes to the border of British Columbia and it is similarly sparse in this border area of the United States. It is not a weed in the northern settlements of Canada or on the acid soils of eastern Quebec.

PROPAGATION

The primary means of reproduction of this species is by seed, but fragments of roots may contribute new shoots. The normal behavior of the plant is the formation of a basal rosette of leaves from a crown in the first year, with a flowering stalk, early or late, in the next season. In a typical season in North America, for example, the plant flowers from July to frost, with first seeds ripe in early August. Flowers, usually 1 or 2 per cluster, open from morning until noon and are shrivelled within 24 hr. The long-distance spread of the species is enhanced by the abundant seed supply and its ability to colonize very difficult, disturbed sites.

Pawlowski et al. (1967–68) in Poland found the average seed production per plant was 6800, with a maximum of 68,000. Korsmo (1930) in Norway found an average of 6500 seeds/plant. Ewart (1908) in Australia was able to germinate seeds known to be 8 yr old. Bruns (1965) tested the longevity of weed seeds in fresh water storage in the western United States and found that many chicory seeds deteriorated within 3 mo but that a few were firm at 54 mo; a small number still germinated at 4 yr.

Maguire and Overland (1959) tested the conditions for germination of chicory seed over a period of 4 yr, always within 1 yr of harvest. In a regime of alternating light and darkness and at alternating temperatures of 20 to 30°C, in alternating light and dark at 15°C, and in full darkness at alternating temperatures of 20 to 30°C, germination was 70 and 50%, respectively. Cross (1931) obtained better germination in the light with alternating temperatures of 20 to 30°C, than at a constant 20°C. Mitchell (1926) found no light requirement in this seed.

Flowering in chicory is normally spread over a long period and this is true in India, but the capitula of some strains of the weed mature in a very short time. Adlakha and Chibber (1963), in a careful examination of seed types, found different forms and strains of chicory from India and France to vary greatly in color, morphology, and germination. The best germination was from heavier, darker seed, which may suggest a particular physiological stage of maturity at the time of harvest. Seed that was less mature was yellow and gave poorer germination.

The historic use of certain types of this species as a food crop in several parts of the world has resulted in considerable research on the physiology of the plant grown for that purpose. Eenink (1981) studied several self-incompatible and self-compatible clones in controlled environment greenhouses at constant temperatures of 10, 14, 17, 20, 23, and 26°C. From experimental studies such as this, we have been provided pieces of information which may have general application, or nearly so, for other types in the species. Eenink found a low germination percentage after self-pollination. The optimum germination temperature was 17 to 20°C. No seeds were found at 10°C. Seed produced in self-compatible clones was viable at higher temperatures. Working with several varieties of cultivated chicory in Belgium, Valette (1978) found that the highest rate and most uniform seed germination occurred between 20 to 25°C. Both pollen germination and seed production decreased as the plant aged and reached the end of its flowering period. Eenink (1981) found that seed production decreased in some clones at temperatures of 26°C.

Marston and Heydecker (1966) and Rutherford and Thoday (1976) have devised methods of propagation from clonal root material for research purposes.

PHYSIOLOGY AND MORPHOLOGY

The literature on the culture, morphology, and physiology of the forms of chicory produced for leaves and other culinary uses is very large, but the types that are weedy, and those with roots ground to be processed for coffee flavoring, seem more closely related in habit. These have received less attention. In India, types that are field cultivated for root harvest and processing can produce 23,000 kg/ha in about 190 days. Up to the normal time of harvest, the root length and girth, dry matter content, and leaf area increased rapidly. Leaves remained functional to this time, but beyond this period they became mature and dry. The plants began to bolt (to produce flowering shoots), the dry matter content decreased, and the roots decreased in commercial quality as they became pithy, fibrous, and hollow (Chaurasia et al. 1972). In northern India, Sirohi, and Suryanarayana (1970) sowed seed on October 1, 10, 20, and 30 and found that the dry matter content of roots was significantly higher with early sowing. Root size was not significantly different in these treatments.

Harada (1966) and Margara (1974) studied flower bud formation *in vitro* with chicory tissue explants. Harada, using stem tissues, found that the initiation of flower buds depends on long-day conditions. The explants were most responsive in the second week of culture and by the third and fourth weeks all of those in long-days were in flower. The total number of flowers was fewer in short-days, but 70% of the explants showed a tendency toward flowering activity. If held in darkness for 2 wk, the tissues lost all ability to flower. Badila et al. (1985) also found chicory to be a long-day plant and reported that red light (660 nm) promoted flowering, and far red light (730 nm) and a combination of red and far red light had no effect on the plant.

Working with types of the species that are grown for leaf harvest, Doorenbos and Riemans (1959) in the Netherlands found that seed vernalization greatly reduced the number of leaves formed and eventually led to decreases in total plant weight. Kohut and Krupa (1977) exposed 11 species of plants to 157 to 294 micrograms of ozone/m^3 for 4 hr at 21°C and 70% relative humidity. In general the plants were quite resistant, but *Cichorium intybus* was one of the most sensitive. Nickell (1960) compiled a list of thousands of plants from which acid and alcohol extractable substances have been prepared and tested for their antimicrobial action. *C. intybus* was found to have activity against gram-positive bacteria, fungi and yeasts.

Knobloch (1954, 1955) and Nikolaeva (1981) studied the developmental anatomy of the roots and stems of chicory. Lecrenier et al. (1955) reported on the general morphology of the species during its development. Bogomolova (1959, 1960) described the embryological stages of this plant. Sharma and Singh (1972) and Sharma and Srivastava (1973) recorded the anatomy of root galls that appear on *C. intybus*.

AGRICULTURAL IMPORTANCE

C. intybus is a serious weed of cereals and horticulture crops in Italy; lucerne in Argentina, Hungary, and Pakistan; pastures in Hungary and Pakistan; sugarcane in the Punjab area of India; vineyards in the former Soviet Union; and wheat in the Madhya Pradesh area of central India. It is especially troublesome in winter crops in Pakistan, where it is also said that "no field of clover is without it." There is legislation proclaiming it a noxious weed in that country.

It is a principal weed in cotton in Iraq, legumes in Egypt, lucerne in India, and pastures in the United States.

It is a common weed of arable fields, especially of wheat in the former Yugoslavia; barley in Canada; beans in Greece; cereals in Canada; maize and mustards in northern India; orchards in Spain and Uruguay; peas in Greece; pastures in Bulgaria; tobacco in India; vineyards of several western Mediterranean countries; and wheat in Canada and the United States.

It is reported as a weed of unspecified importance in the irrigation systems of Australia, Canada, Greece, and India; barley in Greece and Iran; beans in Chile; cassava in Indonesia; cereals in Chile, Jordan, Poland, and Turkey; clover in India and Iran; maize in Indonesia and the United States; forage crops in the United States; legumes in Egypt, Greece, and India; lucerne in the United States; oats in Greece; orchards in the former Soviet Union; pastures in Australia, Canada, New Zealand, and South Africa; peas in India; rape in Chile and India; sugar beets in Iran and Spain; sunflowers in Spain; tobacco in the former Soviet Union; upland rice in Indonesia; and wheat in Chile, Greece, Iran, Italy, Portugal, and the former Yugoslavia.

C. intybus is a very common weed of the agriculture in Jordan. Clark and Fletcher (1909) reported in Canada in an earlier time that the seeds of this weed often moved about with commercial supplies of clover and grass seed. Johnson and Hensman (1910), in a summary of 10 years of inspection of the purity of agricultural seed supplies, found that chicory was being introduced into Ireland with timothy seed. Anderson (1956) estimated that the average yearly loss of oats in Canada during the period 1936 to 1939 because of this weed was 40% of the crop. In northern India it was also found that *C. intybus* was introduced into new lucerne fields by contaminants in the seed supply. Efforts to control the weed included floating some of the seeds away by use of a salt brine, deep plowing to bury seeds shed onto the soil surface, and rotation of crops. Mahto et al. (1970) found that basal or top dressing with 65 kg/ha of P_2O_5 caused more vigorous growth of the crop and brought about a significant reduction of chicory stands.

C. intybus has been used as fodder for cattle and sheep. In Poland and Germany it was formerly grown with clover and timothy hay as forage for animals. In the former Yugoslavia it is considered excellent for pig fodder. The roots of this plant are sometimes dug and stored for cattle food.

It is known, however, that large amounts of this weed ingested by dairy cattle can easily cause off-flavors in milk. Also, Wachnik (1962) in Poland found symptoms of poisoning in pigs 1 wk after feeding them leaves of the plant. Pathological symptoms were loss of appetite, diarrhea, and convulsions. Postmortem examination showed haemorrhagic inflammation of mucous membranes of the alimentary tract and liver degeneration.

At present, several commercial compounds are extracted from the roots of *C. intybus* for use in food preparation. They are used to flavor or to intensify the flavors of many foods we eat. The dried roots can be stored for long periods. A pyrone, maltol, for example, has been approved as a taste-modifying sugar substitute that intensifies the flavor of sugar 30 to 300 times. Taraxacine (a chemical also found in the dandelion, *Taraxacum*), together with the natural sugars carmelized during the roasting process, provides the bitter-sweet taste that is used in coffee-blending. Studies on the phytochemical and pharmaceutical uses of the plant were reported by Balbaa (1973). Steiner (1983) and Lewis (1976) prepared a lively review of the historical medical and culinary uses of the plant from ancient Greece through the Middle Ages.

COMMON NAMES

Cichorium intybus

ARGENTINA	achicoria, radicheta
AUSTRALIA	chicory
BELGIUM	cichorei
CANADA	blue daisy, blue sailors, chicoree sauvage, chicory, coffee weed, wild succory
CHILE	achicoria
DENMARK	cikorie
ENGLAND	chicory
FINLAND	sikuri
FRANCE	chicoree, chicoree sauvage, chicoree amere
GERMANY	Cichorienwegwarte, Cichorienwurzel, Gemeine Wegwarte, Zichorie
GREECE	chicory
INDIA	kasni
IRAQ	chicory, coffee-weed, hindiba, succory
ITALY	cicoria, cicoria selvatica, radicchio
JAPAN	kiku-nigana
LEBANON	chicory, coffee-weed, handab, handabah, shikuriyyah, succory
MOROCCO	chicoree amere
NETHERLANDS	wilde cichorei
NEW ZEALAND	chicory
NORWAY	sikori
PERU	achicoria

POLAND	cykoria podroznik, succory
PORTUGAL	almeirao, chicoria do cafe, labresto, lapsaua
SOUTH AFRICA	chicory, sigorei
SPAIN	achicoria amarga, achicoria silvestre, chicoria, masteguera borda
SWEDEN	vagvarda
TURKEY	yabani hindiba
UNITED STATES	bachelors buttons, blue daisy, blue dandelion, blue sailors, chicory, coffee-weed, succory
URUGUAY	achicoria silvestre
VENEZUELA	achicoria
YUGOSLAVIA	zenetrga

Twenty-Five

Cirsium vulgare (Savi) Tenore

Asteraceae (Compositae), Aster Family

C IRSIUM VULGARE is a robust, spiny, unpalatable thistle that is the scourge of pastures and rangelands in 20 countries. It is a cool-season temperate weed that prefers fertile soils. It is the only member of the *Cirsium* genus with a spiny-winged stem. The weed is in more than 50 countries and troublesome in 20 crops.

FIGURE 25-1   The distribution of *Cirsium vulgare* (Savi) Tenore across the world where it has been reported as a weed.

FIGURE 25-2 *Cichorium vulgare* L.: A. habit; B. terminal portion of inflorescence; C. flower; D. achenes.

DESCRIPTION

C. vulgare (Figure 25-2) is a prickly *annual* or *biennial* herb forming a rosette up to 65 cm diameter its first season; *taproot* stout, fleshy, deeply penetrating, branched; *rosette leaves* oblanceolate to elliptical, coarsely toothed in the first year, stalked, ca 30 cm long, white or gray woolly below; forming a large, flat rosette in the first year; rigid *stems* form in second year, erect, spiny-winged, 1 to 2 m tall, may be branched above, some much branched and spreading from base; *stem leaves* alternate, lanceolate, usually under 30 cm, pinnatifid, green above, frequently with stiff hairs and/or small spines, thinly white woolly beneath, deeply lobed, lobes ending in stiff, robust, sharp, yellow spines with sharp border prickles between them; wavy, crinkled, attached to stem by decurrent leaf base; *inflorescence* involucrate, flower head resembling a single flower, 2.5 to 5 cm diameter at maturity, compact, solitary, or in groups of 2 or 3 at ends of branches, each head or capitulum a composite of numerous, closely packed, very small, purple or reddish-purple tubular florets; *involucre* egg shaped, length 2.5 to 4 cm with numerous spine-tipped bracts; *receptacle* flat, sometimes hairy-bristly; *florets* tubular, bisexual, very shortly stalked; *petals* 5, *stamens* 5, inserted on the petals with the *anthers* united laterally; *fruit* an *achene* elongate to 4 mm, width 1.6 mm, somewhat oblique, oval in cross section, broadest above middle, narrowing toward broadly truncate base and tapering toward apex to a prominent collar; shiny, almost smooth, yellow or yellowish brown with grayish-black stripes; *pappus* plumose of soft white branched hairs, 2 to 5 times longer than achene, deciduous, bristles united at base and fall together as achene matures.

The species can be distinguished by the winged stem with long pointed spines and the spiny leaf surface. It is the only *Cirsium* with a spiny-winged stem.

DISTRIBUTION AND HABITAT

The distribution of *C. vulgare* (Figure 25-1) as a weed is striking—it is almost entirely confined to the north and south temperate zones. In Australia it is in all states and is one of the most widespread thistles in that country, and so it is in New Zealand. It is particularly troublesome in pastures. It is the most common and widespread thistle in western North America, where it is a problem in rangeland, pasture and cereal areas. In Canada it is a burden to farmers all across the south, being worst in British Columbia, Ontario, and Quebec (Howell 1959).

Its habitat is the disturbed area of eroded gullies, ditches, dikes, fence rows, roadsides and wastelands, while in agriculture it is most at home in fertile forage lands and cereals.

McCarty et al. (1984) in the central United States determined that seeds of *C. vulgare* travel with commercial seed supplies of legumes and cereals. In New Zealand, Johnston (1962) reported that these weed seeds, in small quantities, are often contaminants in ryegrass and other pasture seed, but the seeds of *C. vulgare* are regarded as a more serious problem for pastures than some impurities found in greater quantities.

The seed of this thistle is carried by wind and water, transport vehicles and farm machines, in mud on the fur and feathers of animals, in the manure of animals that are on hoof, but the movement with baled or loose hay and forage may be the most common way that large quantities of seeds are carried long distances. The presence of a seed pappus in this species, as in many others, brings many assertions that wind is a primary dispersal agent, but for *C. vulgare* this is of limited help because the pappus usually separates easily and early as the seed matures. There is little doubt that air currents may sweep occasional seeds, with pappus firmly attached, to higher altitudes, perhaps to a distance of several kilometers.

Regarding the speed of migration or dispersal of this species, Forcella and Harvey (1988) studied patterns of migration for 85 weeds (including *C. vulgare*) as they entered the northwestern United States during the past 100 years. *C. vulgare* and many others entered through the then major shipping center at Portland, Oregon in the late 19th century. *C. vulgare* moved east to Montana, then south to Idaho after three decades, and finally migrated east and west from these points of introduction.

PROPAGATION

On average, about 100 seeds per head are produced by *C. vulgare*, although in favorable circumstances there may be 350. One sturdy plant may bear 5000 seeds and exceptional plants have produced 50,000 (Salisbury 1964, Klinkhamer et al. 1988, Michaux 1989). Reports of dormancy vary from immediate germination on harvest to a small amount of seed persisting in the soil for 5 yr. Williams (1966) found populations in England and north Germany that had some dormancy at harvest, yet with 25 and 40% immediate germination, respectively.

The species has the advantage of autumn germination that in many habitats will be followed by rains. Germination seems synchronous with rainfall and movement to the surface by any means. It is possible that the characteristics of a biotype and the conditions of the parent during seed formation may influence the dormant condition of seeds produced. Michael (1968b) reported that in Australia dormancy is important for all major thistles and that it is more pronounced in *C. vulgare* and *Carthamus lanatus* than in most others.

Seven thistles, including *C. vulgare*, were germinated over a wide range of conditions in Australia by Groves and Kaye (1989). *C. vulgare* responded over a wide temperature range from 15/30 to 40/30°C and was one of the least sensitive to moisture stress during the process. Lincoln (1981) found that one-year-old seed germinated very well, with 91% germination at 5/25°C. Germination was reduced at a constant temperature of 15°C. One year after harvest, Maguire and Overland (1959) obtained 40% germination in darkness at 20°C, 80% in the dark at an alternating temperature of 20/30°C, and 72% in alternating light and dark at the same temperatures.

The English and north German partially-dormant seeds referred to just above (Williams 1966) gave almost complete germination when treated with thiourea but did not respond to KNO_3. The English seed sample gave 40% germination with a cold treatment or scarification, but the German seeds did not respond to these treatments.

Fenner (1983) studied the relationships between achene weight, embryo weight and maximum seedling weight in 24 composites, including *C. vulgare*. The latter ranked 3rd, 6th, and 5th in the above characteristics, respectively. In general, the fraction of the seed weight contributed by the seed coat varied from 15 to 60% in the species of this family. Large seeds have relatively small embryos and a large coat (the opposite being true for small seeds), and the relative growth weights of seedlings in the first week was inversely proportional to embryo weight. The root weight ratio of seedlings (dry weight of root/dry weight of whole plant) was inversely proportional to the embryo weight. Fenner postulated that the relatively large seed coats of the big seeds are a defense against predators.

Orchard (1956) in South Australia found seeds of *C. vulgare* to have a very short life in the soil but lasted for 8 yr in dry storage. Van Leeuwen and van Breeman (1980) found that *C. vulgare* seed buried in the soil in the Netherlands had 50% viability after 1 yr. Michael (1968b) reported that all nine major thistles of Australia, including *C. vulgare*, may survive for reasonably long periods in field soil. In England, in field-sown experiments planted in autumn, September to October, 90% of all seed germinated within a year after sowing. Very few of the seeds germinated after the 2nd year, and at 5 years just a few dormant achenes remained (Roberts and Chancellor 1979).

Comes et al. (1978) stored *C. vulgare* and other seeds in fresh water for 60 mo. The *C. vulgare* seeds deteriorated within 3 mo, although when placed in dry storage for the full term 5% were still viable.

C. vulgare favors disturbed sites, and fewer plants are thus seen in undisturbed pasture. Van Leeuwen (1981a) found that the soil microflora was different in those contrasting circumstances and that seedling mortality was higher in the undisturbed sites. He believes this is due to germination caused by microbial activity (fruit coat breakdown and then exudation of growth substances) under conditions that do not favor the survival of the seed. This is in contrast to the results of Klinkhamer and De Jong (1988), who found no difference in seedling mortality between disturbed and undisturbed sites.

In a study of seed predation of *C. vulgare* in the Netherlands, Klinkhamer et al. (1988) noticed that seed production in the flower heads of plants that had no damage to other parts of the plant seemed to vary greatly in a sand dune area. There was also a variance in the plant damage caused by herbivores (rabbits, birds, insects) and together these caused seed losses of 80 and 20% in 1982 and 1984, respectively. Mean seed loss by predation within the flower heads was 3 to 17% for these years. Seed dispersal within 1 m of the mother plant was 50% and only 11% of the total seeds were moved outside this area. After dispersal, small animals consumed 60% of the seed. After 1 yr only 1% of the seed was still viable (see also van Leeuwen 1983). Michaux (1989) in New Zealand found the majority of the achenes remained within a diameter 1.5 times the height of the plant.

Matthews (1963) reported an anatomical study of the seed coat of *C. vulgare* to include all layers, cell characteristics and dimensions of the various tissues.

PHYSIOLOGY AND ECOLOGY

A brief phenology of the annual or biennial *C. vulgare* finds seed germination in late summer–early fall, with seedlings becoming hairy and with many spines at an early age. In New Zealand young seedlings tolerate −2°C (Michaux 1989). The rosette that develops may grow slowly in winter (sometimes reaching a diameter of 65 cm) or may cease growth under severe cold. Under stress from dryness or cold the rosette may be killed in the first season and form again during the late winter or spring. Before spring, and with some winter growth if temperatures permit, an extensive root system develops with some fleshy storage roots. In the second year a flowering stem develops. Flowers and fruits are produced in late spring and summer, then the plant dies.

During a 15-year period, McCarty (1986), in the central United States, studied the phenology of *C. vulgare* plants as they completed the full cycle of growth in the second of their biennial years, with data gathered on the average dates of first occurrences of events (not just those of exceptional individuals). Emergence was on March 20; stem elongation on May 25; first flower bud on July 10; first bloom on August 5; and firm seeds on August 30.

In the Netherlands, Klinkhamer and De Jong (1988) found no persistent reserve of seed in the soil of their area, with the result that disturbance of the soil and vegetation alone, as in stock trampling or small animal burrowing, did little to increase the number of seeds established naturally. If seeds were sown in such areas, small soil disturbances greatly increased the number of established seedlings. There was no difference in seedling mortality between disturbed and undisturbed pastures. This is in contrast to the results of van Leeuwen (1981a) and van Leeuwen and van Breeman (1980) discussed earlier.

C. vulgare is reported as a weed of pastures in 19 countries, far more than in any other crop, and it is more often found in grazed than in ungrazed pastures. Forcella and Wood (1986a) investigated the reasons for the preference of this thistle for pasture land and the nature and sensitivity of its life stages in such locations. The transitional stages of the life cycle are seed to seedling, thence to rosette, and finally to the flowering and fruiting mature adult. Fifteen percent of all seeds produced grew into seedlings and about one-half of all surviving rosettes grew into mature plants. However, the transition from seedling to rosette proved to be the most sensitive period in the cycle, with survival in grazed and ungrazed pastures being only 1 and 0.2%, respectively.

In the Netherlands, Klinkhamer et al. (1987) found natural populations of *C. vulgare* in which 45% of the rosettes 1 yr of age or older were showing delay of the reproductive phase. The tendency to flower increased with size, the amount of growth in a period prior to bolting, and age. Contrary to the general belief that only large biennial plants are vernalized in winter, 80% of the smallest rosettes from a February field collection flowered when placed under optimal growing conditions. The authors suggest that there is no size requirement for vernalization of *C. vulgare*, but that to be able to produce a flowering stalk the plant must attain a minimum size.

In eastern Australia, Forcella and Wood (1986b) observed the flowering patterns of seven thistles, including *C. vulgare*, and in two seasons found a definite sequential order of appearance that was consistent but differed by species. For example, an early flowering species, *Carduus pycnocephalus*, had a brief flowering period, showed a 2-month interval of innate dormancy and germinated poorly at high temperatures. By contrast, *C. vulgare* had a long flowering period, produced some seeds that germinated immediately after maturation and did so over a wide range of temperatures. The authors suggest that early flowering species profit from dormancy by not germinating as the long dry summer approaches. In *C. vulgare*, a dormant period was not a necessity because seeds mature at about the same time the autumn rains begin.

Van Leeuwen (1981b) found that self-pollination in *C. vulgare* and *C. palustre* reduced the quantity of achenes produced but that those formed were heavier than those produced during cross-pollination. With larger achenes the natural establishment of plants is comparatively higher and this helps to explain the beginning of new populations by isolated individuals (perhaps deposited by wind dispersal). Later, as there is increasing population density with more cross-pollination and thereby the development of smaller, lighter achenes, isolated populations of this species may begin to show decline on some sites.

Several researchers in Australia have pointed out that the recent worsening of the *C. vulgare* problem in pastures is coincident with the increase in soil fertility levels as a result of the introduction of subterranean clover and the application of superphosphate. In the words of Wheatley (1971), ". . . this thistle waits to invade millions of acres of valuable pasture as they become favorable."

In the Netherlands, a comparative study was made of growth and nutrient accumulation in two biennials with different patterns of seasonal development: *C. vulgare* and *Cynoglossum officinale* (in the Borage family). Although the two plants had similar dry weights (about 50 g/plant) at the end of the second season, *Cynoglossum* with early germination attained a greater dry weight in the first season, lost much of its nutrient pool from dieback of leaves in winter, then accumulated necessary N, P, and K early in the second season. *C. vulgare*, with a later start, had a dry weight of only 2 to 6% in September of the first year but continued to grow and accumulate nutrients into late autumn. It then acquired the necessary N in early spring and continued to take up P, K, and Ca throughout its remaining lifetime. The reproduction effort for the two species (dry weight of seeds/total plant weight) was 8 to 10% for *C. vulgare* but 30% for *Cynoglossum* (De Jong et al. 1987).

Although *C. vulgare* is widespread in pastures and rangelands, its nutritive value is of no importance for stock animals.

In the laboratory, at 0.4 gm of litter per gm of soil, the litter formed by flowering plants of *C. vulgare* inhibited the growth of seedlings of that plant. N alone and a mixture of nutrients lessened the inhibition but did not remove it—indicating autotoxicity (allelopathy). In field experiments, the litter did not inhibit seedling growth (De Jong and Klinkhamer 1985).

In Britain, on a lowland calcareous grassland, a census was taken of the size and number of rosettes of *C. vulgare* following controlled winter, spring, and summer grazing treatments. Spring grazing significantly increased the thistle rosette numbers and there were always fewer rosettes of 25 to 30 cm size under heavy grazing. Thistle seed planting experiments revealed that more seedlings emerged from large gaps (bare areas) 10 to 20 cm in diameter in the sward than from 5 cm gaps or closed areas. The authors concluded that grazing management of this weed will be most effective if aimed at reducing suitable sites for establishment in spring. Success will depend on suitable growing conditions for the sward. Sudden thistle outbreaks may be expected if the sward is allowed to deteriorate (Silvertown and Smith 1989).

During complete seasons, George et al. (1970) studied the invasion of *C. vulgare* into monospecific grass stands of *Dactylis glomerata*, *Festuca arundinacea*, *Lolium perenne*, and *Phalaris tuberosa* when grazed with 19 or 38 sheep/ha. Invasion was related to vegetation cover with least invasion in *Phalaris* and most in *Dactylis*. On *Festuca* and *Phalaris* pastures they examined the effect of sheep breeds, stocking rates and lambing times on the invasion of the swards. There was significantly more thistle in *Festuca* than *Phalaris* and significantly more in pastures grazed by Merino sheep than Dorset Horn sheep. In pastures grazed by Merinos that lambed in winter there were twice as many thistles as for any other lambing season.

AGRICULTURAL IMPORTANCE

C. vulgare is a serious weed of cereals in Italy, lucerne in Argentina, ornamentals and forest nurseries in the United States, pastures in Australia and Hungary, and wheat in Uruguay. It is a principal weed of barley, maize, oats, sorghum, and wheat in Australia; cereals and orchards in Spain; pastures and rangelands in New Zealand, Scotland, Tasmania, and the United States; and rice rotation schemes in the Murrumbidgee irrigation area of southeastern Australia.

It is a common weed of barley, oats, wheat, and other cereals in Austria; citrus in South Africa; orchards in South Africa and Switzerland; pastures in South Africa, Switzerland, and Uruguay; several winter season crops in Uruguay; and vineyards in South Africa and Spain.

It is also a weed of undetermined rank of cereals in Finland, Greece, South Africa, Tasmania, and Turkey; citrus in the United States; cotton in Greece; linseed in Argentina; maize in Guatemala; orchards in Turkey; pastures in Argentina, Belgium, Canada, Chile, England, Norway, Sweden, and the islands of Hawaii and New Caledonia; potatoes in Argentina; rape in England; vegetables in Tasmania; wheat in Argentina and Guatemala; and vineyards in the former Soviet Union.

A 3-yr study of stock-rearing farms in Scotland, to measure the productive quality of the grasslands, showed that *C. vulgare* and *C. arvense* were the most frequently occurring broadleaf weeds and that 20% of all fields had heavy weed problems (Edinburgh School of Agriculture 1978). In a 2-yr study in New Zealand, Hartley (1983) found a significant negative correlation between *C. vulgare* densities in pastures and sheep live weight gain.

In California, Jordan (1983) found that in citrus trees the trunk and canopy growth, leaf N level, and fruit yield and quality were decreased by competition from weeds, including *C. vulgare*. Soil moisture levels were lower in the weedy plantations.

C. vulgare is on the prohibited noxious weed lists of Australia, Belgium, Ireland, the United Kingdom and Uruguay. In some areas of Australia, *C. vulgare* is listed among species with "vegetable fault," meaning that it contaminates wool with spiny vegetable material that increases the expense of carding and combing operations.

In the past, the treated fleshy roots of *C. vulgare* were prized as bait during times of rabbit pestilence on grazing lands in Australia. They had the advantage of not being attractive to stock animals. They were available in packs of 250, 500, and 1000 baits already mixed with strychnine poison (Parsons 1973).

The 200-year-old agricultural notes of William Pitt in the United Kingdom listed many weeds, including *C. vulgare*, that are still major problems in our fields today (Salisbury 1964).

Harris and Wilkinson (1981), in Canada, detailed the releases and recoveries of the highly host-specific tripetid *Urophora stylata* and its level of control of *C. vulgare*. Redfern and Cameron (1985), with material from Germany and the United Kingdom, described the infestation of the flower heads, and the mortality of the above organism as influenced by the size of the flower head and the time of its development. They found no clear relationship for level of infestation or mortality of predator with plant size or density.

In sum, the dense thistle patches and large rosettes not only reduce the carrying capacity of a field, but the blanketing effect of the leaves makes it more difficult to get closed, dense stands of *Phalaris*, lucerne and other sward plants. In times of drought stress, there is often reduced persistence of even the best pasture species and *C. vulgare* waits in readiness to rapidly invade these areas as the rains come—usually in autumn. If the pasture is fertile, the thistle becomes even more aggressive. The maintenance of a closed perennial pasture, wherever possible, is one of the best tools for preventing the establishment of *C. vulgare*.

COMMON NAMES

Cirsium vulgare

ARGENTINA	cardo negro
AUSTRALIA	black thistle, bull thistle, scotch thistle, spear thistle
CANADA	bull thistle, chardon vulgaire
CHILE	cardo, negro

DENMARK	horsetidsel
ENGLAND	bull thistle, spear thistle
FINLAND	piikkiohdakke
FRANCE	chardon lanceole
GERMANY	Gemeine Kratzdistel
HAWAII	bull thistle, spear thistle
ITALY	cardo asinino
JAPAN	amerika-oni-azami
NETHERLANDS	speerdistel
NEW ZEALAND	scotch thistle
NORWAY	vegtistel
SOUTH AFRICA	scotch thistle, skotse dissel
SPAIN	cardo lanceolado
SWEDEN	vagtistel
TASMANIA	spear thistle
UNITED STATES	bull thistle
URUGUAY	cardo negro

The recent publication of Forcella, F., and Randall, J., 1994, Biology of Bull Thistle *Cirsium vulgare* (Savi) Tenore, *Reviews of Weed Science* 6:29–50 provides important information for researchers interested in *Cirsium*.

Twenty-Six

Cleome gynandra L.

Capparidaceae, Caper Family

CLEOME GYNANDRA is widely distributed in its native continent of Africa and in much of Asia. It occurs occasionally in Latin America and Australia. This tropical and subtropical species is often found in cultivated or fallowed fields, along roadsides, in fence rows, and along irrigation canals and ditches. The caper family is closely related to the mustard family; however, most species are in tropical and subtropical areas. The word *Cleome* is an old Greek name for the plant and *gynandra* is derived from the gynophore, a structure supporting the ovary.

FIGURE 26-1 The distribution of *Cleome gynandra* L. across the world where it has been reported as a weed.

FIGURE 26-2   *Cleome gynandra* L.: 1. root system; 2. flowering branch; 3. ovary, cross section; 4. seed, two views; 5. flower; 6. fruit.

DESCRIPTION

C. gynandra (Figure 26-2) is an *annual* herb with a *taproot; stems* erect, often widely branched, 50 to 100 cm high, glandular-hairy throughout; *stem leaves* alternate, palmately compound with 5 leaflets; *petiole* 2 to 10 cm long; *flower stalk leaves* trifoliate with nearly sessile leaflets; *leaflets* obovate or oblong-obovate, 2 to 7.5 cm long, 1 to 3.5 cm wide with 5 to 8 pairs of nerves; entire or slightly serrulate, fringed with hairs, covered with sticky gland-tipped hairs, fetid; *inflorescence* a terminal raceme borne on 1.4- to 2.5-cm pedicel; *flowers* perfect, with 4 green, lanceolate *sepals* 2.5 to 5 mm long, 0.5 to 2.5 mm wide; *petals* 4, claw-like, white or tinged with purple, 7 to 15 mm long, 1.5 to 4 mm wide; *stamens* 6, borne on an androgynophore; *filaments* purple, 8 to 22 mm long with orange-yellow *anthers; ovary* stalked on *gynophore, fruit* a dry dehiscent *capsule,* borne on long pedicel; cylindrical, 2-valved, 5 mm in diameter, 6 to 10 cm long, containing up to 130 seeds; *seeds* depressed-globular, 1 to 1.5 mm in diameter, black-brown with many concentric ribs and numerous irregular and distinct cross-ribs.

The glandular hairs throughout the plant, the fetid, alternate leaves, and claw-like flowers with four petals are the distinguishing characteristics of *C. gynandra.*

ECOLOGY AND BIOLOGY

C. gynandra adapts to moist soils along rivers and irrigation canals and to semi-arid conditions. It grows from sea level to 2400 m in Africa.

In Colombia, seeds were dormant 4 to 5 mo after maturity, but germination after 6 and 12 mo was 35 and 88%, respectively (Yepes 1978). In India, plants emerge in late July, begin to flower in 15 to 30 days, set fruit in 30 to 50 days and produce mature seed from late September through November (Sen 1981). Yepes (1978) found plant height increased 2.3 cm/day during the fifth and sixth weeks after germination. Plants died at approximately 150 days. Single plants produce over 500 seeds with an average weight of 1.3 mg each (Pancho 1964). Seeds remain viable for long periods.

Leaf length of potted plants in Kenya increased 200 and 300% in 4 and 8 days, respectively, if soil moisture was adequate (Imbamba et al. 1977). Leaves of stressed plants grew half as much in 4 days and no new growth occurred after this time. The highest rate of transpiration (5.2 g $H_2O/dm^2/hr$) occurred with soil moisture of 30 to 39% and photosynthesis peaked (fixing 70 mg $CO_2/dm^2/hr$) at 35% soil moisture. Photosynthesis decreased linearly to 10 mg/dm^2/hr as soil moisture dropped from 35 to 15%. If turgid plants were not watered for 4 days, photosynthesis dropped to 51% and transpiration to 20% of that in non-stressed plants. Stomata and glandular trichomes are found on both leaf surfaces (Puri 1971) and *C. gynandra* is a C_4 species (Imbamba and Tieszen 1977).

Leaves of *C. gynandra* contain seven phenolic acids (Das and Rao 1975). By comparing the phenolic compounds in several **Capparidaceae** and **Brassicaceae** species, they found strong evidence that the former gave rise to the latter family. The chromosome number of *C. gynandra* appears to be variable, with reports of $n = 10$ (Raghavan and Kamble 1979) and $n = 15$, 16, or 17 (Koshy and Mathew 1985).

UTILITY

This species is often used as a leafy vegetable in East Africa. Three *Cleome* species are cultivated in Zambia, but *C. gynandra* is the preferred one and seeds are collected to plant in gardens (Vernon 1983). Plants are an excellent source of vitamins, especially carotene (up to 8900 μg/100 g leaves), and are particularly useful in the dry season when common vegetables are scarce or unavailable (Gomez 1981). In India, bruised leaves are rubbed on affected areas of the body to relieve rheumatism and headaches. The seeds are used to kill internal parasites and are considered antispasmodic (Puri 1971). He also noted that seeds contain 22% oil. In China, seeds are decocted to treat dysentery, malaria and rheumatoid arthritis. Seeds contain cleomin (an unsaturated lactone), tannins and volatile oils, and leaves contain up to 35% protein, 38% carbohydrate, 9% fiber, 2% Ca, and 0.8% P (Duke and Ayensu 1985).

AGRICULTURAL IMPORTANCE

C. gynandra is a weed of 19 crops in over 40 countries (Figure 26-1). It is a principal weed of cotton and pastures in Colombia and maize in Tanzania. It is a common weed of cotton in the Philippines and Sudan; cowpeas, millet, and upland rice in Senegal; maize in the Philippines and Senegal; peanuts and sorghum in Senegal and Sudan; sugarcane in Bangladesh and the Philippines; and vegetables in Thailand.

It is also a weed of unknown rank in edible beans in Tanzania; cacao, cassava, maize, oil palm, rubber, and tea in Indonesia; cereals in Kenya; coffee in East Africa; cotton in Mozambique; legumes in the Philippines; maize in Cambodia, Indonesia, and India; peanuts in Taiwan; rice in Bangladesh, Burma, Cambodia, India, Laos, Malaysia, Thailand, and Vietnam; upland rice in the Philippines, Senegal, Sri Lanka, and Taiwan; soybeans and sweet potatoes in Taiwan; sugarcane in Hawaii, India, and Taiwan; tobacco in the Philippines; tomatoes in Ghana and Puerto Rico; and vegetables in Laos, Saudi Arabia, and Taiwan.

C. gynandra hosts the root-knot nematode that attacks pineapples in Hawaii (Bendixen et al. 1979) and the insect *Crocidolomia binotalis*, a pest of oilseed rape in India (Sen 1981).

COMMON NAMES

Cleome gynandra

AUSTRALIA	spider flower
CHINA	bai hua cai, pinyin
COLOMBIA	platanito
CUBA	volantin
EGYPT	abu qarn, arareng, tamaleekah, tobchangeih
HAWAII	wild spider flower
INDIA	anasoria, bagra, hulhul, naivelai, parhar, surajvarta, vagri, vaminta
INDONESIA	babowan, boboan, enceng-enceng, langsana merah, mamam, mamang

KENYA	akeyo
MADAGASCAR	akendronyaza
MAURITIUS	brede caya, pissat des chiens
PHILIPPINES	apoi-apoian, balabalanoyan, cinco-cinco, hulaya, tantandok
PUERTO RICO	jasmin del rio, volantines de cinco hojas
SOUTH AFRICA	lerotu, lerotho, snotterbelletjie, spider flower, vingerblaatee
SUDAN	tamalaika
THAILAND	phak sian, phak sian khaao, phak som sian
ZAIRE	boanga, isogi, lubanga, mangayamangaya, muhole
ZAMBIA	lubanga, shungwa, suntha
ZIMBABWE	nyeve, spider flower, tsuma, ulude

Twenty-Seven

Conium maculatum L.

Apiaceae (Umbelliferae), Parsley Family

CONIUM MACULATUM is one of the most famous of the approximately 3000 species in the 300 genera of the parsley family. Its poisonous properties have long been recognized and it is believed to have been the plant used to kill Socrates in 399 B.C. The genus name is derived from the Greek word for hemlock and the Latin epitaph describes the spotted stem. The plant is native to Europe, northern Africa and western Asia and was often introduced to new areas as an ornamental garden plant.

FIGURE 27-1   The distribution of *Conium maculatum* L. across the world where it has been reported as a weed.

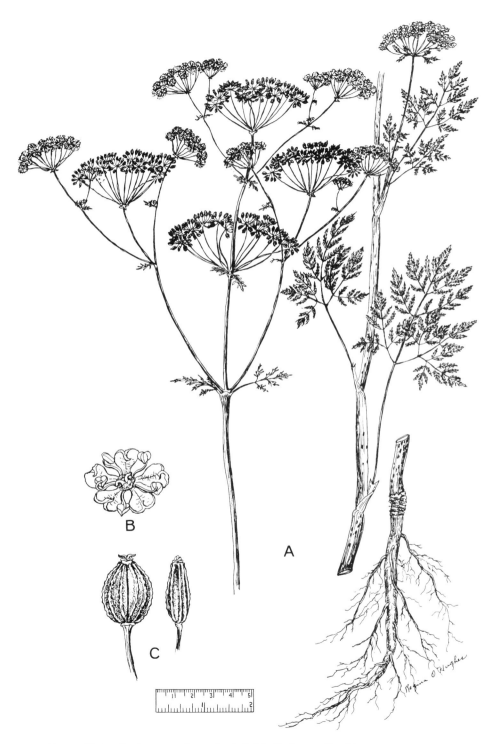

FIGURE 27-2 *Conium maculatum* L.: A. habit; B. flower; C. schizocarps.

DESCRIPTION

C. maculatum (Figure 27-2) is a herbaceous *biennial* plant; *taproot* long, whitish, usually unbranched; *stems* stout, 1 to 2 m tall, branched, smooth, pale green, usually covered with purple spots; hollow except at nodes with fine, shallow, longitudinal ridges; *leaves* borne as a rosette from the crown or alternately on stem; 20 to 40 cm long, 3 to 4 times pinnately compound, segments toothed or deeply cut; *petiole* base tends to sheath the stem; petioles shorter on upper leaves; *inflorescence* in large, open, compound umbels, 4 to 6 cm across, terminal umbel blooming first but soon overtopped by others; *flowers* small in large, loose clusters with a circle of narrow bracts at base; *petals* 5, white, incurved; devoid of sepals; *bracts* of involucre lanceolate, acuminate, inconspicuous; *fruit* a *schizocarp*, oval to circular in outline, composed of two gray or brown *mericarps* (seeds); mericarps narrowly ovate, 1.2 to 2 mm wide, 2 to 3 mm long, slightly extended apex, dorsal side strongly convex with 5 prominent wavy ridges running from top to bottom, inter-rib area granular and light brown.

This species is recognized by the long, whitish taproot, the purple-spotted hollow stem, fern-like leaves, numerous white flowers and the strong "mousey" odor of the plant when crushed.

DISTRIBUTION AND BIOLOGY

C. maculatum inhabits roadsides, stream and river banks, pastures, woodlots, and waste areas and is reported as a weed in North and South America, Europe, western Asia, Australia, and New Zealand (Figure 27-1). It is usually a biennial but can behave as a winter annual or short-lived (monocarpic) perennial. Plants grow best in moist, fertile soils.

Fresh seeds are non-dormant and germinate in both light and darkness (Baskin and Baskin 1988). In England, Roberts (1979) placed freshly harvested seeds in soil in cylinders and monitored the germination monthly for 5 yr. The cylinders were placed out-of-doors and the soil was stirred each spring, summer and fall. Most seeds (26%) germinated within 12 mo of planting, 7.5% germinated the second year, 2.8% the third year and less than 1% germinated each of the following years. Emergence peaked in late winter and early spring, but some seeds also germinated in the summer months. Few viable seeds remained in the soil after 5 yr. However, seed stored dry at room temperature remained viable for 5 yr (Brenchley 1918). A single plant may produce 38,000 seeds (Whittet 1968) and individual seeds weigh 0.5 mg (Korsmo 1935). Seeds usually fall near the parent plant but can be spread by water, rodents and birds (Panter et al. 1988).

In Australia, seeds usually germinate in the fall and plants continue developing through the winter and spring (Parsons 1973). Some plants flower the first spring, but most flower the second year and then die. In the United States, plants flower from June to August. Plants establish readily on disturbed sites and may displace thin forage stands. *C. maculatum* established more quickly when existing perennial grasses were sprayed with paraquat than when tilled, but, the year after seeding, populations were equal for both types of disturbance (Silvertown and Tremlett 1989). Shade enhanced seedling survival. While the initial seedlings rapidly colonized the disturbed site, later emerging plants failed to survive unless additional site disturbance occurred.

TOXICITY

The most widely known and researched aspect of *C. maculatum* is its potential toxicity. It is especially famous as the poison used to kill Socrates. His death from this plant was not an isolated case, as plant extracts were often used to execute criminals and political prisoners in ancient Greece (Parsons 1973).

Human poisonings today usually result because the plant is confused with its **Umbelliferae** relatives parsley (leaves), parsnip (roots), or anise (seeds). All plant parts contain toxic alkaloids and can be fatal, especially to children. Eight alkaloids are found in *C. maculatum* and of these coniine and coniceine are the most active. Their concentration is affected by environmental conditions, season of growth, location, collection within locations and time of day (Panter et al. 1988). Jessup et al. (1986) found the total alkaloid content of *C. maculatum* roots was much higher (5 mg/g dry wt) than that of stems and leaves (0.2 mg/g). The alkaloids in the leaves and stems were 22% coniine, 76% coniceine and 2% others. The roots contained 6% coniine and 94% other alkaloids. Fruits and seeds may contain up to 2% alkaloids with higher concentrations in plants grown in hot, dry regions (Parsons 1973).

Well-fed cattle may tolerate up to 2 to 4% of their body weight as *C. maculatum* in the ration, but young or poorly fed animals may be killed by ingesting only 1 to 2 kg fresh leaves or much lower quantities of seed (Case 1969). It is one of the few green plants in pastures in late winter and may be eaten by hungry livestock, but older animals usually avoid the plant. It is also one of the first plants to green up in the spring and at this time the highly toxic alkaloid coniceine predominates (Panter et al. 1988). The strong odor of the plant reduces fresh consumption, but it can easily poison animals that are eating fresh hay or silage. If they consume it regularly, animals develop a tolerance to coniine just as humans do to a related alkaloid, nicotine. The alkaloids are excreted by the lungs and kidneys, and the breath and urine of poisoned animals have the same mousey odor as the plant.

All domestic livestock and wild animals are susceptible to poisoning, but cattle are the most sensitive, sheep and goats are intermediate and pigs are the least sensitive. Nevertheless, 244 pigs were poisoned by consuming barley grain contaminated with *C. maculatum* seed and 45 died (Panter et al. 1988). The teratogenic effect is more severe in pigs than sheep. The alkaloids are volatile and thus dried or boiled plants are much less toxic. Symptoms of poisoning include listlessness, loss of muscle power, stumbling, heavy salivation, frequent urination, nausea, and convulsions. Death is due to respiratory failure (Kingsbury 1964). Symptoms appear soon after ingestion and if the poisoned animal does not die within 8 hr after symptoms appear, it can often make a complete recovery in a few days. Pregnant cows and sows that consume *C. maculatum* often abort within a few days or may give birth to deformed young (Everist 1974, Hannam 1985).

AGRICULTURAL IMPORTANCE

The greatest impact of *C. maculatum* is its potential toxicity to humans and livestock. Native North Americans have used this feature to their advantage in making poisoned arrow tips, but children using the hollow stem internodes as whistles or pea-shooters have been poisoned (Parsons 1973). Confirmed cases of human and animal poisoning are known in most countries where this weed occurs. In addition to killing livestock, consumption lowers meat and milk production, may cause abortions or deformed offspring and imparts a foul flavor to milk. Australia has banned the importation of any product contaminated with *C. maculatum* seed (Anon. [Australia] 1982).

    C. maculatum is a weed of nine crops in 34 countries (Figure 27-1) and is a frequently reported pasture weed. It is considered a serious or principal pasture weed in Italy, New Zealand, Sweden, and the United States. It also infests pastures in Australia, Brazil, Colombia, and England. It is a common weed of orchards in Bolivia, Brazil, Jordan, Turkey, and Uruguay. It is a weed of unknown rank of cereals in Argentina, Chile, Colombia, and Turkey; lucerne in Argentina; maize in Chile; irrigated crops in Jordan; vegetables in France and Iran; and waste areas of Argentina, Australia, the central and western United States, and the former Yugoslavia.

    The weed hosts virus diseases of lucerne, celery, and carrot in the United States (Howell and Mink 1981). The insect *Agonopcerix alstroemeriana* feeds on the leaves of *C. maculatum* in the northwestern United States. While it has sometimes been employed for medicinal and veterinary purposes, the closeness between therapeutic and toxic levels limits its medicinal uses (Case 1969).

COMMON NAMES

Conium maculatum

ARGENTINA	cicuta, cienta
AUSTRALIA	hemlock, wild carrot, wild parsnip
BELGIUM	dolle kervel, gevlekte scheerling
BRAZIL	cicuta, cicuta da europa, cigue, cuquta maior, funcho selvagem
CANADA	poison hemlock, cigue maculee
CHILE	cicuta, sarrac
COLOMBIA	cicuta
DENMARK	skarntyde
ENGLAND	hemlock
FINLAND	myrkkykatko
FRANCE	grande cique
GERMANY	Gefleckter Schierling
ITALY	cicuta maggiore
JAPAN	doku-ninjin
LEBANON	poison hemlock, shawkaran
NEW ZEALAND	hemlock
NORWAY	giftkjeks
PORTUGAL	ansarina-malhada
SPAIN	perejillon cicuta
SWEDEN	odort
TURKEY	tri baldiran
UNITED STATES	poison hemlock
URUGUAY	cicuta negra
VENEZUELA	cicuta

Twenty-Eight

Conyza canadensis (L.) Cronq.
(syn. Erigeron canadensis L.)

Asteraceae (Compositae), Aster Family

CONYZA CANADENSIS, often called horseweed or mare's tail, is a fleabane, most widely known in the world as *Erigeron canadensis*. It behaves as a winter annual or biennial and may grow to 10 cm or 300 cm depending on its surroundings. As may be seen from the distribution map (Figure 28-1), it prospers as a weed mainly in the north temperate zone although it has worldwide distribution. Salisbury (1964) has observed that

FIGURE 28-1 The distribution of *Conyza canadensis* (L.) Cronq. across the world where it has been reported as a weed.

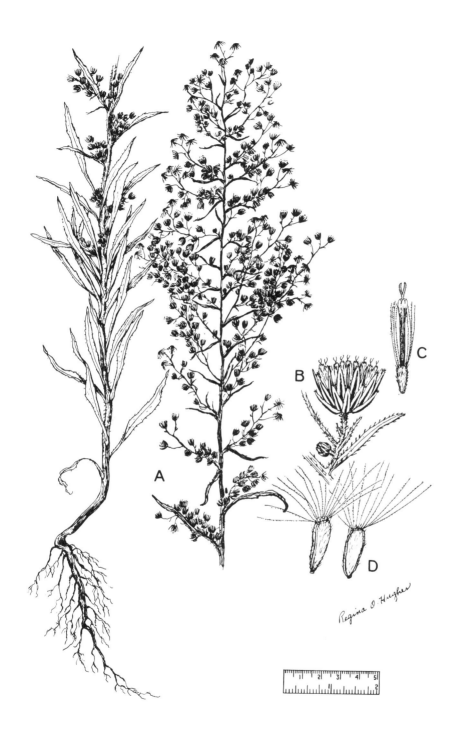

Figure 28-2   *Conyza canadensis* (L.) Cronq.: A. habit; B. flower head; C. disk flower;
D. achenes.

it has an advantage possessed by many widespread weeds in that it has generally unspecialized requirements for growth. For example, it prefers to flower at a definite time in the locality in which it finds itself, but all indications are that it is day neutral.

The weed was moved to the genus *Conyza* (which is mainly tropical) in recent years and the change has been accepted with difficulty, for to this date the taxon *Erigeron* is used far more than *Conyza* for this genus (Heywood 1978).

The weed is in 70 countries and appears in more than 40 crops. It is unique among species in the investment of a very high proportion of its energy and resources into seeds that are admirably suited for dispersal and quick establishment.

Erigeron is from the Greek *er*, meaning spring, and *geron* for old man, an allusion to the hoary-downy covering of parts of this aster-like plant in early season.

DESCRIPTION

C. canadensis (Figure 28-2) is a slender erect herb, winter *annual* or *biennial*, with a long *taproot*; *stem* a few cm to more than 3 m in height, nearly smooth or bristly hairy, unbranched at base, branched near top with many small flower heads; *leaves* alternate but numerous, often appearing opposite, may be light or dark green depending on habitat, without petioles, basal and lower stem leaves 2.5 to 10 cm long, 1 cm wide, strap-shape, entire or toothed, medium and upper stem leaves smaller, sessile, entire, vary narrow, soft hairy at first but becoming harsh on older leaves, some southern Africa types almost glabrous both surfaces but margins rigidly and shortly ciliate; *flower heads* small, numerous on many short branches at top of stem, about 5 mm in diameter, head or capitulum very fluffy at maturity; *involucre* composed of 2 or 3 series of very small, pointed, greenish *bracts* 2.5 to 5 mm long; *receptacle* flat, 1.2 to 2.5 mm broad when bare, *ray florets* very short, inconspicuous, usually concealed by slightly longer involucral bracts around each flower, greenish white to lavender, pistillate, more than 100 per head, about as long as disk florets; *disk florets* numerous, perfect, yellow; *fruit* a dry indehiscent *achene*, cylindrical, elongated, broadest above the middle, somewhat tapering toward scar that has attached light-colored collar, apex truncate, surface is longitudinally grooved and has scattered white hairs, color a greenish, yellowish brown, 1.3 mm long by 0.3 mm wide, *pappus* of 10 or up to 25 hairs, brownish yellow, 1.5 to 3 times longer than achene.

The crushed leaves and other plant parts have the faint odor of carrots.

DISTRIBUTION AND HABITAT

C. canadensis is well distributed in agricultural land throughout the north temperate zone, with a more moderate distribution in the south temperate zone (Figure 28-1). It is present throughout Australia. It is particularly sparse in the equatorial zone. With the exception of Tunisia in the north of Africa and the southern one-fourth of the continent, we have no reports that it behaves as a weed in the vast area between. In eastern Africa there are several weedy, annual *Conyza* species that have the general appearance of *C. canadensis*.

In an earlier time, Voilure coefficients (an allusion to sails or flying surfaces) were applied to seeds and expressed with numbers. *C. canadensis* was found to have a very high coefficient, indicating that it is superbly equipped for efficient seed dispersal (Hitrovo 1912).

In a 4-year study, Kelley and Bruns (1975), in the northwestern United States, found the seed of this fleabane was in irrigation canals and streams and was deposited annually on nearby fields. The weed seeds were counted several times each season from sampling screens placed in irrigation canals designated A and B, as well as in water pumped from the major stream, the Columbia River, itself a source of irrigation water. The different species collected from the above sites numbered 137, 84, and 77, respectively. For the season, the average numbers of seeds found in water equivalent to that needed to place 2.5 cm on one hectare of land were 2,210, 682, and 292, respectively.

C. canadensis ranked among the 15 most plentiful in seeds present among the 137 species found in canal A. Fewer seeds of *C. canadensis* were found in canal B and the river. To extrapolate, the number of seeds of all species disseminated per full season over one hectare in all of the water applied were about 95,000, 10,400, and 14,100 in canals A, B, and the river, respectively. No weed control practices were applied along canal A, but the users along canal B employed several weed control measures and reduced the seed in the water considerably.

It is of interest, however, that soil samples to a 30 cm depth in a non-cropped area along the Columbia River contained no *C. canadensis* seeds and a nearby area cropped for 5 yr had only 7 seeds/m^2. It was estimated that the total seed bank, to a depth of 30 cm, in the uncropped land, contained 125 million seeds/ha. The area cropped for 5 yr was irrigated with water from the Columbia River and contained 500 million seeds in the same volume of soil. Hope (1927) in Canada found this species thriving in fields near irrigation canals, with seed moved into the water by the wind. In one canal 100 seeds of the species passed a check point in 24 hr.

Kasahara (1953) estimated that the widespread abundance of *C. canadensis* in Japan is in great part due to movement of the seed by rail and motor transport. In Canada the earliest appearance of this fleabane was on moist ground in meadows and pastures, but it has now become plentiful on cultivated land.

Michael (1977) of Australia published a brief summary of the current taxonomy of *C. canadensis* and the history of the introduction and spread of the weed in Asia and the Americas, while Wein (1932) prepared similar information for Europe.

PROPAGATION

C. canadensis reproduces only by seed. An interesting tale related by Salisbury (1942) gives evidence of the ever-present supply of seed available for the colonization of newly turned earth. After London was bombed in World War II, observations were made of the earliest arrivals of plants on many of these disturbed sites. Rosebay willowherb (*Chamaenerion angustifolium*) and common groundsel (*Senecio vulgaris*) came quickly to 88% of the sites. It is interesting that the former plant was rather rare in the area before this time, while the latter was plentiful in southern England. *C. canadensis* was ranked with the six species that arrived early in greatest number, being found at 44% of the sites. This weed had been widely distributed in England for more than 200 yr.

While obtaining records of the propagules of the species at the time, Salisbury (1942) found one specimen that produced about 6500 capitula, but he estimated that the average plant formed about 700 when colonizing disturbed soil. The achenes per capitulum ranged from 16 to 49, with an average of 35. The average seed production from such plants would be about 25,000 per individual. The reports of seed weights vary from 0.00004 to 0.6 mg (see also Tateda and Isikawa 1968). Twenty years later Salisbury (1964) revised his estimates upward to an average of 50,000 seeds/plant on a random sample of 50 plants. He found a large specimen with an estimated seed production of a quarter million seeds. Similar estimates were made in Australia (Whittet 1968), and for North America by Bekech (1988) and Kempen and Graf (1981). In Israel the plant is considered an adventive from North America and under good growing conditions it can produce three to four seed crops per year, thus expending much of its energy on reproduction. The thought of a large stand of this fleabane sending this quantity of seed off with the wind into agricultural land on dry autumn days is sobering.

Flowering and seed production vary greatly with distance from the equator, but in the north temperate zone, where the species is most plentiful, these processes begin in July and August and end in October and early November. In Denmark, the germination rate in the field is very high and all seeds emerge within a very short period. In the central United States, seed harvested in early October gave 56% germination, while seed from a late October harvest germinated very poorly.

The uncertainty of one factor—seed size—and its ultimate effect on the dimensions and vigor of the seedling and subsequent young and adult plant has recently come under much careful scrutiny and we are finding it more complex than previously thought. Fenner (1983) recently completed a study of the characteristics of seeds and seedlings in 24 species of **Compositae**, to include *C. canadensis*.

It is often assumed that seedling size may be quite directly related to seed size. Other observations suggest that for survival of a species it may not be the dimensions of the seed but the size of the corresponding seedling that is important. There are indications from Harper (1977) and others that characteristic seed size for a species seems to be a compromise between the requirements for dispersal and for establishment, and this may therefore depend upon the proportion of plant resources allocated to reproduction, as well as the number of seeds per plant. Fenner (1983) studied the weight of seeds, embryos, seed coats, and seedlings of 24 species. *C. canadensis* had the smallest seeds of all species, with the embryo making up 85% of the weight, while *Tragopogon pratensis* was 140 times larger, with only 40% of the seed weight composed of embryo material. The seedling weight to seed weight ratios were 9:58 and 1:37, respectively, for the two species, thus "weight for weight" the larger the seed the lower the return on the initial investment for the plant. In the summary of the data on the 24 species, Fenner concluded there was a clear trend for large seeds to have relatively small embryos and larger seed coats. Fenner's report includes data on predator risks, dispersal, mineral storage by large and small seeds, embryo weight versus resulting seedling root weight, and ecological implications for many matters.

PHYSIOLOGY AND ECOLOGY

Many annuals are ruderal plants, adapted to take advantage of areas temporarily disturbed. They are found in pastures and grain fields, on the sides of roads and ditches, and in forest and ornamental nurseries. They can quickly colonize abandoned fields and new waste areas and remain in all the above places for one to three years until they are replaced by other species. Studies of successional ecology in old fields can tell us something of the characteristics of the weed plants and their competitive ability. For example, Oosting (1942) studied land areas as they were taken out of production in the eastern United States in preparation for a 2000 ha forest planting. *C. canadensis* made up 11% of the species population and *Digitaria sanguinalis* 63% in the first year. The former ranged in height from 120 to 150 cm. In the second year, these species were still important in numbers but had been overtopped by *Aster* and *Ambrosia* species, and the *C. canadensis* was now reduced in height to 15 cm. In the third year, *C. canadensis* was still present, was subordinate to three *Andropogon* species and could only seek space, in a stunted condition, between the clumps of the grass. Booth (1941) and Hancock (1977) in the United States and Kobayashi et al. (1980) in Japan had somewhat similar experiences with this primary invader of abandoned land.

Yoda et al. (1963) in Japan studied the self-thinning process in *C. canadensis* on a sandy, infertile site with a pronounced uniform fertility gradient. Density and dry weight data taken at five harvests during the season revealed that within thick stands of vigorously growing plants, some individuals were constantly being lost. As the season progressed, some populations fell from 125,000 to 1,050 plants/m², resulting in 1% survival of the original adult population. Palmblad (1968) reported a "controlled germination" of the seeds of this species, with a discovery that a smaller proportion of seeds germinated with increased density of seed-sowing!

Many of these ruderal annuals may also become early dominants in spring-planted crops such as maize. Regehr and Bazzaz (1979) in the central United States chose *C. canadensis* for a study of the phenology and ecology of such winter annuals. In the experimental area there was a natural stand of the weed immediately adjacent and upwind from the maize planting. Prior to the experiments it was determined that about 40% of the emergents in this field in autumn were from propagules entering the seed bank in some previous year. With suitable devices they learned that a site in the maize field that was 6 m from the horseweed area received 12,500 wind-blown seeds/m². Another site 120 m from the weed stand received 125 seeds/m². To study the winter toll of individual plants they chose field sites that had received 12,000, 4,000, and 230 wind-blown achenes/m² and that contained rosette plants at the average density of 360, 120, and 10/m² respectively.

There was very little mortality of seedlings up to first frost of late autumn. In winter, however, because of frost heaving of the soil, survival of plants up to early spring was quite low, being 14, 18, and 84%, respectively. Thus we see the plants in the most crowded area with smaller rosettes (360/m²) were most seriously injured. Of the spring germinating plants, 35% survived the growing season without passing through the rosette stage. These plants, and those that germinated in the previous autumn, elongated to give vegetative shoots 1 to 1.5 m in height.

In summary, it is helpful to point out that this particular winter annual, as with some others, is successful in arable crops because of its peculiar phenology. Such plants often germinate in late summer and autumn when many summer annuals are at the peak of seed production; in a maize field they may germinate at times in the midst of a full summer weed community. Seedlings can emerge and find little interference during early growth, and their survival to first frost is high. Sometimes, however, maize rows may be clear because of spring weed control measures. Nevertheless, the crop canopy is there to buffer the new weed seedling from extreme temperature, wind desiccation, and excessive soil erosion. In winter the rosettes are partially protected by crop residues and with suitable light and temperature there may be substantial carbon fixation while potential competitors are dormant (Regehr and Bazzaz 1979). The authors believe that the reproductive success of survivors is enhanced by the lower plant densities that allow larger rosettes. With the high reproductive effort of the species, scattered tall individuals can produce much seed and make it available for wind dispersal.

On the eastern seacoast of the United States, the weed is not often a problem in conventional-till agriculture. Because of recent trends for reduced tillage in arable fields, Bekech (1988) held adjacent experimental fields of maize in no-till and conventional tillage to compare the weed floras after 5 yr. She found that horseweed became the dominant weed in the no-till system and suggests that it can be attributed to the maintenance of "periodically plant-free, open, undisturbed soil," a habitat to which this species is very well adapted. In conventional tillage the spring cultivation kills the horseweed in the vegetative state with additional help from the shade of the crop canopy. Lacking such a cultivation in the no-till system, the weed plants germinating the previous fall were allowed to compete very successfully with spring germinating weeds and maize. The herbicides used in no-till maize suppressed but did not eradicate the *C. canadensis* and other weeds. For the horseweed this means that a single, tall, surviving plant may produce 200,000 airborne seeds that may disperse and supply inoculum for a very large area.

Kapusta (1979) found that *C. canadensis* occurred in no-till soybean fields in the north-central United States but was not a problem in conventional-till with spring cultivation. Brown and Whitwell (1988) had similar results in cotton in the southern United States and found that fall and spring disking controlled the weed in the subsequent crop.

In contrast to the success stories of horseweed as an early colonizer and a dominant in arable fields, the work of Archibold (1981) at lat 55° N in Canadian prairies provides an example of the variability there can be in the life history of a single species when there is a change of habitat to an environment that is more extreme. This weed is widely distributed in Canada and the aim of the research was to estimate the relative numbers of buried propagules in four types of agricultural areas: native prairie, never cultivated; a moist, grazed pasture, never cultivated; a 10-yr lucerne field broken and seeded to wheat in the previous season, now a stubble field; and a wheat-fallow rotation cultivated four times per season. There were no *C. canadensis* propagules in the prairie or grazed pasture. Only a trace of the weed was found in the fallow-rotation. Out of 19 species of annuals and biennials studied, and in spite of the abundant seed production by *C. canadensis*, it ranked among the lowest third in seeds present in wheat stubble. We thus see that the power to colonize aggressively and to produce abundant seed may be greatly limited by a harsh and stressful environment, if at the same time the plant has to compete with weeds better adapted to the area.

Kutschera (1960) in Germany has provided an illustration of the root system after excavating a single plant. A strong single taproot extends downward for the first 30 cm. Below this level, it is divided into several major branches, each with short fibrous roots. The entire system reaches downward to 100 cm. In the top 15 cm of the soil, a very fine fibrous system develops from the tap root and reaches out 50 cm in all directions.

Keever (1950) noticed that *C. canadensis* sometimes had poor seedling growth where its own residues were decaying in the soil, with the effect lasting about 2 mo. Kobayashi et al. (1980) found several 10-carbon polyacetylene compounds peculiar to *C. canadensis* in nearby soil that were strong inhibitors of neighboring species and therefore may be ecologically important. Kaben (1963) reported on allelopathic activity by this species.

C. canadensis biotypes resistant and co-resistant to various herbicides have now been reported in ten countries (Casely et al. 1991, LeBaron and Gressel 1982, Solymosi 1988).

Histochemical studies of the seeds and pollen of *Erigeron* species were made by Kasmyova (1966). Cytological investigations of the genus were reported by Montgomery and Yang (1960). The taxonomy of some hybrids of *Erigeron canadensis* with other species was described by Jovet (1966).

AGRICULTURAL IMPORTANCE

C. canadensis is a serious weed of wheat and barley in Korea, maize in South Africa, and forest and ornamental nurseries in the United States.

It is a principal weed of several horticultural crops in Italy, South Africa, and the former Soviet Union; lawns and turf in South Africa; lucerne in the United States; maize in India and Italy; orchards in Germany, India, South Africa, and the United States; pastures and rangelands in South Africa and Taiwan; pineapple in the Philippines and South Africa; rice in India; sugarcane in India and Taiwan; tea in Taiwan; vegetables in South Africa; and vineyards in the former Soviet Union and Yugoslavia.

It is a common weed of bananas in Taiwan; barley in Canada and the former Soviet Union; cassava in Taiwan; cereals in Turkey; several cultivated crops in the former Yugoslavia; forage crops in the United States; flax in Canada; horticultural crops in Bulgaria; irrigated crops in Israel; maize and millet in the former Soviet Union; nurseries in Israel; oats in Canada; orchards in Japan, Taiwan, and the former Yugoslavia; pastures in Australia, Jamaica, and the United States; peanuts in Taiwan; pineapple in Hawaii and Taiwan; potatoes in the former Soviet Union; rangeland in Australia and the United States; upland rice in Taiwan; soybeans in the former Soviet Union; sugarcane in Honduras; sweet potatoes in Taiwan; strawberries in the United States; sunflowers in Canada; tea in India; tobacco in the former Soviet Union; vegetables in Austria, Australia, Israel, the former Soviet Union, and Taiwan; vineyards in Mexico; and wheat in Canada and the United States.

C. canadensis is reported as a weed of major crops, importance not specified, in the following countries: bananas in Honduras; barley in Japan and the former Soviet Union; cassava in the Philippines; cereals in England, Germany, Jordan, Poland, Romania, and the former Soviet Union; citrus in Japan and the United States; coffee in New Guinea; cotton in Mexico, the former Soviet Union, and the United States; new forest plantings in the United States; lucerne in Czechoslovakia; maize in Honduras, Mexico, the Philippines, the former Soviet Union, Taiwan, and the United States; oil palm in Surinam; orchards in Bulgaria, France, Iran, Iraq, Israel, and Spain; pastures in Brazil, Colombia, India, Japan, and New Zealand; potatoes in Honduras and the United States; rape in Canada and Japan; rice in Indonesia, Japan, and Portugal; rye in the former Soviet Union; soybeans in the United States; sugar beets in Germany and Romania; sugar cane in Australia, Mozambique, and South Africa; tea in Iran, Japan, New Guinea, and the former Soviet Union; tomatoes in Israel and the United States; vegetables in China, Honduras, Iran, Iraq, and Vietnam; vineyards in France, Hungary, and Italy; and wheat in China, Iran, Portugal, and the former Yugoslavia.

As mentioned earlier, horseweed has the propensity for entering the waste or border areas near man-made structures (buildings, ditches, roads), but it should also be mentioned that a standing dry crop of the weed reaching to 2 m in height is a very serious fire hazard for many of these places. It is interesting that the fires of spring-burned pastures in the United States have not interfered with stands of the weed.

Horseweed is so widespread that the literature holds an unusual variety of reports on crop problems, manner of movement, and its coextensive association with many of man's activities. For example, the oils extracted from the leaves have significant biological and medicinal activity and this has resulted in the listing of the species in the *Pharmacopoeia*, an official book about drugs, their chemistry, and method of preparation (Maurya et al. 1973). In the central United States the butter made from the milk of cows feeding on horseweed may have a foul taste within 48 hr (Olson et al. 1953). In Sweden, there appeared a stand of horseweed adjacent to a logyard of imported timber. Petterson (1940) found seeds that had traveled in the fissures of bark and in soil clods from the middle reaches of the Vistula River in Poland where the trees were cut. The weed is found in the gardens of Bedouins in the very dry desert area of northern Sinai. Some have entered Israel from this source and continue to spread rapidly in irrigated crops and gardens (Dafni and Heller 1980).

Zanardi (1962) in Italy found that the growth of new spring buds of grapes was 28% less when *C. canadensis* was a serious competitor. In the Philippines, the weed constantly reinfests pineapple fields because of wind and water movement of seed from adjacent uncropped lands. Sarpe and Torge (1980) in Germany found that severe competition from horseweed reduced sugar beet yields 64%. In North Dakota in the north-central United States, horseweed is very troublesome in seed production fields of the native grasses *Agropyron* and *Bouteloua*. Kasahara (1953) prepared a list of 200 weeds found in the major agricultural areas of Japan and ranked *C. canadensis* as one of the most harmful.

This species has been included in weed control experiments on solarization (soil heating by the sun) in Israel and found to be quite resistant to injury in this procedure (Horowitz et al. 1983b).

COMMON NAMES

Conyza canadensis

AUSTRIA	Canada fleabane
BELGIUM	Kanadese fijnstrall
CANADA	blood-stanch, butterweed, Canada fleabane, colt's tail, fireweed, hogweed, horseweed, mare's tail, pride weed, vergerette du Canada
COLOMBIA	venadillo
DENMARK	kanadisk, bakkestjerne
ENGLAND	Canadian fleabane, horseweed
FIJI	horseweed, fleabane
FINLAND	Kanadan koiransilma
FRANCE	vergerette du Canada
GERMANY	Kanadisches, Berufkraut
HAWAII	small-leaf horseweed, Canada fleabane
INDIA	Canada fleabane, jarayupriya
IRAQ	Canada fleabane, fleabane, mare's tail, thail el-faras
ITALY	impia, saeppola
JAMAICA	Canadian fleabane, daisy, dead weed
JAPAN	himemukashiyomogi
MADAGASCAR	sarijamala
MAURITIUS	herbe gandi

MEXICO	cola de zorra, hierba del caballo, jarilla
NETHERLANDS	Kanadese fijnstraal
NEW ZEALAND	Canadian fleabane
NORWAY	hestehamp
PHILIPPINES	horseweed
POLAND	przymiotno Kanadyjskie
PORTUGAL	avoadinha
PUERTO RICO	pascueta, orozuz
SOUTH AFRICA	armoedskruid, Kanadese skraalhans, tall fleabane
SPAIN	altabaca, canem bord, olivarda, zamarraga
SWEDEN	kanada-binka
TRINIDAD	Canada fleabane
TUNISIA	erigeron du Canada
TURKEY	sifa otu
UNITED STATES	butter weed, flea wort, horseweed, mare's tail, mule tail
YUGOSLAVIA	repusnjaca

Twenty-Nine

Corchorus olitorius L.

Tiliaceae, Linden Family

THE GENUS *CORCHORUS* has about 40 species found largely in the tropics. *C. olitorius* and *C. capsularis* are herbaceous and have become important in world agriculture for their stem bast fibers (jute), which rank second only to cotton as world vegetable fibers. Most jute is grown in the subtropics and is used for cordage and sacking. Varieties of *C. olitorius* are widely grown as pot-herbs in the warm regions, and it is biotypes of these plants that have escaped to become weeds in 28 crops in 50 countries. From the linden family we also have the woody basswoods and limes.

FIGURE 29-1   The distribution of *Corchorus olitorius* L. across the world where it has been reported as a weed.

FIGURE 29-2 *Corchorus olitorius* L.: 1. habit; 2. portion of stem with stipule; 3. flower; 4. stamen; 5. ovary, vertical section; 6. same, cross section; 7. petal showing hairy base; 8. capsule; 9. seed, two views.

DESCRIPTION

C. olitorius (Figure 29-2) is a herbaceous *annual*, glabrous except on petioles; *taproot*; *stems* 30 to 100 cm and much-branched when growing as a weed or vegetable culture, when grown for fiber *stems* straight, slender to 4 m, there are many types; *leaves* alternate, light green; *stipules* 2, linear, up to 1 cm long, deciduous, *petiole* to 2 cm long; *lamina* lanceolate 5 to 12 by 2 to 5 cm, serrate, 2 lower teeth prolonged into fine, pointed auricles, tips acuminate; *flowers* solitary or in few flowered cymes, opposite the leaves, *sepals* usually 5, free, narrow, as long or shorter than petals; *petals* usually 5, yellow, 4 to 5 mm long, short *corona* separates petals from insertion of stamens; *stamens* 10 to many, free, filaments short, *anthers* small, bilobed, *style* short, *stigma* flat, *ovary* superior, 5-locular with numerous ovules; *fruit* a long, cylindrical, 10-ridged, beaked *capsule*, glabrous, 5 to 10 cm long, 0.5 to 0.8 cm in diameter, 5 to 6 chambers formed by transverse septa, 25 to 40 seeds per chamber with 140 to 200 in each fruit; *seed* pyramidal, 1 to 2 mm long, color varying with variety from grayish-blue or green to brownish-black. Wild *C. olitorius* types have black seeds.

C. capsularis may be distinguished from *C. olitorius* by its smaller yellow flowers and a globular, much-wrinkled capsule that is flattened at the top. It has been apparent to those who have tried to improve the crop that a more ecologically adaptable plant would result if the characteristics of the two species could be combined. Thus far, they have been crossed only with great difficulty (Swaminathan 1961). The wild species used by early man tend to be low and branched. From this, it seems likely that selections were commonly made in search of taller, unbranched plants with ever shorter growing periods.

DISTRIBUTION AND HABITAT

This is principally an Old World weed and there is little doubt that it was used as a vegetable in South Asia, the Middle East, and North Africa back to 1500 B.C. Its long history of use as a food plant may account for much of the uncertainty about its origin. It is found, either as a crop or weed, over most of Africa and in a broad arc from the eastern half of the Mediterranean area through southern Russia, Iran, India, Thailand, Indonesia, the Philippines, and down to Australia. It is also in the north of Latin America and in Hawaii. (See Figure 29-1.)

The largest production area of the *Corchorus* jute has always been in the Ganges-Brahmaputra Delta in India, with most of the remainder in the Yangtze Valley in China. The crop remains in the hands of small farmers, it is very labor-intensive, and a certain and adequate supply of water is necessary for retting. The retting process for *Corchorus* jute is now so costly that several countries have been searching for other fiber-producing species suitable to their climates. Strangely, one of those under study is Congo jute (*Urena lobata*), also an important world weed.

The details of habitat requirement for jute and the management of the crop are not important here, but the response of these plant types to different factors of environment may help us to know what to expect in the weedy types (Sarma 1969).

Sarma (1969) finds evidence in reports from across the world that, although the jute plants can be grown on most soil types, they prefer a sandy loam, a slightly acid or alkaline *pH*, with an optimum at 6 to 6.5. They profit from a good supply of N and organic matter. It is not a soil-exhausting crop, responds to N, but is not likely to respond to P and K without the addition of N. It fares poorly on lateritic and gravelly soils. The best locations, again and again over the world, have been on alluvial riverain soils that are flooded frequently and thus enriched with silt. Much of the world's jute is grown below 30 m in elevation.

When in cultivation, the best growth is made during the rainy season at temperatures of 21 to 38°C and a relative humidity of 60 to 95%. Growth is satisfactory at 100 to 250 cm of annual rainfall, but 150 cm are optimum. Young plants are sensitive to waterlogging. Wild species types are more tolerant of salty soils than cultivated types.

PROPAGATION

Despite the widespread distribution of the weedy forms of *C. olitorius* in crops and regions of the world, there is very little information on their propagation, physiology, and morphology. However, a large fund of such knowledge exists on the taller forms of the species grown for commercial fiber production. Information from such studies can supply general data about the patterns and habits of development within the species and thus help us to understand the wild and weedy species.

Modiwala and Dubey (1976) found that the viable seeds found within the very hard coat eventually germinated in the field to provide heavy competition to crops. A significant number of seedlings grew from a depth of 9 cm. Juliano (1940) in the Philippines reported that seeds of the weed held in moist sand germinated for several months after collection. Newly harvested seed placed in sterile sand in inverted glass vials and buried in soil were viable for 6.5 yr. In a laboratory, 4% of the seed in bottles containing naphthalene still germinated at 19 yr.

Freshly harvested seed is delicate and with its 15 to 20% moisture content at collection time will easily lose viability if not dried quickly. If the seed is dried in full sun, the moisture content can be reduced to 7% in 4 days. In commercial jute production, the best quality seed is that taken at the full ripe stage. If seed harvest is delayed to enter into a damp period, a mold develops on the capsule and reduces the seed germination rate.

Van Rijn (1968–1969) in Australia confirmed the hard seed coats of the weedy *C. olitorius*. In his area, 7 mo after harvest a 90% germination rate was obtained with a 30-min soak in H_2SO_4 and a subsequent period in a dark chamber at 27°C. Alternating temperatures did not increase germination. For many of the main weeds in cotton in Australia the best germination occurs in the top 1.5 cm of the soil, but for *C. olitorius* the best depth was 3 cm, with no seedlings arising from below 8 cm.

Moursi et al. (1979) reported that freezing the seed for 6 to 10 wk increased germination, but after 20 wk of freezing there was no germination. Chavan and Trivedi (1962) reported that cracking of the seed was the most successful of several treatments for stimulating seeds to germinate.

To study drought resistance in the germination and subsequent seedling development, Kor (1944) placed seeds in an environment that was wet for 3 hr and then dry for 21 hr for 10 days. He compared them with controls (soaked overnight before planting) and found germination similar in both circumstances, but the treated seeds sprouted earlier, seedlings were taller, and when planted in a soil at 3% moisture, with no added water for 10 days, showed less wilting, greater recovery when watered later, and flowered 6 days earlier.

Because jute seed producers store unsold seed, sometimes for years, Jain and Saha (1971) studied the effect of length of storage on the viability of seed. Dry seed stored in a laboratory for 14 yr showed that a decline in viability varied with age. Older seed sprouted slowly. Viability varied with the variety, but all the seeds were dead at 4 yr.

MORPHOLOGY AND PHYSIOLOGY

The time from seed germination to maturity in commercial varieties of *C. olitorius* varies from 100 to 130 days. For the best quality of fibers, harvesting often takes place midway through the flowering period. Because a long vegetative growing period favors increased yields, jute breeding programs and plant selections favor the types with delayed flowering or with insensitivity to the photoperiodic stimulation of flowering. For this reason, much effort has been devoted to studies on the physiology of responses to temperature and photoperiod. Beyond these studies on jute varieties, biological information is sorely lacking on the weedy species of *C. olitorius*.

The plants are responsive to short-days for the stimulation to flowering and the young plants are more sensitive to the light period than the old ones. The critical dark period for several common varieties is 12 hr, 30 min. Some of the cultivars continue to flower for 8 to 10 wk and during this time there may be periodic flushes of vegetative growth (Sarma 1969). In Bengal, where an early-sown crop may flower too quickly, it was found that a strain brought from Sudan (a lower latitude) did not flower under the similar conditions and was thus useful in breeding programs (Gupta and Dargan 1970).

Bose et al. (1973) found that a 30-day, low temperature seed treatment markedly stimulated flower initiation in short-days in the plants that grew from these seeds. The organ that sensed the short-day was the leaf and the upper leaf was the most sensitive. Removal of part of a leaf prevented flowering in short-days. In India, Sen Gupta and Sen (1952) demonstrated that a 10-hr light period caused some varieties to flower in 21 days instead of 125 days as they do when held under the normal outside light period. Fourteen cycles of 10-hr light caused flower induction. Flowering was delayed in a 16-hr day, or was nil, and plants that had flowers bore no fruit.

The vegetative development of the plants was greatly influenced by photoperiod and temperature (Sen Gupta and Sen 1944). Plants in short-days were shorter with fewer nodes and leaves but with more branches and smaller stems. Thus, at flowering time they are shorter and more bushy. Jute varieties of *C. olitorius* grown at a temperature of 24 to 32°C showed greater plant height and basal stem diameter. Below 22°C there was no response to photoperiod and plants were much shorter. Leaf area was greater on plants in short-days and high temperature than in long-days with low temperatures. A high temperature of 24 to 27°C promoted early flowering in short-days, while a lower temperature delayed it.

When behaving as a weed in Australia, the species gives the most intense competition during the wet season. This is an amazing species, for the types grown for vegetable use in the Middle East and North Africa thrive in hot, arid climates.

Okusanya (1979) in Nigeria surveyed the influence of temperature, salinity, and photoperiod on a commercial variety of *C. olitorius*. Light was necessary for seed germination and high constant or high alternating temperatures enhanced germination. The seeds germinated in 60% sea water, but the rate of germination fell as salinity increased, as did time to first germination. No seedlings survived a salinity of more than 50% sea water. Long daylengths produced the best growth in total dry weight and root development. In contrast to the findings of Sen Gupta and Sen (above), he found that a long daylength produced greater leaf area. Seedlings were poor and stunted at low temperatures. Seedlings grew well in a loamy humus soil but poorly in clay and sand.

Using radiophosphorous, Goswami and Saha (1969) traced the *Corchorus* roots to a depth of 60 cm. The laterals were mainly in an area 60 cm in diameter surrounding the plant, with the principal absorbing roots clustered in a 20-cm area near the plant. Datta et al. (1966)

and Singh (1976) made cytotaxonomic studies of different *Corchorus* species. Ghosh and Datta (1975) and Datta and Chakraborty (1975) studied seed morphology of *Corchorus* species. Gunn and Ritchie (1988) presented line drawings of the seed embryo and transections of the seed.

Stomata are present on both leaf surfaces, but they are most plentiful on the lower surface. The *C. olitorius* jute varieties have fewer stomata and a thicker cuticle than their mates in *C. capsularis* and some believe that this reduces transpiration and helps prevent water loss (Sarma 1969).

The taproot is highly developed in *C. olitorius* and this helps to provide drought resistance at early stages of growth. The pith collapses early, so that at maturity the stem is hollow. Induction of flowering was associated with this stem-thickening in some varieties (Sarma 1969).

AGRICULTURAL IMPORTANCE

C. olitorius is a serious weed of cotton in Mozambique; cowpea, maize, millet, peanuts, upland rice, and sorghum in Senegal; upland rice in the Philippines; and sorghum in Saudi Arabia and Thailand.

It is a principal weed in cotton in Australia, Egypt, and Sudan; dryland arable crops in Australia and Saudi Arabia; jute in Bangladesh; peanuts and wheat in Sudan; and soybeans and sorghum in India.

It is a common weed of cassava in Nigeria; cotton in Ivory Coast; several cultivated crops in Uganda; jute in Nepal; maize in India and Egypt; orchards in Saudi Arabia; peanuts in India; sugarcane in Australia, Bangladesh, India, and the Philippines; and vegetables in Turkey.

In addition to the above crops, it is a weed of unknown rank in cereals, pastures, potatoes, upland rice, transplanted rice, rubber, sugar beets, sweet potatoes, and tobacco in several of the above countries.

C. olitorius is a troublesome weed in sorghum on the coastal farmlands and the midlands (300 to 825 m elevation) in the south and west of Saudi Arabia. It is a problem in other crops on arable land and in orchards. It is becoming a serious threat to sugarcane in Queensland, Australia. In North Africa, it is a popular pot-herb in Egypt, but also a weed of arable crops, while in Uganda it is ubiquitous and troubles many crops.

Cobley (1967) found that varieties of *C. olitorius* are grown in almost every garden in the Middle East, Egypt, and Sudan as a vegetable. The plants may be only 30 cm tall, quick-maturing, and quite branched. They enjoy heat and will give several harvests of leaves from a single plant. In 4 wk some of the varieties grown in Southeast Asia can produce a plant that has sufficient growth to prepare a green, boiled vegetable for the table. Perhaps it is some of these types that have escaped to become weeds throughout the tropics.

Corchorus plants and seeds contain physiologically active glycosides that are of interest for treating patients with chronic cardiac insufficiency (Sharaf and Negm 1969; Samilova and Lagodich 1977). These are cardiotonic agents, similar to digitalin, that increase the force of heart muscle contraction without a concomitant increase in O_2 consumption, thus tending to make the heart a more efficient pump.

The potential of leaves for the supply of minerals, vitamins, and supplemental proteins makes them of critical importance to the health of people who are largely dependent upon starchy tubers and cereals as dietary staples. Schmidt (1971) in Nigeria made a comparative study of the composition of eight leafy vegetable crops, including *C. olitorius*, grown at two fertility levels.

COMMON NAMES

Corchorus olitorius

EGYPT	Jew's mallow, meloykhia
ENGLAND	tossa jute
GHANA	sigli
INDIA	banpat, chanal, harawa, koota, pata parinta, perumpunnhu, perumpunnkku poondu, titapat, tossa jute
INDONESIA	gedangan, rami cina
JAPAN	taiwan tsunaso
MADAGASCAR	tsihitafotora
NIGERIA	oyo
PHILIPPINES	pasau na haba, saluyot, tagabang
SAUDIA ARABIA	malukhia
SIERRA LEONE	krenkre
SUDAN	khudra, mol okhta
TAIWAN	tsanaso
ZAMBIA	lusakasaka, wild jute

Thirty

Coronopus didymus (L.) Sm.

Brassicaceae (Cruciferae), Mustard Family

CORONOPUS DIDYMUS is a foul-smelling plant with creeping shoots radiating from the crown of a tap root to form a round mat. Across the world its familiar name is cress, with an antecedent adjective or noun peculiar to the region or site: hogs, twin, bitter, wart, or lesser swine cress. Because of its habit, it is seldom a vigorous competitor of crop plants whose stature is tall and spreading, but its excessive seed production and the persistent, tangled network of vegetative branches that develop can be a menace to pastures, cereals and especially vegetable and small fruit crops. It is a spoiler of milk and is

FIGURE 30-1　The distribution of *Coronopus didymus* (L.) Sm. across the world where it has been reported as a weed.

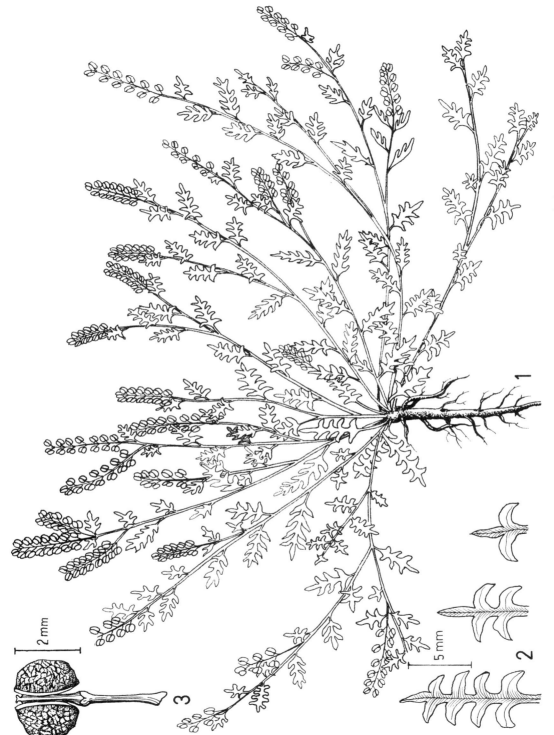

FIGURE 30-2 *Coronopus didymus* (L.) Sm.: 1. habit; 2. leaf forms; 3. fruit.

now present in many dairying countries. It imparts a strong, tainted off-flavor which is intensified when butter and other dairy products are made.

DESCRIPTION

C. didymus (Figure 30-2) is a freely branching *annual* or *biennial* herb with a strong, disagreeable odor; *stems* spreading, prostrate or nearly so, sometimes hairy, matting, 15 to 80 cm long, radiating from the crown of the taproot; *leaves* alternate, 1 to 3 cm, pinnately divided into very fine, short, entire or toothed segments, the upper leaves may be sessile or short-petioled and the basal long-petioled; *flower* minute, white or greenish-white petals or petals missing, crowded on terminal or axillary racemes to 5 cm in length; *stamens* 2, flowers self-pollinated; *fruit* a silicle (short pod), small, 2-seeded, conspicuous and finely wrinkled, maybe kidney-shaped, 2 to 2.5 mm long and 1 to 1.5 mm wide, with deep crease to make the pod appear to be 2-lobed. Average seed output in Australia is 16,000 per plant, with up to 18,000 on a large plant.

DISTRIBUTION AND HABITAT

C. didymus is on all continents and tends to be concentrated in the temperate zone and subtropics (Figure 30-1). It reproduces by seeds that are moved by wind, water, in mud on the feet of birds, animals, and by various activities of man. It generally appears in fields in early spring and autumn, and may be seen on new, sown and overgrazed pasture, around gateways and watering places, in animal yards, and in many types of cultivated crops. Ramirez and Romero (1978) found *C. didymus* seeds mixed with detritus and seeds of more than 100 other species floating in the salt water along the Pacific Ocean beaches of south-central Chile. In a study of the seed movements of the region they found a general shifting of seeds from north to south in the coastal currents and from east to west with the flood waters seasonally.

Ouren (1959) reported that *C. didymus* was one of 70 agricultural weeds to enter Norway at the shipping ballast dump sites near Frederikstad in south Norway. Most of the weed seeds came from European and Mediterranean areas, but it is believed that *C. didymus* was introduced from South American ports.

BIOLOGY AND AGRICULTURE IMPORTANCE

Very little is known of the biology of this member of the mustard family. In cropping systems it appears in early and late season, but once established it seems to prosper whenever growing conditions are satisfactory. Flowering continues the full growing season in several regions and the plant produces much seed. Matthews (1975) in New Zealand believes the weed is gaining in importance because it is tolerant of many cropping herbicides. In India, Jaitly and Srivastava (1970) reported on the embryology and on the structure of the seed coat in *C. didymus*. Chauhan (1979) has studied pollination of the weed by ants.

There is evidence that *Coronopus* is very easily stimulated to germinate by many events that take place in the upper layers of the soil throughout the growing season. This may explain in part why studies of weed seed storage at different soil depths have shown that this species has greater survival at greater depths than many arable land weeds. In New Zealand, it is one of the weeds of greatest significance after early spring cultivations. Later in the season the seedlings of *Chenopodium album* and *Solanum nigrum* become more numerous; later still the annual grasses take over (Harris 1959, Rahman 1982).

Also in New Zealand, Levy (1940) reported that areas that have been in grass for 40 or more years, if plowed in spring or autumn, show germination of many annual and perennial weed seeds as they are turned up to the light. *Coronopus* is among these weeds.

There are several countries of the world that are particularly troubled by this weed and a summary of the crops in which it appears and their appraisal of its importance will provide an appreciation of its place in agriculture. In Brazil, it is reported to be a principal weed of onion and pea fields, but it is in so many vegetable and small fruit crops that it is generally considered to be a serious weed for the country. In New Zealand, it is a common weed of onions, potatoes, and other vegetable crops. It is also found in cereals, fodder beets, soybeans, strawberries, and vineyards. In Australia and New Zealand, it is a common weed of new-sown pastures and badly managed established pastures and causes serious problems with off-flavors in milk products. In some areas it ranks as a serious weed for this reason. In Australia, it is also a weed of carrots, lucerne, onions, orchards, papaya, peas, potatoes, and vineyards. It is a principal weed of cereal and horticultural crops in Italy, and a common weed of tobacco and vegetable crops in Argentina, where it is also found in other horticultural crops, in lucerne, potatoes, and wheat. It is a principal weed of vegetable crops in Hawaii, is common in banana and other horticultural crops, and is also found in papaya and sugar cane. In India, it is a principal weed of potatoes and is also in fields of carrots, cereals, lucerne, orchards, peas, sugar beets, and wheat. Other crops that are troubled are cotton in Egypt, where it appears as a late winter weed, taro in Tonga, and nurseries and safflower in the United States.

In many places in the world domestic animals, especially beasts-of-burden, require large areas devoted to grazing to supply the necessary nutrients, and this makes them serious competitors of man for land devoted to cropping or for harvests of plant material. This shortage of nutrients for animals often necessitates the use of weeds and other noncrop plant materials. Sharma et al. (1973), in India, were prompted by the luxuriant growth and succulence of *C. didymus* to assess its palatability and nutritive value for animals. The weed has a level of crude protein comparable with the standard legumes grown for animals in the area. The palatability for rams was analogous to the best quality green forage and the digestibility coefficients and nutritive values were satisfactory when compared with the standard available feed.

Herbicides with short residual activity, if used early in the growing season, may still allow considerable seed production by *Coronopus* later in the season and thus magnify the weed problem because of additions to soil weed seed reserves. In warm areas where two to three crops can be grown yearly, it is sometimes the practice to use a very low rate of triazine herbicides on one of the crops, for example, to avoid excessive soil carry-over to following crops, thus also permitting heavy, late-season weed growth. This prompted Singh and Saroha (1975) in India to seek an appropriate, inexpensive herbicide to apply at critical stages of seed development, in order to measure the effect on later seed viability. The herbicide 2,4-D was chosen and applied at 1 kg/ha at 50% flowering and at 1-wk intervals for 5 wk thereafter. For two or three years, *Coronopus* was studied with ten each of rainy and winter season species. Mature seeds studied later revealed that there was no germination of seeds from a *C. didymus* mother plant treated at 50% flowering time. This was the most sensitive species and the seeds would not germinate even when the treatment was made 3 wk after mid-flowering time. Untreated seeds of *Coronopus* showed 10% germination each year. Some of the species whose untreated seeds gave 70 to 90% germination in the following season had no germination with herbicide treatment of the mother plant at 50% flowering. In general, for all species, each week of delay in spraying allowed the development of greater numbers of viable seeds. The authors believe the plants were more resistant to the chemical after the zygote had completed its development.

Off-flavors in milk and dairy products can be caused by onions, bad silage, several mustard crops, musty hay, or several species of weeds in pastures. As an example, Armitt (1968) in Queensland, Australia, reported that 20% of all butter submitted for grading was tainted by *C. didymus*, *Raphanus raphanistrum*, and to a lesser degree by other species. The taint in milk products from harvested forage and supplements can be controlled by withholding such animal feed, but those caused by weeds in pasture require specialized management, a more difficult task. Some off-flavors are removed during milk-processing; others are intensified. The spoilage is magnified in the areas where large tank trucks make bulk collections and mix the milk of all suppliers. These off-flavors have been a problem for some time in Australia and New Zealand and they are now becoming more frequent along the Atlantic and southern coasts of the United States.

Park (1965), Park and Arnett (1969) and Walker and Gray (1970) have studied the chemistry and break-down products of the mustard oil glucoside known to cause some of the off-flavor resulting from the ingested *C. didymus*. They reported that consumption of 50 g of such plant material by a cow can be detected in dairy products.

In heavily grazed pastures during wet periods there is much trampling and pugging (pounding and packing of soil). This, together with insect and disease attacks on sward plants, can leave many bare places for *C. didymus* to gain a foothold. For such locations, strip grazing, feeding platforms, and indoor feeding are sometimes necessary (Walker and Gray 1970, Whittet 1968).

COMMON NAMES

Coronopus didymus

ARGENTINA	calachin, mastuerzo, quimpe, yerba del ciervo
AUSTRALIA	bittercress, carrot weed, hog's cress, land cress, lesser swinecress, twin cress
BRAZIL	mastruco, mentruz
EGYPT	rashad el-barr
ENGLAND	lesser swinecress
FRANCE	coronope pinnatifide
GERMANY	Zweiknotiger Krahenfuss
HAWAII	swinecress, swine watercress
INDIA	garjri
JAPAN	karakusa-nazuna
NEW ZEALAND	twin cress
NORWAY	ramkarse
PARAGUAY	mastuerzo

PERU	huamicara, pichicara
SPAIN	mastuerzo silvestre
SWEDEN	hamnkrassing
UNITED STATES	swinecress, wart cress
URUGUAY	mastuerzo hembra

Thirty-One

The Obligate Parasitic Weeds

Cuscuta
Convolvulaceae, Morning Glory Family

The evolutionary development of a few angiosperms has enabled them to live partially or totally on other angiosperms in a parasitic mode. The *Cuscutas*, *Orobanches* and *Strigas* are chief among these parasites that affect agriculture and they are quite unlike other seed-bearing plants.

The *Cuscutas*, most widely known as "dodders," are semiparasitic, have filamentous stems with leaves reduced to small scales, and resemble a tangled bundle of small threads, many coiled about the host stem or one another. The *Orobanches*, called broomrapes, are total root parasites, lack chlorophyll and have an erect aboveground axis covered with scale-like leaves and bearing inflorescences near the top. The biology and distribution of the *Strigas*, root parasites, were summarized by Holm et al. (1977). All of these parasites remove great quantities of water and assimilates, causing serious losses of many different food and fodder crops.

PARASITIC WEEDS

Cuscuta campestris Yuncker and *Cuscuta epithymum* (L.) Murr.
Convolvulaceae, Morning Glory Family

The **Convolvulaceae** is a family of twining, prostrate herbs that has about 1000 species in 40 genera, of which only one genus, *Cuscuta*, is parasitic. Yuncker (1932) revised this genus and recognized 158 species worldwide. *C. campestris* and *C. epithymum* are the most widely distributed in man's crops and the former is the most troublesome. Because of their broad host ranges, these two species must be considered among the most dangerous of the genus for world agriculture. A collection of geographic names such as *california*, *japonica*, *rhodesiana*, and *tasmanica* has accumulated and one must ask whether a single taxon may have received several names across the world. There are few vegetative characters that remain constant enough that they may be used for identification. Flowering material is normally

FIGURE 31-1 *Cuscuta campestris* Yuncker: 1. habit; 2. seed, two views; 3. flower, 4. same, opened.

required to trace identity to the species level. *C. campestris* is reported to be a weed in 25 crops in 55 countries. *C. epithymum* is a weed in 25 crops in 13 countries.

Because the dodders are so unusual and strikingly different when compared with other weeds, and because they are difficult to identify whether viewing an infested crop or using a proper key, it has become the habit in speaking and writing to refer to them all as "dodders," much in the way the word "weed" is used loosely. For example, there are numerous accounts in the literature of seed germination, growth regulator studies, herbicide treatments and other matters performed on "dodder"—no taxon specified. This should not continue, for even though the dodders are similar in some respects, they are all unique in morphology and physiology.

There is, however, some advantage in all this for students. Because there are so many species so widely distributed in agriculture, we have been fortunate in having very good research reported at times on pieces of biology of species not widely known or seen. It is this collected wisdom that has helped us to understand the general biology of this interesting genus. Wherever possible in our account of the dodders we will indicate those experiments and results that apply specifically to *C. campestris* and *C. epithymum*.

DESCRIPTIONS

Cuscuta campestris

C. campestris (Figure 31-1) is normally an *annual*, although haustoria may overwinter within a host; *stems* terete, slender, glabrous, yellow-white, may be closely entwined about the host, some stems may be 1.5 mm long, there are *haustoria*, sucker-like attachments to the host stem; *leaves* reduced to minute scales without function; *flowers* white or reddish, up to 2 to 3 mm long from base of flower to corolla sinuses, 1 to 1.5 mm in diameter, in compact globose clusters, smooth or with scattered, pellucid, gland-like cells, on pedicels mostly shorter than the flowers; *calyx* just about enclosing corolla tube, lobes ovate to oval-ovate, mostly over-lapping when young; *corolla* lobes triangulate, acute tips often inflexed, about equaling the shorter companulate tube; *stamens* shorter than the lobes, filaments slightly subulate, inserted in corolla throat, as long or slightly longer than the oval anthers, *infrastamineal scales* reaching the filaments, ovate, abundantly fringed, exserted, bridged below the middle; 2 free *styles*, slender or somewhat subulate, as long or longer than the globose superior *ovary*; *stigmas* capitate; *fruit* usually depressed globose, membranous *capsules*, length 1.5 to 3.5 mm, width 0.8 to 1.5 mm, with withered corolla at base, 2-celled, 4-seeded, splitting irregularly; *seed* ovate in outline, about 1 to 2 mm long, hilum short, seed flattened, usually on one side, oblong, embryo slender with about 2 coils, the seed of the biotype in California in the United States is quite smooth, dull pink or gray-tan color, in South Africa gray-brown and verrucose, in the former Soviet Union yellow brown, weight of 1000 seeds, 0.87 gm.

Cuscuta epithymum

C. epithymum (Figure 31-2) is normally an *annual*; *stems* slender, sometimes reddish or purplish, bearing reduced scale-like leaves without function; *haustoria*, sucker-like attachments grow on the host stem; *flowers* pinkish to reddish, 2 to 3 mm long from flower base

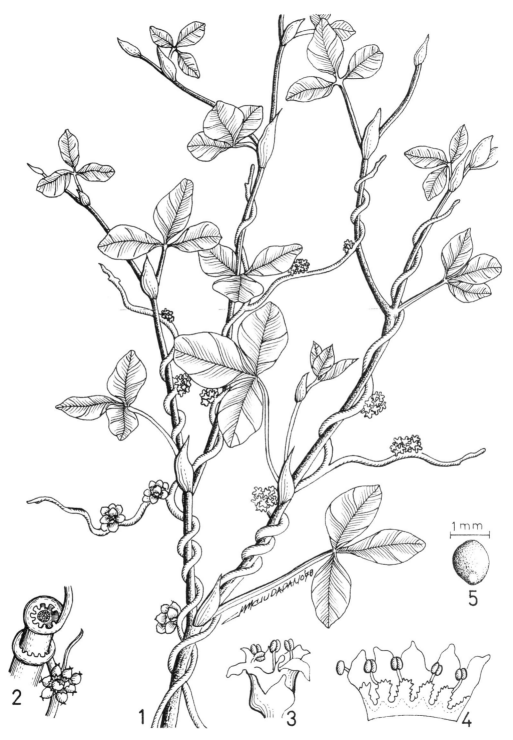

FIGURE 31-2 *Cuscuta epithymum* (L.) Murr.: 1. habit; 2. fruit cluster and haustoria; 3. flower, 4. same, opened; 5. seed.

to corolla sinuses, 5 parted, numerous, sessile, in dense compact clusters; *calyx* as long or shorter than corolla tube, lobes triangular, sometimes purplish; *corolla* lobes triangular, acute, shorter than companulate tube, scales more or less spatulate, shorter than the tube, fringed about the upper part, bridged at about one-third their height; *stamens* shorter than the lobes, filaments longer than oval anthers; *stigmas* oblong, not capitate as in *C. campestris* and *C. suaveolens*; *ovary* globose with slightly thickened apex, styles and stigmas about twice as long as ovary; *capsule* globose, circumscissile, capped by withered corolla; *seed* about 1 mm long, rough, coarsely granular and pitted, angled and compressed-ovoid, usually 4 in a capsule, hilum short, oblong, transverse, dull gray or gray-brown like particles of earth, 0.5 to 1 mm in diameter, weight of 1000 seeds, 0.3 gm. (Kothekar 1970).

DISTRIBUTION AND HABITAT

Annotated bibliographies on the biology, distribution, and control of the dodders have been prepared periodically by the Weed Research Organization of England. Numbers 32 and 146 cover the period 1923 through 1982 (Weed Research Organization 1923 to 1982). *C. campestris* and *C. epithymum* are generally distributed all over the range of the genus and throughout the agriculture of the warm and temperate regions (Figures 31-3 and 31-4). In general we may say that a suitable habitat for a dodder species need only be that of a compatible host; however, there remains much to be learned about the limits of dispersal, the habitats, and the biogeography of most dodder species. Yuncker (1935), after 20 years of research on the *Cuscutas*, reported that the north-south range of *C. campestris* is from Chile and Argentina to Canada in the Americas and from the Cape of Good Hope almost to the Arctic in the Old World. *C. campestris* is recorded at lat 60° N in Sweden and *C. epithymum* was found at lat 65° N and in mountains at 2200 m in the former Soviet Union by Kothekar (1970). Francois (1930) found *C. epithymum* above 2000 m in the mountains of France. Bloomfield and Ruxton (1977) reported that dodder species came into legumes and grasses grown in Saudi Arabia as new areas were used for land reclamation crops under saline conditions in arid land agriculture. In the east of India in Bengal, *C. campestris* was introduced in 1965 and in only 8 years it had spread to south India.

Figure 31-3 shows that several regions are not troubled with *C. campestris*, but they may very well be concerned about other dodder species. For example, *C. campestris* and *C. epithymum* are reported to behave as weeds in only a few agricultural areas of Central and South America and the Pacific Islands, and yet Yuncker (1932) found them in the floras of Argentina, Martinique, Puerto Rico and also in Fiji, New Caledonia and Tahiti in the Pacific. Surely they have also been brought into other areas in these regions along with agricultural supplies.

Propagules are plentiful, with one plant of *C. epithymum* reported to produce 16,000 seeds. Surely the principal means of dispersal is with crop seeds, for those of the parasite are similar to and often difficult to separate from some of the major agricultural fruits and seeds. Early, simple devices for seed cleaning were the use of velvet rollers to which the rough, craggy seed coats adhered, and iron dust to impregnate the crevices and pores of the seed coat for later removal with magnets. Seed of some dodders remains viable while passing through the animal gut and must be considered important in the spread of the weed.

FIGURE 31-3   The distribution of *Cuscuta campestris* Yuncker across the world where it has been reported as a weed.

FIGURE 31-4   The distribution of *Cuscuta epithymum* (L.) Murr. across the world where it has been reported as a weed.

PROPAGATION AND REPRODUCTIVE BIOLOGY

The flowers of the parasite are borne close to the point of attachment to the host. Those of *C. campestris* are normally self-pollinated but can be cross-pollinated. Those of *C. epithymum* are normally cross-pollinated but in the absence of insects may be self-pollinated. The flowers and inflorescences of these plants are the taxonomic characters used for identification and separation of species. Gaertner (1950) and Golova (1967) have provided keys for seed identification of some dodder species.

Baldev (1962) and Jacob (1966) reported that a short-day photoperiod is required for flowering of *C. reflexa*. Fratianne (1965) studied the relationship of flowering in *C. campestris* and two long-day plants (*Matricaria* and *Hyoscyamus* species) and two short-day plants (soybean and *Xanthium* species). When held in inductive and noninductive photoperiods, the parasite did not prevent flowering and the numbers of flowers on the host were about the same whether parasitized or not. Dodder flowered only on hosts that were in flower. With host defoliation and other experiments, he tried to show that a naturally produced flowering hormone was involved in these flowering relationships. Such hormones have never been characterized and Baldev (1962) and Jacob (1966) found no evidence for a flowering hormone in experiments with *C. reflexa*.

Seeds of *C. campestris* will germinate in light and in dark, do not require a chemical stimulant from a host for germination and are not dormant at harvest time, although Hutchison and Ashton (1979, 1980) suggest that they only need a few days of maturation and then germination may slow. As they begin to dry, they are quickly deprived of moisture by the development of an impervious layer in the testa of the seed coat. The seeds are ready to grow whenever this barrier is breached by natural forces or by man in the laboratory (Hutchison and Ashton 1979). Many researchers speak of hard seed and soft seed, referring perhaps to the degree of permeability of the seed coat. *C. epithymum* does not require a host stimulant for seed germination.

In dry storage and in the field, the seeds of *C. campestris* may survive 10 to 20 yr and *C. gronovii* for 30 yr (Dawson et al. 1984). *C. cuspidata, california, indecora,* and *pentagona* may survive 50 yr or more.

Gaertner (1950) found satisfactory germination of freshly harvested seed of *C. campestris*, but in a few days, as the seed coat began to dry, germination became more difficult. On older seeds a 65-min treatment with sulfuric acid resulted in 75% germination, while an 80-min treatment of 20-yr-old seeds gave 80% germination. Ashton and Santana (1976) obtained 100% germination of *C. campestris* seeds by rubbing them between layers of fine sandpaper.

The optimum temperature for germination of this species in the laboratory is 30 to 33°C, with a lower limit of 10°C and some decrease in activity above 40°C (Stojanovic 1959, Allred and Tingey 1964, Stojanovic and Mijatovic 1973, Hutchison and Ashton 1980). In a study of seed germination in three dodder species in the western United States in spring, Allred and Tingey (1964) found that the main period of germination for *C. approximata* began when soil temperature rose to 5°C, while *C. campestris* and *C. indecora* could not germinate until the temperature was 10°C. These patterns serve to explain the prevailing dodder problem in lucerne in that area. Whether cut for seed or hay, the early germinating *C. approximata* caused serious infestations in the first lucerne crop. The later germinating species continued to emerge all through the summer, giving some trouble in the first crop but much trouble in all subsequent cuttings. *C. epithymum* germinates best at 15°C in the greenhouse; in the field it begins to emerge 2 wk after the soil temperatures reach 10°C. The optimum temperature for germination and the period of longevity in soil varies with each *Cuscuta* species.

Flowering and seed production of *C. campestris* and *C. epithymum* normally continues for several months and they may be shedding seeds as crops are harvested. In the northwestern United States, Dawson (1965) sowed known quantities of seed of *C. campestris* in controlled field and greenhouse experiments. Emergence was recorded weekly for 2 yr. From his results it is clear that any successful control effort must be effective over several months of each growing season and infested fields must be monitored for sporadic germination over several years.

Seeds of *C. campestris* were sown under simulated field conditions and emergence was recorded for 5 yr by Hutchison and Ashton (1980). Less than 10% of the total seeds planted ever emerged, most in the first 2 yr and none in the 5th yr. This great loss in viability suggests that these seeds do not persist long in working fields. There is the possibility, of course, that some dormant seeds still remain in the soil. Allred and Tingey (1964) buried seeds of *C. campestris* from 1 to 7.5 cm deep in a sandy loam soil and found that the earliest germination and greatest total emergence occurred from the most shallow depths. Hutchison and Ashton (1980) buried seed at intervals to 20 cm and found the greatest germination in the top 3 cm, with none emerging below 6.5 cm. Stojanovic and Mijatovic (1973) in the former Yugoslavia, however, reported that seed depth did not greatly influence germination. Seeds on the surface germinated in 3 days and those at 4 to 5 cm emerged in 6 days. In Armenia, Karapetyan (1972) found maximum emergence of dodder seeds 4 to 6 yr after field burial. In the former Soviet Union, Gruzdev and Prishchepo (1984) found that seed ripening on the soil surface resulted in the formation of hard seed coats that could provide seed germination over a period of several years. Seeds buried at 50 cm depth survived longer than those buried 10 cm.

In the western United States *C. campestris* seeds still gave 50% germination after being submerged in a bag in a canal for 5 yr (Comes et al. 1978). The response of hard and soft seeds of *C. campestris* to fumigants, a high temperature of 45°C to simulate a hot sun exposure, and the herbicide pronamide were studied by Horowitz et al. (1983a) in Israel. All treatments affected the soft seeds. The hard seeds later germinated immediately when scarified with acid.

Dodder stems stripped from a host may regenerate and grow (Truscott 1958). *C. campestris* may be seen growing on detached pieces of a suitable host (Olifirenko 1959, Urton 1945).

HABIT OF GROWTH

The detailed observations of the life of a *Cuscuta* plant by Lyshede (1985) in Denmark present the opportunity to first glance across the full cycle of growth and thus become acquainted with some special events which we must discuss more fully.

As the radical emerges from the seed near the hilum region it swells enormously and then collapses in a few days. Meanwhile the tip of the seedling, still within the seed coat, absorbs all of the nutrients, emerges to an erect stance and begins to nutate (wave about) as though in search of a foreign object to which it may become attached. In a few days the seedling lowers to the soil and begins to move across the surface toward the light source of highest intensity. It extends with new growth at the apex as the basal portion wilts, thus always retaining a segment of the stem that remains alive. Lyshede found the seedlings, with no host present, could survive up to 4 wk if the ground was moistened daily. In his experiment he used *C. campestris* and *pedicillata*, which behaved similarly.

The seedlings, about 1 to 1.5 cm tall, look like fine yellow threads and are difficult to see. If the soil is dry they may emerge from a crack. No part of the plant is deeper in the soil than the seed, but the first stem-like structure seems to absorb moisture as roots do. Later the dodder-soil contact seems mainly for anchorage until connection is established with a host (Kuijt 1969, Dawson et al. 1984).

The seedling is succulent, resists desiccation and does not seem to be stressed for moisture in its early life. Hot dry winds may however damage it before connection to a host. Dependent upon parasite species, age, weather and other environmental factors, if a suitable host is not available, the parasite may shut down most activities while waiting for a new, nearby, host seedling to appear (Dawson 1987).

Lyshede observed that the dodder sometimes grew near suitable hosts without making contact. Placing dodder stems upon the host did not often cause a suitable contact to be made and resulted in a shunning of the parasite, which then grew on. He observed that plants of a compatible host *Trifolium alexandrinum*, when less than 3 wk old were not attractive to the dodders. Sitkin (1976) found that placing host seedlings more than 3 cm from the parasite greatly reduced chances of contact. In crop fields, workers have reported that other weed plants may host a parasite until it can reach a crop. Again, one dodder plant may have working contacts with more than one host species.

Recently Muller et al. (1993) reported on a method of collecting stimulants and inhibitors exuded from roots of cowpea and millet via trays with recovery by use of resins. The *Cuscutas* were not used in their trials, but the germination of seeds of the parasites *Alectra* and *Striga* was affected by the exudates of the above crops. The quantitative release of these and other compounds could be measured. Presumably these methods could be used to determine the existence of the host-released attractants or germination stimulators that have been the subject of much conjecture.

In the event of an encounter and ultimate connection with a compatible host there is a marked change in the growth habit of the parasite. In *C. campestris* and *C. pedicillata*, Lyshede (1985) reported the cessation of stem growth as the haustorium developed and the loss of contact with the soil. At the apex, differentiation of the scale leaves and buds became apparent and soon the main shoot resumed growth and developed side branches. The shoots of active dodders may extend 50 mm or more in one day. In Hungary, once established, the dodders grow most vigorously at sites and in seasons of warm, dry, sunny weather.

Dean (1937) found that *C. gronovii* could establish one or more close coils around a host within 5 hr of contact, prehaustoria in the 2 days following, and in 5 days haustoria growth invaded the host cortex. The spread of field dodder appears as scattered patches at first, but soon the crop may be blanketed with filamentous biomass that kills it or greatly reduces yields. A single plant may cover a patch more than 3 m in diameter in a season. Dean (1942) recorded almost 75 m of branching growth from a single dodder plant in one season in the central United States.

In the experiments of Lyshede (1985), as the host showed signs of weakening, the parasite began to flower. Some of the haustoria attached to such plants may die and decay, leaving a hole in the host plant to which insects and microorganisms are attracted. As the host *Trifolium alexandrinum* was overcome by the parasite and finally killed, some dodder plants were able to survive on the dead plants for many days.

Dodders are generally considered to be annuals, but Dean (1954) summarized evidence from Germany, Mexico, and the United States for overwinter survival of *C. epithy-*

mum. He also demonstrated with *C. gronovii* on squash (*Cucurbita pepo*) and *C. polygonorum* on willow (*Salix nigra*) that galls formed at the haustorial sites in the host and enabled the parasites to survive the winter and produce shoots in the spring. In another example, Stojanovic and Mijatovic (1973) found that *C. epithymum* overwinters in the crowns of red clover, lucerne and weeds in areas or seasons when the winters were not severe.

Seeds of *C. campestris* will germinate in dark and upon emergence will grow toward the highest light source. During its full life cycle, in reduced light, *C. campestris* shows a decrease in total dry solids, protein and phosphorus in its filament biomass. The response of the host plant is often similar but less pronounced (Setty and Krishnan 1970). Dawson (1966) found that, when they were growing in the shade of lucerne, the attachment of the parasites to the crop was reduced by 90%, the process was delayed by 1 wk, and the growth and maturity of the dodder was seriously delayed.

ANATOMY AND MORPHOLOGY
HAUSTORIUM AND OTHER PLANT STRUCTURES

After germination and seedling growth, the plant soon loses its connection with the soil and must soon establish contact with a host. The *haustoria* of the parasite develop on the coils on the side adjacent to the host stem. Twining and haustorial formation are induced in natural light but not in darkness. If these processes are initiated in white light they continue if plants are placed in darkness. Red light inhibits twining and haustorial formation, far red light promotes it and Pizzolongo (1966) found blue light to be the most effective region of the spectrum for initiation of these events (Zimmerman 1962, Lane and Kasperbauer 1965).

The dodder haustorium was the first to receive special study (Guettard 1744). Small superficial protuberances develop at the sites where coils are in contact with the host and these grow to fill uneven places in the host stems. On the parasite coil, at the point of contact, some cells elongate rapidly and press onto the host, forming a prehaustorium. Following this, meristematic cells form a cushion-like wedge or cone of cells that push through the prehaustorium and into the host (Thoday 1911; Thompson 1925; Truscott 1958; Kuijt 1969, 1977; Kuijt and Toth 1976). Tsivion (1978a) used a cotton string impregnated with cytokinin, benzyladenine, as a substitute for the host and found the haustorium initials grew and penetrated the prehaustorium and entered into the string.

The penetration of these early cells soon ceases and then the leading cells of the haustorium, especially those near the tip of the wedge, begin to extend and form separate filaments or *hyphae*. These structures proceed by dissolving small openings in the parenchyma cell walls of the host. The hyphae tips then enter the cells, grow to the opposite side, and penetrate into other cells. Some hyphae grow along the middle *lamellae* of the host cells.

These "searching" hyphae travel out in several directions in the foreign tissues and some, by chance, contact the conducting elements of the host. There is no direct evidence that they are "drawn" toward specific tissues of the host, as has often been claimed.

During this time, in the haustorial tissues, some cells begin to differentiate to form xylem and phloem elements (Israel et al. 1980). Dorr (1987) found that these conducting tissues are not derived from procambial strands but seem to differentiate from normal haustorial cells. This development proceeds acropetally from the *Cuscuta* stem.

The "searching" hyphae now reach the vicinity of the vascular bundles and the tips develop elongated contact cells that become attached to either the xylem or phloem strands of the host. Then, in 1980, Israel et al. (1980) reported that the haustoria of *C. odorata* and *C. grandiflora* show continuous traces of sieve elements connecting the phloem of the host with that of the *Cuscuta* shoot. This was determined by callose fluorescence after staining with aniline blue. Then the fine structural criteria for sieve tubes were analyzed by electron microscope with special attention to sieve pores, P-protein, and a distinct wall-standing smooth surfaced endoplasmic reticulum.

Dorr (1987) reported that haustorial filaments can easily penetrate host parenchyma cells and readily establish plasmodesmata in these foreign cell walls. Three *Cuscuta* species on five different host plants have all shown the ability to place plasmodesmata in the host cells (Dorr 1987). It is not yet known how the sieve tube constituents or segments that lie within the haustorial cells are connected to the structures of the host and parasite at the points of contact. These interfaces are probably the points of transfer for water and assimilates. The mechanisms of transfer and actual pathways are still to be elucidated.

Dorr (1969, 1987) reported that we do not yet know if there is a direct, open connection between the haustorium and the xylem of the host.

The earliest major effort to extend the study of the anatomy and morphology beyond the haustorium was by Mirande (1901) almost a century ago and these mysterious but fascinating plants have been the subject of many examinations since that time. Yuncker (1932), in a revision of the genus, provided the following illustrations of the reproductive structures (without which identification is impossible for most species) of the 158 species recognized at the time: entire flower, corolla and calyx openly displayed, pistil or mature capsule or both, individual scales, and a seed and a bract for some species. Major structures of the dodders have been studied and illustrated by Smith (1934), Melikyan and Khandzhyan (1968), Kuijt (1969), Lyshede (1985), and Heide-Jorgensen (1987).

Dawson (1984) discovered that careful observation of vegetative characters may disclose differences that are useful in separating similar species. *C. campestris*, *C. indecora*, and *C. planiflora* look much alike, and sometimes grow in the same area. He found that a tendril that arises outside the axil of the scale leaf at each node of *C. campestris* and *indecora* twines about the leaves and stem of the host plants. The primary stems do not twine but continue to grow forward and spread over large areas of a crop. In contrast, *C. planiflora* does not bear tendrils and it is the primary and lateral stems that twine about the host. This habit results in smaller, more dense patches of the parasite.

Johri and Tiagi (1952) and Johri (1987) have completed extensive studies of the embryology of *C. reflexa* and other *Cuscuta* species and have provided excellent photographs of the reproductive process. Fedortschuk (1931) investigated the embryology of *C. epithymum* and *C. monogyna*. The seeds of dodder were studied by Ashton and Santana (1976) and Lyshede (1984) and their reports are well illustrated with electron photomicrographs. Dean (1937, 1954) described the anatomical changes of the host-parasite as haustorial tissues overwinter within *Cuscuta*-induced galls.

PHYSIOLOGY

Mac Leod (1961a,b) examined the pigments found in dodders and was one of the first to show that the plants fix CO_2. He made quantitative measurements of chlorophylls a and b and carotenoids in *C. campestris* and *C. reflexa*, reporting their locations within the cell and in various parts of the plant. *C. campestris* often appears yellow or orange because great concentrations of carotenoid pigments mask the chlorophylls. Photosynthesis has been confirmed in the seedling stems of *C. epilinum* and *C. australis*, together with the flowers of the latter. Light and dark fixation of CO_2 takes place in *C. pentagona*.

Pattee et al. (1965), using radioactive carbon and manometric methods, studied CO_2 uptake in light and darkness in *C. campestris*. They found low levels of photosynthesis overall, with seedlings having the highest rate. Photosynthesis decreased as the plant became parasitic. The authors believe that under ordinary day and night conditions the photosynthate produced in the light period would probably not be sufficient to maintain the dodder through the nighttime hours. The experiments of Ciferri and Poma (1963a,b), however, gave results somewhat different from earlier reports. Using chromatographic methods on plant extracts following the assimilation of $C^{14}O_2$, the radioactivity was detected in areas corresponding to dark fixation products such as organic and amino acids rather than photosynthetic products such as 3-phosphoglycerate, sugars and sugar phosphates.

It now appears that dodders are more self-sufficient than we had believed earlier. We know that they are dependent upon the host for moisture and inorganic nutrients. We know that they can photosynthesize to some degree whether attached to a host or not. We are aware that they eventually die if the connection with the host is severed. The degree to which they are dependent upon the host for the products of primary metabolism, other than sugars, or the products of secondary metabolism, however, are questions that need a great deal more research. For example, although we categorize the *Cuscutas* as obligate parasites, Baldev (1959) grew *C. reflexa* through a *full life cycle* on aseptic media.

The finding of Lyshede (1985), related earlier, that in early life an unattached dodder plant was capable of growth for weeks on moist soil while maintaining a shoot segment of constant length is surprising. Enzymatic activities of various kinds have been reported in several dodders and this caused Nandakumar and Krishnan (1976) to wonder if parasitism resulted from missing links in metabolic systems. They made comparative studies of the enzyme systems associated with the metabolism of starches, sugars, amino acids, and phosphorylated compounds in resting, mature seeds of *C. campestris* and other species. They found that the activity of various enzymes sustained low rates of respiration using carbohydrates. There was a potential capacity for accelerating the metabolism on imbibition of the seed. They learned that the metabolism of such seeds has features quite similar to the seeds of autotrophs. They speculate that perhaps the enzyme systems operating in the seedling may hold the key to the need for parasitism (see also Charles et al. 1982). The nitrogen metabolism of *C. campestris* and *C. reflexa* was studied by Mac Leod (1963) to determine the degree to which these parasites were able to put together organic nitrogen compounds needed for protein building and to inquire into the need for host-derived compounds of this nature. He selected glutamic dehydrogenase and transaminase because of their roles in the metabolism of glutamic acid, which can serve as a precursor of amino acids in protein synthesis.

Of 16 amino acids in the test, only aspartic acid showed appreciable transamination with α ketoglutarate in *C. campestris*, with moderate activity in alanine, valine, asparagine, and methionine. One-half of the amino acids registered no activity. When experiments included dodder growing on several different hosts, and the hosts as well, he found that *Cuscuta* had favorable transamination levels as compared with the hosts. He wondered whether host enzymes released by rupture of cells by growing haustoria may have traveled through phloem or xylem to reach the parasite. However, the extracts of the hosts, *Vitis* and *Pelargonium* species, registered no transaminase activity, while such activity was shown in the extracts of *Cuscuta* plants attached to these hosts.

Perhaps all this suggests that the seat of synthesis of the enzymes is within the parasite. We have already seen that it can photosynthesize and here again we find it more capable than we had supposed, for it may be that there are certain inorganic and organic compounds acquired from the host that it can use in its metabolic system to produce some of the building blocks it needs for its own maintenance and growth.

At those sites in the host stem where absorbing hyphae seem to be attached to xylem and phloem, we find contact or transfer cells that appear to be especially adapted to the exchange of water and solutes between host and parasite. Several workers have shown that the movement of dyes and labelled inorganic and organic material from host to parasite can be accomplished in minutes (Harvey 1930, Mac Leod 1961b, Allred 1966, Littlefield et al. 1966, Salageanu and Fabian-Galan 1968, Wolswinkel 1975). Movement is usually from host to dodder even when metabolism of the former is at a low level, but Littlefield demonstrated solute movement in the opposite direction as well.

After many decades of research in laboratories across the world, improved techniques and new instruments have recently assisted in clarifying some of the questions about the structures and mechanisms involved in the movement of water and solutes in parasites. For example, Dorr (1987) concluded from her studies based on excellent photomicrographs that at the point of xylem contact we do not yet know "whether there is an open connection between the two systems or whether the passage is of tracheidal nature."

We may not yet understand the transfer of nourishment to the parasite, but we do know many things about the exchange. Wolswinkel (1974a) found that most of the C^{14} labelled assimilates of the host accumulate in the parasite and with this there is a cessation of development of the host fruits. Fruits are normally strong "sinks" for metabolites, causing Wolswinkel to label the parasite a "supersink" that can drain away many food reserves from the host.

In several studies, Wolswinkel (1974b, 1975, 1977) challenged the oft-held opinion that there is a passive leakage of materials through the host sieve tube plasmalemmas and that this is influenced by the parasite. He established that there is a metabolically controlled release mechanism for host assimilates by demonstrating its alteration with metabolic inhibitors and low temperatures.

Long ago, Thompson (1925) concluded from nutrition studies on *C. reflexa* that the well-formed xylem connections from host to parasite could be the main channel of both organic and inorganic food supply for the parasite. Much later, Peel (1974), having reviewed the large body of research on solute transport in plants, pointed out that all mobile substances in plants may be in both phloem and xylem and that they often move between the two conduit systems. Tsivion (1978b) speculated that this may happen in the host-parasite relationship. Organic and inorganic substances needed by the parasite may cross the xylem bridge and a later exchange of transport routes in the haustorium must then be considered.

Viruses can be moved from host to parasite in the laboratory by using dodder as a bridge between two compatible hosts. The pathway by which this occurs is unknown.

Tsivion (1978a,b) believes that the parasite withdraws resources from the host according to its degree of dependence on that host and that there may be a nonmetabolic withdrawal of nutrients through the transpiration stream and perhaps some by diffusion. There is probably also a complex of activities which is in part metabolic to regulate movement across membranes in the host cells.

ECONOMIC IMPORTANCE

C. campestris is a serious weed of cabbage, lucerne, and other legumes, peppers, potatoes, and tomatoes in Hungary; carrots and onions in Switzerland; legumes in Pakistan; lentils in Syria; lucerne in Australia, South Africa, the United States, and the former Yugoslavia; sugar beets in the former Yugoslavia; and tomatoes and other vegetables in the United States. It is a principal weed of carrots in Italy; clovers and other legumes in the former Yugoslavia; both irrigated and dryland crops, including vegetables, in Australia; lucerne in Saudi Arabia; and tobacco in the former Soviet Union. It is a common weed of carrots in England; clovers and other legumes in Czechoslovakia, Saudi Arabia, and the former Yugoslavia; maize in Bolivia; lucerne in Bulgaria, Mexico, and Turkey; and onions and other vegetables in Bulgaria and Turkey.

C. campestris is found in many other crops for which we have no rank of importance. For example, the preference of this parasite for forage legumes makes it a pest in Australia, Chile, Czechoslovakia, India, Italy, and Jordan. It parasitizes beans, beets, peas, and other vegetables in Canada, Czechoslovakia, India, Israel, Japan, the Netherlands, Pakistan, the former Soviet Union, and Switzerland. It is found on safflower in Italy; lowland rice in some areas of the Philippines; in sugar beets in Chile, the former Soviet Union, and Turkey; and pastures in South Africa and Uganda.

The list of crops parasitized by *C. epithymum* is similar to that of *C. campestris* but is not as extensive. It is again a serious or principal weed in lucerne and other legumes in Australia, Hungary, Italy, and Turkey. It is serious in cabbage, peppers, potatoes, and tomatoes in Hungary. It is a principal weed of clover and other legumes in Italy. Additional crops troubled by this parasite are flax, orchards, ornamentals, and pastures. Belgium, Egypt, New Zealand, Romania, Spain, and Venezuela have trouble with this weed in one or more crops.

It is interesting but not surprising that these two dodder species are not widely represented as weeds in the crops of Latin America, Western Africa, China, and eastern Asia. But this does not mean that dodders are absent. For example, in one of China's main crops, soybeans, there has long been a dodder problem, and in Argentina these weeds have been serious pests in lucerne for decades, but these problems are caused by other *Cuscuta* species.

In reviews of the world's parasitic weed problems, Parker (1978) and Parker and Wilson (1986) expressed the belief that *C. campestris* is the most widespread of the *Cuscutas* and the most aggressive and troublesome in our economic crops.

Legislation in 25 countries lists the dodders as "declared noxious weeds," with seeds and plant material denied entrance. In the United States, it is the only weed seed whose movement is prohibited in every state. In the former Soviet Union, *C. campestris* and *epithymum* are among the most troublesome dodders; in Australia *C. epithymum* is the most important; in South Africa, which has 12 indigenous species of dodder, both of these species are active but *C. campestris* is the most aggressive. The dodders have now begun to invade natural grazing lands. They are among the ten species indigenous to Canada, with *C. campestris* mainly in Ontario and Quebec, and *C. epithymum* in British Columbia and Ontario. The latter is not as vigorous in these northern regions.

It is quite generally agreed that the movement of unclean crop seed has been the greatest contributor to dispersal throughout the world; however, very little study has been devoted to other means of dispersal.

The physical competition for space, light and nutrients offered by *C. campestris* and other dodders, and the long-term contamination of fields is a serious matter. In the production of crop seeds, the dodders impose a severe limitation because of difficulty of removal of their seeds when the crop is graded out, thus reducing yield and quality. To this must be added increased cost of harvesting and cleaning.

There are other difficulties peculiar to regions and localities. For example, in South Africa some of the areas ideally suited for lucerne seed production have very low rainfall, and irrigation is so expensive that other crops cannot be grown profitably. Now some of these areas have to be abandoned because of severe dodder infestations in lucerne and there is no other way for people to earn a living (Nel 1955).

In the former Yugoslavia there are ten species of dodder that infest 20 crops and attack a total of 60 known plant species. *C. campestris* ranks as one of the top three weeds in lucerne *Medicago sativa* and red clover *Trifolium pratense* production. In some years 80% of these crops may be infested and 20% of the acreage abandoned. For this reason it is a serious obstacle to cattle production (Stojanovic and Mijatovic 1973, Daams 1975). In some years the profitability of growing sugar beets is now questioned because these weeds are known to reduce yields by 10 to 60%, sugar content 20 to 55%, and seed germination by 12%. Because the dodders are often on upper and middle plant surfaces of crops, and to protect soils from further additions to the weed seed bank, the plant material is cut just above the soil and destroyed.

In the Kirghiz region of the former Soviet Union, *C. campestris* is one of the worst weeds of field crops. Efforts to reduce losses include use of herbicides, harrowing sugar beets 3 to 4 days before emergence, and harvest of beet leaves with dodder for processing into vitamin-rich meal or flour. Radio and television warnings are given during a month-long campaign about the dodders and colored leaflets are dropped from airplanes. In some valleys, 80% of the sugar beet monocultures are stricken with the weed and 75,000 seeds/m² have accumulated in the soil. Reduction of yields and sugar content are similar to those for the former Yugoslavia (Rogachev 1969, Lukovin and Kitenko 1974, Lukovin and Rudenko 1975). Also in eastern Europe, *C. campestris* and *epithymum* in Czechoslovakia cause great damage in lucerne and other legume seed and fodder crops and may wipe out entire stands in some years. Of late, one-third of the fields of legumes used for seed production have been unacceptable at market because of dodder, and a lowering of grade of 40% of all seed production crops has taken place (Frolisek 1987).

Stomach, intestinal and blood disorders in cattle and horses, and symptoms of toxicity and poisoning have been reported from laboratory and field ingestions of dodders. Little firm evidence of serious problems is available (Azarian 1954, Kingsbury 1964, Movsesian and Azarian 1971, Parsons 1973).

There is no widely accepted use of biological control for *Cuscuta* species, although a few organisms show promise (Baloch et al. 1967, Protosenko 1981, Cooke and Black 1987). Gall formation caused on *C. pentagona* by feeding *Smicronyx* weevils was reported in the central United States a half century ago by Yuncker (1935). Recently there has been renewed interest in certain species of this insect for dodder control in the Kirghiz area of the former Soviet Union. The weevils are restricted to *Cuscuta*. There is some concern about parasites that have been attacking the weevil and decreasing its effectiveness (Lekic 1970b, Tyurebaev 1977, Khan and Zafar 1981, Horvath 1983).

In north China, conidial suspensions of the plant pathogen *Colletotrichum gleosporioides* gave very effective control of *C. australis* and *C. chinensis* which cause severe losses in soybeans (Li 1987).

Using *Fusarium tricinctum* and an *Alternaria* species, two pathogens of dodder, Bewick et al. (1987) have recently reported very promising results for the control of swamp dodder *Cuscuta gronovii*. There are severe infestations of this dodder on vegetables on organic muck soils in Wisconsin in the north-central United States, and in cranberries in Massachusetts in the northeastern United States. Bewick et al. (1988) later developed a degree day model for predicting the emergence time of this dodder.

HOST RELATIONSHIPS

Citing firm numbers of hosts for these two widespread *Cuscutas* from the literature is a futile exercise, for one can seldom discern whether the perspective is for a country or a region and whether the data refer to mixed economic crops and wild hosts in these places. Figures 31-3 and 31-4 give the geographical distribution of these species. In addition, the degree of susceptibility will depend on the age and physiological condition of the host observed, as well as the race or biotype of the dodder species under study. Suffice it to say that *C. campestris* and *C. epithymum* are troublemakers and each can attack several dozen hosts. Only rarely does *C. campestris* parasitize grasses and other monocots. *C. epithymum* grows well on several grasses and other plants in the **Gramineae** and is probably more widespread than any other dodder. It may also attack more host species than *C. campestris* but it is not as destructive.

Some examples of the economic crops that are favorites of *C. campestris* are asparagus, carrots, chickpea, various clovers, grapevines, honeydew melons, linseed, lucerne, mangels, onions, potato, sugar beet, tobacco, tomato, and turnips. Many of these are also parasitized by *C. epithymum*, which in addition attacks the following: blue grass *Poa pratensis*, maize, lentils, *Origanum* species (marjoram) and ryegrasses. It is of course found on thyme, from which its species name is derived.

Gaertner (1950) reviewed the literature and studied host relationships experimentally for 609 species in 75 families for 10 dodder species. She found no single dodder species that was specific for a single host. See also Dean (1934, 1935) and Allred and Tingey (1957).

A *Cuscuta* plant does not thrive equally well on all plants that it parasitizes. It may grow exceptionally well, may survive, produce seed quickly and die, or may simply remain attached and wait for a better host, and all the while its welfare may depend on the vigor and well being of its host. Dodders may parasitize other dodders. Instances of self-parasitism are known.

COMMON NAMES

Cuscuta campestris

AUSTRALIA	dodder
CANADA	field dodder, cuscute de champs
ENGLAND	field dodder
FRANCE	cuscute de champs
GERMANY	Nordamerikanishe Seide
INDIA	swarnalata
MADAGASCAR	tsihitafototra
MOROCCO	cuscute de champs

NETHERLANDS	veldwarkruid
SAUDI ARABIA	dubbay, hamool
UNITED STATES	angel's hair, common dodder, field dodder, strangle vine

Cuscuta epithymum

ARGENTINA	cuscuta
AUSTRALIA	European dodder
BELGIUM	klaverwarkruid
CANADA	clover dodder, cuscuta du thym
DENMARK	klover-silke
ENGLAND	dodder
FINLAND	apilanvieras
FRANCE	cuscute du trefle
GERMANY	Kleeseide, Quendel-Seide
ITALY	cuscuta del trifoglio
NETHERLANDS	duivelsnaaigaren
NEW ZEALAND	clover dodder, devil's gut
NORWAY	timiansnikjetrad
PORTUGAL	cabelos
SOUTH AFRICA	klein dodder, lesser dodder
SPAIN	epitimo
UNITED STATES	clover dodder

The recent publication of Dawson, J., Musselman, L., Wolswinkel, F., and Dorr, I., 1994, Biology and Control of *Cuscuta, Reviews of Weed science* 6:265–317, provides important information for researchers interested in the *Cuscutas*.

Thirty-Two

Cyperus brevifolius (Rottb.) Hassk. and Cyperus haspan L.

Cyperaceae, Sedge Family

BOTH *CYPERUS BREVIFOLIUS* and *C. haspan* are herbaceous perennial sedges common in wet, poorly drained areas in many tropical and subtropical environments. The generic name is from the Greek for reed or sedge; the specific name *brevifolius* refers to the short leaves. *Kyllinga brevifolia* is a synonym for this species. Fifty-five countries have reported these species as weeds and yet very little is known about their biology and growth habits.

DESCRIPTIONS

Cyperus brevifolius

C. brevifolius (Figure 32-1) is a mat-forming *perennial* herb spreading by means of slender, creeping *rhizomes* 1 to 3 mm in diameter covered with reddish-brown scales; *stems* slender, 3-angled, 5 to 50 cm tall (often 10 cm or less) and 0.5 to 1.5 mm wide; smooth, with reddish-brown sheaths at the base, *leaves* 3 to 6 from each stem, linear, 10 to 20 cm long, 3 mm wide or less, margins scabrous on upper part; *inflorescence* a single globose to ovoid terminal head, 5 to 10 mm in diameter, rarely with 2 or 3 smaller, sessile heads at the base; heads at first greenish, turning whitish with age; subtended by 3 or 4 (rarely 5 to 6) *involucral bracts*, spreading to reflexed, 5 to 10 cm long, longest bract upright or obliquely upright when plant is young; *spikelets* numerous, 2 to 4 mm long by 1 mm wide, 1- or 2-flowered, bunched into heads of many spikelets; heads 6 to 7 mm in diameter, elliptic-oblong or oblong-lanceolate, detaching as a whole; *glumes* as long as spikelet, strongly compressed, membranous, acutely keeled with 2 or 3 nerves on the sides, wing-like more or less spinulose, *keel* green with tip somewhat recurved; *stamens* 1 or 2; *stigmas* 2; *fruit* a biconvex *achene* obovate or elliptic, brown, 1 to 1.5 mm long, 0.5 to 0.75 mm wide.

The distinguishing characteristics of *C. brevifolius* are the small, green, globose heads subtended by three bracts, the slender, weak stems and the creeping rhizomes.

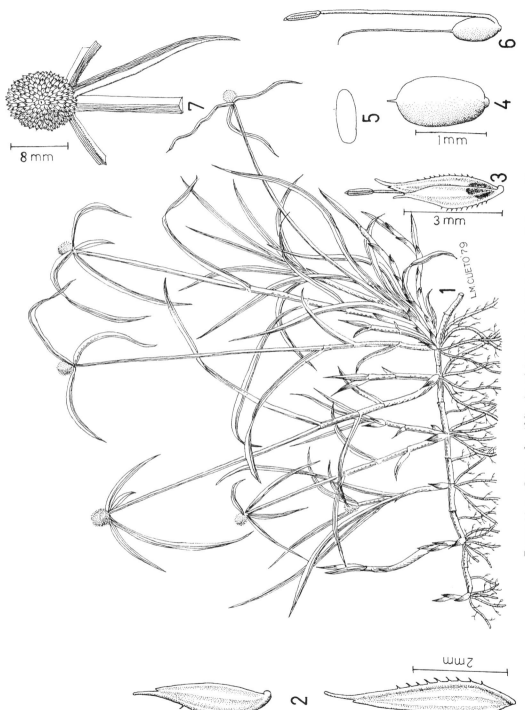

8 mm

1 mm

3 mm

2 mm

L.M.CUETO'79

FIGURE 32-1 *Cyperus brevifolius* (Rottb.) Hassk.: 1. habit; 2. glumes; 3. flower with glumes; 4. achene, 5. same, cross section; 6. flower, the glumes excised; 7. inflorescence.

Cyperus haspan

C. haspan (Figure 32-2) is also a *perennial* herb; *rhizomes* short and somewhat creeping; *stems* 20 to 40 cm tall, solitary or tufted, sharply triangular, often with a median rib on each side, rather flaccid and the base slightly tuberous; *leaves* few, basal, 2 to 10 cm long, 3 to 5 mm wide, often as long as stem, sometimes shorter, lower sheaths brownish, purplish or reddish; *inflorescence* simple or compound, umbellate, flower-bearing rays up to 15 cm long, terminal on stem apex, loose to rather dense, variable size 5 to 15 cm across, slender; *involucral bracts* few, oblique to widely spreading, short but one or two longer than rest, longest one up to 8 cm, slightly overlapping the inflorescence; *spikelets* digitally arranged in clusters, few to many, 8- to 25-flowered, 3 to 15 mm long, 0.8 to 1.5 mm wide, green, linear or linear-lanceolate, strongly compressed to axis, acute, persistent; *glumes* 1.2 mm long, 0.5 to 0.75 mm wide, suberect, keeled, oblong-ovate, closely overlapping with broad, green midrib, membranous sides and sharp tip; *stamens* 1 to 3; *anthers* linear-oblong, 0.5 mm long; *stigmas* 3; style 3-branched; *fruit* a triangular *achene*, broadly obovate, shortly apiculate, densely granular to verrucose, whitish becoming yellowish to pale brown, 0.5 mm long.

C. haspan can be recognized by the purplish or reddish lower leaf sheaths, short rhizomes and the one or two involucral bracts that are longer than the others.

HABITAT, BIOLOGY, AND PROPAGATION

C. brevifolius and *C. haspan* occur in the tropical and subtropical regions around the world (Figures 32-3 and 32-4). Both are found in somewhat temperate areas of Japan and the United States, particularly in poorly drained, wet areas; along the shores of ponds, canals, marshes and streams; in ditches; and in rice and fallowed fields. *C. brevifolius* can be found in lawns in Australia and along footpaths between rice fields in Japan. In the eastern United States, this species occurred only in intertidal fresh water and not in the slightly brackish intertidal waters (Ferren 1973). *C. brevifolius* was described in India as spreading to the inside of ponds and reservoirs, making them "swampy."

C. haspan can be a true aquatic and does well in acidic soils in the United States (Eyles and Robertson 1963) and Brazil (Bertels 1957). The latter author found this species to be less demanding of swampy conditions that other **Cyperaceae** in Brazil. In Surinam, it was more prevalent in sandy than clay soils (Dirven 1970).

Both species reproduce by seed and rhizomes. Plants of *C. haspan* collected in a rice field in India contained 52,440 seeds each and 1000 seeds weighed only 14 mg (Datta and Banerjee 1976). In the Philippines, Pancho (1964) counted 18,720 seeds/plant growing under similar conditions. Plants of *C. haspan* that start as seedlings may flower during the first year of development, but rhizome formation usually does not occur until the second year (Tadulingam and Venkatanarayana 1955). Plants appear in jute fields in India after the first and second weedings have been done (Saraswat 1980). In Japan, this species flowers from August through October (Numata and Yoshizawa 1975). Florets at the base of the spikelet mature first; flowering then begins on the mid and upper sections; fruits are shed as the spikelet elongates and while flowering continues (Godfrey and Wooten 1979).

C. brevifolius flowers 10 to 12 wk after germinating and seeds mature 3 wk after flowering. Fresh seeds are not dormant (Sumaryono and Basuki 1986) and seeds are disseminated by wind and water. This species has the C_4 photosynthetic pathway (Elmore and Paul 1983).

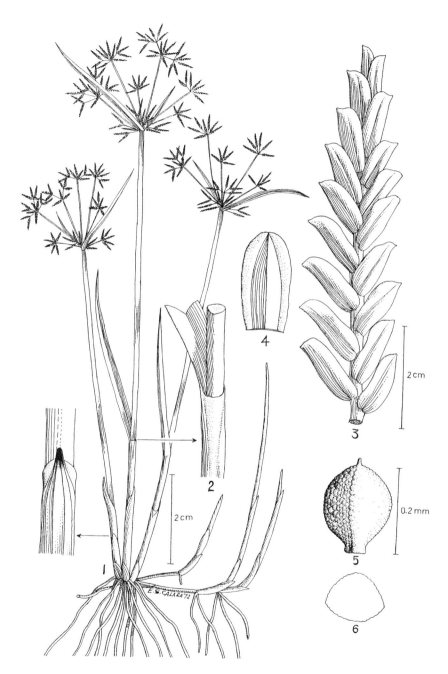

FIGURE 32-2 *Cyperus haspan* L.: 1. habit; 2. portion of leaf sheath; 3. spikelet; 4. glume;
5. achene, 6. same, cross section.

FIGURE 32-3   The distribution of *Cyperus brevifolius* (Rottb.) Hassk. across the world where it has been reported as a weed.

FIGURE 32-4   The distribution of *Cyperus haspan* L. across the world where it has been reported as a weed.

AGRICULTURAL IMPORTANCE

C. brevifolius and *C. haspan* are most often found in and around lowland rice fields. *C. brevifolius* is reported weed of 17 crops in 43 countries (Figure 32-3). It is a principal rice weed in Cuba, Ecuador, Peru, Surinam, and Taiwan, and a common rice weed in Bangladesh, Brazil, Cambodia, Indonesia, Laos, and Thailand. It is an unranked weed of rice in China, India, Madagascar, Malaysia, Nepal, the Philippines, Sri Lanka, and Vietnam. It is a serious or principal weed of coffee in New Guinea; pastures in Colombia, Dominican Republic, the Philippines, and the former Soviet Union; rubber in Malaysia; and vegetables in Australia.

It is a common weed of citrus and coconut in Malaysia; jute in Bangladesh; orchards in India and Sarawak; pastures in Hawaii, Jamaica and Sarawak; pineapple in Hawaii; and rubber in Thailand.

C. brevifolius is also reported as a weed of abaca in the Philippines and Sarawak; bananas in Samoa Islands, Surinam and Taiwan; coffee in New Guinea; macadamia nuts and vegetables in Hawaii; maize in Taiwan; pastures in Australia, Surinam, and Taiwan; pineapple and sugarcane in Taiwan; rubber in Indonesia; taro in Hawaii and Samoa; tea in Indonesia and Taiwan; and tobacco in the Philippines.

C. haspan is a reported weed of 12 crops in 39 countries (Figure 32-4). It is a serious or principal rice weed in Bangladesh, Brazil, Dahomey, India, Indonesia, Peru, Sri Lanka, and Vietnam; a common rice weed in Cambodia, Dominican Republic, Ghana, Laos, Pakistan, and Surinam; and also infests rice in Burma, China, Honduras, Ivory Coast, Malaysia, Nepal, Nigeria, the Philippines, the former Soviet Union, Taiwan, Thailand, and the United States.

It is a principal weed of rubber in Malaysia and a common weed of cacao in Sarawak; citrus and bananas in Sudan; jute in Bangladesh; sugarcane in Ghana and India; and tea in India. It is an unranked weed of bananas in Surinam; jute in India; maize in Brazil and Honduras; orchards in Brazil; pastures in Surinam; sorghum in Honduras; and sugarcane in Honduras and Indonesia.

C. haspan is an important new rice weed in Indonesia (Rahan et al. 1975) and can host the ring nematode (*Criconemoides onoensis*). When nematicides were applied in rice, potential yield increases were off-set by increased weed competition from *Echinochloa* spp. and *C. haspan* since they were no longer affected by the nematodes (Hollis 1972). *C. brevifolius* is host of the oriental sheath and leaf blight (*Corticium sasakii*) (Roy 1973).

Some indigenous groups in East Africa utilize *C. haspan* by preparing salt from the ashes of this species (Uphof 1968). Pigments called "cyperquinones" have also been found in *C. haspan*. Allan et al. (1969) studied 35 **Cyperaceae** species and only four contained quinones. Two were identified in the roots and rhizomes of *C. haspan* and represented 0.5% of the dry weight of these tissues. The quinones have some biological activity, as they were weakly active on some gram positive organisms.

COMMON NAMES

Cyperus brevifolius

AUSTRALIA	mullum bimby couch
BRAZIL	capim de uma so cabeca
CUBA	cortadera
HAWAII	green kyllinga, kyllinga
JAPAN	himekugu
MALAYSIA	short leaved kyllinga
PHILIPPINES	bibi-inok, kadkadot, pugo-pugo

Cyperus haspan

BRAZIL	tiririca roxa
INDIA	chali thuga, motha
JAPAN	ko-azegayatsuri
MADAGASCAR	herana
MALAYSIA	sheathed cyperus
PHILIPPINES	balabalangutan

Thirty-Three

Datura stramonium L. var. chalybaea Koch

Solanaceae, Nightshade Family

Datura stramonium is a tall, erect, rank-smelling annual herb in a family that has 85 genera and 3000 species. The species has become notorious because of the long history of man's use of it for good and evil. Its origins have become veiled by the many conflicting claims of time and place, but early Sanskrit and Chinese legends tell of a magic narcotic plant, used for hypnosis, that seems very like the "dhaturas." The species is

FIGURE 33-1   The distribution of *Datura stramonium* L. across the world where it has been reported as a weed.

FIGURE 33-2   *Datura stramonium* L.: A. habit, upper part of plant; B. cauline leaf; C. ripe capsule; D. seeds.

becoming increasingly troublesome as a weed. It is in more than 40 crops and is now a weed in almost 100 countries, making it more widespread than *Cyperus rotundus*, the world's worst weed. It is often called jimson weed.

DESCRIPTION

Datura stramonium (Figure 33-2) is a smooth, rank-smelling *annual* herb, 0.5 to 2 m tall; *stem* usually erect, simple or branched, glabrous, stout, green to purplish; *roots* shallow, extensively branched or in some soils and areas a stout *taproot*; *leaves* alternate, ovate-oblong, glabrous, thin, soft, dark green, unevenly toothed, 6 to 20 cm long and half as wide, often with unequal base; *petiole* 1 to 10 cm long, leaves and petioles unpleasant to smell when crushed; *flowers* usually erect, solitary on short *peduncles* in axils of branches, 5 to 11 cm long; *calyx* tubular, pale green, distinctly 5-toothed apex, lobes with a sharp taper 0.25 to 0.75 cm long; *corolla* 5-lobed, funnelform, white or purplish, 5 to 9 cm long, fetid, 5 *stamens* attached to inside of corolla tube, long *style* with 2-lobed *stigma*, single *ovary*; *fruit* a *capsule*, 3.5 to 6.5 cm long, hard, oblong, with prickly surface of soft spines that harden when ripe, regularly dehiscent by 4 valves from apex downward, numerous seeds; *seeds* 3 to 3.5 mm long, dark brown to black or in some areas gray, kidney-shaped, wrinkled network of thick veins with small, shallow interspaces, weight 6 mg.

The normally erect flowers, the green to purplish stems and branches, rank-smelling leaves and flowers, prickly pods, and the kidney-shaped, wrinkled seeds are distinguishing characteristics of this species.

A taxonomic account of *Datura* in Australia was published by Haegi (1976). Debourcieu (1977) used thin-layer chromatography to study the chemotaxonomy of *Datura*. Confirming earlier reports, his results indicate that *D. stramonium* and *D. tatula* are identical. Variants of *D. stramonium* having $2n = 12, 25, 26, 36$, and 48 chromosomes have been described. Tetraploid races have smaller capsules with a more spherical shape, fewer leaves, but larger leaves and flowers (Blakeslee 1921).

DISTRIBUTION AND HABITAT

This weed requires disturbed sites for establishment and thus is found on cultivated land, in animal camps, barnyards, on roadsides, and in areas laid waste by man's activities. It prefers rich soil and plentiful rainfall but can survive in sandy pastures and many such difficult places. In the past two decades it has become increasingly troublesome in *Solanaceous* crops of potatoes, peppers, tobacco, tomatoes and if uncontrolled causes severe reduction in the yield of soybeans in central North America. It is spread in agricultural seedstocks, in field grains, in the packed soil on the wheels and frames of farm machinery, and in the mud that clings to the fur and feathers of animals. Capsules and seeds can float for 10 hours. As seen in Figure 33-1, the weed is very widely distributed in the temperate and tropical areas. It may be seen at sea level but it also grows to 2750 m in the Himalayas from Kashmir to Sikkim. Norway received new infestations of *D. stramonium* with imported soybeans on several occasions. One infestation resulted from a shipwreck of a soybean cargo on the Norwegian coast (Ouren 1959). Parsons (1977) in Australia reported that it is a contaminant of grain sorghum because of the similarity of seed shapes and sizes. The weed may be seen at Trondheim, Norway, which is near the Arctic Circle, and it extends to New Zealand and Chile, the very southernmost agricultural areas of the world.

The dispersal of *Datura* is almost wholly by seed. In heavily trampled pastures and cultivated fields, lower portions of older plants may regenerate when bruised or broken. It is, however, a very heavy seed producer, with isolated, well-nourished plants capable of producing up to 25,000 seeds. A capsule may contain several hundred seeds. Van der Pijl (1969) suggested that the spines of the fruit have no direct relation to dispersal of the weed but at most they are a deterrent to being eaten prematurely by animals.

PROPAGATION

In the central United States, Martin (1943) found that the average spring germination time for jimson weed varied from April 4 to May 15 over a 7-yr period. Non-dormant seed capsules of field grown jimson weed harvested at 2-wk intervals after anthesis showed increasing seed germination 2 to 6 wk after that event, with no additional increase after 10 wk. Germination was highly correlated with seed weight (Pawlak et al. 1990).

Gill (1938), Hohn (1952), and others have studied after-ripening of the seed following its separation from the mother plant. Gill harvested seed at several stages of maturity, from immature to very ripe, to study germination. Tests were at 22°C in dark and light in an incubator, and also near a window in the fluctuating light and temperature of a laboratory. Immediately upon harvest, very ripe seeds germinated 100%. Thirty-five percent of the seed was green and wrinkled when taken from partly ripe, green capsules and it did not germinate. The remaining seed was black and gave 67% germination. One month after collection, the very ripe seeds would not germinate, but the black seeds from the partly ripe green capsules now germinated at 100% and retained this capacity throughout the winter and following summer. Gill's conclusion is that the very ripe seeds became dormant because of an impermeable seed coat. Removal of the covering caused immediate germination. The black seeds from the immature capsules did not have the impermeable seed coat and thus germinated freely.

Reisman-Berman et al. (1988) found mature seeds of jimson weed to be dormant at harvest. After harvest and during after-ripening, the response to light and temperature alternation increased according to the dormancy level that characterizes that particular population. The more dormant the seed population, the more temperature cycles and the more extreme the temperature alternations required to stimulate dark germination. In a low dormancy population, germination was achieved with only one cycle of alternating temperature.

Monaghan and Felton (1979) found seeds of *D. stramonium* and *D. ferox* to be dormant 5 to 11 mo after harvest. Seeds were scarified, pinholed, sterilized and decoated, but only the latter brought a germination response (50%) on 1-mo-old seeds.

The research on seed dormancy in this weed has been carried out in many countries and the age of the seed, the precise temperature and moisture conditions, type of germination medium, and the quality, intensity, and duration of light have varied widely and often are not even specified in the reports. From the many experiments we learn, however, that the seeds of several ecotypes will germinate immediately upon ripening but very soon develop an impermeable seed coat that then makes germination very difficult for months and years. Removal of the seed coat allows germination (Martin 1943). Some, but not all workers, obtained slightly better germination with an alternating temperature of 20 to 30°C (Steinbauer et al. 1955, Maguire 1959). After the onset of dormancy, physical and chemical treatments give little help and germination percentages remain low. Holm and Miller (1972) found no response to temperature, sonication (use of sound waves), freezing with liquid nitrogen, or exposure to infrared light. There was a slight response to gibberellic acid and thiourea, but not to 2-chloroethyl phosphonic acid.

Hocombe (1961) in East Africa found that changing flush water (in which the seeds were immersed) every 15 min for 3 days raised germination from 35 to 80%. Lauer (1953) obtained 70% germination at 35°C but none at 30 or 40°C. She obtained 60% germination at an alternating temperature of 10 to 25°C.

In the north temperate zone, Stoller and Wax (1973) buried seeds of jimson weed and other weed species in fields for a 2-yr study of periodicity of germination. Seeds were placed at several levels down to 15 cm depth in autumn 1966 and 1968 to study spring germination April through August. There were two convincing flushes of germination for *Datura* in May and July of 1967 and all were from the first 5 cm of soil. There was only one flush of germination in 1969. Germination from 10 cm or below was insignificant for both years. Fifty to eighty percent of all *Datura* seed for both years had hard coats and did not germinate. *Datura* can thus be a late and uncertain germinator. In this study, the early germinators, such as *Ambrosia* and *Polygonum* species, were not considered to be as serious as those that give significant emergence later in the season. The early seedlings are usually killed during the tillage and planting operations, whereas those that appear after crop planting and emergence usually require more difficult methods of weed control. In general, in early spring in the central United States the stimulus to germination comes with soil warming. After May 1 the response seems to be to favorable soil moisture after a rain.

Stoller and Wax (1974) buried seeds of *Datura* and several other weed species in saran (plastic) envelopes in a silt loam soil in the central United States, at 2.5, 5, 10, 15 cm in November, 1966, and at 2.5 and 10 cm in October, 1968. Seeds were also placed in dry storage in a laboratory at the latter time. The seeds of the 1966 experiments were tested in April 1969 and at yearly intervals thereafter. The seeds to be tested were obtained in darkness during the night cycle and kept moist and dark until morning, when germination preparations were made. An alternating temperature of 20 to 30°C was used for germination and all germinated seeds were recorded and removed periodically during 28 days. *Datura* seed stored in the laboratory after-ripened and improved in germination from 40 to 90% during 1968 to 1971. This has significance for the parallel case in which weed seed contaminants of crop seeds may be held under dry storage for varying periods of time, moved with the crop seed, and planted under ideal conditions. Jimson weed developed an absolute light requirement for germination during the 12 mo following the 1966 burial, but this did not happen to seeds buried in 1968. Burial depth did not influence the germination light requirement. The seeds of all but two species germinated better in light than in darkness after one winter of burial.

To study the effect of seed burial, seeds were planted at several depths from 1.8 to 18 cm in a silt loam soil. At 5 cm and above, emergence averaged 90% and required about 9 days. Below these depths, several more days were required for emergence. The number of seedlings was reduced with increased depth of planting. There was no emergence from 18 cm. Thus, with quite good seedling emergence from upper soil layers, most soil-applied herbicides will not be effective unless they are incorporated with machines or are carried to the seed by rain or irrigation.

Seeds decayed faster at 2.5 cm below the soil surface than at 10 cm, but some viable seeds were recovered from all depths. Hard seeds remaining after germination tests did not respond to a 1-mo cold treatment at 2°C. The authors remind us that *Datura stramonium*, after 39 years of burial at 34 cm, still germinated at 91% in the Duvel test (Toole and Brown 1946), but Stoller and Wax believe their results indicate that their jimson weed would not last nearly that long at a 10 cm depth.

MORPHOLOGY AND PHYSIOLOGY

D. stramonium germinates in the field in early summer and flowers from summer through autumn. In the north temperate zone, for example, it flowers May through September and produces ripe fruit from August until frost in November. It is a moderate to vigorous competitor for space and nutrients and in addition has allelopathic properties.

This species has so many exceptional characteristics that it is not surprising to find that an entire book has been written on its biology. This is truly a rarity for weed plants. Avery et al. (1959) prepared an account of the genetic investigations in the United States on the genus *Datura* by A. Blakeslee over a period of 40 yr. During that time it is likely that the genetics of no other organism, plant or animal, had received so much attention, and much of the experimentation was with *D. stramonium*. This single organism was studied from so many points of view that much was contributed to our general knowledge of heredity during those four decades. The program was so comprehensive that it included all experiments on form and function in the traditional fields of botany and it has extensive bibliographies. Conklin (1976) brought the information up to date in 1976.

Cell division and histochemical studies of the shoot apex during transition to flowering were reported by Corson (1969) and Corson and Gifford (1969). The flowers of *D. stramonium* are normally pollinated and fertilized within 48 hours, ovary growth is completed in about 15 days, embryo growth in 30 days and capsules may open 50 days after pollination (Conklin 1976, Rietsema et al. 1955, Weaver and Warwick 1984). *D. stramonium* is used often in the experiments above because it is not induced to flowering by alternations of the photoperiod, but can be counted on to form a terminal flower after producing 7 or 8 leaves.

Sharma (1972) made a detailed study of the flower of this species, including the morphology of its nectary, and the influence of these parts on bee behavior. In some regions of the world this plant is said to open its flowers mainly at night, but in this area of India, during December and March, the corolla unfolded with the morning sun before 0800 and the bees visited until the temperature became high at midday. The corolla tube is fully ensheathed by the calyx and a foul-smelling fluid is between them. There are five stamens attached to the base of the corolla. The anthers may dehisce before the flower opens. A five-lobed nectariferous disc encircles the ovary at the base, the lobes alternating with the stamens. The lobes are free from the ovary at the upper half but are fused to the ovary wall at their bases where they are supplied with traces.

The sugary nectar is secreted by the lobed disc to the inside of the flower where it mixes with the dehisced pollen and agglutinates on the inner corolla wall in "pollen pellets." The bees alight on the mouth of the corolla and anthers, collect pollen from the latter and may crawl down the filaments and onto the inner corolla wall. They depart with the pollen and sweet nectar. It is well to remember, however, that there is now evidence that some of the honey may be toxic.

Sanders (1948) studied embryo development in four *Datura* species following self and hybrid pollinations. Kondrateva-Melvil (1986) reported on the comparative morphology and anatomy among *D. stramonium* and several weeds and crops. Palomino et al. (1988) studied the cytology of five *Datura* species, including *D. stramonium*.

Weaver and Warwick (1984) suggest that several morphological characteristics contribute to the success of *Datura* as a weed. The large, fleshy cotyledons and the capsules with spines have chloroplasts and thus contribute much photosynthate both early and late in the life cycle. The indeterminate growth, the broad leaves, and the sympodial branching pattern make possible the rapid shading of nearby plants.

Weaver (1985) and Weaver et al. (1985) reported on the variation with changing geography of several characteristics of five populations of *D. stramonium* ranging from the central United States to Ontario, Canada.

Kutschera (1960) described a root system excavated from a well-aerated black soil over loess. The total root system is cylinder-like and in a mature plant may extend to a 65 cm depth in the soil. In the upper soil layers the roots may occupy an area 70 cm in width.

Smith (1972), working in the eastern United States, examined several aspects of the growth and development of this weed on a silt loam soil. He planted seeds in the field 12 times at 2-wk intervals beginning in late April. He obtained about 90% germination on average for all plantings. The emergence time varied from 8 to 15 days, with an average of 11 days overall, and the time was not dependent on the planting date. The number of days from emergence to flowering decreased as the season progressed from a high of 68 days at the April 22 planting to just 30 days for a planting at the end of July.

Dehiscent capsules were eventually formed on all plantings made through mid-June, and the average time required was 44 days from fruit set. Plantings made after July 1 produced no dehiscent fruits and those after September 1 did not produce flowers.

Dry matter production and plant height were greatest from the first planting and gradually decreased with seedings made later. Thus, the plant has become a serious pest because it can emerge during an entire growing season. Satisfactory control measures must take this into account.

To study the effect of shading, plants were grown outdoors, where those in full morning sun received 39,000 lumens/m² and those in 25, 50, and 75% shade received ca. 27,000, 18,000, and 9,000 lumens/m². Those grown in 25% shade were taller and heavier plants at 70 days; at 120 days they were heavier than those in other treatments and taller than most. Plants in 75% shade had significantly less dry matter at both 70 and 120 days. At 50% shade those grown for 70 days had less dry matter than those in full sun, while those grown for the longer period were not seriously affected. All shaded plants were more succulent than those grown in full sun. This tells us that *Datura* may be benefited by some shading and thus may easily grow through some crop canopies before the crops close the rows and provide complete shade.

In a field survey of the soybean crop and seven annual weeds, including *Datura*, Patterson and Flint (1983) found that the latter had the lowest dry matter production at 29 days of age. The stomata of *Datura* were the most sensitive to water stress.

The weed is a day neutral plant and will flower in photoperiods of 8 to 16 hr. Smith (1972) grew them at 13- and 16-hr photoperiods in two temperature regimes: 31°C day with 18°C night and 27°C day with 13°C night. Plants grown at both photoperiods were higher in dry weight at the cooler temperatures. Regardless of temperature, the plants in the 13-hr photoperiod flowered in 34 days and those in 16-hr photoperiod in 38 days. In the 13-hr photoperiod dehiscent fruits were produced at 76 and 86 days in the warm and cool regimes, respectively. At the 16-hr light period, there were flowers but no fruits. These experiments indicate that *Datura* flowers readily after a period of vegetative growth and without respect to day length and is favored by the cooler temperatures of the early and late summer in temperate zones.

Frazee and Stoller (1974) compared the early growth rates and competitive ability of seven dicotyledonous weeds, including *Datura*, with maize and soybeans. The species were grown in 14 hr of light with three temperature regimes of 18/12, 24/18, and 30/24°C during day and night, respectively. *Datura* grew more slowly than maize, and it grew more slowly than soybeans until the weed was about 15 cm in height, at which time the latter two species grew at the same rate. The curves of growth rate had about the same shape at all temperatures but the pace quickened as the temperature increased. *Datura* emerged more quickly at high temperatures but it was one of the latest to surface among all of the crops and weeds. In agricultural practice, seedbed preparation is done just before planting, with a resultant stimulation of weed growth, so it is important to know that maize and soybean can stay ahead of several annual weeds for the first 40 days.

Buchanan et al. (1975) studied the growth of *Datura* in two sandy loam soils with *pH* ranges from 4.7 to 6.3. The weed showed significantly less growth at *pH* 4.7 to 5.2, where some interveinal chlorosis could be seen. The composition of the weed flora of a region will thus vary with soil *pH* and individual species may be poor competitors when growing slowly because of an unfavorable soil reaction.

Hoveland et al. (1976) studied the response of ten warm season and seven cool season weed species to phosphorus and potassium on a fine sandy loam taken from a fertility experiment that had been in progress for 25 yr. The soil *pH* was 5.9 and the P levels ranged from 8 to 95 kg/ha and K levels from 40 to 213 kg/ha. The growth response was measured by means of dry herbage yields. *Datura* was among the most responsive to P of all the warm season weeds, thus confirming results of Smith (1972). Species that gave a high response to P showed extreme P deficiency when placed on low P soils. They were stunted and characteristically reddish-purple in color. In these experiments, *Datura* was among the warm season weeds most responsive to K also and was severely stunted on low K soils, although Smith (1972) did not find this. The authors remind us that over the long term, difference in response to fertility is one of the factors operating to influence the composition of the weed flora in our fields and that this has been demonstrated for decades in long-term fertility studies. The competitive advantage from weeds like *Datura* that can be very responsive to high P and K levels in certain soils and areas is that they may become predominant as weeds of agricultural crops on such fertile soils. It is well to be aware that not all shifts in weed floras and populations are due to herbicide.

On a high fertility silt loam soil, *Datura* was quite responsive to superphosphate (P_2O_5) but not to additions of NH_4NO_3, KCl, or a complete fertilizer. Because the weed is often present around barnyards and animal holding and feeding yards, it is commonly thought that it is responsive to nitrogen fertilization when in fields, but this was not the case in this experiment (Smith 1972).

In the eastern United States, *Datura* and soybean plants were grown together at several densities in rows 40 to 80 cm apart. Beans kept weed free for only 4 wk suffered 20% reduction of crop yield regardless of row width. Weed competition throughout the season at different densities caused 50 to 90% yield reductions in both narrow and wide row spacing (Chitapong and Ilnicki 1982). In the past decade several experiments similar to the above have been done to explore the competition offered by *Datura*, some with an effort to study threshold densities required for crop yield reduction, most often in soybeans. See Bacanovic

(1986), Felton (1979), Hagood et al. (1981), Henry and Bauman (1985), Kirkpatrick and Bazzaz (1979), Kirkpatrick et al. (1983), and Weaver (1986).

In the former Soviet Union, Beilin (1967) demonstrated that *D. stramonium* is immune from attack by the parasitic weed *Cuscuta*. Extracts of *Datura* placed on *Cuscuta* while it was attached to a host killed the parasite but not the host. Gressel and Holm (1964), Retig and Holm (1971), and Retig et al. (1972) have shown an allelopathic relationship between *D. stramonium* and several crop plants. Intact seeds of the weed significantly inhibited the germination of alfalfa, cabbage, carrot, lettuce, pepper, and radish. They inhibited the root growth of these crops by 20%. *Datura* was one of the two most toxic weeds tested. Marked qualitative and quantitative changes were observed in the peroxidases of cabbage seedlings when grown in the presence of *Datura* seedlings. Cell elongation was inhibited and there was disruption of the epidermis and disorganization of the root tissues in cabbage. The biochemical interaction that altered enzyme patterns and injured the roots may have altered normal functions of the root such as nutrient uptake. In concurrent experiments, crop root uptake of organic compounds was altered when crops were grown with the weed species. There are implications here for the ecological relationships of plants both in agricultural and native habitats, and for *D. stramonium* in particular, for it has interesting biochemical interactions with crops, insects, and pathogens. For more recent allelopathic studies on *Datura* in Australia, see Lovett et al. (1981), Levitt et al. (1984), and Lovett 1986.

THE CHEMISTRY AND BIOLOGICAL ACTIVITY OF SOME BY-PRODUCTS OF *Datura* METABOLISM

D. stramonium is one of the major narcotics and poisons among the world's worst weeds. For thousands of years, different members of the *Datura* genus, often themselves confused in taxonomy, have been smoked, sniffed, or otherwise ingested as solid or liquid concoctions. It was the hope of those who used the plant, or forced it upon others, that it would bring divinatory stimulus, relief from physical pain or mental suffering, mind control, or simply the purposeless delirium of witchcraft. Schultes (1970), a plant explorer, reminded us that only a few members of the plant kingdom have been used to induce visual, auditory, tactile or other hallucinations. The constituents of some of the plants known to be sacramental in aboriginal religions were never known and there are surely other toxic and hallucinogenic plants of which we are not yet aware. Our present knowledge seems to indicate that such organisms are generally found among the fungi and the angiosperms.

Atropine, hyoscyamine, and hyoscine are the principal *Datura* alkaloids used in medicine. A slight change in the structure of one of these alkaloids makes a profound difference in the response of humans and animals. In *D. stramonium*, the major site of synthesis of the alkaloids seems to be in the root, but the process can go forward in leaves and other parts. The structure and production of these chemicals is quite variable and the effect of biotype, geography, plant age, time of harvest, and growing conditions is quite well documented.

Another dimension of plants such as *Datura* reminds us that they also contribute to man's well-being, they may be remedial during injury or illness and some may assist him in his work. There is positive evidence now of promising help with pest control problems in agriculture and elsewhere. It is true that some may be used or misused as stimulants and depressants. There remain today in some cultures, herbalists, shamans, and witch doctors, many of whom have spent many years in preparation for a life of therapy and healing among their fellow men. In our sophistication in this latter day, we sometimes regard them lightly—as purveyors of magic—in contrast to M.D.'s and Ph.D.'s, who "do scientific things." We ought to remember, however, that illiterate farmers and housewives in Europe used one of our weeds, foxglove (*Digitalis*), for centuries to increase the contractibility and improve the tone of heart muscle. Today, still, 3 million persons in the United States alone use the same constituent of this same plant, by doctor's prescription, to stay alive.

Less than a century ago mental illness was thought to be caused by witches. There is now renewed interest in hallucinogens of *Datura*, not only because of the age-old problem of their misuse, but also because of the desire to explore potentially valuable drugs for experimental or even therapeutic psychiatry. They are potential tools for research in seeking explanations of the biochemical origins of mental illness. Avery et al. (1959), Burkill (1935), Kreig (1964), Schultes (1970), and Watt and Breyer-Brandwijk (1962) have brought together stories of practices in which these drugs played a central role. Today, somewhat chastened because heart problems, mental illness, cancer, inherited disease, and many other standard maladies persist, we are willing to explore more open-mindedly all of the aspects of healing. The pace of the world-wide search for herbalistic records of past centuries, including plants that ultimately became weeds for man's agriculture, has now quickened.

Watt and Breyer-Brandwijk (1962) cite experiments in which leaf extracts of *Datura* successfully controlled plant aphids (*Aphis*). In a closely related genus of the nightshade family, Williams et al. (1980) found that wild tomato, *Lycopersicum hirsutum* f. *glabratum* contained 2-tridecanone, a nonalkaloid insecticide that killed *Lepidopterous* larvae and aphids (*Aphis*) when confined on treated filter paper. The compound was 72 times more abundant in wild than in cultivated tomato.

POISONING

An overdose of tea or any preparation of the *Datura* plant, or its alkaloids, or of several plant parts that may contaminate forage and feed grains, may poison humans and animals. Four or five grams of crude leaf or seed may contain enough atropine to kill a child. Symptoms in humans and farm animals have much in common and will vary with the relative amounts of the different alkaloids ingested. Symptoms may appear in minutes or hours, followed by thirst, flushed skin, blurred vision, fever, weak but rapid heartbeat, and then perhaps convulsions and coma. Humans become irritable, may be delirious and incoherent, and given to foolish picking and waving of arms.

For overviews of world-wide poisoning incidents by *Datura*, see Everist (1974) and Watt and Breyer-Brandwijk (1962). For evidence of poisoning of specific livestock, see Chesney (1956), Haraszti et al. (1956), Whittet (1968), Evers and Link (1972), Leipold et al. (1973).

Human loss of life is often caused by overdoses of chemicals contained in unclean crop seed used to prepare bread and other foods and is often termed "bread poisoning." The crop may be beans, buckwheat, kafir corn, maize, rye, or wheat. Deaths in dormitories, orphanages, and military camps are usually from contaminated bread flour (Steyn 1933). Honey from the nectar of *Datura* may be toxic (Parsons 1973). During World War II, military units in East Africa lost more than 1500 men from alkaloid poisoning. Thus, in recent times we seem to have more cases of human than animal poisoning.

Nitrate poisoning is also involved in the history of the toxicity of this species. It takes a heavy toll of livestock, particularly cattle and sheep (Case 1957, Stahler and Whitehead 1950).

AGRICULTURAL IMPORTANCE

D. stramonium is a serious weed of beans in Tanzania; cereals in Kenya; cotton in Peru; lucerne in Chile; maize in Guatemala, Kenya, Peru, South Africa, Tanzania, and Uganda; potatoes in Afghanistan; sugarcane in Peru; soybeans in the United States; and wheat in Guatemala.

Also it is a principal weed of edible beans in Kenya; cassava in Madagascar; cotton in Mozambique and the United States; several dryland crops in Australia; forage crops in Kenya; horticultural crops in the former Soviet Union; irrigated crops in Australia; lucerne in Kenya; maize in Madagascar; pastures in Brazil and Zimbabwe; peas in Ethiopia; sorghum in South Africa; soybeans in Brazil and Australia; sugar beets in France; and vegetables in Bulgaria, Indonesia, and the former Soviet Union.

It is a common weed of barley in Tanzania; cotton in Egypt, Mexico, Sudan, Tanzania, and Turkey; several cultivated crops in Brazil, the United States, and the former Yugoslavia; of horticultural crops in Italy, South Africa, and Spain; legumes in India; maize in Brazil, India, Mexico, Spain, and the United States; millet in India; orchards in Egypt and South Africa; pastures of Hawaii, Italy, and the mainland United States; peanuts in Australia, Sudan, and the United States; pineapple in Hawaii and Swaziland; potatoes and tomatoes in the Arabian peninsula; sorghum in Brazil, Mexico, Sudan, and Tanzania; soybeans in Canada; sugarcane in Hawaii, Mexico, Natal, and South Africa; tobacco in the former Soviet Union and the United States; vegetables in Australia, Cuba, South Africa, and Arabia; vineyards in South Africa; and wheat in Sudan and Tanzania.

In addition, *D. stramonium* is a reported unranked weed of forage and table beets, coffee, mangoes, onion, pyrethrum, sweet potato, sunflower, tea, and turnip in one or more of the above countries but may also be in these and other crops in Angola, Argentina, Bangladesh, Czechoslovakia, Colombia, Greece, Honduras, Iran, Iraq, Ireland, Israel, New Zealand, Norway, Portugal, Puerto Rico, and Switzerland.

Import of seed of this species is prohibited in Belgium and Egypt. It is in several upland crops in Brazil and sometimes causes much damage. Forty percent of the farmers in northern New South Wales (Australia) report it to be a troublesome weed. It is in high density crops in central and eastern Saudi Arabia and Yemen, and it is in the midlands and uplands up to 2700 m in southwestern Arabia. In North Carolina and Virginia (eastern United States), jimson weed is one of the ten most costly weeds. In Iraq, the weed is in fields, gardens, orchards, wastelands, ditchbanks, and along railways. In Bulgaria, it is one of the main weeds in beds for growing tobacco and vegetable transplants and it also comes in with the manure used to cover beds.

As a result of 30 yr of land reclamation and intensive land management, including use of fertilizers and pesticides, a decline in the number of weed species has occurred in the Transcarpathian and on the southwest slopes of the Ukranian Carpathian mountains. Several weed species, including *D. stramonium*, are on the verge of extinction (Gamor 1988).

In conventional and no-till soybeans in North Carolina, Brust and House (1988) offered seeds of wheat and four weed species, including *Datura*, to seed feeders (arthropods and rodents) in a free choice design. The predators consumed 2.3 times more seed overall and 1.4 times more large seeds as a group in the no-tillage soybeans.

Copper et al. (1960) found no viable *D. stramonium* seeds in the feces of chickens receiving such seeds in their ration. Flunker et al. (1987) reported reduced food intake and egg weight from chickens receiving 3% ground *Datura* seed in their ration.

For a review of the insects, fungi and viruses associated with Canadian *Datura* plants and the role of the weed as an alternate host to several insect pests and diseases in *Solanaceous* crops, see Weaver et al. (1985).

COMMON NAMES

Datura stramonium

ARGENTINA	chamico grande, estramonio
AUSTRALIA	thorn apple
BANGLADESH	dhutura
BELGIUM	doornappel
BOLIVIA	chamico, cajon del diablo
BRAZIL	estramonino, figueira do inferno, quinquilho
CANADA	jimsonweed, stramoine commune
CHILE	chamico azul
COLOMBIA	chamico, tapete, peo de fraile
CUBA	chamico
DENMARK	pigaeble
DOMINICAN REPUBLIC	belladona del pobre, estramonio
EGYPT	datoura, nefer, semm el-faar, tatoura
ENGLAND	thorn apple
ETHIOPIA	atafaris
FIJI	datura, thorn apple
FINLAND	hulluruoho
FRANCE	datura stramoine, pomme epineuse
GERMANY	Stechapfel
HAWAII	jimsonweed, kikania haola
INDIA	dhatura
INDONESIA	kecubung lutik, kecubung wulung
IRAN	tatoore, tatoorah
ITALY	stramonio, noce spinosa
JAMAICA	devil's trumpet, thorn apple, trimona
JAPAN	shirobana-chosen-assgao
LEBANON	daturah, Jamestown weed, jimsonweed, nafir, thorn apple
MADAGASCAR	ramiary
MEXICO	toloache

MOROCCO	pomme epineuse
NATAL	stink blaar
NETHERLANDS	doornappel
NEW ZEALAND	purple thorn apple
NORWAY	piggeple
PERU	chamico
POLAND	bielun dziedzierzawa
PORTUGAL	estramonio, figueire do inferno
PUERTO RICO	belladona del pobre, chamico, datura, estramonio, peo de fraile
RHODESIA	chohwa, jimsonweed, stinkbaar, *stramonium*, thorn apple
SAUDI ARABIA	datura, tatoora
SOUTH AFRICA	common thorn apple, gewone stinkblaar
SPAIN	estramonio, manzana espinosa
SUDAN	sakaran
SWEDEN	spikklubba
THAILAND	lampong
TURKEY	seytan elmasi
UNITED STATES	jimsonweed
VENEZUELA	nongue morado
YUGOSLAVIA	tatula
ZAMBIA	thorn apple, jimsonweed

Thirty-Four

Daucus carota L.

Apiaceae (Umbelliferae), Parsley Family

D AUCUS CAROTA is a herbaceous plant, identical in nomenclature to the cultivated vegetable, carrots. This genus is one of 300 in the **Umbelliferae** family. The weedy types in English are called wild carrots, bird's nest (from the shape of the inflorescence as the seeds reach maturity) or Queen Anne's lace. The latter name is attributed to the similarity of the compound inflorescence of *D. carota* to the delicate lace collars popular during the reign of Queen Anne of England (Crockett 1977). The finely divided leaves were also inserted into women's hair and used in floral bouquets during that period

FIGURE 34-1   The distribution of *Daucus carota* L. across the world where it has been reported as a weed.

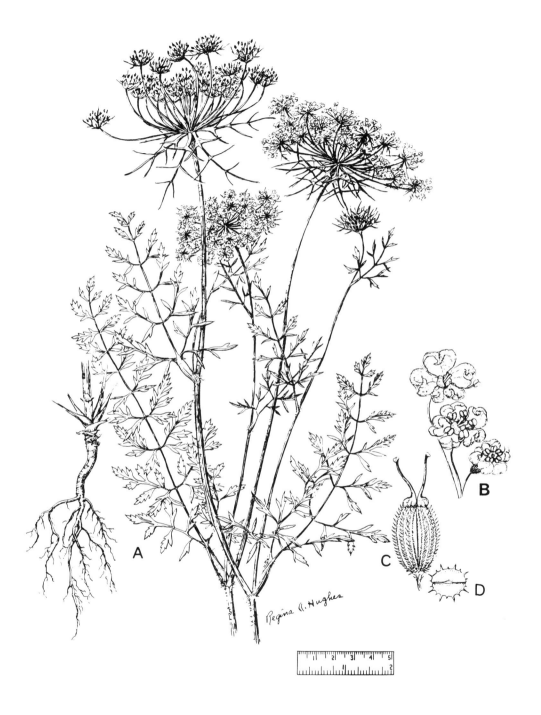

FIGURE 34-2 *Daucus carota* L.: A. habit, upper part of plant; B. flowers; C. fruit; D. cross section of fruit, showing two mericarps.

(Zimdahl 1989). The binomial names are Greek derivatives, *dauc* for umbelliferous plants and *karoton* for carrot. The species is widely distributed in temperate regions and in the highlands of equatorial countries. Its origin is reportedly in Asia, Europe and North Africa.

DESCRIPTION

D. carota (Figure 34-2) is a *biennial* (usually) herb; *taproot* deeply penetrating, tough, usually white; *stems* 30 to 100 cm tall, slender, erect, bristly hairy, branching, hollow, and ridged; *leaves* basal or alternate; basal leaves long-petioled, bi- or tri-pinnately dissected, pubescent with carrot-like aroma when crushed; upper leaves also pubescent, but smaller, less divided and either sessile or on short stalk with sheathing base that may nearly encircle stem at the node; *inflorescence* a large flat-topped compound umbel, terminal on main and lateral branches, 5 to 12 cm across, becoming concave as fruit matures; *umbellets* 20- to 30-flowered with *pedicels* 1.5 to 2.5 cm long; *involucral bracts* 3 to 5 at the base of each compound umbel, cleft or pinnatifid into narrow segments 3 to 5 cm long, white-margined at the base; *flowers* perfect; *corolla* with five small, white or rarely pinkish petals except central one of each umbellet often purple; *stamens* 5, *pistil* 1, *styles* 2; *fruit* a dry *schizocarp* composed of two mericarps (seeds) joined on flattened faces; *mericarps* bristly, grayish to brownish in color, subspherical to ellipsoidal, 2 to 4 mm long, 2.2 to 2.5 mm wide, dorsal side convex, 5-ribbed with 4 rows of large, hooked spines; ventral side flattened.

This species may be recognized by its hollow, ridged stems, the umbel inflorescence composed of numerous white flowers and one central purple flower in most umbellets, its bristly and ribbed fruits and the carrot-like aroma present in the leaves and fleshy roots.

HABITAT

D. carota frequently inhabits old pastures, fallowed fields, roadsides, waste areas and similar environments free of cultivation. Occasionally it infests clover or lucerne fields, vineyards and orchards. It is frequent in the grassy stage of old field successions, but seldom found in cultivated areas. However, occasional disturbances are necessary to maintain *D. carota* populations.

The species has a cosmopolitan distribution except for the warm tropics and arctic regions. It requires at least 120 frost-free days and annual precipitation of 80 to 100 cm. In temperate areas, *D. carota* grows from sea level to 450 m (Dale 1974). It occurs in the highlands of equatorial regions and as far as lat 65° N in Sweden; thus it is adapted to nearly any photoperiod. In a world-wide survey compiled by Duke (1979), *D. carota* was found in areas with an average rainfall of 117 cm (31 to 410 cm), a mean temperature of 18.4°C (3.6 to 25.8°C) and a mean soil *pH* of 6.4 (4.2 to 8.7). He considers the average to reflect its optimum conditions and the range its limits of adaptability.

D. carota seeds have been dated to the Neolithic Age and Bronze Age in Switzerland and to the Iron Age of Sweden (Renfrew 1973). The plant has been in the United States for 150 yr and in Canada for over 100 yr. It is not known how the wild types of the species were introduced, but it was probably as a seed contaminant with either cultivated carrots or other agricultural commodities. In the late 1800s, *D. carota* was in one county in a four-state region of the northwestern United States. Nearly 100 yr later, it had invaded 25 counties of 199 in the area (Forcella 1985). Most of the spread occurred from 1921 to 1960, which coincides with the period when large quantities of exotic crop and vegetable seed were imported into the area.

Since *D. carota* is a frequent roadside plant, Giles et al. (1973) used it to determine the lead content of plants located 15 m or 480 m from a major highway in the eastern United States. Leaf and stem lead concentrations were 367% higher in plants close to the highway as compared with those farther away.

BIOLOGY

One interesting aspect of the biology of *D. carota* is its life cycle. The plant is generally classified as a biennial. However, its genetic variation allows some individuals to behave as annuals and others as short-lived perennials (usually monocarpic, or dying after fruiting), resulting in natural stands with a mixture of plant ages (Harper 1977). Field studies in Michigan (United States) found that 3.5% of the seedlings emerging in a first-year fallow flowered, while no plants flowered during the first year in older fallows (Holt 1972). Thus both the environment and genetic makeup influence the flowering behavior of *D. carota*.

This influence was further documented for maternal phenotype and nutrient level (Lacey 1986). Seed was collected from annual, biennial or monocarpic plants. Offspring of annual plants had the greatest percentage of flowering plants in the first year and those of monocarpic mothers had the highest percentage of plants that flowered after the second year. This was due to the larger offspring formed by annual mother plants, allowing more plants to reach the critical size needed to induce flowering. Earlier flowering occurred in nutrient-rich environments for all seed sources. This is consistent with the observation that *D. carota* flowers sooner in recently undisturbed, highly fertile soils than in marginal land or in fields in mid-succession. The latitude of origin also influences flowering age (Lacey 1988). The age when plants flower increases from south to north in North America. This variation apparently developed after the introduction of *D. carota* into North America in the 17th century.

Holt (1972) noted that in the second year, 37% of the plants in a young fallow with bare ground flowered, while only 7% of the 2-yr-old plants in the older, grassy fallow flowered. This resulted in 21,000 and 1540 seeds/m^2 in the young and older areas, respectively. Seed production was linearly and inversely proportional to the percentage grass cover in the area. The environment is suitable for *D. carota* establishment after plowing in young fallows, but, as soon as other plants are present, fewer wild carrot plants become established. Also, when other plants are present in the community, flowering is delayed up to 4 or 5 yr. Thus the population of *D. carota* is dependent upon periodic disturbance for "bursts of reproduction" among periods of otherwise "slow attenuation" (Holt 1972).

Other studies found that *D. carota* is common 4 to 7 yr after field abandonment in Michigan, in the United States (Gross and Werner 1982). The ability of wild carrot seedlings to establish in areas with ground cover may be related to the vertical growth of their cotyledons and young leaves. More plants flower the first year in young fields than in older fallows, and the density of flowering plants decreases with field age.

The flowering and dispersal times of the parents affect progeny germination, growth and flowering time (Lacey and Pace 1983). Growth rates are the highest for offspring arising from early dispersal and from early-flowering parents. Thus the fate of individual plants is affected by the environment of the previous generation as well as the one it grows in.

Not all seedlings and plants survive from one season to the next. The root crown diameter is highly correlated to total plant dry weight and can be used to predict the likelihood of plant survival (Gross 1981). The probability of death for root crowns 0.05 cm or less in diameter was 0.75; for plants 0.06 to 0.2 cm in diameter, the probability of dying dropped to 0.24. Nearly all plants with crowns 0.2 cm in diameter or larger survived. The likelihood of flowering among the surviving plants was also closely related to root crown diameter. For example, only 13% of those with crowns 0.06 to 0.2 cm in diameter flowered, while 86% of the plants with 0.3 to 0.4-cm diameter crowns flowered. Lacey (1988) observed that high seedling density reduces crown diameter, which then increases plant mortality. Rosettes less than 0.2 cm had the greatest loss before flowering, while all rosettes greater than 0.3 cm in diameter survived.

In greenhouse studies over a wide range of soil fertility levels, germination was 16 to 20% in soils with low to moderate levels of fertility and dropped to less than 5% at very high fertility levels (Parrish and Bazzaz 1982). Survival was also related to fertility levels. Ninety percent of the seedlings in the very low, low and moderate fertility levels survived. Only 25% of those at the high level and 5% at the very high level survived to flowering. No changes in the root to total plant weight ratio occurred. They note that *D. carota* is a C_3 plant.

Seedlings emerge throughout the growing season if conditions are favorable. Flushes of germination are triggered by summer rainfall (Harrison and Dale 1966). Seed size and soil cover affect germination and emergence (Gross 1984). Seeds averaging 0.26, 0.71, and 1.13 mg each had 4, 34, and 87% germination, respectively, in the light and 0, 18, and 30%, respectively, in darkness. Seedling emergence increased as seed size increased and when the soil was covered with litter, vegetation or both as compared to bare ground. Plant growth, however, was 100-fold greater when no vegetation was present.

Method of killing the ground cover and shade interact with *D. carota* establishment and survival (Silvertown and Tremlett 1989). Killing vegetation with either herbicide or tillage and seeding in the fall gave nearly 100% seedling abundance the next year. However, when vegetation was killed by herbicide without soil disturbance, seedlings established over two seasons. In tilled plots no seedlings established the second year because shade from taller species reduced seedling survival in the tilled but not the herbicide treated cover.

Plants can be severely affected by freezing and thawing, particularly in poorly drained soils, and thus are more common on well-drained soils. Studies with cultivated carrots show that even 12 hr of soil saturation at the root tips of 6-day-old seedlings can cause shorter, more highly branched and discolored roots compared to those in normal soil moisture levels (White and Strandberg 1979). These effects were still detectable in root length and weight 78 days after the initial exposure to excess soil moisture, but plant height was not reduced. The optimum temperature for root growth is from 20 to 24°C. Roots grow faster in length than the tops, but the tops produced more biomass in the early growth stages (White and Strandberg 1978).

Roots of cultivated carrots show visible thickening 28 days after planting and become a sink for photosynthates during the vegetative growth phase. At 35, 49, and 67 days after planting, the taproot contained 15, 30, and 42% of the total plant weight, respectively. The corresponding percentages for the shoot dropped to 65, 55, and 48%, respectively (Benjamin and Wren 1978).

Flowering in *D. carota* is influenced by several factors. Litynski and Peplinska (1970) encountered two biotypes. One produced a single, dominant main stem and another gave rise to several stems approximately equal in height to the main stem. The latter biotype formed more umbels, produced more seed and matured more uniformly than the former.

Vernalization is usually required to induce flowering. The best vernalization temperature for cultivated *D. carota* is 5°C for 10 wk (Hiller and Kelly 1979). Growth temperature during the first year and photoperiod in the second year do not affect bolting or flowering. Under post-vernalization temperatures of 27/32°C (night/day) the seed stalk height was reduced but flowering and seed production were equal to those of plants grown at 15/21°C.

Temperature, growth regulators and photoperiod affect flowering of wild and cultivated *D. carota*. Wild lines flower at higher vernalization temperatures than the domesticated lines and flower regardless of day length. Gibberellic acid substitutes for the cold requirement for 95% of the wild and 55% of the cultivated lines. Kinetin does not affect bolting or flowering (Wahlquist 1969).

Wild types of *D. carota* are cross pollinated (Dale 1974). However, the species is self-fertile and pollination from nearby flowers is enhanced by the long filament of the anthers. The early umbels have fewer staminate flowers than the lateral and sublateral umbels. In Ontario, Canada, Judd (1969) found 65 species of insects on wild flowering *D. carota*. Most were nectar and pollen feeders, some were predators of other insects and none were economic pests. Flowering begins in mid-summer in temperate areas and continues until the first killing frost (Dale 1974). Annual plants may flower as early as 6 wk after germination. Flowers open in sequence from the outer whorls to the center.

Dauman (1973) conducted an interesting experiment to see if the central purple flowers play a role in pollination or protection. By removing the purple flowers from numerous plants and observing the visiting patterns of insects, he concluded that the purple flowers neither attracted nor repelled insects. Nor did they protect the umbel from grazing animals by resembling stinging insects.

D. carota densities in grass pastures can be manipulated by clipping and grazing (Harrison and Dale 1966). Two clippings (June and August) were very effective; a single clipping in July, when plants were in full bloom, stopped seed production and, even though many plants flowered a second time, no seeds were formed. As grazing intensity increased, percentage germination, number of seedlings, and number of flowering plants decreased.

D. carota was one of the first species to exhibit biotypes resistant to herbicides. Whitehead and Switzer (1963) confirmed the presence of a 2,4-D resistant (R-) biotype along the roadsides in Ontario, Canada. The R-biotype comprised less than 1% of the total population, but could become dominant after 5 yr of consecutive 2,4-D applications. No morphological differences were found between the R- and susceptible (S-) biotype, nor were any differences in 2,4-D absorption measured. A physiological means of resistance was proposed but not confirmed. Mulligan (1965) suggests that *D. carota* can become a principal weed in pastures if herbicides are used to remove other weeds. A shift from S- to R-biotypes may also be responsible for the population increase in pastures.

The appearance of R-biotypes of weeds may allow us to incorporate this trait into cultivated lines. Gressel (1979) has used cell culture techniques to screen suspensions of *D. carota* cells and isolated strains 100 times more tolerant to 2,4-D than others. To be totally successful, the cells must then be grown to reproductive plants and the progeny of self pollinated plants must maintain the resistance.

Seed production varies greatly for *D. carota*. In the United States, Lacey (1981) reported that plants yielded several hundred to 15,000 seeds, while in Poland Pawlowski et al. (1967–1968) counted an average of 94,900 seeds/plant. In Denmark, isolated plants produced 111,000 seeds, but those growing in pastures yielded only 4000 seeds each (Dorph-Petersen 1925). Each flower cluster can produce 700 to 1300 seeds with an average weight of 68 to 106 mg/seed (Dale and Harrison 1966). In Great Britain, over 11 million seeds/ha were found in the upper 18 cm of soil under grassland areas (Milton 1943), but none were found in cultivated areas (Champness and Morris 1948).

The terminal umbel flowers first and produces the earliest, heaviest and most seeds with a higher germination percentage than those in other umbels (Dale 1974). At pollination, the flower head is still concave or flat, but as the fruits swell while still green, the outer branches of the umbel curve inward and give it a bird's nest appearance. As the fruits dry and mature, the umbel opens and the ripe fruit is dispersed. The umbel branches open and close in response to drying and wetting, respectively. Umbels with mature fruit close when relative humidity rises (Lacey 1980). Umbels vary in rate of response to changes in humidity. Those that respond more quickly lose their seeds sooner and dispersal distance is less than in umbels that respond more slowly. At high humidities, no dispersal occurs. Umbels that slowly respond to humidity changes retain some seed that can disperse when falling onto snow in the winter.

Earlier flowering plants also have earlier seed drop (Lacey 1982). However, dispersal rate is similar across flowering time and plant age. Younger plant populations disperse seeds sooner than older stands, which improves the likelihood of local population growth, because the ground is not snow covered to facilitate dispersal over a greater distance. Later dispersal in older populations, therefore, increases the likelihood of new site colonization.

Many seeds drop during the midsummer and fall seasons. Seeds on late-developing umbels may remain on the plant into the winter. Seed dispersal studies by Lacey (1981) in the United States found that seeds would not stick to the fur of animals with fine hair such as rabbits and mice, but did adhere to those with coarse fur (raccoons, badgers, skunks). Each mericarp has four rows of spines with one to several barbs at the tip of each spine. The spines aid in wind dispersal even though spineless seeds are lighter. In natural conditions, seeds were found an average of 2.2 m from the parent plant. The greatest dispersal distance of 6.25 m occurred with an average wind speed of 10.4 KPH and gusts to 26 KPH. Seeds dropped onto snow moved more than 16 m with a 25 to 40 KPH breeze. She also reported that *D. carota* seeds have been found in deer and horse excretions and may comprise from 0.5 to 2% of the diet of mice, rats, grouse and pheasants. Krack (1959) fed *D. carota* seeds to birds and then measured seed viability. Sparrows killed all seeds that passed through their digestive system, but 10 to 20% of the seeds passing through pigeons and pheasants survived.

Numerous studies on seed germination of *D. carota*, both as a crop and as a wild species, have been done. In North America, Martin (1943), Dale and Harrison (1966), and Dale (1970, 1974) have examined germination of wild types in field and laboratory environments. Most seeds germinate in the spring, but flushes of new seedlings appear in the summer and early fall, especially after soaking rains. As many as 272 plants/m^2 may emerge, but many are killed during the winter. Seeds planted in October germinate in a few weeks at lat 36° N in North America but not at lat 42° or 45° N (Lacey 1988).

Less than 1% of freshly harvested seeds germinate, while over 80% germinate by the next growing season whether overwintering in dry or wet conditions. Seed collected from 70 Canadian and United States sites exhibited considerable variation in total germination and in germination pattern. Some lots germinate completely within 7 days, others require 7 to 14 days and some as many as 21 days. Seeds that remain on the plant longer exhibit higher germination percentage than those dehiscing earlier (Dale 1970). Maximum germination occurred in 16 hr of light at 25°C. Lower temperatures and complete darkness reduced germination. In contrast, Maguire and Overland (1959) noted good germination under many conditions and obtained the highest level (84%) in complete darkness and alternating temperatures of 20 and 30°C. Rogers and Stearns (1958) noted that light enhances the germination of freshly harvested seed, while darkness promoted germination of 2-yr-old seed. Germination increases when the endosperm surrounding the radicle area of the embryo is carefully removed (Dale and Harrison 1966). However, hot water treatment or acid scarification reduce *D. carota* germination (Gardner 1921).

Gray (1979) found that early harvest of a cultivated variety of *D. carota* delays seed germination. Seeds from the primary umbel germinated sooner than those on secondary umbels and germination increased with age: 79% of the seed harvested on July 10 germinated compared to 94% of those collected on August 7. Thus age and position on the plant affect germination and these interact with temperature. It is obvious that *D. carota* germination is highly variable and complex.

Seed development occurs at the same rate across latitudes of 36° N to 45° N (Lacey 1984). However, plants at the southern latitudes developed far fewer seeds than those in northern areas. Seeds from all locations germinated better 80 days after harvest than at 140 days, and germination was highest for seeds from the most northern area and least for those from the most southern area. Seed viability followed the same pattern: 81% for the most northern source and 34% for the southern source. The latitudinal differences are due only to environmental conditions, because reciprocal planting found no link between parental origin and germination and offspring viability. Greater insect predation and high temperature stress in southern areas may affect seeds during their relatively long embryo development period.

Seeds can germinate and emerge from as deep as 10 cm below the surface, but most emerge from 6 to 8 mm (Dale and Harrison 1966). Seeds immersed in water survive up to 24 mo but then lose viability (Comes et al. 1978). However, when buried in the soil, 44% germinated after 3 yr (Dorph-Petersen 1925) and 24 and 8% germinated after 15 and 20 yr, respectively (Madsen 1962). In dry storage, 1-yr-old and 5-yr-old seed has 60 and 3% germination, respectively (Kjaer 1940).

D. carota seeds contain inhibitors that retard the growth of carrots and other members of the **Umbelliferae** family (Chaturvedi and Muralia 1975). Dried foliage of *D. carota* mixed in the growth media of potted black locust (4 g/L of vermiculite) inhibited locust dry weight 77% after 68 days. The number of nodules was reduced 60% and the N-fixing rate was 72% less than that of the controls (Larson and Schwarz 1980). In contrast, *D. carota* residues did not affect red clover biomass production and stimulated nodule production and the N-fixation rate.

UTILITY

The evolution and selection within *D. carota* to give us our cultivated carrot varieties is interesting and well documented (Simmonds 1976). While most of the world only knows the deep orange-colored roots of today's carrots, an Afghanistan biotype of *D. carota* ssp. *carota* with purple roots is believed to be the progenitor of our crop. Roots of wild types also vary in the degree of branching and fleshiness, and centuries of selection have resulted in the succulent, smooth and non-branched varieties we now have. The cultivated anthocyanin type moved eastward along with the yellow-colored mutant. *D. carota* was grown in Asia in the 10th and 11th centuries, in Spain in the 12th, in northwest Europe in the 14th, England in the 15th and in Japan by the 17th century. The popularity of the purple root diminished in Europe because it gave soups an unappetizing brownish-purple color. Thus the yellow types became more prevalent and the orange-yellow color common in cultivated carrots today was selected in the 1600s in the Netherlands. Crossing between wild and cultivated types has continued and a range of plant characteristics can be documented (Wijnheijmer et al. 1989).

Detailed taxonomic studies of *D. carota* found clear differences in root brittleness, palatability, branching and pigmentation; leaf number and erectness; and fruit size between the wild and cultivated types (Small 1977). Domesticated carrots also followed a definite biennial growth cycle and fewer of the umbels had a central purple flower. Subsequent physiological experiments found that cultivated lines of *D. carota* have more stomata and a higher photosynthetic efficiency than wild types (Small and Desjardins 1978).

Both wild and cultivated types of *D. carota* have been used for many purposes. One of the more interesting is the pioneering tissue culture work done with this species (Wetherell 1969, Collins and Wetherell 1970, Dougall and Wetherell 1974). Future tissue culture and genetic engineering research may see the utilization of genetic traits such as herbicide or disease resistance in wild *D. carota* lines in the development of new cultivars.

Tea from the leaves is reported to have stimulant, diuretic and laxative properties (Spencer 1940), but claims that it reduces blood sugars are not true (Lewis and Lewis 1977). These authors list *D. carota* as a plant that can cause photodermatitis in humans. Seeds may prevent flatulence (Crockett 1977) and possess a weak estrogen (coumarin) that can upset the hormonal balance in female white rats so that implantation of fertilized eggs is inhibited (Kaliwal and Appaswamy 1979). Roots reportedly have diuretic properties and are used to treat ulcers (Duke and Ayensu 1985).

Cattle will graze plants of *D. carota* until the late flowering stage. Forage analyses in Canada revealed that the foliage contains 14% protein, 1.8% Ca, 0.24% P, and 16% fiber. Interestingly, the results were similar for seedlings and flowering plants (Harrison and Dale 1966). The authors conclude, however, that palatability may be a problem. In Europe, it is classified as a plant of low nutritional value (Dietl 1982). Eleven lots of *D. carota* seed had an average of 17% protein, and 22% oil with no alkaloids or tannins (Earle and Jones 1962).

AGRICULTURAL IMPORTANCE

D. carota is a reported weed of 16 crops in more than 55 countries (Figure 34-1), but it is seldom a weed of cultivated fields. Nevertheless, Guillerm and Maillet (1982) reported that 71% of the cereal fields in France and 28% of those in Spain were infested, suggesting that perhaps it is becoming adapted to European cropping systems. It occasionally infests no-till maize and soybeans in the north-central United States.

It is a serious or principal weed of cereals in Tunisia; horticultural crops in the former Soviet Union; lucerne in Canada, Hungary, and Turkey; onions in India; pastures in Sweden and the United States; and vineyards in France.

It is a common weed of cereals in Turkey and the former Yugoslavia; cotton and onions in Egypt; horticultural crops in Italy; pastures in England, Germany, and Italy; sugarcane in Mauritius; vineyards in the former Soviet Union; and wastelands in the United States.

D. carota is also an unranked weed of barley and sugar beets in Iran; edible beans in China; carrots in England; cereals in France and Spain; clover in England; horticultural crops in Greece; orchards in Chile, Iraq, the former Soviet Union, and the United States; pastures in Australia, Belgium, Canada, Chile, France, and Switzerland; tobacco in the former Soviet Union; vegetable crops in China, Iran, Iraq, the former Soviet Union, and Tunisia; vineyards in Greece; wheat in Chile, China, Iran, and Portugal; and wastelands in Australia, Iraq, and South Africa.

Since both wild and cultivated types of *D. carota* often grow in the same areas, cross pollination may occur. This would have potentially serious implications in regions of carrot seed production. For example, the annual flowering trait found in wild carrot can be introduced into cultivated carrots, resulting in "bolters" during the first year of growth (Wijnheijmer et al. 1989). Such crossing can also reduce root flavor and tenderness. Similarly, the wild types can serve as hosts for carrot pests such as *Meloidogyne incognita*, *M. hapla*, and *Pratylenchus penetrans* (Bendixen et al. 1979) and carrot thin leaf virus, celery mosaic virus and lucerne mosaic virus (Howell and Mink 1981). It can also host the tarnished plant bug that attacks celery, beets, strawberries, and flowers (Anderson 1956).

COMMON NAMES

Daucus carota

AUSTRALIA	carrot
BELGIUM	carotte sauvage, Wilde peen, Wilde wortel
BRAZIL	cenoura selvagem
CAMBODIA	carot
CANADA	carotte sauvage, Queen Anne's lace, wild carrot
CHILE	zanahoria silvestre
DAHOMEY	vild gulerod
DENMARK	wild gulerod
DOMINICAN REPUBLIC	zanahoria silvestre
ENGLAND	wild carrot
FINLAND	porkkana
FRANCE	carotte sauvage, daucus carotte, pastenade
GERMANY	Mohrrube, Wilde Mohre
INDONESIA	bokti, wortel
IRAN	havijk
IRAQ	jazar barri
ITALY	carota, carota salvatica, dauco marino, pastinaca selvatica
JAPAN	nora-ninjin
MAURITIUS	carotte sauvage
NETHERLANDS	gele peen, gele wortel, wilde peen
NEW ZEALAND	wild carrot
NORWAY	vill gulrot
PERU	zanahoria silvestre
POLAND	marchew zwyczajna
PORTUGAL	cenoura, cenoura brava
PUERTO RICO	zanahoria
SPAIN	zanahoria silvestre
SWEDEN	morot

THAILAND	phakchi-daeng
TUNISIA	carotte sauvage
TURKEY	havuc
UNITED STATES	Queen Anne's lace, wild carrot
VENEZUELA	zanahoria silvestre
YUGOSLAVIA	mrkva

Thirty-Five

Digitaria longiflora (Retz.) Pers. and D. velutina (Forsk.) Beauv.

Poaceae (Gramineae), Grass Family

BOTH *DIGITARIA* species presented in this chapter are common weeds in Africa; *D. longiflora* also occurs in much of Asia, Australia and several of the Pacific Islands. They are most abundant in light, well-drained soils and can obtain high population densities in both annual and perennial crops. Occasionally, either species is used as a forage. In spite of numerous reports of their behaving as weeds, few comprehensive studies on the growth and development of these species are known.

DESCRIPTIONS

Digitaria longiflora

D. longiflora (Figure 35-1) is an *annual* or short-lived *perennial* grass; *roots* fibrous; *stems* prostrate to ascending, 20 to 40 cm tall, often rooting at the nodes, runners copiously branched, smooth; *flowering stems* with 4 to 5 nodes; *leaf sheath* smooth or sparsely hairy; *ligule* membranous, 0.7 to 1.5 mm long, more or less truncate; *blades* 1 to 4 cm long on flowering stems, 3 to 6 mm wide, flat, smooth on both surfaces, bluish-green and rounded at the base; *inflorescence* usually 2 (sometimes 3) digitate, curved, spike-like racemes, 3 to 8 cm long, arising from stem apex; *spikelets* numerous, pale green, 1.2 to 1.5 mm long and 0.7 mm wide, elliptic, minutely hairy, narrow at tip, singly or in twos or threes on short stalks of varying length; when in pairs, one spikelet pedicellate and one subsessile; *floret glumes* empty, unequal; *first glume* absent or very reduced; *second glume* as long as spikelet or nearly so, brownish or purplish when mature, usually 5-nerved with lines of hairs along margins and between nerves; sterile *lemma* 7-nerved with two rows of hairs and a hairy margin, equal to second glume in length; *fertile lemma* 1.8 mm long and 0.8 mm wide, broad at middle, narrowing to a point at apex with regular rows of punctate dots; *fruit* a dry, indehiscent *caryopsis* or grain, yellowish-brown to brown.

    D. longiflora can be recognized by its extensively creeping and mat-forming stolons, the inflorescence with two or three curved spike-like racemes, the absence of the empty

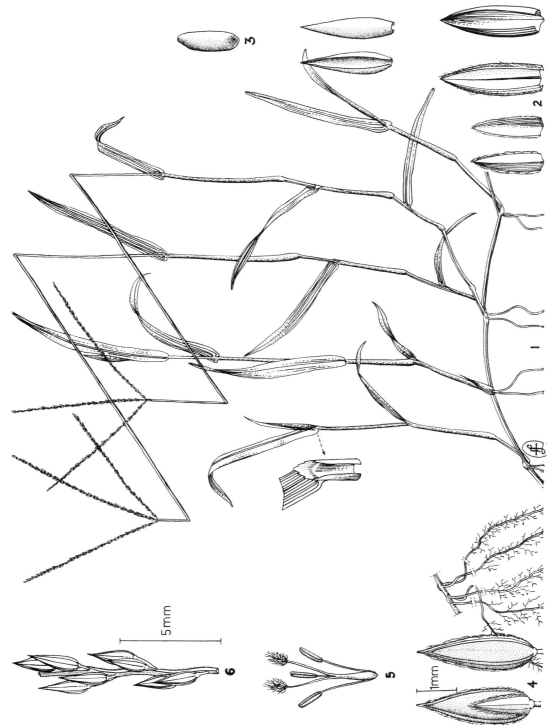

FIGURE 35-1 *Digitaria longiflora* (Retz.) Pers.: 1. habit; 2. glumes; 3. grain; 4. spikelet, two views; 5. flower; 6. portion of raceme.

first glume (or if present very minute) and the 7-nerved lemma that is as long as the spikelet.

Digitaria velutina

D. velutina (Figure 35-2) is a short-lived loosely tufted *annual* grass; *roots* fibrous; *stems* slender, erect, 30 to 75 cm tall, branched, and sparsely pubescent in upper part; *leaves* broadly lanceolate, acute, 4 to 8 cm long and 7 to 8 mm wide, sparsely hairy with subundulate margins; *ligule* membranous; *inflorescence* composed of 8 to 12 spike-like racemes along elongated axis; lower racemes in clusters of 2 to 4 in a whorl, upper racemes solitary, not hairy at the base; *rachis* three-angled, winged, often with long, spreading shiny hairs; *spikelets* ovate-lanceolate, pointed, 1.5 to 2 mm long, one-third as wide; green to brownish purple; *first glume* a broadly triangular scale; *second glume* two-thirds as long as spikelet, acute, 3-nerved, with appressed hairs between nerves and along margins; *sterile lemma* nearly as long as spikelet, central area between 5 nerves glabrous; *fertile lemma* shortly acuminate-apiculate, bright yellowish in color and striate; *fruit* a dry indehiscent *caryopsis* or grain, yellowish or brown.

This species is characterized by the membranous ligule, the 8 to 12 spike-like racemes of the inflorescence and the 3-nerved glume with appressed hairs.

TAXONOMY

While the taxonomy of *D. longiflora* is generally consistent in the literature, that of *D. velutina* is often confusing and contradictory. Since the genus contains over 300 species, some confusion can be expected. The most frequent exchange of synonyms is between *D. velutina* and *D. horizontalis*. For example, the drawing of *D. horizontalis* in Hubbard's book (1926) later appears in books by Hutchinson and Dalziel (1936) and Andrews (1956), with *D. velutina* as the preferred name and *D. horizontalis* as the synonym. A later edition of the *Flora of West Tropical Africa* by Hutchinson and Dalziel (1968) omits any drawing and reverts to placing *D. velutina* as a synonym of *D. horizontalis*, adding the comment that "This closely allied species (*D. velutina*) is confined to East Africa."

Several taxonomists have attempted to clarify the classification of this genus. The *Monograph of the Genus Digitaria* by Henrard (1950) reviews the *D. velutina* descriptions given by earlier botanists. He concludes that *D. velutina* and *D. horizontalis* are "quite different and distinct species." However, it is doubtful that Henrard's opinion is universally accepted and the serious student or researcher of *D. velutina* will need to monitor future taxonomic developments. Because we have considered *D. velutina* as a distinct species, this chapter includes no information on *D. horizontalis*.

DISTRIBUTION AND HABITAT

D. longiflora (Figure 35-3) is found in central and southern Africa, most of Asia, central and eastern Australia and several of the Pacific Islands. It is often the dominant grass in upland crops 2 or 3 yr after the fallow period. *D. velutina* is found in Africa and Costa Rica (Figure 35-4). Both species are most common in light textured soils. They often appear

FIGURE 35-2   *Digitaria velutina* (Forsk.) Beauv.: 1. habit; 2. glumes: a. upper, b. lower lemma; 3. caryopsis; 4. ligule with portion of leaf sheath and blade; 5. portion of inflorescence; 6. portion of raceme after spikelets have fallen; 7. spikelet, three views.

FIGURE 35-3   The distribution of *Digitaria longiflora* (Retz.) Pers. across the world where it has been reported as a weed.

FIGURE 35-4   The distribution of *Digitaria velutina* (Forsk.) Beauv. across the world where it has been reported as a weed.

along roadsides and in waste areas. In Cuba, *D. longiflora* is common in tobacco seedbeds with sandy soil (Sanchez and Uranga 1990). In Senegal, *D. velutina* is present in the central region, where annual precipitation is from 500 to 900 mm (Hernandez 1978). In southeast Asia, *D. longiflora* is found from sea level to 1200 m (Lazarides 1980), and in Zambia it occurs in regions with over 900 mm of annual precipitation (Vernon 1983). It survives in open scrub, deciduous forests and bamboo forests and on rice bunds in Asia. The species occurs in many crops in Taiwan and is more abundant in the first season than in the second.

BIOLOGY

Very few biological studies have been done on these species. *D. longiflora* is an octaploid species with $2n = 72$ and has regular meiosis (Mary and Malik 1971). Cytology studies by Srivastava in India (1978) detected silica bodies in the leaf epidermis. No leaf hairs were found; stomata averaged 29 microns in diameter with an average of 175/mm² on both the upper and lower leaf surfaces. This was the highest stomata density of the seven *Digitaria* species examined.

In Nigeria, *D. longiflora* seeds are spread by wind, water and animals. Its luxuriant initial growth and ability to regrow after cutting made it particularly competitive (Komolafe 1976). *D. longiflora* was a minor weed in competition trials with soybeans, maize and peanuts in Malaysia 2 wk after planting (Woo and Pushparajah 1971). However, at 4 and 14 wk after planting, it was second in abundance only to *Eleusine indica*. Their trials were done in sandy loam soils with *pH* of 5.4 to 6.1, indicating a tolerance to acidic soils.

D. velutina grows in many soil types. It was observed in red lateritic clay loam soils along with *Cyperus rotundus* in Tanzania (Terry 1970) and in grey volcanic silt loam soils (Green and Kalogeris 1967). It often appears in flushes after the first rains and is tolerant of moisture shortages. Clifford (1959) collected mud from vehicles that had traveled unpaved roads in Nigeria and found that seeds of *D. velutina* represented 6% of the total seeds found in the early wet season and 1.7% of the total in the early dry season. Not surprisingly, it was frequently observed along the roadside. In Kenya, seeds of *D. velutina* were found as a contaminant in wheat and forage grasses (Bogdan 1965, 1966). Over 50% of the Rhodes grass (*Chloris gayana*) lots contained *D. velutina* seeds and of the 555 seeds present in 18 lots, 522 (94%) remained after seed cleaning. The weed seed was much more readily removed from the other forage species. Also in Kenya, Popay and Ivens (1982) found *D. velutina* to be one of the major species among the 2292 seeds/m² in a field soil.

AGRICULTURAL IMPORTANCE

D. longiflora is a reported weed of 19 crops of 37 countries (Figure 35-3) and often infests rice, tea, and rubber plantations. It is a principal weed of cowpeas and peanuts in Gambia; peanuts, maize, and soybean in Malaysia; and tea in Indonesia and Sri Lanka. It is a common weed of cowpeas, maize, millet, peanuts, sorghum, and upland rice in Senegal; maize in Zambia; rice in Bangladesh; tea in India; and vegetables in Sarawak and South Africa.

D. longiflora is also a weed of unknown rank of cassava, peanuts, soybeans, sugarcane, sweet potatoes, tea, and vegetables in Taiwan; coffee in Nigeria; jute in India; maize in the Philippines; pineapple in Malaysia and Zambia; upland rice in India and Laos; lowland rice in India and Taiwan; rice in Cambodia, Indonesia, the Philippines, Thailand, and Vietnam; rubber in Malaysia; taro in Samoa; and tea in the former Soviet Union.

D. velutina is a reported weed of 15 crops in 14 countries (Figure 35-4) and often infests coffee, cotton, and maize. It is a serious or principal weed of coffee in Kenya and Tanzania; cotton in Tanzania and Uganda; cowpeas, maize, millet, and sorghum in Senegal; peanuts in Senegal and Uganda; and upland rice in Ivory Coast and Senegal.

It is a common weed of barley, edible beans, maize, and wheat in Tanzania; maize in Tanzania and Zambia; sesame and summer season crops in Sudan; and sorghum in Sudan and Tanzania. *D. velutina* is a weed of unknown rank in irrigated crops in Zimbabwe; pineapple in Ivory Coast and Zambia; and tea and wheat in Kenya. The repeated use of phenoxy herbicides in wheat and seasons of prolonged rainfall enhance the appearance of *D. velutina* in Tanzania (Terry 1970).

At times these species have been utilized as forages. In Tanzania, *D. velutina* analyzed as a forage contained 10.5% crude protein, 28.1% crude fiber, 2.4% K, and 0.43% Ca (Sreeramulu and Chande 1983). In Uganda, it was described as a nutritious, palatable but short-lived forage (Fiennes 1940). *D. longiflora* is also considered to be a good forage for cattle and has also been used as a lawn grass (Gilliland 1971).

D. longiflora closely resembles *D. exilis*, which is grown as a crop ("hungry rice") in much of the savanna of West Africa (Purseglove 1972). *D. exilis* is sometimes considered to be the oldest indigenous cereal of the region and is perhaps a descendent of *D. longiflora* since no wild forms of *D. exilis* are known.

In the southern United States, Ratcliffe and Oakes (1982) found two geographical populations of *D. longiflora* highly resistant to the nymphs and adults of the yellow sugarcane aphid (*Sipha flava*). They propose that this species could provide a source of resistance to this pest for *D. decumbens*, an important forage grass. In India, *D. longiflora* hosts the ergot fungus (Kulkarni et al. 1973).

COMMON NAMES

Digitaria longiflora

INDONESIA	djampang piit, gendjoran
MALAYSIA	lesser crabgrass
PHILIPPINES	sasamon
SRI LANKA	cosy pilla, nandukkal pillu, sugam pilla
TAIWAN	tyabo-mehisiba
ZAMBIA	nsangani

Digitaria velutina

EGYPT	dafira, eilaab
KENYA	majina ya kawaida, velvet finger grass

Thirty-Six

Drymaria cordata (L.) Willd. ex Roem. & Schult.

Caryophyllaceae, Pink Family

DRYMARIA CORDATA occurs in many tropical and subtropical countries as a low growing herb of predominately moist soils. The species is native to tropical America and its tropical distribution is highly atypical of the pink family. While seldom a weed of cultivated areas, it invades plantation crops such as tea and coffee, as well as pastures, lawns, gardens, riverbanks, ditches, and even sandbars in rivers. The genus name

FIGURE 36-1   The distribution of *Drymaria cordata* (L.) Willd. *ex* Roem. & Schult. across the world where it has been reported as a weed.

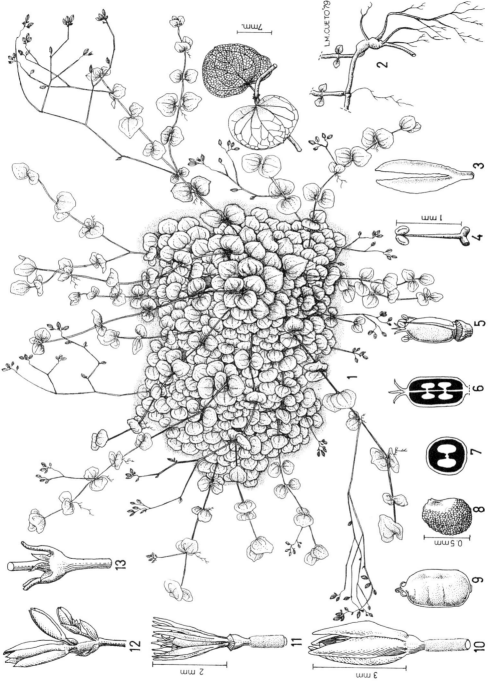

FIGURE 36-2 *Drymaria cordata* (L.) Willd. *ex* Roem. & Schult.: 1. habit; 2. root system; 3. petal; 4. stamen; 5. flower, perianth removed; 6. ovary, vertical section, 7. same, cross section; 8. seed; 9. fruit; 10. flower, 11. same, sepals removed; 12. inflorescence; 13. portion of stem to show stipule.

comes from the Greek for forest and reflects its ability to tolerate shade. The species name refers to the heart-shaped leaves. The genus contained four species when established in 1819 and by 1960 over 120 had been classified (Duke 1961). Some species are desert plants, while *D. cordata*, one of the most advanced of the genus, thrives in moist environments.

DESCRIPTION

D. cordata (Figure 36-2) is an *annual* or *perennial* herb; *root* fibrous, many *adventitious roots* formed at nodes; *stems* 30 to 60 cm long, highly branched, spreading, prostrate to erect, smooth, slender with swollen nodes; *leaves* opposite, circular to heart-shaped or ovate, 5 to 25 mm long, equal to or slightly greater in width, green above, light green below, smooth, weakly 3-nerved with short or nearly absent *petiole* with *stipules* 2 mm long with whitish setae; *inflorescence* a small terminal or axillary cyme, repeatedly forked; *pedicel* 2 to 15 mm long, often girdled by dense band of glandular hairs; *flower calyx* glabrous or shortly glandular-pubescent with 5 *sepals* 2 to 4 mm long, 3-nerved; *petals* 5, white, entire, 2 to 3 mm long, deeply bifid, 1-nerved, enclosed by calyx lobes; *style* bifid or trifid beyond middle, barely exserted from the calyx; *fruit* a 3-valved *capsule* 3 mm long with 5 to 7 seeds; *seed* dark red to blackish, more or less circular, flattened, with grainy surface, 0.9 mm long and 0.7 mm wide.

The key features of this species are the opposite, heart-shaped to circular leaves and the small white flowers with split petals that are shorter than the sepals.

ECOLOGY AND BIOLOGY

D. cordata is found from sea level to 1500 m, especially in shaded areas with moist soil (Ridley 1930). Plants exhibit considerable morphological variation (Malick and Majumdar 1974), some of which is correlated with elevation (Mizushima 1957). Plants readily root at the nodes and also reproduce by seeds. Single plants typically produce 156 fruits with an average of 4.4 small seeds (giving 686 seeds/plant). Seeds are very small and 1 g has over 5700 seeds (Pancho and Kim 1985). At 25°C plants flower 90 to 120 days after planting in continuous light, in 110 to 160 days with 16-hr days and in 125 to 190 days with 10-hr days, reflecting a day-neutral plant (Mathon 1980).

D. cordata plants have been used to treat asthma, diarrhea, vomiting, and urinary problems in India (Majumder et al. 1978, Neogi et al. 1989), snakebites in China (Duke and Ayensu 1985) and contain an anti-leukemia substance, cordacin (Lin and Yang 1974). This compound is very specific against leukemic cells but has little effect on fungi, bacteria and viruses. The LD_{50} of cordacin to mice varied from 1750 to 2200 mg/kg body weight according to their size and age. The toxic effects are not accumulative. Other reported medicinal uses of this species include treatments for liver and kidney ailments, headaches, constipation, fever, boils, and coughs (Duke 1961, Duke and Ayensu 1985).

AGRICULTURAL IMPORTANCE

D. cordata is a weed of 31 crops in more than 45 countries (Figure 36-1) and is frequently reported a weed of tea. It is a serious or principal weed of pastures in Australia and Jamaica and of tea plantations in Indonesia, India, Nepal, and Sri Lanka.

It is a common weed of bananas in Hawaii and Mexico; citrus in Mexico; coffee in Costa Rica, Mexico, Nicaragua, and Tanzania; irrigated crops in Australia; jute in Bangladesh; maize in Costa Rica, Mexico, and Nepal; ornamentals and turf in the southern United States; papaya in Hawaii; pastures in Brazil; potatoes in Central America and India; rice in Brazil; lowland rice in Indonesia and Sri Lanka; roselle in Indonesia; sugarcane in Costa Rica and Hawaii; tea in Taiwan; and vegetable crops in Central America, Hawaii, Laos, and Vietnam.

It is an unranked weed of edible beans in Honduras and Mexico; cacao in Honduras and Indonesia; cassava, coconut, and oil palm in Indonesia; coffee in Honduras, New Guinea and Venezuela; cotton in Honduras; maize in Guatemala, Honduras, Indonesia, and Nicaragua; pastures in Colombia and the United States; peanuts in Honduras and Taiwan; pineapple in Hawaii and the Philippines; potatoes in Costa Rica, Honduras, Nicaragua, and India; rice in Honduras, India, the Philippines, Taiwan, and Thailand; rubber in Indonesia; sorghum in Honduras; sugarcane in Honduras, Mexico, the Philippines, and Taiwan; tea in China; tobacco in the Philippines; and vegetables in Australia, Indonesia, the Philippines, and Taiwan.

It has been tried as a living mulch in tea plantations in Kenya but it often climbs into the bushes (Kasasian 1971b). *D. cordata* has become a serious problem in some irrigated and fertilized pastures of Australia, particularly when they are overgrazed (Hawton et al. 1975). The weed forms a dense sod that covers and kills weakened forages. Applying 250 kg/ha of ammonium sulphate without herbicides increased the percentage of ground covered by *D. cordata* from 45 to 80%. Herbicides maintained the level of infestation at 10% or less with or without nitrogen fertilizer. Because it is intolerant of dry soils, cultivating and reestablishing heavily infested pastures in the dry season is suggested. A related species, *D. pachyphylla*, is highly toxic to livestock (Duke 1961), but *D. cordata* is neither palatable to nor consumed by cattle.

COMMON NAMES

Drymaria cordata

AUSTRALIA	tropical chickweed
BRAZIL	estrelinha, jaboticaa, mastruco do brejo, pego pinto
COLOMBIA	golondrina, nervillo, pajarera
EL SALVADOR	chischina
HAWAII	drymaria
HONDURAS	palitaria
INDIA	laijabori, mecanachil, thei phelwangi
INDONESIA	jukutibun, rond nu-nut, tjebungan
MADAGASCAR	anatarika
PHILIPPINES	bakalanga, kamra-kamra
PUERTO RICO	drimaria, yerba de estrella
TRINIDAD	chickweed
UNITED STATES	heartleaf drymary, West Indian chickweed
VENEZUELA	chicharillo, golondrina

Thirty-Seven

Eleocharis acicularis (L.) Roem. & Schult., Eleocharis dulcis (Burm. f.) Henschel, and Eleocharis palustris (L.) R. Br.

Cyperaceae, Sedge Family

THERE ARE ABOUT 200 species in the genus *Eleocharis*, with more than 100 of them living as aquatic or semi-aquatic plants. The three above, often called the spikerushes, are the most troublesome as weeds in man's wet fields. The hydrophytes in the genus *Eleocharis* inhabit bogs; stream, ditch, and canal banks; shallow water ponds and reservoirs; salt marshes; and low portions of pastures and arable fields from the tropics to the polar regions of both hemispheres. Sculthorpe (1967) believes that *E. acicularis* and *E. palustris* are among the most widely distributed aquatic plants in the world.

Although the major share of man's food, and much feed for animals, is contributed by the grasses, it is not generally appreciated that the closely related and similar sedges (**Cyperaceae**) have very few species that enter into the service of man. In a very early time, *Cyperus papyrus* was used to make a paper-like material on which to write and later the swollen underground tubers of *C. esculentus*, sometimes called chufa nuts, were used for food in the Old World. *E. dulcis*, called water chestnut, has unusually crisp, sweet, edible corms that are now increasingly used as a food of the poor and rich across the world and it seems likely that this plant of the **Cyperaceae** may presently be the largest contributor to man's welfare in that family. This family does, however, provide a richness to the floras of the world, both terrestrial and aquatic.

It is to be remembered as well that the world's most serious weed, *C. rotundus*, together with many other weeds in the family, cause significant annual food losses in agriculture. In recent surveys in south and east Asia, the area that produces more than 80% of the world's rice, *E. acicularis* has been ranked among the five most serious weeds in that crop when it is grown in paddy culture.

308

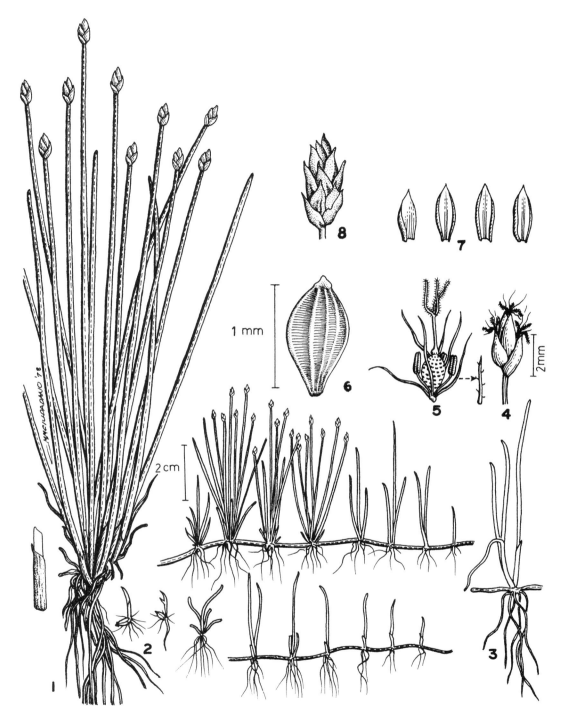

FIGURE 37-1 *Eleocharis acicularis* (L.) Roem. & Schult.: 1. habit; 2. seedling; 3. detached plantlet; 4. spikelet; 5. flower; 6. achene; 7. bracts; 8. spike.

DESCRIPTIONS

Eleocharis acicularis (syn. *Scirpus acicularis*)

E. acicularis (Figure 37-1), often called slender spikerush, is a variable, tufted *perennial* sedge with small rhizomes that creep extensively, allowing the formation of mats or turf; *rhizomes* 0.3 to 0.6 mm thick; *roots* not fleshy; *culms* erect, slender, filiform, may be somewhat flattened, usually 4-angled with lengthwise grooves, smooth, 2 to 25 cm tall, 0.25 to 0.5 mm wide, in running water may be taller; *leaf sheath* thin, membranous, loose, summit may be subtruncate, reddish below, pallid or hyaline terminally; *spikelets* ovate to lanceolate, or may be linear, sometimes flattened, sessile, spirally arranged, usually 5 to 10 flowered but variable, about 3 to 6 mm long and 1 to 1.5 mm wide; *glumes* keeled or 1-nerved, oblong-ovate, midrib green, often with reddish or purplish sides, 1.5 to 2 mm long; *bristles* slender, up to 4, equaling or exceeding the length of the achene (nut), sometimes reduced or absent, *stamens* 2 or 3, anthers 0.5 to 1 mm long, *style* 3-parted; *achene*, obovate-oblong, obscurely trigonous or nearly round in cross section, up to 10 longitudinal ribs with valleys of horizontally elongate cells in a longitudinal series, 0.5 to 1 mm long, about 0.5 mm in diameter, weight 0.5 mg, apical *tubercle* minute, conic, skullcap-like, with bristles or lacking, color may be pearly white, yellow, pale gray or light brown.

Eleocharis dulcis (syn: *E. plantaginea*) (syn: *E. tuberosa*)

E. dulcis (Figure 37-2) is a herbaceous *perennial* tufted sedge with elongated, slender, branching *stolons* and *rhizomes* which bear *tubers* 1 cm or larger; *culms* erect tufted, slender, cylindric, conspicuously transversely septate, smooth, 30 to 200 cm tall and 3 to 10 mm in diameter; *basal sheath* leaf-like, oblique at apex, purplish margins, 5 to 20 cm long; *spikelet* terminal, solitary, cylindric, sessile, as broad or somewhat broader than stem, 1.5 to 6 cm long, 3 to 6 mm in diameter, many-flowered; *glumes* numerous, spirally arranged, densely imbricated (overlapping) obtuse, broad-ovate, finely nerved with distinct midnerve, may have papery margins, 4 to 6.5 mm long, and 2 to 3 mm wide; *stamens* 3; *bristles* 6 to 8, as long or twice as long as the nut, retrorsely barbed; *style* 2- or 3-parted; achene (nut), biconvex, obovate or broadly ovate, 1.5 to 2.5 mm long, persistent apical *tubercle*, 0.8 to 1 mm long, flattened or rarely trigonous, shiny, yellow brown to yellow, with very fine reticulations. This species extremely polymorphic.

Eleocharis palustris

E. palustris (Figure 37-3) is a loosely stoloniferous or rhizomatous *perennial* with extensively creeping rootstocks, *rhizomes* black to chestnut brown in color; *culms* generally round or slightly compressed, 10 to 100 cm or taller, 0.5 to 5 mm in diameter; leaf *sheaths* obliquely truncate, reddish or brownish; *spikelets* ellipsoid or cylindric, sessile, 5 to 25 mm long and 2.5 to 7 mm thick, straw to chestnut brown in color, many flowered; *glumes* ovate-oblong, spirally arranged, may be reddish brown with green midnerve, margins broad, translucent or whitish; *bristles* 4 to 6, retrorsely barbed, equal to or exceeding the tubercle at the apex of achene, sometimes shorter or wanting, slightly scabrid, brown; *stamens* 2 or 3; *style* 2-parted; achene (nut) usually 3-angled, slightly flattened, somewhat

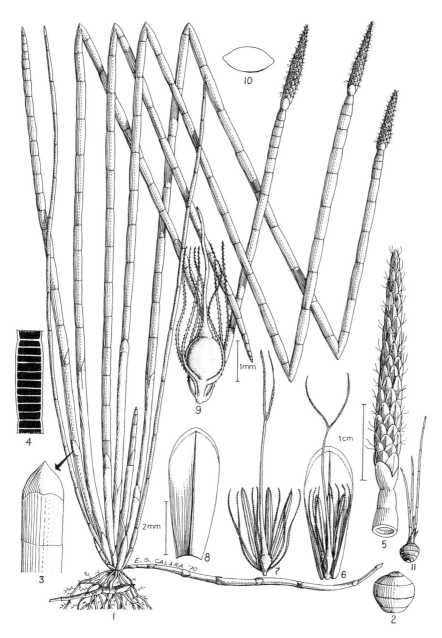

FIGURE 37-2   *Eleocharis dulcis* (Burm *f.*) Henschel: 1. habit; 2. corm; 3. leaf sheath;
4. stem, vertical section; 5. inflorescence; 6. flower with glumes, 7. same, without glumes;
8. glume; 9. immature achene with attached bristles, 10. same, cross section; 11. germinating corm.

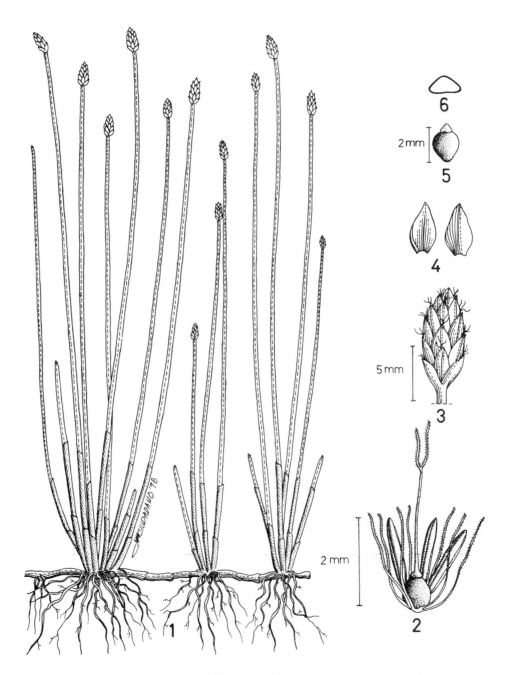

FIGURE 37-3   *Eleocharis palustris* (L.) R. Br.: 1. habit; 2. flower; 3. spikelet; 4. bract, two views; 5. achene, 6. same, cross section.

lenticular (lentil shaped), 1 to 2 mm long and 0.8 to 1.5 mm broad, persistent *tubercle* at apex is conical or triangular, constricted at base, may be faintly cross-striated, bristles pale, longer than achene, color yellowish to brown, shiny, nuts may be found without tubercle or bristles.

The plants of the genus are characteristically without leaves, the photosynthetic activities having been transferred to leafless, erect, short and long culms. Because these plants do not have the mosaic of foliar variations exhibited by leafy plants, a great part of the taxonomic work has been dependent upon the achenes and their tubercles. To distinguish between many of the species in the genus normally requires a great amount of practice and expertise, and without it the three species we are here concerned with may be more easily confused with other *Eleocharis* species than with one another. The achene of *E. acicularis* sets it apart from the other two species in our group because of the pronounced longitudinal ribs with the horizontally elongate or hexagonal cells of the pronounced longitudinal valleys placed between them. *E. dulcis* is easily recognized among the three by the large central cavity of the stem that is divided into several chambers by distinct transverse septa and, in many types, by the large underground tubers. *E. palustris* is set apart from the above species by the pronounced basal constriction of the persistent tubercle on the seed. The three species are remarkably variable across the world, requiring great skill and care for positive identification down to species. Gilly (1941) has described several of the small spikerushes and has pointed out several of the characteristics that help to distinguish between them.

Distribution and Habitat

Although Sculthorpe (1967) suggests that *E. acicularis* and *E. palustris* are among the most widely distributed hydrophytes in the world, a glance at Figures 37-4, 37-5, and 37-6 reveals that they are not so generally troublesome as weeds in all continents. *E. dulcis* in a host of forms and varieties (some cultured for food) is moved about the world more and more by man, although, with the exception of Asia, it behaves as a weed mainly between the latitudes of the Tropics of Cancer and Capricorn (Figure 37-5). *E. acicularis* is a very short plant, *E. palustris* is somewhat taller, but some forms of *E. dulcis* may reach to more than 150 cm. These habits of growth weigh heavily in their ability to obtain sunlight and their tolerance, or lack of it, of other vegetation.

The three species exhibit, as individuals, an interesting array of extremes to which they readily adjust. *E. palustris* is found at 3750 m in the western Himalayan mountains, while *E. dulcis*, which prefers warm surroundings, is found at 1000 m in Indonesia. In acid-polluted waters near mining operations, *E. acicularis* grows very well in water of *pH* 2.8— a rare feat for spermatophytes (Rothrock and Wagner 1975)! *E. dulcis* can thrive in salt water or fresh, but often prefers brackish areas. The three species are mainly pests of rice, but *E. acicularis* and *E. palustris* are often troublesome in coastal grazing lands and wet areas of meadows and pastures. On occasion, they thrive in low areas of cultivated crops that do not dry up for long periods. It is held that they are so prolific that they may form stands so dense that they impede the flow of water, yet *E. acicularis* and other small spikerushes have been under lengthy and serious investigation as plants that can form such a thick, tight, underwater turf that many other more troublesome weeds may be excluded! The spikerush thus serves as a biological control of other unwanted vegetation. There is also speculation that allelochemicals given off by the spikerushes may aid in reducing the

FIGURE 37-4   The distribution of *Eleocharis acicularis* (L.) Roem. & Schult. across the world where it has been reported as a weed.

FIGURE 37-5   The distribution of *Eleocharis dulcis* (Burm. *f.*) Henschel across the world where it has been reported as a weed.

FIGURE 37-6   The distribution of *Eleocharis palustris* (L.) R. Br. across the world where it has been reported as a weed.

growth of other aquatic weeds as they attempt to pass through the mats. *E. coloradoensis*, a very close associate of *E. acicularis* in morphology and behavior, possesses a terpene lactone, dihydroactinidiolide, a potent growth inhibitor (Putnam and Tang 1986). In some regions, *E. acicularis* is viewed as an inhabitant of languid currents and backwaters, yet in some areas of the United States it may be seen in water flows of 100 cm/sec.

All are inhabitants of muddy river banks, vernal pools, lake shores and margins, marshes and shallow ponds and reservoirs, ditches, coastal lowlands and in deep or shallow water, depending upon the season, stage of growth, wave action or competition. They are species that can infest the margins of open water bodies initially, then spread inward as conditions permit and finally contribute to the swamp–marsh-building process.

E. acicularis is very widely distributed as a weed north of the equator but behaves as a weed only in central Argentina, Chile, Indonesia and Australia below the equator (Figure 37-4). It is present in the floras elsewhere in South America and in Africa but does not disturb crops. It may grow in patches and tufts or as an underwater turf or sward. In England, it is regarded as a reed swamp dominant in waters from 8 to 55 cm deep. Rothrock and Wagner (1975) in the United States reported monospecific stands of the weed and areas with *Sparganium* species interspersed in some colonies. One of the most interesting characteristics of this species is the potential of a single plant to grow either as a terrestrial form with short, stiff, often fertile culms, or in a submerged fashion that is more elongate, flaccid, and often with sterile culms. They studied reciprocal transplants of these two forms and found that terrestrial forms placed in a submerged environment developed a "submergent" form and vice versa. The original culms died back on both types, but new shoots appeared and all grew well. The internal structural changes in the terrestrial type that was moved to a submerged condition involved a decrease in the quantity of epidermal fibers, stomata, vascular tissue and mesophyll, with a simultaneous increase in lacuna size. There were no stomata on the submerged culms and lacunae made up about 70 to 80% of the cross-sectional area, whereas these normally occupied a maximum area of 20% in terrestrial culms. In a study of 10 submerged mats, the mean water depth was 37 cm, although one colony was found to be growing in 64 cm of water. Water flow at most of these sites measured 0 to 8 cm/sec; however, healthy colonies at two sites were living in currents of 100 cm/sec. At such sites the plants surely serve as a buffer to erosion of substrate soil. These plants grew in acid-polluted streams near mining operations and, as mentioned above, they were found to survive at very low *pH*s. The authors found them very capable of regrowing quickly if buried by silt. The latter seemed a good, general substrate, for it allowed these short plants to emerge quickly, to put some photosynthetic structures upward into the light and to thus begin production of new material promptly.

Harris (1957) in Minnesota in the United States designed water drawdown experiments to study vegetation changes and wildlife use in altered environments. *Eleocharis* species (probably including *E. acicularis*) were killed out by 3 yr of flooding at the 38 cm water level.

The culms of the terrestrial form of the plant are rather easily killed by frost, but new growth emerges quickly if plants are moved to warm temperatures.

With the exception of general distribution over South America and an area in South Africa, *E. palustris* is a weed in crops only near the Tropic of Cancer and in the North Temperate Zone (Figure 37-6). It is in the floras of Africa from south to north but behaves as a weed only in Egypt. There are many *Eleocharis* species in rice in Southeast Asia, but this one is not reported to be a problem and has thus very likely been excluded by other plants. It is a marshy plant that generally prefers to be in a few centimeters of surface water. With many other reeds and rushes having little or no leafy structure, *E. palustris* tolerates persistent wave action. There are mixed reports from different areas about its ability to grow in flowing water, but wherever it is found it tends to anchor the soil and prevent erosion with its dense underground rootstock proliferation. When it appears in wet portions of croplands or cultivated lands, it disappears quickly if the area is drained.

Walters (1949), in a study of the biology of *E. palustris*, suggested that the plants generally called by this name in south and east Europe are of subspecies *microcarpa*, while in northern and western Europe the subspecies *vulgaris* is common, although *microcarpa* is also present. The habitats occupied by *E. palustris* in Europe are those sites that will not place it in competition with taller species and Walters feels that a lack of shade tolerance is one of the critical factors limiting the distribution of the species over a range of environments. On sites where taller species such as *Juncus* come in, or as peat accumulation raises soil levels, the *Eleocharis* may decline. It was found growing well on peat, mineral soils of high organic matter content, and on sandy and gravelly lake shores. The species can be seen on moist, acid, sandy soils, but it seems to prefer alkaline or neutral substrates. It is rarely found on acid peats. It can tolerate salty soils.

The types found in England accommodate to a fairly wide range of water levels up to 50 cm, yet they will continue in places where the water table is several centimeters beneath the soil surface in summer. Water at or above the surface is needed in spring as regrowth starts. Sites in running water were uncommon in the observations of Walters. Haslam (1978), in a study of the response of several aquatic species to flow and substrate, has observed that *E. palustris* has good holding capacity and, because of its extensive underground systems of roots and rhizomes, it would not easily erode away.

E. palustris does not persist where soils dry out in summer. In the very tall grass prairies of Kansas on the plains of North America, it may become a dominant species in wet areas that hold water until July. It can be dominant in areas where aquatic vegetation is routinely cleared and is quite often found in marshy coastal areas that are continuously grazed and where the water is slightly brackish. The species, once it enters an area, seems to be able to proliferate into many large and small wetlands. A large number of marshes in North Dakota near the Canada–United States border (an area that becomes very cold in winter) had 100 wetland species and *E. palustris* had one of the highest frequencies across all locations.

E. dulcis, the water chestnut, behaves as a weed in much of Asia and down through the Pacific Islands into Australia. It is plentiful in west and south Africa, the west and south United States, but is rarely seen as a weed in South America. Its cultivation as a food crop is similar to that of paddy rice and it seems likely that in the future it may stray out of its present zones to occupy areas that resemble those where paddy rice is grown in the warm temperate regions. The plants may reach to 1.5 m in dense grass-like stands. Large reserves of underground carbohydrates permit it to survive periods of environmental stress and thus persist for long periods.

Hodge and Bisset (1955) prepared an excellent summary of the requirements for cultivation of this species (to be discussed later) and the extensive research work done on these plants does help to inform us about the habitats required for successful growth. The young plants are very susceptible to frost, which explains their inclination to remain within the thermal tropics. The plant tips usually begin to die back as flowering begins in late summer, and then corm production begins. These organs are fully enlarged by the time of the first heavy frost of late fall. The forms of the cultivars differ from the "wild" weedy types, just as the natural forms differ among themselves in this variable species.

PROPAGATION

The multiplication and dispersal of these three sedges are frequently described as an asexual process within fields, while long-distance transport is thought to be by seed. These perennials are quite good seed producers and possess rhizomes and stolons with tubers and corms that can give rise to new plants. Because they thrive in open water or wetlands, flooding and stormy disturbances may fragment the rootstocks and move them quickly to quite distant places. We are unable to find records of experimental data on the relative proportions of new plants that emerge annually in designated fields from vegetative material versus that from seeds. The question of the source of the new plants that are introduced to natural or cultivated sites at the beginning of new growing seasons thus seems to remain unanswered.

In Japan the majority of the winter buds carried on overwintering stolons and rhizomes of *E. acicularis* are usually found in the upper 3 cm of the soil. Sprouting from below that depth is believed to be uncommon (Shimojima 1967). In the experiments of Shimojima, a one-node section of a winter rhizome, 56 days after sprouting, produced 225 new plants with 450 stems and 1300 roots. The sprouting of winter buds was highest at 30 to 35°C, while the total range of emergence varied from 5 to 45°C. If flood water exceeded 6 cm, the number of winter stems on stolons was reduced and the production of winter rhizomes was greatly reduced. Reduced lighting of 25 to 33% (such as the shading offered by rice) inhibited the growth of the weed by 50%. When the weed had grown in the shade of the rice, if the temperatures remained above 20°C at harvest time, the formation of winter rhizomes was slowed.

In India, Misra (1969) studied the behavior of *E. palustris* rhizomes and tubers and observed that vegetative multiplication was most satisfactory in waterlogged soils and was inhibited in drier soils. The tubers were round to oval in form and each had three to five nodes. Damaged tubers often continued producing new shoots, and so experiments were performed in which cut tubers were planted. They were cut longitudinally and horizontally so that each piece retained at least one bud at a node. On the longitudinal pieces, 75% of the apical buds but none of the lateral buds sprouted in 4 days. Lateral buds were still quiescent at 30 days, but by the end of that period the new plant had several new shoots at the apex. On the tuber pieces that were sliced horizontally, a bud sprouted quickly on each apical section. On the basal sections, a bud sprouted from each if there was a healthy node-bud on that half-section.

Stevens (1957) reported that 1000 seeds of *E. acicularis* weighed 0.5 g, with seed production of 2000 seeds/plant. Rothrock and Wagner (1975) studied the germination of the seeds of *E. acicularis* gathered in the eastern United States. Seeds were taken in late November, some were tested immediately, others were placed in distilled water in test tubes at 6°C for up to 5 mo. The germination tests were conducted in an 18-hr photoperiod at 20°C under 250 foot-candles of light. During the tests the seeds were placed in water or on agar plates having a thin film of water but with the seeds exposed to air. The seeds placed in water and tested immediately upon harvesting germinated readily. Those held for 2 mo showed 80% germination in the first week of the test, while those held for 4 mo or longer germinated well, but the sprouting period was much prolonged following the initiation of the germination test. When seeds were placed on agar and held for 2 or 3 mo in the cold, the seeds germinated well and some lots exceeded 85%. In these tests there was a noticeable breakdown of the seeds after 3 mo.

Walters (1949) found abundant fruit set on *E. palustris* in England. It was many-flowered, developed seeds from about one-half the blossoms, and spikes averaged 15 to 40 nuts each. He assumed the barbed bristles at the base of the nuts had a role in seed dispersal. Ridley (1930) reported evidence that large quantities of seeds from *E. palustris* were found in the stomachs of ducks. Walters observed that this species quickly appears in newly dug ponds and ditches to begin colonization of the area, an indication that seed dispersal is very efficient. In germination tests, 80 to 90% sprouting was obtained after 6 mo of storage in a laboratory room. The germination period was very short and almost no seeds germinated thereafter. At 2 days the seedlings had a cotyledon consisting of sheath and bristly lamina, with a primary root just beginning to appear. At 7 days the root was well established, had already been superseded by adventitious roots and the first shoot was well developed. Seeds planted at the water's edge produced few flowers the first year, but all plants flowered the second year. Shade and increased water depth discouraged flowering.

To avoid repetition, the propagation of *E. dulcis* will be discussed later in a summary of cultural methods.

PHYSIOLOGY, MORPHOLOGY, AND ECOLOGY

The cespitose (mat-forming) *E. acicularis* is similar to many small sedges in possessing long slender culms 5 to 15 cm in height, filiform and almost thread-like. The leaves are reduced to basal sheaths and so the photosynthetic function is transferred to these culms. The capillary rhizomes are long and slender, with a small bore. Primary culms arise singly at each node and then, by production of additional culms from buds arising near the base of that culm, new individuals arise asexually.

E. acicularis, slender spikerush, has lately attracted attention for its ability to displace other weeds in ponds, canals, and lake bottoms. Yeo et al. (1985) studied the reproductive morphology of the plant with light and scanning-electron microscopes. The pericarps of the seed had large amounts of a wax-like substance. The seed coat was made up of three convoluted integuments; the innermost was cutin-like. The cotyledonary sheath emerged first, then the first culm, followed by the plumule and radical. Finally, numerous culms and roots were formed to provide a complete plant.

Spikes were formed at culm apices and bore three to 15 flowers. Only one to six achenes formed on each inflorescence. Emersed plants in wet soil flowered in April or May in California in the United States. Submersed plants could be induced to flower in 2 to 4 wk by lowering the water level to the soil surface.

Flowering was indeterminate. The seeds were yellow and the fresh achenes were enclosed in the outer tissue of the exocarp. As they dried the exocarps withered and ruptured easily, and as these tissues were removed a pattern typical only to slender spikerush was revealed. The intricate longitudinal and transverse ridge patterns were described in our description section. Excellent microphotographs accompany this report by Yeo and colleagues.

The information is important if seed production is sought for the species when biological control work is to be undertaken by limiting emergence and growth of other species. Management of water levels allowed the authors to make up to three harvests in one season.

Seedling growth is initiated by elongation of the cotyledon to 2.9 cm, at which time the first emerging culms are already visible, and a bit later adventitious roots appear near the shoot base. The authors suggest that this type of early development is well suited to silty environments because it enables the young plant to quickly place its photosynthetic apparatus above the accumulated silt. In their experience and observation, the submerged plant reproduces mainly through the formation of rhizomes and by fragmentation of such structures. The terrestrial plants produced much seed and it had a high germination rate with and without cold treatment. They and others report that good seed crops may be sporadic. We are unable to find data on the portion of the seed that is normally viable in *E. acicularis*.

Extension of the rhizomes is by a sympodial type of growth in which increase in length is by successive development of lateral buds just behind the apex. Sculthorpe (1967) observed that the capillary rhizomes are long, tender, and quite vulnerable, as is the case with many small hydrophytes. This, however, seems to be compensated for by extensive branching and an enormous array of fibrous roots from the nodal region. Rothrock and Wagner (1975) chose to examine ten submerged mats of *E. acicularis* and the growth of their rhizomes as influenced by the physical characteristics of the several environments. The average water depth for the sites was 37 cm, with one of them at 64 cm. The current flow averaged from 0 to 8 cm/sec, with two sites thriving at rates of 100 cm/sec. In such flows the plants successfully buffered erosion in their areas.

They observed that plants developed best in a mixture of fine clay and silt and that the very slender rhizomes seemed unable to penetrate sand. Experiments were designed for a natural area using a mosaic of sand and silt-clay zones. Rhizomes that reached a sandy zone turned sharply, grew along the edge, and upon reaching silt clay they entered it. Rhizomes placed beneath 1 cm of sand grew sideward until they could enter silt-clay and thus emerge to the surface. The streams in the area experience heavy siltation as the mining operation removes vegetation, thus allowing soil to wash into the streams. The authors recorded sections of streams that received several centimeters of silt within one rainy period. *E. acicularis* can, by elongation of internodes and the formation of new culms, penetrate 1 cm of silt in 2 to 5 days and 4 cm in 7 to 10 days. The *pH* of the water at the 10 sites varied considerably and ranged from 2.85 to 7.1. The *pH* of the substrates varied from 4.4 to 6.9 and was equally varied. There was little available P in either water or substrate, yet the plants grew well. In general, many aquatic plants are eliminated at *pH* 5. Few spermatophytes could survive the lower *pH* range found in this study. Most fish will not tolerate a *pH* of 5 and many aquatic insects fail at *pH* 4 and below (Appalachian Regional Comm. 1969).

The experiments of Yeo (1986) found that seeds of *E. acicularis* had a pericarp induced dormancy and a low temperature after-ripening requirement. Seeds that were scarified for 2 hr in NaOCl and then incubated at 10 to 18°C gave 60% germination. About the same result was obtained by excising the seed from the pericarp and then incubating at 30 to 35°C dry or chilled and wet at 4°C for 2 mo and then incubating at 15°C. The fastest rate of germination was obtained with seeds excised from their pericarps, stored dry for 2 mo and then incubated at 35°C.

Suzuki and Suto (1975) studied the emergence of different species in the field and found that when the air temperature reached 8°C and the water 13°C, *Alisma* and *Callitriche* species began to appear in rice fields. The last to emerge were *Monochoria* and *Vandellia* species at air and water temperatures of 15 and 19°C respectively. *E. acicularis* sprouted midway through the emergence season at air temperatures of 9 to 10°C and water temperatures of 14 to 15°C.

Overwintering is made possible through the formation of cold-resistant buds near the substrate. In shallow water these buds tend to become brown and chlorotic. They seem to have no dormancy, for if removed to favorable conditions they immediately begin to grow. At 6°C the growth continues but very slowly (Rothrock and Wagner 1975). The terrestrial forms of the species are also killed back by the cold, but they too grow immediately when taken to a warm place in midwinter.

Ashton and Bissell (1987) studied the growth of transplants of *E. acicularis* and *E. coloradoensis*, a very similar small spikerush, for 8 wk under several submerged light and temperature conditions. At ten incremental temperatures from 3 to 37°C and five light intensities (high to very low), they found that *E. acicularis* grew better at lower light, and lower temperature conditions and *E. coloradoensis* grew better at higher light, higher temperature conditions. The results were discussed in relation to species selection to establish competitive stands for biological control of other aquatics on specific sites.

Barclay and Crawford (1982) studied shoot extension and survival of 20 species of aquatic weeds under anoxia in an incubator for 7 days at 22°C. Five species, including *Scirpus maritimus* and *Typha angustifolia*, survived and maintained shoot extension growth for the entire period, while seven species were killed. *E. acicularis* and seven other hydrophytes survived but were unable to continue shoot production.

In the east-central United States, the acid drainage from mining operations is a critical water pollution problem in several states. The acidity of streams and ponds becomes so great at times that most life is eliminated from such waters. In one of these areas, Ehrle (1960) reported bright green mats of *E. acicularis* growing on the sides and bottoms of some streams. Rothrock and Wagner (1975) completed a comprehensive study in 1973–75 of the life history of the robust little sedge, with a view toward its possible use in the revegetation of such damaged areas. Surface and deep-shaft mining substrates rich in pyrites are exposed to oxidation, which results in the formation of ferric hydroxide, sulfuric acid, and other compounds. These chemicals seep into nearby waterways, drastically altering their chemical composition and causing *pH*s to plunge downward. Flocculates of iron compounds eventually cover rocks, banks and bottoms and the *pH*s may drop to the range of 3 to 5.

The composition of hydrophytes has meaning only by direct comparison with other similar plants or terrestrial species. Boyd (1968, 1969a, 1974) and Boyd and Scarsbrook (1975) made a thorough study of hydrophytes, including *E. acicularis*, and those who are interested may consult those reports.

Hines (1971) studied the cytology of *E. acicularis*.

A record of the life history of *E. palustris* was published by Misra (1969) in India. Plants shed much seed in March and April and as the rains came in July new growth began with leafless culms emerging from the rhizomes. After 3 to 4 mo of vigorous growth, terminal flowering spikes appeared in November and December, with a second possible period between February and April. In England and the United States, new growth begins as weather warms in late March and April, terminal spikes are seen in May and June, with a smaller flowering period in late summer. Walters (1949) in England found the earliest flowering period to be short and closely synchronized for any one population.

In India, the plants prefer several centimeters of surface water but they will not grow in depths exceeding 30 cm. Plants first appear at the water's edge and then move forward into the water body as the level recedes. Patches of the weed may be seen pressed to the moist or dried substrate. Here again the form of the plant differs depending on whether it is found in dry habitats or water-logged soil or a cover of standing water. With receding water levels, flowering that was somewhat suppressed by inundation now begins. Misra found the tallest culms on water-logged and inundated soils, but the largest numbers were on drier soils where plants were shorter and produced many more stems. Regular grazing by animals invigorated growth on drier soils. More flowering spikes were produced on drier than on very wet soils.

Dry matter production was maximum in water-saturated soils but was reduced 25 and 90% by inundation and in drier soils, respectively. The culms elongated from 47 to 63 cm in length in 25 and 55 cm of water, respectively. The light intensity in this instance was 40% lower at the 55-cm water depth. At a 100-cm depth the culms were much reduced because of the low light. The plant in general preferred some standing water for much of its life cycle and, as the rainy season began, large areas were quickly covered with dense stands of new stems. Misra (1969) grew *E. palustris* plants in 6-, 8-, 10-, 12-, 15-, and 24-hr photoperiods, and found no significant differences in dry matter production, length of aerial shoots or roots, or total number of culms. It is a short-day plant that produces the most inflorescences at 3.5 mo when held in a 10-hr day. A few flowers appeared in 6- and 12-hr photoperiods but none at 15- or 24-hr periods.

Walters (1949) placed plants at the water's edge in a natural area and found that only a few plants flowered in the first year. Almost all of them flowered in the second year of growth. Upon dissection, he found the rudiments of flowering spikes in the young culms of the perennating growing points during the resting stages of winter. He believes that these were laid down in autumn. Only a few culms produced flowering spikes from these initials. The culms that had preceded these particular spikes and those that followed at any one growing point produced a few poorly developed spikes. Most of the culms at these centers produced only vestiges of spike material. The flowers are normally cross-pollinated, are protogynous (flowers whose stigmas become receptive before pollen is shed from anthers of the same flowers), and there were no signs of apomixis.

The rhizome is structurally a sympodium. Tufts of culms arise at the base of each primary culm that develops from the rhizome. These tufts can, in turn, produce rhizomes if the main growing center is damaged and when growth conditions are especially favorable. In autumn the rhizome growth ceases and the growing points, together with all of the subsidiary growing points that have their origin in the developing buds at the culm bases, now begin to perennate. These become very frost resistant. In the second year the links between plants decay and the older tufts now become independent units. In a water site with good growing conditions, a new rhizome network may cover several square meters in one season. In grazed areas, the plants become cespitose, and tufts with short, dead rhizomes are commonly seen.

The species is quite variable across the world, but there are only a few satisfactory records of the responses of biotypes to natural environmental parameters or the manipulation of habitats by man. Misra (1969) gathered plants from lat 26° and 27° N in India and found that the northern plants flowered one full month earlier when both sets of plants were grown at the same location. Walters (1949) found some ecotypes that grew very well in salt marshes, while others prospered in inland fresh water.

Large areas of the Prairie Provinces of Canada are marked by countless small depressions that hold water for at least part of the summer, thus resulting in a mixed flora of hydrophytes. The level and duration of the water varies greatly from year to year. Millar (1973) recorded the behavior of several wetland species, including *E. palustris*, with variations in water depth, land use and other changes. His observations were recorded over a 10-yr period in more than 70 shallow marsh wetlands. Almost 75% of the stands retained their basic shallow marsh character during this period. About one-half of them evidenced changes in vegetation density at some time during the study. His observations indicated that plants in a weakened condition that were required in spring to send new growth through a considerable depth of water were subject to die-off of the species eventually. He chose May 1 as the date for recording water levels as spring growth began. He noted that high water levels in the early spring of the preceding season often contributed to the weakened condition of the plant. *E. palustris* could survive 5 to 6 yr of continuous flooding but was weakened if water levels exceeded 30 cm in early spring. The species re-established itself in 1 yr on a wetland area that was cultivated one to three times. It suffered no apparent damage in areas that were burned one to four times.

Kvet (1975) in Czechoslovakia studied the daily course of the transpiration rate and the water content of seven hydrophytes growing on the sandy shores of a fish pond. *E. palustris* ranked with the lowest in total daily transpiration of water from dawn to dusk. This species ranked highest, however, in the percentage difference between highest and lowest average water content during the day (termed daily maximum water saturation deficit). This is perhaps to be expected in a plant that can grow in such varied wet habitats.

The polluted waters of mining areas of the eastern United States were studied by Gale and Mohr (1976) to assess the ability of fish to spawn in sites that had been so altered. Large amounts of iron had increased water turbidity, lowered light penetration, and coated stream bottoms, banks and sometimes fish eggs with iron deposits. Pollutants had reduced the periphyton, phytoplankton, and benthic organisms, causing loss of food and suppressing fish populations. *E. palustris* was found growing in one of the most heavily polluted areas and large numbers of carp (*Cyprinus carpio*) were spawning in these beds in June.

During the past decade there has been a surge of activity in assaying N_2 fixation by non-nodular plants in different habitats from both the temperate and tropical zones. There are indications that this process may be enhanced by wet soils. Tjepkema and Evans (1976) reported N_2 fixation in *E. palustris* on wetland soils in Oregon in the northwestern United States.

Following an oil spill on the east coast of the United States in the early 1970s, Burk (1977) studied the changes in vegetation in a freshwater marsh. The oil caused general decline in plant diversity in the first 2 yr, followed by a 2-yr recovery as the oil broke down and was flushed away. Observations before and after the spill showed that *E. palustris* became more abundant immediately after the spill and then returned to its normal level. From an area in the northeastern United States, Muenscher (1933) reported that *E. acicularis* and *Potamogeton epihydrus* were the only species of higher plants able to grow in an area heavily polluted with oil and a variety of other wastes.

The C_4 syndrome in plants is based on possession of the Kranz type of anatomy and certain carbon isotope ratios, and this is present in only six of 118 species of *Eleocharis* examined by Ueno et al. (1989). *E. palustris* and *E. acicularis* proved to be C_3 plants.

Exhaustive studies of pollen development in *E. palustris* have been reported from Sweden. Electron microscopic analysis of the ultrastructure and ontogeny of pollen were made by Dunbar (1973), and of cytokinesis and microspore degeneration by Strandhede (1973). Morphological, embryological and cytological studies on this species have been completed by Hakansson (1954), Lewis and John (1961), Shah (1964), Strandhede (1965–66–67), and Harms (1968).

A domesticated form of *E. acicularis* has been cultivated for its unusually crisp, edible corms in the warm temperate parts of China for centuries and they are presently in demand the world over. Wild, weedy, natural forms with smaller corms are also used as food, particularly in Southeast Asia. The chestnut brown color, white flesh, and the nutty flavor and texture prompted the name water chestnut. There are many gradations of morphology and behavior between the domestic and wild types, with a history of numerous taxon binomials coined by persons who believed they had found distinctly different plants, often based heavily on corm morphology and some culm difference (Hodge and Bisset 1955, Hodge 1956). The general habit of the domestic types is a more vigorous growth of taller, thicker stems and larger corms. Hodge (1956) believes that it is commonly accepted that *E. plantaginea* and *E. tuberosa* are included in *E. dulcis*.

It was natural for man, during the many centuries of water culture of rice, to be aware of tuberous wild plants that invaded his crop. *E. dulcis* has become the most popular of these tuber-like domestic foods, but there are also others in the *Acorus*, *Nelumbo* and *Sagittaria* genera, with special mention of *Trapa natans*. The latter is a floating aquatic plant with rosettes up to 45 cm in diameter and with its own water chestnut. After centuries of cultivation in Southeast Asia, missionaries were the first to carry them to other regions in the 16th century.

Little time was given to the study of wild, weedy types of *E. dulcis* since domestic types were emphasized and so we must depend on the study of domestics as we try to understand the general morphology and physiology of the species. The plant is similar to *E. acicularis* and *E. palustris* in being able to grow well on muck (peat) and mineral soils high in organic matter. The optimum performance in trials in the United States was at a *pH* range of 6.9 to 7.3 and it did not do well on acid soils. The plant requires 10 to 15 cm of surface water at the beginning of a new growing season.

The general habit resembles others in the genus with lack of true leaves and cylindrical, tapered, septate culms. In the first 6 to 8 wk the rhizomes grow directly away from the mother plant to form satellite plants at their tips. Later, after active growth has ceased and flowering has started, another type of rhizome appears. These produce the corms and they now grow downward at an angle of 45°, placing some corms at depths as great as 13 cm below the surface of the soil. The swelling of the tips may be seen very early and they continue to enlarge as the rhizomes grow downward. The large corms sprout first and exhibit the most vigorous growth. When the new growth begins, the shoot must travel upward a considerable distance from the corm. It forms a crown at the soil surface and adventitious roots develop from this center.

Plants die back in normal fashion as flowering begins in late summer in the United States. The corms reach full size between early fall and the first heavy frost. Domestic types need a 220-day growing season and as it comes to an end the corms are in various stages of maturity. Young corms are whitish and the older, mature ones are chestnut in color. Corms taken early are low in sugar and are not as palatable. The general composition of the corms of domestic types is about 22% total solids, 19% carbohydrate, 1.5% protein and 1% fiber.

The morphology and anatomy of the species has been studied by Govindarajalu (1974) and Osotsapar and Mercado (1976). Gunn and Ritchie (1988) presented line drawings of the seed embryo and transections of the seed.

E. coloradoensis, or dwarf spikerush, another low-growing perennial sedge, is not an important world weed but deserves mention because it is similar to several of the other short, slender spikerushes, and since much is now known about this species it may inform us about these types of rushes. Yeo has pointed out that these more diminutive sedges are often very difficult to identify and separate. It is therefore possible that *E. coloradoensis* is more widespread than we know but is confused with other species.

From 1966 to 1978 Yeo and Dow (1978), Yeo and Thurston (1979), and Yeo (1979, 1980a,b) in California in the western United States studied the life history and ecology of dwarf spikerush, a sedge that can form a dense sod. It is reported that it is able to displace other aquatic weeds growing in canals and reservoirs. If appropriate methods of propagation and establishment could be worked out, this plant might serve as a biological control for rooted aquatic weeds. It could therefore be an alternative to expensive chemical and mechanical weed control practices and would be available for use in sensitive areas where herbicides could not be applied.

A final life history containing all of the pertinent research results on the species was published in 1980 and the similarities of some of its growth habits to those of *E. acicularis* will be obvious (Yeo 1980a). Each plant in a mat of *E. coloradoensis* is made up of individual rosettes connected by rhizomes, and plants may reproduce by seed as well as corms and subterranean tubers. It was shown to be a prolific seed producer, with up to 65% germination following a cold treatment or scarification with sodium hypochlorite. There is a dormant period that may be caused by an impermeable seed coat. Through manipulation of water levels to promote flowering, Yeo and his associates learned to produce three seed crops per year yielding a total of 80 kg/ha.

Extensive morphological and anatomical studies were made of the developing and germinating seeds and tubers of this spikerush and excellent photographs have been published from their work with light and scanning-electron microscopes. More rosettes, culms and inflorescences were produced at 14-hr than at 11- or 17-hr photoperiods, this in contrast to the 10-hr photoperiod preferred by *E. palustris*. The plants are normally cross-pollinated by insects, wind, or direct contact with other plants. Flowering began in April in California with mature seed gathered 30 days later. Tubers were formed in September and October, they were placed 1 to 6 cm below the hydrosoil surface, and 30 days of active growth were required to bring them to maturity. An individual plant produced 351 new tubers in 1 yr, sometimes at a density of 7/cm². Plants started from tubers, rosettes and achenes expanded to cover areas 150, 127, 99 cm in diameter, respectively, in 6 mo.

Under natural conditions in California, if water levels recede, it is possible that seeds and tubers must endure temperatures that fluctuate between −13 and 54°C. In experiments, damp-dried seeds were exposed to −196°C for 14 days and 72°C for 21 days and still showed 60 and 25% germination, respectively. Damp-dried tubers exposed to the same cold treatment and to 49°C for the 21-day period showed 20 and 49% germination later. If seeds and tubers were submersed in water and given much less severe temperatures, there was little or no survival.

Culms immersed in 0 to 100% sea water for 30 days showed injury at 30% and were killed by 40% sea water. Some tubers were able to germinate in 80% sea water. When held in wet conditions at 4°C for 4 yr, achene germination fell from 48 to 32% and tubers from 100 to 46%.

Potamogeton nodosus, P. foliosus, and *Najas quadalupensis* are among the species most quickly eliminated by *E. coloradoensis* when it becomes established as a thick turf. In all instances the process moved more rapidly if the target plant was placed under a stress such as improper water level, etc.

Johannes (1974) has shown that dwarf spikerush actually offers mechanical resistance to the germination of other species. The germinating propagules of several other aquatic weeds were unable to penetrate the mats of *E. coloradoensis* to become established. As previously mentioned (see distribution and habitat) there is speculation that allelochemicals given off by these plants may assist in reducing growth of the other aquatic plants.

E. acicularis and *E. parvula,* closely related to *E. coloradoensis,* were not displaced by the latter. The former two species have also been observed by Yeo and Johannes to displace rooted submersed aquatic plants in some areas.

AGRICULTURAL IMPORTANCE

Because of not only the similarity in appearance of these three *Eleocharis* species but also their peculiarities in adjusting to seasonal stimuli, water fluctuations, water depths and soil saturation, an effort will be made to treat them as individuals in their behavior as weeds in cropping situations.

E. acicularis is reported as a weed in 47 countries of the world (Figure 37-4). It is very troublesome as a weed in rice in south and east Asia and in Oceania. It is a serious weed in paddy rice in China, Japan, Taiwan, and a principal weed in South Korea and the New Territories of Australia. In Australia it is infrequently found as a weed in upland rice. In a study of the history and origins of the major weeds of Japan, Kasahara (1953) listed *E. acicularis* as one of the most harmful weeds in rice. This was confirmed by Noda (1970), who reported that it still ranked second in importance behind *Echinochloa crus-galli.* Fifteen years later, Takeuchi (1985) reported that it continues to be one of the dominant perennials in paddy fields throughout Japan. This is a remarkable record of persistence in spite of man's best efforts to control it.

Chisaka and Noda (1983) ranked this spikerush as one of the principal weeds in rice throughout East Asia. Takematsu et al. (1976) were invited to make a survey of weeds in paddy rice in mainland China and found *E. acicularis* to be one of the most troublesome. Chang (1973) recorded all weeds of rice in Taiwan, found 154 species, and selected 12 that were of greatest economic importance. Included in the 12 species was *E. acicularis.* He believes it is one of the most difficult weeds to manage in transplanted rice. In 1980 a survey was made of all wetland weeds in Southeast Asia, with *E. acicularis* found in Hong Kong, Japan, Malaysia, the Philippines, Thailand, and Taiwan. It was recommended that this weed be given a high priority in research programs (Glass 1971).

Rice covers almost 50% of the arable land in Japan and because of less hand weeding, more mechanical cultivation with rotary tillers, a decrease in the growing of winter crops and a trend toward greater control of annual weeds with herbicides, *E. acicularis*, *E. kuroguwai*, and *Cyperus serotinus* have become the most important perennial weeds in rice paddies. *Scirpus maritimus* and *S. triangulatus* are also troublesome sedges (Nakagawa et al. 1973). *E. acicularis* is especially dense in early transplanted rice and although the plant is short, the thick carpet-like stands reduce rice yields. Shimojima (1967) suggested that its competition with rice is mainly between root systems and that 20% crop reductions can be expected.

The weed emerges in late March–early April before the soil is flooded and it continues to grow until the tillage operation for transplanting. The buried plants die but some on or near the surface may revive and quickly expand into the crop. In this area, tuber production is initiated in mid-September by shortening days, lack of nutrients and falling temperatures.

In the New Territories of Australia, *Echinochloa colonum* was the most serious problem in drill-sown irrigated rice in the 1970s. *E. acicularis* often entered these fields from the spoon drains and moved into the fields by the spreading of rhizomes. Greater numbers of weeds, including *E. acicularis*, had to be dealt with as aerially sown rice was planted under natural rainfall conditions. Many of the weeds emerged before the soil became thoroughly saturated with water, but this species was among those that delayed emergence until the soil was thoroughly wet.

It is sometimes a principal weed in pastures in Australia and is a weed of wet grazing lands in the United States and northern Europe. It is a common weed in low places in rubber plantations in Thailand and a weed of unknown rank in Hawaii, the former Soviet Union and Vietnam. In countries outside of south and east Asia it is mainly a nuisance in the irrigation canals, reservoirs and drainage ditches that serve agriculture and other human activities.

Sculthorpe (1967) has pointed out that, in the aquatic species of this genus, the achenes usually remain enclosed in an air pocket formed by one or more associated bracts and they can therefore float freely in irrigation canals and be carried considerable distances in streams before they become waterlogged.

Rothrock and Wagner (1975) suggested from their research on the species that it should be studied for use as a stream improvement plant, to include measurement of stream productivity of all life forms after mats become established. They found that algal growth often covers the culms and that aquatic insects become more abundant as they grazed on the algae. As in most ecological niches, one might therefore expect that the insects in turn may encourage and support other forms of life.

E. acicularis is known to provide food and shelter for wading shore and marsh birds and larger waterfowl. Cattle will graze it and the rhizomes and tubers are eaten by pigs, goats, sheep, and rodents.

E. palustris is a weed in 40 countries of the world (Figure 37-6). It is widely distributed as a weed in the subtropics, the temperate zone north of the equator, and in South America, where it is a troublesome weed of aquatic sites and waterways. It is a major weed of rice in California in the United States and in Romania. It is a common weed of rice in Chile, China, and Brazil and is found in that crop in Egypt, India, Japan, and Portugal. It is interesting that this species appears in the floras of countries in the major rice areas of

Asia but seems unable to compete successfully with other weeds of those fields and the rice itself under paddy conditions. It is present in wet pasture land several places in the world and it is found in cultivated fields that are poorly drained.

In Canada, England, India, and the United States, this weed interferes with man's use of water. The species creates local problems in water bodies and because it is tall and forms dense, pure, or mixed stands, the flow of water is impeded, the silt is filtered out, and these processes contribute to flooding. Such interference may be in sectors where water flow is reduced in streams, in irrigation tributaries and their reservoirs, drainage ditches may be filled, and the accumulations with time on the shallow shores of ponds and lakes reduce the size and volume of useful water holding areas.

The experiments revealing the vigorous sprouting of cut tubers, reported earlier, inform us that efforts to control the weed in pastures, fields, or channels where water is drawn down may only tear the tubers and rhizomes and move them to new areas where they will quickly re-establish. When time between crops is sufficient and weather is suitable, some rootstocks may be destroyed by frequent tilling of the top soil layer, for the organs shrivel and dry rather quickly.

E. palustris is one of the plant species grazed by phytophagus fishes in trials in Europe.

The water chestnut, *E. dulcis*, is a weed of more than 45 countries (Figure 37-5) and is another of the sedges that may be as harmful to agriculture for the interference it brings to the waterways needed for irrigated agriculture and wetland management, as for the damage it does through crop competition. It is a serious weed of paddy rice in India and Japan, and a principal weed of rice in Bangladesh, south Borneo, Burma, Cambodia, Chile, Laos, Madagascar, Puerto Rico, Thailand, and Vietnam. It is a common weed of taro in Samoa.

It is a constant problem in the rice fields of the Tonkin Delta in Southeast Asia and is a principal weed problem in south Borneo, where it occurs with several other sedges on poor soils low in organic matter. As double-cropping of rice increased in north Malaysia, it was necessary to establish a network of ditches and irrigation channels, and to keep them weed-free, in order to supply sufficient water for the two crops. *Eichhornia crassipes* became the principal problem and *E. dulcis* was among the other aquatic weeds that proved most troublesome. In contrast to some of the cultivated types that cannot tolerate acid soils, the wild types of *E. dulcis* in north Malaysia were particularly bad in acid soil areas. In a recent survey of 100 rice fields on South Andaman Island (south of Burma in the Andaman Sea), 40 weed species were found on clay and clay loam soils. *E. dulcis* was found only on clay. Another sedge, *Fimbristylis miliacea*, was a predominant weed on both soil types (Singh and Gangwar 1987).

In Australia the species is sometimes a problem in sugarcane drainage ditches and along tram lines. It is a principal weed on the high plateau of Nepal, where several crops are grown. It is reported as a weed with crops unspecified from Gambia, Indonesia, Sri Lanka, and Taiwan.

McCord and Loyacano (1978) studied the effect of *E. dulcis* on water quality and the growth of channel catfish (*Ictalurus punctatus*) in small, controlled, earthen ponds in the southern United States. The weed reduced the level of nitrate and ammonium nitrogen sufficiently that phytoplankton levels were not a problem and fish production was improved. From their experiments, they calculated that the plants removed 108, 7, 1000, 245, and 140 kg/ha of N, P, K, Ca, and Mg, respectively.

As a food, *E. dulcis* is prepared or made available in several forms. It is served sliced and boiled, canned, pickled, made into cakes and puddings, used for the extraction of starch that is then used much like the starch from maize, or the large tubers may be cooked and offered on skewers in trains, ships or on the street.

COMMON NAMES

Eleocharis acicularis

CHINA	neu-mao-chaon
GERMANY	nadel-simse
JAPAN	matsubai
KOREA	soetulgel
MEXICO	pelillo
UNITED STATES	slender spikerush, needle spikerush

Eleocharis dulcis

CHINA	matai, pi-tsi, wu-yu
HAWAII	water chestnut
INDONESIA	beguu, cay-nan, co-nan, peperetan, tembang
PHILIPPINES	apulid
THAILAND	haew soeng kratien, ya-chongkatiam
UNITED STATES	Chinese waterchestnut, ground chestnut, waternut
VIETNAM	nang kim, nang ngat

Eleocharis palustris

BELGIUM	scirpe des marais, waterbies
CHINA	chung-nin
DENMARK	almindelig sumpstra
ENGLAND	common spike-rush
FINLAND	suoluikka
FRANCE	souchet des marais
GERMANY	Gemeines Sumpfried, Sumpf-simse
ICELAND	votasef
ITALY	giunco tondo
NORWAY	sumpsevaks
PORTUGAL	junco-marreco
SPAIN	junco de espiga
SWEDEN	knappsav
UNITED STATES	creeping spikerush, spikerush, wiregrass

Thirty-Eight

Elodea canadensis Michx.
(syn. Anacharis canadensis Planch.)

Hydrocharitaceae, Frog's-Bit Family

E LODEA CANADENSIS is a submerged weed, very widely distributed, found from the north coast of the Gulf of Bothnia, which is 1° from the Arctic Circle (66° 30'N), to lat 40° to 45° S in Tasmania and New Zealand. The name is derived from the Greek *holodes*, meaning marshy. Upon entrance into a new area, the plant has often multiplied explosively. Dispersal throughout the world has been via vegetative fragments carried by men and birds. It has become weedy in 45 countries.

FIGURE 38-1   The distribution of *Elodea canadensis* Michx. across the world where it has been reported as a weed.

FIGURE 38-2 *Elodea canadensis* Michx.: A. habit, pistillate plant; B. flower and leaf detail, pistillate plant; C. flower and leaf detail, staminate plant, flower fully expanded, sepals and outside anthers fallen; D. flowers female, male before full expansion, with all anthers upright; E. capsules; F. seeds.

DESCRIPTION

A submerged aquatic plant (Figure 38-2), rooted, made *perennial* by large quantities of brittle, fragmented stems; dichotomously branched leafy shoots becoming leafless toward the base; *roots* in mud, slender, white or pale, usually unbranched; *adventitious roots* at branch nodes and basal ends of fragments; *leaves* sessile, lower opposite, ovate and small, 7 to 15 mm long, 1 to 4 mm wide; middle and upper leaves in whorls of 3, oblong-ovate or ovate-lanceolate, very finely serrated with dark-tipped teeth; dormant apical *winter buds* with heavy cutin form in late summer; *flower* trimerous, dioecious (perfect flowers seen only rarely); *staminate* plants with *spathes* in upper leaf axils, lower half narrowed to peduncle-like base, inflated and ellipsoidal or ovoid above with gaping mouth bearing 2 acute teeth at summit, 7 mm long, 4 mm wide, single flower per spathe, *hypanthium* elongates as a thread-like *pedicel* to carry flower to water surface, 10 to 20 cm, sometimes breaking; dark *sepals* striate, elliptic, 3.5 mm long, 2 mm wide; *petals* white or pinkish, linear-lanceolate, slender-clawed, narrower than sepals, 5 mm long, 0.3 to 0.7 mm broad; *stamens* 9, smooth, 3 inner filaments united and raising anthers on common stalk, 6 outer ones falling backward onto perianth at anthesis, *anthers* 2 to 3.5 mm long, bilocular, locules dehiscing by a split at axial side of connective to form one wide-spreading valve; *pistillate* plants with flowers appearing before the staminate flowers, *female spathes* on upper leaf axils, cylindric, broadly and evenly 2-toothed at apex, *flowers* fragile, 1 per spathe, exserted on tubular *hypanthium*, 2 to 15 cm (sometimes 30 cm) long, dark striate, oblong-elliptic *sepals* 2 mm long, 1 mm wide falling at anthesis, *petals* white to purple, delicate, membranous, elliptic-spatulate, 2.5 mm long, 1.3 mm wide; *staminodes* 3, opposite petals, *stigmas* 3, broad, 4 mm long, 2-cleft at apex for one-third of total length, *style* single and as long as hypanthium; *ovary* lance-ovoid, 3 mm long, enclosed by base of hypanthium, 3 or more erect *ovules*; *fruit* a sessile *capsule*, 6 to 9 mm long, ovoid, long acuminate, 2 to 3 mm thick, 1 to 6 seeds; *seed* 4.5 mm long, slenderly cylindric, acuminate at summit, subglabrous.

Bisexual flowers, when present, like the female, but with stamens. The plant is water pollinated.

Populations of *Elodea bifoliata*, *E. nuttali*, *Egeria densa* and *Hydrilla verticillata* are often confused with forms of *E. canadensis*. *H. verticillata* can be distinguished from *E. canadensis* by conspicuously toothed leaves. *E. densa* differs in having leaves in whorls of 4 or 5 instead of 3.

The dormant apical winter buds are sometimes called turions, but Sculthorpe (1967) suggests they are not sufficiently differentiated to warrant use of that title.

DISTRIBUTION AND PROPAGATION

E. canadensis behaves as a weed mainly in the north temperate zone but is also a weed in the thermal tropical zone in Mexico, Argentina, Egypt, Mauritius, Thailand, and from north to south in India. The inhabited land masses of the Southern Hemisphere are positioned much closer to the equator so that only the southern half of Argentina, a very small portion of the southern tip of Africa, the southern third of Australia and New Zealand are outside the thermal tropics. In southeast Australia and New Zealand, *Elodea* is as troublesome as anywhere else in the world. It is a weed of a few countries in Africa and South America and is not yet a problem in the Pacific Islands (Figure 38-1).

It is generally assumed that the plant has been dispersed by movement of vegetative fragments. Over-wintering buds and brittle slender branches are easily detached by waves, currents, animal foraging, and boat traffic to be carried away to establish new stands. New roots appear quickly on the nodes of fragments, giving advantage over annuals struggling to get started. The commercial movement of plant pieces to be used for decorative aquaria and ornamental pools has assisted the spread of this plant. Birds on the wing carry pieces of *Elodea* stems, root and stem pieces are found in nests and some birds are believed to consume the entire plant.

Joyce et al. (1980) reported little evidence for the passage of viable fragments of *Elodea* through the gut of waterfowl. Johnstone et al. (1985) in New Zealand studied movement of small boat traffic among 100 lakes and learned that 5% of the rigs carried vegetative weed fragments, including *Elodea*, and 27% of these weed carriers arrived from other lakes. Departing boat trailers carried fragments only when haul-out stations were near significant weed beds. Recreation activities were deemed to be more responsible for the spread of such aquatic weeds than birds and wind in this area. In some respects the species is surprisingly sturdy and can quickly recover from a 24-hr exposure to drying in open air.

The explosive increase and subsequent decline of *Elodea* in England is one of the well-known examples of this characteristic of the plant upon gaining entry into a new and favorable site. The species came from North America to Belfast in Northern Ireland in 1836, was found in Edinburgh by 1842 and Birmingham by 1847. At the latter time, it was also found at Market Harborough, a thriving strategic crossroads of the English canal system. It is said that one river in the system became so full of plant material that the water level increased by 10 cm. Within 12 mo it was found in profusion in surrounding counties and it spread to southwest England, France, Germany, Belgium and the Netherlands by 1870. Late in the 19th and early in the 20th century, it moved through Scandinavia, into Russia and into southeast Europe. At most sites of introduction there was a rapid build-up followed by a decline or die-off. *Elodea* has recently appeared in Lake Baikal in eastern Russia, the world's deepest fresh water body (Kozhova et al. 1985).

With increased attention given to water weeds in the 20th century, we are now aware of similar behavior patterns in several other aquatic species in various places in the world. With *Elodea*, the period of expansive growth varied from a few months to 5 to 7 yr in Europe. The period of abatement for *Elodea* often followed a similar pattern, with the result that the weed became a common member of the exotic flora and was not excessively troublesome. This species came into New Zealand's large Lake Rotorua, quickly became dominant, and in turn was soon displaced by *Lagarosiphon major. E. canadensis* is a light-demanding plant and there is general agreement that bicarbonate as a carbon source, iron in reduced form, and a plentiful supply of P are required if it is to become dominant in a community (Brown et al. 1974).

These species may again exert themselves if the environment is altered to encourage them to become dominant. Herbicide trials in central England continue to list *Elodea* as a principal weed in that area (Way and Moore 1969). Reported observations of 40 designated localities along a 100 km reach of the River Wear in northeast England in 1967 and 1977 recorded that *E. canadensis*, with other species, increased in extent during the decade (Holmes and Whitton 1977). Not all infestations of *Elodea* exhibit the decline after the rapid growth of colonization. After 15 yr of vigorous growth and spread in Australia the weed is still extending its range.

Elodea can grow in a wide range of habitats but prefers quiet ponds, lakes, and slow-moving streams with a peaty or muddy silt substrate. It can be found in swift streams but only if there are sheltered banks with silty substrates. With diving equipment, Pip and Simmons (1986) in Canada and Sheldon and Boylen (1977) in the United States made *in situ* observations of maximum depths of water inhabited by 38 species of rooted, submerged aquatic plants. The maximum for any species was the 12 to 14 m depth for *E. canadensis*. They found the light at that depth was 1% of that at the surface.

More recently Penuelas and Verdaguer (1987) found *Elodea* at 14 m in a reservoir in the Pyrenees region of Spain. It should be remembered that most angiosperms do not go beyond 6 m and the average may be 4 m.

Elodea offers only moderate hydraulic resistance because it is quite streamlined. It is very easily eroded, is readily broken, but quite tolerant of battering and tangling in turbulent but not fast water. The plant will tolerate moderate shade but not turbidity (Brown et al. 1974). In North America it is found in fresh to slightly alkaline waters inland and fresh to slightly brackish coastal waters. In northern Germany it frequents ditches and canals in lowland peat and marshlands where the soil is most fertile.

McCombie and Wile (1971) examined the plant material, water quality, and physical characteristics of 19 natural and man-made ponds and lakes in southcentral Ontario, Canada, as part of an extensive study on the design and management of small multi-purpose impoundments. The specific conductance of the water bodies ranged from 100 to 450 micromhos/cm^2. *Elodea*, which was dominant in several lakes, flourished in the middle of the conductance range between 224 and 300 micromhos/cm^2.

E. canadensis is dioecious and, because of the changing distribution maps of regions and sites occupied by male and female plants, and perhaps because the physiology of sexual reproduction and the conditions which favor this method are not well understood, there is a general acceptance that propagation and dispersal depend primarily on vegetative propagules. The plant fragments root well and can quickly produce very large amounts of vegetative material to discourage other competitors.

Any portion of the axis with a dormant bud can form a new plant. Fragments produce roots at nodes and basal ends of broken pieces. Vegetative growth proceeds most rapidly in warm seasons, during which time older stems blacken and perish.

When both staminate and pistillate flowers are present at a site, the reproductive structures of both are pushed from the spathes, raised to the water surface by thread-like hypanthia, and anthesis and pollination occur. At dehiscence the anthers open explosively and scatter pollen over the water, where it drifts to the stigmas. It is believed that only one or two of each tetrad of microspores ever germinates. These events are the same throughout the genus. Pollination, fertilization and seed formation in the field are believed at present to be very rare because of infrequent and irregular flowering and the differing abundance of the two sexes in nature (Ernst-Schwarzenbach 1945a,b; Sculthorpe 1967; Lawrence 1976; Spicer and Catling 1988). Flowering was recently observed in the area between the Ural Mountains and Moscow in Russia (Rakov 1971) as well as in the Ukraine (Semenikhina and Balashev 1978).

The one-celled inferior ovary remains within the spathe, under water, as anthesis takes place at the surface. Fruits mature underwater and are indehiscent. A few ovules may mature in each ovary. Pistillate plants are found much more frequently than staminate plants. The spread through Europe was believed to be by female plants, male plants having been collected rarely. Douglas (1880) found plants with male flowers near Edinburgh, Scotland; that population persisted until 1903. During several decades the dispersal of the species in New Zealand was believed to be from pistillate plants, until male plants were discovered in 1975. Just across the Tasman Sea, Mitchell (1978) reported that staminate plants are the cause of serious problems in the irrigation systems of New South Wales and Victoria, Australia. Parsons and Cuthbertson (1992) report that no female plants have yet been found in Australia. Flowering plants are infrequent in North America; males are more scarce than females. It is unusual to find male and female populations growing together.

In cool regions and during periods of unfavorable growth, *E. canadensis* and other plants with floating or suspended vegetative organs may not be able to survive and such plants perennate by forming modified buds that are freed and fall to the substrate. Arber (1922) reminds us that the characteristic that most distinguishes many aquatic angiosperms from their strictly terrestrial counterparts is the development of a wide variety of overwintering organs.

In *E. canadensis* these propagules are formed as the apices of lateral and terminal shoots cease to elongate in late summer (or when conditions become unfavorable) and a short shoot becomes tightly wrapped with a cluster of dark green leaves. These buds are dormant apices containing much starch and they are normally quiescent until spring. Bowmer et al. (1984) found 5000 buds/m^2 of sediment. During a mild winter in the north temperate zone the new plants from these buds may begin to grow in November and December. Dale (1956, 1957b) in Canada found that 18°C for 3 days prompted germination and growth of winter buds. The buds sank as the new growth began. Dormant apices can survive cold or unfavorable conditions if buried in mud, even if there is no water cover.

PHYSIOLOGY AND ECOLOGY

Elodea begins growth in the spring seasons of the temperate zones of both hemispheres as the temperature reaches 10 to 15°C. Seasonal growth thereafter is normally interrupted only by the approach of dry conditions or cold temperatures. A range of temperatures from 16 to 28°C for optimum growth are in the literature for different sites and plant types across the world. Francois (1951) worked with plant material for which the maximum temperature for development was 18°C, while Barko (1982) reported an increase in biomass up to 28°C when light was plentiful. In the experiments of the latter, shoot density was directly correlated with biomass production under all combinations of light and temperature, but shoot length increased with temperature and decreased in high light. Barko believes these responses of *Elodea* are expressed in its latitudinal distribution, its accommodation to depth of water and in the duration of seasonal growth.

Haag (1979) and Haag and Gorham (1977) studied the response of *Elodea* to temperature changes in a field site in central Alberta, Canada, near lat 55° N, where the species is uncommon. It was a dominant weed over an entire lake in summer and continued development in winter in bays near the thermal effluent of two electric generating stations. The water body was 80 km^2 in area and was covered with ice 5 mo each year, with the exception of the 25 to 100 ha of warmer water near the generating stations. The size of the ice-free area was dependent on the severity of the winter. The temperature of the stratified water varied from 22°C at lower to 28°C at upper levels. The effluent from a station opened in 1970 was diverted from the lake in 1975, allowing the ice-cover to return, with the result that the *Elodea* population was reduced to a trace within two years.

The populations of many species can remain constant beneath the ice because there is little turbulence. It is so with small ice-free areas as well, because the short reach of open water limits the influence of the wind. In this field site, *Elodea* was the first of 30 aquatic species to grow in spring and in an experimental observation in April, 1977 a large mass of mature plant fragments moved into the surrounding lake from the ice-free area. They were known to be immigrants because they were unrooted. Very few of the fragments perished in severe weather in the open water area and the resulting winter standing crop quickly developed into a greater biomass than other species and so dominated the lake. Stuckey et al. (1978) in the central United States reported that whole, intact *Elodea* plants survived in water at 1 to 4°C for 2 mo, under ice, with 12.5 cm snow cover. Marchand (1985) in Finland reported that photosynthesis continued in plants living under ice and snow. Laboratory and field studies have shown that *Elodea* lacks a dormancy mechanism and can grow at any time conditions are favorable.

The extent to which aquatic plants themselves alter the temperature of their surroundings is less well known. The daily cycling of increasing and decreasing radiant energy may cause marked changes in the temperature profile of a water body in the presence of a biomass of plant material. Dale and Gillespie (1977) studied the temperature gradients in the water columns of more than 35 sites in a lake in south central Ontario, Canada where *E. canadensis* and similar plants were present. In August, at midday, in clear weather the temperature gradient from 10 cm below the surface to the lake bottom was 10°C/m with a large macrophyte biomass present. It was 0.2°C/m when fewer plants were present.

Reinhardt et al. (1980) examined the toxic levels of the heavy metals Cd, Cu, and Zn for *Elodea*, with a view toward using this plant to detect the presence of these ions in water. The deplasmolysis times of *Elodea* protoplasts were affected by concentrations of 0.05, 0.0005, and 0.005 mg/L for Cd, Cu, and Zn ions, respectively. The response of the plants was influenced by the time of year, water hardness, and the presence of more than one of these or other heavy metals.

The aquatic environment is so complex and the habits of plant species and ecotypes vary so greatly that the mechanisms for nutrient uptake are constantly under discussion. Brown (1913), working with *Elodea* plants growing in three substrates containing differing amounts of organic matter, decided that this species does not depend on its roots for the absorption of inorganic nutrients. In his view, the roots were organs of anchorage to hold the plants near the sediments in the proximity of the most plentiful supply of gases. He believed that the growth of *Elodea* in the eastern United States in summer was more likely to be governed by the supply of CO_2 available than by variations in inorganic nutrition. Carignan and Kalff (1980) in Canada used an experimental apparatus that isolated the leafy stems of *Elodea*, growing in open water containing unlabeled P, from the root systems growing in P^{32}-labeled sediments. Once prepared, the plants and suitable control containers were returned to their original locations on a mesotrophic lake bottom. The *Elodea* plants in these experiments obtained all of their P from the sediments. Only in hypereutrophic lakes, seldom encountered, was there significant P uptake from the open water.

Long-term observations of *Elodea* and other aquatic weeds in a lake in the northwestern United States indicated a close relationship between seasonal decline of the macrophyte population and the onset of planktonic *Cyanobacteria* blooms (blue green, photosynthetic). There was good agreement in laboratory and *in situ* on levels of radioactive phosphorus translocated from sediment to open water for senescing plants. In actively growing plants there was some release (leakage) of P into open water. There was evidence that the internal cycling of sediment phosphorus in such a lake may influence and control the pattern, timing, and community composition of planktonic production in the whole water body (Moore et al. 1983). Carpenter and Gasith (1978) reported that plants injured during the harvest procedure allowed little escape of N and P. Rorslett and Berge (1986) found a significant release in 3- and 4-yr-old plants. See also Peverly (1985) on accumulation and release of major nutrients in streams in the central United States.

Mulligan et al. (1976) studied the response of four species of submerged aquatic plants to low and high levels of added inorganic nutrients in experimental ponds. The high levels caused striking increases of phytoplankton populations. *Elodea* and *Potamogeton crispus* survived under these conditions, but *Myriophyllum spicatum* and *Ceratophyllum demersum* were eliminated. At low fertility levels the growth of benthic plants and macrophytes was similar to the controls. Ryan et al. (1972) fertilized ponds containing *Elodea* with N, P and K but found the best growth in the unfertilized experimental ponds. The growth of algae in the enriched waters suppressed the growth of *Elodea*. It is commonly believed that increasing movement of inorganic nutrients from cities and farms into waterways has enhanced the growth of all aquatic plants. Peltier and Welch (1970) found little relation between the year-to-year growth of several aquatic plants and the N and P content of the water in a natural site in the southern United States.

In Europe it is believed that the most important propagule in maintaining *Elodea* populations over the long term is the dormant apex, and to a lesser extent the turion. Janauer (1981) in Austria studied the composition of the plants and their dormant apices in different seasons and in water bodies of high and low fertility. Plant material from more fertile water had lower starch levels and higher total cation and anion content than plants in less fertile surroundings. As storage organs, the dormant apices had the highest starch concentrations and very low levels of sugars and ionic components. Succinate, the anion of an organic acid, that was not present in parent plants, was abundant in these apices. Before vegetative development began and during spring growth, Best (1977) in the Netherlands found a high percentage of the N is available in the form of protein, suggesting a high rate of enzyme synthesis. The starch accumulated in winter was metabolized during spring growth. Ca and Mn contents varied with the season but Fe and Mg did not.

For further information on the composition and mineral nutrition of *Elodea*, see Gortner (1934), Fish and Will (1966), Udel'nova et al. (1971), Adams et al. (1973), Muztar et al. (1978), and Rorslett and Berge (1986). For analytical studies of most inorganic elements, ash content, carbohydrates and crude fiber and protein in *Elodea*, see the Food and Agriculture Organization (FAO-United Nations) *Handbook of Utilization of Aquatic Plants* (Little 1979). The water content of *E. canadensis* is in the range of 85 to 95%, comparable to that of terrestrial plants.

Luther (1951) in Finland studied plants in an estuary near the sea and found that *Elodea* extended from reaches of fresh water seaward to a salinity of 3000 ppm, or about one-tenth of the concentration of sea water.

Bastardo (1979) in Poland studied the decomposition of seven species of submerged littoral macrophytes, including *E. canadensis*, in laboratory experiments. *Elodea* had the most rapid decay rate, a loss of 50% of its weight in 7.3 days, with the most rapid decline in the first half of this period, followed by two *Potamogeton* species that averaged about 13 days. More than 90% of the *Elodea* material decomposed within a month. About 90% of all Ca, Mg, K, Na, P, and N leached out within the first 4 days and caused a marked change in the ambient water. The pattern of decay for this species was the same at different sites, but material taken during cold weather periods decomposed more slowly in the laboratory than that growing vigorously in warm weather.

While growing in water polluted by radioactive wastes in southeast England, *E. canadensis* and several other species accumulated isotopes in living tissues and showed high levels of β activity. It was pointed out that the sudden release of such activity from a large biomass of the weed as it deteriorates could constitute a serious hazard (Dept. of Scientific and Industrial Research, London 1958).

E. canadensis is very widely utilized for laboratory studies in cellular physiology and the literature is therefore quite extensive on its use as a source of chloroplasts, for experiments in protoplasmic streaming, photosynthesis and respiration, uptake of isotopes from solution, and investigations of nuclear membranes and cell structure and content with the electron microscope. Selected research papers of interest to those studying the physiology and biochemistry of this weed, and particularly photosynthesis and respiration, are Brown et al. (1974), Tolbert and Osmond (1976), DeGroote and Kennedy (1977), Hough (1974, 1979), Maberly and Spence (1983), and Catling and Wojtas (1986).

MORPHOLOGY

Leaf morphology is very often used to differentiate between closely related species in the genus *Elodea* because these plants may not flower at all in some areas or may flower very briefly and infrequently. With environmentally induced changes so common in the morphology of plant parts (leaves for example) such taxonomic criteria for distinguishing between related species in mixed populations may become ineffective.

The basal nodes of the *Elodea* plant, which are formed when the apex is young and small, bear only two leaves, while the distal node that is formed when the apex is larger bears three leaves. The *staminate* male plants differ from the *pistillate* female plants in having longer sepals, petals, and internodes, and narrower leaves at successive nodes toward the distal stem end. In some sites the habit of growth of female plants may become disturbingly similar to that of male plants, raising again the question of the advisability of using vegetative characters alone to distinguish between plants of different sex.

Lawrence (1976) mapped the variation in leaf morphology in *Elodea* species at different temperatures. Leaf sizes in *E. canadensis* were reduced as temperature increased until they fell within the range of leaf sizes for *E. nuttali*. Upon examination of 20 populations of these two species in the field in the eastern United States, it was found that four could not be distinguished using this leaf characteristic.

Ernst-Schwarzenbach (1945a,b) described fertile crosses of *E. canadensis* and *E. nuttali* and he believes that some unclassifiable *Elodea* populations may be hybrids of such crosses. Wylie (1904) provided a most methodical account of the interesting sexual reproduction process in *E. canadensis* and the role of the surface water film during this event. The work is accompanied by detailed anatomical descriptions and illustrations of the reproductive organs, beginning with the development of the floral tube.

The mesophyll tissue is totally lacking in *Elodea* leaves, the two epidermal layers being contiguous. There is little or no cuticle on the surface and there are no stomata (Solereder 1913). In subterranean monocotyledonous stems there is extreme reduction of the vascular cylinder because of the failure of cells to differentiate or because of deterioration of those which have begun the process. In mature stems of *E. canadensis*, it is quite normal to find an extensive lacuna in the internode and a few annular or spirally thickened tracheides at the nodes. A similar reduction of the vascular tissues is seen in the leaves (Dale 1957a). The few slender, unbranched roots that form at the nodes make up about 2% of the biomass. *Elodea* belongs to the group of plants that does not develop root hairs in open water but does form them if roots are in a substrate or in water in complete darkness (Cormack 1937).

Wilson (1957), Buvat (1960), Currier and Shih (1968), and Ancibor (1979) have reported anatomical and cytological studies of *E. canadensis*.

INTERFERENCE WITH HUMAN ACTIVITIES

Van Zon (1973) of the Netherlands may have touched upon the characteristic of major importance in the ecology and spread of *E. canadensis* as a weed when he pointed out that one-half million km of ditches and canals in his country become weedy and are cleaned up to six times yearly with hand labor—as they have been since the Middle Ages—and that in all of this time such a method has proven ineffective for elimination or eventual control of *Elodea* and other submerged weeds. The populations of these plants almost invariably increase following hand-cutting and pulling. In a simple experiment that demonstrates the remarkable survival capability of this species, Mason (1960) kept 45-cm stem fragments in 1-liter glass jars in his laboratory at room temperature, and after 9 mo all original leaves were lost, new buds were formed, and the fragments increased in length by 8 cm.

In Australia, *Elodea* is one of the main problems in 8000 km of ditches and canals in the farm areas of Victoria (Bill 1969). The plant is regarded as a threat to agricultural production and is on the Australian Plant Quarantine List of prohibited weed plants (Anon. [Australia] 1982). In New Zealand, *E. canadensis* is sold in markets for use in home aquaria, plant fragments are used in school laboratories to demonstrate O_2 production, and it is used for packing fish and fish eggs for short-term transport, with the result that infestations now appear throughout the country.

Between 1960 and 1970 four submerged weeds, including *Elodea*, reached epidemic proportions in Lake Rotorua, one of the largest lakes on the North Island of New Zealand. In farming areas near Christchurch on the South Island, it is one of the most abundant weeds in drains and ditches and must be removed routinely. Elsewhere in the world, the plant can reduce water flow in canals and streams by 60 to 80%, interfere with river traffic, disturb hydroelectric and urban water supplies, limit recreational water use, and alter the aquatic environment.

Across the world it is regarded as a serious weed in Australia, and a principal weed in Denmark, England, Germany, Italy, New Zealand, Netherlands, Norway, Poland, Puerto Rico, Scotland, Sweden, and the United States. It is also a weed of irrigated areas in Bulgaria, China, Portugal, and Romania. In all of these areas, it interferes with water movements and in some cases the supply needed for lowland rice fields.

Bowmer et al. (1979) reviewed all of the practices used in recent times for the control of *Elodea* in Australia and elsewhere and concluded that the only practical, affordable herbicide available for temporary cleaning of large irrigation canals is acrylaldehyde (acrolein). Non-chemical methods have proven unsatisfactory because of the high cost of labor and machines and because of the fragmentation that eventually causes more rapid spread of the weed. Thus far, the only promising biological control agent is the grass carp *Ctenopharyngodon idella*, which is very fond of *E. canadensis*. Using grass carp in the central United States, Mitzner (1976) reported an 85% reduction in the populations of four submerged macrophytes, including *E. canadensis*, in small lakes in a 3-yr period. The water quality was not significantly altered and shoreline fishing was considerably improved. Successful control of the weed with this fish species has been obtained in England also. Dense beds of *Elodea* are, however, a help in providing food and cover for fish, ducks, insects and other aquatic organisms.

In a study of Danish streams that contain *Elodea* and similar aquatic weeds, Dawson and Kern-Hanson (1979) noted reductions in biomass proportional to the quantity of light at the water surface. This finding suggests that appropriate shade plantings of trees and shrubs on stream banks may help to alleviate aquatic weed problems.

In a study of the influence of ten fresh water plants on mosquito larvae in western Canada, Angerilli and Bierne (1974) found that six macrophyte species, including *Elodea*, and one alga markedly reduced the number of adult mosquitoes emerging from experimental tanks.

COMMON NAMES

Elodea canadensis

ARGENTINA	elodea
AUSTRALIA	elodea, Canadian pondweed
BELGIUM	waterpest, peste d'eau
CANADA	Canada waterweed, elodee du Canada
DENMARK	vandpest
ENGLAND	Canadian pondweed
FINLAND	vesirutto
FRANCE	elodee du Canada
GERMANY	Wasserpest, Kanadier Wasserpest
ITALY	peste d'acqua
JAPAN	kanadamo
NETHERLANDS	brede waterpest
NEW ZEALAND	blackweed, Canadian pondweed, oxygenweed, riverweed, yankee-weed
NORWAY	vasspest
PORTUGAL	estrume novo
PUERTO RICO	elodea, tomillo de agua
SWEDEN	vattenpest
UNITED STATES	American elodea

Thirty-Nine

Emilia sonchifolia (L.) DC. ex Wight

Asteraceae (Compositae), Aster Family

EMILIA SONCHIFOLIA is an annual herbaceous plant common in both cultivated and undisturbed areas. The species name refers to "sowthistle-like leaves" and in some ways it resembles the *Sonchus* genus. However, it is a more delicate plant and never has yellow flowers. It is native to the Old World tropics and now occurs in the tropical and subtropical areas of 54 countries (Figure 39-1), often as an early colonizer of disturbed sites. It has been described as extremely common but not troublesome, which may explain the scarcity of research on this species.

FIGURE 39-1   The distribution of *Emilia sonchifolia* (L.) DC. *ex* Wight. across the world where it has been reported as a weed.

FIGURE 39-2 *Emilia sonchifolia* (L.) DC. *ex* Wight: 1. habit; 2. flower; 3. syngenesious stamens; 4. stigma; 5. achene with pappus.

DESCRIPTION

E. sonchifolia (Figure 39-2) is an *annual* herb; *root* a branched taproot; *stems* weak, erect or often branched at the base, smooth or sparingly hairy, 10 to 60 cm tall; *lower leaves* deeply and irregularly pinnately or bluntly toothed; lobes nearly round, kidney-shaped, ovate, triangular-ovate or obovate, 4 to 16 cm long, 1 to 8 cm wide with narrowly winged petioles; *upper leaves* smaller than lower leaves, alternate, usually entire, sometimes coarsely dentate, sessile and somewhat clasping the stem; *inflorescence* a terminal, involucrate flower head resembling a single flower, 12 to 14 mm long, 4 to 5 mm wide, urn-shaped, long-peduncled; flowering branches usually dichotomously branched with 3 to 6 heads, each head or capitulum a composite of numerous florets; *involucre* green, cylindrical, somewhat inflated below, in a single series; inner *florets* perfect, outer ones pistillate, 30 to 60 per head, flowers purple, scarlet, red, pink, orange, white or lilac; *ovary* inferior, one cell, one *oval* with basal placentation; *fruit* a dry indehiscent *achene* prismatic, 2.4 to 3 mm long, narrowly oblong with 5 shortly hairy ribs alternating with indistinct, smooth ribs, outer achenes reddish brown, inner ones off-white; *pappus* white, abundant, 8 mm long.

This species is recognized by the sowthistle-like leaves, the long-peduncled, usually dichotomously branched inflorescence and the single ring of involucral bracts that are somewhat inflated below.

HABITAT, ECOLOGY, AND BIOLOGY

E. sonchifolia occurs in open grassy or waste areas, dry stony areas, roadsides, plantation crops such as tea and bananas, and cultivated annual crops. It grows from sea level to 1000 m and inhabits many soil types. Plants grow in the partial shade of coffee or in full sunlight in the Dominican Republic (Camilo and Jurgens 1975). In Malaysia, *E. sonchifolia* is one of several **Compositae** to invade newly cleared peat land (Wee 1970). Even with a soil *pH* of 3.2 to 4.8, over 53,000 plants/ha were observed 3 mo after clearing if the site was not weeded.

E. sonchifolia can be crossed with *E. coccinea* (Olorode and Olorunfemi 1973) and chromatographic analysis of the leaves can be used to identify the parents and hybrids of this cross (Nwankiti et al. 1976). Flower color of *E. sonchifolia* varies greatly around the world, but this trait is not correlated with the phenolic distribution within the plant (Nwankiti et al. 1976).

One hundred seeds weigh about 70 mg. The outer circle of florets have only the female parts and form achenes that differ in seed coat color from those of the perfect inner florets (Marks and Akosim 1984). The outer achenes are reddish-brown while the inner ones are off-white. At 27°C, all of the outer achenes germinated and 90% of inner ones did. Germination of both types was only 25% at 30°C and nil at 35°C. When placed under a banana leaf, only seeds from the outer florets germinated. These differences in germination response help maintain a seed reservoir capable of germinating in varying conditions.

At a constant temperature of 25°C, 80% of the seeds in light germinated, while only 60% of those in the dark germinated. In Sri Lanka, germination extends over a 5-wk period (Pemadasa and Kangatharalingam 1977). Detailed studies comparing a "normal landing" (with the achene touching the surface) or with the pappus touching the surface revealed that 88% of the achenes making a "normal landing" germinate, while only 46% of the others germinate. Only 8% of the seeds germinated if the pappus touched the surface and seeds are kept in the dark. The rate of achene hydration was always greater when a "normal landing" occurred; the presence or absence of the pappus did not affect germination. Seeds as deep as 4 cm in the soil may germinate (4%), but only seeds at 0.5 and 1 cm are able to emerge (29 and 3%, respectively).

Seedlings of *E. sonchifolia* occur throughout the growing season in Nigeria if soil moisture is adequate (Marks 1983). Seedlings develop rapidly after germination and tolerate intense rainfall. Flowering plants occur throughout the dry season and individual plants complete their life cycle in about 90 days. Both leaf surfaces are thick and waxy and the upper and lower surfaces have 114 and 140 stomata/mm^2, respectively (Veeranjaneyulu and Das 1984). The chlorophyll a to b ratio is 2.75 and the CO_2 compensation point is 75 ppm CO_2.

AGRICULTURAL IMPORTANCE

E. sonchifolia is a reported weed of 29 crops in 54 countries (Figure 39-1) and frequently infests bananas, cassava, maize, pineapple, rice, sugarcane, and vegetables, reflecting its ability to invade many crops. It is a serious or principal weed of cassava in Brazil and India; cotton, maize, and lowland rice in Brazil; oil palm and rubber in Southeast Asia and West Africa; papaya in the United States; peanuts, sweet potatoes, and tomatoes in Hawaii; pineapple in Hawaii and Malaysia; and taro in Samoa Islands.

It is a common weed of banana in Hawaii and Surinam; edible beans in Cuba; cassava in Ghana and Surinam; cacao and rubber in Indonesia; citrus and rice in Surinam; coffee, potatoes, and tomatoes in Costa Rica; cotton in Peru; maize in Ghana, Hawaii, and Peru; oil palm in Indonesia and Surinam; papaya and sorghum in Hawaii; pineapple in Taiwan; soybeans in Brazil; sugarcane in Bangladesh, Costa Rica and Hawaii; taro in Tonga; tea in India, Indonesia, and Taiwan; tobacco in the Philippines; and vegetables in Bangladesh, Hawaii, and Surinam.

Also, *E. sonchifolia* is a weed of unknown rank in asparagus, avocado, and nurseries in the southern United States; bananas in Honduras, Samoa, and Taiwan; edible beans in Brazil and Colombia; cassava in Indonesia, Nigeria, and Taiwan; cacao in Dominican Republic and Honduras; citrus in Costa Rica; coconut in New Caledonia; coffee in Venezuela; cotton in Colombia and Paraguay; irrigated dryland crops in Australia; horticultural crops in the United States and Venezuela; macadamia nuts in Hawaii; maize in Honduras, Indonesia, Paraguay, the Philippines, Taiwan, and Venezuela; oil palm in Solomon Islands; papaya in Honduras; pastures in Australia, New Guinea and Nigeria; peanuts in Brazil, Indonesia, and Taiwan; pineapple in Honduras, the Philippines, and Venezuela; potatoes in Taiwan; rice in Guatemala, India, Malaysia, Sri Lanka, Thailand, Venezuela, and Vietnam; upland rice in Indonesia, Nigeria, and Taiwan; sugarcane in British Guiana, Dominican Republic, Honduras, Nicaragua, the Philippines, and Taiwan; sorghum in Colombia and Nicaragua; soybean in Indonesia and Taiwan; sweet potatoes in Costa Rica, New Guinea, and Taiwan; tobacco in Honduras and Nicaragua; and vegetables in Cambodia, Honduras, Laos, the Philippines, and Taiwan.

This weed can host the yellow-spot virus of pineapple that is transmitted by onion thrips (Frohlich and Rodewald 1970), the root-knot nematode and the *Pratylenchus penetrans* nematode (Bendixen et al. 1981).

The young leaves of this plant are eaten with rice and in soup in Java (Uphof 1968), as edible leaves in Puerto Rico (Martin and Ruberte 1978) and as salads and for home remedies in Brazil (Lorenzi 1982). Plants are used in India to treat fever, asthma and diarrhea. In China, leaf tea is used for dysentery and whole plants in cases of abscesses, boils, colds, influenza, scalds, and snakebites (Duke and Ayensu 1985). Leaves are edible as a vegetable and have 22% protein, 11% fiber, 2.2% Ca and 0.6% P.

COMMON NAMES

Emilia sonchifolia

AUSTRALIA	emilia, purple sow thistle
BARBADOS	red groundsel
BRAZIL	brocha, falsa, mirim, pincel, serralha
COLOMBIA	borlitas
CUBA	chavel chino
DOMINICAN REPUBLIC	pincel de amor, pincelillo de poeta
HAWAII	floras paint-brush, red pualele
INDONESIA	djawi rowo, djombang
JAMAICA	cupid's paintbrush
JAPAN	usubeni-nigana
MADAGASCAR	tsiontsiona
MALAYSIA	cupid's shaving brush, tambak-tambak merait
PHILIPPINES	cetim, kipot-kipot, lamlampaka, taguilinau, yagod-no-kang kang
PUERTO RICO	huye que te cojo, yerba socialista
THAILAND	flores paint brush, hu-plachow
TRINIDAD	consumption weed, cupid's paintbrush, cupid's shaving brush
UNITED STATES	red tassel-flower
VIETNAM	co chua le

Forty

Eragrostis pilosa (L.) Beauv.

Poaceae (Gramineae), Grass Family

ERAGROSTIS PILOSA, an annual grass, is a heavy seed producer and is found in quite varied habitats in the crop fields of 55 countries of the world. The genus *Eragrostis* is large, is taxonomically difficult, and it is estimated that about 250 of the 300 species are in the Old World. Because of the arduous task of identifying members of the genus, some species, including *E. pilosa*, have an unusually large number of synonyms and this adds to the burden of studying their biology. These grasses certainly prefer the warmer climates, but in some areas they extend well into the temperate zones. Some species across

FIGURE 40-1   The distribution of *Eragrostis pilosa* (L.) Beauv. across the world where it has been reported as a weed.

FIGURE 40-2   *Eragrostis pilosa* (L.) Beauv.: 1. habit; 2. lower glume, three views; 3. upper glume, two views; 4. portion of inflorescence; 5. flower; 6. grain, two views.

the world are used for fodder and in East Africa they are important grains for human consumption. There has been much speculation among botanical writers, who often copy one another unthinkingly, about the derivation of *Eragrostis*. It is most frequently assumed that the Greek *eros* for love and *agrostis* meaning grass were suggested by the lovely, dancing, spikelets of *E. pilosa*. This species and others in the genus often have the common name "lovegrass," accompanied by a descriptive adjective.

DESCRIPTION

E. pilosa (Figure 40-2) is an *annual*; *culms* slender, erect or ascending from a decumbent base, base straw-colored, striate, glabrous, sometimes suffused with purple; *leaf sheaths* 2.5 to 5 cm long, striate, appressed, glabrous with a few long hairs near the blade; *blades* flaccid, flat or convolute, 5 to 15 cm long, 1 to 3.5 mm wide; *ligule* a narrow rim with tufts of fine hair on the auricles, especially of the lower leaves; *inflorescence* a panicle, terminal, open, delicate, erect or inclined, somewhat diffuse, often narrow, 5 to 20 cm long; *rachis* terete, smooth, branches very slender (capillary), flexuous, ascending or spreading, finally somewhat tangled (implicate), lower ones whorled, sparsely long-pilose in axils; *spikelets* 3 to 6 mm long, 6- to 8-flowered, green, sometimes suffused with purple, loosely arranged, *rachilla* visible, tough, smooth, flexuous, about 0.5 mm long; *pedicels* mostly longer than spikelets; *lower glume* minute, acuminate, translucent *upper glume* acuminate, faintly 1-nerved, scabrid on back of mid-nerve; *lower glume* less and upper glume more than 1 mm long; *palea* 1.2 mm long, 2-nerved, the margins infolded, scabrid on back of nerves; *stamens* 3, 0.1 mm long; *ovary* with 2 feathery *stigmata* branched from the summit; *lodicules* (basal scales) minute; *grain* brownish-yellow, 0.6 mm long, the point of attachment serving as an apicula (short, sharp, flexible tip).

The straw-colored base, sometimes suffused with purple, the translucent glumes, lemma, and palea and the infolded margins of the palea that are scabrid on the back of the nerves are distinguishing characteristics of this species.

DISTRIBUTION AND HABITAT

As may be seen in Figure 40-1, the interesting distribution of *E. pilosa* as a weed places it in most coastal countries of all of the agricultural areas of the world. It is found inland as well but tends to avoid croplands in the cooler areas of the north temperate zone. Fifty percent of the *Eragrostis* species are reported to be native to Africa and a special crop, *E. tef*, which is grown regionally in East Africa and particularly in Ethiopia, may have evolved from *E. pilosa* and *E. aethiopica*. Lazarides (1980) has pointed out that *E. pilosa* is in the floras of most of the areas of south and east Asia and it is thus possible, as agriculture changes, that the weed may enter cropfields wherever suitable systems of culture or niches are introduced.

Its varied habitats are also interesting from an ecological view. Although it prefers moist pastures and open, disturbed ground, it also frequents roadsides and waste places that are often seasonally dry and only infrequently disturbed. In Africa it is found in association with scattered steppes of *Acacia* and other woody plants. It may appear at altitudes of 500 to 3200 m. The plant prospers during the May to September season, when rainfall is 1100 mm on average. It grows from Gabon north through Chad and Niger and over to

Sudan. In California, in the United States, it enters lateral canals in rice fields and impedes water flow. In Australia, it is found in coastal Queensland and the Darwin area.

In spite of its world-wide occurrence, observation of the seed reveals no special adaptation for dispersal. Water, wind, and soil movement are the most likely dispersal agents, with help from man. It spreads with hay movement and perhaps in crop seed. Koch (1974) believes that, as a weed, the plant is surely spread about by machines and commercial traffic. In his studies, when plants were found beyond their normal range, they were often associated with trucking and railroad routes and yards where they had been introduced and from which they were apparently unable to move out and establish elsewhere on their own. Similarly, the weed is an adventive of Poland and the dense stands are in and along the railroad facilities of the Warsaw region. There are several *Eragrostis* species in the flora of the Hawaiian Islands, including *E. pilosa*, but the latter does not rank as a problem weed there. Carlquist (1967), in a study of the long-distance dispersal of buds and seeds, believes that these grasses were brought into the islands, perhaps repeatedly, in the gut of birds.

PHYSIOLOGY AND ECOLOGY

Koch (1974) has examined an *Eragrostis* complex consisting of seven taxa in the central United States. He distinguishes between *E. pilosa* var. *pilosa* and a variety *perplexa*. The former is a weed that is now pan-tropical; the latter is not a weed and is rare in the area. The members of the complex are all annuals, they flower in July and August in the north temperate zone, have a life cycle (seed to seed) of about 60 days in the greenhouse, and perennation under cultivation is rare. In Brazil they flower from November to June and fruit from December to February. Seeds weigh about one-half gram and one plant may produce 4000.

The plants usually die when most panicles are mature, even when growing conditions are quite favorable. Under dry conditions, the completion of the reproductive cycle is accelerated, the plants become stunted, and viable caryopses are few.

The seeds are dormant, as is often the case in grasses. The *Eragrostis* seeds will not grow when released by the plant, but after 6 to 8 mo of storage 100% germination is sometimes seen in 1 wk. The seed will germinate to some extent during the first 6 mo if the apical end of the seed is removed following soaking. Koch obtained some germination from 5- and 7-yr-old herbarium specimens. In his experiments the seedlings that appeared in late spring had progressed to panicle production in 1 mo, and these were produced until the death of the plant, which sometimes still bore half-emerged panicles.

Fujii and co-workers (1962, 1963a,b; 1965) and Isikawa et al. (1961) made very extensive studies of seed germination in *Eragrostis* using several species, but mainly *E. ferruginea*. Seed coats were relatively impermeable to gases and moisture at harvest, with increasing permeability during after-ripening. Desiccation and puncturing made the seed coats more permeable to oxygen, and these procedures as well as after-ripening made it possible to germinate seeds in darkness. They detected an early light requirement that decreased as after-ripening progressed and in the final stages the seed would germinate either in continuous light or total darkness. They concluded that the limitation of the oxygen supply, which makes the seed light sensitive, implies that photocontrol is obligatory for germination in species where the inner parts of the seeds are kept under a condition in which there is a very limited supply of the oxygen needed for the respiration of the seed.

It is of interest that in *E. pectinacea*, a species similar to and closely related to *E. pilosa*, the flowering process lasts only about 90 min from first noticeable separation of the lemma and palea to the closing of the floret. The styles and filaments elongate rapidly and become exserted. Upon dehiscence, the anthers are so close to the plumose stigmas that self-pollination is inevitable, the lemma and palea soon begin to close, and it is often seen that one (or more) anther or stigma is left wholly outside the flower.

E. pilosa var. *pilosa* is either apomictic or self-fertile in bagged plants in the greenhouse, but this does not preclude outcrossing in a natural setting. If the latter process does occur, Koch (1974) believes its frequency must be low (barring the presence of an internal mechanism favoring the development of alien pollen) because pollination is made virtually certain by the manner in which the anthers dehisce.

Chandra (1976) and Mukherjee (1978) have reported on the cytology and embryology of several species of *Eragrostis*, including pilosa.

AGRICULTURAL IMPORTANCE

This weed is found in more than 30 crops of almost every type grown by man in more than 50 countries. It is a serious weed of cotton in Brazil and of rice in Indonesia. It is a principal weed of barley and wheat in Korea; of upland rice in the Dominican Republic; of sugarcane in Taiwan; of several dryland crops of India; of pastures in Italy; and of vineyards and other crops in the Ukraine.

It is a common weed of sorghum and several orchard crops in Mexico; of maize, cowpea, millet, peanut, upland rice, and sorghum in Senegal; of jute in Bangladesh; of pastures in Brazil and Hungary; of sugarcane and vegetables in the Philippines; of sorghum and sesame in Sudan; of sugar beets in Spain; and tea in India.

It is a weed of unranked importance in cereals, cotton, lucerne, rice, and tobacco in the former Soviet Union; sugar beets, beans, and coffee in Brazil; maize and sugarcane in India and rice in the west Bengal area of that country; maize, peanuts, and soybeans in Indonesia; onions, rice, soybeans, and tobacco in the United States; a widespread weed in several crops in Nigeria; and in several other crops in 35 other countries. If seed cleaning is done carelessly, this species quickly becomes a contaminant of commercial grass seed in the United States and elsewhere.

In Uganda, the weed is in the savannah and in arable crops. Because soils are poor, with little organic matter and low water retention, crops of short duration are planted as the monsoon breaks in the Bihar region of India near the Nepalese border. Annual grasses, including *E. pilosa*, are among the most troublesome weeds. Here crop seeds are sown broadcast, thus making hand-weeding difficult. On irrigated farms in south and west Mongolia, numerous annual weeds, including *E. pilosa*, make up the main weed flora (Hilbig 1982). In the Punjab region of India, *E. pilosa* is in the sand and sandy loam fields near lowland marshy areas. In Portugal and Spain, repeated use of herbicides such as the triazines in maize fields usually takes care of annual weeds but allows for the entry of resistant perennial weeds. These fields are then subject to extensive populations of a few annuals such as *E. pilosa* in some years ahead (Guillerm and Maillet 1982).

About one-half of the Sudan is desert or semi-desert and roughly one-half of this dry area bears patchy vegetation made up of a mixture of grass and broadleaved weeds around woody scrub bushes. *E. pilosa* and *Dactyloctenium aegyptium*, two of the world's important weeds, are among these desert grasses (called the "hummers"), on which several types of domesticated ruminant animals depend during dry seasons. One of the important animals is the desert sheep. The grass mixture is sparse and it is of low palatability and nutritional value, but the sheep survive and reproduce on it during periods of stress when there are forage and drinking water shortages (Osman and Fadalla 1974).

Nomadic people in the central Sahara in North Africa still practice some Neolithic food habits in the gathering of fruits and seeds. *E. pilosa* is one of the wild plants on which they depend, although analyses have shown that it is low in lysine and therefore not a good protein source (Gast et al. 1972).

E. pilosa is eaten by cattle when available, but it is not very nutritious and yields of herbage are low. A few other *Eragrostis* species, such as *E. curvula*, are important fodder grasses in local areas, but the majority of the genus is neither palatable nor nutritious.

Costanza et al. (1979) reviewed the taxonomy, nature, and some of the cultural characteristics of *E. tef*, commonly called "t'ef," a native Ethiopian cereal which has about 35 cultivars grouped into six complexes. *E. pilosa* and *E. aethiopica* are putative ancestors of *E. tef*. *E. pilosa* is morphologically quite variable but it is very similar to t'ef. They suggest that selected specimens of *E. pilosa* or *E. pilosa*-like plants may have been planted and harvested over a long period, with the result that the domestic cereal *E. tef* came into being.

The cereal is an annual, grows to about 80 cm, and has two main types. The white-seeded Hagaiz gives the best yields but requires 5 mo to mature. In the shorter growing seasons above 2500 m the brown-seeded Beddia variety is grown. It matures in 3 mo, gives lower yields, and tolerates rainy seasons. This crop has become adapted to a wide range of soils that are well drained and are not compacted. The best yields are on very light soils. Jones et al. (1978) pointed out that in Ethiopia it is second only to barley in yield, but t'ef is the most important cereal and perhaps supplies two-thirds of the protein for the peasantry. T'ef was introduced to Sri Lanka as a cereal and forage but has now disappeared. *E. pilosa* occurs in some crops, is not considered a problem weed in most regions, and is sometimes used as herbage. *E. tef* is a forage in Australia, India, and South Africa. Both *E. tef* and *E. abysinica* have been taken to several regions of the world to be used as fodder and many types have been selected for use in the different localities.

COMMON NAMES

Eragrostis pilosa

AUSTRALIA	soft lovegrass
BRAZIL	barbicha-de-alemao, capim-barbicha-de-alemao, capin atana, capin panasco, penasco
FIJI	indian lovegrass
PARAGUAY	kapii, rague
SAUDI ARABIA	heelaagoog
UNITED STATES	India lovegrass, pilose eragrostis, small tufted lovegrass, spear grass
VENEZUELA	grama de fidoeos

Forty-One

Euphorbia helioscopia L.

Euphorbiaceae, Spurge Family

THE SPURGE FAMILY has approximately 300 genera and includes the crops of cassava, rubber and castor bean. The largest genus, *Euphorbia*, has about 2000 species. The genus is from the Greek meaning "good plant," but it also refers to an African plant named for King Juba's (King of Mauritania) physician, Euphorbas. *Helio* means sun and *scopia* is from the Latin for broom-like. *Euphorbia* plants have a highly specialized inflorescence called the cyathium: a cup-like structure from which a female flower arises in the center, surrounded by numerous male flowers. The conspicuous glands at the base of the cyathi-

FIGURE 41-1   The distribution of *Euphorbia helioscopia* L. across the world where it has been reported as a weed.

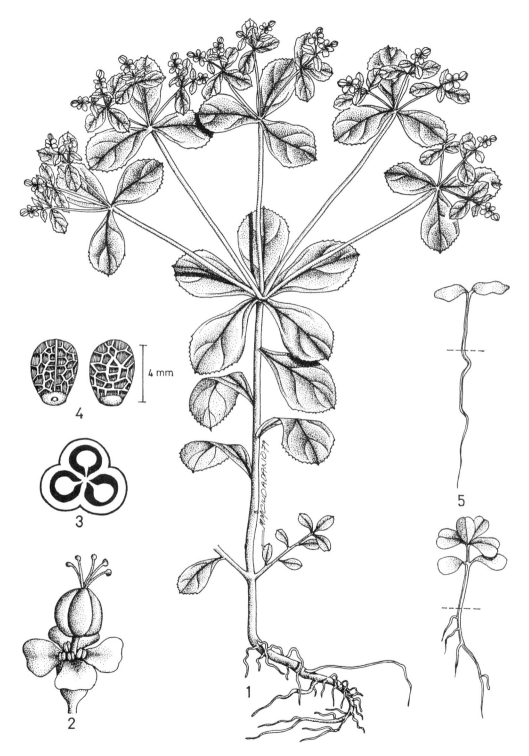

Figure 41-2 *Euphorbia helioscopia* L.: 1. habit; 2. cyathium; 3. ovary, cross section; 4. seed, two views; 5. seedling.

um are a noteworthy feature of the genus. Most members of the genus occur in tropical and subtropical regions, but *E. helioscopia* is widely distributed in Europe and the cooler regions of Asia, where it is a cosmopolitan weed of cultivated crops, gardens and roadsides.

DESCRIPTION

E. helioscopia (Figure 41-2) is an *annual* monoecious herb with milky sap throughout; branched *taproot* up to 80 cm long; *stems* simple or branched at base, yellowish-green or sometimes purplish, glabrous, erect or ascending 15 to 60 cm tall, bearing terminal flower clusters; *leaves* alternate, 1 to 3 cm long, 1 to 1.5 cm wide, terminal leaves often in whorls of 5, simple, sessile, serrulate, obovate or rounded at apex, margins entire or finely toothed at apex; *inflorescence* composed of 5 umbel-like *cyathia* (cup-like receptacles, each containing a flowering group), subtended by whorl of 5 leaves, smaller than stem leaves and not as narrow at base; each branch divides into 3 branches of second order and then 2 of third order with terminal flower cluster; *involucre* urn-shaped, with 4 rounded glands; *flowers* without petals, unisexual, flowering group with a single, central *pistillate flower* with a *gynoecium*: a long stalk with 3 *styles* and 3-celled *ovary* that extends beyond involucre after anthesis; surrounded by 10 to 12 simple *staminate flowers* each consisting of single *stamen* with small bract at base; *fruit* a dry, dehiscent *schizocarp* 4 to 5 mm in diameter with 3 carpels; at maturity carpels open violently; *seed* obovate to ovate in outline, circular in cross-section, 2 mm long, 1.5 mm wide, dark brown to orange-brown, with surface roughened by raised fine-meshed network; *hilum* kidney shaped, white and very conspicuous.

The species is recognized by its milky sap throughout, flowers in terminal umbels of branched cymes, each surrounded by a whorl of five leaves, and the sharply reticulate seed surface.

HABITAT, ECOLOGY, AND BIOLOGY

E. helioscopia is native to the temperate regions of Eurasia but has adapted to subtropical conditions. It occurs to 3000 m in India and Pakistan and is found to lat 69° N in Europe and Canada. It behaves as a winter annual in Japan, flowering from April to May (Numata and Yoshizawa 1975). In India, plants flower from December to April on the plains and in May in hilly regions (Mehra and Choda 1978). It is often associated with light textured soils.

The plant has C_3 leaf anatomy (Welkie and Caldwell 1970), with stomata on both leaf surfaces (Korsmo 1954). Korsmo also gives a thorough anatomical description of this species. The $2n$ chromosome number is 42 and its pollen is 100% fertile (Mehra and Choda 1978).

All *Euphorbia* are unique because the starch grains present in the laticifers are quite distinct from those in other plant parts (Biesboer and Mahlberg 1978). These laticifers form a continuous non-septate system throughout the plant and contain the viscous latex composed of rubber, terpenoids, glycerides, waxes, starches, flavenoids, and alkaloids.

Single plants produce an average of 650 seeds, each weighing 2.9 mg. Seeds germinate primarily at 1 to 5 cm deep (Korsmo et al. 1981).

Seeds are disseminated from the parent plant by being "shot" from exploding capsules. They can survive 90 yr or more in the soil in forced dormancy conditions (Odum 1965), but most seeds germinate within a few years. Seed bank populations of 49 to 56 seeds/m² were found from 0 to 25 cm deep in Czechoslovakia (Kropac 1966). Under controlled conditions, germination occurred over a temperature range from 2 to 38°C, with a peak of 94% at 20°C. This is perhaps part of the reason *E. helioscopia* has adapted to sub-tropical conditions. In England, peak emergence in the field occurs between May and August (Roberts and Feast 1972). Most seedlings emerged the year of planting and declined by 50% per year for the next 5 yr. If the soil was tilled, 69% emerged after 6 yr; if untilled, only 30% emerged. Seeds 2.5 cm deep emerged equally well with or without tillage, but, at 7.5 and 15 cm, tillage enhanced emergence.

AGRICULTURAL IMPORTANCE

E. helioscopia is a reported weed of 23 crops in nearly 50 countries (Figure 41-1) and is most often reported in cereals, vegetables and vineyards. It is reported as a principal weed of barley and wheat in Korea; orchards in Turkey; pastures in Italy; potatoes in Poland; vegetables in Italy and Sweden; and wheat in Iran.

It is a common weed of cereals in India, Scotland, Spain and Tunisia; cotton and sugarcane in India; flax in the Netherlands; potatoes in Scotland; vegetables in Hungary, the Netherlands and Scotland; vineyards in Hungary and Spain; and wheat in India and Pakistan.

E. helioscopia is also a weed of unknown rank in barley in Greece; cereals in Bulgaria, Germany, Greece, Iran, Italy, Pakistan, Portugal, and Turkey; citrus in Cyprus, Lebanon, and Spain; cotton in Iran and Iraq; lucerne in France; maize, peanuts, soybeans, and sweet potatoes in Taiwan; orchards in Germany, Iraq and the former Soviet Union; pastures in Argentina and England; potatoes in Belgium, Iraq, and Taiwan; lowland rice in India and Japan; sugar beets in Iran; vegetables in Argentina, Belgium, Bulgaria, England, France, Germany, Iran, and New Zealand; and vineyards in France, Greece, Portugal, and the former Soviet Union.

Seeds of *E. helioscopia* may contaminate harvested grain. While occasionally cited as a toxic plant, it is usually unpalatable to livestock. The latex can cause a severe skin rash or temporary blindness if it comes in contact with human eyes (Everist 1974). The toxin causes severe inflammation of mucus membranes and the eyes of livestock due to a high molecular weight aliphatic ester in the aerial parts of plants (Schmidt and Evans 1980).

The plant is used medicinally in Pakistan for its anthelmintic properties; seeds are used to fight cholera and fever, and oil from the seed is employed as a purgative (Baqar et al. 1966) and has potential as an industrial oil. In China, *E. helioscopia* is used as a febrifuge and vermifuge. It is also cooked with pork to form a broth for patients with boils and is believed to have anti-cancer properties (Duke and Ayensu 1985).

COMMON NAMES

Euphorbia helioscopia

ARGENTINA	lechetrenza medicinal
AUSTRALIA	sun spurge
BELGIUM	euphorbe reveil-matin, kroontjeskruid
CANADA	euphorbe revelle-matin, sun spurge

CHILE	lechetrenza
CHINA	ze qi
DENMARK	skaerm-vortemaelk
EGYPT	saa'da
ENGLAND	sun spurge
FINLAND	viisisateinen
FRANCE	euphorbe reveil matin, tithymale
GERMANY	Sonnen Wolfsmilch, Sonnenwendige Wolfsmilch
ITALY	erba calenzola
JAPAN	todaigusa
LEBANON	rummadah, sa'dah, sun spurge
MOROCCO	reveille-matin
NETHERLANDS	kroontjeskruid
NORWAY	akervortemjolk
PAKISTAN	gunda buti
PORTUGAL	maleiterir, titimalo dos vales
SOUTH AFRICA	son euphorbia, sun euphorbia
SPAIN	lechetrezna comun, lecherina, lecheruela, mamona
SWEDEN	revormstorel
UNITED STATES	sun spurge

Forty-Two

Euphorbia heterophylla L.

Euphorbiaceae, Spurge Family

EUPHORBIA HETEROPHYLLA is the most widespread of the three members of this genus we are considering. Having originated in tropical America, it now occurs in much of Africa and Asia. Its use as an ornamental plant helped it spread in the United States and Colombia. The red or white color of the upper leaves is the reason this weed is called wild poinsettia. The species name denotes the leaf variation the plant expresses. This characteristic has made classification difficult, because authorities differ in their interpretation of the degree of variation acceptable to define species and synonyms.

FIGURE 42-1   The distribution of *Euphorbia heterophylla* L. across the world where it has been reported as a weed.

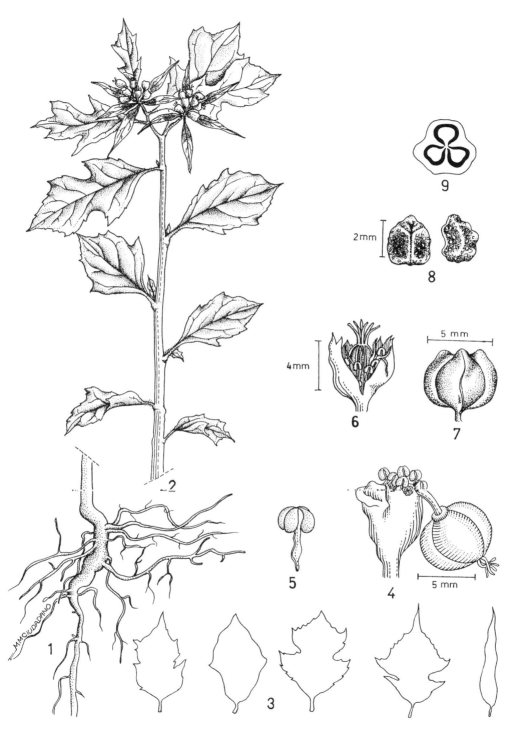

FIGURE 42-2 *Euphorbia heterophylla* L.: 1. root system; 2. fruiting branch; 3. leaf outline, various forms; 4. cyathium; 5. stamen; 6. cyathium, opened; 7. capsule; 8. seed, two views; 9. ovary, cross section.

DESCRIPTION

E. heterophylla (Figure 42-2) is an *annual* monoecious herb with latex in all parts; root a *taproot*; *stems* 30 to 80 cm tall, erect, smooth to somewhat pubescent, branched, hollow with angular ribs; *leaves* highly variable, larger ones pinnately lobed to fiddle-shaped; many oblong-ovate, 5 to 10 cm long, 3 to 5 cm wide; lower leaves alternate, upper leaves opposite or whorled, smaller, green with bright red or whitish base or entirely red; *petiole* 0.5 to 3 cm long; small leaf-like *bracts* subtend; *inflorescence* a cluster of numerous shortly stalked, green, 5-lobed *cyathia* at ends of branches; each cyathium with conspicuous funnel-shaped gland on one lobe; *flowers* apetalae, imperfect, flowering clusters with solitary, central, *pistillate flower* (a *gynoecium*) with split *style*, surrounded by 10 to 12 *staminate flowers*; *fruit* a dry dehiscent, hard-coated, nodding, 3-lobed *schizocarp* (capsule), 5 to 6 mm wide with 3 seeds; *seeds* ovoid, 2 to 2.5 mm in diameter with rough surface, dark brown to black.

This species is distinguished by the red or whitish base of the upper leaves and bracts and the milky sap throughout the plant.

HABITAT, ECOLOGY, AND BIOLOGY

E. heterophylla grows from sea level to nearly 1800 m but is only a weed in warm climates. It has adapted to subtropical conditions. It inhabits cultivated crops, vegetables, pastures, and wastelands and is a particularly troublesome weed in soybeans in several countries (Figure 42-1).

Seeds germinate over extended periods in the field. Flowering may start 20 to 30 days after emergence and seeds "explode" from the capsules 20 to 25 days later. Single plants live for about 80 days in Nigeria (Egunjobi and Kupoluyi 1973). In Brazil, flowering plants can be found all year and plants have an extended flowering period. Pollination is done by insects attracted to flowers by copious amounts of nectar produced by the glands on the cyathia. After pollination, the pedicels elongate, pushing the developing fruit up and beyond the cyathium. The pedicel then bends, placing fruits beside or below the involucre (Heywood 1978).

Plants vary greatly in leaf shape, both within and between populations (Wilson 1981). *E. heterophylla* has C_3 leaf anatomy (Welkie and Caldwell 1970), a $2n$ chromosome number of 56 (Mehra and Choda 1978), and stomata on both leaf surfaces ($128/mm^2$ above and $96/mm^2$ below) (Inamdar and Gangadhara 1978). The latex contains rod-shaped starch grains soon after germination. Biesboer and Mahlberg (1978) found no useful function for this potential source of energy. Plants have a high level of nitrate reductase enzyme in both young and older leaves (Ilangovan et al. 1990).

Plants decapitated below the cotyledonary node in the cotyledon or four-leaf stage form adventitious shoots within 5 days. New shoots appear not at the cut surface but along the hypocotyl, with as many as eight buds appearing in a 1-cm segment of hypocotyl. One or two buds form shoots; if these are killed, other buds sprout (Langston et al. 1984). Mixing freshly chopped plants with soil reduced tomato germination and growth 15 and 60%, respectively (Mohamed-Saleem and Fawusi 1983). *E. heterophylla* did not affect the growth of *Celosia argentia*. Water extracts of *E. heterophylla* greatly increased the germination of the parasitic weed *Striga hermonthica* (Ibrahim et al. 1985). Washing soils greatly reduces or eliminates the allelopathic effects of this weed, suggesting the presence of water-soluble inhibitors. Water extracts of rape or lupines affected *E. heterophylla*. The weed's root growth was reduced 83 to 94% by extracts of many crops (Almeida et al. 1984).

Single plants may have over 100 seeds at a given time (Rodriguez and Cepero 1984) but can produce 4500 seeds during a full season (Celis 1984). Seeds are rich in protein (25%) and oil (37%) but lack starch (Earle and Jones 1962). In tropical areas, fresh seeds lack dormancy, as up to 96% germinate with alternating temperatures of 25 and 35°C in darkness and light. In warm temperate regions, freshly harvested seeds are dormant. This prevents germination prior to the onset of cold temperatures (Wilson 1981). Storage at 5°C induces dormancy. Seed viability decreases rapidly if seeds are stored with 10.8% or higher moisture content, but is maintained for at least 9 mo at 7.7% moisture. Seeds buried at 5 cm for 9 mo had a 73% germination rate, while germination of those at 15 to 30 cm was reduced dramatically (Bannon et al. 1978). Emergence is greatest (40 to 47%) from seeds placed 0 to 8 cm deep and drops to 22% at 10 cm, 12% at 12 cm and none emerged from 14 cm (Cerdeira and Voll 1980). *E. heterophylla* is a weed in both conventional and no-tillage systems in Nigeria (Ayeni et al. 1984).

AGRICULTURAL IMPORTANCE

E. heterophyll is a reported weed of 31 crops in 56 countries (Figure 42-1) and is frequently reported a weed of soybeans, maize, sugarcane, and other plantation crops. It is a serious or principal weed of edible beans in Cuba and Mexico; cassava in Ghana and India; cacao in Ghana; cotton in Brazil and Peru; cowpeas in Nigeria; maize in Brazil, Ghana, India, Mexico, and Peru; pastures in Ghana, Italy, and Nigeria; peanuts in Ghana and Jamaica; plantation crops in Brazil; rice in Ghana and the Philippines; rubber and oil palm in Ghana; sorghum in Mexico; soybean in Bolivia, Brazil, Mexico, Nigeria, Paraguay, and the United States; and sugarcane in Peru.

It is a common weed of bananas and oil palm in Surinam; cassava in Nicaragua and Surinam; cotton in Bolivia, Mexico, and Sudan; maize in Bolivia; pastures in Dominican Republic; peanuts in Sudan; rice in Mexico and Surinam; sesame in Sudan; sorghum in Brazil and Sudan; sugarcane in Bangladesh, Cuba, India, Indonesia, and Nigeria; vegetables in Italy and Surinam; and vineyards in Mexico.

E. heterophylla is also a weed of unknown rank in abaca in the Philippines; bananas in Honduras, Mexico, and Nicaragua; edible beans in Costa Rica, Dominican Republic, and Honduras; cassava in Nigeria; cacao in Brazil, Honduras, and Nigeria; citrus in Mexico and Surinam; coffee in Cuba, Honduras, Mexico, Nigeria, and El Salvador; cotton in Nicaragua, Tanzania, and Uganda; maize in Honduras, Nigeria, the Philippines, and El Salvador; oil palm in Nigeria and the Philippines; papaya and peanuts in Dominican Republic; pineapple in Honduras; rice in Honduras, India, Indonesia, Ivory Coast, Puerto Rico, Sri Lanka, and Thailand; sorghum in Honduras, Nicaragua, and Nigeria; sugarcane in Australia, Bolivia, Colombia, Costa Rica, Dominican Republic, Honduras, Mexico, and Nicaragua; sweet potatoes in Honduras, Nigeria, and Puerto Rico; tobacco in Nicaragua; and vegetables in Costa Rica, Dominican Republic, Honduras, Mexico, and Nicaragua.

E. heterophylla infests over 25% of the Brazilian soybean fields. However, soybeans tolerate higher populations of this weed than would be expected. In Brazil, densities of 75 plants/m^2 reduced yield only 12%; densities of 300 and 600 plants/m^2 decreased yield 23 and 33%, respectively (Hoffmann et al. 1979). Yield losses occur primarily by reducing soybean pod numbers and some varieties compete better than others (Chemale and Fleck 1982). Greater losses were found in the southern United States. Eight plants/m of crop row for 8-wk, 12-wk and full-season competition reduced yield 19, 21, and 33%, respectively. Densities of 50 plants/m often resulted in crop failure (Nester et al. 1979), but 6 wk without competition after planting is adequate for maximum soybean yield (Langston and Harger 1983). The sticky sap of late emerging or noncompetitive levels of this weed contaminates beans with dirt and trash during harvest and may raise the grain moisture content. Seeds are spread on machinery, in the harvested crop and by birds (Wilson 1981).

Cowpea yield in Nigeria was reduced by 25 and 53% for a semiprostrate and an erect variety, respectively, when 10 *E. heterophylla* plants/m^2 competed all season. Plants that emerged 20 or more days after planting had no effect on yield, but uncontrolled plants that emerged with the crop completely shaded the crop in 6 wk (IITA 1977).

E. heterophylla is considered a toxic plant. It hosts the whitefly-transmitted mosaic virus, the bacterial blight of cassava, and other crop diseases in several countries. In some areas, leaves and stems are used as a drastic purgative and the latex as a localized treatment for erysipelas.

COMMON NAMES

Euphorbia heterophylla

ARGENTINA	lecheron
AUSTRALIA	painted spurge
BOLIVIA	escoba lechosa, gota de sangre, leche de la virgin, turujero
BRAZIL	adeus brasil, amendoim bravo, cafe do diablo, flor de pelota, leiteira, parece-mas-nao-e
BRITISH HONDURAS	redhead
COLOMBIA	escoba lechosa, gota de sangre, lechecilla
CUBA	corazon de Maria, hierba lechosa
DOMINICAN REPUBLIC	leche vana, yerba lechera
ECUADOR	lechosa, mata ganado
EL SALVADOR	hierba del duende, pascuita
FIJI	wild poinsettia
GUATEMALA	copal, hierba mala de pascua
HAWAII	fire plant, various-leaved euphorbia
JAPAN	shyojoso
MEXICO	golondrina erecta, leche de sapo, lechillo, lechilla, noche buena
NIGERIA	egela
PARAGUAY	lechetres, nana kamby
PERU	huachapurga, lechera, pascua
PHILIPPINES	kanaka
UNITED STATES	painted spurge, wild poinsettia
VENEZUELA	benba de negro, lechosito, pascuita

Forty-Three

Euphorbia prunifolia Jacq.
(syn. E. geniculata Orteg.)

Euphorbiaceae, Spurge Family

EUPHORBIA PRUNIFOLIA is an annual weed found in cultivated fields, plantation crops, gardens and noncropped areas. The species name refers to its prune-shaped leaves and that of the synonym to the bent appearance of the branched stem.

FIGURE 43-1   The distribution of *Euphorbia prunifolia* Jacq. across the world where it has been reported as a weed.

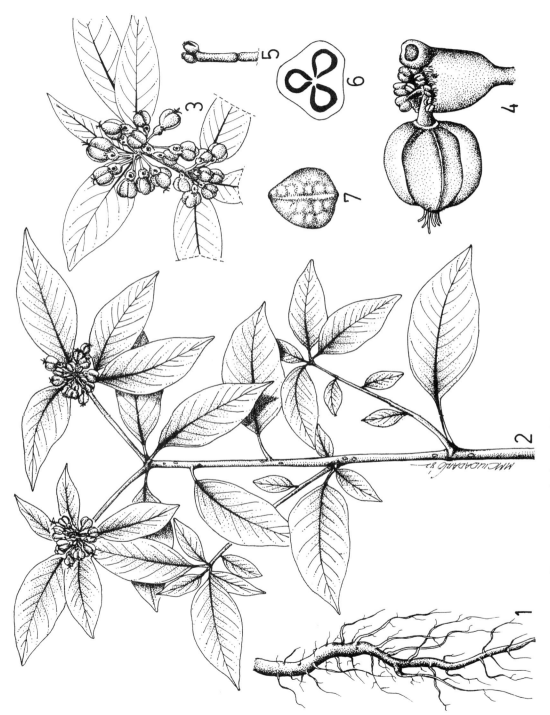

FIGURE 43-2 *Euphorbia prunifolia* Jacq.: 1. root system; 2. flowering and fruiting branch; 3. fruiting branch enlarged; 4. cyathium; 5. stamen; 6. ovary, cross section; 7. seed.

DESCRIPTION

E. prunifolia (Figure 43-2) is an erect *annual* monoecious herb with latex throughout; root a *taproot*; *stem* hollow, round, up to 75 cm tall, repeatedly forked towards apex; *leaves* 5 to 10 cm long, 1 to 3 cm wide, entire or shallowly dentate-serrate, upper surface green with narrow fringe of hairs along margin, whitish beneath; lower leaves alternate or spirally arranged, upper leaves opposite, *petiole* 2.5 to 4 cm long; *inflorescence* a terminal, dense, corymbose cyme of 5-lobed *cyathia*; 3.5 to 4 mm high with yellow or red obconical glands; subtended by 2 (rarely 3) opposite leaves; *flower* imperfect, each flowering group with a single, central, apetalae *pistillate flower* surrounded by cyme of small *staminate* flowers; *fruit* a dry, dehiscent, 3-lobed *schizocarp* (capsule) 3.5 to 5 mm in diameter with 3 seeds; *seed* 2 to 3 mm, nearly triangular, blackish to dark grey with white marks and with minute protuberances on the surface.

This weed is characterized by its hollow stems, milky sap, and leaves that are whitish beneath.

TAXONOMY

Taxonomists are divided on the classification of this and the preceding species. Some consider *E. prunifolia* simply a synonym of *E. heterophylla*. All recognize a wide range in morphological characteristics, especially in leaf shape (Wilson 1981). Mehra and Choda (1978) state, ". . . taxonomic status of this genus is in a state of confusion. There is no general agreement about its delimitation between any two taxonomists." Weed scientists in most countries continue to report them as separate species and we will treat them as such. We include *E. geniculata* as a synonym of *E. prunifolia*.

DISTRIBUTION AND HABITAT

E. prunifolia is native to the tropical Americas but is widespread in eastern Africa and Asia (Figure 43-1). It is one of the most common *Euphorbia* in Egypt and is spreading rapidly in Israel. It is found from sea level to 1500 m in India and is most abundant during the rainy season. Plants grow in rich and poor soils. *E. prunifolia* was a dominant species 14 yr after clearing a native forest in Thailand and growing maize annually without fertilization and minimal weeding (Nemoto and Pongskul 1985). As many as 940,000 plants/ha were recorded in maize by Chin and Ali (1981) in Malaysia. It was introduced into Israel in 1941 and spread very little for 20 yr. Now it is increasing rapidly, especially in cotton fields.

ECOLOGY AND BIOLOGY

Plants have a 2*n* chromosome count of 28 (Mehra and Choda 1978) and C_3 metabolism (Noda et al. 1983). Stomata are present on both leaf surfaces (Inamdar and Gangadhara 1978). *E. prunifolia* transpires twice as much water as maize in normal light and three times more if both species are shaded (Teerawatsakul et al. 1987). Stomata of the weed close more slowly than those of maize. Young leaves of *E. prunifolia* have higher transpiration and photosynthetic rates than older leaves. Aqueous extracts from roots, stems, leaves, and seed reduced wheat seed germination by 25 to 50% in petri dishes (Sugha 1979). Water extracts stimulated germination of the parasitic weed *Striga hermonthica* (Ibrahim et al. 1985).

E. prunifolia completes up to four generations a year and plants can regrow after young shoots have been cut (Dafni and Heller 1980). This occurs because adventitious buds in hypocotys form new shoots, as with *E. heterophylla* (Kigel et al. 1992). Such damage is common with hand weeding and contact herbicide use in cotton.

Plants flower about 1 mo after germination and seeds are formed at 2 mo (Chin and Ali 1981), which is a very short life cycle. Stigmas are receptive to pollen by the third day of anthesis. The anthers dehisce between 8:00 and 10:00 A.M. and nectar is principally a mixture of glucose and fructose. Principal pollinators are ants, wasps, and beetles (Reddi and Reddi 1984).

E. prunifolia has a determinate growth habit. At the flowering stage, the tip of the main stem forms a cyanthium. Subsequently, the axillary buds of the two involucral leaves develop short branches with terminal second order cyanthia. This pattern continues and is unaffected by photoperiod (Kigel et al. 1992). *E. prunifolia* is a short-day plant and growth is reduced by day/night temperatures below 22/17°C.

In Malaysia, single plants competing with maize produced 720 seeds and, if free from competition, over 7000 seeds (Chin and Ali 1981). Seeds weigh 6.8 mg each and they remain viable in the soil for long periods. Soil samples to 10 cm taken from cultivated fields contained up to 28 million seeds/ha. Seeds were more concentrated in the top 10 cm (2190 seeds/m^3) than in 10 to 15 cm depth (1240 seeds/m^3) in a field producing annual crops for 5 yr (Sastroutomo and Yusron 1987). *E. prunifolia* seeds in the soil germinated within 2 wk after receiving favorable conditions.

Low temperatures break seed dormancy and favor uniform germination in the spring (Lior et al. 1985). Emergence is greater from seeds 3 cm in the soil (72%) than on the surface (25%) (Popay and Ivens 1982). Fruits collected in the milk stage do not produce viable seeds, but 80% of the seeds in green fruits can germinate soon after maturing (Chin and Ali 1981). In Israel, fresh seed varies greatly in dormancy from year to year. Temperatures below 10 to 15°C inhibit germination and the optimum temperature is 25 to 30°C (Lior et al. 1985). Light stimulates germination of fresh seed (Noda et al. 1983). In Israel, Kigel et al. (1992) buried seeds at 5 and 20 cm in December. Even though soils were wetted continuously by winter rains, no seedlings emerged until April, when minimum and maximum air temperatures were 10 and 25°C, respectively. Seeds germinated but no seedlings emerged from 20 cm. Thus deep burial does not induce enforced dormancy in *E. prunifolia*. This is in contrast to many annual plants and seed bank depletion would be rapid if *E. prunifolia* control is effective.

AGRICULTURAL IMPORTANCE

E. prunifolia is a reported weed of 27 crops in nearly 30 countries (Figure 43-1) and frequently infests plantation crops, cotton and maize. It is a serious or principal weed of cassava and pastures in Thailand; cacao and tea in Indonesia; coffee in India; cotton in Brazil, India, Israel, and Thailand; and maize in New Guinea and Thailand.

It is a common weed of maize, sorghum, and soybeans in Brazil; maize and upland rice in Sri Lanka; orchards in Egypt; pineapple in Hawaii; sugarcane in Hawaii; and wheat in India.

It is also a weed of unknown rank in abaca in the Philippines; cassava in Indonesia; citrus in Brazil; coconut in Sri Lanka; cacao in Solomon Islands; dates and vineyards in Saudi Arabia; maize in India, Indonesia, and Sri Lanka; oil palm in Indonesia and the Solomon Islands; orchards in India; pastures in the Philippines; peanuts in Madagascar and Sri Lanka; pineapple in the Philippines and Thailand; rubber in Indonesia and Thailand; sugarcane and soybeans in Thailand; and sweet potatoes in India.

While not considered poisonous to livestock, bees foraging for nectar and pollen on *E. prunifolia* are seriously affected. They arrive at the hive semiparalyzed and frequently die (Deodikar et al. 1958). Fortunately, bees only forage on this plant when other food sources are unavailable. Plants host the root knot nematode in India and Brazil. Its year-round presence serves as a ready source of infection for bacterial wilt of Solanaceous crops in Malaysia (Abdullah 1980).

COMMON NAMES

Euphorbia prunifolia

AUSTRALIA	spurge
BRAZIL	amendoim bravo
EGYPT	laban el-homa, sharba
HAWAII	wild spurge
MADAGASCAR	Jean Robert
SOUTH AFRICA	gekleurde de euporbia, painted euphorbia

Forty-Four

Fumaria officinalis L.

Fumariaceae, Fumitory Family

THIS VERY ANCIENT companion of man once had the common name "fumus terrae," smoke-of-the-earth, an allusion to the scent that is experienced as earthy or smoky. It is now called "fumitory" many places in the world. It is a weed of almost all agricultural regions in the large countries of Australia, Canada, China, the former Soviet Union, and the United States. It is also a weed in 45 other countries, where it is found in 33 crops, often favoring cereals, vegetable crops, and vineyards.

FIGURE 44-1   The distribution of *Fumaria officinalis* L. across the world where it has been reported as a weed.

FIGURE 44-2 *Fumaria officinalis* L. 1. habit; 2. flower unopened; 3. fruit; 4. seed, two views.

DESCRIPTION

An erect to sprawling, slender, herbaceous *annual* (Figure 44-2), freely branching, to 60 cm tall or more when bushy; *stems* green, smooth striate to angled, sometimes jointed at nodes; *leaves* alternate, long-stalked, bipinnate, finely dissected, up to 8 cm long, ultimate pinnae obovate 1 to 1.5 cm long, deeply lobed; *inflorescence* in long axillary or terminal racemes, opposite leaves; *flowers* irregular, perfect, tubular, *sepals* 2, minute, dentate; *petals* 4, the upper spurred, flesh-colored to pinkish with purplish tips, 8 to 10 mm long; *pistil* 1, *stamens* 6, *ovary* superior, bracts at the base of the pedicel much shorter than the spreading pedicels; *fruit* a one-seeded indehiscent globular *capsule*, nutlet-like, lenticular, 2 to 2.5 mm in diameter, slightly compressed, somewhat indented at the apex; *seed* reddish-brown, glabrous, dull, weight 3.4 mg.

DISTRIBUTION AND HABITAT

As may be seen in Figure 44-1, fumitory is principally found as a weed in the temperate zones. It has the unusual ability to make slow but continued growth at temperatures near freezing, and thus is one of the earliest weeds to emerge. As a result, in areas of the far north-central United States, for example, in crops that are planted early but cannot be cultivated or properly managed because of prolonged, cold, wet weather, this weed may easily overshadow the crop and offer severe competition. In England, the weed is chiefly found in crops grown on chalk soils where it may dominate; it is frequently found on light, sandy soils also, but seldom on heavy clays.

Fumitory is a weed in the north of Finland and Sakhalin Island in the far east of Russia. In the south it is in Tasmania and New Zealand.

The weed was in Britain in the last phase of the Stone Age (Neolithic period) 8 to 9000 B.C. (Salisbury 1964). Odum (1965) recorded on-site species germination and obtained soil samples containing seeds from excavation sites in northern Europe that were occupied by human settlements as early as 200 A.D. and as late as 1928. These species were found in connection with the inhabited areas of former times under circumstances which gave reason to suppose that the seeds had remained viable for very long periods. Some of the seeds were tested in greenhouse experiments. Germination was obtained in *F. officinalis* seeds gathered from sites dating back to 1300.

In four independent surveys of dicotyledonous field weeds of eastern and country-wide Britain from 1962 to 1967, fumitory was one of the 12 most frequently recorded, but it was recorded less often than most others in the group (Fryer and Chancellor 1970).

The density of the seeds of fumitory is such that they are very poor floaters; at best they may float about 12 hr. Since the plants do not usually develop in sites near running water, the distribution by this means is probably not important (Ridley 1930).

The dormancy and germination of this species were studied by Jeffery and Nalewaja (1970, 1973) in North Dakota (United States). They found that many standard treatments for promoting germination were ineffective on fumitory, namely: alternating temperatures, high temperature heat treatments, red to far red light, puncturing the seed coat, complete pericarp removal, gibberellic acid, and scarification. Stratification for 60 days at 4°C gave very good seed germination. Soaking in water or leaching with water prior to stratification increased the time required for germination. The proper temperature was critical; stratification at 1°C allowed only a few seeds to germinate after 60 days. Lauer (1953) in Germany found that 7°C was the optimum low temperature to encourage germination of the species. There was no germination above 25°C.

Courtney (1966–67) mixed fumitory seeds in 1.25 cm layers of soil placed at surface, and 1.25 cm layers of soil with seed placed just above 5, 10, and 15 cm depths in upright cylinders of soil. Seedling emergence was recorded, and at bimonthly intervals, some cylinders were removed from the soil to test the dormancy of the species remaining at each depth. The seedlings emerged largely from the upper 5 cm of soil.

Roberts and Stokes (1966) and Roberts and Feast (1970, 1972) sampled soil to a depth of 15 cm under 58 old vegetable fields on several soil types. Most of the areas had been in vegetable crops for many years—some for more than 60 yr. Fumitory was not present in great numbers, but was found in 20% of the fields. By contrast, *Stellaria media* and *Poa annua* were found in all fields. They studied seasonal emergence patterns of 20 species of annual weeds by placing the seeds in cylinders of soil in the ground and thoroughly mixing the soil several times each year. *F. officinalis* emerged largely during the period November though May. Seedlings were seldom seen during the June through October period. In similar experiments, seeds were planted in the cylinders at levels of 2.5, 7.5, and 15 cm below ground level. One set of cylinders was never disturbed. In another set, the soil was thoroughly disturbed to the deepest depth four times yearly. After 5 yr, 70% of the *Fumaria* seeds placed at 15 cm had germinated and 85% of those at 2.5 cm in disturbed soil areas. In the undisturbed areas, 30% of the seedlings germinated from the deepest layer and 60% from the 2.5-cm layer.

ANATOMY AND MORPHOLOGY

Ryberg (1960) made an exhaustive morphological study of aerial vegetative shoots, of flowers and fruit parts, and underground organs of **Fumariaceae**, including studies on *F. officinalis*. He has discussed the taxonomic significance of the vegetative and reproductive structures and the problems of classification in the family.

Jeffery and Nalewaja (1973) found that once dormancy was broken in fumitory achenes, growth occurred even when the seedlings were held at 4°C. This prompted a study of the sequence of anatomical and biochemical changes that occurred in the seeds during low temperature after-ripening and the relation of these to the germination process. Seeds stratified in moist sand each 15 days during a 60-day period revealed that the embryo imbibed moisture and became globular in the first period; in the next period, there was rapid cell division with elongation of the hypocotyl root axis, and a time of quiescence for the cotyledons. In the third period, embryo growth consisted mainly of cotyledon elongation, and finally there was marked thickening and elongation of both the cotyledons and root axis. Now, at 60 days, the radicles were 0.5 to 1 mm in length; some had broken their seed coats.

Following 30 days of stratification, no achenes germinated when placed at 20°C, while at 45 and 60 days germination was 65 and 82%, respectively. Lipid fractions were steady during after-ripening, carbohydrates were steady until they increased sharply at 45 days when the embryo began rapid growth, and amino acids increased to 45 days then decreased. The significance of these findings for the diminishing dormancy is discussed.

Kutschera (1960) excavated and prepared a drawing of a root system of this species which was shown to penetrate 60 cm into the soil and was 60 cm in breadth.

PHYSIOLOGY, ECOLOGY, AND COMPETITION IN FIELD SITES

In Finland, Ervio (1981) found that in spring cereals and sugar beet fields fumitory has a long period of emergence that begins in May and continues through July and August. The peak emergence was from the end of May to the first week of June. In central Italy, emergence is only in spring. During 1961 through 1964, Raatikainen and Raatikainen (1972) in central Finland studied the weed populations of 150 fields (then in spring cereals) that had been under cultivation for 1 to 70 yr or more. In fields that had been in cultivation for 20 to 30 yr, *Fumaria* was among the weeds normally present. In general the seed load from all species was 40,000 seeds/m^2 in the top 20 cm of the soil and there were 700 to 800 individual annual seedlings or shoots of perennials in each square meter. They believe that the seeds of many of the weed species came into the fields with manure or contaminated crop seeds.

Raatikainen et al. (1985) measured the air dry biomass of aerial parts of 173 weed species found in more than 500 winter cereal fields in Finland. Fumitory was found in 12% of all fields, ranking among the top 30 species present in the largest number of fields.

The Norwegian Plant Protection Institute reviewed the change in weed floras for five sites in their country during 1950 to 1970 (Stuanes 1972). Several crops were grown at the sites during the 20 yr. Several species increased in numbers, but notably *F. officinalis*, the perennial *Agropyron repens* (couch or quackgrass), and *Agrostis gigantea*. As the use of herbicides increased, these species were generally resistant to the chemicals in use, and they were thus able to colonize land previously occupied by weed species more easily controlled by the herbicides.

In a summary of the changes in the composition of the weed flora of Sweden during 1952 to 1977, Gummesson (1979) reported that *F. officinalis* is increasing in spring cereals. Fumitory also increased as a weed problem in Czechoslovakia during the period 1960 to 1990. In the former Soviet Union, Petunova (1995) reported the development of resistance to the herbicide 2,4-D by *Fumaria* and dicotyledonous annual weeds in wheat following long-term application of the chemical.

To assess the effect of tillage treatments on the weed flora of a sandy loam soil planted to winter cereals, Pollard and Cussans (1981) used plowing (P) to a 22-cm depth in autumn, deep-tine cultivation (DT) to 16 cm, shallow-tine cultivation (ST) to 8 cm, and direct drilling (DD) followed by harrowing. During the period 1971 to 1976, with the exception of the treatment DD above, all plots received the same management, and 32 weed species were assessed each spring prior to a general herbicide treatment for control of broadleaved weeds. The total number of weeds was not reduced after five yr; there was a general tendency toward fewer weeds in treatments with greater degrees of cultivation. *Fumaria* and *Polygonum aviculare* were favored by the P and DT treatments. *Fumaria* was not present in excessive numbers and was absent from DD plots in the first two yr and from the ST plots in the third year. In the final year, there was no great difference in the numbers of weed plants appearing in any of the various cultivation treatments.

There are also instances of the decrease of fumitory in certain crops and types of tilling. During 1960 to 1972 fumitory showed a decrease in German fodder beet fields but was still a widespread weed problem. In an assessment of weed problems of the next decade for Britain, Chancellor and Froud-Williams (1986) pointed out that in the previous 10 yr there was a major shift from spring-sown to autumn-sown cereals that resulted in a decline of fumitory, *Sinapis arvensis* and *Polygonum* species in the fields. In Spain, in the absence of herbicide use in direct drilled cereals, Fernandez-Quintanila et al. (1984) found a rapid increase in weed populations when compared with cereal fields under conventional tillage. Several weed species were encouraged by direct drilling, but the growth of *Fumaria* was discouraged in these experiments. In competition experiments in Scotland, Lawson and Wiseman (1974) found that a full infestation of *Stellaria media* in a field reduced the yield of marketable heads of cabbage by 40%. In a similar experiment in which the above weed was removed, a flush of germination of *F. officinalis* plants dominated the field, resulting in a 62% yield loss. The unweeded check plots in the experiment reduced yields 75%. The *Fumaria* quickly grew above the crop and shaded its foliage.

In the literature there are scattered allegations of harm to animals by *F. officinalis*, but thus far there are no reliable clinical data to substantiate such claims.

Green and yellow commercial dyes are extracted from this plant.

AGRICULTURAL IMPORTANCE

F. officinalis is found in cereals (including one or more of the following: barley, millet, oats, winter and spring wheat) where it is a serious weed in Tunisia; a principal weed in Australia, Finland, New Zealand, Norway, Scotland, Spain, Sweden, and the United States; a common weed in Bulgaria, England, the former Soviet Union, and Turkey; and a cereal weed of unknown rank in Chile, France, Germany, Greece, Italy, Portugal, South Africa, and the former Yugoslavia.

It is a weed of fruit crops (including one or more of the following: citrus, orchards, strawberries, and vineyards), in which it is serious in Scotland; a principal weed in South Africa; a common weed in Greece, Spain, and Uruguay; and a fruit crop weed of unknown rank in Belgium, Cyprus, England, France, Jordan, Lebanon, New Zealand, the former Soviet Union, and the United States.

Fumitory is a weed of vegetable crops (including one or more of the following: beans, beets, cabbage, carrots, onions, peas, and tomatoes), in which it is a serious weed in Argentina; a principal weed in Australia, England, New Zealand, Norway, Spain, and Sweden; a common weed in France, Germany, and the former Soviet Union; and a weed of unknown rank in Canada, Greece, Italy, Poland, Spain, Switzerland, Tasmania, and Tunisia.

It is also a serious weed of linseed in Argentina, and sugar beets in Algeria, Czechoslovakia, England, and Spain; and a principal weed of irrigated crops in Spain; of maize in England; of potatoes in New Zealand, Norway, Scotland, and Sweden; of rape in Spain; and of sugar beets in Finland.

It is a common weed of irrigated crops in Australia; of legumes in England, South Africa, and Tunisia; of ornamental crops in the United States; of potatoes in England and the former Soviet Union; and of sugar beets in France and Germany.

Fumitory is also present in avocado in the United States, flax in the former Soviet Union, linseed in Poland, and maize in Canada, France, Norway, New Zealand, and the former Soviet Union. It is mentioned as an occasional weed of pastures and lucerne in several regions of the world. It is found in rape in Argentina, Australia, Canada, and England; in sugar beets in Italy, the Netherlands, and New Zealand; in sugarcane in Argentina; in sunflower in France and Spain; and in tobacco in Belgium and the former Soviet Union.

COMMON NAMES

Fumaria officinalis

ARGENTINA	flora de pajarito, yuyo paloma
AUSTRALIA	common fumitory, red flowering fumitory
BELGIUM	duivekervel, fumeterre officinale
CANADA	fumeterre officinale, fumitory
CHILE	hierba de la culebra, hierba del salitre
DENMARK	laege-jordrog
ENGLAND	fumitory
FINLAND	peltoemakki
FRANCE	fleur terre, fumeterre, fumeterre officinale
GERMANY	Echter Erdrauch, Gebrauchlicher Erdrauch, Gemeiner Erdrauch
IRAN	shatareh
ITALY	feccia, fumaria, fumosterno
LEBANON	fumitory, kusfarat el hhimar, sataraq
MAURITIUS	fumeterre
NETHERLANDS	duivekerval, gewone duivekerval
NEW ZEALAND	fumitory
NORWAY	jordrok
PORTUGAL	fumaria ou erva moleirinha
SOUTH AFRICA	drug fumitory, gewone duiwekerwel
SPAIN	capa de reina, colomina, conejitos, gallocreste, gitanillas, pendientitos
SWEDEN	jordrok
TURKEY	sahtere
UNITED STATES	fumitory, hedge fumitory
URUGUAY	flor de un pajarito
YUGOSLAVIA	dimmjaca

Forty-Five

Heliotropium europaeum L.

Heliotropiaceae, Heliotrope Family

H ELIOTROPIUM EUROPAEUM was until very recently held to be in the large
Boraginaceae family of about 100 genera and 2000 species of annual and perennial herbs, shrubs, trees and a few lianas. It is still held by some to be in the borage family. These plants are mainly residents of the subtropics and the temperate zones,
although some of the weedy species of the family thrive in tropical agricultural as well.
There are several weeds in the borage family that trouble man's fields and his animals. This
weed, heliotrope, infests 26 crops in 39 countries.

FIGURE 45-1 The distribution of *Heliotropium europaeum* L. across the world where it
has been reported as a weed.

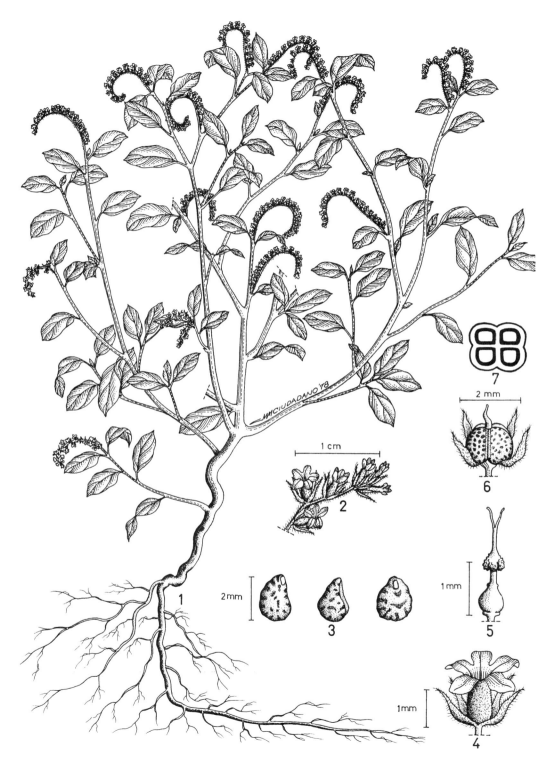

FIGURE 45-2 *Heliotropium europaeum* L.: 1. habit; 2. portion of inflorescence; 3. seed, three views; 4. flower; 5. pistil; 6. nutlet; 7. ovary, cross section.

There are about 250 species in the genus *Heliotropium*. The garden heliotropes are old-time favorites, some being used as early spring indoor pot plants. *H. europaeum* is most notorious as a member of a group of plants containing pyrrolizidine alkaloids that are very toxic to many types of stock animals. In a time when there is increasing discussion about the development of crop plants that will tolerate the herbicides needed in those crops, *H. europaeum* has a distinction of its own. It is perhaps the first weed about which there is speculation that sheep breeds may be developed to have the metabolic capability of detoxifying enough of the alkaloids in the rumen so that heliotrope may be grazed without harm to the animal (Lanigan et al. 1978).

The family supplies us with medicinal plants, about 30 species are used for dyes and some members of the family are poisonous to humans and animals. One species, *Alkanna tinctoria* is the source of a well-known bright red dye used to stain marble and wood, to color medicines, waxes, oils and cosmetics, and as a chemical indicator in industrial research.

The name of the plant is from the Greek *helios* for sun and *trope* for turning, an allusion to the turning of leaves and flowers to the sun. It is now recognized that this is not the habit of *H. europaeum*.

DESCRIPTION

H. europaeum (Figure 45-2) is an erect or semi-prostrate branched *annual*, 20 to 30 cm tall, has a well-developed taproot; the aerial portion of the plant covered with coarse white hairs; *leaves* alternate, grey-green, lighter color below, rough, ovate with rounded tip, prominent veins beneath, 1 to 5 cm long, abruptly narrowed at base into slender stalk that may be from one-third to as long as the leaf; *inflorescence* a cyme; *flowers* small, white, numerous, crowded, in two rows on upper side of narrow, curled spikes that straighten out as seeds ripen; *calyx* divided almost to base, the segments spreading after the flower has fallen; *corolla* tubular, 5-lobed, usually swollen below the middle, hairy on the outside, *style* terminates in a thick cone; *fruit* has 4 nutlets with fine wart-like protuberances; *seeds* brown, 2 mm long, 1 mm wide.

Some biotypes of the weed may be ill-smelling.

DISTRIBUTION AND HABITAT

H. europaeum is quite cosmopolitan in the agricultural areas of the world, with the exception that it tends to avoid the cooler parts of the temperate zone (Figure 45-1). There is a cluster of sites from west to east across south Europe and North Africa and extending into the west and south of the former Soviet Union. Another grouping of locations reaches from east India to south China, down through Southeast Asia and the Pacific Islands. The weed is widely distributed in Australia, is a troublesome problem in many crops in Sudan, and is found on the east coast of Africa. In the Americas, the weed is troublesome mainly in the United States and scattered places in South America. A related species, *H. indicum*, is widespread in Latin America and there may be confusion between the two species. With such an extensive distribution, it is obvious that the heliotrope is adapted to many climates. It is also true that its success in a particular locality will depend on finding cropping patterns favorable to its establishment, as well as on the amount of competition it encounters in fields, pastures, waysides, and natural areas. It can thrive on several soil types.

It is known that the ballasts of sailing ships were carriers of the seed of this weed and aided in its distribution throughout the world. There are records of its appearance in ballast material dumped near Philadelphia in the United States. The weed was distributed along the east coast of the United States as chrome and manganese ores and coal were brought in and stored near the shore. It was brought in with pumice from Italy. In an earlier time the number of species of weeds being introduced into New Zealand by this means was cause for alarm and ship captains were ordered to put out to sea to dump their ballast. For some seeds these precautions were of course futile, for they could simply float to shore. An inspection of just one ship uncovered 18 species of weeds in the ballast material.

Carlquist (1967) suggests that it is well to remember that the seeds of heliotropes float for a long time and that there may have been some long-distance dispersal by this method.

BIOLOGY

The most informative study of the life cycle and the field ecology of this species on agricultural land was completed by Moore (1956) in southeast Australia during 1945 to 1949. Moore and others are quite convinced that their particular types of common heliotrope were brought from the Mediterranean area of Europe, probably Italy or France. The weed was first recorded more than a century and a half ago in the southern areas of Australia. It has become a particularly costly problem in animal husbandry, but it is also found in cultivated fields and is generally distributed on roadsides and waste places.

The species produces a large amount of seed, some of which can remain dormant in the soil for a long period. Germination tests to determine seed viability are often disappointing and this may be due to harvesting and testing of propagules that are at many stages of maturity. The inflorescence is indeterminate (continues to develop) and ripe seed may be shed from lower portions while green unripe seed is being formed in the upper portions. The plant develops rapidly after germination and sends a taproot far into the deeper, more moist soil layers. Once established, and with a greater access to soil moisture, it can persist in dry weather when grasses with shallow root systems and biennials fall under severe stress.

The plants normally continue growth until a killing frost in autumn. Some plants at some stations in southeast Australia survived the entire winter.

The inflorescence is a cyme, usually forked, and the first one to appear usually comes from the terminal bud after the plant has produced five to seven nodes. After development of the first cyme, leafy axillary shoots are formed. These then produce terminal inflorescences and shoots of tertiary and higher order. This process normally continues until the death of the plant. Moore (1956) observed that greenhouse plants produced flowers 3 wk after the appearance of the cotyledons, and this was confirmed in agricultural fields. Bull et al. (1956) observed flowering 9 days after germination in the greenhouse. This heliotrope is thus able to complete a reproductive cycle in a very short growing season. In a season of satisfactory temperature and rainfall, flowering may continue all summer.

At 19°C there was no seed germination, but at 24, 30, and 35°C the results were 23, 26, and 30%, respectively. A cold pretreatment enhanced germination. At a germination temperature of 24°C, seeds given a prior 24-hr cold period of 0°C gave 35% germination, 13% higher than the controls that had no cold treatment. At a 35°C germination temperature, a 10°C pretreatment of seeds for 1 wk resulted in 48% germination, a 17% increase over the controls (Moore 1956, Vasconcelos et al. 1984).

In the field, Moore (1956) found that the amount of litter is critical in the establishment of this weed. Pastures with vegetation that provided only sparse litter and patches of open ground after heavy winter grazing did not encourage the emergence of heliotrope seedlings with the first early light rains of spring. In contrast, nearby paddocks of natural pastures with large numbers of winter annuals and light grazing provided plenty of litter in spring and there were large numbers of emerging weed seedlings, because the early rains came and the soil surface was protected from extensive evaporation by the litter cover. Moore's report also offers detailed observations of the interrelationships of rainfall, pasture composition, and weed growth, including *H. europaeum*, during a 4-yr period and over a much larger area.

Sahay (1974) reported on the pollen morphology of 14 species of *Heliotropium*, including *H. europaeum*.

TOXICITY

Members of the genus *Heliotropium*, other members of the **Boraginaceae**, together with *Senecio* species in the **Compositae** are responsible for heavy stock losses in various places in the world. Pammel (1911) in the United States recorded that *H. europaeum* contained a toxic alkaloid, heliotropine, and that it was to be considered a poisonous plant. In the early 1930s the two alkaloids heliotrine and lasiocarpine were isolated and identified from *H. lasiocarpum*.

The first outbreak of a disease in sheep, later recognized as heliotrope poisoning, occurred in 1925 in South Australia in the Merino breed. Because the pathology of the disease had not yet been described, the deaths were reported to be due to atropic hepatosis, probably from chronic phosphorus poisoning. *H. europaeum* was under suspicion at the time and later, as the story of the chemistry unfolded, it became clear that the outbreak in South Australia had been caused by this weed.

The hazard goes beyond the grazing of natural stands of vegetation. Losses of pigs and poultry sometimes occur when contaminated grain is used to make prepared rations for these animals. When the weed seeds containing these alkaloids are harvested with grain for human consumption, sometimes after being made into bread flour, they have caused serious illness and death.

The toxic chemicals involved are pyrrolizidine type compounds or their derivatives. The disease has several manifestations, but ultimately the deterioration of the liver, resulting in its altered metabolic activity, or the loss of kidney function, becomes fatal. Secondary reactions such as altered copper and nitrogen metabolism bring on other pathological disorders which in themselves may cause death. Culvenor (1978), in a summary of the problem in Australia, has emphasized that under conditions of large landholdings and high labor costs it is not likely that herbicides or other methods can be used economically for the control of these weeds, nor is it feasible to control access of stock to infested areas. He estimates that about 100 million sheep are exposed to *H. europaeum* on about 52,000 km^2 in just the southeastern part of the country. The losses may begin after two or three heavy exposures or the life span of the sheep may be shortened from 8 to 5 or 6 yr.

Good reviews of the literature on heliotrope poisoning in Australia may be found in the book of Newsom (1952) on sheep diseases, in Bull et al. (1956), in the published papers of Lanigan and co-workers (1970 through 1978), and Seaman (1987).

The two principal alkaloids, heliotrine and lasiocarpine, undergo some destruction when in contact with bacterial and plant enzymes in the rumen, but that which reaches the liver causes cells to enlarge, to have increased death rates and to lose their regenerative powers. The disease develops slowly even with continued ingestion. The atrophy of liver tissues is accompanied by a small amount of fibrosis.

It seems unusual that in most cases the animals can survive the first season, even after consuming large amounts of heliotrope. Some or many may appear to be in good condition. In such animals, however, liver cell changes may be seen upon histological examination. The changes remain and predispose the animal to serious poisoning in the next season, when there is frequently loss of condition and evidence of changes in blood composition and metabolism which are characteristic of liver damage.

Yet another clinical syndrome may result. In sheep, this is characterized by sudden hematogenous (carried by way of the blood) jaundice. In these cases the liver is found to have an excess of copper and death may result from copper toxicity.

Symptoms and lesions associated with photosensitization have been recorded. In severe cases lesions have been seen on lungs and rarely on kidneys.

In Australia, it is widely held that Merino sheep do not care to eat *Heliotropium*, but they are also less susceptible to the poisoning than the British breeds and cross-breeds. Some believe that cattle and Merino sheep eat the heliotrope only as a last resort. In 1981 Israel reported the first case of heliotrope poisoning in calves, caused by the ingestion of rations containing heliotrope plant material and seeds. Broiler chickens, ducks, and pigs have been poisoned because their rations have been contaminated with seeds of this weed (Jones et al. 1981, Pass et al. 1979).

What can be done? With stock animals the problem is so large, the losses are so high, and the prospects of an economical control for the weed are so small that some management systems now recognize that some loss must be expected. The heliotrope ranges are grazed with animals destined for slaughter. Sometimes supplemental feed is supplied to reduce the ingestion of fodder from heliotrope areas and thus lower the alkaloid intake. Some graze the weed only when it is small and the quantity consumed is small in the total diet.

In Australia there has been much good research on prophylactic measures that would allow grazing but avoid poisoning. Although no system appears to be especially promising at the moment, there are interesting ideas at work. With the knowledge that about 90% of the hepatotoxic alkaloids of *H. europaeum* were already detoxified in the sheep rumen, Lanigan (1971) reasoned that only a small increase in the rate of the alkaloid metabolism was needed to reduce the amount of pyrrolizidines reaching the livers of animals to the point where they might be spared much of the damage that begins to show in the first year of feeding on the weed. His subsequent studies on the metabolism of pyrrolizidine resulted in the use of iodoform in controlled doses and showed promising trends for the relief of liver damage and for prolonging the lives of some of the experimental animals. The iodoform, at the levels needed, is itself hepatotoxic under some conditions, but the experimental results hold out hope that other preparations or forms of administering the chemical, or perhaps other chemicals, may bring help to the animals. Lanigan and his co-workers suggest that there is sufficient promise in these results that perhaps selective breeding may provide a means of developing a strain of sheep with increased resistance to the toxicity of the pyrrolizidine alkaloids (Lanigan et al. 1978).

While working in Afghanistan in 1975, one of the authors (Holm) became aware of stories of bread poisoning from the Gulgran area northwest of Herat. The trouble developed during the drought famine years of the early 1970s when food, especially wheat, was in short supply and people began using marginal supplies of this and other grains. The sickness was known in this area from earlier times, was no stranger in north India and

Pakistan, and it was accepted by some that weed seeds harvested with the wheat were the cause of the illness. It was also suspected that, in famine years, the wheat was not cleaned as well because the people needed all of the bulk they could get.

Professor J. Young, who was stationed in Kabul with an agricultural team from the University of Nebraska (United States) journeyed to the region to interview people who were stricken, to discuss the harvest procedures with field workers, and to obtain contaminated grain samples and plants from the fields. The specimens were taken to the government herbarium in Leiden, the Netherlands, plants were obtained from seed, and the first indications were that *H. rechingeri* and *H. europaeum* were the weeds involved. Some seed was sent, however, to Dr. H. Riedl at the Historisches Museum, Botanische Abteilung, in Vienna. A specialist on the taxonomy of *Heliotropium*, Dr. Riedl later determined that the species was *H. popovii* subsp. *gillianum*. Firm estimates are often difficult to obtain in such prolonged periods of suffering, but it is possible that about 4000 people became ill from the bread (a very large part of the diet) that had been made from wheat contaminated with this heliotrope and that it was fatal for about 1000 of them.

AGRICULTURAL IMPORTANCE

H. europaeum is a serious weed of pastures in Australia and Italy, and of cotton in Iran. It is a principal weed of cereals in Jordan; of cotton, peanuts, sorghum, and sesame in Sudan; of melons in Italy; and of sugar beets in Iran. It is a common weed of cotton in Spain; of maize in Italy; of peanuts in Israel; of tobacco and several other cultivated crops in the former Yugoslavia; of vegetables and other crops in southwestern Saudi Arabia; and of several cultivated crops in France.

It is also a crop weed of unknown rank in the following: beans, tomatoes, and other vegetable crops in Iran; cereals, lucerne, and winter-sown crops in Australia; citrus and cucumbers in Cyprus; maize, sunflowers, tobacco, and vegetable crops in the former Soviet Union; orchards in Italy and Spain; sugar beets in Spain; rice, sugarcane, and irrigated crops in Indonesia; vineyards in Czechoslovakia, the former Soviet Union, and Switzerland; and wheat in Afghanistan and Portugal. The weed is generally distributed throughout the agriculture of Hungary, particularly in rice, non-irrigated annual and perennial crops, with vigorous growth in stubble fields. It is not yet a problem in cereals or root crop cultures.

The management of cultivated lands infested with the weed in Australia is complicated by the uncertainty of the quantity and distribution of rainfall within a season or over several seasons when fallow is involved. If the weed is unchecked it can cause significant reductions in the current season's crops because the deep root system can provide moisture to give it a competitive edge. Fallow land is ideal for heliotrope because the loose soil allows roots to penetrate easily and the number of competing plant neighbors is usually less during this pattern of field use (Delfosse and Cullen 1980). The practice of using sheep to clean up fallow may be very dangerous if there is abundant heliotrope.

Heliotrope is of greatest concern because of the severity of animal losses, for which there are at present no practical or economical solutions. After many years of difficulties and losses of hundreds of millions of dollars from the mortality of sheep grazed on this weed, some farmers have had to shift from a wool production system to the production of fat lambs. Those who must graze sheep on heliotrope land often sell the animals after one season's grazing, before losses occur. Ewes are thus sold at 3 to 4 yr instead of the preferred age of 6 to 7 yr. Yet, this does not solve the problem of the weed on the land. With such a forced change in the management system, which sometimes doubles the rate of flock turnover, Delfosse and Cullen (1980) estimate that the weed may be costing farmers in southeastern Australia 20 to 30 million dollars per year.

Biological control of the weed offers one more hope. Work has been in progress since the mid-1950s, with several surveys in the Mediterranean and north African areas to find an insect suitable for release and for the control of *H. europaeum*. A flea beetle specific to the genus *Heliotropium*, *Longitarsus albineus*, is the most promising agent thus far. Releases were begun in several areas of Australia in 1979 and results are pending (Delfosse and Cullen 1982).

Grechkanev and Rodionov (1971) reported benefits from mixing 1 to 2 kg/ha of wild heliotrope seed with several legumes as they were sown. They claimed 30 to 70% control of weeds and a reduction of other plant pests as well.

COMMON NAMES

Heliotropium europaeum

AUSTRALIA	barooga weed, bishop's beard, caterpillar weed, heliotrope, potato weed
EGYPT	afeen, afein, aqrabana
ENGLAND	heliotrope
FRANCE	heliotrope
GERMANY	Sonnenwende
IRAN	aftab parast, akreer, heliotrope
IRAQ	European heliotrope, European turnsole, i'jairbeh
ITALY	eliotropio
LEBANON	afayn, European heliotrope, hhash el agrab, sakran, samiryuma, turnsole
MADAGASCAR	anangeaika
MOROCCO	heliotrope d'erope
NETHERLANDS	europese heliotroop
NORWAY	ugrasheliotrop
PORTUGAL	erva das verrugas, tornassol
SAUDI ARABIA	karee
SPAIN	verrucaria, verruguera
TURKEY	akrep otu, bambul otu
UNITED STATES	European heliotrope
YUGOSLAVIA	suncanac

Forty-Six

Hibiscus trionum L.

Malvaceae, Mallow Family

H IBISCUS TRIONUM is a member of the **Malvaceae**, a cosmopolitan family of herbs, trees, and shrubs that contributes many weeds to man's fields but also supplies important economic products. The family is composed of 80 genera, about 1000 species, and *Hibiscus* is the largest genus with about one-third of the species. Cotton (The Gossypiums) is by far the most important economic crop of the family, but from it we also have okra, *Hibiscus esculentus*, a vegetable of warm climates and the fibers of China jute, *Abutilon avicennae*; and aramina from *Urena lobata*. The hollyhocks *Althaea*; the mallows

FIGURE 46-1   The distribution of *Hibiscus trionum* L. across the world where it has been reported as a weed.

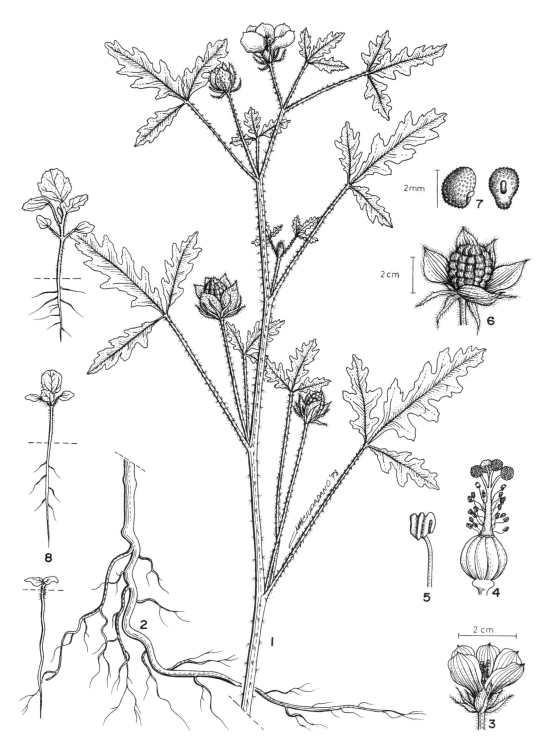

FIGURE 46-2 *Hibiscus trionum* L.: 1. flowering and fruiting branch; 2. root system;
3. flower; 4. pistil; 5. stamen; 6. fruit; 7. seed, two views; 8. seedlings.

Malva; and the bright, lively, colorful *Hibiscus* cultivars provide us with many delightful ornamentals. *H. trionum* is a weed of 27 crops in 48 countries (Figure 46-1).

DESCRIPTION

H. trionum (Figure 46-2) is an *annual* plant, erect or low-spreading, often much branched at the base. The *root system* varies with soil and region, is a long, stout taproot in South Africa, while in Germany Kutschera's (1960) excavations show it to be a dense, fibrous system with several major branches extending in many directions and some reaching to 100 cm in depth. *Stems* green to brown, sometimes purplish, cylindrical, striate, densely to sparsely bristly with whitish hairs; *leaves* alternate, simple, remarkably variable in size and shape, densely to sparsely pubescent, upper and lower surfaces may be of different shades or colors, sometimes reddish at the margins, usually deeply, palmately 3-lobed, middle lobe longer, lateral lobe often redivided, lobes coarsely and irregularly-toothed, some leaves may have up to 7 lobes, *petioles* to 4 cm, more or less bristly; *flowers* solitary in the axils of leaves, open one to a few hours, petals falling quickly, stout bristly pedicels as long as petioles; *corolla* very often sulphur yellow, cream to yellow in South Africa, white in Egypt, with purplish-black eye at center (base), 7 cm or more in diameter, *anthers* yellow, *calyx* of five joined, conspicuously veined membranous lobes, inflates when in fruit to become a nearly transparent bladder that may be up to 4 to 5 cm in diameter; *fruit* enclosed in the bladder, dark green to blackish, bristly, globose, 5-valved capsules, each locule 2 seeds; *seed* to 3 mm in length, 2.2 mm in width, kidney-shaped to triangular, depression at hilum with a short, dark funiculus curved at tip, dark brown to black, surface finely porous with scattered, warty yellow-brown protuberances. One thousand seeds weigh about 3 gm.

DISTRIBUTION AND HABITAT

In general, the **Malvaceae** are scattered over most of the world, with the exception of areas that are very cold. The largest genus, *Hibiscus*, is mainly in the tropics and subtropics; *H. trionum* (Figure 46-1) is at home in these regions but is also becoming more of a weed problem in the temperate zones of both hemispheres. It is plentiful in the south and east of Europe; is found over much of Africa except the arid northwest, and is widely dispersed across the mid and upper mainland of Asia, though it is not prominent in the south. It is troublesome in Canada and the United States, and in areas of better rainfall and on irrigated lands in Australia. With the exception of Chile, we have no reports that this species behaves as a weed in Central and South America or in southern Asia and the Pacific Islands.

The plant is often troublesome in maize and other grains, in arable crops of several kinds, but it is seldom a weed of pastures and perennial plantation crops. It is an adaptable weed, appearing on the heavy arable soils of Canada and the United States, on the banks of the Nile River from the southern border of Egypt to the Mediterranean Sea and on the semi-desert soils areas of Sudan. It is in the arable lands and orchards of the midlands and uplands (to 2700 m) in southwest Arabia, and to the south in Madagascar. It is in the upland crops on the High Plateau of the mountains of Madagascar.

The weed frequents fallow land, roadsides, and waste places in all of these regions (Figure 46-1).

BIOLOGY AND AGRICULTURAL IMPORTANCE

The germination of the seed of *H. trionum* is restricted by the hard seed coat. Martin (1943) reported 12% germination of freshly harvested seed with coat intact, but 65% if the covering is entirely or partially removed. Everson (1949) obtained 90% germination of 2-month-old seed after a 20-min treatment with concentrated H_2SO_4 followed by incubation at a regimen of 20°C for 16 hr and 30°C for 8 hr daily.

The details of the morphological development of each floral part and of the pollen grains were studied by Heilman (1960). Buttrose et al. (1977) studied the pollination procedure of this very short-lived flower. As with several others in the **Malvaceae**, it possesses flowers with prominent styles that can reflex during the first hours after flower-opening, thus allowing the stigmas to make contact with the anthers. This self-pollinating mechanism is interrupted if the flower is pollinated before or during the bending. Should this occur, the style remains erect and selfing does not take place.

Kimmell (1936) studied the anatomy of the seedling of *H. trionum*.

In Uzbekistan in the southern part of the former Soviet Union, monocropping with cotton has increased the weed problem. Shodiev (1980) studied the seeds of 15 weed species, including *H. trionum*, in the top 40 cm of such cotton soils. Most seeds were in the top 20 cm, and total seed numbers in autumn always exceeded those present in spring. The number of *H. trionum* seeds in the top soil layers ranks with those of such prolific seeders as *Amaranthus retroflexus* and *Chenopodium album*.

In an Australian study of the effect of residues of mature crops on weed seed germination and growth under field conditions, Purvis et al. (1985) found that the stand of *H. trionum* plants increased significantly in plots where rape, sorghum, and sunflower residues had been incorporated.

Majatovic and Loranovski (undated publication) in the former Yugoslavia reported that surveys of weeds in maize and small grains from 1952 through 1982 revealed a considerable reduction in species diversity. In spite of the use of herbicides and other changes in farming practices, *H. trionum* and several other main weeds increased in abundance.

During research on factors governing the rate of development of herbicide resistance, Currie and Peeper (1986) found that hand-harvested seed and machine-harvested seed of *H. trionum* gave 0 and 40% germination, respectively, at harvest time. There was no gross visual difference in the seeds. They estimate that fields treated with herbicides and later harvested by machine could reduce the time required for the appearance of herbicide-resistant types by 50%.

In soybeans, Eaton et al. (1973) studied the effect of density and duration of *H. trionum* competition in field experiments. The crop was planted in rows 75 cm apart on a silty clay loam. They placed single weed plants at intervals from 7.5 to 60 cm in the row. They also planted 30 to 40 cm wide bands of weeds in and between the rows, and left undisturbed natural weed stands of 334 plants/m^2 of *H. trionum* in some plots. They harvested weeds at intervals from 15 to 90 days (full season), at which time all weeds were removed and weighed, with the crop remaining free of weeds thereafter.

The results were as follows:

- Full season weed competition in some cases destroyed 75% of the crop.
- Bands of weeds reduced soybean yields much more than single weeds in the rows.
- Bands of weeds left in the crop 40 days reduced yields sharply.

- Natural weed stands reduced yields most sharply and this treatment was the only one that lowered yields when left in place for 30 days.
- In general, crop reduction was greatest for those treatments that kept weeds in the plots through the reproductive growth stages.

A similar experiment compared the relative competitiveness of *H. trionum*, *Abutilon theophrasti*, and *Sida spinosa*, all in the family **Malvaceae**. *Abutilon* reduced soybean yields almost three times more than the other species. Weeds planted in a manner that they would emerge *at the same time* as the soybeans reduced yields by 1000 kg/ha, while in treatments that included weed emergence 10 days *after* the beans emerged the loss was 500 kg/ha. *Abutilon* produced ten times more dry matter than the other two weeds and was the only species to have foliage above the beans.

H. trionum and several other members of the **Malvaceae** have offered ever-increasing competition in cotton in the United States since the 1960s. Chandler (1977), in the southern United States, planted weeds to emerge with the cotton or 2, 4, and 6 wk after. Several weed densities of 0 to 64 plants/12 m of row were used, and these were maintained by hand weeding at emergence and throughout the season. In this crop, *H. trionum* did not compete well with the taller cotton because of its lack of plant height and its limited capacity to increase the size of the vegetative plant. *H. trionum* did not reduce the yield of cotton at any density or duration of competition.

H. trionum is a serious weed of cotton in Iran; and a principal weed of barley in Korea; cotton in Sudan and the United States; maize in Australia, India, and South Africa; peanuts and sesame in Sudan; sugar beets in Iran; sorghum in Australia, South Africa, and Sudan; soybeans in the United States; wheat in Iran, Korea, and the former Yugoslavia; several horticultural crops in Italy; and garden and irrigated crops in Australia.

It is a common weed of several arable and nursery crops in the United States; of cereals, maize, and other cultivated crops in the former Yugoslavia; cotton in Egypt; dryland crops in Australia; horticultural crops in South Africa; maize in Chile, Romania, and South Africa; onions in Hungary; orchards in Egypt; pasture in Australia and Uganda; peanuts in South Africa; pineapple in Swaziland; sesame in Sudan; upland rice in Chile; vegetables in Australia, Bulgaria, Chile, Hungary, and the United States; and vineyards in Iran and Korea.

It is also a weed of beans, cereals, cotton, orchards, peanuts, rapeseed, and sunflowers in Australia; beans in Iran; cereals and maize in Hungary, the former Soviet Union, and the United States; cotton in Egypt; orchards and other horticultural crops in the United States; soybeans in Canada and Iran; sunflowers in the former Soviet Union and the former Yugoslavia; tobacco in the former Soviet Union; upland rice in Portugal; vegetables in the former Soviet Union; and vineyards in Czechoslovakia. It is a weed in orchards, pastures, upland rice, sunflowers, tobacco, and vineyards in one or more of the following countries: Australia, Czechoslovakia, Iran, Portugal, the former Soviet Union, the United States, and the former Yugoslavia.

Ubrizsy (1968), in Hungary, reported that the use of herbicides for 20 yr without rotation (changing of herbicides) decreased the number of weeds, but the diversity of the species was significantly increased. In surveys of major weeds present in the agricultural provinces of Sudan, Walter and Koch (1984) found in the White Nile area that *H. trionum* was a weed problem in 85% of fields studied. In Kashmir in northern India, *H. trionum* is found in 50% of the maize fields. This weed is present in almost all maize in Romania and the maize and wheat fields are troubled by *Hibiscus* in the former Yugoslavia.

COMMON NAMES

Hibiscus trionum

AUSTRALIA	bladder ketmia
CANADA	flower of an hour, ketmie trilobee
EGYPT	shebbet, teel sheitaani
LEBANON	bladder hibiscus, flower of an hour
MADAGASCAR	telorirana
NEW ZEALAND	hibiscus trionum
RHODESIA	flower of an hour
SAUDI ARABIA	shebbet, teel-sheitani
SOUTH AFRICA	bladder hibiscus, terblansbossie
TURKEY	seytan keneviri
UNITED STATES	bladder ketmia, flower of an hour, ketmia, venice mallow
ZAMBIA	kombwe, likulu, lumanda, mukukwa, sansamwa

Forty-Seven

Hordeum murinum L.

Poaceae (Gramineae), Grass Family

HORDEUM MURINUM is an annual weed of disturbed, open habitats, pastures, cereals, roadsides, railways, and wasteland. It is native to the Mediterranean but occurs throughout Europe, in both Americas, Australia, and New Zealand. The genus name, Latin for barley, means bristly in reference to the awns. The species name is derived from "murus" for wall, as this plant is found in the cracks and on tops of walls. The common name in several countries is wall barley, which reflects its adaptation to a unique environment.

FIGURE 47-1   The distribution of *Hordeum murinum* L. across the world where it has been reported as a weed.

FIGURE 47-2   *Hordeum murinum* L.: 1. habit; 2. portion of inflorescence; 3. spikelet.

DESCRIPTION

H. murinum (Figure 47-2) is a tufted, *annual* or *winter annual* grass; *roots* fibrous, shallow; *stems* 10 to 50 cm tall, erect or decumbent at base, smooth with 3 to 5 nodes; *leaf sheaths* loose, smooth, shorter than internodes with well developed *auricles*; *ligule* membranous, truncate, to 1 mm long; *blades* 4 to 10 cm long, light green, somewhat erect, often twisted; apex acuminate, smooth or sometimes rough above; *inflorescence* a dense, bristly, cylindrical spike 5 to 10 cm long, often partially enclosed in an inflated leaf sheath; *rachis* brittle; *spikelets* in groups of 3 at each joint on rachis, each one stalked, lateral spikelets male or sterile; central spikelet fertile forming caryopsis; *glumes* of central spikelet and inner glume of lateral spikelets lanceolate, 3-nerved, ciliate on both margins, with a stiff barbed *awn* 2 to 2.5 cm long; outer glumes also awned but margins smooth; *lemmas* similar to barley but flatter and narrower, length 10 to 12 mm; *fruit* a one-seeded, dry, indehiscent *caryopsis* (grain) 5 to 7 mm long, yellow, hairy at apex.

This species is characterized by the twisted leaves with membranous ligules and prominent auricles and the spikelets in groups of three with long, stiff, barbed awns.

ECOLOGY AND BIOLOGY

H. murinum successfully colonizes undisturbed areas. In Britain, it is most abundant in areas of low rainfall (less than 90 cm annually) and warm temperatures (Davison 1970, 1971a, 1977). Plants at altitudes of 320 and 560 m flower much later than those at 91 m. Plants form equal numbers of fruits per spike at all elevations, but highland plants have 30% fewer spikes. Seeds from lowland plants germinate more rapidly than those from highland plants, but 95% or more of all seeds germinate. The slower germination of highland seeds would result in smaller seedlings when winter arrives, reducing the number of spikes formed the next summer. Seeds of highland plants shatter from the spike less readily, preventing close soil/seed contact of seeds remaining in the seedhead, thereby lowering total seed germination. Thus the failure of *H. murinum* to survive at elevations above 300 m is not due to a single catastrophic event such as a frost, but rather to the cumulative effects of adverse conditions.

Most seedlings emerge in early fall and by the end of winter these plants have one to six tillers (Davison 1971a, 1977). Each plant forms 10 to 15 spikes that appear in June, followed by seed drop in July and August. Seedlings that appear in late fall flower later and form half as many spikes as those that emerge earlier. Plants require vernalization to flower. If seeds are planted in the spring, only vegetative growth occurs the first season. In Britain, flowering occurs in abundance the second year, yielding 45 spikes/plant, 29 seeds/spike and 82 seeds/g.

H. murinum is often found in association with *Poa annua* and *Lolium perenne*, but it is not able to compete with established vegetation. Davison (1971a) planted *H. murinum* alone or with *Dactylis glomerata* or *L. perenne* and monitored its growth for four seasons. Forage grasses reduced *H. murinum* seed production and seed size by 50% in the first year. In the second year, *H. murinum* without competition produced 10,000 seeds/m^2 but, with competition, no seeds were formed, and in subsequent years the weed was not present. Shade affects *H. murinum* and with 80% light reduction, growth ceases. Seeds formed under 40% shade have high viability but germinate slower than those produced in full light. With 66% shade, germination drops and at 75% shade no viable seeds are formed.

H. murinum grows best in loam soils and is frequently found in soils with *pH*s of 7 to 7.5. It grows poorly if soil *pH* is below 5. Thus the variation in *H. murinum* density among sites from year to year is due to the combination of growth conditions plants require (high soil fertility and *pH*, freedom from competition and full sunlight).

H. murinum is more than a ruderal plant in New Zealand, where it has invaded thousands of hectares of pasture land. Soils high in N, P, K, Ca, Mg, and organic matter favor *H. murinum* infestations (Meston et al. 1971). High populations of this weed in areas of high soluble salts is an indirect relationship: the desired forages are less salt tolerant than *H. murinum* and the weed increases as growth of the forage is inhibited (Popay and Sanders 1982).

The invasion of *H. murinum* often starts around stock camps and then spreads into other areas of the pasture. Hartley (1976) explained the population dynamics of *H. murinum* in New Zealand fields. The weed is under-grazed by sheep in the spring because abundant forage is available. In the summer, dry weather reduces the forage supply, but now *H. murinum* is much less palatable and the presence of the bristly awns deters animals from consuming the weed. This results in even heavier grazing of the forage grasses, further reducing their competitiveness and allowing a new flush of the weed to germinate in the fall.

Over-grazing in the winter and spring forces sheep to consume all vegetation in the area (Gunning 1966). Sheep also eat vegetative *H. murinum* plants with immature seedheads in the early summer and two seasons of heavy grazing greatly reduce infestations. Thus over-grazing can be both a cause and a cure for *H. murinum* in pastures.

Morphological traits vary greatly between plants. An in-depth electophoretic enzyme analysis, however, found very uniform enzyme systems across diverse morphological types (Giles 1984). Baum and Bailey (1984) and Giles and Lefkovitch (1986) have thoroughly reviewed the taxonomy of this species. Plants are usually tetraploid with a $2n$ count of 28 but diploid plants occur (Morrison 1958). The species is highly inbred and pollination occurs within the unopened flower. In fact, spikes have viable seeds before they emerge from the boot stage. In pastures, each plant forms approximately 10 spikes with 50 seeds each. Densities of 43 plants/m^2 are common, producing 21,500 seeds/m^2 annually (Harris 1959). Seeds are nondormant and over 90% of the seeds between 0.2 and 10 cm deep in the soil germinate. However, seeds deeper than 5 cm below the soil surface seldom emerge. Only 27% of the seeds on the surface germinated (Popay and Sanders 1975). Most seeds germinate in light and darkness between 5 and 20°C, but darkness gives maximum germination (Popay 1981). However, if seeds are harvested when immature and seedheads still have chlorophyll and the seeds are dried in darkness, light is required for germination (Cresswell and Grime 1981).

Seeds are dispersed by awns adhering to passing animals and by the wind. The three spikelets at each joint of the spike break off as a unit. This means the seed is more readily blown by the wind since two sterile spikelets offer wind resistance but are very light (Ridley 1930). This perhaps explains its ability to reach the tops of walls and towers to 25 m high.

AGRICULTURAL IMPORTANCE

H. murinum is a reported weed of 11 crops in over 40 countries (Figure 47-1) and is frequently reported a weed of pastures, cereals, and wastelands. It is a serious or principal weed of lucerne and pastures in New Zealand; pastures in Italy and South Africa; and wheat in Afghanistan.

It is a common weed of cereals in Turkey; lucerne in New Zealand, Spain, and the United States; orchards and vineyards in Spain; pastures in Australia, Hungary, Turkey, and the United States; and wheat in India.

It is also a weed of unknown rank of barley in Egypt; cereals in Bulgaria, Jordan, South Africa, Spain, and Tunisia; citrus in Cyprus and Spain; maize in Italy; orchards in Iraq and Italy; pastures in Argentina, Belgium, Chile, England, Tasmania, and the former Yugoslavia; sugar beets in Spain; vegetables in Chile, Iran, and Iraq; vineyards in Germany and Italy; and wheat in Iran, Jordan, Portugal, and Syria.

H. murinum causes its greatest economic impact in sheep pastures of New Zealand. Losses are caused by reduced forage availability but, more importantly, by physical injury to the sheep. Mature seeds can penetrate the eyes and mouths of grazing animals. Seeds in the eyes are painful and often result in at least temporary blindness. Those in the mouth and stomach can cause ulcerations due to the unidirectional barbs on the awns and the sharp point of the fractured rachis (Hartley 1976).

Seeds can go through the wool and hide and become embedded in the meat. This results in serious quality losses for all three products. Hides with seed holes are classified as "seedy" and cannot be used for high-quality sheepskin products. The level of damaged pelts along the east coast of the South Island rose from 9% in 1961 to 26% in 1967 and remained at 23% in 1971 (Shugg and Vivian 1973). Nearly 10% of all the hides on the island were downgraded because of seed damage.

Hartley and Atkinson (1972) used chemical and cultural control and reduced *H. murinum* from 15 to 1% of a pasture's biomass. Comparing sheep performance in weedy and nearly weed-free pastures, they found that the incidence of eye injury dropped from 70% to less than 5%, wool production increased 25% and live weight gains jumped from 25 kg/animal to 31 kg after 60 days of grazing.

Plants also cause indirect economic losses by hosting the gall mite, brome streak mosaic and several viruses of wheat, oats, and barley.

COMMON NAMES

Hordeum murinum

ARGENTINA	cola de zorro patagonica
CHILE	cebadilla
DAHOMEY	gold-byg
ENGLAND	wall barley, wild barley
FINLAND	hiiren ohra
FRANCE	orge des rats, orge queue de rat
GERMANY	Mause-Gerste
HAWAII	wild barley
IRAN	jow piyazee
IRAQ	shwaired
ITALY	forasacco, orzo selvatico
JAPAN	mugikusa

LEBANON	abu-stirt, sha-ir-ud-dib, wild barley
MADAGASCAR	arge
MOROCCO	orge des rats
NETHERLANDS	kruipertje, mausegerste
NEW ZEALAND	barley grass
NORWAY	musebygg, villbygg
PORTUGAL	cevada dos ratos
SOUTH AFRICA	mouiswildegars, mouse barley
SPAIN	cebada ratonera, cebadilla, pixaca
SWEDEN	vildkorn, bolmort
TUNISIA	orge des rats
TURKEY	duvar arpasi, yabani, arpa
UNITED STATES	barley grass, mouse barley, wall barley

Forty-Eight

Hydrilla verticillata (L.f.) Royle

Hydrocharitaceae, Frog's-Bit Family

HYDRILLA VERTICILLATA is ranked by Soerjani (1986) as one of the three most important aquatic weeds in the world. It is a much-branched, herbaceous, annual or perennial submersed weed that frequently goes unnoticed because it closely resembles *Egeria densa* and *Elodea* species. *Hydrilla* is generally regarded as a monotypic genus, with most forms being referred to the exceedingly variable *H. verticillata*. It can photosynthesize at very low light levels, is rather insensitive to water quality, produces several distinct types of propagules and is thus well equipped both morphologically and phys-

FIGURE 48-1   The distribution of *Hydrilla verticillata* (L. *f.*) Royle across the world where it has been reported as a weed.

393

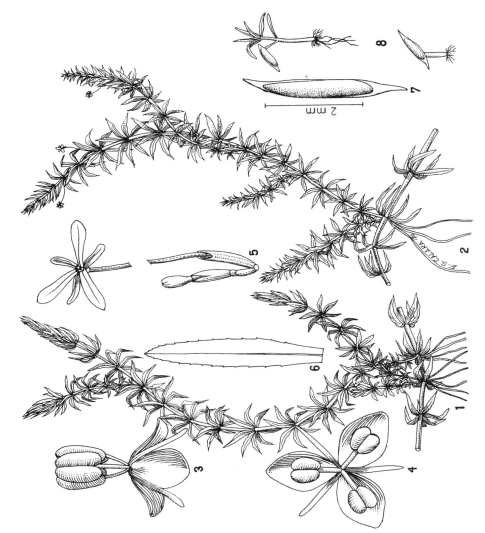

FIGURE 48-2 *Hydrilla verticillata* (L. f.) Royle: 1. staminate plant; 2. pistillate plant; 3. staminate flower, side view; 4. same, top view; 5. pistillate flower; 6. leaf, enlarged; 7. seed; 8. seedling.

iologically to survive and prosper, and can be an aggressive competitor in mixed communities of submersed weeds. These characteristics have assisted in an accelerated dispersal to 60 countries across the world in recent decades. Because of frequent difficulty or carelessness in its identification, we may expect this spread to continue.

DESCRIPTION

H. verticillata (Figure 48-2) is a submerged freshwater herb in still or slow-moving water, forming large masses, *annual* or *perennial*, monoecious or dioecious; *roots*, the underground stems and some of their exposed nodes normally develop *adventitious roots*, 1 to 12 mm long, 0.5 mm in diameter, roots that anchor in substrate may be 200 mm by 1 mm; *stems* slender, smooth, round, freely branched near water surface, may be creeping, subterranean or erect, a few centimeters to several meters in length; *leaves* may be opposite on stolons or bases of stems and branches, or in whorls of 2 to 10 elsewhere, whorls more widely spaced on stems on lower part of plant, linear to lanceolate, prominent central vein with several abaxial multicellular emergences terminating in a prickle hair, causing leaf to have a rough feeling, blades green, with or without red-brown dots and stripes, chloroplasts abundant on both surfaces, young leaves thin, rough to touch, older leaves becoming dull green with pinkish-brown margins, 8 to 40 mm x 1 to 5 mm, margins sharply serrate dentate, each serration terminating in a spine-like prickle hair, plant has no aerial leaves; two *axillary scales* develop at base of each leaf, 0.25 to 0.5 mm long, narrowly triangulate to lanceolate, hyaline, fringed with orange-brown hairs (Yeo et al. 1984); *flowers* solitary or in pairs, imperfect, solitary within spathes; *male spathes* formed from 2 united bracts, solitary in leaf axils, *peduncles* to 1 mm, round or pear-shaped with small knob at top, splits distally to liberate flower; *male flower* shortly pedicelled, obovate, 1.5 to 3 mm long, released as a bud below surface to float upward and open in air; *petals* 3, free, narrow-linear, 0.6 to 1.3 mm, reflexed, color white, red, or brown; *sepals* 3, free, ovate-elliptic, 1.2 to 3 mm long, convex at anthesis, whitish-red or brown; *stamens* 3, with very short filaments, 4-celled *anthers*, about 1 mm, dehiscing explosively to throw pollen grains into the air as the perianth opens; *female spathes* formed from 2 bracts, usually solitary, borne in leaf axil, sessile, cylindrical, bifid at apex, hyaline or reddish-brown, occasionally with lateral wings, ruptured by growing flower; *pistillate flowers* sessile, ca 0.5 mm long; *petals* 3, free, 0.5 to 2.5 mm long; *sepals* 3, oblong-ovate, free, 1 to 4 mm long, withering after anthesis, sepals and petals white to light green with red lines, membranous, fused below to form *hypanthium*; *styles* enclosed in the latter and these lengthen as it elongates; *stigmas* 3, triangulate-lanceolate, 1 to 1.5 mm long; *ovary* cylindrical, tapering gradually, distally, into hypanthium, a single locule of 3 united carpels, parietal placentas, 8 to 11 mm long and 1.5 mm in diameter, cavity may be filled with a viscous fluid; *ovules* acorn-like when young (Yeo et al. 1984), up to 10 per ovary, a few forming seeds, *fruit* softly echinate, cylindrical, length varying according to numbers of seeds formed; *seeds* oblong-elliptic, 2 to 3 mm long, testa smooth, dark brown.

Yeo et al. (1984) suggest that a simple test to distinguish *Hydrilla* from *Elodea* and *Egeria* is to draw the foliage through the hand. The latter two feel smooth while *Hydrilla* feels harsh and scratchy. When using vegetative parts for identification of this species, one must be aware of the wide variations in form and color. Internodes may be long or short, leaves wide or narrow, branching extensive or sparse, color light or dark green with reddish cast and there may be 2 to 10 or more leaves in each whorl. Cook and Luond (1982) described in detail the variations they found in biotypes collected from several places in

Africa. Wolff (1980) presented illustrations of leaves of *Hydrilla* and several species of *Elodea* and discussed features that are useful in comparing these plants. Scannell and Webb (1976) report that there are about 15 specific epithets in the literature for this plant but they believe that few are specifically distinct from *H. verticillata*. The persistent variation of the form and physiological behavior of this plant is a recurrent theme in the literature across the world.

DISTRIBUTION

There is a common but incorrect belief that *Hydrilla* is a tropical species. It persists above lat 50° N in Ireland, in the former Soviet Union, and it has extended its range significantly to the north in the United States (now at lat 45° N) in the last decade. In the Southern Hemisphere, the weed is in the Murray River in Victoria, Australia, as well as in New Zealand. It has the potential to continue to colonize new territories in the tropics and in colder regions.

In Figure 48-1 it may be seen that *Hydrilla* is in the upper Dnieper River in western Russia, above lat 50° N on the Irtysh River in N.E. Kazakhstan and in the Ussuri and Amur rivers in the former Soviet Maritime territories in Far East Asia. These may be its most northerly extensions at this time (Keldibekov 1972). The weed is in the countries bordering the oceans of west, south, and east Asia, with many locations inland as well. It is in several Pacific Islands down to Australia. In the New World it is in Mexico, the United States, Jamaica, and Panama.

Hydrilla is strangely absent from much of South America or has been overlooked because it grows in mixtures with several similar species. It is in northern Europe, and in several places on the east and west coasts of Africa, but it is sparsely distributed about the Mediterranean Sea.

Because of the mistaken identity of this species over time and across the world, Scannell and Webb (1976) prepared an overview of its distribution and taxonomic difficulties. For example, the weed was brought into the southeastern United States before 1960, was noticed and given the name "Florida elodea," *Elodea canadensis*, and was not correctly identified as *Hydrilla* until 10 years later when it had already become widely dispersed and was a major weed of waterways. It is still spreading vigorously in the United States (Blackburn et al. 1969a).

Another example of the invasive character of the weed was seen in Fiji about the same time. A massive aquatic weed infestation, dominated by *Hydrilla*, developed in Fiji's main river system (the Rewa). The tidal waters reached inland 40 km, with *Hydrilla* occupying the upper 25 km during low water. The weed increased in abundance with distance from the sea. The river was slightly acidic and when the water was high, *Hydrilla* grew to a 3 to 5 m depth, but made its best growth at low water when the *pH* was alkaline (Hughes 1971).

Because *Hydrilla* has several systems of propagation, there has been much speculation, but little proof, that animals, particularly migrating birds, are important in dispersal. Joyce et al. (1980) in Florida, in the United States, studied throat to gizzard sections, gizzards, and the gizzard exits to the anus of several species of ducks that overwintered in lakes infested with *Hydrilla*. For some species this weed was a preferred food. The authors found turions in the upper digestive tract but none in the intestines, suggesting that this method of spread may not be important. In a study of more than 100 lakes in New Zealand, Johnstone et al. (1985) found that the dispersal of lengthy, submersed, vegetatively reproduced weeds, including *Hydrilla*, is much more closely related to human activity, particularly boating and fishing, than it is to spread by natural vectors such as birds and winds.

Hydrilla grows and prospers under such a remarkable range of conditions that it seems more fitting to delineate its particular habitats in connection with later discussions of light, temperature and water conditions, as well as other environmental factors that are optimum for it.

ANATOMY, MORPHOLOGY, AND REPRODUCTIVE BIOLOGY

This plant is very adaptable to periods of stress and to a wide range of ecological habitats. In a typical life cycle, the plant may grow as an annual or a perennial, losing those structures above the hydrosoil during different seasons or in regions where it may become desiccated or very cold, while exhibiting year-round growth when inhabiting the tropics. It is comparatively insensitive to water conditions and quite capable of adjusting its physiology to the light and temperature of its surroundings. Toward the termination of the principal growing season, sexual reproduction takes place in some areas. Later the plant fragments, with some pieces bearing overwintering propagules that may be carried long distances to establish new plants in the next season.

Vegetative propagation is the principal form of increase of this weed and its later dispersion. Because a complex floral biology and a large array of different asexual propagules are involved and to avoid repetition, it is necessary to discuss the propagation of the species with the morphology and physiology of the structures and processes.

Ernst-Schwarzenbach (1945a) completed one of the first major studies of the biology of *H. verticillata*, with particular emphasis on the development of the floral structures. A major study of the morphology of the plant was concluded in 1984 by Yeo et al. (1984) using scanning electron microscopy and light microscopy with several types of tissue preparation. They discovered these structures that had not previously been reported: small dormant axillary buds at the base of larger dormant axillary buds; asexual reproductive structures at the base of vertical stems (now termed lateral stem buds); and abscission layers at the bases of turions and the lateral stem buds. Attention to each of these new structures will serve to lessen the confusion in identifying this weed which is similar to other species.

Stems are produced with various types of orientation to bear the leaves and asexual and sexual reproductive structures. Erect stems that later bear both types of reproductive structures originate in nodal buds on horizontal stems, usually several stems at a node. The internodes above the hydrosoil may reach 15 cm in height. Near the surface the stems are more stocky and are much-branched with internodes only 0.5 cm in length. Horizontal stems (in *Hydrilla* variously referred to as rhizomes, stolons, runners) usually grow from buds of newly germinated asexual reproductive structures. Yeo et al. (1984) found that such stems also formed on branch cuttings placed in the hydrosoil.

Two upright axillary scales may be seen compressed against the stem at the base of each leaf, at the bases of young leaves of turions, and at stem *apices*. These have long, tubular, thick-walled secretory cells filled with tannins. Ancibor (1979) believes these are for secretion of a protective, mucilaginous substance.

With the advent of decreasing light and temperature, and/or a change in photoperiod, subterranean stems grew from buds at the bases of erect stems, and traveled out and down into the soil to a depth of 1 to 15 cm. Subterranean turions formed on such stems.

The anatomy of such stems was similar, with little if any epidermal cuticle and a central cylinder that contained sieve tubes and companion cells with large lacuna walled off by a single row of cells. No xylem elements were present.

The plants root well at the bases of erect stems, sometimes on branches of such stems, and on the nodes of floating fragments. Roots may be green or white, up to 2 mm in diameter on larger plants, with a long, tapering root cap to protect the meristem.

Seehaus (1860) in Germany first made us aware of distinct biotypes of *H. verticillata*. As we are able, more and more, to gather live plant materials of a single species such as *Hydrilla* from across the world to be cultured and compared in one place, we have come to appreciate the polymorphism of those plants that must live beneath the water surface. They have adapted to a life in basins and streams offering many depths, light conditions, rates of flow, substrates, salinities, and nutrient supplies. As waters recede or floods occur, the conditions above are altered, and under stress the plant is changed. *Hydrilla* type collections for study have been brought together in the Netherlands, Switzerland, and the United States. Because of the extreme variability, strains and biotypes have been assigned to *H. verticillata* for more than a century, yet recently the common wisdom seems to be that this species is so highly plastic that taxonomic recognition need not have been given to many of the environmentally induced alterations in morphology (Scannell and Webb 1976, Cook and Luond 1982).

Research has recently turned to studies of the genetic differences among the types, but thus far as many questions have been raised as answered by this work, some of which is excellent. A few examples will be adequate to highlight the present status of this research. Cook and Luond (1982) have described a group of plants found in alkaline lakes in Africa and Pakistan that have short, leathery, ovate to widely ovate leaves and long or very short internodes. The plants are sterile. Scannell and Webb (1976) described plants from Ireland and Poland that are morphologically very different from the strains found in the tropics and subtropics. Langeland (1989) examined karyotypes of *Hydrilla* populations from 11 geographical regions of the United States and found that standardized chromosome lengths and arm ratios were not significantly different.

The major infestation of *Hydrilla* in Fiji was caused by dioecious plants that produced only male flowers. Oki et al. (1989) collected *Hydrilla* plants from many areas of Japan and reported all were dioecious, with male and female plants present. The early infestation in the southern United States was consistently reported to be caused by female plants. Recently, monoecious plants have been found in several places in the United States. The plants of Australia are monoecious and dioecious. Those of the Far Eastern Maritime Territories of the former Soviet Union, of northwest Russia, and northeast Kazakhstan are monoecious (Keldibekov 1972, Probatova and Buch 1981).

In still another example of the versatility of the species, plant types were brought together from Kunming, China, and Bogor, Indonesia to be grown together in the latter place. The Bogor types were either monoecious or produced only female flowers and initiated flowers only under short-days. The strains from Kunming produced only male flowers and did so in both long- and short-days (Pieterse 1981).

In a controlled environment, Steward and Van (1987) found the biomass of monoecious biotypes declined under short-days, while subterranean turion production was greatest at this daylength. Growth responses to temperature changes were similar in all monoecious and dioecious plants. Germination of the turions could take place at lower temperatures in monoecious types. The authors believe that the tolerance to lower temperatures and the abundant production of propagules may make it possible for monoecious types to extend farther north than dioecious types.

Cook and Luond (1982) reported that plants collected from the tropics tended to flower in short-days, while those from temperate areas were indifferent to daylength but flowered mostly in long-days. In addition, they believed that plants growing in tropical climates tended to be monoecious and those of temperate zones dioecious, although we are finding exceptions to this of late. They further point out that monoecious plants on which the male and female flowers develop at separate whorls, or perhaps on separate branches, may in cultivation produce flowers of one sex in the ensuing season. Thus, careful observation continues to inform us of the wonderful variability of the species.

Studies on the genetic make-up of the plants across the world are equally interesting. Thus, while diploid ($2n = 16$) and triploid ($2n = 24$) plants are most plentiful and seem randomly distributed, a tetraploid ($2n = 32$) has recently been reported in the United States. Recent research has turned to isoenzyme analysis, an examination of the proteins of *H. verticillata* by electrophoresis. Verkleij and co-workers (1983) used this tool to examine geographically disjunct populations in the world and found large genetic differences. *Hydrilla* exhibits more genetic variation than other aquatic plants they have studied thus far. Fifteen to 18 of the enzymes analyzed were polymorphic. Holmberg et al. (1993) examined the structure and biochemical characteristics of the seeds of monoecious *Hydrilla* plants from Penang Island in the Malacca Straits and those from a cross of this plant with dioecious female plants from Florida in the southeastern United States. Buffered seed extracts were stained for enzymic activities and protein. Starch grains and proteins were distributed differently throughout the embryos and endosperms of the two biotypes. Seeds had detectable alcohol dehydrogenase activity and the patterns of the gels could be used to identify the biotypes. The profiles were invariant in the seeds of the biotypes, but extracts of turions had different patterns for the major proteins. The patterns could also be used to identify the progeny of the cross between the two types.

Populations so examined in the United States, for example, with one exception, have similar banding patterns, thus suggesting that they are still ramets of the same clone. Ryan (1988, 1989) reported on partial characterization of a major family of proteins in the turions of *Hydrilla* and isozymic variability in monoecious plants across the United States.

The isoenzyme banding patterns are not well correlated with variations in morphology and chromosome number. In general, banding patterns of strains in the tropics differ from those in the temperate zone. Wain et al. (1985) summarized the use of this tool for studying plant variation and have summarized results obtained in several plant species (see also: Pieterse et al. 1984a, 1985; Vierssen, van 1986; Verkleij and Pieterse 1986; Steward and Van 1987).

The general anatomy of *Hydrilla* has been studied by Caspary (1858), Ancibor (vegetative organs, 1979) and Pendland (to include ultrastructure, 1979). Chaudhuri and Sharma (1978) reported on cytological studies in relation to the morphological and ecological characteristics of the species. Maheshwari and Johri (1950) and Lakshmanan (1965) reported on the embryology of the species. Anatomical and/or morphological studies of several plants were made by Lakshmanan (1951), Mitra (1955, 1956, 1964), Cook and Luond (1982). Probatova and Buch (1981) reported on the morphology of staminate and pistillate flowers, the structure and development of fruits and seeds, and the methods of dispersal of *Hydrilla* in the former Soviet Far East.

The several types of asexual propagules are described below:

a. Single buds in the axils of leaves on erect stems may give rise to branches that form roots. As these become separated from the stem, they form new plants.

    b. As autumn approaches, the internodes at the apical ends of erect stems and their branches may shorten and the leaves envelop the meristem. The new structures can remain dormant and attached during winter, or if separated from the terminal sections may develop into new plants in the following season.

    c. The plant undergoes a natural fragmentation at season's end. Non-terminal, free-floating stem fragments may develop roots, form branches from axillary buds on the stems and become independent plants. Forty percent of fragments with one or two nodes show successful regrowth; of those with four or five nodes, 70% form new plants (Langeland and Sutton 1980).

    d. Yeo et al. (1984) discovered that short-days and cool temperatures caused special buds to form near the basal nodes of erect stems. These were later called *lateral stem buds*. The buds were 1 to 5 mm long, were covered with tight clusters of dark green leaves with aristate tips, and they abscissed and over-wintered on or in the subsoil.

    e. *Axillary turions* are formed on upright stems and free-floating stem fragments. *Subterranean turions* are formed at the apices of underground stems. Although they are sometimes described as over-wintering structures, they are nevertheless very common in warm regions during dryness or other stress. Their length varies from 3 to 15 mm and the color and external morphology varies with the point of formation—above or below the ground.

Blackburn and Weldon (1969b) found 1100 turions/m^2 in the subsoil in the southeastern United States. Swarbrick et al. (1982) reported that turions are not common in Australia but both types are seen occasionally. In most places the production of subterranean turions exceeds that of axillary turions 10 to 20 times. The fresh weight of axillary and subterranean turions of monoecious and dioecious plants varies considerably, but axillary turions usually weigh less. When grown under similar conditions, the subterranean turions of dioecious plants are heavier than those of monoecious plants (Spencer et al. 1987). Yeo and McHenry (1977) reported that turions may remain dormant in the soil for several years. Ninety percent of the sprouting of both types of turions takes place between 18 and 32°C.

Basiouny et al. (1978b) dried *Hydrilla* plants and turions in an experimental chamber at 30 and 40% relative humidity. Apical and subapical sections of plant material were still physiologically active at 16 hr. The sprouting of axillary turions decreased sharply from 0 to 8 hr, but subterranean turions showed 17% germination after 64 hr.

AXILLARY TURIONS

The axillary turions are formed with a short stalk, are green, cylindrical, ovate or slightly conical in shape, 3 to 12 mm long, 2 to 3.5 mm wide. They usually develop in leaf axils, but some may form at branch terminals. The leafscale encloses a small dormant structure with compressed internodes and several well-formed branch buds. Yeo et al. (1984) found that an abscission layer formed at the base in the autumn prior to the release of the turions that eventually settle to the bottom. The central conductive tissues of the structure were similar to those of the erect stems. Internodes had large intercellular spaces.

How do the turions differ from vegetative buds? At the point of origin of the former, two scales are present; they are colorless, thicker, and less flexible than foliage leaves. The vegetative buds arise where there are three to four leaf primordia in a whorl, the colorless scales resemble foliage leaves; the cells contain chloroplasts. In India, the vegetative buds require no rest period, but the turions have a resting stage and do not grow until conditions are favorable (Mitra 1955, 1964).

Mitra (1956) found green axillary turions in the upper layers of the hydrosoil. Upon germination they had one shoot each, whorled leaves, short internodes, and roots. Turions formed better on floating, unattached fragments than on plants anchored in soil. In India, axillary turions were plentiful in December and January, some shedding was seen in April, but mainly in May and June. Germination, which requires 7 to 14 days, takes place in late May and early June. Haller et al. (1976) in the southeastern United States found that axillary turions formed with the advent of shorter days and cooler waters in late summer. They were plentiful from October through April, and 80% had fallen and germinated by the end of May. Axillary turion formation was reduced as plant growth declined in winter when the plant was forming subterranean turions.

Klaine and Ward (1984), working with plants rooted in a substrate, concluded that turion initiation was heavily dependent upon a short photoperiod (about 10 hr) and was little affected by temperature variation. The phytochrome system was involved, for no buds or turions formed if there was a 1-hr red light interruption of the dark period following a 10-hr light period. A period of far red light following the above red light interruption restored turion formation. Blue and green light reduced plant dry weight and bud production, but yellow light did not.

In the eastern United States, chilling treatments of 40 days at 4°C of freshly harvested turions resulted in 92% germination. There was no germination without the cold treatment (Carter et al. 1987). In Japan, the dormancy of turions was broken in a 16-hr photoperiod at 2°C in 7 to 30 days, with greater root and top growth of the resulting plants following the longer treatment periods. Red and far red light given *after* the cold period promoted germination, while blue and green light inhibited sprouting. Gibberellic acid and indoleacetic acid promoted germination of non-cold treated turions (Basiouny et al. 1978a, Sastroutomo 1980a).

SUBTERRANEAN TURIONS

These turions form at the terminal nodes of the stems that turn downward and penetrate to 10 to 15 cm in the subsoil, where they begin to store food during autumn. The morphology, as in axillary turions, is that of a shoot with compressed internodes and with branch buds forming. The turion is covered with thick leaf scales, normally white, but turning green under light. Some scales may be several cells thick, with heavy cuticle on the outer walls of the epidermis (Yeo et al. 1984). In India, Mitra (1956) detected elongated internodes as the propagules germinated with shoots reaching for the surface. Roots were produced after the shoots reached the surface. Steward (1969) found starch reserves were sufficient to support turion growth for 85 days in darkness.

Subterranean turions formed November to March in India, with vigorous germination in May and June. In the southeastern United States, Van et al. (1978) found that no subterranean tubers formed from May to August when the vegetative growth was at the maximum rate. The turions then formed from October to April, with germination from April through November. Mature tubers formed within 4 wk from planting apical fragments of *Hydrilla*. They formed more readily on free-floating than attached fragments of stems. In growth chambers they found increased growth and subterranean tuber formation as temperatures were raised from 10 to 30°C. At 9°C no turions formed after 5 wk in a 10-hr day. They believe the greater size and quantity of such turions was due to a more abundant supply of photosynthate as the temperature increased.

Miller et al. (1976) found increased sizes and numbers of turions at five increasing water depths (0.3 to 1.5 m) in a lake in the southeast United States. This is in contrast to the finding of Mitra (1964) in India. When grown in continuous light or darkness the best sprouting was from tubers taken from depths of 0.6 to 1.2 m. Bruner and Batterson (1984) grew *Hydrilla* on sediments from sand through marl with increasing levels of fertility. Subterranean turions formed on all sediments but in increasing numbers at higher fertility levels.

Spencer and Anderson (1986) grew monoecious and dioecious biotypes from subterranean turions under several photoperiods and found in a 10-hr day that after 28 and 56 days the monoecious plants produced 38 and 100% new turions, respectively. No turions were formed at 14- or 16-hr photoperiods or by dioecious plants grown at any photoperiods. However, Van (1989), using monoecious plants grown from subterranean turions, did obtain turion formation in a 16-hr photoperiod, although in much reduced quantity. Under similar conditions dioecious plants in an 10-hr day produced turions in 56 days but did not produce turions at the longer daylengths.

Mitra (1964) and Van and Haller (1979) found that removal of most of the leaf canopy from a dense stand of *Hydrilla* stimulated the germination of subterranean turions, and that the propagules were much more responsive when growing in gravel and sand than in clay. This may be related to the finding of Miller et al. (1976) that decreasing tuber germination was observed as CO_2 levels increased in the substrate.

Haller et al. (1976) found that 80% of the subterranean turions formed during a season were germinable by May of the following season. The optimum temperature for this process was 15 to 35°C. When turions were incubated for 14 days, the following rates of germination were observed:

- Immature tubers still attached to submerged stem, 13%.
- Detached turions, 7 to 14 mm in length, 30 to 60%.
- Larger turions, fewer in number, no germination after 6 wk.

Several workers found that subterranean turions sprout and begin to grow in complete darkness but also that light may enhance this process. Sudarmiyati (1975) found good germination at low light intensity, with optimum continued growth at 40 to 60% of full sunlight.

In southern New South Wales, Australia, plants continue to grow much of the winter in experimental pools, and in northern Queensland they grow over a range of 10 to 35°C. Plants in India behave similarly. In the southern United States, *Hydrilla* plants survived after 10 days of being covered with ice.

Thus, light and temperature regimes alone exert an influence on the sprouting of resting turions, but several kinds of chemical treatments have also been effective. Calcium nitrate, ethylene, gibberellic acid, indoleacetic acid, and thiourea promote the germination of subterranean turions (Steward 1969, Sahai and Agrawal 1975). Efforts have also been made to destroy the turions by the prevention of sprouting. Sutton (1986) found that nine allelopathic chemicals of known structure inhibited the germination of the turions, but he cautions that—with the exception of one, salicylic acid—the usefulness of these compounds for *Hydrilla* management may be limited by the high cost of large amounts of such chemicals. Klaine (1986) reported that low concentrations of thiadiazuron inhibited germination of all turions in his tests for 7 wk.

SEXUAL REPRODUCTION

Ernst-Schwarzenbach (1945a) and Yeo et al. (1984) have provided the most detailed and complete studies of the floral biology of *H. verticillata*. What follows is an abbreviated account of their description of the major events from flower formation to seed production.

In spring, Yeo et al. (1984) in California obtained monoecious plants from the eastern United States and placed them in tanks, where flowering began in September at the approach of short-days and ceased in November. The male flowers were usually borne above the female flowers on the stem. The lobes of the enclosing spathe broke open as a bubble formed within, probably as a result of photosynthetic activity. The bud abscised and rose to the surface, where it rested for an hour. As the perianth parts curved backward, three anthers sprung from a horizontal to vertical position, explosively discharging the microspores upward to finally descend on and about the flowers.

The female flowers, usually found on main stems and branches on the upper parts of the plant, resemble an inverted bell filled with a gas bubble. As the hypanthium elongates (as much as 10 cm) the flower bud is carried to the surface. The bubble protects the stigmas from wetting as the structure moves upward and, upon reaching the surface, sepals and petals spread to form a cavity kept dry by action of the surface tension between parts of the perianth. Cook and Luond (1982) noted that the perianth segments are limp and pliable and, as ripples pass, the flower closes around the air bubble, keeping the stigmas dry. As the water level recedes the flower reopens. Ernst-Schwarzenbach (1945a) believed that pollination occurred when the microspores were discharged upward and then fell directly onto the stigmas, and those that fell into the water were therefore wasted.

Yeo et al. (1984) discovered that a second flower bud sometimes opened at the base of a mature flower, thus prolonging the flowering period. Also, late in the flowering period female flowers sometimes formed above the male flowers on the stem. They made histological sections of certain ovules that had a seed-like appearance to search for evidence of fertilization. They found none.

After fertilization, the perianth tube decays and a smooth, bristly, or barbed fruit may develop within the submerged spathe. The fruit may contain up to five dark brown, smooth seeds that are occasionally slimy.

To illustrate the breadth of sexual reproduction by this plant across the world, seeds have been collected in the former Soviet Union, from plants growing in rice field paddies in West Bengal in India, and in southern California, in the United States. Datta and Banerjee (1976) collected weed seeds in rice paddies in West Bengal and found 95 seeds from 37 fruits on one *Hydrilla* branch. The seeds weighed 0.57 g/1000.

H. verticillata was brought into the United States before 1960 and it was believed that all subsequent dispersal was from the same ramet that was dioecious and provided only female plants. In 1982 monoecious plants, shown to be genetically distinct, were found in several places in the eastern United States. Very soon this resulted in a large number of investigations on the growth and behavior of the two types of plants within the country as well as in Europe. Because published reports, both before and after 1982, often refer quite simply to the plant "*Hydrilla*," with subsequent generalization about the species (sans any recognition of the genetic type under discussion) it may be useful to attempt to summarize the principal differences between the monoecious and dioecious biotypes. Because of the present state of our knowledge of these genotypes, and with a sensibility of range of climates and habitats involved, and the diversity of experimental procedures, much of this is tentative, ongoing, and often contradictory. Most of this recent research has been done in controlled environments and/or in small containers. The situation in natural sites has yet to be addressed.

CHARACTERISTICS OF MONOECIOUS AND DIOECIOUS PLANTS

Characteristics	Monoecious	Dioecious
Vegetative growth:	Upon germination produces extensive amounts of horizontal stems, root crowns, and a higher vertical shoot density near the hydrosoil. Appears later at the surface.	Upon germination grows rapidly toward the surface and spreads to make a mat. During growth, total biomass generally increases with longer photoperiods and higher temperatures.
Reproduction:	By sexual or asexual means.	By vegetative means from stem nodes, rhizomes, root crowns and turions.
Dry matter production:	There are various reports of 2 to 15 times more dry matter production from monoecious plants.	During a 16-wk summer season in the southeastern United States, the dry matter yield of *Hydrilla* infested area averaged 4250 kg/ha.
Production and tuber weight:	May produce tubers all year long.	Tuber production only in winter season in warmer climates. Tubers are larger and heavier than those of monoecious plants.
Response to photoperiod:	Tubers produced in 4 wk in 10-hr photoperiod. The total number was sevenfold higher than with dioecious plants. Some tubers were produced in a 16-hr photoperiod but fewer than in short-days. We found no reports on the effect of photoperiod on flowering.	Tubers were not produced until 8 wk in a 10-hr photoperiod. After 10 wk there were tubers in a 16-hr day.

CHARACTERISTICS OF MONOECIOUS
AND DIOECIOUS PLANTS

Characteristics	Monoecious	Dioecious
Response to temperature:	Monoecious plants may germinate at lower temperatures and thrive better in cooler climates. They show a tendency to move deeper into the cooler parts of temperate zones.	
Response to salinity:	Will tolerate some salinity.	Will tolerate some salinity.
Longevity and survival when held below ground:	The number of intact viable tubers declined from 100% in one year to zero at 36 mo. Axillary turions germinated readily or expired in one year.	Tubers remained intact longer and showed higher germinability.

LIGHT AND PHOTOSYNTHESIS

We have discussed the influence of light in the reproductive processes, but its most important role is in photosynthesis. With their work on the physiology of *Hydrilla*, Van et al. (1976, 1978) have provided an excellent, detailed summary of the photosynthetic characteristics of this species. They have pointed out that the environment of a subtropical lake with a dense *Hydrilla* stand shows very large diurnal fluctuations of several photosynthetically related parameters. For example, in a closely packed *Hydrilla* stand on a bright summer day, levels of free CO_2 and HCO_3^- may be close to zero, while the O_2 level may rise to more than 200% of air saturation. Temperature and quantum flux densities in excess of 38°C and 2000 microeinsteins/m^2/sec, respectively, are common at the water surface. In their experiments, the optimum temperature for photosynthesis was about 36°C.

When studied together, they found that *Hydrilla*, *Ceratophyllum*, and *Myriophyllum* have light and CO_2 saturated photosynthesis rates of 50 to 60 micromols O_2/mh chlorophyll/hr at 30°C. At air levels of CO_2 the rates were less than 5% of those achieved by terrestrial plants. All species could use HCO_3^- ions as a source of carbon for photosynthesis, but at saturating CO_2 levels there was no indication of the use of this ion. The rate of photosynthesis was lowered indirectly because of decreased CO_2 supply as *pH* was increased from 3.1 to 9.2. For these plants, the maximum photosynthesis rates were similar at *pH* 4 and 8 when a saturating level (0.5 mM) of free CO_2 was available.

The CO_2 compensation point for *Hydrilla* was 44 microliters/L, while the levels for *Ceratophyllum* and *Myriophyllum* in the same experiment were 41 and 19, respectively. Some "dark" respiration could be detected in the light. Salvucci and Bowes (1981) reported that in *Hydrilla* and other high CO_2 compensation point plants tested, photorespiration as percent of net photosynthesis was about equivalent to terrestrial C_3 plants.

In the experiments of Van and co-workers, light saturation of photosynthesis occurred at 600 to 700 microeinsteins/m²/sec in full sun. *Hydrilla*, as compared with *Ceratophyllum* and *Myriophyllum*, has the lowest light compensation point and requires the least irradiation to achieve the half-maximal photosynthetic rate.

Conditioned by season, age of plant, and the parameters of the surrounding environment, especially light and temperature, *Hydrilla* may exhibit some characteristics of both C_3 and C_4 pathways. In the southern United States, for example, *Hydrilla* shows the C_4 type metabolism in summer and C_3 in winter, with a correlative adjustment of photorespiration and CO_2 compensation point (Bowes et al. 1977a,b; Holaday 1979; Salvucci 1979; Jana and Choudhuri 1979; Holaday and Bowes 1980). C_3 and C_4 plants often differ in leaf anatomy, with chloroplasts generally distributed throughout the leaf in C_3 plants, while in C_4 plants they are usually in bundle sheaths and adjacent mesophyll cells. The leaves of *Hydrilla* appear to be anatomically more similar to C_3 plants.

These are its major photosynthetic characteristics and we need to bring them to bear on the behavior of *Hydrilla* in the ecosystem of the field if we are to understand its rise to become a dangerous weed in so many places in the world. Reviews of the general physiology and ecology of the species have been published by Mitchell (1978), Pieterse (1981), Cook and Luond (1982), and Swarbrick et al. (1982).

To observe the weed in large water bodies with its bounteous profusion of undulating green meadows of vegetative growth and its ability to dominate most other submerged species, is to be convinced that this plant possesses a very powerful photosynthetic machine. Experiments in many places have informed us, however, that *Hydrilla* and many other submersed aquatics may have only 5% of the productivity of many terrestrial plants. This weed does not, however, need to compete with terrestrial plants, but must make its way under water amidst great changes in light quality and quantity and temperature regimes that are greatly buffered against change by the surrounding medium. The success of *Hydrilla* is attributable to several aspects of its behavior: it can photosynthesize at very low light intensities; its photosynthetic systems are quite adaptable to diurnal and seasonal changes at its place of anchorage; with its morphological features (including the production of large numbers of vegetative propagules) and its exploitation of areas of low light intensity where most other macrophytes cannot exist, it is a very aggressive competitor; and finally, for a submersed plant, it is very productive and examples of this will be given.

For this plant, the lowest light intensity recorded at which it can increase in dry weight is 10 to 12 microeinsteins/m²/sec (Bowes et al. 1977b). The ability to extend its canopy quickly in spite of a low photosynthetic rate is due in part to the low dry to fresh weight ratio of *Hydrilla*. Thus it can enlarge the canopy with fewer resources and less energy than is required by other nearby species. The dry weight is about 8 to 9% of fresh weight, whereas some terrestrial crops may have as much as 20% dry weight (Van et al. 1976). In view of these seeming disadvantages, it is surprising to find that it can become the dominant species in many freshwater canals, lakes and streams.

Bowes et al. (1977b) found that *Hydrilla* can adapt its photosynthetic activity to changes in light intensity during its life cycle. When irradiance was low, the light compensation and saturation points were low, and this made it possible to make maximum use of the light received. Haller (1974) and Van et al. (1977) found that *Hydrilla* has a lower chlorophyll a:b ratio than terrestrial plants and believe this may be an important factor in its productivity. This lower ratio was evident when plants were grown in green light. There was a difference in the levels of the two chlorophylls between lower plant parts and those at the surface. They suggest that the higher levels of chlorophyll b tend to absorb more of the longer wavelengths that penetrate to greater depths. The dense surface canopy provides the species with an advantage over most other submerged plants in that the general concentration of chlorophyll in the upper plant portions is greater than that in stems and leaves that are lower (Finlayson 1980).

Sutton and Barlow (1981), Haller and Sutton (1975) and Van et al. (1976) compared the photosynthetic characteristics and productivity of *Hydrilla* with several species of submerged freshwater macrophytes. The low light required for favorable net photosynthesis rates is one of the principal reasons for the success of *Hydrilla*. In *Hydrilla*, carbon fixation can thus begin in early morning when CO_2 is highest and most photosynthesis takes place in dense stands of submerged vegetation. The low light requirement would seem to provide the plant with an exceptional advantage over nearby competing species.

At the beginning of each season or after periods of stress, regrowth from the hydrosoil can be initiated and growth carried forward successfully at greater depth and under canopies providing greater shade because of the same low light requirement. As the plant reaches the surface, the extensive branching occupies greater surface area and inhibits growth of other species below it. In Lake Rawa Pening in Java, *Hydrilla* makes up 50 to 100% of the weed stand to a depth of 3 m. In 1 m^2 of this vegetation, the leaves and stems provide 55 and 100 m^2 of total plant surface area, respectively (Sudarmiyati and Ikushima 1978).

The ability of *Hydrilla* to colonize patches quickly, extend its surface canopies, and produce vegetative beds covering several depths of water gives it further advantage, especially in times and places of great fluctuations of water level. Haller and Sutton (1975) in Florida, in the United States, reported that penetration of photosynthetically active radiation decreased by 29% in the upper 30 cm of weed-free water; with a *Hydrilla* canopy present, radiation decreased from 1500 to 70 microeinsteins/m^2/sec in the same distance, a loss of 95%.

Numerous studies have been published on the general productivity of this weed, but they were done in various latitudes, with different biotypes, in waters of different fertility, during many seasons with plants of different ages, and under a host of different light conditions. A comparison between such experiments is therefore difficult and only a few examples will be mentioned. Sinha and Sahai (1973) reported that dry matter of this species in a north Indian lake peaked at 40 g/m^2/day in July and August, and 1.3 g in January–February. The total aboveground photosynthetic biomass increased from 0.9 mt/ha in winter to 4.5 mt in summer. The canopy of the lake provided by *Hydrilla* was 13% in winter and 32% in summer. In the southern United States, a biomass of 1.8 mt dry weight/ha was reported by Haller and Sutton (1975). Johnson and Manning (1974), also in the United States, recorded an enlargement of a *Hydrilla* bed from 5 to 10 ha in just 6 wk.

In outdoor experiments, Sutton et al. (1980) reported the dry matter production from a planting of one shoot was equal to that from 16 shoots. In 8 wk the dry matter increased 1500 times. In Indonesia, much better growth was obtained from plants grown from subterranean turions than from seeds in the greenhouse experiments. Neither produced fruits in 100 days, but both male and female flowers were produced by each type of propagule.

NUTRITION

The influence of seasons, the fluctuations of water levels with drought and flood, the accumulation of organic material that deposits in ponds and streams because of wind, soil erosion and human activity, and the natural shedding of senescent plant parts all cause wide variation in water and substrate fertility levels. *Hydrilla* seems to grow well over this wide range of available nutrients and obtaining sustenance for its seasonal growth is not often a problem (Steward and Elliston 1973, Van et al. 1976).

Pietsch (1981) gathered *Hydrilla* from 17 sites in northern Germany to study the hydrochemical conditions of each area. In general, the waters were alkaline (an average *pH* of 7.5), biocarbonates were very dominant among the anions, with low chlorides, nitrates and iron, and very low levels of sulfates. Steward (1973) confirmed a low P requirement for *Hydrilla*. In experiments that permitted P^{32} labeled hydrosoil to be isolated from the water above, Bole and Allan (1978) in Canada found that this weed obtained most or all of its P from the hydrosoil when the water contained 0.015 micrograms of P/ml, a level not uncommon in oligotrophic lakes in eastern and western Canada (see also Denny 1972).

In a study of the uptake of N, P, and K from open water and from different sediments, Barko (1982) reported most of the K needed by *Hydrilla* comes from the water, whereas N and P are readily obtained from many different sediments. The uptake of K from some sediments was insufficient to support the best growth of *Hydrilla*. Steward (1984) found that N and K were adequately supplied by either water or rooting medium and the production of plant biomass was not closely tied to P levels.

In the former Soviet Union, Keldibekov (1972) reported that *Hydrilla* grows equally well in river water or that pumped from deep wells. Mitra (1960) in India found that free-floating *Hydrilla* plants could survive with difficulty for 6 mo when growing in unchanged well water, but promptly began to grow better if a layer of clay was added to the culture. These plants would not grow in sand cultures, but would tolerate 25 to 50% sand in mixtures with clay. Vats (1984) also measured the growth of plants in water and substrates gathered from several parts of India. He decided that *Hydrilla* prefers soil with a medium texture and high organic matter. The presence or absence of available P and calcium carbonates did not seem to influence the distribution of the species. McFarland and Barko (1990) reported that tuber formation was unaffected by sediment types used in their experiments.

Sinha and Sahai (1973) examined *Hydrilla* growth in northern India in non-polluted waters and in areas polluted by raw sewage effluent and washing activities on river and pond banks. They found a 30% reduction in growth in polluted waters.

Silver et al. (1974) reported that significant quantities of N_2 are fixed under anaerobic conditions by rizospheres of *Hydrilla* and some other macrophytes. They believe this may help to explain the lush growth obtained in oligotrophic waters that are low in N. Pieterse et al. (1984b) found a stimulation of flower and axillary turion production at low levels of N and P.

In lakes and ponds of Australia, India, Indonesia, and the United States, *Hydrilla* grows well at *pH* 6.5 to 10. Trent et al. (1978) grew the species at *pH* 3, but Sudarmiyati (1975) could not grow it at *pH* 4 to 5; however, his plants did well at *pH* 7 to 8, about the level of many water bodies in Java.

Hydrilla prefers fresh water but tolerates some salinity in the lower reaches of some rivers across the world. Hughes (1971) in Fiji reported that plants in fresh water were a lighter, brighter green than those in saline conditions in which leaves become darker and stems began to blacken.

Steward and Van (1987) found that salt tolerances were similar in monoecious and dioecious biotypes, with an injury threshold of 13 ppt. In the experiments of Haller (1974), plants failed to grow after 4 wk at 6.6 ppt and died at 10 ppt (Haller et al. 1974). Carter et al. (1987) found germination of both types of turions was limited by salty conditions; there was 95% germination in freshwater, 5 to 20% germination at a salinity of 5 to 9 ppt, and no germination above 9 ppt. Vegetative growth decreased at 7 to 9 ppt. The biotypes of the former Soviet Union also grow in weakly salted conditions.

FLOW RATE AND WATER DEPTH

Hydrilla is normally found in still or slow-moving water. Hughes (1971) in Fiji found that it would not survive at flow rates greater than 0.3 m/sec. van Dijk et al. (1986) reported a two-fold increase in growth of *Hydrilla* in moving water with a turnover time of 2 to 5 hr.

Most of this species, when anchored to the substrate, are found in shallow water of 1 to 3 m depth, but, depending on basin morphometry and growing conditions, large biomasses may develop outside of this range. It is found in rice paddies in several parts of the world.

Hughes (1971) recorded plants at 5 m in Fiji and Haller found them at 12 to 15 m in the clear Crystal River on the west coast of Florida. In Indonesia, Sudarmiyati (1975) found that best growth was below the 10-cm depth and speculates that temperatures may be too high for *Hydrilla* above this level. It is found in rice in Indonesia but has not been a problem, again because temperatures may be too high for the weed in the shallow water of such cultures.

Canfield et al. (1985) gathered data on more than 100 lakes of Finland and the north-central and southeast United States, and demonstrated that there is significant positive relationship between water transparency, as measured with the Secchi disk, and the maximum depth of colonization by aquatic macrophytes. *Hydrilla* colonized the deepest parts of several lakes when the percent transmittance of full sunlight was only 0.46 to 1%, much lower than most species studied. The authors developed a model for predicting the way in which basin morphometry, nutrition and human activity will affect light penetration and thus the establishment of weed stands.

ECONOMIC IMPORTANCE

Soerjani (1986) lists *Hydrilla* second only to water hyacinth, *Eichhornia crassipes*, as a menace to world waterways and crops. He regards the weed as one of the three most important in the waters of Southeast Asia. Of the submersed weeds, it is possible that it causes more trouble worldwide than any other species. In rice it is a serious weed in the United States, a principal weed in China, India, and Malaysia, and a common weed in Indonesia and Thailand. It is a serious weed of irrigation systems in India and a principal weed in Australia, Indonesia, Japan, Malaysia, and the United States. As a more general problem in many of a country's water resources, it is said to be serious in Australia, India, and the United States and a principal weed in Indonesia and Panama.

In peninsular Malaysia, a heavy growth of weeds must be managed in irrigation canals and small streams because of run-off and leaching of fertilizer in rice-growing areas. *Hydrilla* is one of the three dominant weeds in these waters. In northeast India, it is the worst submersed weed and in West Bengal it ranks as one of the most devastating and dominant aquatic weeds in the region. In the former Soviet Union, it is reported to develop very quickly, soon chokes out other aquatic weeds, and then sends out its extensive canopies to cover large areas. As one of the examples of the rate of colonization, Haller (1977) recorded a 1-ha infestation of *Hydrilla* in a reservoir in northern Florida, in the United States, in 1971; by 1975 it had grown to 120 ha. *Hydrilla* became the number one aquatic weed in Florida in less than 10 yr after its introduction. By 1987, in that state there were 16,000 ha of public waters infested with the weed and control activities on one-half of that area cost $3.5 million (Schardt 1987).

The weed blocks piers and is a menace to ferries and boats that get stuck in it and may damage or burn out their power plants trying to free themselves. It harbors large numbers of epiphytic algae that are a favorite food of mosquitoes that serve as vectors of human and animal diseases (Biswas and Calder 1936). The *Hydrilla* canopies can form a complete cover over ponds and thus deny light for fish culture in Asia and Africa. The weed plugs irrigation pumps, chokes channels and fouls hydroelectric systems.

This weed is not easily controlled with commonly used and affordable herbicides. Its presence in the often fertile waters of centers of habitation has further hampered extensive use of herbicides. The review of Pieterse (1981) and his extensive bibliography covers much of the research done with specific herbicides and the mechanical devices used for vegetation removal.

Insects and pathogens have been studied for the control of the weed but biological control with the grass carp, *Ctenopharyngodon idella*, and smaller fishes has received the most attention and is most widely used. This fish feeds on many aquatic plants, preferably on submersed vegetation, and forages readily on *Hydrilla*. It is believed that the carp only breeds naturally and successfully in its native China and Siberia. There are worries that if the fish is freely released it may compete for the habitats of native preferred sport fish. It can now be artificially inseminated in fishery laboratories. Also, a sterile hybrid, with male bighead carp, *Hypophthalmichthys nobilis*, has made it more likely that the population can be regulated in natural sites. The F1 hybrid has a somatic chromosome number of $2n = 72$, whereas both parents are $2n = 48$. The triploid hybrid thus has reduced potential for reproduction. The triploid carp is now widely used for the control of *Hydrilla* and other aquatic weeds in Florida's lakes and ponds (Vandiver and Sutton 1988).

For stocking rates, efficiency of conversion to fish flesh, and selectivity of feeding in the presence of a mixed flora, see Sutton (1974), Sutton et al. (1978), Pheang and Muchsin (1975), Venkatesh and Shetty (1978), Pieterse (1981), and Decell (1983). For a general review of the use of herbivorous animals for aquatic plant control, see National Academy of Science United States (1976b).

In a 2-yr survey, Balciunas and Minno (1985) collected more than 17,000 insects associated with *Hydrilla* in the southern United States. They point out that in general most aquatic insects are predacious or feed on detritus or algae, and their survey revealed that only a few of the thousands of insects from *Hydrilla* mats were actually feeding on the living tissue of the plants. Nevertheless, research on biological control with insects and pathogens moves forward at a steady pace, for the management of this weed of our waters will surely, over the course of time, require a combination of methods suitable for various times and locales. Haller (1989) in Florida reported that there was much research activity on the use of insects and pathogens for biological control of *Hydrilla* but no operational controls with these organisms were in use at the time. See Pieterse (1977, 1981); Charudattan and McKinney (1977); Charudattan and Walker (1982); Julien (1982); and Bernhardt and Duniway (1986).

As with other aquatic weeds that produce great masses of organic matter, there is the inevitable quest for information about usefulness as a source of protein and mineral nutrient for men and animals, as a forage in animal husbandry or for water purification by nutrient removal. Studies of the chemical composition of the weed have shown the crude protein and several major and minor elements to be present at about the same level as in terrestrial plants. Ca, Na, Cu, and Fe concentrations are relatively high. The Ca:P ratio is high (about 30) and the plant is therefore questionable as feed for cattle. See Boyd (1969a, 1974), Boyd and Blackburn (1970), Steward (1970), Tan (1970), Hentges et al. (1971), Stephans et al. (1973), Easley and Shirley (1974), Boyd and Scarsbrook (1975), and Little (1979).

COMMON NAMES

Hydrilla verticillata

AUSTRALIA	hydrilla, water thyme
BANGLADESH	jhanji, kureli
CHINA	hae-chao
FIJI	water weed
INDIA	jala, kurelei
INDONESIA	ganggeng, gayanggang runti, saray
JAPAN	kuromo
LAOS	nae pawng han
NETHERLANDS	indishe waterpest
NEW ZEALAND	hydrilla
PHILIPPINES	inata, ginga, lumot-lumotan, lusai
THAILAND	sarai hankarok
UNITED STATES	hydrilla
VIETNAM	rong la ha, thuy thao

Forty-Nine

Ipomoea aquatica Forsk.

Convolvulaceae, Morning Glory Family

IPOMOEA AQUATICA is a marginal, creeping, perennial aquatic weed that may spread over the surface of a pond or of an irrigation or drainage ditch. It interferes with fisheries, impedes water flow, and is a troublesome weed of rice and other crops. It is a weed of more than 20 crops in 60 countries and major regions, yet is cultivated in the Old World tropics as a fresh, green vegetable for human consumption, is used for local medicines, and is also food for farm animals, especially pigs. In Southeast Asia and elsewhere, this plant is known as water spinach and water cabbage.

FIGURE 49-1 The distribution of *Ipomoea aquatica* Forsk. across the world where it has been reported as a weed.

412

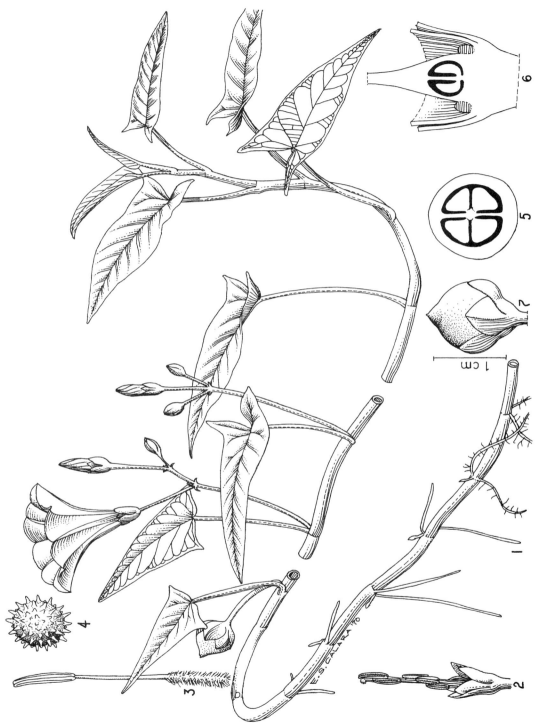

FIGURE 49-2 *Ipomoea aquatica* Forsk.: 1. flowering branch; 2. flower, corolla removed; 3. stamen; 4. pollen grain; 5. ovary, cross section 6. same, vertical section; 7. fruit.

DESCRIPTION

I. aquatica is an aquatic herbaceous, glabrous *perennial* or sometimes an *annual* when growing in an unfavorable site (Figure 49-2); *stems* creeping on mud or floating on ponds or ditches, may be 3 m in length, hollow or spongy, often rooting at nodes; *leaves* alternate, variable, oblong-ovate, or lanceolate, with base hastate, cordate, or truncate, basal lobes may be rounded or acute, apex acute or obtuse, margins may be slightly sinuate, 3 to 15 cm long and 1 to 10 cm wide, long-petioled 3 to 20 cm; *flowers* axillary, erect, perfect, large and showy; *pedicels* usually 1- or 2-flowered, 2 to 10 cm long with minute bracts at base; *sepals* 5, united at base, glabrous, persistent, 8 mm long, oblong, obtuse or acute, usually equal in length, may be brownish-pink; *corolla* funnel-shaped; *petals* united, 3 to 5 cm long, 2.5 cm or more in diameter, pink or pale lilac or purple (rarely white), often with dark purple center, 5 lobed; *stamens* 5, alternate to corolla lobes, inserted on corolla near base, shorter than petals; *filaments* slender and hairy at base; *anthers* dehisce longitudinally, pollen globular; *ovary* superior, glabrous, 2-celled (sometimes 4) with 4 ovules; *style* simple; *stigma* capitate and simple with 2 or 3 rounded lobes; *fruit* a spherical or ovoid *capsule* 6 to 10 mm long, thin walled, surrounded by persistent sepals, dehiscing by 4 (rarely 6) valves, or irregularly; *seeds* 4 or less, grayish, densely pubescent or at times glabrous.

DISTRIBUTION AND HABITAT

There are about 500 species of *Ipomoea* found from salt marshes to mountain tops, many with a creeping or climbing habit. *I. aquatica* can behave as an aquatic, semi-aquatic, or a terrestrial plant with reduced leaves and stems in dry months. When soil moisture is lacking, it may appear to be in hibernation. It can be found in flooded lowland fields and marshes, in dense masses in rice field ditches, or wherever there is soggy soil. Above all else, it is a principal marginal creeper on the banks of muddy streams and ponds, awaiting the opportunity to reach out over the water surfaces to form mats with other vegetation.

The weed extends from the tropics well into the warm temperate zone (Figure 49-1). It cannot tolerate frost or snow and grows poorly when cold. In times of plentiful water, its nodal roots may hang downward to anchor in the hydrosoil. In a monsoon climate, as the water level rises, the creeping branches float upward to give the plant survival as the floods begin. Carlquist (1967) suggests that it has been dispersed over the world in part by ocean drift of seeds and plant pieces. It is found from savannahs to lakes and rivers in Africa. It is very plentiful in both the wild and cultivated forms over southeast Asia.

The plant forms mats on the water with *Eichhornia*, *Pistia*, and *Salvinia*. In some Malaysian lakes, *I. aquatica* and *Salvinia* are the most plentiful aquatic weeds. They are found in similar habitats but in distinct ecological niches. The latter occupies spaces between the taller *I. aquatica* plants and is sheltered. Water levels affect the production of both, with *I. aquatica* showing greater tolerance of adverse conditions (Chin and Fong 1978).

PROPAGATION

New plants of *I. aquatica* arise from seeds, cuttings, or fragments. Fresh seed would not germinate but, if dried immediately, gave 80% germination in 3 days. If the fresh seed was stored for 2 wk, a secondary dormancy set in and the hard seed coat had to be broken with chemical or mechanical means to obtain germination. In the field, it is possible that the hard coat is eventually penetrated by the action of microorganisms, by animal ingestion or by abrasion by soil particles. The authors noted much germination of seed of unknown age in mud at the edges of streams and ponds as the monsoon rains arrived.

Gunn and Ritchie (1988) presented line drawings of the seed embryo and transections of the seed.

I. aquatica has a range of tolerances toward many varied habitats, with a corresponding range of morphological adaptations in responding to them. In India, Datta and Biswas (1973) have completed anatomical studies to examine in greater detail the changes taking place as the plant adjusts to different habitats.

This plant has many adventitious roots at each node if it is near moist soil or water. At times it grows very rapidly and within a few weeks, by means of long rope-like stems, can form a vegetative network to completely cover a water or soil surface. When growing in water, the plant has short green roots and large thin leaves developed from spongy elongated stems. If parts of that same plant are in a more xeric environment, there may be extensive brown roots and small thick leaves on short stems (Datta and Biswas 1973).

Jos (1963) studied details of the development and structure of *I. aquatica* and others in the genus and compared them with other members of the **Convolvulaceae**. He concluded that the structure of the seed coat was quite the same throughout this large family. This is a remarkable characteristic of the family when we consider the contrast of the tall woody trees with tender trailing herbs and the fact that habitats vary from salt marshes to high mountains.

Chan and Hillson (1968, 1971) have made detailed studies of the embryogeny of *I. aquatica* and of the development of the mega and microsporangia. Ashby (1948) studied the morphogenesis of leaf shape, area, and cell size in the genus.

V. Singh et al. (1974) examined the leaf surfaces of 17 species of *Ipomoea* and found the upper and lower surfaces covered with a smooth, thin, uniform cuticle layer. On veins and in other areas of leaves of *I. aquatica*, he found some stomata that were twice the normal size. This species had the most stomata per unit area on the lower leaf surface and had the second highest number on the upper surface. When growing on a pond or lake it does not increase water loss significantly over that of a free surface (Brezny et al. 1973).

Muller (1936) reported that the stem and root show air cavities like those of marsh plants, with the pith replaced by a central air passage divided into sections by nodal diaphragms. Upon injury to an internode, the cells surrounding a medullary lacuna (an air space extending radially) give rise to a phellogen layer (cork cambium) that produces a suberized layer of cells that serve as a protective sheath to prevent water from entering the wound. Toward the vascular ring the phellogen produces a non-suberized, spongy tissue of living cells with prominent air spaces.

At lat 20° N in India, for example, the plant thrives at 130 cm of annual rain falling largely between June and October, with temperature ranging from 40 to 20°C, May to January. The plant makes most of its new growth during these periods. The amount of plant material produced during an annual growing cycle was measured near Cuttack, India, by Patnaik (1976). The weight varied from 0.5 to 2.5 kg/m², with maximum growth during winter and early summer and least growth during the monsoon period. Some plants grew to 23 m in length, were much branched, and had one to ten roots at each node. The roots varied from 15 to 45 mm in length. There is normally a single leaf at each node. Internodes vary from 20 to 200 mm in length. Vegetative propagation is common as pieces of branches are separated from the main plant and become self-sufficient.

On ponds and land areas that are not disturbed, fruit development is vigorous and every node of a single shoot produces three to five fruits with up to four seeds each. The flowers are stalked, large, showy and thus well adapted for insect pollination. The hairs on the seed provide buoyancy for water dispersal, but the seeds are also spread when plants are harvested for human and animal consumption.

Flowers appear in September in Hong Kong and in October and November in central and south-central India. Forty to fifty days are required from emergence or planting to maturation of the fruit. In India, Datta and Biswas (1970, 1973) found abundant seed production in fields, with about 175 to 250 produced per plant.

In India, the species frequents loamy to heavy clay soils with *pH*s of 5 to 7. Nitrogen and phosphorous are important for the development of *I. aquatica* and a preference is shown for ammonium-N (Chin and Fong 1978).

In Malaysia, Low and Lee (1979) found *I. aquatica* to be an active accumulator of Pb. In a commercial field bordering a busy highway the plants contained two to four times more Pb than vegetables planted at a distance from the highway. Washing removed 10 to 50% of the Pb from the plant parts. Damaging Hg levels were present in the floating stems and leaves of *I. aquatica* harvested for pig feed near a caustic soda factory in Thailand. High Hg levels were also present in the fish in nearby waters. The local inhabitants are thus endangered because both pigs and fish are used as sources of food (Suckcharoen 1978).

AGRICULTURAL IMPORTANCE

I. aquatica is a serious weed of rice in Mozambique and of aquatic systems in India. It is a principal weed of abaca in Uganda; of aquatic systems in Malaysia and the Philippines; of bananas in the Philippines; of irrigated areas and jute in India; of maize in the Philippines and Thailand; of papaya in the Philippines; of rice in Dahomey; of lowland rice in Bangladesh, India, and the Philippines; and in Uganda it causes trouble in many crops almost everywhere in the country. It is a common weed in lowland rice in Indonesia, Peru, and Thailand; and of sugarcane in India.

It is a weed of unknown rank in aquatic systems in Australia, Hawaii, Zimbabwe, Sudan, Thailand, and Volta; a weed of cocoa and jute in Indonesia; the large irrigation schemes in Sudan; legumes in India; oil palm in Indonesia; pastures in Australia; peanuts in New Guinea and Nigeria; rice in Cambodia, Indonesia, Nigeria, the Philippines, Thailand, and West Africa; lowland rice in Gambia, Malaysia, and Vietnam; upland rice in India and the Philippines; rubber in Indonesia; sugarcane in Australia and Mozambique; savannahs in Nigeria and Uganda; soybeans in the Philippines; and tea in Indonesia.

The vigorous production of vegetative matter causes *I. aquatica* to create problems similar to those of water hyacinth, *Eichhornia*. On Volta Lake, a man-made lake in west-central Africa, *I. aquatica* is prominent in the environs of the water body and its tributaries. It also becomes an emergent member of the weed communities that form on *Vossia* sudds. It is a prohibited weed in the United States. In Thailand, it harbors snails that are vectors of human diseases. In the Philippines, rats feed upon the *I. aquatica* infestations in rice fields.

I. aquatica provides a green vegetable for millions of people in the south China area and elsewhere in southeast Asia. Each area favors its own varieties, harvests are made every 7 to 10 days, with ten harvests per season. Plantings are relatively hardy and free from pest problems. The crop responds well to fertilizers and water management. In general, water levels in excess of 15 cm are avoided for crop areas. Hong Kong is said to use 3 to 5 million kg/yr of *I. aquatica*, and some fields have yields of 90,000 kg fresh weight/ha/yr.

Oyer (1976) reported yields of 20 to 40 metric tons fresh weight/ha in 42 days. A good field may produce 1 metric ton fresh weight/ha/day containing 10 kg of protein. Samson (1972) in Surinam reported 60 metric tons/ha.

COMMON NAMES

Ipomoea aquatica

AUSTRALIA	pink convolvulus, potato-vine
BANGLADESH	kalmi-sak
CAMBODIA	trakoun kantek
CHINA	ong tsoi
FIJI	ota karisi
HAWAII	creeping swamp, morningglory
INDIA	kalami sag, kalmisak, keerai (Tamil), vellai, ganthian
INDONESIA	trakuon
JAPAN	yosai
LAOS	phak bung
MADAGASCAR	lalandy
MALAYSIA	kangkong ayer
NIGERIA	demo
PHILIPPINES	galatgat, kangkong
TAIWAN	yosai
THAILAND	phak buong
UNITED STATES	swamp morningglory

Fifty

Ipomoea triloba L.

Convolvulaceae, Morning Glory Family

THIS TWINING, FAST-GROWING herbaceous plant is troublesome in a very large number of man's crops. It may have been native to tropical America but is now widespread in the tropical areas of the world. It is found in upland cultivated crops, grasslands, waysides and waste places, and because of its creeping, twining habit, may overwhelm other vegetation in farmers' fields and in natural areas. It is found from sea level to 750 m altitude. The most recent systematic revision of **Convolvulaceae** places *Ipomoea triloba* in section *Batatas* with *I. batatas*, the common sweet potato grown world wide.

FIGURE 50-1   The distribution of *Ipomoea triloba* L. across the world where it has been reported as a weed.

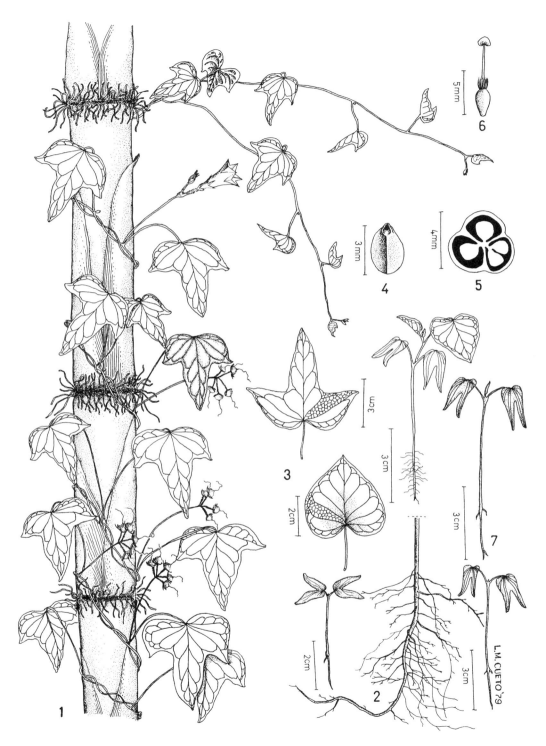

FIGURE 50-2 *Ipomoea triloba* L.: 1. flowering and fruiting branch; 2. root system; 3. leaf, two forms; 4. seed; 5. ovary, cross section; 6. pistil; 7. seedling.

DESCRIPTION

I. triloba (Figure 50-2) is an annual herb with twining stems, 1 to 3 m long, glabrous except the inflorescence; *stems* somewhat angled, about 3 mm thick, milky; *leaves* broadly ovate to orbicular in outline, entire, coarsely dentate to more or less deeply 3-lobed, center lobe may be pointed, base broadly cordate, 4 to 11 cm long, often nearly as wide; *petiole* slender, 3 to 10 cm, glabrous or sometimes minutely tuberculate; *inflorescence* axillary; *peduncle* shorter to longer than the petiole, angular, minutely verrucose toward the apex, one-flowered or cymosely few to several-flowered; branches of the cyme very short; *flowers* aggregate; *pedicels* minutely verrucose or glabrous, 2.5 to 8 mm, closing before noon; *sepals* slightly unequal, 7 to 8 mm long, the outer ones a little shorter, oblong to narrowly elliptic-oblong, glabrous or sparsely hairy on the back with distinctly fimbriate margins; *corolla* is 5-lobed funnel-shaped, 1.5 cm long, glabrous, color variable around the world, pink or pale red to purple in the Philippines, and in Costa Rica may be pale red to violet, or white with a deep red-violet throat with contrasting white stamens and stigmas; *stamens* inserted in tube of corolla; *filaments* hairy at the base; *ovary* 2- to 4-celled, conical, densely pubescent; *ovules* 2 to 4; *fruit* a *capsule*, depressed globose with sharp point, bristly hairy; *seeds* 4 or less, 3.5 mm long, diameter 6 mm, hard, shiny, brown.

Distinguishing features of the plant are 3-lobed leaves, stems with milky sap, and the hirsute or hairy ovary. In Brazil, stems have white to transparent hairs.

BIOLOGY AND AGRICULTURAL IMPORTANCE

I. triloba behaves as a weed on all of the continents and it troubles man in more than 40 of his crops. It is a weed in more than 40 countries and it is interesting that almost all of these countries are within 15°C isotherms north and south of the equator. Europe, almost all of the land mass of the former Soviet Union, and much of North America are outside this zone and we have only scattered reports of weediness of this species for these areas. It is most prominent in Central America and the Caribbean area, as well as south and east Asia and Australia (Figure 50-1).

Despite the widespread distribution of *I. triloba* across the world and its presence in so many of man's major crops, little is known of its biology. It reproduces by seed, is self-fertile, and can produce about 180 seeds/plant. Gacutan (1979) in the Philippines reports that the best methods for obtaining seed germination are nicking the seed coat with a knife, rubbing with sand to scarify (although some seed is damaged by this process), and holding the seed in soil at 40 to 80% soil moisture. Juliano (1940) in the Philippines obtained 50% germination when seed was held in moist sand for 2 wk after harvest. In Brazil, the weed tends to prefer crops on sandy soils. In Costa Rica, the plants begin to flower in mid-October and continue through December. Gunn and Ritchie (1988) have presented line drawings of the seed embryo and transections of the seed.

In Indonesia, *I. triloba* reduces sugar cane stalk numbers and sugar yields and is considered one of the four main weeds in this crop. In the Philippines, where it is one of the main weeds in upland rice, seedlings appear 4 days after the rice is planted, and if left uncontrolled will eventually smother the crop. One of the best legumes for pasture use in that country is Townsville stylo, *Stylosanthes humilis*. As the crop grows from seed it develops slowly at the onset. If the rapidly germinating, vigorous *I. triloba* is present it can dominate the legume in the early growth stages (Briones 1976).

In the sugarcane fields of the Herbert River district of northeast Australia, *I. triloba* germinates in flushes after spring and early summer rains as well as during any wet season (Myatt 1971). In young cane the control is normally by cultivation, but as the stalks lengthen and machinery can no longer enter the fields, an understory of weed spreads and can envelope the standing crop if left undisturbed. Late season weed problems have increased with the advent of machine harvesting and vine weeds are among those to prosper with this change. Overhead boom and aircraft applications of herbicides are used, but if sprays are delayed to give maximum cover of the weed foliage, it is quite likely that some weed seed will already have been produced and the problem is thus perpetuated.

I. triloba is most troublesome in maize, peanuts, upland rice, and sugarcane. It is a serious weed of maize in Brazil and sugarcane in the Philippines and Indonesia. The plant is a principal weed in bananas in Honduras; dry beans and peanuts in Jamaica and the Philippines; maize, upland rice, sorghum, soybeans, and tobacco in the Philippines; and sugarcane in Australia.

I. triloba is regarded as a troublesome, very common weed in bananas, coffee, pastures, pineapple, potatoes, rice, sugarcane, and sorghum in Nicaragua, and in neighboring Costa Rica it is also common in dry beans, cassava, maize, and sugarcane. It is a common weed of dry beans and tobacco in Argentina; of cotton in Mexico; of jute in Bangladesh; of maize in Bolivia and India; of orchards in Bolivia; of lowland and upland rice in Indonesia; of sugarcane in Argentina, Bangladesh, Hawaii, and India; and of vegetables in the United States. It is also a weed of unknown rank in Cambodia, Colombia, Cuba, Ivory Coast, Laos, Nepal, New Guinea, San Salvador, Samoa, Senegal, Thailand, and Venezuela.

In Cuba and throughout the Caribbean, this weed is known as one of the "aguinaldos," meaning gift of honey. Several of the *Ipomoeas* are important honey-bearing plants in this region and *I. triloba* is one of the most prolific producers (Ordtex 1949).

COMMON NAMES

Ipomoea triloba

ARGENTINA	bejuco, enredadera
AUSTRALIA	pink convolvulus, potato-vine
BRAZIL	campainha, corda-de-viola, corriola
COLOMBIA	batatilla, campanilla
COSTA RICA	churristate
CUBA	aquinaldo marrullero
EL SALVADOR	campanilla
HAWAII	aeia morningglory, little bell
HONDURAS	campanilla
INDONESIA	injeh-injehan, ki papesan, malingan, tingkil
JAPAN	hoshi-asagao
MALAYSIA	kong kong bulu, selepat tungau
MEXICO	puyui
PANAMA	campanilla
PHILIPPINES	aurora, kamokamotihan, kamkamote, muti-muti, sagikat
UNITED STATES	three-lobe morningglory

Fifty-One

Lamium amplexicaule L.

Lamiaceae (Labiatae), Mint Family

THIS SPECIES BELONGS TO the **Labiatae**, the more familiar family name, or to the **Lamiaceae**, a more recent designation for the mint family. The two names are equally admissible under the International Code of Botanical Nomenclature. The mint family is large, with about 3500 species, and it is notable for the characteristic odors of particular species. The essential oils of the group are used in medicine, perfumery, and confection, necessitating commercial production and processing systems on several continents. There are many widespread weeds in this family, some of them with a preference for

FIGURE 51-1   The distribution of *Lamium amplexicaule* L. across the world where it has been reported as a weed.

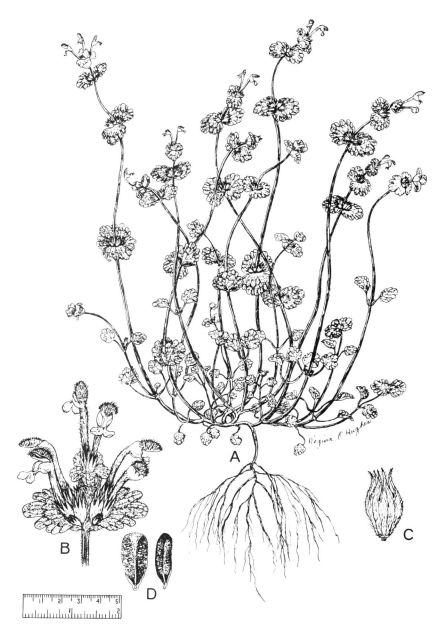

FIGURE 51-2 *Lamium amplexicaule* L.: A. habit; B. flower cluster, showing very short upper internodes; C. calyx surrounding nutlets; D. nutlets.

the temperate zones. *Lamium amplexicaule* is at home in more than 50 crops and countries and the contiguous ditch banks, roads, and headlands that are necessary to agriculture. It may be toxic to farm animals under certain conditions. The species demands our respect, for it has survived all of the major changes in agriculture for more than a century, and persists today across the world. The papers of Buckman (1855) indicate that it was a common weed in fields across England in that early time. Often referred to as a nettle, or as henbit, the plant derives its name from the Greek *laimos* for throat, a reference to corolla shape, and from the Latin *amplexo* meaning to encircle or clasp (the stem).

DESCRIPTION

L. amplexicaule (Figure 51-2) is an *annual* or *biennial* herb, height variable may be erect to 30 cm, decumbent at base with numerous upright branches that root readily at nodes when in contact with the ground; *stems* 4-angled, may be finely pubescent, forming *adventitious roots* on lower nodes; *leaves* in opposite pairs at intervals along the stem, often with more frequent leaves near apex, may be hairy, palmately veined, rounded or ovate, coarsely toothed or lobed, 1 to 2 cm long, lower leaves may have short or long petioles, upper sessile and clasping the stem, broader than long, may be larger than lower leaves; produces open (chasmogamous) and closed (cleistogamous) *flowers* in 1, 2, or 3 compact whorls in leaf axils, usually toward top of stem; *corolla* pink to purplish, tubular, much surpasses calyx, 2-lipped, upper lip may be lobed or entire, forming hood, bearded, the lower 3-lobed, spotted, 1 to 1.5 cm long; *calyx* narrow, 5 to 6 mm long, tubular, may be densely covered with white hairs, with 5 nearly equal awl-shaped teeth; *fruit* a group of 4 small, pear-shaped, angled, nutlets at base of persistent calyx tube, separating at maturity; *seeds* nutlet-like, 2 mm long, sharply 3-angled, obovate oblong, truncate (appearing to be cut off at apex), grayish-brown, surface slightly shiny with grayish-white spots, weight 0.6 mg to 3.5 mg.

The rounded, coarsely toothed, palmately veined leaves; the 2-lipped tubular, pink to purplish corolla; the bearded upper lip; and the lower 3-lobed spotted lip are the distinguishing characteristics of this species.

DISTRIBUTION AND HABITAT

L. amplexicaule is generally distributed throughout the major agricultural regions of the temperate zones, and is notably absent, with few exceptions, along the equator (Figure 51-1). It is interesting that it is on the African continent but troubles crops only in the far north of the area. The plant may be found on rich, arable soils in New Zealand and Australia, the fertile flood plain of the Nile River, or the light sandy or chalk soils of Great Britain. During excavation of an area in a monastery in Denmark, Odum (1965) found germinable seed in soil that was presumed to be undisturbed from the time of construction in the Middle Ages.

Kutschera (1960) in Germany excavated the root system of a summer plant that was 30 cm tall. The root system extended to a 20 cm depth; the first 10 cm had many branches extending 10 cm horizontally from the plant in all directions. The lower 10 cm of the system tended to be a tap root with very short branches.

PROPAGATION

In a spacious environment or a suitable cropping system, henbit can produce enormous amounts of seed. Stevens (1960) in the north-central United States reported on a rapidly spreading biotype of the species with pale yellow flowers having a purple center. The seed of one large plant was collected daily and it produced 60,000 seeds in the season. Other records of field weeds have registered 2000 or more per season for this species.

Jones and Bailey (1956), in the central United States, found that newly harvested seeds were dormant and they believed the inhibition was caused by a water-soluble substance obtained from an extract of crushed seeds. The extract inhibited the growth of tomato and non-dormant *Lamium* seeds. The germination of non-dormant, moist seeds was considerably reduced by light of 1 foot-candle intensity. Higher light intensities, if continued for 72 hr, inhibited the germination of all seeds. The inhibitory effect was temporary, depending to some extent on the intensity of the light used. At low light intensities, for example, recovery was marked within 24 hr and was complete in 48 hr. The seeds are light-sensitive for only a limited period in the early stage of the germination process. Far-red radiation prevented seed germination and this was reversed by red light. The effect of an alternating sequence of red and far-red light treatments was determined by the final treatment in the series. Maximum sensitivity to light occurred when seeds had imbibed water for 12 hr.

Baskin and Baskin (1981) confirmed the complete postharvest dormancy of seeds of this species when harvested in spring and autumn in Kentucky in the central United States, and studied the seasonal variation in germination of seeds during a burial period of more than two yr. In 1978, spring-produced seeds were promptly placed in pots of soil in an unheated greenhouse. Some seeds were removed at monthly intervals and germination tests were conducted in the light of a 14-hr photoperiod and in dark at temperatures similar to those in the environment in which the *Lamium* plants grow from early spring to late autumn.

From the reproductive strategy of *L. amplexicaule* that comes to light in these experiments, Baskin and Baskin have very ably drawn some lessons about the species that help to explain its continuing success as a weed of arable crops. A summary of the germination behavior of the species informs us as follows:

1. Seeds produced in spring and autumn are dormant at harvest.
2. In late spring, seeds produced in spring or autumn will germinate only in light at alternating temperatures such as 15/6 and 20/10°C if they have been in the soil one or more winters.
3. In the high temperatures of summer these seeds after-ripen and come out of dormancy to germinate in the autumn at high percentages in light and over a wide range of temperatures.
4. In late autumn the seed reserves in the soil consist of (a) non-dormant seeds that after-ripened during the summer, and (b) dormant seeds that were produced during the current autumn.
5. In the winter which follows, the non-dormant seeds lose their ability to germinate at high but not low temperatures in light. In darkness at low temperatures the germination increases. Dormant seeds also now gain the ability to germinate at low temperatures in the light. After-ripening can thus occur at low temperatures in these autumn-produced seeds.

The authors suggest that use of experimental temperatures which resemble those in the field allows for some extrapolation of laboratory results to field behavior in the timing of germination. Newly dispersed spring seeds do not germinate upon their release but can pass quickly to a partial dormancy in June, July, and early August; under laboratory conditions, some of them can germinate at temperatures from 15/6 to 30/15°C. The average mid-summer environmental temperatures (35/20°C) are, however, above those for optimum germination. By late August some seeds that are in moist soil and in partial shade can germinate, but by September and October the environmental temperatures are favorable and seeds germinate rapidly in the light. Seed germination is restricted as temperatures fall too low in late autumn and winter in the field, but seeds that fail to germinate in autumn may do so in spring in the light and to a limited degree in the dark, for March–April temperatures are now favorable. As temperatures move higher in summer, germination is inhibited, and the cycle begins again.

Seed germination has a late winter or spring peak, but some emergence continues in summer and autumn. In Kentucky, the seeds of this species that germinate in spring do not usually cause serious problems in summer row crops because, with the advent of hot, dry weather, the plants senesce and die. Although short-lived, plants produce large numbers of seeds. It is important to remember that effective control of *L. amplexicaule* requires the destruction of seedlings in both spring and autumn to prevent the seeds of both seasons being added to the soil seed reserve.

The seed viability in these experiments remained very high. There was no loss of viability in the seeds buried in 1979. About 15% of those buried in 1978 were dead at the end of the 27-mo experiment, but some of these were lost through germination while buried. These results were confirmed in the southern United States by Standifer (1980), who also arranged various cropping systems that permitted fields to be idle at different seasons of the year. As would be expected, he found seed production dropped dramatically when crops occupied the land in spring and autumn, the most important seasons for germination and growth of *L. amplexicaule*.

Brenchley and Warington (1930) in England studied weed seed reserves in the soil of many arable fields and recorded that *Lamium* was present in a few of them. They noticed that there was no periodicity of seed germination through the year and that the seeds were all cleared from the soil within 12 mo. Later, Roberts and Stokes (1966) in England examined the seed population of 58 fields that had been in continuous commercial vegetable production, many for 60 yr or more. *L. amplexicaule*, found in ten locations, was not one of the most widespread, but the soils at six of the sites contained about 2.5 million seeds/ha and one exceeded 8 million seeds of this species. In a continuation of such studies on a sandy loam, Roberts and Ricketts (1979) compared the numbers of weed seedlings emerging after seed bed preparation and the numbers of viable seeds in the top 10 cm of soils in the same area. On average, 3 to 6% of the seed reserve germinated when moisture was adequate, with reduced numbers when dry weather followed the initial tillage. *L. amplexicaule* was not among the species with the highest numbers of seeds in the soil but it was encountered frequently. This species and *Veronica persica* showed no periodicity of germination but emerged promptly after each cultivation. At times, seedlings of *Lamium* made up 10% of the emerging population.

In Denmark, Jensen (1969) examined the weed seed reserves, by species, in the top 20 cm of the soil of about 60 fields of cereals and root crops. *L. amplexicaule* was among a group of annual weeds whose viable seeds numbered 0.5 to 2 million/ha. In the same fields, for comparison, 15 to 30 million seeds/ha were found for some species, and the seeds of *Juncus bufonius* numbered 270 million/ha.

In a study of seed production by weeds of arable fields in England, Leguizamon and Roberts (1982) recorded almost 100 million viable seeds/ha in the top 10 cm of a sandy loam soil. After a cultivation in early April, about 3% of the seed reserve emerged and about one-half matured by mid-summer. Seeds of these plants were permitted to disperse until November, when it was found that about 1.3 billion seeds/ha had been added to the soil.

The main contributors to the original seed bank were *Lamium* species (mainly *L. amplexicaule*), *Poa annua*, *Veronica persica*, and *Stellaria media*. These plants contributed 87% of the total seed load to the soil. *L. amplexicaule* made up about 10% of the total seed bank. This species began to shed seed in mid-June and was dead by mid-August.

The experiment included herbicide treatments for some of the plots. Nitrofen and propachlor decreased seed numbers by about 90% and the latter was particularly effective against *Lamium* species. Methazole on the other hand was not as effective for weed control and the *Lamium* species and *Veronica persica* were the main surviving species. These plants died during the summer, having accounted for 75% of the final weed seed bank in these particular plots.

Enomoto (1985) in Japan monitored the floral and edaphic progression of events on a newly reclaimed polder on the Inland Sea as agriculture began and new weeds appeared. He concluded that *L. amplexicaule* came into the fields with transplants of crop species.

Stryckers et al. (1979) found that urea herbicides at 100 ppm were very effective in breaking dormancy of seeds of *L. amplexicaule*. Taylorson and Hendricks (1976) found that low levels of gibberellic acid administered to henbit seeds at the onset of imbibition stimulated germination. Sensitivity to this growth regulator was quickly lost under far-red light, following a pretreatment in dark at 15°C, if held in darkness above 25°C, or if held at 5°C.

L. amplexicaule produces inconspicuous, self-pollinated, cleistogamous (closed) flowers and chasmogamous (open) flowers, or both, as the season progresses and environmental factors change. Salisbury (1964) in England reported that commonly more than half of the flowers were cleistogamous. This varies with biotype and geography, for sometimes only 15% of the flowers are closed. The closed flowers produce nuts freely.

In the central United States, where the species behaves as an annual, the main period of seed germination is in September and early October, depending on the soil moisture conditions, but some seeds may germinate earlier in August or in the next year in March and April. The plants germinating in late summer and autumn behave as winter annuals; those from seed which germinate in spring are short-lived summer annuals.

Chasmogamous flowers are produced in late summer and early autumn from seeds germinating in August, and ripe seeds from such plants are shed in mid-October. Cleistogamous flowers are present on these plants from late autumn to early spring, but the plants die in March and April without producing more open flowers.

Plants germinating in September and October have closed flowers, and seeds may be produced from late December until March, when open flowers are again produced. If seeds germinate still later, the plants will not flower but will produce cleistogamous flowers in late March, and then produce chasmogamous flowers again in mid to late April.

The summer annual plants from March and April seed germination produce both open and closed flowers and then die with the onset of hot, dry weather in late May and June (Baskin and Baskin 1981).

In the warmer climate of California on the west coast of the United States, the major portion of the flowers produced by this annual weed are cleistogamous, but in the long, hot days of summer some chasmogamous flowers are produced as well. Lord (1980a, 1982a) and others have shown that the type of flowers produced depends, in part, on the photoperiod, the temperature, and possibly other physiological controls. In the cool, short days of winter in California, closed flowers are produced, but the addition of gibberellic acid to the main shoot axis of plants growing in short-days resulted in the production of open flowers. When CCC, an inhibitor of gibberellin synthesis, was added to the soil of seedlings growing in long-day conditions, the treated plants were dwarfed and bore only closed flowers. The subsequent addition of gibberellic acid to these plants reversed the inhibition and open flowers were again produced.

Cleistogamy and other types of dimorphism in flower production are common among angiosperms. Lord (1979, 1980b, 1981, 1982b) has explored the use of cleistogamy, with emphasis on *L. amplexicaule*, as a tool for the study of floral morphogenesis, function, and evolution.

Bernstrom (1952, 1953, 1955) has studied the cytogenetic relationships between annual species of *Lamium*.

PHYSIOLOGY AND ECOLOGY

Beyond the seed physiology and ecology of this species, we know little of its general morphology, anatomy, physiology, and ecology, or of the weedy biotypes that may exist, but it seems likely that its tremendous capacity for seed production, the ability to form adventitious roots at the lower nodes, and its ability to develop slowly through winter months in many areas, have weighed heavily in its persistence as a common or sometimes serious nuisance through more than 150 years of changing agriculture. The dormancy which dissipates quickly, the penchant for germinating in both early spring and late autumn, and the lack of periodicity in its seed germination so that it can emerge almost any time the soil is tilled—all of these are also important to its survival. With all of these biological advantages, it becomes a difficult weed to manage in most agricultural systems.

Continuing research in Israel on the use of solar heating, or solarization, to control annual weeds such as *L. amplexicaule*, and other soil-borne organisms, has shown very promising results. The method has thus far shown no interference with the growth of subsequent crop plantings, and may be considered a replacement for herbicides. It could eventually become a successful treatment for cucurbitaceous and solonaceous vegetables and other crops for which efficient and safe weed control methods are not yet available (Horowitz et al. 1983b; see also Katan 1981 and Rubin and Benjamin 1983).

The method requires moist soil, intense solar radiation, and transparent plastic sheets to cover the crop area. The cover prevents evaporation and thus diminishes heat losses from the soil. Very high temperatures may be attained at 5 and 10 cm soil depths. The physiological disorganization of seed cells and tissues as a result of the high temperatures is little studied, but one may speculate that irreversible metabolic and structural changes may take place.

In one experiment begun in early summer, the maximum temperature at the 5 cm soil depth increased 17 to 19°C under clear plastic and the temperature reached and exceeded 45°C on most days during 4 wk of solarization. Differences were similar but smaller at the 15 cm depth.

Following the removal of the plastic, the reduction in weed seedling emergence in solarized plots was quite remarkable. In autumn, 4 mo after removal of the sheets, the number of *L. amplexicaule* plants in the control was 210/m², but in the solarized plots there were none. In another experiment in which the plastic was in place for only 2 wk in early summer, there were four plants of this species in the treated area and 133/m² in the control 8 mo later. Under Israeli summer conditions, solarization for 2 to 4 wk can result in appreciable reduction of annual weeds in fields one year later. In one of the hottest parts of the country, Sde Eliyahu, a solarization period of only 1 wk in August greatly reduced several sensitive annual weeds.

In these experiments, imbibed dormant seeds of *L. amplexicaule* were subjected to solarization and failed to germinate several months later. The seeds of many species tend to go into a secondary dormancy at high temperatures but these seeds seem to be permanently inhibited or destroyed. Broomrape *Orobanche* species, an obligate parasite, has been controlled in more than one experiment without other established plants being present.

Horowitz points out that it is generally understood that seeds are very heat-resistant when dry, for some of them can germinate in hot regions of the earth when dry top soil reaches 50 to 60°C. Moisture beneath the plastic increases soil heat conductivity and sensitizes the seeds to high temperatures.

Plant species vary widely in their response to heat in the soil. Many common annual weeds are sensitive but most perennials are not affected because of regenerative underground organs which lie below the zone of intense heat. Other species may escape because of impermeable seed coats or because they can emerge from depths that are not heated by the sun. The authors have also presented the results of their experiments with different types of plastics, information on temperatures at varying depths in soil, data on soil gases, and for experiments conducted during different seasons.

In summary, this system of weed control shows great promise for areas with sunny, hot growing seasons, and the method may yet become more effective when we have a more complete understanding of many physiological events that have a role in the process.

The influence of soil fertility on annual weed populations was studied by Banks et al. (1976) in Oklahoma in the central United States on an experimental area established in 1892 to study continuous wheat production without fertilization, on a red prairie soil. In 1929 long-term fertility plots using N, P, K, lime, and manure were included and the same treatments were continued for almost 50 yr. *L. amplexicaule* was a dominant weed in the plots. Generally the lowest plant densities were found on soils receiving no fertilizer treatment. The number of grass weeds increased significantly with the addition of any nutrient to the plots and they were significantly higher when lime was added to the N, P, or K treatments. There was a significant decrease in the numbers of broadleaf weeds per m² in the most complete fertility treatment (N + P + K + lime), while in all other plots they were similar to the control. *L. amplexicaule* populations were lowest on the plot receiving no fertilizer and in the two plots receiving the most complete fertility treatments.

AGRICULTURAL IMPORTANCE

Upon becoming acquainted with the world-wide behavior of *L. amplexicaule*, it is interesting to consider whether there is a character, perhaps termed "weediness," which may be ascribed to plants in varying degrees. This weed is in 50 countries and appears in almost as many crops. With the exception of a few long-term plantation crops such as rubber, oil palm, and coconut, it is generally the case that it appears in almost every kind of agriculture. It prospers on clay or sandy loam, it seems as pleased to be in root crops as in wheat, it is at home on rangeland and pastures, and in managed forage crops as well, and it can be found somewhere in the world in most vegetable crops. It is in many specialized crops such as orchards, vineyards, ornamental and forest nurseries, and in other plantation crops, such as tea. It is in four of man's most important food crops (maize, potato, rice, and wheat) and it frequents rugged, competitive sugarcane fields.

A recitation of each combination of crop and country for *L. amplexicaule* would be tedious; therefore, only those that are most helpful from our data will be cited. It is a serious weed of potatoes and sugar beets in Poland and of vegetables in Australia; a principal weed of linseed, lucerne, and wheat in Argentina; of wheat and other cereals in Australia; of sugar beets and of peppers and other vegetables in Belgium; of peas in Bulgaria; of wheat in Iran; of winter wheat in some areas of Germany; of cereals, rape, and sugar beets in Sweden; and of cotton and forage crops in the United States.

It is a common weed of cereals in the Netherlands, Poland, Scotland, Tasmania, Tunisia, and the United States; of orchards in Uruguay and the former Yugoslavia; of sugar beets in France and Germany; of vegetable crops in Germany, Hungary, Scotland, Tasmania, Tunisia, Turkey, and the United States; and of crops as different as lucerne, sugarcane, peas, vineyards, and turnips in ten countries of four continents.

Finally, we have reports that *L. amplexicaule* is a weed of unspecified rank in 30 countries on the five continents and Oceania, and they tell of a very cosmopolitan plant species. Vegetable crops are troubled by this weed in places as widely separated and as varied as England, Iceland, Iran, Nepal, Spain, Switzerland, and Tunisia; and it is found in wheat from Finland to China to the United States. It is found in other cereals in Canada, Chile, Germany, Jordan, and New Zealand.

L. amplexicaule is a weed of upland rice in Japan and of range land in Korea. In Cyprus, it is a principal weed of citrus and is one of three dominant weed species in winter. In Hungary, this weed is generally distributed in annual and perennial crops, in cereals, and in stubble fields. In Egypt, it is largely a winter weed but is a problem on all cultivated land. In the south of the United States, it is one of the most common of the winter weeds in sugarcane.

The reduced yields of wheat caused by competition with annual weeds was studied by Wells (1979) of the Wheat Research Institute in Victoria, Australia. It is estimated that the loss of wheat because of weeds is 1.3 million tons annually, or about 9% of the crop. Unpublished data in Victoria indicated that losses may exceed 60% in some situations when annual weeds are not controlled. As elsewhere, it is believed that early season weed competition may be most damaging.

In 1970 (July), 4 wk after sowing wheat, five uniformly infested sites were selected, each with a pure stand of a different weed species, including *L. amplexicaule*, and each was thinned with a special "thinning boom" (using a herbicide) to 0, 25, 50, 75, and 100% of the original weed population. Each of the plots was divided into three nitrogen treatments of 0, 20, and 50 kg N/ha. In late spring (October) weed density and dry matter were recorded, and, at maturity of the crop, grain yield and total crop dry matter were measured. Other weeds in the experiment, for comparison, were *Amsinckia hispida*, *Brassica tournifortii* (one of the wild turnips), *Fumaria parviflora*, and *Lithospermum arvense*.

The results of the experiments were as follows:

1. Weed dry matter increased with weed density and applied N had only a small effect.
2. Wheat dry matter was decreased by all weed species.
3. There were large differences in competition offered by different species.
4. For *Lamium* and two other weeds, the losses in wheat dry matter were much larger than the weed dry weights, but for the *Lithospermum* and *Brassica* species, the loss was equal to the weed dry weight.
5. When measured on a plant number basis, *Lithospermum* was the most competitive in causing grain yield losses. However, the very high population density of *L. amplexicaule* (almost 1000 plants/m^2) caused the greater overall decrease in grain yield (0.75 ton/ha).
6. Applied N increased grain yields at all sites but weed competition was not affected.

Wells reminds us that, in practice, weed control decisions are rarely based on objective assessments of weed densities and their ability to offer competition. It is likely that this is due in great part to the lack of information on the factors that might affect the competitive ability of different weed populations. For example, variation in the amount of available moisture and nutrients might be able to swing the balance of competition in favor of either the weed or the crop, or perhaps have no effect, as was found for the nitrogen treatments in each weed species in the present experiments. Wells emphasizes that a weed like *Lithospermum*, which appears in severe infestations only occasionally in this area, must be controlled, for it is very competitive in wheat and can become a major problem. *L. amplexicaule*, which is widespread on clay soils in the area, dies out early in the season and many farmers do not take steps to curb it early in the wheat-growing season. These results emphasize the damage to the wheat crop in early season and the large crop losses that can result from ignoring seemingly insignificant weeds.

This species is a common winter weed in pastures and waste places in the southern United States and it has recently been reported as a host of *Sclerotinia sclerotiorum*, which causes crown and stem rot in winter forages (Welty 1977).

In Australia, cattle, horses, and sheep are reported to be affected by this weed only when driven or moved during a change of location, and sheep are most often troubled. Animals rarely show symptoms of injury when resting in pasture. Grazing of cereal stubble with *Lamium* present in a mature stage is perhaps the greatest danger.

If animals have been ingesting the weed for a time, they tend to lag behind during a drive and appear to be stiff in the rear legs, heads are pushed forward, and backs are hunched. Eventually they stop, breath rapidly, and if driven will soon stop again and begin to shiver and tremble in fore- and hindquarters, or sometimes over the whole body. At rest they may recover, but if the drive continues they often collapse and die.

Four ewes and lambs that consumed 128 kg of mature *Lamium* over a period of 2 wk began to show symptoms on the 6th day and these persisted until 3 wk after the feeding ceased. Symptoms may last longer in some animals (Everist 1974).

In Great Britain, the species is one of the weeds that offers wholesome grazing in sheep pastures for a time but causes staggers under some circumstances. It is most toxic during early stages of growth and at the time of seed production (Chesney 1956).

Aqueous extracts of five weed species, including *L. amplexicaule*, were found to inhibit root hair development of seedlings of *Picea abies*. Air dried material was more inhibitory than fresh material, the toxicity varied with plant part, with plant age, and with several other factors (Schutt et al. 1975).

COMMON NAMES

Lamium amplexicaule

ARGENTINA	flor azul, flor rubi, lamium, ortiga mansa, pata de gallina
AUSTRALIA	dead nettle
BELGIUM	hoenderbeet, lamier amplexicaule
BRAZIL	menta selvagem
CANADA	henbit, lamier amplexicaule
CHILE	lamium
DENMARK	lidentvetand
EGYPT	fomm el-samakah, taqiyit el-ghoraab
ENGLAND	henbit, henbit dead-nettle
FINLAND	sepivapeippi
FRANCE	lamier amplexicaule, ortie rouge aux feuilles rondes
GERMANY	Rundblatterige Taubnessel, Stengelumfassende Taubnessel
IRAN	dead nettle
ITALY	erba ruota
JAPAN	hotokenza
LEBANON	bee nettle, dead nettle, henbit, kurrays-uj-jaji
MOROCCO	lamiera feuilles embrassantes
NETHERLANDS	hoenderbeet
NEW ZEALAND	henbit
NORWAY	mjuktvitann
PORTUGAL	chuchapitos
SPAIN	conejitos, gallitos, lamio, morrones dobles, ortiga de hojas, abrazantes, ortiga muerta
SWEDEN	mjukplister
TUNISIA	lamier
TURKEY	renkli ballibaba
UNITED STATES	bee nettle, blind nettle, henbit
YUGOSLAVIA	krvavac

Fifty-Two

Lemna minor L.

Lemnaceae, Duckweed Family

THE LEMNACEAE FAMILY has four genera with about 40 species and contains the morphologically simplest green vascular species and the smallest floating plants. Although not a fern, the thalli of duckweeds are often referred to as fronds. The genera *Lemna* and *Spirodela* are in the same subfamily and are distinguished by *Lemna* having a single root on each frond while *Spirodela* has two. *Lemna* species have been used extensively in laboratory studies due to their simple nature, genetic uniformity of clones, and the ease of growing them aseptically, free of bacteria or other microorganisms.

FIGURE 52-1   The distribution of *Lemna minor* L. across the world where it has been reported as a weed.

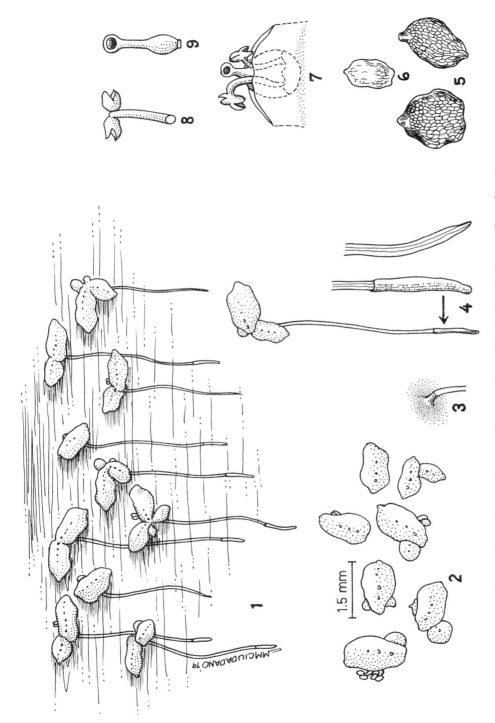

FIGURE 52-2 *Lemna minor* L.: 1. flowering plant with rhizoid; 2. thalli group from above; 3. root emergence on thallus underside; 4. lateral view of single thallus; 5. dorsal surface, two views; 6. seed; 7. sheath with inflorescence; 8. staminate flower; 9. pistillate flower.

1.5 mm

MMCIUDADANO '79

Lemna minor is found throughout the temperate regions of the Northern and Southern Hemisphere, in parts of Southeast Asia and in Hawaii, especially on calm or slowly moving bodies of water. It grows rapidly in the spring and summer and quickly covers open areas of water. This species presents many of the problems associated with floating aquatic weeds. Nevertheless, *L. minor* shows promise in purifying sewage effluent and other polluted waters, and as a source of animal feed. The family name, "duckweed," refers to the fact that these plants are readily consumed by ducks and other water fowl. They can also be used to shade and kill algae and submerged aquatic plants. The name *Lemna* is derived from the Greek meaning a type of water plant.

DESCRIPTION

L. minor (Figure 52-2) is an *annual* herb that occurs either as single floating plants or as colonies of up to 5 or more connected fronds; one *adventitious* root per frond, free of root hairs, unbranched, less than 0.5 mm in diameter, 10 cm long (occasionally 14 cm); tips covered with a conspicuous, non-winged, obtuse root cap; *thallus* or *frond*, a small flat vegetative plant body, leaf-like, obovate to elliptical, symmetrical, 3 to 5 mm long, 1.5 to 4 mm wide, pouch on each side of frond, uniformly green above and pale below, sometimes surface suffused with red or purple; upper surface convex or slightly flattened with low median ridge often covered with small *papillae*, 1- to 5-nerved; when 4- or 5-nerved, outer ones connect to inner nerves at some distance from frond base; lower surface flattened or slightly convex with a deep root furrow; *inflorescence* minute; *flowers* imperfect, rarely seen, inconspicuous, emerging from "pouch" on the frond margin, 2 male and 1 female in each sack-like spathe; *pistil* with relatively long style, *ovule* 1; *fruit* symmetrical, wingless, with 1 indehiscent seed; *seed* ovoid, ribbed.

DISTRIBUTION AND HABITAT

L. minor is a cosmopolitan plant of world-wide distribution (Figure 52-1). It adapts to a wide range of environmental conditions. It is found in still or slightly moving water and thrives in stagnant ponds, sloughs, lakes, canals, and roadside ditches rich in organic matter. It is a free-floating plant but can survive 20 mo or more on wet mud with no change in external appearance (Guppy 1894). *Lemna* grows between *pH* of 5 to 8.2, with an optimum at or below *pH* 7. Lower and upper survival limits are at *pH* 4 and 10, respectively (McLay 1976). Plants tolerate up to 2.5% NaCl. However, if salinity is greater than 10o/oo, growth is reduced and plants become chlorotic (Haller et al. 1974). *L. minor* can be found in water with much variation in conductivity and Ca, Mg, N, P, K, and Na concentrations (Landolt 1975). Haslam (1978) studied the correlation between *L. minor* occurrence and water characteristics and found correlations with biological oxygen demand; Cl, NO_3-N, NH_4-N, and PO_4-P levels; *pH*; total dissolved solids; and total hardness of the water. Populations generally increase as water nutrient content and shelter increase.

Haslam (1978) has described the behavior of *L. minor* in rivers and streams. It is most frequently observed in waters with peat, mud, or silt bottoms and grows in turbid or colored water regardless of water depth. It is less common in rivers over 18 m wide. Populations fluctuate as the water flow rate changes. For example, during rainy periods *L. minor* populations may be washed downstream or out to sea; in dry periods plants are often abundant in the slow-moving waters of rivers and tributaries. *L. minor* may be one of the first species to invade after a canal has been dredged and can predominate for 1 or 2 yr. Plants can also colonize quickly to take advantage of temporary standing water. Plants tolerate chemical and industrial pollutants and can be found in polluted, species-poor, eutrophic channels.

L. minor is often found in association with other **Lemnaceae** species, *Azolla*, *Eichhornia*, and *Nymphaea* (Hillman 1961), but taller plants may shade it out. It can be found up to 3200 m (Biswas and Calder 1936) and enriches the aquatic environment with bacteria, metazoans, protozoans, and free amino acids (Coler and Gunner 1969). As *Lemna* density increases, *Salvinia* populations may decrease (Varshney and Rzoska 1976). *L. minor* dies rapidly if removed from water. One hour after removal from water, 50% of the population was dead (Keddy 1976). After 1.5 hr, 90% had died and all fronds were dead at 2 hr.

BIOLOGY

Lemna has been used in numerous physiology studies, providing a wealth of information on its growth and development. Most research on the species has been done in North America, India, England, and Australia, primarily because of its suitability for laboratory studies on a whole-plant system. Hillman's review (1961) summarizes much of what is known on this species. *L. minor* reproduces principally by vegetative budding. New fronds arise from "pockets" or "pouches" on the margins of mother fronds. Daughter fronds are produced alternately on either side of the mother frond, near the frond base. Each mother frond produces many daughters; fronds may remain attached through several generations and this gives rise to colonies of *L. minor* plants. Active budding starts when the mean water temperature is 4°C for 1 wk (Guppy 1894) and growth continues until the onset of winter or drought stress.

The growth of a *L. minor* population appears to be uniform. However, each plant has a definite cycle of senescence and rejuvenation (Ashby and Wangermann 1951 and Wangermann and Ashby 1951). Small, short-lived fronds produce a daughter that is much larger than the mother frond; this pattern continues for several generations until maximum frond area is obtained. Then, the reverse sequence begins: daughter fronds of large mother fronds become progressively smaller. The cycle shifts after approximately five generations, when the fifth daughter frond is about one-fifth the size of a large mother frond. Small fronds formed late in the life of a mother frond produce daughters larger than themselves and the percentage increase in frond size from one generation to the next is greater, for the smaller, not larger, mother fronds. Individual fronds live about 4 wk and decompose in approximately 2 wk. Thus the life span of one generation is around 6 wk.

The number of generations to complete the rejuvenation cycle is the same (four or five), regardless of light and temperature conditions. The age of the mother frond when daughter fronds are produced affects the daughter's frond area, longevity, and number of fronds produced. Reductions or increases in frond size are due to changes in cell number rather than cell size. Fronds are larger when left attached to their mother. Removal of the mother frond root or even most of the frond does not affect daughter frond growth, indicating that the number of cells formed by a daughter frond is determined by a substance produced by the mother frond and then translocated to the daughter frond.

Lemna exhibits three growth phases when introduced in open water. First an exponential growth phase occurs, followed by slower growth once the surface is covered with fronds. Stable growth typifies phase three: older fronds at the bottom of the mat die and new ones form at a similar rate (Harper and White 1974). At low plant densities, frond doubling times are 2.5 to 6 days but, at high densities, 14 to 70 days are needed (Reddy and Debusk 1985). Total annual dry matter production in open water in the southeast United States was nearly 16 ton/ha.

The rate of reproduction is influenced by environmental factors. Twice as many fronds are produced under high temperature (30°C) than under low temperature (20°C), and frond production doubles by increasing the light intensity from 170 to 500 ft candles (Wangermann and Ashby 1951). Light has a direct effect on the multiplication rate beyond that of the assimilation rate (Ashby and Oxley 1935), and frond numbers increase exponentially as light and temperature increase (Wilkinson 1963). Frond production increases as red light intensity increases from 8 to 45 ft candles (Wilkinson 1964). Frick and Mohr (1973) also noted an increase in frond production by treating plants grown in the dark with red light. The effect was reversed by far red, indicating a phytochrome mechanism in vegetative reproduction.

Numerous detailed studies by Rombach (1976) confirmed earlier work on the effects of light on *L. minor*. He also found that the rate of cell division, frond expansion and frond multiplication rate increased as illumination increased. Sugar uptake from the growth solution was constant and independent of light intensity. Frond multiplication rate peaked at 28°C under high light intensity but was constant between 17 and 30°C at low intensities. Frond shape was not changed by light intensity or kinetin level. Plants can survive with only 2 to 3% of full sunlight, thus control by shading from other plants is unlikely (Wilkinson 1964).

Treatment with abscisic acid reduced *L. minor* cell division and elongation by 60% (Newton 1977). The effect was reversed by cytokinins. The levels of these substances in mother and daughter fronds controls *L. minor* growth and differentiation. Abscisic acid increases the number of abscission zones in *Lemna* fronds and hastens senescence (Ostrow-Schwebel 1979).

Light intensity and ambient temperature affect dry matter production in surprising ways. At low light intensities, temperature increases do not increase biomass production, but at high intensities, dry weight increases as temperature increases (Wilkinson 1963). Hodgson (1970) obtained maximum assimilation at 17.5°C and a 10°C temperature increase reduced assimilation per plant 30%, even though frond area tripled. Apparently, there was more competition for assimilates among fronds at the higher temperature. As with biomass increases at low temperature, light did not affect frond area. In contrast, at high temperatures frond area ratios decreased as light increased. Hodgson (1970) concludes that light is the ultimate limiting factor in determining the growth of *L. minor* and that temperature influences the overall photosynthetic surface through its effects on the size and rate of frond formation.

The adaptability of *L. minor* to its environment is reflected in its ability to obtain over 60% of the carbon used in photosynthesis from the air under laboratory conditions, while only 15% is obtained from the air in natural conditions (Filbin and Hough 1985). Photosynthesis in *L. minor* is highly correlated to light and temperature. Plants kept at constant temperature and light for long periods still expressed rhythmic growth with the maximum in the summer and the minimum in the winter (Bornkamm 1966). Plants had higher protein concentrations in the summer and higher carbohydrate contents in the winter.

L. minor shows characteristics of both C_3 and C_4 plants. Photosynthesis is saturated by about one-third of full sunlight (typical of C_3 plants) but the photosynthetic rate does not decline as temperatures rise above the optimum for photosynthesis (typical of C_4 plants) (Wedge and Burris 1982). However, due to the lack of Krantz anatomy and a low level of C_4 biochemistry, the species is regarded as a C_3 plant. Fronds are primarily composed of chlorenchyma cells with large intercellular spaces called air chambers that give the plant buoyancy. The upper surface is highly cutinized, has stomata and is unwettable. Because fronds float horizontally at the water's surface and are shaped like an oblate spheroid, they intercept light efficiently from any angle above horizontal (McIlraith et al. 1989).

Growth of *L. minor* is influenced by nutrient levels and other water quality factors. Nutrients are absorbed primarily through the lower frond surface (Hillman 1961) and the root is not essential for uptake. Joy (1969) found the maximum growth of *Lemna* occurred when N was supplied as nitrate and a mixture of amino acids was available. Wangermann and Lacey (1955) obtained maximum growth with 1 mg N/L of water. Low N levels increased frond life by reducing the rate of respiration. Hillman (1961) also reported reduced vegetative reproduction and frond respiration, increased starch content, and longer roots at low N levels. The optimum nitrate level increased as light intensity increased. Roots are usually colonized by firmly attached N-fixing epiphytes. Older plants are more readily colonized and subsequently degraded by the microflora (Zuberer 1984).

Phosphorous levels also determine *Lemna* growth rates. Fekete and Riemer (1973) observed a 10-fold increase in frond numbers as the P concentration increased from 0.031 ppm to 0.31 ppm. Maximum dry matter production was at 3.1 ppm. Root length decreased from 51 mm at 0.1 ppm P to 19.5 mm at 3.1 ppm P. *L. minor* could be used as a bioassay species to measure P concentration in water (Fekete et al. 1976). Potassium and Ca concentrations affect root length, multiplication rate, and frond area (Hillman 1961).

Morphological variation between *L. minor* populations is primarily ecological, but genetic differences also occur (Wozakowska-Natkaniec 1977). Plants in one region of Poland formed 91% left-handed plants and those in another had only 15%. Averaged over 19 sites, the proportion of 2-, 3-, and 4-frond plants was 23, 47, and 30%, respectively. The number of 2-frond plants increased as water K levels increased.

It is apparent that *L. minor* grows over a wide range of environmental conditions, leading Sculthorpe (1967) to state that optimum growth occurs when there is a suitable balance between light, temperature and nutrients. An increase or decrease in one factor will be reflected by changes in growth or reproduction rates.

The maximum growth of *L. minor* has been estimated by several researchers. Varshney and Rzoska (1976) counted 18,250 to 84,000 fronds/m^2 in natural infestations. The highest biomass production (170 g/m^2) occurred with high temperatures and long days. Most estimates place the productivity between 3 to 5 g dry matter/m^2/day. Hillman and Culley (1978) reviewed the data of many studies and estimate that *Lemna* can yield up to 7 ton/ha/yr on a dry weight basis. DeBusk and Ryther (1981) harvested 13.5 ton/ha/yr but found that yields of cultivated *L. minor* were three times greater than yields in natural environments. At low densities, the specific growth rate (percent weight increase per day) of *Lemna* can reach 35%, nearly twice that of other aquatic plants. However, productivity based on area and time was less than that of *Eichhornia* and *Hydrilla*. No morphological differences appeared when *L. minor* was grown at densities from 5 to 40 kg fresh wt/m^2. Similarly, cell wall material, protein content and available carbohydrates were unchanged by plant density. Thus, if *L. minor* is grown as a crop, the proper density should be based solely on growth rate, because quality will not vary (Tucker 1981).

Flowering in *L. minor* is rare and has never been observed in some regions. Nevertheless, Bennink et al. (1970) determined that it is a long-day plant that shows a weak flowering response with 10.5 hr of light, and a peak response (25% flowering) with 13- to 14-hr light periods for 23 to 32 days. Only one flower per colony was observed. Guppy (1894) noted flowering when the mean air temperature reached 18°C. In Sweden, flowering occurred in sunny and shady areas only in stagnant water, not in moving or wind-disturbed sites. Fronds of flowering colonies were somewhat smaller than those of non-flowering plants, but no other morphological changes were seen (Martinsson 1984). A Polish biotype flowered only in long-days (20 to 30%) and all flowers were in the right pouch (Krajncic 1974). However, Sculthorpe (1967) noted that flowers often arise in the left-hand pocket of fronds.

The inflorescence is often described as having one female and two male flowers in the same membranous spathe. The carpel lies between the stamens and therefore Plas (1971) considers the flowers perfect. Male and female parts may not appear simultaneously. The pistil and stamen emerge in late spring and summer from the same pouch that would normally produce a new frond and rise above the water (Hillman 1961). Both self- and cross-pollination are possible. Detailed cytological descriptions and drawings of the vegetative and flowering reproductive tissues are presented by Caldwell (1899).

Seeds may float on the surface and germinate immediately, but they usually sink to the bottom with the turions (winter buds) in the fall. Seeds are nondormant and germinate when conditions are favorable. As they germinate, the plumule appears first; it is green and rootless and does not look like a normal frond (McCann 1942, Plas 1971). The plumule then produces the first frond (which may be rootless) and then vegetative reproduction proceeds normally and the remains of the seed detach from the first frond.

Some strains of *L. minor* produce turions that also aid in survival of the species. Turions form in the fall and overwinter on the bottom until conditions favorable for growth to resume occur. These buds are identical to those formed in the spring and summer but lack sufficient air space to cause them to float. When ambient conditions are favorable, turions develop air spaces, fronds rise to the surface and growth resumes (Caldwell 1899).

AGRICULTURAL IMPORTANCE AND UTILITY

L. minor causes problems typical of other floating aquatics in over 60 countries (Figure 52-1). It is considered a principal rice weed in Guyana, India, and Indonesia; and also it is reported to infest rice in China, Malaysia, Nepal, Pakistan, Portugal, Spain, Thailand, and Vietnam. In many countries it interferes with the flow and pumping of irrigation water.

L. minor may be used as livestock feed, to produce fish, as a source of biogas and to purify water. Plants have a constant and rapid growth rate; they have no serious pest problems; the root is only a small fraction of the plant; and much of the plant consists of metabolically active, non-structural cells (Hillman and Culley 1978). However, plants contain at least 95% water and must be dried. They require relatively calm water and may concentrate elements such as boron up to ten times the amount found in other aquatic species (Nat. Acad. Sci. 1976a).

The composition of *L. minor* is very favorable for use in livestock rations. Protein content varies from 14 to 37% and the amino acid composition and metabolizable energy in *Lemna* are comparable to lucerne, and it contains more carotene than lucerne (Burton et al. 1977). Little (1979) reports that the amino acid composition of *L. minor* is similar to that of hen's eggs and the fiber content 7 to 10% lower than that of most forages, but its relatively high ash content (16 to 18%) is undesirable.

Up to 10% *Lemna* in chicken rations was equal to a corn and soybean meal diet, with no evidence of toxicity (Muztar et al. 1976). Harvesting the plants early and washing them improved their quality. *Lemna* is used to feed cattle and pigs in tropical Africa, southeast Asia, and India (Nat. Acad. Sci. 1976a). Harvey and Fox (1973) calculated that 4 to 5 ha of *Lemna* would provide feed for 20,000 to 30,000 hens for 6 to 8 mo. Chickens and ducks actually preferred *Lemna* to lucerne and it has been found equal to or better than lucerne in poultry and swine rations. *Lemna* is readily eaten by ducks and other water animals and they aid in disseminating fronds to uninfested waters.

L. minor is consumed by white omer catfish (*Tilapia zillii*) and grass carp (*Ctenopharyngodon idella*). In India, grass carp may consume 60 to 77% of their body weight daily. In fact, 1000 to 2000 grass carp/ha controlled *Lemna* (Little 1979). In China, grass carp feed on *L. minor* and, in India, the plant is used to kill algae blooms in ponds before releasing carp (Alikunhi et al. 1952). *L. minor* kill the algae by shading and increase the zooplankton in the water which also help the carp fry survive. *L. minor* can be used as feed for fish in fish ponds and to control submerged aquatics by shading (van Zon 1973).

The water-purifying ability of this plant has also been studied. It is an efficient consumer of boron and is 10 to 45 times better than other aquatics as a bioaccumulator (Glandon and McNabb 1978). One kilogram of *Lemna* may contain as much Al as 660,000 L of the water it grew in, as much Mn as 461,000 L, as much Fe as 307,000 L, and as much Cu as 79,000 L (Nat. Acad. Sci. 1976a). Plants can accumulate 0.64 mg B/g dry wt with no symptoms of B toxicity (Frick 1985).

The removal of P from sewage effluent was 90% complete after 4 wk of *Lemna* growth when 6% effluent was in the water, but only 14% complete when grown in undiluted effluent (Sutton and Ornes 1975). *Lemna* biomass production increased up to 25% effluent and the P concentration increased from 3 ppm in the controls to 12.4 ppm in *Lemna* grown in 75% effluent. Protein content was 29.6% in plants grown on 75 or 100% sewage effluent after the first week and biomass accumulation peaked at the third week, indicating that a continuous supply of effluent is needed for sustained, rapid growth and weekly or biweekly harvests are necessary to obtain a high-quality product for feed. Thus *Lemna* reduces the P content in sewage effluent and the rate of removal depends upon the plant population, the concentration of P in the effluent, and the time of contact. *Lemna* can also remove 236 mg N/m^2/day from wastewater and could be integrated into *Typha* systems because of its ability to survive in low light conditions (Reddy and Debusk 1985).

In China, dried *L. minor* plants are used to treat swollen feet, measles, as a diuretic and to improve circulation (Duke and Ayensu 1985).

COMMON NAMES

Lemna minor

ARGENTINA	lenteja de agua
AUSTRALIA	common duckweed
BANGLADESH	khudipana
BELGIUM	klein kroos
BRAZIL	capa rosa, lentiha da agua, pasta miuda, pesca miuda
CANADA	common duckweed, lenticule mineure

CHINA	fu ping
COLOMBIA	lenteja de agua, lentejilla
DENMARK	liden andemad
ENGLAND	common duckweed
FINLAND	pikkulimaska
FRANCE	petite lentille-deau
GERMANY	Kleine Wasserlinse
HAWAII	duckweed
INDIA	chotopana, pacha
ITALY	lenticchia d'acqua
JAPAN	ko-ukilusa
NETHERLANDS	klein kroos
NEW ZEALAND	duckweed
NORWAY	andmat
PAKISTAN	khudipana
PORTUGAL	lentihas de agua menores
SOUTH AFRICA	duckweed, eendekroos
SPAIN	lentejuela de agua
SWEDEN	andmat
UNITED STATES	common duckweed, lesser duckweed, water lentil

Fifty-Three

The Ludwigias
Ludwigia adscendens (L.) Hara,
Ludwigia hyssopifolia (G. Don) Exell,
and Ludwigia octovalvis (Jacq.) Raven

Onagraceae, Evening Primrose Family

FIGURE 53-1   The distribution of *Ludwigia adscendens* (L.) Hara across the world where it has been reported as a weed.

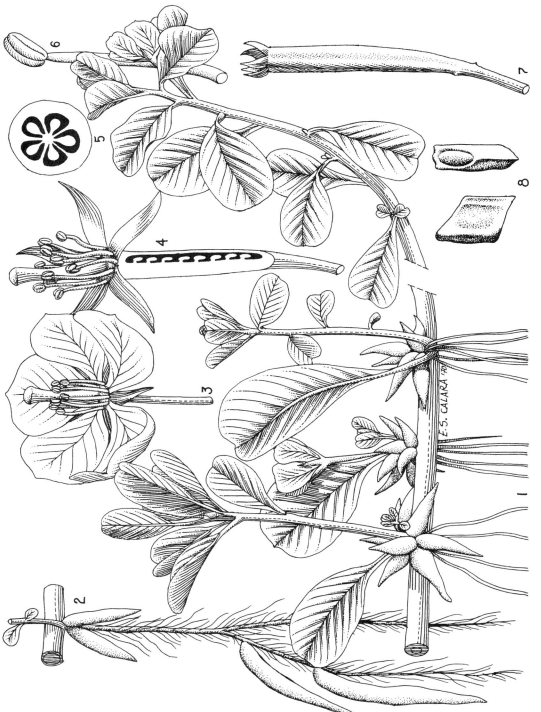

FIGURE 53-2 *Ludwigia adscendens* (L.) Hara: 1. habit; 2. root with pneumatophores; 3. flower, 4. same, petals excised, ovary sectioned vertically; 5. ovary cross section; 6. stamen; 7. fruit; 8. seed, two views.

MEMBERS OF THE ONAGRACEAE are found over all of the land area of the earth, with three small exceptions: internal Greenland, the driest areas of the north African desert, and the dry areas of Australia. Most are herbs, but some are shrubs and aquatics. Most are found in open habitats, wet or dry. The family is best known for the "evening primroses," the *Oenothera*, that have been the subject of intensive cytogenetics work, and for the *Fuchsias* and *Clarkias* among our ornamentals. The weedy *Ludwigias* are often called "primrose willows," their flowers having some of the color of the primroses and the leaves of some species having a resemblance to the willow. Hybrids are rare between recognized species of *Ludwigia*. *L. adscendens* and *L. octovalvis* have relatively large flowers and there seems to be some outcrossing as a result of insect visitations.

There are 18 genera in the **Onagraceae** and all of them can be found in the western United States, leading some to believe that the origins of these plants were in the Western Hemisphere. The preferred sites for these three aquatic weeds seems to be hot lowlands, open water, or the littoral of nearby wet soils subject to water fluctuations. Many of the aquatic weeds now in *Ludwigia* were formerly known by the more familiar name, *Jussiaea*, for they were once held to be distinct. The former has relatively short capsules and the stamens, petals, and sepals are of equal number, while the latter has longer capsules and the stamen number is twice that of the petals or sepals. In the past quarter-century, however, some workers have shown that a distinction based on these characters, as well as general appearance, breaks down upon close examination. Thus, in recent times, some, but not all, have come to regard *Jussiaea* as a synonym of *Ludwigia* (Hara 1953, Raven 1963, Jash and Sharma 1970). The latter authors reported on the cytotaxonomy of the Indian **Onagraceae**.

As a group, the three *Ludwigia* species discussed here are among the most widespread weeds of the world.

Ludwigia adscendens

DESCRIPTION

L. adscendens (Figure 53-2) is an aquatic or sub-aquatic *perennial* herb that may be emergent, may be anchored, with horizontal extensions over the water surface, or may be free floating; *stems* to 1 m, horizontal stems to 4 m, normally glabrous but if water recedes, plants may survive on dry ground where they are densely villous and seldom flower, horizontal stems with long, fibrous roots, as well as adventitious, modified, spindle-shaped, nodal aerophores or air roots, that grow erect and may extend above the water surface, in South Asia stems are yellow-green or reddish in some areas; *leaves* alternate, broadly oblong-elliptic, rounded or obtuse at apex, up to 10 cm long, 4 cm wide, narrowed at the base to a distinct petiole which may be red; *flowers* borne singly at upper leaf axils, 5-merous, pediceled; *calyx* pubescent or sometimes glabrous; *petals* obovate, bright yellow to very pale yellow or white, up to 2 cm long; *stamens* 10, the epipetalous ones are slightly shorter, *filaments* white, 2.5 to 4 mm; *anthers* are 1.2 to 1.8 mm long shedding pollen directly onto stigma at anthesis; *style* white, 4 to 8 mm, densely long hairy on lower half; *stigma* globose, green, upper two-thirds receptive, *ovary* inferior; *fruit* a *capsule* thick-walled, woody, 2 to 3 cm long and 3 mm in diameter, more or less cylindrical, often somewhat curved, surmounted at apex by calyx, glabrous or with soft long hairs, 5-locular, light brown with 10 conspicuous darker brown ribs, seeds evident as bumps between the ribs, irregularly dehiscent, base narrowed; *seeds* pale brown, many in orderly rows, some 4-angled and some prismoid, 1 to 2 mm in size, firmly imbedded in coherent cubes of woody endocarp which are fused to capsule wall.

In the southeastern United States, the sepals and leaves may vary from dark green to dark red and the weed is known as "red ludwigia." This species is distinguished from *L. hyssopifolia* and *L. octovalvis* by its broader, more rounded leaves.

This plant was familiar in a former time as *Jussiaea repens.*

DISTRIBUTION AND HABITAT

In the families of terrestrial plants, it is not unusual to find a group that has become adapted to wet or aquatic sites. It is so of the *Ludwigias*, and *L. adscendens* is one of the most widely distributed. Sculthorpe (1967) gathered data from many sources for preparation of a list of the most widely distributed hydrophytes. In his list of 65 plants, he found that less than 25% were dicotyledons. *L. adscendens* is one of the latter.

L. adscendens is a weed on all continents, being found in 58 countries and quite generally distributed in fresh water over many of the world's waterways (Figure 53-1). It tends to shun the cooler parts of the North Temperate Zone, but, in the Southern Hemisphere, it is in many places in South America, Africa, and Australia. Its peculiar adaptability is interesting to observe. In general, the *Ludwigias* try to avoid the areas of the world with low humidity and dry soils. It is found in the canals on the Nile Delta in Egypt, but is not found south of Cairo. Deserts are inhospitable for it, but plants are found around oases of the Libyan desert. In another example, in south Asia during the rainy season the weed frequents irrigation channels, tanks (artificial ponds for water storage), small lakes, and cultivated crops such as rice and jute. It may be seen from sea level to 1600 m. The plant thrives on a variety of soils in the rice paddies of the world. In one area of India it prospers on a peat soil of *pH* 5 underlain by heavy clay.

PROPAGATION

Propagation is mainly by seed, but extensive creeping stems, on mud or water, may help a single plant to colonize a significant area. If the water level recedes, the stems resting on soil produce roots, and a bud at each node may provide a new shoot. On drying soils, plants are smaller and more hairy. Propagation from broken pieces of floating stems is quite normal.

Pancho (1964), in a study of seeds produced by rice field weeds, reported more than 125,000 seeds produced per plant, with a weight of 88,400 seeds/g.

PHYSIOLOGY AND MORPHOLOGY

In the Cuttack area of south India, Singh et al. (1967) found that *L. adscendens* flowered abundantly in March–April and frequently during May–June. It flowered abundantly again in the short photoperiods of September–October, tapering off in November. Fruiting was almost confined to the September–October season. After pollination, the pedicel bends downward and the fruit ripens in the water. When the fruit decays, it releases the cork-winged, buoyant seeds onto the water.

The plant has three types of roots: long unbranched anchor roots; short, much-branched feeder roots; and the spindle-shaped, erect aerophores.

Some remarkable cases of aerenchyma development are seen in the **Onagraceae**. *Ludwigia peruviana* has been most widely studied because submerged parts of its shoots are clothed in it and it develops on normal shoots that enter mud. The development in *L. adscendens* is similar, but on this plant the "air roots" are usually seen at nodes. The aerenchyma cells arise from a pericyclic phellogen (cork cambium). The phellogen initials produce layers of small cells by periclinal divisions, and at intervals around the circumference some cell layers begin to enlarge rapidly in a radial direction, thus pushing outward all of the layers that are external to them. Air chambers are created that run parallel with the axis of the root. A transverse section of an air root thus reveals that the stele is surrounded by a wide zone of aerenchyma. The usual interrelation of these structures is that they can transport more oxygen more quickly to organs beneath water or mud than would be possible if the gases had to diffuse from aerial foliage through long stems to the same parts.

A great deal more research time has been spent in observing the insect visitors of this species than upon its physiology. Alam and Karim (1980) and Sankaran et al. (1974) have reviewed the potential of four insects, *Haltica caerulea*, *H. foveicollis*, *Mompha ludwigiae*, and *Nanophyes nigritulus*, for the biological control of *L. adscendens*. Lahser (1967) studied the use of the fish *Tilapia mossambica* for biological control and found that *L. adscendens* was killed through the destruction of roots and stems even though the plant material was not ingested in large amounts. The fish were most interested in the periphyton on the surface of the plant foliage and rocks, and the destruction and consumption of plant material was incidental to the removal of the periphyton. There was a definite preference for plant species, although the composition of the periphyton was quite the same on all of them.

A very promising development for the biological control of weeds with pathogens has been reported recently from Arkansas, in the United States, in experiments on *Ludwigia* species growing in rice and soybeans. Boyette et al. (1979) have obtained excellent field control of *Ludwigia decurrens* using the fungus *Colletotrichum gloeosporioides*. Control was obtained with 1 to 2 million spores per ml in 94 L of water/ha. There has been no damage to crops or other *Ludwigia* species in the area. To date it is one of the best examples of biological control of weeds with pathogens.

Khan (1942) made an extensive investigation of the embryology of *Jussiaea repens* (now *L. adscendens*) with its unique 4-nucleate embryo-sac. Outside the **Onagraceae**, Khan reported that this was rare and known to occur only in *Plumbagella* in the **Plumbaginaceae** at that time.

Ludwigia octovalvis

L. octovalvis is equal in importance as a weedy member of this genus. It is troublesome as a weed in about the same areas as *L. adscendens* and it appears to have the same temperature limitations. It is found in upland crops more often than the latter species.

DESCRIPTION

L. octovalvis (Figure 53-3) is an erect, stout, well-branched, robust herb of damp or flooded areas, may be woody at the base and shrubby at times, to 4 m, *annual* or *perennial*, with long stiff hairs sometimes appressed and oriented in one direction; *stems* may be red-brown and

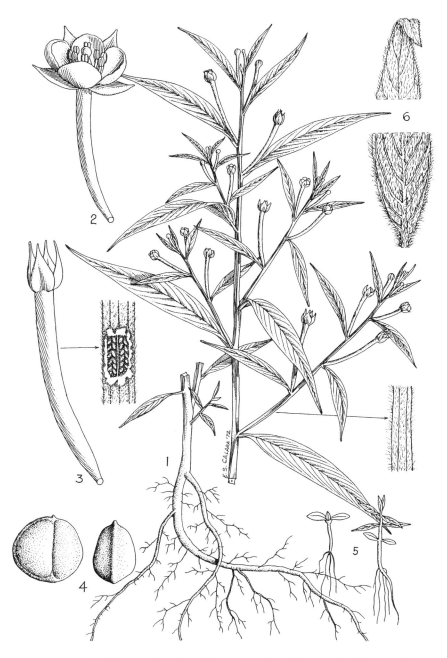

FIGURE 53-3 *Ludwigia octovalvis* (Jacq.) Raven: 1. habit; 2. flowers; 3. fruit; 4. seed, two views; 5. seedlings; 6. leaf.

lignified at base; *leaves* alternate, light green, may turn red upon aging, narrowly lanceolate to ovate, up to 15 cm long, 4 to 40 mm wide, densely pubescent both sides, attenuate at base and apex, 12 to 22 veins each side of midrib, short *petiole*; *sepals* 4, ovate or lanceolate, 8 to 13 mm long by 1 to 7.5 mm wide; *flowers* solitary in axils of leaves and at terminals; *petals* 4, pale to bright yellow, 1 to 2 cm long and 4 to 17 mm wide, broadly ovate and may be emarginate at apex; *sepals* 4, 8, to 15 cm; *stamens* 8, filaments 1 to 4 mm long; *anthers* 1 to 4 mm long, white, hairy, sunken nectary surrounding base of each epipetalous (and shorter) stamen; *style* 1.5 to 3.5 mm long with stigma subglobulose and shallowly 4-lobed; *fruit* a thin-walled, 4-angled, narrowly cylindrical, 8-ribbed *capsule*, 3 to 5 cm long, 2 to 8 mm in diameter, pubescent, irregularly loculicidal, terminated by persistent calyx lobes, color may vary from green to pale or reddish brown, or purplish, pedicel up to 1 cm; *seeds* rounded, beaked, in several indistinct rows in each locule, free, each with inflated raphe equal in size to body of seed, 0.6 to 0.75 mm in size, brown.

L. octovalvis differs from *L. adscendens* by its more erect habit and larger, lanceolate leaves that are somewhat acute. This species was formerly well known as *Jussiaea suffruticosa*.

DISTRIBUTION AND HABITAT

L. octovalvis (Figure 53-4) is a weed on many Pacific islands, in south and central Asia, Australia, over much of Africa, and in the warm areas of the Americas. It frequents a very wide range of humid, wet places and is found in marshes, fresh water lakes and streams, ditch banks of all kinds, along railroads, and on gravelly riverbeds and sandy or silty flood banks. It is found in paddy rice over much of the world and grows in damp, occasionally flooded grasslands. It may be seen on floating logs and it helps to colonize floating islands in lakes. It is found at sea level, up to 1000 m in the Celebes and in Indonesia, and up to 1400 m in New Guinea.

PHYSIOLOGY AND MORPHOLOGY

L. octovalvis reproduces by seed and may also occupy new areas by sending out runners and rhizomes. Pancho (1964) reported that the plant flowers all year in the Philippines and is a very prolific seed producer. He found that the weed can produce more than 375,000 seeds/plant, with about 4000 seeds/g.

Wulff and Medina (1969), Wulff et al. (1972), and Wulff and Briceno (1976) found that this plant has an absolute light requirement in the 10 to 40°C range during germination. Dark germination is zero in this range. The seed coat must be punctured or removed to obtain germination under any circumstance in the dark. High levels of germination are possible in continuous illumination. The light reaction is mediated by the phytochrome system, for it can be repeatedly reversed by short exposure to red and far-red light. If germination is attempted in an atmosphere of pure O_2, the promotive effect of light is lessened. Exposure to cycles of 1 hr of light and 24 hr of darkness at 20 and 35°C stimulated germination. KNO_3 and kinetin enhanced the response to light, but had no effect in the dark.

In later experiments, seeds exposed to continuous light, without previous imbibition, had a bimodal temperature response: germination was high at 25°C and again at 40°C and was very low in the 30 to 35°C range. Both preincubation in darkness at 35°C and high light intensity (15,500 lux) tended to eliminate the bimodal temperature response.

FIGURE 53-4   The distribution of *Ludwigia octovalvis* (Jacq.) Raven across the world where it is reported as a weed.

From the tiny seed, very small cuneiform-shaped cotyledons appear and become 4 to 5 mm in length. The seedling may have a reddish tint on stems. The plant grows very slowly in early life and may flower at 8 wk from emergence. If behaving as an annual, it has a life span of several months. As with *L. adscendens*, the aerophores or breathing roots may be seen floating or protruding at the surface. These were formerly thought to be floating devices. Further investigation has shown that they disappear when water recedes or the plant is stranded on mud and they then seem to revert to normal root functions. It was also shown that, with removal of these roots, the plant continues to float (Biswas and Calder 1936).

Ormond (1973) has described in considerable detail the appearance and Brazilian distribution of two varieties or subspecies, *octovalvis* and *sessiliflora*, that are found in the literature of many parts of the world. Many intermediate forms of these two types seem to exist in Brazil as well. All biotypes are self-fertilized and the various forms remained distinct when transplanted into different areas.

Sheriff and Mahalakshmi (1969) studied the cytology of the species and reported a diploid form ($n = 8$) in India, a tetraploid form in the United States ($n = 16$), and a hexaploid form in Taiwan ($n = 24$).

Ludwigia hyssopifolia

A third species of this genus, *L. hyssopifolia*, is also a troublesome weed that is quite generally spread across the world in the manner of the two species above, but has a greater tendency to remain in warmer regions (Figure 53-5). Raven (1963) feels that it has become very difficult to know the native country of this widespread pantropical weed, for it seems to have no close relatives.

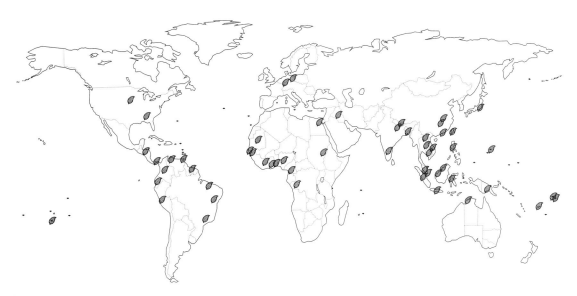

Figure 53-5   The distribution of *Ludwigia hyssopifolia* (G. Don) Exell across the world where it has been reported as a weed.

DESCRIPTION

L. hyssopifolia (Figure 53-6) is an erect, *annual* herbaceous, marshy, or aquatic plant, at times seen on drier land, to 3 m high, sometimes persisting and becoming woody at the base; *stems* nearly glabrous, green but may have reddish or purplish coloration, marked with striations, usually branched above, may appear 3- or 4-angled, young growth and inflorescence minutely pubescent; *leaves* lanceolate to linear lanceolate, narrowly cuneate at base, acute to acuminate at tip, may be red or green, up to 10 cm long, 1 to 3 cm wide, *petiole* short, midrib may be white-green, margin may be serrulate, glabrous or with few short hairs at base of leaf; *flowers* small, axillary, solitary, sessile; *calyx* a tube surrounding the inferior ovary, forming at the top 4 lanceolate, acuminate *sepals*, 2 to 4 mm long, pubescent; *petals* 4, yellow or white fading to orange-yellow, ovate to elliptic, a little larger than sepals; *style* and *stigma* simple, style pale greenish-yellow, *stigma* globose; *stamens* 8, in this species filaments of the epipetalous stamens are 0.5 to 1 mm long, those of the episepalous, being 1 to 2 mm long; *fruit* a *capsule*, cylindrical, 4-celled, up to 3 cm long, 1 to 0.2 mm wide, pubescent, subsessile, somewhat enlarged at top; *seeds* of two types: those of the upper part of capsule numerous, several rows per locule, ovoid, about 0.5 mm long, free, more pale brown than lower seeds; in lower capsule 1 row per locule, about 0.75 mm long, brown, each imbedded in a corky disc. Gunn and Ritchie (1988) have presented line drawings of seed, embryo, and transections of the seed.

This plant may be distinguished from the former two *Ludwigias* by its unusual dimorphous seeds. In a former time, this plant was known as *Jussiaea linifolia*.

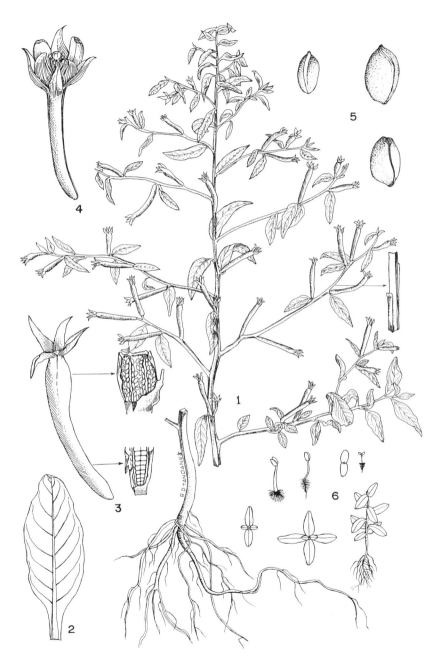

FIGURE 53-6 *Ludwigia hyssopifolia* (G. Don) Exell: 1. habit; 2. leaf enlarged; 3. fruit; 4. flower; 5. seed, three views; 6. seedling.

BIOLOGY

Except for comments about seeds, there is probably no published research on the biology of this species. It is known to frequent pools, shallow ditches, and river edges. It grows in rice and in fallow garden lands and wastelands in humid areas. In Borneo, it prospers in clearings on both heavy clay and coarse white sand, as well as in pools in eucalyptus savannahs. It has been found at 1000 m in old volcanic mudstreams on Java.

Although it produces interesting dimorphic seeds, there is no information on the relative germination behavior of the two types. Pancho (1964) found that a single plant growing in rice in the Philippines may yield 75,000 seeds, with 16,000 seeds/g. Also in the Philippines, Juliano (1940) collected seed in March and November and buried it the following December in inverted but open vials containing sterile sand. Lots of seed were tested every 6 mo for 3.5 yr and *L. hyssopifolia* was still germinating at the end of that period.

Sauerborn et al. (1988) found that seeds of *L. hyssopifolia* would germinate in light but not in dark. In their experiment, seeds would not germinate when placed below the soil surface. The lower temperature range limit for germination was 10 to 20°C, the upper limit was 40°C, whereas the optimum temperature range for germination was 15 to 35°C.

On watery sites, as the wall of the fruit decays, both kinds of seeds from this plant are gradually released to the water surface, where they float for about 2 weeks and then sink.

There are scattered reports that aerophores can be found on shallow roots.

AGRICULTURAL IMPORTANCE OF THE LUDWIGIAS

L. adscendens is a serious weed in rice in India, Laos, and Madagascar. It is a principal weed of rice in Indonesia, of jute in India, and of aquatic systems and waterways in Ghana and the United States. It is a common weed of rice in Brazil, Nicaragua, the Philippines, Thailand, and the United States. It is a troublesome weed of unknown rank in rice in Bangladesh, Cambodia, Chile, China, Indonesia, Malaysia, Nepal, Peru, Sri Lanka, and Thailand; legumes in the Philippines; reforestation practices and savannahs in Uganda; and aquatic water systems in Argentina, Columbia, India, Thailand, and Zambia.

L. hyssopifolia is a serious weed of rice in India, Malaysia, and Sri Lanka. It is a principal weed of rice in Indonesia and Trinidad and a common weed of maize in India, rubber in Thailand, and aquatic systems in Thailand and India. It is a troublesome weed of unknown rank in rice in Malaysia, the Philippines, and Thailand; irrigated crops in Indonesia; sorghum and pineapple in Malaysia; taro in Samoa; and sugarcane and the general waterways in Thailand.

L. octovalvis is a serious weed of rice in Gambia and taro in Samoa. It is a principal weed of rice in Dominican Republic, Nigeria, the Philippines, and Sri Lanka; pastures in Fiji and New Caledonia; and sugarcane in Trinidad. It is a troublesome weed of unknown rank in rice in Bangladesh, Burma, Cambodia, Hawaii, Indonesia, India, Laos, Madagascar, Nepal, Nicaragua, Thailand, and the United States; cabbage in Nicaragua; coconut in Brazil; dryland farming, irrigated crops, and pastures in Australia; pastures in the Philippines; sorghum and maize in Mexico; taro in Hawaii; and aquatic systems in Hawaii and the mainland United States.

To obtain information on species that survived initial weed control practices in lowland rice in Luzon, the Philippines, Pablico, and Moody (1985) surveyed over 500 fields at the time of flowering to heading. *L. octovalvis* appeared in 60% of all fields and was one of the weeds encountered most frequently.

In a later study of the weed species flora as affected by planting pre-germinated seed or transplants in rain-fed areas or irrigated rice fields, they found *L. octovalvis* to be a dominant weed that grew equally well under all of the above conditions.

Several *Ludwigias* are used in China for treatment of inflammation, cuts, boils, abscesses, and snakebite.

COMMON NAMES

Ludwigia adscendens

ARGENTINA	duraznillo de agua
AUSTRALIA	water primrose
BANGLADESH	kassaradam, kesra, malcha
CAMBODIA	kamping pauy, kraping puoy
COLOMBIA	clavito, clavo de agua, mimbra
EGYPT	arous el-bahr, forga'a, freikaal, kharaawa, lorq, moddad
INDONESIA	krangkong, kambang pendjit, nenang belanguh, pangeor, rubah sila
JAPAN	mizukinbai
LAOS	pak pawd
MADAGASCAR	volondrana
MALAYSIA	floating Malayan willow herb, maman pasi, tingir bangau
PHILIPPINES	gabi-gabi, kangkong dapa, singa ng-dagat
PUERTO RICO	yerba de clavo acuatica
THAILAND	paeng puey
UNITED STATES	creeping waterprimrose, red ludwigia
VIETNAM	rau dua trau

Ludwigia hyssopifolia

CAMBODIA	mimbra
CELEBES ISLANDS	kayu ragi
COLOMBIA	mimbra
INDONESIA	anggereman, cacadean, lombokan, meligai
MALAYSIA	inai pasir, jinaleh
PHILIPPINES	barigaua, manakatud, pasau-hupai, taklang-duron
THAILAND	tian na

Ludwigia octovalvis

AUSTRALIA	willow primrose
BRAZIL	cruz de malta
CUBA	clavellinas
DOMINICAN REPUBLIC	culantrillo, yerba de nicotea
FIJI	false primrose, yellow willow herb
HAWAII	kamole, primrose willow
INDONESIA	gaga busan, urang aring
JAPAN	kidachikinbai
MADAGASCAR	volondrano
MALAYSIA	buyangsamalam
MAURITIUS	gandia narron, herbe la mare
NEW GUINEA	ewo
PERU	calavo cimarron, clavo silvestre, flor de clavo
PHILIPPINES	balakbak, malapako, pachar, talangkau, tayilaktan, water willow
UNITED STATES	water primrose

Fifty-Four

Marsilea quadrifolia L.

Marsileaceae, Water Clover Family

THIS FAMILY OF FERNS has three genera with 70 species of emergent, submersed and floating-leaved plants found mainly in the warm regions, but with some species hardy in temperate areas. These aquatic pteridophytes differ from most other ferns in being heterosporous, that is, producing their spores in a specialized organ, the sporocarp. They vary in form from small rush-like plants that resemble the **Juncaceae** to the four leaf clover-like plants of *Marsilea quadrifolia*. They do not resemble the familiar woodland ferns. *M. quadrifolia* is a major weed of paddy fields and a troublemaker in ponds, lakes and irrigation systems in more than 40 countries.

FIGURE 54-1   The distribution *Marsilea quadrifolia* L. across the world where it has been reported as a weed.

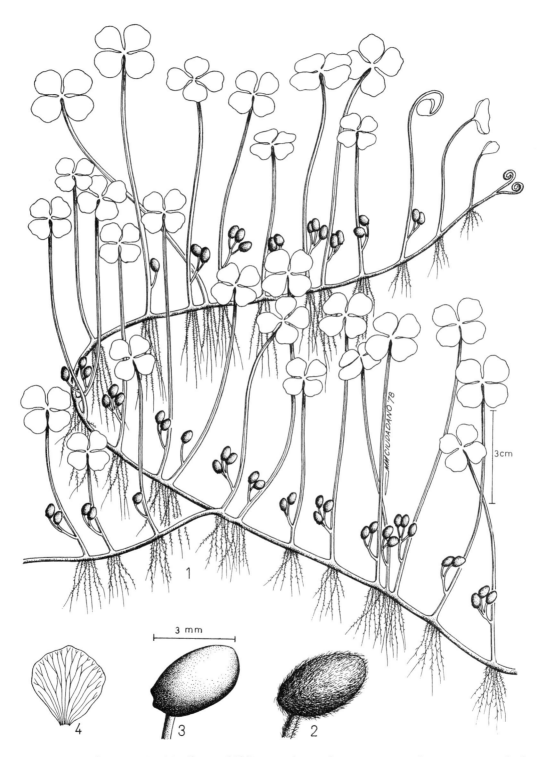

FIGURE 54-2 *Marsilea quadrifolia* L.: 1. plant and sporocarps; 2. and 3. sporocarps; 4. leaf.

DESCRIPTION

M. quadrifolia (Figure 54-2) is an herbaceous, heterosporous, *perennial*, widely distributed aquatic fern, sometimes seen creeping on mud after water recedes; *stems* filiform, *leaves* 4-lobed, floating on water surface, may choke entire areas near margins of ponds; *rhizomes* slender, long, creeping, 1.5 to 2 mm in diameter, irregularly branched; stems brownish-yellow, while very young with appressed to ascending soft hairs; *petioles* arising from rhizomes, projecting above the water, 7 to 17 cm long; leaflets sessile, deep green, somewhat round at apex, entire, smooth, 1 to 1.5 cm long; *sporocarps* 1 to 3, more or less bean-shaped body forms on short stalk at axil of leaf, hard, 4 to 5 mm long, borne at base of or laterally on pedicel, containing 2 rows of indusiated (covered) *sori*, each *sorus* containing several *sporangia*, some with many *microspores* and some with a single *megaspore*.

DISTRIBUTION AND HABITAT

M. quadrifolia (Figure 54-1) is of circumpolar distribution. It is found over much of Europe but is most troublesome in the west, southeast, and the northern Mediterranean area. It is disappearing in a number of localities in northern Europe because of channelization of rivers and the draining or other destruction of standing water bodies in the river alluvia. The weed was formerly in Poland, but is already extinct there (Husak and Otahelova 1986). It is in the western part of the former Soviet Union and is widely distributed in west and east Asia, the Pacific islands, eastern Australia, and New Zealand. The monographic survey of the genus *Marsilea* in Africa in 1968 did not record *M. quadrifolia*, but it is now reported from Zaire and Madagascar (Launert 1968).

    M. quadrifolia can float, stand above the water, or grow where there is no water. When torn apart by storms, waves or currents, the rhizome fragments drift to new areas to re-establish. In Orissa (east India), in summer, the weed is found in canals, tanks, irrigation channels, and on water-logged and swampy land, but not in cultivated crops such as jute. It frequents paddy crops and warm, shallow, muddy edges of fresh water ponds. In Pakistan it seeks out the margins of ponds and irrigation reservoirs in the same manner as *Ipomoea aquatica*, with which it is often associated. When the monsoon rains come, *M. quadrifolia* and others in the genus break out all over India.

    In eastern Czechoslovakia, it grows in slightly eutrophic water in loamy-clay soils of slightly acid to neutral reaction. The soils contain only small amounts of organic matter. The work of Gopal (1969a) earlier in India also found the weed on loamy soils rich in nutrients but in that area also rich in organic matter.

    There is much speculation about the means of long-distance dispersal of *Marsilea* spores, with adherence to the external surface of birds and movement by wind frequently suggested. The former has yet to be demonstrated and the latter seems unlikely because of the weight and size of the sporocarps. Malone and Proctor (1965) studied the effect of the avian digestive system on the viability of spores of *M. mucronata* (now *M. vestita*), a species similar to *M. quadrifolia*. They found that the sporocarps generally remained uncrushed and quite viable following passage through certain ducks and marsh birds. The retention times in the digestive tracts were sufficient to permit long-distance dispersal during migrations. Spore viability after passage differed widely with differing bird species.

    Seed analysts have been aware that the exterior appearance of the sporocarps of *M. quadrifolia* and other family members can be easily confused with seeds and other structures, such as the fruiting bodies of the bird's nest fungus, **Nidulariaceae** (Danielson 1962). In an interesting case of long-distance dispersal, the sporocarps of a member of the genus *Pilularia* were transferred across the Pacific to the United States with seed lots of subterranean clover (*Trifolium subterraneum*). This raises the likelihood that the smaller sporocarps of *M. quadrifolia* may also travel with rice seed in areas of the world where such seed is not well cleaned.

PROPAGATION

M. quadrifolia, and all of the *Marsileas*, reproduce vegetatively by means of creeping rhizomes or following dispersal and establishment of rhizome fragments. It reproduces sexually through spores formed in aerial sporocarps found in the lower petiole area, and only when the plant is floating or emergent. As with many emergent hydrophytes, when the plant comes under stress from receding water levels, temperature extremes or other pressures, the plants die back to the swollen, food-storing rhizomes which then form dormant terminal and lateral buds. The profusely branched network of runners or rhizomes can then produce new plants from buds at the nodes as proper growing conditions are restored.

In India, for example, the sporocarps and vegetative buds begin to germinate and produce new sporelings and young plants soon after the rains come and when the water in the ponds settles to a depth of 0.5 to 1 m. The young fern plants pass through the well-known juvenile stages during the hot summer. From careful observation and from growth records, it is believed that most new plants in India arise from vegetative buds and that there is a very low percentage of spore germination and establishment (Gupta 1962).

The sporocarps are quite rugged and very resistant to environmental disturbances because of heavy, thick walls in the hypodermis, much as in the hard seed coats of angiosperms. It is not unusual for mature sporocarps to remain closed for 2 or more yr until the stony cell layers have decayed. Bloom (1974) has reported the germination of spores from 51-yr-old sporocarps.

When water finally enters the sporocarp, gelatinous layers inside the walls enlarge vigorously, break the structure and within 20 min a sorus-bearing ring, a sorophore, protrudes and continues to expand in worm-like fashion. In a few days the spores are liberated from the sori and they normally germinate immediately (Sculthorpe 1967). With Indian biotypes, Bhardwaja and Mohammad (1967) have shown that emergence of the sorophore takes place only in darkness.

The sporocarp, with its contents, is remarkably adapted to long-term survival for the species. Bloom (1955) summarized experiments on the surprising resistance of *M. quadrifolia* sporocarps to aging, drying, alcohol, and herbarium poisons. In later experiments he found that newly-harvested spores, when dried for 2 days at 65°C, would still germinate. Some lots of sporocarps were held in the laboratory until the following spring, when they germinated normally. Upon boiling them for 2 hr, he found that numerous gametophytes developed and later produced sporophytes.

However, upon further investigation of heat resistance by the sporocarps later in the year, the sporocarps could not tolerate boiling for 5 min. Bloom speculated that the structures may have taken up excess moisture in the laboratory storage during a very humid summer. The sporocarps were again dried to constant weight at 65°C (losing 8% moisture), boiled for periods to 2 hr and autoclaved at 15 lbs pressure for 15 min, scarified with a file, and gametophytes developed following all treatments.

Sporocarps of all ages show some loss of viability, probably due to failures during development and maturation. Those containing viable spores show a high percentage of megaspore viability, at times close to 100% over several years. Microspores appear to be more susceptible to aging effects than megaspores.

MORPHOLOGY AND PHYSIOLOGY

The biology of this heterosporous fern (one that produces two kinds of spores representative of the two sexes) is interesting for its amphibious habit and its morphological diversity. Because it is so widespread in the world, it persists in colonizing new niches and from these sites new variations in forms and biotypes are often collected, differing in both vegetative and reproductive structures. Perhaps because of these characteristics, much of the biological work has emphasized the developmental morphology and anatomy of the plant.

The contrast in appearance is greatest between plants from aquatic sites and those from drier sites on shores and mud flats. As water recedes, the internode and petioles are shorter, the new leaves become ever smaller and their margins crenate instead of entire. Alterations of form may be so extreme that Gupta (1962) has found that specialists often fail to recognize that specimens from wet and dry sites in a given region are indeed the same species. The limits of variation are, however, fixed for the species.

The anatomy and morphology of the conductive tissues of the rhizomes and/or petioles were studied by White (1961–1963), Allsopp (1963), Miller and Duckett (1979), Bhardwaja and Baijal (1977), Loyal and Singh (1978), and Vasilevskaya and Prokopenka (1982). Schmidt (1978) found four distinct types of leaves on the plants: juvenile, submerged water leaves, floating water leaves and fertile land leaves. Mickel and Votava (1971) and Noda and Eguchi (1973) reported on the anatomy of the leaves. Reports in the literature by Pandeya (1953) on the variation in leaf forms in *M. quadrifolia* should be viewed with caution, for they were later found to be those of *M. minuta* (Gupta 1962).

Marschall (1925), Demalsy-Feller (1957), Rice and Laetsch (1967), and Dunn (1977) studied the embryology of *M. quadrifolia*. Johnson (1898) made a very extensive study of the development of the leaf and sporocarp of this species. Gupta (1962) published a very thorough study of the taxonomy and morphology of the Indian species of *Marsilea*. Launert (1968) prepared a comprehensive systematic treatment of the genus in Africa and Madagascar two decades ago.

Because of its amphibious habit, Gopal (1968) studied the effect of water depth and soil moisture on the morphology and productivity of *M. quadrifolia*. Plants grown from rhizome pieces were held in containers of soil at several moisture levels: water level at container surface (water-logged), water applied every day, or water each 3rd, 4th, or 5th day. The soil water was brought to saturation for each watering in the latter four treatments. Four other *Marsilea* species were included in the experiments.

Root length and fresh and dry weight increased with moisture levels in *M. quadrifolia*, and internode and petiole length increased as well. There was an increase in shoot dry weight even when water-logged, while other species stopped growing with water applied each 3rd or 4th day. Sporocarps were formed in *Marsilea* only in water-logged condition, whereas some other species formed them at all moisture levels and still others only at medium or low moisture levels.

M. quadrifolia thus appears most suitable for growing in a truly aquatic environment, while still being able to develop (although not reproduce sexually) with less moisture. In experiments in which the species were held at several submerged water levels, sporocarps developed on *M. quadrifolia* plants to the 10 cm depth but failed to form on other species at that place. *M. quadrifolia* accumulated more dry weight at 10 cm depth than in the water-logged condition of the previous experiment. In a study of the floodplain of a Czechoslovakian river that had been extensively channelized, Husak and Otahelova (1986) found the greatest aboveground emergent biomass in 0.22 m of water, while the greatest underwater biomass was at 0.3 m. The lowest above and underwater biomasses were found at 0.5 m.

Gopal (1969a) planted *M. quadrifolia* and four other species of the genus in experimental pots of a heavy, clay garden soil, or the garden soil mixed with an equal amount of sand, or a sandy soil. *M. quadrifolia* showed optimum growth and dry matter production in the clay garden soil, with declining growth as sand was added to the mixture.

It is believed that sporocarp development is favored by high light intensity. Allsopp (1951) found that *M. quadrifolia* plants on a culture medium in low light could be induced to form sporocarps with additions of sucrose to the medium.

In India, this species grows in a very wide temperature range, and has even survived in Kashmir, where temperatures may be well below freezing. To explore this hardiness, Gopal (1969b) placed different lots of *M. quadrifolia* and four other *Marsilea* species at −13°C, in a single exposure, for 30 min and intervals up to 24 hr. All species could tolerate 2 hr of cold but all of them, except *M. quadrifolia*, showed 50% mortality if held in the cold for 4 hr. At 8 hr, *M. quadrifolia* suffered 50% mortality; by that time most other plant material was dead. At 12 hr only *M. quadrifolia* had some surviving plants, but at 24 hr all were killed.

The extreme penetration of *M. quadrifolia* into the temperate zone is thus explained by its adaptability to several substrates and its ability to develop over a wide range of temperature and moisture conditions.

AGRICULTURAL IMPORTANCE

M. quadrifolia is a weed of crops and waterways in more than 40 countries. It is a serious weed of rice in Bangladesh, China, and India and a declared noxious weed in Taiwan. It is a principal weed of rice in Cambodia and Korea. All of these are major Asian rice-growing countries in the area of the world where the greatest quantity of rice is produced. In paddies of Guyana, Japan, Portugal, and Thailand, it is less important but still a very common weed. It is a rice weed of unspecified importance in Bulgaria, Burma, Cambodia, Hungary, Indonesia, Iran, Romania, and Spain. In 1948, *M. quadrifolia* was reported as a weed of cotton, wheat and winter arable crops in China, presumably in the irrigation systems for such fields (Chi 1948). Other countries in which it is troublesome in waterways, irrigation reservoirs, canals and furrows, and crops, are shown in Figure 54-1.

In Taiwan, where it is one of the three most important weeds in rice, Chang (1970) found that this weed is equally troublesome in both first and second crops and in sites of high and low fertility. It is both a pre- and post-transplanting weed, emerging 5 to 10 days following transplanting and quickly becoming a serious competitor of rice. The seasonal competition it can offer is therefore equal to that of *E. crus-galli*, the world's major weed of rice. In Japan, it is not one of the most important weeds but is one of three perennial broadleaved weeds that offers strong competition to rice (Noda 1969). Noda feels it is very difficult to attack because of thick walls in the epidermal cells and a very poor vascular transport system, which limits the effectiveness of many herbicides. Ali and Sankaran (1981) report *M. quadrifolia* as one of two main weeds in puddled (transplanted) rice in south India. To prevent yield loss, 50 and 130 weed-free days are needed in the monsoon and summer seasons, respectively.

Moderately successful control of this weed in paddies and ditches has been obtained by draining them and letting them dry out. This is only possible if a region has an extended dry spell or if there is an effective drainage system.

In Bangladesh, the plant is relished as a vegetable. Ducks and shore birds consume all parts of the plant.

COMMON NAMES

Marsilea quadrifolia

BANGLADESH	susni-sak
CAMBODIA	chantol phnom
CHINA	ping, sui-mien
FRANCE	fougere d'eau
GERMANY	Vierblattriger Kleefarn
INDIA	arai keerai, pepperwort, sush uni
IRAN	pepperwort
JAPAN	denjiso
MADAGASCAR	anatsiriny
NETHERLANDS	drijfblad
PORTUGAL	trevo de quatro folhas
SPAIN	aigret, viola
UNITED STATES	European pepperwort
VIETNAM	ran bo

Fifty-Five

Matricaria chamomilla L.

Asteraceae (Compositae), Aster Family

SEVERAL HEAVILY-SCENTED plants of *Matricaria* and *Anthemis* are loosely referred to throughout the world by the vulgar names "mayweed" or "chamomile" without regard for their systematic characterization. The Greek word *chamomile* refers to pyrethrum-like, heavily-scented plants. They tend to have a similar appearance and are often poorly identified because the leaves are very finely, pinnately dissected.

With the advent of herbicides, it was thought that the weedy *Matricaria chamomilla* would soon disappear, but in the mid-1980s it was still a dominant weed in many cereal

FIGURE 55-1   The distribution of *Matricaria chamomilla* L. across the world where it has been reported as a weed.

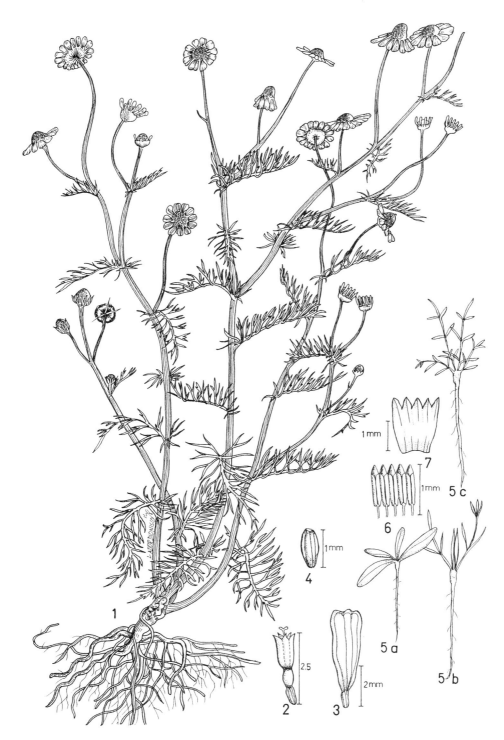

FIGURE 55-2 *Matricaria chamomilla* L.: 1. habit; 2. disc flower; 3. ray flower; 4. achene;
5. seedlings; 6. syngenesious stamens; 7. petal of disk flower opened.

fields of Belgium, England, Finland, Germany, Hungary, Italy, the Netherlands, Poland, Spain, Sweden, and elsewhere. A long list of synonyms for each of several closely related *Matricarias*, often cross-listed within the group, gives evidence that the taxonomy is mixed. *M. recutita* is frequently assigned to this well-known wild chamomile and, recently, *Chamomilla recutita* as well (Toman and Stary 1965, Rauschert 1974).

A curious mode of travel was discovered by Loktev (1958) in the former Soviet Union when he found up to 3 seeds of *M. chamomilla* traveling about with the seed of *Bromus secalinus* (cheat grass) as they lodged in longitudinal slits of those seeds. The latter species, a brome grass, is used for hay and forage in some areas of the world.

DESCRIPTION

M. chamomilla (Figure 55-2) is an *annual* herb, erect, branched, up to 1 m tall, with a strong odor when the plant is bruised; *leaves* alternate, soft, 2 to 3 pinnatipartite (pinnately-parted) with slender segments; *flower head* large, solitary on 2 to 8 cm long grooved peduncles; *receptacle* glabrous, hollow, conical about 5 to 7 mm high and 2.5 mm wide; *ray flowers* 1 seriate, white, 7 to 10 mm long and 2 to 3 mm wide, deflexed nocturnally and after pollination; *disk flowers* numerous, yellow, 2 mm long; flowerheads give off characteristic chamomille odor when crushed; *fruit* is an *achene* with pappus small or absent, elongated, curved, oval in cross section, tapers to basal end, apex has collar with central beak, ventral side with 5 long ribs, dorsal with fine longitudinal grooves, surface dull, color yellow-brown to brown with lighter ribs; small seed is 1.1 mm long by 0.4 mm wide, weight is 0.07 gm per 1000 seeds.

DISTRIBUTION AND HABITAT

M. chamomilla (Figure 55-1) is found in eastern Australia, New Zealand, and the several countries of South America in the south temperate zone and behaves as a weed in most agricultural areas of the north temperate zone. It is not a weed of consequence in Southeast Asia or the Pacific Islands. It is found in pastures at 1650 m in Switzerland.

From reports across the world, it is obvious that this weed can succeed on many soil types. Hanf (1983) reports the weed to be abundant on arable land of all kinds in Europe, particularly in cereals. It is found along cattle paths and in waste places. It is present mainly on fertile clay or sandy loams that are lime free. The plants will tolerate some salinity. In the former Yugoslavia, Tucakov (1957) found this weed grew best on loamy soils at an optimum *pH* of 8 and with a tolerance at *pH* 9 if NaCl was not in excess. In New Zealand, the weed is found in poor pastures and cultivated fields, and Matthews (1975) believes that it enters grazing areas at points where cattle trample and break the turf. He does not believe it will be troublesome in well-managed pastures.

Ridley (1930) reports that the seed surfaces have a mucilaginous exudation from hairs and glands when moist and this helps in seed dispersal.

PROPAGATION

Reproduction of *M. chamomilla* is by seed, with flushes of germination in spring and fall. Seedlings that emerge in late autumn behave as winter annuals and overwinter in rosette form. A plant in favorable surroundings can produce 5000 seeds.

On a 15 hectare area, Roberts (1958, 1962) in England initiated a 6-year experiment on the persistence of weed seeds in vegetable crop fields. For the 8 previous years the site had been in cereals, one root crop, and one year in a mixed grass-legume pasture. The fields held an average of 515 million total weed seeds/ha in the top 15 cm of soil at the out-set, one-half of them from *M. chamomilla* and *Poa annua*. After 6 years of mixed vegetable cropping, the *M. chamomilla* seed bank of the soil was reduced to 4% of the original, and the total seed content of the fields had been reduced by 80 to 90%.

In a study of weed seeds consumed by cattle, Hansen (1911) in Norway learned that a single cow in a weedy field may ingest one-half million *M. chamomilla* seeds in one day and pass one-fourth of these in feces, with 27 percent remaining viable. As with many species, such seeds remain dormant in the dung heaps until the material is sufficiently decomposed that the seeds can germinate.

Wagenvoordt and Opstal (1979) stored seeds of this species at 20°C in a laboratory and found 100% germination after 3 years. Klein (1956) found that 1°C was the lowest temperature at which one-half of the *M. chamomilla* could germinate and produce normal cotyledons and radicals.

The careful work of Kolk (1962) in Sweden on the seeds of *M. inodora*, a species close-ly related to *M. chamomilla*, is of interest here because of the scarcity of information on germination, dormancy, and longevity of the seeds of the latter. Newly harvested seed ger-minated in the light but had very low germination in the dark. Following overwintering or after aging for 2 years the seeds became less dependent on light. Alternating temperatures caused a slight increase in germination. Temperatures over 20°C or placement in moist sites out-of-doors retarded germination. In his experiments, seeds exhibited a moderate dormancy for more than 3 years. The optimum depth for emergence in a sandy loam was at 0.5 cm for old seeds, and there was no germination below 2 cm.

In long-term experiments with seeds buried in soil, Salzmann (1954) obtained ger-mination of 89, 81, 77, and 73% after 1, 2, 3, and 11 years, respectively.

MORPHOLOGY AND PHYSIOLOGY

Rusch (1965a,b) prepared keys and plant diagrams to assist in the identification of all of the mayweeds, *Matricaria* and *Anthemis*, of Germany. Karawya et al. (1968) made a histo-chemical study of *Matricaria* and Korsmo (1954) has published excellent illustrations of the anatomy of all parts of *M. inodora*, a closely related species.

In stands of *M. chamomilla*, flowering proceeds from May to September in the north temperate zone, with some plants having two flowering periods per year. Roberts and Feast (1974) in England found that several mayweeds that may emerge from January to June, including *M. chamomilla*, required progressively shorter periods to first flowering as days become longer, reaching a minimum of 40 to 50 days. After midsummer the time from emergence to flowering became longer. Plants emerging in late summer–early fall remained in rosette form over the winter and flowered the next spring. In plants held at 8, 13, 15, and 17 hours of daylength in a glasshouse, flowering was hastened at the longer photoperiods.

AGRICULTURAL IMPORTANCE

M. chamomilla is a very versatile weed and appears in 24 crops in more than 50 countries. It is a serious weed of cereals in England, the Netherlands, Poland and Spain; of peas in the

Netherlands; of potatoes and other vegetables in England; of rape and sugar beets in Spain; of sugar beets and vegetables in Germany; and of wheat and several winter season crops in Uruguay. It is a principal weed of barley in Germany; of beans in France, Germany, and India; of fodder beets, table beets, and sugar beets in Belgium; of cereals in Belgium, Hungary, and Finland; of winter and spring cereals in Sweden; of flax in France; peas, potatoes, and other vegetables in Belgium; of peas in Greece; of rape in France; of sugar beets in Belgium, France, and Italy; of wheat in Italy; and of winter wheat in Belgium and Germany. It is also ranked as a principal weed of unspecified crops in Afghanistan, Austria, and Tunisia.

It is a common weed of barley in France and Canada; of cereals in Bulgaria, Germany, South Africa, Switzerland, and Tunisia; of maize in France; of flax in the Netherlands; of legumes in Tunisia; of oats in Canada; of pastures in Poland and New Zealand; of peas, potatoes, and sunflowers in France; of potatoes and rye in Germany; and of wheat in Canada, France, Spain, and the United States.

M. chamomilla is also reported to be a ubiquitous weed, with crops unspecified, in Albania, Argentina, Brazil, Bulgaria, Chile, Colombia, Costa Rica, Czechoslovakia, Cyprus, Denmark, Egypt, Hawaii, India, Iran, Iraq, Israel, Japan, Jordan, Norway, New Zealand, Peru, Portugal, the former Soviet Union, Turkey, Venezuela, and the former Yugoslavia.

This weed is an important competitor in several crops of central and southern Europe and is troublesome regionally elsewhere on the continent. In Poland, in 1984, the mayweeds *M. chamomilla* and *Anthemis cotula* were found to infest 60 to 70% of the cereal-growing areas and yield losses amounted to 10 to 35% (Rola and Rola 1984). On a severity scale of 1 to 5, *M. chamomilla* ranks 3 in importance in cereals in Tunisia. Raatikainen and Mukula (1985) found that 8% of the biomass of the aerial parts of plants in 540 winter cereal fields in Finland was made up of weeds, with *M. chamomilla* ranking third in weight among the winter annuals. In more than 170 areas surveyed in northern Italy, Ferrari et al. (1984) found that regardless of the recent use of shorter rotations, less fertilizer and more limited soil tillage, *M. chamomilla* was one of seven annual weeds that had become dominant again.

Rademacher in Germany long ago predicted that *M. chamomilla* would become a dangerous weed of cereal lands. In 1970 he and co-workers reported on shifts in the weed flora after 15 years of changes in farm machinery, management systems, and modern weed control methods. *Matricaria* was a weak competitor in very weedy fields but was quick to fill in the vacant places left by other weed species more easily controlled by herbicides, thus profiting by the removal of weed competition (Rademacher et al. 1970). In a subsequent evaluation covering an additional 10 years in the same regions, Petzold (1979) reported that there had now been a general reduction in the density and the numbers of weeds, but with increases evident in 5 species, including *M. chamomilla*.

Perhaps related to this was a report by Petzold (1959) on the dispersal of weed seeds by several types of machines and harvesting systems that were coming into use in cereal fields. On average, 60 to 80% of the weed seeds were found in the grain as it was harvested with combine machines. The blow chaff (resulting from the cleaning operation inside the combine) contained 10 to 25 percent of the weed seed (that was sometimes returned to the ground). *M. chamomilla* was among the four species found in greatest quantity in the chaff.

Hunyadi (1973) in Hungary reported on a nationwide survey of weeds in cereals and found that *M. chamomilla* was again on the increase. Similar results were reported by Ramson et al. (1982) concerning winter wheat from the German Democratic Republic.

In the experiments of Bonfiq and Lindner (1981) in Germany, it was found that short-strawed varieties of spring wheat, sown at standard rates, were highly competitive to *M. chamomilla*. In fields infested with *Matricaria* and *Stellaria media*, Paul (1984) in Germany found that new, high-yielding rye cultivars were less competitive than traditional varieties. Rademacher and Ozolins (1952) worked with many biotypes of *M. chamomilla* and found in general that weed seedling emergence was lower in rye than in wheat fields, suggesting an allelopathic influence. However, no reliable detrimental effect of rye seedlings on the germination capacity of the weed could be found in laboratory experiments.

M. chamomilla is considered a medicinal plant in several areas of the world and there is considerable chemical research on various constituents that have biological activity. For example, its oils are studied for their inhibition of the growth of several fungi and bacteria (Aggag and Yousef 1972). The plant is cultivated in Eastern Europe and elsewhere because it is used in the manufacture of cosmetics and as a flavoring for tea, tobacco and liqueurs. If ingested, *M. chamomilla*, *Anthemis cotula*, and other mayweeds taint the milk of cows, being most troublesome in early winter and spring. In some cultures, extracts of the plant and its parts are used as treatments for inflammation, spasms, and worms of the intestinal tract.

COMMON NAMES

Matricaria chamomilla

ARGENTINA	manzanilla
BELGIUM	camomille echte kamille
BRAZIL	camomila dos alemaes, camomila vulgar, mecanilha
CANADA	matricaire camomille, wild chamomile
CHILE	manzanilla
DENMARK	vellugtende kamille
EGYPT	babouning
ENGLAND	scented mayweed, wild chamomile
FINLAND	kamomillasaunio
FRANCE	camomille ordinaire, fausse camomille, matricaire camomille
GERMANY	Echte Kamille, Feldkamille, Kamille, Mutterkraut
IRAQ	baboon, baboonij
ITALY	camomilla, capomille
JAPAN	kamitsure
NETHERLANDS	echte kamille
NEW ZEALAND	wild chamomille
NORWAY	kamilleblom
PERU	manzanilla comun
PORTUGAL	margaca das boticas, matricaria
SPAIN	camomila, magarza, manzanilla, manzanilla bastarda, manzanilla de aragon, manzanilla loca
SWEDEN	kamomill, sotblomster, sotkamomill
TUNISIA	camomille, matricaire
TURKEY	makikipapatya

UNITED STATES	wild chamomile
URUGUAY	manzanilla
VENEZUELA	manzanilla
YUGOSLAVIA	kamilica

Fifty-Six

Melastoma malabathricum L.

Melastomataceae, Melastoma Family

THIS WEED IS A MEMBER of the large family that favors tropical and subtropical climates but has an occasional representative in the temperate zones. The family, made up of 3750 species, is very large and ranks about 10th in number of species per family in the plant kingdom. With the exception of some cultivation for its colorful flower, the plant is of no economic importance. The species ranks as an important world weed because it is so widespread and competitive in the agriculture of tropical and subtropical Asia, particularly in all kinds of perennial plantations and orchards and also in forest plantings. It is an early invader, is persistent, and cannot be eliminated except by the removal of the entire plant.

FIGURE 56-1   The distribution of *Melastoma malabathricum* L. across the world where it has been reported as a weed.

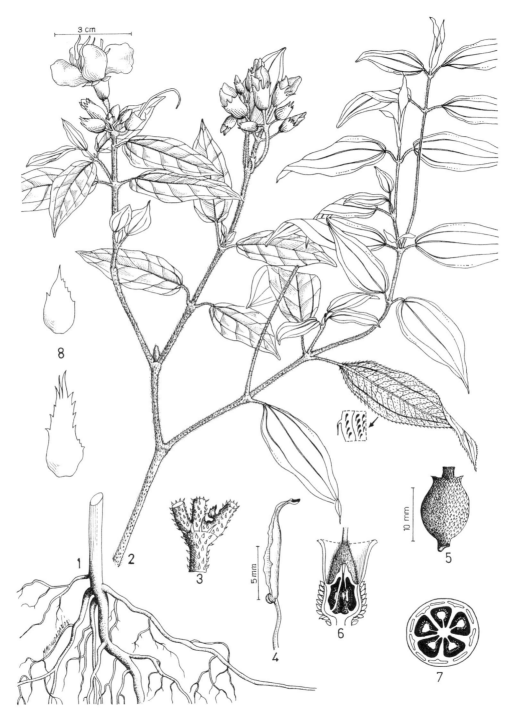

FIGURE 56-2   *Melastoma malabathricum* L.: 1. root system; 2. flowering branch; 3. portion of stem enlarged; 4. stamen; 5. capsule; 6. ovary, vertical section, 7. same, cross section; 8. two kinds of scale, enlarged.

DESCRIPTION

M. malabathricum (Figure 56-2) is a *perennial* erect shrub, 30 to 150 cm, or a slender small tree; *stems* branching, square, reddish to brownish hue, rough with small bristly scales; *leaves* opposite, ovate to lanceolate to narrow, rough both sides, scaly or covered with flat-lying or erect hairs, 3 to 5 strikingly prominent leaf veins, 5 to 10 cm by 2 to 4 cm, *petioles* short; *flowers* cymose, terminal or axillary, 2 to 8 cm in diameter, clustered on short stalks, opening out flat, *pedicel* stout, 6 to 18 mm in diameter, *petals* large, white to cream-colored, deep magenta-pink, light violet, or purple; *hypanthium* green with close-set chaffy scales; *sepals* broadly ovate, acute, glabrous within, 6 by 14 mm, with reddish tinge in Malaysia; *stamens* 10, 5 larger with yellow stalk and curved purple upper part; *anther* 1 cm or longer; *style* pink, long, with green tip; *fruit* berry-like, light brown, about 6 mm in diameter, set with scales; *calyx* bristle-tipped; fruit bursting irregularly when ripe to expose seeds buried in red pulp; *seeds* minute, numerous, spiral or semicircular in shape, pale-cream or black, at times lightly covered with sweet, red astringent, may be shiny or have scale-like appearance except near hilum, 0.5 to 0.7 mm in size.

This is an extremely variable species. A general description of the weed as it is seen across Asia would be that it is a branching shrub to 150 cm with a rough brown-reddish stem and green, rough leaves with prominent veins. Attractive flowers of several colors are borne at terminals or in axils, with rough berry-like fruit bearing minute seeds.

DISTRIBUTION AND BIOLOGY

As a weed, *M. malabathricum* is of concern from Mauritius through Sri Lanka and India, across southern Asia and north to Taiwan (Figure 56-1). It is in Hawaii and is common throughout Polynesia (Parham 1958). While found in north and west Australia, it appears not to be of concern there. The plant thrives on poor soil, tolerates dry, waste places, lends itself to cultivation as an ornamental for its lovely flowers, but quickly becomes dominant when it enters fields and plantations if not properly cared for.

When the seedlings of this species become established, they initiate flowering when quite small and then flower and fruit throughout the year. Rao and Chin (1972) found an average of more than one thousand seeds per fruit from plants near Singapore. They harvested fresh seeds and planted them within 24 hr on moist paper, a thin layer of water or moist sand. All germinating vessels were held at 24 to 28°C in low light intensity. They obtained 65% germination in the first 10 to 15 days and 80% at 4 wk.

A prominent enlargement near the hilum gave the first visible evidence of embryo growth in the seed on the fifth day. The testa soon ruptured, a broad, blunt radical emerged, and root hairs began to form within 12 hr. At the end of the third week lateral roots developed.

Small seeds of this bushy shrub come up in great abundance in open country in India and Malaysia. The weed has an inconspicuous pink berry which dehisces to show a black viscous mess full of very small seeds. Birds relish the black pulp, swallow it in great quantities, and thus help to spread the propagules. The weed can germinate and grow in fields of the perennial grass *Imperata cylindrica* and displace the grass and eventually prepare the land for reforestation (Ridley 1930).

In west Malaysia, pineapple is grown exclusively on peat soils that are prepared by ditching (channeling) before the trees are cut, dried, and burned. Tree stumps and large logs litter the area and the cost of the subsequent weeding by hand or with herbicides, or a combination of the two methods, is often a major portion of the production cost. Wee (1970) and Lee and Enoch (1977) reported on the weed successions in such fields. Wee selected areas having three different ages and management histories. Area *A* had been in pineapple for 10 yr and weed records were taken from plots that had been unweeded for 6 and 24 mo. Area *B*, a 4-yr-old pineapple field, had been without weed control for 5 mo in one area and 24 mo in another. Area *C* was a newly cleared planting with weeds unattended for the 3 mo prior to first planting.

In the 10-yr-old planting, the woody *M. malabathricum* and two *Cyperus* species were early invaders and still dominant species in an area unweeded for 6 mo. *M. malabathricum* was three times more plentiful than any other weed. When the area was allowed to go unattended for 2 yr, *M. malabathricum* plants were still the most troublesome weeds and some were more than 3 m tall. This weed stand was equivalent to more than 27,500 plants/ha, while no other species numbered more than 125.

In the 4-yr-old pineapple field, unweeded for 5 mo, many herbaceous weeds were recorded, while *M. malabathricum* was 10-fold more plentiful than any other woody species.

The peat soils of these areas were often more than 3 m deep and very acidic, with a *pH* of 3.2 to 4.8. Sedges were among the dominant early invaders and if unattended they soon formed a complete soil canopy. In this shade the seedlings of *M. malabathricum* survived the very early periods of establishment and after that only complete removal, including roots, would eradicate it. The weeding practice of top-removal only served to cause formation of a copse of new shoots. In these experiments the plants began to flower and fruit when they were 2 m tall and 5 mo of age. The weed may grow to 3 m in 2 yr.

Corner (1952) feels that the preference of this species for poor and acidic soils contributes to the success of its establishment and spread. Its small seeds pass unharmed through the digestive tracts of birds. Its rapid growth and effective distribution of seeds by birds assures its dominance.

Nicholls (1973) studied weed successions on land cleared for pasture in Hawaii and found that *M. malabathricum* was one of the species that favored southern slopes with full exposure to the sun.

AGRICULTURAL IMPORTANCE

M. malabathricum is a serious weed of pastures in Hawaii, New Caledonia, and Sarawak; of pineapple in Sarawak in east Malaysia; and of crops on peat soils in west Malaysia. It is the number two weed in rubber in some parts of Malaysia and a serious weed of rubber in Indonesia. It is a principal weed of oil palm in Malaysia and elsewhere in Southeast Asia; of rubber and other plantation crops in Brunei and Sabah in east Malaysia; of rubber in Sri Lanka; and of tea in Thailand.

It is a common weed of coconut in Cambodia, Laos, the Philippines, and Vietnam; of sugar cane in Hawaii; and in the northern and southern tea-producing areas of India. It is a weed of cassava in Melanesia and of rice fields in India and Indonesia.

It is a weed of other unspecified crops in Mauritius, Taiwan, Solomon Islands, New Caledonia in Melanesia, Palau in the Caroline Islands (Micronesia), and Fiji in West Polynesia.

M. malabathricum has no forage value, but in grazing land it forms dense thickets and crowds out preferred species. It is common in the dry zones of Fiji, although presently it does not show signs of becoming a serious pest. It is a close relative of one of the serious weeds in the islands, *Clidemia hirta.*

Riepma (1964) pointed to the lack of good data on the depression of rubber yields by weed competition; it is known, however, that *M. malabathricum*, along with *Eupatorium*, *Ficus*, and *Mikania* species, causes considerable reduction in the girthing of the trees. Such inhibition of growth prolongs the time until first tapping and may ultimately reduce the return per acre.

In Malaysia, when preparing jungle lands, old rubber fields or land covered with *Imperata cylindrica* for new rubber plantings, often by burning or other means, the soil may remain bare for months unless a cover crop is established. If it is left bare, a mixed scrub vegetation of *M. malabathricum*, ferns, *Mikania*, and more *Imperata* will eventually come in and will aid in checking erosion in the early stages. When established, however, these plants then compete severely with the new rubber crop (Watson 1963).

COMMON NAMES

Melastoma malabathricum

FIJI	kaunisiga
HAWAII	melastome
INDIA	phutuka
INDONESIA	harendong, kloeroek, senggani
MALAYSIA	sendudok, Singapore rhododendron, straites rhododendron
PHILIPPINES	malatungau, tungao-tungao, yagomyum
THAILAND	kadu-du, khlong-khleng-khi-nok, mang kre
UNITED STATES	Banks melastoma

Fifty-Seven

Momordica charantia L.

Cucurbitaceae, Gourd Family

MOMORDICA CHARANTIA is in the gourd family, which has many species that are grown as crops. Fruits of this family are among the largest in the plant kingdom. *M. charantia* is native to the old world tropics but is now a weed in the tropical and subtropical regions in most of Latin America, all of Asia and parts of Africa. It was probably introduced from Africa into Brazil with the movement of slaves (Walters and Decker-Walters 1988). As with many of the approximately 700 species found in 90 genera of this family, plants are monoecious and form sprawling vines with tendrils. The *Momordica* genus contains about 40 species and its name is derived from the Latin *mordeo*

FIGURE 57-1   The distribution of *Momordica charantia* L. across the world where it has been reported as a weed.

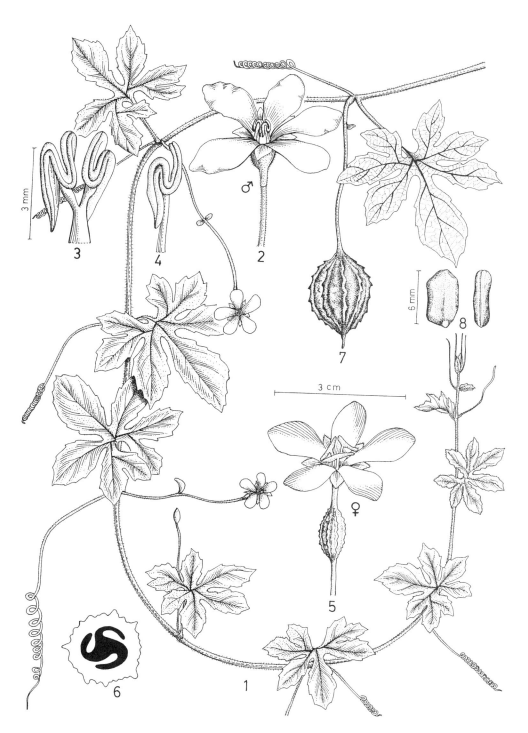

FIGURE 57-2 *Momordica charantia* L.: 1. flowering vine; 2. staminate flower; 3. stamens enlarged, 4. same detached; 5. pistillate flower; 6. fruit, cross section; 7. fruit; 8. seed, two views.

(to bite), in reference to the ridged surface and jagged margins of the seeds. The species name is from the Greek and means beautiful flower.

DESCRIPTION

M. charantia (Figure 57-2) is an *annual* creeping or climbing, herbaceous vine with a strong, foul odor; *root* a taproot; *stems* 2 to 3 m long, often forming a dense carpet over other plants, highly branched somewhat angled or furrowed with simple axillary *tendrils*; *leaves* alternate, petioled, 2.5 to 10 cm in diameter, cut nearly to the base into 5 or 7 oblong-ovate, variously lobed segments with heart-shaped base, margins notched; *flowers* axillary, long-peduncled with 5 pale to bright yellow petals 1 to 1.25 cm long and sepals 3 to 9 mm long; monoecious, *staminate flowers* with lobes 15 to 20 mm long, 8 to 13 mm wide, the peduncle subtended by an orbicular, green *bract* about 1 cm in length in the middle; *pistillate flowers* on shorter peduncle than male flowers, with *bract* at base of peduncle; *stigma* deeply 2-lobed or one entire style, *ovary* long-beaked; *fruit* an orange to orange-yellow, pendulous, egg-shaped berry covered with small warts, 2 to 7 cm long in wild forms, to 30 cm in cultivated forms; 8 to 10 longitudinal ridges marked with prominent triangular tubercles, dehiscing from the apex downward in 3 irregular valves to reveal 15 to 20 scalloped, variegated seeds; *seeds* light brown to black, embedded in sticky, moist, crimson pulp (*aril*), 5 to 9 mm long, 2.5 to 6 mm wide with ridged or pitted surface and thick ragged margin as though carved.

The distinguishing characteristics of this species are the climbing habit, foul odor, stems with tendrils, imperfect flowers, and the orange, ribbed fruit with seeds surrounded by a bright red pulp.

HABITAT AND BIOLOGY

M. charantia grows from sea level to nearly 1000 m. It grows where annual precipitation is as low as 480 mm to as much as 4100 mm, where mean temperatures are as low as 12.5°C to as high as 25°C, and in soil with *pH*s from 4.3 to 8.7 (Duke 1979). It is especially common in Latin America and Asia (Figure 57-1). Plants grow rapidly and quickly cover the supporting vegetation or structures. The tendril tips curl around the nearest object. The rest of the tendril then coils like a spring, pulling the stem to the support object (Heywood 1978).

M. charantia leaves have a wide array of trichomes: from wart-like to filiform types, with or without a conical hook at the apex, and some with glands at the base (Inamdar and Gangadhara 1975). The species has the C_3 pathway (Prieto and Leon 1975) and its $2n$ chromosome count is 22.

Flowering can begin 30 to 35 days after planting and fruits mature 15 to 20 days later (Purseglove 1968). Male flowers are larger and develop sooner than female flowers (Deshpande et al. 1979). Flowers open between 3:30 and 4:30 A.M., and anthesis starts between 4:00 and 7:00 A.M. and is complete by 6:00 to 10:00 A.M.. Ghosh and Basu (1983) noted that a higher proportion of female flowers are produced in short days (8 to 9 hr of light) than in long days. Treating plants with IAA or GA₃ also enhances female flower production. Plants often flower over several months and flowers and fruits are commonly seen year round in tropical areas.

The bright red aril which surrounds the seed may attract birds and mammals which then eat and disperse the seeds (Ridley 1930). The aril is moist and sweet, while the orange wall of the fruit is bitter. This is an unusual adaptation among the cucurbits because the fruits of many species are edible. Seeds kept in dry storage maintained 70 to 80% germination for 6 mo, 60 to 70% for 8 to 12 mo, and 20 to 30% for 24 mo (Doll et al. 1976). No further information about seed biology was found, which is surprising, because the plant propagates only by seed and is frequently grown as a crop.

UTILIZATION

The most widespread use of *M. charantia* is as a vegetable and occasionally as an ornamental. Leaves or fruit are eaten in several Asian and Latin American countries. Because the fruit is bitter unless very ripe, it is often blanched or steeped in salt water before it is eaten. Rodriguez et al. (1975) recorded a 100-fold increase in the carotenoid content of the seeds and pulp as they passed from the green to mature stage. The bright crimson color of the pulp is due to the very high proportion (96%) of the carotenoid lycopene, which is red. The fruit, young shoots and flowers are used as flavoring, the leaves as greens and the pulpy arils as sweets. The bitter substance is momordicine and the fruit is rich in iron, phosphorous and ascorbic acid (Walters and Decker-Walters 1988).

Numerous medicinal uses of *M. charantia* have been recorded. In China, seeds are used to treat halitosis and as an aphrodisiac (Duke and Ayensu 1985). It is considered an abortifacient in the Americas and the fruit is used as a soap substitute in Colombia and Cuba (Morton 1967). Brazilians use it as an antihelminthic, a purgative, to reduce pain during difficult menstrual periods, and to treat hemorrhoids and colics caused by parasites (Lorenzi 1982). In Sri Lanka, skin rashes are treated with leaf extracts and the fruit is considered a tonic to cure rheumatism, gout and liver diseases (Chandrasena 1936).

An intriguing aspect of medicinal uses is the potential of *M. charantia* to treat certain cancerous tumors. The lectin proteins found in this plant can induce selective killing of tumor cells (Lewis and Lewis 1977). Leukemic cells were selectively killed by seed extracts within 2 hr after treatment, whereas normal human lymphocyte cells were unaffected (Takemoto et al. 1982).

Another important use of *M. charantia* is as a hypoglycemic agent to treat diabetes (Khanna et al. 1981). Seeds and fruits are used for this purpose in India and the Chinese have developed pills from dried fruits. Eighteen grams per day are administered to treat diabetes mellitus (Duke and Ayensu 1985). The plant does not induce insulin secretion but seems to speed carbohydrate utilization by affecting cell membrane lipids (Welihinda et al. 1982).

M. charantia is found in pastures in several countries. Nuwanyakpa et al. (1983) analyzed the forage value of several pasture weeds in Ecuador during the dry season when they would possibly be consumed. *M. charantia* had the highest crude protein (18.1%) of the seven species tested, but was the lowest in digestible dry matter. It contained 6265 ppm of nitrate and was also relatively high in Ca, P, and K. However, cattle seemed to avoid eating this weed, probably due to its offensive odor.

AGRICULTURAL IMPORTANCE

M. charantia is a weed in 22 crops in over 50 countries (Figure 57-1) and is frequently reported in sugarcane and other plantation crops. It is a principal weed of bananas in Surinam; cacao in Ecuador; citrus in the southern United States; cotton, soybeans, and sugarcane in Bolivia; maize and pasture in Colombia; oil palm in Indonesia; sesame in Venezuela; and taro in Samoa Islands.

It is a common weed of bananas and maize in Costa Rica; edible beans in Cuba and Mexico; cacao in Dominican Republic; coconuts in Trinidad; coffee in Brazil and Dominican Republic; cotton, peanuts, and sorghum in Sudan; pastures in Brazil; pineapple in Hawaii; rice in Guatemala and Mexico; and sugarcane in British Guiana, Hawaii, Jamaica, Nicaragua, and Trinidad.

M. charantia is also a weed of unknown rank of bananas in Honduras, Jamaica, and Mexico; edible beans in Brazil and Colombia; cassava in Ghana and Nicaragua; citrus in Surinam; cacao in Brazil, Honduras, New Guinea, and Nigeria; coffee in Honduras, Mexico, and Nigeria; cotton in Colombia and Honduras; maize in Colombia, Ghana, India, and Mexico; pastures in New Guinea; pineapple in Honduras; rice in Colombia, Costa Rica, Honduras, Mexico, and Nigeria; sorghum in Mexico; soybeans in Colombia; and sugarcane in Australia, Brazil, Colombia, Dominican Republic, and Honduras.

In Florida (southern United States) it grows to the top of citrus trees and seriously shades the trees in late summer and fall. It also spreads into vegetable fields in this area and is of added concern because it hosts viruses and leafhoppers of celery, papaya and watermelon. Similarly, it can host *Cercospora* and *Fusarium* diseases and is attacked by the rootknot nematode (*Meloidogyne* spp.) in the United States and the Philippines. Its high susceptibility to nematodes may provide a natural means to slow its spread in the southeastern United States (Bistline and Rhoades 1984).

COMMON NAMES

Momordica charantia

ANGOLA	mimbuzu
AUSTRALIA	balsam pear
BANGLADESH	korolla
BARBADOS	carilla, cerassea, miraculous bush
BOLIVIA	balsamina
BRAZIL	erva de lavaderia, melao de Sao Tana, melaozinho
BRITISH GUIANA	coryla vine
CAMBODIA	moreas
CHINA	ku gua
COLOMBIA	archucha, balsamina
COSTA RICA	sorosi
CUBA	cundeamor
DOMINICAN REPUBLIC	cundeamor, sorosi
ECUADOR	achochilla
EL SALVADOR	balsamito, balsamo
FIJI	balsam pear, bitter gourd, kerla
GHANA	kakle, nya nya, nyinya

GUATEMALA	paroka, sorosi
HAWAII	balsam apple, peria
HONDURAS	calaica
INDIA	kakara, karela, kuraila, pagel, pava kai, sushavi
INDONESIA	pare, paria, peria
JAMAICA	cerasea
LIBERIA	ga ge su lu
MADAGASCAR	morogozy
MALAYSIA	kyet-hin-ga, peria, peria laut
MALI	lumba-lumba, manamat
MAURITIUS	margose
MEXICO	cunde amor, cunde amor grande, pepino
NIGERIA	akban ndene, daddagu, ejirin, garafuni, lele duji
PANAMA	balsamino
PARAGUAY	andi mi, calabacita
PERU	balsamina, papayilla
PHILIPPINES	ampalaya, ampalia, palia, paria
PUERTO RICO	cundeamor
SENEGAL	barbouf, beurhoh, liane merveille, zara
SRI LANKA	pahal-kai
SUDAN	abu eloffein
SURINAM	wilde sopropo
THAILAND	mara pah
TRINIDAD	carilla, cerasee bush
UNITED STATES	balsam apple
VENEZUELA	cundeamor, maravilla
VIETNAM	muop dang hoan, muop dong

Fifty-Eight

Myriophyllum spicatum L.

Haloragidaceae, Watermilfoil Family

IN RECENT DECADES, *Myriophyllum spicatum*, an aggressive invader, has become one of the dreaded, submersed, halophyte weeds of the Northern Hemisphere and around the world. There is no suitable classification of the genus and this results in much confusion in field identification and with field research. There are about 40 species in the genus and they all tend to stay "at home," with the exception that *M. verticillatum* and *M. spicatum* have become widespread in the world. The latter is reported as a weed problem in more than 50 countries, while the former is troublesome only occasionally. Long-distance

FIGURE 58-1 The distribution of *Myriophyllum spicatum* L. across the world where it has been reported as a weed.

FIGURE 58-2   *Myriophyllum spicatum* L.: A. habit; B. whorl of leaves; C. part of flower spike, with pistillate flowers below and staminate flowers above; D. immature fruits; E. mature fruit.

dispersal is believed to be due to the aquarium and aquatic nursery commercial trade and the migration of birds. Within a region, fragments are moved about by the flow of water and recreational vehicular traffic.

DESCRIPTION

M. spicatum (Figure 58-2) is a *perennial* or *biennial*, submersed, aquatic herb; *stems* flexible, sparsely or much branched, slender, becoming leafless toward base, 1 to 4 m length, with extreme of 12 m reported from western Himalayas in Asia; *adventitious roots* on lower side of stem when on or in mud with additional at the upper surface prior to fragmentation; *leaves* dimorphic, grayish-green, in whorls of 4 to 5, usually with 14 to 24 pairs of filiform obtuse segments, 6 to 12 mm in length, extending outward from axis to give a feather-like appearance; *bracts* inconspicuous, shorter than stem internodes; *inflorescence* borne on terminal spike of main stem and branches, 5 to 20 cm long, usually pink, below the spike are 5 to 20 nodes with diameter twice that of remainder of stem, rigid, lying parallel to water surface, spike erect at anthesis, parallel to water surface at fruit set; *flowers, staminate flowers* on upper axils; *pistillate flowers* below, often with *bisexual flowers* in the transition zone, flowers verticillate in whorls of 4, 2-ranked, lower 2 to 4 whorls of *floral bracts* usually comb-like, often longer than flowers, upper bracts entire, broader than long and shorter than flowers; staminate flower *sepals* ovate to triangular, 0.5 by 0.3 mm, erect, *petals* wine red, auriculate, 2.5 mm long, falling at anthesis, *stamens* 8; pistillate flower *sepals* strongly reduced, semiorbicular, erect, 0.2 to 0.3 mm, *petals* spreading, 0.5 to 0.3 mm, falling soon after anthesis; bisexual flower *sepals* and *petals* as in pistillate flowers, *petals* reddish; *fruit* muricate (a rough surface with sharp projections), globoseovoid, about 2.5 mm long, 4-grooved with 2 somewhat wrinkled ridges adjacent to lines of dehiscence, separating into 4 nut-like fruits.

For more detailed information on *M. spicatum* and similar plants, see Patten (1954), Love (1961), Aiken et al. (1979), Aiken and McNeill (1980), and Cook (1985).

DISTRIBUTION, HABITAT, AND PLANT DISPERSAL

M. spicatum is reported as a weed almost exclusively in the Northern Hemisphere, where it sweeps westward in a band from Japan through heavily populated regions of Asia, then northward through North Africa to all of Europe, to include the western part of the former Soviet Union. It is present over much of Canada and the United States. It is troublesome in Indonesia and the south of Africa (Figure 58-1).

Paleobotanical studies have shown that *M. spicatum* has been a long-time resident of Europe. Fossil remains 8000 years old were found in bottom clays of Finnish lakes. It was present in Britain about the same time (van der Knaap 1985).

M. spicatum is found near the Arctic Circle north of Moscow, and above lat 70° N in Alaska and Canada (Holmquist 1971). From paleobotanical studies, van der Knaap (1985) reported that the plant was formerly present near lat 80° N. in Spitzbergen north of Norway. Milfoil was reported in North America by Linnaeus in 1814 and was introduced again through ballast dumped from ships in the eastern United States in the late 19th century. The weed, however, did not attract attention until the 1960s, when it began to spread rapidly in North America. In a recent survey, Couch and Nelson (1985) found 400 populations of *M. spicatum* in three Canadian provinces and 33 states of the United States.

Mitchell and Orr (1985) recently reported that *M. spicatum* is not a serious problem in Australia.

Northeast of New Delhi, India, in the foothills of the Himalayas, *M. spicatum* was found at 2000 m (S. Singh 1981) and at about the same elevations in the former Yugoslavia and Canada (Aiken et al. 1979). In most research papers, watermilfoil is found rooting and anchored at a depth of 2 to 4 m, but S. Singh (1981) in India and Pip and Simmons (1986) in Canada found it at 12 m or more. As it approaches the surface, the plant branches profusely, spreading horizontally to form large masses called "milfoil meadows" that may be several kilometers in size. Some masses are several decimeters in thickness. The spread is influenced by water movement and chemistry, substrate, and by snow cover in winter periods. In Canada, it was noticed that milfoil grows poorly in shallow water (less than 1 m depth) because of wave action, large temperature fluctuations, variations in water levels, and high light intensity (British Columbia Ministry of Environment 1981). Kimbel (1982) reported that colonization, in terms of growth and mortality, is best in late summer, shallow water being preferable, and it is favored by the plentiful nutrients and optimum light and temperature of the period. Colonization is poorest in early autumn.

Except for brief periods during sexual reproduction, milfoil remains beneath the water surface, but in India and elsewhere it can become almost a terrestrial plant, surviving during dry months in subswampy areas and in nearly dry habitats (Sharma 1978b).

Growth of this weed in fresh to brackish waters has been reported from Canada, Corsica, the Scandinavian countries, and the United States. There is general agreement that it will tolerate 10 to 15 ppm of salt or about one-third the concentration of sea water (Luther 1951, Steeman-Nielsen 1954, Anderson et al. 1965, Hinneri 1976, Aiken et al. 1979, Marshal 1984).

M. spicatum prefers to grow in eutrophic lakes and in streams that receive high levels of nutrients. Its presence is often correlated with a substrate of medium grains or particles and of soft mud, but its habitats across the world include a variety of substrates. In the former Yugoslavia, it grows on bottoms of alluvial sand deposits, thick peat, mud deposits and black marsh soils. Spence (1964) studied growth in lakes where sediments graded from rocks to coarse sand at the shore to sandy mud at a 120 cm water depth. As sediments improved and wave action lessened with distance from shore, shoot height and total plant cover increased. Barko and Smart (1985, 1986) reported less growth on sediments with a high concentration of organic matter. They believe that the response to sediment texture and organic matter may be largely related to mineral nutrient availability.

The plant will tolerate some water turbidity as well as a coating of silt or epiphytes. It survives in areas of considerable water level fluctuation and where waves reach a height of 1 m. A study of many English rivers found the plant partial to wide streams with water of medium depth. The roots can descend to 15 cm in the substrate. The roots and rhizomes may grow quickly in and over soft substrates, but in such areas there are large plant losses during storms. Plants that are much-branched near the surface offer much resistance to water flow. The plant can survive intermittent spates but suffers tearing and dislodging during continued fast flows. In experimental studies, milfoil growing in a substrate of medium texture was dislodged by pulling on shoots with a force of 250 to 750 g (considered a moderate tension) (Haslam 1978).

Aiken et al. (1979) of Canada reported that *M. spicatum* plants grew very well on sand or acid peat in highly alkaline waters of *pH* 9 to 11. Anderson et al. (1965) in the eastern United States collected plants growing in waters with temperatures of 0.2 to 30°C and *pH*s 5.8 to 9.5. Butcher (1933) in England found that the preference of *M. spicatum* with regard to water hardness ($CaCO_3$ content) was for non-calcareous to moderately calcareous conditions with alkaline *pH*s.

In several places in the world, entire plants of watermilfoil can survive the winter in cool waters and thus be prepared for spring growth much earlier than most aquatic macrophytes. The species can drive out most submerged aquatic weeds 2 or 3 yr after becoming established in a new area. Aiken et al. (1979) believe that only *Hydrilla verticillata* can compete favorably with milfoil.

Haslam (1978) in England studied the effect of storms on *M. spicatum* growing in a medium-sized stream with a substrate of mixed particles somewhat consolidated and covered by a silt layer. A storm causing 2.5 times the normal flow rate tore out some milfoil plants, but at 4 times the normal flow, one-half the plants were torn out, many small plants disappeared and shoots 2 m in length lost one-half their length. Chabreck and Palmisano (1973) studied species composition and plant coverage, including *M. spicatum*, in many areas of the active delta of the Mississippi River 1 yr before and 2 wk after a destructive hurricane with winds exceeding 200 km/hr and tides to 5.2 m. The force of wind and water uprooted, tore apart and washed away so much vegetation that there was no significant recovery after 1 yr. The salinity of the fresh water areas increased significantly after the storm but declined within a year and probably had minimal effect on plant life.

The vegetative propagules are the principal means of dispersal of this species. In 25 yr of recorded observation and samplings in the littoral zones in the TVA (Tennessee Valley Authority) area, a flood control scheme covering several states in the central United States, no seedlings were ever detected in natural sites. Seeds gathered from plants or substrates germinated readily when taken into laboratories (Patten 1956, Davis et al. 1974, Aiken et al. 1979, Coble and Vance 1987, Madsen and Boylen 1989).

Patten (1956) believes the dispersal of *M. spicatum* propagules is largely caused by wind and water movement. Fragments that adhere to the feet of birds, aided by a sticky glucoside layer on some terminal leaves, may account for long-distance dispersal. Fragments and small buds that adhere to the feet and feathers of birds may move propagules to the north during migrations in the Northern Hemisphere, just as seeds may be carried south in autumn. Couch and Nelson (1985) believe that vendors who sell worms (for fish bait) and use *M. spicatum* for fresh packing material may be important distributors of the weed locally.

Mature fruits (with seeds) normally separate and fall from the spike, but sometimes, as decay takes place, the spikes may float on the surface for a time, and thus spread the propagules during water movement. The achenes normally sink upon release, but those adhering to fruits, some of which may also float freely for a time, may travel to distant places.

Sprouts on rhizomes are an additional means of spread in the vicinity of the plants.

The spread of this plant can be phenomenal. In 1965, in the eastern United States 40 ha were seriously infested and 200 to 400 ha were in a phase of early establishment. One year later the figures were 3000 and 26,800 ha, respectively (Nichols 1975, Nichols and Mori 1971).

On the west coast of Finland (Gulf of Bothnia), above lat 64° N, two nuclear power plants are discharging warm water (used for cooling reactors). The coastal waters are normally ice-covered for 3 to 5 mo and *Myriophyllum* and a few other species may survive (at times with green above-water stems and leaves) in the large areas of open water. These plants quickly regenerate and enhance the spread of weed stands very early in the spring (Keskitalo and Heitto 1987, Keskitalo and Ilus 1987).

VEGETATIVE AND SEXUAL REPRODUCTION

Complete plants may continue to photosynthesize and grow all winter in some areas, exhibiting a luxurious growth toward spring that gives them a competitive advantage. Aiken et al. (1979) believe that such winter survival is dependent on water temperatures of 10°C or above. Elsewhere the plants die back to propagating root crowns that bear adventitious shoot buds that elongate quickly in spring. In the central United States, some growth may be detected in January, but the growth of new reddish meristems and leaves is usually seen in early March (Bates et al. 1985). The longevity of the root crowns is unknown, with the result that we cannot be sure whether populations are biennial or perennial. Overwintering crowns store non-structural carbohydrates to the extent of 20 to 25% of their dry weight (Titus 1977).

Peak periods of autofragmentation in the central United States occur in spring and again in autumn after flowering has ceased. Whether formed by abscission, cutting, or tearing, the leafy stem pieces quickly begin to produce adventitious roots and new buds and leaves. Roots can form before fragments are released from the parent plant and while stems are floating free. Zutshi and Vass (1976) reported the formation of adventitious roots on cut ends of fragments in less than 24 hr. In the laboratory, shoots doubled in length in 2 to 3 wk.

After floating for a time, the fragments sink, the roots quickly penetrate most substrates, and they may grow into cracks in rocks. As cool weather approaches in late autumn, the plant begins to branch extensively and to form adventitious rootlets. Now another type of vegetative propagule appears in the form of an unusual, axillary, small, easily detached, vegetative bud. Such buds overwinter and are released in late winter and spring.

In the eastern United States, Patten (1956) denuded a quadrat area 1 x 4 m², including a 1 m border. After 20, 38, and 52 days, 15, 58, and 80 individuals were recorded in the test area, respectively. In April of the following year, the denuded site was indistinguishable from the rest of the area and no other species had appeared.

The small, late-forming vegetative axillary buds are called turions by some workers, but Patten (1956) believes them to be intermediate between the turionate and aturionate conditions in the genus. Turions usually form on terminals and are larger because of stored reserves. Upon separation, the small buds of milfoil quickly produce new plants and are responsible for much revegetation of spring growth. The abscission of these buds and stems of *M. spicatum* in all seasons takes place in ill-defined separation zones of partially lignified cells.

Sexual reproduction is far less important in the propagation process and in the colonization of new areas (Patten 1956, Davis et al. 1974). However, experience with other species has taught us not to be premature in our decision that because we have *not yet seen them* nature does not permit seedling survival in this species. It is entirely possible that we shall yet learn of seedlings produced in areas not yet studied.

In the central United States, a few flowers may be seen in May, but peak flowering is usually at the end of July or early August. In the former Yugoslavia, the peak is one month earlier. Flowering continues for 2 or 3 mo and in September and October the fruiting spikes are seen just below the water surface. There are reports from several regions of the world that the time of anthesis may be quite different in adjacent water bodies having similar habitats.

The inflorescence is aerial. It is a terminal, naked, interrupted spike. A plant may have several flowering stems, each with several lateral flowering branches. Plants may have all bisexual, all male, or all female flowers, or they may be polygamous, with bisexual and uni-sexual flowers. They are, however, usually functionally monoecious, with staminate flow-ers on the upper stem and pistillate flowers below. The flowers on the main stems bloom before the laterals. The first evidences of flowering in ponds and lakes are the small, com-pressed spikes near the water surface. Each of these structures is partially covered by the last leaves of the vegetative terminal. When in bud, these leaves are covered with trichomes that secrete a protective glucosidic slime. A *pH*-sensitive anthocyanidin contained in the slime becomes bright red in acidic conditions and may indicate the acidity of local sites on a water body.

The usual sequence is an elongation of the spike, an upward turning to raise the spike above the surface, pollination, and then submergence. As this happens the internodes become longer below the spike, the spike axis thickens, becomes more succulent, and all this assists in the floatation of the flowering structures. The flowers on the upper stem por-tion tend to be staminate with pistillate below, the latter maturing first. One strong and two more delicate bracts enclose and protect the young flowers, opening gradually as the spike elongates and the fruits mature.

Data are lacking, but most workers speculate that a significant portion of the pollina-tion is by wind; there is some pollination by insects (Patten 1956). In watermilfoil beds in the eastern Transvaal of South Africa, Guillarmod (1979) reported that workers observed sudden puffs of pollen rising to 2 m above ripe anthers in late afternoon on sunny days. Spikes that are held temporarily below the water by turbulence or other conditions may not set seed. Cross-pollination is favored by the ripening of the stigmas as the spikes emerge, with stamens maturing later. A small amount of crossing may occur if the late-maturing pollen is released by main stems as lateral stem flowers, emerging later, present receptive stigmas. It must be remembered that usually many plants are packed together in a dense weedbed and a mixing of pollen is assured because of the variety of flower sequences.

After pollination, the staminate structures decline, some abscise, and the pistillate portions move below the surface, where the leaves assist in buoying them up. Now that it is autumn, some stems and leaves are sloughed off, the spike decreases in thickness, and as it begins to disintegrate some of the fruits remain attached for a time. Finally the rotting spike releases the achenes passively. Some achenes may remain on the plant until late and must pass the winter encased in ice. The spikes carry three to ten whorls of pistillate flow-ers and on satisfactory sites may produce 10 to 40 seeds per spike. The watermilfoil seeds are indehiscent and the endocarp is made up of stony, lignified, sometimes mineralized cells. The micropyle is sealed with a plug formed of integument tissue and this must be dis-lodged before germination can proceed (Sculthorpe 1967, Aiken et al. 1979). The primary root is very delicate and favorable conditions are required for the survival of the seedling.

Guppy (1894–1897) in England and Bates et al. (1985) in the central United States obtained immediate germination of most of freshly harvested seeds. The remainder of the seed germinated in the second season. Patten (1955) in the eastern United States found very low germination following harvest. Higher germination was obtained with combina-tion treatments of freezing in tap water and drying. Seeds kept in storage 1 yr improved in germination. Davis et al. (1973) obtained 30% germination of seeds kept in dry storage for 7 yr. Patten believes that seed will not germinate below 10°C, thus in nature low water tem-peratures and occasional freezes will subdue germination. Meanwhile, after-ripening goes on to enable the plant to germinate promptly in spring. The pericarp is believed to contain an inhibitor causing germination delay and seed treatments help to remove this inhibition. In water the seeds will germinate in dark and light (Patten 1955).

More recently, Coble and Vance (1987) reported no dark germination. Germination was also inhibited in blue light (445 nm), while 97% was obtained in red light (725 nm). Light measurements showed a loss of 50 to 60% at the longer wavelengths at about 0.5 m. At this longer wavelength there was a significant decrease in germination. The inhibition was partially overcome by increasing the light intensity.

For seeds found to be dormant, the following treatments have been reported to enhance germination: freezing in ice water for 2 wk, partial removal of the endocarp (inner fruit wall), drying for 1 yr, scarification, exposure to high H^- ion concentrations, and prolonged exposure to low temperature (Guppy 1894, Patten 1955, Aiken et al. 1979).

PHYSIOLOGY AND MORPHOLOGY

Smith and Barko (1990), in a review of the ecological research published in the 1980s, prepared a summary of the factors influencing growth and morphology of watermilfoil, including parameters of water clarity (light), temperature, carbon sources, nutrients, sediment texture, water movements, cold, and desiccation. From this background, they suggest that milfoil does not appear to achieve greater biomass production than similar submersed weeds; nor does its initial entry into a water body necessarily portend a great explosion of biomass productivity. Its photosynthetic capabilities are not extraordinary. Nevertheless, it remains one of the most vigorous and aggressive of the submersed weed species. The morphology and habit of growth that enable development in water bodies with wide ranges of water clarity, the natural inclination to grow to the surface and form a canopy of horizontal stems early in the season to shade out competitors, and the ease with which it can adapt to changes in water level, depth, and turbidity are all characteristics that favor productivity in crowded places.

M. spicatum is one of the most dynamic competitors of all submerged macrophyte weeds. Smith (1971) reported from the central United States that repeated propagation of one stem fragment could give rise to 250 million watermilfoil plants in a eutrophic freshwater lake. Nichols and Mori (1971) found 253 stems/m^2, with a dry weight of 385 g. At peak season such plants could produce 56 kg of dry wt/ha/day. To try to understand its dominance of the waters it occupies in so many places in the world, researchers have concentrated on physiological studies of the conditions necessary for maximum photosynthesis, the source of required nutrients, and the reproductive systems (discussed below).

Grace and Wetzel (1978) made an extensive review of studies on the production biomass ratio as affected by seasonal growth of milfoil, depth of water, canopy formation as the plant begins to branch profusely when nearing the surface, and sloughing of plant parts beneath the dense vegetative canopy.

When compared with terrestrial plants, submersed aquatic weeds, including watermilfoil, have very low rates of net photosynthesis. Their success seems to result more from the habit of elongating quickly to form a canopy to cover the water surface than from the production of massive quantities of biomass, and this puts bioproductivity in a new light.

Terrestrial plants may be designated C_3 or C_4 plants on the basis of the characteristics of their photosynthetic pathways. From the studies of submerged plants thus far, it seems doubtful that true C_4 plants will frequent aquatic environments. The production and later metabolism of glycolate to CO_2 is characteristic of several C_3 plants. Glycolate is produced in milfoil, although at lower rates than in most C_3 plants, but at higher levels than in most C_4 plants. An anatomical arrangement of large, starch-storing chloroplasts in the bundle sheaths, called "Krantz" anatomy, is found in many C_4 plants and is present in an altered form in *M. spicatum*. In spite of such similarities (together with the absence of rapidly formed C_4 acids), as well as the low levels of phosphoenolpyruvate carboxylase, it seems unlikely that this photosynthetic pathway (C_4) is important to this plant (Stanley and Naylor 1972, Adams et al. 1974, Grace and Wetzel 1978).

Golubic (1963) established that *M. spicatum* does not occur in the clear-water lakes of the former Yugoslavia at depths receiving less than one-fourth of the photosynthetically active radiation (400 to 700 nm) incident on the lake surface. Steeman-Nielsen (1947) and Van et al. (1976) found that free CO_2 is the preferred source of carbon for the plant. At high *p*Hs, however HCO_3^- ions may be the important source of C for photosynthesis.

Both dark respiration and photorespiration operate in *M. spicatum*. Photorespiration appears to be of lesser magnitude than the level found in terrestrial C_3 plants or many other submersed aquatic angiosperms (see also Salvucci and Bowes 1983).

In a saline solution with a concentration one-third that of sea water, the photosynthetic rate of watermilfoil was reduced by 35% within 20 hr. There was no effect on respiration. Both photosynthesis and respiration were severely reduced in plants held for 10 days in salinities one-sixth that of sea water (Davis 1972).

Adams and McCracken (1974), Nichols and Mori (1971), Titus et al. (1975), and Howard-Williams and Davies (1978) studied the details of biomass production in different environments and point out that milfoil gives the impression of being very productive during the peak of vegetative growth because of the very dense masses of stems and foliage just below the water surface.

Stanley and Naylor (1972) found maximum photosynthesis at 30 to 35°C, with the process continuing at 10°C. Growth of the plant increases in a water temperature up to 32°C.

Barko and Smart (1982) studied the performance of milfoil at six light ranges from 5 to 75% of full sun and five water temperatures from 16 to 32°C. Low light and high temperatures promoted shoot extension and the growth of the associated canopy. High temperature stimulated growth and shortened the growth cycle. The CO_2 compensation point decreased with increased temperature. The plant exhibited metabolic acclimatization to light but not temperature over broad ranges. Biomass production and C metabolism were influenced more by temperature than by light.

In experiments on the tolerance to cold, greenhouse grown plants were exposed to winter cold outdoors or subfreezing temperatures in incubators for varying periods of time. All plants were then returned to the greenhouse for 60 days before biomass measurements were recorded. The results indicate that the subsequent growth was related to the total cold received within each treatment (Stanley 1976).

When fully developed, with its deep, dense canopy covering large areas of water, this plant can greatly alter the ecology of all life below the surface. Dale and Gillespie (1977) found that it was one of the submersed macrophytes that could alter temperature profiles in shallow lakes by as much as 10°C.

Research on the uptake of P and N in lab and field by submersed plants such as *M. spicatum* is performed on many substrates, in many kinds of water, and with quite variable light and temperature conditions. Phosphorous seems easily available by root uptake from sediments, but the species can also extract the mineral from the ambient water (Carignan and Kalff 1980, Chambers et al. 1989). The uptake of N is less well studied. Nichols and Keeney (1976) have shown that N can be absorbed as NH_3 and NO_3 from the surrounding water or as NH_3 from the sediment. They believe that milfoil prefers NH_3.

Mantai and Newton (1982) grew watermilfoil in decreasing concentrations of N and P in a nutrient medium, causing tissue levels of these elements to decrease, although not to a level of shortage. The lower N and P tissue levels resulted in a dramatic increase in root growth.

Enrichment of a natural weed bed of milfoil with N caused an increase in plant length and number of shoots and thus a greater biomass. There was no response to P and K (Anderson and Kalff 1986).

Loczy et al. (1983) in Canada measured C uptake under a range of *pH* and dissolved inorganic carbon levels. After 4 to 8 wk in sediments containing labelled C^{14} as $NaHCO_3$, less than 1.5% of the total carbon in the watermilfoil shoots came from root uptake. The authors suggest that root uptake varied with the extent of root development and that C uptake from sediment is restricted to small, rosette-shaped plants growing in poorly mineralized soil.

Ryan et al. (1972) added N, P, and K fertilizer to experimental plots and examined the inorganic mineral content of the water and sediments with time. The concentrations of NO_3, NH_3, P, and K in the water rose sharply to 7 days after treatment and then declined rapidly. At the end of the second year, the top 1.3 cm of the sediment layer showed an increase in cation exchange capacity, organic matter, total N and available P in all treatments. The underlying sediment layer was unchanged. Plant growth was best in the control plots because the fertilizer caused dense algal growth. Barko and Smart (1986) studied the role of Na, K, Ca, and Mg in watermilfoil and suggest that these cations will normally not be limiting unless there is low inorganic carbon availability.

In Lake Balaton in Hungary, it was found that 10 microelements (some of them present because of pollution) could be accumulated by *M. spicatum* at 10 to 100 times the concentrations found in the external water or the sediments (Kovacs et al. 1984). Anderson et al. (1966) have supplied additional information on the regulation of ion uptake by working with plants in fresh and brackish waters. Growing in fresh water with 10 to 20 ppm of Ca, K, Na, and Mg, watermilfoil contained 350, 2700, 1200, and 50 ppm (fresh wt) of these elements, respectively. When in brackish water containing Ca, K, Na, and Mg at 150, 125, 2700, and 40 ppm, respectively, the milfoil contained 2500, 1600, 2100, and 140 ppm, respectively.

Overall, *M. spicatum* seems to be at home from midway in the range of nutrient-rich sediments and water to those aquatic areas that are more impoverished. The large surface area of the stems and leaves in the great beds of milfoil enables the uptake of significant quantities of nutrients in fertile waters. These are also conditions that provide optimal growth of phytoplankton, with the resultant loss of water clarity for the great meadows of *Myriophyllum* (Spence 1964, Waisel and Shapiro 1971, DeMint and Frank 1974, Best and Mantai 1978, Bole and Allan 1978).

Carpenter (1980) reported that one-half of the continued movement of dissolved total P and dissolved organic matter from the littoral to the pelagic zone was accounted for by *M. spicatum* in a hard-water lake in the north-central United States. Decay of plants provided a major source of biologically available dissolved total P and organic matter for the pelagic community of the lake. The release of these materials from *M. spicatum* was quite continuous through summer and autumn (see also Peverly and Brittain 1978). In the same area, Prentki et al. (1979) studied sedimentation rates in the pelagic zone and in a watermilfoil weedbed. In the weedbed, it was calculated that, over a 20-yr period, 1.4 g of P would be lost /m²/year at the rooting depth. This rate of loss seemed to be about 70% more than the reserves available from sedimentation in the area. The authors suggest that the major source of P in the water column in summer was not from external loading but from uptake of P from sediments, incorporation into tissues, and release during senescence and death of older plants.

Several decades ago, Lohammar (1938) of Sweden made an exhaustive study of the chemical ecology of the lakes and seas of his country. More recently, Hutchinson (1970) examined these data to study the performance of three species of *Myriophyllum* that are known to be present in waters of different ranges of chemical composition. *M. spicatum* and *M. verticillatum* can occupy waters with higher calcium content than *M. alterniflorum*. *M. spicatum* behaves as a calciphile in most of Europe, but Spence (1967) found it in both calcareous and noncalcareous waters of high *pH* and suspected that this distribution is related to its capacity to use bicarbonate in photosynthesis. *M. spicatum* can also do well at low *pH*s, but Hutchinson suspects that other physiological properties may enable this. *M. verticillatum*, which does not use bicarbonate as a source of C, is often found at lower *pH*s than those preferred by *M. spicatum*. In some circumstances, when *pH* and calcium were quite low, and where *M. verticillatum* was absent, *M. spicatum* was able to occupy soft-water niches where the former species would normally be found.

Bastardo (1979) gathered plants of *M. spicatum* and six other species of submerged macrophytes from Polish lakes and immediately submerged them in envelopes for decomposition studies during a 32-day period. During the first 4 days the plants lost, by leaching, 85 to 95% of the initial amount of Ca, Mg, K, Na, and total N and P. Watermilfoil showed the greatest weight loss. The *pH*, O_2 content and electrolytic conductivity of the surrounding water were significantly changed during the experiments. Carpenter and Adams (1979) found that N enrichment significantly increased the decay rate of watermilfoil in field and laboratory, but the addition of P did not. The decay rate for shoots and leaves increased at temperatures to 28°C and declined thereafter.

Watermilfoil is widely distributed in North America, and the development of several biotypes might be expected. Aiken et al. (1979) gathered plant materials from eight places in North America and grew them in a common chamber in the northern United States. Their growth was identical. Plants from England and the Netherlands were included and "showed a slightly different cast." Is there a common clonal origin of the North American plants?

The morphology of the plant varies with the environment, exhibiting short, firm shoots in flowing water and very slender stems in standing pools (Sculthorpe 1967). The land form appears as a dense turf of dwarf, much-branched stems that root profusely at the nodes. The leaves are smaller, broader, thicker and fewer in number than when submerged. When again covered with water, they quickly revert to the aquatic form (Schenk 1885).

In Canada, *M. spicatum* has two seasonal growth forms. Above 15°C, the summer form is characterized by a fine, hair-like root system and rapid top growth (2.5 to 3.7 cm/day), while the winter form, below 15°C, shows a coarse, fibrous root growth and a deep, red-pigmented top that grows slowly (Anon. [Canada] 1979b).

There is little cuticle on the stems but somewhat more on the leaves. In milfoil and some other aquatics, chloroplasts are more frequent in the epidermis than in any other tissue. In such plants the epidermis becomes the active site of photosynthesis, while the mesophyll and/or cortex serve as the main storage areas for starches and oils (Sculthorpe 1967).

Using light and scanning electron microscopy, Diez et al. (1988) studied the pollen structure of 15 species of aquatic angiosperms, including *M. spicatum*. The pollen of the latter is of taxonomic importance because of its unusual morphology.

Haslam (1978) found that an anchored, submerged plant of watermilfoil, under difficult conditions, can survive for a year or more with only 1 to 3 cm of live stem material. He pointed out that, when under stress in storms and fast water, the plant can tolerate much battering and perhaps recover slowly if it remains anchored. If it is uprooted, it may not find the undisturbed conditions needed for re-establishment.

Beginning in 1962, the heavy infestation of *M. spicatum* in some areas of Chesapeake Bay in the eastern United States showed a decline of 90%. The malady became widely known in the literature as the "Lake Venice" and "Northeast" disease, names chosen for locations where the disease was prevalent. Viruses and/or bacteria were thought to be the infectious agents, but by 1969 there was still no evidence for a virus, and transmission of the "disease" in the laboratory was not achieved (Bayley et al. 1968, Bayley 1970, Bean et al. 1973).

ECONOMIC IMPORTANCE

M. spicatum is a principal weed in the waterways of some areas of West Bengal, England, Turkey, and the former Yugoslavia. It is ranked from common to number one weed in waterways and irrigation systems of the United States. It is a weed of rice in China, the Philippines, Portugal, the United States, and the former Yugoslavia. In eastern and southern Saudi Arabia, where rainfall is about 10 cm/year, most agriculture is under irrigation and here *M. spicatum* has become a problem in ditches and reservoirs.

In North America, the weed has covered more than 75% of some lake surfaces. For details on the invasive behavior and replacement of other species, or lack of it, see Nichols and Mori (1971), Keast (1984), Lillie (1986), Madsen and Boylen (1989), and Smith and Barko (1990).

This vigorous, robust aquatic plant with its dense, tangled canopy can support the weight of small animals and may drive out the flora and fauna living beneath it. Growth of shellfish is inhibited and fishing is seriously interfered with. During spates of fast water or windstorms, the canopy is shredded and the free strands clog water intakes and flow-meters for irrigation and flood control, and beaches become littered with rotting vegetation. Boating, swimming and general recreation are interfered with, while the accumulated refuse becomes very unsightly. In the former Yugoslavia the weed not only impedes water flow but causes very severe bank erosion (Hulina 1987).

At some sites, milfoil beds provide choice fishing locations for selected species, suitable habitats for crustaceans, and spawning beds for fish. Because it is present in large quantities near centers of human activity, many attempts have been made to find uses for it, frequently with limited success. Gortner (1934), Muztar (1976), Burton et al. (1977), and Muztar et al. (1978) examined the potential of *M. spicatum* as a forage additive by determination of levels of organic acids, crude fiber, protein, pigments, and amino acids, and by ensiling the weed as well as washing it to try to reduce its very high mineral content. Feeding studies were carried out on several animals. Anderson et al. (1965) concluded that there was no economical use for the weed as fertilizer. Because of high salt levels and *pH* problems, Wile et al. (1978) found it difficult to prepare milfoil as a compost.

Sculthorpe (1967) reported an inorganic ash content of 17 to 20% of dry weight for this species. Most high-quality forage plants contain less then 2.3% dry weight of tannins, compounds which interfere with protein digestibility. In a study of many species of plants, Boyd (1968) found a tannin level of 3.2% (dry wt) in milfoil, whereas the content in most aquatic plants was about 7%. Boyd and Scarsbrook (1975) reviewed and summarized a large number of research studies on the organic and inorganic constituents of many aquatic weeds, including *M. spicatum*.

Painter and Waltho (1985) and Painter (1988) in Canada harvested watermilfoil in October in an attempt to control it, and found a short-term reduction in productivity in the next season. An October harvest in the western United States, where temperatures are warmer in autumn, did not delay the plant in the next season. A harvest at this time caused a significant decline in total non-structural carbohydrates, but these were replaced in winter and the plants grew well in the following spring (Perkins and Sytsma 1987).

In heavily used recreation areas in western Canada, Maxnuk (1985) applied bottom-tillage treatments to manage *M. spicatum*. In the central United States, ponds and reservoirs are sometimes over-filled with water and subsequently drawn down to abandon fragments of milfoil on dry soil for desiccation.

In British Columbia on the west coast of Canada, Dearden (1983, 1984), a geographer, reported an excellent case study of the public perception of the development of *M. spicatum* in their water bodies as the weed slowly evolved into a nuisance of epidemic proportions in a recreation area centered on Okanagan Lake and Valley. As conflicts arose within and around advisory groups and government agencies, it became obvious that biological research specialists with limited competence in the social sciences were making unfortunate management decisions, resulting in some wasting of resources.

Experiments involving biological control of aquatic plants with fishes do not easily lend themselves to comparison because of variations (often extreme) in types of water bodies, climates, age, and rate of stocked fish, the quantity and species composition of available plant food, the taste preferences of the fish, as well as the varieties of experimental methods used to gather data. *M. spicatum* is not the first choice of several fishes and researchers worry that this avoidance can lead to monocultures of the dangerous weed. Hauser et al. (1976, 1977), Legner (1979), and Legner and Murray (1981) found in laboratory experiments that the fish *Tilapia zillii* did not prefer *M. spicatum* when it was the only species available. Some tender new leaves were eaten, leaving the stems that made up much of the biomass. In canals where several plant species were present, however, the fish seemed unable to distinguish between species and ate enough milfoil to keep it quite well under control.

In a 4-yr trial in Florida in the United States, 58 grass carp/ha (*Ctenopharyngodon idella*), controlled most species of aquatic weeds. Three years were required for control of *M. spicatum* (Miley et al. 1980). In Arkansas in the south-central United States, a stocking rate of 25 grass carp/ha controlled most species of aquatic weeds but not watermilfoil (Newton et al. 1979).

For a detailed survey of control methods for this species, including the use of fishes, see *The 1989 Annotated Bibliography of the Biology and Control of Watermilfoil* by D. Helsel and Alan Baker (1989).

Schultz et al. (1983) found that chemicals released from *M. spicatum* in upper levels of the water column were toxic to mosquitoes when they touched the surface water film. When water extracts containing the chemical were displayed in cups, other insects were attracted and drowned in the solution.

COMMON NAMES

Myriophyllum spicatum

BELGIUM	aarvederkruid, myriophylle en epi
CANADA	Eurasian watermilfoil, myriophylle en epi

CHINA	nih-chain
ENGLAND	spiked watermilfoil
EUROPE	Eurasian watermilfoil
JAPAN	hozakinofusamo, kingyomo
SOUTH AFRICA	parrots-feather, waterduisendblarr
UNITED STATES	Eurasian watermilfoil
VIETNAM	rong toc tien

Fifty-Nine

Najas graminea Del. and Najas marina L.

Najadaceae, Najas Family

AJAS IS A GENUS of small, submerged, aquatic annual or perennial plants distributed over the temperate and tropical regions. It is the lone genus of the family and contains about 50 species, many of which are difficult to identify. Linnaeus named the genus for the Latin *naiad*, or water nymph. Several in the genus have become weeds, but *Najas graminea*, *N. marina* and *N. minor* are the most troublesome in water bodies and paddy crops. Each of the former two species is in about 40 countries of the world and has varying degrees of economic importance. They are ranked among the most highly dispersed aquatic weeds in the world. These two species will be reviewed as examples of the weedy *Najas* species.

The *Najas* species can venture into widely different environments, some of them quite extreme. *N. marina* can prosper in fresh, brackish, or highly alkaline water. *N. tenuifolia*, often confused with *N. graminea*, lives in the sulfide-rich waters of a volcanic lake in Java at a temperature of 60°C.

DESCRIPTIONS

Najas graminea

N. graminea (Figure 59-1) is *monoecious*, very slender, much branched, rooted, submerged, herbaceous, grass-like, bright green, 10 to 60 cm long; *roots* may become long, creeping in soft mud; adventitious roots form at nodes of stems; roots are of uniform diameter full length, tawny-orange color; *leaves* flat, acicular, acute, often densely tufted on short lateral shoots giving a plumose habit, 1.8 to 3.5 cm long and 0.7 to 1.5 mm wide, minutely serrate with 40 to 60 inconspicuous, sharp, yellowish-brown teeth on each margin, leaf widens at base to broad sheath with 1 to 2 auricles half-clasping stem; *sheath* 0.3 to 5 mm long, 2 to 4 mm in width with 10 to 30 spines either side; *auricles* mostly long, triangular, about 1/2 the total sheath length, apex acute, rarely acuminate or obtuse, entire, rarely lobed, bearing up to 10 prominent spines; *flowers* often 3 together in different stages, spathes absent in all flowers; *anthers* 4-celled, elliptical, rarely ovate to oblong, 1 mm long, 0.4 to 0.7 mm wide, pollen pale yellow and produced in abundance; *stigmas* 2; *fruit* 2 to 4 in axils of leaves

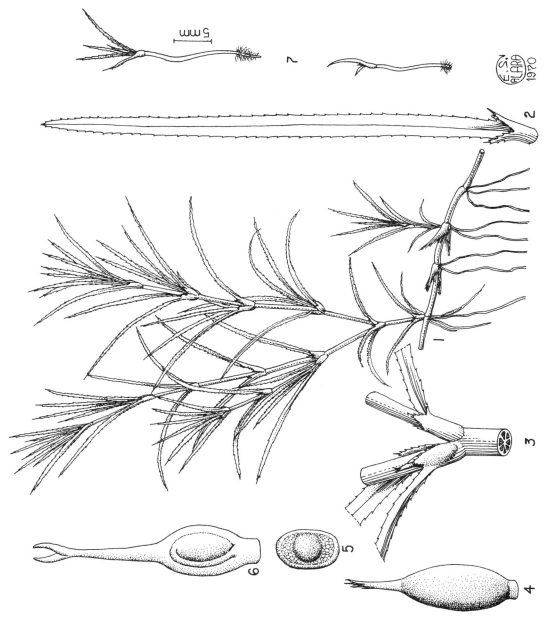

FIGURE 59-1 *Najas graminea* Del.: 1. habit; 2. leaf, enlarged; 3. leaf base, enlarged; 4. staminate flower; 5. pollen grain; 6. pistillate flower; 7. seedlings.

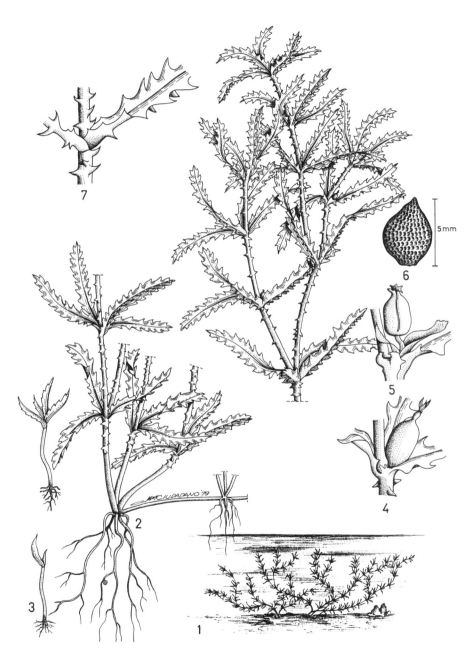

FIGURE 59-2 *Najas marina* L.: 1. habit; 2. vegetative branch 3. seedlings; 4. pistillate flower; 5. staminate flower; 6. seed; 7. vegetative portion, enlarged.

of small shoots, ellipsoidal; *seeds* ovate, raphe conspicuous, 2 mm long, testa with 20 to 30 lengthwise rows of angulate aereoles.

African types of *N. graminea* are often recognized in the field by a very lax (almost gramenoid) appearance, with long, minutely toothed leaves.

Najas marina

N. marina (Figure 59-2) is an herbaceous, *dioecious*, bright to pale green, submerged, rooted, quite variable aquatic plant growing to 80 cm, may be extremely brittle, *adventitious roots* from base and lower nodes; *stems* stout, dichotomously branched, spreading or ascending, may be glabrous sparsely toothed; *leaves* flat, almost always fleshy and sometimes triangular in cross-section, 0.5 to 4.5 cm long, 1.5 to 3.5 cm wide, tip acute to blunt, serrate with 5 to 10, rarely 40 marginal spines or teeth each side; spines may be greater than, equal to, or less than leaf width; dorsal leaf surface mostly with 1 to several spines; *sheath* with or without 1 to 5, rarely 10, mostly inconspicuous spines; *auricles* absent, or about 0.02 mm long if present; *flowers* solitary; staminate flower enclosed in spathe, spathe apex with or without a few minute spines, *anthers* 4-celled, 2.5 to 3.5 mm wide; pistillate flowers, 2 to 4 *stigmas*, 0.9 to 2 mm, spathe absent; *fruit* 1-seeded, plump, often reddish, finely reticulate, slightly asymmetrical, may have scurphy surface; *seed* elliptic to ovate, narrowing toward the tip, somewhat compressed, about 4 mm long and 2.5 mm wide, with rather irregularly arranged isodiametrical shiny testa patterns.

Haynes (1977) expressed the view that many *Najas* species, including *N. marina*, have been divided into numerous varieties based on leaf size, number of internodes and spine numbers, all of them variations to be found in one species at one location but not sufficiently different that they warrant taxonomic recognition.

DISTRIBUTION AND HABITAT

N. marina behaves as a weed over much of the Asian continent (Figure 59-3). It is not yet a serious problem in most of the Pacific Islands or the former Soviet Union. In the dry climate of the Arabian Peninsula, it is present at several sites in the southeast region, presumably in irrigation systems. It is present in the northern Mediterranean area and continues on northward to southern Finland, Norway, and Sweden. It is found at high altitudes in India, at Chamoli in the northwestern Himalaya Mountains near the northern border of Nepal.

It is generally distributed over the United States, Jamaica in the Caribbean area, and in scattered sites in South America. We have no reports of it as a weed problem in the Central American mainland. In the Southern Hemisphere, it is in Argentina, Africa, and Australia. As a weed, the species does not frequent the warmest parts of the tropics.

The weed inhabits saline, alkaline and fresh waters of ponds, lakes, reservoirs, and slow-moving streams and canals. Few species of aquatic weeds are aggressive in colonizing brackish waters (between fresh and salt water) but *N. marina* is conspicuous in doing so. In the north-central United States, for example, this species is one of the constant inhabitants of the standing water of shallow lakes where evaporation exceeds precipitation and the *pH* ranges from 8 to 9. These waters carry rich loads of 150 ppm or more of sulphates, with Ca and Mg as the main cations. In the high volcanic lakes of El Salvador and the

FIGURE 59-3   The distribution of *Najas marina* L. across the world where it has been reported as a weed.

FIGURE 59-4   The distribution of *Najas graminea* Del. across the world where it has been reported as a weed.

southwest United States, the plant may be found where solute concentrations exceed 25,000 ppm (Moyle 1945). In England, Barry and Jermy (1952) usually found *N. marina* in brackish waters or salt springs in 0.5 to 2 m of water. The plants can colonize a mud patch or grow in mixtures with *Phragmites communis* in reed swamps or with *Myriophyllum verticillatum* in submerged sites. In monoculture it produces dense beds and, once established, they become brittle with age and begin to break up. Feeding ducks tear the plants apart and assist in dispersal. Agami and Waisel (1988) have shown that some of the hard-coated seeds of *N. marina* may remain in the digestive tract of fishes for 65 hr before release and still be in viable condition, thus playing a role in distribution of the weed in connecting water bodies.

N. graminea is found in east and west Australia, in several Pacific islands, thence across tropical Asia, through the Middle East to the Mediterranean and northeastern one-third of Africa. In the Americas, it is found in northern Argentina, Brazil, and the United States. *N. graminea* (Figure 59-4) tends to seek a somewhat warmer environment than *N. marina*. A local infestation in Italy is the result of importation of the weed seed with rice from Egypt. In England, a local infestation existed in the warm effluent of a factory for a time. It is believed that the seed was removed from Egyptian cotton by carding machines and subsequently found its way into canals and ditches.

From fossil records, it is known that this is one of several aquatic weeds that moved north into Europe during interglacial periods and were later lost as the ice sheets advanced.

In Southeast Asia, the weed is found most frequently in shallow, stagnant freshwater ponds and ditches. In North Africa, it is most frequent in the Nile valley and Egyptian oases. Rantzien (1952) believes *N. graminea* is one of the most important *Najas* weeds in North Africa, although *N. pectinatus* may have the widest distribution. The latter, because of its rapid and vigorous vegetative growth, is also regarded as a noxious weed of waterways in tropical Africa. *N. graminea* is in the general floras of all of the Americas but only a few areas are reporting it weedy to this time.

PROPAGATION

Adequate seed production and the rooting of fragments insures renewal and survival of *N. marina*. With so many biotypes of the species across the world, there are few general statements to be made about its reproduction. For example, most workers do not find or report overwintering buds or tubers on this species, but in some regions, such as Israel, turions carry the plants through difficult seasons (Agami et al. 1984).

The sequence of events during sexual propagation for most aquatic plants carries one or both of the sex organs to the surface where animals, wind, insects, waves, or surface tension influences the transfer of pollen. *N. marina* and most *Najas* species are among the few that are truly hydrophilic (the flowers remain fully submerged). Arber (1922) reported an observation of a submersed aquatic animal that helped to pollinate *N. graminea*. A colony of the family **Vorticellidae** became attached to a leaf and the constant sweeping motion of the marginal cilia helped to move the pollen in the direction of the stigma.

Muenscher (1930) in the United States, Forsberg (1965) in Sweden, and van Vierssen (1982) in the Netherlands studied the germination of seeds of *N. marina* and found, in general, that a long pre-treatment in the cold in darkness and under anaerobic conditions at 20 to 25°C gave the best germination. Agami and Waisel (1984) in Israel observed no germination of fresh seed and assumed growth was inhibited in the first season. Barry and

Jermy (1952) in England, however, brought whole plants into the laboratory in October, held them in an aquarium, and found that they deteriorated during about the same time as plants at the natural site from which they were taken. They noted that just before the plant broke up, seeds fell to the detritus below and some germination took place in the thin cover.

For those studying *N. marina*, the most helpful seed germination experiments to this time are those of Agami and Waisel (1984) with plants in Israel. Because alternating temperatures yielded only 15% germination after 12 wk, they began to experiment with whole and cracked seeds in the laboratory, in water and soil, with various light and temperature regimes, and with anaerobic conditions as well. Similar lots were taken to field sites and tested at several water depths.

The best laboratory germination was 50% with cracked seeds in darkness under anaerobic conditions. In the natural sites, the germination increased with depth, and when seeds were covered with soil 65% germination was realized. Cracking of the seed coats may thus replace the long cold treatments used by other experimenters. Because the plant is widely used by waterfowl and fishes, the authors assume some seed coats are cracked or removed during the feeding process or in the digestive tract. It is interesting that with this species the maximum germination that can be obtained is 60 to 65% in all of the above conditions. Agami and Waisel (1984) assume that about 40% of the seed remains in the soil seed bank. They found seeds viable after 4 yr of dry storage in a laboratory. The survival of the population in difficult times is thus served well by the long period of seed viability.

S. Singh et al. (1967) made a thorough study of flowering and fruiting in *N. graminea* and several other aquatic weeds in eastern India. They found a distinct period of sexual reproduction, with abundant flowering beginning in September and lasting through February; fruits developed freely from September through December. *N. graminea* flowered at a younger age than most aquatic weeds, with some flowers showing at 4 to 6 wk. This species increases by vegetative reproduction as well and may do so by growth of stolons or the rooting of scattered, broken stem fragments (Chokder 1958). The primary period for such propagation in India is July through September.

MORPHOLOGY AND PHYSIOLOGY

N. marina is the most morphologically distinctive of the *Najas* species in North America and, although it is quite variable, the teeth on leaf margins are conspicuous on even the smallest, most slender plants (Hotchkiss 1967, Stuckey 1985). Barry and Jermy (1952) in England found long roots with well-developed root hairs and speculated that these organs were effective in absorbing most of the plant's nutrients from the substrate. Sauvageau (1889), Venkatesh (1956), and Lodkina (1977) have studied the anatomy of various organs of this plant, Jain (1987) studied the development of the staminate flower of this species, and Cheadle (1942) has shown that the stems are almost completely lacking in vascular tissue but are filled with air-spaces that are separated by rays as in the spokes of a wheel. Fotedar and Ray (1972) and Viinikka (1975, 1978) reported on the cytology of several of the Najadaceae, and Serbanescu-Jitariu (1986) and Swamy and Lakshmanan (1962) on the embryology. Gunn and Ritchie (1988) presented line drawings of the seed embryo and transections of the seed. Casper (1979) recently surveyed the taxonomy of the *Najas* species.

Campbell (1897) made perhaps the most thorough morphological study of the genus *Najas*. The work is of interest here even though he studied *N. flexilis*, because the morphology of *N. marina* is very similar. Because of the worldwide distribution of so many *Najas* species, there is very much variation in morphology and the extreme simplicity of the flowers makes the limits of each species, including *N. marina*, very hard to define.

Following his study of the *Najas* species in Africa and comparison with species elsewhere, Rantzien (1952) concluded that there is little valid, organized information across the world about the variation of these species, including *N. marina*. Many barren specimens now reside in herbaria collections but they are not helpful, for it is necessary to have male and female flowers for identification efforts. In nature, these are only available for short periods, or are rarely seen at some locations.

In many submerged hydrophytes, the leaf mesophyll cells are quite homogeneous and lack differentiation into palisade and spongy tissues. In *N. graminea* (and also *Elodea*) there is further reduction and simplification, with a lack of mesophyll altogether and with only two layers of epidermal cells on either side of a single vein. The roots are few, slender and usually unbranched.

In the English types of *N. graminea*, Bailey (1884) found stems to 70 cm in length. Flowers appeared after five leaves were produced and the majority of the plants produced both types of flowers, with female flowers being more numerous. Male flowers were often solitary, but females occurred in groups of 2, 3, or 4.

Each male flower has but a single, sessile anther which is borne aloft at anthesis. The female flower has a solitary, sessile carpel with two stigmas (V. Singh 1965b). It has been observed that the germination of microspores is often underway when they are released. The plant is normally monoecious and, as heavy, intertwined mats are formed, the two types of flowers are often in close proximity. The extended pollen tubes of the floating microspores serve to increase their effective area and they are caught at random by the elongated stigmas.

Sinha and Sahai (1973) studied seasonal changes of standing crops of two dominants, *N. graminea* and *Hydrilla verticillata*, in a large but shallow lake in north India. The *N. graminea* plants covered 20% of the area in midwinter and twice that in summer. The total above-ground biomass increased from 2 metric tons dry matter/ha in winter to 4.6 in summer, and that produced below ground from 0.36 to 0.95. The average daily rate of dry matter production peaked in July–August at 53 g/m^2/day, followed by sharp losses as senescence and decay set in during November–December. The biomass production of *Hydrilla* followed a similar pattern.

In the same region, the zonal distribution of the biomass of this species was studied with depth of water in a large water body 1 to 2 m deep. The top 20 cm contained 50% of the biomass and 30% was in the 60 to 80 cm zone, thus accounting for 80% of the photosynthesis. The vertical distribution of the chlorophyll content was similar to the dry weight distribution. Stems and petioles contributed little to total production (Ambasht and Ram 1976).

It is frequently assumed that because the roots of submerged aquatic plants are such a small part of the total biomass (often about 10% or less) these organs are not of great importance to the development of the plant. *N. marina* differs in that its roots may make up one-third of the total biomass. Waisel and Agami (1983) have shown that the need for and use of roots by *Najas* is dependent upon environmental conditions. *Najas* plants that have developed in the soil have active roots and their removal inhibits shoot growth. Roots that have developed in water are not very active and their removal does not affect growth.

In Israel, Agami et al. (1980, 1984) demonstrated that *N. marina* is comparatively tolerant of low light because of the low light compensation and saturation points for photosynthesis. In field studies, however, they found the plants could only continue to develop and produce seed when midday light levels were far above the photosynthetic compensation points they had been working with. This spread between light levels needed for photosynthesis and those for growth and development is critical for seasonal or long-term survival, especially when the light attenuation of a water body changes unpredictably. To explore this behavior they suspended containers of plants at five depths down to 225 cm in a natural site. To a depth of 75 cm, growth increased until August, the plant then flowered, seeds were produced, growth ceased, and plants deteriorated in late November. At the 125-cm depth the growth rate was high only to mid-July, at which time the standing crop began to decline. The growth period was shorter at the 225-cm depth, with all plants decayed before August. An analysis of water and light characteristics at various levels revealed that increased turbidity from the growth of phytoplankton was the cause of the decline in growth in summer.

In a study of the effect of temperature and photoperiod on the growth of *N. marina* in Israel, Agami and Waisel (1983) concluded that the restricted annual growth of *N. marina* in summer months is caused by a combination of day-length and temperature, with temperature having the greatest influence. The optimal temperature for summer growth was 25°C, while growth was inhibited at the 13°C temperature of the natural habitat in winter. In all experiments conducted at high and low temperatures, the growth of the *Najas* plants in a long-day was superior to those held in short-day conditions. Undoubtedly the longer duration of photosynthesis in long days contributed greatly to the success of the plants.

In the central United States, *N. marina* plants growing in a pond at *pH* 9 were placed in a laboratory aquarium for 12 days and then different lots were subjected to different *pH* levels by adjustments with H_2SO_4. The plants did not survive below *pH* 4.7, they continued growth above *pH* 6.2, with the optimum at *pH* 8.1 (Stuckey 1985).

In 1965, a fresh-water bay in southern Finland was cut off from the sea by an embankment and Hinneri (1976) studied the changes in the aquatic flora and water quality for the following 10 yr. The *pH* of the reservoir was quickly lowered because of the inflow of sulphates from clay deposits in the catchment area. The *pH* of the water fell to 4.8 in 10 yr. *N. marina* was in the original flora but disappeared during the 3rd year of closure, along with *Myriophyllum* and *Potamogeton* species.

N. marina and some other fresh-water plants are found almost exclusively in brackish waters in Finland. Luther (1951) observed that at high salinities these plants could be seen at both calm and turbulent sites, but at low salinities they grew only where there was turbulence. On further study, he concluded that in Finnish waters it is only in brackish water that the *pH* is high enough to make available an adequate supply of bicarbonate ions. He found very low bicarbonate concentrations in calm water of low salinity, but that turbulence stimulates the renewal of bicarbonate ions in these waters and this enhances the gradient for diffusion into the plant.

In eastern England, Barry and Jermy (1952) studied the effect of salinity on *N. marina* in the brackish waters of different rivers as they widen near the sea, and found a range from 85 to 2800 ppm NaCl with *pH* at about 8. In one river, all of the *N. marina* was killed when the salinity rose to 32,000 ppm (sea water being 35,000 ppm) during a sea flood, perhaps in part because some plants were buried or uprooted. The *N. marina* was completely restored with time, and the authors speculated that the seed bank in the soil may have provided the plant material.

Plants of this species in Israel are found mainly in fresh water but they respond favorably to additions of NaCl up to 35 to 55 ppm.

Waisel et al. (1982), in Israel, studied uptake and transport of four inorganic ions by four submerged aquatic species, including *N. marina*. The rates of uptake by root and shoot tissues varied with the species but, in general, the aboveground shoots made the largest contribution to the mineral nutrition of all of the species.

To compare the hydrochemical conditions of two similar aquatic plants, Pietsch (1981) in Germany measured the *pH* and mineral content of many stands of the plants, *N. marina* and *H. verticillata*. The *pH* averaged about 7.5 in the waters of both species, with high Ca, Mg, SO_4, Cl, and CO_3 in the *Najas* stands. Bicarbonates were very dominant among the anions in *Hydrilla* stands, with a very small proportion of sulphate ions and with low Cl, NO_3, and Fe.

Fossil records have shown that *N. marina* disappeared from Scandinavian fresh waters during the latter part of the post-glacial period. This was coincident with the lowering of the electrolyte concentration of the water which resulted from the process of land uplift; therefore, today in this region the plants are mainly found in brackish water. The species requires water of high ionic concentration because it cannot accumulate sufficient electrolytes when the concentration falls below a minimum approximately equivalent to 300 micromhos/cm^2 (regarded as an average for the vegetative period) (Forsberg and Forsberg 1961).

The water content of *Najas* tissues is in the range of that in terrestrial plants. The thin, linear-leaved plants can survive for only a short period when removed from the water. Burton et al. (1977) reported the ash, inorganic, organic, protein and amino acid composition of several *Najas* species.

The *Najas* species are among those plants that often become encrusted with marl deposits in alkaline calcareous sites. This phenomenon has several causes, but it is likely that CO_3 ions are absorbed and transferred through the leaves, with excess ions migrating back to the surface to react with hydroxyl ions to produce carbonates that are then precipitated.

Sahai and Sinha (1976) examined the growth of several species, including *N. graminea*, in nonpolluted water and that polluted by raw sewage effluent from shore communities, as well as washing activity at stream banks. The production of dry matter was reduced by 85% as a result of the pollution.

AGRICULTURAL IMPORTANCE

Each of these two *Najas* species causes problems in about 40 countries as they choke streams and canals, expand into great tangled masses of plant material that hinder fishing, fish culture, the movement of boats and ships, and interfere with rice production in Bangladesh, Burma, China, Egypt, Hungary, India, Indochina, Malaysia, the Philippines, Romania, Thailand, Vietnam, and the United States. Wild (1961) of Zimbabwe pointed out that the *Najas* species are readily observed in alarming quantities in pools and ponds and piling up behind dams, but that the real danger is the insidious and gradual reduction of water flow in irrigation furrows, canals and drainage ditches. From this it follows that there will be greater water loss through evaporation and leakage from dikes and ditches, with the resultant water-logging of nearby fields and salting up of the plow layer as nutrients are moved to the surface.

One or both species are regarded as major problems in Australia, Italy, Pakistan, and the United States and as widespread general nuisances in Japan, the Philippines, and Taiwan. In northern India, *N. graminea* ranks among the five most important aquatic weeds in crops and waterways. In that area it also causes the stagnation and prevention of drainage of ponds and pools that then become mosquito-breeding sites. The species is one of the most abundant weeds in reservoirs, streams, and irrigation systems in Thailand, and of irrigation canals and oases in Egypt.

Attempts are made to control the *Najas* species by soil tillage following drawdowns. Pakistan has reported successful control by cutting plants at the soil levels three or four times per year. Experiments in control using plant-eating fishes are very difficult to compare, for in the complex aquatic environment many factors cannot be controlled in natural sites. With *N. graminea* there are reports that fish both prefer it and avoid it, yet these data may be influenced by the single, simple choice among several to many species of plants available at the various experimental sites. Cure et al. (1970) in Romania studied the use of fish to control weed vegetation in a water body overgrown with 30% soft, submerged and floating weeds such as *N. marina* and 70% fibrous emergent types. There was 95% removal of the weeds in one year, with total absence of *N. marina* and other soft species and a remaining vegetation of a few fibrous species such as *Phragmites communis*.

These two weeds provide fish with food, shelter, shade, and spawning areas. Ducks, marsh and shore birds, and other animals forage on them; some animals eat the entire plant. They are used for green manure and, because they are easily gathered, they are used for packing, with a resultant dispersal of seeds.

COMMON NAMES

Najas graminea

BANGLADESH	jhaojhanji, kanta jhanji
JAPAN	hossumo
PHILIPPINES	aragan
VIETNAM	thuy kieu hoa ban

Najas marina

DENMARK	stor najade
ENGLAND	hollyleaf naiad
FINLAND	meri-nakinruoho
FRANCE	naide marine
GERMANY	Grosses Nixenkraut
ITALY	spini da ranocchi
JAPAN	ibaramo
NETHERLANDS	groot nimfkruid
NORWAY	stivt havfrugras
PORTUGAL	galiroa
SWEDEN	natesarv
UNITED STATES	bushy pondweed, hollyleaf naiad, marine naiad, spiny naiad, water nymph
VENEZUELA	marite

Sixty

Nicandra physalodes (L.) Gaertn.

Solanaceae, Nightshade Family

N ICANDRA PHYSALODES is mainly a weed of arable land, is in 35 crops, and is of world-wide distribution. The seeds of the weed germinate early in the growing season and then sporadically through the cropping period. It is capable of producing millions of seeds per hectare.

FIGURE 60-1 The distribution of *Nicandra physalodes* (L.) Gaertn. across the world where it has been reported as a weed.

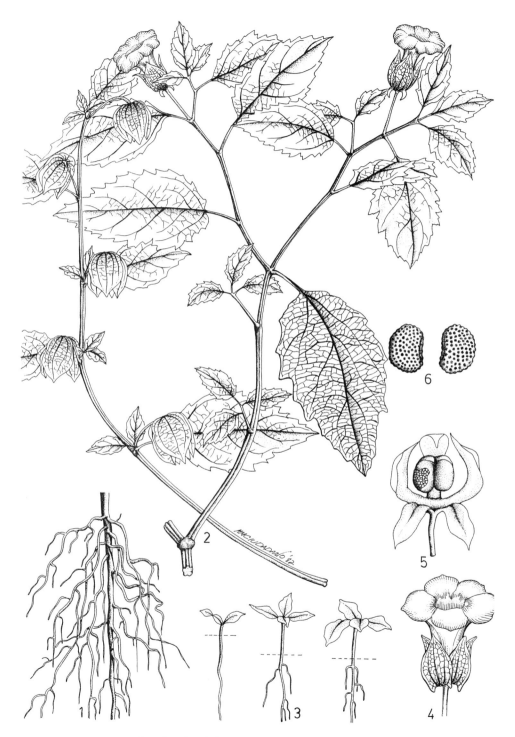

FIGURE 60-2   *Nicandra physalodes* (L.) Gaertn.: 1. root system; 2. flowering branch;
3. seedlings; 4. flower, 5. same, with petals and stamens removed; 6. seed, two views.

DESCRIPTION

N. physalodes (Figure 60-2) is an erect, branched *annual* which can grow to 2 m; *stems* strongly angular, grooved or furrowed lengthwise, hollow; *leaves* alternate, simple, ovate-oblong abruptly contracted into a long decurrent base, irregularly or shallowly lobed or cut, both surfaces bright green, very sparsely pubescent; 6 to 25 cm long, 2.5 to 18 cm wide, *petioles* 1 to 20 cm long; *flowers* solitary in axils of upper leaves, erect during anthesis, drooping afterward; *corolla* campanulate with lobes spread to 4 cm in diameter, pale blue or white, or blue with white center; *pedicels* 1 to 4 cm long; *calyx* 1 to 3 cm long, membranous, more or less 5-winged, enlarging to a bladder enclosing the fruit, green at first then turning brown and papery; *stamens* 5 in apical part of the corolla tube, equal; *fruit* a *berry*, yellowish, smooth, globose, 1 to 1.5 cm in diameter, more or less lenticular, glabrous, containing many seeds; *seeds* light brown, 1.25 to 1.5 mm in diameter, light brown, glabrous, finely pitted testa.

DISTRIBUTION AND BIOLOGY

N. physalodes is a weed of arable land in 35 countries and, as may be seen from Figure 60-1, it is found in agriculture from lat 50° N (Poland and eastern Canada), to lat 35° S (South Africa and Victoria, Australia (Kummer 1951)). It is most troublesome in southern and eastern Africa and in Australia, but it is widespread in the eastern Mediterranean, India, Central America and the central latitudes of South America. It is found most often in cultivated fields but prospers as well on roadsides and waste places.

As the black soils of virgin lands of Western Australia were opened to agriculture, *N. physalodes* was one of the troublesome early weeds and it was presumed to have been in the land before it was cultivated. After several years of irrigated agriculture, it was replaced by other species. In quite another environment, the wet tropical coasts of north Queensland, Australia, *Nicandra* can cause heavy losses in newly sown tropical pastures.

In East Africa, where it is more troublesome than elsewhere in the world, it is a characteristic weed of fertile, arable land. An equally serious weed, *Rottboellia exaltata*, germinates slightly earlier as the growing season begins but is readily curbed by one or two cultivations. In these situations *Nicandra*, which is not easily eliminated by cultivation, quickly fills in and grows vigorously to become a tall competitor. Ridley (1930) believes the dispersal of *N. physalodes* on the African plains has been due in part to the movement and belowground storage of the seed by ants.

The majority of the research on the physiology and ecology of *N. physalodes* has been devoted to seed production and seedling behavior.

The species is an annual, reproducing by seeds only. Studies in East Africa have shown that in pure stands this weed can produce 22,000 million seeds/ha or about 4,400 kg/ha. Average seed produced per plant was 16,000, with a high of 44,000 (Schwerzel 1967, 1970b, Thomas and Schwerzel 1982). In that area, for example, the seeds begin to germinate in late December and new seedlings appear sporadically throughout the growing season. Late-germinating plants are less competitive to crops. Favorable moisture and weather may enable field seeds to sprout in 5 days. The time from germination to flowering ranges from 43 to 54 days and to seed ripening, 53 to 64 days.

The discrepancies in the reports of presence or duration of seed dormancy may be of little consequence, because it now seems that until the seed coat is removed or broken the seed cannot sprout. Hocombe (1961) obtained 55% germination following a 15-min treatment with H_2SO_4. Some seed lots are reported to be 90% viable. Darlington and Janaki-Ammal (1945) have shown that the presence or absence of an iso-chromosome in this species determines whether a seed will germinate readily ($2n = 20$) or remain dormant ($2n = 19$). A garden variety of *N. physalodes* that had been lost was restored when some chromosomally deficient seed types became available after remaining dormant during a burial of 28 yr. This may be a dormancy characteristic that goes unrecognized in agricultural fields.

An 8-year experiment on 13 weed species was conducted in Zimbabwe (then Rhodesia) to study periodicity of germination when seeds in fields were subjected to regular tillage in rain-grown summer maize. Known quantities of weed seeds were incorporated into the soil at the outset. *Nicandra* germinated year round, produced five times more plants in summer than winter, and produced more seedlings than any other species (Schwerzel et al. 1980–81).

A study was made of the longevity of seeds of four common weeds of crops in Zimbabwe, including *N. physalodes*, that were buried at various soil depths. Seed of *Nicandra* placed below 75 mm was still viable after 5 yr, suggesting that deep plowing as a control measure may only help to increase its survival (Schwerzel et al. 1980-81). In Zimbabwe, in a season of normal rainfall, *Nicandra* is ranked among the six main weeds of crops and is one of three highest in seed production. In a long-term experiment with these weeds, their seeds were incorporated into the soil and the land was the cultivated to a depth of 22 cm at monthly, quarterly or yearly intervals and some plots were undisturbed. Frequent cultivations exhausted the supplies of seeds of *Nicandra* within 10 yr. In soil disturbed once per year, 3.6% of the *Nicandra* seeds were still germinating after 15 yr. (Schwerzel 1970a, Schwerzel and Thomas 1979, Schwerzel et al. 1980-81).

In an experiment on the management and control of 30 weeds of Zimbabwe, Schwerzel (1983) cut some weeds near the ground line when they were 8 cm in height and others were cut when half-grown or full grown. *Nicandra* was killed when cut at the earliest stage. In a weed competition experiment in cotton in Zimbabwe, Thomas and Schwerzel (1968) studied the effect of *Nicandra*, a principal weed, together with other weeds for 2, 4, 6, and 8 wk after planting. The crop suffered critical damage if the initial weed stand was allowed to remain more than 2 wk. In a crop hand-weeded for 4 wk, the weeds emerging subsequently, such as *Nicandra*, did not lower the yield. The authors believe the competition for light in this crop is more important than that for water or nutrients.

Experiments on embryology (Crete 1959, Saxena 1973) and cytology (Pal 1979) have been reported, and Schafer (1969) studied the anatomical structure of the gynoecium of this species. Kaniewski (1965) studied fruit histogenesis in *Nicandra*, and Prasad and Singh (1978) have reported on a detailed examination of gametophyte formation and the development of the seed.

In the past decade, interesting new chemical compounds have been extracted from and characterized for *N. physalodes*. The withanolide, nicandrenone, has shown cytotoxicity against certain cancerous cells in mice and humans (Subramainan et al. 1973, Gunasekera et al. 1981). New alkaloid and terpenoid compounds found in *Nicandra* have been shown to inhibit the feeding of several insect species (Romeike 1965, 1966; Begley et al. 1972). It is interesting that the new chemistry of this plant is a reflection of its name. Nikander, a poet of Asia Minor who lived about 100 B.C., wrote of the medicinal uses of this species. *Nicandra* has its name from this man.

AGRICULTURAL IMPORTANCE

Nicandra is a serious weed of beans in Tanzania; of cotton, maize, peanuts, sorghum, and wheat in Zimbabwe; of maize in Australia, South Africa, and Zambia. It is a principal weed of barley, coffee, cotton, forage legumes, maize, pastures, sorghum, and wheat in Tanzania; of beans, coffee, and pastures in Kenya; of beans, peas, potatoes, and soybeans in Zimbabwe; of cotton, sorghum, and soybeans in Zambia; of several dryland crops, irrigated crops, linseed, rice, safflower, sorghum, soybeans, vegetables, and established forage and legume crops in Australia; of maize in Nicaragua; and of sugarcane in Peru.

It is a common weed of beans, cotton, maize, and soybeans in Brazil; of beans, soybeans, and tobacco in Argentina; of cotton, maize, and sugarcane in Peru; of maize, peanuts, and wheat in Kenya; of maize and rice in Guatemala; of orchards, sorghum, and vineyards in South Africa; of newly sown pastures and tomatoes and several other summer crops in Australia; of pastures, pineapple, and sugarcane in Hawaii; of sugarcane in Natal and wheat in Angola.

Nicandra also appears as a weed of unknown importance in the crops listed above in Costa Rica, Honduras, India, Indonesia, Mozambique, Nepal, and the former Soviet Union. The species is troublesome in fodder beets, lettuce, lucerne, papaya, pepper, and sweet potatoes in one or more places in the world.

The harvests of grass and legume seed crops grown in East Africa become contaminated with seeds of *Nicandra* and separating them from some of the crop seeds is difficult. Because the seed contains more than 15% protein, it is used as feed for caged birds in some regions. Poland has experimented with *Nicandra* plants as fodder for animals (Czekalski 1981).

COMMON NAMES

Nicandra physalodes

ANGOLA	Margarita, onigahongula
ARGENTINA	Margarita, farolito
AUSTRALIA	apple of Peru
BOLIVIA	farolita, capuli cimarron
BRAZIL	balao, bexiga, falso joa de capote, joa de capote, quintilho
HAWAII	apple of Peru
INDONESIA	tjeploekan
KENYA	apple of Peru, Chinese lantern
MADAGASCAR	bereda
NATAL	Peru apple
NEW ZEALAND	apple of Peru
PERU	capuli cimarron, capuli de la costa, toccoro
SOUTH AFRICA	apple of Peru, basterapplliepie
TANZANIA	Chinese lantern

THAILAND	apple of Peru
UNITED STATES	apple of Peru
ZAMBIA	wild gooseberry
ZIMBABWE	apple of Peru, mubumacembere

Sixty-One

Orobanche ramosa L. and Orobanche minor Sm.

Orobanchaceae, Broomrape Family

O ROBANCHE RAMOSA, branched broomrape, is surely the most widely distributed and dangerous of the weedy broomrapes. Our records indicated that we must also emphasize the distribution and biology of *O. minor*, clover broomrape, recognizing that Chater and Webb (1972) found this taxon so variable that ten taxa of the weedy *Orobanches* that seem to be conspecific were placed into an *O. minor* group or *complex* (hereafter referred to as *O. minor*) that has no formal taxonomic standing. Some believe the complex has very wide distribution in the world but this may be because of its variability and the difficulty in defining its taxonomic limits.

O. ramosa and *O. aegyptiaca* are regarded by some as a continuum from the smaller forms of *O. ramosa* to the more robust forms of the larger *O. aegyptiaca*. Some believe the latter is the form of *O. ramosa* that has adapted to hot, dry areas. Data on this "complex" (also without formal taxonomic standing) will be referred to under *O. ramosa* where appropriate (Musselman 1982, 1986; Parker 1986).

O. ramosa and *O. minor* are each in 45 countries, with the former in 25 crops and the latter in 14 crops. For the sake of brevity we have used the collective terms clovers (*Trifolium* species) and vegetables often, with only occasional examples given for specific crop designations. The *Orobanches* are so invasive in these crop forms that repetition becomes confusing.

DESCRIPTIONS

Orobanche ramosa

O. ramosa (Figure 61-1) is a herbaceous *annual* or *perennial* root parasite without chlorophyll. Some time after considerable growth underground, a main stem emerges; stem erect, small, thin, richly branched, brown or yellow straw-colored, glandular pubescent, 10 to 30 cm

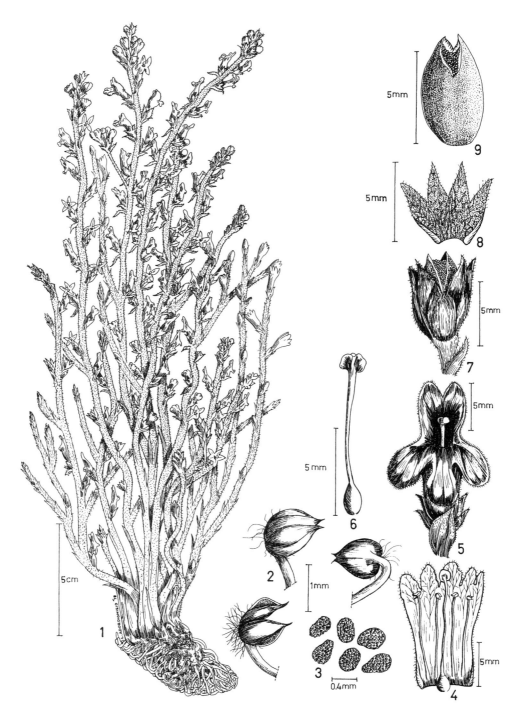

FIGURE 61-1 *Orobanche ramosa* L.: 1. habit; 2. capsule, three views; 3. seeds; 4. flower open, 5. same, front view; 6. pistil; 7. capsule enclosed with bracts; 8. bracts, opened; 9. capsule.

high; *leaves* reduced to purplish scales; branched stems terminate in *flowering spikes*; *flowers* perfect, *calyx* 4-lobed, not divided, with triangular teeth, acuminate, shorter than corolla tube, 3 bracteoles present at base of calyx, *corolla* about 15 mm long, tubular, curved, may be constricted above ovary, 2-lipped, upper erect and 2-lobed, lower spreading and 3-lobed, usually violet or may be yellow tinged with violet, subtended by one ovate *bract* and 2 linear *bracteoles*; *stamens* 4, 2 long and 2 short, inserted on corolla tube; *pistil* superior ovary, 2-celled, *style* long, *stigma* large, *fruit* a *capsule*, one-celled with 4 placentae, many seeded; *seed* minute about 0.3 mm long, ovate, dull, yellowish brown, netted veined.

Similarities of *O. ramosa* and *O. aegyptiaca* in morphology, behavior, and chromosome number ($2n = 24$) make them difficult to separate (Musselman 1986). Hepper (1973) of Kew Gardens separates these types on the basis that *O. aegyptiaca* has a larger flower with longer corolla and anthers that are densely hairy in contrast to the glabrous condition of those in the *O. ramosa* flower. At times the flowers of the former are heavily scented. The former also seems the more vigorous of the two.

Orobanche minor

A herbaceous *annual* or *perennial* root-parasite, without chlorophyll (see Figure 61-2); *main axis* erect, unbranched, slender, often tall (may be up to 80 cm in South Africa), nearly cylindrical, sticky-pubescent, purplish or reddish brown, sometimes clustered and covered with growth of soft whitish hairs, stem swollen near base at contact with host; *leaves* reduced to scales or bracts, ovate-acuminate, also purplish-brown, up to 1.5 cm long, scales overlapping near base but more sparse as they proceed upward on stem; *flowers* in dense terminal spikes, 2.5 to 3 cm in diameter, covering the upper half of the stem, each subtended by a purplish-brown bract as long as corolla, no bracteoles present, *calyx* divided almost to base into two lateral sections which are again cleft part way down; *petals* united into broadly tubular *corolla* that is curved, has no constriction, divided at tip into shallowly 2-lobed upper lip and 3-lobed lower lip, corolla violet-purple above, yellow below (in Egypt blue-violet), 1.5 cm long, viscid-pubescent outside; *stamens* 4, attached to corolla tube; *ovary* bearing 2-lobed *stigma*; *fruits* oblong-ovoid, brown, *capsules*, membranous, splitting into two valves at maturity, very many black, glabrous *seeds* less than 0.5 mm long.

The most extensive treatments of the systematics of the *Orobanche* genus are those of Beck-Mannagetta (1890, 1930). Musselman (1986) believes little progress has been made toward a "modern taxonomic synthesis" within the genus *Orobanche* during the last 50 years.

DISTRIBUTION AND HABITAT

Annotated bibliographies of the distribution, biology and control of the *Orobanche*, which include several hundred references, have been prepared periodically from 1940 onward by the Weed Research Organization in Great Britain (Weed Research Organization 1940 onward). It is important to include here the beautiful book, "South African Parasitic Flowering Plants," by Johann Visser (1981). The descriptions of form, color, and habitat are supported by superb color photography.

It has been customary to look to the Mediterranean area, Near East, and Central Asia as the preferred home of the agricultural broomrapes. *O. aegyptiaca* is often said to be one of the most widespread of all weeds in Central Asia. In Figure 61-3, however, we may see

FIGURE 61-2　*Orobanche minor* Sm.: A. habit; B. enlarged flower spike; C. flower diagram; D. capsules; E. seeds.

FIGURE 61-3   The distribution of *Orobanche ramosa* L. across the world where it has
been reported as a weed.

FIGURE 61-4   The distribution of *Orobanche minor* Sm. across the world where it has
been reported as a weed.

that *O. ramosa* has moved into the New World, with some scattered reports of weed problems in Central and South America. There are some serious infestations in Cuba and Mexico, although Hammerton (1989) reports that they are seldom seen elsewhere in the Caribbean area.

Several *Orobanches* are now generally scattered over Africa, and serious infestations are found in south India, Australia, Tasmania and New Zealand. There are few reports of weed problems with these particular root parasites in the Pacific Islands, Japan and China, although other species are reported to be at work in those areas. Clover broomrape, *O. minor*, has quite a similar world distribution but with additional locations in the Indian Ocean islands and with troublesome infestations in Australia and New Zealand (Figure 61-4).

Both species are found over Europe, which brings them to lat 50° N, with *O. minor* at lat 60° N in Sweden. In the South Temperate Zone they are below lat 30° S in Africa and below 40° S in Asia. In sum, the crops and fields of the entire Mediterranean area, the Near East, and Central Asia, along with southern Europe and most of Africa, are the most severely infested with *O. ramosa* and *minor*. Both species tend to avoid the hot tropical areas, except at high elevations. Branched broomrape is found in heavily settled areas above 1800 m in Uganda and in the highlands of Ethiopia (Masefield 1939).

Movement of the weedy *Orobanche* parasites has been almost exclusively from the Old World to the New World. The tiny seeds are dispersed by wind, water, agricultural machinery, and on the clothing and shoes of workers. Boskovic (1962) reported that *Orobanche* seeds can travel long distances as contaminants of sunflower seed. They remain viable after passage through the digestive tracts of cattle and goats and are moved about by those kinds of roving animals.

Many workers find that the heaviest *Orobanche* infestations and the most serious crop losses occur on poor soils. Beilin (1967), Abu-Irmaileh (1981) and others have shown that increases in fertility result in decreases in *Orobanche* development. Branched and clover broomrapes attack a broad range of host crops in many regions of the world on an array of soil types, yet we have no definitive research with which to distinguish between the soil preferences of the parasites. Some workers believe the *Orobanches* grow more vigorously in fields that have alkaline soils (Bischof and Foroughi 1971).

We know of no experiments on *Orobanche* seed germination and longevity at carefully controlled levels of soil moisture and this has led to mixed reports about the requirements for differing levels of soil moisture during several phases of the development of the broomrape. Some reports in the literature suggest that low moisture favors broomrape development, leading to subsequent host injury. In southern Spain, Cubero (1986) reported that damage to bean fields was most serious in the dry areas where some crop areas have now been abandoned. It was just here that there is the greatest need for good protein for their cattle.

Beilin (1967) reported that branched and clover broomrapes grew poorly on wet and waterlogged soils. In Egypt it was observed that a parasite problem did not appear in broad bean (*Vicia faba*) fields rotated with wet paddy rice. In tests of preplanting floods of bean fields, Zahran (1982) found that a 20-day water cover delayed parasite emergence and reduced the number of plants parasitized, improving crop yields. In retrospect Zahran believes that in times before the Aswan High Dam was built on the Nile there was much less problem with *Orobanche* on fields covered for months with flood waters of the river. It is possible as well that some seeds were buried deeply in silt deposits and could not germinate.

PROPAGATION AND REPRODUCTIVE BIOLOGY

Research efforts to understand the biology of reproduction in the *Orobanches* have favored the study of stimulants of seed germination and the period of development immediately following. Harper (1977), in his studies of population dynamics, has reminded us that in contrast to their green neighbors, parasites such as the broomrapes have exchanged the necessity to carry large quantities of seed food reserves for the possibility that very large numbers of tiny seeds will perchance place some propagules near a host that will promptly stimulate germination and quickly become a supplier of nutrients to the parasite. The very small propagules have been called "dust seeds" at times and Harper referred to them as "little more than a few dried cells" and "tiny bags of DNA."

The parasitic *Cuscutas* and the *Orobanches* are examples of different parasitic modes: the former, with somewhat larger seeds and traces of chlorophyll, can survive for a few days while growing and searching for a suitable host, whereas members of the latter genus must have a host to supply food almost immediately after germinating.

A prelude to the production of this enormous amount of seed, of course, is the necessary array of environmental requirements that govern flower initiation and development in all angiosperms. Of these conditions we know little, but they will be explored before we embark on a discussion of the complex state of our knowledge of the natural and synthetic stimulants currently under study.

In England, Holdsworth and Nutman (1947) reported that *O. minor* flowered only in long-days and only when its host flowered. Other workers have found that *O. minor* and *O. ramosa* can flower independently of the host. *O. ramosa* flowers all season long in the United States (Garman 1903, Kribben 1951, Musselman 1980). Cross-pollination of *O. ramosa* by large Hymenoptera insects, especially bumble bees, is normal, but the plant may be selfed in the absence of insects.

Very large numbers of seeds are produced by several weedy broomrapes from many countries, with up to 1 million seeds per plant being recorded (Kadry and Tewfic 1956a, Walker 1966, Strelyaeva 1978, Pieterse 1979). It is commonly believed that *Orobanche* seed persists in the fields from 1 to 12 yr, even though there is little experimental evidence to confirm the survival or viability of such seed through these years (Bischof 1984). Seeds produced by *O. ramosa* in California during summer and fall were 10% viable. Laboratory storage survival is often stated to be 3 to 5 yr, with conditions seldom specified.

With centrifugation of wet soils, Ashworth (1976) detected seeds of *O. ramosa* at a level of 5 per 500 g of infected field soil. In Germany, Kachelreiss (1988) determined seed number by centrifuging soil in an $MgSO_4$ suspension (specific gravity = 1.16 g/ml) to which kaolin was added. The supernatant was sieved at 500 micrometers, placed on a graduated petri dish, and examined under a 16 x 16 microscope. At a 15-cm depth, some fields held 170,000 seeds/m². Wilhelm (1954) in California dried soil from an *Orobanche*-infested field, in the laboratory, for 3 and 6 mo and found a drastic reduction in germinating seeds at 3 mo, with no germination at 6 mo. These conditions may be extremes not reached in field soils and do not necessarily contradict the report mentioned earlier of Cubero's (1986) research showing greater parasite crop damage in the dry areas of Spain.

Linke (1987) and Sauerborn (1990) in Germany found that the distance to the host root at which the germination of parasitic seeds still occurred was enhanced by higher soil moisture levels. The germ tubes were 0.3 mm in dry conditions and 3 mm in saturated soil. They also found that higher rainfall meant greater production of seed by the parasite as well as increased viability. In these instances a plentiful supply of moisture seems very important for stimulation of germination.

Vasyura (1975) in the former Soviet Union placed *O. ramosa* seed at several depths to 50 cm in warm, moist Crimean soil during the period June to September. Parasitization of tomato was at 100, 27, 7, and 0% at 10, 20, 30, and 40 cm, respectively. In an *O. ramosa*-infested California tomato field on clay loam soil with a distinct plow sole layer at 15 cm, all seed was in the top 23 cm, with most above 15 cm and the greatest amount in the top 4 cm (Wilhelm and Benson 1954). Kasasian (1973) prepared a potting soil that, with the exception of the top 2.5 cm, was uniformly mixed with *O. crenata* seeds. Broad beans planted at 2.5, 5, and 7.5 cm were all infested to some degree and were dead at 10 wk.

There are several different patterns of response to light and darkness during germination of the different *Orobanche* species. Izard and Hitier (1953) detected no difference in the germination of branched broomrape in light or dark. Ter Borg (1986) reported *O. ramosa* indifferent to light, and the complete inhibition of germination of *O. aegyptiaca* in light. Hiron (1973) found germination of *O. crenata* in dark much better (55%) than in light (10%). Ter Borg (1986) has pointed out some of the ecological consequences of the response to light. Seeds at or near the surface that may be triggered to germinate in the presence of light have little chance to find a host root, and a seedling beginning at such a location would soon dry out. This would be especially true in the warm, dry climates that are the favorite of *O. aegyptiaca*. In obligate parasites such as *Orobanche* and *Striga*, Sahai and Shivanna (1982) believe that, because the seeds must germinate very close to the host root for survival in the field, it is unlikely that there will be a light requirement.

An optimum temperature of 20 to 25°C for seed germination has been reported for *O. ramosa* and several other species of the genus in various parts of the world (Racovitza 1959, Privat 1960, Sunderland 1960, Beilin 1967, Kasasian 1973). ZH Elev (1987) found that seed germination in *O. ramosa* began at 10°C, was optimum between 18 to 30°C, and ceased at 35 to 40°C. Linke (1987) in Germany kept air dry seeds at 40 to 80°C for 20 days and found them very heat tolerant. Survival fell sharply beyond 20 days. At 50°C seeds lasted only 48 hr when fully imbibed. Kasasian (1973) preconditioned *O. aegyptiaca* and *O. crenata* seeds (while moist) at several temperatures from 1 to 33°C, then applied a *Vicia faba* root exudate and placed the seeds in the dark to incubate at the same temperatures. For pretreatment and germination there were also treatments at all possible combinations of the temperatures. There was no germination of either species at 1°C or of *O. crenata* at 33°C. There was some germination at all other treatments, including combinations. Maximum germination was at 5 days on average unless the temperature was below 13°C.

The temperature requirements are variable between and within species at different locations. Kasasian (1973) found the same temperature was often satisfactory for *O. aegyptiaca* in both the pretreatment and incubation periods, and the optimums were higher than for *O. crenata*. The latter, however, seemed to prefer an incubation temperature that was lower or higher than its optimum pretreatment temperature. In studying these and other data, ter Borg (1986) pointed out that some practical helps become available for management of *Orobanche* if temperature responses are taken into consideration. For example, in *O. ramosa* the optimum germination temperature has been reported to be 18, 20, and 25°C in the United States, southern Germany, and Lebanon, respectively. This suggests that in the Mediterranean region, where the *Orobanche* species are often weeds of winter crops, if the temperature becomes too low, the seeds of the parasite may not germinate or may wait until spring. Thus, in late-sown crops, host stimulant may arrive too late to promote seed germination of the parasite. In contrast, Jacobsohn (1986) in Israel found that parasitic seeds may germinate and cause trouble in carrots in winter but there is no problem in summer.

Most researchers recognize three stages for the *Orobanche* germination process: after seedfall a dormant stage, then a pretreatment stage during which the seed must be moist, and finally an incubation stage in which germination can be induced by stimulants. The dormant stage may continue for days or years (Linke 1987).

For several *Orobanche* species, a period of several days or months in a soil or other moist medium must precede germination. The stimulants, to be discussed below, are effective only after such a treatment—dry seeds do not respond (Sunderland 1960). *O. ramosa* required 1 wk of moist treatment and became less active thereafter (Abu-Shakra et al. 1970). *O. minor* required 21 days at 25°C in a moist condition for maximum response to stimulants (Sunderland 1960). Brown (1965) reported that on a moist medium *Orobanche* seeds may remain for months and *Striga* seeds for weeks without further development. Ninety percent germination occurred in 24 hr for *Striga* and 96 hr for *Orobanche* when a stimulant was applied. Sunderland (1960) reported that the effect of the moist treatment was reversible in *O. minor*. Seeds that had reached maximum germination capacity did not retain it when dried, but upon re-moistening germination began again. The physiological changes that take place during pretreatment are not fully understood. They are temperature sensitive, and they do not take place in the absence of O_2, but it is not likely that long storage periods would be required to increase the permeability of this small seed. There is little evidence for the leaching of inhibitors, although metabolic blockages within the cells may be removed during this period without our knowledge.

There are many reports of pretreatment experiments but two will suffice to acquaint us with the complexities of such research. In the experiment of Abu-Shakra et al. (1970), a high seed germination percentage was obtained when the pretreatment water contained gibberellic acid and incubation was carried out on a flax root diffusate agar medium. The reverse of this reduced germination. Chun et al. (1979) found that pretreatment of *O. ramosa* seed in moist field soil was a prerequisite for optimum germination. When temperatures were below 20°C, excessive soil moisture reduced germination. Some non-host plants may produce germination stimulants and Chun found, following pretreatment of *O. ramosa*, that four to nine host species stimulated the seeds. Mung bean (*Vigna radiata*) root exudate caused 76% more germination than the pretreatment conditions alone, and gibberellic acid used during incubation (while variable) sometimes brought nearly complete germination. Chun found slight help with ethylene and Linke (1987) reported no response.

Spontaneous germination (without stimulants) is on average 2% for several *Orobanches*, but these data are largely from laboratory studies and the situation in the field is not yet understood (Garman 1903, Krenner 1958, Nash and Wilhelm 1960, Cezard 1973a, Kumar 1977, Pieterse 1979, Riopel 1983). It should be remembered that the ethylene mentioned above as a stimulant is given off from decaying crop residue and other organic materials of several kinds in the soil. Among the hundreds of other chemicals released naturally into the soil there may also be stimulants for parasitic seeds that we are not yet aware of (Bartinskii 1940, Musselman 1980).

The seeming chemical interactions between hosts and parasites has been recognized for more than a century. In the 1950s research turned to the administration of inorganic salts, disinfectants, vitamins, plant hormones such as indoleacetic acid, and amino acids (Izard and Hitier 1958, Domini 1959, Cezard 1973b). Later coumarin derivatives, kinetin and other substituted purines, gibberellic acid and ethylene were tried (Worsham et al. 1962, Egley and Dale 1970). Abscisic acid inhibits germination.

In 1972 a germination stimulant of *Striga* was extracted from an exudate of cotton roots and the structure was determined (Cook et al. 1972). It was later given the trivial name strigol. It is a tricyclic molecule with a connecting unsaturated lactone. In nature, strigol has thus far been obtained only from cotton. Extraction and purification are difficult and Vail et al. (1985) estimated that by 1984 only a total of 5 g of strigol had ever been isolated.

The first total synthesis of strigol was reported by Heather et al. (1974). Since 1976 many analogs of the compound have been produced (Johnson et al. 1976, Dailey et al. 1987). Brooks et al. (1985) recently achieved total synthesis of strigol and some analogs using methods that are significantly cheaper than previous procedures and may possibly lead to large-scale synthesis.

Certain numbered analogs are prefaced with GR, the initials of G. Roseberry, the scientist who first made them. The most active thus far is GR-24. Strigol and some analogs stimulate the germination of *O. ramosa* in the range of 0.01 to 1 ppm, but the structures of the active compounds in the root exudates of principal hosts of the *Orobanches* are unknown (Zwanenburg et al. 1986).

We know that both inhibitors and stimulators are present in the exudates and crude extracts of roots and other plant parts that sometimes serve as a source of stimulation (or inhibition) for parasitic seed germination. Further, results reported from several places in the world indicate that a single plant species may produce more than one stimulant (and/or inhibitor). Different host species may produce different chemical stimuli, thus giving us a display of species specificity by parasites as they respond.

To further complicate matters, each cultivar of a single crop species may have its own distinctive chemical compounds for promoting germination, perhaps helping us to understand the regional differences in the crop-parasite relationships. Finally, this array of variability must now be coupled with the knowledge that the parasite species themselves may have segregated into biotypes, often by regions. This matter is little studied, but field reports from the former Soviet Union for several decades tell of standard or sometimes resistant crop varieties being moved between geographic regions only to be constantly challenged by new races of the same parasitic species.

The potency, or lack of it, of all these chemicals can at present be measured only with bioassays. The activities in this field of research are in the normal state of uncertainty that always exists in biology when the structures and identities of enormous numbers of biologically active compounds are as yet undefined. At the same time it is obvious that the chemistry of an *Orobanche* and its host(s) has become very important to an understanding of the interspecific relationships within these particular plant communities. Many of these uncertainties will vanish when structures of some of the base compounds are known (Whitney 1986).

Pieterse (1979) has recently reviewed dozens of research reports concerning root exudates or extracts of them. Because we do not know the nature of the chemicals, it has not been possible to standardize the extraction procedures and the bioassays, thus making it impossible to compare and verify the results obtained with important *Orobanche* species in different laboratories. Some of these results are quite contradictory. For the purpose of discussion there is no need to enumerate all the papers. We have chosen instead to illustrate with examples some of the strange but interesting behavior of these unusual parasites and to emphasize some of the complexities making them so difficult to work with at present.

Some *in vitro* studies have shown that the exudates of flax, sorghum and tomato will stimulate the germination of *O. ramosa* only if collected under sterile conditions. This may help to explain the contradictory reports of particular crop species that cause germination in some studies but not in others in both laboratory and field (Ballard et al. 1978, Musselman 1982).

Gold et al. (1979) found some California tomato soils suppressive of *O. ramosa* and discovered that *Rhizoctonia solani*, which is non-pathogenic to tomato, can cause severe stem rot of the parasite, fewer shoots, and a lowering of viable seed production. The soil is a very lively medium, and whether by chemical or microbial action, there appears to be some level of inactivation of biologically active substances given off by the host roots (Bischof and Koch 1973).

It is commonly accepted that *Orobanche* species tend to occur on the poorest soils, but the reasons for this are unclear—perhaps it is only that the crop is under severe stress from several causes and therefore susceptible. It is believed by some that increased soil fertility reduces this parasite problem, and that added K and P tend to do this by maturation of the crop (Beilin 1967, Kasasian 1971a). Racovitza (1959) found that adding superphosphate to a culture of caraway (*Carum ajowan*) caused an increase in the amount of root exudate, with resulting better parasitic seed germination and expanded parasite problem.

Because of the small amount of host stimulant needed to provoke a response, it is difficult to determine whether it causes a direct stimulus to germination of the seed, or whether it triggers the production of a chemical within the seed that then brings about germination. For example, Baird and Riopel (1980) suggest that host signals may sometimes be very important in species with very narrow host limits, such as *Conopholis americana* (Family **Orobanchaceae**) found only in association with oak trees (*Quercus* spp.). They found many germinated seeds and early host penetration stages in the field, but the requirements for seed germination remain unknown. They could not get parasite seed germination in the laboratory even in the presence of oak root exudate.

Strangely, Zaki and Tewfik (1974) in Egypt found that aqueous extracts of stems, roots and tubercles of the parasites themselves, such as *O. crenata* and *O. ramosa*, can serve as stimulators of germination for parasitic *Orobanche* seeds. This calls into question the rigidity of some of the hierarchies of the parasite-host plant specificity patterns that are much written about.

Whitney and Carsten (1981) have given us an insight into a possible way that both high and low concentrations of exudates may serve to increase the likelihood of successful contact between host and parasite. Having arranged a concentration gradient of the root exudate extract of *Vicia faba*, they placed seeds of *O. crenata* on the gradient for germination and found that at high concentrations the stunting was so severe that the radicle could scarcely break out of the testa. At different concentrations of the extract, the radicle size varied and the direction of growth was influenced. There was a definite chemotropic response of the radicle at the point on the gradient where the best germination occurred. The authors speculate that cells of the radicle on the side nearest the host, where the concentration is high, may be inhibited, causing the radicle to turn toward the host. If at a distance from the host, the radicle may receive a lower concentration (perhaps with less inhibitor?) and thus be expected to grow to greater length to reach the host (Whitney 1986).

The above are representative illustrations of continuing inquiries as efforts are made to unravel the puzzling behavior of these strange flowering angiosperms as they begin life. Whatever the effect of the stimulators, it seems clear that they act quickly and in very low concentrations. Their biology becomes more fascinating as the story unfolds, but there is urgent need to understand the chemistry of the donor-receptor responses that lead to masses of parasitic plants and the resulting crop destruction. If the germination stimulators can some day be synthesized and produced in sufficient quantity for field application, it would seem a major breakthrough in control technology. It must be remembered, however, that the *Orobanche* seeds may endure for a decade or more in the fields and continuing treatment will be required.

The treatments for *Orobanche* control cannot be too costly for many of the crops and localities cannot afford expensive inputs. Riopel (1983), Visser (1989) and Foy et al. (1989) have provided recent, extensive lists of chemicals that stimulate and inhibit the germination of seeds of *O. minor*, *O. ramosa* and other *Orobanche* species.

The concentration of synthetic compounds in general use for *in vitro* experimentation are as follows: 2,4-D 0.0001 ppm, ethylene 5 ppm, gibberellic acid 5 to 100 ppm, napthaleneacetic and indoleacetic acid 0.01 to 0.1 ppm and strigol 0.01 to 1 ppm (GR-7 and -24, 1 to 10 ppm).

PHYSIOLOGY AND HABIT OF GROWTH

In a study of the life cycle of *O. ramosa* on two tobacco soils, a red ferratic and a black gley soil (possessing a sticky subsurface layer), Gonzalez and Rodriguez (1981) in Cuba found the cycle duration was about 50 to 55 days on the former soil and 60 to 65 days on the gley soil. The seed germination period was 20 to 30 days and emergence of the parasitic shoots was 50 to 55 days after transplanting tobacco. The parasite developed underground for the first 20 to 25 days in red soil; 5 days longer in black soil. Maximum growth occurred 1 wk before and 2 wk after emergence. Flowering began 6 to 9 days after emergence and there was a similar period between final flowering and fruit ripening. The fruits dried in one wk. In Turkey, ratoon tobacco crops are believed to be less susceptible to this parasite than the original transplants. Linke and Vogt (1987) used a unique plexiglass container that permitted observation of the germination and early development of *O. ramosa* on several hosts without destroying the plant material. The plants were observed for several weeks as they grew to a depth of 18 cm. For this parasite, the first host infections were seen about 8 days after the parasitic seeds germinated.

In eastern Australia, *O. minor* first appears in mid to late spring in the form of yellow-brown stems rising above the pasture. Soon great quantities of seed are produced to be moved about by wind and rain. The above-ground phase of growth is completed by early summer (Evans 1962, Edwards 1972). The seeds remain in the soil until next season and must then be near the root of subterranean clover (*Trifolium subterraneum*) or other host if it is to germinate. Haustoria form on the host roots and may remain alive in summer after the parasitic stems have dried and under favorable conditions behave as perennials by surviving until the next growing season. The plant behaves as an annual when the dry, hot weather of late summer causes the haustorium to decay. The authors found the seed production period of the parasite to be a time of great stress, when lack of water and nutrients will soon cause the plant to perish.

With *O. ramosa*, an emerged shoot count may give an incomplete picture of the severity of the infestation, for there may be large numbers of underground clusters without above-ground shoots (Racovitza 1960, Kropac 1973). In Australian pastures, however, where *O. minor* causes severe reduction of subterranean clover stands, the number of aerial parasite stems, regardless of size, is a more important factor in the prediction of yield reduction than is the actual weight of these stems on a given area of clover. In a search for resistance among 12 cultivars of *Vicia faba*, Aalders and Pieterse (1986) found that the most vigorous crop plants with the greatest shoot and root biomass had the higher number and the more advanced stages of the development of tubercles, independent of inoculum density.

Rakhimov (1967) in the southern part of the former Soviet Union found high transpiration rates in *O. aegyptiaca* and similar species. The greatest loss of water was from scale leaves with a rate 3 times greater than from stems and flowers. Several types of melons with *Orobanche* infections had increased transpiration in the morning, with decreased water loss in the afternoon (Mukumov 1974). Faizieva (1978), also in the former Soviet Union, found a decrease in morning transpiration in similarly infected tomatoes. The turgidity of the host plants was not greatly altered in these cases.

Kolyadko (1972) examined the nutrient content of *O. ramosa* and the hemp (*Cannabis sativa*) that it parasitized, and found the broomrape stems had 3, 7, and 22 times as much N, K, and P, respectively, as the hemp stems. Ismail and Obeid (1976) and Lotti and Pardossi (1977) have shown that *O. ramosa* can acquire some water and minerals directly from the soil by absorption through the non-haustorial portion of its own roots. This matter may require further examination, for Bischof (1977) reported that he could not find uptake of materials directly from the soil.

An enormous effort has been poured into studies of the chemical interrelationships of host and parasite at the time of awakening of the broomrape seed. Perhaps for this reason the data on the physiology and biochemistry of the metabolic systems of the host and parasite still remain scattered and incomplete. Following a review of about 50 of the principal papers on metabolic activity, Pieterse (1979) concluded that the broomrapes alter the physiology of their host plants very much. They cause reductions of stored carbohydrates, proteins, total P, and the organic acids tartaric, citric, malic, fumaric and succinic. Bound amino acids, N, Ca, and Mg tend to increase in the host. Using labelled P^{32}, Abou-Raya (1970) found that P absorption was more or less parallel for host and parasite.

Pieterse (1979) believes the level of activity of certain enzyme systems and/or their presence or absence may account in part for the parasitic nature of these angiosperms. The levels of individual organic acids and various sugars seem to vary with species and may suggest different patterns of metabolic activities. The research of Singh and Krishnan (1971a,b; 1977a,b) on the characteristics of the mitochondria of *O. cernua* found no evidence of basic abnormality in their biochemical properties related to the parasitic life. They were as functionally active in the Krebs cycle, electron transport and the necessary enzyme pathways as were non-parasitic plants. Despite this, there appears to be a general lowering of the level of several primary processes by several of the *Orobanches* (Press et al. 1986).

In the experiments of Singh and Krishnan (1971a,b), parasitism by *Orobanche* lowered the nucleoprotein content in the host stem but not the root, and reduced the chlorophyll content as well. Finally, in all of the principal weedy parasitic angiosperms, the *Cuscutas*, *Orobanches* and *Strigas*, we find a general inability to incorporate inorganic N and C and thus there is a critical demand on the host for life-sustaining organic compounds.

The increased production of phenolic compounds in *Cuscutas*, and *Orobanche* and some other parasites, particularly in the tissues of the host, suggests an important role in this parasitic relationship.

Fedotina (1973) in the former Soviet Union reported a mycoplasma-like plant pathogen that causes the big bud disease of tomato to be present in *O. aegyptiaca* when it is parasitizing that crop. Khanna (1968) showed that tobacco mosaic and potato *X* virus could not be transmitted to broomrape either from tobacco or by direct inoculation.

There is much work to be done on the physiology and biochemistry of normal processes of these strange plants before we can wisely and efficiently plan for control measures, including the breeding of resistant host crops.

A special project to define research strategies for *Orobanche* control in legume crops and to develop effective means of control was conducted by K. Linke and J. Sauerborn from 1987 to 1992 at the International Center for Agricultural Research in Dry Areas (ICARDA) in Aleppo, Syria and at the University of Hohenheim in Stuttgart, Germany. Two publications that summarize this research experience are *Biology and Control of Orobanche in Legume Crops* by J. Sauerborn and K. Linke and *An Orobanche Field Guide* by K. Linke, J. Sauerborn and M. Saxena. They may be obtained from the Institute for Plant Production and Protection in the Tropics and Subtropics at The University of Hohenheim.

The Deutsche Gesellschaft fur Technische Zussammenarbeit (GTZ) has recently established a special division on "The Ecology and Management of Parasitic Weeds" at the Institute for Plant Production in the Tropics and Subtropics at the University of Hohenheim, Germany, J. Kroschel, Director.

ANATOMY AND MORPHOLOGY OF THE HAUSTORIUM AND OTHER STRUCTURES

The seeds of *O. ramosa* are thick, cutinized and have reticulate surface patterns (Abu-Shakra et al. 1971). Musselman and Mann (1976) and Joel (1987, 1988) in Israel used the scanning electron microscope to study surface patterns of *Orobanche* seeds. Joel additionally used fluorescence microscopy to develop a key for the identification of the seeds of the principal agricultural broomrape species in Israel.

The seeds are ovate in shape, with the micropylar region of the seed at the narrow end and chalazal area at the other extremity. The endosperm is located at the micropylar end with the elongated embryo structure buried in it. The embryo is a mass of undifferentiated cells with no obvious preliminary forms of cotyledon, radicle or plumule (Abu-Shakra et al. 1971). Sunderland (1960) described the embryo of *O. minor* as globular with variations of size and staining density of cells in different regions; again no organ differentiation. With pretreated moist seeds he found that a 30-sec exposure to a root exudate of linseed *Linum* species was sufficient to initiate the germination process. In several *Orobanches* the emerging radicle may be seen about 96 hr after exposure to a suitable stimulant (see also Chabrolin 1938).

Aseptically cultured seeds of *O. aegyptiaca* germinate without a root exudate upon addition of certain ingredients to the medium. Coconut milk or yeast extract caused roots and shoots to emerge from the morphological radicular end of the seed. With auxins, cytokinins, gibberellin or strigol in the medium, the shoots originated at the plumular pole and the roots at the radicular pole (Kumar 1977).

The source and nature of the signal to begin haustorial development has not been studied in *Orobanche*. Okonkwo (1966) showed that a host stimulus was required for this process in *Striga senegalensis* and Riopel (1979) reported cultures of *Striga asiatica* that never formed haustoria without a host stimulant. With a stimulant, haustoria were formed on host roots overnight. He feels this to be the most rapid cellular response recorded for any multicellular organ in the angiosperms.

When the parasitic radical emerges it attaches to the host root at the most active region for elongation and absorption, and undergoes rapid cell division while thickening to form a primary haustorium. The first probing growth of the host root is made by polymorphic cells with epidermal coverings. There are no traces of xylem or phloem in these early cells. In a study of fine structure, Dorr and Kollmann (1974, 1975, 1976) could distinguish between the host and parasite tissues with the latter having densely structured protoplasts with many ribosomes, a highly organized rough endoplasmic reticulum, and many cell organelles. *O. ramosa* had cells containing spherical bodies 60 nm in diameter. Some had tail-like appendages that served as markers. As the apical cells force their way into the host root, the intrusion seems to proceed by dissolution of nearby cell walls (Dorr and Kollmann 1974). Nuclei on both sides of the union migrate toward the cell walls, a papilla-like structure of the parasite makes a small pore in the host root, and the cell contents are emptied into the host cell in ameboid-like form. Other advancing fingers proceed in the same fashion, penetrating the pericycle, and growing toward the central cylinder of the host. Finally the haustorial tissue surrounds the host's vascular system. As haustorial growth progresses, cell division begins in the host roots and there is a tendency toward lignification, as though in self-defense. Ultimately the entire union is similar to a graft fusion (Kadry and Tewfic 1956b, Dorr and Kollmann 1974, 1975, 1976; Pennypacker et al. 1979).

Dorr and Kollmann (1974, 1975, 1976) studied the fine structure of the assimilate conducting cells of *O. ramosa* at an intermediate stage of haustorial formation. The phloem had typical features of sieve element differentiation with disintegration of nuclei and tonoplasts, structural changes in plastids and mitochondria, and a plentiful supply of ribosomes. A smooth endoplasmic reticulum near the cell wall seemed to be specific for sieve elements and the best development was in the parasitic cells near the sieve tubes of the host. There was always an intermediate contact cell with a normal protoplast of high density between the host and the special assimilate conducting cell of the parasite. Transfer cells developed adjacent to xylem elements of the host and these eventually seemed to differentiate into haustorial xylem to represent a kind of xylem link-up of host-parasite. They found no evidence of open connections between the lumina of the host and the parasitic xylem cells. Salle (1987) summarized a literature survey on the existence of true xylem tissues in the absorptive organs of parasitic flowering plants and the structure of phloem tissues in species of *Orobanche* (including *ramosa*), *Striga* and *Cuscuta*.

For decades the search for direct connections—open pipelines—between host and parasite, or for other mechanisms for the exchange of assimilates between transgenic plants, has been wearisome and not very rewarding. Of late, with improved microscopic equipment and techniques, a few such open linkages have been found. Elsewhere in the plant world there are recent discoveries that may some day inform us about the movement of assimilates and large bodies between adjacent plant cells. Using microspectrofluorometry, Goff and Coleman (1984) demonstrated that the small red algal parasite (*Choreocolax* species) can insert some of its own nuclei into the cells of a distantly related algal host *Polysiphonia* species. The metabolism and morphology of the invaded cells are greatly modified. The nuclei persist for weeks in the new environment and the invaded cells function for extended periods with the foreign nuclei scattered about in their cytoplasm. Wolf et al. (1989) investigated the role of a tobacco mosaic virus protein, called movement protein, which affects the spread of the virus between plant cells. In the absence of the movement protein, the plasmodesmata could accommodate particles in the range of about 800 daltons (atomic mass units) while in its presence molecular masses of 9400 daltons could pass between cells.

Those parts of the *Orobanche* seedling that are external to the host form an enlarged, elongated swelling or protuberance, sometimes called a tubercle, that attaches to the host root. There are further smaller protrusions on this lump, and one, slightly larger, becomes the terminal bud of the shoot that will bear the bracts and inflorescence. Ungurean (1973) in Rumania believes the swollen tubercle is a reduced seedling since it assists fully in the formation of the parasitic plant. In *O. aegyptiaca* such shoots may live 30 to 40 days (Kabulov 1966).

The other protrusions on the tubercle are of different structure and some form roots to 5 cm in length. Together all of these organs give the early tubercle a crumb-like appearance. In *O. ramosa* the tubercle is sometimes much less pronounced than in *O. minor* and may soon be hidden by the mass of roots originating on it. Some of the protrusions grow toward lateral host roots and produce secondary haustoria; others may infect host roots already attacked by primary haustoria. These "crown roots" at the stem's base may also attack nearby crop or weed plants.

Attawi (1977) and Attawi and Weber (1980) studied the development of secondary haustoria in 15 species of *Orobanche* and reported a general pattern similar to the above. They also found that the larger the number of host secondary roots crossing an area near the parasite the greater the number of secondary haustoria present. Roots of *Orobanche* plants can attack one another. Several unusual haustorial types were found among this array of species. Meta haustoria seemed to have failed in contacting roots, or to have lost contact. Wart haustoria appeared to have failed to differentiate from cortical to haustorial cells. There were no root hairs on haustorial, adventitious, or lateral roots.

Young parasitic plants have phloem elements and some xylem vessels with helical thickenings. Starch grains are present in young shoots but not mature stems. Cross-sections of bracts reveal a simple structure with a spongy mesophyll and vascular traces with the whole surrounded by an epidermal layer (Saghir et al. 1973). The stomata are very much reduced and have lost all function. Trichomes cover the surface of peduncles, allowing for release of excess water through hydathodes (Rakhimov 1967).

Moreno et al. (1979) reported on the meiotic behavior of five populations of *O. crenata* and from his results postulated that the hybridization may be occurring between different strains and/or interspecific crosses.

AGRICULTURAL IMPORTANCE

O. ramosa is a serious weed of beans in Egypt; eggplant in Bulgaria and Jordan; flax in Bulgaria; peppers in Jordan; rape (*Brassica napus*) in Hungary, Lebanon and elsewhere in the eastern Mediterranean area; sunflower in the former Yugoslavia; *Taraxacum koksaghys* (grown for rubber production) in the former Soviet Union; tobacco in Bulgaria, Cuba, Hungary, Jordan, eastern Mediterranean area, Mexico, Nepal, the former Soviet Union, and Switzerland; and tomato in Egypt, Hungary, the eastern Mediterranean area, Jordan, Lebanon, Sudan, and the United States.

It is a principal weed of carrots in Egypt and occasionally elsewhere in the world; chickpeas in the Near and Middle East; eggplant in Lebanon; several legumes in Italy; lentils in the Near and Middle East; peppers in Lebanon; tobacco in Lebanon, Rumania,

Turkey, and the former Yugoslavia; tomato in Iraq, Iran, Jordan, and Saudi Arabia; and several other vegetables in Sudan.

In several of the above crops, branched broomrape is of lesser or undetermined rank, also in beans in Ethiopia; eggplant in Israel; flax in France; peppers in the United States; sunflower in Hungary and the former Soviet Union; tobacco in the United States, Germany, Czechoslovakia, India, Italy, Lebanon, Rumania, and Sudan; tomato in Czechoslovakia, the former Yugoslavia, Rumania, the former Soviet Union, and Ethiopia; and vegetables in India. It is also a weed in cabbage, cauliflower, celery, clover, hemp, onion, rape, and pastures in one or more of the following areas: Cuba, England, France, Switzerland, the western part of the former Soviet Union, eastern Europe, the eastern Mediterranean, the United States, and South Africa.

O. minor is a serious weed of beans and peas in Egypt; clover, rape, and tobacco in New Zealand; and legumes in Czechoslovakia. It is a principal weed of legumes in Italy, Egypt, and Australia; and grassland in Uganda and elsewhere in East Africa. It is a common weed of lucerne in Turkey and New Zealand; legumes of several kinds in Hungary; and vegetables in Saudi Arabia.

It is a weed of lesser or undetermined importance of lucerne and clover in Belgium, England, Germany, Sweden in northern Europe, and in the former Yugoslavia, Lebanon, Jordan, and Egypt in the Mediterranean area, as well as in the United States. It also infests beans in Ethiopia and South Africa; carrots, ornamentals, and tobacco in the United States; pastures in Austria and Australia; and vegetables in Turkey. In Australia it is reported in the following clovers: alsike, berseem, crimson, hop, red, subterranean, white, and also black medic. *O. minor* has a wide host range but tends to prefer **Leguminosae**, where it is especially troublesome in clover.

O. aegyptiaca, as mentioned previously, is believed by some to be a form of *O. ramosa* that replaces the latter in hot, dry areas. It is a more robust plant, with heavily scented flowers. As expected, *O. aegyptiaca* shows up on many of the crops listed for *O. ramosa* and is also listed more often on cotton, melons, peanuts, vetch, and the *Brassica* mustard and oil crops.

The *Orobanches* are rarely found on monocots, but there are scattered reports of it on maize in Bulgaria, Cuba, and elsewhere (Bailov and Slavkov 1974, Torres 1986). Kasasian (1971a) reported that maize, *Pennisetum* and *Setaria* species can be used as trap crops for branched broomrape.

Before and after harvest, weeds such as *Amaranthus retroflexus, Capsella bursa-pastoris* and *Xanthium spinosum*, with other native plants, can prosper on roadsides and ditchbanks while hosting some of the *Orobanches*, and thus ensure the continuing survival of the parasites in intensively cropped areas of susceptible crops. The parasite is also said to survive on remnants and residues in sugar beet fields.

There are many pairing lists for the *Orobanches* and their hosts, but some must be viewed with caution, for each of the broomrape species seems to have several biotypes or strains, and some of these physiological races are known to be more harmful to certain crop plants than other races. Some may not attack the crop plant at all (Petrov 1970, Bailov and Slavkov 1974, Mijatovic and Stojanovic 1973). In addition, all of our crop plants, through breeding and selection, have cultivars and therefore may vary greatly in their own right in the ability to resist infection by a particular parasite species that may devastate the same crop elsewhere. An example from India illustrates this. A turnip strain of *O. cernua* would not germinate when planted with a mustard closely related to turnip. Further, a strain of the parasite growing on a closely related mustard would not germinate when planted with turnip (Singh and Pavgi 1975). Vranceanu et al. (1986) reported on development of physiological races of *O. cumana* on sunflowers in Rumania in relation to breeding of sunflowers resistant to parasites and the response of individual sunflower genotypes.

Thus, host range lists tend to be full of contradictions and omissions. For working purposes, the discussion of importance by parasitic species, crop, and country at the beginning of this section is sufficient portrayal of "pairings." One further credit must be given to branched broomrape to emphasize its exceptional host range. Several crops well known to us but important only to local diets and economies may be parasitized by *O. ramosa*, among them hops, paprika, parsnips, pyrethrum, etc.

Sauerborn (1991) has estimated that 4 to 5% of all the world's arable lands are presently threatened by the *Orobanches* and the *Strigas*. Yield losses due to *Orobanche* infections have reached levels of 25 to 75% for *O. ramosa* in tomatoes in Hungary and 30% for sunflower, with an attendant reduction in oil quality (Hodosy 1981); one-third of the crop in tomato in the United States and sunflower in the former Yugoslavia (Cordas 1954); and 40% in vegetables in Afghanistan (Alekozai 1969). With 80% of the fields infested with *O. ramosa*, sowing of beans and peas has been abandoned in some areas of Malta, Morocco, and Sicily. The growth of the parasitic plant biomass below ground is so vigorous at times that it may weigh several times more than the crop to which it is attached.

Because the *Orobanche* plant is so complex in its behavior and in the response to its neighbors, the management and control of the different species, in the field, will surely have to be a combination of methods and systems. Long-term control efforts must give high priority to the reduction of parasitic propagules in the soil seed bank, the prevention of new additions, and a concerted attempt to arrest the spread of this plague to new areas.

Trap cropping uses plant species that cause parasitic seed germination but are not themselves parasitized. Catch crops promote seed germination, are themselves parasitized, and are then destroyed before the desired crop is planted. There are problems with the latter system, for early generous periods of rainfall are often needed to get a sufficiently good stand of catch crops to make the effort worthwhile. In seasons when rains continue too long, it is often difficult to get into the field to plow down the catch crop and replant the desired crop.

Trench or deep plowing has been used to bury the weed seed in Bulgaria, New Zealand, and the former Soviet Union. With this method, Kabulov (1966) reported 80 to 90% reduction of the parasite infestation in 3 yr in some areas of the former Soviet Union. From several regions of the world, less *Orobanche* trouble is reported when crops are planted early. In Egypt, direct-seeded tomatoes were more resistant to attacks by *O. ramosa* than transplanted tomatoes.

Jacobsohn et al. (1980), Braun et al. (1987) and Sauerborn and Saxena (1987) have recently reported promising results for destroying *Orobanche* seeds in the field with soil heating under polyethylene sheeting.

The fly or midge *Phytomyz orobanchia* is reported to give almost complete control of broomrapes in the fields of some countries of eastern Europe and parts of the former Soviet Union. The fly feeds on developing fruit and damages stems, thus causing desiccation. Increases in yields of sunflower, tobacco, and tomato have been reported with the use of *Phytomyza* in the former Soviet Union and the former Yugoslavia (Lekic 1970b, Chalukov 1973, Klyueva and Pamukchi 1978, 1982).

The chemical stimulation of parasitic seed germination in field soils to reduce infestations does not hold promise of practical use by farmers at this time. Research on the use of herbicides to control broomrapes is increasing, but Jacobsohn (1986), after a broad review of these studies, feels that practical use of such chemical measures is not widely accepted because of cost, lack of selectivity among crops, etc.

Finally, there seems to be general agreement that the use of crop varieties resistant to the broomrapes is at this time the principal control measure for bringing help to large areas of crops. In spite of the difficulties of a constantly shifting pattern of virulence within the physiological races of a particular *Orobanche* species, together with changes to improved cultivars in principal crops (for better disease resistance and higher yields but sometimes with less resistance to broomrapes), there has been scattered evidence following decades of selection and breeding for the existence and usefulness of resistant varieties in several crops. Cubero (1986) believes that suitable resistant varieties (for certain regions) have thus far been developed in sunflower (*Helianthus annuus*), faba or broad bean (*Vicia faba*), and eggplant (*Solanum melongena*). In the former Soviet Union, Avdeev, and Shcherbinin (1976), after sorting 200 cultivars, announced the discovery of a tomato variety very resistant to *O. aegyptiaca* in the Caspian Sea area. Such varieties have often been the diligent work of scientists from Egypt, eastern Europe, and the former Soviet Union.

Two examples are illustrative of some of the difficulties in this work. In Israel, Shalom et al. (1988) have demonstrated that varieties of sunflower resistant to three *Orobanche* species expressed this characteristic only in spring and summer. In winter plantings the varieties became susceptible. This climate-dependent resistance has also been shown for carrots in Israel. Varieties of sunflower known to be resistant to *O. cernua* in Israel are known to be susceptible to that parasitic species in other countries.

Mijatovic and Stojanovic (1973) of the former Yugoslavia pointed out long ago that, although *O. cumana* remains a threat to sunflower, for some periods the parasite populations have been held to low levels by use of resistant varieties. However, some of the parasite-resistant sunflower selections are more susceptible to pathogenic fungi, necessitating the search for both broomrape and disease resistance or a shift to other control methods.

Recent extensive reviews for the control of the *Orobanche* have been published by Cubero (1986), Ramaiah (1987), and Foy et al. (1989).

Kamel (1956) in Egypt reported some deaths in cattle and goats from acute gastroenteritis following ingestion of shoots of *O. minor*. The problem was less serious in dogs and cats. *Orobanche* shoots are grazed in pastures in Australia and elsewhere, are fed to milk cows in India, but are reported to be foul-smelling and unpalatable to animals in several places in the world.

COMMON NAMES

Orobanche minor

BELGIUM	klavervreter
CHILE	orobanche
DENMARK	klover-gyvelkvaeler
ENGLAND	common broomrape
FRANCE	orobanche du trefle, orobanche mineure
GERMANY	Kleeteufel, Kleine Sommerwurz, Tannli, Zapfen
ITALY	succiamiele della carota

PORTUGAL	erva-toira-menor
SOUTH AFRICA	clover broomrape, klawerbesmrapp
SPAIN	rabo de lobo
TURKEY	vinagrillo
UNITED STATES	clover broomrape

Orobanche ramosa

CUBA	yerba de sosa
EGYPT	halouk
ENGLAND	hemp broomrape
FRANCE	orobanche rameuse, orobanche du chanvre
GERMANY	Astige Sommerwurz
IRAN	gole jeez
ITALY	succiamiele ramoso
LEBANON	branched broomrape, haluk-rihi
NETHERLANDS	hennepvreter
PORTUGAL	erva-toira-ramosa
SAUDI ARABIA	halook
SOUTH AFRICA	branched broomrape, vertakte besmraap
SPAIN	hierba tora
TURKEY	mavi cicekli canavarotu
UNITED STATES	branched broomrape

Sixty-Two

THE WILD RICES

Oryza sativa L.,
Oryza punctata Kotschy ex Steud.,
Oryza rufipogon Griff.,
Oryza barthii A. Chev.
(syn. O. breviligulata A. Chev. et Roehr.),
and Oryza officinalis Wall. ex Watt.

Poaceae (Gramineae), Grass Family

RICE (*ORYZA SATIVA* L.) is the world's most important crop. It provides nearly 80% of the calories for 2 billion people in Asia and one-third of the caloric intake of 1 billion in Latin America and Africa (Chang 1984). Nearly 100,000 varieties are grown in over 100 countries, on every continent except Antarctica, to latitudes as far north as Manchuria, to as far south as Uruguay, South America, and New South Wales, Australia (Hargrove and Chang 1978). *O. sativa* has been used as a food since 5000 B.C. in Thailand and *O. glaberrima* was domesticated in Africa around 1500 B.C. While the latter species is less diversified and cultivated than *O. sativa*, thousands of varieties are found in west Africa and it offers several unique adaptations less common in *O. sativa*. The wide dispersal of rice around the world and its long history of cultivation probably make it the most genetically diverse cereal crop in the world.

After reviewing the information on "wild rices," we felt it was impossible to either limit this chapter to one species or to cover all those mentioned in the literature. Naturally, the meaning of the term "wild" varies among scientists. Plant breeders see wild types as precious genetic reservoirs and indeed they are. Production agronomists and weed scientists, however, generally use the term to denote a weedy plant type. The spontaneous occurrence of nondomesticated rices in nature may or may not mean that they are weeds. Only if wild types interfere with human activities would they be considered as weeds. And

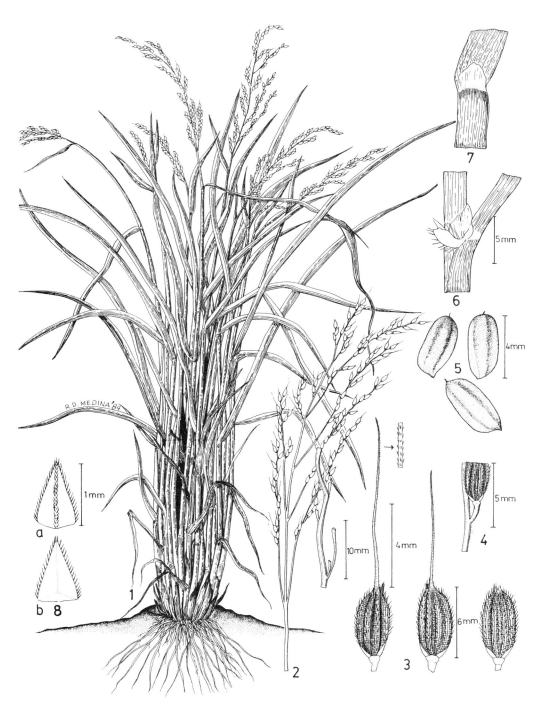

FIGURE 62-1 *Oryza punctata* Kotschy *ex* Steud.: 1. habit; 2. panicle; 3. spikelets, 4. basal part of spikelet, enlarged to show pubescence; 5. caryopsis; 6. leaf collar, 7. front view to show ligule; 8. sterile lemmas: a. back view, b. front view.

even this criteria varies from region to region and from season to season. In parts of India, for example, red rice is planted as a desired variety, but in most areas, any non-white rice is considered undesirable and treated as a weed. Where *O. sativa* has been introduced into Africa, volunteer plants of *O. glaberrima* are considered as weeds (Parker and Dean 1976). During years of drought, the grain of spontaneous rices may be used as food or the plants used as livestock forage.

Both Greek and Latin names for rice correspond to the genus name and there are over 20 *Oryza* species recognized by taxonomists and plant breeders specialized in this area (Tateoka 1964, Sampath 1973, Bezancon et al. 1978, Ogbe and Williams 1978, and Chang et al. 1982). In the next section we will briefly review the origin and taxonomy of rice as a background to the remainder of this chapter and because it is a fascinating evolutionary story.

ORIGIN AND TAXONOMY

Perhaps no other crop in the world has been as intensely researched as rice. It is the principal cereal of the world and is a major crop in nearly all tropical and subtropical regions. Many species are known and the study of the origin of our cultivated types is most interesting, as it reveals the importance of both natural and human influences on crop evolution. Weed scientists would have a much better appreciation of species biotypes if we knew even the mere beginnings of evolutionary changes that have occurred in our important species. In the case of rice, we have a general understanding of the sequence of events that led to our cultivated and weedy types.

Research and a review by Sampath (1973) in India suggests that *O. perennis* is the common ancestor of both cultivated species, *O. sativa* and *O. glaberrima*. The oldest known evidence of rice used as a food was in Thailand, where it was consumed around 5000 B.C. Both *O. perennis* and *O. rufipogon* are found in Thailand, Burma, and Cambodia. Natural crosses between different *O. perennis* populations, followed by several generations of self-pollination, could have formed *O. rufipogon*. The occurrence of mutations to give awnless, non-shedding grains and the selection of grain types by prehistoric agriculturalists could have resulted in the *O. sativa* that we now know as cultivated rice. Sampath cites supporting evidence on the evolution of cultivated rice in Africa. If populations of *O. barthii* (the African ancestor of cultivated rice) are self-pollinated for two or three generations, some of the resulting progeny are new plant types and can be classified as *O. breviligulata*, and these may have mutated into the cultivated types of *O. glaberrima* found in this part of the world.

The excellent review on the origin of rice by Chang (1976) suggests parallel forms of evolution in Asia and Africa as follows.

ASIA

O. rufipogon (wild perennial) —-> *O. nivara* —-> *O. sativa* (and "*spontanea*" forms)

AFRICA

O. longistaminata (wild perennial) —-> *O. barthii* —-> *O. glaberrima* (and "*stapfii*" forms)

In each case, the sequence originated with a wild perennial, went to a wild annual and then to a cultivated annual. These changes were caused by differences in both human preference and population pressures. Chang stated that the annual weedy types are "conglomerates of natural hybrids of all intergrades among the above three" species cited for each region. He believes that the weedy types in Asia are *spontanea*, while in Africa they are *stapfii* (considered by others as a synonym for *O. barthii*).

Several changes occurred during the evolutionary process. Plants became taller, the leaves longer and the stems thicker; there was a decrease in pigmentation, rhizome formation, dormancy, photoperiodic response and low temperature sensitivity. The frequency of cross pollination decreased so that the crop is more inbred than the wild types. Chang believes that both the *O. sativa* and *glaberrima* complexes are undergoing continual and dynamic changes and that "pure" forms of *O. rufipogon* and *O. nivara* are conceptual and no longer exist in nature. He also estimates that there are over 100,000 cultivars of *O. sativa* alone in the world (Chang 1984).

The review of the rices of Africa by Bezancon et al. (1978) reveals several aspects of interest. *O. glaberrima*, the cultivated species, has a lower yield potential than *O. sativa* but is more tolerant to deep water, drought, rice blast and diopsids. *O. breviligulata* (considered as a synonym to *O. barthii*) is primarily a self-pollinated annual type with grains that mature and shatter early and are strongly dormant after maturity; it crosses with *O. glaberrima*, giving rise to hybrids that are intermediate in grain shedding and other characters. *O. longistaminata* is the highly adapted wild type. It is found in salt marshes, deep water, standing or running water, dry and sandy fields and occasionally in forests. *O. breviligulata* dominates in cultivated fields. When the field is abandoned, *O. longistaminata* often takes over.

Shastry and Sharma (1974) provided an excellent review of the development of rice into a crop and organized the *Oryza* genus into three sections and seven series. They readily distinguished between species across a series but often found it difficult to do within a series. They also believe that continual crossing among species occurs and define a "hybrid swarm" as the result of crosses between cultivated and wild types. Roy (1921) found 24 "types" of rice based only on leaf sheath color (red, green, or purple), whether the pedicel was enclosed by the flag leaf, and glume color. Katayama (1969a) studied the surface features of glumes and leaves of 22 *Oryza* species. Detailed descriptions of the cell shape, nature of surface hairs (if present), characteristics of both the upper and lower leaf surfaces and stomatal arrangement are given. He believes that such morphological studies can be used to help clarify the taxonomy of this genus.

Chang et al. (1982) notes that in recent decades it has become increasingly difficult to classify rice varieties into their ecogeographic races based on morphological traits and grain characteristics. Even between species, the taxonomy of the *Oryza* genus appears to be more of an art than a science. Ogbe and Williams (1978) state that ". . . most of the species (of *O. sativa* and *O. glaberrima*) group into complexes the delimitation of which is a matter of opinion." Harlan et al. (1973) are even more direct in stating that, "Inept classifications have probably caused more difficulty in understanding the origin and evolution of cultivated plants than any other factor." Thus weed scientists will find confusion in the literature regarding the wild rices. This should not discourage us from conducting the necessary research on those species behaving as weeds in our cropping systems.

Other genera also contain species called "wild rice." The species *Zizania aquatica* is native to North America and has been cultivated as a deep water crop by native Americans for centuries (Johonson 1969). *Zizaniopsis miliacea* is called "southern wild rice" and is sometimes a problem weed along the edges of reservoirs or where it impedes the flow of water or traffic (Tarver et al. 1979). *Z. aquatica* is an annual with stems 1 to 3 m tall, according to the water depth. The panicle is 30 to 50 cm long and the male flowers are found on the lower portion of the panicle. The spikelets are 2 cm long and without glumes. Several varieties of *Z. aquatica* are recognized. In addition to being a cultivated crop in the Great Lakes region of the northern United States, California (in the western United States), and southern Canada, it is also harvested in parts of China and Japan. *Z. miliacea* is a perennial growing 1 to 3 m tall with short, scaly rhizomes. The panicle has pistillate and staminate flowers on the same branches. The spikelets are 5 to 8 mm long and the second glume (there is no first glume) has numerous nerves (Tarver et al. 1979).

DESCRIPTIONS

The species described here are those frequently cited as wild or weedy rices. Others could also be included in this group. Perhaps in this genus more than any other, the continual crossing among types and species gives a wide array of morphological characteristics. Those presented describe the "typical" plants of each species, but some variation is to be expected. All *Oryza* species have these characteristics in common: spikelets of one floret with six stamens, loosely arranged on branched, elongated panicles; one to three glumes are present but the first and second are often very minute; the third glume is 5-nerved, hard, keeled and awned or awnless; the palea is linear and as long as the glume, 3-veined with membranous margins. The spikelets are 5 to 10 mm long, approximately 4 mm wide and are covered with two hard scales, one partially enfolding the other and are covered with minute dots.

Oryza sativa (no illustration)

The red seed coat of some strains of *O. sativa* is very undesirable in many countries. The annual "red rice" of the United States, and Central and South America, and the "black rice" of Brazil are invariably referred to as *O. sativa*. In addition to the red pericarp, the undesirable types are characterized by early shattering seeds, a greater degree of dormancy, plants taller than cultivated varieties with a weaker straw and the presence of pubescence and relatively long awns on the lemma (Craigmiles 1978). Plants are annuals, with erect stems, 80 to 120 cm tall, tillered, glabrous and have a well-developed membranous ligule. Further distinctions can be made between the strawhull and blackhull red rices (Sonnier 1978). Strawhull types have a normal-colored lemma and palea and produce relatively open plants with few tillers and drooping panicles with awned or awnless lemma. The blackhull types have a blackish lemma and palea and dense, compacted plants with 50 to 75 tillers; the panicles may not emerge completely from the boot and the lemmas have awns. Blackhull types are also taller and slower to reach anthesis than strawhull types.

Oryza punctata

O. punctata (Figure 62-1) is an *annual* tufted grass; *root* system fibrous; *stems* to 1.5 m tall, 4 mm or less in diameter, the base usually spongy and thick; *leaves* flat, 30 to 60 cm long, linear-lanceolate, not exceeding 2 cm in width, tapering from the middle to a fine tip; *ligule* membranous, triangulate, 3 to 5 mm long, soft, whitish, not fringed; small *auricles* clasp the stem; *inflorescence* loose panicle with spreading branches, the axis slightly woolly pubescent at the origin of branches, the rest entirely glabrous, smooth or scabrid; *spikelets* laterally compressed, pedicelled, elliptic 5 to 6.5 mm long, 2 to 2.5 mm broad; *glumes* rudimentary; *lemmas* 1st and 2nd sterile, triangular and acute, 1 mm long; *awn* terminal, almost straight, 3 to 7 mm long, with rather rigid bristles; *fruit* a *caryopsis* 4 mm long.

This species is often confused with *O. eichingeri*, from which it differs in having spreading panicles, straight or flexed awns with rigid bristles, and sterile, triangular lemmas. It is found widely in Africa, from the Ivory Coast to Kenya and south to southern Zimbabwe and Madagascar.

Oryza rufipogon

O. rufipogon (Figure 62-2) is a *perennial*, tufted grass; *stems* erect, to 1.5 m tall, spongy below; *leaf sheath* terete, loose, quite glabrous, with clearly defined *auricles* at junction with blade; *blades* linear, acuminate, flat, up to 40 cm long, to 12 mm wide, scabrid on margins and main veins; *ligule* well developed, foliose, up to 5 cm long, acutely bifid; *inflorescence* a strict, terminal, exserted panicle, up to 20 cm long, finally nodding, main axis angular, scabrid on the angles; *spikelets* pedicelled, 8 to 9 mm long, 2 to 2.5 mm wide; *glumes* rudimentary; *lemmas* one and two sterile, 2 to 4 mm long, one nerved, keeled, 3rd lemma fertile, 7 to 9 mm long, 5-nerved with terminal *awn* up to 7 cm long, hispid-scaberulous; *fruit* a *caryopsis* 6 mm long, oblong, brown.

It occurs in ponds, ditches and other places with stagnant or slow-moving water. It often grows side by side with cultivated rice, and closely resembles it in vegetative characters. It is difficult to eradicate from cultivation and is common in eastern India, Madras, Burma, Thailand, Malaysia, and Indonesia.

Oryza barthii

O. barthii (Figure 62-3) is an erect or spreading *annual* grass; *stems* to 1.5 m tall; *leaf sheaths* open, somewhat shorter than the internodes or equal to them with distinct venation and small ciliated auricles at the base of blade; *blades* linear-lanceolate, those near base 30 cm or more long, 11 mm wide, tapering from middle to a fine tip and narrow base, upper surface scabrous, lower surface minutely serrate-acicular along edge; *ligule* membranous, yellow green, 3 to 12 mm long with blunt or rounded, sometimes notched to pointed tip; *inflorescence* a rather dense or open panicle, sometimes producing tertiary branches, rising slightly above the leaves, up to 15 cm long, the axis ribbed, glabrous or woolly-pubescent with the lower part sharp-scabrous; *spikelets* pedicelled, strongly compressed from the sides, 7 to 11 mm long, with *awns* 5 to 18 cm long, covered with rather course, hard, sharp bristles; *pedicel* short, 1 to 4 mm long ending in oblique cup-shaped enlargement representing the rudiments of the lower pairs of empty glumes; *fruit* a *caryopsis* up to 7 mm long, oblong, compressed from the sides, brown.

This species is related to *O. glaberrima*, the African cultivated rice, from which it differs in having secondary or tertiary branches in the panicles, longer grains and awns with stiff bristles. It is also confused with *O. longistaminata*, but the latter is perennial and rhizomatous. It is widely distributed in Central Africa, especially within the limits of irrigation by the river Niger in Sudan and the bogs southeast of Lake Chad.

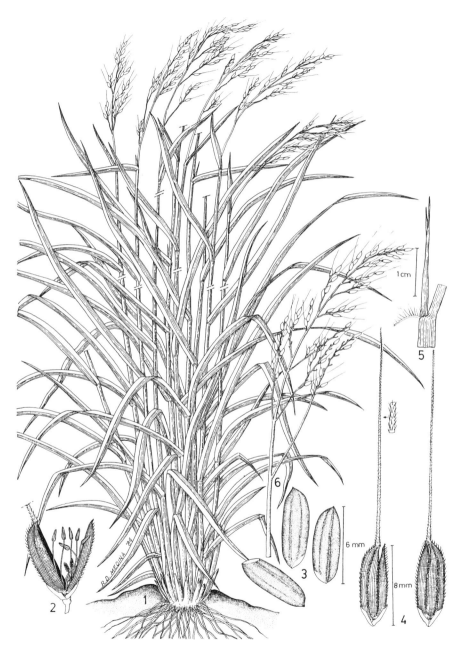

FIGURE 62-2　*Oryza rufipogon* Griff.: 1. habit; 2. spikelet open to show flower; 3. caryopsis, three views; 4. mature spikelet; 5. leaf collar showing auricle and ligule; 6. panicle.

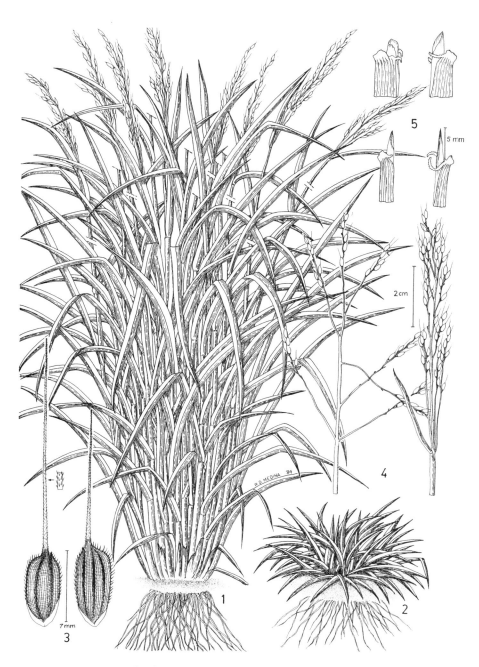

FIGURE 62-3   *Oryza barthii* A. Chev.: 1. habit; 2. seedling; 3. mature spikelet, two views;
4. panicle, open and closed types; 5. ligule, four views.

Oryza officinalis

O. officinalis (Figure 62-4) is a *perennial* grass; *roots* fibrous, occasionally rhizomatous; *stems* erect or ascending, up to 1.5 m tall, somewhat inflated at nodes; *leaf sheath* terete, quite glabrous; *blades* linear, acuminate, 15 to 70 cm long, 7 to 17 mm wide, smooth or scabrid; *ligule* 1 to 5 mm long, lacerate or not, glabrous or ciliate; *inflorescence* a panicle with the lower half or more upward parts of the branches naked and somewhat descending; *spikelets* less then 2 mm wide, the length always less than twice the breadth, turning dark brown or black at maturity, shedding easily; *awn* up to 2 cm or awnless; *fruit* a reddish-brown to grayish *caryopsis*.

This species is similar to *O. minuta* but differs in being diploid ($2n = 24$) while the latter is tetraploid ($2n = 48$). In addition, the mean spikelet breadth of the diploid is less than 2.1 mm and that of the tetraploid is more than 2.2 mm. The length is always less than twice the breadth in the diploid, while in the tetraploid the length is almost always more than twice the breadth (Tateoka and Pancho 1963).

This species is found in marshy or swampy areas, ditches, shallow ponds and rice fields from New Guinea to India. In vegetative form it is difficult to distinguish from cultivated rice.

BIOLOGY AND ECOLOGY

The following section will present the important aspects of the biology and ecology of the wild rices we encountered in the literature. As previously discussed, the taxonomy of the *Oryza* genus is by no means clear or conclusive. The Latin names presented in the remainder of this chapter will be those given by the authors.

As a crop, *O. sativa* is highly adapted to a wide range of environmental conditions. It grows from lat 53° N to 40° S; some types are adapted to dryland, wetland and deep water culture. *O. glaberrima* is less diversified and has a narrower north-south distribution. The wild rices naturally share in this range of adaptation.

One characteristic often found in wild rice is the red pericarp. Its presence requires additional milling that reduces the quality of the milled rice and results in more broken grains. Varieties of *O. sativa* and *O. glaberrima* with red pericarps exist. Many of the wild species also have red seed coats. The red pigmentation is a dominant character (H. Leitao et al. 1972) and is controlled by more than one gene (Wirjahardja et al. 1983).

Early seed drop is another characteristic of wild rices. In studies done in India, Chalam (1942) found that the slightest contact with *O. sativa* var. *fatua* or *O. coarctata* caused shattering when the seed had hardened. The long awn found on many wild rices causes the wind to hasten seed drop. His anatomical studies discovered that the attachment of the spikelet to the pedicel in non-shattering varieties was similar to a ball-and-socket joint. The spikelet and pedicel arrangement of shedding types more closely resembled two discs, one on top of the other. However, the main difference was in the abscission layer. In cultivated varieties, this layer of cells is not fully formed and bands of lignified tissue around the central vascular bundles provide protection and bind the spikelet to the pedicel. In both *O. fatua* and *O. coarctata*, the abscission layer forms more fully and earlier.

Seed shattering and a red pericarp are dominant traits (Sastry and Seetharaman 1978). They are controlled by two genes, one of which is located on the same chromosome for prostrate growth, a recessive trait. The *2n* chromosome number of rice is 24. Many

FIGURE 62-4   *Oryza officinalis* Wall. *ex* Watt.: 1. habit; 2. panicle; 3. mature spikelet, three views; 4. ligule, two views; 5. caryopsis, three views; 6. spikelet opened to show flower.

species are diploid, while others are tetraploid (Tateoka and Pancho 1963, Shastry and Sharma 1974).

Even though rice is generally a self-pollinated crop, the small degree of out-crossing allows weedy traits like red pericarps and shattering seeds to contaminate domestic varieties over time. Similarly, efforts to use the purple leaf trait in cultivated varieties to separate them from wild rices failed, because this characteristic soon appeared in the weedy types, thereby making it impossible to distinguish between wild and cultivated types when hand weeding (Harlan et al. 1973).

Plant breeders have long studied the dynamics of crossing among and between species. Oka and Chang (1959) compared three populations of *O. sativā* f. *spontanea* and noted that the degree to which a genotype of a population approached that of cultivated rice is the degree to which the habitat has been disturbed by humans. The overall gene flow is from cultivated rices to the wild types. They found a population of wild rice in the Central Province of India with several domesticated traits, including weak dormancy, uniform germination and reduced shattering. Oka and Morishima (1971) grew crosses of *O. perennis* and *O. sativa* for several generations and learned that *O. perennis* has several genes of cultivated rice (especially nonshedding and larger grain size) that increased rapidly under cultivation. They conclude that this selection has been the result of human manipulations, while natural selection resulted in a higher degree of self-pollination in cultivated rice.

The flowering process in wild and cultivated varieties was examined by Roy in India (1921). The florets of wild rice open between 8:00 and 9:00 A.M. and remained open longer than those of cultivated varieties (1 hr or more). The stigmas emerge when the florets open and the anthers burst when warmed by the sun for 2 to 5 min. The likelihood of cross-pollination is higher in wild rices than in cultivated varieties. Katayama (1970a,b) observed the flowering traits in 76 strains of 24 species. Flowering occurs in a regular sequence in the panicle of all species. Namely, it begins in the top rachis of the panicle and proceeds downward to the lowest rachis. On a given rachilla, most species (16) flowered in this order: top spikelet, lowest spikelet and then flowering moved upward from the next lowest to the top in sequence. In four species, after the uppermost spikelet flowered, flowering moved down the rachilla. Seven species flowered regardless of climatic conditions, seven responded to climatic conditions, and nine species were controlled primarily by day length. Viable red rice seed is formed 15 to 18 days after anthesis.

Wild and cultivated rices formed flower buds 30 days before heading (Katayama 1974). Factors that influence flowering of photoperiodic sensitive species include the plant's age (older ones are less sensitive), the day length (short photoperiods enhance flowering) and the origin of the material (strains from higher latitudes are more sensitive). Wirjahardja and Nurfilmarasa (1975) report that *O. perennis* is a strongly photosensitive species of wild rice. *O. sativa* var. *fatua* was considered similar in flowering response to the long-day varieties of cultivated rice.

The blackhull red rice has a black or darkened lemma and palea and a red aleurone layer. The black color starts developing in the terminal spikelet 9 to 12 days after anthesis and then progresses randomly through the remainder of the spikelet as it matures. The lemma and palea of red rice in Brazil were more tightly bound to the caryopsis than in white rice (F. Leitao et al. 1972).

Red and wild rice seed is more dormant at maturity than the seed of cultivated rice. The degree of dormancy is influenced by the time of removal from the panicle after heading. Blackhull and strawhull seed harvested 21 days after anthesis had 40 and 70% germination, respectively, when stored at 20°C for 2 wk after harvest (Helpert and Eastin 1978).

Germination was 90% for both types when harvested 30 days after heading. Thirty three days after heading, 50% of the red rice seed had shattered. The early shattering characteristic may partially explain the greater dormancy of wild rice as compared to cultivated (nonshattering) varieties.

Studies by Cohn and co-workers (1981, 1982, 1983) provide further details on red rice dormancy. Removing the hull reduces seed dormancy. Chemical inhibitors are partially responsible, as evidenced by the inhibition of lettuce seed germination by the leachate from dormant rice seed (Oka and Chang 1959). Cytokinin imbibition for 2 hr breaks red rice dormancy, especially in dehulled seeds. Sodium nitrite gives similar effects and germination is equivalent under light and dark conditions. Treatment of *O. sativa* f. *spontanea* seeds with a 14% HCl solution breaks dormancy (Takahashi 1961).

The length of dormancy has been estimated in several countries. In Brazil, red rice seeds remained viable up to 3 yr (H. Leitao et al. 1972); in Swaziland, *O. punctata* was dormant for more than 12 mo (Armstrong 1968); in the United States, viable red rice seed persisted for 2 yr (Klosterboer 1978); and in East Africa, *O. punctata* seeds remained dormant for up to 5 yr (Majisu 1970).

Katayama (1969b) studied the germination behavior of 20 *Oryza* species, including *sativa* and *glaberrima*. The 18 wild species were categorized into five groups as follows: (1) germination occurred within 2 to 3 days (*O. stapfii* and *subulata*); (2) germination had started in 2 to 3 days and peaked at 6 days; final germination was greater than 50% (seven species, including *O. barthii*, *minuta*, *latifolia* and *punctata*); (3) similar to the previous group but germination was less than 33% (two species); (4) germination occurred up to 9 days and was greater than 60% (six species, including *O. perennis*, *officinalis* and *sativa* var. *spontanea*); and (5) like group 4, but total germination was less than 50% (*O. breviligulata*). His long-term germination studies were conducted over 334 days with 50 strains of 11 species. After 30 days, 51% of the seeds had germinated, after 60, 90, 180, 240, and 334 days, the germination values were 62, 72, 80, 92, and 100%, respectively. These data clearly show the delayed germination trait present in many wild rices. He concludes, however, that there are no clear relationships between the germination characteristics and the taxonomy of the *Oryza* genus.

Both blackhull and strawhull red rice types have a higher percentage emergence and produce taller plants 3 days after emergence than cultivated rice. Emergence is greatest when seeds are planted 1 to 4 cm deep. Some seedlings of both strawhull and blackhull rice emerge from 8 and 12 cm (Eastin 1978, Helpert and Eastin 1978). The optimum germination temperature is 30 to 35°C, but red rice seed will sprout from 15 to 40°C. Red rice germinates 1 day earlier than cultivated rice; and on a given day, red rice sprouts at 5°C lower than cultivated rice. Storage at high temperatures (40 to 55°C) also reduced red rice dormancy (Eastin 1978). Blackhull red rice biotypes produced 27% more tillers and 18% more straw and mature later than strawhull types. Both types emerge sooner, grow taller, have more panicles per plant and shatter more than cultivated rice (Diarra et al. 1985b).

The anatomy of cultivated and red rice seeds and seedlings was analyzed with a scanning electron microscope (Hoagland and Paul 1978). The awn of red rice and the presence of numerous spines along the axis and apical end distinguish it from cultivated rice. However, the arrangement of stomata in parallel rows and the presence of epicuticular rodlet wax structures on both surfaces of the coleoptile were the same in both rices. Hoagland (1978) found that red and cultivated rices metabolize propanil in the same manner.

In Indonesia, Wirjahardja and Nurfilmarasa (1975) compared the growth of *O. perennis* and *O. sativa* var. *fatua* and found the latter species produced much more biomass. When single nodes of both species were planted, 80% of the *fatua* and 47% of the *perennis* nodes developed shoots, indicating a notable potential for vegetative regeneration if plants are disked or cultivated into moist soil.

Very little information exists on nutrient uptake or accumulation by wild rice. Naturally those species and types closely related to cultivated ones would be keen competitors for the elements essential for rice growth. Great variations in tolerances to low and high soil *pH* have been observed (Howard-Williams and Walker 1974).

AGRICULTURAL IMPORTANCE AND CONTROL

Wild rice is a weed in over 50 countries (Figure 62-5). Countries that consider wild rice a serious or principal weed in rice include Argentina, Brazil, Colombia, Costa Rica, Gambia, Guyana, Indonesia, Korea, Mexico, Peru, and the United States. It also infests rice in Guyana, Honduras, India, Japan, Malaysia, Madagascar, New Guinea, Nepal, Nicaragua, Nigeria, Pakistan, Panama, the Philippines, Senegal, Sri Lanka, Surinam, Taiwan, Thailand, Venezuela, and Vietnam.

In addition, it infests jute and peanuts in Taiwan; maize in Thailand; soybeans in the Philippines, Thailand, and the United States; vegetables in Tonga and the United States; and wheat in India.

The principal problems caused by wild rice are the reduction in rice yield (since the wild types shatter) and rice quality (due to the red pericarp in many wild rices), and the added expense required to mill red rice to the point where the colored aleurone layer has been removed. In several countries a lower price is paid to the producer if red rice contaminates the harvested grain.

FIGURE 62-5   The distribution of wild rices (*Oryza* spp.) across the world where they have been reported as a weed.

Considering the wide distribution of the problem, relatively few competition studies have been done. Baldwin (1978) in the United States reported that 32 red rice panicles/m^2 reduced white rice yields 64%. Greenhouse studies in Brazil revealed that the red rice root system was 12% greater in fresh weight at maturity than white rice when each was grown in equal ratios in pots. Red rice also formed more tillers than white rice and increased the percentage of infertile spikelets in white rice (H. Leitao et al. 1972). A field competition study was done by Diarra et al. (1985a) in the southern United States. Two rice cultivars were seeded at 100 kg/ha and red rice was seeded at 0, 5, 108, and 215 plants/m^2. At 60 days after planting, red rice produced 63, 270, and 388 tillers/m^2 at densities of 5, 108, and 215 plants/m^2, respectively. Red rice at 108 plants/m^2 or higher reduced white rice stem numbers up to 49%. Red rice densities of 5 plants/m^2 reduced grain yields of white rice by 22%; densities of 108 and 215 red rice plants/m^2 reduced yields 74 to 82%. Low red rice densities did not affect panicle number or increase the percentage of empty florets in white rice. Higher densities affected these parameters and all red rice densities reduced white rice straw dry weight and grains per panicle. The medium-grained, longer season white rice variety competed better with red rice than the long-grained, shorter season variety.

In Indonesia, dried leaves of *O. perennis* and *O. sativa* var. *fatua* reduced the root but not shoot growth of the variety IR-5 (Wirjahardja and Nurfilmarasa 1975). Wild rices are often excellent alternate hosts for common rice insect, disease and nematode species (Aldrick et al. 1973, Babatola 1980).

The level of wild rice infestation is often quite high. In British Guiana, 90% of the rice land is reportedly infested (British Guiana 1959). Over 5000 seeds/m^2 were found in the top 15 cm of soil in infested fields in Surinam (Keisers 1985). Red rice was reported in North and South Carolina, in the United States, in the 1840s (Smith 1981). A survey conducted in the United States in 1929 found that 54% of the tested rice samples had red rice and the average level of contamination was 62 red rice seeds/kg of rice (Goss and Brown 1939). Smith (1981) estimated the losses caused by red rice in only the southern United States to be $US 50 million. Oka and Chang (1959) reported up to 30% contamination by wild rice in India, but 3% was more typical. In Guyana, 80% of the marketed rice samples contained more than 2% red rice; 8% of the sample contained over 40% red rice (Rai 1973). The practice of growing two rice crops per year in Colombia has lead to a rapid increase in red rice infested fields (Grist 1975). Huey and Baldwin (1978) have demonstrated how rapidly a red rice infestation can multiply. One uncontrolled red rice plant can theoretically yield 45 g of seed in one season (1500 seeds) and this can result in 61 kg of seed (2,250,000 seeds) the second season. This example assumes that each plant forms 10 tillers, each panicle yields 150 seeds and all seeds germinate.

The spread of red and wild rice is almost always as a contaminant in rice seed. It is impossible to mechanically separate wild rice seed from cultivated varieties unless there is a significant difference in size or weight. It is conceivable that birds might help disseminate wild rice seeds. However, studies done by Powers et al. (1978) in the United States show that this is not the case for ducks. They fed up to 615 red rice seeds to individual ducks and no viable seeds were excreted. Viable seeds of other rice weeds (*Leptochloa fasicularis* and *Polygonum pennsylvanicum*) were excreted and thus could be spread by ducks. Thus waterfowl may actually reduce the severity of wild rice infestations by eating the seeds.

Hand pulling wild rice in cultivated rice is impractical because it is very difficult to distinguish between the two until heading occurs. Up to 50% of the crop was destroyed in India when hand weeding was practiced (Roy 1921). This author suggested using purple-leaf crop varieties as a means of marking the crop for easy identification. Subsequent workers adopted the idea and produced purple-leaf commercial varieties with yields equal to green-leaf varieties (Singh and Saini 1960). Since the wild rices eventually inherit the purple leaf character, a rotation of green- and purple-leaf varieties is usually practiced so that seedling with the "wrong" leaf color are rogued each year (Grist 1975). Mechanical control of wild rice is seldom feasible unless the land can be fallowed and disked four to six times for at least 2 yr (Klosterboer 1978). Quicker results may be obtained by deep tillage of perennial wild rices such as *O. longistaminata* (Parker and Dean 1976). Even if infested fields are rotated to pastures and mowed, it is difficult to prevent red rice from seeding (Sonnier 1978). Pastures required at least two clippings at 28- to 42-day intervals to keep most plants from producing seed.

Chemical control is also very difficult due to the close relationship between the wild and cultivated rices. Applying dalapon and glyphosate prior to land preparation or seeding can be appropriate in some situations. Some work to find antidotes that would protect the crop has been done (Wirjahardja and Parker 1977) but no commercially feasible treatments have been found.

In addition to using crop seed free from wild rice, the best control is obtained from the cultural practices of crop rotation and water management. Excellent reviews of practical red rice management systems were prepared by Baker and Sonnier (1983) and Smith (1989). Crop rotations involving soybeans and sorghum for two or three seasons greatly reduce red rice infestations in the southern United States. Several preplant incorporated and postemergence herbicides give excellent red rice control in soybeans. When rice is grown, soil puddling and precise water management reduce red rice infestations. Red rice will not germinate if a puddled soil is kept flooded. Since this is often impractical in the southern United States, an intermediate level of water management is recommended. After soil puddling and seeding pregerminated seed, the field is drained until the rice seedling is well rooted. Then water is brought into the field and maintained until the rice matures. The influence of water management on red rice was studied by Sonnier and Baker (1980). With continuous flooding, 37 red rice plants/m^2 emerged. With a brief period of drainage after planting, 140 plants/m^2 germinated, and if the field was drained for 2 wk or more, 895 seedlings/m^2 appeared. The percentage of red rice in the harvested grain for these systems was 20, 31, and 69%, respectively.

Difference in red rice infestations also occur between upland and flooded rice. In India, 13% of the plants in dry seeded fields were red rice plants; 7% of the plants were red rice when the field was puddled and planted with pregerminated seed and 0.01% of the plants were red rice when rice was transplanted into puddled fields (Singh and Saini 1960).

Cultural practices of using high seeding rates (100 to 200 kg/ha) and selecting competitive cultivars will also favor the production of white rice in red rice infested fields (Baker and Sonnier 1983, Diarra et al. 1985a). For example, tall-statured varieties (115 cm tall when mature) are more competitive with red rice than short-statured varieties (Kwon et al. 1991).

Smith (1981) reported that red rice in the United States was more sensitive to molinate than cultivated rice. In an integrated control study, he found that 3.4 kg/ha of molinate produced United States grade no. 1 rice when the field was kept flooded, but that 6.7 kg/ha of the herbicide was necessary to obtain no. 1 grade rice if the field was drained after seeding. The use of carefully controlled water management and molinate gave up to 93% red rice control. The use of continuous flooding, molinate and a zero tolerance of red rice in certified rice seed in California, in the western United States, are the principal reasons red rice infestations have decreased substantially in this region (Baker and Sonnier 1983).

UTILIZATION

Certainly the wild rices have been and will continue to be evaluated and used by plant breeders to incorporate possible beneficial traits into commercial varieties. In this sense, the wild rices are a great natural resource and a large collection of wild rice strains is maintained at the International Rice Research Institute in the Philippines.

Straw from wild rice has been used as livestock feed and as thatching material in India and the grain is eaten routinely by the poor or by the general population during famines (Biswas and Calder 1936, Lazarides 1980). Red rice is grown commercially as a crop in some areas of India. Its yield potential is less than that of white rice varieties, but it can be somewhat higher in protein content (Deosthale and Pant 1970). *O. barthii* was analyzed as a forage in Zambia and found to have 2.24% K, 0.18% P, 2.8% N, and 0.32% Ca in the leaves, with an apparent digestible protein level of 12.5% in the leaves during the rainy season (Rees 1978). *O. sativa* var. *fatua* had 13% protein and *O. perennis* had 17.6% when tested as forages in Indonesia (Wirjahardja and Nurfilmarasa 1975).

COMMON NAMES

Oryza sativa

ARGENTINA	arroz colorado, arroz macho
AUSTRALIA	wild rice
BOLIVIA	arroz rojo
BRAZIL	arroz vermelho, arroz preto
CAMBODIA	sragne
COLOMBIA	arroz rojo
COSTA RICA	arroz rojo
CUBA	arroz rojo
ECUADOR	arroz rojo
GUYANA	red rice
HONDURAS	arroz rojo
INDIA	birhni, karga, reesa
INDONESIA	padi ketek, paparean
KOREA	salebyeo
MADAGASCAR	vary
MEXICO	arroz rojo
NICARAGUA	arroz rojo
PANAMA	arroz rojo
PARAGUAY	arroz rojo
PERU	arroz rojo
PUERTO RICO	arroz rojo
THAILAND	klao
TURKEY	pirinac

UNITED STATES	red rice
VENEZUELA	arroz rojo
VIETNAM	lua ma
YUGOSLAVIA	pirinac
ZIMBABWE	wild rice

Sixty-Three

Oxalis latifolia H.B.K.

Oxalidaceae, Wood Sorrel Family

O*XALIS LATIFOLIA* is a unique perennial weed, particularly because it is highly unusual to encounter dicotyledonous plants with bulbs. Its prolific production of bulb and bulbils makes it very difficult to control. Most of the nearly 900 species in the **Oxalidaceae** family are in the *Oxalis* genus. The Greek derivation of *oxys* means sour or bitter and refers to the acidic taste of the leaves given by oxalic acid. The species name denotes broader leaves than many other species in the genus. *O. latifolia* is native to the Americas. It

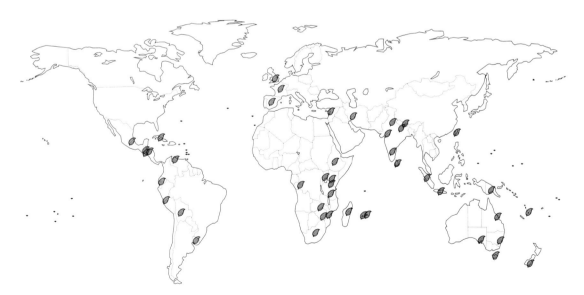

FIGURE 63-1 The distribution of *Oxalis latifolia* H.B.K. across the world where it has been reported as a weed.

548

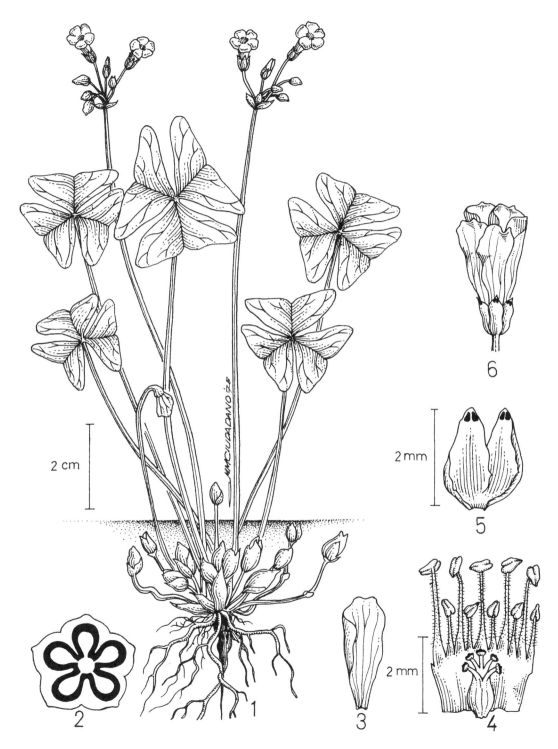

FIGURE 63-2 *Oxalis latifolia* H.B.K.: 1. habit; 2. ovary, cross section; 3. single petal;
4. basally connate stamens opened and pistil; 5. imbricate sepals; 6. flower

is now widely distributed in the tropical and subtropical regions around the world and also occurs in several European countries with temperate climates.

DESCRIPTION

O. latifolia (Figure 63-2) is a stemless *perennial* herb; *taproot* up to 6 cm long, carrot-like, waxy-white; *bulbs* found on top of taproot, 1 to 2 cm in diameter, composed of lanceolate *scales*, outer ones brown and papery, inner ones white, fleshy; bulbs form *rhizomes* up to 10 cm long with terminal *bulbils* 5 to 6 mm in diameter; *petioles* arise from bulb, erect, slender, glabrous, 10 to 25 cm long, bearing 3 smooth, distinctly triangular *leaflets*, 2 to 5 cm wide; leaflets about twice as wide as long, with smooth edges, rounded corners; apex notched up to one-third the length of leaflet; *peduncle* arises from leaf axil of bulb, 15 to 20 cm tall, usually exceeding petiole length; *inflorescence* 5 to 12 flowers borne in slender, drooping umbels, bluish-purple, pinkish-purple or purple-violet; *flowers* perfect; *calyx* of 5 oblong-lanceolate *sepals* 4 to 5 mm wide, each with two small orange glands at apex; *corolla* of 5 overlapping *petals*, twisted in bud, free, green below, purpled above, 12 to 15 mm long; *stamens* 10 in two series of 5 each in lower, middle or upper positions relative to stigma; *ovary* 5-locular with 5 *styles*; *fruit* rare, if present a longitudinal *capsule*, green until maturity, with small, oval, orange to dark yellow *seeds* 0.7 by 1 mm, with 2 longitudinal and several transverse ribs giving seed coat a wavy appearance.

This weed is recognized by the taproot below the scaly bulb, numerous bulbils formed on rhizomes, the notched, triangular leaflets and the purplish flowers with orange glands at the calyx apex.

DISTRIBUTION AND HABITAT

O. latifolia is found in Mexico and much of Central and South America (its native region), on the slopes of the Himalaya Mountains in India, many east and south African countries and in Oceania (Figure 63-1). It is most common in gardens, orchards, plantation crops, nurseries, and any intensely cultivated area. Plants are shade tolerant and thrive in the highlands of eastern and central Africa. In Colombia it is found to 3000 m. The weed grows in medium and heavy textured soils in Bolivia but is common in the light-textured, low organic matter soils of Mauritius (Peng 1984). Occasional cultivation increases *O. latifolia* populations, but it can be displaced by cover crops or more aggressive perennials like *Cynodon dactylon*.

ECOLOGY AND BIOLOGY

The most studied structures of *O. latifolia* are its bulbs and bulbils, perhaps due to their uniqueness on a dicotyledon. Bulbs are usually 2 to 3 cm long and the central cone of tissue in bulbs is a true stem (Jackson 1960). Several types of scales are formed and all originate from this cone. The membranous ones are colorless, moderately thick at the center and thinner at the margins and have rudimentary leaves and a petiole at the tip. These are closely appressed and may completely encircle the bulb. Another type of scale is thick, fleshy, brownish, somewhat triangular in cross section and relatively narrow. The third kind of scale, found at the base of bulbils, is thin, of irregular shape and does not form leaves but may give rise to rhizomes.

Robb (1963) in England described the bulbils as numerous papery scales arising spirally from the stem disc. The brown external scales form a protective sheath around the fleshy inner scales. She observed cavities with tannin-like substances in the scale leaves but not in foliage leaves. The fleshy root contracts from the upper end during moisture stress and at senescence, pulling the bulb and bulbils downward. If the drought stress is severe, the root eventually collapses. This contractile response is viewed as a survival mechanism because the reproductive structures are placed more deeply in the soil during dry weather and at the end of the growing season. An anatomical description of *O. latifolia* roots in general and contractile root growth in particular is given by Estelita-Teixeira (1978).

Bulbs can emerge from 24 cm below the soil surface, but most shoots originate from bulbs in the upper 12 cm. No bulbs emerge from 40 cm (Esler 1962). Rhizomes dehydrate rapidly on the soil surface but the starchy bulbs tolerate these conditions very well (Rivas 1960). Even bulbs left unwatered on the soil surface or at 4 cm deep for 50 days sprouted readily when watered (Wetala and Sambi 1977). Buried bulbs sprouted sooner than those on the surface, but 6 wk after watering over 90% in both conditions had sprouted. Cutting the bulbs in half also delays sprouting but has little effect on their sprouting ability. These studies suggest that the contractile root is of small importance to long-term bulb and bulbil survival.

Bulbs lie dormant during the winter and early spring months in New Zealand (Hunter and Linden 1958). Sprouting begins when the soil warms to 15°C. Chawdhry and Sagar (1974a) investigated bulb dormancy and determined that storage at 5°C for 8 wk and then a 4-hr treatment with 45°C heat gave 71% sprouting, while cold treatment alone gave only 9%. Exposing bulbs to −15°C for 6 min resulted in 40% sprouting, but 30 min of exposure killed them. Thus *O. latifolia* will probably not survive in areas where soils freeze to 5 to 8 cm deep.

O. latifolia growth has been widely studied (Jackson 1960, Robb 1963, Chawdhry 1974, G. Marshall 1987, Marshall and Gitari 1988). Growth and development occur in several phases. First, a crown of delicate adventitious roots arises from the base of the stem tissue of the bulb. Usually one of these roots begins to thicken early in the season and eventually becomes a taproot. Then the first petiole and leaf emerge from a membranous (inner) scale. Petioles are curved at the tip. The leaflets are folded at the midribs and are tightly appressed to the petiole during emergence. Pulvini at the base of the petioles react to stimuli and control the sleep movements of the leaflets. Hot, dry conditions also cause leaflets to fold. Each bulb usually produces 10 to 14 leaves. Peak leaf formation is 5 to 6 wk after planting and then reproductive growth begins.

When taproot formation starts, lateral rhizomes arise. These are white and fleshy, reaching 10 cm in length before terminating in a bulbil. Rhizomes may branch to form more than one bulbil or new rhizomes may arise from the bulbil, giving rise to primary and secondary bulbils. Upon separation from the parent plant, they are referred to as bulbs. Bulbils seldom have roots. Most of the early formed bulbils develop leaves, but beyond 8 wk after planting only 25 to 35% do (Marshall and Gitari 1988). Each plant may produce up to 28 primary rhizomes and 45 leaves.

Peduncles develop in the axils of membranous (outer) scales. The umbels are borne on the tips of peduncles and droop until the peduncle is fully formed. The number of rhizomes and inflorescences formed is independent of day length. In the final growth phase, aerial plant parts begin to die and the taproot starts contracting. Simultaneously, bulbils

increase rapidly in size and differentiate thin, brown protective scales from the outer membranous scales.

In the first season, bulbils form 30 to 40 true scales inside the membranous scales. Rhizomes decay and the bulbils become separated from the parent plant. As many as 60 bulbils/plant are produced in Kenya (Chawdhry 1974) and 194/plant in India (Muniyappa et al. 1983). The number of new bulbils formed can be as many as the number of true scales formed the year before and thus often varies greatly between bulbils.

Maximum aerial and underground biomass production occurs approximately 14 and 18 wk after planting, respectively (Chawdhry 1974). The subterranean biomass is nearly 75% of the total plant weight (Muniyappa et al. 1983, Marshall and Gitari 1988). Researchers in India measured the biomass of *O. latifolia* for two seasons. The weed produced an average of 30 ton/ha fresh weight (2 ton dry matter) and its foliage removed 68, 4, and 48 kg/ha of N, P, and K, respectively (Misra and Sharma 1980).

Chawdhry and Sagar (1973) fed plants $C^{14}O_2$ at ten growth stages to monitor carbohydrate accumulation in *O. latifolia*. Plants appear to live on reserves of the parent bulb until the 5-leaf stage. During the 6- to 25-leaf stages, considerable C^{14}-assimilate moves to the taproot and new bulbils. At later growth stages, translocation is primarily into new, well-developed bulbils. New bulbils are initially fed by assimilates from leaves; as the season ends, reserves are translocated from the taproot into bulbils. Chawdhry (1974) also determined that the parent bulbs are rich in starch and actually gain weight over a 16-wk growth period. A detailed study of *O. latifolia* shoot anatomy was done in Brazil by Estelita-Teixeira (1982).

Flowering occurs over several weeks. Sepals have secretory canals in the apical region and nectaries are often present at the base of the first whorl of stamens (Estelita-Teixeira 1984). Kumari and Narayana (1980) give a detailed account of the embryology following fertilization, but the species seldom produces seeds. It exhibits "trimorphic heterostyly," which means biotypes with three floral forms exist. One type has stigmas in the lower position relative to one set of anthers in the middle and another set in the upper position. A second type finds the stigma in the middle position with anthers above and below. The third type has stigmas above and a set of anthers in the middle and lower locations. Flowers with similar floral forms are incompatible (Weller and Denton 1976).

Since *O. latifolia* dispersal from its region of origin (the tropical Americas) was most often by vegetative propagules, homogeneous populations were introduced into most regions and therefore little seed production occurs. If formed, they are "shot" 20 to 40 cm from the capsule as the valves split open (Rivals 1960). Plants coming from seed are able to form a small bulb the first season. Diploid and triploid forms are found in Mexico and the $2n$ chromosome count is 14 (Weller and Denton 1976).

AGRICULTURAL IMPORTANCE

O. latifolia is a weed in more than 37 countries in nearly 30 crops (Figure 63-1) and is frequently reported in tea and other plantation crops. It is particularly troublesome in India, New Zealand, Australia, South Africa, and Uganda. It is a principal or serious weed of cassava, maize, upland rice, tea, and vegetables in Indonesia; cereals in Ethiopia; coffee in Zaire; cotton in Uganda; maize, potatoes, and tea in India; orchards in Australia; sugarcane in Mauritius; tea in Sri Lanka; and vegetables in Australia, Spain, and Tasmania.

It is a common weed of coffee in Kenya, Tanzania, and Uganda; maize in Guatemala and South Africa; nurseries in New Zealand; orchards and sugarcane in India and South

Africa; tea in Kenya and Uganda; vegetables in New Zealand and South Africa; and vineyards in South Africa.

O. latifolia is a weed of unranked importance of edible beans in Honduras; cacao in New Hebrides; citrus in Saudi Arabia; coffee in Mexico and El Salvador; cotton and peanuts in Kenya; maize in Honduras and Tanzania; orchards in Honduras and Nepal; upland rice in India; rubber in Indonesia; sorghum and sweet potatoes in Honduras; soybeans in Tasmania; sugarcane in Bolivia and Indonesia; vegetables in Honduras; and wheat in Mozambique and South Africa.

Its introduction into several countries was intentional. Nursery operators imported it into New Zealand as a rock garden plant and as an ornamental into East Africa. It was introduced into Uganda in the 1920s as a cover crop in coffee. While still used for this purpose, it is very harmful to other crops, especially in the early growth stages (Wetala 1978). Uncontrolled *O. latifolia* reduced maize yields 56% in India (Atwal and Gopal 1972). Hand weeding early in the season allows the crop to compete effectively during the later stages. Without crop competition, Cox (1978) found that even repeated sprays of glyphosate allowed a 17-fold increase in bulbs over the initial populations he planted in a previously uninfested area. In the nontreated areas, populations reached 125 million bulbs/ha that weighed 34 ton after two seasons!

Because it occurs in many crops and countries, control measures have been investigated for many years. Recommendations in the 1920s included spraying a 10 to 20% solution of sulfuric acid (Young 1958). *O. latifolia* suppression has been obtained with dinitroanaline, substituted urea, uracil and thiocarbamate herbicides, but long-term control from herbicides alone is unlikely.

The weed spreads on field tools, boots and in soil dug with plants for transplanting. Using power rotary cultivators hastened its spread in Great Britain. Smothering with plastic or straw mulches was suggested as a control measure in New Zealand (Hunter and Linden 1958).

Eradication via mechanical or chemical defoliation requires intensive efforts. Chawdhry and Sagar (1974b) clipped plants each time they reached the 4- or 10-leaf stage and noted that five clippings reduced plant dry weight by 93%. Reductions were 82 and 54% when plants were clipped at the 20- and 30-leaf stage, respectively. Clipping at the 30-leaf stage eventually resulted in a nearly constant plant biomass, so control measures must be done on a more frequent schedule. They found the timing of the first defoliation after plant emergence the most important: the earlier the first one, the more effective were subsequent clippings.

Plants have some medicinal uses in Mexico (Mendieta and Amo 1981) but the high oxalate content limits its use as food or feed. *O. latifolia* hosts several *Puccinia* rusts and some nematodes that may infect crops. Its seriousness as a weed resulted in Australia declaring it a prohibited species in all imported goods (Anon., Australia 1982).

COMMON NAMES

Oxalis latifolia

AUSTRALIA	purple-flowered oxalis, shamrock
BOLIVIA	taru-taru
BRAZIL	trevo

COLOMBIA	acedera, trebol falso, trebol de jardin
CUBA	vinagrillo
INDIA	khati-buti, phiphru, tipatia weed
INDONESIA	tjalintjing gede
MADAGASCAR	kodidimborona
MAURITIUS	oseille, trefle
MEXICO	acedera, acederilla, trebol
SOUTH AFRICA	red garden sorrel, rooituinsuring
SPAIN	trebol de huerta
SRI LANKA	puliyarai
UGANDA	katanpuni
VENEZUELA	vinagrillo

Sixty-Four

Papaver rhoeas L.

Papaveraceae, Poppy Family

PAPAVER RHOEAS is a winter annual or annual plant closely related to the opium poppy, *P. somniferum*, which also provides the poppy seeds used in baking. *P. rhoeas* occurs in every continent but is most abundant in Europe where it originated. Plants are easily recognized by their colorful, showy flowers. There are 25 genera and over 200 species in the family; the *Papaver* genus contains nearly 100 species and subspecies. The genus name refers to the thick, milky latex found in the stems and the species name may be a derivative of the Greek *rhoe* to denote the quick-falling sepals, petals and seeds.

FIGURE 64-1   The distribution of *Papaver rhoeas* L. across the world where it has been reported as a weed.

FIGURE 64-2 *Papaver rhoeas* L.: 1. lower part of plant; 2. flowering and fruiting branch; 3. ovary, cross section; 4. capsule, 5. same, face view; 6. seed, two views.

DESCRIPTION

P. rhoeas (Figure 64-2) is an *annual*, sometimes *winter annual*, herbaceous plant with a branched *taproot*; *stems* with milky sap, erect, 10 to 90 cm tall, branched, covered with stiff unbranched hairs; *leaves* initially formed in rosettes, deeply pinnately lobed, light green; *stem leaves* few, alternate, upper leaves sessile, lower leaves petiolate, all leaves pubescent; *inflorescence* solitary on long unbranched peduncles arising from leaf axils; *flower buds* nod while stem elongates; *flowers* perfect, regular, 3 to 10 cm in diameter; *sepals* hairy, usually 2, dropping as the buds open; *petals* 4 in two dissimilar pairs, 2 to 6 cm long, the wider pair enclosing the narrower one in the bud; deep scarlet, bright red, purple or bluish, occasionally white-margin, often with a dark spot at petal base; *stamens* numerous; solitary *pistil* with nearly flat *stigmatic disc* with conspicuous membrane; *fruit* a smooth, tan to brown, globose *capsule*, 1 to 2 cm wide and nearly twice as long with 8 to 18 apical *pores* below edge of *stigmatic disc*; *seeds* numerous, 0.7 to 1 mm long, 0.5 mm wide, kidney-shaped with reticulate surface, dull purplish gray or dark brown.

This species is identified by the spreading hairs on all plant parts except the capsule, the milky latex in the stems, the crimson or purplish flowers, and the capsule with pores under the edge of the stigmatic disc.

HABITAT AND ECOLOGY

P. rhoeas is found in annual crops (especially winter cereals), gardens, meadows, nurseries, roadsides, wasteland, and disturbed sites. Pastures that have not been disturbed for years may become a sea of red *P. rhoeas* flowers when tilled.

Plants have existed in Britain since the Bronze Age (Harper 1966) and the species has been extensively studied in Great Britain. It is found to lat 70° N in Scandinavia. *P. rhoeas* is usually a lowland weed, ascending to only 300 m in Scotland. Several species of *Papaver* often appear in the same habitat. *P. rhoeas* is the most abundant species in Europe and frequently is the only one encountered as a single species (McNaughton and Harper 1964). When growing alone, high plant densities reduce the number of capsules produced per plant and the chances of a given seed forming a plant (Harper and McNaughton 1962). From another perspective, an eightfold increase in seeding rate never gave more than a twofold increase in mature plants. *P. rhoeas* was the most aggressive of the four species examined. Nevertheless, it was a poor competitor against barley and *Sinapis alba* (Haizel 1972). Even in pure stands, its growth 12 wk after planting was two and four times less than that of *S. alba* and barley, respectively. If grown with barley or *S. alba*, the weed was a weak competitor for 8 wk and was totally displaced by the crops after 12 wk.

P. rhoeas is highly responsive to environmental conditions. Without competition, individual plants become quite large and form many capsules. Densities of 270 plants/m^2 resulted in six capsules per plant. When competing with wheat, plants were greatly suppressed but each one flowered and produced at least one capsule with seed (Harper 1966). Interestingly, *P. rhoeas* formed two to three capsules per gram of plant dry weight at maturity and this ratio was nearly constant over a wide range of densities. Harper (1959) also encountered plants with 400 capsules containing 2000 seeds each and as many as 4300 capsules/m^2.

Plant growth is reduced by poor soil fertility, shade, waterlogged soils, and interference from other plants, but plants survive in fairly dry conditions (McNaughton and

Harper 1964). Flower size and number varies with environmental conditions, an unusual feature in angiosperms. Seed size, however, remains constant over a wide range of conditions. Petal color and leaf shape often vary markedly within and between populations.

BIOLOGY

P. rhoeas seeds are highly dormant when fresh, except for the cultivated variety, Shirley, that germinates readily when harvested (Harper and McNaughton 1960). Alternating day/night temperatures of 10/30°C stimulate germination, but some seed remains dormant. Harper (1966) describes this trait as "polymorphism in germination requirement," which is beneficial to survival of the species because a given environment induces only a portion of the seeds to germinate. Seeds may germinate between temperatures of 2 and 35°C but the optimum is between 7 and 13°C (Andersen 1968). Light, nitrate and chilling treatments often interact to enhance *P. rhoeas* germination (Vincent and Roberts 1977, 1979). These researchers also recorded more emergence at 1 cm than 3 cm in the soil. Seed scarification does not enhance germination (Harper 1966).

   P. rhoeas seeds placed in 1.5, 3.3, and 5.2-cm diameter clods of soil had 50, 20, and 8% emergence, respectively, in hard clods; and 55, 35, and 20%, respectively, in soft clods. Most of the seeds remaining in the clods were dormant. Thus fields with large, hard clods will have more dormant *P. rhoeas* seeds than those with a fine-textured seedbed (Terpstra 1986).

   Roberts and Boddrell (1984) seeded *P. rhoeas* to 10 cm and recorded 4% emergence that fall. Most seedlings emerged from February to April, with a secondary flush in August to October, resulting in 21% emergence of all seeds planted that year. Only 1 to 7% of the remaining seeds emerged over the next 3 yr, accounting for 38% of the seeds. Seeding depth also influences the emergence pattern. Froud-Williams et al. (1984a) placed seeds at 0, 2.5, and 15-cm depths. No germination occurred for 3 mo at 0 and 2.5 cm. Those placed 15 cm deep were dug at 3-mo intervals and 15% germinated in the fall and 40% the following spring, but none germinated in the summer months. They obtained 20% germination from seeds kept in darkness for 7 wk and then given alternating light and dark periods. Feast and Roberts (1973) discovered that drying field soil with *P. rhoeas* seeds for 2 mo prior to a germination test markedly improved germination and that twice as many seedlings emerged when the soil was kept in 1-cm layers as compared to 3-cm.

   Roberts and Feast (1973) monitored seed populations under simulated tillage practices. Seeds were mixed with potted soil from 0 to 15 cm. The soil was "tilled" or not five times annually for 6 yr. The number of viable seeds remaining at the end of the year in the cultivated soil dropped 20 to 26% annually; the seed loss was much slower in the nontilled soil. This left 21% of the original seed in the undisturbed soil after 6 yr as compared to 7% in the cultivated soil. Nearly four times as many seedlings emerged in the cultivated soil as in the noncultivated (34% vs. 9%). Seeds were mixed to 2.5, 7.5, and 15 cm in the soil and the soil was either tilled or not (Roberts and Feast 1972). More seeds emerged the second year than the first year and soil disturbance always increased emergence. After 5 yr, 64, 45, and 37% of the seeds emerged at 2.5, 7.5, and 15 cm, respectively, with cultivation as compared to 20, 18, and 7% for these depths if the soil was undisturbed.

   Seed banks can contain millions of *P. rhoeas* seeds. Kropac (1966) found 4,760,000/ha in the top 30 cm of soil in Czechoslovakia. In England, Roberts and Neilson (1982) found half the vegetable fields with *P. rhoeas* had more than 2.5 million seeds/ha while some had nearly 20 million. Salisbury (1964) reported over 280 million seeds/ha. Long-term studies from Denmark (Kjaer 1948, Madsen 1962) recorded 35% germination for seeds buried 7 yr, 31% after 11 yr, 25% after 20 yr, and 13% after 26 yr.

Fallowing rapidly decreases *P. rhoeas* seed bank populations (Brenchley and Warington 1945). A reasonable program seemed to be to fallow fields every fifth year, because populations after 4 yr of wheat and 1 yr of fallowing were reduced to 56, 25, and 7% of the initial levels at 5, 10, and 15 yr, respectively. However, failure to control *P. rhoeas* in a single season of wheat production increased the seed bank from 580 to over 21,000 seeds/m^2 (Roberts and Chancellor 1986). Intensive vegetable production systems reduced the seed reservoir by 72% in 5 yr (Roberts 1962). Also, *P. rhoeas* seeds have a half-life of 11 yr in undisturbed grass sods and thus persist for many years in such sites (Chancellor 1986).

The root of *P. rhoeas* is described as a taproot, but it can become highly branched below 15 cm and may penetrate 1 m or more (Kutschera 1960). Young plants grow slowly, but once stem elongation starts, development is rapid. Kohji et al. (1979, 1981) investigated the bending movements of *P. rhoeas* stems. They are erect upon emergence, nod downward 180° for a period and then become erect again. The initial bending starts when the stem is approximately 12 mm long and the entire process of nodding and then straightening takes about 12 days. They concluded that the initial bending is due to the weight of the flower bud. Both the concave and convex sides of the stem continue growing during both bending periods. The straightening process is controlled by hormones released by the flower buds.

Once the flower on the primary stem reaches the bud stage, axillary shoots arise. They form sequentially, starting with the uppermost leaves and proceeding downward (Nanda 1961). Plants have a well-developed system of secretory canals that produce latex (Heywood 1978). Korsmo (1954) notes stomata are found on both leaf surfaces and he gives excellent anatomical descriptions of the plant. Plants vary noticeably in leaf form, petal color, capsule shape and growth habit (Rogers 1971). Capsule shape and pore number change appreciably, even among those formed on the same plant. While most descriptions cite the presence of a dark blotch at the base of *P. rhoeas* petals, Rogers found only 2% of the plants expressed this characteristic. Acheson et al. (1956) found two anthocyanin pigments in *P. rhoeas*. Changes in their relative concentrations probably explains the variation in flower color we observe.

As flowers open, the sepals drop, allowing the crumpled petals to open. Flowers produce no nectar but have abundant quantities of pollen. The species has long been known to be self-incompatible (McNaughton and Harper 1960, Lawrence et al. 1978). *P. rhoeas* flowers later than *P. argemone* and *P. dubium* in England, but it continues to flower for 2 to 4 mo longer than the other species. Nevertheless, mixed populations of *Papaver* are in bloom simultaneously for long periods. Thus hybridization could occur but seldom does. Pollen of *P. rhoeas* is mature in the bud stage, but if it falls on the stigma, few if any germinate and those that do never form a long pollen tube (Rogers 1969b). Stigmas are receptive to pollen in the bud stage and remain so for 7 days after the bud opens. Honey and bumble bees are the most frequent visitors of *P. rhoeas*' flowers and most bees consistently visit the same species of *Papaver* in mixed stands during a flight (McNaughton and Harper 1960). This helps assure cross-pollination for the completely self-incompatible *P. rhoeas*. The 2*n* chromosome count of *P. rhoeas* is 14 and it crosses readily with *P. dubium* (2*n* = 42). Progeny of this cross have virus-like symptoms and plants are sterile (Harper 1966).

P. rhoeas is a prolific seed producer. Salisbury (1942, 1964) determined that a single plant may form 50 capsules (a maximum of 342 was noted!) with 1300 seeds each and vigorous plants yielded 14,500 to 19,500 seeds. Seeds are two to three times smaller than the pores of the capsule and 1000 seeds weigh only 120 mg (Harper 1966). Thus they can be readily dispersed from the capsule. Van der Pijl (1969) described this dispersal as the "censor mechanism" because the swaying action of capsules on long peduncles distributes seeds away from the parent plant. The effectiveness of such a catapulting action varies with the height of the capsule above the ground. Capsules 58-cm high disperse seeds up to 3 m from the plant (Salisbury 1942). Seeds are also dispersed by birds (Ridley 1930) and some survive passage through their digestive tract (Salisbury 1964).

AGRICULTURAL IMPORTANCE

P. rhoeas is a reported weed of 23 crops in 43 countries (Figure 64-1) and is frequently reported a weed of winter wheat and other cereals. It is a serious or principal weed of barley in Greece, Iran, the former Soviet Union, and Spain; cereals in Germany, Scotland, the former Soviet Union, Spain, Sweden, and the former Yugoslavia; oats in Greece; rye in Poland; and wheat or winter wheat in England, France, Germany, Greece, Hungary, Iran, Italy, Morocco, Poland, and Spain. It is also a serious or principal weed of lentils and lucerne in Spain; peas in Greece and Ireland; oil seed rape in England, France, and Spain; and sugar beets in Italy, Spain, and Turkey.

It is a common weed of beets in Spain; cereals in Bulgaria, Israel, Switzerland, and Tunisia; horticulture crops in England; legumes in Tunisia; maize, millet, orchards, and vegetables in the former Soviet Union; oats in Spain; potatoes in Poland and Scotland; vineyards in the former Soviet Union and Turkey; and wheat in Czechoslovakia.

It is reported to infest barley in Germany; beans in France and Germany; carrots in England; cereals in Turkey; flax in Belgium; hops in the former Yugoslavia; legumes in Greece; lucerne in France and Italy; oats in the United States; onions in Italy; orchards in Turkey; pasture in England; peas in England and France; oil seed rape in France; sugar beets in England, Germany, and Ireland; vegetables in England and Switzerland; vineyards in Spain; and wheat in Belgium, Portugal, Italy, the United States, and the former Yugoslavia.

Yield losses in small grains are seldom severe. Densities of 500 to 1000 plants/m^2 did not affect yields of spring sown cereals, as the weed emerged later than the crop and other cereal weeds (Blackman and Templeman 1938). *P. rhoeas* can compete effectively with winter cereals. Single plants of *P. rhoeas* weigh nearly four times less than a winter wheat plant at harvest and yield loss per plant per square meter is 0.10%, up to a maximum loss of 43% at extremely high densities (Wilson and Wright 1990). Even though it is easily controlled by 2,4-D and related herbicides, its long dormancy in the soil assures its persistence and seriousness for many years.

Applying N fertilizer to wheat decreased *P. rhoeas* populations in Italy (Covarelli 1974). Leachate collected after over-watering *P. rhoeas* in sand culture inhibited barley and oil seed rape growth (Weinberger 1963). However, when the weed was already established and crops were planted into the same pots, oil seed rape seed germination was reduced, while barley's increased. Removing *P. rhoeas* from the pots and planting oilseed rape was not inhibitory, suggesting a short persistence of its allelochemicals. Plants can host a wide range of nematode species (Bendixen et al. 1979) and yet flowers contain nematicidal compounds (Mohammad et al. 1981).

While *P. somniferum* has been used for centuries as a medicinal plant, *P. rhoeas* has few reported uses. The *Papaver* genus contains rhoedine alkaloids, but *P. rhoeas* has very low levels, with none in the seed (Frohne and Pfander 1984). Flowers of *P. rhoeas* are used in China to treat jaundice and it is believed the plant contains an anticancer agent, chelerythine (Duke and Ayensu 1985). Seeds have been used as a tonic for horses and the petals as a source of red ink (Renfrew 1973). Seeds contain over 21% protein and 47% oil (Earle and Jones 1962).

COMMON NAMES

Papaver rhoeas

ARGENTINA	amapola silvestre
AUSTRALIA	field poppy
BELGIUM	coquelicot, klaproes, kollebloem
CHILE	amapola roja
CHINA	li chun hua
COLOMBIA	amapola
DENMARK	korn valmue
EGYPT	deydahaan, zaghleel
ENGLAND	common poppy, field poppy
FINLAND	silkkiunikko
FRANCE	coquelicot, pavot coquelicot
GERMANY	Feldmohn, Feuermohn, Klapperrose, Klatsch-mohn, Klatschrose, Wider Monhn
ITALY	papavero salvatico, rosolaccio
LEBANON	corn poppy, field poppy, shaka'ik-un-naman
MOROCCO	coquelicot
NETHERLANDS	klaproos
NEW ZEALAND	field poppy
NORWAY	kornvalmue
PORTUGAL	papoula ordinaria, papoila-das-searas
SPAIN	amapola
SWEDEN	kornvallmo
TUNISIA	coquelicot
TURKEY	gelincik
UNITED STATES	corn poppy
YUGOSLAVIA	bulka

Sixty-Five

Paspalum distichum L.

Poaceae, Grass Family

PASPALUM DISTICHUM is a perennial grass native to South America. It thrives in wet areas of tropical and subtropical regions and often invades cropland from irrigation canals and ditch banks. It is most troublesome in Asia and Latin America and is a weed in over 60 countries (Figure 65-1). The genus name comes from the Greek *paspalos*, a type of millet, and the species is derived from the Latin *distichus*, referring to the seeds on the rachis in two opposite rows.

FIGURE 65-1   The distribution of *Paspalum distichum* L. across the world where it has been reported as a weed.

FIGURE 65-2 *Paspalum distichum* L.: A. habit, with a young shoot; B. ligule; C. back of
leaf, showing fringe of long hairs at base of blade; D. spike; E. florets.

DESCRIPTION

P. distichum (Figure 65-2) is a spreading, mat-forming *perennial* grass with shallow *rhizomes* and creeping, extensively branched *stolons* with *adventitious roots* at nodes; flowering *stems* 25 to 60 cm tall; internodes short; nodes thickened, often pubescent; *leaf collar* with membranous *ligule* up to 2 mm long, truncate; *blades* 3 to 10 cm long, 2 to 6 mm wide, sparsely hairy on margin and usually hairy at base; *sheath* loose, keeled, often hairy near ligule; *inflorescence* terminates with 2 (rarely 3 or 4) spreading spike-like racemes 2 to 7 cm long, one side of rachis with two rows of tightly packed spikelets; *spikelets* light green, subsessile, ovoid, acuminate, 2.5 to 4 mm long, 1.3 to 2.5 mm wide; *floret anthers* purple, protrude beyond glumes; *first glume* absent or greatly reduced, more or less triangular, to half the spikelet length; *second glume* minutely hairy toward apex; *sterile lemma* 5-nerved, smooth; *fertile lemma* hairy at apex and nearly as long as spikelet; *fruit* an ovate to elliptical *caryopsis* with dark yellow to brown *seed coat*.

The dense mat of stolons and shallow rhizomes, membranous ligule, short internodes and two rows of tightly packed spikelets on the underside of both racemes are the key features of this plant.

HABITAT, TAXONOMY, AND ECOLOGY

P. distichum abounds along irrigation canals and streams, on rice levees, and in swamps, drainage ditches and similar areas with wet to shallow flooded soils. It originated in tropical America, but has become widely dispersed to subtropical and even temperate climates of Japan, Great Britain (Good 1964) and in Washington state, in the United States. Plants survive the winter in Japan even when ice forms on the water's surface (Shibayama and Miyahara 1977). The leaves above the ice are killed but some buds survive and sprout in the spring.

The species is often classified as an anchored, emergent aquatic weed. Plants can survive in 50 cm of water but flowering is delayed as water depth increases. Flowers appeared 30, 42, and 52 days after stem elongation in saturated soil and 10 and 15 cm of water, respectively (Manuel et al. 1979). Interestingly, seeds matured 20 to 30 days after flowering in all water levels.

P. distichum is taxonomically similar to *P. vaginatum* and is synonymous with *P. paspaloides* (Jovet and Guedes 1972). Godfrey and Wooten (1979) consider *P. distichum* and *vaginatum* very closely related and they can only be separated "with considerable training." A thorough anatomical comparison of the leaves of both species revealed sufficient differences to justify their classification as separate species (Ellis 1974). These species are also distinguished by the glabrous second glume of *P. vaginatum* in contrast to the hairy one of *P. distichum*.

Eighteen biotypes of *P. distichum* from Iran, South Africa, Uruguay, Taiwan, and Japan were grown in Japan (Ikeda and Oyamada 1982). Raceme length of most biotypes was 4 to 5 cm, but two biotypes were shorter and one was longer. Spikelet number was proportional to raceme length, with 40 to 60 present on the 4- to 5-cm racemes. Comparisons of 235 specimens from the United States were made on the degree of leaf pubescence (Allred 1982). The most pubescent type is classified as var. *indutum*. The degree of pubescence increases from the Atlantic to the Pacific coast of the United States, but there is surprising similarity in all other morphological features. Among two Japanese biotypes, one adapted to a wider *pH* range than the other (Okuma et al. 1983a). A Pakistan biotype tolerated a *pH* of 8.3 (Sheikh 1969).

P. distichum populations found on mine tailings deposits and in normal soil in Hong Kong were collected and studied. Both types grew in soil *pH* of 4.5 to 7.7. When grown for 4 wk in normal soil, plants from the tailings contained 30% more Mn and 25% more Cu in the foliage and 85% more Fe in the roots than the population from normal soil. It appears that after 80 yr of adaptation, *P. distichum* has become nearly twice as tolerant to heavy metals and could be used to stabilize tailings areas and to remove these contaminants before they leach into the sea (Wong et al. 1983).

BIOLOGY

P. distichum propagates vegetatively via long, slender, many-noded stolons and rhizomes. Cut stolons can form new plants in only 36 hr. Growth is favored by warm temperatures. Stems elongate up to 3.3 cm/day at 30°C. This is three times faster than rice elongates (Noda 1969). The rate drops to 1.8 and 0.6 cm/day at 25 and 18°C, respectively. The rate of sprouting, rooting and early growth of both single-node rhizome and stolon segments of *P. distichum* increases to 30°C, plateaus between 30 and 40°C, and then declines above 40°C (Huang et al. 1987). Rhizome and stolon segments die at a constant 45°C temperature but survive alternating temperatures (either 16/8 or 8/16 hr) of 45 and 22°C. There is little growth at 10°C or less. Stolon segments generally sprout and root faster than rhizome segments.

P. distichum growth was compared with that of turf grasses in the southern United States (Busey and Myers 1979). Its average daily growth rate of 6.9% was second only to *Cynodon dactylon* at day/night temperatures of 32/16°C for 46 days. They calculated that segments planted 1 m² apart would form a complete sod in 138 days. *P. distichum* that was planted to cover a creek bank in Japan did so in 2 to 3 yr (Okuma et al. 1983a). Growth rate was correlated to the NH₄-N concentration of the water.

One-node rhizome and stolon segments were planted nine times during the year in Portugal (Moreira and Vasconcelos 1979). All plants survived, but those planted in August to February grew little until the following spring. When averaged over planting dates, rhizome-originated plants produced more stem growth while stolon-originated plants produced more rhizome growth. Nevertheless, both organs showed a high regenerative ability. Maximum stolon growth was 25 to 30 cm/wk during the summer and plants produced three to five times more stolon than rhizome biomass. Rhizome formation did not begin until the new plants had more than 20 leaves. Rhizomes originating from either source were identical and had 1- to 1.5-cm internodes. All rhizomes were formed in the upper 17 cm of soil and most were in the upper 10 cm. Flowering occurred in July for nearly all planting dates.

The internode size varies with position on the stolon and this influences the growth of plants arising from single node cuttings (Hsiao and Huang 1989a). When 15-node stolons are cut into 1-node segments, the apical 1 to 7 internodes are 2 to 3 times shorter than internodes 8 to 15. Twenty days after planting, new shoots from nodes 1 to 7 were half as tall as shoots of nodes 8 to 15. When 15-node segments were buried intact, 90% of the apical nodes produced shoots. Sprouting decreased linearly to node 8 (10 to 15%) and then increased linearly to node 15 (70%). This pattern was similar even when the two youngest nodes were decapitated.

In the Philippines, one-node rhizome segments form new shoots 25 days after planting (Manuel and Mercado 1977). The growth rate between 20 and 120 days averaged a 400% increase in plant dry weight for each 20-day period! The large increase in shoot number is principally from the branching and rooting of stolons rather than from rhizome buds. While rhizome internodes are half the length of stolon internodes, stolon segments with equal numbers of nodes as rhizomes weigh twice as much as the rhizome segments on both a fresh and dry weight basis. Apical dominance is expressed by *P. distichum* stems. After 30 days, one-, two- and three-node stem pieces formed 9, 10, and 13 sprouts, respectively, which means that most buds on the two- and three-node segments remain dormant. All nodes except the terminal ones sprout readily, especially after overwintering (Okuma et al. 1983b).

Placing 3- to 5-cm stolon segments at 0, 3, and 5 cm in the soil gave 100, 15, and 0% plant establishment, respectively (Noda 1969). Rhizomes are produced deeper in a well-drained soil (13 cm) than in flooded soils (6 cm) (Ikeda and Oyamada 1980).

Roots of *P. distichum* are also relatively shallow. In Pakistan, maximum penetration was 37 cm, with 70% of all root and rhizome biomass in the upper 8 cm and 90% in the upper 16 cm (Sheikh 1969). Root surfaces often have orange-brown deposits, indicating that oxygen is escaping from the roots and reacting with iron to form iron oxides. Anatomical examination found large intercellular spaces in leaves, stems and particularly root cortexes. The proportion of corticular space increased as root depth increased, an adaptation allowing oxygen to move from the aerial plant parts to the roots so that plants can grow in saturated soils.

The sprouting and rooting capability of 1-, 3-, and 7-node rhizome segments is not suppressed by flooding in the light but is in the dark (Hsiao and Huang 1989b). In fact, shoot growth is sometimes greater in flooded than non-flooded conditions. Submerged leaves of *P. distichum* use the CO_2 dissolved in water to maintain photosynthetic activity and plants can survive complete submersion for 15 days. However, root flooding and stem submersion do not support maximum plant growth.

P. distichum is a C_4 plant and fixes 16 g $CO_2/dm^2/hr$ (Yamasue et al. 1983). Plant growth is very sensitive to shading. Reduced growth was evident in diffuse light in only 20 days, and after 120 days shaded plants produced 60% fewer shoots than those in full sunlight (Manuel and Mercado 1977). Nearly all biotypes have a $2n = 60$ chromosome number (Katayama and Ikeda 1975). Pollen fertility is high but seed production is low due to chromosome irregularities often encountered during the meiotic phase of cell division.

Only 5 to 10% of the flowers form seed, which reflects the relative unimportance of seed propagation of this species (Okuma and Chikura 1984). Seeds remain viable in water, however, and could start an infestation if moved to new areas. *P. distichum* seeds were found in 4% of 375 samples immediately after threshing in the Philippines (Rao and Moody 1990). Seed processing on the farm failed to completely remove the weed seed from any of the rice samples.

Dormancy is broken by stratification at 5 to 10°C in Japan. Germination occurs between 20 and 40°C, and 30°C is the optimum temperature. In the western United States, soaking seeds in sulfuric acid 30 to 60 min or in sodium hypochlorite for 1 to 8 hr gave 53 to 95% germination. In darkness, 11% of untreated seed germinated, while in light 40% germinated (Huang and Hsiao 1987). The hull and seed coat membranes regulate germination of *P. distichum* seeds.

AGRICULTURAL IMPORTANCE

P. distichum is a weed of 20 crops in 61 countries (Figure 65-1) and is frequently reported a weed of lowland rice, irrigation systems and orchards. It is considered one of the seven most important weeds of China. It is a serious or principal weed of citrus and cotton in the former Soviet Union; citrus, horticulture crops, and pastures in South Africa; horticulture crops and irrigation systems in Australia; maize in Portugal, South Africa, the former Soviet Union, and Spain; orchards in Israel, Pakistan, South Africa, and Spain; rice in Bangladesh, Belize, Colombia, Cuba, Japan, Morocco, Pakistan, the Philippines, Portugal, and Taiwan; sugarcane in Pakistan; tea in Iran and the former Soviet Union; vineyards in South Africa; and wheat in Nepal.

It is a common weed of bananas in Surinam; edible beans in Mexico; citrus in the United States; irrigation systems in Brazil, South Africa, and the United States; lucerne in South Africa; maize in Mexico and Nepal; orchards in Egypt; pastures in the United States; rice in Brazil, Chile, China, Dominican Republic, Nepal, Peru, Spain, and the United States; sugarcane in South Africa and Spain; and wheat in China.

P. distichum is a weed of unknown rank in barley in Iraq; cereals in Jordan; cotton in Greece, Iran, Iraq, and Spain; maize in France, India, and Taiwan; orchards in Chile, Greece, Honduras, Iraq, and Japan; pastures in New Zealand and Surinam; peanuts and sweet potatoes in Taiwan; rice in Argentina, Egypt, France, India, Indonesia, Iran, Iraq, Italy, Laos, Sarawak, Sri Lanka, Surinam, Swaziland, Thailand, and Vietnam; soybeans in Taiwan and the United States; sugarcane in Australia, Honduras, and Mexico; tea in China, Japan, and Taiwan; vegetables in Honduras, Iran, Iraq, and Portugal; vineyards in Chile, France, and Portugal; and wheat in Honduras, India, and Iraq.

A survey of rice weeds in the Philippines found *P. distichum* in 50% of the fields with transplanted rice and 61% of the wet-seeded fields (Pablico and Moody 1986). Infested fields average 8 and 18% cover by this weed for transplanted and wet-seeded rice, respectively. *P. distichum* often encroaches from irrigation canals and levees. Occasionally Japanese farmers plant it in paddy fields as a forage following rice harvest. As noted, it has vigorous growth and responds to N fertilization. Its nutritive value is high (Ikeda and Emoto 1973, Yoshida et al. 1979) and maximum production is obtained with two cuttings per year (Ehara and Ikeda 1972). Its extensive network of branching stems makes it a very effective soil protector. Biotypes that produce more tillers and fewer stolons have been found and should be selected if *P. distichum* is used as a crop in rice-growing areas (Ikeda et al. 1988).

However, few countries view *P. distichum* as compatible with current cropping systems. It has been declared a noxious species in Taiwan and seriously affects the efficiency of operation and water losses in irrigation districts. If uncontrolled in rice, yields were reduced 34% with short-statured varieties while medium-statured ones were more competitive (IRRI 1977). In potted experiments, IR-42 rice was the most competitive variety. Four rhizome segments/pot reduced IR-42 growth 43% as compared to the 74% reduction of the most sensitive rice variety, IR-36 (Manuel et al. 1979).

The density of transplanted rice influences the competitiveness of the weed. Rice planted in a 15×15-cm spacing eliminated competition from *P. distichum*, while the standard spacing of 20×20-cm or greater resulted in a 45% yield loss. Water depths of 10 to 15 cm also reduce *P. distichum* growth, but it thrives in soils with up to 5 cm of water. Delayed rice planting also reduces *P. distichum* competition in Japan (Ikeda et al. 1983).

Tilling fields to 15 cm in the fall and spring controls stolon and rhizome regrowth if the stems are desiccated to 35% moisture or less. Even if not dried, temperatures of 45°C for 9 days or 50°C for 3 days kill rhizome buds (Vasconcelos et al. 1979).

Effective annual weed control and increased use of N in rice favor *P. distichum* encroachment. Thick cell walls increase the plant's tolerance to many herbicides (Noda 1969), but it can be killed by glyphosate (IRRI 1976). Once established, the plant competes with upland crops, especially cotton, maize and sugarcane. As tillage is reduced, *P. distichum* becomes more abundant in soybean fields in the United States and in upland fields in the Philippines. It can become a dominant weed in only two seasons of no-till methods. Thorough tillage controls it in a single season but reduced tillage should be avoided in infested fields unless *P. distichum* is controlled with herbicides (IRRI 1976).

In addition to reducing yields, *P. distichum* hosts rice viral diseases, bacterial leaf blight, the rice hispa (*Dicladispa armigera*) and spider mites. Inflorescences host ergot that contains alkaloids potentially toxic to cattle (Everist 1974), and plants accumulate NO_3 when fertilized in upland, but not in lowland conditions (Yoshida et al. 1979).

COMMON NAMES

Paspalum distichum

ARGENTINA	gramilla, gramilla blanca, gramilla del tiempo, gramilla dulce
AUSTRALIA	water couch
BRAZIL	capim da praia, grama de forquilha, grama doce
CHILE	chepica
CHINA	shrun-sue-chio-bye
COLOMBIA	paja amarga
CUBA	rapiente
EGYPT	abu'oqeila, moddeid
EL SALVADOR	grama colorado
ENGLAND	water couch
FIJI	knotgrass
INDONESIA	asinan
IRAQ	shalhaw
ISRAEL	paspalon du-turi
ITALY	paspalo distico
JAPAN	kishu-suzumenohie
MADAGASCAR	fandrolakana, mahabanky
MEXICO	grama colorado
MOROCCO	paspalum a deux epis
NEW ZEALAND	mercer grass
PAKISTAN	naru
PHILIPPINES	bakbaka, dagat, malitkalabaw, panluilui, luya luyang

PORTUGAL	alcanache, graminhao
PUERTO RICO	saladillo, salaillo
SOUTH AFRICA	couch paspalum, kweek paspalum
SPAIN	gram d'algua
SRI LANKA	knotgrass, water couch
SURINAM	watra adroe
TAIWAN	shuang-suei-tsue-bai
TURKEY	kanalli dari
UNITED STATES	knotgrass
URUGUAY	gramilla brava
VENEZUELA	grama

Sixty-Six

Passiflora foetida L.

Passifloraceae, Passion-Flower Family

P ASSIFLORA FOETIDA is a foul-smelling, climbing or scrambling perennial weed that is kin to the pleasant passion fruit of commerce. The weed is largely confined to the tropics and subtropics. Strangely, although it is a serious or principal weed of seven of the most important crops in the tropics, with the exception of a few studies on embryology and on the histogenesis of tendrils, the biology and ecology of the species as it occurs in agricultural fields has not been studied. The plant contains glycosides that yield HCN on hydrolysis and is reported to be harmful to stock animals. It is in 20 crops in 49 countries.

FIGURE 66-1   The distribution of *Passiflora foetida* L. across the world where it has been reported as a weed.

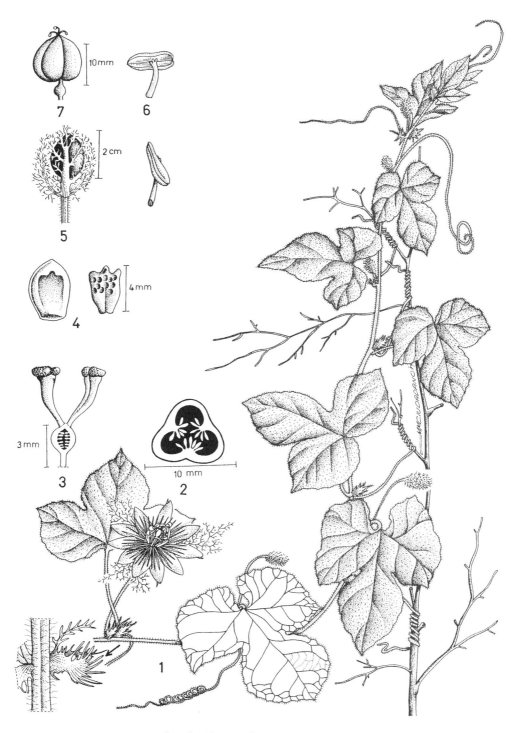

FIGURE 66-2 *Passiflora foetida* L.: 1. flowering vine; 2. ovary, cross section, 3. same, vertical section; 4. seed, two views; 5. fruit, surrounded by involucre; 6. stamen, two views; 7. fruit, without surrounding involucre.

DESCRIPTION

P. foetida (Figure 66-2) is a fetid, herbaceous, hairy, *perennial* vine, scrambling or climbing to 5 m or more by axillary, unbranched, coiling tendrils with soft to hard, yellow to brown hairs; *stems* slender, green, round, covered with yellowish fine hairs; *leaves* alternate, thin, ovate to ovate-oblong, 4.5 to 14 cm long, 3.5 to 13 cm wide, 3-lobed with central lobe slightly longer than others, base cordate, pale green or yellowish, soft but densely hairy, venation distinct; *petiole* 2 to 10 cm long; *flowers* solitary in leaf axils, on stalk 3.5 cm long, white to pale-purple or pinkish, about 3 cm across, within corolla is a collar or *corona* of 2 rows of purple filaments with white tips, spreading out flat and nearly as long as petals, flower subtended by prominent *involucre* of 3 pale green *bracts* that are 1- to 3-pinnately divided into numerous segments, the ultimate segments glandular; *sepals* 5, white, linear, 1.5 cm long, pale; *petals* 5, linear; *stamens* 5, *anthers* large; *filaments* united in a tube; *carpels* 3, syncarpous; *pistils* 3, each with 2- or 3-lobed *stigma*; *ovary* intermediate, 1-locular with many *ovules*; *fruit* an indehiscent *berry* or capsule, yellow, red or orange, globular, dry inflated, 2 to 3 cm long, surrounded by the shaggy involucral bracts; *seeds* numerous, wedge-shaped to ovate, about 4 mm long, with coarse reticulate pattern centrally each side, seeds covered with white, sweet pulp.

The filamentous corona with purple base and white in upper half, the prominent and persistent involucre of bracts that are pinnately divided, and the disagreeable odor of all parts when crushed are distinguishing characteristics of this species.

DISTRIBUTION AND BIOLOGY

P. foetida (Figure 66-1) behaves as a weed from India southeastward through much of Australia and is widely distributed in the Pacific Islands. It is in the Middle East, in the western countries of Africa, but rarely in East Africa, the islands of the Indian Ocean and the Middle East. It is reported from Tanzania, Madagascar, Reunion, and Syria. In the Americas it extends from the southern and western United States southward through the Caribbean Islands and Central America to Peru, and is in southern Brazil as well. Good (1964) places it with a small group of species most widely distributed in the tropics.

The plant thrives on many soil types, including peat, and prefers moist tropical areas and wet seasons in Australia and Hawaii, while frequenting drier areas in Fiji. It is found most often in plantation crops, grows vigorously in neglected plantings, and because it tends to infest work roads and field borders the weed may spread into crops. It is common on seashores, river banks, bushland, highway borders, wastelands, and seeks out disturbed areas.

In plantation crops of the tree habit, the weed tends to be most severe in mature plantings where there is some shade.

The species reproduces only by seeds. The seeds are eaten by birds and may be carried long distances. Ewusie and Quaye (1977) reported that the flowers open with the early light of morning and close with the high light of midday. Raju (1954) in India reported that anthesis occurs for a very brief time in early morning when the atmosphere is relatively cool.

The pollination mechanism and the development of gametophytes, ovules and seeds has been studied by Padhye (1963), Padhye and Deshpande (1960), Raju (1954), and Singy (1962). The histogenesis and morphology of tendril development was studied by Shah and Dave (1970). The adaptations for climbing in the axillary structures are interesting. The leaf subtends three bud initials placed in a triangular pattern: the single uppermost is vegetative and may become a branch shoot, one of the lower becomes a flower and the other a tendril. On any given shoot all buds on the left or all buds on the right become tendrils, but each branch has its own orientation (Anon. [Malaysia] 1964).

AGRICULTURAL IMPORTANCE

P. foetida is the number one weed in maize in some regions of Malaysia and is a serious weed of rubber in Indonesia and Malaysia. It is a principal weed of coconut in New Guinea and elsewhere in the Pacific region, of maize in Thailand, of cotton in Peru and Thailand, of several dryland crops in Sarawak, of oil palm in Indonesia, of sugarcane in Australia and Thailand, and of taro in Samoa.

It is a common weed of bananas in Surinam, coconuts in Sarawak and Thailand, cocoa in Indonesia, cotton in Nicaragua, dryland crops in Australia and the Philippines, irrigated crops and pastures in Australia, maize in Mexico, pineapple in Malaysia, several plantation crops in Ghana and Malaysia, upland rice in Indonesia, rubber in Sarawak, Thailand and Sri Lanka, sugarcane in Bangladesh, Fiji, Hawaii and Nicaragua, tea in Indonesia, tobacco in the Philippines, and vegetables in Australia.

In Colombia, the weed is found in beans and cotton, in Honduras in cotton, pineapple, and sugarcane, in the Philippines in abaca, coconut, pastures, and sugarcane, in Samoa in coconut, in Tanzania in cotton, in the Solomon Islands in oil palm, in Peru and Reunion in sugarcane, and in New Caledonia in vegetables. In northwest Mexico, it is plentiful in shifting cultivation and particularly where the soil has been opened up or disturbed.

In an earlier time, the species was recommended for some areas as a competitive plant to smother the perennial grass weed, Imperata *cylindrica*, and other weeds, but this is no longer deemed to be effective. *Passiflora* has not been successfully controlled in trials with many standard herbicides.

The plant contains cyanogenetic glycosides (yielding HCN upon hydrolysis) in all above-ground parts of the plants except fully ripe fruits. The highest concentration of HCN is in leaves and immature fruits and these are alleged to have caused the death of goats and fowl in Queensland, Australia (Hurst 1942). Noting that the fruits are eaten several places in the world, Dalziel (1937) has warned that immature fruits can be inadvertently mixed with those thought to be fully ripe and this can lead to serious illness.

COMMON NAMES

Passiflora foetida

AUSTRALIA	stinking passion flower, love in a mist, mossy passion flower
BRAZIL	maracuja-da-pedra
CAMBODIA	sav mao prey
DOMINICAN REPUBLIC	caguazo, mariballa
EL SALVADOR	granadilla colorado, granadilla montes, sandia de culebra
FIJI	wild passion fruit
HAWAII	love in a mist, scarlet fruited passion flower
HONDURAS	granadilla

INDIA	banchathail, mukkopeera
INDONESIA	ceplukan blunsun, katjeprek, lemanas, permot, rambaton blunsun
JAMAICA	granadilla, love in a mist
JAPAN	kusa-tokeiso
MADAGASCAR	tsipopoka
MALAYSIA	love in a mist, pokok lang bulu, timun dendang, wild water lemon
MAURITIUS	poc-poc sauvage
NETHERLANDS	marie-goujeat
NICARAGUA	catapanza
PERU	granadilla cimarrona
PHILIPPINES	kurunggut, lupok-lupok, masaflora, melon melonan, pasionariang-mabaho, prutas taungan, stinking passion flower
PUERTO RICO	flor de pasion silvestre, tagua tagua
REUNION	petite grenadille, poc poc
SRI LANKA	dalbattu, kodimathulai, madahalu, udahalu
THAILAND	ka-thok-rok
VENEZUELA	parchita de culebra, parchita de montana
VIETNAM	chum bao

Sixty-Seven

Phyllanthus niruri L.

Euphorbiaceae, Spurge Family

T HIS SPECIES IS ONE of over 600 tropical and subtropical members of the large and diversified *Phyllanthus* genus. Now pantropical in distribution, it is believed to have originated in the West Indies. *Phyllanthus niruri* emerges with the first rains and competes with a wide range of annual and perennial crops. It is particularly troublesome in Asia. The genus name reflects the unique arrangement of the flowers on the leaf branches. In Greek *phyllon* refers to leaf and *anthos* to flowers, thus describing the flowers hanging from the leaves.

FIGURE 67-1   The distribution of *Phyllanthus niruri* L. across the world where it has been reported as a weed.

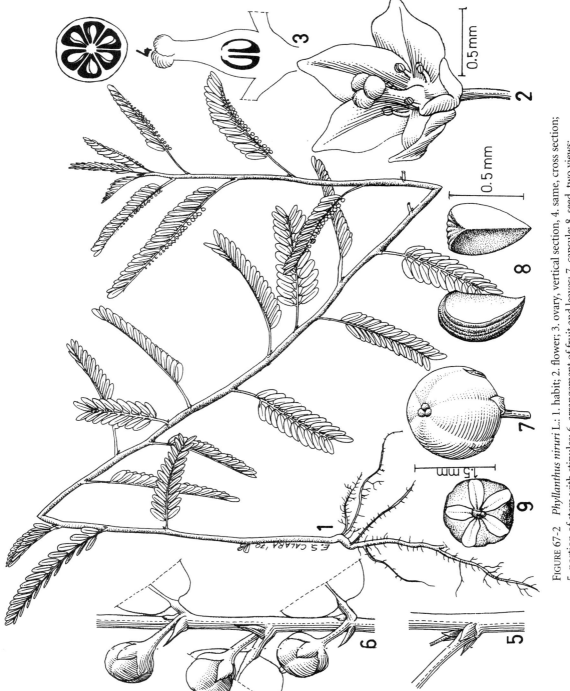

FIGURE 67-2   *Phyllanthus niruri* L.: 1. habit; 2. flower; 3. ovary, vertical section, 4. same, cross section; 5. portion of stem with stipules; 6. arrangement of fruit and leaves; 7. capsule; 8. seed, two views; 9. capsule, dorsal view.

DESCRIPTION

P. niruri (Figure 67-2) is an erect, slender, branched *annual* herb, 10 to 60 cm tall; *taproot* slender, wiry, with lateral branches evenly distributed; *stems* woody at base, green, cylindrical, smooth, numerous; *leaves* on lateral branches giving the appearance of pinnately compound leaves; 15 to 30 leaves arranged alternately in two rows along a 6- to 12-cm angular branch; small, simple 5 to 10 mm long, 3 to 4 mm wide, oblong to asymmetrically ovate or elliptic, pale green above with clearly visible veins below, on very short stalk subtended by small narrow triangular *stipules* of unequal length, to 1.5 mm; *flowers* minute, borne in leaf axils, appear in a row hanging below the length of the leafy stalk; monoecious with green or whitish 6-lobed *perianth*; *staminate flowers* with 1-veined *calyx* lobes, *stamens* 3 with *anthers* split horizontally; *pistillate flowers* with 5 green *sepals*; 3-celled *ovary*; 3 bifid *styles*; *fruit* a dehiscent 3-celled *schizocarp* or capsule, smooth, globose, 1.5 to 2.5 mm across, borne on 1.5 to 2 mm pedicels, 2 seeds per cell; *seeds* wedge-shaped, 1 concave and 2 flat sides, 1.5 to 1.8 mm long, dark brown and longitudinally ribbed on back.

The key characteristics of this plant are the numerous small leaves, the monoecious flowers that arise in the leaf axils, and the dehiscent, 3-celled capsules.

TAXONOMY, HABITAT, AND ECOLOGY

P. niruri has been confused with similar species, especially *P. amarus*, *P. fraternus* and *P. stipulatus* (Webster 1957, 1970). Floral characteristics are quite similar and pollen and seed morphology are often more helpful in identifying each species. *P. niruri* pollen has a microreticulate surface with a large polar axis and a distinctly circular mid-section (Punt and Rentrop 1973). In India, Mitra and Jain (1985) consider *P. niruri* to be a mixture of three species (*P. amarus*, *P. debilis* and *P. fraternus*). After describing the characteristics of each, they combine these species into a *P. niruri* complex.

Plants are found in cultivated fields of cotton, rice, and maize as well as perennial crops of sugarcane, coffee, and bananas. They occur in gardens and roadsides and thrive in full sunlight or partial shade from sea level to 1800 m.

P. niruri is a pioneer species and is one of the first to appear at the start of the rainy season. It grows in wet soils and mature plants tolerate complete flooding for several days without injury (Singh et al. 1983). Plants can grow as epiphytes in the leaf axils of oil palm trees (Ridley 1930).

BIOLOGY

Plants have slender, wiry taproots with lateral branches more or less uniformly distributed along the main root. The lateral roots are the primary site of water and nutrient uptake (Shetty and Maiti 1978). The fungal flora in the rhizosphere of *P. niruri* in India consisted of 18 species during the species' life cycle (Mishra and Kamal 1972). The greatest fungal diversity occurred during the seedling stage, while the highest populations developed when plants matured. Singh and Singh (1939) observed the greatest nutrient uptake at the preflowering stage when plants contained 2.4% N, 1.5% P_2O_5, 1.8% KO_2, 2.6% Ca, and 0.5% S. The species is considered rich in calcium because it had the highest levels of five **Euphorbiaceae** species tested.

Leaves have 144 and 580 stomata/mm^2 on the upper and lower surfaces, respectively (Das and Santakumari 1977). *P. niruri* has a transpiration rate of 28.4 mg water/cm^2/hr and a transpiration ratio of 582 g water/g dry weight produced. Singh (1956) thoroughly described embryo and endosperm development of *P. niruri*. The species is a C$_3$ plant with a 2*n* chromosome number of 36, but its cytology is not well researched (Webster 1970, Holm-Nielsen 1979).

Over 250 seedlings/m^2 emerged after cotton was planted in the Sudan (Idris and Beshir 1979). Some of the initial plants died but newly emerged seedlings kept the population at the original density for 6 wk. The population declined to 170 plants/m^2 after 8 to 9 wk and then dropped rapidly as plants matured 10 to 12 wk after emergence. The first true leaf appeared 3 to 4 days after emerging, flowering started at 18 days, the first fruits were formed at 38 days and plants senesced at 86 days. If soil moisture became limiting, the life cycle was shortened to only a 5- to 6-wk period.

Single plants can produce 3175 seeds with a mean weight of 0.17 mg each (Pancho 1964). Seed populations in the soil of the Sudan were 245, 50, and 25 seeds/m^2 at 0 to 15, 15 to 30, and 30 to 45 cm, respectively. *P. niruri* seeds represented 30% of the total broadleaf weed population. During dry weather, cracks in the heavy-textured soils allowed seeds to penetrate to 45 cm (Idris and Beshir 1979). Additional studies discovered that germination was highest in the rainy season (10.0 vs. 1.5% for dry season) and higher in moist soil than in dry soil (8.4 vs 3.8%). Twice as many seeds germinated on the surface than at 2- or 4-cm depths. Seed stored for 7 yr maintained an 8% germination rate.

AGRICULTURAL IMPORTANCE

P. niruri inhabits various weed-crop habitats in tropical and subtropical regions. It is reported as a weed of 32 crops in 59 countries (Figure 67-1), and is most frequently reported in sugarcane, maize, upland rice and plantation crops. *P. niruri* is a serious or principal weed of beans in India and Jamaica; cassava in Indonesia; cotton and peanuts in Sudan; maize in India and Mexico; cotton, millet, orchards, peanuts, peas, rice, sesame, soybean, sugarcane, and sunflower in India; pastures in Thailand; rice in Mexico and Sudan; sorghum in Colombia and Sudan; taro in Samoa Islands; vegetables in Jamaica and Samoa Islands; and wheat in Sudan.

It is a reported common weed of bananas in Hawaii and Surinam; barley and wheat in Peru; beans in Mexico; cassava and citrus in Surinam; coffee in Costa Rica; jute in Bangladesh and India; maize in Malaysia, Nepal, and Taiwan; nursery crops in Australia; oil palm in Surinam; peanuts in Taiwan; rice in Central America, Indonesia, Mexico, and Surinam; sugarcane in Bangladesh, Indonesia, Mexico, Nicaragua, and Trinidad; tea in India; and vegetables in Surinam and Tonga.

P. niruri is also a weed of unknown rank of bananas in Central America and Mexico; beans in Brazil, Colombia, and Nicaragua; cassava in India and Nicaragua; citrus in Ghana and Mexico; coffee in Honduras, Mexico, El Salvador, and Zaire; cotton in Colombia, Tanzania, and Thailand; dryland crops in India; maize in Angola, Cambodia, Central America, Colombia, Indonesia, the Philippines, and Thailand; oil palm in Ghana and Malaysia; peanuts in Indonesia; pineapple in Central America, Malaysia, and Taiwan; rice in Nepal, the Philippines, Puerto Rico, Thailand, and Vietnam; rubber in Ghana, Indonesia, and Sri Lanka; sorghum in Central America and India; soybean in Indonesia, the Philippines, and Taiwan; sugarcane in Colombia, Honduras, Nepal, the Philippines,

Taiwan, and Thailand; sweet potatoes in Honduras, Puerto Rico, and Taiwan; tea in Indonesia, Sri Lanka, and Taiwan; tobacco in Central America; and vegetables in Australia, Central America, Hawaii, New Caledonia, Sudan, Taiwan, and Thailand.

Weed surveys in upland crops over a 4-yr period in Sudan revealed that *P. niruri* comprised 8 to 18% of the total weed population (based on plant counts), making it one of the principal weeds (Wilson-Jones 1958). When *P. niruri* was the dominant weed in dry-seeded irrigated rice trials in Sudan, yield losses ranged from 10 to 70%, with a 50% loss common without weeding (Ghobrial 1981). Three hand weedings achieved maximum yields.

The plant may also be allelopathic. Water used to wash whole, fresh roots was placed in petri dishes with seeds of leguminous crops. The leachate significantly reduced green gram germination and soybean, peanut and green gram root and hypocotyl length (Tiwari et al. 1985). Additionally, *P. niruri* hosts the root-knot nematode in the Philippines (Pancho and Obien 1983), the cotton white fly (Yassin and Bendixen 1982), and a *Xanthomonas* bacterial leaf disease (Sabet et al. 1969).

Several beneficial uses are known for *P. niruri*. In India, pharmaceutical companies manufacture a preparation from it for use as a diuretic and to treat jaundice, dropsy, gonorrhea, urinary tract infections, and asthma (Anandalwar and Venkateswara 1981). Brazilians use it as a diuretic, to treat diabetics and to remove kidney stones (Lorenzi 1982). Row et al. (1966) characterized the bitter principal in *P. niruri* as the lignin phyllanthin and the non-bitter component as hypophyllanthin. Useful flavenoids have been found in the plant's roots (Chauhan et al. 1979).

COMMON NAMES

Phyllanthus niruri

ARGENTINA	phyllanthus
AUSTRALIA	lagoom spurge
BRAZIL	erva pombinha, quebra pedra, saxifraga
COLOMBIA	bolsilla, viernes santo
DOMINICAN REPUBLIC	quininito
HAWAII	niruri
INDIA	badisnla, bhoomyamalaki, bluinanvolah, hazardana, jaramla, keela nelli, nela usiti
INDONESIA	meniran
JAMAICA	carry me seed, quinine weed, seed underleaf
MADAGASCAR	anakalsotsy
MEXICO	cabeza de arricra
PARAGUAY	para-para'i
PHILIPPINES	kurukalunggai, sampasampalukan, san pedro, talikod
PUERTO RICO	quinino del pobre
SUDAN	surib
TRINIDAD	seed underleaf
VENEZUELA	flor escondida

Sixty-Eight

Physalis angulata L.

Solanaceae, Nightshade Family

P HYSALIS ANGULATA is a widely distributed tropical and subtropical weed. Several closely related species (*P. minima*, *P. peruviana*, *P. pubescens* and *P. viscosa*) also occur in crops, but *P. angulata* is the one encountered in most countries. While native to tropical America, it is now found in over 63 countries. It infests primarily annual crops but also occurs in orchards, nurseries, fallow land, roadsides and waste areas. The genus name is derived from the Greek *physa* for bladder in reference to the inflated calyx, and the species name refers to the angular stem. In spite of its distribution and frequency as a weed, relatively few studies have been done on this species.

FIGURE 68-1   The distribution of *Physalis angulata* L. across the world where it has been reported as a weed.

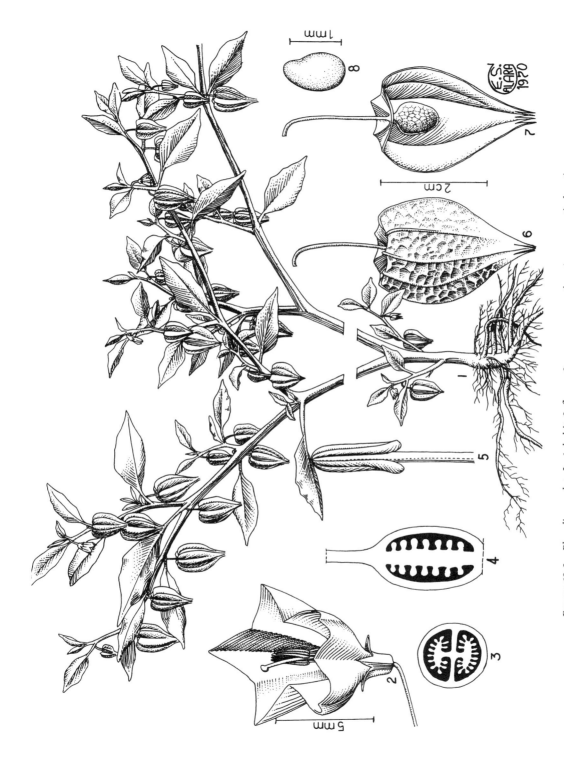

FIGURE 68-2 *Physalis angulata* L.: 1. habit; 2. flower; 3. ovary, cross section, 4. same, vertical section; 5. stamen; 6. fruit, 7. same, partly excised; 8. seed.

DESCRIPTION

P. angulata (Figure 68-2) is an erect, smooth, highly branched, fleshy *annual* herb 1 m or less high; *taproot* shallow; *stems* angled, ribbed and hollow; *leaves* alternate, bright green, ovate-oblong, acute or acuminate, 5 to 10 cm long, 2 to 4 cm wide, base often acute, margins entire, wavy, with pointed apex; *petioles* 1 to 5 cm long, sometimes purplish; *inflorescence* composed of solitary flowers borne in upper leaf axils on slender pedicel 1 to 3 cm long; *flowers* perfect, *corolla* pale yellow, tubular, spreading to 1 cm in diameter, about 6 mm long, appressed-hairy outside, interior base of tube often brownish; *stamens* 5 with blue *anthers*; *calyx* 5 mm long, partially fused as fruit develops; *fruiting calyx* grows to form large, membranous, 5-sided bladder-like "lantern" enclosing berry, 2 to 3 cm long with 10 prominent purplish veins; *fruit* a spherical *berry*, 1 cm in diameter, fleshy, yellow when mature with numerous seeds; *seeds*, kidney or lens-shaped, golden brown, 2.5 mm in diameter.

This species is recognized by its angular, hollow stems, the yellow corolla with a brownish base, and the pendulous berries surrounded by the inflated lantern-like calyx.

ECOLOGY AND BIOLOGY

P. angulata grows best in moist, fertile soils and is tolerant of partial shade (Lorenzi 1982). In Colombia, plants are found to 3000 m when temperatures are above 10°C in habitats as varied as from annual and perennial crops to waste areas and pastures (Gomez and Rivera 1987). When 8-cm-tall plants were cut just above ground level, only 11% died. If cut when 25 and 50 cm tall, 40 and 92% died, respectively. A second cutting killed plants at all heights (Schwerzel 1983).

In Zimbabwe, Thomas (1982) seeded *P. angulata* in the field and then either tilled and irrigated or did not till or irrigate. More *P. angulata* seedlings emerged on tilled, non-irrigated land (16%) than in non-tilled nonirrigated fields (10%). Only 3 to 5% emergence occurred with irrigation. Similar populations emerged in cropped and non-cropped areas and emergence dropped for all treatments during the 5 yr after seeding (Thomas 1982).

P. angulata seeds failed to germinate at constant temperatures of 10 and 40°C. Temperatures of 20, 25, and 30°C gave 6, 39, and 44% germination, respectively. Alternating temperatures of 10 hr at 21°C and 14 hr at 30°C gave 96% germination (Bell and Oliver 1979). Emergence decreased from 84% for seeds 0 to 1.2 cm deep to 60% at 5 cm deep. No seedlings emerged when seeds were planted 10 cm deep. Seeds germinate in both light and dark, and while germination is greatest at *pH*s between 6 and 8, seedlings are less vigorous at *pH*s below 6 (Thompson and Witt 1987).

Plants free of competition grew 80 to 100 cm tall before flowering in the United States; but with high intraspecific competition, flowering began when plants were 25 to 35 cm tall (Bell and Oliver 1979). Single plants produced 13,100 seeds in Taiwan (Peng 1984), 22,000 in Zimbabwe (Schwerzel 1967), and 30,875 in Peru (Celis 1984). *P. angulata* is a C_3 plant (Prieto and Leon 1975) with a $2n$ chromosome number of 48.

Viable seeds are present 2 wk after anthesis, with maximum viability at 4 wk (Thompson and Witt 1987). By 8 wk after flowering, some seeds became dormant (Bell and Oliver 1979). Seeds can be spread by birds and cattle that ingest the berries and the fruits can float in moving water inside the inflated calyx (Ridley 1930).

AGRICULTURAL IMPORTANCE

P. angulata is a weed of 29 tropical and subtropical crops in 63 countries (Figure 68-1) and is frequently reported a weed of summer annual and perennial plantation crops. It is a principal or serious weed of cotton in Mexico and Venezuela; jute, upland rice, and sweet potato in Taiwan; maize and pineapple in South Africa; pasture and peanuts in Ghana; sesame in Venezuela; soybean in Australia, Mexico, and Taiwan; sugarcane in Indonesia, South Africa, and Taiwan; and taro in Samoa.

It is a common weed of bananas in Surinam; beans, coffee, and cotton in Brazil; maize in Brazil, Indonesia, Nigeria, Peru, and Zimbabwe; millet in Sudan; pastures in Brazil and Surinam; pineapple in Swaziland; rice in Guatemala, Mexico, and Surinam; lowland rice in Indonesia and Senegal; upland rice in Fiji, Indonesia, and Senegal; sesame in Sudan; sorghum in Mexico and Sudan; soybean in Brazil; sugarcane in Bangladesh, Mexico, and the Philippines; and vegetables in Bangladesh and Jamaica.

P. angulata is also a weed of unknown rank in abaca in Malaysia and the Philippines; bananas in Samoa and Taiwan; beans in Colombia; cassava in Ghana, Indonesia, and Nigeria; cereals in Kenya and Tanzania; cacao in Nigeria; cotton in Colombia, Honduras, and Nicaragua; cowpea in Nigeria; legumes in the Philippines; maize in Cambodia, Colombia, Ghana, Honduras, Mexico, Natal, the Philippines, Taiwan, Venezuela, and Vietnam; orchards and pineapple in Honduras and South Africa; peanuts in Natal and Taiwan; potato in Taiwan; rice in Gambia, Honduras, Indonesia, Ivory Coast, and Nigeria; lowland rice in the Philippines; upland rice in the Philippines and Vietnam; rubber in Indonesia; sorghum in Brazil and Honduras; soybeans in Bolivia and the United States; sugarcane in Angola, Colombia, Mozambique, Natal, Nigeria, and Peru; sweet potato in Cambodia, Madagascar, New Guinea, and Nigeria; tea in Indonesia; tobacco in Honduras; and vegetables in Cambodia, Honduras, Laos, and the United States.

Perhaps its resistance to dinitroananlins and tolerance to 2,4-D explain its presence in many crops. For example, *P. angulata* produces seed on levees in rice fields in the southern United States and it becomes a serious weed when these fields are planted to soybeans. However, substantial yield losses may not result every year. Eight weeks after crop emergence, Bell and Oliver (1979) noted a leaf area index for soybeans of 5.2, while that of *P. angulata* was only 1.8, giving soybeans a great competitive advantage over the weed. In one trial, densities of 20, 40, and 60 *P. angulata* plants/m^2 did not reduce yield, but in another, soybean yield was reduced 3-fold by uncontrolled *P. angulata*. Only plants that emerged within 2 to 4 wk of soybean planting complete their life cycle (Thompson and Witt 1987).

Losses can also occur when stems, leaves and fruits clog harvest equipment and berries contaminate the grain. *P. angulata* hosts viruses found in lucerne, tobacco, potato, pepper, okra, and other crops as well as *Pythium* wet rot of cowpeas and several species of rootknot nematodes (Barbosa et al. 1983). The related weedy species, *P. minima*, hosts the parasitic weed *Orobanche* spp. (Bhargava et al. 1976).

Many **Solanaceae** plants have food and medicinal uses and *P. angulata* is no exception. The leaves and fruits are consumed in several countries (Martin and Ruberte 1978) and its leaves have nearly 5% N (Byers 1961). The plant has been used to treat malaria in Peru (Ferreya 1970), toothaches in Puerto Rico (Velez and Overbeek 1950), liver ailments and rheumatism in Brazil and also as a diuretic and relaxant in Brazil (Lorenzi 1982). Many organic compounds known as "physalins" have been identified in *P. angulata* (Row et al. 1978). Alkaloids in the plant are poisonous to cattle (Gomez and Rivera 1987).

COMMON NAMES

Physalis angulata

ARGENTINA	alkekenje
AUSTRALIA	annual groundcherry
BOLIVIA	motojobobo embolsado
BRAZIL	balaozinho, bucho-de-ra', camapu, camaru
COLOMBIA	mullaca, vejigon
CUBA	huevo de gato
DOMINICAN REPUBLIC	tope-tope
ECUADOR	popoja
EL SALVADOR	bomba, huevillo, huevo de tortuga
FIJI	wild cape gooseberry
GHANA	wild gooseberry
GUATEMALA	meltonate
HONDURAS	tomatillo
INDONESIA	cecendet, ceplukan, tjeplukan
JAMAICA	gooseberry, hogweed, poisonous cape, wild cherry, wild tomato
JAPAN	sennari-houzuki
MEXICO	tomatillo
NIGERIA	koropo
PERU	bolsa mullaca, capuli cimarron
PHILIPPINES	putok-putokan, tino-tino, toltolaya
PUERTO RICO	sacabyche
SOUTH AFRICA	wild gooseberry, wild physalis, wilde appelliefie
TRINIDAD	hogweed
UNITED STATES	cutleaf groundcherry
VENEZUELA	huevo de sapo, topotopo
ZAMBIA	wild gooseberry
ZIMBABWE	wild gooseberry

Sixty-Nine

Poa annua L.

Poaceae (Gramineae), Grass Family

POA ANNUA IS ONE OF THE smallest species of secondary weeds and yet one of the most studied, probably due to its extensive distribution, its adaptation to numerous habitats and to the presence of both annual and perennial types within the species. A native of Europe, *P. annua* is found around the world in temperate and alpine climates. It is a very successful colonizer, is found in both disturbed and undisturbed sites, and tolerates varied environmental conditions. Its importance in agriculture is due more to its persistence through high seed populations and its presence in numerous crops than to substantial yield losses.

FIGURE 69-1 The distribution of *Poa annua* L. across the world where it has been reported as a weed.

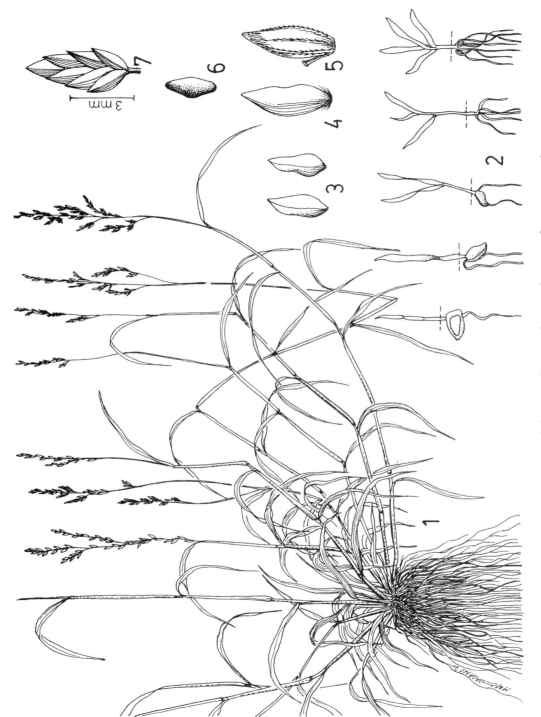

FIGURE 69-2 *Poa annua* L.: 1. habit; 2. seedlings; 3. glumes; 4. lemma; 5. floret; 6. caryopsis; 7. spikelet.

P. annua may have evolved through the crossing of *P. infirma* and *P. supina* (Tutin 1952). Annual types are often referred to as variety *annua* and the perennial as variety *reptans*. Its survival as a weed is due to high genotypic and phenotypic variability, rapid germination, survival when uprooted, tolerance to compacted soils, and small, light seeds that are readily spread by birds and transported on shoes, tools, mowers, and other equipment (Warwick 1979).

DESCRIPTION

P. annua (Figure 69-2) is an erect or ascending *annual* or nearly prostrate, short-lived *perennial* grass; *roots* fibrous; *stems* 5 to 25 cm long with 2 to 4 nodes, light green; perennial types frequently rooting at nodes; *leaf sheaths* smooth, compressed, keeled, loosely surrounding culm; *ligule* membranous, thin, white, up to 4 mm long, obtuse in lower, more acute in upper leaves; *blades* smooth, v-shaped, 3 to 10 cm long, 2 to 4 mm wide, with boat-shaped tips; *inflorescence* a terminal panicle, triangular in outline, sometimes more or less 1-sided, 2.5 to 10 cm long; *spikelets* 3- to 6-flowered, crowded beyond middle of branch; *upper glume* elliptic or oblong, 2 to 4 mm long, 3-nerved; *lower glume* lanceolate to ovate, 1.5 to 3 mm long, 1-nerved; *lemmas* overlapping, keeled, 5-nerved, smooth or hairy on nerves toward base, nerves not extending to apex; *palea* with hairy (rarely glabrous) keels, slightly shorter than lemmas; *anthers* pale yellow, 1 to 1.5 mm long; *stigma* white; *fruit* an elliptical, bright amber *caryopsis* 1.5 to 2.5 mm long, dorsally keeled and pointed at both ends.

    P. annua is characterized by the boat-tipped leaves, often with wrinkles in young leaves, the flattened leaf sheath, membranous ligule and 5-nerved lemmas.

HABITAT AND DISTRIBUTION

P. annua occurs in a multitude of habitats in over 80 countries with temperate climates and in mountainous regions of tropical countries (Figure 69-1). It invades gardens, lawns, foot paths, bowling greens, flower beds, golf courses, and cracks in sidewalks and pavement. *P. annua* can be found at the margins of ponds and streams as well as in agronomic and horticultural crops and pastures. Because it has poor drought tolerance, it is not found in semiarid regions, but it is known to exist in both Arctic and Antarctic regions (Walton 1975). It grows from sea level to over 1200 m in the British Isles (Hutchinson and Seymour 1982). *P. annua* occurs in areas of 90 to 430 mm annual precipitation; average minimum and maximum temperatures of 4.9 and 27.4°C, respectively; and soil *p*Hs from 4.5 to 8.2 (Duke 1979).

    P. annua grows on a wide range of soils, tolerates trampling, and is a frequent weed in areas heavily trafficked by livestock or humans. Its root system is quite shallow in these conditions, but when grown in noncompacted soils, its rooting depth is similar to that of the perennials *Poa pratensis* and *Cynodon dactylon* (Beard 1970). Warwick (1980a) compared trampling tolerance of perennial (prostrate) and annual (erect) *P. annua* biotypes. Total biomass production was reduced 50 and 70% for "light" and "heavy" trampling, respectively, for each type. Trampling causes plants to use relatively more energy in vegetative than reproductive growth.

ECOLOGY AND BIOLOGY

An amazing feature of *P. annua* is the presence of annual and perennial types. As would be expected, each occurs in environments best suited for its growth and development. Annual types are usually erect and flower within 44 to 55 days after germination, while perennial types are prostrate to semi-erect, semi-stoloniferous and slower to flower (Tutin 1957). Annuals are the predominant type in cultivated areas and perennials thrive in closely mowed, well-managed areas such as golf courses, pastures, and bowling greens.

Warwick and Briggs (1978) selected plants from highly managed bowling greens and from adjacent flower beds in England. The ratio of annuals to perennials in the flower beds was 2:1, but winter collections had a higher proportion of annuals than spring collections. Ninety-six percent of the plants from bowling greens were prostrate. Both types produced progeny of the same type as their parents, regardless of the environment of the first generation of plants. Erect and prostrate plants flowered 55 and 80 days after planting, respectively.

P. annua has a $2n$ chromosome count of 28 and plants are normally self-pollinated, with 0 to 15% outcrossing in natural populations (Ellis 1973). Plants collected from different habitats maintained their morphological differences and habitat preferences for 6 yr (Tutin 1957). He observed that anthesis starts at the panicle apex and also at the tips of spikelets. Anthesis peaks 2 to 3 days after the process starts, is complete in 6 to 7 days, and occurs in darkness (between 10:00 P.M. and 4:00 A.M.) (Liem 1980). Maximum anthesis occurs at 20°C and is more rapid in very short days (2 to 8 hr of light) than in longer days (10 to 12 hr of light). The response to environment in the anthesis cycle did not occur for two perennial grass species also studied and reflects another adaptation of *P. annua* to specific conditions. At temperatures of 29°C or more, pollen or anthers of *P. annua* are killed and this may explain its absence from tropical climates (Hovin 1957). Seeds are viable in only 1 to 2 days after pollination (Beard 1973).

P. annua plants usually become established in the late summer or early fall, often from seeds produced the same year. Plants resume growth earlier than other grass species in the spring. Perennial types produce numerous tillers and prostrate stems that usually form adventitious roots at the nodes. Most tillers die without flowering. Annual types have few nodal roots because they are generally erect.

P. annua is day neutral and flowering begins in early spring in the Northern Hemisphere. Seed head production peaks in May and June and continues at a lower level thereafter (Wells 1974). Annual plants die after flowering, but not all tillers on a plant mature uniformly. Ong and Marshall (1975) discovered several unique physiological features of *P. annua*. The inflorescence biomass increases for 3 to 4 wk after emergence, but then inflorescences lose weight as seed drop occurs, even though they are still green. Most of the assimilates produced by the inflorescence go into the grain and only 25% of the assimilates in the inflorescences are "imported" from other plant parts. Thus the panicle of *P. annua* contributes a very high proportion of assimilates to the seed, as compared to annual cereal grasses. Equally noteworthy is the fact that the inflorescence remains active even after seeds drop and even if green leaves are still present. While all leaves on a stem send assimilates to the inflorescence, most are provided by the flag leaf. If seeds are removed before maturity, all translocation is diverted to other plant parts. After normal seed drop, assimilates from the inflorescence move into the root system and not into other tillers. Net assimilation of CO_2 by the inflorescence drops in half after seed drop.

Prostrate plants have nearly twice as many stomata on the upper leaf surface as erect types (220 vs. 125/mm^2). They are arranged in double rows on the upper epidermis, while on the lower epidermis and sheaths they are in single rows (Hutchinson and Seymour 1982). *P. annua* is a C$_3$ plant and has a higher rate of photosynthesis in short (8-hr) than long (16-hr) days (Burian and Winter 1976). Its overall growth rate was among the fastest of 132 species tested, indicating it is very competitive during its active growth period (Grime and Hunt 1975). However, early season crops compete effectively with *P. annua*. Fifty and 150 pea plants/m^2 reduced *P. annua* biomass 63 and 94%, respectively (Topham and Lawson 1981).

Annual and perennial types respond differently to cutting and competition. McNeilly (1981) found that *P. annua* collected from closed habitats (such as lawns) dominated *Lolium perenne* when clipped but not if unclipped. *P. annua* from open habitats did not compete well with *L. perenne* when clipped every 2 wk, but grew better than lawn biotypes if unclipped. He concludes that population differences in *P. annua* occur in very short distances in response to environmental conditions.

In Australia, Lush (1989) studied the morphological and physiological traits in populations of *P. annua* from golf course greens, fairways and roughs. Populations from fairways and roughs were similar, but these varied greatly in growth habit, biomass production, flowering, seed size, and germination as compared to populations in golf greens. Golf green plants were shorter but had more tillers, produced less biomass, flowered later, had smaller seeds and germinated without being chilled. Thus the transition from the green to the fairway/rough was a sharp one and few genotypes are common to the green and surrounding areas. Harper and White (1974) describe the species as one with an indeterminate growth system, well suited to unpredictable environments; if the season is unusually short, it will readily form seed. In longer seasons, it keeps on growing.

P. annua tolerates close mowing. Plants cut to 0.5 cm can still produce 360 seeds each (Beard 1973). While they easily survive close cutting, maximum dry weight and tiller production occur at 2.5 cm (Bogart and Beard 1973). *P. annua* has little heat or drought tolerance. Its abundance in golf courses and lawns during the summer is usually due to frequent irrigation, close cuttings, and fertilizer applications. Of 115 collections of *P. annua* tested for heat tolerance in Canada, only 22% had fair to good tolerance (Cordukes 1977). There was no correlation between growth habit and heat tolerance. Heat injury was greater at 100% relative humidity than at 70 to 80%. Plants grown under intense management were more heat sensitive than those in low management systems (Wehner and Watschke 1981). *P. annua* was less heat tolerant than *P. pratensis* but equal to *Lolium perenne*.

Plants that emerge in the fall in the northern latitudes may be winter killed. Beard (1964) noted that all plants kept at −4°C for 90 days survived if cold was the only stress present. No plants survived 15 days when frozen in ice at the same temperature. If flooded and kept under a layer of ice, plants lived 60 days, but after 90 days, 50% had died. If flooded and kept at 1°C, over 90% survived for 90 days. Cold hardiness also varies with the season. Plants are more cold sensitive in the spring than in the fall and *P. annua* was the least tolerant of six species tested to the combined effects of shade, low or high soil moisture levels, low or high temperatures, compaction, and smog (Couch 1979). Beard (1970) generally concurs with these observations but found *P. annua* relatively well adapted to shade and soil compaction.

Annual types of *P. annua* flower at all day lengths, have a moderate nodal rooting capacity and mature in 3 to 4 mo. Perennial types flower more abundantly in short days with cool temperatures, have a high rooting ability and can live 1.5 to 4 yr (Wells 1974, Netland 1984). Year-round growth can occur in coastal areas of Scandinavia even during periods of very short days.

P. annua responds well to N, P, and K fertilization (Beard 1970, Hoveland et al. 1976). High nutrition hastens panicle development, increases tiller production, and results in relatively more biomass accumulation in the inflorescence than in the roots (Ong et al. 1978).

The population dynamics of *P. annua* in the absence of other species were studied in England (Law 1981). After the first summer, over 2500 plants/m² were present, but after the second year populations did not exceed 4500 plants/m². Highest densities were noted in the spring and fall. Initial plants formed up to 13 inflorescences per month, but by late summer they averaged 1 per plant per month. Such tremendous and rapid population increases in open areas explain its ability to quickly colonize open niches in a wide array of environments. Less rapid but equally dramatic population explosions were noted in production fields over a 6-yr period (Chancellor 1976). Wells and Haggar (1984) conclude that *P. annua* is not an invader that displaces other plants, but rather a highly opportunistic colonizer.

P. annua's response to stress is also found in the appearance of herbicide-resistant biotypes. Twelve years of repeated triazine use in France (Darmency and Gasquez 1981), 10 yr of repeated paraquat treatment in England (Harvey and Harper 1982), and 14 applications of metoxuron during 5 yr (Holliday et al. 1976) resulted in resistance. Darmency and Gasquez (1981) found the resistant type was semi-prostrate and susceptible ones were erect, and thus the resistant ones would be less competitive. The triazine resistance trait is maternally inherited in *P. annua* and resistant biotypes have also been found in western the United States, the Netherlands and Belgium. Several countries also have a *P. annua* biotype resistant to amitrole. A biotype resistant to both paraquat and simazine exists in England (Clay 1989).

SEED VIABILITY, GERMINATION, AND DYNAMICS

P. annua seeds generally have a short after-ripening period before they will germinate. However, great variation may exist. Seeds from original collections in the eastern, southern and northern United States were grown at the same southern location for 3 yr. Freshly harvested seeds were stored in moist soil at 30°C for 2 wk. Seeds from a southern collection did not germinate at a range of temperatures between 5 to 25°C and storing imbibed seeds did not break dormancy. Freshly harvested seed from the eastern location germinated readily (78%) at 10°C. Imbibed storage reduced germination to about 50% at temperatures of 5 to 20°C. More than 50% of the freshly harvested seed from the northern location germinated at all temperatures and imbibed storage had no effect on germination. These responses show that the eastern and southern populations have dormancy mechanisms adapted to avoid high summer temperatures but that the northern population behaves as a summer annual (Standifer and Wilson 1988).

Naylor and Abdalla (1982) collected plants from 18 locations in Scotland and grew them to maturity in greenhouse conditions. At 20°C, freshly collected seeds gave 0 to 100% germination. Populations of after-ripened seed responded differently to constant temperatures. One population failed to germinate at constant temperatures between 2 and 30°C. Another population had 56, 92, 71, and 18% germination at 5, 15, 20, and 25°C, respectively. Both populations had 95% germination at 15/25 or 20/30°C night/day temperatures. Radicles emerged twice as rapidly in fluctuating than in constant temperatures. If needed, one day of chilling broke dormancy. With alternating temperatures, seeds did not respond to changes in light or dark periods.

A 4-day chilling period gives optimum germination (Roberts and Benjamin 1979). Seeds respond to light, nitrate and alternating temperatures before chilling, but only to alternating temperatures after chilling. The best range of alternating temperatures is 19°C (Thompson and Whatley 1984). If the difference between high and low temperatures exceeds 24°C, germination drops markedly. Sgambatti-Araujo (1978) compared seed germination of annual and perennial biotypes. Seeds from perennial plants are not dormant, but four stages of dormancy exist in annual plants: (1) 0 to 1 mo with no germination unless stratified at 4 C; (2) from 1.5 to 2.5 mo, germination is controlled by the lemma and palea; (3) between 2.5 and 8 mo, light favors germination, and (4) seeds older than 8 mo germinate readily.

Germination is also controlled genetically. Fresh seeds obtained from two reciprocal hybrids varied in germination speed at 20°C but not at 10 or 15/25°C, nor when seeds had aged (Darmency and Aujas 1988). Differences in hormonal regulation of germination between seeds is indicated and this could favor adaptation to specific niches. In Australia, *P. annua* produces "persistent" seeds (live more than one year) and "transient" (germinate within one year) seeds (Lush 1988). Most seeds are transient and germinate in a big flush after flowering. In a golf green, the persistent component of the seed bank averaged 30,000 seeds/m^2 and the transient population reached 210,000/m^2 in the spring.

Placing seeds in sealed vials and exposing them to 50°C for 14 days in light increases germination from 21 to 46% (Taylorson and Brown 1977). Only a slight enhancement occurs if seeds are kept in the dark at 50°C. Standifer (1983) stored seeds in wet or dry soil at seven temperatures between 5 and 35°C. After 4 wk, seeds stored at 25°C or higher in moist soil had low germination. After 8 wk in moist soil, germination was 100% for seeds kept at 25°C or higher. Seeds stored at lower temperatures in moist soil required longer periods to germinate. Seeds in dry soil did not begin to germinate until 12 wk of storage, and, in this case, seeds kept at the lower temperatures germinated first. *P. annua* germination varies with its own seed density or with that of other species. Irrigation and mowing practices influence *P. annua*'s germination response to temperature in California, in the United States (Wu et al. 1987). Seeds from plants on golf greens (watered and mowed daily) germinate readily (90 to 98%) at 12 and 25°C. Seeds from plants in the rough (not irrigated and infrequently mowed) have less than 10% germination at 25°C and germination peaks at 70% at 12°C. Seeds from fairway populations (irrigated and mowed moderately) have 50% germination at 25°C and 85% at 12°C. This species exhibits rapid genetic differentiation in temperature-enforced dormancy among populations at the micro-ecological level, even on golf courses where mowing and golfers disperse seeds readily. The preservation of distinct genetic differences between green and rough populations suggests the selection pressure is both high and persistent.

Germination increased rapidly as soil moisture content increased from 20 to 40% (Koch 1968). No additional increase occurred up to field capacity. Under field conditions in England, most *P. annua* germinates in the fall (Chancellor 1964), especially if annual tillage is done. Over one-third of planted seeds germinate the first year and, after 5 yr, 60% of the seeds have emerged (Harris 1961). Maximum emergence of imbibed seeds occurs at 1 cm (92%), with 45% emergence at 0 cm and 25% at 3 cm (Williams 1983). When seeds were mixed with soil to 2.5-, 7.5- and 15-cm depths and tilled, 71, 68, and 63%, respectively, had emerged after 5 yr (Roberts and Feast 1972). Emergence was 25% less when the soil was left undisturbed. Viable seeds were present after 5 yr, especially in the untilled soil.

Individual plants can produce abundant quantities of seed. Estimates usually range from 1050 to 2250 seeds/plant, with weights of 0.1 to 0.2 g/1000 seeds (Stevens 1957,

Pawlowski et al. 1967–68, Pancho and Kim 1985). Over a 9-month period, Cordukes (1977) obtained an average of 1.8 and 2.6 g of seed from single plants of annual and perennial biotypes, respectively. Assuming 0.2 g/1000 seeds, the perennial type produced approximately 13,000 seeds/plant.

Numerous researchers have measured the soil seed population of *P. annua* in the seed bank and the numbers are incredibly high. Standifer (1980) found 422 seeds/m^2 to 15 cm in the southern United States; Harris (1961) reported 3230/m^2 in a pasture and 118,600/m^2 in a sports turf; Jensen (1969) found 6800/m^2 in Denmark; and in Scotland, Warwick (1984) noted 3500/m^2. A survey of 64 fields in England found a range of 625 to 35,550 seeds/m^2 to 15 cm and over 25% of the fields had more than 2500 seeds/m^2 (Roberts and Chancellor 1986). *P. annua* often constitutes a major portion of the seed reservoir of arable fields.

Roberts and co-workers monitored the changes in the soil seed bank for several decades (Roberts 1958, 1962, 1963; Roberts and Stokes 1965, Roberts and Ricketts 1979, Roberts and Potter 1980, Roberts and Neilson 1982). The population of *P. annua* seeds in the soil increased from 15 to 38% of the total seed bank in vegetable production fields. Deep plowing reduced seed populations more than disking (900 vs. 3300/m^2 to 40 cm). Large increases in seed population occur in years of high rainfall because cultivations are much less effective. *P. annua* seeds became 62% of the total seed bank after 9 yr of vegetable cropping. When *P. annua* did not produce seed and no crops were grown, the rate of seed loss over 5 yr was 22 to 26%/yr in non-tilled areas and 30 to 36%/yr in tilled areas. Rate of seed loss reached 56%/yr when soils were disturbed seven times annually.

P. annua biomass in the field is a poor indicator of seed bank populations. Jensen (1969) found it comprised only 7.2% of the weed biomass in vegetable fields, but it represented 23% of the soil seed bank. It was only a trace of the vegetation in a pasture, but the soil contained 13,260 seeds/m^2, equivalent to 5.9 kg/ha of *P. annua* seed (Champness and Morris 1948). Cropping systems also influence *P. annua* populations. Fifteen years of effective chemical or manual weedings in maize and spring barley reduced soil seed densities 94 and 63% of their original levels, respectively (Roberts and Neilson 1981a). Seed bank populations of *P. annua* increased 54% in carrots and 35% in wheat, indicating that it was impossible to prevent seed production in these cropping systems.

Germinating seeds tolerate 46°C for 6 hr but are killed at 49°C (Wells 1974). Covering soil with clear plastic for 40 days in the summer killed all seeds in the top 6 cm of soil, but those below 8 cm survived (Standifer et al. 1984). If done after beds are formed and planting is done without soil disturbance, *P. annua* should not affect vegetable production.

Seeds are dispersed by human activity, water, animal consumption (especially livestock and birds) and wind. *P. annua* seeds were the most abundant of all species found in the mud on footwear (Clifford 1956) and are a common contaminant of forage crop seeds (Tonkin 1968b). Only a 1% (w/w) contamination of *P. annua* in forage seed would result in seeding approximately 90 seeds/m^2 (Sagar and Mortimer 1976). The glume serves somewhat as a wing to aid in wind dispersal, seeds can float in water, and birds may use the panicles to build nests (Ridley 1930).

AGRICULTURAL IMPORTANCE

P. annua is a weed of 38 crops in 80 countries (Figure 69-1) and is most frequently reported a weed of vegetables, cereals, turf, sugar beets, potatoes, and orchards. It is a serious or principal weed of edible beans and cabbage in England; barley and oil seed rape in Japan; cereals in Alaska, Belgium, Scotland, Sweden, and Tasmania; lucerne in Argentina, Germany, Mexico, South Africa, and Spain; maize in Ecuador; millet in India; onions in Australia, England, and Poland; orchards in Alaska, Spain, and the United States; pastures in Iceland; peas in Ireland; potatoes in Belgium, England, India, and Mexico; rice in Portugal; sugar beets in Belgium, England, Germany, and Spain; strawberries in Canada; taro in Samoa; turf in South Africa, Tasmania, and the United States; vegetables in Alaska, Argentina, Belgium, Finland, Indonesia, Mexico, Scotland, Spain, and the United States; and wheat in Italy, Japan, Korea, and Portugal.

It is a common weed of barley in Canada, India, Nepal, Peru, and Spain; edible beans in Mexico; cabbage, carrots, and lettuce in Nicaragua; cereals in Ecuador, England, the Netherlands, Poland, Tunisia, and Turkey; cotton in Spain; forage crops in France; flax in Canada; legumes in India; maize in India, Mexico, and Peru; oats in Canada and Mexico; orchards in Australia, Bolivia, and South Africa; pastures in England, New Zealand, Sarawak, and South Africa; peas in England; potatoes in Ecuador, France, Iceland, Nicaragua, and the United States; oil seed rape in Canada and France; rice in India; sorghum in Honduras; sugar beets in Austria; sugarcane in South Africa; sunflowers in Canada; turf in Australia; vegetables in Australia, Germany, India, Poland, South Africa, Taiwan, and Tasmania; vineyards in Australia, Germany, and South Africa; and wheat in Canada, Colombia, France, India, Mexico, Nepal, Peru, and Spain.

In addition, *P. annua* is frequently cited by many countries as a weed of unranked importance in nearly all of the above crops.

The environment most affected by *P. annua* is that of turf areas used as golf courses, bowling greens and lawns. It is a weed in turf because of its light green color, continual seed head production, shallow root system, drought and low and high temperature sensitivity, and annual or short-lived perennial life cycle. However, if grown as a single species and frequently irrigated and fertilized, it makes an excellent turf grass for putting greens. It tolerates close mowing, compacted soils and heavy traffic and has a very rapid germination and growth rate. Thus, with careful management, it can be a useful component of turf areas.

In spite of its wide distribution and frequency, quantitative studies on yield losses caused by *P. annua* are lacking. Because populations increase as tillage is reduced (Pollard and Cussans 1981), it is likely to become even more abundant. It rose from the fourth most abundant weed in British vegetable fields in 1953 to the most important in 1975 (Davison and Roberts 1976).

The seriousness of *P. annua* in grass forages is not great. While protein and mineral levels decline as plants mature, *P. annua* has acceptable levels of Ca and Mg at all growth stages and of P in several stages, does not accumulate nitrates or oxalates, is palatable to livestock, and responds to fertilization (Gupta et al. 1982). Pastures receiving 170, 40, and 40 kg/ha of N, P_2O_5 and K_2O, respectively, for 8 yr had 21% *P. annua* in the harvested biomass and 5600 seeds/m^2 in the soil, while unfertilized pastures had 1% *P. annua* in the forage and 185 seeds/m^2 (Williams 1985). Yield of *P. annua* was equivalent to *L. perenne*, and a mixture of these species gave higher yields than monocultures, with no negative effects on nutritive value (Wells and Haggar 1974). Invasion of *P. annua* into established pastures indicates that over-grazing reduces the vigor of sown species through excessive defoliation and perhaps trampling. Reducing grazing pressure allows sown species to dominate *P. annua*.

P. annua competes aggressively with newly seeded lucerne, especially in the fall, and it can jeopardize successful legume establishment if not controlled. Tremendous increases in seed populations in the soil often occur within several years of legume seeding (Roberts and Chancellor 1986). *P. annua* may host tobacco rattle virus and *Xiphinema* or *Pratylenchus* nematodes (Bendixen et al. 1979), ergot of wheat, stripe virus of rice, and *Puccinia epiphylla*, as well as many other insects and diseases (Hutchinson and Seymour 1982).

COMMON NAMES

Poa annua

ALASKA	annual bluegrass
ARGENTINA	pastillo de invierno, pasto de invierno, pelillo
AUSTRALIA	annual poa, goose grass, winter grass
BELGIUM	paturin annuel, straatgras, tuintjeagras
BRAZIL	capim pe de galinah, pelo de chancho
CANADA	annual bluegrass, paturin annuel
CHILE	hierba de la perdiz, pasto de las liendres, pata de perdiz, piagillo, piojillo
COLOMBIA	pasto azul anual, pata de gallina, piojillo
DENMARK	enaarig rapgraes
ECUADOR	poa
ENGLAND	annual meadowgrass, annual poa
FINLAND	kylanurmikka
FRANCE	paturin annuel
GERMANY	Einjahrige Rispe, Einjahriges Rispengras, Jahrige Rispe, Spitzgras
GREECE	poa
HAWAII	annual bluegrass
ICELAND	varpasveifgras
INDIA	ghas
ITALY	fienarola annua, gramigna delle vie
JAPAN	suzumeno-katabira
MALAYSIA	annual bluegrass
MEXICO	zacate azul, zacate poa
MOROCCO	paturin annuel
NETHERLANDS	straatgras
NEW ZEALAND	poa annua
NORWAY	tunrapp
POLAND	wiechlina roczna
PORTUGAL	cabelo de cao
SAUDI ARABIA	sameeha
SOUTH AFRICA	annual bluegrass, eenjarige blougras
SPAIN	cebadilla, espiguilla, hierba de punta, pel de ca, pelosa, poa
SRI LANKA	annual meadowgrass
SWEDEN	vitroe

SWITZERLAND	Einjahriges Rispengras, paturin annuel
TAIWAN	chao-soo-ho
TASMANIA	winter grass
TURKEY	buy, salkim otu
UNITED STATES	annual bluegrass
URUGUAY	pastito de invierno, pelo de rata
YUGOSLAVIA	enoletna latovka, jednogodisnja livadarka, vlasnjaca

Seventy

Polygonum aviculare L.

Polygonaceae, Buckwheat Family

POLYGONUM AVICULARE, a native of Europe and Asia, is an ubiquitous species found in most temperate and subtropical countries. It commonly forms mats in areas of heavy foot traffic where other species have been eliminated but is also a frequent weed in cropland. The family has about 30 genera with approximately 700 species. The genus name, *Polygonum*, means "many knees" and refers to the jointed nature of the stem due to the enlarged nodes of most species. The specific name, *aviculare*, means "small birds," as the seed is eaten readily by poultry and small birds (Spencer 1940).

FIGURE 70-1   The distribution of *Polygonum aviculare* L. across the world where it has been reported as a weed.

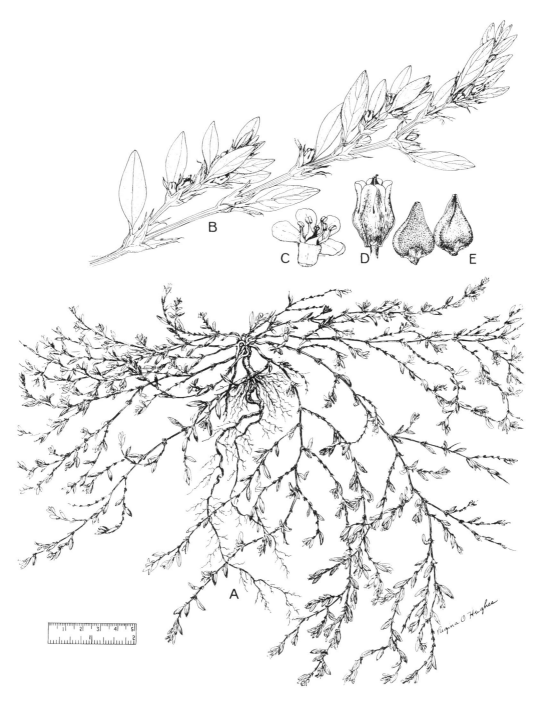

FIGURE 70-2 *Polygonum aviculare* L.: A. habit; B. flowering branch, enlarged; C. flower;
D. fruiting calyx; E. achenes.

DESCRIPTION

P. aviculare (Figure 70-2) is a low, mat-forming *annual* herb; *taproot* strong, relatively shallow, with branched fibrous roots; *cotyledons* united at the base forming a small cup, often with whitish bloom on the surface; *stems* prostrate to decumbent, 10 to 100 cm long, highly branched, slender, wiry, striated, smooth with somewhat enlarged nodes; *leaves* alternate, bluish-green, entire, lanceolate to oblong-lanceolate with sharp-pointed to rounded tips, 1 to 3 cm long, 2 to 8 mm wide; lower leaves usually larger than those on the flowering stems; *petiole* short; *ochrea* cylindrical, silvery, transparent, papery, loose, often with lacerated margins, torn by the expanding fruit; *inflorescence* composed of small inconspicuous flowers in axillary spike-like clusters of 1 to 6; *flowers* small, greenish or red, perfect, with 8 *stamens* united with perianth at base; *style* trifid; *stigmas* capitate; *carpels* 3-united; *ovary* 1-ovuled; *perianth* 2 to 3 mm long, green with whitish or pinkish margins, 5 or 6 lobes united only at base, persistent; *fruit* an *achene* surrounded by remains of the perianth, 2 to 3 mm long, 1 to 2 mm wide, triangular, broadest one-third of way from base, angles smooth, shiny, somewhat rounded, sides slightly concave, faces dull, somewhat roughened, dark mahogany-brown to almost black.

This species can be recognized by the presence of the papery ochrea at the nodes that encircle the base of the petiole, the longitudinal lines or striation on the wiry stems, the green perianth with pink or whitish margins, and triangular seeds.

HABITAT AND ECOLOGY

P. aviculare is a common weed in trampled areas such as footpaths and animal trails, in lawns, along the edges and in cracks of sidewalks and other paved surfaces, along roadsides, and especially in fields of cereal crops. It is found on dark and sandy loam soils rich in N but also grows well on infertile soil. It grows in soils with *pH*s of 5.6 to 8.4 (King 1966). In Poland, Borowiec et al. (1972) encountered *P. aviculare* in 41% of cereal crop fields with very poor soil and in 58% of the fields with very good soil. It was the eighth most frequent weed species in agricultural fields in Finland, occurring in 47% of the fields (Paatela and Ervio 1971), and in England it occurred in 38% of the cereals (Fryer and Chancellor 1970).

P. aviculare is a variable species with many growth forms and varieties. In full sunlight, plants remain prostrate and can form dense mats of wiry stems or the main stem remains flat and the branches may be somewhat erect. In partial shade, it is nearly erect, reaching 30 to 40 cm tall. It is one of the first species to appear in the spring. It invades bare ground and competes well with grasses such as *Poa annua*. It can survive among growing crops (especially cereals) and then grows rapidly after harvest until frost occurs.

BIOLOGY

Seedlings can emerge from 6 cm, but the optimum depth is 0 to 2 cm (Froud-Williams et al. 1984a). While it is common in trampled soils, Kollman and Staniforth (1969) observed the lowest emergence of *P. aviculare* from compacted soils of the four species studied. Roots and shoots grow at similar rates up to 10 cm. Most roots are found in the upper 6 cm of soil but they can penetrate to 60 cm. *P. aviculare* requires 678 ml of water to produce 1 g of dry matter (Black et al. 1969).

The variability in *P. aviculare* growth has been documented by Hart (1980) in the United States and Meerts and Lefebvre (1988) in Belgium. Plants from different locations had 80 to 160 leaves at 6 wk, began flowering 5 to 11 wk after emergence and varied in seedling height, biomass accumulation, seed production, seed size, and competitive ability with rye. While the time to flower varied greatly between populations, it was quite constant within a population. Leaf size decreased as the season progressed for all populations. Flowering continues until the first killing frost. Photoperiod apparently has no effect on flowering. The diversity in morphology and chromosome number ($2n = 40$ and 60) of Canadian biotypes caused McNeil (1981) to propose that the $2n = 40$ plants be classified as *P. arenastrum* and those with $2n = 60$ be classified as *P. monspeliense*. These biotypes also differ in leaf shape and uniformity of size, perianth size, pollen types, and seed size and shape.

Flowers are normally self-pollinated and each plant can produce 6380 seeds if competition is light, or as few as 160 seeds under heavy competition, with an average of 4600 seeds/plant (Stevens 1957). In Sweden, plants produced an average of 53 seeds/plant when in competition with barley and 1109 seeds without competition (Fogelfors 1972). Seed weights have been reported at 900 to 1000 mg/1000 seeds (Stevens 1932, Hart 1980).

SEED DYNAMICS AND GERMINATION

P. aviculare germinates early in the spring and then ceases to emerge. Seedlings appear in mid-March in Iowa, in the United States. Martin (1943) and Courtney (1968) observed that emergence occurs from late February to May in England, with peak emergence in March and April. Soil disturbance increased emergence from 4 to 21%, but did not affect the duration of emergence. After 2 yr, only 10% of the seeds added to the soil were present and viable. Soil disturbance did not affect dormant seeds but enhanced germination of nondormant seeds. The mean annual decrease in viable seed at 0 to 5 cm was 66% in disturbed soil and 26% in undisturbed soil.

Roberts and Ricketts (1979) observed peak germination after March and April cultivations. However, only 9% of the seeds in the soil produced seedlings. *P. aviculare* planted in July does not emerge until the next spring (Roberts and Feast 1972). Emergence of seeds placed 7.5 and 15 cm in the soil was greater the second year than the first, while the opposite was true for those at 2.5 cm. After 5 yr, more viable seeds were recovered from the undisturbed soil (21%) than the tilled soil (2%) and from 15 cm (22%) than 2.5 cm (2.5%). Therefore deep, undisturbed seeds are the most likely to remain dormant.

Freshly harvested seeds are dormant, and may not germinate for 60 days after harvest (Justice 1941). Seeds stored at 2 to 4°C for 5 mo had 26% germination. Storage in cold water gave the highest germination, and scarification in sulfuric acid or physically removing the pericarp greatly increases germination by reducing the after-ripening period. Light does not affect germination and aged seed has a lower cold requirement than fresh seed. Hammerton (1964) compared the germination of *P. aviculare* seeds harvested at different locations in the same year in England and found significant variations in the chilling requirement. Some seed lots required 3 wk and others 12 wk of chilling to achieve maximum germination. Some seeds failed to germinate after 5 mo of cold treatment. Thus the degree of after-ripening varies between seed sources.

Seeds of *P. aviculare* placed 30 cm deep in river water reached maximum germination (46%) after 9 mo (Comes et al. 1978). Fifty percent of the seeds were still firm after 5 yr but only 1% germinated.

The degree of dormancy varies between seed within the same lot, and those with seed coats require three times as long to after-ripen as those with seed coats removed. In fact, if the seed coat and aleurone layer are intact, germination will not occur even if the cold requirement has been satisfied (Ransom 1935). Fewer seeds emerge in darkness than in lighted conditions and emergence requires more than a 4.8°C fluctuation in day/night temperatures (Thompson and Whatley 1984). Fluctuating temperatures of 14.4 and 19.2°C gave maximum emergence.

The length of dormancy in the soil has been estimated to be 10 yr (Thurston 1960), 20 yr (Odum 1974), and 58 yr (Brenchley 1918). *P. aviculare* emerges sporadically and appears to "miss" germinating some years (Thurston 1960). This is perhaps due to the variation in after-ripening requirement and fluctuations in the length and severity of winter from year to year.

After-ripened seeds become dormant again if exposed to temperatures of 23 to 25°C (Courtney 1968). Seeds removed from 0 to 1.5 cm of soil in May did not germinate, while those removed from 9 to 14 cm germinated because they had been in a cooler environment. Seeds removed from any depth in June failed to germinate. He speculates that the 20% of viable seed in the soil that did not germinate has a greater cold requirement than the other seeds. The seasonality of *P. aviculare* germination is influenced by temperature and light conditions. Baskin and Baskin (1990) buried freshly harvested seed in the fall and exhumed samples monthly for 28 mo in the central United States. Seeds were given light (14 hr) or kept in darkness in a range of alternating temperatures. During autumn and winter, seeds began to germinate, peaking in March (95 to 100% in light at all temperatures and 7 to 61% in darkness). During the summer, germination declined and the germination requirements became more specific. In the light, with warm temperatures (30/15 and 35/15°C), 15% of the seeds germinated. In darkness and at cooler temperatures in the light, less than 10% germinated. By September, nearly 65% of the seeds were dormant. The germination pattern was similar the second year.

Many investigators have estimated the seed population of *P. aviculare* in the soil. The population varies with crop, tillage and weed control methods. Brenchley (1940) reported a loss of 76 and 96% of the seeds in the soil with 1 and 2 yr of fallowing, respectively. Brenchley and Warington (1945) observed the number of *P. aviculare* seeds in a field from 1925 to 1940. After fallowing from 1925 to 1929, the seed population remained low for several years; then the population increased, but not to the original level. Roberts and Dawkins (1967) monitored the population of *P. aviculare* seeds for 6 yr when no plants were allowed to go to seed and no crops were planted. The original population of 6.9 million seeds/ha declined exponentially in the first years. Nearly all germination occurred in the spring in both tilled and nontilled areas. Tillage increased seedling emergence as compared to no tillage, but there was no difference between 2 or 4 cultivations/yr. Seed populations increased greatly after 15 yr of continual barley production in England but not in maize or carrot fields (Roberts and Neilson 1981a). *P. aviculare* germinates readily when barley is planted in the spring and, due to its prostrate growth habit, plants are hardly affected during harvest. Thus it produces seeds abundantly in mid to late spring.

Most seeds are in the upper 5 cm of soil, but some occur as deep as 30 cm (Kropac 1966). Champness and Morris (1948) found 660,000 seeds/ha in pasture land and 2.2 million in arable fields. An original population of 48 to 84 million seeds/ha was reduced by 20% after 2 yr in vegetable production (Roberts 1958). Deep or shallow plowing did not affect seed populations, but the use of rotary tillers (shallow tillage) slightly increased seed numbers (Roberts 1963). Jensen (1969) observed an average of 8.2 million seeds/ha in 57 fields and found correlation between the amount of vegetative growth of *P. aviculare* and the seed population. *P. aviculare* was the eleventh most frequent species in terms of seed numbers in the soil in southern and central Finland (Paatela and Ervio 1971). Infested fields averaged 7.5 million seeds/ha in the top 20 cm. If a cereal crop was grown the year before sampling, the seed populations were 38% higher than if the preceding crop was pasture.

In contrast, Heard (1963) found more *P. aviculare* in wheat planted after 3.5 yr of pasture than after a rotation of tilled crops. Pasture management also influenced the following infestation. More *P. aviculare* occurred where pastures were cut and harvested than when they were grazed; perhaps frequent grazing reduced seed production. More seedlings appear in deep-tilled fields than in shallow or non-tilled fields (Pollard and Cussans 1981). Chancellor (1976) observed dramatic increases in the seedling population of *P. aviculare* between 1962 and 1969 in arable fields because it was unaffected by the herbicides used in crops during this period. Over 40 and 85% of the arable fields in Scotland and England, respectively, contained *P. aviculare* seeds in the 1970s (Warwick 1984, Roberts and Chancellor 1986). Seed populations averaged 2.7 million/ha, the sixth highest of all species detected in Scotland.

Seeds are spread by birds, other animals, water and through human activity. Thirty-three percent of the seeds sprouted after passing through cows, and 10 of 36 grain samples had viable seeds of *P. aviculare* after grinding (Dorph-Petersen 1925). Hope (1927) found 606 seeds of *P. aviculare* in a 24-hr period in the top 4 cm of irrigation water in Alberta, Canada, and 2.7 seeds/254 kl of water were collected in irrigation canals of Washington, in the United States (Kelley and Bruns 1975).

P. aviculare seeds frequently contaminate harvested grain and forage seeds. It was among the five most common weeds in lucerne grown for export in Argentina (Mascazzini 1939) and in England Tonkin (1968a) found 6, 4.9, 9.5, and 8.8 *P. aviculare* seeds in each 50-g sample of wheat, rye, barley, and oats, respectively. It was more common in wheat and barley in this period than in the early 1950s.

UTILITY

P. aviculare seeds were used as food in prehistoric times (Renfrew 1973), as a source of meal by the American Indians (King 1966) and for flour during the Middle Ages in Poland (Dembinska 1976). Swine consume the plants and in Japan plants yield a blue dye resembling indigo (Brenchley 1920). Wild birds feed extensively on *Polygonum* species. *P. aviculare*, *P. lapathifolium*, *P. persicaria*, and *P. convolvulus* comprised 88% of the autumn diet of gray partridge in England in the mid 1930s. However, by 1968 these species were only 44% of their fall diet. Using herbicides to control *Polygonum* species in cereals and increased burning of cereal stubble contributed to this decline (Potts 1970).

P. aviculare plants are readily consumed by poultry and cows (Spencer 1940). The aerial portion of plants contains 70% stem and 30% leaf tissue on a dry weight basis. Grazed plants were somewhat lower in digestibility, N, and ash content than lucerne, but ungrazed plants matured and were unsuitable for use as a forage (Jones et al. 1971).

The reported medicinal uses of *P. aviculare* include treatment for lung ailments, hemorrhoids and rheumatism (Uphof 1968); use in obstetric and gynecologic practice as hemostatic agents in the postpartum period and in uterine hemorrhages after abortion; in folk medicine as an astringent, diuretic and hemostatic (Penkauskene and Shimikunaite 1973); and the preparation of *P. aviculare* tea to stop diarrhea (Spencer 1940).

AGRICULTURAL IMPORTANCE

P. aviculare is a weed of 37 crops in 67 countries (Figure 70-1) and is frequently reported as a weed of cereals, vegetables, sugar beets, and pastures. It is one of our most widely distributed weeds and can be invasive in many temperate climate crops.

It is a principal or serious weed of barley in Denmark, England, and France; edible beans in Chile, England, and France; cereals in Australia, Belgium, Bolivia, Ecuador, Finland, Hungary, Italy, Poland, Scotland, Tasmania, and the United States; cotton in Australia and Iran; flax in Argentina, Brazil, and France; irrigated dryland crops in Australia; linseed in Argentina, Australia, and Spain; lucerne in Argentina and Mexico; maize in France and Hungary; onions in Australia, England, and Italy; orchards in the United States; pastures in Alaska and Argentina; peas in Argentina and New Zealand; potatoes in Belgium, Bolivia, Chile, Ecuador, England, and France; oilseed rape in Japan and Spain; upland rice, soybeans, and sweet potatoes in Japan; rye and vineyards in the former Soviet Union; sugar beets in Belgium, England, France, Iran, Italy, Poland, and Spain; sunflowers in France, Rumania, and Spain; vegetables in Bulgaria, Scotland, Spain, and Tasmania; wheat in Argentina, Mexico, New Zealand, Uruguay, and the former Yugoslavia; and winter wheat in England, Japan, Spain, and South Africa.

It is a common weed of barley in Finland, New Zealand, and Peru; edible beans in Mexico; field beets in Belgium, France, Germany, and Spain; cabbage in Iceland; cereals in Bulgaria, Germany, Iran, the Netherlands, and Tunisia; citrus in South Africa; cotton in Mexico; flax in the Netherlands; legumes in Tunisia; lucerne in Spain; maize in Honduras, Mexico, Peru, Rumania, and the former Yugoslavia; oats in Mexico; onions in Spain and South Africa; orchards in Chile, Poland, and South Africa; pastures in Australia, Chile, and Tasmania; peas in England, France, the Netherlands, and New Zealand; potatoes in Iceland, Peru, and Poland; rice in China and Mexico; sugar beets in Tunisia; sugarcane in South Africa; tobacco in the former Soviet Union; vegetables in Finland and Germany; vineyards in South Africa; and wheat in Finland, France, and Peru.

Also, *P. aviculare* is frequently cited as a weed of unranked importance by many countries in nearly all of the above crops.

P. aviculare has increased in severity in fruits and vegetables in England because it tolerates most herbicides in these crops. In 1953, it was not on the list of the 10 most important weeds; in the early 1960s, it was in 9th place and by the 1970s it was the 4th most frequently encountered weed in vegetable crops (Davison and Roberts 1976).

Even though *P. aviculare* is a prostrate or low-growing weed, it can reduce crop yields. Barley reduced the growth of this weed by 95% because it is poorly suited to compete for light; nevertheless, barley yields were reduced (Fogelfors 1977). After barley harvest, *P. aviculare* resumed active growth. When grown without barley competition, *P. aviculare* produced 132 plants/m^2 and 18 g dry matter/plant. In competition with barley, these values were 129 plants/m^2 and 0.9 g dry matter/plant. Moisey (1974) suggests that it competes with sugar beets for soil factors. Applying N to wheat may increase *P. aviculare* growth (Welbank 1963, Covarelli 1974). The weed reduced the N content and growth of wheat.

Hammerton (1962) compared the competitive effects of three *Polygonum* species. *P. aviculare* was the least competitive, and high densities of kale eliminated its competitive effects. Kale reduced the dry weight of *P. aviculare* 40% and the weed had no effect on the N content of the crop (Welbank 1963). Studies by Hewson (1969) and Hewson et al. (1973) found the critical period of *P. aviculare* competition in onions to be the first 5.5 wk of growth. There was no benefit from weeding after 7.5 wk of competition. Broadbeans, however, are more tolerant of competition, and weeding can be delayed 3.5 to 5 wk after 50% of the crop has emerged before losses are observed. Losses from *P. aviculare* in pastures were measured in Argentina (Lopez and Mattiacci 1983). Populations of lucerne and fescue decreased as the weed density increased. Each 50 g/m² increase in *P. aviculare* dry matter reduced forage yield by 20% up to weed levels of 150 g/m².

A biotype of *P. aviculare* resistant to simazine was found in England (Anon. [United Kingdom] 1979) and the Netherlands (Oorschot and Straathof 1988). A strain resistant to amitrole is found in Belgium (Bulcke et al. 1988).

P. aviculare contains soluble allelochemicals that inhibit lettuce seed but not ryegrass germination. Extracts reduced growth of annual *Medicago* species by 50%. Leaves and green stems are more inhibitory than roots or woody stems, and rainfall and cultivation minimize the effect (Kloot and Boyce 1982). Studies by Alsaadawi and Rice (1982a,b) determined that the plant as well as its exudates and the soil under *P. aviculare* were very inhibitory to several species, including *Cynodon dactylon*, cotton and sorghum. Four inhibitors were isolated and determined to be phenolic compounds that can persist in the soil for 4 mo.

COMMON NAMES

Polygonum aviculare

ALASKA	knotweed
ALGERIA	gerda
ARGENTINA	chilillo, cien nudos, huichun, pasto chanchero, sanguinaria
AUSTRALIA	hogweed, knotweed, wireweed
BELGIUM	cinnudos, lenguade pajaros, trainasse, varkensgras
BRAZIL	sempre noiva dos passarinhos
CANADA	prostrate knotweed, renouee des oiseaux
CHILE	huichun, pasto del pollo, sangrina, sanguinaria
COLOMBIA	caminadora, gonorrea, cien nudos
DENMARK	honsegraes, vej-pileurt
ECUADOR	coloradilla
EGYPT	qoddaad, qordaab
ENGLAND	hogweed, ironweed, knotweed, knotgrass, wireweed
FINLAND	pihatatar
FRANCE	centinode, herbe aux cochons, renouee des oiseaux, trainasse
GERMANY	Blutkraut Wegetritt, Vogelknoterich
GUATEMALA	corredora, hierba de chivo
HUNGARY	madar keserufu
ICELAND	blooarfi, hlaoarfi
IRAN	khorfe
IRAQ	massalah
ITALY	centinoda, coreggiola

JAPAN	michi-yanagi, niwayanagi
LEBANON	assa-er-rai, batbat, door weed, knotweed, shabat al ghul
MADAGASCAR	ahitrakely
MEXICO	alambrillo, huichuri, sangrina, sanguinaria, verdolaga
NETHERLANDS	varkensgras
NEW ZEALAND	wireweed
NORWAY	tungras
PARAGUAY	correguela, sanguinaria
POLAND	rdest ptasi
PORTUGAL	cemtinodia, erva muda, sanguinha, sempre noiva
SAUDI ARABIA	batbat, shabat el ghul, turnah
SOUTH AFRICA	koperdraadgras, prostrate knotweed, voeduisendknoop
SPAIN	cien nudos, correguela de los caminos, herbe de las calenturas, lengue de pajaro, sanguinaria mayor
SWEDEN	tramport, tranpgras
SWITZERLAND	renouee des oiseaux, trainasse, vogelknoterich
TUNISIA	renouee des oiseaux
TURKEY	coban degnegi
UNITED STATES	prostrate knotweed
URUGUAY	sanguinaria
YUGOSLAVIA	dvornik oputina, dvornik pticji, pticja dresen, tro skot

Seventy-One

Polygonum hydropiper L.

Polygonaceae, Buckwheat Family

P OLYGONUM HYDROPIPER, an annual plant native to Eurasia, is commonly encountered in shallow marshes, poorly drained fields, canal and ditch banks, and other areas of wet soils. Several *Polygonum* have a very acrid, bitter taste in their leaves and stem. Indeed, the English common name "smartweed" for many species of this genus refers to the "smarting" sensation that results when sensitive areas such as the eyes are exposed to crushed leaves and stems or when plants are eaten. The species name *hydropiper* refers to its occurrence in water (*hydro*) and the peppery (*piper*), acrid taste of the leaves and stem.

FIGURE 71-1   The distribution of *Polygonum hydropiper* L. across the world where it has been reported as a weed.

FIGURE 71-2 *Polygonum hydropiper* L.: A. habit; B. node showing ochrea; C. spike; D. flower; E. achenes.

DESCRIPTION

P. hydropiper (Figure 71-2) is an erect or ascending *annual* herb; *roots* branched, to 120 cm deep; *stems* branched at base, 15 to 80 cm tall, smooth, somewhat flattened, green, often with a reddish ring above the node that becomes completely red as plants mature, internodes 3 to 6 cm long; *nodes* slightly enlarged, surrounded by a brown membranous *ochrea* 0.5 to 1 cm long with a few bristles less than 5 mm long on the margin; *leaves* alternate, short petioled, simple, lanceolate to ovate-lanceolate, 4 to 10 cm long, 1 to 3 cm wide, smaller near the top of the plant, glabrous, glandular punctate with margins shortly ciliate and entire to wavy; *inflorescence* nodding, slender panicled-racemes on a long, slender peduncle or the lower ones concealed by the ochrea; *flowers* perfect, solitary or in clusters of 2 to 4, subtended by funnel-shaped bracts; *perianth* of 3, 4, or 5 *tepals*, united at base, 2 to 4.5 mm long, 2 to 2.5 mm wide, greenish at the base, white to pinkish above, conspicuously covered with dark, sessile glands, persistent; *stamens* 6 to 8, united with perianth at base; *ovary* 1-ovuled, *fruit* an *achene*, mostly triangular but also lenticular in shape, 2 to 2.5 mm wide, 2 to 3.5 mm long, acuminate, minutely roughened, dark brown to black in color and dull, perianth often remains attached.

The annual habit, acrid or peppery taste of the leaves and stems, greenish flowers in loose racemes, dotted calyx and the cylindrical, truncate, fringed sheathes above the slightly swollen nodes are the distinguishing characteristics of this species.

HABITAT AND BIOLOGY

P. hydropiper is a summer annual commonly found in moist soil or standing water. It is often included in aquatic weed flora but also occurs in crops and pastures with poorly drained soils. It grows in most temperate and subtropical climates of Europe, North America, and Asia. Common habitats include stream and canal banks, edges of marshes and swamps, wet fields, and other sites with damp soils. It may replace pasture grasses lost in waterlogged areas and it appears in gardens.

P. hydropiper grows well in most soils, including peat and muck. It tolerates a wide range of soil *pHs* but often occurs in acidic soils. Timson (1966) found it in soils with *pHs* of 5.7 to 6.0 and in water with *pHs* of 5.9 to 7.6. After 6 mo, 3 and 66% of the seed in sand and loam soil, respectively, remained viable. All seeds in peat died during this period.

Seeds survived from 4 mo (Shull 1914) to 36 mo (Comes et al. 1978) underwater and 50 yr buried in soil (Darlington 1951). Seed populations were greatest in organic soils and averaged 69/m^2 to a 20-cm depth in Finland (Paatela and Ervio 1971).

Freshly harvested seeds do not germinate because they have an after-ripening requirement. Stratification at 2 to 4°C for 18 wk can give greater than 90% germination (Justice 1941). Removing the seed coat, alternating the germination temperature, and providing light stimulate more seeds to germinate (Nakamura 1970). Seeds do not respond to gibberellin, but far-red light inhibits and red light stimulates germination. Germination often varies between seed lots. *P. hydropiper* has an oxygen requirement for germination equal to that of *Echinochloa crus-galli* var. *practicola* (Kim and Kataoka 1978), which is not surprising, because both species are common in wet soils.

P. hydropiper germinates in the spring and flowers in early to midsummer in all habitats. Flowering continues until the plant is killed by frost or drought. Fruits are shed from about August until death in the Northern Hemisphere. The plant is self-pollinated and little phenotypic variation occurs (Timson 1966). *P. hydropiper* was the most allelopathic species to rice seedlings of 22 **Polygonaceae** tested. The inhibitory substance was identified as polygodial (Harada and Yano 1983). Plants have a $2n$ chromosome number of 20.

P. hydropiper seedlings are used to garnish white-fleshed fish in Japan and the purplish-red color is desirable. The degree of pigmentation varies in response to plant age and light intensity. Miura and Iwata (1979, 1981) studied the effect of N, P, and K on anthocyanin production. High N levels reduce anthocyanin and carbohydrate levels and increase protein content. P and K do not affect seedling color or growth. The optimum temperature range for anthocyanin synthesis is 5 to 10°C.

The degree of stem branching decreases as *P. hydropiper* density increases. Stomata occur almost exclusively on the lower leaf surfaces. Reproduction is by seeds, but if stems are trampled and touch the soil surface, they can root at the nodes (Timson 1966). Individual plants produce 385 to 3300 seeds that weigh 1 to 2.5 mg each (Datta and Banerjee 1973).

Seeds can be spread in poultry feed (Johnson and Hensman 1910) and small grass seed and by other human activities. Seeds float in water and have been screened from irrigation canals and rivers in Washington, in the United States (Kelley and Bruns 1975).

UTILITY

Plants are rarely consumed by wildlife or domestic animals because of the acrid taste. However, *P. hydropiper* was evaluated as a potential forage and found promising based on protein content (Matai 1976). Perhaps it loses some of the peppery flavor when dried, but this is doubtful, as leaves of *P. hydropiper* are used as a condiment in Southeast Asia. It can cause dermatitis in livestock and another serious concern of using this species as a forage is its antifertility effect. Dried and ground stems and leaves reduced fertility of male and female mice and caused temporary sterility in guinea pigs (East 1955). Alcohol and ether extracts were 100% effective as antifertility treatments in rats (Garg et al. 1978).

In parts of India, plants are used to poison fish so they can be caught (Neogi et al. 1989). Its medicinal uses include treatment of internal and hemorrhoidal bleeding in Europe and as a hemostatic in Russia. *P. hydropiper* also has diuretic, sedative and analgesic properties and affects gram positive and gram negative bacteria (Nickell 1960).

AGRICULTURAL IMPORTANCE

P. hydropiper is a weed of 25 crops in nearly 52 countries (Figure 71-1) and is frequently reported a weed of lowland rice and wheat. Many reports are from the United States, China, India, Taiwan, and Japan. It is more common in the temperate climate of the Northern Hemisphere but also occurs in Argentina, Australia, Brazil, Chile, and New Zealand.

It is a serious or principal weed of barley and wheat in Finland; cereals and sugar beets in Poland; flax, potatoes, rape, sweet potatoes, and tobacco in Taiwan; maize in the former Soviet Union; onions, peas, and rice in Brazil; and lowland rice in India and Korea.

It is a common weed of cereals in Italy and the Netherlands; irrigated crops in Australia; maize and soybeans in the eastern United States; potatoes in the Netherlands; rice in Honduras; sugarcane in India; vegetables in Bulgaria and the southern United States; and winter wheat in Japan.

P. hydropiper is also an unranked weed of barley in Ireland; edible beans in Nepal; beets in Germany; cereals in Germany, Jordan, and Switzerland; citrus and coffee in Mexico; cranberries in the former Soviet Union; irrigated crops in Indonesia and the United States; maize in India and Taiwan; oats in Rumania; pastures in Belgium, New Zealand, and the former Yugoslavia; peanuts, soybeans, sweet potatoes, and tea in Taiwan; potatoes in Nepal and the United States; rice in Bangladesh, China, India, Japan, Malaysia, Nepal, and Portugal; sugarcane in Mexico; tobacco in the United States; vegetables in China and Switzerland; and wheat in India, Nepal, and the former Yugoslavia.

COMMON NAMES

Polygonum hydropiper

ALGERIA	felfel el ma
AUSTRALIA	water pepper
BANGLADESH	bishkatali, pakurmal, panimarich
BELGIUM	poivre d'eau, waterpepper
CANADA	marshpepper smartweed, renouee poivre d'eau
CHINA	pinyin, shui-liao
DENMARK	bidende pileurt
EGYPT	qordaab, qordeyb, qeddaab
ENGLAND	marshpepper smartweed, water-pepper
FINLAND	katkeratatar
FRANCE	persicaire acre, poivre d'eau, renouee poivre d'eau
GERMANY	Pfeffer-Knoterich, Wasserpfeffer, Wasserpfeffer-Knoterich
HUNGARY	borsus keserufu
INDIA	bishkatal, packurmul
IRELAND	red shank
ITALY	erba pepe, idropepe, pepe b'acqua
JAPAN	yanagitabe
MEXICO	chillo
NETHERLANDS	waterpepper
NEW ZEALAND	water pepper, willow weed
NORWAY	vasspepar
PAKISTAN	water pepper
PARAGUAY	caatai
POLAND	rdest ostrogorzki
PORTUGAL	persicaria mordaz, pimenta de agua
SAUDI ARABIA	fulful el ma, zangabil et kilab

SPAIN	persicaria picante, pimienta de agua, resquemona
SWEDEN	bitterpilort
SWITZERLAND	Wasserpfeffer-Knoterich
THAILAND	pahk pai, phak phai nam
UNITED STATES	marshpepper smartweed
YUGOSLAVIA	dvornik papreni, dvornik tankoklasni

Seventy-Two

Polygonum lapathifolium L.

Polygonaceae, Buckwheat Family

P OLYGONUM LAPATHIFOLIUM is an annual plant native to Europe and now widespread through temperate regions. It is common in cultivated land, roadsides and waste areas, especially along streams, ditch banks and in other wet and poorly drained areas.

FIGURE 72-1   The distribution of *Polygonum lapathifolium* L. across the world where it has been reported as a weed.

FIGURE 72-2 *Polygonum lapathifolium* L.: 1. root system; 2. seedlings; 3. flowering branch;
4. flower, open; 5. spike; 6. node showing ochrea; 7. achene, 8. same, cross section.

DESCRIPTION

P. lapathifolium (Figure 72-2) is an *annual* herb; *stems* weak (ascending) or stout (erect), 30 to 120 cm tall, green or reddish, jointed, swollen above the nodes, hollow, branched, smooth; may root at lower nodes; upper stems rough or gummy due to presence of glands; *ochrea* cylindrical, membranous, smooth, greenish, often tinged with red, strongly veined, 1 to 1.5 cm long, devoid of apical hairs; *leaves* alternate, broadly lanceolate, 5 to 16 cm long, long-pointed at apex, wedge-shaped at base; margin fringed with hairs and sunken, pellucid glands on lower surface; upper leaf surface nearly smooth, often with a dark triangular spot near the center; petiole to 3 cm long; *inflorescence* a densely flowered spike, drooping or nodding, terminal or axillary, 3 to 10 cm long on slightly glandular *peduncles*; *flowers* perfect, greenish white or pinkish; *stamens* 5 to 7, longer than perianth; *perianth* 4- or 5-lobed, glandular, persistent, with raised anchor-shaped veins on outer segments; veins longer than fruits and fold around achenes forming air-filled "beak" over remains of stigma; *fruit* an *achene*, usually lenticular, 1.5 to 3 mm long, 1.3 to 1.8 mm wide, broadly ovate to circular with apex elongated to a point, flattened with thickened edges, brown shiny black and finely granular.

The hollow stem that is swollen above the nodes, leaves with sunken glands on the lower surface, nodding spikes and flattened seeds are the distinguishing characteristics of this plant.

ECOLOGY AND BIOLOGY

P. lapathifolium, a native of Europe, is a common weed in cultivated fields and other disturbed areas throughout temperate regions from sea level to 2100 m (Figure 72-1). Plants tolerate many edaphic conditions and climates (Simmonds 1945), and are often found along streams and river banks, growing best in loose, slightly acid, nutrient-rich soils high in organic matter. *P. lapathifolium* was used as a source food during the Iron Age in Denmark and the Bronze Age in England and Holland. One liter of seed was found in a burnt house from the Iron Age in Denmark, suggesting that it was considered a food plant (Renfrew 1973) and that seeds probably spread through Europe as people migrated in the region.

The species is highly variable in form and many biotypes have been observed. This is reflected in seed germination studies with *P. lapathifolium*. Dorph-Petersen (1925) obtained 85% germination with fresh ripe seed and 99% germination the following spring. Sixty-two percent of fresh unripe seed germinated, and unripe seed lost its viability in 3 yr and ripe seed in 7 yr. In contrast, Justice (1941) found freshly harvested seeds to be dormant. Hammerton (1967a) and Hammerton and Jalloq (1970) studied the reasons for such variability. Germination of fresh unchilled seed in various locations in England ranged from 0 to 75%. No correlations with climate or mean seed weight were apparent. Seed from some populations responded to chilling while others did not. Neither removing the perianth nor KNO_3 treatment affected germination but acid scarification with H_2SO_4 broke dormancy in all *P. lapathifolium* populations. Seed weight and germination also varied significantly between plants collected at the same location.

Seed buried outdoors for 90 days showed a dramatic increase in germination, whether on the soil surface (80%) or at 25 cm (83%) (Horng and Leu 1978). Germination of buried seed remained high for 240 days but decreased for those on the surface. Seeds that failed to germinate in the laboratory often germinated when exposed to sunlight in the greenhouse.

Pretreatment with light improved germination, as did fluctuating temperatures of at least 15°C (Watanabe and Hirokawa 1975a). Staniforth and Cavers (1979b) found *P. lapathifolium* to be less dormant than two other *Polygonum* species and that it exhibited both innate and induced dormancy. These authors, Timson (1965c) and Justice (1941), found 4°C the best temperature to break seed dormancy when stored in water. Comes et al. (1978) determined that 59% of the seed remained firm after storage in water for 60 mo and it maintained a 63% germination rate. The nutrient level and degree of competition between parent plants have no effect on seed germination of *P. lapathifolium* (Hammerton and Nuttall 1971).

In Canada, most seeds fall to the soil and subsequent flood water carries them downstream (Staniforth and Cavers 1979a). The air sack formed by the perianth enables the seed to float. In calm water, 75% of fresh seeds with intact perianths floated for 6 mo; only 28% of those with the perianth removed floated as long. If seeds dried on the soil surface before flooding, as usually occurs, 99 and 61% of the seed with and without perianths, respectively, floated for 6 mo. Seed either sank immediately or floated for long periods. In agitated water, all seeds sank in 84 hr. Estimates are that many seeds could float 3.5 days in streams and rivers with flow rates of 15 km/hr. Kelley and Bruns (1975) found up to 104 seeds/254 kl of water in the Columbia River (Washington, in the United States) with a 40% germinability. On the shores of river islands of England, *P. lapathifolium* seeds germinate in periods of low tide. Seedlings are not dislodged by tidal scour (Shimwell 1973).

P. lapathifolium accumulates large seed reservoirs in the soil. Jensen (1969) reported 560 seeds/m² to a depth of 20 cm and Kropac (1966) found 697 seeds/m² distributed more or less uniformly to a depth of 25 cm. Seeds emerge from 10 cm (Takabayashi and Nakayama 1979). Over a 3-yr period, 13% of *P. lapathifolium* seed in undisturbed soil and 38% of the seed in cultivated soil formed seedlings (Watanabe and Hirokawa 1975b). The number of viable seeds decreased exponentially by 36%/yr in undisturbed soil and 72%/yr in cultivated soil. Emergence begins when the air temperature reaches 7 to 10°C and peaks at 10 to 15°C. Higher temperatures tend to induce dormancy. Most seedlings emerged the first year after production, but some emerged through 5 yr (Roberts and Neilson 1980).

In several *P. lapathifolium* populations, heavier seeds were produced by late flowers than by early flowers, while the reverse was true for other populations (Hammerton and Jalloq 1970). Later planting resulted in consistently smaller seeds, and the percentage of viable seed was higher from seeds planted in March or April than from those planted in May. Seed from March and April plantings had a 95% emergence rate; 30% of the seed from May-planted plants emerged. Larger plants resulted from seedlings that emerged early, but both early- and late-emerging plants produced approximately 2400 seeds/plant. The authors conclude that variation in germination and dormancy help *P. lapathifolium* survive and adapt to many environments, and variability in seed weight may favor dispersal in different crops.

Germination occurs in the spring and early summer, and stems begin to branch 3 wk after emergence. The first five to seven leaves are often pubescent on one or both surfaces. Pubescence decreases with plant age and some populations are more pubescent than others (Hammerton 1969). Roots are highly branched and can penetrate to 80 cm, but most are in the upper 30 cm (Kutschera 1960). Plants have a 2*n* chromosome count of 22.

P. lapathifolium flowers 4 to 6 wk after emergence and is either self-pollinated (enhanced by the curved nature of the stigmas) or cross-pollinated by insects (Simmonds 1945). The number of seeds produced per plant varies tremendously. Stevens (1957) found 19,300 seeds/plant when grown without competition, and Hammerton and Nuttall (1971) reported 1131 seeds/plant produced by well-fertilized plants and 151 seeds/plant at low nutrient levels. Larger seeds and more seeds are formed in temperatures of 20 to 26°C than at 9 to 12°C (O'Donovan 1985).

Seeds can be disseminated as feed and crop seed contaminants (Johnson and Hensman 1910) and have also been eaten and spread by rabbits (Staniforth and Cavers 1976, 1979a). Over 4% of 1500 seeds eaten by rabbits were excreted as viable seed. Most passed through the animals within 8 hr, but excretion continued for 48 hr.

AGRICULTURAL IMPORTANCE

P. lapathifolium is a weed of 31 crops in 54 countries (Figure 72-1) and is frequently reported as a weed of wheat, barley, and vegetables. It is concentrated in the Northern Hemisphere but is also found in Australia, New Zealand, Chile, and Argentina.

It is a principal or serious weed of asparagus in Korea; barley and wheat in Canada and Korea; beets, irrigated crops, and lucerne in Germany; carrots and flax in Canada and the former Soviet Union; cereals in Hungary and Sweden; maize in France, Hungary, Portugal, the former Soviet Union, and the former Yugoslavia; oats and oilseed rape in Canada; onions in the former Soviet Union; pastures in New Zealand; potatoes in France, Germany, and Sweden; rice in Morocco and upland rice in Japan; sugar beets in Poland; sunflower in Canada and France; tomatoes in Portugal; and vegetables in Germany and Scotland.

It is a common weed of cereals in England, Italy, the Netherlands, Scotland, Tunisia, and the former Yugoslavia; flax and peas in France; hemp in the former Soviet Union; maize in Spain; potatoes in Chile, Kamchatka, the Netherlands, and the former Soviet Union; rice in China; sugar beets in France, the Netherlands, and Tunisia; tomatoes in France; vegetables in Bulgaria and the United States; and wheat in the former Soviet Union and Turkey.

In addition, *P. lapathifolium* is an unranked weed of barley in Australia, England, Finland, the former Soviet Union, and Sweden; edible beans in Chile; beets, millet, oats, and tobacco in the former Soviet Union; cabbage in Taiwan and the United States; carrots in Germany; cereals in Finland, Germany, Norway, and Switzerland; irrigated crops in Australia and the United States; jute in India; maize, peanuts, oilseed rape, sugarcane, and sweet potatoes in Taiwan; orchards in Belgium, Iraq, and the former Soviet Union; pastures in Taiwan and the former Yugoslavia; peas in Belgium and Taiwan; rice in India, Japan, Portugal, Spain, and Vietnam; lowland rice in China and Taiwan; rye in Ireland; sugar beets in Belgium, Czechoslovakia, England, Italy, and Japan; soybeans in Taiwan and the United States; sugarcane in Taiwan; sunflowers in Hungary; tea in Indonesia; tobacco in the former Soviet Union; tomatoes in the United States; vegetables in Belgium, China, Czechoslovakia, England, Iraq, Switzerland, and Tasmania; and wheat in China, Finland, and India.

P. lapathifolium competes effectively with many crops. Aspinall and Milthorpe (1959) and Aspinall (1960) observed less tillering in barley when grown in competition with *P. lapathifolium*, even though the dry weight of barley was not significantly affected. *P. lapathifolium* did not branch during the first 4 wk of competition with barley. Later, stems branched at the higher nodes. As the barley matured, this weed continued to branch and grow. When grown separately, *P. lapathifolium* grew faster than barley due to a greater leaf area ratio. Barley reduced the net assimilation rate of *P. lapathifolium* but the reverse was not observed at normal crop and weed densities. Barley root competition affected weed growth more than *P. lapathifolium* reduced barley root growth. At low nutrient levels, barley tillered less and *P. lapathifolium* reduced barley root growth. Aspinall also concludes that both light and nutrient competition occur. Hammerton (1962) observed that stress reduces the weed's growth but it is highly adaptable to crop competition.

Kutuzov and Stepanenko (1968) found that *P. lapathifolium* reduced barley yields 8.7% and ryegrass 17%. These crops reduced the weed's growth by 57 to 60%. Root exudates of barley were inhibitory to this weed. Evenari (1949) found that the sap in *P. lapathifolium* leaves inhibited the germination of other species and Borner (1960) reported that a recirculated nutrient solution from this weed inhibited potato growth.

In Taiwan, *P. lapathifolium* competes with cool season vegetables grown after rice (Horng 1980). After emergence, up to 1000 *P. lapathifolium* seedlings/m² were detected; the population dropped to 400 plants/m² at 10 wk. Five weeks of competition with cabbage reduced yield and, after 6 wk, the number of marketable heads dropped. Yield losses from competition were reduced if cabbage was transplanted before rather than after the rice harvest.

Biotypes of *P. lapathifolium* resistant to triazine herbicides have been reported in France (LeBaron and Gressel 1982). Application of atrazine in 3 out of 6 yr resulted in a resistant population. Biotype variations in susceptibility to 2,4-DP have been observed in England (Hammerton 1966), and morphological biotypes occur in Ireland (MacNaeidhe and Curran 1982).

COMMON NAMES

Polygonum lapathifolium

ALGERIA	arakilioun
ARGENTINA	duraznillo, pimienta de agua
AUSTRALIA	pale knotweed
BELGIUM	viltige duizend knoop
CANADA	pale smartweed, persicaire pale
CHILE	duraznillo
DENMARK	bleg pileurt, knudet pileurt
EGYPT	qardaab, qeddaab, qoddaad, qooddaaby, qordaab, qordeyb
ENGLAND	pale persicaria, willow weed
FINLAND	ukontatar
FRANCE	renouee a feuilles de patience, renouee noueuse, saulcette
GERMANY	Ampfer-knoterich, Ampferblattriger Knoterich
HUNGARY	lapulevelu keserufu
ICELAND	loblaoka
IRAQ	mwaisilah
ISRAEL	arkuvit hacktamim
ITALY	persicaria maggiore, persicaria salcerella, poligono a foglia di romice, salcerella
JAPAN	sanaetade, o-inu-tade

LEBANON	hummaydah, ghadar, knotweed, pale persicaria
MOROCCO	bet-bet
NETHERLANDS	knopige duizendknoop, vitige duizendknoop
NEW ZEALAND	pale willow weed
NORWAY	gront honsegras, raudt honsegras
POLAND	rdest kolankowaty, rdest szczawiolistny
PORTUGAL	erva-pessegueira-bastarda, mal-casada
SAUDI ARABIA	ghadar
SPAIN	duraznillo, persicaria mayor, poligono pata de perdiz
SWEDEN	knutig pilort, rodkhaa, vanlig pilort
SWITZERLAND	ampferblattriger knoterich, renouee a feuilles de patience
THAILAND	phong phot, pong pode
UNITED STATES	pale smartweed
YUGOSLAVIA	dvornik veliki, scavjelistna dresen, uzlati dvornik

Seventy-Three

Polygonum persicaria L.

Polygonaceae, Buckwheat Family

P OLYGONUM PERSICARIA is native to Europe but is now widely distributed throughout
the world. It is adapted to many edaphic and environmental conditions and is most
common in moist soils, disturbed sites, waste areas and cereal and vegetable crops.
It may grow so densely as to completely crowd out other plants. The triangular water spot
on most leaves is the basis of its common name of spotted persicaria or lady's thumb in
several countries.

FIGURE 73-1   The distribution of *Polygonum persicaria* L. across the world where it has
been reported as a weed.

FIGURE 73-2 *Polygonum persicaria* L.: A. habit; B. spike; C. ochrea; D. achenes.

DESCRIPTION

P. persicaria (Figure 73-2) is an *annual* herb; *root* branched, 10 to 20 cm long; *stems* 30 to 120 cm tall, ascending or decumbent, simple to highly branched at base, often rooting at lower nodes, green to reddish or purplish, fleshy, swollen above the nodes, smooth or occasionally hairy; *ochrea* encloses the petiole base at the nodes, fringed with short bristles 1 to 2 mm long, thin and membranous, covered with appressed hairs; *leaves* short-petioled, alternate, variable in size, 4 to 15 cm long, 0.5 to 3 cm wide, narrowly to broadly lanceolate, pointed at both ends, usually smooth with a reddish to purplish triangular spot near the middle; *inflorescence* erect, dense, pedunculate, terminal and axillary flowering spikes, 1.5 to 4.5 cm long; secondary spikes much shorter; *flowers* perfect, tend to overlap; *perianth* of 5 *tepals*, united at base, persistent, glandless, pink, purplish or green, rarely white, 2 to 4 mm long, with prominently netted-veined bases, vein ending not anchor-shaped as in *P. lapathifolium*; *stamens* 6 to 8, united at base with perianth; *carpels* 2-united, *ovary* 1-ovuled, *styles* 2 or 3, *fruit* an *achene*, 1.5 to 3 mm long, 1.5 to 2 mm wide, broadly oval and tapering to a point, flattened or sometimes 3-angled, shiny, black, smooth, microscopically pitted, remnant of perianth often remains attached to base.

The dark triangular spot near the middle of the leaves, the ochrea with short bristles on the fringe, and the lack of glands or anchor-shaped vein endings in the perianth are the distinguishing features of this species.

HABITAT AND BIOLOGY

P. persicaria is most commonly found in moist, undisturbed areas such as ditches, waste areas, roadsides, and canal and river banks and in over 30 crops. It is found on nearly all soil types and occurs from the subarctic region to the warm temperate areas of Japan and to 4000 m altitude in the Himalaya Mountains. *P. persicaria* is often encountered in communities with other *Polygonum* and *Rumex* species (Simmonds 1945).

Seeds germinate in early spring. Peak germination occurs in April and May in England. *P. persicaria* germination continues through July, which is longer than for other *Polygonums*. This may explain why *P. persicaria* has relatively large seed populations (2790 seeds/m^2 to a 15-cm depth) compared to related species (Witts 1960). Other studies have found 600 seeds/m^2 to 20 cm (Jensen 1969), 2717 seeds/m^2 to 18 cm (Milton 1948), and 2014/m^2 to 15 cm (Roberts and Stokes 1966).

As with most *Polygonum* species, a cold treatment breaks dormancy of *P. persicaria* seed. Storage in cold water for 1 to 3 mo is usually sufficient (Justice 1941, Timson 1965c, Staniforth and Cavers 1979b). Constant cold temperatures from 2 to 4°C are better than alternating temperatures. Gibberellic acid does not affect germination. Nitrate or sulfuric acid scarification may enhance germination (Bayer 1958, Vincent and Roberts 1979). Germination is greater in light than in darkness (27 vs. 15%) at 25°C but equal in both regimes at 15°C (3.5%).

P. persicaria seeds can survive for many years in the soil. Forty percent of the seed buried in the eastern United States for 20 yr germinated. After 30 yr, 9% germinated but none were viable after 40 yr (Toole and Brown 1946). Seed buried for 10 yr in peat maintained 15% viability (Lewis 1963). After 20 yr, seed buried in peat germinated up to 32%, while in a mineral soil the maximum germination was 2% (Lewis 1973). *P. persicaria* seeds in dry storage died after 6 yr (Dorph-Petersen 1925) and seed stored in silage also lost viability (Zahnley and Fitch 1941). Seed placed in canal water reached maximum germination at 3 yr (54%), and 24% were viable after 5 yr (Bruns 1965). However, the longest period of seed survival was recorded in Japan. Seeds 4000 yr old were excavated from an archaeological site in the Akita Prefecture and several germinated (Umemoto 1974).

In England, half the fresh seeds in the soil germinated the following spring and emergence continued for over 5 yr (Roberts and Neilson 1980). A linear decrease in seed population of 54%/year occurred, leaving 10% of the original population in the soil after 5 yr. Freshly harvested seeds were buried at 10 cm, removed periodically, placed in petri dishes and given conditions favorable for germination over a 2-yr period (Karssen 1980–81). No germination occurred initially, but the innate dormancy was completely gone by early spring. During late spring and early summer, seeds developed secondary dormancy and by late summer the first year no seeds germinated. Seeds remained dormant until early spring of the second year, when the pattern of germination followed by dormancy was repeated.

Soil disturbance stimulates *P. persicaria* emergence and one cultivation is as effective as monthly cultivations (Chancellor 1964). Soil texture affects *P. persicaria* germination. After one winter, 33, 40, and 50% of the seeds in a peat, sand, and loam soil, respectively, germinated (Timson 1965c).

Germination varies between populations of *P. persicaria* and even seeds from the same plant may have different germination requirements (Hammerton 1967b). Trigonous seeds are less dormant than biconvex seeds and some seeds have a chilling requirement longer than the winter season in England. Fewer seeds of *P. persicaria* than of *P. lapathifolium* germinate at low temperatures. Some populations germinate well after three wk of chilling, while others require 6 or 9 wk to reach maximum germination. However, there is much less variation in chilling requirement between populations of *P. persicaria* than with *P. lapathifolium*. Germination is enhanced by light and by a KNO_3 solution in darkness (Karssen 1980–81).

Soil moisture level influences *P. persicaria* germination but not its emergence. Germination increases as field capacity increases from 43, 65, and 85% (Yamamoto and Ohba 1977). Seeds do not emerge from depths greater than 6 cm (Lovato and Viggniani 1974). *P. persicaria* tolerates acidic soil, but growth increased three-fold with a *pH* change from 4.0 to 4.5. Further increases to 6.0 had no effect on dry matter production (MacNaeidhe and Curran 1982).

Plants arising from seed sown in April have higher fresh weights (149 g/ plant), more inflorescences (118), and greater seed production/plant (4470) than those sown in May, June, or July (Hammerton and Jalloq 1970). Plant weight is positively correlated to seed weight and number.

P. persicaria produces twice as many leaves and over 70% more biomass in 18-hr days as compared to 12-hr days. In contrast, short-days induced flower buds in 23 days, while plants in long-day environments required 50 days to form buds (Regan and Bell 1964). Plants in 15-hr photoperiods and night/day temperatures of 18 and 23°C, respectively, formed 40% more leaves and required 9 days more to reach the budding stage than did 12 and 18°C night/day temperatures. When growing in the field without competition, plants are generally decumbent to prostate but, with competition, they are erect.

Plants flower approximately 6 wk after germination. Very little nectar is produced and insect pollination rarely occurs. *P. persicaria* is almost exclusively self-pollinated because the stamens curve inward toward the stigma (Simmonds 1945). While reports of many hybrids of this species exist, they are rare (Timson 1965a,b). However, since its $2n$ chromosome number is 44, it could be an autotetraploid of *P. lapathifolium* ($2n = 22$). The absence of cross-pollination accounts for the retention of the basic characteristics of *Polygonum* species growing in close proximity to each other.

P. persicaria is a highly variable species, which probably explains why hybridization was thought to occur freely. Hammerton (1965, 1967b) studied the physiological and polymorphic variations and observed differences in foliage color and clarity of the water mark. Some populations flowered in June, while most flowered in July. Dry weights were similar among populations during the growing season, but leaf area and relative growth rate varied. Hammerton speculates that these differences may have evolved in response to the wide range of environmental adaptability in the species.

P. persicaria produces numerous seeds. Estimates range from 500 to 1500 (Stevens 1957) to over 4400 seeds per plant (Hammerton and Jalloq 1970). Seed weight varies from 1.65 to 3.91 mg (Hammerton 1967b; Kelley and Bruns 1975; Simmonds 1945). In Japan, a pure stand of *P. persicaria* had 86 plants/m^2 that yielded 382 g dry wt/m^2 and over 144,000 seeds (Hayashi 1984).

Seed shape also is highly variable. Hammerton (1967b) found the quantity of trigonous seed averaged 42% but varied from 25 to 80% between populations. Later-planted plants produced a higher proportion of trigonous seeds. For some populations of *P. persicaria*, the ratio of trigonous to biconvex seed was inherited, while in others it was not. Flowers with two styles and lenticular ovaries produced biconvex seeds and those with three styles and trigonous ovaries produced triangular seeds (Timson 1965a). More trigonous seeds are formed on older plants (up to 73%, while the normal proportion is 22% trigonous to 78% biconvex) and trigonous seeds are usually heavier than biconvex seeds (Timson 1965a, Hammerton and Jalloq 1970).

Seeds of *P. persicaria* can spread as a contaminant in harvested seed crops (Simmonds 1945, Harper 1959, Tonkin and Phillipson 1973) and by animals and water. Rabbits consume 95% of the seed placed before them within 2 hr (Staniforth and Cavers 1977). Most seeds are excreted between 2 and 8 hr later, and 2.1% of the excreted seeds are viable. Smaller seeds are less likely to lose viability than large seeds.

P. persicaria seeds are disseminated in water. Nearly half the water samples collected in irrigation canals in the western United States had *P. persicaria* seeds and they floated for more than 130 hr in calm water (Egginton and Robbins 1920). Over half sank in agitated water after 1 hr, 74% sank after 10 hr, and 90% after 20 hr. If dropped into water from 1.5m, 80% of the seeds floated. Hope (1927), Kelley and Bruns (1975), and Staniforth and Cavers (1976) also documented and studied the dispersal of *P. persicaria* in water. The latter authors attribute the seeds' ability to float readily and for long periods to the air space between the remnant of the perianth and the seed. Fresh or dry seeds floated for 6 mo in calm water. Either over-wintering or physical removal of the perianth greatly reduces the percentage of floating seeds.

AGRICULTURE IMPORTANCE

P. persicaria is a weed of 35 crops in 50 countries (Figure 73-1) and is frequently reported a weed of cereals, maize, potatoes, sugar beets, and vegetables. It is a serious or principal weed of barley, beans, oats, oilseed rape, and tomatoes in Canada; field beets in Belgium, Germany, and New Zealand; cereals in Belgium, England, Italy, New Zealand, and Sweden; flax in Canada, Germany, Ireland, and New Zealand; pastures in New Zealand; maize in Canada, England, France, and New Zealand; onions in Ireland and Spain; peas in Ireland

and New Zealand; potatoes in Belgium, Chile, France, Germany, New Zealand, and Sweden; sugar beets in Albania, Belgium, Chile, England, Italy, and Poland; sunflowers in Canada and France; vegetables in Canada, England, Germany, Italy, New Zealand, Portugal, and Scotland; wheat in Canada, Germany, New Zealand, and the former Yugoslavia.

It is a common weed of barley and legumes in England; edible beans in France; carrots in New Zealand; cereals in Poland, Scotland, Tasmania, and Tunisia; lucerne in Canada; maize in the United States and Spain; onions in New Zealand and the United States; orchards in Belgium and Brazil; potatoes in England and the United States; oilseed rape in Japan; soybeans in Canada and the United States; sugar beets in France and Tunisia; tobacco in the United States; vegetables in Brazil, Spain, and Tasmania; and winter wheat in Japan.

P. persicaria is also an unranked weed of the crops already mentioned and others in many countries of the world.

In Scotland, *P. persicaria* occurred in nearly 40% of the sampled fields throughout the country, with an average density of 2900 seeds/m^2 (Warwick 1984). The species is more competitive with kale than wheat and reduces the leaf nitrogen content of both crops at low soil nitrogen levels (Welbank 1963). *P. persicaria* shows little response to nitrogen.

Jahn-Deesbach and Vogt (1960) encountered more *P. persicaria* in barley fertilized with N, P, K, Ca, and manure than when nutrient levels were low. When barley growth was reduced by low nutrient levels, competition from this weed increased. The weed grows to maturity after barley harvest. *P. persicaria* was allelopathic to flax and potatoes (Harper 1960). When the weed was grown for 60 days and then nutrient solution was flushed through the soil and used to water crops, their growth was reduced by more than 50%. A biotype of *P. persicaria* resistant to triazines is found in France (Barralis et al. 1979). Plants serve as a host to several species of nematodes (Bendixen et al. 1979).

This weed may have some use in human and animal diets. Seeds of *P. persicaria* are similar in nutritional value to rice and maize (Bayer 1958) and have been found in the stomachs of prehistoric man (Renfrew 1973). The foliage contains 3.12% N, 1.16% P, and 3.12% K and has been fed to cattle and horses (Long 1911). Perseca et al. (1976) found high amino acid levels in *P. persicaria* leaves and suggest that it may be a suitable forage. Leaves and stems have been used to treat hemorrhoids and diarrhea in Brazil (Lorenzi 1982).

COMMON NAMES

Polygonum persicaria

ALGERIA	araktiooun
ARGENTINA	persicaria
AUSTRALIA	persicaria
BANGLADESH	panee marich
BELGIUM	perzikkruid
BRAZIL	erva de bicho, persicaria de pe vermelho
CANADA	lady's thumb, renouee persicaire
CHILE	duraznillo
COLOMBIA	barbasco

DENMARK	fersken pileurt, ferskenbladet pileurt
EGYPT	qeddaab, qordaab, qordeyb
ENGLAND	spotted lady's thumb, persicaria, redshank, willow weed
FINLAND	hanhentatar
FRANCE	persicaire douce, pied rouge, renouee persicaire
GERMANY	Floh-Knoterich, Gemeiner Knoterich, Pfirschblattriger Knoterich, Pfirsch-Knoterich
GUATEMALA	chileperro
HUNGARY	baracklevelu keserufu
ICELAND	floajurt
INDIA	panee marich
IRELAND	spotted persicaria
ITALY	persicaria
JAPAN	harutade
MEXICO	chillo
NETHERLANDS	perzikkruid
NEW ZEALAND	willow weed
NORWAY	honsegress, vanleg honsegras
POLAND	rdest plamisty
PORTUGAL	erva pessegueira, persicaria
SCOTLAND	persicaria, redshank
SPAIN	cristas, duraznillo, persicaria, pimentilla, poligono pejiguera, presseguera
SWEDEN	akerknaa, akerpilot, vanlig pilort
UNITED STATES	ladysthumb smartweed
YUGOSLAVIA	breskova dresen, dvornik veliki

Seventy-Four

THE POTAMOGETONS

Potamogeton pectinatus L.,
Potamogeton crispus L.,
Potamogeton natans L.

Potamogetonaceae, Pondweed Family

POTAMOGETON, WITH ALMOST 100 species, is the largest genus of flowering plants in which all members are aquatic in habitat. In this genus, *P. pectinatus* is the one most often encountered by man, and it is the most widespread in the world. Biswas and Calder (1936) found it from the low plains of India to 5200 m in the Tibetan highlands. Vekhov (1988) found *P. pectinatus* at lat 70° N in the Yakutsk area of the former Soviet Union. Several of the species have quite general distribution on all continents.

These plants are monocotyledons, submerged or floating, most are perennials, mainly found in fresh water and rarely marsh or bog plants, with a few species that will tolerate quite brackish water. They are weeds of man's ditches, waterways, and impoundments but serve also as excellent forage for fish and waterfowl, provide protection and cover for fish, and are centers of colonization for aquatic flora and fauna. The names of the three species of interest here are derived from the Latin *pecten* (comb or rake), *crispus* (curly or wavy), and *nato* (swim or float), while the genus and family names come from the Greek *potamo*, denoting river plants.

DESCRIPTIONS

These three *Potamogetons* are all submersed *perennial* herbs with *rhizomes* creeping above and below the mud and with fibrous roots on the lower side of each node. Stems and rhizomes often 3 to 4 m long, richly branched, leaves alternate. The small perfect flowers are on pedunculate axillary spikes, fruiting carpels are one-seeded, indehiscent seeds are without endosperm, the embryo with a large "foot," and the plumule enclosed by the cotyledon.

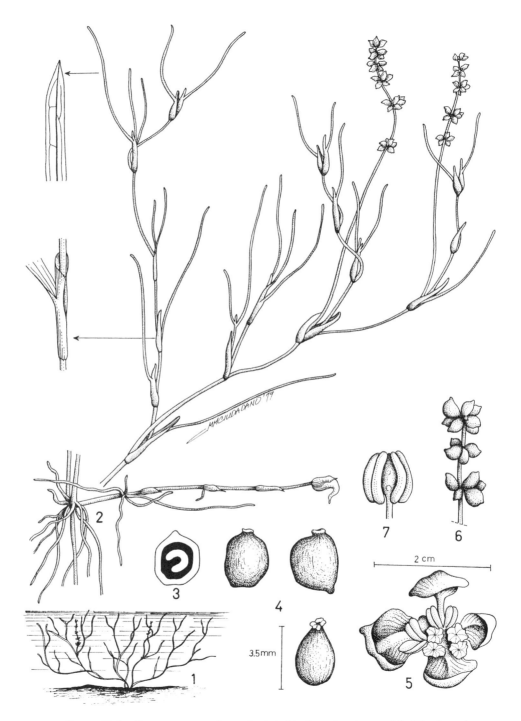

FIGURE 74-1 *Potamogeton pectinatus* L.: 1. habit; 2. root system and fruiting branch; 3. fruiting carpel, vertical section, 4. fruiting carpel, three views; 5. flower; 6. fruiting spike; 7. anther with perianth segment removed.

Potamogeton pectinatus

In *P. pectinatus* (Figure 74-1) the *leaves* are narrow-linear, entire, apex tapering to an acute point, greenish or brownish, 5 to 35 cm long, 0.5 to 2 mm broad, adnate at the base to the stipular sheath; *sheath* with its lower portion 0.5 to 2.5 cm long and encircling the stem, the upper portion, 3 to 15 mm, forming a distinct ligule; inflorescence a *spike* 1.5 to 6 cm long when in fruit, interrupted, 2 to 6 unequally spaced groups of usually 2 flowers; *peduncle* slender, flexuous, 5 to 25 cm long, often thread-like, elongating to carry flowers to water surface; *stigma* broad and wart-like; *anthers* 0.5 to 1 mm long; *fruiting carpels* 2.5 to 4 mm long and 2 to 3 mm wide, globular to ovoid, laterally compressed, brownish, smooth, 3 obscure longitudinal keels on dorsal surface, short beak, sometimes almost recurved. Long keels are present in Australian species (Aston 1973) but only obscure lateral keels with dorsal keel absent on biotypes found in the United States by Correll and Correll (1975).

Potamogeton crispus

In *P. crispus* (Figure 74-2) the slender *stems* are laterally compressed, tending to be 4-angled with furrows on broader sides that are 0.5 to 2.5 mm wide; *rhizomes* may be buff or reddish in color; *leaves* alternate, sessile, narrowly lanceolate to linear-oblong, obtuse, serrulate, undulate to strongly wavy at margins, bright green to dark green, may be reddish, 0.75 to 1.5 cm wide, 10 cm long, free stipular sheath, *stipular sheath* 5 to 15 mm long, truncate, often disintegrating; *inflorescence* in 3 to 5 whorls of flowers, spike 1 to 2 cm long; *fruiting carpels* 2 to 7 mm long, 1.5 to 3 mm wide, dark olive to brownish, sometimes with strongly developed dorsal keel, conspicuous or somewhat curved beak, fruit body with smooth to strongly tuberculate sides.

Potamogeton natans

In *P. natans* (Figure 74-3) the simple *stems* branch up from the horizontal rhizomes and those beneath the water surface bear very thin *linear leaves* reduced to phyllodia, 10 to 30 cm long, 1 to 2 mm wide; *floating leaves* broadly elliptic to oblong, may be subcordate at base, usually widest midway between base and tip, broadly rounded at apex, petiole longer than blade; *stipules* 5 to 12 cm long, linear-lanceolate, membranous; *flowering spikes* in axils of leaves, 3 to 6 cm long on stout peduncles, 2 to 3 times as long as spike; *fruits* 2.5 to 3.5 mm long, 2 to 2.5 mm wide, beaked, with prominent keels.

Identification of *Potamogeton* species is notoriously difficult. Those with ribbon- or thread-like leaves require very careful study but they are well understood, well-described, and can be named with some certainty. Some species are extremely variable when growing in different environments. *P. gramineus*, for example, has so many leaf forms and branching habits that it has been registered in many varieties and forms. The three species of interest above are easily distinguished by their difference in leaf characteristics. Wehrmeister (1978) found that much of the variation characterizing varieties and hybrids could be found among the seasonal growth forms within a single population of plants over the course of one year.

Ogden (1943) surveyed the broad-leaved species of *Potamogeton* of North America north of Mexico.

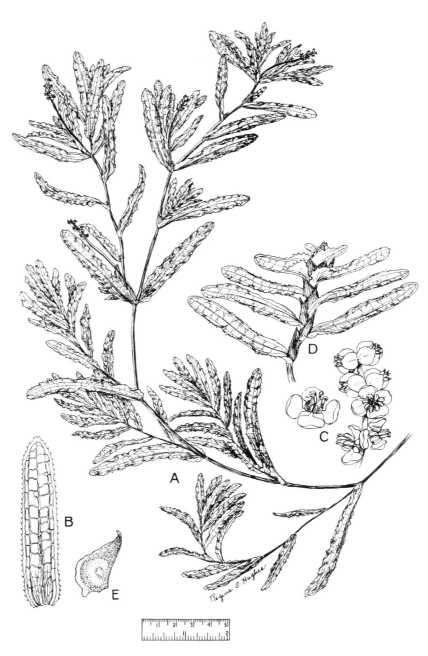

FIGURE 74-2   *Potamogeton crispus* L.: A. habit; B. leaf venation; C. flowers; D. winter bud;
E. achene.

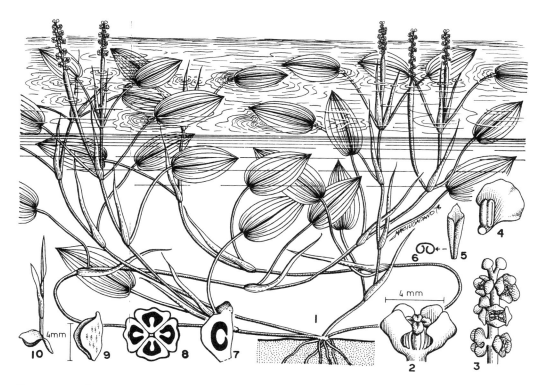

FIGURE 74-3   *Potamogeton natans* L.: 1. habit; 2. flower; 3. portion of inflorescence;
4. stamen, adnate to perianth; 5. young leaf, 6. same, cross section in diagram; 7. ovary,
vertical section, 8. same, cross section; 9. fruit; 10. seedling.

DISTRIBUTION AND HABITAT

Several *Potamogeton* species are very widespread in the world and may be among the oldest of the hydrophytes. They are found in the ditches and streams of hot, arid, or humid
regions but also thrive in some of the coldest waters of the North Temperate Zone. The
world distribution of *P. pectinatus* and *P. crispus* is quite similar (Figures 74-4 and 74-5).
It is interesting that *P. pectinatus* is found far out in the harsh and stormy environment of
the Aleutian Chain in the Andreanof Islands (Adak Island) between North Asia and North
America, a place that gives birth to much of the weather that eventually sweeps southeastward across North America. *P. natans* (Figure 74-6) tends to remain quite well north of the
equator and the Tropic of Cancer but with introductions reported in islands east of
Madagascar and of Australia.

   They are found at sea level and ascend to mountainous areas. *P. pectinatus* is found at
4880 m in Kashmir, 5200 m in Tibet, and at 1900 m on the equator in Kenya. We consider them freshwater species, but all will tolerate some brackishness. *P. pectinatus* is capable
of sustained growth in waters of very high salt content. *P. pectinatus* and *P. crispus* are
among the world's most widespread hydrophytes.

FIGURE 74-4   The distribution of *Potamogeton pectinatus* L. across the world where it has been reported as a weed.

FIGURE 74-5   The distribution of *Potamogeton crispus* L. across the world where it has been reported as a weed.

FIGURE 74-6   The distribution of *Potamogeton natans* L. across the world where it has been reported as a weed.

P. pectinatus is the most cosmopolitan of the three species, and this is in part because it is one of the few hydrophytes with the capacity to form dense, closed communities that discourage the growth of competitors. Its success comes also from the ability to colonize areas of deep water or other places where native vegetation is sparse: shaded places, swift flowing waters, and sometimes ditches and ponds that are badly polluted. Extensive meadows of this species are at times seen in very saline waters. Butcher (1933) points out that some types of hydrophytes are very efficient in trapping silt from soil run-off and sediments from sewage effluent, while avoiding burial by the material. The long, smooth, narrow leaves of *P. pectinatus* are agitated by the slightest motion and tend to keep themselves free of the particles that are passing or settling in the water. On establishment, they become traps for finer particles that they screen from the water to be added to the subsoil beneath. They now contribute organic material from their own structures. Pearsall (1920) found *P. natans* growing on soil containing 74% organic matter.

P. crispus shares several similar characteristics but has fashioned a life cycle of very early spring development, with dormant apices sometimes finished off by late June. This allows maximum use of the resources of a pond or river before life becomes crowded, and it avoids the heavy season of midsummer competition. This will be discussed in detail later.

The *Potamogetons* are fond of canals, irrigation ditches and other waters near man's agriculture. In central and northern India, as the dry season approaches and waters recede, some of the exposed areas are quickly planted to crops appropriate to the region and soil type. The jheels (ponds) and swampy pools that form nearby are often dominated by *P. pectinatus* that comes in quickly. The species is troublesome in the irrigation systems of east and south Australia and is the curse of such waterways in the western United States. In the irrigated Gezira scheme of Sudan, three *Potamogetons* are included in the eight most common aquatic weeds, and *P. natans* and *P. pectinatus* are among them. Across the Mediterranean Sea in Europe, *P. natans* is a weed in transplanted rice. Sutton (1977) made a survey of the use of fish for aquatic weed control in eastern Europe and the former Soviet Union and recorded as well the location of many hydrophytes. In the great Kara Kum canal that is under construction in the south of the former Soviet Union, and which is to be 5000 km in length, *P. pectinatus*, *P. perfoliatus*, and *Myriophyllum spicatum* caused many of the serious weed problems in the early years. It is reported that deepening the infested stretches to 4 m was very helpful in controlling growth of these species.

In studies of other species, it has been pointed out that the nature of the stream bottom is determined in part by the rate of current flow, and this influences the communities that can become established at different sites. Butcher (1933) found this to be true in a study of several rivers in England. In rivers arising in low to high hills, with water of high *pH*, medium current flow, no sudden flooding, but water sometimes turbulent, there were scattered patches of fine silt and fine gravel, and *P. crispus* was found to thrive on these. In rivers arising in low-lying land, with water of neutral *pH*, slow current, and with no sudden changes in water level, the bottoms were generally covered with a very fine mud. There was much weed vegetation here and *P. natans* was found in very mixed communities.

Haslam (1978) reported that following dredging and clean-up of ponds and streams, *P. pectinatus* and *P. natans* came in quickly and easily found their place among the dominants in a population within 2 or 3 yr. On the flats and shallows of the muddy coasts of Lake Vrana in the former Yugoslavia, Golubic (1961) found "seaballs" (or lake balls) composed of *P. pectinatus*. Similar spheres of other species have been reported elsewhere. Wave action and nearly level ground are required for the formation of these oddities. Toward the outer edge of each ball, he found a distinct zone in which blue-green algae were imbedded in the plant remains. The depth of the zone was limited by the extent to which light could penetrate.

P. crispus shows a surprising ability to maintain active growth under very cold conditions. Vladimirova (1968) has recorded growth under ice in the area of Lake Baikal in the former Soviet Union. In ponds in the central United States, the vegetative plants remained in a photosynthetically active state under relatively thick ice and snow cover. The light intensity for some of these plants was 120 foot candles or less (Wehrmeister 1978).

P. pectinatus is pleased to live in alkaline, calcareous, polluted water and is one of the most tolerant of the submerged weeds to saline conditions.

PROPAGATION AND REPRODUCTIVE PHYSIOLOGY

The most exhaustive study of the biology of a *Potamogeton* species is that for *P. pectinatus* by Yeo (1965). Over a period of four years, he studied flowering, fruiting, the development of seeds, the formation of tubers above and below the soil surface, and the germination and longevity of both sexual and asexual propagules. This work serves well as a background for a discussion of reproduction and propagation. His research was done in Montana in the northwestern part of the United States, where data could be recorded from May 1 to October 15. The site of the weed infestation was an irrigation channel 3.7 m wide and 1 m in depth with continuous flow.

Shoots began to emerge the first week in May, in spring, when air and water temperatures were 10°C. Foliage growth was slow to mid-June when light intensity and air and water temperatures began to increase rapidly toward summer maximums. Inflorescences began to form during this warming period, foliage growth ceased about July 1, open flowers were seen the last week in June, and fruit formation was seen by mid-July. Light energy and water and air temperatures decreased rapidly from August 1, mature fruits were shedding from the plants by early August, and by early September new growth of leafy shoots or axillary tubers could be seen in the leaf axils of the terminal one-half of the shoots. The axillary tubers were well developed by October 1. From early to late September, the water and soil temperatures were similar and fell from 10 to 6°C, resulting in the death of the foliage.

In Australia, *P. crispus* flowers November to May, while *P. pectinatus* generally produces flower buds and flowers from October to May and fruits November to May. In some warm areas, it can fruit most of the year. In Japan, Kunii (1982) followed the life cycle of *P. crispus* plants in shallow freshwater ponds from turion germination from the subsoil in autumn through the next growing season and found the pattern for this species similar to that in California, as described above. Turion dry weight accounted for 42% of the total plant biomass.

Rogers and Breen (1980) studied the development of *P. crispus* in small lakes on a subtropical flood plain of the Pongola River in South Africa. Because the lakes are flushed out by flooding during summer and isolated in winter, growth is very seasonal, starting in autumn (April), and with the maximum standing crop in early spring (September). Plants are generally absent in summer. The stands are almost monospecific in spring and winter. Wehrmeister (1978) found that *P. crispus* in the central United States exists in a dormant state from mid through late summer, remaining thus because of vegetative dormant stem tips that form in late spring and begin to grow in early fall. The leaves of the winter form are then flat, blue-green, and narrow in contrast to the wider, undulate margined, redbrown leaves of plants with spring growth. In early spring, the flowering and fruiting was much more prolific than is generally suggested in the literature. The dormant apices show a seasonally earlier onset of germination and growth if the water level is drawn down and if surrounding plants of other species are removed from the vicinity of the dormant, vegetative stem tips. He believes that these structures must have a cold treatment or period and a minimum threshold light intensity before they will germinate. The dormant apices could be initiated with a 16-hr day at 25°C. In an 8-hr day, there was no initiation.

Whatever the total daily light dose, Chambers et al. (1985) found few turions formed in long, warm days at low photon fluence rates or at low red:far red ratios near 1; production of turions increased as these were raised. Thus, they found turions were formed from June through August in the upper 1.5 m of a freshwater lake where photon fluence rates and red:far red ratios were high.

Hoogers and van der Weij (1971) found that *P. natans* showed continued growth of well developed and richly branched rhizomes in deep mud all winter in ditches and canals of the Netherlands. No typical winter buds were observed. *P. crispus* plants began to develop from winter buds in spring. Both of these plants can make some growth in winter.

The spike of the monoecious flower of *P. pectinatus* is formed on a peduncle at the end of a leafy shoot, and, as the florets develop, the peduncle and rachis elongate. The structure is raised to the water surface. The florets, averaging about 11 per spike, are compressed and enclosed by two leaves. A mature flower consists of four 1-celled pistils with sessile, orangeyellow stigmas that extend slightly above the four large 2-locular anthers. Four large sepal-like connective tissues extend under the anthers and protect the florets in the early stages of development. The pollen is buoyant, oblong, transluscent, with white caps at each end. Pollination, fertilization, and fruit development are at the water surface. Once pollinated and fertilized, the ovaries swell and usually two of four pistils develop. The mature fruit, a drupelet (sometimes called achene or nutlet in research reports) consists of a white seed with seed coat, leathery endocarp and mesocarp, and fleshy exocarp. Seeds remain on the rachis until late fall in still water but may be stripped and dispersed to other areas in flowing water (Yeo 1965). Azarova and Artemenko (1979) have published excellent illustrations of the seeds of 18 *Potamogeton* species.

Many aquatic plants have one-seed indehiscent fruits such as nuts (with a hard exterior) or drupes (a fleshy exterior), as in the *Potamogetons*. Most of the aquatic angiosperms have an extended dormancy, and it is often due to the mechanical confinement within a testa or pericarp. In the *Potamogeton*, we usually find a stony, hard, close-fitting scleridial endocarp in which the micropyle is normally sealed so that germination will not go forward until the wall is ruptured or the seal removed (Sauvageau 1894, Crocker 1907). For most angiosperms, animals, man, wind, and water bring about dispersal, but the fruits and seeds of water plants have special significance, for as they float for a few days or a few weeks, they are often moved away from the mother plant and, if caught in flood water, may go long distances. The buoyancy results from large intercellular spaces in the pericarp or air-filled lacunate tissues, as in *Potamogeton*, *Pontederia*, *Alisma*, and others.

P. pectinatus not only spreads very rapidly during the vegetative phase but it produces great quantities of all of its various propagules in a very short time. Yeo (1966) studied the production of propagules by the three species of concern here, with plots in the states of California and Montana in the western and northwestern United States. Plants were grown in containers of sizes varying in surface area from 0.65 to 22.7 m², with 10 to 15 cm of clay soil on the bottom and a water cover of 25 to 50 cm. He gathered data on the production of propagules per season from single tubers, turions, and seeds planted in spring. In general, the period August through October was the period of greatest propagule production. *P. pectinatus* plants produced no seed in small (0.65 m²) containers when started from seed, but yielded 110, 1380, and 6000 seeds from tuber plants when grown in containers of 0.65, 2.6, and 22.7 m², respectively. In a culture started from one seed in California, 63,300 seeds were produced in a container of 7.5 m² in surface area. In a container of 6 m² surface area, one of the turions of *P. crispus* produced a plant that had 1000 seeds. *P. natans* did not flower. It is of interest that one plant of horned pondweed, *Zannichellia palustris*, that was started from seed produced more than 2 million seeds in one of the small containers.

Kelley and Bruns (1975) harvested weekly or biweekly screenings of seeds in three irrigation systems and the Columbia River in the northwestern United States. A few seeds of *P. pectinatus* were taken in irrigation ditches but none from the river.

There is a general belief that the *P. crispus* type(s) of Europe is a heavier seed producer than the type(s) found in North America. Hunt and Lutz (1959) found excellent seed production in 8 to 30 cm of water in a marsh to the west of Lake Erie in North America. They estimated that there was sufficient seed in a 0.4 ha plot to feed 500 to 1000 large ducks for one day. They found this seed in 11 of 15 ducks examined. Pending further experiments, they suggest that this species will produce much more seed if water levels decrease or are drawn down to 8 to 30 cm in spring and remain there during the period of growth.

In the experiments of Yeo (1965) described above, it was learned that in *P. pectinatus* rupture of the seed coat, low temperature, abrasion of outer integuments, alternate wetting and drying, and overwintering on a canal bottom improved seed germination. The drupelet has a hinged opening on the dorsal side that has been called a "trapdoor." Upon opening, one finds a white, curved seed with a long cotyledon and a slightly swollen embryo. Opening this door, or rupturing the coat of a healthy seed to allow entry of water, gave 100% germination in some cases. All other methods were much less effective. Crocker

(1907) had reported this earlier but also noticed that if the seed was harvested in a green condition (unripe) and kept in cold water it would not germinate. If kept at room temperature, germination could soon be obtained. Yeo found that green seeds had to be held at room temperature for 2 or 3 mo before the "trapdoor" opening was completely formed. He also found that dry storage of seed near freezing temperatures gave 30% germination, while wet storage at this temperature, or wet or dry at room temperature, was less satisfactory. Maguire (1934) harvested seed of the same species from large numbers found in water near the shore in a freshwater lake in Utah in the United States. He also found much dry seed above the water line. The seeds from the water germinated well, but the dry seeds were no longer viable.

Guppy (1894–97), in some very early work on *P. crispus* and *P. natans*, found that the former, if held in water after harvest, showed 68% germination in the first year. If placed in mud, only 6% germinated in the first year, with an increase to 25% in the second year. Seeds of *P. natans* placed in water or in mud in the laboratory continued to germinate for 4 mo. Seeds held dry for 4 mo germinated freely, but after 30 mo there was no germination and the seeds rotted. Harvested seeds fed to ducks and recovered gave 60% germination in the next spring. Guppy found that seeds were able to germinate in light and darkness but believed that darkness enhanced the process. Muenscher (1936b) could get no germination of this species when seeds were held dry at room temperature up to 12 mo. In water at 3°C, germination was 7% at 3 mo and 40% at 12 mo. Teltscherova and Hejny (1973) in Czechoslovakia found 40% seed germination of *P. crispus* seed in Bohemian fishponds. Rogers and Breen (1980) say there are no reports of seed germination under natural conditions in North America. See also Wehrmeister (1978).

After the sexual cycle of reproductive growth, the plants begin another period of expansive growth. The asexual propagation of *P. pectinatus* is mainly by subterranean tubers that develop from specialized tissues at the ends of branches. They are borne singly or in chains of two or more, swell rapidly, and store large amounts of starch. These propagules enable winter survival, and they form new plants in spring. The swollen parts of the two halves of the tubers are internodal tissue. On the upper part of the tuber is formed a long shoot bud consisting of two nodes and internodes. Stolons and roots grow from these nodes, and at the terminal node there is an apical meristem surrounded by leaves. An internode separates adjacent tubers. A small dormant shoot bud is also formed on the upper surface of each tuber and is stimulated to growth if the long terminal shoot is lost or damaged. All shoots in a chain eventually grow (Yeo 1965).

In September, leafy branches or axillary tubers form in the leafy axils of the terminal areas of the summer-growing shoots. These tubers are like the subterranean tubers but smaller in diameter, occur singly or in chains of two, and are formed at the tips of short branches. When the foliage dies off at the season's end, these axillary tubers fall to the bottom and produce new plants in spring.

In the experiments of Yeo (1966) referred to earlier, in which he started plants from the three types of propagules, those grown from tubers grew more vigorously than those from seed until the water warmed in July. A representative selection of the results with the asexual propagules shows, for example, that the plant from a single subterranean tuber grown in the smallest container produced 2000 subterranean tubers. This increased to 36,000 in the largest container. Axillary tuber production was 40 and 8000 and seed production 110 and 6000, respectively, for these two containers. In a small container planted with a single seed initially, no seeds or axillary buds formed, but 300 subterranean tubers were produced. In the container of 7.3 m², there were 15,000 subterranean tubers, 63,000 seeds, and no axillary tubers. In another comparison, a single subterranean tuber placed in a container of 6 m² surface area produced 8500 similar tubers at season's end, but a plant from a single seed in a similar pool formed 13,500 tubers.

Wehrmeister (1978) reported that non-rooted plants that had been released from the substrate developed dormant apices irrespective of the long days and warm temperatures normally required.

Reproduction by these types of propagules is obviously a very complex process. In a general summary of his study on reproductive capacity, Yeo (1966) points out that larger numbers of propagules were harvested where there was free extension of the plant into open areas without interference. In one of the large containers, flowering shoots of one plant migrated outward to cover an area more than 3 m in diameter. Heavy seed production by a single plant often resulted in the production of small tubers on that plant. It may be seen that the potential of *P. pectinatus* for dispersal and establishment through vegetative fragments, stolons, tubers, and seeds is awesome. Bruns and Comes (1965) found 1400 tubers in a 0.03 m³ block of soil at the bottom of a heavily infested irrigation canal.

Haskova and Slavonosky (1968) in Czechoslovakia found that the propagation of *P. crispus* in the warm early growing season was by short, free, stem fragments and by dormant turions (specialized vegetative buds) that developed large parenchyma cells packed with starch. As autumn approached, the partially developed turions, as well as young shoots that had come from rhizomes, became dormant and survived the winter in this condition. In the studies of Rogers and Breen (1980) on *P. crispus* in small pans (lakes) in South Africa (referred to earlier), turions were the most important propagule giving rise to annual growth. The water level in these pans was 4 m at flood in summer and surface evaporation reduced them to less than 1 m in winter. Here, 60% of the turions on a sediment surface of 1,100 m² germinated in April. Some of the first-formed turions from this crop germinated as soon as they were formed, but most entered a period of dormancy that lasted though the summer. The authors feel that the life span of a single plant of *P. crispus* is about 4 to 5 mo in their area. Seed germination at 0.001% is a contributing factor in dispersal but is not significant in the development of the large standing crop. Seed germination increased slightly when a pan dried out and was again wetted.

Major factors that influence new growth of winter bud apices, tubers, turions and seeds in *Potamogeton* species, as in most plants, are temperature and light intensity. In the *Potamogetons*, the dormancy of such propagules can usually be overcome as early as November and December in the North Temperate Zone by placing them in warm water. It is assumed that in natural sites the higher temperatures of approaching spring stimulate new growth, but as yet there is very little experimental evidence to substantiate this. Sahai and Sinha (1969) found that freshly gathered mature winter apices of *P. crispus* gave almost no sprouting. Treatment with appropriate concentrations of potassium nitrate, ammonium sulfate, potassium phosphate, indoleacetic acid, and thiourea gave 30 to 100% sprouting, with the latter compound being most effective (see also Sastroutomo 1980b, 1981).

The rapid radial migration beyond the flower-bearing growth may be observed in *P. pectinatus* (Yeo 1965). A single plant may develop into a large network, with stolons traveling considerable distances. In the United States, stolons have been excavated from 1-m depths. Haslam (1978) has pointed out that our observations may show that small and large stands of aquatic weeds may slowly move to other sites or rearrange themselves. But because most aquatic plants can propagate vegetatively, she believes that the death of such patches from old age is improbable. Rudescu et al. (1965) estimate that the stands of *Phragmites* in the deltas on the Black Sea in Romania may have lived for 1000 yr. Storms that break up aquatic plants may cause them to move to more distant places by the distribution of vegetative fragments. Haslam reports that, to grow again, torn stem fragments of *P. pectinatus* must have a rhizome portion attached. Yeo (1965) photographed and measured the vegetative extension of *P. pectinatus*. The stolons traveled horizontally, produced a leafy shoot at every node, and then the apex turned upward, grew several inches, and formed a node that developed a leafy shoot. This shoot eventually turned downward, entered the soil, grew several inches, and re-emerged. The node that had borne this shoot developed roots and a tuber-bearing branch.

Yeo (1965), in his research with asexual propagules, contributed significantly to our understanding of longevity and winter survival. Since almost all new spring growth in *P. pectinatus*, for example, is from tubers in or on the soil, the hardiness of these reproductive structures is important in the continuity of the species. He found that tubers could not survive temperatures below freezing. During winter in the experimental area, air temperatures fell to −35°C for several days, but temperature measurements in bottom soil in a canal with flowing water and at 2.5, 15, and 30 cm soil depths in a dry channel covered with 15 to 60 cm of snow revealed that soil temperatures were never below freezing during these cold periods. In a study of survival under laboratory conditions, he coated small tubers with paraffin, placed them in opaque containers at 4°C, and then removed 10 of them at two-month intervals and placed them in water at room temperature. All tubers germinated in the first year, but in the second year they began to deteriorate until only 1 of 10 would germinate. In a similar test with large tubers, all sprouted at 24 and 36 mo, but at 48 mo only one-half were still viable.

Catling and Dobson (1985) believe that the life cycle of *P. crispus* is unlike that of any other American pond weed.

ANATOMY AND MORPHOLOGY

There is reliable evidence that the **Potamogetonaceae** may be older than the **Gramineae** (the grasses) or the **Cyperaceae** (the sedges). Several monocotyledons are believed to date back into the Cretaceous period (60 to 130 million years ago) and among them are the **Potamogetonaceae**. The genus *Potamogeton* is not yet found prior to the Oligicene period (beginning about 35 million years ago). These records are now represented by leaves, fruits, seeds, and pollen from England, the former Soviet Union, and other areas (Daghlian 1981).

In describing the morphology of submerged aquatics and in assigning taxonomic status to the many forms in which they appear, there is often confusion between phenotypic and genotypic variation. The plants may be rooted in very deep water with stems and leaves at a depth of one or more meters, some near the surface, others at the surface, and still others may be emergent, and all with varying form and structure. Such vegetative variants are bewildering, and the *Potamogeton* species have many of these. A statement by Sculthorpe (1967, page 222) describes the plight of those who would sort through the species of this genus in an attempt to identify them: "Other genera of infamous taxonomic repute include the *Potamogeton* in which leaf form and anatomy may vary widely with age, water depth, current speed, nutrient supply, light intensity, and perhaps other factors."

Hettiarachchi and Triest (1986) of Belgium collected plants from several areas of Europe and found in *P. pectinatus* that isozyme patterns of peroxidase in leaves, alcohol dehydrogenase in seeds, shikimate dehydrogenase and glutamic-oxaloacetate transaminase in turions showed remarkable intraspecific variations. Some other enzyme patterns in the plants of the collection showed greater consistency.

Among the major research papers describing the anatomy and morphology of these species are those of Gluck (1906), Esenbeck (1914) and Campbell (1939); and Sauvageau (1894) on the anatomy and morphology of *P. pectinatus*; Diez et al. (1988) on the pollen of *P. pectinatus*; Lapirov (1985) on the morphology of the development of the terminal bud in the tuber of *P. pectinatus*; Misra's (1972) cytological studies of some Indian **Potamogetonaceae**; Singh (1964, 1965a) on vegetative anatomy and vascular anatomy of the flower of **Potamogetonaceae**; and ovule ontogeny and seed development in *P. natans* by Takaso and Bouman (1984).

In 1887, in southeast England, during a very hot summer with deficient rainfall, Fryer (1887) found that many drainage ditches became dry; water temperatures rose considerably in water that still remained; and with these circumstances, he encountered an extraordinary growth of land forms of the *Potamogetons*. There was also an unusual development of coriaceous (leathery) floating leaves where water remained. In this genus, land forms are produced only by those species that can inhabit shallow pools and fens that are subject to reduced water levels and drying at some time during each year. Such species, which can survive exposure to dry, free air and hot sunshine for a time, all belong to a section of the genus that has the ability when needed to produce leathery floating leaves. The land forms are noticeably produced in the dry years but are formed to a limited extent annually in the areas where plants come under such moisture stress. Species that are unable to make a minimal growth in such circumstances must cease to exist. Although it is quite likely that the latter species may be seen over a long period of years in such a habitat, it is quite possible that they must be re-introduced after each dry season or each succession of them.

The true land form is a shoot that springs from a rootstock or stolon at some depth in the soil and grows into the open air when the water cover disappears. Usually it appears as a tuft of leaves growing at the apex of an underground stem. Sometimes the stem extends a few inches above the soil, erect, simple, or rarely with one or two short branches. There is no flower production, but the life of a plant is prolonged by a stolon that bears one or more tubers. The land form of *P. natans* is very robust, there is no stem, the leaves form a tuft, and the lower ones (always produced) are linear, longer than upper leaves and are reduced to a thickened midrib. Upper leaves are leathery, slightly auricled at the base, and are broader in proportion to their length than in the usual water form. Lower leaves are 5 to 10 cm long and upper leaves 2 to 5 cm by 4 to 7 cm, with a 1- to 4-cm petiole. When covered by water, this species often retains its upper leaves through the winter, but in land forms it persists only until injured or killed by frost. When plants are re-submerged, all leaves return to the familiar characteristic water form.

When compared with terrestrial plants, a marked reduction in the number of xylem conducting elements and in the degree of lignification is seen in submerged organs. In the stems of species such as *P. pectinatus*, there may be a condensation of most or all of the vascular strands into a central cylinder. True vessels are lacking in many submerged hydrophytes, the conducting elements being long annular or spirally thickened tracheids, some or all of which eventually become disorganized. A bundle may often consist of only a xylem lacuna (an opening) and a phloem strand. In the aquatic monocotyledons, there is usually no cambial activity in mature bundles. There may be temporary cambial activity in very young petioles of *P. natans* and *Sagittaria sagittifolia* (Sculthorpe 1967).

Sculthorpe (1967) has assembled, from several authors, an excellent collection of photomicrographs and diagrammatic illustrations of the internal anatomy of several submerged species. There is a portrayal of the reduction and fusion of vascular bundles of the stem in a *Potamogeton* series beginning with *P. pulcher*, where there are several scattered bundles inside the circumference, through several other species to *P. pectinatus* which shows extreme condensation and bears only a central cylinder. The phloem of the aquatic monocotyledons has not been modified as greatly. In many, the phloem seems to be highly specialized, to the point of having sieve tube members with transverse (rather than oblique) end walls.

In the *Potamogeton*, the rhizomes of many species are slender, fragile, and quite vulnerable, but on the other hand they are well branched, with extensive systems of fibrous roots at all nodes.

In the roots of submerged plants, the stele is centrally located as in land plants, an arrangement that helps resist the pulling, stretching, and dislocation of tissues in an environment subject to much change. The structure of the vascular tissues themselves may be modified in a manner similar to that of submerged stems. In *P. natans*, a pentarch (arising from five points) arrangement is seen in the roots, and the walls of the xylem elements, including some vessels, are thickened. In *P. pectinatus*, the fine protoxylem strands are absent at maturity, and the stele has only an axial, spirally thickened vessel (Sculthorpe 1967).

The "flower" of the **Potamogetonaceae** has been a matter of some controversy. Some have regarded it as a simple flower with four carpels and four stamens, while others propose that it is an inflorescence of four staminate and four pistillate flowers. Singh (1965a) reviewed these arguments and reported on studies of the vascular anatomy of the flower in nine members of this family, including *P. natans* and *P. pectinatus*. He considers this reproductive organ of the **Potamogetonaceae** to be a true flower, not an inflorescence, and presents details and drawings to support his conclusions.

One member of the genus *Potamogeton*, *P. berchtoldii*, can send flowers to the surface from a depth of 2.5 m. For submerged species in general, there are difficult mechanical problems at or above the water surface. In spite of wave action, they must remain above the water for display and cross-pollination. Air currents tend to bend them down, and flowing water currents pull at them constantly. One of the adaptations that is effective may be seen in the *Potamogeton*, whose mat of floating stems, leaves, and peduncles gives support to aerial floral clusters. Mechanical and vascular tissues of the floral axis of underwater species may often resemble those of dicotyledonous land plants that must support their own weight and thus possess greater resistance to bending. In *P. natans*, for example, this may be seen in the arrangement of collateral bundles in the flower structures, in contrast to the condensed cylinder of vascular tissues seen in the rhizomes and vegetative stems (Singh 1965a).

Most members of the genus *Potamogeton* have erect spikes and are wind pollinated. In *P. natans*, the spike is densely flowered, while in others the flowers are few. In *P. pectinatus*, the spike floats on or near the surface, each successive flower being lifted just above the surface. The pollen floats to the stigmas of the same or other inflorescences.

Varying habitats may cause extensive modification of the form of the entire plant. In *P. natans*, the lower leaves are often described as "bladeless" or "phyllodial," and the upper leaves at the surface are elliptical and floating. In a cold, clear lake in northern Minnesota, in the United States, which had a depth of 1.5 m and a rather constant water level, Thieret (1971) found plants with well-developed narrow leaf blades. There were no floating, elliptical leaves, and all leaf material remained 25 cm or more below the surface of the water.

In most of the lakes of northern New York State, in the United States, the *P. pectinatus* plants tend to grow upward in a columnar mass of stems and leaves and with branching predominantly at the base. In one lake in the area with heavy plankton growth and thus little light penetration, each plant put up only a few vertical stems and these branched profusely, but only in the top 30 cm of the water (Forest 1977). See also van Wijk (1986, 1988).

The anatomy and morphology of leaves, which are peculiar to each species, and the age and condition of the leaf will have much to do with the uptake of nutrients and their loss. Mayr (1915) in Germany discovered that several genera, including *Potamogeton*, *Ceratophyllum*, *Myriophyllum* and *Sagittaria* have special epidermal areas in which are located the only cells that are easily permeable to salts. These cells can be detected *in vivo* with special procedures using dyes. He gave them the name "hydropoten." Such cells are not found in the epidermis of organs that normally grow above water but are temporarily submerged. Hydropoten cells have since been found in other genera (McIntosh et al. 1978).

P. pectinatus and *M. spicatum* normally exhibit very rapid rates of growth, yet a significant portion of the leaves die before the maximum biomass is reached. Howard-Williams and Davies (1978) used the scanning electron microscope to study changes in leaf structure from emergence to death. A distinct succession of microflora was found beginning with an already dense community of diatoms and bacteria at 1.5 wk. At 6 wk of growth, they found leaf pitting and the onset of cuticular erosion. The leaves began to senesce at 14 wk, and this deterioration was accompanied by extensive cuticular peeling and epidermal cell wall eruption. They hypothesized that this may prepare the leaf for rapid leaching soon after death.

ECOLOGY AND PHYSIOLOGY

One of the major ecological studies of river plants is that of Haslam. Over a period of many years, she gathered data on almost every aspect of water plant life in relation to habitat in the rivers of England. Her data on the performance of plant communities and of species as they respond to light, temperature, substrate, flow, and turbulence are recorded in the excellent book *River Plants* (Haslam 1978). Selected information from this work is of interest to those who are working with *Potamogeton* species when they are behaving as weeds.

P. natans joins a group of plants which are closely associated with fairly shallow water depths of 30 to 75 cm, while *P. pectinatus* was often found at 80- to 120-cm depths. The behavior of the latter species at different flow rates was quite dependent upon the type of substrate, but it was most often found in stretches with moderate flow and was rather intolerant of spates (river flooding) or very fast flows. *P. natans* and *crispus* were not associated with a particular flow rate, but the latter was more tolerant of rushing water from violent storms because of its superior anchorage and tougher stems. The hydraulic resistance of water plants (resistance to water movement) depends on size (height, breadth) and shape (streamlined, branched, bushy), and the "pull" on the plant is, of course, a measure of such resistance and the possibility for damage. *P. pectinatus* offers medium to low resistance and *P. crispus* low resistance.

The preference of a species for a particular substrate is influenced and altered by other characteristics of the environment, especially rate of flow. With large numbers of observations, however, some associations of plant and substrate are revealed. *P. natans* prefers a peaty substrate but can grow in several soil types, while the presence of *P. pecti-*

natus is best correlated with mud and silt. To maintain a hold on a site, most aquatic species depend on firm anchorage in substrates to which they are adapted. Plants that are torn loose will wash away. If severed at the stem, many types of aquatics have the opportunity to grow again. *P. crispus* breaks at the stem when pulled with a low to moderate force of 200 to 750 g when rooted in a medium to coarse substrate. *P. pectinatus* either breaks at the stem or is dislodged an equal number of times at this force if in the same substrate. If in a medium substrate, it performs this way at 200 g or less, and, on a coarse substrate, a stronger pull of 750 g may be needed to dislodge it.

Plants respond differently to the battering and bruising that results from fast water flows and the attendant pulling at their leaves and stems. *P. pectinatus* and *P. crispus* are intermediate in their tolerance of such treatment, and *P. natans* is very tolerant. Although the former two species may be broken at the stems in the turbulent waters following storms, the damage to such plants often depends upon the seasonal stage of growth. In one instance in a 3-meter-wide stream that was dominated by *P. pectinatus* in the early phase of growth, the plants suffered little injury and were easily replaced after the stream flow was more than doubled by a storm. This species slows in growth in summer and begins to die back in early autumn. A later storm that affected the same stream brought a very heavy increase in flow that removed 80% of the vegetation, and the foliage was not replaced in that year.

From government records in the United Kingdom and with knowledge of species locations in many rivers, Haslam (1978) put together a comprehensive summary correlating nutrients and water quality with plant species distribution. Our three *Potamogeton* ranked together in their preference of alkalinity (as $CaCO_3$) at 170 to 250 ppm, biological oxygen demand at 2.5 to 4 ppm, and for the NH_3 form of nitrogen at 0.1 to 0.3 ppm. *P. pectinatus* and *crispus* were similar in their preference for a *pH* above 8 and for total dissolved solids above 500 ppm, but beyond this the species were quite individualistic in their requirements. *P. pectinatus* had its best correlation with NO_3 nitrogen above 6 ppm, NO_2 nitrogen above 0.1 ppm, Cl at 65 to 100 ppm, PO_4 phosphorus at 0.3 to 1.2 ppm, and a total water hardness ($CaCO_3$ plus $MgCO_3$) of over 350 ppm. *P. natans* showed its best association with water containing Cl at 35 to 65 ppm, PO_4 phosphate below 0.3 ppm, total dissolved solids below 350 ppm, and a total hardness of 100 to 350 ppm. Many of the species studied were not consistent in their preference for the various nutrients found in river water. For additional detailed information on the range of each component of the total water chemistry and for a further similar attempt to correlate species distribution with inorganic nutrients present in the silt substrate, see Haslam (1978) and Hellquist (1980).

Haslam's work examines another aspect of plant distribution in rivers. She has summarized the species' preference for sites across channels (bank to bank) of many rivers, preference along the channels, downstream changes, the influence of shading from above, behavior in the turbulence caused by wire and bridge structures, and finally the various changes in stream plants with topography and geology as the water courses through hard calcareous rock, soft sandstone, clay chalk, and other geologic materials.

In a large field and laboratory study of the Tennessee Valley Authority river scheme, a large power development project in the central United States, Peltier and Welch (1969) found that *P. pectinatus*, a principal weed, grew as well in tap water as it did in river water that was several times richer in nutrients. This suggests that other factors had greater influence on biomass production. For example, the net change in the weed biomass production dropped from 8 g/cm^2/day in the 3-wk period following April 12, to 1.8 g for the 3 wk following May 5. Light measurements showed that available light decreased by 25% during this time frame.

In Israel, Waisel (1970) studied the effect of temperature on the growth of ten submerged aquatic plants. Nine of the ten, including *P. pectinatus*, were thermophilic, with very high growth rates in the warm summer. When the temperature fell below 20°C, the plants produced turions and were dormant. The growth of *P. crispus* was restricted to cooler water temperatures; growth stopped at 30°C and turions were produced.

In Great Britain, it is a standard practice to cut *P. pectinatus* and other species one or more times per season. Some species respond with flushes of growth from the remaining plant material but *P. pectinatus* does not. In unusual seasons when nutrients are very high and with very favorable growth conditions, three or four cuttings may be necessary for all species (Haslam 1978).

Jupp and Spence (1977) studied the growth of *P. pectinatus* in exposed and sheltered sites in a lake in Scotland where biomass production was quite low when compared with other published data on this species. Wave action and waterfowl grazing led to decreases in biomass productivity, and this was confirmed by transplanting individuals between sheltered and protected sites. At season's end, the production was 80% less in disturbed sites as compared with protected areas. They believe the fine particles of mud that accumulate on the substrate of sheltered sites contain nutrients that promote plant growth.

Jana and Choudhuri (1979) studied photosynthesis, photorespiration, and dark respiration in three submerged species, *P. pectinatus*, *Hydrilla*, and *Vallisneria*, in distilled water in the laboratory. Dark and photorespiration were highest in *P. pectinatus*, and they suggest that this may explain, in part, the less vigorous growth of the species when it must compete with *Hydrilla* and some other submerged species. It is assumed that all of the species are basically C_3 plants.

In Japan, the optimum temperature for photosynthesis in *P. crispus*, *Ceratophyllum*, and *Cabomba* was 30°C. The maximum rates of apparent photosynthesis for these three species were, respectively, 4.43, 4.5, and 3.86 μl O_2/dry weight mg/hr (Saitoh et al. 1970). CO_2 is the carbon source normally used, but a significant amount of bicarbonate may be assimilated under alkaline conditions (Kadono 1980).

The speed of water movement has a profound effect on the distribution of water plants because it influences the characteristics of the bottom substrate, turbidity, temperature, and many other factors. Metabolic rates are usually higher in flowing water than in still water and sometimes by a factor of 10. Using laboratory apparatus, Westlake (1967) studied photosynthesis rates at water velocities of 0.02 to 0.5 cm/sec, rates lower than those in open, flowing water but comparable to water movement in lakes and streams with beds of weeds. At the lower velocities, photosynthesis increased rapidly with velocity, but the rate fell off at higher flow rates.

The size and carbohydrate content of different organs of *P. pectinatus* were studied by Hodgson (1966) in a chamber under controlled conditions. He found that new plants must grow at least 16 days before they become self-sufficient. Plants were grown at 21°C under 400 foot-candles of light for a 14-hr photoperiod and were harvested daily for 30 days. Unsprouted tubers had a 20% dry weight, with 75% being carbohydrate. The supply decreased by half during each 5-day period, whereas shoots began to grow logarithmically at 11 days and doubled their weight every 4.5 days. Plants grown from average tubers increased 7-fold in dry weight in 30 days.

The communities of plants in the various zones of water bodies normally undergo changes over a period of years. This process is often accelerated when man is near and actively engaged in the pursuit of water for power, irrigation, impoundment for multiple uses, navigation, and other uses. The forces of nature, of which hurricanes and tornadoes are examples, create great winds and waves, cause fluctuations in water level and velocity, and may alter salinity. The domination of an area by adventive fishes, rodents, or other animals and the combination of forces during serious flooding may all bring influence to bear on the structure of the plant communities. Sometimes the changes are slow, subtle, ecological shifts that bring gradual shifts among the species of a community. These are often difficult to explain. At other times, a species or community may suffer a sudden decline over a large area and such striking changes sometimes stimulate investigations that add greatly to our knowledge of water plants. On occasion these are dismissed with such comments as "too much salt" or "too much pollution," etc., but the alterations are seldom simple and are rarely explained by a single cause.

An example of such a change is the decline of *M. spicatum* and other submerged species in Chesapeake Bay on the eastern shore of the United States in the years following 1963. The weed infested about 40,000 ha of the bay but was reduced to a very low level in 4 yr. Accompanying this phenomenon was the decline of *P. pectinatus* and *crispus* as well as *Ceratophyllum* and *Vallisneria*. One portion of the area, the Rhode River, for example, was dominated by a heavy load of *M. spicatum* in 1964, while *Potamogetons*, *Elodea*, and other submerged species were subdominants. In 1965, all of these species grew until they had almost reached the surface in mid-June. By mid-August, a slow decline was obvious, and the species almost disappeared. The stands were reduced by 90% in 1966, and the plants were almost absent in 1967. Diseases, changes in salinity, increased carp (fish) populations, turbidity, and several other explanations have been offered, but alteration in such a large number of species over a large and variable area does not suggest a single simple answer as a cause of such sharp changes. The decline of several species in this area was reviewed in detail by Elser (1969).

For those interested in an intensive study of the zonation of plants, we recommend the very comprehensive survey of literature on this subject by Spence (1982). Data are included on plant behavior in selected freshwater bodies on all continents, with frequent mention of *Potamogeton crispus*, *natans*, and *pectinatus*. Included are the horizontal and vertical variables found in such waters (for example, topography, movement of water, and sediment changes). The distribution of plants in response to these environmental conditions is discussed.

Some believe that plants and animals are the world's best organic chemists and man has taken up an eternal search for their chemical compounds to supply food, shelter, medicines, sustenance for his animals, and chemicals for industry. For our species these may be studied in such documents as "Handbook of Utilization of Aquatic Plants" by Little (1979), in which he has attempted a world summary of important research papers on composition, methods of harvest and processing, and utilization. A small summary of each paper is provided and many tables are gathered. Boyd and Scarsbrook (1975) summarized the literature on the chemical composition of a large number of aquatic weeds of North America, including macro and micronutrients, amino acids, and caloric content. In these and the research papers cited below, *P. pectinatus*, *crispus*, and *natans* are often included.

Gerloff and Krombholz (1966), Riemer and Toth (1969), Hill (1979), Burton et al. (1977), and Rawlence and Whitton (1977) have reported analyses for organic and inorganic compounds in a large number of species of aquatic plants. Kollman and Wali (1976) made a very detailed study of the water characteristics and nutrient dynamics of freshwater lakes across the northern United States. Sharma and Singh (1980) reported on amino acid content of eight aquatic species of weeds of India, including *P. pectinatus*. The nutrient value of aquatic plants for animal feed varies with season, age of plant, the hydrosoil, and several other environmental parameters. Boyd (1968, 1974) has reviewed these uses, and Easley and Shirley (1974) analyzed *P. pectinatus* and other hydrophytes for ten nutrients important for livestock. They found the content of plants from their sites were comparable to those of terrestrial forages. Linn et al. (1975) studied 22 freshwater aquatic weeds for their potential feed value and ran tests on lambs that were fed ensiled alfalfa and ensiled maize mixed with *P. pectinatus*. The dry matter, nitrogen, digestibility and energy supplied were lower when aquatic plants were included in their mix.

SALINITY

The tolerance of hydrophytes to salinity is a remarkable story. The waters of the sea are at a concentration of 35,000 ppm or 3.5% salt. Some plants, including *P. pectinatus*, can stand a considerable quantity of brackish water in their natural sites, but most shy away from 3000 to 4000 ppm. *Halodule wrightii*, a perennial monocotyledon with linear grass-like foliage, normally found in marine waters in tropical regions, was found growing in Texas, in the United States in lagoons that have a salt concentration of more than 60,000 ppm (Conover 1964).

The move from fresh to saline water involves physical and biological interrelationships that are very complex and it is therefore not surprising to find contradictory information on a given species. Luther (1951) in Finland has grouped the aquatic plants of his area according to their salt tolerance. *P. natans* could grow only at 2000 ppm or less, while *P. pectinatus*, which grows elsewhere in both fresh and brackish water, is found only in brackish areas in this country. The latter species was found in both calm and turbulent sites at high salinities but only in turbulent places when salinity was low.

Sculthorpe (1967) reviewed the distribution of certain freshwater aquatic species in salty inland lakes on several continents. *P. pectinatus* is in shallow brackish lakes on surface salt deposits in England and in shallow lakes of the plains of the central United States where water stands on the salt-rich Cretaceous strata of arid regions where evaporation exceeds rainfall. Here Ca and Mg are the main cations, *pH*s are 8.5 to 9, solute concentrations are high, and sulphates may be more than 150 ppm. This species is in four volcanic lakes in El Salvador that are notably high in Cl, SO_4, P, and Na, and in lakes at 1000 m in New Mexico, in the United States, that have a total solute concentration of 25,000 ppm.

Bourn (1932) showed experimentally that dry matter production of *P. pectinatus* on the east coast of the United States was stimulated by increasing salt content in water up to 9000 ppm. In a growth study at several NaCl concentrations, Teeter (1965) found that 1-wk-old plants of this species were severely inhibited at 9000 ppm but recorded a small amount of new growth at 12,000 ppm in 4-wk- to 8-wk-old plants. Low salt concentrations reduced seed germination severely. A concentration of 15,000 ppm (about 43% sea water) killed plants of this species.

Shepherd and Bowling (1973) demonstrated that the roots of *P. natans* actively accumulate Na in their natural environment in a freshwater lake in northern Scotland. Their data indicate that the accumulative process is most active when the external concentration of Na is low. K, NO_3, and Cl were also actively accumulated, while Ca and Mg appeared to be in electrochemical equilibrium with the lake water.

POLLUTION

The rampant growth of aquatic weeds in vast areas of freshwater within the sight of man has become a symbol of our failure to manage our affairs properly. Our attention has been sharply drawn to the role of N and P in the enrichment of these valuable water resources that we assume will be hospitable to all of the aquatic angiosperms because they are required as a life support system for all plant and animal life in watery habitats. If pollutants carry excess N and P, some hydrophytes, once rooted, may prosper.

Thus we see that pollution has two faces. With the sudden mysterious dieback of several aquatic angiosperms over thousands of hectares, as reported for bays of the eastern United States, perhaps in part from pollution, we become alarmed, for they are the principal resource for the prosperity and maintenance of all of the large and small plants and animals in such watery habitats. On the other hand, when streams are no longer navigable because of the excessive growth of the same aquatic plants, the streams are now said to be polluted by weed vegetation.

One of the plants most tolerant of pollution is *P. pectinatus*, and it sometimes proceeds upstream beyond other water plants and may even invade heavily polluted zones at times. Because of its linear leaves, it tends, even when the flow rate is very slow, to free itself from settling particles. It is not generally colonized by filamentous sewage bacteria and fungi. The other *Potamogetons* are not as tolerant as *P. pectinatus*.

The studies of pollution effects on water plants reported in the literature are very difficult to compare because the toxicants and their concentrations are often not specified. To say that a water body carries a small or large level of pollution does not give information for comparisons. For example, Sahai and Sinha (1976) studied the net primary productivity of *P. pectinatus* and *crispus* with several other submerged species in sites with and without pollution in a eutrophic lake in India. Pollutants entered from a stream used for washing by the local inhabitants and in raw sewage from the settlement nearby. *Hydrilla verticillata*, the most tolerant of the species studied, was reduced in growth by 30%, whereas *P. pectinatus*, which is usually very tolerant of pollution elsewhere, was reduced by 93%. *P. crispus* was reduced by 78%. The pollutants and their concentrations were not specified.

Howard-Williams and Davies (1979) in South Africa studied the release of elements from decomposing *P. pectinatus* by collecting leaves before die off, placing them in plastic bags and lowering them in a natural area with the canopy as it sank. The rate of decay was 2% per day and was complete in 158 days. The original supply of K and P leached more rapidly than dry matter in early decomposition. Almost all of the K and 60% of the P were lost in the first 7 days. The proportions of N and P in the decomposing detritus increased significantly in the final stages of decomposition, providing a rich food source for the abundant filter-feeding animals of the littoral zone. The half-life (time needed for initial mass to be reduced to 50%) for *P. pectinatus* is 35 days, which is very rapid as compared to emergent species. By comparison, the decay half-time for several *Typha* species in England varied from 90 to 425 days. It was 11 days for *Eichhornia crassipes*, water hyacinth, in Brazil. The most rapid of those recorded were 2.3 days for *P. perfoliatus* and 2.7 days for *P. lucens* in Poland. The latter disappeared completely in 18 days.

In an effort to shed light on the fate of nutrients as they entered and were recycled in a lake, Howard-Williams (1981) carried out enrichment experiments on an entire community of flora and fauna under controlled conditions. The treatments used were 5, 10, 25 and 100 mg of P and 50, 100, 250, and 1000 mg of N/m^2/wk. The treatments continued for

15 wk for the lower rates and 23 wk for the two higher rates and controls. The highest levels were not sufficient to overload the capacity of this natural community, although there was a slight rise in soluble active P seen after 10 wk in the 100-mg weekly treatment.

In *P. pectinatus*, P is taken up through both roots and leaves. In a later study of P cycling in Lake Swartlei, Howard-Williams and Allanson (1981) found that the sediments have a far larger reserve of nutrients than the lake water and that, during the growing season, more P is taken up by *Potamogeton* than enters the lake from inflows, thus indicating that the substrate is the principal P source for this species. In all of the work, the tissue concentrations of P and N were found to be low, but the very large biomass of the plants in this lake means that, with the exception of the sediments, the macrophytes have the largest reserve, and the major nutrient pathway from these plants is back into the water in soluble form. The results of the studies lead to agreement with the hypothesis of Godshalk and Wetzel (1976) that in warm aerobic conditions there is almost a complete breakdown of macrophytic tissue, with very little sedimenting out as particulate matter. Thus, in the end, the major nutrient pathway is from sediment through macrophytes to the water.

In spite of the input of P from macrophytes during decomposition, a rise in soluble reactive P or total dissolved P could not be detected in the water even when the sampling intervals were as short as 8 hr. This suggested an efficient mechanism to retain and trap P in the community, and the results, indeed, indicated that epiphytic algae, filter-feeding animals, and the *Potamogeton*-periphyton complex were responsible. As the P is released, it is apparently trapped almost immediately. The littoral zone thus acts as a sieve and a trap for dissolved organic material. It is a nutrient sink, and the major component is the sediment with its surface detrital layer. The larger reservoir of nutrients in the littoral zone plays a vital role in the life of the lake.

Mulligan et al. (1976) planted several submerged vascular species in 0.1-ha ponds and supplied them with low and high fertility for 1 yr. In the high level, 75 and 7.5 mg/L of N and P, respectively, the phytoplankton bloom eliminated *Myriophyllum spicatum*, while *Elodea canadensis* survived and made some growth. *P. crispus* was not harmed and proceeded to form large quantities of healthy winter buds.

ECONOMIC IMPORTANCE

In India, *P. pectinatus* is a serious weed of general waterways, including the mains and canals of irrigation systems and small and large lakes, sloughs and jheels. It is a principal weed of such water bodies in Australia, Egypt, the United Kingdom, and the United States. It is also troublesome in Brazil, Canada, and Hawaii. *P. crispus* is a principal weed of general waterways and irrigation schemes in Australia, Bangladesh, Czechoslovakia, Egypt, Germany, India, Sudan, and the United Kingdom, and it is a common weed of such sites in the United States. It is a troublesome weed in aquatic places in Brazil, Japan, the Netherlands, New Zealand, and the Philippines. *P. natans* is a principal water weed in India, a common weed in Australia, and is a troublesome weed in Brazil.

In rice, *P. crispus* is a principal weed in China and a weed of unknown rank in Bangladesh, Hungary, Iran, and Portugal. *P. natans* is a principal weed of rice in Madagascar, a common weed in China, and present but of unknown rank in rice in Hungary, Portugal, and Spain. *P. pectinatus* is a weed of unknown rank in China, Hungary, India, and Iran.

The *Potamogetons* are major weeds worldwide in the reservoirs of municipal water supplies, in recreation waters, the water used for industrial power and steam, and navigable waters. In the Nile River, *P. pectinatus* is one of the three most prevalent aquatic weeds north of Cairo. In Egypt, regular cleaning of the canals has promoted submerged aquatic weed growth and *P. natans* and *pectinatus* are among the most troublesome.

P. pectinatus is one of the common weeds at altitudes of 1600 to 4000 m in northern India (Kaul et al. 1973). In Australia and the United States flow reductions of 95% are caused by dense stands of these weeds. As the temperature rises in spring in the Netherlands, *P. crispus* is one of the aquatic weeds that must be controlled. *Potamogetons* rank among the troublesome weeds in the waterways of Poland.

These species are important elements of the aquatic environment as direct suppliers of food, shade, shelter, and spawning sites for fish, waterfowl, and the insects necessary for many small animals. The buds and foliage are relished by partridge, pheasants, deer, beaver, and muskrats. Anderson and Low (1976) believe these weed species may be the most important food for waterfowl in North America. In study areas in the wild, they found that waterfowl harvested 40% of foliage and buds in one season.

The fish *Tilapia zillii* has become important for control of these and other weeds in the western United States, particularly in the canals of the Sonoran Desert area. It has also become an important game fish for the region (Legner and Murray 1981). In the Chambal irrigation scheme in northern India, the grass carp, *Ctenopharyngodon idella*, has a high preference for *P. pectinatus*.

For information on mosquito larval habitats in the dense mats of *P. pectinatus*, as well as an extract of the weed found to be toxic to the mosquito, see Balling and Resh (1985) and Graham and Schooley (1985).

COMMON NAMES

Potamogeton crispus

AUSTRALIA	curly pondweed
BANGLADESH	pata jhanji
BELGIUM	gekruld fonteinkruid, potamot crepu
CANADA	curly-leaved pondweed, potamot crepu
CHINA	shar-choa
DENMARK	kruset vandaks
EGYPT	ghazl, hillis, khass zelf
ENGLAND	curled pondweed
FINLAND	poimuvita
FRANCE	potamot crepu
GERMANY	Krauses Laichkraut
ITALY	lattuga ranina
JAPAN	ebimo
NETHERLANDS	gekroesd fonteinkruid
NEW ZEALAND	curled pondweed
NORWAY	krustjonnaks

PORTUGAL	carvalhas
SWEDEN	krusnate
UNITED STATES	curlyleaf pondweed

Potamogeton natans

BELGIUM	drijvend fonteinkruid, potamot negeant
DENMARK	svommende vandaks
ENGLAND	broad-leaved pondweed
FRANCE	potamot
GERMANY	Schwimmendes Laichkraut
ICELAND	blookunykra
ITALY	lattuga ranina
MADAGASCAR	valatendro
NORWAY	vanleg tjonnaks
PORTUGAL	colher de folha larga
SPAIN	espiga de agua, llengua d'oca
SWEDEN	gaddnate
UNITED STATES	floatingleaf pondweed

Potamogeton pectinatus

ARGENTINA	espiga de agua
AUSTRALIA	fennel pondweed, sago pondweed
BELGIUM	kamfonteinkruid, potamot pectine
CANADA	potamot pectine, sago pondweed
CHILE	huiro, luchecillo
DENMARK	borstebladet vandaks
EGYPT	'alaaq, sha'ar el bint, sha'er el hosaan
ENGLAND	fennel-leaved pondweed
FINLAND	hapsivita
FRANCE	potamot pectine
GERMANY	Kammformiges, Laichkraut
JAPAN	ryunohigemo
NETHERLANDS	schedefonteinkruid
NEW ZEALAND	pondweed
NORWAY	bust-tjonnaks
PORTUGAL	limo-mesto
SPAIN	senill
SWEDEN	borstnate
UNITED STATES	bushy pondweed, sago pondweed

Seventy-Five

Pteridium aquilinum (L.) Kuhn

Dennstaediaceae, Fern Family

THE FRONDS OF A LARGE PLANT of *Pteridium aquilinum* bracken fern resemble the great wingspread of the eagle, hence the specific name from Latin, *aquila* for eagle. The genus *Pteridium* is monotypic; it is on all the continents including Antarctica, and may be one of the most widely distributed vascular plants on earth. It is not found in extremely cold or dry areas. It is a very ancient plant that has become a very successful modern weed. Oinonen (1967a,b) in Finland estimated that some bracken clones may be about 1500 years old. Page (1986) suggested some clones of bracken may be amongst the

FIGURE 75-1   The distribution of *Pteridium aquilinum* (L.) Kuhn across the world where it has been reported as a weed.

FIGURE 75-2 *Pteridium aquilinum* (L.) Kuhn: A. habit; B. pinnules showing marginal
sori; C. marginal glands.

oldest living things in the contemporary landscape. This fern appears to have several chemical compounds that cause very serious illnesses in humans and stock animals. It is a weed of 20 or more crops in 65 countries (Figure 75-1).

DESCRIPTION

P. aquilinum (Figure 75-2) is a *perennial* fern; *rhizomes* cord-like, creeping extensively, repeatedly branched, dark colored or black, 5 to 15 mm diameter, may be several meters long, some varieties (types) may be hairy with others hairy only at tip; *croziers* in groups of 3 with silvery gray hairs; *fronds* (leaves) alternate, scattered on rhizome, coarse, deciduous, not dimorphic, 35 cm wide, often 1 to 1.5 m tall but may be 3 to 5 m in favorable locations; *stipe* (petiole) deciduous, woody, red brown or dark purple brown at base, generally glabrous, may have hairs near base; *blade* pinnately divided, general shape is broad triangular to ovate, somewhat bipinnate to tripinnate, *pinnae* opposite with lower pair larger than the rest and with nectaries at base (an unusual feature in the pteridophytes), leaf segments numerous, revolute (rolled backward at edge), veins free, grooved above, raised and densely hairy below, reaching leaf margins; *sori* marginal, linear, nearly continuous on underside of leaves; *indusia* (these cover or contain the *sporangia*) silvery white, delicate; *spores* extremely small 25 to 30 microns, brown, very finely spinulose, tetrahedral, globose.

The genus *Pteridium* has been viewed as monotypic, with *P. aquilinum* thought to be the only species over the whole range. This view has been challenged of late. The most comprehensive world-wide treatment of the genus was by Tryon (1941), who accepted the monotypic position and designated two subspecies: *aquilinum* with eight varieties principally in the North Temperate Zone, covering Central and North America, Africa, Eurasia, north Queensland, and the Hawaiian Islands; and *caudatum* with three (or four) varieties which was assigned to those plants of the southern hemisphere that occur mainly in a part of Central America, in South America, and throughout Australasia and the South Pacific. Brownsey (1989) reported that *P. esculentum* was the most common and widespread of the bracken ferns in Australia, whereas the second species *P. revelutum* was in northern Australia. He believes that sterile hybrids exist between these two. If so, this would be the first record of wild hybrids in *Pteridium* and it gives further evidence that the concept of a monotypic genus is incorrect.

The distribution of the varieties in the world and their adaptations to their principal range and habitat may be found in Tryon (1941) and Page (1986).

DISTRIBUTION AND HABITAT

As may be seen from Figure 75-1, bracken fern is distributed over most of the world. In cold climates in autumn, late emerging fronds are killed and this shortens the adult life of the plant. In spring the plant may be crippled by a frost-kill of the fronds. If litter is insufficient in winter, freezing may kill some underground rhizome apices and those of differentiating fronds not yet emerged. Aside from these limitations, it has full range over the earth.

It is in the temperate climatic zones of the Andes Mountains in South America and is already colonizing the newly deforested areas of Brazil (Martins and DeCarvalho 1982). It is found at 3000 m in East Africa and Japan, and is at 3250 m in the Rocky Mountains of the United States. The plant tends to avoid extreme heat, yet it is found, for example, at sites a few degrees from the equator in the Galapagos Islands (where craters rise to 1700 m) and in Burundi in East Africa (2800 m).

Bracken has shown the ability to accommodate to a vast range of climatic conditions, exposures, soil types (depth and drainage are important aspects) and *pH* levels. An example would be its acclimatization from the northern United States border to lat 60° N, where the temperature varies from −15 to 21°C mean temperature winter to summer, the rainfall from 60 to 165 mm, and snow depth from 10 to 50 cm (Cody and Crompton 1975).

The plant may often be found on dry, rather sterile stony or sandy soils in open woods and on railroad and highway verges. It is found throughout the former Soviet Union from coniferous to deciduous woods, in brushy thickets on slopes and often on dry sandy soils. In Uganda it is a ubiquitous weed, common in grasslands and in waste places (Tiley 1970). The plant is also found over a large area of dry fields south of lat 17° N in India. Thus we see that this species, so often an inhabitant of cool, moist habitats is also a resident of open, exposed places that tend to be arid. It lives in the latter places at the expense of a lowered photosynthetic rate, for the stomata close quickly during periods of high evaporation, thus limiting CO_2 uptake. Cuticular loss is also reduced. In open, dry, exposed locations the litter may be blown away, resulting in fronds that are undernourished, short, and few in number (Bright 1928, Tinklin and Bowling 1969, Pitman and Pitman 1986, Roberts 1986).

Watt (1976) makes the point that the tallest measured fronds in the British Isles (often 3 to 4 m) are in woods and brush where the plants are sheltered, often with fronds supported by the woody branches of other plants. Page (1976) suggests that in undisturbed areas bracken is not an aggressive species. In woodland areas it operates as a pioneer in locations of open canopy but recedes and disappears as the forest closes in. If the forest is removed by man or because of fire, the bracken again returns to colonize the area. Although bracken has many morphological and physiological characteristics that enable it to prosper in different kinds of areas, Page feels that it is often aided by man's lack of an ecological appreciation of the consequences of his own activity.

Poel (1951, 1960, 1961) and Watt (1964) have shown the sensitivity of bracken to low O_2 levels in soil and thus its almost complete absence from marshes and waterlogged heavy soils. In swampy areas, rhizomes persist by growing around the emerged edges of embedded stones and isolated islands, biding time until evaporation and/or drainage again provide suitable soil conditions with adequate O_2 supply. The vertical distribution of rhizomes in different soil types may be influenced mainly by the O_2 diffusion rates in such soils.

Young sporelings need adequate N, P, and K. Older sporophytes responded more to N and K than to other nutrients (Conway and Stephens 1957). Using several soil series, Hunter (1953) compared nutrient supply with vigor of growth and found little correlation between them. He thought the moisture supply was the controlling factor in growth in many cases.

After a lifetime of work on bracken, Watt (1976) feels that bracken will be found mainly on nutrient-poor, acidic soils. It can also prosper on rich soils if they have not already been secured by man in his own interest for crops and animals. It is rare on calcareous soils in the British Isles, often with chlorosis on the fronds. Conway and Stephens (1957) have shown that the presence of calcium in larger or smaller amounts, however, is not the primary factor controlling the amount of bracken on such an area. Bracken types with a preference for calcareous soils are reported from the former Soviet Union (Komarov 1968).

In a summary of the management of troublesome weeds of meadows and pastures in Japan, Nemoto (1982) pointed out that bracken is encouraged by frequent mowing in semi-natural pastures, presumably because it tolerates the practice better than other species in the community. In the grasslands of the European Alps, bracken thrives in permanent pasture that is undergrazed, and was one of the few plants that had better competitive ability in areas left unfertilized (Dietl 1982).

The advancement of bracken into so many new areas was encouraged in the late Neolithic period (about 50,000 years ago) as the wandering nomadic life declined and there arose more permanent communities with pastures and cropland nearby. With these came deforestation for buildings and fuel. This altered human activity permitted greater encroachment by the fern. There was need for land for husbandry, but in medieval times the larger animals such as cattle, horses, large sheep and goats tended to keep bracken under control by foraging and trampling. Today's smaller sheep are more selective in foraging, cannot tolerate bracken, and do not trample and crush the fern as the larger animals had done (Taylor 1988).

BIOLOGY

Professor Alex Watt (1882–1985) of Cambridge University in England devoted 60 years of his life to the study of bracken and we are all indebted to him for our basic understanding of the biology of bracken fern. With other researchers, he was influential in arranging a Linnaean Society symposium on *The Biology of Bracken*. The record was published in the Botanical Journal of the Linnaean Society (volume 73) in 1976 and is a significant help for those interested in morphology, physiology, ecology and the complex structure and behavior of the very large and old clones of this plant. In his studies of population biology, Harper (1977) suggested that the most detailed study of the structure and population dynamics of the parts of a clone-forming plant may be that of Watt (1945, 1947, 1970). In the above symposium, Watt (1976) summarized some of the major observations and findings of his lifetime of research on bracken. Salient points from this and others of his publications are included in the biology that is summarized below (Watt 1940, 1942, 1950, 1954, 1955, 1964, 1967, 1969, 1971). For other reviews on bracken biology, see Cody and Crompton (1975), Rymer (1976), Page (1976, 1986), Fletcher and Kirkwood (1979), Smith and Taylor (1986), Taylor (1986), Jones (1987), and Lawton (1988).

The bracken fern can quickly colonize an area by means of underground roots and rhizomes, but the long-range dispersal is by spores. Under suitable conditions, the germinating spore gives rise to a small sexual plant called prothallus, about 1 cm in size. This bears the reproductive cells, forming male gametes, the spermatozoids, in antheridia; and female gametes, the oogonia, in archegonia. Under moist conditions, the spermatozoids are released and propelled by flagella to the archegonia, where fertilization takes place. In extended dry periods, fertilization may be restricted, for the prothallus is but one cell thick and sensitive to desiccation. Prothalli can produce new sporophytes in 6 wk, following which new rhizomes and fronds develop, with the new plant capable of spore production in the next season. Clones of the fern are remarkable for their long life; some have been estimated to be several centuries old.

VEGETATIVE AND SEXUAL REPRODUCTION

Depending on environmental circumstances, the bracken rhizome biomass is composed mostly of large rhizomes at greater soil depths (often referred to as long shoots) that produce few fronds, and smaller rhizomes near the surface (referred to as short shoots) that produce most of the fronds. There are also intermediary branches that may explore both depths and can develop into either of the above types. The deep, long shoots are the main storage organs and may extend 30 to 200 cm in one season, while the short shoots are often 1 to 2 cm long. In excavations, Watt (1976) found dense, branching rhizome systems with 9 m of total length underlying each m^2 of ground. On some podzols in Great Britain, Watt estimated that rhizomes in some bracken stands were 70 years old and only one-half of that in soils where decay was more rapid. As previously mentioned, Oinonen (1967a,b; 1968) in Finland found that war, with its accompanying fires, provided ideal places for spore germination. From historical records, he has estimated that some clones covering 15 ha may be 1400 years old.

The rhizome may overwinter if insulated by sufficient litter, the depth of which may vary from 0 to almost 1 m. Conway (1952) in Scotland constructed special trenches for the accurate measurement of rhizome growth by the season. Rhizomes grew most vigorously in autumn, when large numbers of frond buds were also initiated. In spring, those fronds which are to emerge first complete the extension of the petiole before the lamina unfolds. In Australia, O'Brien (1963) found rhizome branching reached a maximum in late spring and early summer. He also learned that many frond primordia do not survive the summer. Hellum (1964) in the United States found that bracken emergence times in spring were so closely correlated with the prevailing temperature that an unusual warm spell in May triggered early emergence. Such events, when followed by a frost, can damage new growth and be a severe setback to the plant. Watt (1940) found that the terminal bud of the rhizome may be dormant for one year or it may produce two internodes per year.

Daniels (1985) planted different types of rhizome segments and found the overall capacity for regeneration was about the same for all of them. Renewal capacity was the same with or without an apical bud on the segment. All pieces produced new rhizomes, lateral buds, and fronds in the first season; however, the patterns of growth that followed regeneration differed with the type of rhizome piece and its origin. For example, more new lateral buds were produced from segments without an apical bud.

Conway (1952) buried a small rhizome fragment in spring and it grew 32 cm in length and produced seven side branches in 22 wk. The original piece had one frond bud, but now the plant had two expanded fronds and 25 frond buds. Some frond buds remain in reserve in case of fire, drought or mechanical damage. Subsequently the plants in Conway's experiment produced 45, 136, and 300 fronds in years 2 to 4, respectively.

Colonies of bracken vary greatly in quantity of spores produced; some produce no spores. After a survey of several years, Conway (1957) found that individual fronds within a colony varied from 0 to 90% in spore production. A large, healthy frond can produce 300 million spores (Conway 1952). In general the lower, early fronds are sterile, whereas the heaviest production takes place on large fronds, often on 2nd and 3rd pairs. Spore dispersal may begin on lower branches while sporangia above are still maturing. Sporulation times vary greatly and often influenced by short-term weather conditions. In Canada, for example, Cody and Crompton (1975) found that earliest sporulation times varied from June 24 in central Canada (Ontario) to August 23 in far eastern Newfoundland. If spore production is late, fewer spores, or none, may be produced. The process is influenced by age of colony, soil fertility and climate. Increasing shade or the presence of a plant near a rapidly advancing front may reduce sporulation.

As the spores, which are 25 to 30 microns in size, are ejected from sporangia (1 to 2 cm paths) in dry weather, they may be caught up in air currents and remain suspended for a long period, perhaps moving long distances. The spores of fern species are difficult to identify, with the result that firm, definitive data are lacking on short- and long-term dispersal of viable fern propagules and their place of origin. In the North Temperate Zone, the number of spores in suspension seems to peak in August and early September. Large deposits may be expected with rainfall at these seasons. There is evidence that spores are not always dispersed and deposited randomly but may move seasonally in formless clouds.

At the Rothamsted Experiment Station in England, spores were collected 2 m above ground for a full season, with a mean daily count of $4/m^3$. In favorable periods, the count may be in the millions. A small patch of bracken was at a distance of 2.5 km from the trap site, but there were no large areas for several kilometers. Spores have been collected from high altitudes over mid-ocean in the North Temperate Zone. Air pollution studies have found that survival of such spores requires a tolerance of temperature extremes, humidity, and atmospheric pressure, as well as several types of radiation (Wolf 1943, Polunin 1951, Reed 1976). Spores approximate the size of some of the fine particles released at the time of the world's largest volcanic eruption, that of Krakatau in Indonesia in 1883. It is believed the material from that event remained suspended long enough to be carried twice around the world. The importance of spores of various kinds as viable propagules is often measured by the promptness with which they appear on virgin soil from landslides, bomb craters, volcanic eruptions, and the like. Eleven species of ferns, including bracken, were thriving on Krakatau 3 years after the eruption. Only two were species from nearby islands (Polunin 1951). A volcanic eruption formed the unique island of Surtsey off the south coast of Iceland in November, 1963. The first vascular plant appeared in 1965 and 24 species were present in 1988, but *Pteridium* was not yet among them (Fridriksson 1989).

Conway (1957) found no prothalli or sporelings in a bracken stand where the floor was covered with spores, but when pots of soil were placed in the rain of spores and removed to a greenhouse, they germinated in 7 to 10 days. Sporelings appeared at 6 wk. Smith (1938), however, believes that in nature spores do not germinate until the second season. Sporelings may be produced in several kinds of habitats, although they are usually in moist places, in the open, with little competition. Page (1976) has stated, ". . . sporelings are never found to begin life, and survive, in any community of closed vegetation." In the wild, sporelings may be seen growing in cracks in walls on old buildings, but especially in natural areas ravaged by fire (Conway 1949). Conway believes that the scarcity of prothalli in nature is in part due to fungi and **Collembola,** an order of wingless insects called springtails. It may also be that a very specific set of physical and chemical conditions, perhaps rare, must be available in a microsite for a spore to germinate and survive.

Sporelings planted out on good soil in spring produced 22 fronds and a rhizome 140 cm in length by October (Conway 1949). There are no data on the number, age, and viability of bracken spores that survive different types of microsites. Smith (1938) germinated bracken spores 50 yr of age.

Miller (1968) reported that the highest temperature that permitted fern spores, including bracken, to germinate is 30 to 35°C. There are reports of bracken spore germination just above 0°C. Because of biotype variability in bracken, an optimum is difficult to state, but it seems to be about 10 to 20°C.

In laboratory cultural conditions, Conway (1949) found the optimum *pH* range for bracken spore germination to be 5.5 to 7.5, with inhibition setting in at a declining *pH* value of 3. Spores from plants on limestone had higher optima.

In laboratory experiments, spore germination varies with light quality and darkness, different temperatures, and with age of the parent plant when the spores were produced

(Page 1976). If other germination conditions are satisfactory, spores of bracken will germinate in very low to high light intensities (Dubuy and Neurnberg 1938, Page 1976, Howland and Edwards 1979). Nagy et al. (1978) in Hungary found that bracken did not need light for germination, but for continued normal development afterward both light and active phytochrome were required. In the laboratory, long periods of illumination favor spore germination; continuous light is better than alternation of light and darkness. A long period of illumination is better than a short period of light at very high intensity.

Apospory, the production of a gametophyte from a sporophyte by a vegetative process, thus without spore formation or meiosis, has been reported often in bracken and other ferns (Whittier and Steeves 1960; Whittier 1964, 1971; White 1979; Sheffield and Bell 1981a,b; Sheffield 1984). Whittier (1966) suggested that all such cases of "natural apospory" with loss of sexual function should be carefully investigated, for he found "prothalloid" outgrowths or galls were abnormalities that were caused by two *Eriophyes* mites.

MORPHOLOGY AND ANATOMY

On grassland and other open sites, an active bracken clone may exhibit a pattern of zones or stages of top growth. Beneath all this there is an enormous biomass of rhizomes and roots; Watt (1976) found 3 m of rhizome for each actively growing frond in some instances. His description from front to rear of such a clone is as follows: first a band of scattered short fronds (sometimes termed vanguard); next a more dense stand of taller fronds with long petioles; then the crest, a zone of the tallest fronds (in the Canary Islands fronds may be 4 m tall). Behind the crest is a zone approximately 30 m wide of fronds that are shorter. To the rear of all this, the hinterland, are patches of bracken representing several ages and stages of the plant. At the leading edge of this total biomass there may already be an extension of the rhizomes to 1 m with no fronds yet showing. Other species of plants disappear where the canopy is tall and dense and litter accumulates to protect the clone from erosion, wind, and frost (see also Harper 1977).

The rhizome is an axis dying at one end, growing on the other and with alternating branches to right and left. The long shoots can grow in any direction, short shoots generally grow upward, and this orientation is retained if a shoot changes to the other type. A basal bud at the foot of the frond is normally dormant or quiescent for an unknown number of years, but may become active if the main shoot is damaged. Fronds can reach full height in two months. After the first frond emerges, another begins to develop from the short shoot, grows slowly during summer, and then emerges early in the spring. Watt believes that mature plants normally produce one frond per year but that young sporophytes may produce more.

Watt (1976) found that rhizomes under heavily grazed heath were at a depth of 18 to 34 cm, with roots on each side. The roots radiate out in all directions, with two-thirds originating on the lower half of the rhizome. Descending roots (3 mm in diameter) have short branches and may go down to 80 cm, while upper roots quickly become thread-like (1 mm in diameter) and may move up to within 8 cm of the soil surface. As the shoots rise toward the surface, their roots may be 4 to 5 cm in length. There are no adventitious roots. Little is known about the duration of the functional life of a bracken root.

Chemotaxonomy efforts are increasing as attempts are made to sort out the genetic variations of the different kinds of bracken biotypes seen across the world. Cooper-Driver (1976) looked at two-dimensional chromatographic patterns of flavanoid compounds in bracken plants from most areas of the world. The patterns were almost identical no matter where the sample came from. He concludes that bracken is a single species with many varieties.

Isozymes are single gene markers that can be used to sort individuals that are genetically different, providing a sort of "fingerprint" of an individual. Sheffield, Wolf, and co-workers (Sheffield et al. 1989, Wolf et al. 1988) used isozyme analysis to study genetic variability between bracken types and to determine the dimensions of clonal areas occupied by a single genotype. Lee and Oh (1987) in Korea used a morphological taxonomic study to resolve taxonomic problems in working with 15 species of ferns, including *P. aquilinum*. Anatomical and morphological studies of various phases of reproductive development have been reported by Bell and Muhlethaler (1962), Bell and Duckett (1976), Tourte (1975a,b), Elmore and Adams (1976), Demaggio (1977), and Sheffield and Bell (1979). General morphology of the bracken fern has been studied by Gottlieb (1958), Gottlieb and Steeves (1961), Webster and Steeves (1958), and Dasanayake (1960).

PHYSIOLOGY AND ECOLOGY

Page (1986) has called bracken fern "the permanent ecological opportunist." Its polymorphism, coupled with an exceptional tolerance to a broad range of climates, environmental parameters, and edaphic factors, has made this plant the most successful of the ferns and fern allies. This freedom to exploit such an assortment of climates and conditions is an unusual characteristic among pteridophytes.

The carbohydrate reserve of the frond-bearing rhizome is rapidly exhausted from May until early July in the North Temperate Zone and further needs are then drawn from storage rhizomes. At the time of the unfolding of the second pair of pinnae, photosynthesis increases until the plants reach full height. These assimilates, and later transfer of nutrients from senescing fronds, replace the carbohydrate reserves by the end of September (Williams and Foley 1976, Watt 1976).

N, P, and K peak in mid-season, while Ca rises slowly then maintains a steady state until autumn (Fletcher and Kirkwood 1979). Conway and Stephens (1957) reported a beneficial effect of plentiful N, P, and K on foliar bud initials. Hunter (1953) has examined the major and trace element constituents of bracken. Smith and Agiza (1951) examined amino acid content of this fern and compared it with several forage plants. There are some anomalies, in that bracken was very low in threonine and phenylalanine and had no tryptophan.

The ferns have been evolving for about 200 million years, and bracken or near relatives for 55 million years, with the result that they display some resistance to insects and diseases and are not often challenged by severe losses. The insect-moulting hormones, ecdysones and ecdysterones, have been isolated in relatively large quantities from dry bracken pinnae (Kaplanis et al. 1967). These hormones interfere with the growth of insect predators and may discourage foliar feeding. These and other compounds with similar effect have been reviewed by Fletcher and Kirkwood (1979). Jones and Firn (1978) also reviewed the status of such chemicals and in addition made extractions from bracken fronds for use in insect feeding trials. They concluded that during the May–October growing season levels of such compounds are not sufficient in the plant to prevent insect feeding on bracken by the seven insects they studied. The role of insect-feeding deterrents is not well understood for bracken at present.

Bracken does, however, deter invasions by other plants. Gliessman (1976) and Gliessman and Muller (1978) have shown that allelopathic compounds are released from standing fronds in the summer and from decaying vegetation in autumn and winter. These compounds and the physical dominance of the large plant structures serve to weaken and discourage other competitors (see also J. Frankland 1976). For several reasons, the bracken community may thus become monospecific, but the studies of Sparke (1979) have shown that there is a larger number of seeds of a greater variety of species in the soil under this fern than in nearby areas. Removal of the fern, without having a plan for continued land maintenance, may therefore result in an increase in the number and percent of weed species in the sward that follows.

Studies of the litter have shown that it is low in nutrients. Berry (1917) found 2.5% crude protein, 0.8 to 1.3% K, and 0.065% P, with quantities dependent on the nature of the frond and the condition of the habitat. In a 5-yr study on six soil types, J. Frankland (1976) found that decay rates vary with soil types. Most nutrients leached from litter in the first few months and final decay of dry matter required 11 to 23 yr. The majority of the fungi at work were cosmopolitan to litter in general and the population became less specialized as the decomposition proceeded. Pearsall and Gorham (1956) and Watt (1976) found that dry weight production of litter may vary from negligible to 14,000 kg/ha in places where bracken stands are monospecific.

Under very good growing conditions, bracken litter production may exceed decay and become a victim of its own success, finally degenerating and giving way to other species. The rate of gain or loss depends on the site, climate, and fitness of the plant. The layer may vary from zero to almost a meter, but there may be degrees of thickness (even within a single stand) as losses occur from wind, erosion and the influence of man.

Extremes of weather cause weak fronds to break near the ground, where they may more easily join the decaying litter layer, but tall, vigorous fronds may break some distance above ground, supporting one another and making a different type of suspended canopy in a manner that is not favorable for decay (Watt 1970, 1976).

As has been previously mentioned, the roots and rhizomes of bracken tend to rise upward in the soil as the community develops, and the plants thus become more and more dependent on a thinner layer of soil and their own litter. Watt (1976) cites a period of extreme dryness in Great Britain during which surface roots shriveled. In one area the invading front of bracken was a green band 2 m wide, while behind all was yellow. All of the rhizome system was in mineral soil. Because of so much cutting, burning, trampling and soil disturbance over decades, Watt believed there had been no analysis of bracken plants with all rhizomes and roots existing in the litter. In his studies, he became aware of an area where bracken had existed but was subsequently entirely absent for 34 yr, although there was still evidence of bracken remains in the soil. In his phrase, "a bracken plant forced to live on its own remains is forced to grow on a wasting capital," because some nutrients are simply washed away in winter. If the bracken is in a poor soil area, survival may be difficult.

In full natural light and 25% light (shade) at several fertilizer levels, Daniels (1986) found that P alone had no influence, high N increased the number of fronds in shade but not in full light, and low N produced more fronds in full light. Combinations of N and P, or N, P, and K increased rhizome and frond production with greatest response in full light. Only the latter fertilizer treatment increased rhizome dry weight. Fronds in shade differed as follows: they had decreased thickness with thinner cuticle, wider pinnae, a less well developed palisade layer and a more open mesophyll with large air spaces.

BRACKEN TOXICITY

Historical records tell of poisoning from bracken in the last century. Although there is renewed interest in the toxicity to humans and stock animals of late, the weed scientist need not be a specialist in the discovery and definition of chemical compounds responsible for the several types of bracken disorders exhibited by different animal species. The chemistry of these toxic compounds (some quite unstable) and the clinical evidence of injury is fast becoming quite complex. However, short- and long-term management plans for this very widespread weed demand that injury to man and animal be kept in mind at every step. For our purposes, the discussion can only outline the nature and size of the toxicity problem and the research currently under way. Clinical signs may be helpful for those faced with the sick animals of owners who have little understanding of the bracken disorders.

Vitamin B_1 deficiency was one of the first disorders noticed when animals on bracken land became ill. Simple-stomached animals such as horses, mules and pigs must obtain thiamine from their diet; ruminant animals such as cattle and sheep are provided with some of this vitamin by virtue of microbial action in the rumen. It was soon discovered that there are variable and sometimes high levels of thiaminase in some geographical areas and in some strains of bracken. The green fronds and rhizomes seem to be most toxic for this disorder. Horses exhibit staggering and uncertainty as they move, they tire easily, their pulse is rapid but weak, and they lose appetite. Death is preceded by muscle spasms. Reduced blood thiamine levels are recorded.

This acute bracken poisoning is less dramatic in pigs, but when they are afflicted they deteriorate quickly and heart damage is evident upon examination. When diagnosed early, some of these non-ruminant animals can be saved by removing the fern from the diet and by the administration of strong doses of thiamine (Fenwick 1989).

An acute hemorrhagic syndrome, thought to be associated with bracken feeding, was described in ruminant animals (cattle and sheep) at the end of the 19th century. In part because of confusion with anthrax, little research was done on this illness until the mid 20th century (Evans and Evans 1949, Evans 1964). There is a progressive failure of blood-forming bone marrow, with reduced blood platelet numbers and a consequent increase in blood coagulation time. Symptoms in calves are loss of appetite, oral and nasal mucous discharges, heavy breathing, and high temperatures. In addition, in older animals, rumination may cease and the feces may be bloody. Finally, as the number of white blood cells decreases, the animals become susceptible to pathogenic bacteria. There is extensive hemorrhaging of the internal organs and mucous membranes. Sheep are less susceptible to this malady. Another disorder, "bright blindness" in sheep, has been studied by Watson et al. (1965, 1972) and McCrea and Head (1981). This ailment is caused by a constriction of blood vessels, with progressive retinal atrophy, following sustained bracken feeding.

Chronic bovine haematuria (blood in urine) has been reported in Central and South America, the Balkans, Turkey, India, and Scotland, and in water buffalo in China, Indochina, and Taiwan. Hemorrhaging occurs in the urinary bladder mucosa and in bladder wall tumors in later stages. In early stages, the disease is intermittent; it increases in severity as tumors form and there is depression of bone-marrow activity, with reduced levels of red and white blood cells. The time of exposure to bracken, amount consumed and age of the animal influence the development of this sickness.

Most of the above illnesses may also result from ingestion of bracken fronds contained in dry hay or bedding made from bracken fronds.

Bracken fern has shown carcinogenic activity in experimental feeding trials in many places in the world. The plant has caused urinary bladder cancer in cows, rats, and guinea pigs, intestinal adenocarcinomas and sarcomas in rats and Japanese quail, and pulmonary adenomas in mice.

Rosenberger and Heeschen (1960) in Germany provided the earliest evidence for carcinogenicity from bracken. Among the chemical compounds isolated and tested since then are flavanoids, a complex series of inandones (pterosins, pterosides), shikimic acid, tannins, pterolactam and, recently, ptaquilosides. Several of these compounds are now in question because of inconsistencies in the results over several animal species. Research on others has not been acceptable to the International Agency for Cancer Research because of limited evidence or inconsistencies in the results on experimental animals. The isolation procedures and bioassays of these substances have been reviewed by Hirono (1981), Evans (1984) and Fenwick (1989). Soeder (1985) made an extensive review of the literature on the chemical constituents of ferns (including bracken) during 1966 to 1984. Emphasis was on the toxicity to humans and domestic animals.

Hirono (1981) believes there are several reasons for the difficulties encountered in research on bracken toxicity. There is an absence of specific acute toxicity in small laboratory animals, whereas bracken poisoning is easily shown by simply feeding it to cattle. There is no evidence that the factor involved in the acute cattle poisoning illness is the same as that which causes carcinogenic activity, although many carcinogens do produce a similar acute toxicity in the early stages. An additional problem is the necessity of using the larger, expensive animals in greater numbers. Such experiments also require much longer time periods. Further, it is known that bracken carcinogenesis varies with geographical region, with animal species and even within strains of the same species. Working with *P. esculentum*, Smith et al. (1988) of New Zealand studied two sites and found that ferns of one area contained four to seven times more carcinogenicity than the other.

In Canada, China, Japan, Siberia, and Wales, bracken is sometimes grown for human consumption or for herbal remedies. In much of Europe, the plant was only consumed in times of food shortage. In Japan in 1986, 13,000 tons of bracken were imported in salted form. Young bracken is the most popular edible wild food in the country. High incidence of gastric and esophogeal cancer in humans and/or stock animals has been reported from more than one region in Japan and also from Brazil, Costa Rica, Scotland, and Wales. The plant is often cooked, pickled, or processed in some other way, with the result that some of the carcinogenic substances are removed or inactivated. Most studies show that variable amounts remain after these procedures.

A fraction with carcinogenic activity can be obtained in water extracts. This has given rise to the concern that watersheds with dense stands of bracken may pollute local water supplies. Galpin and Smith (1986) completed an extensive study of the influence of environmental factors on the pattern of mortality from gastric cancer in a community in Wales. They found no positive correlation between such deaths and the extent of bracken infestation in the watershed area of the community. It is known that the chemical(s) can be transferred to milk. Here again the concern about local milk supplies from bracken-infested pastures becomes apparent. Can the toxic material be transferred to infants with mother's milk? The question remains open. Many communities now have milk stations where milk is bulked and possibly heat-treated or processed in a way that will dilute or inactivate the carcinogenic activity.

There is no evidence at present that the carcinogen(s) is transferred to the meat of cows, pigs or sheep. Evans (1986) recently reported that bracken spores are carcinogenic and this of course has far-reaching implications for humans and animals.

IMPORTANCE TO HUMANS

Bracken is a serious weed of pastures and rangelands used for forage in Bulgaria, England, Japan, New Zealand, Scotland, and the United States. It is a principal weed of cassava in Colombia; of pastures and grasslands in Brazil, Colombia, Fiji, Ghana, and Uganda; of pineapple in Malaysia; of rubber in Indonesia; of tea in India and vineyards in Greece.

It is a common weed of pastures and grasslands in Austria, Costa Rica, Dominican Republic, Italy, Kenya, Norway, and Spain; of beans and cassava in Madagascar; and of blueberries in the eastern United States.

Also, bracken is a weed of unknown rank in the following crops: pastures in Australia, Belgium, Canada, Colombia, East Africa, Ecuador, Finland, France, Germany, Greece, Panama, South Africa, the former Soviet Union, Switzerland, and Taiwan; maize in Bulgaria and Honduras; tea in Japan and Taiwan; as well as beans, cassava, coffee, orchards, upland rice, sugarcane, sorghum, sweet potatoes, several vegetables, vineyards, and wheat in some of the above countries. Thus we may see that in addition to the stress this fern puts on the land and its flora and fauna, it competes directly with the food and forage plants of agriculture.

As a general nuisance, it is ranked as a serious weed in the United States and a principal weed of Germany and New Zealand. It is a major weed of field crops in West Africa (Akobundu 1987). In a survey of weeds in cassava in Colombia on almost 300 farms in five regions, with data gathered three times during the cropping season, bracken fern was the most frequently listed troublesome weed (Doll et al. 1977). In New Zealand, it is the most widespread weed affecting forestry. In eastern Canada, bracken growth is detrimental to the germination and early survival of spruce, *Picea* spp., and balsam fir, *Abies balsamea* (Place 1953). The control of bracken has been attempted by plowing and cultivating, crushing fronds, applying herbicides, burning and by research on biological control. The location of the bracken stand, accessibility, and the usefulness for agriculture will influence the choice of methods. For example, in the northwestern United States, Angell (1950) reported that the seeding of open, accessible spaces with greater birdsfoot trefoil, *Lotus major*, alta fescue, *Festuca arundinacea*, and red fescue, *F. rubra*, effectively crowded out bracken in 4 to 5 yr.

As for most of the world's bracken, however, there now seems to be a firm conviction that there is little hope of an absolute kill or control until the deep and widespread underground rhizome systems are destroyed or disabled to the point where they are no longer capable of promoting or sustaining frond growth. It is a formidable task—O'Brien (1964) writes of an area in Australia where bracken was defoliated 13 times in one season and still produced new fronds the next spring.

At present the choices are largely mechanical or herbicidal treatments. On suitable terrain, land can be plowed early to mid-summer when nutrient reserves have been reduced throughout the plant, and then cultivated for several years to destroy new fronds arising from rhizome fragments. If a plow cannot be used, the fronds can be cut, otherwise damaged, or burned at about the same time, with additional similar treatments during the season being helpful. By late summer the food reserves of rhizomes are restored and mechanical treatments after this time will not be effective.

Asulam has been used on bracken for more than two decades and is the most successful herbicide treatment for bracken thus far known. Combinations of chemical and/or mechanical treatments are required as follow-up procedures to obtain practical control. Recent newcomers for chemical control are chlorsulfuron (Chancellor and Froud-Williams 1986, Davies and Williams 1987), and glyphosate (Williams 1987, Fenwick 1989).

The experiments of Lowday (1987) in England during six growing seasons provide examples of the use of combined chemical and mechanical control efforts. A treatment with asulam in August reduced the standing bracken by 99% in the first year. Without further treatment, the fronds recovered to the pre-spray level in 6 yr. There was severe damage to frond buds and rhizome apices, but the rhizome network remained intact. In asulam plots and those that received only cutting, new sections of frond-bearing rhizomes developed on the storage rhizomes deep in the soil.

Cutting the bracken once per season in July in the years following the initial spray resulted in an 83% stand reduction of bracken (as compared with untreated plots) at the end of 6 yr. Plots cut once per year developed a closed canopy of fronds by July in the same season. Lowday (1987) pointed out that, without proper follow-up, any of these treatments can cause severe damage to frond-bearing rhizomes (short shoots) at the upper soil levels, with the result that similar new structures may arise deeper in the soil on storage rhizomes (long shoots). The latter can produce vigorous, early emerging fronds. He suggests that, without suitable after-care management of treatments such as those above, there may be an increase in vigor of bracken stand in the long term.

Much of the biological control research on bracken fern has been done in Great Britain. There is no biological control practiced at present. Lawton (1988) recently reviewed the distribution, life histories, and status of two South African moths, *Conservula cinisigna* and *Pantima* sp. near *angularis* (previously referred to *Parthenodes angularis*), as the best-qualified predators for liberation in Great Britain.

After several years of research on biological control of bracken, Lawton (1988) warns that it is not reasonable to expect that such an energetic, robust, and widespread weed will be controlled with a single species of insect. It is his view that no biological control agent has ever completely eliminated a host plant and eradication of bracken is inconceivable. It therefore seems that the release of promising, well-studied insects for control purposes poses much less a threat to native organisms than the continued rapid bracken encroachment on valuable lands, or in massive aerial spraying or extensive reforestation of lands, some of which land may be much more useful to man for other purposes. Lawton has reviewed the environmental, socio-economic, political, and legal constraints involved in the control of bracken by any method. Thus, the final management system for bracken control may be combinations of methods adapted to the site, climate and the pressures of nearby human activity.

There is one more characteristic of this expansive, adaptable, pioneering species as it moves across the world, about which we know little. The polymorphism which is its habit may provide a wide range of biotypes that will be both more resistant and more susceptible to the several control methods we may need. The systems of bracken control have been about the same for decades and we have as yet no affordable, satisfactory controls. If we must change our basic approach to the management of the species, early in our thinking we must surely come to know more about the biotypes within local bracken communities, as well as those creeping across the world's parks, pastures, grasslands and cultivated fields.

The losses from bracken are inestimable for the world because of the plant's manifold ways of interfering with the activities of humans and animals. The husbandry of animals suffers from loss of land, from direct poisoning, and from the increased difficulty of shepherding caused by dogs and stock animals being hidden in bracken. This plant is now a major source of land pollution, it drives out animals and many other plants that are deemed more desirable than the bracken weed, and the cost of reclamation of such lands is very high. It is likely that some areas can no longer be recovered for agriculture because of the high costs of clean-up and restoration. Finally, the plant contains carcinogens that affect the lives of human beings and their animals.

COMMON NAMES

Pteridium aquilinum

AUSTRALIA	bracken
BELGIUM	adelaarsvaren
BRAZIL	feio, feto, pluma grande, samambaia
CANADA	bracken, eagle fern, eastern bracken, grande fougere, fougere d'aigle
COLOMBIA	helecho
DENMARK	ornebregne
ECUADOR	helecho
EL SALVADOR	crespillo, palma
ENGLAND	bracken
FIJI	mata, quato, qato cuva
FINLAND	sananjalka
FRANCE	aquiline, fougere aigle, grande fougere, pteris aigle
GERMANY	Adlerfarn
HAWAII	bracken fern
INDONESIA	pakis gemblung, paku gila, paku rincang
ITALY	felse aquilina
JAPAN	warabi
MADAGASCAR	apanga
NEW ZEALAND	bracken
NORWAY	einstape
PHILIPPINES	pakong buwaya
PORTUGAL	feto-ordinario
PUERTO RICO	felpa, helecho alambre, helecho marrano
SPAIN	helecho comun
THAILAND	kut kin
UNITED STATES	bracken
ZAMBIA	luputu, mukochi, mushilu, ngoni

Seventy-Six

Ranunculus repens L.

Ranunculaceae, Buttercup Family

R ANUNCULUS REPENS is common in pastures, fields and other areas with wet soils in temperate climates. It is found in 40 countries, most in and near its continent of origin, Europe. Because plants propagate by stolons and seeds, many population dynamic studies have compared this species with other common buttercups.

The buttercup family has 50 genera with approximately 1800 species. Those in the *Ranunculus* section have a nectary scale attached to the flower base and compressed achenes with a distinct beak. The genus name is derived from the Latin *rana* for frog, as most

FIGURE 76-1   The distribution of *Ranunculus repens* L. across the world where it has been reported as a weed.

664

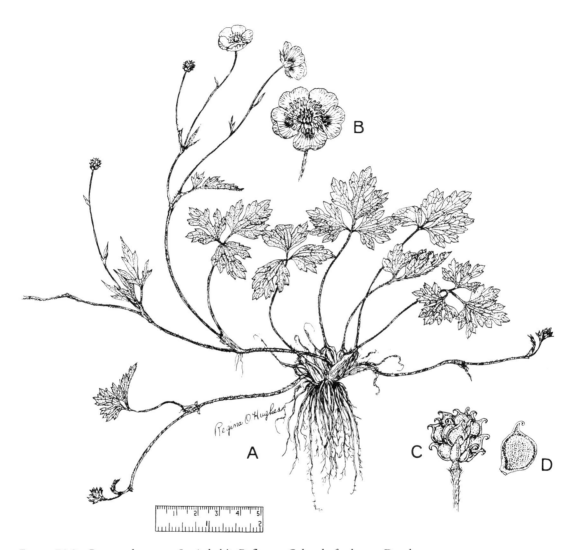

FIGURE 76-2 *Ranunculus repens* L.: A. habit; B. flower; C. head of achenes; D. achene.

species grow in moist areas where frogs are common. The species name refers to the creeping stolons that form daughter plants. Farmers used to believe the bright yellow flowers imparted their color to butter if consumed by cows and this may have contributed to the family's common name, buttercup.

DESCRIPTION

R. repens (Figure 76-2) is a creeping, low growing *perennial* herb with fibrous *roots*; *adventitious roots* arise from swollen stem bases and stolon nodes; *stems* coarse, branched, hairy, rarely glabrous, to 50 cm long, strongly 5-ribbed near the tip; *stolons* arise from leaf axis and have 3 to 6 nodes; internodes 4 to 8 cm long; *leaves* alternate, hairy, dark green, sometimes with light spots, 3-divided or 3-lobed, segments broadly ovate to nearly rounded in outline, sharply toothed; *basal* and *lower stem leaves* pinnate, long petioled; center lobe also long stalked, extending beyond others; lobes further divided into 3-toothed segments; blades 1.5 to 6 cm long, 2 to 8 cm wide; *upper leaves* sessile, irregular, palmately trisect with lanceolate lobes; *inflorescence* cymose, irregular, with single terminal flower on hairy, furrowed *peduncle* to 10 cm long; *flowers* perfect, solitary or in corymb-like clusters, 2 to 3 cm in diameter; *sepals* 5, hairy, green, not reflexed, separate; *petals* 6 to 9, bright yellow, with nectaries at base, 8 to 15 mm long, two-thirds as wide; *stamens* numerous; *carpels* numerous, separate with short recurved *styles*; *fruit* in globular heads as clusters of 20 to 50 achenes; *achenes* 2.5 to 3.5 mm long with beveled margin, short hooked beak .7 to 1.2 mm long at the tip, light brown to blackish brown with unevenly pitted surface.

The key features of *R. repens* are the creeping, hairy, stolons; the alternately compound leaves with toothed margins; the bright yellow flowers; and beaked achenes with beveled margins.

DISTRIBUTION, HABITAT, AND ECOLOGY

R. repens is concentrated in Europe and other temperate climate regions between lat 38 and 50° N, but also occurs from lat 70° N to the Nile River delta and from sea level to 1000 m above sea level (Harper 1957). It also is found in Australia, Chile, Argentina, South Africa, and New Zealand (Figure 76-1). The species is best adapted to pastures and waste areas with fertile, poorly drained soils but is also a weed of arable land. Plants tolerate trampling and grazing and are especially competitive with crops after pastures are plowed. This species is an effective colonizer and thus has followed the movement of civilizations. *R. repens* is common in wetlands and along the margins of ponds, ditches and streams and is also found in forest edges and clearings.

An excellent example of species adaptation to microenvironments is found in three *Ranunculus* species. Grazing often forms natural terraces in pastures on sloping land. *R. bulbous* occupies the upper part, *R. acris* the side and *R. repens* the bottom of these terraces, reflecting each species' preferred niche (Harper 1958). All three species are found in flatland pastures, too, and their distribution is usually associated with micro-topographical differences that influence the rate of drainage and speed of soil drying during dry periods.

R. repens is frost tolerant and survives moderate droughts. The basal stem region has several intercellular spaces that form air canals. Smaller ones are found in the roots and these help plants survive in wet soils (Korsmo 1954).

Thorough population dynamic studies have been done in England and Wales. Sarukhan and Harper (1973) monitored populations at eight sites in a 50-yr-old pasture for 3 yr. Population changes varied from +74 to −228% of the original densities, with an average loss of 30% over all sites. Only 8% of the plants survived 2 yr and the annual percentage mortality was 67%. Estimated time for complete population turnover was 2.8 yr. The highest ramet mortality was for plants between 6 to 12 mo and 18 to 24 mo of age (i.e., spring and summer). Few died in the fall and winter months. Life expectancy dropped as plant density increased. Plants originating from seed have even shorter life expediencies, generally less than 6 mo.

Soane and Watkinson (1979) used field data to develop a computer model to simulate population dynamics of plants derived from seeds and stolons. Plants from stolons lived only 1.2 to 2.1 yr and the death rate increased as reproduction increased. *R. repens* from several localities were grown at one site and all survived successfully during the observation period. They postulate that if only 3% of the total population originates from seed that genetic diversity will be maintained.

Grasslands management affects *R. repens* populations. Fields cut once or twice annually in the Netherlands for 9 yr experienced an increase in *R. repens* density. Seedlings emerged after the July cutting but not after September's. Thus populations in fields cut in only September are maintained vegetatively, while those in fields cut in July or July and September are seed-maintained, because the summer cutting destroys stolons. Plants devoid of stolons produced more and larger seeds than those with stolons (van den Berg et al. 1985).

A series of studies by Doust (1981a,b,c; 1987) compared the population dynamics and growth of *R. repens* in wooded and grassland habitats. Higher populations were encountered in the woods (186 vs. 81 plants/m^2) but the age structure and stolon number per plant were similar in both habitats. The soil contained over 1000 seeds/m^2 but few seedlings appeared in either site. Surprisingly, birth rates were not correlated to population density but death rates were. Plants from the woods were planted in a pasture and vice versa, or dug and replanted in their original environment. Ramets grew best in their original habitats, especially those from the woods. This biotype in its natural environment has stolon internodes 8.3 cm long, but in a grassland they were only 4.2 cm in length. *R. repens* from pastures had internodes 5.5 and 5.8 cm long when grown in grassland or wooded habitats, respectively. Woodland plants form more leaves and ramets per plant than grassland plants. Ramets farthest from the parent have the fewest leaves and shortest internodes. The number of leaves per ramet is generally constant for a given position away from the parent. Ramets rely on the parent plant for water and nutrients. If ramets are separated prematurely, growth and stolon development are reduced, while the parent then forms more leaves and uses the added energy for stem and inflorescence development.

When light and nutrients are limiting, woodland plants allocate proportionately more biomass to ramet roots. In contrast, grassland plants invest proportionately more biomass to roots of the parent rosette. These studies carefully analyzed the important considerations in genotype by environment research and conclude that it is inappropriate to say certain properties are genetic and others are environmentally induced. Rather, we can determine the relative plasticity of traits, and if a single genotype is studied, we measure the amplitude of the phenotype (Doust 1987).

BIOLOGY

A thorough review of the biology of this species is found in Doust et al. (1990). Seed propagation is less important for *R. repens* than for other closely related species. Nevertheless, seed often accounts for long-distance dissemination and gives rise to new plants in most environments. Seeds germinate and seedlings grow under water-logged conditions (Harper 1957, Sarukhan and Harper 1973). In continuous light or with alternating 18 hr of light and 6 hr of darkness, 50% of the seeds germinate with only a 1°C temperature fluctuation. In continuous darkness, a 5°C fluctuation is necessary for 50% germination (Thompson and Grime 1983). *R. repens* seeds average 2.32 mg each and were among the largest of the 112 species tested. They theorize that large-seeded species germinate with small temperature fluctuations because they can emerge from greater depths than small-seeded ones. However, Williams (1983) found 17% emergence at 1 cm, 4% at 3 cm and none at 5 cm over a 1-yr period in undisturbed soil. Seed viability was correlated with soil depth because 60, 73, and 75% were viable at 1, 3, and 5 cm, respectively.

Roberts and Boddrell (1985) placed 1000 seeds in cylinders with a loam soil that was disturbed to 7.5 cm three times a year. Seeds were planted in July and, by December, 3.5% emerged. For the next 5 yr, 19, 14, 11, 10, and 4% of the seeds germinated annually. The remaining seeds were highly resistant to decay. Flushes of emergence sometimes followed soil disturbance, but not always. Months of active emergence were April, May, September, and October (24, 8, 23, and 15%, respectively). Under field conditions in England, emergence was enhanced by monthly or quarterly tillage (Chancellor 1964). In a field that had been a pasture for 30 yr; 56, 51, 35, and 19 seeds/m^2 emerged during 2 yr when tilled monthly, quarterly, annually or left undisturbed, respectively. More seed germinated in the second year than in the first. Most germination was between May and September, although some occurred every month except December.

Seeds remain viable for many years. Lewis (1973) buried seeds at 13, 26, and 39 cm in a mineral soil. After 20 yr, germination was equal to that at 4 yr (54%) and the seeds responded as though freshly harvested. Seeds were less persistent in peat, as only 4% germinated after 20 yr of burial. Seeds from archeological sites in Denmark dated between 1300 and 1800 A.D. were viable (Odum 1965). Odum (1974) estimated the minimum age of *R. repens* seeds in the soil that were over 20 yr old to be 80 yr.

Long seed persistence is reflected in high seed populations. Chippindale and Milton (1934) found 90 to 11,400 seeds/m^2 under many field conditions. Higher levels were observed in pastures cut for hay in the summer and grazed in the fall than in those that were only grazed. Populations in grassland were much greater than those in arable land (Milton 1943, Champness and Morris 1948). The number of seeds in the soil is enormous compared to the number of plants present. Populations of 16 million seeds/ha are not uncommon. An average seed weight of 2.4 mg each (Korsmo 1935) gives 38.4 kg seed/ha.

Stolon production starts in May on overwintering rosettes (Sarukhan and Harper 1973). One to two stolons per plant are common but some plants have up to five. Secondary branching may occur. Internodes range from 5 to 15 cm in length. One or two leaves and a pair of root initials form at the nodes. Once plants are anchored, more leaves and roots are produced. Stolon production peaks in mid summer. Stolons separate naturally from the parent plant by autumn, and grazing animals often hasten the detachment process. Most new plants (usually called ramets) are independent by September and parent plants usually die by year's end. Stolon production is especially responsive to environmental conditions. Short stolons are formed in dense turf and much longer ones in open fields (Harper 1957).

R. repens expresses great morphological variation. Leaves on overwintering rosettes are more finely divided than those formed on stolons. All plants collected across Europe had a 2*n* chromosome count of 32 and readily crossed with each other (Coles 1977). Stomata are present on both leaf surfaces (Korsmo 1954) and young plants are especially high in nickel (Sapek et al. 1980).

R. repens exhibits sharply exponential growth between April and June (Sarukhan 1976). After stolon formation begins, dry matter accumulation ceases. Only 1 to 5% of the total plant biomass goes toward seed production, while 47 to 53% is directed to vegetative reproduction.

R. repens growth was optimal in a nutrient solution with 50 ppm nitrogen. Shoot to root ratios were 2.0, 4.7, and 7.6 at nitrogen levels of 10, 50, and 200 ppm, respectively. Stolon numbers tripled as nitrogen increased from 10 to 50 ppm. Nitrogen deficiency greatly reduces formation of secondary and tertiary stolons. In this way, plants can "sample" a number of sites as stolons develop and those in the more favorable microenvironments respond with rapid colonization. This can be considered a trial-and-error method of habitat exploration (Ginzo and Lovell 1973a,b).

R. repens responds to favorable habitats by forming more stolons through branching. When nitrogen is limiting, stolons seek favorable conditions far from the parent by remaining unbranched and long-distance assimilate movement is necessary. Photosynthates are readily transported throughout the plant system. A single plant growing without competition formed 28 m of stolons with 179 nodes in one year (Coles 1977).

Most flowers have five petals, but this may vary from four to 13 per flower. Cunnell (1964) thoroughly studied the spiralled arrangement of five-petaled flowers. Highly consistent patterns of overlap were found for inflorescences of the same type (lateral or terminal), from the same sites and from year to year.

Flowering peaks in early summer and fruiting follows within 2 wk. Sarukhan (1974) noted that only 20% of the plants flowered and of these 75% failed to set seed and 66% of the plants form only one flower. Nevertheless, infested pastures had 31 flowers/m^2 that produced 83 seeds/m^2. Salisbury (1942) observed an average of five flowers per plant and 30 seeds per fruit, while Korsmo et al. (1981) report 140 seeds per stem. Seed production in *R. repens* is more variable than vegetative reproduction, but this is inconsequential because seeds have extremely long "half-life" in the soil.

Most flowers open by 9:00 A.M. Ninety-nine percent of the youngest flowers close by 4:00 P.M., while older flowers remain open longer. They do not open on rainy days, but, if rain falls after flowers open, they do not close. Pollen shed peaks between 10 and 11:00 A.M. and continues 4 to 9 days. Flowers average 63 stamens and shed 3.4 mg of pollen each. Anthesis occurs readily at 11°C or higher, especially on sunny days (Harper 1957). The well-developed nectaries and bright color attract insects. Flowers are insect-pollinated and self-pollination is uncommon. Outcrossing is favored because ovaries are immature when a flower has ripe pollen (Heywood 1978). Cross-pollination to closely related species never occurs (Harper 1958). After flowering, the plant often dies and a new ramet usually establishes in the same site. Seeds are dispersed by birds (Collinge 1913), by adhering to animals with the hooked spine, and in water. The seed coat is unwettable and the surface tension created allows seeds to float (van der Pijl 1982). Seeds trapped in ice during severe winters sink when the ice melts. Wellington (1957) discovered that up to 9% of the forage grass seed lots sampled were contaminated with *R. repens* seeds.

AGRICULTURAL IMPORTANCE

R. repens is a reported weed of 11 crops in 40 countries (Figure 76-1) and is frequently reported in pastures, cereals and temperate plantation crops. It is a serious or principal weed of barley and wheat in Finland; cereals in England; and pastures in Belgium, England, Italy, Norway, Scotland, Sweden, and the United States.

It is a common weed of cereals in Canada, Iran, Poland, Tunisia, and Turkey; horticulture crops in England; legumes in Tunisia; orchards in the Netherlands and Spain; pastures in Australia, Bulgaria, Hungary, and the Netherlands; rye in Finland; sugar beets in Poland; and vegetables in Iceland.

R. repens is also an unranked weed of cereals in Germany; forage crops in the Kamchatka peninsula of the former Soviet Union, and the United States; horticultural crops in South Africa; nurseries in Germany; orchards in England and Sweden; pastures in Austria, Chile, France, Germany, New Zealand, and the former Yugoslavia; rangelands in France, Germany, and the former Yugoslavia; rice in Portugal; strawberries in Ireland; vegetables in Sweden; vineyards in France; wheat in Italy; and wastelands in Australia and India.

Fertilizing and intensive cutting or grazing pastures increases the competitiveness of *R. repens* (Dietl 1982). It is considered a noxious species in grassland if it is more than 5 to 10% of the forage because it has low nutritive value. While *R. repens* is sometimes considered toxic, it is only mildly bitter and livestock will eat it (Harper 1957). Plants have less of the glucoside ranunculin than closely related species, so animal poisoning is unlikely. Ranunculin is lost when hay is dried, so poisoning is only possible if fresh plants are eaten.

The sap of *R. repens* also contains protoanemonin, a blister-causing compound. This is the active ingredient used by indigenous people in western Canada to treat boils, cuts, abrasions, muscle aches, colds, and headaches (Turner 1984).

COMMON NAMES

Ranunculus repens

ARGENTINA	boton de oro, ensalada de ranas
AUSTRALIA	creeping buttercup
BELGIUM	kruipende boterbloem
BRAZIL	botao de ouro
CANADA	creeping buttercup, renoncule rampante
CHILE	boton de oro
DENMARK	lav ranunkel
ENGLAND	creeping buttercup
FINLAND	ronsyleinikki
FRANCE	bouton d'or, renoncule rampante
GERMANY	Kriechender Hahnenfuss
IRELAND	creeping buttercup
ITALY	cresione selvatico, pie di nibbio
JAPAN	hai-kinpoge

NETHERLANDS	kruipende boterbloem
NEW ZEALAND	creeping buttercup
NORWAY	krypsoleie
PORTUGAL	erva belida
SPAIN	boton de oro, boton de oro rastrero
SWEDEN	revsmorblomma
UNITED STATES	creeping buttercup

Seventy-Seven

Raphanus raphanistrum L.

Brassicaceae (Cruciferae), Mustard Family

I N THIS SPECIES, widely known as wild radish, we have a close relative of the common vegetable radish, *Raphanus sativus*, which varies so much in form as it is grown all over the world for food for men and animals. *Raphanus* is the Latin word for the Greek *raphanis*, a vegetable grown from antiquity. Inferred here is the Greek *ra* meaning quickly, and *phainomai*, to appear, thus providing a description of the quickness in growth of these plants each season.

FIGURE 77-1   The distribution of *Raphanus raphanistrum* L. across the world where it has been reported as a weed.

FIGURE 77-2   *Raphanus raphanistrum* L.: 1. habit; 2. seedling; 3. flower; 4. open flower; 5. silique; 6. seed.

The weed does not have the thickened root of the garden radish. Its leaves are typical of those of the mustard family but are rougher, more hairy, and with a thicker cuticle. Pods of the wild radish are larger and more seed is produced.

Private and public journals on agriculture in England from the period 1800 to 1850 mention wild radish as one of the worst weeds of arable fields. In the decades following and with the advent of herbicide use, it maintained a presence but was only regarded as a major weed in a few areas of the world. In the past two decades, it has reappeared in the unstable weed communities that accompany limited tillage and herbicide resistance, and it has again become a cause for concern. Where present, this weed becomes the nemesis of man's grain crops. It is now in more than 45 crops and 65 countries.

DESCRIPTION

R. raphanistrum (Figure 77-2) may behave as an *annual, winter annual,* or *biennial* and may have a large basal rosette of leaves; *root* (see full description later); *stems* erect or spreading (striate to angled in South Africa), much branched, 30 to 100 cm (to 200 cm in Australia), short, stiff hairs especially at base (a type in California, in the United States), almost glabrous; *leaves* alternate, rough, lower deeply lobed with much enlarged terminal segment, upper narrower, entire to slight indentations, 8 to 20 cm long; *flowers*, perianth with four free segments, in long, terminal, corymbose racemes, petals pale yellow, rarely white, purple veins (occasionally petals reported to be pinkish or purplish, may be straw-colored in Scotland), 1 to 2 cm across, pedicels 1 to 2 cm; *fruit* fleshy *pod*, spongy, long, narrow, cylindrical, 5 to 10 mm in diameter, 2 to 7 cm long, terminating in 1 to 2 cm pointed beak, longitudinally ribbed, indehiscent, 2 to 10 seeds, constricted but without septum between seeds, lower pods often small and seedless, sections with seed break apart at constriction when mature, are difficult to clean from grain crop seed supplies; *seeds* globular, ovoid, reddish to orange-brown (dark brown in South Africa), 2 to 4 mm in diameter, covered with fine network of veins with shallow interspaces.

At maturity, wild radish pod does not split longitudinally as does wild mustard *Brassica kaber* and its relatives.

In addition to *R. raphanistrum*, there are two other wild radishes, *R. maritimus* and *R. landra*, and it is likely that all three contributed to the evolution of the crop radish that is believed by some to have its origin in the eastern Mediterranean area (Simmonds 1976). Radish types with very large roots are much in use in all of East Asia, where they are eaten raw, cooked, stored, pickled, canned, and dried, yet they probably did not come to the area until about two millennia after they were in use in the Middle East and Europe. The mougri-radish, which does not have fleshy roots, is grown in Southeast Asia for its leaves and young seed pods that may reach 20 to 100 cm in length. Also without fleshy roots is the fodder radish grown for foliage and used as animal fodder or green manure. This type grows very rapidly and has been of interest lately in northern Europe.

The wild species of *Raphanus* are variable and difficult to identify. Panetsos (1963) suggests that this condition is further aggravated by escapes of the crop radish which have become weedy, a condition seen in the crop oats (*Avena sativa*) and other crop species. The cultivated form may have been assisted in this reversion to weediness by introgression from the already weedy *R. raphanistrum*. The new escapes have acquired deeply penetrating taproots, they pass quickly to the flowering stage, have regained a seed dispersal system, and have a harder fruit wall to give a measure of protection from birds and a brief "dormant" period while the wall is deteriorating in the mixture with other trash on the soil surface.

DISTRIBUTION AND HABITAT

R. raphanistrum is a weed in much of the agricultural world (Figure 77-1), but strangely has not been troublesome in man's fields in tropical Western Africa or South and East Asia. At present, it is a common to serious problem in small grains, especially wheat, in many countries, but it was not always so. The records of the Rothamsted Experiment Station at the turn of this century report that wild radish preferred chalk and sandy soils, was often the dominant weed on chalk, was never in wheat, but was always found with oats and barley. Present-day reports from both England and the United States show that the present form of the weed grows in grain crops on many different soil types. Thus not all agree on the soil type favored by radish. Vogel (1926) in Germany stated that this weed may be thought of as an indicator plant that prefers acid soil but also informs us about the physical characteristics of the soil and its lime content. On the other hand, LeFevre (1956) studied the weeds of crops in the Picardy region of France and their relationship to the lime status of the soil. From the literature, he also compiled a list of weeds said to be indicators of acid soils, alkaline soils, or indifference to soil *pH*. He concluded that the relationship between soil *pH* and adventitious plants is a "loose" one and that wild radish is only a modest indicator of a requirement for lime.

To examine the influence of soil type and kind of crop (cereal or root) on the consistency of appearance of a large number of weeds, *R. raphanistrum* included, a large number of field studies were carried out in several regions of Poland (Borowiec et al. 1972). Soils ranged from heavy fertile loams to sands and black soils that were at times eroded or excessively wet. On poor rye soils (light loamy sands), wild radish occurred on more sites (88%) than other weeds in this crop but was less frequent (70%) in root crops. On good rye soils (brown soils on light to loamy sands), the weed was much less frequent in rye and varied with a frequency of 10 to 50% of all sites planted to root crops. On low-lying black turf soils over sand, wild radish was much less frequent in cereals and was one of four predominant weeds in root crops.

Roberts and Stokes (1966) sampled the seed banks of soils in many fields under commercial vegetable production over a large area of England. Some of them had been in constant cultivation for 60 to 100 years. A very small number of *R. raphanistrum* seeds were found in each of only two fields.

The movement and dispersal of wild radish seeds seems closely tied to man's activity. It is one of the dominant species of weed seeds that contaminate wheat and barley seedstocks in the non-irrigated areas of northern Iraq. In Iran, Dastgheib (1989) found that the manure from sheep grazing brought 10 million seeds/ha to the arable fields of Iran and farmer-saved seed of cereals contributed 180,000, while irrigation water carried only 120. Thomas et al. (1984) and Davidson (1984) reported that the movement of hay, grain, and animals to cope with the drought of 1980 to 1984 in Australia caused widespread movement of seeds to new agricultural areas. Many new seed types were found in grain seed supplies, and wild radish was one of the most serious contaminants.

Country and regional regulation of seed purity frequently permit no more than 1% by weight of weed seed contamination. Sowing a cereal crop at 30 kg/ha containing 1% of *R.*

raphanistrum seed would add about 25 seeds/m² (Horne 1953). In Bulgaria, wild radish seeds are among the most serious contaminants of the beds used to produce vegetable and tobacco transplants. Adding to the contamination is the manure hauled to the area for covering the beds. The seeds can pass the gut of several animals, including birds and cattle, with some remaining viable. The proportion of good seed is unknown, for seeds may remain in guts from 2 to 10 days. This period allows for much seed dispersal by moving animals.

PROPAGATION AND FIELD ECOLOGY

Almost all of the studies of the biology of this important weed of cereals have been strikingly repetitive investigations of seed germination. The precise conditions of laboratory testing procedures (light quality and quantity, for example) were not controlled or not defined, and results are thus not very helpful in explaining the field behavior of the weed. We must be grateful to Piggin et al. (1978) and Reeves et al. (1981) of Australia for their recent excellent investigations of the field ecology and physiology of this weed. The information revealed in their reports is most useful, and it is therefore necessary to review only a few of the earlier seed germination studies.

Wild radish is a weed of increasing severity and is found in all the states of Australia. Recognizing that the success as a weed is due to a number of factors and that it is highly unlikely that it will be eradicated from infested areas, Reeves, and Piggin and co-workers studied the biology of the species in the field and laboratory for a period of 3 yr. The weed reduces grain yields, contaminates the grain harvest and may increase its moisture content beyond acceptable limits, and it makes harvesting difficult. As others have found, it is a prolific seeder, sometimes reaching more than 17,000 seeds/m² from a weed stand of 52/m². Because of the ability of this seed to germinate for an extended period each season, there are mixed reports of soil seed bank supplies in various regions of the world. In these Australian experiments, 45,000 seeds/m² were found in some plots. Because only one-half of the seed in the soil germinated in one season, the burden of seed in the soil can be tremendous. As the weed population increased, the number of seeds produced by each plant decreased, but the seed production per unit area increased overall. About 20 to 40% of the seed produced in a season was still viable 12 mo later, and this again foretells a continuing adequate weed seed supply even under the worst conditions of weed seed production in any season. Kurth (1967) in Germany reported *R. raphanistrum* seeds were viable in the soil for 15 to 20 yr.

Germination tests on seed buried at 0, 1, 5, and 10 cm revealed that those at the surface were reduced to 43, 18, and 5% at 6, 12, and 24 mo, respectively. A portion of the above loss was due to germination, of course. There was a slow decline of germination at the 10 cm depth (76 to 53%) during the 6- to 24-mo period. Only 16% of the seed placed at 1 cm was viable after 24 mo. In general, all seeds placed near the surface deteriorated most rapidly.

Because the seed has staggered germination, there is a problem with timing of control measures. Early cultivation and herbicide treatment are often most successful in grain, yet late-germinating weeds may set seed and contaminate the harvest. Late treatments may give clean grain, but yields may be lowered because of weed competition or spray injury. In bad years, more than one treatment may be needed.

When tested in the laboratory, the seed germinated well over a wide range of temperatures (constant or alternating in light or dark) but was most responsive to widely varying temperature fluctuations. Perhaps this explains why the weed germinates so well in the field after autumn rains, when there is great temperature fluctuation, but also provides new emergence with each rain all through the year. In the laboratory, seed vernalized at 5°C in the light and then germinated at a fluctuating temperature of 25 to 5°C in the dark gave improved germination. This light-dark effect may help to explain the large increases in germination in the field following disc cultivation—the seed in the light on the surface is buried and germinates readily.

Mekenian and Willemsen (1975), in the United States, studied the germination of seeds from a noncrop area. Their experiments covered the after-ripening of seeds of *R. raphanistrum* held at room temperature for 6, 8, and 10 mo, germination following leaching at 21°C for 8, 16, and 24 hr, and stratification in moist sand at 5°C for periods from 3 to 15 wk. Germination was studied at four alternating temperatures from 5/15°C to 20/30°C. After-ripening was completed in less than 6 mo in their studies. These results are in agreement with those of Piggin et al. (1978) and Reeves et al. (1981) that germination was generally higher in the dark at all alternating temperatures and storage times. Light germination increased with increasing temperatures. The inhibitory effect of the fruit wall (pod) was detected in their experiments, also.

Stratification generally decreased germination, and all leaching treatments gave about the same results, but with indications of some improvement in the dark and with alternating temperatures. Germination of freshly harvested seed was low, in agreement with the same early innate seed dormancy found in so many summer and winter annuals. Here, as in Australia, the pods that overwinter on the ground seem to have broken and deteriorated to the extent that the seed is released from the chemical and mechanical inhibition, is buried in some fashion, and becomes ready for early spring germination. It seems likely that the establishment of *R. raphanistrum* at any time during the growing season thus depends on seeds produced in a previous growing season.

In the central United States, to overcome a primary dormancy of six month's duration, Steinbauer and Frank (1954) and Steinbauer et al. (1955) recommended placing the seeds of wild radish between blotters moistened with a 0.2% solution of KNO$_3$.

Cheam (1984, 1986) in western Australia found that wild radish populations in southern Australia had a higher level of dormancy than those in northern Australia.

Lauer (1953) in Germany found the minimum temperature for germination of the species was below 5°C, maximum was 35°C, and optimum was 20°C. Several alternating temperatures were tried but none were as effective as a constant 20°C.

Reeves, Piggin, and co-workers found, as others have, that the pod has an inhibitory effect on seed germination and that the sporadic emergence through the years may be the expression of a slow but relentless breakdown of pods and release of seeds on or below the surface.

It was shown in a further study of the phenology of this weed that the planting date had a marked influence on the vegetative and fruiting phases. The shortest time from emergence to elongation (or bolting) was in the earliest seedlings of spring. These also provided the longest seasonal flowering period. Each phase of growth was, however, influenced by the times of sowing, and the total life spans of plants therefore varied from 317 days (planted in January) to 134 days (planted in September–October). The flowering period was almost 300 days for plants that came up in January, but only 90 days if germination was in November.

To determine the relative importance of temperature and day length on the duration of the developmental phases, the statistical method of Fischer (1963) was used. This takes into account the time in days for each phase and the average daily mean temperature for that phase (the thermal requirement). This analysis indicated that the time from emergence to elongation and from elongation to flowering were altered very little when variations in day length were used, thus suggesting that temperature was the major controlling factor. This was not true with the total duration of the flowering phase that seems to be controlled by both day length and temperature.

The management of this weed must surely depend on the control of the seed burden in the soil. The enhanced germination of seeds buried near the soil surface suggests that a shallow preplanting seed covering, followed by cultivation to destroy the seedlings, will be helpful. Successive cropping with minimum tillage also offers promise of a considerable reduction of the soil seed burden. Moldboard plowing (not much used of late) to a depth of 15 to 20 cm has been shown to reduce weed problems considerably because of the depth of seed burial. This practice will dictate succeeding cropping patterns because of the longevity of the seed at that depth and the danger of returning nondormant viable seed to the surface if subsequent cultivations are too deep. Reeves et al. (1981) point out that combinations of the above cultural practices and chemical control methods have been adopted successfully by some farmers in their area of Victoria. The weed has been reduced to manageable levels, but future improvements will depend on the destruction of the supply of seeds in the soil.

In summary, the persistence of the weeds and the difficulty in controlling them are not surprising. They produce thousands of seeds/m^2, can reduce wheat yields up to 20%, and the weed seeds may continue to cause losses in future years.

ANATOMY AND MORPHOLOGY

Pistrick (1987) investigated the taxonomy of the highly variable *Raphanus* genus, including vegetable, fodder, and oil crops. The study was mainly concerned with morphological and anatomical characters and their geographical distribution. Prakash and Hinata (1980) published a review of the taxonomy, cytogenetics and origin of the crop *Brassica*.

Stanton (1984a,b; 1985) and Stanton and Mazer (1986) found the reproductive output of seeds of wild radish was influenced more heavily by seed weight than by the time from planting to emergence of the parents of those seeds. Seeds of 6 mg or more grew more rapidly and produced more flowers than seeds weighing 4 mg. In the greenhouse the original seed size had little influence on plant size at maturity.

The weight and position of each seed borne by six individuals was recorded and they were planted out in the following season for progeny analysis. Seed weight decreased as the number of seeds increased, seed weight varied significantly among maternal plants, and a comparison of average seed weight among the progenies of the six individuals showed a significant genetic component for seed size variation.

Seed weight varied up to six-fold within single plants. The largest seeds were normally near the pedicel or in the middle fruit position. Seed size tended to decrease through the flowering period.

In experimental populations, Stanton et al. (1986, 1989) found discrimination of color (yellow or white) by natural pollinators had no significant effect on relative maternal function (fruit and seed production). Yellow-flowered individuals were much more successful as fathers (pollen donors). This increased attractiveness resulted in more pollen from yellow-flowered individuals being spread among other nearby plants, with a consequent increase in fitness in the yellow population.

Stanton et al. (1987) studied the effect of variation in pollination thoroughness on overall plant growth and yield components in *R. raphanistrum*. Mazer et al. (1986) and Mazer (1987) studied fertilization dynamics and parental effects on fruit development in wild radish with consequent effect on seed size variation. Hill and Lord (1986, 1987) studied the morphology, cytochemistry and ultrastructure of transmitting tissues during pollen tube growth. Lyshede (1982) reported on the differences in seed coat structure between *R. sativus* and *R. raphanistrum*.

Kutschera (1960) found a remarkable root system beneath a mature plant excavated from a fallow field in mid-October in Germany. There was a very extensive fibrous root system to a depth of 20 cm and spreading horizontally to 80 cm in all directions. There were two strong taproots reaching to a depth of 70 cm, at which point they divided into three to four branches and continued to descend. Another fibrous array of roots spread through an area 80 cm in diameter at 120 to 160 cm in depth.

AGRICULTURAL IMPORTANCE

R. raphanistrum is a major weed of cereals in the world, especially wheat, and in the latter crop it is often the winter planting that is most troubled. It is a serious weed of barley in Mexico and the former Soviet Union; of cereals of several kinds in Ecuador, Israel, Jordan, Poland, South Africa, and Tunisia; of horticultural crops of several kinds in Hungary; legumes in Tunisia; maize in Mexico; oats in the former Soviet Union; orchards in South Africa; potatoes in Ecuador; oil seed rape in Mexico and Spain; soybeans in Brazil; sugar beets in the former Soviet Union; vegetables and vineyards in South Africa; wheat in Mexico, Mozambique, Portugal, and South Africa; and when wheat is grown as a winter crop in Argentina, Australia, Brazil, Latvia, Romania, the former Soviet Union, Spain, and Uruguay. Overall it is a serious crop weed in one or more regions of 17 countries.

It is a principal weed of barley in Iran, Iraq, Kenya, Peru, South Africa, Spain, and in Romania when planted as a winter crop; beans in Mexico; carrots in the former Soviet Union; cereals in Australia, Colombia, England, Finland, Germany, Italy, Mexico, and Tasmania; cotton in Peru; of several dryland crops in Australia; fodder beets in Belgium; forage crops in the United States; flax in Germany; horticultural crops in Peru; irrigated crops in Australia and Spain; lucerne in Canada and in the first-year crop in Germany; maize in Argentina, Ecuador, Germany, Hungary, Italy, and Romania; oats in Mexico, South Africa, and the former Soviet Union; onions in Brazil; mixed winter pastures in Queensland in Australia, Colombia, and South Africa; peas in Brazil, Canada, and the former Soviet Union; potatoes in Belgium; soybeans in Bolivia; strawberries in Canada; sugar beets in Belgium, England, and Poland; sugarcane in Peru; summer crops in Sweden; tobacco in Bulgaria; vegetables in Australia, Bulgaria, Tasmania, and the United States; wheat in Hungary, Iran, Iraq, Kenya, Peru, and the former Yugoslavia; and spring wheat in northern Germany.

It is a common weed of several arable crops in Mexico; barley in Finland and the former Yugoslavia; cabbage in the former Soviet Union; cereals in Canada, Kenya, Scotland, the former Soviet Union, Spain, Switzerland, and the former Yugoslavia; coffee in Brazil; hemp in Germany; horticulture crops in Australia and Mexico; legumes in England and Israel; lucerne in Bulgaria, Mexico, and South Africa; lupines in the former Yugoslavia; maize in Brazil, Colombia, France, and the former Yugoslavia; oats in the former

Yugoslavia; olives in Spain; rye in the former Yugoslavia; sunflowers in France; vegetables on the high plain in Madagascar and in Scotland; vineyards in Australia; and wheat in Colombia, Finland, Honduras, and the former Yugoslavia.

In addition, 30 of these crops are present in many of the countries reported above but we have no rank of importance for them. The weed is so ubiquitous in both crop and country that a further extensive listing is of little value. Although not reported above, the weed is also present in crops in Chile, Cyprus, Lebanon, Norway, Turkey, and the Kamchatka Peninsula in the far east of the former Soviet Union.

R. raphanistrum and *Rumex acetosella* are the two most important weeds in wheat in Romania. Bogdan (1965) found seeds of 42 species of weeds in 50 samples of wheat collected from several regions of Kenya. The seeds of eight species, including wild radish, made up 90% of the total seed in all of the samples.

In a study by Wilson and Cussans (1983) in England on weed competition in barley and wheat by *Alopecurus myosuroides*, they noticed that crop yield reduction could be predicted with reasonable confidence from the autumn seedling populations in the field. Later it was learned that the largest yield losses per weed seedling were caused by *R. raphanistrum*, *Galium*, *Papaver*, and *Matricaria* species.

In Queensland, Australia, the weed travels on the routes over which cattle and sheep are driven and may taint milk if ingested with the flora. Wild radish is a problem in Uruguay, where birdsfoot trefoil (*Lotus corniculatus*) and wheat are grown as companion crops, and it is one of the most plentiful plants in forage lots maintained for undomesticated animals, such as deer, in the Netherlands.

In northeastern Germany, after 20 yr of changes and improvements in soil management, Otto and Hilbig (1987) found decreases in several weed species, including wild radish, that had formerly been dominant on strongly acid soils.

Chancellor (1986) reported on the decline of weed species during 20 yr under a grass sward. Of 21 species studied, *R. raphanistrum* showed the greatest decline, with a mean annual reduction of 30%. The author suggests that sowing a weedy arable field to grass for 20 yr will not eradicate the seeds of even the most rapidly declining species. Wild radish decreased in cereal and vegetable fields in Norway from 1950 to 1970 and in sugar beets in Germany from 1960 to 1972.

Roberts and Neilson (1981b) summarized soil seed bank studies for a 16-yr period on the farms of the Weed Research Organization of England. There were paired plots, cropped in monoculture with spring barley, or maize, or carrots, one of each pair receiving a herbicide treatment. Apart from this, all plots of an experiment were treated in an identical manner; weeds were destroyed soon after emergence by hand-hoeing, and the herbicide-treated plots received the same cultivations for weed control as did those left unsprayed. *R. raphanistrum*, present mainly in the barley plots at the outset, declined to a trace in only 2 to 3 yr.

Rubin and Benjamin (1983) in Israel obtained effective control of *R. raphanistrum* with 4 to 5 wk of solar heating of soil under plastic.

In Mexico, leaves of wild radish are harvested for cattle feed and are eaten during food shortages by humans.

Large amounts of some mustard seeds, including those of *R. raphanistrum*, when harvested with wheat for bread, may cause "bread poisoning" if the bread is not baked with intense heat. Moistening and kneading the dough renders water-soluble toxins more readily absorbable by the intestinal mucosa (Nikolaev 1964).

COMMON NAMES

Raphanus raphanistrum

ALGERIA	abou vel bou-quir, lebsan, ravenelle
ARGENTINA	rabano, rabizon
AUSTRALIA	jointed charlock, wild radish
BELGIUM	knopherik, ravenelle
BRAZIL	nabica, nabo, saramago
CANADA	charlock, jointed radish, radis sauvage, wild turnip, wild radish
CHILE	rabano
COLOMBIA	rabano morado, rabano mostaza
DENMARK	kiddike
ECUADOR	rabano
EGYPT	figl
ENGLAND	charlock, runch, wild radish
FINLAND	peltoretikka
FRANCE	radis ravenelle, radis sauvage, ravenelle
GERMANY	Ackerrettich, Hederich, Wilder Rettich
HUNGARY	repcsenyretek
IRAQ	fijaila, fujul
ISRAEL	tznon matzui
ITALY	rafanistro, ramolaccio selvatico, rapastrello, ravastrello
JAPAN	hamadaikon
KENYA	white charlock
LEBANON	aysh wa gubn, fijjaylah, fugl barri, white charlock, wild radish
MADAGASCAR	radia
MEXICO	flor de nabo, jaramado, nabillo, nebo cimarron, nebo silvestre, taramao
MOROCCO	bahamon, ravenelle
NETHERLANDS	knopherik
NEW ZEALAND	wild radish
NORWAY	akerreddik
PARAGUAY	rabanito salvaje
PERU	rabano cimarron, rabano silvestre
POLAND	lopucha poina, rzodkiew swirzepa
PORTUGAL	labresto, saramago
SAUDI ARABIA	aysh wa gubn, fugl barri
SOUTH AFRICA	ramenas, wild radish, wildemostert
SPAIN	jaramago blanco, oruga silvestre, rabanillo, rabaniza comun, rabano silvestre

SWEDEN	akerrattika
TUNISIA	abou vel bou-toum, ravelle
TURKEY	esek turpu
UNITED STATES	wild radish
URUGUAY	mostacilla, rabano silvestre

Seventy-Eight

Rumex acetosella L.

Polygonaceae, Buckwheat Family

R UMEX ACETOSELLA, often called sheep or red sorrel, is a perennial plant that reproduces by seeds and by aerial shoots arising from adventitious root buds. It is normally a dioecious plant, with each sex spreading clonally from its root buds. It is in most agricultural land north of the equator, is troublesome in Australia and New Zealand, and is found on islands in the Arctic and Sub-antarctic regions. One hundred years ago, the government of New South Wales declared that sheep sorrel was the worst weed ever introduced into Australia (Anon. [Australia] 1891). It is now a weed of 45 crops in 70 countries.

FIGURE 78-1   The distribution of *Rumex acetosella* L. across the world where it has been reported as a weed.

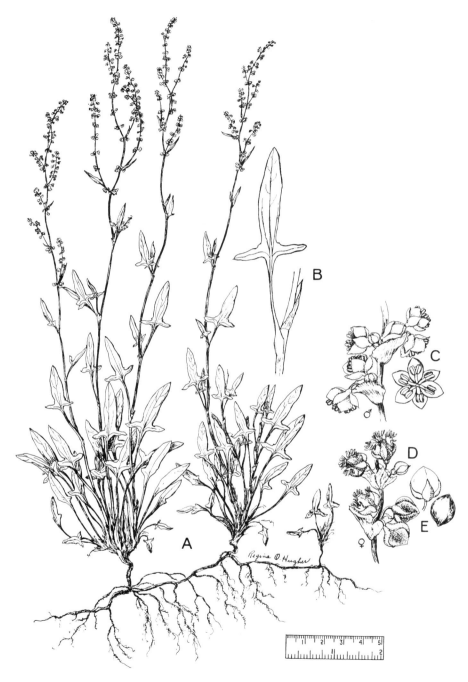

FIGURE 78-2 *Rumex acetosella* L.: A. habit; B. leaf detail; C. staminate flowers; D. pistillate flowers; E. achenes, in and out of calyx.

DESCRIPTION

R. acetosella (Figure 78-2) is a persistent, normally dioecious, *perennial*, 15 to 45 cm tall; *stems* erect, slender, glabrous, branched above; *roots* fleshy red-yellow, persistent, spreading extensively, with *adventitious buds* giving rise to aerial shoots, sexes spreading clonally by root buds; *leaves* acid to taste, alternate, variable in shape and size, lower most halberd-shaped with one or two basal lobes, lobed leaves long petioled with 2 fused stipules forming a silvery nodal sheath (ochrea) as in many **Polygonaceae**, upper leaves may be more slender and without lobes; *inflorescence* terminal in branched panicles; *flowers* borne in large and small clusters; *staminate clusters* yellow-orange, bearing or releasing much yellow pollen; *pistillate clusters* red-orange; *achene*, 1 to 1.5 mm long, almost as broad, 3-angled, smooth, shiny, mahogany-red, usually surrounded by the persistent, reddish perianth.

This species can be recognized by the sour taste of leaves, the red-yellow roots and the halberd-shaped lower leaves with silvery, sheathing nodal ochrea.

DISTRIBUTION AND HABITAT

Sheep sorrel is generally distributed as a weed of agriculture in Australia and New Zealand; Europe; North, Central, and South America; and Asia with the exception of the very warm regions (Figure 78-1). There are some infestations reported near the equator but these are likely to be found in higher mountain valleys. In Africa, it is found in Tunisia and on the east coast from Kenya to South Africa. It is in Greenland and Iceland, and many flowering plants and new seedlings may be seen on Sub-antarctic islands (Walton 1975).

In New Zealand, it is found from sea level to the upper limits of the snow-tussock grasslands, in Sri Lanka to 1800 m, and in France to 1200 m. First introductions of record are 300 yr for North America, 100 yr for Australia, with several introductions to New Zealand in the past 150 yr.

Near Quebec, Canada, the preference of sheep sorrel for different habitats was studied in experimental plots. It could not survive in a hoe-cultivation area, was present in cereals but was not a problem, preferred pastures and young and old prairies, and it avoided abandoned fields (Hamel and Dansereau 1949). In working fields, however, sorrel invades and persists in natural and sown pastures but is also a pest in many fields of fruits and vegetables, orchards, and annual crops of several kinds.

A few examples would be its presence as one of the five most abundant weeds in cereals in Prince Edward Island in far eastern Canada, while in Finland an examination of 150 fields used from 1 to 70 yr for spring cereals showed *R. acetosella* to be a very early, active colonizer. After 20 to 30 yr of growing cereals, some fields had accumulated 40,000 seeds/m². It is believed most initial infestations resulted from seeds in manure or contaminated crop seed (Raatikainen and Raatikainen 1972). It is in East African pastures and can be found in New Zealand in uncultivated tussock grasslands degraded by fire or because of the introduction of herbivores. In the latter areas, the species is sometimes regarded as an economic benefit because it helps in revegetation and soil conservation.

Paatela and Ervio (1971) examined soils to study the seed bank in spring cereal fields in eight grain production districts of south and west Finland. They found the supply of sheep sorrel seeds was much less in fine silt soils than on organic or coarse mineral soils. In New Zealand, where the weed has very wide distribution, it is a strong competitor of established lucerne and one of the worst weeds on light pumice soils. In Ireland, MacNaeidhe, and

Curran (1980, 1982) studied peat bog weed floras before and after conversion to mixed agriculture and found *Rumex* (probably brought in by flood water) already present and one of the species that proliferated rapidly as farming began. It was common on pond edges, near open drains, headlands, and roadsides, and its dispersal was favored by frequent travel of men and machines. *R. acetosella* is a problem in southeastern Australia in non-irrigated annual and perennial pastures and lucerne. When under irrigation, these crops are troubled by other *Rumex* species (docks, etc.). Sheep sorrel is also in potato fields and invades industrial sites and railroad properties. Loktev (1958) in the former Soviet Union found that 7% of the seed in samples of *Bromus secalinus* cheatgrass (sometimes planted as a forage), "carry" seeds of small-seeded weed species (sheep sorrel among them) in the longitudinal slits on their seed coats. All of such weed seeds germinated normally in laboratory and field tests.

The commonly held belief that sheep sorrel prefers acidic and infertile soils has been a controversial subject for a century. Harris (1971) has reviewed the important publications and research on this matter for most of the above period. These new and old reports continue to stimulate research on the growth of *Rumex* after heavy liming of soils, as well as the necessity to apply more complete fertilizer with the lime to stimulate competitiveness of the desired pasture species.

Horne (1953) generally agreed that *R. acetosella* was an indicator of acid soils but pointed out that there was also evidence that the species grows better at a higher *pH*, with ample calcium and other nutrients supplied. The reason for its apparent success on acid, infertile soils is that there is much less competition from crops grown there and from other weed species more sensitive to the acidity. Lefevre (1956) in France found that *pH* of 5.5 to 6 favored the growth of sheep sorrel. Suaghara (1981) in Japan adjusted the soil *pH* downward on an upland field over 4 yr and found that the fresh weight of *R. acetosella*, even in the first year, decreased with decreasing *pH*. The lethal *pH* for sheep sorrel on the site was 5.25.

PROPAGATION

Although sheep sorrel produces abundant seed and has many dispersal agents, it is believed that, within a given field, regeneration is almost exclusively by the extension of roots that then produce aerial shoots (Putwain et al. 1968). The vegetative clones reproduce for unknown periods. Putwain and Harper (1972) speculate that they may last for decades or even 100 yr. Almost the entire root system can produce adventitious root buds with aerial shoots, an advantage for recovery after grazing (Hughes 1938).

The horizontal roots are often mistaken for rhizomes. A fragment of root 1 cm in length is sufficient to propagate a new plant, thus calling into question the use of machine control measures, which may only spread root pieces and produce a more dense weed stand.

The plant does, however, produce much seed and has several means for dispersal. The seed is blown by the wind, moves in water (where it has been found in fissures of floating nuts and in other debris), is carried by several large domestic animals and by large and small birds, especially the sparrow *Passer domesticus* (Collinge 1913, Ridley 1930). Meadly (1965) reported that many sheep sorrel seeds are found undigested in the feces of large stock animals. In Denmark, seed buried 1 m in manure and beet leaves did not survive for 60 days (Anon. [Denmark] 1960). Dorph-Petersen (1925) reported that 40% of the sorrel seeds ingested by pigs and 15% of those eaten by chickens pass through the intestinal tract without injury.

In some areas seeds remain on the flower stalks of *R. acetosella* for a long time and thus may be harvested with timothy and clover seed. The weed has become notorious for its ability to pass undetected in crop seed cleaning operations and thus continues to add to the weed seed reserve of the fields. It is found routinely in seed supplies of timothy, several rye grasses, and several clovers in northern Europe, the United States, Australia, New Zealand, and elsewhere. Nineteen states of the United States prohibit sale of seed containing sheep sorrel seeds (Porter 1936, Johnston 1962, Tonkin 1968b, Tokela 1971).

The successful colonization of new areas by sheep sorrel may depend on the movement of seeds to disturbed or open sites where there will be no intense competition for a time. In seasonal emergence studies in southern Australia, Amor (1985) found that 7% of the seeds of this species, planted outdoors, emerged during the first growing season; 75% of that portion emerged in autumn (April–June). The seeds germinated from the surface to 7 cm following soil disturbance. Hughes (1938) reported that seeds could germinate from a maximum depth of 5 cm in the soil and that results were best on alkaline soils.

When growing in light for 8 to 20 hr, the maximum seed germination was obtained at 16 hr in the presence of a 0.2% nitrate solution as a moistening agent. Good germination could be obtained at 20 and 30°C constant temperature, but it was best at an alternation of these two.

Fresh seed may need 3 to 4 wk to germinate completely, but all seeds germinate in 7 to 8 days following 4 mo of dry storage. Seeds can remain viable for several years in dry storage, but there is a rapid loss of viability after the second year (Povilaitis 1956; Steinbauer and Grigsby 1958, 1960; Kolk 1962; Deschenes and Moineau 1972). Seed scarification favored germination but cold temperature stratification did not.

Dorph-Petersen (1925) studied the weed seeds in the upper 15 cm (plow layer) of the soil of four weedy Danish fields and found *R. acetosella* to be among the five species with the greatest number of seeds. Also in Denmark, Jensen (1969) found the seeds of 55 weed species in the upper 20 cm of soil in more than 50 cereal and root crop fields. Sheep sorrel was among them, with 50 to 200 viable seeds/m^2. Madsen (1962) buried sheep sorrel seeds in soil for 25 yr, found many seeds viable at 10 yr, with 3% germination at the end of the experiment. Stevens (1957) reported the weight of 1000 seeds of this species varied as follows: Norway 0.3 g, Canada 0.45 g, and the northern and central United states about 0.5 g.

Davidson (1984–85) made some interesting observations about seeds during a study of the role and consequences of weeds during and after a severe Australian drought in 1983–84 when much fodder, feed grain and large numbers of livestock were moved between areas. These activities resulted in large numbers of weeds being introduced to the place of final transport. A typical hay bale contained more than 20 weed seeds, with *Polygonum aviculare*, a restricted weed, being the most common, followed by *R. acetosella* and *Avena fatua*. Hay shipments in the east and south contained the seeds of up to 230 species and serious infestations followed. Seeds of 22 weeds were found in feed grains, with a mean total number of 550/kg of grain.

PHYSIOLOGY AND MORPHOLOGY

Archer and Auld (1982) of Australia reviewed the major research on the physiology and ecology of *R. acetosella* through 1982. The detailed work of Harris of New Zealand has contributed greatly to the understanding of the species (Harris 1968; 1969a,b; 1970a,b; 1971; 1972).

In the central United States, the major chronological events in the life cycle of sheep sorrel were recorded each 2 wk for 2 yr by Freeman and Sigafus (1966). One-month old seedlings planted in autumn developed 220 leaves and 40 branches in a 30-cm rosette. At a soil depth of 2.5 to 8 cm, creeping rootstalks extended 33 cm laterally and bore 66 adventitious buds, with some having aerial shoots. At 6 mo the roots extended 68 cm laterally and bore 200 root buds, of which 28 produced secondary plants above ground. At 9 mo, 60 flower stalks 60 cm tall had grown from the original rosette and 200 secondary plants made up one-half the total plant weight, with some now flowering also.

In autumn, after mowing to remove the top growth at maturity, the primary plant rosette decreased in vigor as the secondary plants increased to 670 in number. The latter remained attached to the common root system until after they bloomed at 21 mo (during the month of May). They produced an average of two flower stalks per plant. The crown of the primary plant had almost disappeared by mid-summer of the second year, and after all the top growth was mowed the creeping rootstalks deteriorated and one-half the secondary plants died. Plants that survived initiated new root systems.

It is certain from the work of Harris (1970a) that many ecotypes of this species across the world differ in their response to photoperiod and the thermoperiod of the site. Some may respond by flowering and producing seed in the seedling year or they may use their resources to produce adventitious roots. Carlson (1965) grew sheep sorrel at several photoperiods and found that the short days promoted adventitious root production and long days favored adventitious shoot formation. Plants of the male and female clones also differ in their response to environmental conditions.

The growth cycles of male and female are not the same in a given field. The average ratio of male to female plants in a field is normally 1:1, but soils, competition, and other factors of the environment can alter this (Putwain and Harper 1972, Doust and Doust 1987, Escarre and Houssard 1989). Male inflorescences develop earlier and overlap the later female flower production. As the male flowers decline, the female flower structures continue to elongate and develop. The males have the relatively smaller task of producing pollen, while females must set seed and carry it to completion. The dry weight of the sexes thus differs, with the female directing more of its resources into sexual reproductive tissues (Putwain and Harper 1972). Harper (1977) points out that each of the sexes, while growing as neighbors, makes different demands on the environment, and they may thus behave toward one another as if they were different species. The result is that earlier male growth may be more vigorous than that of females, only to soon be overgrown by the females as development continues. Harris (1968) found that the tussock communities had more male plants and that, in this instance, a greater proportion of the plants' resources were given to vegetative growth, thus giving the competitive advantage to this sex. Male plants have greater drought tolerance than female plants (Zimmerman and Lechowicz 1982).

Johnson and Briggs (1962) described a single plant of this species in Australia that had male, female, and hermaphroditic flowers.

Harris (1972) studied the effect of shading on sheep sorrel by growing it in various mixtures with *Lolium* species and *Trifolium repens*. The rosette habit of the weed gives it little capacity to keep pace with taller plants in lifting photosynthetic tissue upward into the light. It can reorient its leaves from horizontal to vertical but has limited ability to increase the petiole/lamina length ratio in shaded conditions. It is for this reason that many suggested management systems use suitable competitive plants that grow in fertile soils to suppress *R. acetosella*.

Harris (1970b) measured yield and plant height of populations at sea level, 650 and 1400 m. Soil from each location was moved to all other sites in an effort to separate edaphic from climatic factors. The change in climate was found to be the major determinant in plant height.

Plant specimens were gathered from 40 herbaria in Europe and North America and compared with local New Zealand plants. The time of flowering varied because the growing season was delayed at increasing latitudes and altitudes. Seeds from plants of several of the countries that spanned 50° latitude were planted at Christchurch (43° South). Time of flowering for sheep sorrel was correlated with latitude and resulted in some variation caused by montane, continental and Mediterranean climates. Most plants required long days for the stimulation of flowering, but some from higher latitudes could not flower in the first year in the prevailing day length of Christchurch. All populations flowered in the second year (Harris 1970a).

Moore (1950) in New Zealand found that the root systems of overwintering young seedlings of sheep sorrel were subject to breakage from soil heaving during freezing and thawing. Severe breakage killed some plants, some could tolerate mild heaving, while others re-rooted and survived.

Farris (1984) found the mean leaf area of *Rumex* plants from xeric sites (low moisture) on strip mines to be significantly larger than those of plants from mesic sites (moderate moisture) in abandoned fields when both types were grown under water stress or a daily watering. The reduction of leaf area under moisture stress was less for xeric plants (25%) than for mesic plants (42%).

Kiltz (1930) excavated a portion of an extensive root system of *R. acetosella* growing on a fertile silt loam in the central United States where rainfall was 65 cm/yr. A section 1 m long had seven aerial shoots growing from a main horizontal root 10 cm below the surface. The upper 30 cm of soil were filled with a fibrous root system. Many roots descended to 1.5 m, with some to 2 m (Kutschera 1960).

Harris (1968) examined the level of ploidy and organ size in 50 populations of sheep sorrel from Asia, Europe, North America and New Zealand. He found 40 hexaploids, four tetraploids, and one diploid. The correlation between ploidy and organ size was discussed in detail. As an example, there were significant differences among populations but no apparent relationships between seed length and ploidy.

The biosystematics of *R. acetosella* were studied in several European areas by den Nijs and co-workers. These have been reported in an extensive series of papers, the latest of which is by den Nijs et al. (1985). Jensen (1979) provided a key to and descriptions of the fruits of many *Rumex* species. Milkowska et al. (1975) completed anatomical and histological studies of this species.

AGRICULTURAL IMPORTANCE

Sheep sorrel is a serious weed of cereals in Ecuador and Poland; of lucerne in Hungary; of onions in Brazil; of pastures in Italy; of potatoes in Ecuador; and of sugar beets in Poland. It is a principal weed of barley in Korea and Lithuania; of carrots in Australia; of cassava, maize, and upland rice in Indonesia; of cereals in Australia, Belgium, and Canada; of flax in Germany; of linseed and lucerne in New Zealand; of ornamental nurseries in New Zealand and the northeastern United States; of oats in Colombia, Ecuador, and Lithuania; of pastures in Australia, Norway, New Zealand, and Sweden; of potatoes in Chile; of soybeans and turnips in the United States; of vegetables in the Philippines; and of wheat in Korea, Lithuania, New Zealand, South Africa, and the former Soviet Union.

It is a common weed of barley in Finland; of cabbage in Peru and the former Soviet Union; of cereals in Sweden, Tunisia, Tasmania, and the former Yugoslavia; of maize in Mexico, South Africa, the former Soviet Union, and the United States; of forages in Japan; of forest nurseries and plantings in Turkey; of several horticultural crops in Australia and England; of legumes in Tunisia; of oats and peas in the former Soviet Union; of orchards in Australia, Japan, and South Africa; of pastures in Austria, Bulgaria, and Japan; of potatoes in Colombia, Iceland, Mexico, Peru, Poland, the former Soviet Union, and Sweden; of sugar beets in Sweden; of tea in India; of vegetables in Tasmania; of vineyards in South Africa; of wheat in Colombia, Finland, Mexico, and Peru; and of several crops in Madagascar.

Sheep sorrel is present as a weed of unknown rank in barley in England, Germany, and New Zealand; beans and carrots in New Zealand; blueberries in Canada; cereals in Chile, Finland, South Africa, and the former Soviet Union; clover in England, New Zealand, and the former Soviet Union; cranberries in the United States; forages in Ireland, Kamchatka area in the former Soviet Union, and the United States; flax in Lithuania and the former Soviet Union; forest nurseries in Australia, England, and Germany; small fruits in Chile and New Zealand; hay in the former Soviet Union; lettuce in Australia; lucerne in Australia and South Africa; maize in Germany; ornamental nurseries Belgium, Canada, Germany, New Zealand, Sweden, and the United States; oats in Kamchatka area of the former Soviet Union; onions in New Zealand; orchards in Canada, Chile, Costa Rica, New Zealand, and the United States; pastures in Argentina, Belgium, Canada, Chile, Colombia, England, Germany, Scotland, Kamchatka area of the former Soviet Union, Tasmania, the United States, and the former Yugoslavia; potatoes in Australia, Chile, Germany, and the United States; rangelands in England, Greece, Japan, Switzerland, and the United States; oil seed rape and soybeans in Chile; annual ryegrass production in Brazil; sugar beets in England and the United States; strawberries in Belgium, Canada, and the United States; tea in Japan; tobacco in the United States; vegetables in Canada and New Caledonia; vineyards in Australia and France; and wheat in Argentina, England, Germany, and Venezuela.

During most seasons, sheep sorrel is unpalatable to stock animals, but they may consume large or small quantities while eating other forage. The weed often increases under heavy grazing, for its capacity for regeneration from extensive underground reserves helps it to secure new areas as the desirable forage is taken off. Moorland grazing lands in Scotland are often dominated by heather (*Erica* species). Welch (1984) reported that heavy grazing favors the development of *R. acetosella* in these areas.

Experiments and surveys in Germany, Poland, and Sweden suggest that fertility, liming and drainage have caused some decline of *R. acetosella*. In the 1960s sheep sorrel was not very widespread on arable land in Japan, but it became increasingly important as a weed as mechanical and chemical weed control were used more frequently. Kasahara (1982) reported it to be among the most harmful weeds in Japan.

In southeastern Australia, the digestibility of the whole plant of *R. acetosella* compared favorably with similarly managed sown species and was much better than native grasses. The nitrogen content of sorrel was equal to that of lucerne that was cut or ungrazed (Jones et al. 1971).

There are reports of oxalic acid toxicity to stock animals from several parts of the world but conclusive proof is lacking. Everist (1974) and Archer and Auld (1982) suggest that the levels of oxalate accumulated in animals are seldom high enough to cause much harm.

There is evidence that sheep sorrel was prominent among the wild plants and was used for human food around the 9th century in Poland and prior to that in Denmark (Dembinska 1976).

COMMON NAMES

Rumex acetosella

ARGENTINA	acederilla, vinagrillo
AUSTRALIA	sorrel
BELGIUM	petite oseille, schapezuring, veldzuring
BRAZIL	azeda
CANADA	petite oseille, sheep sorrel
CHILE	romacilla, vinagrillo
COLOMBIA	lengua de vaca, sangre de toro
DENMARK	rodknae
ECUADOR	pactilla
ENGLAND	red sorrel, sheep's sorrel, small sorrel
FINLAND	ahosuolaheina
FRANCE	petite oseille
GERMANY	Kleiner Ampfer, Kleiner Sauerampfer
HAWAII	red sorrel
HUNGARY	juhsoska
ICELAND	hudasura
INDIA	khatta palak, pottakanchi, updoli
ITALY	acetosa minore
JAPAN	himesuiba
MADAGASCAR	lavaravina
MEXICO	acederilla, hierba de cristo, hierba roja
MOROCCO	hammonida
NETHERLANDS	schapezuring
NEW ZEALAND	sheep's sorrel
NORWAY	smasyre
PERU	acedera
POLAND	szczaw poiny
PORTUGAL	azdinhas, erva-azeda
SAUDI ARABIA	hhummad saghir
SPAIN	acedera menor, acederilla, vinagrerita

SWEDEN	bergsyra
TURKEY	kucuk labada
UNITED STATES	red sorrel
VENEZUELA	acedera, cizana
YUGOSLAVIA	kiselica mala, mala kislica, stavelj mali

Seventy-Nine

Saccharum spontaneum L.

Poaceae (Gramineae), Grass Family

S ACCHARUM SPONTANEUM is a tropical grass species believed to have played a key role in the evolution of the noble cane, *S. officinarum*. Today *S. spontaneum* is utilized in several sugarcane breeding programs. It is also a weed in 33 countries and is adapted to diverse environments. The genus name in Latin means sugar and the species name refers to its natural occurrence in the wild. It is native to and a serious weed in India (Panje 1970).

FIGURE 79-1   The distribution of *Saccharum spontaneum* L. across the world where it has been reported as a weed.

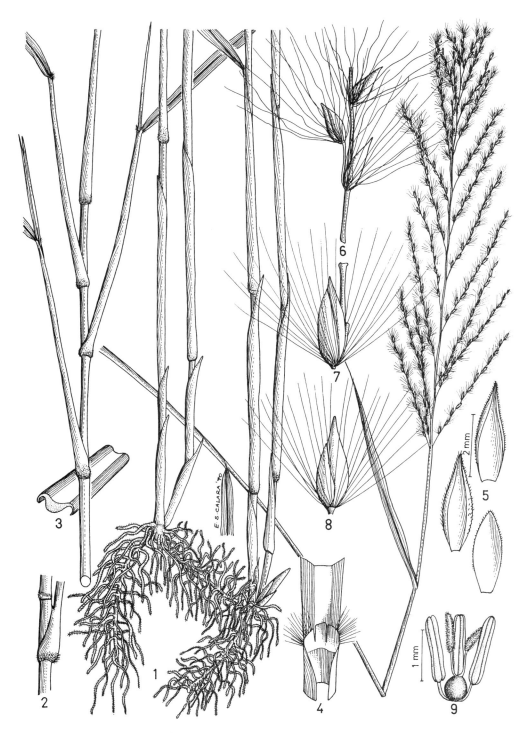

FIGURE 79-2 *Saccharum spontaneum* L.: 1. plant base and flowering culm; 2. culm section; 3. mid portion of blade; 4. leaf collar showing ligule; 5. glumes; 6. portion of inflorescence with spikelets; 7. and 8. spikelets; 9. floret.

DESCRIPTION

S. spontaneum (Figure 79-2) is a deep rooted, tufted or gregarious *perennial*; *roots* fibrous; *stems* stout, fibrous, 1 to 4 cm in diameter, 1 to 4 m (rarely 6 m) tall, unbranched, arising from long, creeping *rhizomes*; *leaf sheath* ciliate along outer margin and along top of inner margin; otherwise smooth, often with reddish or purplish blotches; *ligule* ovate, membranous; *leaf blade* dark green with conspicuously toothed margins, narrowly linear, 0.45 to 1 m long, 6 to 15 mm wide, midrib conspicuous and white; *inflorescence* a panicle, pyramidal or conical, lanceolate, white, 15 to 30 cm (occasionally 60 cm) long; branched, slender, spreading, whorled, fragile, the joints covered with long, silvery hairs; *spikelets* in pairs, one sessile and the other pediceled, both perfect, 3 to 3.5 mm long, awnless, with tuft of long, white hairs at base; *fruit* a dry, indehiscent, 1-seeded *caryopsis* 3.25 mm long, 1 mm wide; basal hairs several times longer than florets and form cottony web encompassing several seeds.

S. spontaneum is a highly variable species but can be distinguished by its stout stems, toothed leaf margins, whitish midrib and large plume-like panicle with numerous fine, white hairs at the base of the spikelets. These silky hairs are absent on *S. officinarum*.

HABITAT, ECOLOGY, AND TAXONOMY

S. spontaneum is found in waste areas, fallow fields, marshes, banks of streams and ponds, on sand dunes, along railroads and highways, and in or around fields. It is a tropical and subtropical species most commonly encountered in central and southeastern Asia (Figure 79-1). In New Guinea, it grows from sea level to 1500 m and tolerates many soil textures and moisture levels (Henty 1969). *S. spontaneum* is an early colonizer and was one of the first species to develop on a volcanic island of Indonesia formed in 1929. Its rhizomes withstood repeated eruptions and considerable accumulation of volcanic ash. To date it is one of the most prevalent species and occurs to within 80 m of the top of the volcano's cone (Suzuki 1984). Repeated burning of cropland results in nearly pure stands of *S. spontaneum* and *Imperata cylindrica* in the Philippines (Siebert 1987). Forest land that is not farmed or burned after clearing has much less perennial grass. *S. spontaneum* is more abundant on the upper slope areas and ridge tops than at lower toposequences.

Biotypes exhibit distinct patterns of root growth. One has deep roots with few lateral branches, another has relatively shallow and diffusely distributed roots, and a third has highly branched roots that penetrate to over 3 m (Negi 1962). Floating roots develop on some biotypes (even on those from dry areas) when they are flooded. They float because aerenchyma tissue forms in response to flooding, and plants can survive under these conditions for over 8 mo (Srinivasan and Batcha 1963b). In contrast, other biotypes are well suited to xerophytic areas (Kehar 1949) and, in Japan, plants have been used to stabilize the landward side of sand dunes (Suzuki and Numata 1982).

S. spontaneum is believed to have crossed spontaneously with *Miscanthus floridulus* to form *S. robustum*, which is one of the parents of noble sugarcane (Simmonds 1976). Due to the great morphological, genetic and physiological differences within *S. spontaneum*, breeders have an abundance of germplasm to develop improved sugarcane varieties. However, this diversity can confuse proper identification of the species. Clones ranging from 0.4 to 6 m in height, from bunch grasses to single stems, and with various stem diameters and other differences were collected in the southern United States and carefully described by Artschwager (1942). A key that could be used to identify clones was also developed. Mukherjee (1957) reviewed the taxonomy of *Saccharum* and related genera and used the characteristic of spikelets at the ends of the tertiary branches of the inflorescence to help identify *S. spontaneum*.

The weedy types of *S. spontaneum* have many rhizomes. However, this trait has not been incorporated into *S. officinarum*. The rhizomatous types originated in India, especially in areas with moderate but prolonged dry periods (Panje 1970). Summer fallowing allows plants to become well established.

BIOLOGY

Sugarcane breeders and plant physiologists have done most of the research on *S. spontaneum*. The $2n$ chromosome number is highly variable: from 40 to 128. The group with $2n = 60$ to 70 is the largest and has the most diversity, including high rhizome production, and thus most of the weedy biotypes are in this group (Panje 1970). Plants can readily propagate by stem pieces because each node has a root band with one or two rows of root primordia (Artschwager 1942). Dry matter production of daughter plants is proportional to the weight of the original seed piece. Among the seven ecotypes tested, three had the greatest biomass production after 14 days at 22°C, two at 26°C, one at 30°C, and one at 34°C (Whiteman et al. 1963). No sprouting occurred at 10°C, and 40°C reduced sprouting of all biotypes.

Factors affecting *S. spontaneum* flowering have been extensively studied. Some biotypes never seem to flower and others flower prolifically. Both genetic and environmental factors are involved and they often interact. Panje and Srinivasan (1959) collected 640 clones from lat 5° to 34° N in India and grew them for 6 yr at 11° and 30° N lat. Those collected between 5° and 19° flowered readily, but those from further north often failed to flower. Nevertheless, even 33% of those from 30° to 34° flowered. Of the 177 clones planted at lat 11° and 30° N, 97 flowered 20 to 60 days later at the more northern latitude and 155 flowered 1 to 80 days later at the northern site. They calculated that flowering is delayed 2.4 days per 1° of latitude. Most flowering occurs the second year after establishment. A brief exposure to light during the dark period delays or prevents flowering.

Extensive studies by Julien (1973) determined that the optimum floral induction photoperiod for many biotypes is 12.5 hr. Different photoperiods may be required for floral differentiation and inflorescence elongation. Daniels (1963) successfully induced flowering by shortening the photoperiod 15 min per week and by maintaining high relative humidity.

Some clones have long, decumbent stems that never flower. When these are in an erect position at the time of flower initiation, some are induced to flower (Srinivasan and Batcha 1963a). In the Northern Hemisphere, flowering may occur from June to December, with peak flowering in September and October in many areas.

S. spontaneum clones vary greatly in sucrose content (Chu et al. 1962, Brown et al. 1969). This trait as well as disease resistance, cold temperature tolerance, high tillering ability, vigorous regrowth capacity, a deep root system and others are sought by sugarcane breeders (Panje 1972). Plants can be self- or cross-pollinated without difficulty, assuming flowers are present on both desired parents. Kainth and Tariq (1969) noted that the inflorescence emerges 5 to 7 days after the boot stage, and that the florets open when the flowers emerge. Stigmas emerge at 5:00 A.M., stamens 45 min later and the florets remain open for 2.5 to 3 hr. Maximum pollen dehiscence occurs between 6:30 and 7:00 A.M., which is also the period of highest seed set. Pollen is readily wind borne and remains viable for 4 to 5 hr. Seed production also varies among ecotypes. In the Philippines, 12,800 seeds/plant were formed (Pancho 1964), while in India 3042 were produced (Datta and Banerjee 1976). Seeds are readily dispersed by the wind.

S. spontaneum is a C_4 plant. Among eight tropical species studied, the chlorophyll content of *S. spontaneum* was more than twice as much as the next highest species (Mall et al. 1973). *S. spontaneum* leaves have fewer stomata on the upper surface compared to other *Saccharum* species (70 vs. 87/mm^2) and those on the lower surface are protected from air movement because they are in the veinal grooves and are covered by a spine-like structure of silica (Rojas and de Castro 1985). These features enhance its drought tolerance.

AGRICULTURAL IMPORTANCE

Nearly all reports of *S. spontaneum* as a weed are from Asia (Figure 79-1). It is a serious or principal weed of forages in Thailand; pasture and pineapple in the Philippines; pasture, sugarcane, and tea in India; and rubber and tea in Indonesia. It is a common weed of sugarcane in Bangladesh and the Philippines; tobacco in the Philippines; and wheat in India; and is an unranked weed of coffee in Indonesia and Kenya; cotton, jute, maize, peanut, rice, and sorghum in India; maize in Bangladesh; rice in Laos, Nepal, the Philippines, Thailand, and Vietnam; rubber in Malaysia; and tea in China, Japan, and Sri Lanka.

The plant has infested nearly 4 million ha in central India, often forcing farmers to abandon entire fields (Sen 1981). Deep plowing followed by several lighter tillage operations helps reclaim fields, but reinfestation occurs unless control measures are continued (Panje 1970). Mulching with sugarcane trash to 10 to 15 cm after sugarcane emergence is beneficial in India (Mathur 1965). Annual grasses like *Rottboellia myurus* dominated and displaced *S. spontaneum* after several seasons (Chakravarti 1963). *S. spontaneum* may be allelopathic to crops. Leachates from rhizomes and roots inhibited shoot and root growth of three wheat varieties in petri dishes (Amritphale and Mall 1978). This weed hosts many sugarcane insects and diseases of economic importance.

S. spontaneum has several beneficial uses. While relatively high in fiber, it can be used as a forage and maintains animal weight without the use of protein supplements (Kehar 1949). When four annual cuttings are taken, dry weight yields of over 5.5 ton/ha are possible. Plants also serve to make brooms, rope and mats, provide material for thatching or fencing, and can be used as paper pulp. Philippinos have several medicinal uses for the plants (Pancho and Obien 1983), and young shoots are boiled and eaten with rice in Indonesia (Uphof 1968). Its slow rate of decomposition makes it an excellent mulch (Wapakala 1966).

COMMON NAMES

Saccharum spontaneum

AUSTRALIA	serio grass
BANGLADESH	kash
CAMBODIA	ampeon prxy
EGYPT	boos, boos el-gezzair, boos giddawi, ghazar
INDIA	kans ghas, kash

INDONESIA	glagah, tobioe
JAPAN	wase-abana
MADAGASCAR	fary
MAURITANIA	canne sauvage
NEW GUINEA	pit-pit
PAKISTAN	kahi
PHILIPPINES	bobang, bugang, sidda, talahib, tigbau
THAILAND	phong
VENEZUELA	cana uba

Eighty

Sagittaria sagittifolia L.

Alismataceae, Water Plantain Family

THE FAMILY ALISMATACEAE is made up of aquatic and marsh plants and is perhaps the most typically amphibious of our water plants. The genus *Sagittaria* has about 20 species and many are viewed with uncertainty by various taxonomists because of the plants' ability to severely alter their morphology to accommodate changes in the environment. The leaves of this weed present the greatest variation in leaf form exhibited by the family. The striking arrow-shaped leaves and bold inflorescences of the *Sagittaria* place them among our most attractive aquatic plants. *S. sagittifolia* prospers near the equator but is also found above the Arctic Circle. It is a weed in about 50 countries of the world.

FIGURE 80-1 The distribution of *Sagittaria sagittifolia* L. across the world where it has been reported as a weed.

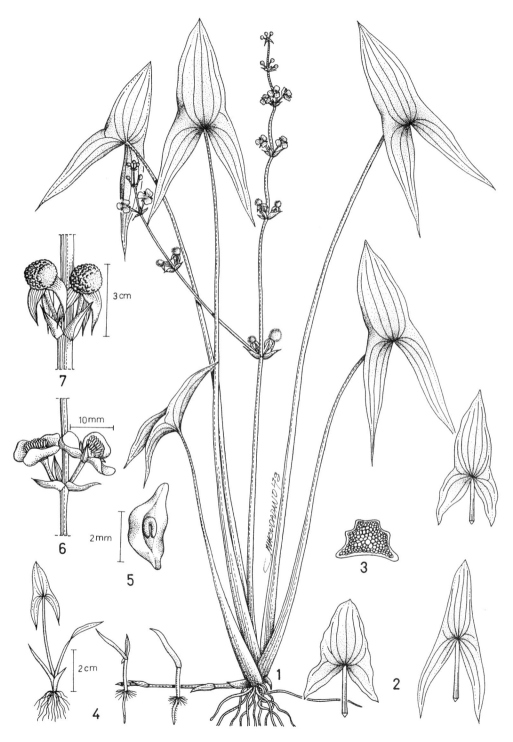

FIGURE 80-2 *Sagittaria sagittifolia* L.: 1. habit; 2. enlarged leaf; 3. petiole cross section; 4. seedlings; 5. achene; 6. staminate flowers; 7. pistillate flowers.

DESCRIPTION

S. sagittifolia (Figure 80-2) is an *herbaceous, perennial* or sometimes *annual* aquatic plant, monoecious or sometimes dioecious, may be anchored beneath the water, growing in marshes, or on mud, 30 to 90 cm tall, erect, *stoloniferous,* with milky juice, perennating by detachable tubers borne terminally on stolons; *tubers* ca 3 cm long, ovoid or subcylindrical, bright blue with yellow spots; *submerged leaves* linear, translucent, sometimes spongy; *floating leaves* lanceolate to ovate, *aerial leaves* long petioled, blades sagittate, 5–20 cm long, acutely attenuate, lateral lobes of equal length with needle-like or blunt tips; *nerves* in terminal lobes 5 to 9 or more, in basal lobes 4 to 5, connected by parallel cross veins and veinlets; *petioles* sharply triangular, 20 to 60 cm long, sheath with broad, scarious margin, racemes *inflorescence* arising from leaf rosette on terminal, solitary, naked *scapes,* usually with several tripetalous *flowers,* monoecious, 2 cm in diameter, petals white with or without purple, carmine, or other basal spot, *petals* larger than *sepals,* suborbicular to broad elliptic, bottom whorls of inflorescence mostly female flowers, upper whorls mostly male, but considerable variation in sexual composition of blooms in two bottom whorls (Sidorski 1984); stamens numerous, filaments glabrous, as long as anthers; *anthers* purple, carmine or yellow; *style* central, stigmas punctiform; *racemes* 1/3 to 1/2 as long as peduncle with 2 to 6 whorls of flowers; *peduncles* 1 to 5, erect, sharply triangular, hexagonal, or polygonal, 20 to 50 cm including raceme and reflexing after anthesis; fruiting heads globular, up to 1.5 cm; *achenes* obovate 3 to 5 mm long and 1.5 to 3 mm wide with broad dorsal or ventral membranous wing; seed light brown.

In the European and North Asian specimens and east in Siberia to longitude 150°, petals are white with distinct purple or carmine basal spot, anthers are purple or carmine, sepals are appressed or spreading after anthesis, and the basal lobes of the sagittate leaves are blunt at the extreme tips. Specimens from South and East Asia, including Malaysia, are distinct with pure white petals, yellow anthers, sepals reflexed after anthesis, the basal lobes of the leaves ending in a very acute, needle-like tip (Bogin 1955). Because of these marked differences in leaves and flowers in the temperate and tropical zones, an effort has been made to assign specific rank to plants for each area. Bogin, however, accepted them as two distinct geographical races with subspecific rank. This opinion is followed here. The temperate taxa are designated as the typical subspecies; the warm temperate to tropical as ssp. *leucopetala.* We have speculated that this controversy may explain in part the paucity of information on the distribution of the species in the Southern Hemisphere.

DISTRIBUTION AND HABITAT

S. sagittifolia (Figure 80-1) behaves as a weed in many of the agricultural areas and waterways of North America. The plant is generally distributed in Europe, where it is found as far north as 69° 30' N near the Norway-Russia border (Okland 1962). It is in Eurasia, south and east Asia, the Pacific Islands and Hawaii and Australia. As previously discussed in the description of the species, the lack of agreement on the designation of the taxa for the plants of the species in the northern and southern hemispheres may be contributing to the lack of information about its role as a weed on the African and South American continents. More than 100 years ago, De Candolle (1855) prepared a list of 100 flowering plants, including *S. sagittifolia,* that tolerate a very wide range of climatic conditions and are spread over more than one third of the earth's surface. The seeds float well and have sticky surfaces that help them cling to feathers and fur (Hroudova et al. 1988).

The species grows in temperate, warm temperate, and tropical regions where it is in rice paddies or found mainly in quiet, shallow, standing water sheltered from winds and waves. It colonizes mostly shallow river banks and quiet bays throughout river basins. It avoids still water with increased mineral content and seldom frequents depressions in fields and roads that dry temporarily. During severe floods, its short, stout stolons are torn from their moorings and washed into ditches, and later come to rest along quiet banks of streams, drains and water bodies of all sizes.

Haslam (1978) in England found that the species prefers eutrophic sites with soft, silty substrates in slow canals, drains and streams coursing through clay soils. The number of plants decreased as sand, gravel or stones became more plentiful in the substrate. Plants are unable to tolerate non-eutrophic pollution. The species is moderately tolerant of shade as measured at the water surface and is quite tolerant of turbidity because it frequently has some leaves above the water. Fast flows and spates are not tolerated. In slow-flowing or quiet waters with inhospitable substrates, should silt and organic matter be released and deposited on the bottom, *S. sagittifolia* is one of the first species to appear.

The plants are moderately susceptible to battering by turbulence, the early leaves being most tolerant. This plant ranks among those aquatics that are deep-rooted, having many roots below 15 cm. The deep, straight roots make the plants capable of tolerating sporadic silt-loading and also the disturbance of the upper silt. Experimental measurements have shown that plants growing on coarse substrates are well rooted and can only be dislodged by high force when they are pulled.

Among several aquatic plants studied by Haslam (1978) in England, *S. sagittifolia* ranks with those that can continue to grow satisfactorily at a 120-cm depth or more. In the rivers, it preferred streams 8 to 18 m in width. These smaller streams, canals, and drains are often dredged to clean them, as excess vegetation and the growth of tall monocots such as *Sparganium erectum* begin to interfere with flow. *S. sagittifolia* and *Potamogeton pectinatus* often become dominant in the early years after dredging. The plant parts of these two species, buried in the undredged soil, may be dormant for many years, with little aboveground vegetation. The restoration of light as the taller vegetation is removed allows renewed growth of the shorter species until they are again shaded out.

ANATOMY AND MORPHOLOGY

The changes in habitat undergone by *S. sagittifolia* are reflected in anatomical adaptations such as differentiation of parenchyma tissues to provide large intercellular spaces in submerged leaves and increases in the number of vascular bundles that are more highly developed in emerged leaves. Supporting tissues are nearly absent in submerged leaves but are plentiful in emerged leaves. Chloroplasts are found in the epidermis of the upper side of submerged ribbon-like leaves, on the dorsal side of floating leaves, and are absent in the epidermis of arrow-shaped leaves (Stant 1964). The variation in leaf shape (usually in response to a particular aquatic site) is surely the greatest change manifested by this species as conditions change.

The lacunate tissues (having air spaces) in the *Sagittaria* are quite fragile, so that bruising and stretching can easily result in waterlogging of stems, petioles and submerged organs. Transverse, water-tight diaphragms that develop at intervals in the lacunae help to prevent some of the injury. The diaphragms are formed from the swelling of wall cells into the cavity, followed by rapid division and extensive branching until a partition wall of loosely arranged cells is completed (Arber 1920, 1922; Sculthorpe 1967). While studying the lacunate tissues of *Sagittaria*, Arber (1922) observed that roots and stolons sometimes break through the diaphragms of the leaf sheaths of living leaves and penetrate as far as 10 cm into the petiole, running parallel to its long axis.

The radical leaves (those arising from stem base near the ground) of *S. sagittifolia* come from an erect, short bulbous and succulent rootstock with very condensed internodes. The position of the shoot apex at the crown of this rootstock changes little from year to year. In deep or fast-flowing water, the leaves produced are long and strap-shaped. One plant may bear 20 such leaves and Arber (1920) reported some 2 m in length. As the water becomes more shallow, transition leaf forms between the simpler aquatic patterns and the aerial types appear in various shapes. The general pattern is a widening of the lamina at the apex to give lanceolate to ovate leaf form. Some of these become floating leaves.

At the water's edge or on mud, the abbreviated plant axis shows further striking changes by producing leaves whose petioles rise into the air, with laminae becoming more and more sagittate at the base until true arrowhead forms appear. Many floating leaves of aquatic weeds are quite durable because of their leathery quality, but leaves of *S. sagittifolia* are thinner, more delicate and so are more easily torn.

Funke (1937) carried out an unusual experiment with this species to demonstrate the very large capacity of the plant to adjust to changing environments. As mature plants from shallow water were transplanted to deep water, petioles resumed growth to carry the leaf laminae to the surface. The increased petiole length resulted from both cell division and extension, and rates of growth of 17 mm/hour were recorded.

Changing environments may also result in a return of the plant to a more juvenile state, calling for renewed production of ribbon-like leaves. Land forms of *S. sagittifolia* that are transplanted to sites in water will revert to the production of ribbon leaves. Forms with only ribbon leaves in water, when transferred to sites on land, begin to produce aerial leaves.

Placement of mature, individual aerial leaves into deep or heavily shaded water will cause the plant to begin production of some ribbon leaves. Weak light, drastic pruning of foliage, or movement of plants to barren substrates or distilled water depletes the carbohydrate and other reserve, with the result that juvenile ribbon leaf production is resumed. Extensive discussions of the morphology and anatomy of stem, petiole and root tissues of *Sagittaria* may be found in Arber (1920, 1922) and Lee and Chang (1958).

REPRODUCTION

Morphological studies of vegetative and sexual reproduction of *S. sagittifolia* are far more abundant than explorations of the physiology and ecology of the species. The propagation of the species and the flexibility and versatility of its adaptations to changing conditions during reproduction are thus appropriately discussed together.

The renewal of the species depends on both seed production and the formation of underground tubers. From the base of crowded leaves on the short main axis, large white underground stolons several nodes in length arise, each with one or more scale leaves, and a terminal bud. The stolons are thicker than the roots. Three altered internodes at the end of the stolon give rise to a tuber and new vegetative plant tip. Tubers range from 0.3 to 3 mm in length. An anthocyanin pigment in the epidermis of the tuber gives it a blue tint.

Small tubers near the surface often originate from lateral stolon branches. All of the above structures form soon after the above-ground plant has developed. Scale leaves cover the tuber, food storage enlarges the organ, and the stolon turns downward to carry it into the substrate. Toward the end of the season the parent plant dies; the tuber remains buried for the winter or for the duration of any unfavorable period (Hroudova et al. 1988).

Tuber formation drops off quickly below 20 cm in the soil; tuber length increases below 30 cm as does average tuber dry weight. Arber (1920) reports that in a favorable site this weed may provide a dense stand of plants producing 2 to 3 L of tubers/m^2 of soil area. Unfavorable times such as aphid attacks, diseases, poor nutrition, and water deficiencies may cause the plant to begin tuber formation.

In the spring, the more basal of the two internodes of the tuber elongates to carry a bud to the surface, forming a new plant from which roots and leaves develop. The adventitious roots that form at the nodes at this time are poorly branched, appear in dense bundles, and grow only to a depth of 0.15 to 0.3 m according to the soil profile. While developing its new stolons and other structures, the new main plant may remain attached to the old original tuber. The latter eventually becomes dry and spongy. The survival time of buried tubers is not known.

The sexual reproduction process rests upon the indehiscent achene. Germination of the seed usually begins in the spring of the season following its formation. These floating seeds may be carried long distances, aided by the flattened mericarps containing sufficient air to make them suitable for dispersal by wind or water. The achenes have large distinct wings with lacunate parenchyma, a large-celled, lightweight epidermis, and a waxy surface layer (Pancho 1964). The fruits may float from weeks to months until frost causes them to sink as the ovary wall becomes waterlogged (Hroudova et al. 1988). Guppy (1894–97) reported the seeds could float 6 to 12 months.

The seeds of *S. sagittifolia* germinate in light or dark; the optimum temperature for the process ranges from 15 to 35°C. There was no germination at 10°C and it was very restricted at 40°C. Seeds remaining in mud below water level for prolonged periods began to germinate as the water temperature rose as water receded. Following 10 yr of storage under water at 5°C, seeds gave 15 to 20% germination when transferred to 20°C (Hroudova et al. 1988).

The seed production of *S. sagittifolia* is responsive to the variability in the large number of habitats available to it. For example, in Czechoslovakia, Hroudova (1980) found that plants usually have more space for growing in littoral communities and often have better growing conditions, with the result that they are more fertile and produce more seeds. Fertility also depends on the ratio of female and male plants in the seed numbers, which varied from 400 to 4000/plant. Pancho (1964) in the Philippines found single plants bearing 9000 seeds. The seeds weighed 0.7g/1000.

Immediate germination seldom occurs in freshly harvested seeds. Hroudova and coworkers (1988) believe the pericarp must be altered by a combination of physical, chemical, and microbial processes in the muddy substratum before germination can occur (see also Crocker 1907). Guppy (1894–97) in Britain did not believe that the seeds of his *S. sagittifolia* plants were "altogether hindered" in their germination by a hard seed coat. He placed seeds in mud immediately after harvest and 25% germinated in the first and second years. Seeds that were dried for 7 wk after harvest, then placed in water, gave 80% germination over a 3-yr period.

Crocker (1907) and Serbanescu (1973) agree that *Sagittaria* seeds ripen above the water. For good germination and establishment, Serbanescu believes the seeds must be ripe before they fall into the water or mud, a matter on which there is little agreement and which needs careful experimentation. The former obtained consistently high levels of germination by cracking or removing seed coats in several ways before planting.

In the experiments of Hroudova et al. (1988), seeds germinated better in quiet water than in aerated water, and they suggest that anaerobic conditions may encourage germination in the substratum. Guppy (1894–97) found that seeds floated on sea water still gave 70% germination in the second and third years. He also found that seeds remained viable after several weeks in ice.

Seeds eaten by fish were viable after spending 48 hr in the gut (Ridley 1930). De Vlaming and Proctor (1968) reported increased germination of seeds eaten by ducks and shore birds. The retention time in the stomach would allow movement of *Sagittaria* seeds up to 1600 km during migrations.

PHYSIOLOGY AND ECOLOGY

The life history of *S. sagittifolia* and its exceptional ability to adapt its leaf forms to different habitats is surely best expressed in the changes made during fluctuating water levels. In a study of 100 sites in Czechoslovakia, and from a survey of reports during 100 yr in France and Germany, Hroudova (1980) decided that most populations were found in 0 to 80 cm of water, with optimum flowering and fruiting at 10 to 80 cm. Fruit-bearing plants were found to 1 m depth. The maximum production of aerial leaves was at 0 to 10 cm and below that a gradual increase in floating leaves. On terrestrial areas where water level was below ground, this weed formed arrowhead leaves almost exclusively and fruit-bearing plants were found at half the sites. The ecological factor most likely to become limiting at greater depth is the loss of light. In 90 cm or more of depth, plants are retarded, but the ability to reproduce sexually throughout its entire depth range is one more evidence of the great plasticity of this species.

Depending on the environment in which it grows, *S. sagittifolia* has very little or negligible cuticle and a thin epidermis. This allows rather free passage of O_2 and CO_2, but there is evidence that, in submerged organs, only certain of the epidermal cells are easily permeable to the salts of the surrounding medium. These localized cells, called hydropoten by Mayr (1915), are not found in leaves of the aerial type that may be temporarily submerged.

In an extensive study of the biology and ecology of the aquatic hydrophytes of British rivers, Haslam (1978) endeavored to relate species' site preference to water quality. In a summary of the characteristics of the water of the preferred natural sites of *S. sagittifolia*, in comparison with other aquatic plants in the rivers, she found the plant in areas of high alkalinity levels (over 250 ppm as $CaCO_3$), and discovered that it has one of the highest biological O_2 demands and favors areas high in Cl, P, NO_3-N, and a *pH* of 7.5 to 8. Now if we turn to the nutrients to which the plant is favorably related in terms of silt chemistry (as compared with other plants), we find the following: low levels of Ca, Mg and K, moderate levels of Cl, Na, P, S, and its presence was poorly correlated with NO_3-N and NH_3-N.

Hinneri (1976) studied the aquatic plant population of a 40 km^2 bay on the southwest coastal area of Finland after it was cut off from the sea by an embankment. The *pH* of the water quickly fell to 4.8 due to the influence of water rich in SO_4 leached from deposits in the catchment area. Several common hydrophytes disappeared in the first 2 to 3 yr as the *pH* fell, but *S. sagittifolia* formed large fields of vegetation on the clay bottoms at depths of 150 to 250 cm. Floating leaves and emergent growth forms prospered in some eutrophic bays of the reservoir. Luther (1951), in south Finland, found that *Sagittaria* extended from the freshwater area of an estuary to reaches of salinity that contain 3000 ppm NaCl (seawater being 35,000 ppm). An analytical study on the organic constituents of the species was reported by S. Sharma et al. (1972).

This weed favors a finely granular substrate, deep muddy sediments, or loamy soils; very poor peaty or sandy soils are sometimes occupied by the weed, but it is rarely found on coarse sand or gravel. It has a wide amplitude of tolerance to soil chemistry, the characteristics of which may change greatly within a single stand. It is not well adapted to increasing mineralization and thus is rarely found in saline habitats. A *pH* range of 6.5 to 8 in the substrate seems satisfactory for growth. Overall, the plant seems adaptable to varying substrates, as it can change its morphological characteristics to meet environmental changes. As may be expected, the total production of biomass and the chemical composition of the material covers a very broad range consistent with the particular site of growth. For further detailed information on the preference of this plant for habitats with varying water quality and substrates, see Haslam (1978) and Hroudova et al. (1988).

ECONOMIC IMPORTANCE

As a weed, *S. sagittifolia* is a general nuisance in the crops, irrigation systems, drains and waterways of more than 50 countries. Its remarkable ability to adapt, both in form and physiology to drastic changes in the environment, conveys a tenacity for survival that enables the plant to reappear again and again as growing conditions become favorable. The species can create closed meadows of green, underwater vegetation to interfere with water flow, or, as an emergent plant, provide extensive stands in drains or along shores of reservoirs and irrigation canals, where it frequently must be removed.

S. saggitifolia is a common weed of irrigation systems in India and Italy and of maize in India. It is a principal weed of rice in India, Italy, and Taiwan and a weed of unknown importance in rice in Bangladesh, Burundi, Cambodia, Sri Lanka, China, Cuba, Hungary, Indonesia, Laos, Malaysia, Nepal, Pakistan, the Philippines, Portugal, Thailand, and Vietnam. It is a weed of taro in Hawaii.

It is regarded as a serious weed in several kinds of waterways in Argentina, Australia, England, Germany, Hawaii, Italy, the former Soviet Union, Sweden, and Taiwan; and a principal weed in Germany and Hawaii. In India, it is a principal aquatic weed and interferes with potable water supplies and the production of fish in ponds. It is a common weed in the aquatic systems of Iran and Portugal. In addition to all of the above places, it is an aquatic weed of 20 more countries as may be seen from the map in Figure 80-1.

In Asia, the tubers are used for food when boiled and seasoned. Freshly harvested young leaves and petioles are edible. Selected varieties of this plant were once cultivated in Japan and China, with some tubers reaching 10 cm at harvest. In several countries, the tubers are fed to cattle and pigs, and the foliage, fruits and seeds are eaten by water birds. The foliage is of moderate importance to fish for shade, shelter, and spawning areas. Phytophagous fish have only a moderate preference for this weed. The plant is extensively used in the aquarium trade and in aquatic gardens.

COMMON NAMES

Sagittaria sagittifolia

AUSTRALIA	arrow-head
BELGIUM	pijlkruid
DENMARK	pilblad
ENGLAND	arrowhead
FINLAND	pystykeiholehti
FRANCE	fleche-d'eau
GERMANY	Pfeilkraut
ITALY	erba saetta
NETHERLANDS	pijlkruid
NORWAY	pilblad
PHILIPPINES	gauai-gauai
PORTUGAL	seta
SPAIN	saeta de aqua
SWEDEN	pilblad
UNITED STATES	chinese arrowhead

Eighty-One

Salsola kali L.

Chenopodiaceae, Goosefoot Family

S ALSOLA KALI, with the oft-used name tumbleweed, or Russian thistle, is one of our most interesting weeds. When mature, it may roll and tumble for hours as it spreads seeds in its path over flat or hilly country. It may be at home as a strand-line (water's edge) species where the sea meets the land or may prosper in semi-desert areas where efficiency of water use is a first requirement.

The taxonomy of the *Salsola* genus is mixed and there is little choice at this date, on a world basis, but to treat this group of weeds as a single taxon for purposes of examining

FIGURE 81-1   The distribution of *Salsola kali* L. across the world where it has been reported as a weed.

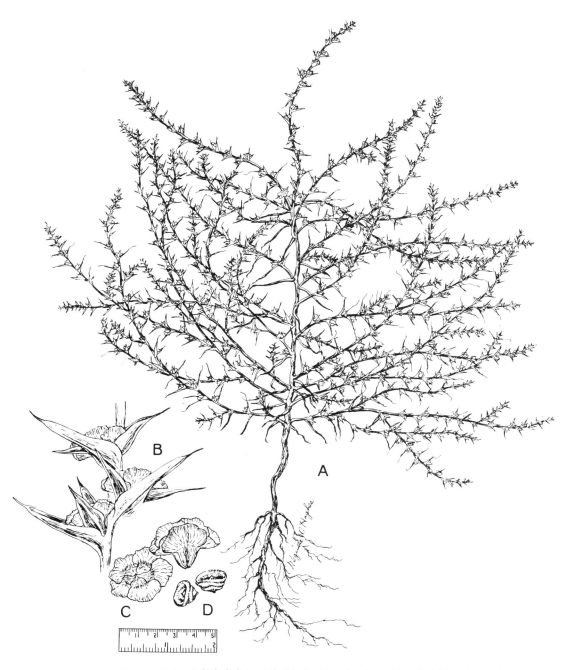

FIGURE 81-2 *Salsola kali* L.: A. habit; B. flowering branch; C. fruiting calyxes; D. achenes.

the behavior on agricultural lands. In Europe, around the Mediterranean Sea and in Central Asia the plant has a variety of forms and has been assigned a large number of subspecies and variety designations. Everist (1974) in Australia states that *S. kali* is quite a variable species, that authors in his country continue to partition the types into several species, and that the group is now in need of revision. The plethora of names continues as we move to North America. Government botanists and experiment station workers in Canada and the United States have reported to us, or recorded in the literature, several different names for the species, among them: *S. iberica*, *S. paulsenii*, *S. pestifer*, *S. kali* var. *tenuifolia*, *S. tragus*, and *S. kali* var. *tragus*. However, Shetler and Skog (1978) of the Missouri Botanical Garden, in the United States, have included only one species, *S. kali*, in their provisional checklist of species for the flora of North America. Beatly (1973) and Aellen (1961, 1964) have recently reviewed the preferred names for the species in the western United States, Europe, southeast Russia, and Central America. Young and Evans (1985) prepared a chronology of the history of the scientific names for Russian thistle from 1810 through 1970. It is rare indeed for a single genus to have many weed species that are troublesome in agriculture.

Because of these uncertainties, the weed will be treated as a single taxon, *S. kali*, and wherever appropriate we will supply other species or variety designations when offered by authors. We have studied most of the biological knowledge about many of these similar weeds and believe that there is a general resemblance of form and behavior and that such an account can provide useful information to work with.

Much of the knowledge we have on biology and control for this species comes from workers in Canada and the United States because the weed moved so swiftly across the western parts of the continent after its introduction 125 years ago. After surveying more than 100 countries, we find that it is in more than 30 crops and 40 countries and is considered to be a major problem in five of the major agricultural countries of the world.

A story related by a traveler to Russia in an earlier time is a tribute to this curious weed. He told of a plant on the steppes east of the Volga River that was large, wiry, interlaced by branches and thorns, and capable of forming into large globular masses with other similar dry plants as the autumn blasts released them from their moorings. Thousands could be seen coursing over the steppes, bouncing, rolling, leaping over the ground, often resembling at a distance a troop of wild horses. It was not unusual for 20 or more weeds to form into a single mass, only to roll away like a huge giant in his seven-league boots. *S. kali* is regarded with the same respect today at several sites in western America (Pammel 1894).

DESCRIPTION

Salsola kali (Figure 81-2) is an *annual*, usually upright herb that becomes woody at maturity, reproducing only by seeds, 5 to 120 cm tall with exceptional plants and some biotypes much larger, Egyptian types sappy and more or less hairy, in Lebanon prostrate or decumbent; *stems* bushy, much branched, rigid, spiny, cylindrical with reddish stripes or becoming reddish later, young stems green and succulent, old stems break off at soil line; *leaves* 1 to 5 cm long, cylindrical or flat on upper surface, rounded below, first-formed leaves opposite, 2 per node, succulent, later leaves alternate, sometimes half-clasping at base (Lebanese types), stiffer, thickened at base and ending in hard, sharp spine, usually one per node, leaves usually bearing young shoot in axil, first-formed leaves drop early; *flowers* small, axillary, solitary or in some regions 2 or 3 per axil, flowers developing from lowest to uppermost parts of plants, petals none, *sepals* 5, pink to greenish-white, sometimes reddish, membranous, winged, persistent; *stamens* 5; *pistil* with 1 or 2 *styles*; each flower in a depression formed by leaf base and 2 rigid, spiny-tipped *bracts*; conical *fruit* forms as ovary becomes dry at maturity and is enclosed by 5 enlarged sepals, each developing a fan-shaped, strongly veined wing on its back, the 5 wings meet and nearly cover fruit; *seed* an *achene*, without endosperm, conical, about 2 mm long, 1.5 mm wide, base that forms tip of cone is truncate; tip of *seed* is somewhat concave with a protuberance in the center, surface dull grayish-brown to brown, seed coat of 2 parts, outer 3-cell layer consists of elongated cells parallel to surface, below this a 3-cell layer of irregular parenchyma cells; coat thin, membranous, sometimes *embryo* visible on one side, other side thicker and at times with abundance of calcium oxalate crystals (Pammel 1894), viable embryo forms 2 coils of unequal size, one within the other, color varies from dark green to yellow, weight 2.9 mg (Korsmo 1935).

DISTRIBUTION AND HABITAT

From Figure 81-1, it may be seen that *S. kali* is adaptable to a wide range of environmental conditions. It can be found from 3300 to 4500 m in western Himalayan mountains (Mani 1979) as well as the littoral zones and beaches of the major oceans. It grows best in high, dry, disturbed sandy soils, is at home on alkaline soils, but performs well on many soil types if they are well-drained. Most ecotypes avoid locations that are wet constantly during the growing season. The plant is seldom seen in permanent shade such as that in medium dense forests and cannot survive under intense cultivation. It is most often found on disturbed waste places, in fallow areas, and on abandoned fields.

This tumbleweed is most troublesome above lat 20° N. It is in croplands in northern Russia, central Siberia, and extends to lat 50° N in Canada. In the Southern Hemisphere it is in temperate zone fields of South Africa, South America, and Australia. With a few exceptions (notably Indonesia and New Guinea), this species is absent, as a weed, from a wide belt in the tropics, from most Pacific Islands, and the east coast of Asia. Its reach into cooler climates is finally interrupted at zones where frosts may kill plants during any part of the growing season. Dewey (1894) suggested that the plant is adaptable to conditions wherever flax and wheat can grow.

In Egypt, it is widespread in agriculture but especially on saline soils near the Mediterranean coasts. In Iraq, it is in wheat fields and prospers on drainage, irrigation, and river banks, on airports, railroads, and roadsides, as well as all abandoned land previously disturbed. In western North America, it is on overgrazed range and pasture, abandoned farms, in fence rows, and along motor and water routes. After a century in California, the weed is still spreading by the wind, in the fur of animals, and the soil on shoes and machines. In that state, the department of transport spends very large sums of money to control growth along highways. Massed balls of tumbleweed (some 8 to 10 m³ in size) cause auto accidents as frightened drivers see the windblown plant material bearing down on them. In one instance, a very large truck was required to remove just four of the giant balls.

Pammel (1894, 1898) suggested that, in the evolution of this tumbleweed, the types with the rounded form and the habit of breaking off at the soil line took advantage of the autumn–winter winds to roll across landscapes in a seed-scattering performance that has now resulted in widespread dispersal and still further adaptations. He was among the first to point out that in some of the types in North America the seeds are held in the axils of the bracts by two minute tufts of coiled hair that regulate dispersal for varying periods of time as the rolling and bouncing continues. He observed that the fruit with the papery calyx, upon separation from the plant, may continue to move along the soil surface or the snow with the calyx serving as a sail. In spring, some seeds may be found in plants that have rolled around all winter.

The dispersal habits of this weed are graphically portrayed in aerial photographs of a large area of productive farmland in Arizona that was not used for a year (Karpiscak and Grosz 1979). The photos revealed striking linear patterns, and a later field investigation showed these to be *Salsola* plants that had grown from the seed of single, rolling tumbleweed bushes. Some lines were continuous for a full kilometer, while others proceeded generally with the wind direction but wandered from side to side, often intersecting the rows (paths) of other tumbleweeds. Those that had lodged against an obstacle proceeded off in a new direction as the wind direction shifted. A striking feature was the decreasing density of the weeds with distance from the starting point because of depletion of the seed supply.

The shedding of seed while the plant remains anchored has been reported for some ecotypes, but in most arid areas seeds are not released until the plants begin to roll, sometimes for scores of kilometres, until they come to rest against an obstacle or are worn away from the friction and bruising of the journey.

The spread of this seed about western America also resulted from several human activities. In Alberta, Canada, it was shown that 75% of wheat seed samples, 65% of the oats, and 55% of the barley samples in drill-boxes were contaminated with *S. kali* seeds. Railroad routes became corridors for spreading tumbleweed seed from bedding straw in cattle cars and from bulk grain leaks and spills. In other instances, plants caught between and beneath boxcars dumped seed on the roadbed, and some seed fell into flowing water as railroads crossed bridges. Hope (1927) placed seed traps at the surface of flowing irrigation water and caught 135,000 seeds in a 24-hr period.

Joel (1929) in Canada studied weed distribution, including that of *S. kali*, across six major soil belts in Saskatchewan, beginning in the semi-arid southwest and ending with better soils to the north. In the first zone, *S. kali* and tumbling mustard, *Sisymbrium altissimum*, were quite dominant weeds on clay, silty clay, loam and light sand, with the former easily the dominant species in the driest years. In the next belt to the north, on a light brown soil, the pattern of weed dominance was the same until approaching a dark brown, more fertile soil. Here the two species dominated only on droughty or well-drained fields in dry seasons. In the next zone, the two species were of minor importance, except on some dry patches of soil, and on the remaining zones, all with better soils, *S. kali* was never a problem. Joel concluded that alkali, soil structure, fertility and other factors were truly determinants of weed habitats, but all were secondary to the influence of soil moisture and efficiency of water use by a species.

S. kali was said by Dewey (1894) to have arrived in eastern North America in the mid-1700s but it did not become a problem. The weed was brought to the plains in mid-America in the late 1800s and it raced across the United States and Canada. It soon covered vast areas, and it was said that no weed of agriculture in North America had ever spread so quickly (Howitt 1908).

PROPAGATION

S. kali seeds respond to favorable temperatures and moisture in an incredibly short time and many of the plants grow to produce tens of thousands of new seeds that have a very brief period of after-ripening. Most of the seeds do not survive longer than six months to a year. The fascination with this plant which can spring to life after only a brief rain shower in an arid place, and later roll as a ball to disperse its own seed, was certain to arouse the curiosity of investigators interested in reproductive biology. Much of the known biology of the species, therefore, tends to be caught up in one or another aspect of its propagation system.

Pammel (1894) in the central United States found 20 to 30,000 seeds on plants with an above-ground dimension of 1 m in diameter and relates that a Professor Fletcher, presumably working in the same region, found that 2 million seeds were produced by a plant 2 m in diameter. All reports of seed counting inform us of this production of very large quantities of seeds, although all seeds are not destined for long-distance dispersal. Chepil (1946a) observed that in heavy stands the plants tend to support and stabilize one another so that they do not readily break off and roll away. There is little shattering of seeds if plants are stationary, the seed vitality is maintained, and the soil seed reserve is kept in good supply unless the area is plowed or burned. Young and Evans (1979) report that a type of plant, said to be *S. paulsenii* or barbwire Russian thistle, is a coarse annual that has a short after-ripening period and disperses its seed without the necessity of rolling free.

Most of the biological research on *S. kali* has been done in the North Temperate Zone, where it tends to bloom for about 2 months beginning in midsummer and begins to produce seeds in August, with maturation in that month and September. On occasion, when the growing season begins early, ripe seed may be taken by early August. Chepil (1946a) in Canada reports that seeds are usually ready when the grain harvest begins and they shatter during that operation. On a scale of shattering tendency, in which complete loss of seeds equals 100%, *S. kali* ranks at 70%.

These seeds can germinate and survive at the soil surface but this is unusual. Because only a centimeter of cover is required for germination, the summer rains and winter snows normally bury enough to provide a later field infestation. Seeds that come to rest in arid or semi-arid sites may have only fleeting chances for germination. These tumbleweed seeds are rather simple, with normally only a thin, membranous cover on the embryo, and they come equipped to take up moisture at the first opportunity. During continuous observation of *S. kali* seeds following wetting, Rhoads et al. (1967) photographed the uncoiling of the embryo and recorded growth data. Germination began in 38 min. It is the experience of workers again and again that this is one of the first species to emerge in various plant communities. This quickness, this propensity to rush ahead of its neighbors, may be thought to assure the germination of a large number of seeds and to take advantage of space and resources which would not be available if water uptake by the seed proceeded at a slower pace. It is also true, however, that this may result in a very heavy mortality of seedlings should the field site become dry soon after germination and before the root can penetrate the soil. Other adverse conditions such as high wind velocities within hours or days may take an additional toll. The waste of seed continues in the soil. Chepil (1946a) in Canada planted 5000 seeds in late autumn of the year of harvest and recorded 1000 and 600 seedlings at the close of the next May and June, respectively, with almost no emergence of any more seedlings in the next 5 yr.

Young and Evans (1972) and Evans and Young (1972) conducted comprehensive investigations on the biology of *S. kali* var. *tenuifolia* in greenhouse and field in the Great Basin area of western North America. This vast expanse lies between two mountain ranges, encompasses the Mojave Desert on the south and the Great Salt Lake Desert in the north, includes all or parts of several states and has no drainage to the ocean. It has frequent and long periods of moisture stress above and below ground. Their examination of microsites for *S. kali* seed germination was done with research techniques more advanced than those used previously (Evans et al. 1970, Young et al. 1970). They have made the largest contribution to the biology of this species and have both altered previous notions and added new information.

They studied the role of temperature through the life cycle, moisture relations, seed dispersal, the timing of seed germination and seedling growth under natural conditions, and the microenvironmental monitoring of the seedbed. They found that the rate of phenological development was directly related to temperature and that the sequence of germination events was the same at all temperatures. Seeds placed at 2°C for 16 hr and 15°C for 8 hr 11 completed germination in 336 hr; if the warm temperature in this procedure was raised to 30°C only 96 hr were required. At a constant temperature of 30°C, germination began in 2 hr, seedlings emerged from bract membranes in 24 hr, and the process was finished in 48 hr.

They learned that *S. kali* could germinate while being held at subzero temperatures for one part of the daily regime and a higher temperature during the remainder of the 24-hr day. These data foretell what may be expected in the field at similar temperature regimes.

A few seeds harvested early (August–September) germinated when held at optimum temperatures, but Young and Evans believe that the bulk of the Russian thistle plants produce seed that will not germinate until October in the field. These temperature dependencies for germination receded during the cold of winter and the seeds were ready to germinate by April. In one test, 30% of the seed germinated with a regime of –6 to 2°C, and some seed held at –9°C germinated when the warm part of the regime was 15°C for 16 hr. The results of Maguire and Overland (1959) were similar.

Because of the required after-ripening, seeds harvested in December and stored inside until April, and seeds left in the field all winter, germinated similarly. This suggests an internal time clock that regulates the after-ripening process and, so far as is presently known, the process is unaffected by external stimuli. Stevens (1943) also found a period of a few weeks after harvest when seeds held in favorable environments would not germinate. The excised embryos of these seeds, however, grew in 72 hr.

Ogg and Dawson (1984) in the northwestern United States made observations for 3 yr of the time of field germination and emergence in the spring for several weed species. They found that *S. kali* emerged at mid-March, much earlier than other species. Most seeds that were able to germinate had emerged by April 1. It was rare to see emergence after May 1. *S. kali* had the most restricted emergence period of all species in the test.

The ability of *S. kali* to extract water from the surrounding medium for germination was studied in the laboratory with special equipment described by Evans et al. (1970) and Young et al. (1970). With this apparatus, germination was 60% under –16 bars of osmotic stress (in their study osmotic pressure was assumed to be equivalent in effect to the water tension in the soil matrix). In a clay substrate, about the same germination was obtained under –15 bars of water tension, while, in sand or loam, germination was greatly reduced at only –2 bars.

Soil and litter samples taken from the field revealed that only 2 seedlings/l00 cm^2 emerged from the soil surface in the space between the plants, while 40 seedlings emerged from an area of similar size beneath the intact Russian thistle plants. This emphasizes the need for this plant to break away and distribute its dehisced seeds more widely. The most viable seeds were found on the soil surface (77%), 16% were in the first centimeter of soil, and only 7% of the viable seeds were found below that level.

The investigations of the soil litter cover, compaction, and depth of burial reveal over and over that, although there are several ways in which this unique plant may get a foothold in the soil, the environment in the first centimeter beneath the soil surface is the best place to begin life. A lower level of germination (but always at least 50%) could be obtained by sprinkling seed onto an irrigated soil surface. It is interesting that the higher night temperatures always provided the best opportunity for germination and seedling establishment whether the seed was buried, or was placed on uncompacted soil or under litter. In the greenhouse, at high temperatures the soil surface dried quickly and within 4 days emergence dropped sharply. The behavior in the field was similar because of the drying. Seeds on compacted soil often showed 80 to 100% germination but then died because the roots could not penetrate the soil to obtain moisture. However, if litter was put on compacted soil before the seeds were spread, there was satisfactory seedling survival at all temperatures because the root tips could now rapidly penetrate the soil. The pieces of litter provided fixed matter for the seedlings to push against as they uncoiled and pressed into the soil. The uncoiling action was also the mechanism of burial for those seeds that chanced to enter spaces in loose soil. When seed was buried at several levels in soil beds in the greenhouse, emergence was best at 1 cm, dropped sharply at 6 cm and ceased at 8 cm.

In some very laborious experiments, Chepil (1946a) in Canada (Saskatchewan) studied the germination behavior and field ecology of 60 species of weeds, including *S. pestifer* (similar to *S. kali*). Fresh seed was mixed with the top 6 cm of each of three soil types and no new seeds were allowed to enter the area. Plots were alternately planted with barley or wheat or left in fallow in succeeding years. Non-emerging seeds in the soil were counted. In late fall plantings, the ground freezes soon and emergence ceases. In an experiment lasting 3 yr, by April 15 almost all seeds had germinated, with few emerging thereafter. There were experiments of different duration, and one has the impression that the carry-over of Russian thistle seed to succeeding years is almost negligible. In this area, through germination or loss of viability, it may be that the soil is quite well cleansed of this seed annually.

At this time, Chepil also tried to determine the germination behavior and longevity of five species, including *S. pestifer*. Before freeze-up in the fall, the following field treatments were put in place:

- Seeds placed on the surface or mixed with the top 6 cm or 15 cm of the soil and never tilled.
- Seeds mixed with the top 6 cm of soil and cultivated monthly for the growing season to come.
- In similar plots, the soil was packed after each cultivation or they were just kept moist through the crop season.
- Finally, seed was mixed into the top 15 cm of soil, the area was plowed to that depth in June, then cultivated monthly to 6 cm.

In summary findings related to most species, it was apparent that the seed placed at the surface gave the highest germination because the rains and snows of 3 yr helped to cover them lightly. For *Salsola*, the seeds placed on top of the loam soil showed 40% germination by the end of June and no seedlings came up thereafter. Seeds in the top 6 or 15 cm gave 20% and 10%, respectively. Over a 5-yr period, germination was always poorest on a sandy loam soil. The plots with seed and soil mixed to 15 cm and cultivated monthly gave a surprising 20% germination.

Burning of field stubble and dried weed plants was tried as a control measure in an earlier time. Pammel (1894, 1898) found that *S. kali* seed germinated well at temperatures from 40 to 55°C. At 58°C some seed germinated in 10 to 15 min. Germination continued at a slower pace up to 70°C, with a thermal death point at 71 to 78°C. Dwyer and Wolde-Yohannis (1972) also showed germination of seed at 68°C.

Bruns (1965) stored *S. kali* and other weed seeds at 30 and 120 cm depths in a fresh-water canal in the northwestern United States. Seeds of *S. kali* survived less than 3 months.

MORPHOLOGY AND PHYSIOLOGY

With their excellent methods of excavation, together with the scale at which they performed such difficult experiments in the field, Pavlychenko and Harrington (1935) in Canada were among the first to help us understand that competition between plants through overlapping root systems takes place long before the plant tops shade one another. With Weaver (1926) and Weaver and Fitzpatrick (1934) in the United States, they have taught us that in lands of great prairies at least one-half of a cultivated crop exists below ground level.

The *S. kali* root systems were found to occupy areas 5.2 m in diameter, as compared with those of wheat, oats and barley that average 0.6 m across. Later Pavlychenko (1937) reported that, at the time of emergence in the greenhouse, a total wheat root system measured 31 cm, but it was twice that long if grown in the field. In the similar experiments, *S. kali* had root lengths of 4 cm and 7 cm, respectively, and was therefore subject to severe inhibition with any damage to the small roots. This helps to confirm the sensitivity of *S. kali* to nearby plants.

Davis et al. (1965) measured the extraction of soil moisture by sorghum and several weed species by determining the removal of soil water at many points throughout the soil profile. *Xanthium pennsylvanicum* and sorghum drew water from the most extensive profile areas, while *S. kali* was of intermediate profile among the ten species.

In a dry sandy soil in a greenhouse, Dwyer and Wolde-Yohannis (1972) planted *S. kali* seeds in separate containers and applied 0.5 to 3 cm of simulated rainfall in 0.5 cm increments. Water was added only once and plant growth was measured each 24 hr. In the lowest rainfall level, one seedling emerged at 14 hr; at all higher levels, 25 to 40% of the seedlings emerged, with more coming up until 48 hr. In some cases, viability was 95%. Seedlings receiving 2 cm of rain died in 5 days, while all others grew rapidly for a like period, slowed in growth for the next 8 days, and all died on day 13.

In a sandy soil, they then determined the amount of water absorbed by *S. kali* plants between field capacity and permanent wilting of the plants (termed "available water"). Water levels at field capacity, 0.5, 0.2, and 0.1% of available moisture, were then established and maintained for the life of the plants. Plant biomass increased with available water, but, interestingly, the efficiency of water use varied considerably. At field capacity, 222 g of water were needed to produce one gram of dry matter, but, in one experiment, at 0.1% available moisture, only 76 g of water were needed to produce 1 g of *S. kali* dry matter. Earlier, Dwyer and DeGarmo (1970) had shown that, on average, four grass species needed 1000 g each and four shrubs 4600 g each of available water to produce 1 g of dry matter.

In the first decades of this century the relative efficiency of water used by plants was studied by Shantz et al. (1927), Maximov (1929), and Dillman (1931). The latter found millet to be the most efficient of several weeds and crops, producing 250 g of dry matter for each 1000 ml of water used. *S. kali* produced about the same result and was the most efficient of the weed species.

It is well to be aware, however, of a quite different habitat for this species. It is common in the littoral zones, or strand-lines, of the sandy ocean shores of northwest Europe. In these unstable habitats, the communities of plants are ever changing because of the excessive disruption brought about by high tides, storms and winds. Nevertheless, some species reappear and are constant in the strand-lines over large areas. Ignaciuk and Lee (1980) in England studied the phenology, germination, and salt tolerance of *S. kali* and other strand-line species in these zones.

In the west of England, near the inlet of the Irish Sea, the highest tides often occur during the spring equinox (the time of the sun's crossing the equator). Because these strand-line species germinate 4 to 8 wk after the equinox, they are not disturbed by such tides. The salinity in the strand soil at the equinox was 340 mM NaCl (sea water being 600 mM in salinity) and this was reduced to 14 mM in early June. There was no germination of any species until the salinity in the zone had fallen to 100 mM.

Working with *S. kali* and several crops, Repp (1961) studied response to salt solutions in cross-sections of the stems by recording plasmolysis and osmotic withdrawal from the large central vacuole. Fifty percent of the cells of *Vicia faba* and *Medicago sativa* perished at 0.25 M NaCl, in *Beta vulgaris*, the edible beet, changes in cell structure appeared at 0.6 M, but *S. kali* showed no stress until 1.0 M.

Ignaciuk and Lee (1980) learned that removal of the enclosing bracts from *S. kali* seeds prompted quick germination. In deionized water there was optimum germination at 30°C, with a rapid decline at 20°C and lower, but if moistened with one-tenth the salinity of sea water there was a significant stimulation at 5 and 10°C, but none at 30°C. This stimulatory germination response was not observed in the other strand-line species but was reported previously by Binet (1964, 1965).

Ignaciuk and Lee (1980) also found that *S. kali* accumulated equal amounts of Na^+ and Cl^- ions, while other strand-line plants such as *Cakile maritima* and some *Atriplex* species took up more Na^+ than Cl^-. All fruits of *S. kali* sunk in 22 days.

The authors speculate that the intact persistent perianth in which the seed is normally enclosed may enforce a type of dormancy that prevents germination during the season of seed formation, but that the abrasion and decay of the protective structures in winter on the strand-line removes the inhibition.

The mechanisms for the low salinity stimulation at low temperatures and the loss at higher temperatures are not understood, but the authors surmise that it may not be a direct temperature sensitivity response but rather could be the result of increasing accumulation and toxicity of the NaCl. For *S. kali*, however, saline stimulation to germination may be a decided ecological advantage.

Rozema et al. (1982) studied the effect of salt spray on the growth of two sand dune strand-line species, including *S. kali*, and two salt marsh strand-line species in experimental sand-compost cultures. All species were resistant to airborne salinity and under conditions of low soil fertility the dry matter production was increased by the spray.

Ungar (1978) gathered information to show that the range of salinities required to completely inhibit the germination of maritime plants may vary from 200 to 1700 mM, and that about 65% of all such plants are completely inhibited at concentrations of NaCl less than that of sea water (600 mM). In the case of *S. kali*, there was again abundant germination in sea water with few seedling survivors.

The first stage of succession of old agricultural lands is usually dominated by weedy annuals for 2 or 3 yr. These are often years of low fertility and seem to serve as a time of preparation for the invasion of perennial species. The brief life of the annual populations is believed to be, in part, due to chemicals released by plants that limit their own growth as well as that of neighbors. This phenomenon is sometimes termed allelopathy. Lodhi (1979) and others have pointed to the similarity in the behavior of the pioneering vegetation of the spoil banks and soils accumulated in strip-mining operations. Wali and Freeman (1973) have shown that *S. kali* is one of the annuals that colonizes mine soils early and then disappears.

When Lodhi (1979) prepared containers with a soil mix containing decaying *Salsola* leaves, and planted with *Kochia scoparia*, sweet clover *Melilotus officialis*, or *S. kali* and let them grow for 6 wk. He found that the dry weights of roots, shoots and whole plants of *Kochia* and *Salsola* were severely reduced; there was little effect on sweet clover. In the same experiment a leachate of fresh *Salsola* leaves, used to water similar pots of the three species, inhibited only the shoots of *Kochia* and sweet clover.

Analytical work with extracts of *S. kali* identified several compounds previously found in other weed plants associated with abandoned old field successions: quercetin, ferulic acid, caffeic acid, and chlorogenic acid and some of its derivatives.

Hepp (1974) in Hungary studied control of *S. kali* by plowing the seed down to 20 (normal), 40 and 60 cm, with all the areas plowed to 20 cm each year. First year control was 20 to 40% for the 40- and 60-cm plow depths, respectively, as compared with normal plowing; second year control was 12% for the 60 cm depth; and in year three there were 10% more weeds than normal from the 60 cm depth.

Pammel (1894) has reported results of several chemical analysis of the components of this weed.

Oxalates that can be toxic to animals are present in *S. kali*. The symptoms are dullness, twitching, trembling of body muscles, frothing at the mouth, and coma prior to death. Death may occur 10 to 12 hr after eating the forage. Upon autopsy, it is found that there is excess fluid in abdominal and chest cavities, hemorrhaging in the digestive tract and serous membranes about the heart, and congestion and swelling of the kidneys. Consumption of 0.1% of body weight of oxalate by starving animals may cause poisoning, but if the same amount is ingested over a longer period of time, several times this amount may be taken without harm. Soluble oxalates of Na, K, and ammonium and insoluble forms (calcium and acid oxalates) are common in plants.

Everist (1974) in Australia found young plants of *S. kali* (under 15 cm) to contain 2 to 11% of soluble oxalates and total oxalates 5 to 16%. Mature plants have a lower oxalate content. Insoluble oxalates are excreted by animals without ill effect, but soluble oxalates are absorbed into the blood stream. Horses generally dislike this weed, but it is normal for cattle and sheep to graze on it without harm when plants are young. There are some recorded deaths in travelling sheep and cattle if they have eaten too much of the weed.

Uptake of oxalate is rapid in the single stomachs of horses, pigs, rabbits and man. The soluble oxalates can be detoxified or decomposed in the rumen; however, most reported cases of field injury have strangely been in ruminants, especially sheep. It is possible that in some cases there was over-consumption of plants high in oxalates at the time. When soluble oxalates are excessively high, oxalate crystals can precipitate out in the tubules of the kidneys and lead to the formation of "kidney stones" in the urinary tract.

The hayfever and dermatitis caused by pollen of *S. kali* is of important allergenic significance in the west and midwest of Canada and the United States (Lewis and Lewis 1977, Powell and Smith 1978). Following visitations or work in areas where contact was made with *S. kali* or *S. pestifer*, some people report skin rashes, burning, and itching skin. It is now known that tiny tips of the spines on the thistle become imbedded in the flesh, and that some relief is experienced if the skin is stripped with adhesive tape to remove them. Powell and Smith (1978) report that these scratches and abrasions are also classed as allergic reactions. Cool compresses and steroid creams may give symptomatic relief and the rash and itching often passes in a couple of days.

Sharp spines of the *Salsola* bush cut the legs of stock animals, causing infections in open sores. In an earlier time, special boots were made to protect the legs of work horses.

AGRICULTURAL IMPORTANCE

S. kali is a serious weed of barley, flax, oats, rape, and sunflower in Canada; of cotton in Mexico; of flax, linseed, and lucerne in Argentina; of pastures in Hungary; and of wheat in Afghanistan, Argentina, Canada, and the United States. It is a principal weed of several other cereals in the United States and several small grains in the former Soviet Union; of pastures in Australia; of rye in Canada; and of vineyards in Spain.

It is a common weed of barley in the United States; of cereals in Spain; of horticultural crops in Italy; of irrigated crops in Australia; of lucerne in Hungary; of maize in Mexico and the United States; of pastures in Belgium, Italy, South Africa, and the United States; rape in South Africa and the United States; of sorghum in Mexico; of vegetable crops in the United States; and wheat in Iraq and Mexico.

This weed must also be controlled in clover, millet, soybeans, sugar beets, and horticultural crops such as asparagus, citrus, eggplant, onion, orchards, pepper, potato, safflower, and tomato in one or more of the above countries, as well as Jordan, Iran, Turkey, and Romania.

From the above it may be seen that one century after the introduction of the weed into the fields of western North America it is still the cereals, grains, and pastures that are most troubled. In an earlier time, efforts were made to plant dense stands of oats as early as possible to try to escape injury from the weed. The vigorous growth of good stands of millet for hay usually made them safe from competition by Russian thistle. In an earlier account of a visit to Russia to observe Russian control efforts, we learned that Russian farmers also tried to sow cereals as early as possible, used varieties that produced the most tillers and thus offered more competition, and plowed immediately after harvest to kill all *S. kali* plants by severing their roots (Pammel 1894). In the tremendous expanse of black soils west of the Volga River, some of the most fertile soils in Europe, farmers were still "fleeing the land in terror of this weed"!

In America, to plow up original vegetation or disturb the land in any way was to invite an infestation of the species. On pastures that were overgrazed, *S. kali* plants became large, some 9 kg in weight, and they eventually crowded out other species. In fall, the large plants rolled away, taking the nutrients from the field with them.

Pavlychenko and Harrington (1934) studied the competition offered by *S. kali* and 12 other weeds of the plains with several cereal crops. Based on a period of several years of work, their general conclusions about the attributes for success, whether of a crop or weed, were that there must be a readiness and a uniform germination under adverse moisture conditions, the ability to develop a large assimilation surface early in the seedling stage, possession of a large number of stomata, and a root system with a mass of fibrous roots near the surface but with main roots penetrating deeply. *S. kali* was grouped with weeds that are serious under some conditions and in certain crops, along with *Chenopodium album, Amaranthus retroflexus,* and *Polygonum convolvulus. S. kali,* under some conditions, does not tolerate competition very well and is not very successful against some crops. In one experiment, when growing alone in a 3 m² plot, it produced 1662 g of dry matter above the ground and hundreds of thousands of seeds, but when competing with barley it produced 0.5 g of dry matter and no seeds.

In a 2-yr trial, Young and Morrow (1984) and Young (1986) reported that winter and spring wheat reduced growth, yield, dry matter production and seed production of *S. kali.* Winter wheat gave the most competition and caused the greatest *S. kali* seedling mortality. In the small grain farming areas of the United States, Russian thistle produces over 90 per cent of its dry weight after crop harvest. A single plant of this thistle may use more than 30 kg of water after harvest and produce 17,000 seeds.

In the extremely dry climates of the southwestern United States, *S. kali* severely limits the use of native grasses for securing the verges and slopes along highways because it competes so fiercely for nutrients and water. Strangely, with its love of dry areas, the species produces biotypes that prefer high water tables if they are not crowded too much. Dewey (1894) described large, vigorous Russian thistle plants along irrigation ditches in the western United States with roots almost in the water, while adjacent plants on higher ground were smaller. Robust plants are also found on sandbanks in the Missouri River where it is so wet that there is no other vegetation.

Occasionally this species and other tumbleweeds are defended because of their efficient water use on arid lands and the necessity to have the young, tender plants for animals in spring seasons when rainfall is lacking. Stock animals do indeed eat the early growth and attempts were made in earlier times to use it for hay and forage. With the awesome spread of the weed and the damage to crops, animals, fields, buildings, and other farmlands there is less effort to keep the weed around. Failure to appreciate the terrible toll already exacted from farmers by this weed still today results in scattered, single-minded research reports on the possibilities of the plant for temporary forage, and when compressed, as a fuel supply.

The weeds become entangled in farm machinery and enormous banks of mature *S. kali* lodge against fences that are then pulled down in windstorms. If such masses of weeds catch fire, fences are burned, sections of windbreaks are destroyed, and flames may spread to farm buildings.

A weed survey of Alberta and Saskatchewan in Canada in 1977 was compared with a similar survey of the same farm areas 30 years earlier. It was found that better methods of weed control and the changes in agricultural land management had caused some decline of the *S. kali* weed problem.

Cushing and Olson (1964) recorded changes during an effort to control *S. kali* by burning masses of the dried weed along an irrigation ditch. When the weed was 200 cm tall, the 40-min burn, covering an area 8 by 50 m, dropped 11.5 kg of ash in the water. The water temperature rose by 10°C, the *pH* from 7.8 to 11, and Ca and Mg increased 2- and 3-fold, respectively, and there was high mortality of juvenile fishes placed in traps at various distances from the burn.

The tender stems of *S. kali* are sometimes cooked and succulent shoots used as "potherb" greens for humans. Small animal feeding trials with ground seed meal indicated weight gains similar to the control diet (Uphof 1968, Coxworth et al. 1969).

Finally, from the Russian thistle we have learned some lessons about the germaneness of the relation between high technology and the total fauna, flora, soil, and water in our environment. The world's first plutonium factory was built at Hanford, Washington in the western United States in 1959. Whether through ignorance or carelessness, there was little regard for a program of radioactive waste disposal in those days.

It was later learned that badgers, rabbits and other small animals came through the fences and into the waste pits to lick salty radioactive chemicals. In a short time they scattered 200 curies of radioactive droppings over 1000 ha of the site. Tumbleweeds growing in this same land accumulate such chemicals and because they can send roots to 6 m they may at times reach into deeply buried waste dumps of strontium-90.

At maturity, plants break off and "tumble" around dry areas spreading radioactive seeds that become available to birds and animals. With all this comes the possibility of surface movement of chemicals or leaching into underground aquifers and thence to the very large Columbia River. In the event of fires on the rangeland, there is the prospect of airborne contamination from burning tumbleweeds and other vegetation (E. Marshall 1987).

COMMON NAMES

Salsola kali

ARGENTINA	cardo del diablo, cardo ruso
AUSTRALIA	buckbush, prickly saltwort, soft roly-poly
CANADA	Russian thistle, Russian tumbleweed, soude roulante
CHILE	cardo ruso, monte espinoso
DENMARK	sodaurt
EGYPT	ashnaan, eshnaan, qalye, shinaan
ENGLAND	prickly saltwort
FRANCE	salsola kali, soude
GERMANY	Kali-Salzkraut
HUNGARY	Russian thistle
IRAN	shooreh
ITALY	erba kali
JAPAN	nohara-hijiki
LEBANON	kali, Russian thistle
MEXICO	chamizo, rodadora
MOROCCO	soude kali
NETHERLANDS	loogkruid
NEW ZEALAND	saltwort
NORWAY	sodaurt
PORTUGAL	soda
SOUTH AFRICA	Russian tumbleweed, Russiese rolbossie
SOVIET UNION	leap-the-field, wind witch
SPAIN	barrilla pinchosa
SWEDEN	sodaort
TURKEY	dikenli soda otu
UNITED STATES	prickly saltwort, Russian cactus, Russian thistle, Russian tumbleweed, tartor thistle

Eighty-Two

Scirpus maritimus L. and
Scirpus mucronatus L.

Cyperaceae, Sedge Family

THESE ARE THE BULRUSHES that provide excellent food and shelter for wildlife and have served as a companion of man for thousands of years. During excavations at Catal Huyuk in Turkey and Ali Kosh in Iraq, it was found that *Scirpus maritimus* was a food of humans in prehistoric times. These were sites of paleoethnobotanical studies of the remains of communities in existence prior to 5000 B.C. (Renfrew 1973). Presently, in a study of the biogeography of the monocotyledonous weeds, excluding grasses, Hafliger (1982) employed a system of 35 geographical world regions and he has found *S. maritimus* in all of them. This is a rare distinction among the higher plants. Forms of this species have been collected from altitudes above 3000 m in Tibet and the western United States.

Some believe that, early in the evolution of the monocotyledons, the Juncaceous rush-like plants separated from the lily lines, and that later the sedges, **Cyperaceae**, and grasses, **Poaceae**, split away from the rushes. The grasses and sedges often tend to look alike, so that it is common for the world's worst weed, *Cyperus rotundus*, a sedge, to be called both "nutgrass" and "nutsedge" across the world. There are several distinguishing morphological differences between the two families, however, and if some simple characters are kept in mind it is seldom difficult to separate them. A cross-section of the culm stem is triangular in the sedges and tends to be spherical in the grasses, the stems are without joints, the internodes are solid, and the leaves are three-ranked in the former, while in the grasses the stems are jointed, hollow, and the leaves two-ranked. There are other differences and there are, of course, species in both families that are exceptions to these large general rules. Some of the sedges thought to be most primitive are rush-like, while those more advanced are more grass-like, and the grasses themselves are thought to be most advanced.

The fodder grasses, the grassy cereals, and the pea family supply a very large portion of the food used by men and animals, but the sedges contribute little of economic importance. We may almost say that none are cultivated. Some sedges are grazed or may provide food for game birds and animals, a small amount of paper and matting are made from them, and a few corms and tuberous rhizomes are eaten by humans.

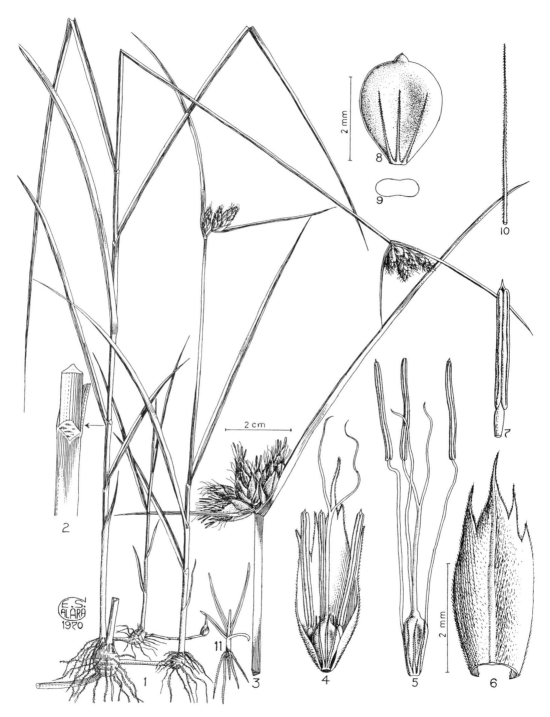

FIGURE 82-1 *Scirpus maritimus* L.: 1. habit; 2. sheath, upper part; 3. inflorescence;
4. immature flower with glume; 5. mature flower, glumes excised; 6. glume, dorsal view;
7. stamen; 8. achene with bristle; 9. bristles transverse section; 10. bristle; 11. seedling.

Scirpus is a large and cosmopolitan genus whose plants frequent marshes and wetlands, are often tolerant of salt, and which vary greatly in habit and morphology. Many rushes are troublesome in rice across the world, and all of the principal species are perennials. *S. maritimus* and *S. mucronatus*, which reproduce by stolons and tubers and by seed in several habitats and regions of the world, are the most important of these. This chapter will explore the biology and distribution of these two weedy species. As will be seen later, the extreme variability of these plants has called forth the usual proliferation of names for the many different forms. Wherever possible the author's choice of name for his type, variety, or subspecies will be given.

Scirpus comes from the Latin designation meaning bulrush, *maritimus* suggests the seaside habit, while *mucronatus* from the Latin *macro*, a sharp point or sword, refers to the spiny tips of the glumes. *Bolboschoenus maritimus* is a synonym found frequently in current and older literature for *S. maritimus*.

S. maritimus and *S. mucronatus* are weeds in 60 and 43 countries, respectively.

DESCRIPTIONS

Scirpus maritimus

Scirpus maritimus (Figure 82-1) is a *perennial*, often tufted, spreading extensively by horizontal creeping *rhizomes* and *stolons* several mm thick with ovoid *tubers* at nodes, 1 to 1.5 cm in size, hard, ligneous, brown to black thin scales; *stems* erect, solitary from tuberous base, slender to stout, triquetrous (3-angled), striate, smooth or scabrid below inflorescence, 15 to 180 cm tall, 3 to 15 mm thick, can grow 1.5 cm/day; *leaves* 3 to 5, well developed, 2 to 12 mm wide, stiff, with revolute margins when dry, upper ones overtopping the inflorescence; *ligule* absent or small-triangular; *sheaths* light; *bracts* may be several, flat, leaf-like, ascending or usually spreading; *inflorescence* umbelliform to capitate, sometimes reduced to a single spikelet, or may be in dense clusters; *involucral bracts* one to several, dilated at base, overlapping inflorescence, the longest usually erect, others oblique, leaf-like; *spikelets* rounded, many-flowered, 1 to 4 cm long, either all sessile or some variously sessile and others peduncled, quite variable; scales 6 to 10 mm long, almost as broad; the dark brown *rachilla* persistent; *glumes* spirally arranged, appressed, not keeled, emarginate or lacerate at top, pubescent outside, 4 to 7 mm long, may be reddish to chestnut brown; *bristles* lacking or 3 to 6 retrorsely barbed; *stamens* 3; *stigmas* 2 or 3; *achene* (nut) two-sided or trigonous, obovate, brown to black, 2.5 to 4 mm long.

The species can be recognized by the appressed, not keeled, glumes that are emarginate or lacerate at the top.

While mapping the circumpolar plants of the northern hemisphere, Hulten (1964) found the different forms and types of *S. maritimus* to be very complex, highly variable, and in his opinion in critical need of taxonomic revision. This seems to be the condition in the rest of the world, and Hulten's attempts at mapping the geographical distribution of the various forms may serve as an example of the manner in which names have proliferated for the species. In brief, *S. maritimus* is found over most of Europe, with the exception that *S. maritimus* var. *robustus* is the name used in Spain, Portugal and on the Mediterranean coast in the south. The species extends eastward below lat 60° N to Yakutsk in Siberia. One site in the Kamchatka Peninsula is in an area of hot springs. In Korea, Manchuria, and the Japanese Islands, the name in use is *S. yagara*, and in much of central Asia, *S. affinis*.

In an area of North America along the eastern coast and near Hudson Bay, the names *S. maritimus* var. *ernaldii* and *S. paladosus* var. *atlantica* are in use. In the Great Plains and near the border of the United States and Canada in the west, the name *S. paladosus* is used. The latter merges with *S. robustus* in the published floras of California. *S. robustus* itself is regarded by some workers as a form of *S. maritimus*.

In 1972, while working with *Scirpus* materials collected by Swedish expeditions in Mongolia and Sinkiang, Norlindh (1972) of the Museum of Natural History in Stockholm experienced considerable difficulties with the taxonomic treatment of the *Scirpus maritimus* complex. From the complex, several taxa have been segregated at the specific level. *S. compactus* and *S. affinis* were probably separated on the basis of the ramification of the inflorescences and the variations in styles and achenes. Beginning with the specimens of Linnaeus, he also examined many plants in herbaria and in fields, reviewed the discussions in the literature, and from all of these he concluded that *S. compactus* and *S. affinis* still belong in *S. maritimus*. Another instance of the variability of this species with changing habitats is given in the study of the forms found in the different places by Robertus-Koster (1969) in the Netherlands. Together, these studies illustrate some of the present-day problems in the comparative biology of the many variable forms and types of plants presently held in this species by different workers.

Scirpus mucronatus

Scirpus mucronatus (Figure 82-2) is a *perennial*, tall, stout, tufted sedge with short *rhizomes*; *stems* sharply triquetrous with more or less concave sides, smooth, 0.5 to 1.5 m tall, 3 to 8 mm wide, with few leaf sheaths at base; *leaves* reduced to 1 or 2 membranous bladeless sheaths; *inflorescence* pseudolateral, almost at the tip, dense clusters of 2 to 25 spikelets, 2.5 to 3.5 cm long, 3 to 4 cm across, *involucral bracts* at first erect, finally often spreading to reflexed, 1 to 10 cm long; *spikelets* sessile, ovoid to oblong-ovoid, terete, rather acute, densely many-flowered, brownish, at maturity 4 to 20 mm long, 4 to 6 mm wide; *rachilla* persistent; *glumes* spirally organized, lightly appressed, concave, ovate or broadly ovate, abrupt apex with spiny tips, reddish, 3.5 to 4 mm long, 2 to 2.5 mm wide; *bristles* 5 or 6, unequal, retrorsely scabrid, slightly to distinctly longer than nut; *stamens* 2 or 3; *styles* 2 or 3, branched; *achene* (nut) dorsiventrally compressed, planoconvex or trigonous, obovate, shortly apiculate, rugulose to smooth, black at maturity.

This species is widely recognized by the bladeless sheaths and pseudolateral capitate inflorescence. It is also a polymorphous species.

Scirpus grossus is another weed of wet rice, river beds and banks, reservoirs, and irrigation systems. It is a large marsh sedge often found in 30 cm of water or in very wet soil. It may grow to more than 2 m. It is a serious problem in rice in regions of Vietnam, India, the Philippines, and the lands in southeast Asia.

The rootstock bears several stolons that terminate in dark-colored, round tubers. From these, at stable water levels, new plants arise and the stolon-terminal tuber sequence is repeated. If the water level drops or if the pond dries, the stolons swell and produce tubers that perennate and remain dormant until the water returns. Several long, linear, acuminate leaves radiate from the flowering axis. Flowers are borne in terminal umbels of brown spikelets (Norlindh 1972). Mullan (1941) has reported on the biology and development of this species.

Detailed descriptions of these and other *Scirpus* species may be found in a comprehensive taxonomic study of the genus published by Koyama (1958).

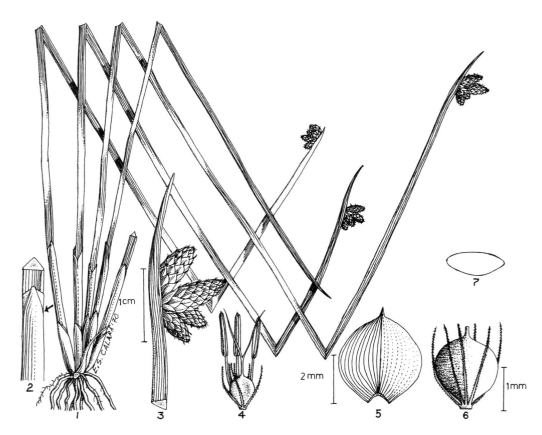

FIGURE 82-2   *Scirpus mucronatus* L.: 1. habit; 2. culm portion with leafless sheath; 3. portion of culm, with inflorescence; 4. flower; 5. glume; 6. achene with bristles; 7. achene cross section.

DISTRIBUTION AND HABITAT

S. maritimus (Figure 82-3) is found as a weed of agriculture and waterways on all continents, with general distribution over Asia, Europe, and North America. It is found in most regions of Africa and South America but it is more sparsely distributed there. This plant is seen less commonly as a weed in the equatorial zone. *S. mucronatus* (Figure 82-4) is not encountered as frequently but its general distribution resembles that of *S. maritimus*. *S. maritimus*, along with *Potamogeton crispus*, *P. pectinatus*, *Eleocharis acicularis*, *Spirodela polyrhiza*, *Najas marina*, *Typha latifolia*, and *T. angustifolia* are believed by Sculthorpe (1967) to be the most widespread aquatic species of the world. He found relatively few higher plants to be habitual colonists of brackish waters. In the species-poor communities of the brackish habitats of the north temperate zone, *S. maritimus* and members of the *Najas*, *Ruppia* and *Zannichellia* genera are the most conspicuous occupants.

FIGURE 82-3   The distribution of *Scirpus maritimus* L. across the world where it has been reported as a weed.

FIGURE 82-4   The distribution of *Scirpus mucronatus* L. across the world where it has been reported as a weed.

The two *Scirpus* species are semiaquatic plants found in coastal swamps and along rivers and streams, infesting poorly drained rice fields, irrigation canals, drainage ditches, and reservoirs. They compete with rice to lower crop yields and impede the flow of water. They occupy many unusual niches because they are so widespread. In the Netherlands, for example, *S. maritimus* is one of the weedy species of the plant communities that develop in pastures that are inundated in winter and early spring. It may be found at water holes in deserts. In Europe, it is seldom found above 600 m elevation, yet in Tibet it is recorded at 3000 m. In the Rocky Mountains in the United States, the form called *S. paladosus* is found at a similar elevation. This designation is regarded by some as synonymous with *S. maritimus*.

The taxon designations of all variable species bring special problems to studies of world distribution of weeds. For example, In Egypt, *S. mucronatus* is present in the Nile Delta up to Cairo, yet *S. maritimus*, which is in most countries nearby, is not recorded for Egypt. *S. tuberosus* is, however, widespread in the country and it is regarded elsewhere as another form of *S. maritimus*. Australia is a special case, for it appears that *S. maritimus* is seldom weedy there. In Hulten's (1964) work on the floras of the world, however, *S. maritimus* is recorded over much of the South Pacific, including east and south Australia and Tasmania. It was also recorded on the islands of Mauritius and Madagascar and in the deserts of Africa and Asia.

PROPAGATION

The intact plants of these perennial *Scirpus* species renew themselves and spread in the main by extension of stolons and rhizome-bearing tubers, or by the disturbance and relocation of plant parts within a field or adjacent fields. When propagules enter a field, the routine agricultural practices will insure rapid distribution, to be quickly followed by dense infestations of the weed. Viable seeds are produced in some areas and under some systems of field management, but for the most part the production of tubers is of most serious consequence for the farmer.

The growth and development of the tuber will be fully explored in later discussions of this weed, because almost all of the studies on physiology and ecology begin with or are principally concerned with this propagule.

In greenhouse experiments in the Philippines, Cao (1974) found no flowers on shoots of the first generation of original tubers. After the death of the mother shoot, and about 25 wk after germination of the original tuber of the network, about 2% of the shoots produced by secondary stolon tubers began to flower shortly before they themselves perished. At this time, in the period of March through May, some flowering shoots could now be seen in rice fields. Visperas and Vergara (1976), also in the Philippines, observed no flowering in plants they held for 30 wk.

It is a general observation that flowering occurs in the field after rice harvest (the weed shoots being severed with the crop). In pot experiments, Visperas and Vergara (1976) cut weeds at ground level at 100 days and at subsequent intervals of 10 days through 140. With the exception of those cut at 100 days, an average of 33 new shoots were produced in other plots and a few formed inflorescences. Uncut plants showed mostly dying shoots and put out very few new shoots after 150 days. In other experiments (Anon. [Philippines] 1974) there was 100% flowering in plants cut at 140 days. Plants cut at 100 days produced many shoots but all were vegetative. Visperas and Vergara (1976) speculated that both vegetative and reproductive buds are formed during development but the latter do not normally grow until the vegetative shoots die, or are cut or damaged. This adaptation may, therefore, be a survival mechanism that serves when vegetative reproduction cannot proceed.

The reports of *S. maritimus* seed germination studies by different workers vary from complete success or failure in greenhouse and laboratory to a very successful system of mass pre-germination of seed for planting in wildlife habitats. Seed germination in fields and natural areas is well documented. Dorph-Petersen (1924) in Denmark placed seeds in incubators that simulated outside temperatures and obtained 98% germination. Isely (1944), using *S. paladosus*, stored the seed in water for 6 mo and found good germination when the seed was transferred to water at 32°C in bright light. Cao (1974) placed freshly harvested dry seed on moist filter paper in light and dark but obtained no germination after 3 mo.

Ryang et al. (1978) in Korea found that scarification by scraping or soaking in NaOH or HCl increased seed germination. Kaushik (1963) found reduced germination when seed was moistened with a 1.5% NaCl solution. Guppy (1893), on the other hand, while studying the River Thames in England as a seed dispersal agent, found that the seeds of this species will germinate after "months" of storage in a salt solution more concentrated than that of sea water (3.5%). Guppy also reported that most seeds of *Scirpus* "sink like a stone" but those of *S. maritimus* float for "some time" and that this, of course, aids in dispersal.

Lieffers and Shay (1982a) found satisfactory seed germination at about 1.5% NaCl, which is about the salinity of the mud flats on the prairies of Canada, but discovered that higher salt concentrations inhibited germination. When such seedlings became older and more established, they could tolerate higher salinities and greater water-level fluctuations. These authors recorded satisfactory seed germination at 19 of 24 sites in the prairies from mid-January to late July. The plants emerged from mud flats or in water of 5 cm depth or less. Upon examination of their data from a large number of sites, they concluded that saline wet areas support germination and seedling establishment successfully only on the upper part of basin slopes where the salinities of the mudflats during drawdowns and after precipitation are below a critical level. Thus, these concentrations of salt are a factor in the distribution of *S. maritimus* in prairie wetlands. Kawashima et al. (1977) found a few primary shoots that came from buried seeds in spring in Japanese rice fields.

The seeds of *S. maritimus* are eaten by many species of birds and it has long been recognized that the bulrushes are valuable as food and cover for many kinds of wildlife. Until recently, however, the dormancy and germination problems with *Scirpus* species have prevented their use in seeding marshes. Stratification and scarification programs have shown some success, and O'Neill (1972) in California reported on a procedure for breaking dormancy and for pre-germination of large quantities of seed of "alkali bulrush" to be used in planting hundreds of hectares of marshes. The seeds in their experiments were probably a mixture of *S. paludosus, robustus* and *tuberosus*; all are either forms of or near relatives of *S. maritimus*.

The seed was placed in shallow, plastic-lined earthen pits holding a 0.05% solution of NaOCl. The pits were in a sunny location and were covered with transparent plastic that was removed daily for stirring after the first 3 days. At times, temperatures exceeded 55°C in the pits. The seed color changed from light to dark brown as the impervious seed coat was penetrated by moisture. On the 7th day the bottoms of the liners were punctured to allow the solutions to drain. The first sprouts were seen in 12 days. To prevent injury to the seeds and their sprouts it was necessary to plant as soon as the first seeds showed germination. Seeds were sown into shallow water by aircraft or by broadcast seeders on the ground at the rate of 1.4 to 2.3 kg/ha. Subsequent to establishment, successful water management allows use of the area for cattle grazing, haying, waterfowl nesting, and in autumn water-fowl hunting programs.

PHYSIOLOGY AND ECOLOGY

Scientists who are interested in and concerned with the biology of *S. maritimus* and its control will find a substantial body of knowledge already in existence. We are especially indebted to workers in the Philippines and Canada for their systematic portrayal of the growth and development of the plant. The research in the Philippines was conducted by Mercado et al. (1971), Cao (1974), Lubigan and Mercado (1974, 1976–77), Visperas and Vergara (1976), Vergara et al. (1977), and in Canada by Lieffers and Shay (1981, 1982a,b). Many of the biological findings are in agreement and for this reason a synthesis of their findings will be more satisfactory and less repetitive than a detailed account of more than a score of experiments.

The first shoot (mother shoot) from the original tuber (mother tuber) normally appears in 3 to 5 days from planting. This tuber may produce up to 3 shoots 35 to 70 cm in height at 3 to 7 wk, respectively. In the field, the plant reaches to 100 to 125 cm, maintaining the height for 3 to 4 wk, when it then begins to senesce before death. The number of leaves per shoot increases up to 7 or 8 wk, reaching an average of 10 to 13, with decay and yellowing setting in at 11 wk.

As the mother shoot reaches 6 to 8 cm, a fibrous, white root system develops at the base of the shoot and this darkens until maturity. Stolons appear at the base of the mother plant 3 wk after germination. The mother shoot lives for 11 to 12 wk but does not flower in the Philippines. The lower portion of the shoot remains attached to the tuber that was the original propagule, and this may remain in place or be moved by tillage operations or flowing water to a new site where it can grow again if conditions permit.

When the stolons appear at the junction of the mother shoot and tuber, they extend for a time and then form a terminal tuber which is considered to be without dormancy, for it also bears a shoot. The new white stolons and new tubers have a fibrous root system; at 4 wk the new tubers produce stolons and tubers. With age, the underground organs darken to a blackish hue. Stolon lengths vary from 2 to 35 cm, with internodes of 2 to 6 cm. Within 15 wk after planting, an average of 70 tubers may form from the original mother plant. As the mother shoot dies, dormant tubers begin to form but do not produce shoots at this time. All shoots from the original system may be dead in about 25 to 27 wk, thus concluding the first generation. When most of these old shoots are gone, the dormant tubers send up new shoots as a new generation begins at some distance from the original plant.

Most of the *S. maritimus* tubers bear one shoot at the onset; if two or more are formed they come much later. Shoot loss or damage quickly stimulates replacement.

Roots penetrate to 55 cm, and stolons and tubers to 40 cm below the soil surface. This level is beyond the normal plow depth and is below that which can be reached by many herbicides.

The work of Visperas and Vergara (1976) provided interesting insights on tuber productions during the most aggressive periods of growth of this semiaquatic but emergent weed. Diagrams of the growth systems of 140-day-old plants revealed that on average each mother tuber produced six stolons. Some remained very close to the mother tuber and were often inconspicuous. As the shoots grew, the tuber enlarged and darkened. Some tubers without shoots continued to fill out and increase in size, indicating that food is translocated from plant to plant through the stolons. These were pot studies, but at 40 days the plants had produced 70 units each and were connected by 4.5 m of stolons. In a rice field, with much greater freedom to expand, it is understandable that serious infestations can develop quickly.

The fresh and dry weight production by this plant proceeds slowly in the early stages and reaches a maximum at about 20 wk, followed by a decline as shoot material begins to decay and die. On average the fresh weight may be about 360 g and 160 g dry weight at maximum size. Visperas and Vergara suggested three distinct stages of material synthesis. For the first 3 wk, production is slow, with only the shoots synthesizing dry matter. The shoot number reaches a maximum at about 15 wk. The second stage, 3 to 17 wk, is a period of rapid dry matter increase as the leaf number and area reach a maximum and as tuber production, somewhat delayed, also increases rapidly. In an experiment with potted plants, the maximum leaf area, 3900 cm^2/plant, was reached at 9 wk. In competition with rice, the foliage of *S. maritimus* contributed 70% of the canopy. In such competition, the vigor and dry matter production of rice declined, surely having been influenced by the shading of the weed canopy. Cao (1974) found about the same tuber production rate as Visperas and Vergara. There was a linear increase in production for 20 to 180 days, then a leveling off. In the end, the total number of tubers in the plant network was three times the number of shoots, thus indicating the high percentage of dormant tubers formed. Toward the close of this period of rapid leaf and tuber growth, some senescence can be detected in the shoots.

The third stage continues until about 30 wk, with root, stolon, and shoot weight declining, as tuber growth accounted for about 50% of the dry weight. At the end of the life of this plant network, most of the dry matter of the plant is stored in tubers.

In spite of its slow start, *S. maritimus* should be considered a vigorous, fast-growing weed. In greenhouse experiments, the average daily growth in height was 2.7 cm. The maximum height of 80 cm was reached in about 6 wk, and this very rapid, early extension can offer significant competition to semi-dwarf rice varieties.

In the cultivation of fields, the network of plants is always torn into single- or multiple-organ fragments. We are unable to find reports of new buds or shoots forming on isolated stolon or rhizome pieces with or without a connected plantlet. Cao (1974) in the Philippines made a random collection of tubers from rice fields, sorted them into three sizes, and obtained 30, 47, and 80% germination for small, medium, and large tubers, respectively; medium and large organs produced two or three shoots per tuber.

Kawashima et al. (1981) noticed that the distribution of *S. maritimus* tubers in Japanese paddy fields differed greatly between adjacent fields. In an effort to explain this, he studied the location of tubers below ground and found about equal numbers above and below the 10 cm depth in the soil. He also found that tuber emergence continued for about 1 mo and that those in the top 4 cm emerged much more easily than the rest. Most tubers had three to five buds, with one or two sprouting, usually the larger sizes first. If sprouted buds were removed, one or two more became active.

Ryang et al. (1978) in Korea found that tubers more than 3 cm deep in the soil would not germinate in areas that were covered by 3 cm or more of water. When placed at the surface of the soil, germination was satisfactory in up to 5 cm of surface water, but was markedly reduced at 7 and 10 cm of water. Some standing water was required for all germination, salinities of 0.1 to 0.5% favored germination and a *pH* of 7 was optimum.

It appears that tubers will not germinate if their moisture content falls below about 16%. Germination is retarded and finally seriously reduced as the moisture content falls below 30%. Twenty days of air drying in the greenhouse reduced the moisture content of tubers to 16% (Visperas and Vergara 1976). This agrees with the results of Cao (1974), who could get no germination of tubers dried for one month in a greenhouse. In the field, this means that the number of viable tubers can be reduced by cultivation practices that bring them to the top of the soil for exposure to the sun. The authors feel that this may explain in part why *S. maritimus* is more common in irrigated than in rainfed rice.

In their work on the wetlands of the Canadian prairies, Lieffers and Shay (1982a) found that this species has some long-lived clones. Some tuber mortality occurs under ice in winter, but generally the propagules go dormant in dry or highly alkaline soil and sprout only when the stress has been removed. They examined dormant buds on over-wintering tubers and found no floral bud primordia, suggesting that the initiation of such buds occurs at the time of, or after the beginning of, vegetative growth.

The general pattern of development of *S. maritimus* during its life cycle has also been studied by Dykyjova et al. (1972) in Czechoslovakia, Ghosh et al. (1971) in India, and Kawashima et al. (1977, 1981) in Japan.

Visperas and Vergara (1976) pointed out that the very wide distribution of *S. maritimus* in the world places it in agriculture from lat 45° S to lat 55° N and confirms that it must be comfortable over a considerable range of temperatures and photoperiods. They placed plants in photoperiods of 10, 12, 16, and 24 hr for 90 days and could find no effect on flowering. Examination of bud material revealed no flower primordia. At these photoperiods, the plant heights were 1.05, 1.35, 1.8, and 2 m, respectively. In previous experiments, there was no flowering in plants held up to 210 days at natural daylength. At higher latitudes the canopy of shade will therefore be too much for successful rice culture if this weed is in competition with the crop.

Photoperiod significantly affects the allocation of the plant's resources. The growth of below-ground parts is greatest in short photoperiods, while longer photoperiods (over 12 hr) give greater above-ground growth. The tuber dry weight at a 10-hr photoperiod was significantly greater than at other daylengths. The total plant dry weight, however, did not vary significantly with changes in daylength.

In short photoperiods, a larger number of shoots and tubers are produced, and it may therefore be expected that in southeast Asia, where the days are long during the main cropping season for rice, fewer *Scirpus* tubers will be formed. The tubers that develop during this period are, however, larger and it is the general finding that large tubers germinate more readily.

The authors point out that, in the field, *S. maritimus* seems to have several different patterns in its competition with rice and they vary with the circumstance. In the longer photoperiods of higher latitudes, the rapid growth rate and the great height of plants will make light the limiting factor. In the lower latitudes where days are shorter, the rapid growth rate, the large number of shoots, and the production of large germinable tubers will also bring severe competition. Rice may generally have a shorter duration of growth in a short photoperiod and so it may also be shorter in stature. Where this is the case, the weed need not be as tall and yet may offer competition.

The effect of different light intensities was studied by placing plants in full sun and in 60 and 30% of full sun for the first 40 days after sowing. The total dry matter production was reduced by 4 and 70%, respectively, at the latter light intensities. The numbers of organs and their dry weights were reduced by shade, with tubers and roots most severely affected. This explains in part the greater success of taller rice varieties against the weed.

When the weed plants were placed in temperature regimes of 20/20, 26/18, 29/21, 32/24, and 35/27°C, the growth was about the same for the first 40 days. At 80 days the tallest plants were found in the 29/21°C temperature regime, and there was a general tendency for plants to be shorter at lower temperatures. Smaller tubers are produced in higher temperatures, but the numbers of shoots and tubers are favored by such temperatures and this may give a competitive advantage in tropical areas as compared with temperate areas. Total dry matter accumulation was generally better at higher temperatures, with the exception that the 20/20°C regime equaled the yield of the highest temperature. The accumulation of food reserves was favored by lower temperatures, and it was found that the dry weight of tubers and underground parts increased under these regimes.

Visperas and Vergara (1976) studied the N uptake of *S. maritimus* and found that it was rapid in the first 60 days and then leveled off until harvest time, even though the dry matter content mounted steadily. It was not clear from these experiments whether most of the required N was taken up early or whether N was limiting in the soil. It was obvious, however, that the plant could make very rapid increases in dry weight while drawing upon its own resources for most of the N needed. They followed the percent of N in each of the plant parts in the early stages and found that it decreased for the first 80 days in the tubers and then leveled off, while in the shoots there was a steady decline until final sampling. The authors believe these data suggest that, if the rice crop is well fertilized, the N response will be strong in *S. maritimus* and competition would certainly then be increased.

To study the effect of salinity on the growth of *S. maritimus*, Mercado et al. (1971) surveyed saline soils in two large rice-growing areas of the Philippines for electrical conductivity (EC), *pH*, Na$^+$ content of soil extracts, and irrigation water. They found that the EC of some soils was eight times greater than in non-saline areas and that of the soil extracts was frequently five times higher. The *pH* levels of irrigation water and soil extracts were about neutral in both types of areas and the Na$^+$ content of the irrigation water was four times higher in saline areas. Rice plants in saline areas had the typical symptoms of stunting, old leaves drying while young leaves were still erect and turgid, and if bearing fruit the grains were empty. The *S. maritimus* plants were green, growing vigorously, and much taller than the rice.

Fresh, firm tubers were obtained from saline soils and placed in petri dishes with 0.2, 0.4, or 0.5 M NaCl or mannitol. At 9 days only tubers in the 0.2 M NaCl solution had germinated, with some additional germination when tubers were removed and placed in distilled water for 8 days. Tubers germinated well in all mannitol concentrations and there was a slight improvement when they were moved to the distilled water treatment.

Tubers were also placed in pots of garden soil to which 0, 0.2, 0.4, 0.6, 0.8, and 1% NaCl were added and which were maintained under lowland culture conditions. Plants at the four highest salt levels produced a larger number of shoots and more and larger tubers than those at 0.2% salt or no salt. At the low concentration, the plants were pale green and spindly, while others had larger bases, more chlorophyll, and were taller.

Thus, in the Philippines, *S. maritimus* is a salt-loving plant. Although it grows better in saline soils, it is not a halophyte, that is, one confined to salty places, for it occupies a wide variety of habitats here and elsewhere in the world. In these experiments, as the NaCl concentrations increased the uptake of Na$^+$ and Cl$^-$ was generally greater, but at the higher concentrations the increment of uptake was minimal, indicating, as others have found with other species, that *S. maritimus* may have a regulating mechanism that monitors and maintains the uptake of these ions at a level that is non-toxic. Hayward (1956) has suggested that lack of salt tolerance in most crops may be due to an inability to control salt uptake and to a protoplasmic sensitivity to accumulated salts.

In North America, Lieffers and Shay (1981, 1982a,b), and Shay and Shay (1986) studied the biology and ecology of *S. maritimus* (the variety reported to be *paladosus*) in the Canadian prairies, where it is found in saline, closed basins, marshes and wetlands that have large fluctuations of water level (and therefore salinity) within and between seasons. The species is generally found in shallow, sometimes dry, areas around the wetlands but is tolerant of extreme changes in water level. New plants appeared in spring from tubers and from seeds. One dramatic example of the effect of a change in growing conditions was recorded at a particular site, Porter Lake, in Saskatchewan. In this shallow basin, *S. maritimus* grew rapidly, produced many new shoots, and had extensive floral development in a year when the lake was constantly flooded and only moderately saline. Tillering was vigorous in summer and by mid-August the above-ground biomass peaked with a 22-fold increase over what it had been one year earlier. From their studies, the authors believe most of the variability on the prairie sites, between years, can be accounted for by fluctuations in water depth and salinity.

To obtain detailed information on the effect of water level on growth, they placed tubers in a clay loam soil in pans that were held in large tanks of fresh water. The pans were positioned at increments of 10 from 10 cm above the water surface to 50 cm below. With controls on temperature and day length, and with simulated rainfall, an effort was made to match the conditions prevailing on the prairies. Almost all tubers sprouted within 6 days, some with more than one shoot, and at 0 and +10 cm all culms developed normally. At least one sprout per tuber emerged and began normal development at all levels, but at −40 and −50 cm, one-third of all shoots aborted before reaching the water surface. Tillering began at 24 days at upper levels and at 52 days at −50 cm.

Culm height increased with water depth and averaged 83 cm at the +10 cm level and about 125 cm at the −40 and −50 cm levels. The time of inflorescence appearance was affected by water depth. Floral buds appeared at 28 days at −10 and −20 cm, but at −50 cm and at +10 cm they were delayed to more than 40 days. Vegetative tiller biomass, below-ground biomass, and total biomass decreased with water depth. In sum, the biomass of rhizomes, tubers, and roots per stem were greater in shallow water, but by contrast the inflorescence biomass was greater in deep water.

We recognize in many plants a habit of changing from vegetative growth to seed production with alterations in temperature, light, moisture, injury, crowding, etc. In the experiments of Lieffers and Shay, the shift from vegetative to reproductive growth came with increasing water depth. Plants growing at the surface of the water or above had greater shoot survival and clonal expansion by rhizomes and tillers. In the prairies, shifting to seed production may be an important survival mechanism because of cyclic wet and dry periods that cause great changes in water level and salinity. It has been noticed that *S. maritimus* disappears from basins when a large increase in water depth takes place. The species cannot be productive then, and competition from other emergents increases in these non-saline conditions. Thus, if *S. maritimus* uses available energy for seed production in the deeper, relatively fresh water, it may survive longer, for the seeds are known to float for several days and this promotes dispersal to new sites. Because some seeds have long dormancy, this too helps the plant to pass unfavorable periods. During falling water levels, exposed mud flats are often rapidly colonized by *S. maritimus* seedlings.

Distribution in these closed wetlands, then, depended on the degree of salinity during germination and seedling establishment. On hyper-saline wetlands, the plants begin on the upper slope of the basin in a narrow band where the mud flat's salinity is low enough to allow successful germination. This leaves a central, open area.

On saline wetlands, germination takes place in a broader area of the middle and upper slopes. On moderately saline basins, the species is usually out-competed by fresh-water species but may dominate the center of the basin after several years of low water. The species showed large phenotypic growth responses to differing environmental conditions. Under usual water level regimes of flooding in spring and drying in autumn, *S. maritimus* was frequently found in monospecific stands in saline and hyper-saline wetlands. In years when there was little spring runoff water entering the basins, the *Scirpus* areas usually became dry and very saline. Now tubers stayed completely dormant or the few that sprouted had very short nonflowering culms. Other species then invaded the area.

In shallow water there was reduced salinity, individual stems were larger, and stem density and above- and below-ground biomass were at a maximum. In water more than 40 cm deep, with low salinity, individual stems and inflorescences reached maximum size, but the much lower stem density resulted in a total biomass reduction. It was found that seed production may be influenced by the previous year's water level. At sites that were dry but flooded in the subsequent year, more stems flowered and the inflorescences were larger than at sites that had been flooded continuously.

Deep inside the tissues and organs of large plants, and in some plant parts at various levels when in flooded soils, total or partial anaerobiosis is not unusual. The toxic or excessive concentrations of metabolic by-products from microbial activity, or from the higher plants themselves, are a further consideration in growth where oxygen is limiting. Flooding tolerance therefore requires a number of physical and metabolic adaptations. Barclay and Crawford (1982, 1983) studied the growth and survival of 20 plant species kept under total anoxia in an anaerobic incubator at 22°C for 7 days. Three-fourths the species died or survived without growth until they were returned to aerobic conditions, at which time normal metabolic processes resumed. *S. maritimus* was among the few plants to continue the production of new, healthy shoots during anaerobiosis and to rapidly green up and grow normally on return to air. Further work revealed that this species, under anoxia, can sustain normal growth from unextended buds for at least 8 wk. In the first 7 days the shoot elongation rate lagged behind that in air, but once metabolic pathways were adjusted the growth rate was similar to that in air. *S. maritimus* under aerobic conditions exhibits shoot growth with dry weight increases, but under lack of oxygen shoot growth was normal but there were no dry weight increases.

Sabnis (1921), D'Almeida and Ramaswamy (1948), Khanna (1965), Juquet (1966), Metcalfe (1971), and Govindarajalu (1976) have reported upon the embryology and anatomy of *S. maritimus* and *mucronatus*. Hwang et al. (1981) reported on a crude water extract of *S. mucronatus* that inhibited the growth of mouse leukemia cells.

AGRICULTURAL IMPORTANCE

In spite of the increasing availability of knowledge of weeds throughout the world, there are now on record many examples of single-minded approaches to control programs that only result in more damaging weed problems. In some areas, the annual grasses and annual broadleaved weeds of rice and sugar cane, for example, were targets for control on large and small fields with crop management systems that employed herbicides. The removal of the annual weed vegetation resulted in a shift to perennial grasses and sedges. These then became permanent inhabitants by the rapid production of underground vegetative propagules containing large amounts of reserve food stored for later use.

Hand pulling of these organs or rupture of plant systems and movement by machines during tillage permits fragments to develop new plants and also helps the weed to spread to new areas. Top removal often increases the number of plant units because several new vegetative buds may be stimulated to growth. In some perennial species, the vegetative propagules may grow downward to levels that cannot be reached by tools, machines, or herbicides. Very often these shifts to more troublesome species are simply the result of ignoring the principles of plant biology and field ecology that are already known. *S. maritimus* and *S. mucronatus* have become predominant in many rice fields for the reasons cited above. Acquaintance with existing knowledge about the biology of the plant and control methods can reduce the severity of the weeds and limit their spread.

During the only international conference ever held on weed control in world rice, De Datta (1983) expressed the belief that *S. maritimus* is perhaps the most important and most investigated weed in wetland rice, being of a serious nature in the Philippines and many other Asian countries. Noda (1977) prepared a list of 30 weeds important for transplanted rice and 40 for direct-seeded rice. He believes that *S. maritimus* and *S. mucronatus* are principal weeds in both types of rice culture but that the latter is less troublesome in transplanted than in direct-seeded rice.

S. maritimus is a serious weed of rice in Italy, Korea, the Philippines, Romania, and Spain; and a principal weed in India, Morocco, Peru, Portugal, Senegal, Thailand, and South Vietnam. In Hungary, it is a very serious problem in rice as the result of a very rapid spread in the 1970s. It is also found in the rice fields of China, France, Iran, Japan, and in the Odessa region of the former Soviet Union. It is a troublesome weed in irrigation canals and drainage ditches, ponds, reservoirs and river banks. These problems are reported in the wet tropics, in the drier Middle East, in Europe, in southern Africa and in Oceania. The species is troublesome in tea in Indonesia at times. Although the crops are not specified, we have reports that *S. maritimus* is a serious weed elsewhere in the former Soviet Union, also a serious weed in Afghanistan, a principal weed in Cambodia and Iraq, a common weed of agriculture in Bangladesh and France, and a troublesome weed in aquatic sites in the Punjab in India. The weed is in England, where it was shown to be very susceptible to the herbicide glyphosate when applied as the weed reaches 1.5 m in height.

S. mucronatus is a serious weed of rice in Portugal and Spain, a principal weed of rice and other crops in Bangladesh in winter and summer, and a common weed in the Philippines. It is a weed of rice in France, India and the United States; and a weed in the jute-producing area of Bangladesh. In other unspecified crops, it is regarded as a principal weed in Indonesia and Italy and a common weed in Bulgaria, Malaysia, and the United States. *S. mucronatus* and other sedges that love wet places are troublesome in low areas and in water-logged planting rows of rubber and other plantation crops, and they tend to grow with abandon along ditches of all kinds. In a natural stand of weeds in an experimental field of jute in Bangladesh, there were 75 plants/m² of *S. mucronatus*, comprising about 20% of the total weed vegetation. Eighty-five percent of the weed vegetation was made up of *Scirpus*, *Echinochloa crus-galli*, and *Cyperus rotundus*. In another area, this weed, along with *Jussiaea decurrens* and *Monochoria hastata*, made up 75% of the total weed vegetation in wetland rice, often surrounding each rice hill with eight weed plants (Ahmed et al. 1986, Gaffer 1981).

S. maritimus is said to infest more than 80% of the rice fields in the southern half of the Korean peninsula. The weed sprouts and sends up shoots both before and after transplanting, and heavy infestations may reduce rice yields by 50% (Ryang et al. 1978). Rice is produced in ten countries of southern Europe, but Italy raises about 50% of it. In this area, both *Scirpus* species are principal weeds, but *S. maritimus* is the most troublesome. Both *Scirpus* species are widespread in Europe, are generally not a problem in the north, but are major problems in certain regions of the south, as cited above.

Vega et al. (1971) treated the same rice field plots with the same herbicides for three successive seasons to study the effect on rice yields and changes in the weed species populations. Seven recommended herbicides were applied singly and in mixtures. *S. maritimus* was among four dominant weeds in the field plots. At the close of the experiments, *S. maritimus* had survived all chemical treatments except propanil and had become dominant in all other plots.

To study the effect of *S. maritimus* density on rice yield, Lubigan and Mercado (1974) in the Philippines placed 20 12-day-old rice seedlings in field plots that were 1 m^2 and seven days later added tubers of the weed with a single sprout at various quantities from 20 to 100. The competition was so severe that the experiment was repeated with quantities of weeds from 5 to 30 plants/m^2. There were no other weed plants or tubers in the plots and other species were removed on appearance.

In the first experiment, 20 and 40 weed plants/m^2 caused 80 and 100% reductions in yield, respectively. Five weed plants that later increased to twice the number of the rice plants, or 40/m^2, caused no significant reductions in rice yields. In this instance, the competition of the large number of shoots of *S. maritimus* in the latter part of the season was not important. Control methods that allow the survival of more than 5 weed plants/m^2, however, will cause yield reductions in this area. In this region, *S. maritimus* is more competitive in the field than the annuals *E. crus-galli* and *Monochoria vaginalis*. Kim and Moody (1980) identified eight different weed communities growing in transplant rice in experimental fields in Korea. Each community of weeds influenced rice growth in its own way and time during the season. As an example, a *Monochoria-Echinochloa* community increased its competition with rice from 40 days after transplanting to rice maturity, while a *S. maritimus* community exerted its influence on the rice in the first 40 days after transplanting and thereafter its effect was less. The highest reduction in rice yields, 42%, was caused by an *Echinochloa-Scirpus* community. By comparison, other weed communities caused 10 to 20% yield decreases. The use of *Azolla pinnata* as a weed suppressant in the Philippine transplanted irrigated rice fields did not control *S. maritimus* (Janiya and Moody 1984).

Visperas and Vergara (1976) designed *S. maritimus*–rice competition experiments to be conducted in boxes 1 m^2 and 25 cm deep containing 25 20-day-old rice seedling and 16 tubers of the weed. Both rice and weeds were taller in competition, but the weed grew faster and was taller than the rice. Presumably this aspect of competition would be much worse as the number of weeds in the field increased.

The competition caused a greater decrease in rice tiller number than in the weed shoot number. The weed shoots were eventually seen around the edges of the boxes as they tried to spread outward. The tillers of the rice and the shoots of the weed were, however, fewer than when each was grown alone.

The production of dry matter by the weed was greater than that of rice whether grown alone or in competition with the crop. Dry matter production was 396 and 244 g/m^2 for *S. maritimus* and rice, respectively, when the plants were grown alone. Actually, when they were in competition, the dry matter of rice was reduced 46%, while that of the weed increased slightly, indicating that the latter competed successfully with the crop. In mixed populations, the rice produced 24% of the total dry matter of the plot, the weed 76%.

For two full cropping seasons De Datta et al. (1979) and Bernasor and De Datta (1981) in the Philippines compared minimum and zero tillage systems with conventional methods for transplanted rice. The ten different minimum tillage treatments were combined with preplant herbicide applications and flooding. Each gave grain yields similar to conventional tillage methods and significantly higher grain yields than the zero tillage treatments. Conventional, minimum, and zero tillage methods were used over four successive crops, and, after two crops with zero tillage, the plots were dominated by *S. maritimus* and *Paspalum distichum*. A single application of 2,4-D at 20 days after transplant greatly reduced the stand of *S. maritimus*.

In a series of 14 consecutive rice crops, different cultivars and tillage systems were studied to observe changes in weed communities. As various tillage treatments were altered toward the zero tillage system, weed communities shifted toward perennial plants, with *Paspalum distichum* dominant through the fifth crop and *S. maritimus* in the ascendancy thereafter. There was no consistent difference between rice cultivars in perennial weed control across the 14-crop series. However, the weed weights in the plots with intermediate-statured semi-dwarf rice varieties tended to be less than with shorter varieties, suggesting that such varieties can offer more competition to perennial weeds.

De Datta and Jereza (1976) suggest that proper land and water management and various combinations and rotations of dry-land crops with wetland rice can effectively control this weed with some help from rotary weeders, herbicides and hand weeding.

Following several years of work on one of the most intensive studies ever done on the biology of *S. maritimus*, Vergara et al. (1977) translated their results into some practical suggestions for control:

1. If handweeding is done it must be repeated often.
2. A timely re-harrowing is necessary after the first tillage of the field.
3. If possible use tall rice varieties.
4. Use rice varieties with a long duration of growth whenever possible.
5. Plow the field 10 to 20 days after harvest.
6. Bring tubers to the soil surface often for desiccation.
7. Use crop rotations.
8. Use herbicides where possible.

In some areas of the world various organs of *S. maritimus* are eaten raw or dried and ground into flour for bread making. The pollen is sometimes added to the bread. Several Indian tribes in North America use these plants for food. In some areas of the former Soviet Union where *S. maritimus* is plentiful, the plant is processed and made into cardboard paper.

COMMON NAMES

Scirpus maritimus

DENMARK	strand-kogleaks
ENGLAND	sea club-rush
FINLAND	merikaisla
FRANCE	scirpe maritime
GERMANY	Gemeinestrandbinse, Meer-Sime, Meer Binse

ITALY	erba nocca
JAPAN	ko-ukiyagara, sea clubrush
MADAGASCAR	kierana
MOROCCO	scripe maritime
NETHERLANDS	zeebies
NEW ZEALAND	purua grass
NORWAY	havsevaks
PHILIPPINES	apulid, bawang-bawang, buslig, marabawang
PORTUGAL	triangulo
SPAIN	erbe nocca, Jonca, serrada mayor
SWEDEN	havssav
THAILAND	kok ta krap
UNITED STATES	saltmarsh bulrush

Scirpus mucronatus

BANGLADESH	chechra
ENGLAND	roughseed club-rush
FRANCE	scirpe mucronee
GERMANY	Stachel-Teichsimse
INDONESIA	bimpolu, login ajaui, mendongan, walini
MALAYSIA	rumput kumbah, rumpt kerechut
PHILIPPINES	kanubsuban
PORTUGAL	castanho, erva do espeto, espeto
SOVIET UNION	sea scirpus
SPAIN	punxo
THAILAND	chut mu
UNITED STATES	roughseed bulrush

Eighty-Three

Senecio vulgaris L.

Asteraceae (Compositae), Aster Family

S*ENECIO VULGARIS* is a slender annual herb, often called groundsel, found primarily in unstable environments. It belongs to the largest genus of flowering plants, and one which is believed to cause more livestock poisoning and death than all other poisonous plants combined (Heywood 1978, Lawrence 1981). The species is a weed of more than 40 crops in 65 countries. Groundsel was the major species of study during the early discovery of herbicide resistance in plants.

FIGURE 83-1   The distribution of *Senecio vulgaris* L. across the world where it has been reported as a weed.

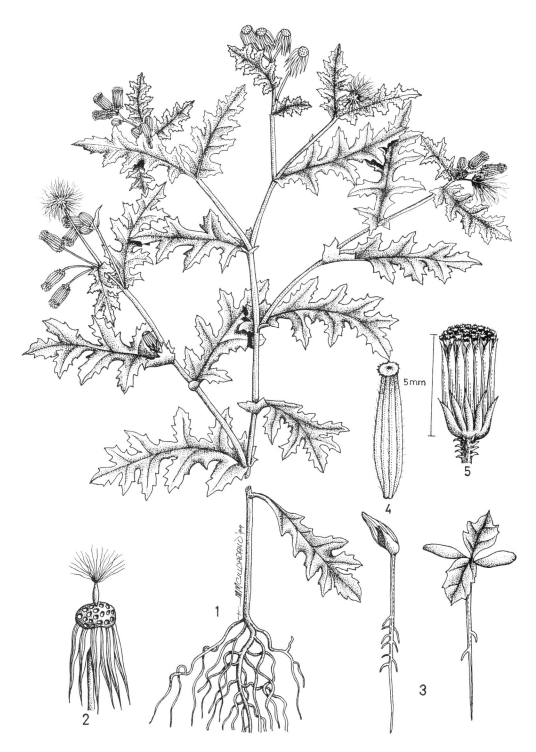

FIGURE 83-2 *Senecio vulgaris* L.: 1. habit; 2. mature flower head; 3. seedlings; 4. achene without pappus; 5. flower head.

DESCRIPTION

S. vulgaris (Figure 83-2) is a slender *annual* (sometimes biennial) herb reproducing only by seed; *stems* simple or branched, erect or decumbent, ribbed, somewhat fleshy, smooth, or with cottony hairs primarily on upper portions, 10 to 60 cm; *leaves* alternate, 2 to 10 cm long, 0.5 to 5 cm broad, slightly fleshy, shape variable from smooth and almost without teeth to shallowly or deeply lobed with margins finely to coarsely and irregularly toothed, may be sparsely hairy on veins on lower surface, lower leaves stalked and tapering to a point, upper leaves stalkless, often clasping stem; *inflorescence, flower heads* stalked in corymbose clusters, at ends of stems and branches, each head 5 to 10 mm across, cylindric or conic; *disk florets* yellow, *ray florets* absent (some ray floret populations have been reported in local areas); *involucral bracts* linear in single row, overlapping, usually with black tips; *peduncle* somewhat cottony, 0.5 to 4.5 cm long with few small linear *bractlets* at base; *seed* an *achene*, somewhat hairy, 3 to 4 mm long, apex truncate with about 10 vertical ridges, reddish-brown to gray-brown, with prominent white hairy *pappus* that may be 2 times seed length. Seeds and fruits may become sticky when wet (Good 1964).

DISTRIBUTION AND HABITAT

With the exception of the warmest regions of the world, *S. vulgaris* is very widely distributed in all of agriculture (Figure 83-1). The seeds are dispersed by wind, water, and in the gut or on external surfaces of birds. Dorph-Petersen (1925) in Denmark found a 5% survival rate in the animal gut. The plant thrives on many soil types and in a wide range of habitats. In commerce it is known to have traveled from Poland to Sweden in the bark and mud on timber shipments (Petterson 1940).

Groundsel was found in most of the cultivated fields of England by 1855 (Buckman 1855). Roberts and Stokes (1966) in that country examined the seed banks of 60 fields that had been in commercial vegetable production for 60 yr. Of 40 species studied, *S. vulgaris* was found to be among the four most widely distributed. It ranked sixth in abundance of seed in the soil, with some areas having 40 million seeds/ha. A long-term experiment over a 16-yr period was carried out at the Weed Research Organization in England to study the effects of herbicides on crops and soils (Fryer and Kirkland 1970). The experiments also provided the opportunity to assess the pattern and rate of decline of populations of viable seeds present in the soil. In an area where carrots were grown in rotation for 9 yr on land that was previously in agronomic crops, *S. vulgaris, Poa annua, Stellaria media,* and *Capsella bursa-pastoris* together accounted for 70% of all viable seeds found in the soil. (See also Roberts and Neilson 1981a.)

In an extensive survey of soil weed seed banks in 50 cultivated areas over Denmark, Jensen (1969) identified 90 annual species, *S. vulgaris* among them. As germination tests were conducted in field and laboratory, he found that groundsel did not contribute a major share of seeds to soil reserves, but he questioned whether the ready germinability of the seed may have annually provided a significant portion of the growing weed vegetation in the fields, thus preventing entry into the seed bank. He placed this species with a group that regularly supplied 50 to 200 seeds/m². By contrast, some heavy seed producers provided 1000 seeds/m².

There are mixed reports of the role of *S. vulgaris* in the soil seed reserves under grassland and long-term pasture, with Chippindale and Milton (1934) and Champness and

Morris (1948) finding relatively few viable seeds. Milton (1948) later found as many groundsel seeds under undisturbed sward as in nearby fields planted to potatoes. He speculated that the seeds arrived in the sward in stockyard refuse hauled to the sward, in the gut of animals moved to the area for grazing, and in bundles of grain (containing weed seed) transported to the pasture to provide additional feed.

PROPAGATION

S. vulgaris is a prolific seeder, and there are many reports of 1100 to 1800 seeds per plant, depending upon site and biotype. Kempen and Graf (1981) found in California beet fields that some plants averaged 45 seeds/flower head and 38,000 seeds/plant. Seed weight is 190 mg/1000 seeds. Many such figures may not be meaningful, however, for this species can complete a life cycle very quickly and thus produce several generations per year in some climates. Using seed traps and soil cores, Archibold and Hume (1983) studied the annual rain of seeds added to the soil at ten stations scattered over 1300 km^2 in the plains of western Canada. Groundsel registered the largest number of seeds (of 40 weed species) found in any trap, in part because of its seed production on one of the weediest fields. With the exception of *Amaranthus retroflexus* and *Setaria viridis*, groundsel supplied the largest number of seeds to the soil cores. There was some variability by species between stations.

Achenes capable of germination may be present in the capitula 5 days after flowering and ripe seeds in 11 days. The interval gradually increases to 20 to 25 days by November. Ripe seeds may be present 5 to 6 wk after emergence of seedlings (Salisbury 1942). Gill (1938) severed groundsel plants when at the flower bud stage, full flower stage, and when seeds were fully ripe. Seeds from flowering plants and the fully ripe stage gave 35 and 90% germination respectively.

Senecio exhibits flushes of germination during a 12-month period and these may come at different times in different years. In the temperate zones, the greatest germination is in early to mid-spring and again 3 months later. Many of the seeds produced by groundsel are capable of immediate germination, but for the survival of a population a portion (usually small) is equipped with a mild dormancy. This seed dormancy decreases in dry storage but may be prolonged during soil burial.

Popay and Roberts (1970a,b) in England made some of the most detailed studies on the response of *S. vulgaris* seeds to several factors of the environment. They found that most of the seeds would germinate only if given some light, and that even intermittent low levels of daylight were sufficient. The phytochrome system is involved in the light response (see also Morgan and Smith 1979, Hilton 1983).

In the light, when the temperature gradient for imbibed seeds was raised from 3 to 30°C during a 10-wk period, the greatest flush of germination was at 9°C. In germination tests at several constant temperatures, 25°C proved to be optimum. Lauer's results (1953) agree with the latter and she also reported the maximum temperature for germination to be above 35°C. The few seeds that germinated in the dark were favored by lower temperatures, with the optimum being 10°C. At 4°C, there was very little light and no dark germination. When light was present for germination, prior low temperature stratification gave no advantage [see also Koch (1969) on chilling requirements for *S. vulgaris* and other annuals].

In a literature review of experiments on the germination of *S. vulgaris* and other annuals, Koch (1970) reported better germination with alternating high and low temperatures, as did Popay and Roberts above; however, the latter suggested that the germination performance may be related to the total time spent in the high temperature.

Karssen (1980–81) in the Netherlands buried ripe seeds from field-gathered wild plants of *S. vulgaris* (and other species) and measured dormancy over a 2-yr period. Germination was studied by bringing the seeds into standard laboratory conditions. The seeds were buried at 10 cm deep to provide conditions that prevented germination in the field. They exhibited a clear pattern of dormancy change with: (1) no innate dormancy at harvest or when buried in the field in November, (2) in late winter and early spring they were fully ready to germinate, and (3) in late spring and early summer they developed a deep dormancy leading to a complete loss of germination. The pattern was the same in the second season. He believes the high temperature of summer contributed to the development of the summer dormancy. The germination capacity changed between full dormancy and absence of dormancy both in light and dark, but the seeds responded to some light requirement in periods connecting the two extremes.

Seeds of groundsel that have a dormant period may continue in that state if buried and protected from light. Wesson and Wareing (1969a) found that seeds of this species did not grow during a 50-wk dark burial in soil but grew immediately upon removal to light. In the soil environment, however, it is likely that a combination of factors exert an influence on the seed reserves. Popay and Roberts (1970a) found that a combination of darkness, 10% O_2 and 4% CO_2 suppressed the germination of groundsel at all temperatures from 4 to 25°C. Upon removal of the seeds to normal light and atmospheric conditions, all of the inhibition was released immediately.

More recently, Hilton and Owen (1985) studied the respiration of germinating seeds under different light conditions, including red, far-red, and darkness. For *S. vulgaris* and several other weed species, they found no significant effect of light on the O_2 uptake prior to germination.

Brenchley and Warington (1930) in England studied the number of viable seeds on light sandy and heavy clay experimental plots that had been in continuous spring-sown barley and autumn-sown wheat for 50 and 75 yr, respectively. Preceding the weed seed studies, the areas had been in fallow briefly for weed control purposes. High levels of *S. vulgaris* seed were found at both sites and the germination was monitored under controlled conditions for 3 yr. Most of the seed reserve germinated in the first year and few of the original seeds remained after 3 yr.

PHYSIOLOGY AND MORPHOLOGY

Stebbins (1957) pointed out that *S. vulgaris*, together with other similar annuals that are widely distributed in the world, can seldom maintain a population of constant size in agriculture because of crop rotations and the annual preparation and destruction of suitable weed habitats as single-season crops are grown. Such species are therefore required to have a very high reproductive capacity and be well adapted to quickly building large populations as opportunities are presented. Self-fertilizers are often homozygous individuals and, if they have initially colonized an area without difficulty, they may readily transmit their adaptive traits to their offspring and continue to be successful.

Because groundsel and many other annuals can set seed and produce new seedlings several times during a growing season, they are well suited to short-crop, unstable, ever-changing cycles. If a season is abruptly shortened, some seed will usually have been produced; if it is favorably extended, the plant can continue to build up reserves (Harper and White 1974). Many of these species have indeterminate growth patterns. Death results from flood, drought, cold, or deterioration of the environment, causing plants to slowly rot away while still trying to produce more flower buds. Because they do not normally require narrow, restrictive conditions for the stimulation of flowering, they seem always prepared to take advantage of complex and unstable field conditions.

The variation in vegetative and reproductive structures of *S. vulgaris* throughout the life cycle when grown under various levels of stress, and the allotment of resources to the different organs under these conditions, were studied by Harper and Ogden (1970). The stress treatments were imposed by growing the groundsel from seed in poor soil in containers of different sizes. The distribution of dry matter to the various organs was followed during the growth cycle. Conversion factors were used to transform the dry weights of plant parts to calories and thus produce a net energy budget. Reproductive effort was deemed to be total seed production per total net production × 100. When expressed as total calories, the "reproductive effort" for *S. vulgaris* was 18 to 24%, which is comparable to that found for other annual composites. The annual **Compositae** that have been used for crops, such as sunflower *Helianthus annuus* and safflower *Carthamus tinctorius* have about the same reproductive efficiency as the weedy composites studied thus far.

Fenner (1986) used *S. vulgaris* to determine how a parental nutrient shortage affects allocation of specific nutrients to seeds. The plants were grown from seeds in various concentrations of nutrient solutions. The relative biomass allocated by parent plants to the reproductive structures was constant in spite of the large differences in plant weight at the various nutrient levels, so that the final structure of the seed proved to be quite well buffered from the nutrient status of the parents. K, Ca, and Fe were less concentrated and N, P, and S were more concentrated in the seeds than shoots, and overall the fraction of the parent plant's total content of any one element that was allocated to the seeds varied widely. In the high levels of the nutrient solution, this ranged from 4% of the total K to 38% of the total P, while at the low nutrient level, the range was 2.5% Fe to 52% of total P.

Lambers (1976), Garcia-novo and Crawford (1973), and Lambers et al. (1979) have reported on the flood tolerance and metabolic adaptation to flooding in *Senecio* species.

There is increasing concern about plants subjected to high salt concentrations during the de-icing of motorways, as well as to the salt stockpiles near them, and the pollution by leaching and washing as a result of these operations (Davison 1971b, Lumis et al. 1973, and Westing 1969). In greenhouse and water culture experiments with *Senecio*, Briggs (1976, 1978) found indications that salt-tolerant variants were present on the salt-saturated areas. Some variants were tolerant to both lead and salt, while one was tolerant to lead only.

In the irradiation of a forest (oak-pine) and weed community that developed in a field after cultivation ceased, no member of the forest community survived 360 roentgens/day of gamma radiation. *S. vulgaris* withstood several 1000 roentgens/day (Woodwell 1963).

A very detailed study of the anatomy of vegetative and reproductive organs of *S. vulgaris*, with excellent illustrations, was completed by Miejers (1963) of the Netherlands. Lawrence (1981) reported on the cytogenetics, morphology and reproductive biology of the *Senecio* species of Australia. Drury and Watson (1965) have discussed the gross vegetative morphology of the genus *Senecio* and the need for taxonomic revision. In a detailed study of the role of phytochrome in the developmental responses of plants of open and shade habitat, Morgan and Smith (1979) found that *S. vulgaris* was extremely responsive to even very low levels of supplemental far-red light. They have discussed the alteration of the growth patterns as a result of this sensitivity.

In north Germany, Kutschera (1960) excavated a complete root system of *S. vulgaris* from a sugar beet field in early July. The roots extended 20 cm to all sides in the upper layers of the soil, with some roots descending to 45 cm. The majority of the system was in the upper 15 cm of the soil.

AGRICULTURAL IMPORTANCE

S. vulgaris appears as a weed in so many crops and countries that a detailed accounting would serve no useful purpose. It behaves as a weed from Mongolia and Iceland in the north to New Zealand on the far side of the world. In general, the reports of major trouble with this weed are from Europe and North America, but there are some important exceptions, as will be seen below.

It is reported to be a serious weed of maize in Canada, of woody plant nurseries in England, Norway, and Sweden; and of horticultural crops such as vegetables and small fruits in the Netherlands, Norway, and Sweden; and of strawberries in Scotland. It is a principal weed of most irrigated crops in Mongolia, of legumes in Hungary, of maize in England, of woody plant nurseries in the United States, of vineyards in Hungary and Italy, of wheat in Hungary and Korea, and of many vegetable crops, small fruits, and some orchards in Belgium, Canada, England, Finland, Germany, Hungary, Ireland, New Zealand, Spain, Turkey, and the United States.

In addition to the above locations, the weed is troublesome in more than 26 other countries on all continents in more than 30 additional agronomic, horticultural and plantation crops. In such places, groundsel is either ranked as a common weed, appearing generally throughout a country in several crops, or we know it is present but of unranked importance. The crops range from barley in Canada, to cereals near the equator in Kenya, citrus in Cyprus, cotton in Spain, flax in Argentina, orchards in Uruguay, pastures in Chile, tea in Japan, tobacco in the former Soviet Union, vineyards in Switzerland, and wheat in Iran. In Yemen, for example, it is a troublesome weed throughout the country but is a very serious weed in cooler montane regions. Likewise, in Saudi Arabia it is found in arable fields and orchards in the midlands and from 1000 to 2700 m in the uplands, sometimes forming a cover so thick that crops are overwhelmed. It is a common weed of forest nurseries in Madagascar as well as several other crops on the high plateau.

In Kashmir in the north of India, it is a common weed in all types of crops. The extensive weed surveys by Kasahara (1953) reported *S. vulgaris* to be one of the most widespread and harmful weeds of the upland fields in the whole of Japan. A survey by Enomoto (1985) thirty years later found the situation unchanged. It is the most troublesome in the cooler parts of the country. Much farther north, in the Kamchatka Peninsula of the former Soviet Union, it is a ruderal weed found around centers of habitation and in some grazing lands, but it is not a problem on arable fields.

In Egypt, where most agriculture borders the Nile, groundsel is generally distributed through most cultivated crops. In eastern Europe, in Hungary for example, it is in root crops, stubble, and cereals in most annual and perennial crops and thus covers much of the country's agriculture. It is very plentiful in central Europe, where for decades it has been considered a universal weed of root crops. In a recent survey, *S. vulgaris* was found to be one of the worst weeds of vineyards and soft fruits, especially strawberries, in European countries (Clay 1987). To proceed northward into Finland, Raatikainen et al. (1985), in a survey of more than 500 cereal fields, reported that groundsel was present over the country but its frequency in fields and the biomass produced ranked low among the 175 weed species studied.

In Canada, Groh and Frankton (1949), following an extensive weed survey across the continent, also reported that groundsel was generally distributed over the country but was of low frequency in most fields. In California, in the United States, only 3 to 8 groundsel plants/m² reduced yields of broccoli by about 25% (Agamalian 1983). In the same area, Norris (1981) reported that groundsel reduced the yield of seedling lucerne by 50% at first cutting.

S. vulgaris is such a pervasive and enduring inhabitant of the world's agriculture that it seems to find a strategy for being a continued nuisance even in the face of considerable change in field management. Cussans (1966) in England reported a general decrease in density of annual dicotyledonous weeds with the beginning of direct drilling and minimum soil disturbance systems, but some species, including *S. vulgaris*, tended to increase in relative importance. Nielsen and Pinnerup (1982) in Sweden made twice-yearly weed counts in spring barley grown with reduced tillage and found that *S. vulgaris* was one of the weeds that could increase in such a system. As new black peat soils are opened to agriculture in Ireland, groundsel, with the seeds probably blown in by the wind, increases quickly during the nutrient-rich early cultivation stages but tends to diminish in numbers thereafter. Rola (1979) reported on a 10-yr study of the weed flora of degraded black soils in Poland, where a combination of suitable cropping and use of herbicides caused the disappearance of seven weed species including *S. vulgaris*.

As mentioned previously, the *Senecio* species may become especially serious as weeds of pasture because they are said to cause more livestock deaths than all other poisonous plants combined (Heywood 1978). Cattle, horses, and several other livestock animals are susceptible. The reports of Robertson (1906) and Qualls (1980) inform us about these types of tragedies. It is important to mention here as well that several species of *Senecio* have been implicated in reports of the loss of human lives in disasters called "bread poisoning" over many decades. The deaths are usually the result of the presence of seeds or other parts of the *Senecio* plants in wheat used for human food (Steyn 1934).

Plants containing pyrrolizidine alkaloids (PA), including *Senecio* species, are found everywhere in the world and are implicated in the poisonings and losses because of the damage they cause to liver and lungs, and because they may have a part in carcinogenesis. The final products involved in the toxicity have been elusive because of the many intermediate metabolites, some of which are very reactive and difficult to characterize. Using senecionine, a PA derived from *S. vulgaris*, Segal et al. (1985) and Lessard et al. (1986) have recently given examples of the *in vivo* pathology of metabolites isolated during these chemical procedures (see also Bull et al. 1968 and Mattocks 1972). The literature on this subject is very large.

HERBICIDE RESISTANCE

Special mention must be made of the major role of *S. vulgaris* in the discovery and elucidation of herbicide resistance in plants, and particularly to the triazine compounds. Some believe that, in the decade following the first reports of herbicide resistance in *S. vulgaris* in the early 1970s, we came to know more about the mechanism of resistance (to triazine compounds) than we do about any other case of pesticide resistance (LeBaron and Gressel 1982).

The richness of the accumulated biochemical and biological knowledge learned from these studies has already benefited mankind. *S. vulgaris* was the major species of study in the early research on resistance in that decade.

Plants, with their remarkable capacity to protect themselves against adverse natural or man-made conditions, sometimes need additional assistance in our agricultural fields and we have tried to help them by selecting or breeding resistant crop varieties, removing competition, applying pesticides and in many other ways. Because of their surprising adaptability, many weeds, diseases and insects remain with us; often reasserting themselves following our best control efforts. Pesticide resistance by insects and diseases was first noticed soon after 1900 and became widespread with the introduction of synthetic organic pesticides in the 1950s. Few worried about resistance to herbicides until Ryan (1970) reported that the owner of an ornamental nursery in the northwestern United States discovered that high levels and repeated applications of the herbicide simazine no longer controlled *S. vulgaris*. Susceptible populations were normally controlled with 1 to 2.5 kg/ha, but in some fields even 18 kg/ha were no longer effective. This biotype was later shown to be resistant to several other triazine herbicides (Ryan 1970, Radosevich and Appleby 1973a). It is now known that triazine-resistant biotypes of *S. vulgaris* are in Canada, California, Oregon and elsewhere. Within a few years of the first discovery, resistance was found in more than 50 species across the world.

Later, Radosevich and Appleby (1973b), using isolated chloroplasts derived from *S. vulgaris*, demonstrated that simazine and related compounds inhibited photosynthesis in susceptible (S) but not in resistant (R) biotypes. In the triazine R-biotypes studied thus far there is a modification in the 32-k-D herbicide-binding polypeptide of the photosystem II that prevents triazine-binding and the plant is therefore resistant to the herbicide. In S-plants the herbicide binds to this protein and electron transport in photosystem II is inhibited (Radosevich et al. 1979, Radosevich and Holt 1982, Arntzen et al. 1982). Warwick (1980b) used S- and R-biotypes of *S. vulgaris* to establish that the former, which had occupied the fields prior to the advent of simazine use, had done so because they were much more able and therefore aggressive in that environment. As they were removed by simazine, the less productive but herbicide R-types occupied the area.

By the mid-1980s, there were several reports suggesting that triazine-resistance and reduced productivity were linked in some way. Holt (1988) in California used field collected biotypes of groundsel with identical environmental histories, to examine whether reduced productivity and competitiveness accompany the trait of triazine-resistance. Growth and development, resource allocation and photosynthetic efficiency were measured in competitive and non-competitive experiments and it was found that in both types of plantings S-plants produced more total dry weight and reproductive output than did R-plants. No differences were detected in number of leaves, root-shoot ratios, total leaf area, relative growth rate or net assimilation rate. Under non-competitive and competitive conditions, R-plants produced relatively more leaf area tissue and a greater leaf area ratio, but less reproductive tissue, than S-plants.

In summary, the work agrees with previous work that S-biotypes are usually greater producers of biomass and reproductive structures. Holt cautions that while a reduction in the efficiency of photosystem II in R-plants probably results from altered functioning of the electron acceptor that also acts as the binding site in S-plants, it is possible that future nuclear-genome controlled traits could mask the intrinsic difference between biotypes due to the chloroplast mutation itself. This photosynthetic difference is only one part of the whole-plant productivity and there is no reason to expect that plants sensitive to the triazines, for example, should be more vigorous or competitive relative to resistant ones in any trait not linked with resistance itself.

Gressel (1989) reminds us that common groundsel, one of the first species to show resistance to the triazines, has evolved this resistance in orchards, nurseries, and roadsides where there is little or no mechanical cultivation—but not in cultivated maize fields where the propagules are incorporated into the soil seed bank to remain viable for several years. Seeds that fall onto such undisturbed soil at season's end will likely germinate and die in that season or early in the following season. Thus, this species has evolved resistance where there was the lowest average seed bank lifetime and is consistent with predictions of standard population dynamics models.

Watson et al. (1987) studied changes in achene behavior of triazine S- and R-biotypes under different management practices. He found that R-types have greater longevity than S-types at soil depths of more than 2 cm, while at 0 to 2 cm depths both biotypes showed differential longevity depending on management practices (see also Putwain et al. 1989).

COMMON NAMES

Senecio vulgaris

ARGENTINA	hierba cana, senecio comun
AUSTRALIA	groundsel
BELGIUM	klein kruiskruid, senecon commun
CANADA	common groundsel, senecon vulgaire, staggerwort, stinking Willie
CHILE	hierba cana
COLOMBIA	cineraria, yuyito
DENMARK	almindelig brandbaeger
EGYPT	morrar
ENGLAND	groundsel
FINLAND	pelovillakko
FRANCE	herba aux charpentiers, senecon commun, senecon vulgaire
GERMANY	Gemeines Kreuzkraut, Gemeines Greiskraut, Gewohnliches Greiskraut, Kreuzkraut
ITALY	calderugia, erba calderina
JAPAN	noborogiku
LEBANON	common groundsel, moraar
MADAGASCAR	anadraisoa
NETHERLANDS	gewoon kruiskruid, klein kruiskruid
NEW ZEALAND	groundsel
NORWAY	akersineblom
POLAND	starzec zwyczajny
PORTUGAL	cardo morto, tasneirinha

SAUDIA ARABIA	moraar
SPAIN	buenvaron, hierba cana, lechocinos
SWEDEN	korsbo, vanlig korsort
TURKEY	kanarya otu, sofeira
UNITED STATES	common groundsel

Eighty-Four

Setaria geniculata (Lam.) Beauv.

Poaceae (Gramineae), Grass Family

THE *SETARIA* GENUS is in the **Paniceae** tribe and has approximately 120 species in temperate, subtropical and tropical areas, including several important millet crops and weedy species. *Setarias* are identified by the presence of rough bristles (modified panicle branches) that remain attached to the rachis after seed drop, and spikelets with two florets, the lower one being either male or sterile. *Setaria* is derived from the Latin *seta* meaning bristle or bristle-like. The species name refers to the bent or jointed stem bases of *S. geniculata*. This weed occurs in 46 countries in tropical and subtropical climates. Unlike many perennial rhizomatous grasses, *S. geniculata* reproduces and spreads primarily by seeds.

FIGURE 84-1   The distribution of *Setaria geniculata* (Lam.) Beauv. across the world where it has been reported as a weed.

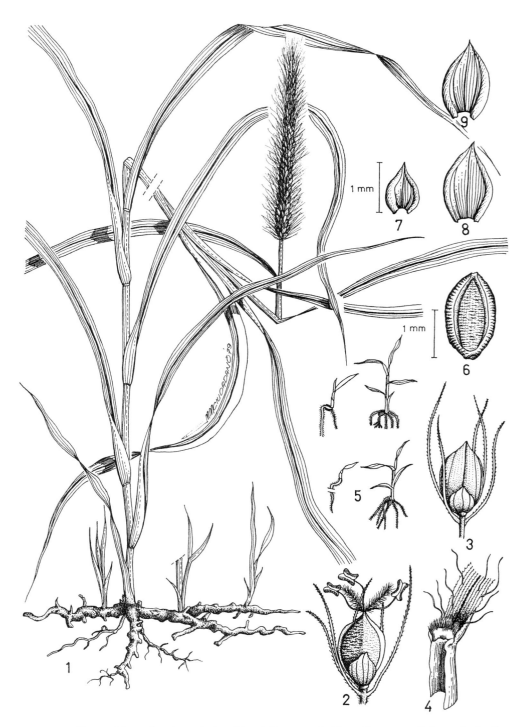

FIGURE 84-2   *Setaria geniculata* (Lam.) Beauv.: 1. habit; 2. floret; 3. spikelet; 4. leaf collar showing ligule; 5. seedlings; 6–9. glumes.

DESCRIPTION

S. geniculata (Figure 84-2) is a slender, loosely tufted, erect *perennial* grass; *stems* 40 to 75 cm tall, compressed, geniculate, branched at base; *rhizomes* short, knotty, branching; *leaf sheath* 4 to 6 cm long, smooth, cylindrical to slightly flattened; *ligule* reduced to rim of stiff hairs, 0.5 to 1 mm long; *blade* flat, 4 to 8 mm wide and up to 18 cm long, smooth except may have few hairs at base; *inflorescence* a cylindrical, dense panicle, erect to slightly nodding, 5 to 10 cm long, 1.5 cm in diameter, including the 4 to 12 rough, persistent, yellowish, green, orange or purplish *bristles* at base of each spikelet; *spikelets* 2 to 3 mm long, green or purplish; *lower glume* hyaline, acute, 3-nerved, 0.7 to 1 mm long; *upper glume* hyaline, 5-nerved, 1.2 to 1.5 mm long; *sterile lemma* 7-nerved, 1.6 mm long, indistinctly keeled; *fertile lemma* indurate (hardened), transversely rugose, yellowish-green to brown, often black-tipped, boat-shaped, 1.6 mm long; *palea* also indurate; *stamens* 3, *stigmas* 2; *fruit* a *caryopsis* 2.5 mm long, half as wide, tapering above middle to a long-pointed apex transversely ridged; yellow to yellowish brown.

This species is distinguished by the short, knotty rhizomes, the short, hairy ligule, the knee-like joints at the stem base and the typical foxtail inflorescence.

HABITAT, ECOLOGY, AND BIOLOGY

While present in several European countries, *S. geniculata* is principally a weed in the Americas and Asia, and is conspicuous by its absence in Africa (Figure 84-1). *S. geniculata* is found in perennial and annual crops, pastures, roadsides, gardens, orchards, ditch banks, lake borders and waste areas. It is native to the tropical Americas and grows from sea level to over 3000 m in this region. It was an important wild cereal in Mexico before the advent of agriculture (Dewet and Harlan 1975). Though replaced by maize around 5000 B.C., *S. geniculata* never lost its natural seed dispersing ability and persists as a weed. Both wild and weedy types are found in Mexico. *S. geniculata* is the only perennial *Setaria* in the central United States. It is a sparse but persistent species in prairie environments. It survives burning on about a four-year cycle and its relatively small size (as compared to dominant prairie grasses) may favor dispersal to appropriate microhabitats (Rabinowitz 1978). In greenhouse conditions, *S. geniculata* competes well with dominant prairie grasses when grown in equal proportions, but it grows best when surrounded by dominant plants, which is its normal habitat (Rabinowitz et al. 1984). Part of its competitive ability may result from its C_4 metabolic pathway (Elmore and Paul 1983).

Southern Brazil is considered a secondary center of *S. geniculata* evolution (Freitas-Sacchet et al. 1984). In this region, plants are nearly equally divided with $2n$ counts of 36 or 72 chromosomes. Plants are wind pollinated, and pollen from both genotypes is highly fertile. The wind-induced harmonic oscillations of its compacted panicle enhance the likelihood of pollen reaching a floret on the same inflorescence (Niklas 1987).

Freshly harvested seeds are dormant, but they germinate readily in the spring. Established plants flower from early July through September in the central United States, and seeds drop from August to December (Rabinowitz and Rapp 1980 and 1981). Seed drop in a prairie was 104 seeds/m² and the "seed rain" was more similar to the seed bank than the latter was to the plant density of *S. geniculata*. In the Philippines, single plants produced 850 seeds with a mean weight of 3.1 mg each (Pancho 1964). In Brazil, plants can set seed 60 days after emergence (Lorenzi 1982). Plants are considered palatable to livestock when they are young, but the bristles on the inflorescence injure the mouths of cattle if they are eaten when mature.

AGRICULTURAL IMPORTANCE

S. geniculata is a reported weed of 27 crops in 46 countries (Figure 84-1) and is a frequently reported weed of cotton, maize, pastures, and sugarcane. It is a serious or principal weed of cotton in Peru; maize, pasture, potatoes, rice, and soybeans in Brazil; pastures in Colombia, Ecuador, and Hawaii; rice in Brazil and Peru; and sugarcane in Argentina.

It is a common weed of citrus in Jamaica; cotton in Bolivia and Colombia; maize in China, Mexico, and Nicaragua; pastures in Jamaica; pineapple in Hawaii and Nicaragua; lowland rice in Thailand; soybeans in Bolivia; sugarcane in Bolivia, Hawaii, and Mexico; and vegetable and nursery crops in the southern United States.

S. geniculata is also an unranked weed of alfalfa in Argentina; bananas in Honduras, Mexico, and Taiwan; edible beans in Colombia and Honduras; cacao in Honduras; cassava in Colombia, Indonesia, and Taiwan; coffee in Brazil, Costa Rica, Honduras, and Mexico; cotton in Greece, Honduras, and Paraguay; flax and lucerne in Argentina; maize in Argentina, Colombia, Greece, Honduras, Indonesia, Paraguay, the Philippines, and Venezuela; pastures in New Zealand and Nicaragua; peanuts in Colombia, Honduras, and Taiwan; pineapple in Honduras and Venezuela; rice in Honduras, Indonesia, the Philippines, Sri Lanka, Taiwan, and Thailand; soybeans in Colombia and Taiwan; sugarcane in Colombia, Honduras, Laos, Mexico, the Philippines, and Taiwan; tobacco in Argentina, Honduras, and the Philippines; and vegetables in Australia, Brazil, Honduras, and Taiwan.

COMMON NAMES

Setaria geniculata

ARGENTINA	cola de zorro, paiten
AUSTRALIA	slender pigeon grass
BARBADOS	bristlegrass
BOLIVIA	cola de zorro
BRAZIL	rabo de raposa
CHILE	pega-pega
COLOMBIA	gusanillo, munchira
CUBA	gusanillo
DOMINICAN REPUBLIC	pajon blanco
EL SALVAROD	gusanito, gusano
MALAYSIA	verbena
NEW ZEALAND	bristlegrass, knotroot
PARAGUAY	cola de zorro, pasto setaria
PERU	chilena, chilicua, grama, rabo de zorro
PUERTO RICO	deshollinador, rabo de zorro

SRI LANKA	kavalu
TAIWAN	hsio-li-gou-wei-tsao
TRINIDAD	bristlegrass, knotroot
UNITED STATES	knotroot foxtail
URUGUAY	cola de zorro
VENEZUELA	limpia botella

Eighty-Five

Setaria glauca (L.) Beauv. (syn. S. lutescens (Weig.) F.T.Hubb.)

Poaceae (Gramineae), Grass Family

S ETARIA GLAUCA is a widely distributed annual grass found in diverse habitats. It originated in Europe and was used centuries ago to produce flour and groats, especially during the Middle Ages when wheat was in short supply (Dembinska 1976). It has spread throughout North America, the Andean countries of South America, Australia, and Asia. Terrell (1976) reviewed the taxonomy of this plant and concluded that *S. glauca* is the

FIGURE 85-1   The distribution of *Setaria glauca* (L.) Beauv. across the world where it has been reported as a weed.

FIGURE 85-2 Three *Setarias* commonly found in the same areas are presented to aid in species identification.: A. *Setaria faberii* Herm. a. habit, b. spikelet showing subtending bristles, c. ligule, d. caryopsis. B. *Setaria viridis* (L.) Beauv. a. habit, b. spikelet, c. ligule, d. caryopsis. C. *Setaria glauca* (L.) Beauv. a. habit, b. spikelet, c. ligule, d. caryopsis.

preferred name. The species name in Latin means bluish-green or bluish-gray in reference to the leaves, and the synonym *lutescens* means yellowish, which describes the inflorescence and is part of the common name used for it in several countries, yellow foxtail.

DESCRIPTION

S. glauca (Figure 85-2) is an *annual* tufted grass, branching at base; *stems* erect or ascending, 50 to 100 cm tall, often with reddish or purplish base; *leaf blade* glaucous-green, linear-lanceolate, flat, 6 to 30 cm long, 4 to 10 mm wide, several long, prominent silky hairs on the upper surface at base, 3 to 10 mm long; *leaf sheath* glabrous, split, the lower portion flattened; *ligule* a fringe of ciliate hairs, 1 to 3 mm long joined at base; *inflorescence* an erect spike-like panicle, cylindrical, dense, 5 to 14 cm long, 9 to 14 mm wide, axis densely pubescent, yellow at maturity; *spikelets* 3 to 3.5 mm long, awnless but subtended by 4 to 12 yellow, orange or tawny bristles 2 to 3 times as long as the spikelet with forward-pointing barbs; *glumes* broadly ovate, *lower glume* 3-nerved, up to half as long as spikelet; *upper glume* 5-nerved, two-thirds as long as spikelet; *fertile lemma* strongly and transversely rugose; *fruit* an indehiscent *caryopsis*; broadly ovate, 2.5 to 3.3 mm long, 1.5 to 2.2 mm wide, flat on one side, strongly convex on opposite; glumes remain attached and cover lower half; surface wrinkled crosswise with prominent edge from overlap of upper and lower glumes; yellowish brown; slightly translucent; apex often somewhat 3-toothed.

The key characteristics of *S. glauca* are the long, silky hairs at the base of the leaf blade and the coarsely wrinkled lemma of the seeds. (Note: Figure 85-2 includes the related species *S. faberii* and *S. viridis*.)

HABITAT AND ECOLOGY

S. glauca is a weed of cereals, vegetables, root crops, pastures, roadsides, and waste areas. It is the most widely distributed *Setaria* in the United States but is conspicuously absent in most of Africa (Figure 85-1). It grows from sea level to 3000 m in India and is adapted to a wide range of environments.

Plants are most common in disturbed sites. Gregg (1973) plowed a fertile pasture and 1 yr later, tall, healthy *S. glauca* plants predominated. If soil disturbance continued, plants maintained vigorous growth, but without tillage the few plants that emerged were stunted and unbranched. When a native prairie was plowed five consecutive years, *S. glauca* comprised 0, 0.2, and 13% of the foliage cover in the first, third, and fifth season, respectively (Penfound and Rice 1957). Populations also vary with plowing date. Peak emergence in the field is in late April to early May in the eastern United States and soil disturbance at later dates reduces the population (Gregg 1973). Crop rotation also affects *S. glauca* density. Kommedahl and Linck (1957) recorded 670 plants/m^2 following 10 yr of oats and 325/m^2 following 10 yr of flax, with intermediate densities for maize, wheat and soybeans.

Biotypes of *S. glauca* have been noted in many countries. One Indian biotype is common in moist soils around ponds or along ditch banks and has a long panicle; a short-panicled type is found in well-drained soils (Ramakrishnan 1963). Biotypes in the United States are also well documented. Seed collected at eight sites over a 160-km radius in the eastern United States produced prostrate (25-cm tall) or erect (over 50-cm tall) plants, leaf widths from 2 to 5 mm and 13 to 27 tillers per plant. Some biotypes dropped 70% of their seed by August 18, while others had shed none. Biotypes also varied in susceptibility to dalapon (Santelmann and Meade 1961).

Schoner et al. (1978) grew biotypes from the western, central and eastern United States in California. The three western collections were identical to each other but distinct from the rest. California biotypes were prostrate in growth habit but the others were erect. Seedlings of the California biotype were erect initially but plants soon assumed a horizontal position and remained prostrate until maturity. The foliage resembled the rosette-type growth common in some broadleaf plants. After pollination, the last two nodes bend upwards and the last four internodes elongate rapidly. The horizontal type may have been selected in irrigated lucerne fields that are mowed repeatedly. Biotypes with prostrate growth would successfully produce seed, while erect biotypes would often be clipped before seeds matured. Other differences were also noted. An eastern biotype had yellow-green leaves, while the others were blue-green. One eastern biotype produced the most heads per plant, while another had the fewest. Steel et al. (1983) observed a dwarf biotype in Canada common in dry or infertile soils.

S. glauca is adapted to a wide range of soil textures and grows in soils with *pH*s of 6 to 8. When *S. glauca* was grown with other *Setaria* species, it always persisted, but at levels of 5 to 15% of the total population (Schreiber 1977). It was the only species to survive in stands of *S. faberii*.

BIOLOGY

S. glauca seeds are dormant upon maturity but germinate readily when after-ripened for 3 to 4 months. Removing the lemma and palea enhances germination of stored seed and more seeds germinate at a constant 20°C than at 30°C (Povilaitis 1956, Rost 1975). Hard seed coats inhibit germination and account in part for seed persistence in the soil (Peters et al. 1963). Even fresh seed has 50% germination when scarified in sulfuric acid for 5 to 10 min and more seeds germinate in continuous light (76%) than in darkness (2%) (Ramakrishnan 1963). Ultracold temperatures (–96 C) enhance germination of *S. glauca* (Jordon 1981), but the cool, moist environments of fields in the winter is sufficient to break the dormancy of most seeds. Abscisic acid in the seed coat inhibits germination of excised embryos (Kollman and Staniforth 1972).

Germination varies between seed lots and plant biotypes. Taylorson and Brown (1977) collected seed from four sites in the same vicinity in the eastern United States for several years. Fresh seeds in one lot failed to germinate, but 81% germinated after 14 days of exposure to 50°C in sealed tubes. Germination of another seed lot decreased from 60 to 0% with the same treatment. Seeds collected in an east-west transect across Japan varied greatly in germination. There were clear biotype and environment interactions that make predicting the germinability of seed difficult (Shibata 1981).

Germination was more consistent when biotypes were grown under identical conditions in the western United States. Western biotypes had 85% germination after 4 mo of storage, while eastern biotypes had less than 35%. Stratification for 2 mo reduced germination of a western biotype from 92 to 43%, while eastern biotypes increased from 34 to 57% with this treatment. The optimum germination temperature was 20 to 25°C for all biotypes, but the western type emerged 1 to 4 days sooner than the eastern biotypes (Norris and Schoner 1980).

Seeds germinate within 48 hr in optimum conditions and the radicle grows several centimeters per day initially. A detailed and excellent description of the germination process is given by Rost (1975). Germination decreases more for *S. glauca* than for *S. viridis* as soils dry. Without moisture stress, germination after 72 hr at 25°C was 70 and 40% for *S. viridis* and *S. glauca*, respectively. In −4 and −8 bar osmotic potential solutions, germination was 70 and 31%, respectively, for *S. viridis*, and 12 and 1%, respectively, for *S. glauca* (Manthey and Nalewaja 1987).

Emergence is greatest (87%) from 1.5 mm and declines to less than 6% at 10 cm (Gregg 1973). Shallow-planted seeds emerge in 4 days and those at 10 cm require 15 days. At a given depth, most seedlings emerge within 1 to 4 days after the first ones appear, but a few emerge sporadically for 30 to 35 days after the initial flush. Under natural conditions, the mean emergence depth is 1.4 cm in untilled and 1.8 cm in tilled fields. Maximum emergence depths were 13.7 cm for untilled and 9.2 cm for tilled fields.

Seeds buried in the fall in the central United States emerged between April 22 and May 20, with no consistent relationship to degree days. Greatest emergence was between 1.3 and 5.1 cm (Stoller and Wax 1973). Vengris (1963) planted *S. glauca* at 2-wk intervals from May 15 to September 15. Seedlings emerged in 7 to 8 days from mid-June to early September and in 10 to 13 days for earlier or later plantings. Days to heading and maturity declined continually from 59 to 40 and from 86 to 51, respectively, during the season. Heading and maturity were delayed 4 to 6 days when *S. glauca* competed with maize. No plants formed seed heads when planted on September 1 with maize or on September 15 without maize. Plant height and total biomass decreased as seedling date was delayed.

Populations are self-regulating. In greenhouse trials, 100 to 1000 plants/m² had no mortality, but 58, 66, and 84% died at densities of 2,500, 5,000, and 10,000 plants/m², respectively (Gregg 1973). Plants grow slowly until they are 5 to 8 cm tall; then growth is rapid until heading.

Plants tiller 10 to 20 days after emergence and continue tillering for 70 to 85 days. Total plant weight is highly correlated with the number of tillers, and secondary and tertiary tillers are common. Peters et al. (1963) found 75 tillers on plants spaced 20 cm apart, 26 tillers at a 5-cm spacing and only two tillers on plants in dense stands. Late emerging and nutrient deficient plants tiller less. Adventitious roots may appear at the lower nodes.

Shading also reduces tillering and delays heading by more than 1 wk (Bubar and Morrison 1984). The number of tillers dropped from 25/plant in sunlight to 16 with shade. When plants grow in full light 1 mo before shading occurs, an 80% reduction in light has only a slight effect on plant dry weight (Lee and Cavers 1981). Shade affected *S. glauca* the least of the three *Setaria* studied.

Greenhouse research found tiller numbers only slightly reduced by dry soil conditions. However, shoot dry weight was reduced over 50% at 6 wk after emergence and total root length per plant dropped from 2610 to 305 cm in dry soil (Nadeau and Morrison 1983). *S. glauca* has a high N and moderate P requirement (Gregg 1973). Flowering plants had 1.4% N, 0.3% P, 3.6% K, and 0.21% Ca, while seeds had 2.6% N and 0.36% P. This species had the highest leaf area per plant of five *Setaria* studied and the leaf area doubled as Hoagland's nutrient solution increased from one-half to 3x strength (Schreiber and Orwick 1978).

S. glauca is a day neutral plant, but, as day length is shortened, fewer tillers are formed and plants flower and mature more rapidly. Under continuous light, plants do not flower (Santelman et al. 1963, Gregg 1973) or, if they do, many florets are sterile (Listowski and Jasmanowicz 1969).

S. glauca has C$_4$ metabolism (Elmore and Paul 1983) and a 2*n* chromosome count of 36 (Kawano and Miyake 1983). Counts of 2*n* = 18 and 72 are also known. Plant biomass is distributed as follows: 8% roots, 28% stems, 19% leaf blades, 3% rachis, and 24% seed. Flowers are wind- or self-pollinated and are highly fertile. Biotypes resistant to triazine herbicides occur in France (LeBaron and Gressel 1982).

This species may be allelopathic. Water extracts from 60 g of *S. glauca* seeds/L of water were used to germinate eight crops. Germination was reduced from 80 to 20% for lucerne, 67 to 32% for cabbage, and 79 to 44% for radish. Extracts had no effect on timothy, carrot, pepper, tomato or turnip and whole seeds did not inhibit crop germination (Gressel and Holm 1964). Root washings reduced the germination of soybeans from 86 to 66% and of mungbean from 94 to 60%. Roots and hypocotyls of both crops were stunted, but peanut germination and growth were unaffected (Tiwari et al. 1985). Roots and shoots can be equally inhibitory (Peters et al. 1963).

In the biotron, *S. glauca* shoot residues in the growing medium inhibited maize and soybean growth. The effect was greater at low temperatures for maize and at higher light intensities for soybeans (Bhowmik and Doll 1983). Under greenhouse conditions, *S. glauca* residues in the soil lowered the N and P concentration of maize but increased the K content, perhaps due to the high levels of K in the weed residue. Under field conditions, residues from uncontrolled, dense *S. glauca* stands the previous year had no effect on maize or soybean yields (Bhowmik and Doll 1984). *S. glauca* exhibits no autotoxicity (Gregg 1973).

Seed production per plant depends upon the number of tillers per plant and seeds per inflorescence; both characters fluctuate greatly among biotypes and environments. Estimates vary from 92 seeds/plant in India to 8460 in the United States. The average of seven reports is 2575 seeds/plant. Seed weight varies from 0.68 to 4.9 mg/seed, with an average of 2.4 mg. Long-panicled biotypes in India produced 538 seeds/plant and short-panicled biotypes yielded 92 (Ramakrishnan 1963). Single plants free of competition formed 47 seed heads with 180 seeds each (8460 seeds/plant) (Santelman et al. 1963). In natural stands, seeds per seed head range from 30 to 400 and dense infestations produce nearly 36,000 seeds/m^2 (Gregg 1973).

Seed productivity also varies among crops. In Russia, *S. glauca* forms the most seeds in potatoes and fodder beets and the least in winter rye and maize. Seed production drops with rising altitudes and varies between populations collected at several sites and grown in the same location (Hamor 1978).

Seeds spread as grain contaminants and are carried by beetles, birds and water (Ridley 1930). *S. glauca* was found in two of 156 irrigation water samples in the western United States. Over 90% of the seeds floated when dropped into water from 1.5 m (Egginton and Robbins 1920).

Seed burial studies in Europe and North America found *S. glauca* seed survived up to 30 yr in the soil (Toole and Brown 1946, Kivilaan and Bandurski 1973). Most seeds in the soil either germinate or die within 13 yr (Dawson and Bruns 1975). Seed bank populations can be very high. Schweizer and Zimdahl (1984) found 22 million seeds/ha of *S. viridis* and *S. glauca*. Effective control in maize reduced the seed reservoir by half in one season and to 1 million *Setaria* spp. seeds after four seasons.

Seeds ensiled with forage crops or maize are killed during the fermentation process. Zahnley and Fitch (1941) placed *S. glauca* seeds at four positions in silos for 7 yr. Seeds removed from all levels were nonviable at all sampling dates.

AGRICULTURAL IMPORTANCE

S. glauca is a reported weed in 63 countries (Figure 85-1) and infests a wide array of 50 crops in the Americas, Europe, the former Soviet Union, and Asia. It is particularly common in annual row crops like maize, soybeans, and cotton but also occurs in small grains, sugarcane, tree crops, and pastures. It is a serious or principal weed of avocado in the southern United States; barley in Korea; edible beans in Canada; citrus in Israel; cotton in Egypt and Israel; flax, lucerne and sugar beets in the United States; jute, peanuts, and dryland crops in India; maize in Austria, Australia, Canada, Czechoslovakia, France, Germany, India, Italy, Rumania, the former Soviet Union, the United States, and the former Yugoslavia; millet in the United States; pastures in Ecuador and the United States; potatoes in India and the former Soviet Union; upland rice in India and Sri Lanka, and lowland rice in India; soybeans in Canada, India, and the United States; strawberries in Canada and the former Soviet Union; vegetables in Bulgaria and the former Soviet Union; and wheat in Korea and the United States.

It is a common weed of bananas in India and Mexico; citrus in Mexico and the former Soviet Union; coffee and rice in Mexico; cotton in Colombia, India, and the United States; hemp, millet, and soybeans in the former Soviet Union; horticultural crops in Dominican Republic; legumes in India; maize in Mexico, Portugal, and Spain; orchards in India, Spain, and the former Soviet Union; pineapple in Hawaii; potatoes in Italy and the United States; sorghum, sunflowers, tobacco, and vegetables in the United States; sugar beets in Canada and the former Soviet Union; sugarcane in Bangladesh, India, Mexico, and the Philippines; taro in Samoa and Tonga; and vegetables in the United States.

S. glauca is also a weed of unknown rank in barley in Iraq; edible beans in Chile and the United States; cassava in Indonesia; cereals in Germany, Jordan, and Switzerland; clover in Ireland; cacao in Dominican Republic; coffee in Dominican Republic and Venezuela; cotton in Greece, Iran, Spain, and the former Soviet Union; irrigated crops in the former Soviet Union and the United States; macadamia plantings in Hawaii; maize in Bulgaria, Hungary, and Indonesia; pastures in New Zealand and the former Yugoslavia; peanuts in Australia; rice in Portugal; rye in Ireland; sorghum in the former Soviet Union; soybeans in Chile; strawberries in the United States; sugar beets in Iran; sugarcane in Hawaii, Mauritius, and Peru; tea in India, Japan, and the former Soviet Union; and vegetables in Hawaii, Iraq, Iran, and Rumania.

Competition studies found that 20 to 100 plants/m of row reduced sunflower yield only 6 to 12% (Nalewaja et al. 1972). *S. glauca* was less competitive than *Brassica kaber* on a plant-to-plant basis, but the grass is often more abundant than the broadleaf. Staniforth (1957, 1961, 1965) noted the greatest interference of *S. glauca* in maize at low N levels. Without N, yields were reduced 21%, but with 63 and 126 kg/ha N, losses were only 10 and 5%, respectively, even though the weed biomass increased as fertilizer rates increased. *S. glauca* competition reduced the yield of later maturing maize varieties more than earlier maturing varieties. In soybeans, each kilogram of *S. glauca* biomass (dry weight basis) reduced soybean grain yield 0.15 kg. This species produced less biomass in soybeans than *S. viridis* or *S. faberii* and thus was less competitive than these species.

Zimdahl (1980) reported that 225 plants/m^2 produced 2300 kg dry matter/ha and that each kilogram of *S. glauca* reduced sorghum yield by 0.64 kg. Sorghum yield losses were 28% with 6 wk of competition and 53% if *S. glauca* was uncontrolled all season.

S. glauca has long been found in cereals. Ten percent of the weeds in an eleventh-century European granary containing rye was *S. glauca* (Kosina 1978). It has been disseminated as a contaminant of cereal and forage seeds (Johnson and Hensman 1910). In the state of North Dakota, in the United States, *S. glauca* infests 90% of the cropland and over 400,000 ton of *S. glauca* and *S. viridis* seeds are harvested as contaminants of small grains and flax annually. However, if the grain is used as livestock feed, the contamination may not be significant. In fact, swine can consume up to 40% *S. glauca* instead of barley with no ill effects (Harold and Nalewaja 1977). Seeds have 4.44 kcal/g gross energy, 16.8% protein, 7.5% fat, 0.38% P, 0.8% Ca, 0.89% K, and 0.45% Mg. The protein is low in lysine and tryptophane, but the seeds were the highest in zinc (1738 ppm) and iron (1671 ppm) of the 15 species tested.

S. *glauca* is also widespread in the small grain region of Canada. Average densities are 113 plants/m². Morrison and Murice (1980) discovered that it took 200 or more plants/m² to reduce wheat yields. At 600 plants/m², production dropped 30%. At high *S. glauca* seed densities, fewer plants emerge than at lower densities, suggesting a self-regulating population mechanism.

Greenhouse research by Peters et al. (1963) showed that *S. glauca* reduced lucerne growth 60%, while the crop only reduced weed growth 25%. Lucerne did not respond to fertilizer in the presence of *S. glauca* but the weed responded both with and without lucerne present, and the percentage of P and K in *S. glauca* leaves and stems was equal at all fertility levels and both with or without lucerne.

Nevertheless, *S. glauca* has more protein than timothy in harvested hay (Peters et al. 1963), is as palatable as oats to sheep, and the levels of Ca, P, K, and Mg are above the minimum required for ruminants (Marten and Andersen 1975). As *S. glauca* matures, its acceptability as a forage drops rapidly due to increased fiber and lower protein levels (Bosworth et al. 1980). Mature plants become unpalatable to livestock, but if forage is scarce and plants are consumed, the seedhead bristles can cause painful lesions in animals' mouths, can predispose ruminants to hypomagnesemia, and can cause stomatitis in cattle and horses (Steel et al. 1983).

S. *glauca* is a valuable wildlife food, especially as a source of seeds for birds, but it can host ergot, aphids and downy mildew (Steel et al. 1983). It can also host maize dwarf mosaic, army worms and northern corn rootworm.

COMMON NAMES

Setaria glauca

ARGENTINA	cola de zorro amarilla
AUSTRALIA	pale pigeon grass
AUSTRIA	Gelbe Borstenhirse
BANGLADESH	halud shiallja
BURMA	sat
CANADA	setaire glauque, yellow foxtail
COLOMBIA	cola de zorro, gusanillo, limpia frascos
CUBA	rabito peludo
DENMARK	blagron skaermaks
DOMINICAN REPUBLIC	rabo de zorra

EGYPT	deil el-faar, faar, safeea, shar el-far
ENGLAND	yellow bristle grass
FIJI	mongoose tail, yellow bristle grass
FINLAND	sinertavapantaheina
FRANCE	setaire glauque
GERMANY	Fuchshirse, Gelber Fuchsschwanz, Gelbe Borstenhirse, Gilb-fennich, Graugrune Borstenhirse, Rote Borstenhirse
HAWAII	yellow bristle grass, yellow foxtail
HUNGARY	fako muhar
INDIA	banara, banari
INDONESIA	ekor andjing, uler-uleran
IRAN	asb vash
IRAQ	dukhain
ISRAEL	ziphan khalhal
ITALY	pabio, panicastrella, panicastrella scura, panico glauco, setaria
JAPAN	kin-enokoro
LEBANON	bristlegrass, yellow foxtail
MADAGASCAR	ahipody, taindalitra, taindambo
MEXICO	cola de zorra amarilla, rabito
NETHERLANDS	zeegroene naaldaar
NEW ZEALAND	yellow bristle grass
NORWAY	bla busthirse
PAKISTAN	chiria-ka-dana, kangni, lundi
POLAND	wlosnica sina
PORTUGAL	milha amarela, milha glauca
SPAIN	almorejo glauco
SRI LANKA	kawalu
SWEDEN	gra kolvhirs, grahirs
SWITZERLAND	Graugrune Borstenhirse, setaire glauque
TAIWAN	chin-se-gou-wei-ysao
THAILAND	yaa haangmaa noi
TURKEY	sari tuylu dari, sican saci
UNITED STATES	yellow foxtail
VENEZUELA	limpia botella, rabo de zorro
YUGOSLAVIA	sinjo proso, sivi muhar

Eighty-Six

Setaria pallide-fusca (Schumach.)
Stapf & Hubb.

Poaceae (Gramineae), Grass Family

S ETARIA PALLIDE-FUSCA is an annual weed often found in its native Africa and parts of
Asia and Australia. The species name refers to the variable color of the inflorescence,
from light or pale yellow "*pallid*" to reddish brown or purple "*fuscus.*" This is the
least studied of the *Setarias* considered as secondary weeds. The taxonomy of *S. pallide-
fusca* is based on spikelet length and this too is a variable trait (Simon 1984). Some authors
place it as a subspecies of *S. pumila*.

FIGURE 86-1   The distribution of *Setaria pallide-fusca* (Schumach.) Stapf & Hubb. across
the world where it has been reported as a weed.

FIGURE 86-2 *Setaria pallide-fusca* (Schumach.) Stapf & Hubb.: 1. habit; 2. seedlings; 3. leaf collar; 4. portion of inflorescence showing persistent bristles and rachis; 5. spikelet; 6. caryopsis.

DESCRIPTION

S. pallide-fusca (Figure 86-2) is a tufted *annual* grass with fibrous *roots*; *stems* erect, 25 to 60 cm tall, smooth, slender, often rooting from lower nodes; *leaf sheath* 3 to 8 cm long, glabrous; *blade* 10 to 15 cm long, 6 to 10 mm wide, smooth except for few hairs at base, tapering to a fine tip; *ligule* a shallow membrane topped with stiff *bristles*, 1.2 to 1.5 mm long; *inflorescence* an erect, cylindrical spike-like panicle 2 to 10 cm long with successive short clusters of 2 spikelets (one fertile) each subtended by involucre of 6 to 10 pale yellow, golden, orange or reddish brown to purple persistent *bristles*; *spikelets* 2 to 2.5 mm long; *lower glume* 1- to 3-nerved, 1.4 mm long; *upper glume* 5-nerved, 1.6 mm long, the nerves joining towards tip; *lower floret* usually sterile, with flat, obscurely 5- to 7-veined *lemma* and flat, membranous *palea*; *upper floret* fertile, stamens 3, stigmas 2; *lemma* boat-shaped with prominent transverse wrinkles; *palea* nearly flat, finely wrinkled; both lemma and palea hard and leathery when mature; *fruit* a *caryopsis* 1.4 mm long with coarsely rugose back, nearly flat face and punctiform *hilum*; apex 3-toothed, dark.

This species is characterized by the smooth, fine-pointed leaves, hairy ligule and purplish red bristles of young inflorescences that turn yellow to golden brown when mature.

ECOLOGY AND BIOLOGY

S. pallide-fusca infests dryland crops, roadsides, waste areas, ditches and occasionally grasslands. It is adapted to a wide range of soils and climates and is especially well suited to dry soil conditions (Rochecouste 1967). In Japan it occurs on sandy textured soils (Kawano and Miyake 1983), while in India it is found on poorly drained clay soils (Hodd and Hodd 1982). When grazed it becomes more prostrate in habit and seed heads are 2 cm long; seed heads on erect forms are 10 to 12 cm long.

Most seeds (84%) emerge within 15 days of planting and the rest within 30 days (Deat et al. 1978). Plants allocate nearly 30% of their biomass to seed formation, 24% to stems, 16% to leaf blades, 15% to leaf sheaths, 11% to roots, 3% to the rachis and 1% to bristles (Kawano and Miyake 1983). Most plants are octaploids with a $2n$ count of 72 and they produce seeds three to six times larger than the diploid *S. viridis* ($2n = 18$). Self-pollination is very effective, as even isolated plants have very few empty spikelets. The bristles usually remain attached to the rachis and may serve to protect florets and seeds from predators. *S. pallide-fusca* is a C_4 species (Gaudet 1979).

Plants produced over 5000 seeds each in a tropical environment in Zimbabwe (Schwerzel 1967) but only 80 per plant in Japan (Kawano and Miyake 1983). Schwerzel obtained only 7% germination of fresh seed. Light stimulates germination.

AGRICULTURAL IMPORTANCE

S. pallide-fusca is a reported weed in 36 countries (Figure 86-1) and its weedy nature is reflected in the diversity of the 17 crops it infests. It is a serious or principal weed of cereals in Uganda; cotton in Sudan and Zambia; maize in Gambia and India, South Africa, and Zambia; millet in Gambia; pastures in Nigeria; peanuts and sorghum in Gambia and Sudan; sorghum in Sudan; and wheat in Kenya and Sudan.

It is a common weed of cassava in Ghana; cereals in Tanzania; cotton in Zimbabwe;

cowpeas, millet, peanuts, and sorghum in Senegal; jute in Bangladesh; maize in Ghana, Kenya, Senegal, and Zimbabwe; upland rice in Fiji and Senegal; and tea in India.

S. pallide-fusca is also an unranked weed of cassava in Indonesia; coffee in East Africa; cotton in Tanzania; maize in Ethiopia and Indonesia; pastures in India and the Philippines; rice in Bangladesh, India, Indonesia, Ivory Coast, Nepal, the Philippines, Thailand, and Vietnam; sugarcane in Mauritius; tea in Indonesia; and wheat in India and Tanzania.

Gaudet (1979) found 24% of Zambian maize fields infested with *S. pallide-fusca*. Seeds often contaminate harvested wheat in India (Dasgupta 1978) and Kenya (Popay and Ivens 1982). Seeds of this weed contaminated 80% of the lucerne and 10% of the Rhodes grass seed in Kenya and only 12 and 25% could be removed from the legume and grass seed, respectively (Bogdan 1966). Populations increased in sugarcane in Mauritius as repeated use of 2,4-D controlled broadleaf weeds (Rochecouste 1967).

COMMON NAMES

Setaria pallide-fusca

AUSTRALIA	Queensland pigeon grass
FIJI	cat's tail grass
INDIA	nerkka-kora, kuradakorigaddi
MAURITIUS	millet sauvage

Eighty-Seven

Sida rhombifolia L.

Malvaceae, Mallow Family

SIDA RHOMBIFOLIA is a persistent, semiwoody weed common in pastures, roadsides, waste areas and short- and long-season crops throughout tropical and subtropical regions and is described as a pantropic species. It is not the only one of the approximately 200 Sida species to behave as a weed but is perhaps the most widespread, occurring in over 70 countries (Figure 87-1). The genus name means simply "plant" in Greek, while the epithet refers to the rhombic-shaped leaves.

FIGURE 87-1　The distribution of *Sida rhombifolia* L. across the world where it has been reported as a weed.

FIGURE 87-2 *Sida rhombifolia* L.: 1. habit; 2. flower, perianth removed to show staminal tube; 3. ovary, vertical section; 4–5. flower with jointed pedicel; 6. flower, front view; 7. mericarp, 3 views; 8. seed, 2 views.

DESCRIPTION

S. rhombifolia (Figure 87-2) is an erect, semiwoody *perennial* 0.3 to 1.0 m tall with a strong *taproot*; *stems* branched, finely pubescent, woody when mature; *leaves* alternate, broadest in middle, diverse in size, 1 to 4 cm long, 0.5 to 2 cm wide; rhombic, rhombic-oblong to oblong, narrowed toward apex; obtuse to subcuneate at base; margins obscurely dentate, with teeth acute to rounded; pale green, stellate hairy beneath; *stipules* bristly, 1-nerved, linear-lanceolate, as long as *petiole*; *inflorescence* axillary, solitary flowers on slender *pedicel*, 2 to 3 cm long, jointed above middle; *flower calyx* green, cup-shaped, membranous, persistent, ridged at base, with stellate hairs and lobes terminating abruptly into elongated points; *corolla* of 5 pale yellow *petals*, 1.5 to 1.8 cm in diameter; *fruit* a *schizocarp* with 8 to 10 wrinkled or nearly smooth *mericarps*, each about 2.5 mm long, not awned, or with awns 1.5 mm long, wedged-shaped with rounded backs; *seeds* flattened, reniform, 1.25 to 2 mm long, dark brown.

The key characteristics of this weed are the semiwoody stem, stipuled leaves, jointed pedicel, and the persistent calyx surrounding the schizocarp.

TAXONOMY

This species has many morphological forms and taxonomists refer to the *S. rhombifolia* "complex." Several have defined subspecies. Ugborogho (1980) described three subspecies in Nigeria: The subsp. *rhombifolia* is in southern Nigeria, grows to 2 m tall, has stellate hairs on both leaf surfaces and flowers between 10:30 and 11:30 A.M. The subsp. *retusa* is shorter (80 cm), also occurs in southern Nigeria and has stellate hairs on both leaf surfaces, but its flowers are smaller and they open later (12:00 to 12:30 P.M.) than those of *rhombifolia*. The subspecies *alnifolia* is found in both northern and southern Nigeria, has simple hairs only on the upper leaf surface and its flowers open the earliest (9:00 A.M.). In Asia, Pancho and Obien (1983) described subsp. *rhombifolia* as having leaves 1 to 4 cm long, pedicels to 3 cm and awnless mericarps, while subsp. *retusa* has smaller leaves that are pubescent beneath, flowers with shorter pedicels, and beaked mericarps. In Brazil, the variety *Typica* has leaves greater than 1 cm wide that are serrate from the midsection to the tip, while the variety *canariensis* has narrower leaves (F. Leitao et al. 1972).

ECOLOGY AND BIOLOGY

S. rhombifolia grows from sea level to 2000 m above sea level in many soil types and from fertile to degraded conditions. Plants grow best in non-disturbed sites but are also found in cultivated land. When reduced and no-tillage systems are adopted, this species becomes more common in cropland.

Fresh seed is dormant and dry storage (Doll et al. 1976), KNO_3, IAA, GA, kinetin, alcohol, various light regimes and freezing fail to induce germination (Rizk et al. 1969). Acid scarification for 45 min, heating at 90°C for 12 hr and storage at 5°C for 2 to 4 mo break dormancy (Chawan 1971, Chawan and Sen 1973, Smith et al. 1992).

Viable nondormant seeds germinate best between 25 and 35°C in either light or dark (Smith 1977). No seeds germinated at 40°C and, after 3 wk at 45°C, only 21% of the seeds were viable (Smith et al. 1992). Seeds germinated readily at an osmotic stress of −400 kPa and 12% germinated at −800 kPa. Nearly half the seeds on the soil surface germinate and they germinate equally well in *pH*s from 5 to 8. The ability to germinate on the soil surface under a range of conditions favors *S. rhombifolia* establishment and spread from seed and is consistent with the variable habitats where it is found (Smith et al. 1992). Over 80% of the seeds emerge from 0.5 to 2 cm in the soil. Fifty percent emerge from 5 cm but, at greater depths, sprouted seeds fail to reach the soil surface.

The roots are moderately branched, with lateral roots angled acutely downward. Manual or mechanical eradication is difficult because root buds form new shoots if stems are destroyed (Shetty and Maiti 1978). *S. rhombifolia* leaves fold toward the branches at night, leaving only the lower leaf surface exposed. They unfold at dawn and move during the day to be at right angles to the sun (Harper 1959). The plant is a C$_3$ species (Patterson 1985), and both diploid $2n = 14$ and tetraploid $2n = 28$ forms exist (Ugborogho 1982). Plants are highly self-compatible and pollination occurs before or as soon as the flower buds open. Hybridization between diploid types (subsp. *rhombifolia* and *retusa*) can occur, but diploid crossing with the tetraploid *alnifolia* does not take place.

Flowers open only once and all flower parts except the calyx and ovary are ejected the next day (Ugborogho 1980). Cold weather delays flower opening. On warm days, flowers remain open 2 to 5 hr. Petals usually open simultaneously but close in sequence. Each pollen grain forms two pollen tubes (typical of **Malvaceae**) but the sperm is found in only one of the unbranched tubes (Datta 1958). Single plants produce 4000 (Datta and Banerjee 1976) to 11,600 seeds (Pancho 1964) and seeds weigh 1.2 to 1.5 mg each. Seeds can float on water for long periods and have been dispersed by ants in Africa (Ridley 1930).

Maximum growth occurs under very warm conditions (25°C nights and 30°C days) with little growth below 20°C. Plants become dormant with the onset of frost in Australia (Smith 1977) and survive winters as far north as Tennessee, in the United States (Rizk et al. 1969).

AGRICULTURAL IMPORTANCE

Even though *S. rhombifolia* is widely distributed in Africa, it is most frequently reported as a weed in Central and South America and Asia. It is a reported weed of 34 crops in 75 countries (Figure 87-1) and is frequently reported a weed of pasture, sugarcane, and maize. It is a serious or principal weed of bananas in Samoa; edible beans in Colombia; cassava in Brazil and India; coffee in Dominican Republic; cotton, rice, and soybeans in Brazil; maize in India; pastures in Australia, Brazil, Colombia, Dominican Republic, Ecuador, Gambia, Guatemala, Jamaica, New Guinea, the Philippines, and West Africa; and sorghum in Mexico.

It is a common weed of bananas in Costa Rica and Taiwan; edible beans in Costa Rica and Cuba; cassava in Costa Rica; citrus in Nicaragua and South Africa; coffee in Costa Rica, Cuba and Nicaragua; cotton in Colombia, Mexico, Paraguay, and Peru; maize in Brazil, Costa Rica, Mexico, and Peru; peanuts in India; sugarcane in Bangladesh, Costa Rica, Hawaii, India, Mexico, and South Africa; and tea in Indonesia.

S. rhombifolia is an unranked weed of edible beans in Brazil and Honduras; cassava in Colombia, Indonesia, Madagascar, Nicaragua, and Taiwan; coffee in Brazil and Mexico; maize in Colombia, Honduras, Indonesia, Nicaragua, the Philippines, and Taiwan; pastures Cuba, Honduras, India, Mexico, Nigeria, Puerto Rico, and Taiwan; peanuts in Australia, Brazil, and Taiwan; rubber in Indonesia; and sugarcane in Australia, Argentina, Brazil, Colombia, Honduras, Nicaragua, the Philippines, and Taiwan. In addition to the above crops, it is reported as a weed in cowpea, jute, oil palm, orchards, pineapple, sweet potatoes, and taro.

The prevalence of *S. rhombifolia* in both cultivated and undisturbed sites reflects its adaptability. In Colombia the weed was not part of the flora that initially infested a fallowed field, but appeared 3 to 4 mo later (Doll and Piedrahita 1976). It is present in nearly 40% of the no-till soybean fields in Brazil (Wiles and Hayward 1981). Plants may invade rice fields and thus the name "paddy lucerne" in Australia. Little is known of the competitive effects of *S. rhombifolia*.

The awns on many fruits and high stem fiber content cause *S. rhombifolia* to be highly undesirable in pastures. The awned mericarps that contaminate grain crops can also injure livestock when used in the ration (Smith 1977) and young leaves may be poisonous (Gomez and Rivera 1987). Plants host the white fly (a vector of several *Sida* viruses), the spider mite (*Tetranychus yusti*), and *Pratylenchus* and *Meloidogyne* nematodes (Bendixen et al. 1979, 1981; Pancho and Obien 1983).

S. rhombifolia stems are used to make rough cordage and broom heads. Leaves are eaten as green vegetables in Central America (Martin and Ruberte 1978) and are sometimes used to make tea. Stems have a high-quality fiber and were the source of one of the "hemps" sent to Europe from India. The species was introduced into the United States from Australia in the late 1800s as a promising fiber crop (Maiden 1894).

This plant has numerous medicinal uses. Roots have up to 0.05% alkaloids and are chewed with betel nut in New Guinea to cure diarrhea. The shoots and leaves calm upset stomachs and the root has a sedative effect (Holdsworth 1980). In China, roots are used to treat constipation, cramps, fever, rheumatism, and toothache. Shoots are given to cure chicken pox, measles, and swelling (Duke and Ayensu 1985). It is sold in liquid, powder, and oil formulations in India to treat tuberculosis, ulcers, itches, and snake bites. Over 15,000 kg of the plant are used annually in India for medicinal purposes (Anandalwar and Venkateswara 1981, Bariuan 1985).

COMMON NAMES

Sida rhombifolia

ARGENTINA	afata, escoba, escoba dura, mata alfalfa, sida, tipicha guazu
AUSTRALIA	common sida, paddy's lucerne
BOLIVIA	afata, taporita
BRAZIL	guanxuma, guaxima, malva, malva-preta, relogio, vassourinha
CHINA	huang hua mu
COLOMBIA	escoba, escoba negra, escobilla
CUBA	malva de cochino
DOMINICAN REPUBLIC	malva
FIJI	paddy's lucerne
HAWAII	Cuba jute, rhombiod ilima
HONDURAS	escoba, escobilla, malva
INDIA	antibala, berela, saru-sonborial
INDONESIA	idem, sidagoeri

JAPAN	kingojika
MADAGASCAR	tsindahoro
MALAYSIA	lidah ular
MEXICO	escobilla, huinar, malva
NEW CALEDONIA	herba a balais
NEW GUINEA	brumstik
NEW ZEALAND	paddy lucerne, sida
PARAGUAY	typxa guasu
PERU	angosacha
PHILIPPINES	basbasot, baseng-baseng, eskobang-haba, sinaguri, sinutan, taching-baka, ualisualison
SOUTH AFRICA	Pretoria sida
THAILAND	khat-mon, yaa khat
TRINIDAD	broom weed
UNITED STATES	arrowleaf sida
URUGUAY	escoba dura, malvavisco
VENEZUELA	escoba babosa, escoba blanca

Eighty-Eight

Silybum marianum (L.) Gaertn.

Asteraceae (Compositae), Aster Family

*S*ILYBUM MARIANUM is one of hundreds of thistles found across the world. It is sometimes called milk thistle, has delicate, showy, white veins in its leaves because the milk of the Virgin Mary fell upon them, according to a Christian legend. It is also called Blessed thistle, Holy thistle and St. Mary's thistle. The Order of the Thistle was founded in Scotland in the 1500s to confer honorary knighthood upon deserving subjects of King James.

The plant has recently come under intensive study by chemists and pharmacologists because of the discovery of a previously unknown group of chemical compounds that have

FIGURE 88-1   The distribution of *Silybum marianum* (L.) Gaertn. across the world where it has been reported as a weed.

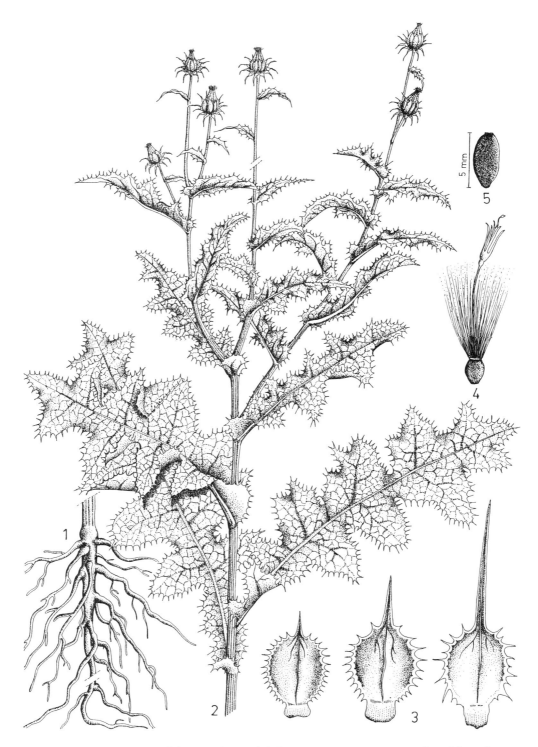

F<small>IGURE</small> 88-2 *Silybum marianum* (L.) Gaertn.: 1. root system; 2. portion of flowering branch; 3. involucral bracts; 4. flower; 5. achene.

shown promise for treatment of mushroom poisoning in humans. It is a weed of 25 crops in more than 50 countries (Figure 88-1).

DESCRIPTION

S. marianum (Figure 88-2) is an erect *annual* or *biennial* to 3 m or more, commonly 1 to 2 m; large taproot; *stems* simple or branched, stout, hollow or pith-filled, vertical ribs without spines or wings but the stem sometimes showing a cottony down; *leaves* large, light to dark green, lower 30 to 60 cm long and one-half as wide, deeply cleft with wavy margins, may be petiolate, upper leaves smaller, may be clasping, also deeply cut, with strong spines of various sizes, yellow, longest at tips of largest leaf lobes, lower surfaces dull and hairy, upper leaf surface shiny with sparse hairs and with a network of fine white veins and white patches giving leaves the characteristic variegated appearance; *flowers* large, showy, globose, solitary at ends of branches, head with large reflexed bracts ending in stiff spines, spines from overlapping bracts may vary from 3/4 to 1 1/2" long, dense clusters of soft purple or white florets in each head, head with bracts may be 10 to 15 cm in diameter; *fruit* an *achene*, oblong, 6 mm long, flat but thick, smooth, shiny, black or brown; *pappus* may be yellowish or white, made up of several series of minutely barbed, silky hairs or bristles 1 to 2 cm long, seeds and pappus may vary in size, and where latter is large enough the seed may be carried some distance by the wind.

DISTRIBUTION AND HABITAT

S. marianum is found on all of the continents, but it is noteworthy that it does not behave as an important problem in three large agricultural areas: Central America and the islands of the Caribbean Sea; with the exception of one report from Morocco in northwest Africa, it is not a problem in western Africa; and with the exclusion of one report from northern China, the Far East from the Kamchatka Peninsula through the rest of China and the islands of the Pacific do not seem to find it a troublesome weed (Figure 88-1). Does it have predators of the large seeds and seedheads in these regions? It is one of the largest of the thistles and it does not seem likely that its reported absence could be from misidentification over large regional areas such as these.

Thistles have attracted man's attention ever since his first attempts at planting and harvesting because they are disagreeable plants to have around habitations and in crops, fence rows, or irrigation schemes where people must labor. In addition, domestic animals usually find them unsatisfactory for grazing and at times of high nitrate content, such as after cutting, the animals may be harmed if they eat the leaves.

In 1851, in Australia, this species was the subject of the first legislation against noxious weeds in that country (Michael 1968). In Tasmania, it is found in feed grains offered to stock animals and in low-grade, uncertified cropseed supplies. Here it is one of the species whose seeds are "prohibited" in the standards for certified pasture seed. Here also the plant seems to prefer fertile soil.

The weed is spread by natural means, by transport vehicles, including farm equipment, by animals, with movement of hay, in mud and water, by accident on sacks and other articles of commerce, and sometimes with intent to use the species for folk remedies or other medical purposes. For example, the pharmaceutical material silymarin (a group of isomers) is obtained from *S. marianum* and it is therefore a suitable cash crop. It is often grown in a rotation with wheat in South Africa (Meissner and Mulder 1974). The seeds that remain in the field later germinate and become a weed problem. The heavy seed is probably not dispersed by the wind.

In his observations of the species in southeast Australia, Parsons (1973) usually found it on soils of alluvial or volcanic origin, on the soils of river flats and in places where N was plentiful. In agriculture and forest lands it was found wherever soil was disturbed, on fire lanes of ranges and forests, on farm roads, around animal camps and yards and near rabbit warrens. Grasslands become susceptible to invasion by the species if dry weather in late summer and autumn results in breaks in the cover so that thistle seedlings become established. In northwest India, this weed grows on sandy loam soils that are high in organic matter and potassium.

In New Zealand, this species is a serious weed in open pastures and waste places, but particularly in coastal areas. Unconsolidated sands and light, stony soils that dry out badly in summer are likely to have good stands of *S. marianum*. Glue and Matthews (1957) found it to be the largest and fastest growing of all the common thistles in this country.

In California, in the western United States, there was a very unusual and rapid dispersal of this weed in the central valleys between the mountain ranges in the 1940s. Young et al. (1978) have studied the ecology of the weed and have pointed out that its movement was a remarkable demonstration of adaptation for colonizing, for it came to dominate a large but discontinuous habitat in a very short time. The agriculture that it entered, and in which it succeeded, had been dominated by alien annual weeds for 150 yr.

The Pampas region of South America is the site of one of the world's most important grasslands. These grasslands were invaded by *S. marianum* and by *Cynara cardunculus*, often called "cardoon." The two species, introduced from Eurasia, grow to great size in the Pampas and in favorable seasons may form an almost impenetrable plant cover over large areas (Darwin 1839, Hudson 1918). Even today, at several places in the world where infestations have gotten out of control, it is not uncommon to travel on farm and range roads with thickets of *S. marianum* towering to 3 to 4 m in height on either side.

S. marianum is a common ruderal plant in Israel, where it is adapted to a life of association with the harvesting-ant *Messor semirufus*. An oil body (an elaiosome) at the tip of the achene attracts the ants and they carry the seeds to the protection of their nests. Later they are carried out and planted with refuse from the nests (dead ants, grains, soil, other plant parts). Rain water and nutrients in the refuse stimulate early establishment of plants that become much larger and produce more seed heads than plants in a control area.

PROPAGATION

S. marianum can propagate only by seeds, some of which may persist in the field as long as 10 yr. The dormancy at harvest usually dissipates rapidly and, as with many species, the seed viability varies a great deal in different growing seasons. Michael (1970) in Australia generally found high viability initially followed by a sudden drop. Parsons (1973), also in Australia, found the mature seed crop to be less than 50% viable at times. Experiments in eastern Australia by Forcella and Wood (1986b) examined the sequential spring flowering of seven thistles common to the area. *S. marianum* was one of the first to flower, had a brief flowering period when compared with late-flowering species, possessed a pronounced innate dormancy at maturation, and avoided germination at high temperatures. It benefited by this pattern of development by avoiding precocious germination in cold, wet springs and by the ability to suppress emergence after rare rains falling at high temperatures during the long, dry summers of the Mediterranean climate of the area.

The seeds are heavy, weighing about 20 mg, with an average of 50 seeds produced per head, and 10 to 50 seedheads per plant. Young et al. (1978) have therefore calculated that if 10 to 50 g of seeds are produced by each of 2 plants/m², theoretically the field production could be 100 to 500 kg/ha of seed.

Cooler temperatures are usually required for germination and we thus find that the peak of this activity is reported to be sometime in autumn in many regions. In Tasmania, it is seen to germinate in spring and summer as well, but only in special situations such as irrigation systems, and presumably this is true elsewhere. The plant grows slowly, produces a rosette, and eventually sends up the stalks on which the flowers are borne. Flowering time varies again by season and by region but generally may be expected in late spring and early summer. The seeds are formed and finished in summer and the after-ripening process must be completed in time for germination as autumn rains and cooler temperatures approach. In the other extreme, in Tasmania it is one of the few thistles able to grow and flower during the winter. The life span of plants of *S. marianum* is usually from autumn to autumn.

There is often little agreement on the role of wind in seed dispersal for species whose seeds bear umbrella-like plumes, and so it is with *S. marianum*. There may be biotypes of this weed whose plumes and seeds vary in size, but on average it seems the heavy seed is destined to remain in its own neighborhood. When the seeds mature at the time of hay and forage harvest, the thistle seeds may be caught up and transported some distance.

In the previous discussion of the distribution of this species, we related the interesting observations of Young and his colleagues (Young et al. 1978) on the remarkable, explosive scattering of this species in the valleys of California, and it is to their work that we must turn for most of our information about the germination behavior of this plant. Their studies have also provided important information on the field ecology of this thistle. It was obvious that *S. marianum* had a great competitive advantage over most annual species in the early stages of growth. Seeds were gathered, placed in room temperature storage for 1 mo and then placed in dark chambers at constant temperatures of 2 and 5°C and all the 5-degree increments through 40°C.

These were tested monthly; at the end of the first month there was germination only at 10 and 15°C. In the second month there was over 50% germination at 5, 10, 15, and 20°C, with only 10% germination at 25°C. At 6 mo there was some germination at all but 35 and 40°C. Thus the after-ripening process was much slower at high temperatures. After 1 yr there was still no germination at 35°C.

When after-ripening was completed, the seeds showed some germination over a temperature range from 0 to 30°C. When 2 to 15°C cold periods at 16 hr were alternated with 10 to 30°C warm periods of 8 hr, optimum germination was obtained. In further tests there was some degree of germination over a very broad range of constant and alternating temperatures. There was even some germination at regimes of 0/30°C and 2/40°C. These temperatures are similar to the 8-hr warm and 16-hr cold periods prevailing in mid-winter in the central California valleys. The situation then is similar to the behavior of seeds in Australia as described above.

In California, the milk thistle seeds usually mature in July at the peak of the summer drought that is a characteristic of Mediterranean climates. This allows 3 to 4 mo of after-ripening before rains begin to come in October; seedbeds are now at 20 to 30°C. By

November the temperatures fall quickly, the seeds germinate in the moist soil, thus helping them to colonize good sites before the first winter annuals can appropriate these favorable places.

Young et al. (1978) remind us that annual grasslands with thin litter cover are largely colonized by rapidly germinating species of *Erodium* with their self-burying seeds.

Young et al. (1978) arranged field plot seed burials at several levels down to 8 cm and found that germination decreased with depth. There was still substantial emergence from the 8-cm depth. This has biological significance for seeds buried in rodent spoils. Without rodent burial, seed survival is poor, because most seeds fall on inhospitable surfaces (Young et al. 1969).

There is another matter yet to be resolved with thistles and other large-seeded species capable of producing large quantities of seed that can become a major food source for several rodent populations. This could increase the disturbance of sites now made more favorable for milk thistle germination. At present there are no data on the nature and periodicity of seed predation by birds and rodents (Young et al. 1978).

In a 4-year trial in the former Soviet Union, Melnikova (1983) found the average seed weight to range from 24.3 to 26.6 mg. The minimum and maximum temperatures for germination were 10 and 35°C, with an optimum of 25°C. Freshly harvested seed required a period of after-ripening. The time required for imbibition of water to 160% of the original seed weight was 18, 3, or 2 days at 10, 20, and 30°C, respectively.

PHYSIOLOGY AND ECOLOGY

As the seedlings develop in autumn, growth proceeds slowly and a rosette is formed. The pace of development quickens as spring approaches. Very early in the seedling stage, *S. marianum* develops a comparatively large leaf area. Under some conditions, the luxuriant growth of the large rosette leaves with undulating, crumpled edges and with much crowding gives the plant a cabbage-like appearance. The rosettes commonly reach 1 m in diameter, coverage of the ground is complete and all plants beneath the mat are destroyed. When the thistle and its remains deteriorate, a large bare spot has been prepared for perhaps unwanted vegetation. Center stems arise from the leafy rosettes in early spring and flowers are borne on the terminals in late spring and early summer. The old plants die in late summer to late autumn and skeletons may be seen in the field for some time. The seeds are large and have a small pappus, so that many are found within a few meters of the parent plant, thus giving rise to dense local stands.

Thistles find it difficult to enter areas that have a permanent, closed cover of desirable species and long, favorable, growing seasons. In contrast, ranges that characteristically have dry periods in late summer frequently have a thinning out of pasture cover and fall-germinating thistles may slowly begin to encroach upon such an area. Pasture fertilization may favor the thistles as well as the sown species. The autumn rains are variable in such climates, but if thistles can become established in one or two favorable seasons, and if viable seed is produced, the area is in trouble.

Dodd (1989) suggests that, in many parts of Australia, the plant is disliked because the large, fast-growing rosettes are very competitive in crops and pastures. Moreover, the plant likes high-fertility land and thus represents a threat to crop production on those places where farms are concentrated. On occasion it is very high in nitrates and can be very toxic to stock animals. Finally, the dense clumps of *S. marianum* harbor vermin, especially rabbits.

In the early 1960s Michael (1968a,b) in Australia launched a 10-yr study on the control of *S. marianum* by proper pasture management. The experimental area was a red-clay loam hilltop campsite in east central New South Wales where the thistle had increased to a dense cover following years of cereal crops and volunteer pasture production with occasional applications of superphosphate. The area also supported several annual dicots, a few annual grasses of moderate importance, and a few other thistles that were not then a problem.

Lucerne (*Medicago sativa*) and *Phalaris tuberosa* were planted in experimental plots in autumn (May) 1958 and spring (October) 1958; other plots planted in autumn 1958 were subterranean clover (*Trifolium subterraneum*), rye grass (*Lolium rigidum*), a mixture of *Phalaris* and clover, and a mixture of rye and clover. Harvests were taken at 4, 12, and 17 mo at the onset, with thistle counts made several times; seeds were counted in the top 10 cm of the soil (from natural reproduction) in 1958 and 10 yr later. Between harvests and for the duration of the experiments, the vegetation was cut occasionally and removed, or the area was given intermittent heavy or continuous grazing.

Four months after the initial autumn sowings, there was no difference in the weights of thistles on the plots (10 ton/ha fresh weight). Twelve months after sowing, the lucerne areas were free of thistles and the *Phalaris* areas had thistle production of 2.5 to 5 ton/ha. The depression of thistle weights in the latter plots appeared to result from a reduction in size and not number of thistle. The lucerne and *Phalaris* plots sown in the spring of 1958 were favorably established, but the *Phalaris* plots did not survive the following winter.

Thistle seed counts were reduced by 85% in the soils of the lucerne and *Phalaris* areas during the 10 yr of the study, thus leaving sufficient seed to cause trouble if these areas were later used for cropping. Michael states that few thistles appeared after this date in any of the plots for the duration of the experiment and he feels that the seasonal variation in environmental factors, the lack of soil disturbance, and the shortage of a new thistle seed supply may be important in the relative sparsity of the thistles on this experimental area. The immediate complete control of *S. marianum* by sowing lucerne in spring is in part because this is the time of year most unfavorable to the germination of the thistle. The ability of lucerne and *Phalaris* to make growth quickly after late summer or autumn rains is a second factor that is important in their ability to hold the thistle at bay.

In a glasshouse study of the seedlings of *S. marianum* and *Onopordum acanthium*, another thistle, Pook (1983) in Australia, reported that growth was systematically reduced with increased shading. Time of initiation of leaves was delayed and leaf numbers were reduced as well. Withal, he believes the seedlings to be quite tolerant of shade because seedling mortality and grass seedling morphology (except for size) were not appreciably affected. Others have shown that a perennial pasture cover is much more effective for thistle control than annual plants and that competition for soil moisture appears to be important in limiting the germination of thistle seeds, especially in warm seasons.

Pook believes, however, that in cool seasons when there is more moisture to favor thistle seedling establishment, shading by sown pasture species may be influential in assisting with thistle control. He estimates, however, that 80% light interception is probably required to weaken them sufficiently. In a comparison of his data with those of Medd and Lovett (1978) on germination and light requirements for *Carduus nutans*, the *Silybum* and *Onopordum* species appear to be less sensitive to shading than *C. nutans*. This could mean that weed replacement by *C. nutans* should be cautioned for those farmers who seek removal of *Silybum* or *Onopordum*.

In late summer in southern Australia, the pastures in dry areas consist mainly of senesced grasses of low protein content and digestibility. During these periods, some weeds grow well and can make a substantial contribution to the green matter available for stock; therefore, many feel that weeds and thistles do not influence animal production unduly unless the weeds become very thick and troublesome. The point at which weediness becomes intolerable because there is no longer enough room for other forage is very difficult to assess. Michael (1972), in a brief study of the past history of weeds in pasture management, came upon evidence that some farmers in the 19th century believed sheep "could do well, even fatten, on *S. marianum* in pastures." Others believed they were the salvation of sheep in very dry weather.

Recognizing that there is experimental evidence to show that weed suppression may increase pasture yield but that there are also data to show that animals can make equally good liveweight gains on weedy and non-weedy pasture, Jones et al. (1971), in Australia, made a study of seasonal changes in the composition of weeds, including *S. marianum*, and pasture species on different sites and under different grazing regimes. The weed species were gathered near Canberra from pastures that were either ungrazed or heavily grazed by sheep.

The percentages of dry matter, ash, cellulose, nitrogen and *in vitro* digestibility of organic matter were determined on total plants and on some plant parts of each species. Taken together, the data for these weed species tell us that they compare very favorably with the components of sown and native pasture species in these difficult circumstances. There are, however, other factors of importance in pasture management, such as weed toxicity and palatability for stock. Experiments are needed to obtain data on animal intake of individual species of both crops and weeds, with accompanying records on liveweight gains.

Langhammer (1969) studied the anatomy of the fruits of *S. marianum* and examined the cells of several of its tissues. He devised a histochemical test that is specific for the flavonoids in the fruit and aids in distinguishing them from similar compounds in the fruit of *S. eberneum*. Singh and Pandey (1984) studied the developmental anatomy of the seeds of this species, and Sharma and Singh (1974) reported on the histology of the seeds as a corollary to their pharmacognostic studies. Carreras Matas (1976) examined the biochemical profiles of the flavanolignans of the shells of fruits and the sterols and fatty acids of embryos to aid in the chemotaxonomic discrimination of the taxa of the genus *Silybum*.

CHEMISTRY AND TOXICITY

The poisoning of livestock as the result of feeding on *S. marianum* is not a special case of toxicity but instead is a routine problem that arises wherever animals are forced to or allowed to graze on species, sometimes crops, that accumulate high levels of nitrate. Stock animals normally have little interest in this formidable plant because of the tough, sharp spines on leaves and flowerheads. They will eat when the plant has been cut and wilted, or when it is standing after being sprayed with a hormone-like herbicide. At times of plant die-off in late summer and autumn, animals may be seen feeding on senescent leaves. If nitrogen is plentiful in the soil and the nitrate is high in the plant tissues the animals can be harmed. For the farmer who is uninformed of this there is danger, and for those who appreciate the problem there is a dilemma, for if a range has a scattering of *S. marianum* or if his animals may suddenly break out into dense patches of the thistle, there is a continuing decision that needs to be made about the quantity they should be allowed to ingest. Often such judgments must be made without knowing the nitrate levels in the plants.

In Australia, it is reported that the field cases of nitrate poisoning are very often in hungry livestock or among animals that are under the stress of mustering, droving, or other handling. There are also many reports of accidental or unexpected exposure to the high nitrate weeds and it may be well to emphasize how quickly the animals become incapacitated and go down, and how swiftly the preparations must be made to treat them if a lifesaving effort still seems a possibility. Parsons (1973) reports a case in southeast Australia of a farmer who put 24 heifers into a paddock that was being plowed in an effort to control the thistle. All of the animals were dead the following morning. The soil moisture was high, the wilted thistles had not been completely covered in the tillage operation, and the animals consumed them in the night.

The first reported case of nitrate poison by *S. marianum* in the United States occurred in central California in 1955 (Kendrick et al. 1955). The weed is widely distributed in the state and at the time of the poisoning it was not unusual to allow cattle to feed on the mature plants in winter. The poisoned animals had been pastured for several months on a grassland of 50 ha containing some stunted *S. marianum* (not over 1 m). A gate was opened to a small field of 0.4 ha that was completely covered with a luxuriant growth of the thistle that was 2 m in height. The next morning nine of the heifers were found dead or dying, while 50 were unaffected. On about one-half of the small area, all of the leaves had been eaten. Laboratory examinations of blood and rumen contents confirmed the nitrate poisoning. The sudden death of these animals allowed no time for treatment.

The losses from high-nitrate plants may be considerable. Hurst (1942) reported that the losses from *S. marianum* poisoning for only a 6-yr period in New South Wales, Australia, were 200 sheep and cattle and several horses.

We do have some knowledge of the conditions that bring on high NO_3 concentrations, and many farmers are wary of these. Very cloudy weather with low light intensity inhibits NO_3 reduction. High soil NO_3 content and/or deficiency in some other element, particularly sulphur or molybdenum, tend to increase NO_3 levels in plants. Some herbicides, notably hormone-type chemicals such as 2,4-D and MCPA, when applied to some plants seem to make them more palatable, while also inhibiting nitrate reductase, with a consequent rise in the level of NO_3. This is known to be the case when *S. marianum* is sprayed with such chemicals.

Certain combinations of environmental factors during a drought may bring about nitrate toxicity. During a drought period, if there is sufficient soil moisture to allow uptake of NO_3 ion at night (at which time nitrate reductase is inactive), followed by days with hot, dry conditions that cause rapid water loss from cells and tissues following sunrise, there may be NO_3 accumulation during darkness with incomplete reduction to other compounds during daylight hours, because wilting also inhibits nitrate reductase. Following several days of such conditions, NO_3 may build up to dangerous levels. Normally, nitrate reductase reduces the NO_3 to NH_3, in which form it begins a further conversion into amino acids and proteins. Factors or environmental conditions that inhibit the activity of this enzyme in plants will thus tend to create a dangerous condition for livestock. The conversion of NO_3 to NO_2 proceeds rapidly in the rumen (or stomach) of cattle, to a lesser degree in sheep, and in the digestive tract of horses. Cattle are usually much more sensitive to high NO_3 levels than other stock animals. The minimum lethal dose of NO_3 for ruminants is reported to be 0.005% of body weight. When a concentration of 1.5 NO_3 is reached (as KNO_3 on a dry matter basis), the plant or tissue is considered potentially lethal. Sublethal toxicity symptoms are seen at 0.5% and above. Maize, lucerne, and other crop plants may, under particular conditions of soil or weather, accumulate sufficient quantities of NO_3 to be harmful. *S. marianum* is one of the species that nearly always gives a positive test for nitrates.

When reduced to nitrates in the animal body, symptoms of low blood pressure, increased heart activity, rapid respiration, muscle twitching, collapse and coma are seen, but the clinical cause of the illness is methaemoglobinaemia. The nitrate produced in the rumen is rapidly absorbed by the blood stream, where it brings about the conversion of divalent iron in haemoglobin to the trivalent methaemoglobin that cannot combine with or transport oxygen. This leads to asphyxiation (anoxia) of all body tissues. At autopsy, the blood is found to be chocolate-colored, liver and kidneys may be congested, and the lungs discolored (Everist 1974).

If the treatment for such poisoning from any plant is begun at an early stage, the suffering animals can usually be relieved with intravenous injection of water solution of methylene blue at a dose rate equivalent to 0.009% of animal body weight. About 100 ml of a 2% solution would be required at an early stage for a 360 kg steer or 10 ml for a 36 kg sheep.

The current interest in the biologically active constituents of *S. marianum* in medicinal chemistry stems from the protective action of the silymarin group of compounds against the toxins phalloidine and alpha-amanitine from *Amanita phalloides*, the poisonous death cap mushroom. For humans this is one of the world's most deadly plants. Vomiting and diarrhea begin following ingestion and finally there is damage to and failure of the liver. Circulatory failure follows in 2 to 10 days, the patient drifts into a coma, and death follows.

The silymarin group of compounds is mainly three isomers: silybin (formerly called silymarin), silydianin, and silicristin. They constitute a new class of chemical compounds and are almost certainly formed in the plant by the coupling of a flavanoid and coniferyl alcohol (Windholz 1983). Information on the nature of the compounds from *S. marianum* and their mechanism of action may be found in studies from several parts of the world: Bandopadhyay et al. (1972), Morelli (1978), Rizk et al. (1970), Trost and Halbach (1978), Voemel et al. (1977), Vogel et al. (1975), and Wagner et al. (1974).

AGRICULTURAL IMPORTANCE

S. marianum is a serious weed in pastures in Australia, Brazil, New Zealand, and the United States; of vegetables in Israel and of wheat in Iran. It is a principal weed of cereals in Australia, Portugal, and Spain; of several dryland and irrigated row crops in Australia; of oats and sunflowers in Argentina; of pastures in Argentina and Italy; of sugar cane in Iran; and of wheat in Iraq and Jordan.

It is a common weed of barley and other cereals in Iran and Peru; of lucerne in Argentina; of orchards in South Africa and Turkey; of pastures in Chili, Tasmania, and Uruguay; of potatoes in Colombia and Iran; of vegetables in Australia; of vineyards in South Africa; of wheat in Argentina, Colombia, Peru, South Africa, and Uruguay; and of winter season crops in Uruguay.

It is also a weed of cotton in Iran; linseed in Argentina; lucerne in Australia; maize in Spain; oats and potatoes in Iraq; sorghum in Israel and Uruguay; sugar beets in Israel and Spain; and wheat in Kenya, Portugal, and Spain.

In Australia, *S. marianum* is a very competitive plant and once it becomes established in a pasture it can drive out most other plants by competing for moisture and nutrients and sometimes by shading them (Parsons 1973). The density of stands of *S. marianum* and other thistles vary from year to year, and Parsons feels this is often traceable to the presence of or the lack of competition offered by other weeds or native or sown pasture species as the *S. marianum* seedlings germinated in the previous autumn. Dispersal of the thistle in Australia was made possible by animals on the hoof, movement of seed in fresh or dry forage, or by natural causes, and had reached the limit of its distribution about 1981 (Medd 1981). Its dispersal was further hastened by the extensive use of subterranean clover and superphosphate after 1940. He believes that the failure to adopt a long-term control practice will inevitably lead to intensification of thistle abundance. In a survey of more than 100 local government areas in 1988, Briese (1988) ranked *S. marianum* fifth among 12 thistles most needing control.

S. marianum has been declared a noxious weed for plant quarantine purposes in Australia, Chile, and New Zealand. In Israel the extensive use of herbicides in the crops preceding sugar beets has resulted in a shift of weed species toward those, such as *S. marianum*, that are more difficult to control.

In Western Australia, mowing and slashing of the thistle is practiced with only partial control because of the seed reserves in the soil and the remarkable development of the seed in capitula after the cutting. Dodd (1989) sought more precise information on seed survival after anthesis begins. He found there was a significant reduction in seed production on all slashed and mowed plots but the problem remained. In slashing, capitula with 20 cm of stem attached produced viable seeds if the cut was made when one-half the florets were open. Viability of the seed ranged from 0.3% in capitula at mid-anthesis to 12% at the end of anthesis. Mowed plots produced viable seeds even when in the advanced flower bud stage and in capitula cut at any stage of anthesis. In irrigated plots, anthesis lasted 5 days and ripe seeds were released 17 days later. There was an average production of 190 seeds per primary capitulum and 114 in sub-terminals. During a 2-month flowering season beginning in November each plant has the potential to produce an average of 55 capitula and more than 6000 seeds, of which 94% may be viable.

The extent of the interference of a community of weeds in human activities, especially agriculture, often tends to be quantified in ways which are much too simple. The assessment of the economic impact of a single species is far more difficult, for individual weed species normally appear in mixed floras, they vary in response to weather changes between growing years, and in their sensitivity to farm management practices.

A precise figure in kilograms for yield reduction of potatoes in a weedy field may seem to clarify rather neatly the economic consequences of this seasonal loss. On a particular farm, however, this lonely figure may ignore the need for chemicals, fertilizers, the efforts to spare excessive wear on harvesting equipment as large clumps of weedy material make their way through the machines, the necessity to prevent seed production that will provide trouble in future years, as well as other needs for land, labor, cash, and physical inputs that must be taken into account (Auld et al. 1979). The authors have provided a bioeconomic model of weeds in pastures in relation to a specific farm system, a hypothetical prime lamb production farm in New South Wales, Australia.

The weevil *Rhinocyllus conicus* was introduced into the western United States as a possible biological control for *S. marianum*. The weevil is found on a limited portion of the range of this weed in Greece and Italy but is not associated with it in Egypt, Pakistan, or the former Soviet Union (Goeden and Ricker 1980). Boldt and DeLoach (1985) found the weevil not entirely satisfactory in the United States because it had a relatively short oviposition of 6 wk and it was not well synchronized with the development of terminal capitula on primary and lateral stems. It was nearly finished by the time that sublateral capitula appeared on lateral stems. Because of the long season and large seed output, the restricted period of oviposition in this insect and the low density of larvae per capitulum might limit its use as a biological control agent in Australia as well.

COMMON NAMES

Silybum marianum

ARGENTINA	cardo asnal, cardo blanco, cardo lechero, cardo mariano
AUSTRALIA	bull thistle, milk thistle, Saint Mary's thistle, spotted thistle, variegated thistle
CANADA	blessed thistle, hardon Marie, lady's thistle, Marian thistle, milk thistle
CHILE	cardo blanco, cardo menchado, cardo santo
COLOMBIA	cardo blanco, miona, poma
DENMARK	marietidsel
EGYPT	likhlaakh, shoak sinnaari, shok el-gamal
ENGLAND	Saint Mary's thistle
FRANCE	chardon Marie
GERMANY	Mariendistel
IRAN	milk thistle
IRAQ	kallaghan
ITALY	cardo della Madonna, cardo Mariano
JORDAN	holy thistle
NETHERLANDS	mariadistel
NEW ZEALAND	variegated thistle
NORWAY	maritistel
PORTUGAL	cardo leiteiro, cardo de Santa Maria
SOUTH AFRICA	blessed milk-thistle, gevlekte silybum
SPAIN	cardo borriquero, cardo gallofer, cardo Mariano
TASMANIA	variegated thistle
TURKEY	mariam anna dikeni
UNITED STATES	blessed thistle, holy thistle, milk thistle, Saint Mary's thistle
URUGUAY	cardo asnal, cardo burro

Eighty-Nine

Sonchus arvensis L.

Asteraceae (Compositae), Aster Family

S ONCHUS ARVENSIS is a perennial herbaceous plant found throughout the temperate regions of the world. A native of Europe, it now occurs in nearly 60 countries. The species is adapted to a wide range of edaphic conditions and its extensive horizontal and vertical root system make it very difficult to control. The Greek derivation of *Sonchus* is from *sonchos*, which means "hollow" and refers to the stems; *arvensis* refers to plants that grow in cultivated fields.

FIGURE 89-1   The distribution of *Sonchus arvensis* L. across the world where it has been reported as a weed.

FIGURE 89-2 *Sonchus arvensis* L.: A. habit; B. achene.

DESCRIPTION

S. arvensis (Figure 89-2) is a deep-rooted *perennial* with milky sap in all plant parts; *roots* creamy-white, fleshy, vertical and horizontal, widely spreading, to 6 mm in diameter; often crooked and easily broken, with buds at close intervals; *stems* erect 0.5 to 1.5 m tall, hollow, smooth on lower part of plant but often glandular-hairy above, often branched above; *leaves* variable in size and shape; rosette leaves up to 30 cm long, petiolate, cut into backward-curving lobes, terminal lobe tips broadly triangular; stem leaves crowded on lower stem with weak prickles on margins; upper stem leaves sparse alternate, small, divided or almost entire, margins weakly prickled, sessile; and clasping the stem; *inflorescence* composed of flower heads of 2 to 5 cm in diameter; in large open corymbose clusters; *flower* florets bright yellow, perfect, ligulate; *involucre* about 1.5 cm long, the bracts linear-lanceolate, obtuse, the outer densely covered with coarse gland-bristles; *peduncle* glandular pubescent or smooth; *fruit* a dark brown to reddish-brown *achene*, 2.5 to 4.5 mm long, narrowly ovate with the base somewhat truncate, the apex with an expanded collar, somewhat flattened with longitudinally 5 prominent ribs on each side, often slightly curved, transversely wrinkled; *pappus* composed of numerous simple, persistent, white hairs to 1.5 cm long.

This plant can be distinguished from other *Sonchus* species by its long, creeping thickened roots with many buds; its relatively large inflorescence of yellow, ligulate flowers; the 5-ribbed achenes; and the presence of glandular hairs on the peduncles of most biotypes. The hollow stem and milky juice in all plant parts separate it from thistles in other genera.

DISTRIBUTION AND HABITAT

S. arvensis is native to Europe and existed before Neolithic man's agricultural activities, but perhaps was present during the period of Paleolithic man's wandering in pursuit of game and food (Salisbury 1964). It is widely distributed in the temperate world (Figure 89-1) and grows to 400 m above sea level and as far as lat 70° 33' N in Europe. It has been in the United States for at least 150 yr (Muenscher 1930). In some areas it was originally a weed of lowland areas such as lake shores and stream banks, but now inhabits many upland environments as well. In Finland, *S. arvensis* tolerates a wide range of soil *pH*s and nutrient levels, and is most abundant in clay soils and soils high in potassium (Borg 1964). Plants grow best in moist to very wet soils and in full sunlight (Zollinger and Kells 1987). Dry weather can reduce the plant's growth. When grown at 30 to 60% of field capacity, *S. arvensis* did not flower and biomass production was reduced 66 to 75%. Aerial parts were more affected than subterranean ones (Swietochowski and Sonta 1962).

BIOLOGY AND PROPAGATION

S. arvensis emerges in the late spring and produces a cluster of rosette-like leaves by early May in most northern regions. In the north central United States, flower stalks form in early June; flower buds appear by mid-June and flowering starts in early July and continues until late August or September (Stevens 1924). Plants are very sensitive to frost and roots acquire dormancy by late summer.

Detailed studies by Hakansson (1969, 1982), and Hakansson and Wallgren (1972a,b) in Sweden provide a thorough understanding of *S. arvensis* growth in both nondisturbed and disturbed conditions. Root segments 12 cm long planted in the fall produce new shoots the following May; thickened roots form by early June. Most of the roots are in the top 10 cm of soil but some grow to 25 cm deep. Seventy to 80% of the shoots emerge by early May and the remainder by late May. Shoots from new roots emerge in July and August but none appear in September or later, suggesting dormancy within the root buds. New shoots may also arise from root segments 2 yr old and from the buried portions of last year's stems. Thin roots are formed in May and thickening begins in late May and June; roots become 4 to 5 mm in diameter. The underground dry weight of *S. arvensis* reaches a low in late May and early June when the new shoots have five to seven rosette leaves. Very rapid root growth and thickening then occurs.

Soil disturbance or defoliation are most effective in killing *S. arvensis* when plants have four to six rosette leaves. Excavating and replanting roots once or twice at this stage stops further growth, but if plants have eight or more rosette leaves, they continue growing. More defoliations than excavations and replanting are required to kill the plants. Three defoliations in the 6-leaf stage or four defoliations in the 4-leaf stage are effective. More cuttings or replantings are required to kill shallowly-planted root segments than deeper plantings.

These researchers also sequentially dug and replanted *S. arvensis* roots during the growing season. New shoots emerge from either new or last year's roots dug until August 25. Cold treatment (storage at 2°C for 1 mo) breaks root dormancy and the accumulation of root reserves is independent of the dormant condition.

The number of shoots produced from root segments buried 5, 7.5, and 10 cm deep is similar, but emergence is delayed as planting depth increases. As expected, shoots on larger root segments can emerge from greater depths than those on smaller segments. The amount of new root production per segment decreases as size of root segments decreases from 24 to 6 cm long. Root pieces left on the soil surface usually die. Exposure for four days at air temperature kills root segments (Ravn 1964), but air drying roots to 25 to 50% of their initial moisture level may not kill them (Gruzdev and Tulikou 1966). *S. arvensis* roots in the soil survive freezing temperatures of −12°C, but nearly 50% die at −16°C and 90% die at −20°C (Schimming and Messersmith 1988). Shoots arising from roots exposed to −16°C had 40% less biomass (dry weight basis) than those produced on non-frozen roots.

Roots as short as 5 mm in length can produce vigorous shoots if a bud is present; without buds, new shoots and roots develop very slowly from the cut surfaces (Stevens 1924). Roots can extend 1 to 2 m in diameter from parent plants in a single season when free of competition, and 70% of the new shoots emerge from roots 0 to 5 cm deep. Few shoots arise from 20 cm or more. Approximately 20% of the rosettes produce flower stalks (Stevens 1924). Bases of stems with seven or more leaves are also capable of vegetative reproduction the following season if not killed during the winter (Hakansson 1969).

Carbohydrate assimilation studies find the reserve energy to be inulin rather than starch (Stevens 1924). The root dry weight as a percentage of the total plant biomass is at its lowest (12 to 14%) in May and June but is over 25% by the end of the season (Arny 1932). Total root sugar content drops sharply from late April (50%) to late June (22%). The readily available and total carbohydrate levels are lowest when plants reach the bloom stage; then levels increase until the end of the season.

Rosette leaves 3 cm in length can translocate assimilates to the roots and translocation generally increases as plants grow in size (Fykse 1974, 1977). During elongation, movement of assimilates to the roots drops, but resumes once flowering occurs. Within 10 min of leaf exposure to $^{14}CO_2$, radioactive assimilates are found in the furthest parts of a single root-shoot system. Very little movement of assimilates from one stem to another occurs, indicating that each stem is self-sufficient in energy production.

Leaves contain a bitter-tasting latex as early as the 1-leaf stage (Kummer 1951) and the stem becomes hollow early in the plant's life (Howitt 1908). Korsmo (1954) gives a very detailed anatomical description of all parts of *S. arvensis* and notes that stomata are present on both leaf surfaces but are most abundant on the lower.

Estimates vary greatly on the number of seeds produced per plant. In Russia, Abramov (1969) reported 35,000 seeds/plant (and a root biomass of over 3 ton/ha dry weight!) while Howitt (1908) found 2000 seeds/plant in Ontario, Canada. In Sweden, each head can form 150 to 200 seeds and each flowering stem over 6000 seeds (Korsmo et al. 1981).

Perhaps a more consistent measure of seed production would be seeds/flower stalk. Stevens (1924) counted 185 florets/flower head but only 30 achenes/head were produced. In pure stands of *S. arvensis*, he observed 2000 seed heads/m², or 60,000 seeds/m². Later data from Stevens (1957) reported 9750 seeds/flower stalk. Seeds weigh 0.5 to 0.7 mg each (Salisbury 1964).

S. arvensis is self-sterile. Few if any seeds are formed if pollen from the same flower head or from flower heads on the same plant is used (Derscheid and Schultz 1960). An average of 58 achenes/flower head were obtained when cross pollinated by bees and these seeds were 80% viable.

S. arvensis produces flowers for several months. The diameter of the flower head increases from 2.5 to 7 cm when fully flowered. Seeds mature rapidly after flowering. Kinch and Termunde (1957) noted that flowers often open over a 2-day period (but would close about noon the first day). When flower heads are cut 4 days after opening, seed germination is very low; it increases dramatically to 34, 60, and 83% when cutting is done 6, 7, and 9 days later, respectively. If flower stalks do not dry out completely after mowing, they can continue producing fresh flowers and viable seed (44%) for up to 1 wk (Stevens 1924).

Detailed research by Sheldon and Burrows (1973) discovered that the pappus cannot fully expand while the achenes are still attached to the flower head. The pappus is arranged in three rings at the achene crown, giving it a denser filament arrangement than that found in *Taraxacum* species. The relatively slow fall of the pappus in comparison to other **Compositae** and the explosive way the achenes break away from the seed head as the pappus fully expands perhaps enhance dispersal of *S. arvensis*. The pappuses of infertile achenes may stick to fertile ones and aid in dispersal. Their paper also thoroughly reviews the importance of the pappus in seed dispersal. Seeds can also be spread by water. In Washington, in the United States, an average of 0.2 seed was trapped in each 254 kl of irrigation water (Kelley and Bruns 1975).

Seeds germinate best when temperatures alternate from 5 to 25°C (Hakansson and Wallgren 1972a) or 20 to 30°C (Andersen 1968). Prechilling at 5°C also enhances germination (Kinch and Termunde 1957). Light can enhance germination, but most seeds germinate in darkness. Germination is similar with or without the pappus, but only half the seeds germinate if the pappus lands in such a way that the achene is not in contact with the soil (Pemadasa and Kangatharalingam 1977).

In the field, seedings may emerge after planting seed 3 cm deep, but most emergence occurs from 0 to 0.5 cm (Hakansson and Wallgren 1972a). Roberts and Neilson (1981a) buried seeds in 0 to 7.5 cm of sterilized soil and placed the pots outdoors in England. The soil was cultivated three times annually. *S. arvensis* germination occurred mainly in the spring and most seeds germinated the first year. Germination decreased exponentially over a 5-yr period and very few viable seed remained after 5 yr.

Seed remained viable for over 3 yr in the soil in Canada (Chepil 1946a) and in England where populations of 19 seeds/m^2 in the upper 15 cm of soil were found (Brenchley and Warington 1933, 1936). In cropped areas, the seed population increased nearly two- to three-fold, while in fallowed areas the reservoir was reduced to 38 and 19% the original level after 1 and 2 yr, respectively.

After emergence in the field, plants grow rapidly. In North Dakota (in the north-central United States), seedlings that emerge in early May have roots 70 cm long by early July. Vertical roots reach 50 cm and horizontal ones up to 1 m, and flowering occurs about 3 mo after emergence (Stevens 1924). Seedlings that emerge in midsummer produce thicker roots but do not flower. Hakansson and Wallgren (1972a) noted that seedlings in the 5- to 6-leaf stage have roots 1 to 1.5 mm thick, and once roots are 1.5 mm in diameter they are capable of vegetative regeneration. Seedlings produce 7 to 8 leaves within 1 mo after emergence and appear similar to the rosettes which originate from vegetative shoots.

The biotypes of *S. arvensis* have been well studied. Perhaps the most diverse biotypes found were those researched by Pegtel (1972, 1973, 1974) in the Netherlands. One biotype grows in arable, upland areas (var. *arvensis*) and the other is found in coastal dunes, salt marshes and areas temporarily flooded (var. *maritimus*). Differences in seed germination are found, but Pegtel concludes the ecotypes differ primarily in the greater root volume of the coastal type, which allows it to survive with very little nitrogen and phosphorous in the soil. Both ecotypes are C$_3$ plants and have the same water requirement and photosynthetic rate. The faster regeneration of the arable ecotype after defoliation or tillage, as well as its ability to emerge from greater soil depths, accounts for its predominance in arable soils.

The existence of glandular-hairy and glabrous biotypes of *S. arvensis* has led to some confusion among taxonomists. While several describe the glandular one as *S. arvensis* var. *arvensis* and the smooth one as var. *glabrescens* (Alex and Switzer 1977), others identify the smooth type as a separate species with the name *S. uliginosus* (Shumovich and Montgomery 1955). The latter authors observed that both types readily cross pollinate, which makes it virtually impossible to separate *S. arvensis* from the hybrids in the fields. They also established that the basic chromosome number of the perennial sow thistles is $n = 9$; the smooth type is a tetraploid $n = 36$ and the glandular one a hexaploid $n = 54$. The smooth variety has been known in Europe for 160 yr and in England since 1873, but Lousley (1968) feels that it cannot be classified as a separate species. Boulos (1961) concurs with what most weed scientists seem to have concluded, namely, that many "races" of the species exist and that *S. uliginosus* is synonymous with *S. arvensis*.

Considerable variation can be found in localized areas. Bell et al. (1968) collected *S. arvensis* plants from three states in the north-central region of the United States and grew them at one site. Differences in leaf margins, leaf texture, color, spininess and even susceptibility to 2,4-D were encountered. They warned that the repeated use of 2,4-D in small grains infested with *S. arvensis* could result in biotype shifts to more tolerant strains.

AGRICULTURAL IMPORTANCE AND CONTROL

S. arvensis is a weed of 33 crops in 59 countries (Figure 89-1) and is frequently reported a weed of cereals, maize, potatoes, and vegetables. It is especially serious in cereal crops. It is a serious or principal weed of carrots and other vegetables in the former Soviet Union; cereals in Canada, Norway, Poland, Sweden, and Turkey; cotton and peanuts in Tanzania; lucerne in Canada and Spain; maize and vineyards in the former Soviet Union; orchards in

Spain; sorghum in Bulgaria; strawberries in England; sugar beets in Poland and the United States; sugarcane in Hawaii; upland crops in Indonesia; and wheat in Afghanistan, India, Iran, Korea, and the former Yugoslavia.

It is a common weed of barley in Canada and Finland; cereals in England, Finland, Italy, the Netherlands, Scotland, Tunisia, and the United States; coffee in Brazil; flax in Canada; legumes in England and Tunisia; millet in the former Soviet Union; maize in Afghanistan and Italy; oats in Canada; orchards in the former Soviet Union; peas in India; potatoes in England, India, Scotland, and the former Soviet Union; oilseed rape in Canada; lowland rice in India; sorghum in Bulgaria; sugar beets in the former Soviet Union; sunflowers in Canada, Mexico, and the former Soviet Union; sweet potatoes in India; tea in India; vegetables in Afghanistan, Tasmania, and Tunisia; vineyards in Spain; wheat in Canada, Finland, Guatemala, Italy, the former Soviet Union, Turkey, and the United States; and wastelands in the United States.

S. arvensis is also an unranked weed of barley in Norway; carrots in Germany and Italy; cassava in Indonesia; cereals in Alaska, Belgium, Bulgaria, Germany, India, the former Soviet Union, and Tasmania; clover in Ireland; flax in the former Soviet Union; nurseries in Finland and Germany; maize in Indonesia, India, Mexico, Rumania, and the former Yugoslavia; onions in India and Ireland; orchards in Bolivia, Germany, India, and Poland; pastures in Brazil, England, and India; peas in Canada, England, and the former Soviet Union; potatoes in Belgium, Germany, Kamchatka, the Netherlands, Norway, Poland, and the United States; pyrethrum in Tanzania; rape in France; rice in India and upland rice in Indonesia; sorghum in Mexico; soybeans in Japan and the former Soviet Union; sugar beets in France and Ireland; sugarcane in India; sweet potatoes in Japan; strawberries in Germany; tea Indonesia; vegetables in Bulgaria and Japan; vineyards in Bulgaria, France, and Germany; and wheat in Czechoslovakia, England, Mozambique, and Norway.

Grain losses from *S. arvensis* and *Cirsium arvense* are estimated at 180,000 ton in Siberia, in Russia (Mokshin 1978). Over 450,000 ha are severely infested and 320,000 ha are slightly infested of the 3 million ha surveyed. In other words, over 25% of the area has some *S. arvensis*. Oat yields were reduced 58% in Canada by *S. arvensis* (Anderson 1956). Populations of 3 to 15 shoots/m^2 reduced wheat yields 4.5 to 27% and significantly reduced the nitrate nitrogen content in tillering wheat (Shashkov et al. 1977). Thirty-nine percent of the oilseed rape fields of the Canadian provinces of Manitoba and Saskatchewan are infested with *S. arvensis* but only 7% of the area is actually infested. The yield loss in these provinces was estimated to be over 15 million kg annually (Peschken et al. 1983). More than 55% of the lucerne fields surveyed in Manitoba were infested with this weed (Goodwin et al. 1986). While *S. arvensis* is similar to forage species in nutritional value, it is less palatable (Marten et al. 1987).

Brenchley (1940) found more *S. arvensis* in fields high in ammonium sulphate. The weed was more competitive with barley at high rather than low nitrogen levels (Hakansson and Wallgren 1972b). Shorter root segments and deeper plantings of *S. arvensis* reduced its competitive ability. A normal crop population reduced the weed's growth significantly. *S. arvensis* competes vigorously with crops under various moisture conditions. In a normal rainfall year, soybeans and garden bean (*Phaseolus*) yields were reduced 49 and 36%, respectively, by *S. arvensis*. In a drought year, yield losses from similar weed densities were over 80% for both crops (Zollinger and Kells 1988). *S. arvensis* may have nearly twice the concentration of N, P, K, and Ca as wheat or barley and three to four times as much Mg. The concentrations of K and Mg were four and two times higher, respectively, in oilseed rape than in the weed (Malicki and Bereciowa 1986).

Russian scientists have shown *S. arvensis* to be allelopathic. Tulikov (1971) found that root and foliage extracts reduced germination of maize, barley, and proso millet. Interestingly, extracts of germinating crop seeds inhibited bud growth of *S. arvensis*. In laboratory studies, this weed inhibited the germination and seedling growth of five pasture grass species but had little effect on the legumes (Ovesnov and Shchekina 1959).

Sow thistle has been described as one of the worst weeds in Canada (Howitt 1908) and was most prevalent in Saskatchewan in grazed pastures, then in wheat stubble, and less abundant in fallowed land (58, 22, and 14 shoots/m^2, respectively) (Archibold 1981). In addition to cultivated land, it infests roadsides and wastelands; it can be found along lake shores, streams and canals and in salt and brackish marshes. *S. arvensis* can host several nematode, mite, and economic insect species (Bendixen et al. 1979, 1981).

Control of *S. arvensis* has been studied for many years. Howitt (1908) noted that sheep (but not cattle) will keep it closely grazed. Muenscher (1930) applied sodium arsenite to an infested field until crops were killed or injured for several years, but this only caused slight foliar burn to the weed and new shoots appeared in the year of treatment.

Derscheid et al. (1961) evaluated control systems that integrated mechanical, cultural and chemical control measures. Summer tillage plus fall cropping for 2 yr controlled *S. arvensis*, as did five deep cultivations at 4-wk intervals and 16 shallow cultivations 2 wk apart. Hakansson and Wallgren (1972b) noted that increased root fragmentation had little effect on root survival. Deep burial, however, reduced plant vigor and growth. They noted that tillage after grain harvest did not reduce the infestation since the roots are dormant by late summer. In Russia, four to five cultivations after deep plowing eradicated *S. arvensis* (Gruzdev and Tulikov 1966). They also observed that repeated cutting of shoots in the 4- to 5-leaf stage exhausted root reserves. Infestations can increase rapidly in zero tillage systems.

Biological control of *S. arvensis* has been investigated. Schroeder (1973) found that *Tephritis dilacerata* prevented seed production in attacked heads but he considered too few heads were attacked to be successful, especially since this species propagates vegetatively. No insect damage to roots was found in Europe.

Subsequent work by Berube (1978) and Shorthouse (1980) in Canada has shown a potential to use *T. dilacerata* to reduce *S. arvensis* infestations. Adult females lay nearly seven clutches of eggs per flower head. These hatch in 4 to 5 days and feed on developing flowers in the immature flower head. The galls appear 5 to 6 days after hatching and button-shaped flower heads result. At least five larvae/head are necessary to assure that no viable seed is produced. In Russia, the rust *Puccinia suaveolens* forms spores only on *S. arvensis* and can completely desiccate plants (Kiselev 1971). The spores washed from ten to 20 infected plants can treat an additional 2000 to 2500 plants.

The potential of *S. arvensis* as a source of natural rubber has been studied and has promise (Buchanan et al. 1978). The seeds contain 31% oil and the plant is used for insecticidal and medicinal purposes in China (Duke and Ayensu 1985). This species and *S. asper* have been used as a salad herb in Europe for centuries because the leaves are high in minerals and vitamin C.

COMMON NAMES

Sonchus arvensis

ARGENTINA	yerba del campo
AUSTRALIA	perennial sowthistle
BELGIUM	akkermelkdistel, laiteron des champs
CANADA	laiteron des champs, perennial sowthistle
DENMARK	ager-svinemaelk
ENGLAND	corn sowthistle, field milk thistle, perennial sowthistle
FINLAND	peltovalvatti
FRANCE	laiteron des champs
GERMANY	Acker Gasedistel, Ackersaudistel, Feld Gasedistel, Milchdistel, Saudistel
INDIA	sahadevibari
INDONESIA	jombang, tempuyung
ITALY	crespione comune, crespione dei campi
JAPAN	hachijona, taiwan-hachijona
NETHERLANDS	akkermelkdistel
NEW ZEALAND	perennial sowthistle
NORWAY	akerdylle
SPAIN	cerraja, cerraja arvense, lechuguilla
SWEDEN	fettistel akermolke
UNITED STATES	perennial sowthistle

Ninety

Sonchus asper (L.) Hill

Asteraceae (Compositae), Aster Family

SONCHUS ASPER is a common annual plant native to Europe but now distributed around the world. It is found in a wide variety of habitats between lat 70° N and 50° S. It is a pioneer species and management is difficult because seeds germinate irregularly and over a prolonged time, and plants develop and mature rapidly and produce many easily dispersed seeds. The species name is from the Latin word for rough.

FIGURE 90-1 The distribution of *Sonchus asper* (L.) Hill across the world where it has been reported as a weed.

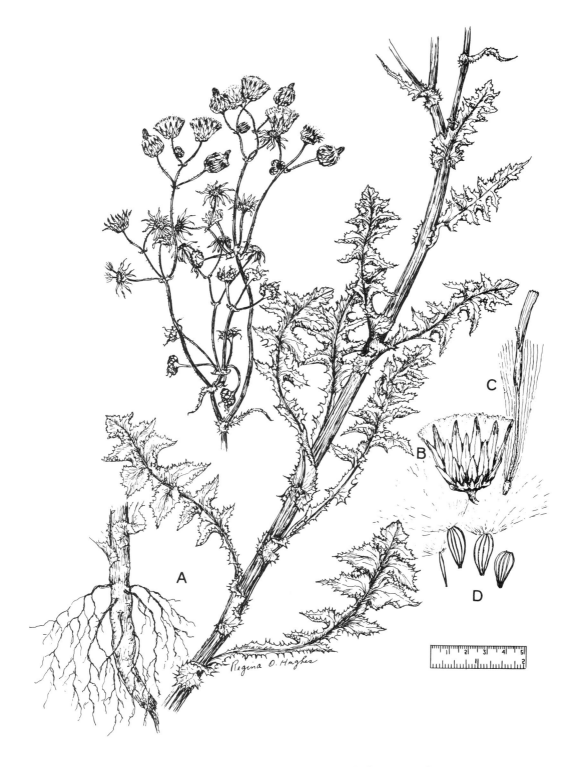

FIGURE 90-2 *Sonchus asper* (L.) Hill: A. habit; B. flower head; C. single flower; D. achene.

DESCRIPTION

S. asper (Figure 90-2) is an herbaceous *annual* or *winter annual*; entire plant contains a sticky, white latex; *taproot* short, bushy with many lateral roots; *stems* erect, hollow, stout, unbranched or slightly branched, 30 to 150 cm tall, often reddish; may have gland-tipped hairs on upper stems; *leaves* alternate, 4 to 18 cm long, 0.5 to 5 cm wide, crisped, many-lobed (5 to 11 lobes on each side) with fewer lobes on upper leaves; ear-like basal lobes clasp stem, tip lobe often broadly triangular, rarely divided to the midrib; margins lined with long stiff spines; sometimes purple on lower surface, dark, glossy green above; *inflorescence* composed of flower heads 1.5 cm long, 1.2 to 2.5 cm in diameter, stalked in a cymose panicle, flask-shaped after opening; *involucral bracts* 9 to 16 mm long, green, with membranous margins, the inner row much longer than the outer; each capitulum with 25 to 150 ligulate, perfect, pale yellow *florets*; *fruit* an *achene* somewhat flat to obovate, orange-brown at maturity, 2 to 3 mm long, 1 mm wide, margined with a narrow wing, usually with 3 (rarely 4 or 5) distinct longitudinal, transversely wrinkled ribs on each face; spaces between the ribs smooth; *pappus* white, composed of numerous unbranched hairs united at base into deciduous ring, about 1 cm long.

This species may be identified by the hollow stems, milky juice, firm many-lobed leaves with spiny margins, the inner row of involucral bracts much longer than the outer, and achenes with longitudinal but no transverse ribs.

HABITAT AND BIOLOGY

S. asper, a pioneer species, invades disturbed sites. With 2 or 3 yr of nondisturbance, this species is usually displaced by others (Bornkamm 1986). More plants become established following spring rather than summer or fall disturbance. *S. asper* achieves more ground cover in silty loam and clay soils than in sandy soils. Plants tolerate saline soils, but not moisture stress. In Colombia, *S. asper* is most abundant from 1000 to 2500 m and at average temperatures between 13 and 23°C (Gomez and Rivera 1987).

Seeds can reach extremely high populations in the soil. Champness and Morris (1948) sampled many fields in England and detected 3.3 million seeds/ha in a grassland area and 4.2 million in arable land. Subsequent surveys found the weed in over 50% of the fields in England, but seeds were not present in large numbers (Roberts and Chancellor 1986). In France, over 60% of the fields examined had *S. asper* seeds and 20% had more than 2.5 million/ha and 99% of the seeds germinated (Barralis and Chadoeuf-Hannel 1987).

Light enhances germination of *S. asper* seed. Wesson and Wareing (1967, 1969b) recovered seeds from soil at night and divided them into two equal portions. Seeds receiving light had a higher germination percentage than those kept in darkness. Freshly harvested seed exhibited similar responses, but, after 25 wk, seeds germinated similarly under light and dark conditions. Light can substitute for the cold treatment normally required to break dormancy (Montegut 1965). *S. asper* seed germinates over a wide temperature range. Lauer (1953) obtained good germination with alternating temperatures of 25/10°C, but constant temperatures from 7 to 35°C resulted in poor germination. *S. asper* begins to germinate when the oxygen concentration reaches 6 to 8% and increases to 75% germination at 12 to 16% oxygen (Mullverstedt 1963a).

Seeds germinate from spring until the fall if conditions are suitable. Most germinate in late spring. Fewer seedlings emerge as the intensity of cultivation increases. For example, the number of seedlings that emerged annually was 43, 26, 18, and 16/m^2 for 0, 1, 4, and 12 cultivations/yr, respectively (Chancellor 1964). Seedling emergence occurs primarily the first year after seed production. Over a 5-yr period, 14% of the seeds emerged and 2% remained as viable seeds in the soil (Roberts and Neilson 1981a). *S. asper* density increases when nitrogen fertilizer is applied (Unterladstatter 1977).

Plants have latex in the veins and midrib by the time they reach the 4-leaf stage (Kummer 1951). Leaves taste rather bitter and the latex turns dark brown on exposure to air. The root system extends laterally to approximately the same extent as the aerial portion of the plant. *S. asper* growing free of competition can produce a root system 68 cm deep and 60 cm across, with stems 120 cm in height and 60 cm in diameter (Cole and Holch 1941). Stomata are found only on the lower leaf surface.

Plants complete their life cycle in 100 to 120 days. They reach the rosette stage about 6 wk after germination. Then they bolt, flower buds appear at 9 wk, and anthesis follows in a few days. Flowers open for several hours on two successive mornings, self-pollination occurs, and mature achenes are formed about a week later (Hutchinson et al. 1984).

S. asper flowers from the summer through the fall. Flower buds go through three stages of development: (1) floral parts differentiate, (2) ovules and anthers develop rapidly, and (3) the corolla tubes, styles and stigmas, and bracts elongate (Berube 1978). Individual plants produce numerous flower heads. Salisbury (1942) found over 100 capitula with nearly 200 achenes each on single plants. Over 20,000 achenes were produced by such plants, but under normal field conditions plants average 2400 seeds each (Sidhu and Baljinder 1983).

S. asper plants often exhibit appreciable morphological variation. Lewin (1948) cites evidence of biotypes based on differences in leaf form, spinyness, and pigmentation. Variation in the presence of gland-tipped hairs on the upper stems ranges from abundant to lacking (USDA 1970). Two subspecies of *S. asper* are found in the Old World, but only one occurs in North America (Hutchinson et al. 1984). The observed variation could be due to crossing of *S. asper* ($2n = 18$) with *S. oleraceus* or *S. arvensis* (both $2n = 36$). Hsieh et al. (1972) found that such crosses are possible, but all F$_1$ hybrids lacked viable pollen and were sterile. Thus crossing with related species is unlikely.

The silky pappus facilitates seed spread, despite its small diameter (5 to 6 mm). The tall stems and dense filamentous arrangement of the pappus bristles offer considerable air resistance, giving achenes a high potential dispersal distance (Sheldon and Burrows 1973). Achenes were collected on a screen by aircraft 600 m above the ground (Glick 1939). Seeds can also contaminate grass seed (Harper 1960) and float readily in water. Egginton and Robbins (1920) detected *S. asper* seed in irrigation canals and no seeds sank when dropped from 1.5 m onto water. Seeds can survive in the digestive system of animals. Dorph-Petersen (1925) reported 27% germination of *S. asper* seeds recovered from cow manure.

BIOLOGICAL CONTROL

Biological control of *S. asper* has been explored. Schroeder (1973) examined 11,000 flower heads and many whole plants over a 3-yr period and found only 16 phytophagous insects. The insect density was never greater than 14% and did not seem to affect either individual plants or populations of *S. asper*. Since this species is an early invader and has erratic populations, it is a poor candidate for biological control with insects.

Berube (1978) studied the effect of gall-forming thrips on *S. asper* and reached similar conclusions. Larvae of *Tephritis formosa* feed on the ovaries and then on the receptacles of *S. asper*. The females oviposit on capitula in a rather narrow size range (average 2.3 mm in diameter). The flower head size selected was important because it must provide sufficient food for the larvae. They rarely laid eggs on *S. oleraceus*. They often laid eggs on *S. arvensis*, but the flowers aborted and no galls were formed. As females did not lay eggs on all capitula, this insect would not reduce seed production sufficiently to control the plant.

In contrast, the leaf-gall fly (*Cystiphora sonchi*) of Europe and the former Soviet Union offers hope of suppressing *S. asper* and *S. arvensis* in Canada (Peschken 1982). Females lay eggs on the undersides of leaves, forming up to 270 galls/plant and this insect was initially released in Canada in 1981.

AGRICULTURAL IMPORTANCE

S. asper is a weed in 26 crops in 64 countries (Figure 90-1) with temperate and subtropical climates and is a frequently reported weed of cereals, vegetables and pastures. It is a serious or principal weed of lucerne in Saudi Arabia; pyrethrum in Kenya; oilseed rape in England; sugar beets in Poland; sunflowers in Argentina; vegetables in Sweden and the United States; and wheat in India.

It is a common weed of beets in Germany; cereals in Iran, Italy, the Netherlands, Norway, Peru, and Tunisia; coffee and soybeans in Brazil; cotton and pastures in South Africa; legumes in Tunisia; lucerne in Argentina and the Netherlands; maize in Peru and the former Soviet Union; orchards in Bolivia and the former Soviet Union; potatoes and sugar beets in France; sugarcane in India, Mauritius, and South Africa; sunflowers in France and the former Soviet Union; tobacco in the former Soviet Union; vegetables in the former Soviet Union and Tunisia; vineyards in France and the former Soviet Union; and wheat in Peru.

S. asper is also reported as an unranked weed of barley in Iran; beets and peas in France; cassava in Indonesia and Madagascar; cereals in Canada, Finland, Germany, Norway, and Tasmania; coffee in East Africa; cotton in Iran, the former Soviet Union and Spain; dates in Saudi Arabia; horticultural crops in Australia, Canada, and Finland; lucerne in the United States; maize in Indonesia, Mexico, and Spain; nurseries in Norway; orchards in Brazil and Chile; pastures in Australia, Brazil, Chile, England, Germany, Spain, and the United States; potatoes in Chile, France, and Germany; upland rice in Indonesia; sorghum in Mexico; soybeans and sunflowers in Spain; sugar beets in Iran and Spain; sugarcane in Argentina; sweet potatoes in Madagascar and New Guinea; vegetables in Belgium, Iran, South Africa, and Tasmania; vineyards in Germany and Portugal; wheat in Iran, Italy, Mexico, Portugal, and the former Yugoslavia; and wastelands in Australia, India, New Zealand, and the United States.

S. asper caused substantial economic losses in sugarcane until 2,4-D and MCPA became available (Rochecouste 1967). No competition studies on *S. asper* were found, but plants contain nearly three times as much K and Mg and twice as much P and Ca as barley (Malicki and Bereciowa 1986).

Plants can host the mongold fly (*Pegomyia betae*) (Pammel 1913), several virus-transmitting aphids, and certain species of nematodes (Bendixen et al. 1979) and can be parasitized by *Cuscuta australis* (Lundberg 1957). Biotypes resistant to triazine herbicides are found in vineyards in France.

Plants are used as a potherb in the Old World and Africa and to purify blood and treat kidney and bladder ailments. Freshly harvested leaves have nearly 3% protein and are rich in calcium (Wehmeyer and Rose 1983). The latex was thought to influence lactation in animals (Lewin 1948). In Colombia, leaves are used on salads and are fed to rabbits, and plants have various medicinal uses (Gomez and Rivera 1987).

COMMON NAMES

Sonchus asper

ARGENTINA	cerraja brava
AUSTRALIA	rough sowthistle
BELGIUM	laiteron apre
BRAZIL	serralha
CANADA	laiteron rude, spiny annual sowthistle
CHILE	nilhue, nilhue caballuno
COLOMBIA	cerraja aspera
DENMARK	ru svinemaelk
DOMINICAN REPUBLIC	lechugilla
ENGLAND	prickly sowthistle
FIJI	sowthistle
FINLAND	otavalvati
FRANCE	laiteron apre, laiteron epineux
GERMANY	Dornige Gansedistel, Dornige Saudistel, Rauhe Gansedistel, Rauhe Saudiste
INDONESIA	delgiyu, jombang
ITALY	crespigno spinoso
JAPAN	oni-nogeshi
MADAGASCAR	beroberoka
MAURITIUS	lastron piquant
NETHERLANDS	brosse melkdistel, ruwe melkdistel
NEW ZEALAND	prickly sowthistle
NORWAY	stivdylle
PERU	cerraja macho
PORTUGAL	serralha aspera, serralha espinhosa
SPAIN	cardimuelle, cardinche, cerraja, cerraja comun
SWEDEN	svintistel
UNITED STATES	spiny sowthistle
URUGUAY	cardo

Ninety-One

Spirodela polyrhiza (L.) Schleiden

Lemnaceae, Duckweed Family

S PIRODELA POLYRHIZA is in the family of the world's smallest seed-bearing plants, the **Lemnaceae**, often called the duckweeds for obvious reasons. Only five of the 25 species of duckweeds produce more than one root and all of these have been placed in *Spirodela*. The plant body is a thalloid, often called a frond, and although it is the largest and most complex of the duckweeds it is only occasionally the dominating species in a mixture of these plant types. *S. polyrhiza* is one of the few duckweeds to clearly differentiate turions, sometimes called winter buds. The species is a weed problem in the world's

FIGURE 91-1   The distribution of *Spirodela polyrhiza* (L.) Schleiden across the world where it has been reported as a weed.

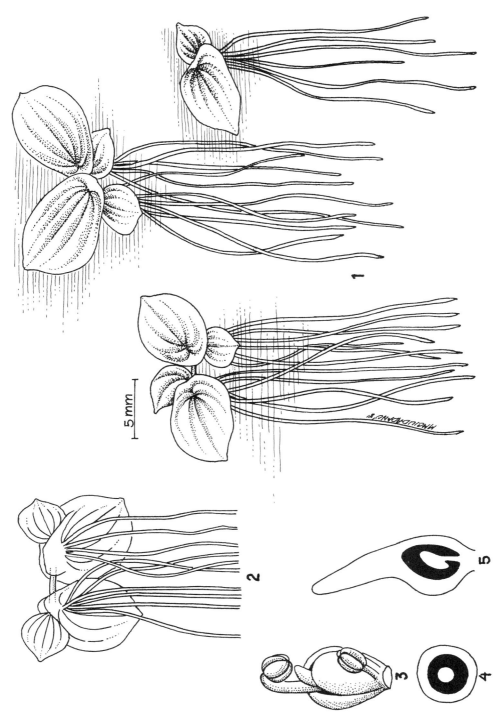

5 mm

FIGURE 91-2 *Spirodela polyrhiza* (L.) Schleiden: 1. habit; 2. dorsal view showing root attachment; 3. flower; 4. ovary, cross section, 5. same, ventral section.

leading rice-producing countries and a troublesome problem in the world's waterways. Because it is the largest of the duckweeds, it is commonly referred to as giant duckweed. It behaves as a weed in 60 countries.

DESCRIPTION

S. polyrhiza (Figure 91-2) is a minute, free-floating, stemless, aquatic herb; *fronds* broadly ovate to rounded, flat, opaque, palmately 5- to 11-nerved, margins entire, size variable from 5 to 10 mm long and 4 to 6 mm wide, apex rounded to obtuse, usually glossy dark green above (may be yellow-green) and purplish to red below, inflorescences when present and off-shoot fronds born in 2 ventral pockets (pouches), fronds attached to parent by slender marginal *stipe*; *roots* 2 to 18, descending, unbranched, usually devoid of root hairs, 3 to 25 mm long, the vegetative propagules (turions), produced very near the place of attachment of roots; *flowers* unisexual, rarely seen in nature, globose, surrounded by small sac-like *spathe*; *inflorescence* composed of 3 flowers, 1 pistillate, 2 staminate; *anthers* 2-celled, dehiscing by slits; ovary with 2 or more *ovules*; *fruit* a *utricle*, 1-seeded; *seed* ovoid, longitudinally ribbed with transverse striations or smooth with spongy outer layer; *turion* a small, modified version of the vegetative plant, round to reniform, 1 to 3 mm long and 0.3 mm thick.

DISTRIBUTION AND HABITAT

S. polyrhiza has a general distribution over much of the area inhabited by man (see Figure 91-1). It seems to be limited by extreme cold but its propagules may survive for several months encased in ice. It does not prosper in cold spring water as does *Lemna minor*. It grows at an altitude of 1850 m in the Kashmir in India (Misra and Das 1969).

Giant duckweed is most often found in quiet permanent waters. In mixtures with other duckweeds, it frequents low-lying roadside ditches, sheltered bays, pockets in floating bogs, and sites where town sewage and farm run-off have made waters nutrient rich. It is often seen in mixtures with larger aquatic species on the vegetation-choked shores of reservoirs, ponds and lakes. The plant loves full sun, but as with *Lemna minor*, it also frequents woodland and tall grass ponds where there is always partial shade. Fast water dislodges large populations and aids in the dispersal of the species (Jacobs 1947).

This duckweed will not tolerate salinity. It can grow in water and on substrates with a wide range of *pH*. In India, plants removed from water and dried for 30 min could not recover when placed in water (Das and Gopal 1969). Plants that are stranded on mud may, if the substrate remains moist, survive and produce new fronds and turions for an extended period. Guppy (1894) reported the survival of such a colony for more than a year. On mud the roots often twist and seem unable to penetrate the substrate. Jacobs (1947) speculates that they do not find sufficient anchorage for the process because they do not develop root hairs. Meijer and Sutton (1987) found that the roots of *Lemna paucicostata* could not penetrate agar. McCann (1942), on the other hand, reported the roots of a population growing in a "slushy" mix of soil and water showed remarkable development, with good subsurface root penetration. The plants were larger and more vigorous than those floating on water.

PROPAGATION

In 1929, Saeger made a search of the evidence for flowering and seed production of *S. polyrhiza* in natural settings and found only nine reports (Saeger 1929). Such reports are equally scarce today, but the manipulation of artificial media to bring plants into flower in laboratories is meeting with some success. The duckweeds are very simple plants; they are members of a family that has moved toward a less complex morphology and with it a decreased frequency of flowering. Arber (1922) has pointed out that even if seed production is successful, some of the seed germinates immediately, a portion of it while still on the parent plant, and so it is of no value in dispersal. This plant has, however, developed marvelous systems for a bountiful reproduction and spread by vegetative means. In some instances, 30,000 plants may be present in one square meter of water.

Having become almost entirely dependent upon vegetative propagules for survival, it is now clear that there are many physiological races of the species throughout the world, all with adaptations to make them fit for survival in these various areas and particular habitats. Thus the conditions which stimulate (a) formation and (b) germination of the propagules may seem almost contradictory in different regions. Further, these events may be interdependent, for Sibasaki and Oda (1979) in Japan demonstrated that different types of dormancy are present in the turions depending upon the temperatures in existence at the time of formation, as well as the date at which the propagule was formed *after* turion formation was initiated. In the material that follows, it should also be remembered that the search for influential environmental factors, when moved into the laboratory, is pursued in many creative ways, but seldom are they standardized so that one can make valid comparisons of results in the reports of different experiments in diverse places.

In India, there are two periods of turion formation, April and May, with germination as soon as the rains come and the temperature rises, and again in November–December, with sprouting in the next season at about the same time as the above (Das and Gopal 1969). Fresh turions, formed in early November and harvested in late November, and placed in the light at room temperature (14 to 23°C), began to sprout in 4 days and reached a maximum in 2 wk. They also sprouted in the dark at 40°C. Thus, there was little or no dormancy.

In the northern United States, turion formation begins in July and continues until plants are killed by frost. Jacobs (1947) believes that few of these propagules germinate in the season of formation, with the exception that extreme temperature fluctuations may cause limited sprouting in late fall. In the field, turion germination normally begins in May in this area. In contrast to the behavior of the propagules in India, fresh turions held under illumination for a 20-hr day at several temperatures between 10 and 30°C gave a small amount of germination after 9 mo at the 25°C level. At 30°C there was 80% germination in 5 mo, indicating that after-ripening does proceed slowly at high temperatures. There are several treatments now known that will break the dormancy of turions formed in the cool temperate zone.

One of the most effective treatments for breaking the dormancy of fresh turions is low temperature. For example, turions held at –4 to –10°C for 2 wk gave prompt germination when moved to any temperature above 15°C (Jacobs 1947). Light was required but the intensity was not critical. There was no germination in the dark. Misra (1969) and Das and Gopal (1969) in India, however, obtained germination in complete darkness. The latter workers gave fresh turions from a December harvest a low temperature of 6°C for different periods from 15 min to 24 hr and recorded 40% germination for an 8-hr treatment.

When this treatment was given to turions in March after 4 mo of storage, the germination was 90%. Turions placed at $-13°C$ for 15 min resulted in 35% germination, and when this short treatment was given for 5 successive days the germination went up to 70%. An exposure of more than 15 min decreased germination. Turions stored from December through March gave 95% germination when placed in the open sun at 37 to 42°C.

As mentioned above, the conditions under which turions are formed influences the measures needed to break the particular type of dormancy present. For example, Misra (1969) found that summer turions formed at high temperatures sprouted promptly when placed at temperatures above or below the temperature of formation, but winter-formed turions would sprout only at higher temperatures. Jacobs (1947) found that old turions required less pre-treatment time and those formed at low temperature required less pre-treatment than those formed at higher temperatures. Turions sprout better at low temperatures under a short photoperiod regime. They germinate better at a high temperature in long photoperiods (Misra 1969). It is generally agreed that the proper treatment fitted to the type of dormancy present will often bring 100% germination.

Jacobs (1947) has pointed out that the early and prolonged dormancy of turions is an important evolutionary characteristic for this species at sites in cool regions of the temperate zone, for the vegetative plants cannot overwinter in such areas. In detailed observations made in early spring, he found that as the surrounding temperature reached 15°C, during the light period, an air bubble pushes out between the pocket sheath and frond surface, quickly pulls the turion to the surface, the gas is released, and the propagule is held aloft by the surface tension. At 20 to 35°C, germination is very rapid at the surface, but if it fails, the organ may sink and rise again as another bubble of gas is formed. Newton et al. (1978) reported formation of the bubble in both light and dark.

As the turions germinate, they swell and become glossy dark green above and pale green or pale red below. Roots appear on the underside and the first off-shoot extends from a pocket.

Lacor (1969) and Czopek (1964) have reported on the influence of gibberellic acid, kinetin and red light for the stimulation of turion germination in the laboratory. Malek (1981) found that a partial desiccation of turions in air or with the use of polyethylene glycol improved germination.

In general, turions are much hardier than vegetative plants. Jacobs (1947) held turions at 50°C for 24 hr without loss of viability. In India, temperatures above this level are lethal for the types of giant duckweed in their waters. Turions encased in ice at $-4°C$ survived for 3 mo without loss of viability, but if held at -8 to $-12°C$ they were killed in a short time (Jacobs 1947). Turions may be held and will germinate at *pH*s from 4.2 to 9.6. They are destroyed in passing through the gut of birds. In cool regions, water depth does not appear to limit turion germination.

The quick entry of the vegetative turions into new water pools and shelters is puzzling but is evidence of a highly effective dispersal system. There is still much conjecture about the carriers. In addition to spread by floods, waves and currents, Jacobs (1947) observed that agents such as muskrats (*Ondatra zibethica*) are very effective in the movement of turions. This particular animal moves nocturnally in low-lying areas where humidity is high, with turions in the mud on fur and feet. There is little consensus on the dispersal of turions by birds in flight. In the higher, cooler latitudes, Jacobs has pointed out that spring-migrating birds have often completed their journeys before the duckweeds make vigorous growth. On the return flights in autumn, water levels are down, large weeds occupy great expanses of open water, mud flats are in evidence and the growth and spread of giant duckweed is retarded. Jacobs (1947) cites an instance of a 6 min flight in which turions held in feathers were desiccated. But in wet mud on feet or lower body parts the turions would last longer, particularly if the flight was in fog or light rain (see also Guppy 1906). Ridley (1930) however suggests that turions can survive for 12 hr beneath the plumage of birds and recover promptly. Thus, a bird in flight at 35 km/hr might assist in providing a long reach in dispersal to distant places. The seed of *S. polyrhiza* has no special adaptation for attachment to bird plumage.

MORPHOLOGY AND PHYSIOLOGY

As we come to know more about the biology of *S. polyrhiza*, there seems a growing consensus that the plant is not a great collection of ecological races but a species with an enormous range of conditions to which it can adapt in different sites, seasons and geographical regions (Jacobs 1947, Landolt 1957, Das and Gopal 1969).

A major physiological and ecological study of a large number of populations of different strains and types in 12 species of the **Lemnaceae** found evidence for great tractability of the plants in adjusting to changing conditions. Jacobs (1947) has given specific examples of the broad ecological amplitude to which this plant can adjust. Plants moved suddenly from shade to bright sun, or from 15 to 45°C, or vice versa, were not likely to survive. When such changes were made gradually, the plants were able to accommodate the new, more extreme, conditions and survive. Plants moved from North America to Varanasi, India, did not grow in the day-night cycle of the new place, but when the cycles in India were reversed they grew well.

Among angiosperms, the duckweeds represent a striking reduction and simplification of the vegetative body; in *S. polyrhiza* this takes the form of a small, leaf-like, flattened, thallus or frond about 10 mm long. The frond is not far different from the floating leaves of some of the larger, more advanced, aquatic plants. It is the termination of a long, slender stolon which extends through the base to a small dense area (centrum) near the proximal end of the frond. The centrum serves as a center of attachment for all organs, is bordered on either side by the reproductive pockets or pouches (sometimes called lids), and bears the simple adventitious roots. Krajncic (1974) in the former Yugoslavia, in a report on flowering in **Lemnaceae**, reminds us that the inflorescence of *S. polyrhiza* is produced in the left reproductive pouch, while in *Lemna minor*, which is more widely distributed in the world, the flower structures are in the right reproductive pouch.

As new off-shoot fronds appear at the pockets, they may remain attached, and with the mother form a clone of four to six fronds. Daughter fronds may mature within 3 to 4 days. As conditions change unfavorably, new developing fronds may take the form of turions, the overwintering vegetative propagule.

The frond may be looked upon as a highly reduced rosette with the vertical axis shortened to three nodes (Das and Gopal 1969). The vascular bundles are greatly reduced (Hillman 1961). The upper and lower leaves have an epidermal covering of small cells with stomata and small chloroplast-bearing guard cells above. The upper surface is cutinized and the lower carries a mucilaginous layer. A spongy mesophyll separates the two leaf surfaces. On the underside, a subepidermal layer of cells with thickened walls gives rigidity to the frond, and it is here that the anthocyanin pigments accumulate to give the reddish color. Rao (1968) studied the ultrastructure of *S. polyrhiza* with special reference to chloroplast development during turion formation. Rimon and Galun (1968) studied the morphogenesis of *S. oligorhiza*, a species quite similar in appearance to *S. polyrhiza*.

Up to 15 roots (usually less) may be found on a frond and lengths may reach 25 mm. They have a persistent root cap, are unbranched, may contain chloroplasts, have no cutin and are devoid of root hairs. The rather stiff roots hang down and seem to serve as a drag anchor to prevent the plant from overturning or drifting around too much (McCann 1942, Hillman 1961). It seems apparent from the work of Hillman (1961) and Muhonen et al. (1983) that the roots have little, if any, role in the uptake of nutrients by this particular duckweed.

In Germany, Hegelmaier (1868) published an early, major monograph of the family **Lemnaceae** but was never able to see *S. polyrhiza* in flower. Later, flowering and fruiting specimens of the species were sent to him from the United States and he then published an account of the sexual reproductive cycle (Hegelmaier 1871). His papers carry excellent descriptions and illustrations of this species (see also Maheshwari and Maheshwari 1963).

In many areas of the world, natural sexual reproduction is infrequent in most of the **Lemnaceae** species; it is rare in *S. polyrhiza*. In literature reports on reproduction of the latter over the past 200 yr, only about 20 cases are cited (Saeger 1929, Hicks 1932, Ivanova 1970). In the decade following 1963, with use of artificial media and aseptic cultures, Czopek (1963), Lacor (1968, 1969, 1970), Krajncic (1974) and Wolek (1974) produced flowering plants experimentally in the laboratory. Lacor obtained flowering in 17 days by adding casein hydrolysate and gibberellic acid to the medium. Flowering was induced to a lesser degree with supplemental sucrose. Sometimes flowers and turions were produced simultaneously from the same pockets. Working with a familiar clone, Wolek in Poland found flowers in all of his cultures on the 39th day.

As mentioned previously, the duckweeds are very simple plants that have assumed a less complex morphology and thus exhibit a decreased frequency of flowering. The flower primordia arise in or near the meristematic area that produces the daughter fronds. Flowers are minute and, as far as is known, a frond produces only one flower during its lifetime. The inflorescence of *S. polyrhiza* consists of two stamens and an ovary (one or two ovules) with style and stigma. Pollen is white, spherical and plentiful. Pollen tubes develop rapidly. If seed is formed it matures, separates from the seed coat, sinks to the bottom and grows in the next season. This is in contrast to the experience of Arber (1922), mentioned previously, who found in a different region that the seeds may germinate immediately. The flowers may be cross- or self-pollinated as plants drift about and contact one another. Wind and water are believed to play little or no role in pollination. Seeds kept dry over winter germinated quickly in spring (Hillman 1961).

Czopek (1963) and Wolek (1974) hypothesize that the inhibition of vegetative growth is the factor directly responsible for the induction of flowering: it may bring about a turn toward sexuality or a shift toward formation of turions. Ecological factors prevailing at the time may thus indirectly influence the course of the propagation method.

Because giant duckweed is so dependent upon turions for survival, a great portion of research on the biology of this plant has been devoted to their formation. The propagule is simply a small and modified version of the vegetative plant and is often called a winter bud, although it often forms in early summer and frequently in places that have no winter. It is unique among the 25 duckweeds in being almost completely dependent upon this structure for winter survival. It is the most specialized and well known of the duckweed turions because it is smaller, thicker, has a dark green or purple color with dull red below, internally fewer air spaces, and an abundance of starch grains.

The turions are concave above, convex below, 1 to 3 mm long and 0.3 mm thick. Stolons bearing turions are shorter and have a well differentiated abscission layer at the turion base. Dormant turions have no roots but bear up to 6 root primordia, some of which elongate during germination. In the northern United States, as turion formation begins in midsummer, at first only a small proportion of off-shoots proceed toward turion formation. Up to six off-shoots can develop from a single *S. polyrhiza* plant and any of them can become turions. Later in the season most plants produce only turions.

There are no records of flowers on turions. Several successive generations of vegetative plants are required before another turion is formed, and under moderate temperature conditions the plant may propagate itself indefinitely without any turion formation (Jacobs 1947).

Perry (1968) conducted experiments on turion formation with two clones from the United States and one each from Argentina and Puerto Rico and found that the latter two could not be induced to form turions with any experimental conditions of temperature, daylength, or nutrition. Newton et al. (1978) induced turion formation in nutrient cultures with the addition of sucrose and $Ca(NO_3)$. Malek and Oda (1979) induced turion formation of plants by reducing the nitrate level of a liquid culture medium. They then grew the plants in red and blue light and found production of turions to be the same at 15 days but twice as great in red light at 35 days.

Changes in the direction of growth and the morphology of the plant are normally the result of an interplay of several environmental conditions with the physiological and chemical responses of the plant cells. In *S. polyrhiza*, an appropriate photoperiod is not a critical factor in the initiation of turions, for Jacobs (1947) found that they were formed at 8, 10, 16, and 20 hr of daylight. Krajncic (1974) collected all of the **Lemnaceae** species from northeast Slovenia and grew them in pre-cultures of long-day (16 hr) or short-day (8 hr) for 30 days. He then put *each* of the above in *both* long- and short-day for 25 to 30 days and recorded flowering. He believes that *S. polyrhiza* is a day neutral plant. In the field it has long been observed that turion formation normally occurs when temperatures are high. Jacobs has shown, however, that in experimental cultures they will form at 10°C, although reluctantly, for if held at a temperature of 7°C the vegetative plant can only survive for three weeks. In his cultures, the maximum constant temperature at which turions would form is 30°C. With various combinations of photoperiod and alternating temperature, however, turions were produced at 44°C.

So it is with light; in nature turion formation is associated with times of high light intensity. In experiments, it soon becomes obvious that light and temperature are interrelated, for with an appropriate temperature, high light is not an absolute necessity for turion formation. In experimental cultures, Jacobs (1947) found that turions were formed at a very low light intensity (50 foot-candles) in a 10-hr day, but only at 10°C, the lowest temperature used. They were also formed at 10°C in all higher light intensities and longer photoperiods (up to 800 foot-candles and 20 hr of light). It is tempting to believe that the total light energy received by the plant (intensity × duration), is the simplest statement of its role in turion formation. Jacobs found that at 15°C the minimum effective amount of light energy for turion initiation was 100 foot-candles for a 20-hr day. The same total light energy, 200 foot-candles for a 10-hour day, failed to induce turions. The distribution of light with time is thus also a factor in controlling turion production.

These and other experiments led Jacobs to speculate that, working together, all of the above factors were indicating that turions tend to form when there is a slowing of the growth rate and a balance between photosynthesis and respiration that provides an excess of photosynthate. He arranged experiments to stimulate photosynthetic activity by adding supplemental CO_2 to the cultures, and to reduce losses of carbohydrate in respiration by use of a cold dark period and a shortage of nitrogen. It was indeed the case that all of these steps favored turion formation.

Wolek (1979) grew *S. polyrhiza* and *Wolffia arrhiza* in uncrowded mono- and bicultures and found the release of metabolites that could bring an allelopathic reaction in their relationship. Both on land and in water this phenomenon may be important as colonization takes place, for such chemicals could be a factor in the inhibition of growth and in the determination of the subsequent path toward sexual or vegetative reproduction.

With all of the fascination of the turion story that has attracted so many researchers, we must not lose sight of the very bountiful supply of the off-shoot or daughter fronds that pours forth during the life of a frond and its offspring. They are produced most rapidly at about 25°C and in the field in India their number can double each 3 to 4 days (Das and Gopal 1969). Singh et al. (1967), also in India, found the weight of plant material increased 35 times and the area covered by 30 times in an 8-week period.

ECONOMIC IMPORTANCE

S. polyrhiza is a serious weed in rice in Korea, a principal rice weed in China, India, Indonesia, and Japan; and a common weed of this crop in Hungary, Malaysia, Nepal, Pakistan, the Philippines, Portugal, Taiwan, and Thailand. It is found in irrigation systems in most warm regions but is a principal weed in India and troublesome in Indonesia. It is a weed of lowland jute in India. In the waterways needed for agriculture and commerce, it is a serious weed in India and is troublesome in Brazil, Puerto Rico, and Thailand because the thick mats interfere with drinking by livestock, pumps become clogged, and navigation becomes impossible as the wind and waves pile it up and push it about in large masses.

Rice is produced in 82 countries of the world. In a survey of rice yield losses due to weeds and of control measures in many of these areas, Smith (1983) stated that *S. polyrhiza* is one of the weeds that "gives moderate reductions of yield and quality and is economically troublesome in certain rice cultures of all the major producing areas." In a 2-year survey of paddy fields in Korea, *S. polyrhiza* was found to be the most widely distributed weed and one of the two most dominant in paddies. The species has long been reported in rice fields and waterways in Japan. In 1982 Kasahara (1982) was still rating it as one of the most harmful weeds in paddy.

A survey by Misra and Das (1969) reported *S. polyrhiza* to be one of the three most important water weeds of Orissa state in east India. In the Kashmir area, this plant is said to be the most troublesome floating plant, covering very large water areas and slowing and stagnating water. The huge masses that form in rice fields render the land unfit for that crop.

There are occasional reports that the duckweeds, including *S. polyrhiza*, "save water" because as they cover a water body the evaporation is less than from a free water surface. Kawabata et al. (1986) in Japan reported that duckweed growth in rice paddy fields irrigated with secondary sewage effluent was effective in removing excess nutrient supplies for the rice crop but also served as a purifier of effluent itself (see also Reddy and DeBusk 1985).

S. polyrhiza is used in aquariums and is eaten by a large number of shore and water birds and fishes. It is used as food for poultry in Poland and fed to pigs and cows elsewhere. Rusoff et al. (1978) reported on the feeding value of giant duckweed for dairy cattle.

COMMON NAMES

Spirodela polyrhiza

AUSTRALIA	large duckweed
BANGLADESH	kuti pana
BELGIUM	veelwortelig kroos
BRAZIL	erva de pato, lentiha d'agua
EGYPT	adas el-moya, ads el-maia
GERMANY	Grosse Wasserlinse, Teichlinse
INDONESIA	kakarewoan, mata lele
JAPAN	tanenanashi, ukikusa
PHILIPPINES	liyang pula
THAILAND	nae yai
UNITED STATES	giant duckweed
VIETNAM	beo tam

Ninety-Two

Stachytarpheta jamaicensis (L.) Vahl

Verbenaceae, Verbena Family

S TACHYTARPHETA is in a family of plants that contributes many useful economic products, notably the durable and water-resistant teak *Tectona grandis* that is used for ship
and boat building. There are about 50 species of herbs and shrubs in the genus. It seems
generally agreed that these plants are native to tropical America. Some of the species began
to appear in the fields of Asia at the end of the 18th century. The four that have become most
weedy in tropical and subtropical agriculture are *S. jamaicensis*, *S. indica*, *S. cayennensis*, and *S.
urticaefolia*. The Greek *stachys*, a spike, and *tarphys*, thick, have contributed the name for this

FIGURE 92-1   The distribution of *Stachytarpheta jamaicensis* (L.) Vahl across the world
where it has been reported as a weed.

FIGURE 92-2 *Stachytarpheta jamaicensis* (L.) Vahl: 1. habit; 2. portion of spike; 3. petal open to show stamens and staminodes; 4. fruit; 5. seed, two views.

genus in which the dense floral spike may be several centimeters in length. The specific name, *jamaicensis*, expresses the native area of the most weedy species. This species causes trouble in plantation crops, arable fields, and in pastures and rangelands.

DESCRIPTION

S. jamaicensis (Figure 92-2) is *annual* or *perennial*, erect, branched, often an undershrub that may be 1 to 2 m high, may be suffrutescent (woody below with herbaceous shoot produced perennially); a strong woody *taproot* with white laterals; *stems* round or younger ones slightly 4-angled, green, sometimes with purplish color; *leaves* opposite, may be widely spaced, elliptic to oblong-ovate, acute, 2.5 to 10 cm in length, 3 to 6 cm wide, dark green, smooth or slightly hairy, puckered (bullate) between secondary lateral veins, veins depressed above, prominent below, consequently conspicuously rugose margins serrate, contracting toward base to short leaf stalk that may be winged; fully extended *floral spikes* at ends of branches and main stems, 20 to 40 cm long, 3 to 4 mm thick, usually greenish, continuous, with 1 to 3 flowers only open at one time; *calyx* small, narrow, oblique, 4-toothed, *bracts* lanceolate; *corolla* tubular, curved outward, 5 to 10 mm across, pale lavender, deep blue, or dark violet, petals 5, unequal, with white throat; *stamens* 2; *ovary* 2-celled; *fruit* a capsule, small, 2-seeded, 3 to 5 mm long, enclosed in calyx, oblong, smooth, and one-half or more of it imbedded in groove in the flower axis that becomes dry and brittle after flowering. Seed a nutlet with inner side flat. Gunn and Ritchie (1988) have presented line drawings of the seed embryo and transections of the seed.

BIOLOGY

Little is known of the biology of *S. jamaicensis*. It was chosen as the representative of this group of weeds because it is believed to be the most widespread. The infestations are centered in two regions on opposite sides of the earth (Figure 92-1). The largest area is bounded by Australia, India, south China, and islands in the Pacific Ocean as far out as the Cook and Samoan Islands. The species is also troublesome on many islands of the Caribbean sea and the countries that border that sea on the north, west, and south. There are scattered infestations that seem to stand alone in Ghana, Hawaii, Madagascar, and Mauritius. The species prefers wet to moderately wet sites, but can also prosper on dry fields and pastures. In Hawaii, it is found from sea level to middle elevations up to 900 m.

In north and east Australia it is found in gardens, parks, vacant lots, and disturbed sites such as roadsides and building sites. It is a weed of moist pastures as well as unirrigated improved pastures. It also appears in unimproved pastures made up of mainly native plants. Its seeds are moved about with hay and soil and may contaminate pasture seed supplies (Swarbrick 1984).

Its widespread dispersal into the tropical regions is difficult to understand, for it is quite unlikely that it would have been transported by man as a food crop. Dried leaves were at one time shipped from Brazil to Europe as "Brazilian tea," but the plant has not become a weed in the latter place. It is doubtful that it was deliberately introduced to new areas as an ornamental, for it has no spectacular display and shows very few florets at one time.

The plant flowers year-round in Sri Lanka and Trinidad and for a period of several months in Puerto Rico in the Caribbean area. Pancho (1964) collected seed of this and other species in the rice fields in the Philippines. The weed seeds were planted in field plots and harvested at intervals. *S. jamaicensis* produced an average of 2000 seeds/plant. There were 430 of the small seeds per gram.

Juliano (1940), also working in the Philippines, gathered seeds of 23 weed species in the spring and autumn of 1933, mixed them with moist sand in open glass vials, and buried them in the ground at a depth of 15 cm. About one-half of the species, including *S. jamaicensis*, were still viable after 6.5 yr of burial.

AGRICULTURAL IMPORTANCE

This species is a principal weed of bananas and pastures in Hawaii, coconut and pastures in the Solomon Islands, pastures in Australia and Taiwan, and of vegetable crops in New Caledonia.

It is a common weed of bananas, cassava, citrus, oil palm, rice, and vegetable crops in Surinam; of coconuts in Trinidad and Indonesia; of oil palm in Malaysia and Indonesia; of pastures in the Dominican Republic and Jamaica; of rubber in Indonesia, Malaysia, and Thailand; of sugarcane in Bangladesh, Mexico, and the Philippines; and of vegetable crops in Australia and Hawaii.

The weed is in abaca, cocoa, coconut, and upland rice in the Philippines; cocoa and coconut in Laos; bananas and taro in the Samoa; maize in India; pastures in New Caledonia and New Guinea; pineapple in Hawaii; upland rice in Indonesia and Taiwan; soybean in Indonesia; sugarcane in Australia, Dominican Republic, Hawaii, and Vietnam; and tobacco in the Philippines.

The species is on the noxious weed register in Hawaii because it spreads so rapidly that it pushes out most other desirable forages in pastures. In addition to its presence in many kinds of agriculture fields, the plant is a common inhabitant of roadsides and waste places. This weed was introduced into Hawaii and by 1967 had spread to 240,000 ha.

In various places in the world, the plant is regarded as useful for treatment of human illnesses. It has been administered for dysentery, and is commonly sold in the shops of herbalists in Southeast Asia, where a broth of leaves is recommended as treatment for malaria.

COMMON NAMES

Stachytarpheta jamaicensis

AUSTRALIA	Jamaican snakeweed, light blue snakeweed
BARBADOS	vervain
COLOMBIA	golondrina, verbena azul
CUBA	verbena cimarona
DOMINICAN REPUBLIC	verbena morada
HAWAII	Jamaica vervain
INDIA	kariyartharani, katapunuttu, semainyuruvi
INDONESIA	gewongan
JAMAICA	vervain

MADAGASCAR	ombimboalareo
MALAYSIA	ramput tahi babi, selaseh dandi
MAURITIUS	queue derat
NEW CALEDONIA	herbe bleue, nettleleaf vervain
PHILIPPINES	albaka, bilu-bilu, bolomaros, Brazil tea, kandi-kandilaan, limbagat, sentemiento, verbena de las Antilles
PUERTO RICO	verbena
SRI LANKA	bulunakuta, hai-or ingi
TRINIDAD	vervain

Ninety-Three

Synedrella nodiflora (L.) Gaertn.

Asteraceae (Compositae), Aster Family

SYNEDRELLA NODIFLORA is an annual herb native to tropical America and now widely distributed in nearly 50 countries. One of its interesting characteristics is the dimorphic seed produced in the ray and disc florets. Each seed type is so distinct that they appear to represent separate species. This weed is an important species in both crop and noncrop land in all tropical continents, yet relatively few studies exist on its biology. Its Latin name reflects the appearance of the inflorescence of this plant. The Greek meaning of *Synedrella* is "seated together" and *nodiflora* refers to the presence of flowers in the nodes of leaf axils.

FIGURE 93-1   The distribution of *Synedrella nodiflora* (L.) Gaertn. across the world where it is reported as a weed.

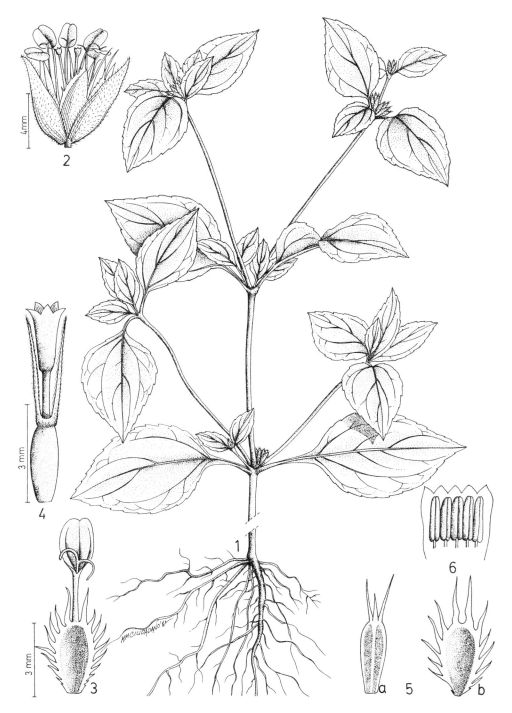

FIGURE 93-2   *Synedrella nodiflora* (L.) Gaertn.: 1. habit; 2. flower head; 3. ray flower; 4. disc flower; 5. a. achene of disk flower, b. achene of ray flower; 6. syngenesious stamens.

DESCRIPTION

S. nodiflora (Figure 93-2) is an *annual* herb; *taproot* branched; *stems* erect, 30 to 80 cm tall with long internodes; dichotomously branched, subangular, smooth to sparsely hairy, *leaves* opposite, somewhat roughly hairy on both surfaces, simple, acute, ovate-lanceolate to elliptic-ovate, with finely toothed margins and 3 prominent veins; 4 to 9 cm long, 1.5 to 4 cm wide; base tapers into a short *petiole*; *inflorescence* composed of small globose, axillary and terminal flower heads in upper third of plant; solitary or 2 to 7 together, sessile or on short *peduncle*; *involucral bracts* in two series; 6 marginal *ray florets* female, yellow, strap-shaped, 2- to 4-dentate; 20 central *disc florets* perfect, yellow, tubular, 3 to 4 mm long with pubescent awns; *fruit* a dimorphic *achene*; ray floret achenes 3.5 to 5 mm long by 2 mm wide, dark brown to black, oblong, flattened, margins with stiff whitish wings with upward pointing lobes; achenes of disc florets smaller, brown, linear-oblong, nearly triangular, covered with thin, short hair-like protuberance with 2 to 4 rigid, oblique awns at the apex that replace the pappus found on many **Asteraceae** species.

This species is recognized by its nearly sessile yellow 2- to 4-dentate ray florets and the dimorphic seeds, the outer ones flattened with winged margins and the central triangular one with rigid bristles at the tip.

HABITAT, DISTRIBUTION, AND BIOLOGY

S. nodiflora is adapted to many environments. It is particularly well adapted to the partial shade found under jute and plantation crops like tea, coffee, bananas, cacao, and rubber. Plants appear in moist soil and along roads and foot trails. It occurs not only in the Americas where it originated, but also in China, Australia, the Caribbean, India, Indonesia, the Philippines, and in several African countries (Figure 93-1).

S. nodiflora can complete its life cycle in 130 to 150 days in Brazil (Lorenzi 1982) and often has two generations annually in Nigeria (Komolafe 1976). Plants often appear soon after annual crops are seeded, are most abundant in moist, shaded areas and are prolific seed producers. This species was described by Adams and Baker (1962) as an example of a plant with "extreme plasticity in the face of variations of water supply" under Ghanian conditions.

Banerji and Pal (1959) conducted an intensive cytological study of *S. nodiflora* and found the $2n$ chromosome number to be 40. They give a detailed description of pollination and early reproductive development. Both the ray (outer) and disc (inner) florets produce viable seeds with well-developed embryos. A single plant can produce 6330 seeds, and 1 gm of seed contains approximately 1400 seeds (Pancho 1964). Seeds are spread by wind, water and animals. The form of dispersal varies between the disc and ray seeds. Seeds from the disc florets have two or three short bristles, are considerably lighter, and detach from the inflorescence earlier than seeds from the ray florets, which often lack dispersal structures (van der Pijl 1969). Also, the seeds produced by ray florets are dormant for several months (unless the seed coat is removed), while those produced by disc florets will germinate as soon as they are formed (Purseglove 1965). *S. nodiflora* seeds germinate well in both continuous light or dark conditions (van Rooden et al. 1970). However, disc seeds germinate in a wider range of conditions than ray seeds and this allows the species to occupy a wider range of niches than if both behaved similarly (Marks and Akosim 1984). For example, seeds from ray florets germinate similarly in a wide range of shades but those from disc florets germinate better as the level of shade increases.

Seeds buried to 15 cm in the soil survived 1 yr in the Philippines (Juliano 1940). Sampling done in a field where maize had been grown for 8 yr in Belize found 5700 viable *S. nodiflora* seeds/m^2 to a 10-cm depth (Kellman 1978). Most seeds were near the surface. Of the 23 species encountered, *S. nodiflora* seed was the fourth most abundant species in the soil reservoir. Similar soil samples taken from a permanent pasture detected only 100 *S. nodiflora* seeds/m^2.

Oladokun (1978) did an intraspecific competition trial in Nigeria in which populations of 5, 10, 15, 20, and 25 plants were grown for 7 wk in pots with 1 kg of soil each. He observed a large drop in root and shoot dry weight per plant from 5 to 10 plants/pot and then a gradual decrease in weights at higher densities. The number of nodes and leaves per plant decreased linearly as density increased, while internode length increased. These responses were similar for plants originating from seeds of ray and disc florets. Thus any ecological or biological advantages of dimorphism appear to lie with the dispersal and germination of this species and not in its growth and reproduction.

AGRICULTURAL IMPORTANCE

S. nodiflora is reported as a weed in over 28 crops in 50 countries (Figure 93-1) and is frequently reported as a weed of tropical plantation crops, maize and upland rice. It is a principal or serious weed of cassava in Nigeria; cacao in Ghana and Solomon Islands; coconut in Trinidad; maize in Colombia; pastures in Nigeria and the Philippines; taro in Samoa; and tea in Taiwan.

It is a common weed of edible beans and soybeans in Brazil; cacao and sorghum in Dominican Republic; cotton in Peru, the Philippines, and Tanzania; maize in Bangladesh, Dominican Republic, and Peru; upland rice in the Philippines; roselle in India; sugarcane in Bangladesh, Peru, the Philippines, and Zaire; taro in Samoa; tea in India; tomatoes in Ghana; and vegetables in Australia.

S. nodiflora is also an unranked weed in abaca, peanuts, and pineapple in the Philippines; bananas in Costa Rica, Honduras, Samoa, and Taiwan; cacao, coffee, cotton, edible beans, maize, orchards, sorghum, sugarcane, tobacco, and vegetables in Honduras; cassava in Nigeria and Taiwan; coconut in the Philippines and Samoa; cacao in Brazil and Nigeria; coffee in Dominican Republic, Nicaragua, Nigeria, and Zaire; cowpeas and nurseries in Nigeria; jute in India; maize in Cambodia, Indonesia, Laos, Nicaragua, Nigeria, the Philippines, and Vietnam; oil palm in Indonesia and Sabah; orchards in Australia and Taiwan; pastures in Australia; peanuts in the Philippines and Taiwan; lowland rice in Taiwan; upland rice in India, Indonesia, Nigeria, and Taiwan; rubber and tea in Indonesia; soybeans in Nigeria and the Philippines; sweet potatoes in New Guinea; sugarcane in India and the Philippines; tomatoes in Costa Rica; and vegetables in the Philippines, Samoa, and Venezuela.

No studies on the interference caused by this species were found, but its wide distribution in many annual and perennial crops of the tropics attests to its importance. It has been described as one of Trinidad's worst introduced weeds. *S. nodiflora* is a host to the root-knot nematode (Godfrey 1935). On the other hand, young leaves of this plant are sometimes used as "lalab," a side dish with rice in Java (Uphof 1968) and for medicinal purposes in Colombia (Gomez and Rivera 1987) and New Guinea (Holdsworth 1980).

COMMON NAMES

Synedrella nodiflora

BARBADOS	porter bush
BRAZIL	barbatana, botao de ouro, vassourinha
COLOMBIA	cerbatana, flor amarilla, venturosa
CUBA	cerbatana, espinillo
DOMINICAN REPUBLIC	selvatana
HAWAII	nodeweed, synedrella
HONDURAS	flor amarilla, guacara
INDONESIA	babadotan, dijotang kuda, gletangan, srunen
JAPAN	fushizakiso
MALAYSIA	rumput babi
NIGERIA	aworo ona
PHILIPPINES	fantakuen, tuhod-manok
PUERTO RICO	cerbatana, sarbatana, scerbatana
TAIWAN	fushizaki-so
THAILAND	phak-khral
TRINIDAD	fatten barrow, porter bush
UNITED STATES	synedrella
VIETNAM	bo xit

Ninety-Four

Tagetes minuta L.

Asteraceae (Compositae), Aster Family

T AGETES MINUTA is an herbaceous weed prevalent in over 35 countries. It is native to South America and is well known for the strong odor that arises from oil glands on its leaves. The oil has been studied for its pharmaceutical, nematicidal and insecticidal properties. The genus name refers to the Latin name for marigold, "Tages," an Etruscan god (grandson of Jupiter) who sprang from the earth as a boy and taught the Etruscan people the art of plowing. The species name refers to the small flowers and not to the plant size.

FIGURE 94-1   The distribution of *Tagetes minuta* L. across the world where it has been reported as a weed.

FIGURE 94-2   *Tagetes minuta* L.: 1. root system; 2. flowering branch; 3. involucre, opened with glandular dots; 4. flower, partly opened; 5. flower head, opened; 6. node; 7. disc flower.

DESCRIPTION

T. minuta (Figure 94-2) is a strongly aromatic *annual* herb, growing to 120 cm or more tall; *stems* with longitudinal channels or grooves, branching in large plants, pale brownish to reddish; *leaves* cauline, to 20 cm long, opposite on the main stem but often alternate on the branches of the inflorescence, deeply pinnafid with 9 to 17 finely serrated lobes; lobes lanceolate to narrowly elliptic, up to 5 cm long, 5 mm wide, dark green; sunken oil glands scattered especially along edges of leaves and on either side of the central vein of each lobe; *inflorescence* composed of terminal, cylindrical, narrow, shortly stalked flower heads, up to 12 mm long, 2 mm wide; in congested corymbs; containing 4 florets; *florets* 2 yellow tubular or disc and 2 cream ligulate or ray; *involucral bracts* joined with five short lobes above, smooth; *fruit* an *achene*, black, 5 to 8 mm long, .6 mm wide, spindle-shaped, flattened, sparsely covered with short brown hairs; apex with 4 pointed scales, one longer than the others; *pappus* a few awn-like bristles of various lengths.

The distinguishing characteristics of this weed are the grooved stems, its strong aromatic scent, deeply divided leaves and the variable length of bristles in the pappus.

HABITAT AND BIOLOGY

T. minuta is found in many tropical and subtropical environments (Figure 94-1). It has been grown as an ornamental in several countries. After many years of such use in Israel, it became a serious weed in the Golan Heights area in the early 1970s (Dafni and Heller 1982). The authors theorize that a "lag" phase of 10 to 30 yr after introduction is necessary for an adventive species to attain a certain level of propagules and initiate a rapid dissemination period. The intensive use of herbicides in orchards may also have created a niche for *T. minuta* in Israel.

It is prevalent in East and South Africa and can reach dense populations after a fire or when forests are cut and burned (Ivens 1967). Plants are abundant at high and low altitudes, and in high or low rainfall conditions (Popay and Ivens 1982). In an ecological study in South Africa, Altona (1972) imposed 12 yr of fallowing in a field that had produced maize for 50 yr. During the fallowing period, levels of zero, low, or high fertilizer rates were applied. *T. minuta* was one of the predominant species in the field when maize was grown, but it completely disappeared under the fallowing system with zero or low fertilizer levels. At the high fertility level but with no crop or tillage, *T. minuta* persisted as a dominant species. *T. minuta* grows in soils with *p*Hs from 4.3 to 6.6 and often responds to P fertilization, especially if the mycorrhizal fungus *Glomus macrocarpus* is present (Graw 1979).

Seeds of *T. minuta* achieve maximum germination at 25°C in the light but none germinate at 10 or 35°C, even when in the light (Forsyth and van Staden 1983). One-fourth of the seeds germinated at 25°C in darkness. Over 80% of the seeds that failed to germinate at 20°C in the light sprouted when placed at 25°C. Thus the optimal germination temperature range is narrow.

Interestingly, seeds imbibed at 35°C show accelerated germination when placed at 25°C (Drennan and van Staden 1989). This effect is maximized with 24 hr of imbibition at 35°C, and these seeds can be desiccated and stored up to 30 days before the accelerated germination response is lost. Seeds that have been imbibed at 35°C in the light, desiccated in the light, and then reimbibed at 25°C in darkness germinated completely in light or dark conditions.

Seeds survive many environmental conditions, but only those near the soil surface germinate. Over 60% of the seeds on the surface can germinate, while most that are 6 mm or deeper remain dormant (Hocombe 1961, Soriano et al. 1963a). Even seeds on the surface under shaded conditions are unlikely to germinate (Fenner 1980). Alternating temperatures, soaking in water, and acid or mechanical scarification increase seed germination (Green 1963, Huxley and Turk 1966). Seeds have no after-ripening requirement and are capable of underwater germination, especially if the water is aerated (Soriano et al. 1963b). Under controlled conditions, plants receiving 13 hr of light flower the quickest (Luciani-Gresta 1975). At low temperatures (20°C) and low light intensities (1200 to 2400 lux), *only* plants receiving 13 hr of light flowered. No flowering was observed with photoperiods of 16 hr or longer.

When grown outdoors in eastern Sicily, *T. minuta* flowered in July. In Zimbabwe, 20 plants produced an average of 29,100 seeds each. Germination of fresh seed was as high as 95% (Schwerzel 1967).

POTENTIAL USES

The strong odor of *T. minuta* may have suggested that this plant had possible medicinal or insecticidal properties. Plants contain a volatile oil that has been examined for many uses. An extensive review of the uses of *T. minuta* (and other *Tagetes* species) by Neher (1968) notes that it has been used as a relish, laxative, diuretic, flavoring, insect repellent, stimulant and snuff. The juice may be irritating to the skin and it reportedly kills maggots found in flesh wounds. It has been used in Brazil for coughs, stomach cramps and rheumatism (Lorenzi 1982). The plant is used in parts of Peru as a vegetable called "huacatay." It is among the group of vegetables with the highest levels of vitamin C (Lopez and Olivera 1970) and is grown as a crop in South Africa, where it provides a source of essential oils for the perfume industry (Drennan and van Staden 1989).

Pharmacological studies in India determined that the LD_{50} of the oil was 450 mg/kg when injected into rats (Chandhoke and Ghatak 1969). At non-lethal doses, the oil has a tranquilizing effect, checks electrically induced convulsions, causes a drop in body temperature, and demonstrates anti-inflammatory and hypotensive properties. Ickes et al. (1973) in the United States identified several organic compounds in flowering *T. minuta* plants that reduce the formation of lung tumors.

In East Africa, Okoth (1973) examined the insecticidal properties of this species. It repelled some ants and killed others. The flowers, and to a lesser degree the leaves, were toxic to adult mosquitoes when they were in close proximity to but not touching the plant. Not all species of mosquito were killed but all were repelled by the plants. Researchers in India report *T. minuta* to be only the second angiosperm with significant juvenile hormone activity. This is very important since it could be easily cultivated as a crop (Saxena and Srivastava 1973). The steam distillate of plants in full bloom applied to nymph wing pods of the cotton stainer bug (*Dysdercus koenigii*) prevented their developing to the adult stage. However, the eggs and larvae of *Aedes* mosquitoes or house flies were not affected. *T. minuta* produces more oil than other *Tagetes* species and the most active juvenile hormone fraction was identified as "tagetone." Maradufu et al. (1978) identified the insecticidal component for ants and mosquitoes to be (5E)-ocimenone, which has been synthesized in the laboratory. In the United States, Jacobson et al. (1975) extracted compounds from *T. minuta* stems, leaves and flowers that killed milkweed bug (*Oncopeltus fasciatus*) nymphs, but the roots had no effect.

Scientists in several countries have studied the impact of *Tagetes* on nematode infestations. Soybean yields in Colombia doubled when *T. minuta* was grown before planting, as compared to soybeans following other crops. Five genera of nematodes were affected, but the greatest reduction occurred with *Pratylenchus* (Yoshii and Varon de Agudelo 1977). In the southern United States, Good et al. (1965) planted *T. minuta* in late summer in a nematode-infested field and chopped it before viable seeds were produced to prevent volunteer growth as a weed the next year. Tomatoes were planted and, of the seven plant species tested, *T. minuta* reduced the nematode population the most and gave the highest number of marketable tomatoes. This plant affected seven of the nine nematode species in the field.

Greenhouse studies with *T. minuta* in Zimbabwe have also shown dramatic effects on nematodes (Daulton and Curtis 1964). Several cropping systems were tested and plants in each system were grown for 35 days. Tomato roots were examined for root-knot infection after the third planting. Three consecutive crops of tomatoes gave the highest index of infection (74). Two 35-day plantings of *T. minuta* followed by tomato had the lowest index (0.6). Two 35-day fallow periods before planting tomatoes gave an intermediate infection level (32). *T. minuta* was a more effective nematicide than *T. erecta* or *T. patula*; all three species prevented the nematode *Meloedogyhe javoneca* from developing beyond the second larval stage. However, under field conditions, growing *T. minuta* three seasons failed to protect tobacco from this nematode species (Shepherd 1969).

Similar results were encountered in Japan (Toida 1972). Water extracts of leaves, roots and stems of *T. minuta* inhibited the hatching of *Meloidogyne* sp. and 2-day immersions killed the second-stage larvae. However, mulberries planted with *T. minuta* in the field were not protected from root gall damage.

Thus the nematicidal effects vary among crop and nematode species under field conditions. Also, the composition of the oil, and certainly other plant components, varies with environmental conditions and the stage of plant maturity, especially before and after flowering (Villiers et al. 1971).

AGRICULTURAL IMPORTANCE

T. minuta is a weed of 19 crops in 35 countries (Figure 94-1) and is especially common in Africa, where it is a frequently reported weed of maize. It is a serious or principal weed of edible beans in Kenya and South Africa; cotton in Brazil and Swaziland; maize in Argentina, Guatemala, South Africa, Uruguay, and Zambia; pastures in Australia, Brazil, Hawaii, and Zimbabwe; potatoes in Zimbabwe; pyrethrum in Kenya and Tanzania; sorghum and soybeans in South Africa; sunflowers in Argentina; vegetables in Brazil and South Africa; wheat in Guatemala and South Africa; and wastelands in Brazil.

It is a common weed of barley in Peru; edible beans in Tanzania; maize in Kenya, Peru, Tanzania, and Zimbabwe; orchards in Bolivia, Brazil, and South Africa; peas in Venezuela; pineapple in Swaziland; soybeans in Argentina and Brazil; sugarcane and vineyards in South Africa; and wheat in Kenya and Peru.

T. minuta is also an unranked weed of edible beans and potatoes in Brazil; coffee in Kenya; cotton in Kenya, Paraguay, and Tanzania; maize in Angola, Belize, India, Natal, and Paraguay; peanuts in Australia, Natal, South Africa, and Tanzania; rice in India; sorghum in Zambia; soybeans in Colombia; sugarcane in Argentina, Australia, and Natal; vegetables in Australia; vineyards in Argentina and the former Yugoslavia; and wheat in Angola and Tanzania.

As noted, *T. minuta* can be a weed in many crops. In some parts of East Africa, it is found in 10% of the maize fields and can completely dominate short-statured crops like beans if uncontrolled. Late-season infestations can seriously impede crop harvest. If consumed by lactating animals, it imparts an objectionable flavor to milk, but it is seldom eaten if other forages are available (Whittet 1968). However, the oil on leaves can adhere to udders and flavor the milk in this manner.

T. minuta seed can be transported as a contaminant of crop seed. In Kenya, 44% of the wheat samples examined contained *T. minuta* seed, and it was the fourth most important species. Contaminants occurred as single achenes or as involucres with seeds and were not easily separated from the grain (Bogdan 1965).

The same author also examined forage seeds (Bogdan 1966) and found 75% of the Rhodes grass (*Chloris gayana*) samples were contaminated with *T. minuta* seeds. Cleaning procedures only removed 5% of the weed seed. Rhodes grass has two awns and a short, hairy seed and the light weight seeds of this weed readily adhere to it. *T. minuta* also contaminated seed lots of the grasses *Setaria sphacelata* and *Melinis multiflora.*

In South Africa, a polyacetylene derivative in the roots of *T. minuta* is allelopathic to crops (Meissner et al. 1986). Aqueous extracts of soil where the weed grew delayed germination of several vegetables, maize, and sunflower. Dry weight and height of crops planted in soil previously infested with the weed were greatly reduced. Polyacetylenes also cause photosensitization in humans and in some animals.

While most of the effects of *T. minuta* on other pests are beneficial, it can host the bean fungus (*Ascochyta phaseolorum*) under natural conditions in Australia (Alcorn 1968).

COMMON NAMES

Tagetes minuta

ANGOLA	ekiabulo
ARGENTINA	chil chil, chinchilla, Margarita, suique
AUSTRALIA	stinking Roger
BRAZIL	chinchila, coora, cravo de defunto, rabo de rajao
CHILE	quinchihue
HAWAII	stinkweed, wild marigold
MADAGASCAR	mavoadala
MALAWI	khaki
NATAL	khali weed
NEW ZEALAND	Mexican marigold
PARAGUAY	agosto, suico
RHODESIA	mbanda, Mexican marigold, stinking Roger
SOUTH AFRICA	lang kakiebos, tall khaki weed
UNITED STATES	wild marigold
ZAMBIA	Mexican marigold, mutanda zyeelo

Ninety-Five

Taraxacum officinale Weber

Asteraceae (Compositae), Aster Family

T ARAXACUM OFFICINALE is distributed in almost every temperate and subtropical region of the world. It is especially adapted to pastures, lawns, orchards, hay fields, roadsides and other areas of permanent vegetation with occasional disturbance. The bright yellow flowers herald the arrival of spring and, soon after flowering, the lightweight seeds float away in the wind. Fifty to 60 species of *Taraxacum* are known (Mitich 1989). The Romans, Celts and Gauls ate *T. officinale* and the plant has many potential benefits.

The genus name is from the Greek *tarassen*, for disorder or confusion, or more likely, a Latinization of the Persian "tarashqun," for bitter potherb (Mitich 1989). The Latin name

FIGURE 95-1   The distribution of *Taraxacum officinale* Weber across the world where it has been reported as a weed.

FIGURE 95-2 *Taraxacum officinale* WebeB: A. habit; B. flower; C. achenes; D. achenes with pappus.

of the species implies that it has long been useful to humans: *officinale* means "official" or "sold in shops." The large tooth-like leaf lobes give rise to the name in English of dandelion, which is a corruption of the French name "dent de lion" or "lion's tooth."

DESCRIPTION

T. officinale (Figure 95-2) is an almost stemless, lactiferous, deeply rooted *perennial* herb; *taproot* thick, branched, deep; *stems* acaulescent, 1 to 2.5 cm, internodes extremely short, at or below soil surface; *leaves* in radial rosettes, usually pubescent, 5 to 25 cm long, highly variable in shape from lobeless to toothed edges to highly incised; if lobed, the lobes point to the leaf base that narrows into a short, hollow *petiole*; every sixth leaf overlaps in the rosette; *inflorescence* involucrate flower head resembling a single flower, 2 to 5 cm in diameter, terminal, solitary on 5 to 45 cm long, hollow, cylindrical, unbranched, glabrous *peduncle* or scape, each head or capitulum a composite of 50 to 250 small bright yellow ligulate or ray florets; *involucre* oval-cylindrical with lanceolate, obtuse, herbaceous bracts, green to brownish, the inner ones of uniform length and 1-serrate, the outer ones unequal, one-third to one-half as long as the inner bracts and many-seriate; all bracts reflexed at maturity; *receptacle* convex, minutely pitted, without paleae; *florets* perfect, irregular, all ray florets, *corolla* of 5 united *petals* with one side prolonged, strap-shaped, golden yellow, 5-notched at the tip; *anthers* 5, fused into tube with sagittate base, filiform basal lobes and obtuse apex; *style* fuzzy beneath point of dividing into 2 *stigmas*; *fruit* a dry, indehiscent *achene* narrowly obovoid-oblong, 3 to 4 mm long, 1 mm wide, 5- to 8-ribbed on each side with upwardly pointed teeth at apex, light brown, apex beaked, topped by pappus; *pappus* composed of numerous hairs, 3 to 4 mm long, mostly white, persistent and connate at the base, forming a short ring.

The sticky, white juice throughout the plant, lobed leaves, hollow naked flower stalk, strap-shaped brilliant yellow ray flowers and white seed heads are the distinguishing characteristics of this species.

HABITAT AND DISTRIBUTION

T. officinale probably originated in Europe and is now found in most countries of the world (Figure 95-1). It is found from near sea level to the mountainous regions in temperate climates and in the higher elevations of tropical countries. It is present in the subantarctic region of the Southern Hemisphere (Walton 1975) and in the arctic tundra area of Russia where farming was attempted. It is one of the most widely distributed weeds of Europe, North America, and Asia.

Plants thrive in hay fields, pastures, lawns, roadsides, and waste areas. However, if left totally undisturbed, densities decline. In farming systems of zero or reduced tillage, *T. officinale* can occur as a weed of field crops or vegetables. It occurs in regions that range from 90 to 2780 mm annual precipitation, from 4.3 to 26.6°C mean temperature, and with soil pH from 4.2 to 8.2 (Duke 1979). Native species of *Taraxacum* occur on all five continents. Richards (1973) suggests that the genus may have reached South America before the continents separated. He traces the evolution of the genus and discusses the cytology, embryology, hybridization, and origin of many of the species in the 32 sections of *Taraxacum*. A later paper reviews the taxonomy of the genus (Hughes and Richards 1989).

Enzyme electrophoretic analysis of 518 plants from 22 *T. officinale* populations revealed 21 distinct allozyme phenotypes in the United States (Lyman and Ellstrand 1984). The only morphological trait linked to specific enzymes was seed color and seven color classes were identified. Based on both allozyme patterns and seed color, 47 clones were detected, which reflects high genotypic diversity both within and among populations. This diversity is probably due to multiple genotype introductions into the United States from Europe.

ECOLOGY

T. officinale is highly adapted to many ecological niches and its growth and reproduction strategies vary among biotypes and with environmental conditions. For example, three morphologically distinct biotypes were collected near Leningrad and planted in the field with 3 or 18 cm between plants in pure or mixed populations. Two years later the number of survivors of each biotype was determined. In pure stands and low densities, 69% of biotype B survived, while 90% of biotype C survived; at high densities, the proportions were reversed: 49% of biotype B survived, while only 24% of biotype C survived. In mixed populations, biotype B was the poorest survivor, while biotype C was the best at both densities. Biotype A was always intermediate to the others. Differences in flowering were also noted. In mixed stands, biotype C produced the most flowers per plant but in pure stands the least (Dobzhansky 1951).

Solbrig and Simpson (1974, 1977) conducted similar studies with four *T. officinale* biotypes in the north-central United States. Isozyme analyses detected four biotypes from three distinct sites in close proximity to each other. Biotypes A, B, and D were most abundant in a specific site, while biotype C was uniformly distributed across all three. Additional competition studies with biotypes A and D were conducted. Whether grown together or separately, biotype A produced more seeds per plant than biotype D (3.3 vs. 1.2 heads/plant/season, respectively). Biotype A had a much higher percentage of flowering plants but biotype D yielded more seeds per head; overall, biotype A produced five times more seed than biotype D, and the researchers speculated that biotype A would predominate in disturbed environments and biotype D in undisturbed conditions. Field studies conducted over 4 yr with pure and mixed stands of biotypes A and D in disturbed and undisturbed conditions confirmed their hypothesis. In the mixed population, 92% of the plants in the disturbed site were biotype A and 84% of those in the nondisturbed site were biotype D. They define biotype A as an r-strategist (invests much energy in seed production) and biotype D as a K-strategist (places more energy in vegetative reproduction). Biotypes B and C were intermediate to A and D.

The ability of *T. officinale* to become established varies not only with biotype but also with management practices and weather. In Canada, Darwent and Elliott (1979) measured *T. officinale* establishment and growth in seven forage grasses over 3 yr in two experiments. The poorest competitor was Russian wild ryegrass (*Elymus junceus*). Weed growth in the other forage grasses was only affected by row spacing, with the most growth in the wider rows. Spacings of 30 cm or less were necessary to reduce the population below 75 plants/m^2 after 3 yr. In general, the density of *T. officinale* increased consistently once the forage was seeded, but varied with weather conditions from year to year.

In grasslands, cutting height and frequency also influence *T. officinale* growth and establishment. In Denmark, Molgaard (1977) clipped grass at 2, 5, 10, 20, and 30 cm on a weekly basis or twice a year at 5 cm for 4 yr on both a clay and a loam soil. In general, the taller the grass, the more difficult the establishment of *T. officinale*. The infestation rate was similar between soil types and was fairly constant from year to year. However, when conditions are right, a population explosion occurs. These conditions are short grass, a moist soil and light. Open soil alone is not sufficient for establishment. The uncut plot had some open areas but these received less than 2% of the available sunlight at the soil surface.

Very few plants become established if the grass is never cut. Two clippings per year allow some plants to establish and results in large plants. This practice is common in pastures and along roadsides and helps maintain the weed population. A few plants clipped at 2 cm produce flowers. Plants in closely mowed areas (lawns) show an r-strategist tendency, while those mowed higher and less frequently exhibit the K-strategist response. This hypothesis is supported by observations in New Zealand that in uncut grasslands *T. officinale* does not flower (Struik 1967).

The establishment, longevity and reproductive strategies of this plant in Wales varies with the site (Ford 1981a,b). Frequent changes in the individual plants occurred in lowland meadows and upland pastures. Densities ranged from 13 to 84 plants/m^2 and a complete population turnover occurred in 16 yr in the pasture and 20 yr in the meadow. The survival potential of plants in the upland pasture was similar for flowering and nonflowering plants, but in the lowland meadow, more flowering plants survived. At the latter site, 13% of the roots had multiple rosettes; none were observed at the upland site. Plants at the lowland site had a 30-fold advantage in total seed production over those in the upland pasture. However, the probability of a seed producing a seedling was 23 times greater (0.014 vs. 0.0006) for the upland than the lowland site. In the final analysis, differences in plant survival, seed production and establishment ratios all interact to give stable populations in both environments.

Ford's second study (1981b) compared the growth and reproductive strategies of ten biotypes in three environments: an unweeded roadside, a bare roadside and an upland pasture. *T. officinale* plants in the unweeded roadside produced 30 times more seeds per plant than those in the pasture, and plants in the bare roadside area produced 50% more seeds per plant than those in the unweeded area. Biotypes reacted differently to the grasses present in the pasture and had a shorter half-life than those in roadside environments due to grazing by cattle and sheep. Plants varied considerably in growth and reproductive characteristics between biotypes and sites, suggesting that the r and K values are dependent upon both factors.

Fertilization practices also influence *T. officinale* populations. Turner et al. (1979) applied several rates of P, K, and limestone for 3 yr to a bluegrass turf free of *T. officinale* and monitored the weed encroachment for 3 yr after the last fertilization. As the P rate increased from 0 to 85, 170, 340, and 680 kg of P$_2$O$_5$/ha, *T. officinale* densities decreased linearly from 11 to 6/m^2. In contrast, increasing K and limestone levels enhanced *T. officinale* encroachment. The most dramatic effect was caused by limestone applications; populations were 4.6 plants/m^2 in the nontreated areas and 12.3/m^2 when 5400 kg/ha were applied for 3 yr. Greenhouse research found that *T. officinale* grew better as soil *pH* increased from 4.5 to 8 (Welton and Carroll 1941). In the field, a soil with a 7.1 *pH* produced 45% more fresh weight per plant and had 67% more plants than a soil with a *pH* of 6.2. However, this species tolerates very acidic soils, as illustrated by the fact that in Japan plants grow in soils with a *pH* as low as 4 (Sawada et al. 1982).

Other researchers have studied the effects of *pH* and P on *T. officinale* growth and found that plants receiving P had higher dry weights and longer leaves than the controls (Zaprzalka and Peters 1982). The response to increasing *pH* (from 4.7 to 6.7) was significant but relatively small in comparison to the effect of P. Plant growth was reduced by more than 20% and the roots were brown, with discolored tips and few branch roots, when the Al level in soil increased from 2 to 8 ppm (Gilbert and Pember 1935). Thus they classified this species as sensitive to aluminum in the soil.

Interestingly, *T. officinale* is not greatly affected by N levels. Plants grown alone in the greenhouse did not respond to N application (Zaprzalka and Peters 1982), while those in a grass pasture in Czechoslovakia were favored by 120 kg N/ha (Kasper 1980). Applying 480 kg N/ha nearly eliminated *T. officinale* by greatly increasing the grass growth.

The use of N fertilizer in lawns is recommended to maintain a competitive, dense turf to reduce the opportunity for *T. officinale* establishment. Before the advent of phenoxy herbicides for broadleaf weed control in lawns, repeated applications of ammonium sulfate were suggested to kill *T. officinale* (Welton and Carroll 1941). The best method was to apply 7.4 kg/100 m² every other week for 4 to 5 mo when the foliage was wet. The fertilizer caused serious burn to the weed leaves without affecting the grasses. This necessitates more frequent mowings and may increase the infestation of annual *Digitaria* species in the lawn.

T. officinale can be found from near sea level in Europe and other regions to 6000 m in India. Habovstiak and Javorkova (1977) in Czechoslovakia measured the effect of altitude on growth and development of this weed. Between 350 and 1000 m above sea level, initial growth of *T. officinale* is delayed 5.5 days for each 100 m increase in altitude. However, elevation had a smaller effect (2.7 days/100 m) on the later stages of development. Plants flowered at soil temperatures of 16.3°C at 350 m and 12.7°C at 1000 m, which shows how they have adapted to each environment. The authors observed that the optimum date for pasture grazing or harvesting at a given elevation coincides with the appearance of the first *T. officinale* flowers.

There are 20 indigenous species of *Taraxacum* in Japan. *T. officinale* is now a naturalized species and is spreading rapidly, especially in urban areas. The introduced species can give rise to 15 times as many seedlings as native species in urban areas (Ogawa 1978). It is also invading apple orchards and often dominates the native species *T. hondonense* (Sawada et al. 1982). They measured dandelions beneath apple trees. The density increased as they went from the center to the edge of apple trees. Light increased from 30 to 50% of the total possible at the center of the trees to 60 to 80% near the edge. Not surprisingly, the number of seedlings per unit area decreased as the number of established plants rose. After mowing the orchard, leaves contain 16% of the *T. officinale* biomass. Forty days later, this increased to 35 to 60% of the total plant weight and was a much more rapid regrowth than observed in *T. hondonense*.

Changes in natural animal populations can influence *T. officinale* stands. Ellison and Aldous (1952) studied the impact of pocket gophers on vegetation in Utah, in the United States. Over an 8-yr period, gophers reduced the foliage dry weight of *T. officinale* ten-fold. This plant is one of the favorite foods of gophers and dried taproots are often the principal food stored in their den. If gophers were excluded from prairie sites, foliage biomass of the weed increased 50% over 8 yr.

BIOLOGY

The biology of *T. officinale* has been investigated around the world, reflecting its global importance. The roots are primarily composed of secondary tissue produced by the vascular cambium (Khan 1973). This results in more phloem than xylem tissue, which is important, because the plant accumulates and stores high levels of carbohydrates in the roots. Latex tubes run parallel to the sieve elements and are arranged in concentric circles. Some researchers have used these rings to estimate the age of *T. officinale* plants, but this is not an accurate method (Ford 1981a). New roots arise from meristems in the pericycle and the conducting tissue of new shoots is rapidly connected to the woody root cylinder (Korsmo 1954). Lateral roots are arranged in two rows that wind clockwise down the root in a loose spiral fashion, and are more or less evenly distributed along the entire root (Gier and Burress 1942).

The species can regenerate from root fragments as well as from seeds. In Canada, roots below the crown were up to 3 cm in diameter and penetrated to 2 m deep (Mann and Cavers 1979). Studies on root regeneration in the field found that roots cut in May and September had the lowest regeneration percentage (20%) and those cut from June through August the highest (65%). Fragments from 1-yr-old plants regenerated slightly less successfully than older plants, and fragments that were placed in their normal upright position regenerated better than those that were inverted. Fragments from the upper part of the root survived better than those from lower sections, but the entire root is capable of regeneration and sections from similar regions of flowering and nonflowering plants regenerated equally well. Fragments left on the surface had the lowest survival rate and 4 days in the sun will kill them (Ravn 1964).

Segments 1.5 mm in length produced shoots but no roots. Segments 2 mm or longer formed both roots and shoots. Shoots were visible 9 days and roots 21 days after cutting. Occasionally, shoots developed without roots but never the reverse (Khan 1969). The initial processes of cell division begin at the same time at each end of a cut root segment. After 48 hr, meristem formation begins at the proximal end; at the distal end, isolated pockets of dividing cells continue forming, but root primordia are found in the callus tissue at some distance from the xylem nodule (Khan 1973). Peroxidase levels peaked 12 hr after cutting and were equal at both ends of the fragment (Khan 1972). Khan (1975) also studied the effect of the carbon and nitrogen sources on *T. officinale* regeneration from callus tissue and found that sucrose had little effect on either leaf or root regeneration, while KNO_3 enhanced the regeneration of both tissues. He describes a technique for successfully tissue culturing this species.

Welton and Carroll (1941) removed the top 5.0, 7.6, 10.0, and 12.7 cm of the root from established *T. officinale* plants in a lawn at several times during the season. Removing 10 cm of the root in the spring when reserves were the lowest gave 90% plant kill but only a 21% kill in the fall. Plants that were not killed sent up eight or more shoots from the remaining root system.

The growing point of seedling plants is 10 mm above the soil surface, but within a few weeks it is at the surface and, by autumn, it is 2 to 3 cm below the surface (Keil 1940). Five types of *T. officinale* roots were found in Germany that were related to differences between soils and plants from site to site.

More detailed attention has been given to the variations in leaf morphology than any other part of the plant. In general, the leaves are arranged spirally around the 1- to 2.5-cm-long stem. The internodes are extremely short and occur at or below the soil surface. Every sixth leaf overlaps and the largest leaves are the lowest ones on the plant. Stomata are present on both surfaces (Korsmo 1954). Chloroplasts have large, dense inclusion bodies that may store protein (Martin and Larbalestier 1977). Leaves formed in sunlight are thicker and greener than those growing in shade (Gier and Burress 1942).

Sanchez (1967, 1971) studied the factors that influenced leaf morphology in *T. officinale*. Rounded and toothed leaves can be found on the same plant. More rounded leaves are formed when plants receive less than 42 cal solar energy/cm²/day. The total energy received and not the photoperiod determines leaf shape. At high energy levels, red and blue light produced plants with dissected leaves; far-red, light or dark conditions yielded round leaves. Twenty minutes of red light were sufficient to reverse the effect of far-red light and produce incised leaves. At low light intensities, all colors resulted in the formation of rounded leaves. He also noted that once a leaf is 15 mm long, the shape cannot be changed, and far-red light increases the leaf length more than its width. This effect could also be reversed by giving plants red light. Plants collected from two regions of Poland varied in leaf size and the degree of leaf incisions (Listowski and Jackowska 1965). Thus biotype and environment influence leaf shape, and morphological variations within populations can be as great as those between populations (Taylor 1987).

Gibberellic acid (GA) retards leaf senescence in any season but is less effective in the winter and spring (Fletcher and Osborne 1966). Fletcher et al. (1969) also noted a drop in GA levels when *T. officinale* flowered and formed seed. At this time, the mature leaves also senesced and then new leaves with high levels of GA appeared. They conclude that leaf senescence is associated with a GA deficiency in older leaves.

T. officinale is a C_3 plant and has its maximum photosynthetic efficiency of 20.8 mg CO_2/dm²/h at 20°C. Plants have a linear photorespiration and dark respiration response between 10 to 30°C and 10 to 40°C, respectively, and a transpiration rate at 20°C of 3.2 g H_2O/dm²/h. Plants collected from 1630, 2375, and 3475 m above sea level in Colorado, in the United States, were similar in photosynthetic efficiency, transpiration, and gas exchange rates. Thus, the species has a broad optimum temperature range for photosynthesis and shows no signs of altitudinal adaptation that contributes to its establishment and productivity in thermally diverse sites (Kemp et al. 1977).

In the eastern United States, Bunce (1981) noted differences in photosynthetic rates between ecotypes of *T. officinale*. In non-stressed conditions, a cultivated variety had the highest rate, followed by the ecotype from an abandoned field, one from a meadow and finally the one from a cultivated field. Interestingly, the order of efficiency was reversed when plants were exposed to moisture stress. The ecotype from the cultivated field had the driest environment and thus reflects its adaptation to this condition.

T. officinale produces a long-chain insoluble sugar known as inulin (Rutherford and Weston 1968). The inulin content of stored roots dropped from 10.5% in freshly harvested roots to 6.3% in 4 wk and 2.0% after 14 wk in storage. The percentage of soluble sugars increased from 3.1 to 7.4% during the 14-wk period. *T. officinale* was one of the first plants used to determine the mode of action of 2,4-D. After treatment, plants exhibited increased rates of respiration and reducing sugar levels and lower levels of sucrose, dextrin and levulin (Rasmussen 1947).

In Russia, the phyllosphere (above-ground portion of the plant) fixed 0.33 mg N_2/m² of leaf surface/hr at three times during the year (Sadykov and Umarov 1980). This was one of the highest rates of N fixation measured among the plants in 13 families that were tested. The authors attribute the fixation to epiphytic microorganisms present on the phyllosphere.

The flowering process in *T. officinale* has been thoroughly researched. In Poland, Listowski and Jackowska (1965) planted seeds in greenhouse pots and observed that flowering occurred between 140 and 240 days after germination. Biotypes differed in flowering times. Plants needed at least 20 to 23 leaves before flowering began and some plants had over 100 leaves. Under artificial light conditions, four types of flowering patterns occurred: (1) plants flower early and then continue flowering for extended periods, (2) same as the previous group but flowering begins later, (3) plants flower early and then flowering pattern cycles, and (4) plants show a low level of bud formation with long periods between flowering. The above differences nearly disappear, however, when plants are vernalized. Vernalization is not required to induce flowering but greatly enhances it. In east-central Nebraska, in the United States, the first bud appears at the end of March. Sixteen days later, the first flower develops and, 11 days after this event, firm seed are formed (McCarty 1986).

A thorough study of flowering under natural conditions in a *Poa pratensis* lawn was done in the central United States by Gray et al. (1973). Capitula were counted and collected before each weekly mowing from April through November. *T. officinale* flowered throughout the year (except when snow was present), with the major peak in flowering between early April and early June (68 capitula/m²). A second peak occurred in mid-September to early October (>10 capitula/m²). Fewer than 10 capitula/m² were present the rest of the year. Flower stalks were longest from the late spring until early fall. Seed production varied from 54 to 172 seeds/capitulum, with generally more seeds/capitulum formed in the spring. Two patterns of flowering were observed. In the early spring, capitula remained open from sunrise to dusk, but in June, July, and August, they were closed by noon. Unusual weather conditions, such as a sudden temperature drop or very cloudy conditions, caused flower heads to remain closed. A capitulum opened for 2.5, 2.1, and 3.2 days in April, October, and November, respectively, and for less than 2 days in the summer. The heads remained closed for 10 days in the early spring and October, 20 days in November, and for 6 to 7 days during the summer.

Each flower head has two rows of involucral bracts at its base (Beal 1898). The shorter outer row is reflexed downward and does not move. The upper row can close to protect the florets at night or on damp, rainy days. During the seed maturity phase, the bracts remain closed until the "bloom" of white pappuses is observed. The upper bracts then resume the practice of closing at night to protect the seeds.

Flower heads open and close in response to temperature and light. Capitula in darkness open when temperatures increase (Tanaka et al. 1987). The higher the initial temperature, the greater the opening response to a given temperature rise. Capitula kept in darkness at 5, 10, and 15°C did not open when given light at these temperatures. However, capitula at 20°C opened upon receiving light without a change in temperature.

Scape development in *T. officinale* also has distinct phases (Chao 1947). The first flowers appear approximately 9 days after the scape is visible. The second phase consists of the time the head is closed and seeds develop, and the final phase starts just before the seed head opens and continues through the dispersal period. He gives detailed accounts of both cellular and organ growth in the scape throughout the flowering process. Korsmo (1954) presents excellent anatomical drawings and descriptions of the scape and other parts of *T. officinale*.

Flowering is influenced by the environment. Peak flowering in plants in lowland sites in Wales occurred 4 wk earlier and finished 10 wk sooner than for plants 300 m above sea level (Ford 1981a). As the degree of competition from grasses increases, less *T. officinale* biomass is found in the inflorescences, and the percentage of non-flowering plants in the population also rises (Molgaard 1977). High altitudes (875 m) and north-facing slopes delayed flowering 13 and 6 days, respectively, as compared to plants in lower pastures (540 m) and south-facing slopes. In the subantarctic, *T. officinale* can grow 75 cm tall and sometimes have fasciated scapes and double-headed inflorescences (Walton 1975).

T. officinale is generally an apomictic triploid plant with a $3n$ chromosome compliment of 24 (Baker 1965). However, variations in ploidy number and the presence of sexually reproducing biotypes are reported in Austria (Furnkranz 1966), England (Valentine and Richards 1967), and India (Gill 1969). It is considered an aggregate species with many microspecies. Harper (1960) states that apomictic species are usually found in "temporary" habitats. In this context, Doll (1981) describes three phylogenetic stages of *T. officinale* evolution. The primitive stage consisted of diploid period of polyploid apomictic evolution. He believes the "resexualizing" phase is now starting for this species.

The bright yellow flower color is due to the presence of the pigment "taraxien," a diester of taraxathin (Booth 1964). Even though seed production usually occurs without pollination, the flowers produce abundant quantities of pollen and nectar (Solbrig and Simpson 1974). If an inflorescence is cut in full bloom, the pappus will not emerge and viable seeds are formed only on mature heads (Gill 1938).

Bostock and Benton (1979) compared the means of reproduction and establishment of *T. officinale* to four perennial weeds in England. They described the plant as one with perenniating buds at the soil surface that are protected by soil or dead plant parts with no "vegetative extension" system. Ninety-eight percent of the ovules form seed and 182 seeds/head and 2170 seeds/plant are produced. Plants maintained 62% of their dry weight during the winter; this was higher than for the other species, since many of the leaves of *T. officinale* survive the winter. Most of the biomass in established dandelion plants is in the support organs (57%), 33% is in the reproductive organs and seeds, and 10% in vegetative organs. Dandelions allocate only 13% of their net production to vegetative reproduction, while 24% is allocated to seed reproduction. Plants produce 3000 times as many seeds as "vegetative daughters." The probability of dandelion establishment for a given seed was estimated to be 0.74, which gave a dry matter cost of 3.1 mg/established dandelion seedling. For each vegetative propagule, the cost was 4260 mg, which was the highest for the species studied.

SEED PRODUCTION, DISSEMINATION, AND GERMINATION

Numerous studies have been done on *T. officinale* seeds. Estimates on the number of seeds produced per capitulum range from 124 to 317 (Roberts 1936, Stevens 1957). The number of capitula per plant varies greatly. Stevens reported an average of 24, which resulted in a total of 3000 seeds/plant, while Roberts counted 93 heads that gave rise to 23,400 seeds/plant. He then calculated that more than 608 million seeds/ha could be produced annually. Seeds weigh approximately .58 mg each (including the pappus), with 45% of the dry weight in the embryo, 35% in the pericarp and 20% in the pappus (Bostock 1978).

The soil can attain very high seed populations. In England, Champness and Morris (1948) found 1,575,000 seeds/ha in the top 13 cm of soil in a grassland area and 2,350,000 seeds/ha in the top 18 cm of an arable field. Earlier studies in England found no seeds in the soil of natural grasslands that had never been cultivated or grazed, 200,900 seeds/ha (to 30 cm deep) in pastures 50 yr old or older, 550,900 seeds/ha in pastures that had been tilled, and 803,400 seeds/ha in grasslands that were harvested for hay during the summer and grazed in the fall and winter (Chippindale and Milton 1934).

Seeds of *T. officinale* are readily disseminated by the wind. Experiments by Small (1918) found that the pappus expands and forms a parachute-like structure at right angles to the main axis of the achene when the relative humidity is 77% or less. The mean area of each pappus is 1.06 cm² and the rate of achene fall is 0.6 KMH in still air. Wind velocities of only 2.3 KMH or more will keep the seed airborne. The bracts on the inflorescence of *T. officinale* open and close in response to relative humidity to protect the pappus (Sheldon and Burrows 1973). The fully expanded pappus gives a wide separation between achenes that favors dispersal of each one. The height of the scape varies greatly according to the height of the surrounding vegetation and this enhances effective wind dispersal. Sagar and Mortimer (1976) in the United States also documented great movement of *T. officinale* seeds by wind. Seed traps were placed in areas with no standing vegetation and the equivalent of 36,150 seeds/ha entered the site.

Wind is not the only means of seed movement. Intact seeds have been found in droppings of sparrows and green finches (Collinge 1913) and in the mud taken from students' boots after a university field trip (Clifford 1956). Undoubtedly the species has also moved great distances when it was purposefully planted as a crop and it would be a frequent contaminant in hay that is sold and transported. Water also disseminates *T. officinale* seeds. An 8.2-cm diameter trap was placed in an irrigation canal in Colorado, in the United States, and seeds of this weed were found in every sampling during May and June (Egginton and Robbins 1920). A maximum of 1844 seeds/hr was recorded and this is equivalent to more than 10 million seeds floating through a 3.6-m-wide canal in 24 hr! Laboratory experiments found that seeds dropped from 1.5 m float readily in water. Seed did not sink immediately with agitation, but after 1, 10, and 30 hr of agitation, 50, 80, and 97% of the seeds sank. In calm water, only 16% sank after 130 hr. Seeds suspended in moving irrigation water lose viability in 9 mo (Comes et al. 1978).

Longevity of *T. officinale* seeds in dry storage at room temperature was less than 3 yr if the seed had more than 5% moisture and greater than 2 yr with 3.9% moisture (Crocker and Barton 1953). Seed stored at 5°C with 3.9 to 7.9% moisture remained viable for 10 yr and seeds stored at −5°C gave 60 to 83% germination after 15 yr in storage. Mezynski and Cole (1974) found that stored seed had a higher optimum temperature than fresh seed and that storage tended to induce seed dormancy. Germination peaked at 45% when fresh seed was at 20°C for 16 hr and at 10°C for 8 hr.

Soil management affects *T. officinale* seed germination. An old pasture was planted to barley for two seasons in England and then tilled monthly, quarterly, once a year or not at all for 2 yr. The highest emergence of *T. officinale* occurred in the undisturbed plots (38/m²) and the least when the site was tilled each month (19/m²). Peak emergence took place in both the spring and fall (Chancellor 1964).

Roberts and Neilson (1981a) buried 1000 *T. officinale* seeds in cylinders and observed emergence for 7 yr. Nearly all seedlings emerged in the first 2 yr after planting, with less than 1% emerging after the third year. Less than 0.5% of the original seeds were viable after 5 yr in the soil.

At harvest, *T. officinale* seeds are nondormant and chilling does not affect germination (Bostock 1978). Dark conditions and far-red light inhibited germination (13 and 6%, respectively), while red light gave 58% and normal light gave 72% germination at 25°C. Alternating temperatures of 10 and 25°C increased germination in the dark from 13 to 61%. At 25°C, seeds germinated in 3.8 days and maximum germination occurred under high moisture conditions. Similar results on the effects of light and temperature on *T. officinale* germination were reported by Maguire and Overland (1959). In Poland, seeds placed under leaf canopies did not germinate in controlled conditions, while 86% of those in natural diffuse light germinated (Gorski 1975).

Germination occurs between 4 and 30°C, and 23°C is the optimum (Russwurm and Martin 1977b). Emergence between 0 and 2 cm of soil was similar, but declined as depth of seeding increased and no seeds emerged from 8 cm. Chepil (1946a) buried seeds in natural conditions and monitored their emergence in three soil types for 5 yr. Peak emergence occurred the first year after burial in the loam and sandy loam soils. Emergence was greatly reduced in the clay soil. Seeds germinated for 4 yr after burial in all three soils but no seedlings emerged the fifth year. No pattern of emergence during the growing season was apparent and he concludes that *T. officinale* has no periodicity of germination.

Sheldon (1974) studied the effect of the position of *T. officinale* seeds on the soil surface germination. Seeds germinated when there was good contact between the substrate and the attachment scar. Removing the beak enhanced germination, but the highest germination (85%) occurred when achenes were buried vertically to half the achene length, and when seeds were at a 45-degree angle to the soil, as they normally are after landing when the pappus is still attached. Soil compaction delayed germination for 3 to 7 wk after seeding, but by 11 wk, 80% of the seeds germinated in all levels of soil compaction. However, only half as many seedlings established in compacted soils because the radicle was often unable to penetrate. After falling on the soil surface, intermittent wetting and drying of the pappus raises and lowers the achene until this ability is eventually lost. This movement changes the position of the achene in relation to the soil and this movement, plus the backward-facing hairs and teeth on the lower section help seeds encounter and maintain good soil contact.

The proximity of seeds to each other also influences germination. Seeds placed singly or in groups of 5, 10, or 25 contiguous seeds had germination percentages of 68, 64, 54, and 41%, respectively (Linhart 1976). This response may be a means of regulating the population under natural conditions.

AGRICULTURAL IMPORTANCE AND UTILITY

T. officinale is a weed in over 60 countries (Figure 95-1). It is most often troublesome in pastures, forages, turf and lawn areas and orchards but can also infest maize, vegetable gardens, strawberries, vineyards, and cereal crops. It is one of the most frequent weeds in lawns in the temperate regions of the world and occurs in all 50 of the United States. It is an aesthetic problem during the flowering and seed production periods and, once established, continues to encroach. In Italy, *T. officinale* reduced the shoot growth of grape vines 20% (Zanardi 1962). It is becoming a more frequent weed in farming systems based on reduced and no-tillage methods. Nearly 100 yr ago, Hillman (1897) reported that *T. officinale* was "fast becoming a most serious weed of Nevada (United States) lucerne fields and lawns."

The presence of *T. officinale* may not cause economic losses. Pollard and Cussans (1976) noted that this weed was favored by no-till methods of wheat and barley production, which illustrates how species adapt to changing cultural practices, but it did not reach an economic threshold under their conditions. McCarty et al. (1974) observed the effects of several pasture management systems for 20 yr in the central United States. The ungrazed areas had the fewest *T. officinale* plants ($1.9/m^2$); mowing without grazing resulted in 6.4 plant/m^2. Rotationally grazed areas had 9.8 plants/m^2 and mowing grazed areas increased *T. officinale* density to 70 plants/m^2. The highest weed population occurred with continuous grazing and mowing (158 plants/m^2). Plots with the most litter and ground cover had the fewest plants. As many as 1300 seedlings/m^2 were found in some years but not all survived. Areas reseeded to cool season grasses had fewer *T. officinale* plants than those seeded with warm season grasses because the latter provided less early season competition.

This weed is among the ten most important lucerne weeds in North Carolina, in the United States. It is becoming an increasingly serious problem in hayfields of Europe and the north-central United States. Dietl (1982) and Doll (1984b) believe that more frequent forage cutting and the maintenance of higher field fertility levels increase the competitiveness of *T. officinale*. The brilliantly colored flowers give fields a weedier appearance than is really the case. On a seasonal basis, Sheaffer and Wyse (1982) found no consistent differences in protein content and in vitro digestible dry matter between lucerne with and without *T. officinale*. However, Doll (1984a) sampled *T. officinale* and lucerne plants at the time of first harvest for four seasons and found that the weed contained 5% less crude protein than the crop. If the harvested forage contained 25% *T. officinale*, approximately 80 kg/ha of protein would be lost. In subsequent harvests, protein contents of dandelion and the crop were similar. Doll reported an increase from 37 to 147 *T. officinale* plants/m^2 from the second to the fifth year of hay production. Lucerne stems decreased from 910 to 293/m^2 in this period. In Germany, this weed composed 10 and 20% of the harvested forage in the second and third years of lucerne production, respectively (Russwurm and Martin 1977a).

Controlling *T. officinale* does not increase total forage yield (Sheaffer and Wyse 1982, Doll 1984b, Moyer 1984). In fact, the biomass in the first harvest may decrease when the weed is controlled; high production usually occurs in the remaining harvests and thus season totals are equivalent in treated and nontreated fields. Approximately 80% of the total *T. officinale* biomass is harvested in the first lucerne harvest, which coincides with the time of rapid spring growth of this weed (Doll 1984b). The effect of the weed on the lucerne drying time was also measured. Freshly cut *T. officinale* had 87% moisture, which was higher than that of lucerne (80%). Over a 4-day period after cutting, forage with 13 to 50% *T. officinale* biomass generally required an additional day to dry to the same moisture level as weed-free forage.

T. officinale has long been the object of chemical control studies. As early as the 1890s, it was treated with salt in Sweden. In the early 1900s in the United States, iron sulphate was tested "at the rate of 45 kg to one barrel of water" (Pammel 1913). Refinement of this method resulted in *T. officinale* management programs in lawns that combined iron sulphate applications with fertilization and reseeding (Munn 1919). Shifting from pastures to annual crops and using broadleaf herbicides caused *T. officinale* to disappear in 3 yr (Fryer and Chancellor 1970). Most phenoxy herbicides control this species, but MCPB and 2,4-DB are ineffective (Matthews 1975).

T. officinale represents perhaps the first documented case of herbicide resistance. Stryckers (1958) noted 2,4-D and MCPA no longer controlled this weed after 10 yr of consecutive treatment in a pasture. Mann (1981) found that a single treatment of 2,4-D killed 76% of the plants but, if he cut the root at the soil surface 2 wk after treatment, only 60% died. Thus treated areas should not be mowed for at least 2 wk after spraying. Roots cut 2 cm below the soil surface killed only 20% of the untreated plants. Welton and Carroll (1941) obtained 94% kill of *T. officinale* by mechanically defoliating plants seven times in one season.

Controlling *Agropyron repens* in a lucerne field in the northern United States gave a two-fold increase in *T. officinale* biomass (Dutt et al. 1983). *T. officinale* invades pure lucerne stands but not a lucerne-bromegrass mixture in Canada (McElgunn et al. 1972). Four annual applications of simazine reduced the weed's population from 56 to 16 plants/m^2 and three seasons of terbacil treatment to 2 plants/m^2 (Waddington 1980). The terbacil applications also increased lucerne seed production 34%. Metribuzin and hexazinone selectively control *T. officinale* in lucerne and the effects of a single application are often evident for 2 yr (Doll 1984b).

As a weed of pastures and hayfields, its forage value has been thoroughly examined (Fagan and Watkins 1932, Schneider 1947, Vengris et al. 1953, Fairbairn and Thomas 1959, Dutt et al. 1982). In comparison to other forage weeds, it is relatively high in K, Ca, Na, Cl, Fe, and Cu. It is lower in P, S, and N than grasses (van der Kley 1956), is palatable to livestock, and has a high level of digestibility. Dietl (1982) actually proposed that a mixture of species in forages (including species often considered as "weeds") is beneficial and that levels of *T. officinale* of 25% in pastures, green chopped forage and silage, and up to 10% in hay are desirable. Van der Kley (1956) compared the mineral content of *T. officinale* and forage grasses at many specific sites in pastures during the season and concluded that grasses with up to 20% legumes and herbs like *T. officinale* would be healthier for animals than pure grass. The weed is a good antidote for scours and acidic urine, and is an excellent source of copper in the diet.

Numerous medicinal uses are attributed to this plant, including treatment for liver ailments, constipation, rheumatism and as a diuretic (Lorenzi 1982), as a blood purifier (Millspaugh 1892), and as a laxative and tonic, and to correct pale skin color (Mendieta and Amo 1981). Reportedly over 45,000 kg of *T. officinale* roots were imported into the United States for phamaceutical uses (Spencer 1940). The plant has shown antimicrobial (Nickell 1960) and antibiotic activity (Chauvin and Lavie 1956). A hot water extract with antitumor properties was isolated from *T. officinale* in Japan (Baba et al. 1981).

Flowers of *T. officinale* produce abundant nectar and pollen and are frequently visited by bees. They produce a dark, strong honey, and much of the pollen is fed to young bees in the hive (Magers 1970). Sugar yields of 77 kg/ha from *T. officinale* are possible but were not achieved in Alberta, Canada (Szabo 1984). With nearly 600,000 flowers/ha/day available for foraging, bee populations are often too low to harvest the available nectar. Controlling this weed in New Zealand reduces pollen and nectar sources for bees in the spring (Patterson 1956). On the other hand, uncontrolled *T. officinale* in orchards may result in less frequent bee visits to fruit flowers. In England, *T. officinale* flowers at lower temperatures (8 to 14°C) than apples (10 to 19°C) and the weed's period of peak pollen availability is from 10 to 11:00 A.M., while the peak for apples is from 12 to 6:00 P.M. (Free 1968). However, bees are conditioned to return to the same plant species they initially visited, even if little food is present. Thus few bees switch their visiting habits from one species to another during the season and only rarely in the same day. Using mechanical or chemical weed control in orchards and moving colonies into a new orchard and releasing bees only after 12:00 P.M. on warm days will result in most bees visiting fruit flowers first.

Seldom can all parts of a plant be eaten by humans. Recipes are available in many languages on the preparation of salads, teas, wines and many other food dishes to utilize *T. officinale* as a human food. Roots can be dried, roasted and ground for use as a coffee substitute (Uphof 1968). Gorini (1982) describes the cultural practices for growing the plant as a vegetable crop in Italy, from the seeding of the nursery, transplanting, pest control and postharvest storage techniques. The level of bitterness in 69 field populations of *T. officinale* and two garden varieties was evaluated by taste testing. On a bitterness scale of 0 to 6, ratings ranged from 1 to 5 and bitterness was relatively constant within each population (Kuusi and Autio 1985). Bitterness levels were higher in the late summer than in the spring, higher under dry, sunny conditions, and were similar for roots and leaves of a given population. Bitterness was not correlated with leaf shape or basal petiole color.

Gardeners in the eastern United States were encouraged to grow their own supply of *T. officinale* seed (Tomson 1918). They were cautioned that only "experienced dandelion growers" should attempt to grow more than for their own needs. Seed yields varied from 165 to 275 kg/ha, with an average value of US $22/kg in 1918. The plant is an excellent source of iron, copper, potassium and other minerals.

T. officinale can host the aster yellows disease that infects lettuce, carrots, celery and potatoes (Anderson 1956), and hosts an array of nematodes, including *Meloidogyne incog-*

nita, *Ditylenchus destructor*, *Pratylenchus penetrans*, and *Xiphinema americanum* (Miller 1980, Bendixen et al. 1979). The nematode *Tylenchus dipsaci* is borne inside seeds of this weed and can infest lucerne stems in Australia (Bendixen et al. 1979). A seed-eating weevil (*Ceutorhynchus punctiger*) was found on *T. officinale* in the eastern United States (McAvoy and Kok 1981). Development from egg to adult was 50 days and each larva consumed an average of 22.8 seeds.

COMMON NAMES

Taraxacum officinale

ARGENTINA	amargon, chicoria, diente de leon, radicha, radicheta
AUSTRALIA	dandelion
BELGIUM	paardebloem, pissenlit
BOLIVIA	amargon
BRAZIL	amargosa, dente de leao, radice bravio, taraxaco
CANADA	dandelion, pissenlit
CHILE	diente de leon, lechugilla
COLOMBIA	chicoria, diente de leon, lechuguilla
DENMARK	maelkebotte
ECUADOR	diente de leon
FIJI	dandelion
FINLAND	rikkavoikukka
FRANCE	dent-de-lion, pissenlit
GERMANY	Gemeiner Lowenzahn, Maiblume
HAWAII	dandelion
INDONESIA	jombang
ITALY	dente di leone, soffione, tarassaco
JAPAN	seiyo-tanpopo
MEXICO	diente de leon
NETHERLANDS	paardebloem
NEW ZEALAND	dandelion
NORWAY	lovetann
PERU	diente de leon
PORTUGAL	dente-de-leao
SOUTH AFRICA	common dandelion, perdeblom
SPAIN	achicoria silvestre, amargon, diente de leon, taraxacon
SWEDEN	maskros
UNITED STATES	common dandelion
URUGUAY	diente de leon
YUGOSLAVIA	maslacak

Ninety-Six

Thlaspi arvense L.

Brassicaceae (Cruciferae), Mustard Family

T HLASPI ARVENSE is a very old companion of humankind's food-gathering efforts, having been found at sites of human habitation reaching back to the time of the Stone Age more than one million years ago. It remains a problem today in 30 crops in 45 countries. It is a very strong competitor because of its prolific seed production and an extensive root system that surrounds those of plants nearby, thus gaining a competitive advantage in the uptake of water and nutrients. In addition, Hume (1984) has shown that it can form germinable seeds in a few days following anthesis. The species has become

FIGURE 96-1   The distribution of *Thlaspi arvense* L. across the world where it has been reported as a weed.

FIGURE 96-2 *Thlaspi arvense* L.: A. habit; B. silicle; C. seeds.

adapted to an extreme range of lat 80° N to lat 45° S. The milk and flesh of animals acquires off-flavors if *Thlaspi* seeds are consumed in feed and forage.

DESCRIPTION

T. arvense (Figure 96-2) is an *annual* or *winter annual*, entire plant glabrous and bright green, with an unpleasant odor when bruised; *stems* erect, 18 to 80 cm tall, simple or branched above; *leaves* alternate, basal leaves narrowly obovate, petioled, soon withering, the middle and upper leaves oblong, entire or irregularly toothed, sessile, clasping stem by 2 ear-lobes, 1 to 1.5 mm long; *flowers* at first in a small flat cluster at top of leafy stem with racemes becoming elongated when in fruit, perfect, regular, 4 *sepals*; 4 white *petals* 3 to 4 mm long, equal, twice as long as sepals; 6 *stamens*, two shorter than others; *silicle* pod-like, borne on slender, upward curving stalks, bright green to yellowish to greenish-orange, as seeds ripen easily seen in crop fields, almost circular, 1.25 cm across, strongly flattened and winged; very short *style* persists in a deep, narrow notch at the top of wings, dehiscent, the 2-winged locules each with 4 to 16 seeds; *seeds* ovoid, 1.2 to 2.3 mm long and 1 to 1.5 mm wide, reddish or purplish-brown to black, unsymmetrically oval in outline, somewhat flattened with several concentric ridges resembling a fingerprint, each face with narrow groove extending from hilum to center of seed. No mucilage found on seed when moist.

It is often recognized by the rank smell when leaves are crushed. Plants resemble *Lepidium densiflorum* in having white flowers, flattened and notched pods and clasping leaves. Flowers of the latter are much smaller and pods contain only two seeds.

DISTRIBUTION AND HABITAT

Figure 96-1 shows that *T. arvense* behaves as a weed in the temperate zones of the north and south but is seldom a problem in tropical crops. Seeds have been found at sites of human habitation in the temperate areas since the Stone Age and there is evidence that the species has been weedy in the agricultural activities of early communities for several thousand years. This extended period has given much opportunity for long-distance intra- and intercontinental movement (Willerding 1981). Climatic requirements do not seem to be a limiting factor in its distribution, for it grows at about lat 80° N in Spitzbergen, from moist valleys to 2700 m in the Rocky Mountains of western North America, and at 4200 m in the Himalayas in Asia (Polunin 1959, Mani 1979).

The weed is dispersed locally by grain combines and other machinery, by mud on the feet of men, animals and birds; and animal dung as it is spread in fields or falls from vehicles during transport on farm roads. Ridley (1930) found the wings of the seed could cause it to sail on the wind for 1 km or more. The seed has a high specific gravity and in water it sinks upon agitation, but Hope (1927) in Alberta, Canada, found significant amounts of the seed moving with the flow in mains and laterals of irrigation systems. The seed travels as a contaminant in cereal and flax seed stocks. In India, it is one of a dozen common weed seeds found in the wheat sold in food shops (Das Gupta 1978).

The species will grow on wet and dry ground and in several soil types, but it prefers fertile sites. Its preferred site is cultivated ground, it prospers in cereal fields, and it is common in gardens, waysides and waste places. Hume and Archibold (1986) in Canada placed seed traps from 1 to 100 m into a fallow field for 12 mo to gather weed seeds as they migrated from a weedy pasture immediately adjacent. Weed seeds decreased with distance from the pasture, with only a few found at 7 m. *T. arvense* was one of four weeds that dominated the fallow field. Fifty species of weeds were found in sunflower fields in Saskatoon, Canada. *T. arvense* was one of four species that occurred in 50% of the fields. It had the highest weed density (5.6 pl/m^2) of any species (Thomas and Wise 1983, 1986).

PROPAGATION

T. arvense reproduces only by seeds that weigh about 0.8 mg and that are produced in quantities of up to 20,000 seeds/plant. Paatela and Ervio (1971) found 20 to 450 seeds/m^2 in the upper layers of the soil of fields in Finland. Batho (1939) reported 1300 seeds/m^2 in Manitoba, Canada and estimated that heavy infestations of the weed in cereals results in a weed seed yield of 1350 kg/ha. He reported experiments with infestations of this weed in grain that was sown at a low seeding rate, without fertilizer, in which the weeds dropped more than 10,000 seeds/m^2 into the grain stubble. Waldron (1904) found that seeds that ripen by autumn, but remain in the pod, are normally dead by spring. He learned from farmers that plowing down plants with green pods in an effort to destroy them was futile, for the green pods and seeds continue to ripen beneath the soil. Hume (1984) found that immature green seeds harvested 6 days after anthesis germinated and produced seedlings. More mature seed from field-grown plants had greater dormancy than seed produced in the greenhouse.

In a report on a 40-year seed burial experiment, Toole and Brown (1946) found that most *T. arvense* seeds germinated in the first 9 yr but 5% were still viable at 30 yr (Duvel 1905). Smith (1917) found a 20-yr life for seeds buried in soil. In dry storage, Kjaer (1940) reported a complete loss of seed viability in 2 yr.

Chepil (1946a) and McIntyre and Best (1975) in Canada, when working in greenhouse and laboratory, found that freshly harvested seeds were non-dormant, gave almost complete germination in light at an alternating temperature of 10/25°C, and did not become dormant in summer heat or winter cold. Salisbury (1964), on the other hand, found good germination of new seed but also a proportion of them with a firm dormancy. Other workers have shown that field results may vary with conditions of the environment and there are indications that the peculiarities of different biotypes could be confusing the matter.

Baskin and Baskin (1988, 1989) in the United States found that in May most freshly matured seeds were dormant. Some of the seeds were conditionally dormant and germinated under limited conditions. Seeds sown on the soil germinated in spring and autumn. For most seeds, after-ripening occurred in summer and seeds became non-dormant by autumn. Seeds entered conditional dormancy in early winter and became dormant in late winter or early spring. Monthly tests in light and dark revealed that buried seeds had an annual dormant–nondormant cycle. When buried, dormant seeds that were kept at various thermoperiods from 5 to 35°C (some with alternating temperatures) gained the ability to germinate at 95 to 100%. Initially dormant seeds germinated 100% after 4 wk at 5°C, with the exception of some held at 35°C. After 18 wk at 5°C, only 19% of the seed germinated at any thermoperiod. These and other findings suggest that seeds of winter annual plants of *T. arvense* are non-dormant in autumn and enter dormancy in winter, whereas summer annual plants are dormant in autumn and become non-dormant during winter.

Hakansson (1983) in Sweden placed the seeds of several weeds, *T. arvense* among them, in soil in fields and climate chambers and tested the germination over a period of 2 yr to gather information on the readiness to germinate at all seasons. Some of the soils were disturbed at intervals to simulate the common tillage routine of the region. Seeds in undisturbed soil in the field and climate chambers had a peak of germination in May, with good germination in April and June. In addition, seeds stored in the field and "tilled" periodically showed a large peak of germination in late summer and early fall. Chepil (1946a) and Koch (1967) reported similar endogenous germination rhythms in this weed in Canada and Germany. It may be that the endogenous rhythms apply only to that portion of the seeds that have a profound dormancy.

The effect of seed burial and tillage operations on germination and survival of this weed have been much studied because of the abundant seed production. Chepil (1946b) recorded emergence of the weed each year for 5 yr with seeds placed on the surface with no tillage, or with cultivation down to 6 or 15 cm with several different tillage machines. On average, only 5% of the seeds survived with a cultivation depth down to 6 cm, and 15% when tilled to 15 cm. Experiments by Roberts and Feast (1972, 1973) during a period of 6 yr are in agreement with the survival of the seed of this weed at different depths and the stimulation of emergence by tillage (see also Zwerger and Hurle 1986). Kolk (1947) in Sweden found the best germination in the upper 2 cm of the soil and recommended cultivation to this depth soon after harvest to destroy some of the emerging weeds. Chepil (1946a) also planted freshly harvested seeds in mid-September in grain fields that were destined for a program of fallow, wheat, fallow in the 3 succeeding years. Tillage was simulated in experimental plots in fallow years. More than 75% of the seeds emerged in the first fallow year, with a few emerging in each succeeding year. Less than 10% of the seeds remained at the end of 3 yr.

In the laboratory, Wehsarg (1918) in Germany reported the average limits of germination temperatures as follows: optimum 28 to 30°C, minimum 1 to 2°C, and maximum 32°C. The more mature seeds had higher maximum and lower minimum temperatures. Kolk (1962), in an extensive literature survey on seed germination of many weeds present in Europe, confirmed the need for alternating temperature for *T. arvense* and was in agreement that the range of germination temperatures increases with age of seed.

Courtney (1967) collected seeds from the field in darkness, maintained the darkness through the germination tests, and obtained only 5% germination. He concluded that increased germination with tillage was due in part to the exposure of the seed to light. He found that cultivation promoted germination in spring, summer and fall.

It was established that on the plains of Canada there are genetically distinct early-flowering (EF) and late-flowering (LF) strains of *T. arvense* (Best and McIntyre 1972, McIntyre and Best 1978). The authors tested the germination of freshly harvested seed in petri dishes in the greenhouse for 14 days under several combinations of light and temperature. The EF and LF strains showed maximum germination in light at 10/25°C alternating temperatures. In darkness only the EF strain germinated and at a very reduced rate. At a constant temperature of 10°C, only a few seeds of either strain germinated, while at 25°C only the EF strain germinated in the light.

Small to spectacular increases in germination of *T. arvense* seed of all ages have been reported with stimulants, both physical and chemical. Koch (1967) found that the seed responded favorably at *p*Hs 4 through 7. Kolk (1947) found optimum germination of the seeds at 60% of the water-holding capacity in sandy soils; germination ceased at 30%. Seeds of many species are restive when soil aeration is poor. Chepil (1946a) and Bibbey (1948) found that germination decreased as atmospheric O_2 dropped from 20 to 12%, with little germination at 9%. Germination ceased at CO_2 levels above 9%.

Germination is stimulated with use of gibberellic acid, soaking in sodium hypochlorite, and seed coat removal or scarification (Hsiao 1980, Corns 1960a,b, Pelton 1956, and

Salisbury 1964). For information on several combination treatments with light, temperature, NO_3, ethephon, and gibberellic acid, see Saini et al. (1987). Hintikka (1988) in Finland found that sand treated with daminozide and chlormequat chloride placed an inhibition on growth of *T. arvense* for one yr. This could be relieved with use of gibberellic acid. For details of many germination experiments, see Andersen (1968), Hofsten, von (1947), Kolk (1962), and Metzger (1983).

Ozer (1982) found that seeds of this species were not affected by passage through the gut of lambs.

PHYSIOLOGY AND MORPHOLOGY

The genetically distinct strains of *T. arvense* that exist in the cereal fields of Canada show differences in lateral branching, leaf number, seed germination and rates of flowering (Anon. [Canada] 1979a). In Germany more than 50 wild populations showed large ecotypic variation, with significant differences in plant and oil seed characteristics (Hondelmann and Radatz 1984). No evidence of hybridization has been reported. The many biotypes and the extreme climatic adaptation have brought forth several versions of the phenology of the species.

The most extensive phenological record of this species was made over a period of 15 yr in the same population at lat 41° N in Nebraska, in the United States (McCarty 1986). The average date for emergence for seedlings or rosettes was March 10, stem elongation April 1 to 10, first buds April 6 to 16, first bloom April 30 to May 4 and production of first firm seeds May 7 to 23.

The average date of 50% emergence for *T. arvense* in grain at lat 50° N on the plains of Canada is April 30, about 4 to 6 wk later than in the above experiment. The average date for ripening and shattering (dropping) seed is July 7, long before the crops are harvested. Hume (1984) in Canada found some seeds fully formed 6 days after anthesis, with the process completed at 15 days. He suggested cultivation within 6 days after anthesis to prevent seed build-up in the soil.

The compact rosette form helps the plant to take maximum advantage of the snow cover and gives some protection from low temperatures and drying winds. With adequate light, stem elongation normally occurs about the time of flowering. Plant morphology differs greatly in different soils and sites. In dry, shallow, infertile sites the plant may be unbranched and 1 cm tall. In a favorable site, many flowering lateral branches are formed, basal buds are produced and stems may reach 80 cm (Best and McIntyre 1975). Late plants that are in flower may be frozen as winter approaches, but Clark and Fletcher (1909) in Canada found many were not seriously injured. They thawed in spring, continued to grow and ripened seed by July.

To study the effect of season of emergence on morphology, seed production and phenology, Klebesadal (1969) in Alaska planted seeds gathered from three areas on ten dates between June 21 and August 31 in an area just below the Arctic Circle. Data were taken for one full year. When planted early, the seed pods were green and plants were 65 cm tall by August 21. Those planted before mid-June produced ripe seeds. When seeded in mid-July and later, only small, leafy rosettes were formed in fall.

In the second season after planting, new growth became apparent on over-wintered plants by mid-April; it was one of the earliest weeds to have new growth. The planting dates of the previous year influence comparative development of the plants in the spring and summer following. By mid-May of the second year, plants from seedlings prior to August 1 of the previous year were in the early flowering stage, while those planted after mid-August were in the bud stage and later flowered by June 1. The morphology of these plants was also altered in the second season. Those planted early in the previous season elongated and made secondary stems from the plant crown; those overwintering in rosette form had few secondary stems. The author concluded that plants emerging in that area before mid-July will grow as summer annuals and should be eradicated before seed production; those coming later are not a threat because seed production will fail.

High yields of viable seeds are obtained from covered plants that are self-pollinating (Knuth 1908, Mulligan 1972). The four longest of the six stamens reach the same or a higher level than the stigma and as their pollen-covered surfaces turn inward at maturity pollination is assured. There is some cross-pollination by insects, but there is little information on this procedure.

This ubiquitous weed may be altered in rate of growth and morphology by the physical factors of the environment, but, except in the extreme, it is not at the mercy of any of them for its vegetative or reproductive growth. Experiments in Canada have shown that both early-flowering (EF) and late-flowering (LF) strains flowered in 8- and 16-hr photo periods, but growth was greatly accelerated in the long-day. The latter effect was increased by growing plants at a reduced N level. Leaf number was increased by reducing day length, increasing the N supply, or reducing the light intensity from 34,000 to 3800 lux (Best and McIntyre 1972). Increasing the day or night temperatures accelerates flowering but reduces the leaf number in the EF strain, while causing an increase in leaf production and delay in flowering in the LF strain.

Vernalization at 2°C for 2 to 4 wk induced early flowering in the LF strain and caused it to behave as a summer annual. A 2-wk vernalization treatment caused flowers to appear first on lateral shoots, while a 4-wk treatment caused most plants to flower first at the main shoot apex.

Working with *T. arvense*, Metzger (1988) reported that the apparent site of perception of the low temperature needed to bring about reproductive development (stem elongation and flower formation) was apparently localized at the shoot tip and in immature leaves. From studies with grafting and organ cultures of *T. arvense*, however, Metzger believes that cells from other locations on the plant may be thermoinductive. He suggests that, if several cell types may be thermoinduced, one must be wary that although the shoot tip *appears* to be the site of perception, it nevertheless remains the only locality associated with the origination of the reproductive structures, while the signal(s) may come from elsewhere.

Fogelfors (1972) in Sweden studied the effect of light intensity on several weed species at six levels under the leaf canopy in crop fields and found that some, such as *Stellaria media*, that remain close to the soil surface, could tolerate the low light and continue to develop. *T. arvense* could not develop under such conditions, while *Sinapis arvensis* with its upright growth was one of the most competitive plants.

This weed is surprisingly inefficient in its use of water, as compared with barley *Hordeum vulgare*, Russian thistle *Salsola kali*, or green foxtail *Setaria viridis* (Anderson and Best 1965). The time schedule for growth of the root system that supplies the water is, however, rather unusual. In a study of the mechanism of weed competition in cereals on the plains of Canada, Pavlychenko and Harrington (1934) recorded total linear root production at 5 and 21 days after emergence in 20 annual and biennial weeds (including *T. arvense*) and 11 varieties of four cereal crops. At 5 days, *T. arvense* made one-half the growth of several weeds but one-tenth the root growth of Hannchen barley and was far behind most crop plants. At 21 days, its root growth was exceeded only by wild mustard *Brassica arvensis* among the weeds, and both were much more prolific than other weeds. Only Trebi barley equaled the root growth of *Thlaspi* at 21 days, with root systems of all other crops being much less extensive. This suggests that within 3 wk from emergence this weed is in a position to gather nutrients and water (albeit inefficiently used) far better than most species it associates with.

An excavation of the complete root system of a 50-cm flowering plant (in July) in a wheat field in Germany showed a much-branched pattern with penetration to 50 cm and most roots within an area 20 cm in diameter beneath the plant (Kutschera 1960).

Hoefert (1979, 1980), Hoefert and Martin (1984), and Prasad (1977) have studied the anatomy and morphology of *T. arvense*.

Wood et al. (1958) and Schroeder et al. (1974) reported on the composition of the seeds and Nickell (1960) on the antimicrobial activity. *T. arvense* may be successful in part because it releases from its leaves allylthiocyanate, which is avoided by the adapted enemies of this and other species of **Cruciferae**, rather than allylisothiocyanate, which is an attractant for many insects (Feeny 1977).

In a study of the allelopathic effect of one seed upon another during germination, Stefureac and Fratilescu (1979) in Romania found that *T. arvense* seeds stimulated the germination and early growth of seeds of the cultivated crops, perennial rye *Lolium perenne*, birdsfoot trefoil *Lolium corniculatus*, and red and white clover *Trifolium pratense* and *repens*. The germination of seeds of wheat *Triticum aestivum* was inhibited by the weed seeds. The authors suggest that the active compounds are released in exudates from the newly-formed roots.

AGRICULTURAL IMPORTANCE

T. arvense is a serious weed of barley, flax, oats, rape, sunflowers, and wheat in Canada; of fodder beets and vegetables in Germany; of barley and wheat in Korea; and of pastures and winter wheat in the United States. It is a principal weed of several crops on arable lands of Mongolia; of asparagus, beets, beans, forage crops, onions, peas, and other vegetable and root crops in Canada; of cereals in Hungary, Norway, and Sweden; of fodder and sugar beets and other root crops in Belgium; of horticultural crops in Germany; of lucerne in Argentina and new seedings of the crop in East Germany; of maize in Hungary and Romania; of pastures in Alaska; of potatoes in Belgium and Germany; of oil seed rape in Sweden; and of wheat in Iran and the United States.

It is a common weed of several crops on arable land in New Zealand and the former Yugoslavia; of barley in Finland; of cereals in Germany, Scotland, Tunisia, and Turkey; of flax in Belgium and the Netherlands; of forage crops in the United States; of horticultural crops in Scotland; of maize in the United States; of peas in the Netherlands; of potatoes in Norway; of sugar beets and other root crops in Poland and the United States; of vegetables in Norway; and of wheat in Finland and winter wheat in Germany and Sweden.

In addition, the weed is present but of unranked importance in several grain and cereal crops in Alaska, Belgium, Bulgaria, Colombia, Czechoslovakia, England, Germany, India, Italy, the Netherlands, Poland, the former Soviet Union, Sweden, and the United States. It is also a weed of unranked importance of beans in Belgium and England; cabbage in Germany; carrots in Poland; cotton in the former Soviet Union; horticultural crops in

Tunisia; onions in England and the Netherlands; pastures in England and the former Yugoslavia; peas in the United States; potatoes in Alaska and Poland; rape in Germany; rice in China and India; several root crops in Switzerland and Ukraine; soybeans in Romania; tobacco in Belgium; arable winter crops in Australia; and vegetable crops in Alaska, England, Poland, and the United States.

This species has been listed with major weeds of arable land for more than 200 yr in Great Britain (Salisbury 1964). Hurle (1974), in a 12-yr experiment in Germany, reported that continued use of herbicides has reduced the amount of seed of this plant, in the soil, by 65%, yet it remains a formidable weed across the world. Later Reuss and Bachthaler (1988) in Germany found in a 3-yr field experiment that there was an increasing density of *T. arvense* plants despite repeated use of herbicides and extensive cultivation. Similar experiences have been reported in Denmark and elsewhere after several decades of heavy use of phenoxy herbicides.

The tenacity of this weed in the face of continuous control efforts is in great part due to the abundant reserves of seed in the soil of infested areas, as well as the propensity to germinate freely when brought to the surface. When buried, it may remain viable for 30 yr or more. Hume (1987, 1988) in Canada reported that although highly susceptible to 2,4-D injury, *T. arvense* and *Chenopodium album* were still dominant in a wheat, wheat, fallow rotation following 36 yr of annual sprays with the herbicide. After a 3-yr experiment with a detailed study of the growth and development of *T. arvense*, Hume suggested ten ways that the plant may manage to survive as a dominant weed in the age of herbicides. Among them are intermittent and frequent production of new seedlings, a short life cycle, the failure of control practices that may allow some individuals to go on to become heavy seeders, viability of immature seed, long-term dormancy, and the possibility of some herbicide tolerance (though not resistance).

In the central United States, the seed begins to shatter from *Thlaspi* plants before the first hay is cut, following which the new weed crop is re-seeded. The number of seeds in grain fields in Canada increased greatly during the first year after fallow, with continued accumulation at a slower rate in the second year after fallow (Budd et al. 1954). Petzold (1959, 1979) ranked *T. arvense* with those weeds that have the greatest seed fall during harvest operations. In a study of the effect of combine harvesting on weed seed supplies at the same agricultural sites over a period of 2 decades, he found a reduction of the number and density of seeds of many weeds, but *Thlaspi* was one of five species that showed increases. In a study of the effect of vegetable cropping on seed reserves in the top 15 cm of the soil, Roberts (1958) found that the initial level of 1,500,000 seeds of *T. arvense* per hectare was reduced by one-half in the first year and two-thirds in the second year.

Paatela and Ervio (1971) surveyed 800 agricultural fields of Finland and found the weed everywhere that crops are grown. Uljanova (1985) in the former Soviet Union reported that *T. arvense* is a basic weed in cabbage, oat, and pea crops in the Maritime Territories of the Far East. The weed is important in the north and south of Europe because it competes with many crops in many types of agriculture. It is a major weed in some western and central European regions. In the plains and the Peace River Valley of western Canada, *T. arvense* is a very important weed of forages, annual cereals, and oil crops (Alex 1982, Hume 1982, Thomas and Wise 1984, 1986).

For several years in Germany, Wahl (1988) compared the weed floras of a conventional cropping system and a so-called integrated cropping system consisting of shallow tillage, N applied at 20% of the normal rate, paired row drilling, and pesticides as dictated by economic thresholds. In the plots of the integrated system, the density of emerged weeds of *T. arvense* and other weeds, and their soil seed reserves, increased as compared with the conventional cropping system.

Because of its potential for enormous seed production, the short life cycle that permits several generations per year, marked by the unusual capability to produce germinable seeds within a few days after anthesis, together with the allocation of resources for rapid growth of roots very early in life, *T. arvense* has a reputation for intense competition and persistence in the face of adversity. For example, in Canada it has been shown experimentally that a light infestation of the weed can reduce wheat yields by 35%; a heavy infestation by 50% (Best and McIntyre 1975). The authors feel that this species is an especially severe problem in the prairies because its root system competes so well for a limited moisture supply. Fall sown cereals usually have fewer weeds than those sown in spring, but winter annual weeds such as *Thlaspi* are very successful when sown as fall seedings (Hay 1970).

T. arvense has not, however, been successful in all plant communities. Kirk et al. (1941) found this species to be a poor competitor with certain forage crops such as crested wheat grass (*Agropyron cristatum*) and smooth brome grass (*Bromus inermis*). They have shown experimentally that the weed may be reduced from 2000 plants/m² at 24 days from emergence to none at 82 days. In the central United States, Burnside et al. (1984) studied many winter wheat varieties for their competitive ability against *T. arvense* and found several, principally the variety "Turkey," that were quite effective.

Wood et al. (1958) studied the proteins of the seeds of this weed and concluded they would make satisfactory feed for ruminants and monogastric animals, with the latter requiring a supplement of suitable S-containing amino acids. There are, however, other problems in processing these seeds for feeds. As with many other mustards, the foliage is usually not toxic to animals, but the seeds are rich in oil glucosides and when ground with feed supplies these can break down to release volatile mustard oils and related compounds. These break-down products cause flavor changes and odors in milk and cause several disorders in stock animals. For example, Smith and Crowe (1987) found that eight pregnant cows from a herd of 220 died within 5 days after feeding on a ration of 100% *T. arvense* plants. Examination revealed massive submucosal oedena (accumulation of fluids) of the wall of the forestomachs, particularly the rumen. The ration was found to liberate allylisothiocyanate at the rate of 250 mg/100 g of feed. See also Steyn (1934), Kjaer et al. (1953), Hawk (1956), Whiting et al. (1958), and Baksi and Case (1971).

COMMON NAMES

Thlaspi arvense

ARGENTINA	carraspique
BELGIUM	boerekers, tabouret des champs, witte krodde
CANADA	bastardcress, fanweed, field penneycress, stinkweed, tabouret perfolie
DENMARK	almindelig pengeurt
ENGLAND	pennycress
FINLAND	peltotaskuruoho
FRANCE	tabouret des champs
GERMANY	Ackerhellerkraut, Ackertaschelkraut, Herzschotchen, Pfennigkraut

ITALY	erba storna
JAPAN	gunbainazuna
NETHERLANDS	witte krodde
NEW ZEALAND	pennycress
NORWAY	pengeurt
SPAIN	carraspique, telaspio
SWEDEN	penningort
UNITED STATES	field pennycress

Ninety-Seven

Trianthema portulacastrum L.

Aizoaceae, Carpetweed Family

TRIANTHEMA PORTULACASTRUM is an herbaceous plant found in many tropical and sub-tropical countries. Many members of this **Aizoaceae** family have adapted to very dry desert conditions. The fleshy leaves and succulent stems of *T. portulacastrum* aid its growth in dry conditions. However, the plant requires abundant soil moisture to germinate and become established. Some plants in this genus may have three flowers or anthers, as the name suggests, but *T. portulacastrum* has neither. The species name refers to *Portulaca oleracea*, another species with fleshy leaves and succulent stems. The generally prostrate growth habit and early season germination make it very competitive with many crops.

FIGURE 97-1   The distribution of *Trianthema portulacastrum* L. across the world where it has been reported as a weed.

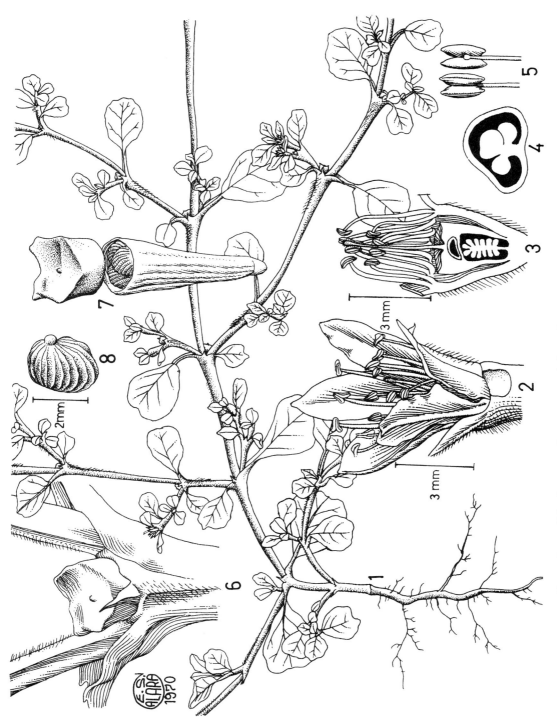

FIGURE 97-2 *Trianthema portulacastrum* L.: 1. habit; 2. flower; 3. ovary vertical view; 4. same, cross section; 5. stamen, two views; 6. portion of stem showing stipules; 7. capsule; 8. seedling.

DESCRIPTION

T. portulacastrum (Figure 97-2) is a prostrate or procumbent *annual* succulent herb; *taproot* firm, well developed; *stems* angular, thickened, succulent, green to reddish or purplish in color, glabrous or finely pubescent, 10 to 50 cm long; much-branched, one branch of opposite pair markedly larger; *leaves* simple, fleshy, dark green to reddish-green, often purple-margined, entire to slightly undulate, opposite with one of the pair very unequal in size; larger ones ovate-obovate-obcordate with cuneate base, 1.5 to 5 cm long, 1 to 4.5 cm wide; smaller ones similar in shape or oblong, 8 to 30 mm long, 4 to 20 mm wide; *petioles* 4 to 30 mm long, membranous with a few short, thick hairs; dialate into a sheath at the base, forming deep axillary pouch containing flowers; *stipules* acute, sparsely covered with short hairs on the midrib, 2 to 2.5 mm long; *inflorescence* small, solitary, sessile flowers in leaf and branch axils; *flower* without petals, 5 petal-like pink or white *sepals*, perfect, *stamens* 10 to 25; *anthers* pale pink or white; *ovary* superior, 1-celled, truncate; *style* solitary; *fruit* a *capsule* hidden in petiole sheath and clasped by persistent calyx; *capsule* with two distinct parts, membranous lower end sunken into axil with 6 to 9 seeds, fleshy top with 1 or 2 seeds and an exserted beak; *seeds* reniform, 3 to 5 mm long, 1.8 to 2.5 mm wide, dull black, concave on both sides with faint wavy ribs.

This species is recognized by its succulent leaves and fleshy, prostrate stems, purple-margined leaves with petioles and uneven sizes within each pair, and the axillary flowers and fruits enclosed by the petiole base.

DISTRIBUTION, ECOLOGY, AND BIOLOGY

T. portulacastrum is found in tropical and subtropical countries of the Americas, Africa, and Asia and in several regions of Australia (Figure 97-1). It is particularly abundant in India. It is generally reported as a pantropic species with no known center of origin. It occurs in wastelands, roadsides, lawns, gardens, upland cultivated crops, and in paddy fields if the water supply is low. Occasionally it is found in perennial crops and pastures, especially in subhumid and semiarid regions.

T. portulacastrum establishes with the first rains of the wet season and often becomes the dominant early season weed. It prefers rich, moist soils as a seedling (Schmidt et al. 1964). Seedlings exposed to a very dry period are easily killed (Sen 1981). Seedlings are also easily killed if flooded. Civico and Moody (1979) transplanted 5-day-old plants into pots and grew them in a well-drained or saturated soil or in 1, 2.5, and 5 cm of water imposed 0, 1, 2, or 3 wk after transplanting. This species was the most sensitive to flooding of those studied. No seedlings survived if the soil was flooded when they were transplanted and only 20% lived when 1 cm of water was imposed 1 wk after transplanting. If flooding was delayed 2 or 3 wk, survival was greater, but weed height, root length and dry weight 6 wk after planting always decreased as flooding depth increased. Thus the plant is poorly adapted to paddy rice culture, and only when the water supply is limiting does *T. portulacastrum* occur in flooded rice.

Over 40% of the seeds on the surface can germinate, but 60% germinate at 1.2 cm, 40% at 2.5 cm, 26% at 5 cm, and 10% at 7.5 cm. No seeds emerge below 7.5 cm (Rao and Reddy 1982, Balyan and Bhan 1986a). Plants tolerate saline soils better than some crops and have up to 4.5% Na, and a high electrical conductivity (Gidnavar 1980). However, it is not as well adapted to alkaline soils (up to *pH* 9) as is *T. triquetra* (Ramakrishnan and

Lekhi 1972), which germinated equally well at osmotic levels from 0.5 to 6 atmospheres. *T. portulacastrum* germination decreased as the salt concentration increased because it was less able to imbibe water.

In India, the number of leaves per *T. portulacastrum* plant and plant dry weight increased progressively until 40 days after planting (Balyan and Bhan 1986b). Plants from a June 30 and a July 20 sowing had more leaves, leaf area and biomass than earlier or later plantings. The number of primary branches increased for 40 days after planting on June 10 and for 50 days at all other dates. Plants from the June 30 and July 20 sowing had the most secondary branches at maturity. Node formation started 10 days after planting and peaked at harvest for all planting dates. Seed numbers per node and time to reach maturity were similar for all planting dates, except the August 10 and 30 sown plants that needed 5 to 7 days longer to mature. Maximum seed numbers resulted from planting on July 20, followed by the June 30 date.

Biotypes of *T. portulacastrum* occur in India. Typical descriptions refer to red and green as well as large and small types. Differences in prostrate and erect biotypes are sometimes observed. Mahajan (1980) noted that the red biotypes also form larger plants: roots may be 0.5 to 1 cm in diameter at the base and the stem has long internodes and is reddish, as are the sepals, bracts, midribs and pods. Roots of the green biotype are only half as large, internodes are considerably shorter, flowers have white sepals and the plant has green bracts and pods. The red biotype is more abundant, but the green one appears earlier in the season.

The species has a high reproductive capacity of 2460 [(average number of seed produced/ plant) × (percent germination/100)]. Germination of fresh seeds from both red and green biotypes increased from an average of 8% when fresh to 93% when stored for 42 wk (Rao and Reddy 1982). Maximum germination for both types occurred in diffuse light followed by darkness (52%) and the least in continuous light (28%), with continuous darkness having 43% germination. Both large and small biotypes have a $2n$ complement of 26 chromosomes (Bhalla and Tandon 1967).

Both red and white varieties grew best under partial shade and thrived in neutral to alkaline soils low in organic matter in India (Chandra and Sahai 1979). Using a replacement series design, Reddy and Rao (1985) found that the green biotype greatly reduced the growth of the red type in either full light or shade conditions. However, when grown separately, the biomass of each biotype was nearly identical in each light regime. The red biotype allocated more energy to sexual reproduction, while the green type maintained an advantage in competitive ability.

T. portulacastrum exhibits the little-studied phenomenon among weeds of solar tracking. Specifically, the leaves have "diaheliotropic" movements: the leaves remain perpendicular to the sun as it moves across the sky. This gives the species great advantage in its daily net photosynthesis rate (Ehleringer and Forseth 1980). The tracking ability is found in both C_3 and C_4 plants (*T. portulacastrum* is a C_4 plant) and in diverse plant families. Solar tracking becomes common among more species as the day length decreases.

This plant is somewhat unusual in another characteristic: the xylem and phloem occur in alternating concentric rings in the root that appear as growth rings (Bhambie et al. 1977). Additional anatomical details are given by these authors. Raghavendra and Das (1976) in India have thoroughly studied the physiology of *T. portulacastrum*. The chlorophyll a/b ratio was 5.0 in the mesophyll and 4.0 in the bundle sheaths, and the bundle sheath chloroplasts were arranged centripetally. The upper and lower leaf surfaces had 54 and 62 stomata/mm², respectively. The transpiration rate was 18.7 mg water/cm²/hr and the transpiration ratio was 313 g water/g dry matter produced (Das and Santakumari 1977).

Plants begin flowering 20 to 30 days after emergence. In Ghana, flowers of *T. portulacastrum* opened on clear days at 8:00 A.M. and closed at 2:00 P.M. Light intensities of 6400 ft-candles induced flowering in February, while flowering occurs at 5800 ft-candles in December. Flowers closed at 14,900 ft-candles in February and at 12,000 ft-candles in December (Ewusie and Quaye 1977). Flowers produce abundant pollen and the pollen tube reaches the embryo sack within 24 hr after germinating (Dnyansagar and Malkhere 1963). The endosperm follows nuclear development. Most seed growth occurs between 9 and 12 days after pollination and most of the embryo growth takes place at 12 to 14 days. Seeds mature 16 to 17 days after pollination. Applying 2,4-D at flowering prevents viable seed formation; applications at 1, 3, and 4 wk after flowering reduced seed viability by 86, 59, and 21%, respectively (Singh and Saroha 1975). When environmental conditions are suitable, flowering plants can be found all year (Sen 1981).

In India, Datta and Banerjee (1976) collected *T. portulacastrum* seeds as they matured from individual plants for over 1 mo and obtained 4825 seeds/plant. Joshi and Nigam (1970) observed plants under various environmental conditions and found 4 to 15 seeds/capsule, with an average of 9.4. Fewest seeds per capsule were found in the erect branches, the highest number in prostrate branches, and intermediate numbers in procumbent stems. Total seeds per plant ranged from 126 to 16,300 and averaged 6940, with a mean weight of 1.2 mg/seed.

Some freshly harvested seeds germinate, but germinability increases up to 9 mo after harvest and can be increased by mechanical or chemical scarification or by washing fresh but not old seeds (Satendra 1980). Additional studies by Ravel and Chatterji (1968) in India noted that fresh seed had a 17% germination rate. When exposed to dry heat of 90°C for 1 hr, germination increased to 90% and resulted in normal seedlings. However, temperatures of 50°C with high humidity damaged the seed. Thus it is not surprising that solarization of the soil with clear polyethylene sheets reduced emergence of *T. portulacastrum* 87% in the southern United States (Egley 1983). Soil moisture levels were high and temperatures reached 66°C when the soil was covered. Many seeds were killed in soil covered for 1 or 2 wk, but 3 to 4 wk were required to approach complete kill.

Seeds germinate readily between 25 and 40°C but not at 20 or 45°C. Germination is complete within 12 days at optimum temperatures. Seed longevity and germination are greater for seeds in the soil than for those in dry storage (van Rijn 1968, Balyan and Bhan 1986a). Germination is lower in continuous light than in darkness (8% vs. 34%) and is even higher (42%) in alternating dark and light conditions (Mahajan 1982).

AGRICULTURAL IMPORTANCE

T. portulacastrum is widely adapted as a weed in 39 crops of more than 40 countries (Figure 97-1) and is a frequently reported weed of cotton, maize, upland rice, and sugarcane. It is a serious or principal weed of edible beans, carrots, cotton, millet, oats, peanuts, potatoes, rice, sorghum, and sugarcane in India; cabbage and onions in the Philippines; cotton in Australia, Mexico, Nicaragua, the Philippines, and Thailand; irrigated dryland crops in Australia; maize in Australia, Cambodia, Gambia, Guatemala, and Thailand; pastures in Australia and Thailand; peanuts in Australia and Gambia; rice in Ivory Coast; sorghum in Australia, Gambia, and Puerto Rico; sugarcane in the Philippines, Tanzania, and Thailand; sweet potatoes in Cambodia; and vegetables in Ghana, Puerto Rico, and Thailand.

It is a common weed of edible beans in El Salvador; cotton in Peru; cowpeas, millet, and peanuts in Senegal; jute in Thailand; maize in Dominican Republic, Mexico, Peru, and Senegal; onions in Nicaragua; orchards in Sudan; rice in Nicaragua and El Salvador; upland rice in Senegal; sorghum in Dominican Republic, Mexico, and Senegal; sugarcane in Argentina, Bangladesh, Indonesia, and Peru; tobacco in the Philippines; vegetables in Cambodia, Sudan, the United States, and Vietnam; and vineyards in Mexico.

T. portulacastrum is also an unranked weed of edible beans in Colombia and Mexico; cassava in Indonesia, Ghana, and Nigeria; citrus in Mozambique and the United States; coconut in Samoa Islands, coffee in Honduras; cotton in Colombia, Guatemala, Honduras, and Mozambique; cowpeas in Nigeria; dates in Saudi Arabia; jute in India; legumes, linseed, lucerne, and tobacco in Australia; maize in Honduras, Indonesia, Mozambique, Nigeria, the Philippines, El Salvador, and Saudi Arabia; orchards in Australia; pastures in Dominican Republic and Honduras; peanuts in El Salvador; pineapple in Honduras, Nicaragua, and Thailand; rice in Burma, Honduras, Malaysia, Nepal, Pakistan, and Thailand; upland rice in Indonesia, the Philippines, Sri Lanka, Thailand, and Vietnam; lowland rice in Ivory Coast and the Philippines; safflower in Australia and India; sesame in Honduras and India; sorghum in Honduras and Saudi Arabia; soybean in Mexico and the United States; sugarcane in Australia and Mozambique; sweet potatoes in Nigeria and Puerto Rico; taro in Samoa Islands; tomatoes in Ghana and India; and vegetables in the Philippines.

Once established, the plant grows rapidly and competes effectively with many crops. Two hand weedings at 20 and 50 days after planting finger millet (*Eleusine coracana*) in India were insufficient to obtain optimum yields (Subbiah et al. 1974). When control was deficient, two additional irrigations were required, indicating a high moisture consumption by *T. portulacastrum*. This weed can remove seven to ten times as many nutrients as maize (Rajan and Sankaran 1974). In Australia, *T. portulacastrum* was the principal weed during 3 yr of competition studies in grain sorghum. When uncontrolled, crop yields were reduced 29% (Thomas et al. 1980). Timely cultivations gave effective control. Van Rijn (1968) noted that once cotton forms a canopy, it competes well with this weed. In the southwestern United States, the repeated use of simazine and diuron in citrus groves has resulted in this plant becoming a dominant weed. It can be hard to kill by hand or mechanical means because the succulent stem resists desiccation (Egunjobi 1969a).

In competition studies done in pots in the greenhouse in the Philippines, *T. portulacastrum* reduced cotton yields an average of 35% over three weed densities. Cotton maturity was delayed, and N and P concentrations in cotton were reduced by 35 and 36%, respectively (Guantes and Mercado 1975). In India, *T. portulacastrum* is a principal weed of maize and produces over 1000 kg/ha of dry matter in 55 days after maize planting (Kumar 1983). This weed forms over 30 kg/ha/day of biomass.

There are numerous countries in the Americas, Asia and Africa that have not observed *T. portulacastrum*. Appropriate measures should be taken to prevent its introduction into these areas. Once present in a country, infestations may be spread by ants (Mahajan 1980) or in manure because seeds can survive passage through the digestive tract of cattle (Sastry 1957).

In India, the plant hosts the chilli mosaic virus that is transmitted by aphids (Mariappan and Narayansamy 1977), and it is host to the cantaloupe disease *Macrophomina phaseolina* in Texas. Sclerotia were found on the weeds roots, but they did not affect its growth. In parts of India, insects may feed heavily on the leaves of *T. portulacastrum*, reducing its severity (Sen 1981). It can also host the parasitic weed *Cuscuta reflexa* which seriously damages the plant (Ravel and Chatterji 1968).

In Australia, the plant is rarely eaten by animals and is reportedly unpalatable (Everist 1974). However, in South Vietnam, plants are commonly chopped and mixed with rice flour or ground maize, soaked in water and fed to swine. Poultry eat it readily without preparation; and cattle, goats and water buffalo graze it on roadsides and in waste areas. Occasionally plants are harvested, dried and stored for livestock feed. The only problem encountered was the appearance of lush *T. portulacastrum* plants after a serious drought, which caused many ruminant animals to bloat and die after grazing fresh plants.

Nevertheless, Schmidt et al. (1964) compared *T. portulacastrum* to lucerne to evaluate its potential as a forage. When both species were well watered, the weed yielded twice as much as lucerne (3.3 vs. 1.5 ton/ha dry matter) and was three times higher in P (0.74 to 0.24%). However, it was considerably lower in protein and calcium. Under dry soil conditions, lucerne was higher than *T. portulacastrum* in yield and all quality factors except P content. In India, *T. portulacastrum* was equivalent to other forages in protein, digestibility, P and Ca content; and male cattle gained 28 g/day when fed only this plant and wheat straw (Singh et al. 1982). Interestingly, the crude fiber content of the weed remained relatively constant as the plant matured, which may be why animals readily consume young or mature plants.

Other uses of *T. portulacastrum* have been reported. It is sometimes eaten as a vegetable (Uphof 1968) and has been used as a medicine for many years. The leaves are sometimes used as a diuretic (Lewis and Lewis 1977). Whole plant extracts have analgesic, antibacterial and anti-inflamatory effects and can be used to treat fevers, inflammatory diseases, respiratory infections and pain (Vohora et al. 1983). In India, Chopra and Chatterjee (1940) compared the medicinal properties of red and white biotypes of this plant to *Boerhavia diffusa*. Both species are commonly used as medicines and the common name "punarnava" refers to either species. Their studies demonstrated that this confusion has little practical importance. Even though the species are members of very different plant families, both appear to contain the same alkaloid known as "punarnavine." The red biotype of *Trianthema* contained the most alkaloid and *Boerhavia* the least, but the difference was not great.

COMMON NAMES

Trianthema portulacastrum

ARGENTINA	verdolaga rastrera
AUSTRALIA	black pigweed, giant pigweed
CAMBODIA	phti thmar
COLOMBIA	verdolaga blanca
DOMINICAN REPUBLIC	verdolagilla
EL SALVADOR	verdolaga de hoja ancha
GHANA	seaside purslane
GUATEMALA	verdolaga de hoja ancha
INDIA	ambatimadu, bishkapra, galjeru, itsit, patharchata, salsabuni, santhi, sarani, swet, vishakapara, yerkugoligery
INDONESIA	krokot, telekan
MEXICO	verdolaga de cochi, verdolaga de hoja ancha

NICARAGUA	verdolaga de hoja ancha
NIGERIA	olowonjeja
PERU	verdolaga
PHILIPPINES	ayam, kantataba, tabtabukol, toston, ulisiman
PUERTO RICO	verdolaga de hoja ancha
SAUDI ARABIA	lanni
THAILAND	phak-bia-hin
UNITED STATES	horse purslane
VENEZUELA	toston, verdolegon
VIETNAM	sam, tamlang

Ninety-Eight

Tridax procumbens L.

Asteraceae (Compositae), Aster Family

TRIDAX PROCUMBENS is native to the tropical Americas but is now found in nearly 60 countries. Of all the *Tridax* species in tropical America, only *T. procumbens* has global importance. It is generally considered a perennial but some refer to it as an annual or short-lived perennial. The species adapts to many environments and can rapidly colonize new areas. The genus name refers to the three lobes of the ray flowers while the species name refers to the prostrate, trailing habit of the stems.

FIGURE 98-1   The distribution of *Tridax procumbens* L. across the world where it has been reported as a weed.

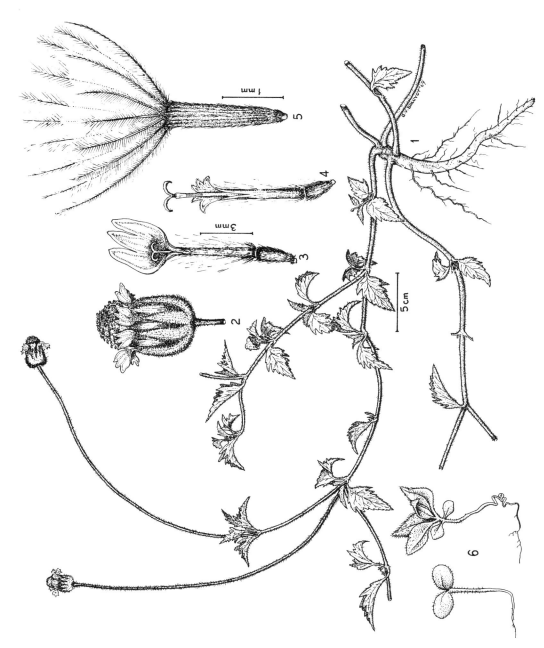

FIGURE 98-2 *Tridax procumbens* L.: 1. habit; 2. flower head; 3. ray flowers; 4. disc flowers; 5. achenes with pappus; 6. seedlings.

DESCRIPTION

T. procumbens (Figure 98-2) is a semi-prostrate *perennial* herb; *taproot* slender, wavy with many lateral branches; *stems* more or less ascending, 30 to 50 cm high, branched, round, sparsely to very hairy; *leaves* simple, opposite, lanceolate to ovate, 3 to 7 cm long, 1 to 4 cm wide, with irregularly toothed margins; base wedge-shaped, shortly-petioled, hairy on both surfaces; *inflorescence* a terminal involucrate flower head or capitulum, 1 to 2 cm across, solitary on erect *peduncle* 10 to 25 cm long; *involucre* 3-seriate, ovate, acute to shortly acuminate, 5 to 6 mm long; *receptacle* with oblong, hairy scales; *ray flowers* 3-dentate, few, pale yellow; *disk flowers* 5-dentate, tubular, yellow to brownish-yellow, with recurved hairy segments; *fruit* a black *achene* covered with fine, pale hairs giving a grayish-brown appearance, 2 mm long, 1 mm wide at apex, base narrow; *pappus* in one row of wide scales, unequal in length, 5 to 6 mm long.

The 3-seriate and hairy involucre, the 3-dentate pale yellow ray flowers, opposite leaves with toothed margins, and semi-prostrate habit are the distinguishing features of this species.

HABITAT AND DISTRIBUTION

T. procumbens occurs throughout the tropical and subtropical belt of the world (Figure 98-1) and is frequently found in annual crops, roadsides, pastures, fallow land and waste areas, and occasionally in lawns, perennial crops and nurseries. *T. procumbens* adapts to many environments. It is particularly well adapted to coarse-textured soils of tropical regions and is found from sea level to 1000 m. It is the most common dicotyledonous plant on Wake Island, a dry atoll in the Pacific Ocean (St. John 1976). When present in cassava fields in Colombia, it was the most abundant species, with densities of 240,000 to 340,000 plants/ha (Doll et al. 1977). Its wide distribution and importance as a weed are due to its spreading stems and abundant seed production (Baker 1965).

It reportedly was introduced into Nigeria as an ornamental in the early 1900s. After many years, the population began spreading to other areas, especially along roadsides and in artificial pastures (Adams and Baker 1962). *T. procumbens* has spread rapidly in Zambia since the 1950s and is becoming a common weed of arable land, except in areas of high rainfall (Vernon 1983).

BIOLOGY AND ECOLOGY

T. procumbens seeds germinate over a prolonged period and in a variable pattern. Only 44% of freshly harvested seed in Nigeria was viable and seed germination in response to light was cyclic (Marks and Nwachuku 1986). Freshly harvested seed required light to germinate (100%), but after 2 mo of burial in soil, half germinated in darkness. The light requirement was reinstated from May onward as the rainy season progressed and declined as the rains ended. This pattern allows more seed to germinate at the start of the rainy season because seeds in darkness below the soil surface can germinate.

Germination is also influenced by the type of "landing" the achene makes (Pemadasa and Kangatharalingam 1977). In normal landings, the achene touches the soil and then 78% of the seeds germinate. If the pappus lands on the soil, germination is 30%, which is less than for other species with smaller achenes. Removing the pappus reduces germination from 79 to 49% because achenes absorb less water when the pappus is absent. If imbibed seeds subsequently dry, germination is delayed but the final percentage is not changed. Fifty-six percent of the seeds on the surface germinated and 30, 11, 5, and 2% of seeds placed 0.5, 1, 2, and 4 cm deep, respectively, germinated. Seeds 2 and 4 cm deep did not emerge and only 6% of those at 1 cm emerged.

Nearly half the seeds exposed to six wetting and drying cycles germinated, while only 16% of the controls did (Fenner 1980). Potted seeds in East Africa germinated very well when they received long rains (not defined) but germination was below 2% when short rains fell (Popay and Ivens 1982). Germination of fresh seed of edaphic ecotypes in India varied from 32 to 53%. All ecotypes germinated best at 30°C and at *pH*s between 6 and 8 (Ramakrishnan and Jain 1965b). Research by Padmanabhan (1968) gives a thorough description of the embryogeny and seedling anatomy of *T. procumbens*.

T. procumbens is sensitive to shade, as plant height, dry weight and leaf area index decline as the level of shade increases. However, this species is less affected by shade than many others and thus crop competition may not effectively suppress its growth (Shetty et al. 1982).

Intra-specific competition studies by Oladokun (1978) in Nigeria and Pemadasa (1976) in India found plant density greatly affects *T. procumbens* growth. Root and shoot weight, plant height and the number of leaves per plant dropped as the plant population increased. Pemadasa (1976) planted 2, 6, 18, and 54 seeds in pots 25 cm in diameter and placed them outdoors. Ninety-five percent of the seeds emerged at all densities, but the establishment percentage dropped from 95% at 2 seeds/pot to 82% with 18 or 56 seeds/pot. Fewer inflorescences were formed at the high populations, while the number of seeds per inflorescence remained constant. The overall production of seeds per pot rose from 450 to 800 at densities of 2 and 54 plants/pot, respectively. Plants partition proportionately less biomass into reproductive structures at high populations. Pemadasa created a heterogenous soil surface and planted seeds on the ridges or in the depressions. Survival was higher among ridge-planted seeds, and this is consistent with the occurrence of this species in relatively dry soils. While *T. procumbens* may be less competitive than other **Asteraceae** species, its adaptability to microhabitats enhances its survival in mixed plant communities.

Plants attain maximum height and biomass 12 wk after germination in Nigeria (Ogbonnaya 1988). The ratio of leaf area to whole plant dry weight peaked 4 wk after germination. *T. procumbens* forms slender, wavy taproots with many lateral branches (Shetty and Maiti 1978). The branches are more abundant near the soil surface and on the upper half of the main root. The lateral roots angle sharply downward and are important in nutrient and water uptake.

Ecotypes of *T. procumbens* were observed on soils with high, moderate and low levels of calcareous parent material in India (Ramakrishnan and Jain 1965a). The Ca content in plants correlated to the levels in the soil. When grown on the same soil at *pH* 7, the differences between ecotypes in Ca content remained.

The leaf surface anatomy of *T. procumbens* has also been studied in India (Das and Santakaumari 1977, Pemadasa 1979, Veeranjaneyulu and Das 1984). Estimates range from 54 to 175 stomata/mm^2 on the upper leaf surface and from 142 to 295/mm^2 on the lower surface. Plants transpire 25.2 mg of water/cm^2/hr, with a transpiration coefficient of 658. Other estimates place this value as high as 1402 (Datta 1959), as compared to sorghum with a coefficient of 430, which means that this species is a very inefficient user of water. *T. procumbens* is a C_3 plant, and has 1.8 mg chlorophyll/g fresh weight, an a/b chlorophyll ratio of 1.2, and a CO_2 compensation point of 65 ppm.

In Sri Lanka, flowering plants can be found all year (Pemadasa 1976). In Indian jute fields, plants flowered from late March through May in 1971; in 1972 they flowered at a similar time and from mid-August through mid-October (Saraswat 1980). *T. procumbens* flowers 35 to 55 days after emergence and seeds ripen within 3 wk of flowering (Popay and Ivens 1982). Single plants can produce 500 to 2500 seeds and one gram contains 1300 seeds with the pappus (Pancho 1964). The pappus is relatively small in comparison to the seed weight and is not likely to aid in widespread seed dispersal (Baker 1965). Achenes formed by tubular (disc) florets are distinct from those of ligulate (ray) florets (Marks and Akosim 1984). Ten achenes (excluding the pappus) of ray and disc florets weigh 5.38 and 3.78 mg, respectively. The pappus comprises 20% of the total weight of seeds from ray florets and 42% of seeds from disc florets. This may give them different dispersal patterns. The total weight of the achene plus pappus is similar for both types, as is their germination.

Cytological studies found seven types of chromosomes with a $2n$ value of 36 (Bhattacharyya and Sharma 1970). Detailed cytological studies of *T. procumbens* reproduction discovered that it is not apomictic and can be either cross- or self-pollinated (Rogers 1969). Florets reach the same stage of development via either form of pollination at equivalent times.

In India, thrips pollinate *T. procumbens* flowers (Ananthakrishnan et al. 1981). As the florets open, thrips begin to inhabit the capitula and the population peaks when the stigmatic lobes are exposed. Each thrip carries 40 to 200 pollen grains on its body and both adults and larvae move frequently. Butterflies, beetles and bees are also found on the inflorescences of this plant.

Das and Pal (1970) in India studied the allelopathic effects of *T. procumbens* to rice. Vapors emitted from leaves did not affect rice seed germination but reduced root and coleoptile length 30%, coleoptile dry weight 31%, and root dry weight 15%. When exposed to *T. procumbens* leaves, rice roots exhibited a proliferation of secondary root growth. The volatile substances of *T. procumbens* were more inhibitory to rice than those from *Cyperus rotundus*.

AGRICULTURAL IMPORTANCE

T. procumbens is a reported weed of 31 crops in 60 countries (Figure 98-1) and is frequently reported in maize, cotton, rice, sugarcane, and pastures. It is a serious or principal weed of cassava in Ghana and India; cotton in India, Morocco, Mozambique, Thailand, and Tanzania; dry-land crops, jute and wheat in India; irrigated crops and vegetables in Australia; maize in Ghana, Guatemala, Nigeria, and Thailand; pastures in Australia and Cuba; peanuts in Ghana, India, and New Guinea; sorghum in Thailand; soybeans in India and Taiwan; and sugarcane in India and Kenya.

It is a common weed of edible beans in Cuba; maize in India and Mexico; pastures in Hawaii; pineapple in Hawaii and Thailand; rice in Nicaragua; upland rice in India and Sri Lanka; roselle in Indonesia; soybeans in Ghana; sugarcane in Nigeria and Thailand; tea in India; and wastelands in Australia and India.

T. procumbens is also an unranked weed of avocado in the United States; bananas in Costa Rica, Honduras, and Taiwan; edible beans in Honduras, Mexico, and Nicaragua; cacao and coffee in Nicaragua and Nigeria; cassava in Colombia, Indonesia, the Philippines, and Taiwan; cotton in Honduras, Kenya, and Nicaragua; cowpeas in Nigeria; dry-land crops in Australia and Ivory Coast; legumes in the Philippines; mango in Mexico; maize in Cambodia, Honduras, Indonesia, Laos, Nicaragua, the Philippines, and Vietnam; oil palm, rubber, and tea in Indonesia; orchards in Australia and Honduras; pastures in Brazil, Dominican Republic, Honduras, India, Nigeria, and the Philippines; peppers and tomatoes in Costa Rica; peanuts in Honduras and Taiwan; upland rice in Honduras, Indonesia, Nigeria, the Philippines, Taiwan, and Vietnam; lowland rice in Indonesia and Ivory Coast; sesame in Honduras and Nicaragua; sisal in Tanzania; sorghum in Honduras, India, Mexico, and Nicaragua; soybeans in Indonesia and Nigeria; sugarcane in Cambodia, Indonesia, Nicaragua, the Philippines, and Taiwan; sweet potatoes in Honduras, Nigeria, and Taiwan; tobacco in Honduras and the Philippines; and vegetables in Honduras.

In Sri Lanka, *T. procumbens* is considered one of the three most troublesome **Asteraceae** weeds on arable fields. Even if plants are hand-pulled or mechanically weeded, their stems often break readily and plants regrow from the lower nodes (Adams and Baker 1962). This weed can interfere with jute harvest in India. *T. procumbens* is a host to the root-knot nematode in India (Upadhyay et al. 1977), the insect *Phalanta phalanta* which defoliates poplar (*Populus* spp.) trees in Nigeria (Akanbi 1971), a virus in India (Shamsher 1979), and the red spider mite (*Tetranychus telarius*), also in India (Choudhury and Mukherjee 1971). The weed is also an alternate host to *Orobanche* and stimulates the germination of seeds of this serious parasitic plant (Sen 1981).

The plant is sometimes used as green feed for poultry in Nigeria (Egunjobi 1969a) and to stop bleeding in certain Indian villages. Kasture and Wadodkar (1971) in India analyzed mature plants and found sugars, sterols, and tannins but no alkaloids or glycosides.

COMMON NAMES

Tridax procumbens

AUSTRALIA	tridax daisy
BRAZIL	erva de touro
BURMA	mive sok ne-gya
COLOMBIA	cadillo chisaca
CUBA	romerillo de loma
DOMINICAN REPUBLIC	piquant jambe
EL SALVADOR	hierba del toro
FIJI	wild daisy
GHANA	white-dirty cream
HAWAII	tridax
HONDURAS	hierba del toro
INDIA	bisalyakarmi, mukkuthipoo, phanafuli, tunki
INDONESIA	gletang, gletangan, sidowolo, tar sentaran
JAPAN	kotobukigiku
MADAGASCAR	anganiay
MALAYSIA	coat bottoms, kanching baju
MAURITIUS	herbe caille
MEXICO	flor amarilla, panquica, rosilla

PUERTO RICO	tridax
TAIWAN	kotobuki-giku
THAILAND	teen tuk kae
TRINIDAD	railway weed
UNITED STATES	tridax daisy

Ninety-Nine

Typha angustifolia L. and Typha latifolia L.

Typhaceae, Cattail Family

TYPHA SPECIES are widespread and troublesome emergent, aquatic, freshwater weeds found throughout the world. They interfere with the use and maintenance of drainage and irrigation canals, and impede water transport, fishing, recreational, and other activities in lakes, ponds, marshes, rivers, and reservoirs. The genus is the only one in the family and its name is from the Greek *typhe* meaning a cat's tail, smoke or a cloud, refer-

FIGURE 99-1   The distribution of *Typha latifolia* L. across the world where it has been reported as a weed.

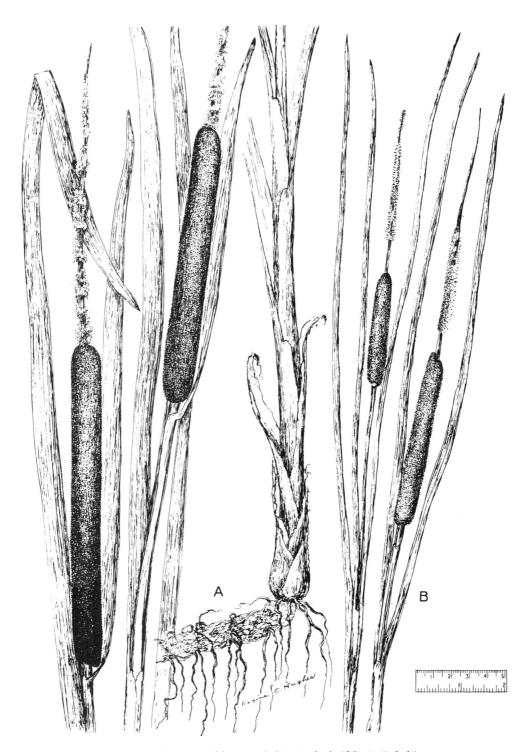

FIGURE 99-2 *Typha angustifolia* L.: A. habit. *Typha latifolia* L.: B. habit.

ring to the plants' appearance when seeds are released. The species names reflect their respective leaf width: "angusti" for narrow, "lati" for broad or wide, and "folia" for leaf.

DESCRIPTIONS

Typha angustifolia

T. angustifolia (Figure 99-2) is a slender *perennial* aquatic to 3 m tall with branched, creeping, stout *rhizomes* 2 to 4 cm in diameter, up to 70 cm long; *roots* fibrous in dense mats at base of stems and from rhizome nodes; *stems* erect, unbranched, round, solid; *leaves* grasslike, linear, 60 to 80 cm long, 3 to 8 mm wide (occasionally 12 mm), deep green, strongly planoconvex, usually less than 10 per stem, sheathing at base; *inflorescence* a cylindrical monoecious *spike* 40 to 70 cm long; *staminate flowers* above, brown to yellowish with single pollen grains (*monads*), separated from female flowers by gap of 10 mm or more; *pistillate flowers* reddish-brown to dark brown, *stigmas* linear, not fleshy, with many whitish to light brown hairs attached to base of pistil, intermixed with dark brown bracteoles; *fruit* an achene, 5 to 8 mm long, subtended by copious white hairs arising above middle, acute base, apex obtuse and broader; *seeds* pendulous with straight, narrow embryo nearly as long as seed.

Typha latifolia

T. latifolia (Figure 99-2) is an erect, rhizomatous *perennial* aquatic to 3 m tall; *rhizomes* creeping, up to 70 cm long, arising from stem base; soft, white, 1 to 3 cm diameter with fibrous scale leaves; terminate in erect, leafy *stems*; stem base 1 to 2 cm in diameter surrounded by persistent leaf sheath; *leaves* 80 to 120 cm long, 8 to 15 mm wide (occasionally to 25 mm), linear, base white, blade light green, spongy, smooth, waxy, flat on underside; *inflorescence* similar to *T. angustifolia* but without gap between male and female flowers; to 30 cm long; *staminate flowers* reddish to blackish-brown, pollen shed in tetrads; *pistillate flowers* dark brown, *stigmas* lanceolate to ovate, fleshy and thread-like; bracts absent on female and uniformly narrow on male flowers; *fruit* an *achene*, one end pointed, other end blunt; subtended by copious white hairs arising at base.

The main differences between these species are in the leaf color and width and in the thinner inflorescence of *T. angustifolia* with the conspicuous gap between the staminate and pistillate flowers in this species versus the continuous spike in *T. latifolia*. Additionally, the leaves of *T. angustifolia* overtop the inflorescence, while those of *T. latifolia* are just equal to or only slightly exceed the height of the inflorescence.

HABITAT AND ECOLOGY

Both species occur in shallow lakes and streams, river edges, ditches, marshes, reservoirs and similar sites. They are found from the Arctic Circle to lat 30° S and to 3000 m (Figures 99-1 and 99-3). *T. angustifolia* tolerates deeper and more alkaline water than *T. latifolia* (Mcmillan 1959, Sale and Wetzel 1983). Leaf tips of *T. latifolia* curl when plants are in 1% salt water, while those of *T. angustifolia* are unaffected.

McNaughton (1966) compared the growth of ecotypes of both species collected from 33 sites along a north-south gradient in the central United States. Environment, not eco-

FIGURE 99-3   The distribution of *Typha angustifolia* L. across the world where it has been reported as a weed.

type, controls *Typha* height. Maximum height for all types was with 14 hr of light at 30/24°C or with 16 hr of light at 30/15.5°C. Northern *T. latifolia* populations formed more rhizomes than southern populations and more than *T. angustifolia* from any site. Rhizome production peaked at 30/15.5°C regardless of photoperiod. Initiation of spring growth was more uniform among biotypes of *T. angustifolia* (within 2 days) than *T. latifolia* (over a 16-day period). An inverse relationship between rhizome formation and flowering was noted: nearly 80% of the *T. angustifolia* shoots flowered but only 28% of *T. latifolia* shoots did. Northern biotypes of *T. latifolia* exhibited greater genetic variability, reflecting the more variable climatic conditions of this zone. *T. angustifolia* was more productive than *T. latifolia* under ideal conditions, but the latter is adapted to a wide range of conditions. Later research lead McNaughton (1975) to consider *T. angustifolia* a "climatic specialist" and *T. latifolia* a "climatic generalist." Other studies (McNaughton 1973, McNaughton et al. 1974) found nearly identical assimilation and transpiration rates for *T. latifolia* from California and Canada and for ecotypes selected across a range of altitudes in the western United States. The main difference observed was that the high-altitude biotype absorbed P more efficiently from cold soils than coastal types.

Several interactions between the species occur as water depth increases (Grace and Wetzel 1981a, 1982). *T. latifolia* predominates in water depths of 15 to 50 cm, while maximum *T. angustifolia* biomass occurs at 80 cm. *T. latifolia* leaves become longer as water depth increases, but *T. angustifolia* leaves are always longer than those of *T. latifolia*. As water level increases, *T. latifolia* forms more leaves per plant at the expense of the parent rhizome. In contrast, *T. angustifolia* sacrifices sexual reproductive biomass to maintain the parent rhizome. Within 2 yr after establishment from seeds, *T. latifolia* and *T. angustifolia* can occupy 58 and 48 m², respectively.

BIOLOGY

T. angustifolia and latifolia often occur as monocultures. Regeneration and spread takes place primarily through rhizome growth, but establishment from seed at the shoreline is also possible, especially when water levels drop. *T. angustifolia* germinates and establishes in saturated soil with up to 10 cm of standing water (Keddy and Ellis 1985). In coarse soils, fewer than 5% of the seeds germinate when the water level is 4 cm below the soil surface, while 25% germinate under these conditions in fine soil (Keddy and Constabel 1986). Soil texture has no effect on germination when 1 cm of water covers the soil.

Intact seeds of *T. latifolia* need reduced oxygen levels, light, or nitrogen in combination with alternating temperatures to germinate (Morinaga 1926a,b). Rupturing the seed coat induces germination. Intact seeds germinate best at oxygen levels between 1 and 18%; no germination occurs in oxygen-free conditions. Yeo (1964) noted that applying pressure on the blunt end of the seed breaks the seed coat and enhances germination. He obtained emergence under greenhouse conditions in 75 cm of water. Some seeds placed 75 cm below the water emerged in the greenhouse. Weller (1975) found that 50% of the *T. latifolia* seeds germinate in 2.5 cm of water, 30% at 15 cm, 20% at 25 cm, and only 15% at 35 cm. Most (95%) germinate within 35 days after planting.

Wetlands are sometimes burned to rejuvenate the vegetation. In darkness, 48% of the seeds germinated in distilled water, and if ash was present, 72% germinated. Green-leaf extracts of *T. latifolia* reduced germination to 15%. Ash overcame most of this inhibitory effect (38% germination). In light, germination was similar in all solutions and in both light and darkness at *pH*s of 4, 7, and 12. After germination, green-leaf extract strongly inhibited root development, even with ash. This may prevent establishment after germination (Rivard and Woodard 1989).

Bonnewell et al. (1983) obtained maximum germination at 35°C and none at 10°C for Canadian *T. latifolia*. Southern biotypes of both species germinate at lower temperatures than northern biotypes (McNaughton 1966). This response protects seedlings from a killing freeze after germination.

After germination, *T. latifolia* forms two to four short leaves and then two to six ribbon-like, floating leaves. Finally, erect leaves emerge. When new leaves are 30 cm tall, a crown develops at the base. Once shoots are 35 to 45 cm long, their growth rate decreases and rhizome formation begins. When rhizomes are 35 to 60 cm long, they turn upward and form shoots. The process repeats itself many times, and in a single season approximately 100 shoots and lateral buds are produced that may cover an area 3 m in diameter. If plants originate from seed, neither species flowers the first season.

Rhizome formation and overall growth patterns differ between the species. *T. angustifolia* forms a few stout, short rhizomes, whereas *T. latifolia* rhizomes are longer and thinner. *T. latifolia* forms twice as many rhizomes per parent node and the rhizomes are usually less than 3 yr old because the crown usually dies after flowering, which destroys the basal meristem (Grace and Wetzel 1982). In contrast, *T. angustifolia* plants regenerate from old rhizomes for several seasons.

In Europe, two peaks of *T. latifolia* rhizome growth occur: one from June to early August and another from late September to October (Fiala 1971). Rhizomes are shorter and thicker in the fall and have many buds that form dense clumps of shoots the next spring. A single rhizome can form colonies 6 m in diameter after two seasons.

In Czechoslovakia, Fiala (1978) compared the growth of both species originating from rhizomes. When grown free of competition, *T. latifolia* formed 2.9 shoots/plant/day in late

August, while *T. angustifolia* formed 0.9 shoots. In the second year, they averaged 9.5 and 6.1 shoots/plant/day, respectively, at the peak growth period in August. In the fall, the rate of shoot formation decreases and reverses: *T. angustifolia* forms 2.4 shoots/day, while *T. latifolia* forms only 1.6 shoots/day from September to November. In the year of planting, both species formed 215 shoots. In the second year, *T. angustifolia* and *T. latifolia* produced 1080 and 1390 shoots, respectively.

Rhizomes grow to 1 m long and form new shoots without branching. Subsequently, a new rhizome develops at the shoot base and grows in generally the same direction. Both species have alternating periods of intense shoot and then rhizome development. In the first year, rhizomes spread to 2 m in diameter for *T. latifolia* and 1 m for *T. angustifolia*. The latter species has its peak rhizome growth in the fall. After two seasons, a single colony of *T. latifolia* covered 54 m² with a total rhizome length of 480 m, and *T. angustifolia* covered 38 m² with 380 m of rhizome. *T. angustifolia* rhizomes survived 7 days under anaerobic conditions (Barclay and Crawford 1982), but most rhizomes deprived of oxygen for 2 wk die (Brandle 1985).

Maximum underground biomass accumulation occurs in late July to early August (over 1 g/shoot/day) with a secondary peak 8 wk later. In the fall, 20 and 26% of the total plant dry weight of *T. angustifolia* and *T. latifolia*, respectively, is carbohydrate. During the summer this value is about 10%.

Three "pulses" of *T. latifolia* shoot emergence are common in the northern United States (Dickerman and Wetzel 1985). Initial canopy formation usually occurs by the end of May. The early appearing shoots are dead by autumn. Most (78%) of those that emerge in midsummer die that year but the remainder form new shoots the following season. Eighty-five percent of the shoots appearing in late summer to early fall survive and grow again the next year. Thus *T. latifolia* populations always have a range of shoot ages. Densities of about 42 shoots/m² are typical in mature stands.

Leaf weight per unit area is similar for both species (Grace and Wetzel 1982). *T. latifolia* has more surface area per unit leaf height and more leaf biomass per plant than *T. angustifolia*. The latter species allocates 20% of its new biomass to sexual structures and less than 5% to lateral ramets. The reverse is found with *T. latifolia*. In both species, lateral ramets form after flowering begins.

T. latifolia crowns form shoots in the upper portion, exposed buds in the central region, and rhizomes from the lower area (Yeo 1964). Each crown forms up to eight shoots and the lateral buds form near the shoots and account for the "generation" pattern of shoot development. If rhizomes are planted, plants do not flower the first year and rhizomes have 25 to 30% carbohydrate. Plants flower the next year and carbohydrate levels drop to 20% (Fiala 1978). If flowering shoots are removed, *Typha* species form more rhizomes.

Productivity of *T. latifolia* varies from 430 to 2250 g dry wt/m²/yr (Boyd 1971, Dickerman and Wetzel 1985). This is equivalent to 8% of the N present in the standing crop. This rate of carbon assimilation is typical of C_4 plants, but *Typha* species are C_3 plants. Both sides of *T. latifolia* leaves are equally active in receiving and using light, which gives the plant high photosynthetic efficiency (Kvet et al. 1969). From March 24 to May 6, nutrient uptake is twice as rapid as biomass accumulation. Plant dry weights increase for 90 to 120 days of the season in the southeastern United States. In growth chambers, *T. latifolia* produced 275% more shoot biomass at 25°C than at 10°C (Reddy and Portier 1987). Root biomass yield was also lowest at 10°C and shoot/root ratios were low (0.7 to 0.8) at 10 to 15°C but increased to 2.3 to 2.6 at 20 to 25°C. In the southern United States, *T. angustifolia* produced 2780 and 2400 g dry wt/m² of above- and below-ground biomass, respectively (Hill 1987). Above-ground biomass accumulation was related to length of the growing season, precipitation, cumulative degree days and cumulative pan evaporation.

Both species allocate more biomass to rhizomes when in sparse populations as compared to dense stands (Grace and Wetzel 1981b). Over 50% of the leaf volume of *Typha* species is air cavities that are more numerous in the basal region (Pazourek 1977). Excluding the cavities, most leaf tissue is parenchyma cells (over 50%), while a relatively low 22% is photosynthetic tissue. Both species have well-developed internal aerenchyma tissue for gas exchange between below-ground parts and the atmosphere (Sale and Wetzel 1983).

Both species accumulate nutrients in high proportions. *T. angustifolia* accumulated 16 to 37 elements at higher levels than the water in which it grew (Kovacs 1982). It was particularly high in Na and Cl. Most N was in root hairs and leaves, and the highest P levels were in leaves. *T. latifolia* had the highest level of 7 of 23 elements measured in six species in a coal-burning power plant basin (Guthrie and Cherry 1979). Concentrations of Se, Mg, Br, Cl, Ca, K, and Mn were 39, 148, 150, 220, 225, 455, and 6070 times higher in plant tissue than in the water. Klopatek (1978) detected 3.8% N, 0.8% P, 3.8% K, 1.6% Ca, and 0.3% Mg in *T. latifolia* shoots. The maximum quantities accumulated by the whole plant were 38, 35, 32, 9.8, and 4.8 g/m^2 of K, N, Ca, Mg, and P, respectively. Nutrient levels drop rapidly when growth begins in the spring.

N and K are the most abundant nutrients in *T. latifolia* (Prentki et al. 1978). Levels of P are twice as high in shoot bases as they are in rhizomes and new shoots, and rhizomes have twice as much P as adult organs. Most of the P in shoots is leached or released into the water during decomposition. Nutrient and biomass accumulation are relatively slow for the first 4 to 8 wk in the spring. Plants then enter a rapid growth period for 4 to 8 wk, and 50 to 80% of the total biomass production and nutrient accumulation occurs. During this period, *Typha* leaves represent 60 to 70% of the biomass and are the primary nutrient sink. As the growing season ends, approximately 40% of the N, 35 to 44% of the P, and 4 to 38% of the K is translocated to the rhizomes (Garver et al. 1988). Seed heads are another sink for N, P, and Mg and contain 30, 39, and 37% of the N, P, and Mg, respectively, in the above-ground biomass at the end of the season (Boyd 1970b).

Both species have high rates of transpiration. Water loss in *T. angustifolia*-infested areas is 50% greater than that of open water in India (Brezny et al. 1973). In Poland, water loss in infested areas is approximately 3000 L/m^2/season for both species (Krolikowska 1978). Peak transpiration occurred at 11:00 A.M. and 3:00 P.M. Younger leaves transpire more than older ones, and the maximum transpiration rates of 600 and 500 mg/g fresh wt/hr for *T. angustifolia* and *T. latifolia*, respectively, occur in July. While their true transpiration rate is low, their high leaf area results in significant water loss.

Ten-day-old leaves of *T. latifolia* are more photosynthetically active than 30-day-old leaves (McNaughton 1973). Maximum CO_2 fixation was 39 mg CO_2/g dry wt/hr for two biotypes studied, which is high for a C_3 plant. Both leaf surfaces have about the same number of stomata (378/mm^2 on the upper and 349/mm^2 on the lower surface) and transpiration was also similar for both biotypes (average of 2.64 g water/g dry wt/hr).

Shades of 40, 60, and 90% reduce growth of both species about 60, 80, and 90%, respectively, as compared to full sunlight. Most plants die after 3 mo in 90% shade. *T. latifolia* competes well with other species for light because of its high leaf area index (Grace and Wetzel 1981b). *T. latifolia* leaves are heavier per unit height, have shorter internodes, and intercept more light when in 15 cm or less of water than *T. angustifolia* (Grace and Wetzel 1982). This species is "exploitive" in its ability to colonize available space readily, while *T. angustifolia* is a "conservative" colonizer by virtue of its lower vegetative spread and longer retention of older rhizomes.

T. latifolia fixes up to 18 kg N/ha/yr in the northern United States (Biesboer 1984). This is equivalent to 8% of the total N present. N fixation peaks after pollination in early August and then declines linearly to the end of the season. Roots have both aerobic and anaerobic bacteria and their populations closely parallel water temperatures. Old rhizomes are nearly depleted of starch in July and August and are not replenished to previous levels. Rather, most carbohydrates accumulate in new rhizomes.

Inflorescences have female flowers above and male flowers below. The lower pistillate flowers are fertile with a central carpel, and the mid-section contains sterile, stalked, club-shaped cells. The terminal flowers are rudimentary and consist of only tufts of hair (Krattinger 1975). *T. latifolia* forms 280 to 420 million pollen grains/inflorescence and *T. angustifolia* around 175 million.

Pollen of *T. latifolia* remains viable for 4 wk, which is nearly the same as the flowering period. Cross-pollination is more frequent with *T. angustifolia* because its pollen is lighter (single-grained). Pollen of both species is wind borne and yet they have a high degree of self-pollination. Hybridization occurs between the two species (Sculthorpe 1967).

Over 50% of the pollinated flowers set seed (Krattinger 1975). Seeds are protected from germinating in the stalk by the swelling of the pistillodes that are distributed throughout the inflorescence. In humid conditions, they swell and keep the spike intact. They can swell 15 to 20% in 15 min in 100% relative humidity. Upon drying, the pistillodes shrivel, air again reaches the seed, and the perianth hairs spread. Their collective pressure causes the inflorescence to burst, releasing the fruits to the air. The hairs serve as parachutes to disperse the seeds. If they fall on water, the hairs close and the pericarp releases the seed which then sinks. However, this process may take 4 days for *T. latifolia* and 4 wk for *T. angustifolia*, allowing for significant dissemination by water (Ridley 1930). Seeds of *T. latifolia* have been collected from water moving in irrigation canals in the western United States (Kelley and Bruns 1975). Each *Typha* inflorescence can produce 200,000 seeds which weigh 10 to 13 mg each. Seeds remain viable for long periods if conditions are not favorable for germination. Comes et al. (1978) noted that seeds kept under water germinated over a 60-mo period and 20% of the seeds were still firm after 60 mo.

Leck and Graveline (1979) collected soil to 10 cm deep from six vegetation types (from stream bank to stream bottom) in December and March in the eastern United States and monitored *T. latifolia* germination in the greenhouse. In soil collected from the *Typha* vegetation zone, they found 5610 and 11,950 seedlings/m² for the December and March samplings, respectively. Only 40 to 210 seedlings/m² appeared in the non-*Typha* sites. Thus the soil holds a great reservoir of *Typha* seed in established colonies.

Biomass of *T. latifolia* decomposes much faster than that of terrestrial plants and is often completed in 2 yr. Thus nutrients are recycled rapidly. Leaves have high C:N and C:P ratios that minimize herbivore activity (Puriveth 1980).

T. latifolia was considered autotoxic by McNaughton (1968) and Szczepanska (1971), but studies by Grace (1983) found that extracts of *Typha* inhibited germination only after mold grew in the media. Live *Typha* plants were not allelopathic to *Typha* seedlings.

Both species have chromosome numbers of $n = 15$ (Roscoe 1927). This is an unusual number for higher plants. Sharitz et al. (1980) found similar isozyme patterns of both species in many locations and believe *T. latifolia* and *T. angustifolia* are the evolutionary parents of *T. glauca*. In Switzerland, colonies of *T. latifolia* are composed of several genotypes, especially in more recently infested areas (Krattinger 1983).

UTILITY AND AGRICULTURAL IMPORTANCE

Both species have many potential uses for humans, livestock, and wildlife. Reviews by Morton (1975) and the National Academy of Science (1976a) highlight the following attributes. *Typha* was often an important food for indigenous people and is considered the most useful emergency crop of all wild plants. Young leaves and shoots are edible and young spikes can be boiled or roasted as a vegetable. Rhizomes can be eaten raw, boiled, or baked and are rich in starch, which can be separated from the fibers to yield flour as rich in protein as maize and rice. Only potato flour has more minerals (Schuessler 1960). *Typha* can yield 7000 kg/ha of rhizomes with up to 25% carbohydrates. Rhizomes are also an important food for wildlife. *Typha* stands provide nesting sites for birds, spawning areas and protection for fish, and protect shorelines from erosion.

Mature leaves have 30 to 40% soft fiber that can be used to make mats, fans, rope, bedding, and baskets, and *Typha* fibers can be used to produce paper. A set of books published in 1765 with *Typha* paper still exists, and a considerable quantity of paper was made from *Typha* in the eastern United States during the mid-1800s. Because the leaves swell when wet, they make a good caulking material.

Flowers can be used to treat burns, wounds, and ulcers (Morton 1975), and the leaf and rhizome contain diuretics, pollen is a stringent and sedative, and flowers treat abdominal pain and hemorrhoids (Duke and Ayensu 1985). The seed "fluff" can be used as fiber to stuff mattresses and life jackets. Mature inflorescences serve as torches and for decorative purposes. Seed has been used as a food by native North Americans, and it contains a drying oil similar in quality to linseed oil.

Typha stands can purify water of oils and minerals. Boyd (1970a) calculated that *T. latifolia* could potentially remove 4570 kg K, 2630 kg N, 1710 kg Ca, 730 kg Na, 403 kg P, 307 kg Mg, 250 kg S, 79 kg Mn, 23 kg Fe, 7 kg Cu, and 6 kg Zn/ha/yr.

Both species are globally distributed and are weeds in waterways, ponds, irrigation canals, and rice fields. *Typha* stands increase silting, impede travel, interfere with fishing and recreational activities, provide breeding ground for mosquitoes, and increase water loss in fields and reservoirs. *T. latifolia* is found in 58 countries (Figure 99-1) and *T. angustifolia* in 72 countries (Figure 99-3). However, few African countries report either species as an important weed. Europe and North America cite them as weeds more than other regions.

T. angustifolia is a serious or principal weed of irrigation systems in Australia, India, and Rumania. It is a common weed in these sites in the United States and an irrigation weed of unspecified rank in Indonesia and Iraq. It is a principal rice weed in Peru, and a weed of unspecified importance of rice in Algeria, Caribbean, Chile, China, Greece, Indonesia, Iran, Laos, Malaysia, Nepal, the Philippines, the former Soviet Union, Sri Lanka, Thailand, the United States, and Vietnam.

T. latifolia is a serious or principal weed of irrigation systems in Australia, India and Rumania; and of rice in Morocco and the former Soviet Union. It is a common rice weed in the United States, and a weed of unspecified rank of rice in Greece, India, Iran, Mexico, the Philippines, and Portugal.

Mechanical control is effective if stems are cut below water level. Cutting foliage above the water has little effect on rhizome oxygen level, but it drops to zero after 8 hr if cut below the surface (Sale and Wetzel 1983). Cutting plants in the spike stage is most detrimental to *Typha* and in most cases a second cutting is required to eradicate the stand (Husak 1978). Even cutting or bending standing dead shoots during the dormant season reduces biomass production and plant height the next season, especially if these disturbances occur early in dormancy (Jordan and Whigham 1988). Natural damage to dead shoots (wind, ice, animal feeding) also influences *Typha* growth and reproduction. Draining infested areas and burning the foliage does not control *Typha* (Smith and Kadlec 1985). In fact, burning may stimulate above-ground biomass production.

COMMON NAMES

Typha angustifolia

ARGENTINA	totora
AUSTRALIA	bulrush, cumbungi
BELGIUM	kleine lisdodde
BRAZIL	partasana, taboa
CAMBODIA	narrow-leaved cattail, quenouille a feuilles etroites
CANADA	narrow-leaved cattail, quenouille a feuilles etroites
CHILE	enea, paja de estera, totora, tutuvaco, vato
COLOMBIA	enea, espadana, junco
DOMINICAN REPUBLIC	enea
ENGLAND	southern reedmace
FIJI	bulrush, deniruve, denisoqe
GERMANY	Schmalblattriges Schild, Sudlicher Rohrkolben
HONDURAS	enea
INDONESIA	purun
JAPAN	hime-gama
MALAYSIA	banat
PHILIPPINES	balangot
PORTUGAL	tabua-estreita
PUERTO RICO	eneas, yerba de enea
THAILAND	kok chaang, thoup susi
UNITED STATES	narrowleaf cattail
URUGUAY	totora
VENEZUELA	enea
VIETNAM	co nen, thuy huong

Typha latifolia

ARGENTINA	totora
AUSTRALIA	bulrush
BELGIUM	grande massette, grote lisdodde
BRAZIL	taboa
CANADA	cattail, quenouille a feuilles larges

CHILE	totora
CHINA	xian pu
COLOMBIA	enea, junco
DENMARK	bredbladet dunhammer
ENGLAND	great reedmace
FINLAND	leveaosmankaami
FRANCE	massette
GERMANY	Breitblattriger Rohrkolben, Breitblattriges Schilf
ITALY	mazzasorda
JAPAN	gama
MEXICO	tule
NETHERLANDS	grote lisdodde
NORWAY	breitt dunkjevle
PORTUGAL	tabua larga
SAUDIA ARABIA	barda
SPAIN	enea, espadana
SWEDEN	bred-kaveldun
UNITED STATES	common cattail
VENEZUELA	enea

One Hundred

Ulex europaeus L.

Papilionaceae (Leguminosae), Pea Family

U LEX EUROPAEUS, widely known as gorse, is a dense, spiny, woody, nitrogen-fixing, legume plant that can successfully compete with pasture because of its growth habit and its prolific production of seeds, some of which are very hard and may persist in the soil for 30 to 50 yr. With little forethought, it was carried by man to all continents for use as an ornamental and a living fence or hedgeplant. In all cases it escaped to form impenetrable thickets, to invade pastures, forests, and rangelands, and to shelter unwanted animals. Some constituents of the seeds are widely used in biochemical and medical research. Gorse is now a weed in more than 30 countries.

FIGURE 100-1 The distribution of *Ulex europaeus* L. across the world where it has been reported as a weed.

FIGURE 100-2 *Ulex europaeus* L.: 1. fruiting branch; 2. root system; 3. seed, three views;
4. flower without perianth; 5. single flower; 6. immature pod; 7. portion of stem.

DESCRIPTION

U. europaeus (Figure 100-2) is a densely branched *biennial* or *perennial* shrub with spiny habit, 1 to 6 m tall; *stems* woody when mature, longitudinally ridged, hairy, with numerous long spines that are modified primary branches, extended branches may have primary, secondary and tertiary spines, stem color changing green to brown when mature, prostrate stems rooting; *root* system fibrous in upper layers of soil but may also form a taproot; *leaves* alternate, about 2.5 cm long, reduced to dorsally flattened spines; *flowers* pea-like, yellow and showy, fragrant, mostly in leaf axils and terminal clusters; *sepals* deeply 2-lipped, yellow, densely hairy, 0.75 to 1.25 cm long, with ovate standard, wings and keel of equal length; *filaments* of 10 united *stamens*; pods hairy, 1 to 2 cm long, containing 2 to 6 seeds; *seeds* 2 to 3 mm long, rounded at one end, broader and shallowly notched at the other, with conspicuous straw-colored appendage over the scar, smooth, shiny, olive-green to brownish.

The species can be recognized by its thorny, impenetrable habit, yellow flowers, and the conspicuous appendage over the seed scar.

Formerly there was much confusion about nomenclature in this species because it is so variable. Some of this was relieved as Rothmaler (1941) in Germany reduced the number of species from ten to three.

DISTRIBUTION AND HABITAT

U. europaeus (Figure 100-1) was carried by man to New Zealand, Australia, and the western coasts of North and South America. It is found on the coasts of Denmark and Germany, the lowlands of western Britain, and in France and Spain. It is unable to tolerate extremes of heat and cold in continental climates, but there are occasional reports that it has survived severe frost at some sites. During some winters in Great Britain there has been severe damage to plants and killing; in the winter of 1962–63 more than 50% of the plants in lowlands in Wales were killed and many froze back to ground level (Rymer 1979).

The species is reported as a weed in the very warm climates of New Guinea, Sri Lanka, and Trinidad, but generally it finds a home in cool mid-temperate zones of the two hemispheres.

The species is not found at high elevations and cannot survive on arid sites. In New Zealand, where it ranks as a major threat to crops, it prospers in medium- to high-rainfall areas. Growth is best on well-drained locations. The bacterial nitrogen-fixing metabolism in the nodules slows down under wet or flooded conditions.

There are reports of ejection of seeds to 5 m as the pods open, but the seeds are heavy and normally fall near the plants. They are washed from hillsides into flowing ditches and streams and thus are moved long distances. They are spread by animals and by man with his transport vehicles and field machines. The seeds are stored by wood ants (*Formica rubra*) and distributed as they are dropped on the way to the nest. The reports of dispersal by birds are controversial, perhaps because there are many different carriers and because investigators do not study the same winged species. Gorse is commonly seen under trees and around fence posts, a tell-tale sign of seed deposit by birds. (Ridley 1930).

Ulex frequents areas disturbed by man and prefers to move into highly productive land. It does fix its own atmospheric N and can therefore colonize areas where little else will grow, such as heterogeneous soil and rock mixtures on mine dumps.

Gorse is frequently said to be a lime-hating plant and to prefer a soil *pH* of 4 to 5; in some places this appears to be essential. The level is also agreeable to the nitrogen-fixing bacteria of the nodules (Hartley and Popay 1982, Thompson 1974). The weed is not confined to any special soil type and so may be seen on light sandy or heavy clay areas. Thus it is found on river banks, in grasslands and open forests, and as hedges or mixed with roadside scrub.

PROPAGATION

The increase of *U. europaeus* is by seed, since regeneration from disturbed root or stem material is possible but rarely occurs. In Galacia in northwest Spain, Puentes et al. (1988) studied the soil seed bank in two shrub bank areas and found 645 and 1045 seeds/m^2 in the different areas. All seeds were in the top 5 cm of soil and were 95% viable. Millener (1961) in New Zealand found 10,000 seeds/m^2 in the upper soil and Parsons (1973) calculated a seed production of more than 35 million/ha/year. There may be two periods of seed production by a plant during a year. A portion of all propagules produced is hard seed and may persist from 1 to 50 yr in soil. The hard coats extend the life of the seed, with the result that they are distributed in time and space as the seed population, under natural conditions, becomes permeable to gases and water at successive intervals.

For experimental purposes, more than 90% germination may be obtained by boiling seeds for 30 to 60 sec and then cooling them quickly in tap water (Millener 1961). Dry heat at 80 to 90°C for a short period may also provide good germination.

Ivens (1983) found the germination rate to increase linearly with temperatures from about 0°C to an optimum at 18°C. Germination then decreased to the maximum temperature of 26°C. Above 35°C viability was lost. Light was not required for germination and the seeds showed no stimulatory response to a wide range of alternating temperature regimes.

In the fields, few seeds germinate in the shade of a gorse canopy, but a flush of seedlings appears upon its removal. The results above of the experiments by Ivens do not support the widespread speculation that increased light intensity and a wider range of fluctuating temperatures cause the abundance of new seedlings. Ivens suggests that moisture may be the important factor, since it is known that a dense canopy intercepts much of the precipitation. Aldridge (1968) has shown that 75% of a 12 mm rainfall is absorbed by the weed canopy.

PHYSIOLOGY AND MORPHOLOGY

Emergence of seedlings is variable and quite responsive to moisture supplies. In an area kept bare after clearing in late fall in New Zealand, there was a flush of emergence with autumn rains, while peak germination came in spring during the two following seasons. Only 25% of the seeds in the top 10 cm of the soil germinated during this time. At a similar site sprayed with herbicides, burned, oversown with pasture and grazed, the seedling number declined by 95%.

On the way to adulthood, the seedlings go through two stages. The first is a quite compact, almost rosette-like habit with leaves being the only obvious lateral appendages. The first leaves are trifoliate (some 1 or 2 foliate leaves present) with thin, expanded leaflets. Rapid stem extension begins as the meristem produces a series of simple leaves that become smaller, narrower, more pointed and later awl-like. Spines (modified primary branches) begin to develop in the axils of simple leaves, to be followed by secondary and tertiary spines (Millener 1961). When mature, the gorse plants may grow to a height of 6 m (although most are less than one-half of this) and may live for 30 yr or more (see also Binet 1958, Boodle 1914, Skipper 1922).

Lee et al. (1986) recorded the growth characteristics of 125 gorse plants over a long period. The growth in stem diameter averaged 5 mm/yr and the height 200 mm/yr. When measured at a point 100 cm above the ground, the average diameter was 217 mm, the height was 7 m, and the average age was 29 yr.

Flowering is quite variable in *U. europaeus* and within a given area it is seldom uniform. In the Southern Hemisphere, the main flowering period is August to October (spring) with some flowers appearing again during fall (March to May). In some areas, flowers may be seen throughout the growing season. Following burning or mechanical brush removal, the emerging seedlings normally require 18 mo or more of growth before flowering. Coppice growth does not flower until 2 yr of age or more. Pollination of flowers is by bees and similar insects. Rooted cuttings from 1-yr-old wood can be made to flower in 6 mo. Seeds begin to ripen shortly after petal fall.

U. europaeus appears to be a day-neutral plant with respect to flower initiation, but Millener (1961) has shown that the photoperiod exerts much control over early vegetative development. When plants were grown in greenhouses in 16- and 8-hr days with low and high light intensity, all of the 8-hr plants were still in the rosette stage at 8 wk and had few or no spines. Almost all plants in 16-hr days were tall and spined at 6 wk, having already passed through the stem extension phase separating juvenile and adult stages. Later all plants developed spines. Those in low light were the last to do so.

In later experiments on ecotypic variation with latitude, seedlings from 16 locations were collected from the far north to the south of Great Britain and grown in one location. Few juvenile leaves were produced on low latitude plants but there were many on high latitude plants. The author postulates that differences in daylength, with latitude, also explains the altered morphological development (Millener 1962).

Bieniek and Millington (1967, 1968) studied the changes that occur in the axillary shoot apex as it differentiates into a thorn. The onset of thorn formation is slightly delayed by short days, but once the process begins it is no longer affected by daylength. Very low light intensity tends to interfere with shoot growth and to suppress thorn formation, but high humidity or high N level did not.

Rolston and Sineiro-Garcia (1974) studied the effect of defoliation (at the cotyledons or sixth or 9th trifoliate leaf stages) and the interaction of these with shading (20 to 80% daylight) in a greenhouse. In general, the removal of leaves and cotyledons reduced growth but the plants survived. If the leaves were removed well down from the growing point the plants died. The gorse plants responded to leaf removal by tending to become prostrate. Shading with or without defoliation reduced and delayed spine formation but did not cause death of the seedlings.

Burning of gorse for control has been practiced for 100 years, usually most successfully following crushing or desiccation with chemicals. Always, the seeds remain. In a study of fires at five locations, most seed was found in the top 6 cm of soil and temperatures below 100°C stimulated germination. Above 100°C the heat was lethal after a short period. In general, a reduction in soil seed reserves of about 33% can be expected from a good fire

(Zabkiewicz and Gaskin 1978a). Repeated fires, however, destroy all vegetation and organic matter and eventually lead to denudation of the area and, in the final stages, erosion.

Miller et al. (1956) made a detailed study of the biological and chemical changes in the ecosystem after a burn. Large quantities of major nutrients accumulated on the soil as ash. After 10 mo, 20 to 25% of the phosphate and cations were still in the unburnt part of the litter and a large proportion of the nutrients that had leached into the topsoil was still there. Thus, a good burn has a beneficial effect on the plant nutrient supply for a year or maybe several years.

The initial effect of burning and pasture establishment was to reduce or destroy litter fauna but did not adversely affect topsoil and subsoil fauna. There was a temporary resurgence of litter fauna, followed by extinction of all but a few groups of soil- and litter-dwelling animals as the supply of litter for food failed. Earthworms in the topsoil were destroyed because of the failure of suitable food supplies. In summary, initial changes caused by fire were followed by a gradual return to conditions similar to those prevailing before the fire.

The roots of most gorse plants are shallow, with no well-developed taproots on most soils. Gorse growing in gravel, shingle, or in very coarse, heterogeneous substrate may send out horizontal branches that creep just below the surface, producing 5-cm roots bearing nitrogen-fixing root nodules. The nodules are long-lived, as compared with other species, and they thrive under very aerobic conditions. The nitrogen-fixing bacteria are inhibited in excessively wet soil. A *pH* of 4 to 5 is very suitable for these organisms. The N content of the bush may rise to 680 kg/ha in 10 yr but, as mentioned previously, much of that N would be lost in a good burn (Egunjobi 1969b).

Zabkiewicz and Gaskin (1978b), with the use of a scanning electron microscope, found a marked seasonal variation in the surface wax and trichomes of *Ulex*. Molloy and Wilson (1969) have reported on the biochemistry of germination in the pollen grains of gorse.

Several protein compounds in the seeds of *Ulex* are used in studies of animal physiology and biochemistry. When these vegetable proteins, known as lectins, contact functional cell membrane glycoproteins with polysaccharide chains, they can combine to form bridges between cells, causing agglutination *in vivo*. They can also introduce preferential killing of tumor cells and stimulate lymphoid cells to divide and mature. As an example, Pirofsky et al. (1981) found reduced growth potential in murine (mouse) lymphoid tumor cells cultivated in the presence of *Ulex* seed extracts.

AGRICULTURAL IMPORTANCE

U. europaeus is a serious weed of forests in New Zealand, of mountain pastures in Hawaii, and of hilly pastures in New Zealand, where it covers one half million acres of potentially productive land (Ivens 1979). It is a principal weed of pastures in Australia, Brazil, Chile, and Tasmania; and of fodder kale in Germany. It is a common weed of forests in Scotland and Spain; and of pastures in Italy. It is a pasture weed of unknown rank in England, Germany, and India.

In England, this plant was reported as a common agricultural weed more than 125 yr ago (Buckman 1855). It is a proclaimed noxious weed in Tasmania and Victoria, Australia, and a Federal noxious weed of New Zealand.

Egunjobi (1971) estimated that the solar energy utility rate by *Pinus radiata*, a principal reforestation species in New Zealand, was 2.2, while gorse was also very proficient at the rate of 1.6 to 2. Egunjobi (1969b) estimated dry matter accumulation by gorse was 77,000 kg/ha at 10 yr.

Some consider the plant to be helpful at times for the prevention of erosion on marginal land, in young stages it may supply emergency feed for stock, and it provides stock shelter. The damage to forests, pastures, rangelands and parklands is, however, overwhelming in the long term.

Gaynor and MacCarter (1981) published an extensive bibliography of papers concerned with gorse control prior to 1977.

Research workers of New Zealand and Australia have contributed a major portion of our knowledge of the biology of this species and they have been pioneers in the development of management systems on vast areas used for animal husbandry. In New Zealand, in spite of decades of burning and mechanical clearing, as well as the use of 13 million liters of herbicides and biological control trials using insects, the absolute gains on reducing gorse are small and costs continue to increase. It is now generally agreed that, for long-term control after land clearing, the sowing of suitable pasture mixtures, addition of fertilizer, good grazing management, and spot-spraying with herbicides at times must all be combined to enable profitable land use. Moss (1959) has warned that clearing must be followed by 10 yr of good management to prevent a resurgence of the weed. He believes that, wherever possible, the gorse seeds in the topsoil should not be dug up or disturbed in any way. In all such efforts, the nature of the soil, the steepness of terrain, and the age and vigor of the brush will influence the outcome.

Because the land is usually bare after clearing, the initial task is to curb the vigorous growth of new gorse seedlings by oversowing pastures with suitable grass-legume mixtures. Ivens (1979) has performed experiments to record the biological nature of the early competition between gorse and several pasture species. On areas adequately fertilized, he found that numbers of gorse seedlings were reduced by 30 to 60% over 12 mo when in competition with *Lolium perenne*, *Agrostis tenuis*, *Holcus lanatus*, *Trifolium repens* and grass mixtures with the latter. When short periods of heavy sheep grazing were added to the above swards, weed seedlings were reduced by 70 to 90%.

In 1980 Ivens and Mlowe (1980) planted gorse and perennial rye (*L. perenne*) in monocultures in 5 planting ratios of the two species. They found that the shoot growth of gorse alone, after 22 wk, exceeded that of rye, but when the species were grown in competition the weed growth was decreased more than the *Lolium* was reduced by the brushy species. During the first 10 wk, the rye in monoculture made 4 to 6 times more growth than the weed so that gorse in competition with rye is subject to shading very soon after emergence. The root system of gorse was smaller than that of rye and was further reduced by competition.

When periodic defoliation was added to the above treatments, both species declined in vigor but rye still out-yielded gorse at harvest. Much of the advantage for rye came in the period of rapid growth just after emergence. Under competition, the gorse initiated a more spreading habit from dormant basal buds. It is well known, of course, that some weed seedlings may penetrate the grass canopy, broaden, and begin to shade the pasture. In such areas spot treatments with herbicides are required.

Hartley et al. (1980) and Hartley and Thai (1979, 1982) studied gorse seedling survival in sheep paddocks after grazing, treading, and mowing treatments of several pasture species. Treading without grazing was accomplished by walking the sheep on otherwise protected areas on different time schedules. Grazing without treading was arranged by fencing with netting in which head-sized holes allowed grass consumption on entire plots.

Open plots supplied normal grazing. Wherever treading was allowed, there was a damaging effect on gorse survival. Mowing was the least harmful treatment to the gorse. Grazing without treading was not as harmful to the gorse as normal grazing or treading alone. Survival for the weed was most difficult in a *Holcus lanatus* pasture, while perennial ryegrass allowed the most vigorous growth of the gorse.

Thompson (1974) in New Zealand found that in gorse-infested areas where the sward was kept short, white clover was a better competitor than ryegrass. The gorse weed seedlings and juvenile plants responded strongly to P and less to K, while N and Ca additions retarded gorse seedling growth. Established gorse responded to N. In his experiments, low N in spring meant low competition from pasture species, confirming observations that gorse readily invades low fertility pastures.

In Tasmania, on 100 ha of steep, gorse-infested ironstone land (from iron-rich sedimentary rock) a program of heavy stocking, satisfactory fertility levels and good grass management increased wool production from 97 kg with six wethers (male sheep)/ha to 1210 kg with nine wethers/ha in 2 yr (Wilson 1968).

In a recent grazing management trial for gorse control in New Zealand, goats and sheep were grazed alone or in mixtures (with two goats equivalent to one sheep) on paddocks of 0.8 ha. Each of the above were also used in set (continuous) stocking or in a rotation comprised of four sub-paddocks grazed on a 28-day cycle. On this area that had been burned, oversown with pasture and fertilized, on the goat only and the mixed sheep-goat rotationally grazed paddocks, the gorse was reduced to negligible levels in 3 yr (Radcliffe 1985).

Salisbury (1929) cites an interesting observation of competition between gorse and bracken fern, *Pteridium aquilinum*. The early shading and heavy mulch formation by the fern, occasionally assisted by a good fire, eventually allowed the fern to become dominant and greatly reduced the gorse biomass. Salisbury observed that a good fire may damage a gorse stand to the point where several years are required before it is again competitive.

On the west coast of the United States and elsewhere, gorse meets many of the requirements for stabilizing sand dunes, but in some areas it is regarded as dangerous because of its highly flammable volatile oil content.

Jobson and Thomas (1964) have reported on the chemical composition of gorse.

In this time when there is a world energy shortage, it is appropriate to mention that in the 1600s in England gorse was sown on farms with poor soil to produce an excellent crop of wood for fuel each 4 to 5 yr. It was also used to provide refuges for game, and because it is evergreen it was used as fodder in winter. "Whin-mills" were developed to crush stems prior to feeding (Rymer 1979).

COMMON NAMES

Ulex europaeus

ARGENTINA	aliaga, tojo
AUSTRALIA	furze, gorse, whin
BRAZIL	tojo
CANADA	ajonc d'Europe, gorse
CHILE	aliaga tojo, corena, espino amarillo, marticorena, pica pica, yaguil
DENMARK	tornblad

ENGLAND	common gorse
FRANCE	ajonc
GERMANY	Europaischer Stechginster
HAWAII	gorse
ITALY	ginestra spinosa
NETHERLANDS	gaspeldoorn
NEW ZEALAND	gorse
NORWAY	gulltorn
PORTUGAL	tojo-arnal
SPAIN	tojo
SWEDEN	arttorne
UNITED STATES	gorse

One Hundred One

Urtica urens L.

Urticaceae, Nettle Family

MANY PLANTS IN THE **Urticaceae** family are known for their stinging hairs and *Urtica urens* is no exception. In fact, both the genus and species names are derived from the Latin *uro*, to burn or sting. The species is native to Europe but is now cosmopolitan, occurring in horticultural crops, gardens, pastures, waste areas and roadsides in over 50 temperate-climate or high-altitude countries.

FIGURE 101-1   The distribution of *Urtica urens* L. across the world where it has been reported as a weed.

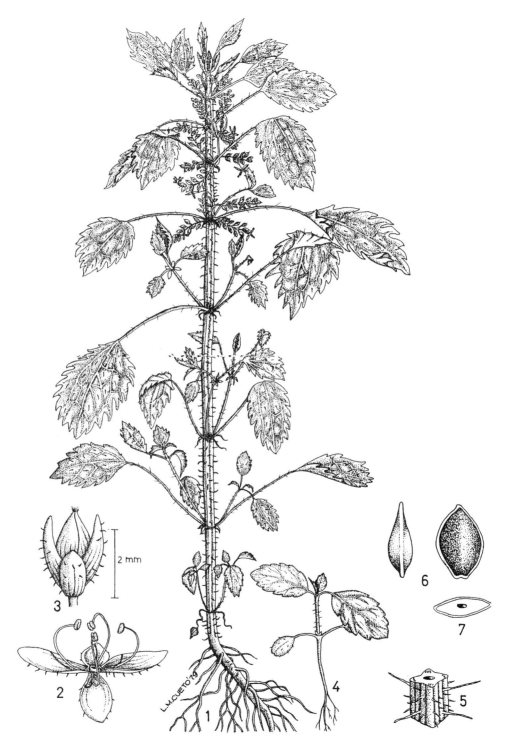

FIGURE 101-2 *Urtica urens* L.: 1. habit; 2. flower; 3. fruit; 4. seedling; 5. portion of stem; 6. seed, two views; 7. seed, cross section.

DESCRIPTION

U. urens (Figure 101-2) is an *annual* monecious herb with a branched *taproot*; *stems* square, tough, simple or branched from the base, 10 to 60 cm tall with stinging hairs; *leaves* opposite, decussate, covered with scattered stinging hairs, elliptic to ovate, deeply inciso-serrate, 1 to 3 cm long, 3- to 5-nerved with short petiole and two oblong *stipules* 1 to 4 mm long; *inflorescence* spike-like, lax and elongate, arising in pairs from each leaf axil; *flowers* inconspicuous, lacking petals, greenish, imperfect, with 4-segmented *perianth*; *staminate flowers* small with 4 equal *sepals*, 4 *stamens* inflexed in bud, straightening quickly as flower opens to eject pollen; more numerous than *pistillate flowers* that have 1 *pistil* with brush-like *stigma*, surrounded by a bell-shaped *calyx* of two pairs of unequal *sepals* with the inner ones much larger and enclosing the fruit; *fruit* a single-seeded *achene* with persistent perianth, 1.6 to 2.0 mm long, 1 to 1.5 mm wide, ovate in outline with pointed tip, somewhat flattened, minutely granular, yellow, tan or brown with reddish-brown dots.

The key characteristics of this monoecious plant are the stinging hairs on the stems and leaves, square stems, opposite leaves, and axillary small spike-like inflorescences with many greenish flowers.

ECOLOGY AND BIOLOGY

U. urens is frequently found in light textured soils, especially those rich in organic matter. In the north-central United States, it is common on the edges of marshes, poorly drained ditches and other lowland sites. It grows at lat 71° N in Europe and to 2000 m in Colombia.

Seeds can remain viable for 20 to 100 yr in the soil (Odum 1965, 1974). Seed populations in soil taken from 58 vegetable fields in England averaged over 92 million seeds/ha, with a maximum of 230 million (Roberts and Stokes 1966). *U. urens* was present in 93% of the fields sampled, but a later survey found the weed in only 49% of the fields, with an average population of 56,800,000 plants/ha (Roberts and Neilson 1982). These researchers (1981b) also observed *U. urens* after 16 yr of continuous maize production but not in barley or carrot fields after this period.

Emergence is enhanced by soil disturbance and is greater in the top 2.5 cm than at greater depths (Roberts and Feast 1973, 1977). Only 4% viable seed remained in the soil after 6 yr with cultivation, compared to 39% viable seed in non-disturbed soil.

Seed germination is optimal at 25°C, decreases rapidly at temperatures below 20°C (Andersen 1968), and is greater in darkness than in light (Soriano et al. 1963b). In England, most seedlings appear in April and May but emergence continues through July. Few plants emerge between August and December (Roberts and Feast 1970).

U. urens is a nitrophylic plant, with whole plants containing over 5% nitrogen. The nitrogen is primarily NO_3^--N and is distributed equally between leaves and stems. At maturity plant biomass is partitioned as 46% stems, 43% leaves, 5% roots, and 6% flowers and fruits (Rosnitschek-Schimmel 1983). Plants have a *2n* chromosome count of 26 (Woodland et al. 1976).

When drought stressed, *U. urens* flowers several days sooner than normal and the number of nodes with inflorescences drops from eight to four per plant (Boot et al. 1986). Drought also gives a large and progressive increase in the root to shoot ratio.

Corre (1983a,b; 1984) studied *U. urens* grown in various light regimes. This species is light-loving and dry matter distribution is not affected by light intensity. Its photosynthetic capacity is 13.5 mg $CO_2/dm^2/h$ and is not affected by the red to far-red light ratio. *U. urens* grown in nutrient solution as a monoculture produced 31, 9.5, and 8 g dry matter in 5 wk at 100, 35, and 15% full sunlight, respectively. When competing with the perennial *U. dioica*, *U. urens* produced 67, 55, and 44% of the total biomass at 100, 35, and 15% sunlight levels, respectively. Thus it is most competitive in full sunlight, while *U. dioica* is better adapted to shade.

This species is adapted to many environments. Sometimes it flowers and sets seed when 8 to 10 cm tall and before the cotyledonary leaves have dropped (Greig-Smith 1948). Several successions of inflorescences are usually found on early emerging plants. Seeds formed early in the season may produce new plants the same year. Plants flower from late May to October in England and are killed by frost.

Pollen release in the *Urtica* genus is unique. Immature stamens are bent toward the center of the flower; when the anthers mature, the stamens suddenly straighten, shooting pollen into the wind. Plants are cross pollinated and produce 100 to 1300 seeds weighing 0.5 mg each (Korsmo et al. 1981). Seeds are rich in oily endosperm and do not float in water (Greig-Smith 1948).

Each stinging hair on *U. urens* is a tapered, elongated cell, constricted just below the tip, with a bulbous base embedded in a multicellular pedestal. When hit, the tip breaks off and the hair becomes a miniature hypodermic needle that penetrates the skin and injects its irritating chemicals. The tip of the hair is high in silica, but the silica concentration decreases toward the base, where it is replaced by calcium. Plants grown in silica-free culture have little "stinging" ability because the hairs are not rigid enough to penetrate the skin. When silica is made available to plants, stinging hairs are present after 2 wk (Thurston and Lersten 1969). Each hair is 100 microns long and has 10 micrograms of fluid which contains histamine and acetylcholine. Stem hairs have 2.5 times more acetylcholine than leaf hairs, while upper and lower surface leaf hairs have equal concentrations. The leaf itself has nearly as much histamine and acetylcholine as the leaf hairs. Crushed leaves can also give a stinging sensation, but are not as irritating as the hairs (Emmelin and Feldberg 1947). The stinging reaction is gone within 1 to 3 hr for most people, but the hairs can remain in tissue and cause pain for 24 to 36 hr. Plants are not considered toxic to livestock but cause the same irritating reaction in all animals (Everist 1974).

AGRICULTURAL IMPORTANCE

U. urens is a weed of 27 crops in 50 countries (Figure 101-1) and is a frequently reported weed of vegetables and orchards. It is a principal or serious weed of cabbage in Germany; carrots in Germany and Ireland; citrus in Spain; legumes, maize, onions, potatoes, and sugar beets in England; peas in New Zealand; and vegetables in Poland, Scotland, Spain, and Sweden.

It is a common weed of beets in Colombia; carrots in the United States; cereals in Italy, Scotland, and Tunisia; citrus in Tunisia; cotton in Turkey; horticulture crops in South Africa; irrigated dryland crops in Australia; lucerne in Spain; onions in Germany; orchards in Czechoslovakia, Hungary, South Africa, and Uruguay; pastures in Bulgaria; peas in England; potatoes in Colombia; sugar beets in Israel and Spain; vegetables in Argentina, Australia, Hungary, Israel, and the United States; vineyards and waste areas in South Africa; and wheat in Colombia.

Also, *U. urens* is a reported unranked weed of beets in England and Germany; cabbage in England; carrots in England and the Netherlands; cereals in Australia, Chile, Colombia, Finland, Germany, and New Zealand; citrus in Brazil, Cyprus and the United States; hops in Germany; horticulture crops in Finland; irrigated crops in the United States; lucerne in Argentina and the United States; maize in Argentina and Brazil; nursery crops Germany; onions in the United States; orchards in Australia, Belgium, Bolivia, and Chile; pastures in Australia, Brazil, and Colombia; potatoes in Argentina, Belgium, and Germany; rangeland in South Africa; rape in New Zealand; sugar beets in Germany and the United States; sugarcane in Argentina; strawberries in England, Germany, and the Netherlands; tobacco in Belgium; vegetables in Belgium, Germany, the Netherlands, Norway, and the former Soviet Union; vineyards in Australia and Germany; and wastelands in Australia and the former Yugoslavia.

Once *U. urens* appears in vegetable fields, populations can increase rapidly. It was the third most frequently encountered weed in vegetable fields in England in the mid-1960s but dropped to sixth place 10 yr later (Roberts and Stokes 1966, Davison and Roberts 1976). Using simazine in orchards favors its buildup. *U. urens* can host the potato aphid, *Pratylenchus* nematodes, viruses, *Verticillium* in hops and the cucumber mosaic virus (Tomlinson 1970, Bendixen et al. 1979).

Seeds can spread with grain and vegetable seeds and can pass intact through the digestive system of cattle (Ridley 1930). Herbal uses of *U. urens* have been known for centuries. Fresh plants have a painful but beneficial effect on rheumatism. Leaves and flowers are reportedly powerful diuretics (Uphof 1968) and in spite of the stinging hairs, young stems and leaves are edible and can be used as a potherb (Martin and Ruberte 1978). In South Africa, plants have 5.2% protein, 0.6% fat, 7% carbohydrates, and 2.9% fiber on a fresh weight basis. Plants are high in calcium, potassium and vitamin A (528, 553, and 4.9 mg/g, respectively) (Wehmeyer and Rose 1983).

COMMON NAMES

Urtica urens

ARGENTINA	ortiga, ortiga brava, ortiga chica, ortiga negra, rupa chico
AUSTRALIA	annual nettle, small nettle
BELGIUM	kleine brandnetel, petite ortie
BRAZIL	urtiga
CANADA	dognettle, ortie brulante
CHILE	ortiga comun, ortiga negra
COLOMBIA	ortiga, ortiga blanca
DENMARK	braende naelde, liden naelde
EGYPT	horreig
ENGLAND	annual nettle, small nettle
FINLAND	rautanokkonen
FRANCE	ortie, ortie brulante, petite ortie
GERMANY	Kleine Brennessel, Kleine Nessel

ICELAND	brenninetla
ITALY	ortica piccola
JAPAN	karafuto-irakusa
LEBANON	hurrayk, shar-el-aguz, small nettle, zaghil
NETHERLANDS	kleine brandnetel
NEW ZEALAND	nettle
NORWAY	smanesle, stornesle
PORTUGAL	urtiga menor
SOUTH AFRICA	bosbrandnetel, bush stinging nettle
SPAIN	ortiga comun, ortiga menor
SWEDEN	brannassala, etternassla
TURKEY	isigan otu
UNITED STATES	burning nettle
URUGUAY	ortiga
YUGOSLAVIA	sitna kopriva

One Hundred Two

Vallisneria spiralis L.

Hydrocharitaceae, Frog's Bit Family

VALLISNERIA SPIRALIS, commonly called eelgrass, is a weed of more than 50 countries and is widely distributed on all continents. It is customarily assigned to the tropics and sub-tropics in the floras of the world, but it prospers as a weed in very cool places in the temperate zones. As a rooted, submerged annual or perennial it can reproduce by seeds, winter buds, or sturdy creeping stolons. It is found in some lowland crops and its ubiquitous presence in irrigation canals and large and small streams impedes the flow of water needed for housekeeping, agriculture, navigation and recreation.

FIGURE 102-1   The distribution of *Vallisneria spiralis* L. across the world where it has been reported as a weed.

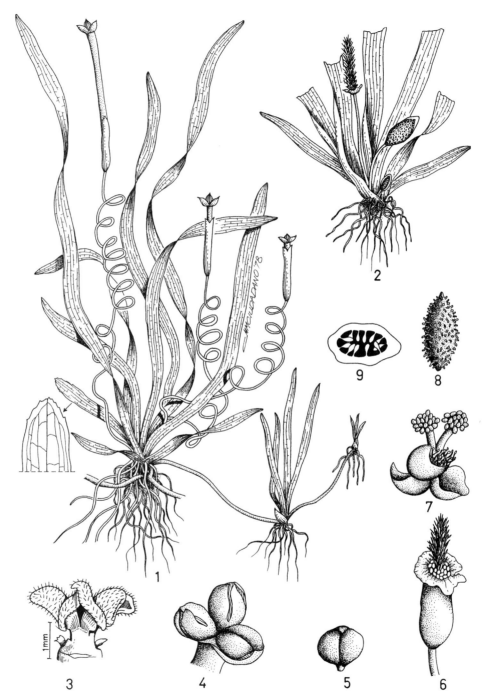

FIGURE 102-2   *Vallisneria spiralis* L.: 1. habit of female plant with ripening fruits on coiled peduncle; 2. male plant; 3. stigmatic lobes of pistillate flower; 4. pistillate flower apex; 5. staminate flower, detached but unopened; 6. staminate inflorescence; 7. staminate flower; 8. seed; 9. ovary, cross section.

DESCRIPTION

V. spiralis (Figure 102-2) is an annual or a *perennial*, submersed, stoloniferous, dioecious plant with *stems* buried in mud; *roots* fibrous; *leaves* ribbon-like, sheathing base, arranged in tufts at intervals along a stolon, 1 to 7 cm broad, 1 to 6 m long, upper portion sometimes floating at the surface, 5 to 9 main longitudinal veins with fine transverse connections, acute to obtuse, edges may be finely toothed toward apex, winged at base with one wing folded over edge of next inner leaf and other wing extended; *pistillate flower* 1.5 to 2.5 cm long, solitary, sessile, within membranous sheath, *peduncle* may be up to 60 cm long as flower bud is raised to surface; *spathe* 1.5 to 2 cm long; *sepals* 3, concave, springing directly from summit of the ovary; *petals* 3, white, alternate with sepals, minute and scarcely visible; *pistil* with 3, 2-lobed nearly sessile *stigmas*; *ovary* inferior, long, cylindrical, unilocular, with mucilage-filled cavity containing numerous crowded *ovules*; *staminate flower* minute, less than 1 mm long and broad, numerous, enclosed by membranous spathe; *spathe* 1 to 2 cm long, terminal on a 7 cm long *peduncle*; *perianth* of 3 sepals, concave, 2 larger than the third; *stamens* usually 3; *petals* absent; *fruit* long, 4 mm broad, many seeds embedded in a gelatinous mass, enveloped by the persistent spathe; *seed* tapering, ellipsoidal, papillate, 1.5 to 3 mm long. Gunn and Ritchie (1988) presented line drawings of the seed embryo and transections of the seed.

V. americana Michx collected at different life stages and over a range of differing environmental sites may show a remarkable similarity to *V. spiralis* or a sharp contrast of certain morphological characters, resulting in disagreement on the appropriate taxa (Good 1964, el Hadidi 1968, Sculthorpe 1967, Svedelius 1932). Because there are parallels of behavior and response of these two closely related plants, for this discussion they will be described together.

It is believed by some that *V. asiatica* and *V. gigantea* in Asia, *V. aethiopica* in Africa, and *V. americana* in the Americas are geographical races of *V. spiralis*.

DISTRIBUTION AND HABITAT

V. spiralis (Figure 102-1) is widely distributed in Asia, in the islands of the Pacific, including Australia and New Zealand, in Africa from Egypt to Tanzania, in central and southern Europe, in Canada and the United States and in northern and southern South America. It is most often found in 0.5 to 3 m of water (reported to 10 m in clear water). The general impression that this species is mainly a weed of the tropics and subtropics is no longer valid, for the map in Figure 102-2 demonstrates that as a weed it is widely dispersed in some very cool regions of the world. In north India, northeast of Haryana, the plant is found at 2500 m in the underwater flora of a lake in the Himalayas. In north India, Vats (1984) reported that eelgrass grew vigorously with the onset of monsoon rains, preferred heavy soils, and was more tolerant of low temperatures than similar water weeds in the area. It is found in fresh waters and in coastal areas can occupy brackish pools and backwaters with salt contents of 0.2 to 1.5 ppt. den Hartog and van der Velde (1986) in the Netherlands found only a few plants that invaded the brackish and fresh-water habits along the coasts. The immigrants, including *V. spiralis*, have been most successful in man-made and heavily disturbed areas.

It is found in lakes, rivers, waterlogged swamps with open water, man-made reservoirs, and irrigation channels. It thrives in streams but is seldom present in fast water. In

England and central Europe, it is believed to have first become established in water artificially warmed by human activities (Ant 1970). It was carried to agricultural areas bordering the Nile River in Egypt on the feet of birds and in feces (el Hadidi 1968).

In India, it is in both temporary and perennial ponds and irrigation tanks and has adapted itself admirably to survival in rapidly fluctuating water levels and to areas seasonally devoid of water. Near Orissa, it is abundant in both winter and summer and may be found in some cultivated lowland crops such as jute and rice.

PROPAGATION

The dispersal of *V. spiralis* is by seed, winter buds, or fragments of rootstocks. Depending on the site, season and region, one or more of the propagules may be important for this widely distributed weed.

Vegetative stolons extend rapidly on or just below the sediment surface and produce new shoots and roots at intervals along the rootstock. The growing point of the traveling runner eventually becomes erect to form a new plant which is again anchored by adventitious roots. Soon a lateral bud on the new, erect plant becomes a runner and the procedure begins all over again. Some of the plants remain connected but many "bridges" are broken by decay.

In Varanasi, India, at 25° N. latitude, plants begin to flower during the shorter days of November with the lower temperatures of approaching winter. The process begins at sites beneath trees or banks in partial shade (Choudhuri 1966). Fruit set always occurs in winter, never in summer, even under photoperiods conducive to flowering. *V. spiralis* behaves as an annual in seasonal ponds that become dry and where it thus depends on seed for its continued presence.

Seeds germinate in ponds at the end of the monsoon in response to shorter days and temperatures that may fall to 30°C. If water levels become too low after the rains cease, the plants die before flowering. In perennial ponds, both seeds and vegetative structures are important. Perennation is by rhizomes that must persist under water during summers when high temperatures cause death of the leaves. As monsoon waters rush in, some rootstocks are dislodged and float or tumble. Those that come to rest in shallow water take root and give rise to another population that eventually recedes with water level.

In nature the seeds mature in the cool dry weather of late winter and seem quite unresponsive to the normal conditions favoring seed germination. Choudhuri (1966) found that clean seed soaked in concentrated H_2SO_4 for 3 min began to germinate in 3 days at 30°C and gave 80 to 90% germination in 10 days. In the normal day-night photoperiod of that season, 90% of the seeds germinated at 30 to 35°C, but only 10% in continuous darkness. Optimum *pH* for germination was 7.5 to 8.

Muenscher (1936a) found no dormancy in seeds collected and stored in tap water at room temperature, with a total of 70% germination obtained in an 8-wk test. When stored at 0°C, 2 to 7 mo were required for 80% germination. Seeds stored dry would not germinate.

In a study of the propagation of *Vallisneria* for areas needing food for wildfowl in the United States, McAtee (1917) found that seeds, winter buds, and rootstocks could be moved at any time if they were carefully protected from drying. Seeds ripened from September to November and fell to the sediment surface. He found that the seed pods could be harvested, immediately broken up into 1.2 cm lengths and planted. Buds or rootstocks moved in fall and spring must be weighted so that roots develop and anchor the plant.

MORPHOLOGY AND PHYSIOLOGY

In *V. spiralis*, as in many land and aquatic plants with a broad, flat shoot apex, the stem is much reduced, internodes are shortened, and leaves arise in tufts and clusters. The ribbon leaves of plants are better adapted to resist tearing than are dissected leaves for the occasional periods of heavy wave action or violent water turbulence. In *Vallisneria* there may be two to four leaves in the rosette or crown between leaves with axillary buds. The leaves are completely closed with no stomata.

The root of eelgrass shows an extreme degree of simplification among aquatics. Aerenchyma forms early, there is a simple central channel surrounded by a ring of cells, three of which are sieve tube cells with companion cells. The mechanical tissues in all organs, including the root, are mostly collenchyma. This living, elastic tissue, together with a lack of lignification of the conducting elements, allows the flexibility needed for life in the water.

Ancibor (1979) reported on the systematic anatomy of the vegetative organs of several members of the **Hydrocharitaceae**, including *Vallisneria*. Wylie (1917–1921) reported on the details of pollination, fertilization, and embryogenesis in *Vallisneria*.

Some aquatic plants are pollinated in air, some under water. Eelgrass is much studied as a transitional species in this respect for it approaches hydrophily. The spathes of the male flowers have up to 2000 individual, tiny flowers, each with two perianths hermetically sealed and containing an air globule. Upon release, these flowers hasten to the surface, and two sepals reflex and serve as buoyant floats. The third stands erect as a sail. Before pollination, the peduncle of the female flower elongates to carry it to the surface. The flower weight results in a slight depression with the central stigmas projecting into the atmosphere. The male flowers, drifting in the vicinity, may approach the female flower and slide into the depression, where the sticky pollen is transferred. The peduncle normally now coils spirally (giving the descriptive name to the species), or shortens with bends and irregular undulations, pulling the flower beneath the water, slowly at first, then more quickly until it is drawn to the plant base (Arber 1922; Sculthorpe 1967; Svedelius 1932; Wylie 1917).

V. spiralis, *Hydrilla verticillata*, and *Potamogeton pectinatus* are often found in competition in the same plant communities. In a study of photosynthesis and respiration in these species, Jana and Choudhuri (1979) found that *Hydrilla* showed minimum dark and photorespiration and maximum apparent photosynthesis, *Potamogeton* showed the reverse, while *Vallisneria* was intermediate in this respect. The authors believe these to be C_3 plants (see also Helder and van Harmelen 1982). *Vallisneria* was similar to terrestrial plants in showing a gradual decline in physiological processes with leaf aging. Their studies also provided information on enzymatic activities and ethylene production as they affect dry weight, protein content of cells, and tissue permeability during the aging process (Jana and Choudhuri 1980, 1982a, 1984). They also studied the effect of chilling temperatures in lowering photosynthetic activity and protein levels of eelgrass leaves, and their restoration with appropriate temperature and light intensities (Jana and Choudhuri 1982b).

The growth of several submerged macrophytes at several levels of photosynthetically active radiation and temperature was also studied in greenhouse tanks by Barko et al. (1982). Experimental light levels varied from 100 to 1500 E/m²/sec and temperatures ranged from 12 to 32°C. At 20°C and above, the biomass and shoot density of *V. americana* increased with increases in light, particularly between low and mid-levels. Shoot length increased with decreasing irradiance, particularly between 20 and 32°C. Shoot and root biomass, and shoot density and length increased with increasing temperatures up to 28°C at mid and high light levels. The growth of eelgrass was severely restricted under 20°C.

Sutton and Barlow (1981) planted *Hydrilla* and *Vallisneria* in a muck-sand mixture in large tanks, alone and in combination. At 12 wk, *Hydrilla* increased from an initial dry weight of 4.8 to 71.1 g. *Vallisneria* increased from 7.2 to 38 g during this period. With both *Hydrilla* and *Vallisneria* in the tanks, dry weights were 67.3 and 6.9 g, respectively.

Both leaf surface area and ratio of leaf length to breadth increased with temperatures to 28°C. These leaf characters of *Vallisneria* were more responsive to temperature and light conditions than those of *Potamogeton nodosus* in the same experiment (Barko et al. 1982).

From an analysis of their own and other data, Barko and co-workers concluded that basic differences in the life cycles, mediated by seasonal light and temperature changes, are important factors in the distribution of submerged macrophytes.

Vallisneria and *Hydrilla* are in the same family but have entirely different growth characteristics, with the former developing from a single meristem and with greater biomass near the substratum. The latter produces a great canopy near the surface where it can take maximum advantage of available light (Haller and Sutton 1975). The dominant meristem of *Hydrilla* is at the shoot apex, as are several lateral meristems that assist in the early establishment of a covering light-shield very near the surface, thus discouraging the growth of all submerged plants beneath it.

Titus and Adams (1979) found that *V. americana* had limited ability to compete with *Myriophyllum spicatum* in a lake in the northern United States where the latter could extend its growing season beyond that of *Vallisneria* by photosynthesizing at lower temperatures.

Carpenter (1980) studied the environment of a hardwater, eutrophic, freshwater lake in the northern United States by making quantitative assessments of nutrients derived from macrophyte decomposition throughout the entire water body. Because the direct, *in situ*, effects of plant decay on water chemistry are the result of many processes, field and laboratory work, and models, were employed to measure or calculate the release of total dissolved P and dissolved organic matter from decaying plants.

He found the dissolved material was transported to open water by a rapid water exchange between littoral and pelagic zones with a resident time of 8 hr for water in the former zone. The timing of release and movement of nutrients from the littoral zone varied with the species composition of the macrophyte stand. He found that *V. americana* senesced late and contributed less to the summer nutrient supply than *P. pectinatus*, for example, which senesced early. Eelgrass decomposition thus took place in colder water and contributed less nutrients to the pelagic zone and more to the sedimentary organic matter than those species that died off in warmer weather.

Lakes and ponds above 35° N latitude are normally ice-covered for several months in winter, but Boylen and Sheldon (1976) found that almost one-half of the 25 submerged species in a lake in the northern United States could remain photosynthetically active. *Vallisneria*, among these species, showed a seasonal pattern of sprouting from rhizomes in mid-June, increasing to 100 plants/m^2 at the 3-m depth by mid August. New rhizomes formed in October and the vegetative plants began to decline and decrease in number through January. In contrast, *Potamogeton robbinsii* remained quite stable, with a population of 100 to 1000 plants/m^2 year round.

The water content of 85 to 95% in *V. spiralis* is closely comparable to that of some herbaceous land plants (Sculthorpe 1967). Pond (1905) reported that this species obtains the majority of its mineral salts by uptake from the substratum. For information on electrolyte exchange between *V. spiralis* and the surrounding medium, see Ariz (1963, 1964).

AGRICULTURAL IMPORTANCE

Vallisneria behaves as a weed in natural and man-made aquatic systems in more than 50 countries. It is ranked a serious weed of irrigation schemes and of aquatic waterways in India. It is ranked a principal weed of irrigation lands in Australia and of many types of waterways in Australia and the United States (Cook 1974, Robson 1976). It is in lowland rice in China, India, and Portugal and jute in India. *Vallisneria*, with *Hydrilla* and *Utricularia*, are the major submersed weeds of Sri Lanka (Kotalawala 1976). The weed is extending its range in Europe (Cook 1974).

The Indian subcontinent suffers more from the interference of this weed with fisheries, irrigation, navigation and recreation than any other area. An extensive survey of Andhra Pradesh found eelgrass to be one of the most widespread aquatic weeds in that state (Ramachandran et al. 1976). Mani et al. (1976) believe it is one of the four principal aquatic weeds in all of India.

The Chambal irrigation scheme in Rajasthan, India commands more than 400,000 ha of farmland, and when aquatic weeds seriously reduced the flow of the canals in the mid-1960s they began to silt up and *V. spiralis* began to grow in several areas. It soon became one of the dominant submerged weeds that further reduced the flow (Mehta and Sharma 1972, 1976). Ten years later, Reeders et al. (1986) reported that this species had replaced *Potamogeton pectinatus* and *perfoliatus* as the dominant weed over the entire Chambal system. As in the Chambal, reduced flow in canals and ditches becomes the major problem in several places in the world and it is frequently caused by mixed populations of submerged, emerged and floating weeds. Mitchell and Orr (1985) reported a particular trio of weeds that interfere with water management in Australia. Populations of *Myriophyllum* species, *Potamogeton tricarinatus*, and *V. spiralis* originate on the channel edges, grow out into deeper water, mix, and may form a biomass of considerable depth that chokes the stream.

Eelgrass is a major weed interfering with fisheries in the Cuttack area. In the Hissar district, it is a principal weed in 2800 km of irrigation canals. It has been customary to close the canals 7 days every 2 mo to enable hundreds of laborers to harvest the weed in knee-deep snake-infested waters (Malhotra 1976). There are mixed reports on the preference of the grass carp, *Ctenopharyngodon idella*, for *Vallisneria*.

V. spiralis is an excellent food for waterfowl and provides good cover for fish that prefer shallow marginal areas for spawning. Analysis of the composition of eelgrass harvested from many sites, and its possible usefulness as animal food, have been reported by Gortner (1934), Easley and Shirley (1974), and Muztar et al. (1978). Heffron et al. (1977) prepared a standard ration in which *V. americana* (dried, milled, and pelleted) replaced 35% by weight of the lucerne meal, and fed it to sheep and pregnant goats for 130 days. There was no significant difference in ration intake, rate of gain, or ration digestibility of the two rations. The aquatic ration was notably higher in ash, and lower in fat, fiber, and energy. All goat offspring were normal.

COMMON NAMES

Vallisneria spiralis

AUSTRALIA	eelweed, ribbon weed
BANGLADESH	pata jhanji, pata showla
CANADA	tape grass
CHINA	kuk-chao
ENGLAND	eelweed
FRANCE	vallisnerie en spirale
GERMANY	Gemeine Wasserschraube
INDIA	patasewla
ITALY	alga di chiana
NETHERLANDS	vallisneria
NEW ZEALAND	eelgrass
PORTUGAL	saca-rolhas
UNITED STATES	eelgrass, ribbon weed, tape weed

One Hundred Three

Vernonia cinerea (L.) Less.

Asteraceae (Compositae), Aster Family

V ERNONIA CINEREA is widely distributed in tropical and subtropical regions. The genus, named for the 17th-century British botanist William Vernon, has 400 species, 25 of which are considered weeds (Holm et al. 1979). Of these *V. cinerea* is clearly the most important. The species name is Latin for ashes or ash colored. *Vernonia cinerea* occurs in nearly 50 countries and is common in gardens, field and plantation crops, pastures, roadsides and waste areas.

FIGURE 103-1   The distribution of *Vernonia cinerea* (L.) Less. across the world where it has been reported as a weed.

FIGURE 103-2 *Vernonia cinerea* (L.) Less.: 1. habit; 2. flower; 3. achene with pappus.

DESCRIPTION

V. cinerea (Figure 103-2) is an *annual*, erect herb; *stems* sparingly branched, ribbed, somewhat woody, pubescent, 20 to 80 cm tall; *leaves* alternate, oblanceolate to obovate, acute or obtuse, shallowly toothed, 2 to 6 cm long and 0.5 to 3.5 cm wide; petioled or the upper leaves sessile; *inflorescence* terminal, in open, lax, branched *corymbs*; *capitula* discoid, peduncled, 0.4 to 0.5 cm wide, surrounded by 4-seriate lanceolate *involucre* 4 to 5 mm long, hairy, often tinged with purple, glandular and 1-nerved; each capitulum with 20 to 25 tubular, bright purple or pinkish-violet *florets*, each twice as long as involucral bracts; 5 petals united into 5-toothed *corolla*; *stamens* 5 with anthers united laterally; *ovary* covered with biseriate hairs and unicellular glands; *fruit* an *achene* 1.5 mm long, covered with appressed, silky hairs, faintly 4- or 5-ribbed; *pappus* of long, white, silky hairs, outer row shorter than others.

This species is recognized by the slender, ribbed stem, shallowly toothed leaves and the branched corymbs with bright purple to pinkish-violet flower heads.

BIOLOGY AND ECOLOGY

V. cinerea is prevalent in tropical and subtropical regions and nearly all research on it has been done in India. Plants exhibit clear morphological variations in height, degree of hairiness and other features. Achenes at the edge of the capitula differ in size, shape and color from those in the center (Singhal and Sen 1981). Tandon and Bhalla (1967–68) did cytological examinations on groups of *V. cinerea* plants with small (3.0 by 4.2 cm) or large (3.8 by 7.7 cm) leaves and with small (0.4 cm diameter) to large (0.5 cm) capitula. All plants were diploids with a *2n* chromosome number of 18. The bivalents (paired chromosomes) were of the ring type. All plants had an equal number of stomata and similarly sized pollen grains. Plants are rich in potassium (3.1% K_2O) and also have 2.6% N, 2.1% CaO, 1.5% P_2O_5, and 0.5% S in the preflowering stage (Singh and Singh 1939).

If moisture is available, plants flower and set seed for many months. Single anthers form 76 pollen grains, or 380 per flower (Mondal and Roy 1984). Tiagi and Taimni (1963) conducted detailed embryological studies and found very little endosperm in the seeds. The relatively long pappus aids in seed dispersal and is hygroscopic. Even if seeds land without touching the soil, many still germinate (Pemadasa and Kangatharalingam 1977). Seeds germinate with or without the pappus when in contact with the soil. Light enhances germination (82% in light versus 62% in darkness) and seeds germinate over a 30-day period at 25°C. Germination decreases from 58% on the soil surface to 36, 19, 12, and 9% at 0.5, 1, 2, and 4 cm, respectively. Seedlings emerge only from 0 on the surface to 1 cm. If seeds receive no moisture for up to 72 hr after germination has started, many still germinate, but the process is greatly delayed.

AGRICULTURAL IMPORTANCE

V. cinerea is most important in Asia, East and West Africa, and the Caribbean countries. It is a reported weed of 27 crops in 47 countries (Figure 103-1) and is frequently reported in sugarcane, upland rice, and tropical plantation crops. It is a serious or principal weed of cotton, peanuts, sugarcane, and wheat in India; pastures in Australia, India, Nigeria, and Thailand; upland rice in the Philippines; and taro in Samoa.

It is a common weed of banana in Surinam and Tonga; cassava, citrus, and oil palm in Surinam; cacao in Indonesia; cotton in the Philippines; maize in India; pastures in Australia, Dominican Republic, and Jamaica; pineapple in Hawaii; rice in Surinam; upland rice in India, Indonesia, and Sri Lanka; rubber in Indonesia and Thailand; sugarcane in Bangladesh, Hawaii, and the Philippines; taro in Tonga; tea in India and Indonesia; and vegetables in Surinam and Thailand.

In addition, *V. cinerea* is reported as a weed but is unranked in abaca, legumes, pastures, tobacco, and tomatoes in the Philippines; cacao and coffee in Dominican Republic; cassava in India, Indonesia, and Nigeria; coconut in Sri Lanka and Surinam; cotton in Mozambique and Tanzania; macadamia nut in Hawaii; maize in Cambodia, Gambia, Indonesia, Nigeria, the Philippines, and Zambia; peanuts in Indonesia and Nigeria; upland rice in Laos, Thailand, and Vietnam; rubber and tea in Sri Lanka; and sugarcane in British Guiana, Dominican Republic, Laos, and Vietnam.

While it is a weed of numerous crops, no competition data was found for *V. cinerea*. It can host the tobacco leaf curl virus (Sen 1981) and the root-knot nematode (Pancho 1964). Medicinal uses of *V. cinerea* in India include treatment of conjunctivitis, dropsy and urinary disorders (Anandalwar and Venkateswara 1981). In the Philippines, an infusion of this plant is used for coughs and skin diseases and to dress wounds. A poultice from leaves reduces headaches, while a root decoction relieves stomachache and diarrhea (Bariuan 1985). One of the active principles in the roots is the bitter glucoside "vernonin" and leaves have some antibiotic activity (Oliver-Bever 1986).

COMMON NAMES

Vernonia cinerea

AUSTRALIA	vernonia
CUBA	machadita
DOMINICAN REPUBLIC	yerba morada
FIJI	ironweed
HAWAII	little ironweed
INDIA	ankari, ankta, pokasungo, sahaderi, sandri
INDONESIA	boejoeng-boejoeng, bujung-bujung, leuleuntjann, sasawi langit
JAPAN	mura-saki-mukashi-yomogi, yambaru-higotai
MALAYSIA	common vernonia, rumput tahi babi
MAURITIUS	ayapana sauvage
NIGERIA	bojure
PHILIPPINES	agas-moro, bulabod, kolong-kulong, magmansi, sagit, tagulinau
PUERTO RICO	rabo de buey, vernonia, yerba socialista
SRI LANKA	alavangu pillu, monara kudumbiya
THAILAND	suea-saan-kha, ya-la-ong
TRINIDAD	ironweed
UNITED STATES	little ironweed

One Hundred Four

Veronica arvensis L. and Veronica persica Poir.

Scrophulariaceae, Figwort Family

V ERONICA ARVENSIS, a winter annual, and *V. persica*, an annual, are native to Eurasia but are now common in temperate and mild-climate regions around the world. Both are low-growing herbs found in gardens, lawns, cultivated fields, roadsides and waste areas. The genus name was given in honor of St. Veronica and is derived from two Latin words that mean true image. The epithet *arvensis* is Latin for "of the field" and *persica* means peach. These and related species are called "speedwells" in English.

DESCRIPTIONS

Veronica arvensis

V. arvensis (Figure 104-1) is usually a *winter annual* herb; *roots* fibrous; *stems* erect or spreading from base and then erect, 10 to 30 cm long, diffusely branched, somewhat pubescent; *lower* and *middle leaves* opposite, petioled, two to four blunt teeth on each side, ovate to elliptic, 6 to 12 mm long, palmately veined, pubescent above and below; *upper leaves* alternate, sessile, smaller, not toothed, lanceolate to linear; *inflorescence* a terminal raceme forming over half the plant; *bracteal leaves* progressively smaller towards tip; *flowers* on very short pedicel (1.5 mm); *sepals* 4, small, lanceolate, very unequal, 3 to 5 mm long; *corolla* 4-lobed, blue to blue-violet, 3 to 4 mm in diameter; *stamens* 2; *style* 8 mm long; *fruit* a 2-celled *capsule*, rounded with a deep notch at top, nearly as broad as tall, ciliate, 6 to 20 seeds per capsule; *seeds* oval, yellowish-brown to brown, 1.0 to 1.25 mm long, slightly convex dorsal side and almost flat ventral side, surface finely tuberculate.

Veronica persica

V. persica (Figure 104-2) is typically an *annual* herbaceous plant; *roots* fibrous; *stems* 10 to 50 cm long, simple or branched, often prostrate with roots at nodes, scattered long hairs;

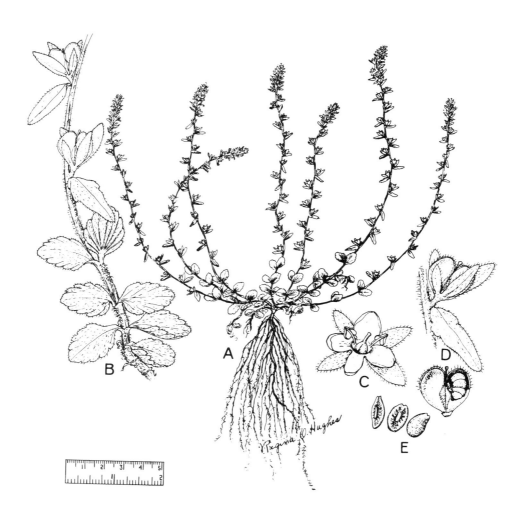

FIGURE 104-1   *Veronica arvensis* L.: A. habit; B. enlarged branch; C. flower; D. capsules; E. seeds.

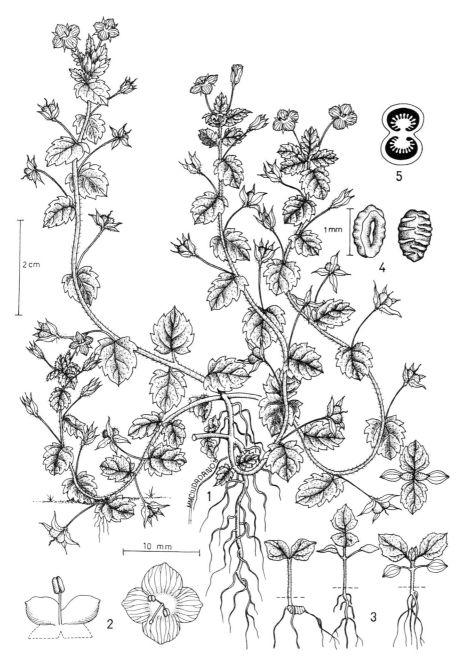

FIGURE 104-2 *Veronica persica* Poir.: 1. habit; 2. flowers, side and front view; 3. seedlings; 4. seed, two views; 5. ovary, cross section.

lower leaves opposite, petioled, coarsely toothed, round-ovate, to 2 cm long; *upper leaves* similar but alternate and sessile, scattered pubescence on all leaves; *inflorescence* axillary on pedicels to 2 cm long (longer than leaves); *flower calyx* 4-lobed, green, 6 to 8 mm long; *corolla* 4-lobed, blue, 8 to 12 mm in diameter, *stamens* 2; *fruit* a 2-celled *capsule*, broadly heart-shaped, lobes point outward with a shallow notch, clearly wider (6 to 8.5 mm) than tall (4 to 6 mm); style and calyx persistent; somewhat pubescent, 7 to 18 seeds per capsule; *seeds* obovoid, brown to brownish-yellow, to 1.5 mm long, one side deeply concave, other rounded, surface tuberculate.

Both species are easily recognized by their spreading growth habit, flower parts in fours, 2-celled capsules, and opposite lower leaves and alternate upper leaves. They are readily distinguished from each other by the somewhat larger size and greater pubescence of *V. persica* and by the differences in their flowers. *V. arvensis* has a terminal raceme of much smaller flowers on very short pedicels, while *V. persica* has axillary flowers supported on pedicels 2 cm long.

ECOLOGY AND BIOLOGY

V. arvensis and *V. persica* can spread rapidly. *V. persica* was first reported in Britain in 1820 and was widely distributed in the region within 50 yr (Harris and Lovell 1980c). As an annual, it grows and produces dense vegetation all year in Brazil. *V. persica* is found in 40% of the fields with root crops and 10% of the cereals in Poland, while the winter annual, *V. arvensis*, occurs in many more cereal than root crop fields (Borowiec et al. 1972). *V. persica* is seldom found above 350 m, while *V. arvensis* grows from sea level to 900 m (Salisbury 1964). *V. persica* favors moist environments and tolerates clay soils, while *V. arvensis* grows best in alkaline and relatively drier soils.

Fischer (1987) gives a thorough review of *V. persica*'s origin and taxonomic characteristics and attributes its wild adaptability to the xeromorphic characters of one parent and the mesomorphic ones of the other. He sees *V. persica* as an ideal weed because it can set seed all year, seeds germinate when mature in a wide range of conditions, and plants grow rapidly to the flowering stage, are self-compatible, and are pollinated by many insect species.

In the United States, *V. arvensis* seeds germinate primarily in the autumn, overwinter as rosettes, then flower and die by early summer. In wheat in England, *V. persica* starts flowering in January or February, and *V. arvensis* in May, and maximum plant biomass is achieved in May and July, respectively (Wilson and Wright 1990). Most fresh seed of *V. arvensis* requires an after-ripening period to break dormancy. The optimum temperature regime for germination of fresh seed in June is 15/6°C (day/night) (15 to 20% germination). By October nearly all seeds germinate at 15/6 and 20/10°C. Few *V. arvensis* seeds germinate at temperatures of 30/15 or 35/20°C, and thus seeds seldom germinate after maturing in the summer months.

Very few seeds of *V. arvensis* germinate at any temperature in the dark (Baskin and Baskin 1983). All fresh seeds of *V. persica* germinated within 3 to 8 days in the light or dark at 24°C. Prechilling at 4°C for 8 days did not affect germination of either species (Harris and Lovell 1980a). *V. arvensis* has nearly a 12-wk after-ripening period (Janssen 1973). Fresh seeds of *V. persica* are not dormant and two generations per year are possible (Salisbury 1964). As with *V. arvensis*, light enhances germination (Wesson and Wareing 1969b). Unlike *V. arvensis*, *V. persica* germinates from early spring into the fall, with a peak in May in England (Roberts and Feast 1970).

In England, 74% of the *V. arvensis* seeds planted in October germinated within 3 mo when placed on the surface, 17% when at 25 mm, and none emerged from 75 mm (Froud-Williams et al. 1984a). Monthly soil disturbance of the surface sown seed stimulated germination (81 vs. 63% if undisturbed). Maximum emergence occurred from 0 to 5 mm. In contrast, 60% of the *V. persica* seeds emerged from 25 mm, while only 20% germinated on the soil surface. Maximum emergence depth of *V. persica* was 50 mm and the optimum was 5 to 20 mm.

Seeds of *V. arvensis* can remain viable in the soil for over 20 yr (Odum 1974) but seed populations in the soil vary greatly with cropping system and tillage practices. Fallowing with tillage reduced seed population 73% in 1 yr, but the population increased to 50% of the original after 4 yr of cropping (Brenchley and Warington 1945). *V. persica* seed can maintain viability for 30 yr or more (Odum 1974) and 29% of the seeds placed 15 cm below the surface were recovered after 5 yr without soil disturbance. Nearly all seeds from 2.5 to 15 cm emerged when tilled annually for 5 yr (Roberts and Feast 1972). Seed population of *V. persica* was unchanged after 9 yr of annual plowing and weeding with standard practices. However, rototilling to 15 cm each year tripled the seed density, and applying manur`e quadrupled the seed population (Roberts and Stokes 1965).

V. arvensis does not form adventitious roots, but leaf cuttings of both species placed in distilled water root readily (Harris and Lovell 1980b). *V. persica* roots at the nodes and a single plant may cover 1.7 m² and have 200 rooting nodes (Salisbury 1962). Therefore plants can easily reroot and continue growing after surface cultivation (Roberts and Stokes 1966). Even though nodes far from the main stem form roots, all stems remain attached to the parent plant (Harris and Lovell 1980a). *V. persica* is a polyploid with a 2*n* chromosome number of 28 and many ecotypes exist (Harris and Lovell 1980c, Fischer 1987).

V. persica does not grow well in the shade. A dense tobacco canopy can reduce its growth 90%, even though the chlorophyll concentration was unaffected by the shade (Fitter and Ashmore 1974). At high densities in wheat, *V. arvensis* and persica produce only 1 to 2 g dry wt/plant. Stomata open in the morning but are nearly closed in the afternoon. Aging reduces the degree of stomatal opening, perhaps in response to the higher K levels in guard cells of older plants (Losch and Krug 1979). Plants growing without competition form stems 60 cm long after 4 mo in England. Seeds drop from mature capsules and new seedlings emerge before the parent has died. Mowing killed *V. persica* transplanted into a pasture and no plants arising from seed in undisturbed pastures reached maturity (Harris and Lovell 1980c).

Both species are self-pollinated and are prolific seed producers. A single plant of *V. arvensis* can produce 870 capsules with 20 seeds each or 17,410 seeds/plant, equivalent to 30% of the above-ground weight. *V. persica* may have 565 capsules that average 11.6 seeds each to give 6540 seeds/plant, equivalent to 15% of the plant's above-ground weight (Harris and Lovell 1980a). Seeds of *V. persica* are larger than those of *V. arvensis* (.38 vs. .10 mg/ seed) and seed weight and number per capsule are relatively constant over a range of environments. *V. persica* has a 4-month "seed rain" and, once seedlings emerge, more than 90% survive if free of competition. Seventy-two plants/m² produced 35,000 seeds in a single year (Leguizamon and Roberts 1982). Most seeds of *V. persica* fall near the parent plant, but a single seed remains tightly attached inside each fruit capsule (Fischer 1987). The flat capsules are readily wind borne and can disperse seed long distances. In addition, plants with intact capsules are moved by wind after senescence and spread seeds in tumbleweed fashion (Harris and Lovell 1980c).

The abundant seed production is reflected in high seed populations in the soil. Roberts and Stokes (1966) found up to 3200 and 450 seeds/m² of *V. persica* and *V. arvensis*, respectively, in English vegetable fields. A later survey found *V. persica* in 40% of the vegetable fields and 20% had more than 250 seeds/m² and the highest population was 1650/m². Seventeen percent of the fields had *V. arvensis*; 7% had more than 250/m² and the maximum was 1480 seeds/m² (Roberts and Neilson 1982). In Denmark, densities of 221 seeds/m² of *V. arvensis* and 825 seeds/m² of *V. persica* were found, but there was little correlation between soil seed reserves and the actual weed vegetation present (Jensen 1969).

AGRICULTURAL IMPORTANCE

Both species are widely distributed in Europe and North America, and are frequently reported weeds of cereal and vegetable crops. *V. arvensis* is a weed of 17 crops in 43 countries (Figure 104-3). It is a serious or principal weed of barley in Korea; cereals in Italy, Spain, and Sweden; maize in the former Yugoslavia; orchards in Spain; oilseed rape in Sweden; and wheat in Chile and Korea.

V. arvensis is a common weed of cereals in Bulgaria and Poland; citrus in Tunisia; horticultural crops in England; lucerne in Spain; orchards in Turkey and Uruguay; sugar beets in Poland; and vegetables in England and Hungary.

V. arvensis is also an unranked weed of barley in Finland and France; field beets in Belgium; cereals in Bangladesh, England, the former Soviet Union, and Turkey; horticultural crops in Bangladesh; orchards in Argentina; pastures in Spain; rape in England, Spain, and Switzerland; vegetable fields in Australia, Belgium, Brazil, China, England, and New Zealand.

FIGURE 104-3   The distribution of *Veronica arvensis* L. across the world where it has been reported as a weed.

V. persica is a weed of 27 crops in 45 countries (Figure 104-4). It is a serious or principal weed of cereals in Italy and Sweden; beets and potatoes in Germany; horticultural crops in England; oilseed rape in Sweden; sugar beets in Czechoslovakia, England, and Poland; sunflowers in Argentina; vegetables in Germany and England; and wheat in Iran.

It is a common weed of barley in Peru; cereals in Bulgaria, Ecuador, England, France, Germany, the Netherlands, and Scotland; maize in Colombia and Ecuador; flax, potatoes, oilseed rape, sugar beets, and sunflower in France; horticultural crops in the Netherlands; oats in India; orchards in Turkey and Uruguay; vegetables in Hungary and Tasmania; and wheat in Colombia and Peru.

V. persica is also an unranked weed of the following: barley in Colombia; edible beans in England; beets in France and Italy; cereals in Poland; coffee in Mexico; lucerne in Italy and the United States; orchards in Argentina, Bolivia, and Spain; potatoes in Belgium and Colombia; oilseed rape in England and Japan; sugarcane in Australia; tobacco in Argentina; vegetables in Argentina, Australia, Iran, New Zealand, and Switzerland; vineyards in Bulgaria and the former Soviet Union; and wheat in Belgium, Czechoslovakia, England, Italy, and Japan.

Both species reportedly compete with cereals for N but seldom cause yield losses (Welbank 1963). In England, densities of *V. arvensis* from 80 to 1965 and of *V. persica* from 45 to 3685 plants/m^2 did not affect wheat yield (Wilson and Wright 1990). *V. persica* increases in abundance in cereals in England when urea-based herbicides are used for grass control and its presence can predispose the crop to lodge even though it dies before harvest. Continual triazine use in maize in France has led to the development of tolerance (but not classical resistance) after 14 yr (Grignac 1978). *Veronica* can host aphids, nematodes and viruses (Bendixen et al. 1979, 1981).

FIGURE 104-4   The distribution of *Veronica persica* Poir. across the world where it has been reported as a weed.

COMMON NAMES

Veronica arvensis

ARGENTINA	menta silvestre, veronica
BRAZIL	mentinha
CANADA	corn speedwell, veronique des champs
CHILE	veronica
DENMARK	mark-aerenpris
ENGLAND	speedwell, wall speedwell
FINLAND	ketotadyke
FRANCE	veronique des champs
GERMANY	Feld-Ehrenpreis
ITALY	ederella
JAPAN	tachi-inunofuguri
LEBANON	wall speedwell
NETHERLANDS	veldereprijs
NEW ZEALAND	field speedwell
NORWAY	bakkeveronika
SPAIN	veronica arvense
SWEDEN	faltarenpris, faltveronika
UNITED STATES	corn speedwell

Veronica persica

ARGENTINA	canchaagua
AUSTRALIA	Persian speedwell
BELGIUM	grote ereprijs, veronique de Perse
BOLIVIA	adaluzia
BRAZIL	mentinha
CANADA	bird's eye speedwell, veronique de Perse
CHILE	veronica
COLOMBIA	golondrina, violettilla
DENMARK	storkronet aerenpris
ECUADOR	veronica
ENGLAND	common field speedwell
FINLAND	Persian tadyke
FRANCE	veronique de perse
GERMANY	Acker-Ehrenpreis, Grosser Ehrenpreis, Persischer Ehrenpreis
ITALY	veronica querciola, occhietta della madonna
JAPAN	o-inunofuguri

NETHERLANDS	grote ereprijs
NEW ZEALAND	scrambling speedwell
NORWAY	orientveronika
PERU	tutahuira
SPAIN	borroneillo
SWEDEN	tradgardsveronika
UNITED STATES	Persian speedwell

Glossary

abaxial.   Facing away from the axis of the plant.

absciss.   To fall off, as with leaves.

acaulescent.   Stemless, or apparently so.

achene.   A small, dry, hard, one-seeded fruit.

acicular.   Needle-shaped.

acropetal.   Ascending (e.g., blooming in succession from the basal portion toward the apex).

actinomorphic.   Flowers that are radially symmetrical.

acuminate.   Tapering to a slender point.

adaxial.   The side toward the axis.

adnate.   The union of unlike parts (e.g., stamens to petals).

adventitious.   Originating from an abnormal position.

adventive.   Introduced but not well established.

aerenchyma.   Parenchyma with large intercellular spaces.

after-ripening.   Metabolic changes that must occur before dormant seeds can germinate.

aleurone.   Granules of protein found in endosperm of cereals.

allelopathy.   Biochemical inhibition or stimulation between organisms.

ambient.   Relating to the environment at a particular time.

anatropous.   Ovary bent over against funicle so hilum and micropyle are close together.

androgynophore.   A stalk bearing both stamens and pistil above the point of perianth attachment.

antheridium.   The male organ of the sexual generation in bryophytes and pteridophytes.

antherozoid.   A small, flagellated, male sex cell.

anthesis.   The time of full flower expansion.

apiculate.   Ending in a short, pointed tip.

apomictic.   Capable of producing seed without any form of fertilization or sexual union.

archegonium.   The female sex organ in bryophytes and pteridophytes.

aristate.   Bearing a stiff, bristle-like awn.

articulate.   Jointed.

auricle.   An ear-like lobe at the base of various leaves and petals.

autotetraploid.   A tetraploid with four identical sets of chromosomes.

autotroph.   An organism that makes its own food.

axil.   The angle between a branch or a leaf and the stem.

axillary.   Situated in, growing from, or pertaining to an axil.

baccate.   Pulpy throughout, like a berry.

benthic.   Organisms that live on or attached to the bottom of aquatic habitats.

biennial.   A plant that normally requires two growing seasons to complete its life cycle.

bifid.   Forked; two-cleft.

biotype.   A group of individuals with the same genotype.

bipinnate.   Twice pinnate.

bolting.   The abnormal formation of stems on plants which normally have a rosette growth habit.

bract.   A modified, often much reduced leaf subtending a flower or inflorescence.

bullate.   Having blistered, swollen or puckered appearance.

callus.   Soft parenchymatous tissue that forms over any wounded or cut surface of a stem.

calyx.   The outer whorl of usually green leaf or bract-like structures called sepals.

campanulate.   Bell-shaped, as a flower.

capillary.   Very slender, hair-like.

capitate.   Clustered together into a dense head.

capitulum.   A congested head of flowers.

capsule.   A dry dehiscent fruit composed of more than one carpel.

carpel.   The ovule-bearing structure of a flower.

caryopsis.   An achene with the pericarp and testa inseparably fused, as in grasses.

centripetal.   In inflorescences, blooming from the outside inward, or from the base upward.

chasmogamous.   Referring to pollination which takes place in open flowers.

chlorosis.   Yellowing caused by loss of chlorophyll.

ciliate.   Fringed with fine hairs.

circumscissile.   Splitting along a circular line, as the lid of a capsule.

cleistogamous.   A flower that does not open and is self-pollinated.

clone.   A group of individuals resulting from vegetative multiplication.

coleoptile.   A protective sheath-like structure enclosing the epicotyl in seeds of grasses.

collenchyma.   A flexible supporting tissue composed of elongated living cells with unevenly thickened primary walls.

connate.   Union or fusion.

contiguous.   Touching without fusion.

coriaceous.   Thick, tough and leathery.

corm.   A shortened (compressed) usually subterranean stem enclosed by dry, scale-like leaves.

corolla.   The petals of a flower.

cortex.   The zone of tissue lying underneath the epidermis.

corymb.   Short and broad, flat-topped, indeterminate inflorescence, outer flowers opening first.

crenate.   Having the margin cut into rounded scallops.

culm.   The jointed stem of a grass or sedge.

cuneate.   Triangular with the acute end at the point of attachment.

cyathium.   A cup-like involucre enclosing flowers.

cyme.   A broad and more or less flat-topped determinate inflorescence. The central flowers open first.

decumbent.   Reclining on the ground with tip turned upward.

decussate.   Opposite leaves alternating at right angles with those above and below.

dehisce.   To split open when ripe.

dentate.   Toothed, with the teeth more or less perpendicular to the margin of the leaf.

dichotomous.   Branching by repeated forking in pairs.

dioecious.   Having staminate and pistillate flowers on different plants of the same species.

dorsal.   The lower or under surface of a leaf.

downy.   Covered with short, weak hairs.

drupe.   A fleshy, pulpy, or fibrous fruit with a hard endocarp (the stone) enclosing a single seed.

ecotype, ecotypic.   A biotype resulting from selection in a particular habitat.

emarginate.   Bearing a shallow notch at the apex.

emersed.   Having part of the plant aerial and the rest submersed.

endocarp.   The inner layer of the pericarp or fruit wall.

endoplasmic reticulum.   An extensive system of double membranes present in the cytoplasm, dividing it into compartments or channels.

endosperm. The nutritive tissue of most seeds.

entomophilous. Pollination by insects.

epipetalous. Having stamens attached to the petals or corolla.

epiphyte. An organism that grows on another plant but is not parasitic on it.

eutrophic. A water body rich in organic and inorganic nutrients.

exsert. Protruding beyond some enclosing organ or part.

fasciated. Stems and branches malformed and flattened.

fetid. Stinks.

filament. The part of a stamen that supports the anther.

fistular. Hollow and cylindrical.

follicle. A dry, dehiscent fruit derived from one carpel that splits along one suture.

frond. A fern or palm leaf.

gametophyte. The generation that bears the sex organs.

geniculate. Bent abruptly like a knee.

genotype. The genetic constitution of an individual.

glabrous. Having a surface without hairs.

glaucous. Covered with a bluish or whitish bloom.

glume. One of the two, empty, chaffy bracts at the base of the spikelet in grasses.

gynoecium. A collective term for all the carpels (female parts) in a flower.

hastate. Arrow-head shaped with the basal lobes spreading at nearly right angles.

haustorium. An outgrowth of roots or stems of parasitic plants that penetrates the host plant to draw food and minerals.

heterocyst. A clear cell occurring at intervals on filaments of some blue-green algae.

hilum. The scar or point of attachment of the seed.

hoary. White or grayish-white pubescence.

hyaline. Thin and translucent or transparent.

hydathode. Epidermal structure for secretion or exudation of water.

hypha. A single, thread-like filament which is the structural unit of fungi.

hypocotyl. The portion of the stem below the cotyledons in the embryo.

hypodermis. A layer or layers of cells beneath the epidermis.

imbricate. With margins of structures overlapping.

incompatibility. Genetically determined inability to mate successfully.

indehiscent. Not dehiscent.

indusium. An epidermal outgrowth which covers a sorus in some ferns.

in situ. In the natural position.

involucre. A whorl or rosette of bracts, often resembling an ordinary calyx, subtending or support-ing a flower cluster or fruit.

isodiametric. Having equal diameters.

keel. A prominent dorsal rib or ridge.

lactiferous. 1. Having a milky sap or juice. 2. Bearing latex.

lacuna. A space between cells.

lanceolate. Shaped like the head of a lance.

lemma. In the grasses, the lower of usually two bracts immediately enclosing the flower.

lenticels. An opening in the periderm to facilitate gas transport.

lenticular. Shaped like a double-convex lens.

ligule. A thin membranous outgrowth at the top of the leaf sheath where the sheath and leaf meet.

littoral zone. At the seashore, the region between high and low tide.

locule. A compartment, chamber or cavity; as in an ovary.

lumen. The space within a plant cell bounded by the cell wall.

megaspore. The larger spore of heterosporous plants that gives rise to the female gametophyte.

mesocarp. The middle layer of cells of the pericarp or fruit wall.

mesophyll. The photosynthetic tissue between the upper and lower epidermis of a leaf.

mesophyte. Plants in environments that are neither very wet nor very dry.

micropyle.   A small opening in the integuments of an ovule through which the pollen tube enters.

microspore.   The cell from which a pollen grain develops.

monoecious.   A plant with separate male and female reproductive structures occurring on the same plant.

mucro.   An abrupt point or tip at the end of an organ.

mutation.   An inheritable change in the genetic material of a cell.

nectary.   Any structure which secretes nectar.

oblanceolate.   Inversely lanceolate; with the broadest portion nearest the apex and tapering toward the base.

obligate parasite.   Parasites that cannot exist independently of a host.

obovate.   Inversely ovate.

obovoid.   Inversely ovoid, as a rounded object that is obovate in outline.

obtuse.   Blunt or rounded at tip.

ochrea.   A sheathing or tubular stipule.

oligotrophic.   Water bodies low in nutrients and organic matter.

ovary.   The ovule-bearing region of a carpel in a simple pistil.

ovate.   Egg-shaped, with the broadest end downward.

ovoid.   A solid object that is oval in outline.

ovule.   A structure that develops into the seed after fertilization.

palea.   The upper or inner of the two bracts that enclose the grass flower.

palmate.   Having lobes, veins or divisions radiating from a common point.

panicle.   A lose, irregularly compound inflorescence with pedicellate flowers.

papilionaceous.   Descriptive of the "butterfly-like" flower of the legumes.

pappus.   A ring of hairs or bristles at the top of an achene.

parenchyma.   Soft, thin-walled plant cells, relatively undifferentiated.

pedicel.   The stalk of an individual flower in an inflorescence.

peduncle.   The stalk of an inflorescence or a solitary flower.

pellucid.   Nearly transparent in transmitted light; clear.

perianth.   The floral envelope of a flower.

pericarp.   The ripened wall of the ovary when it becomes a fruit.

pericycle.   A layer of tissue located inside the endodermis which forms a cylinder around the vascular tissues.

petiole.   The stalk attaching a leaf blade to a stem.

phenology.   The study of periodicity in organisms as related to climatic events.

phloem.   The principal food-conducting tissue of a vascular plant.

phytochrome.   A blue protein pigment found in the cytoplasm of green plants. It acts as a photoreceptor for red/far-red light.

phytoplankton.   Small marine or freshwater plants and animals drifting with the surrounding water.

pilose.   Pubescent with long soft hair.

pinnate.   A compound leaf that has the leaflets arranged on each side of a petiole or rachis.

pistil.   The female reproductive organ of a flower, composed of an ovary, style and stigma.

plasmodesmata.   Minute cytoplasmic connections that extend through pores in the cell walls between protoplasts of adjacent living cells.

plumule.   The first bud of the embryo above the cotyledonary node.

polymorphic.   Having several to many variable forms within the same species.

prothallus.   The minute, reduced gametophyte of ferns and their allies.

proximal.   Situated near the point of reference, usually the stem.

pteridophyte.   Ferns.

pubescent.   Hairy.

raceme.   A simple intermediate inflorescence of pedicelled flowers on a common, more or less elongated axis.

rachis.   The axis of an inflorescence or of a compounded leaf beyond the petiole.

radicle.   The embryonic root.

ramet.   An individual member of a clone.

receptacle.   In angiosperms, the portion of the axis of the flower stalk on which the flower is borne.

reticulate.   In the form of a network.

retrorse.   Bent or directed downward or backward.

rhizome.   Any underground root-like stem.

rhizosphere.   The region in the soil surrounding the roots.

ruderal.   A plant growing on rubbish or in disturbed places.

rugose.   Wrinkled.

sagittate.   Like an arrow head, with the basal lobes pointing back.

scabrid.   Rough to the touch.

scape.   A peduncle arising at or beneath the ground.

scarification.   The use of hot water, acid, or scraping of the seed coat to hasten germination.

scarious.   Thin, dry, scale-like, membranous, not green.

senescence.   The aging process.

sepal.   One of the leaves of the calyx.

septum.   A dividing cross wall or partition.

serrate.   A leaf with the sharp teeth pointing forward on the margin.

sessile.   Not stalked.

sieve element.   A cell of the phloem concerned mainly with the longitudinal transport of food materials.

silique.   An elongate, many-seeded, two-celled fruit with two parietal placentae, usually with two valves that separate from the partition on dehiscence.

sorus.   A cluster of spores and/or sporangia.

spathe.   Sheathing lateral organ(s), usually open on one side, enclosing an inflorescence.

spermatophyte.   A seed plant.

sporangium.   A hollow, unicellular or multicellular sac-like, spore-producing structure.

spore.   A reproductive cell capable of developing into an adult without fusion with another cell.

sporocarp.   A hard, multicellular, nut-like receptacle which contains sporangia in heterosporous ferns.

sporophyte.   The spore-producing (also often seed-producing) generation, each cell with $2n$ chromosomes.

stele.   The central cylinder of the plant that comprises the vascular system and associated ground tissue.

stigma.   The part of the pistil that is adapted to receive pollen.

stipule.   Appendages at the base of the petiole.

stolon.   A horizontal stem at the surface of the ground, that takes root and gives rise to vegetative shoots.

stratification.   Exposure to moist media (warm or cold) to overcome embryo dormancy of seeds.

style.   The slender, stalk-like extension of a pistil which extends from the ovary to the stigma.

subulate.   Awl-shaped, tapering from base to apex.

suffrutescent.   A perennial plant which is slightly woody only at the base.

syncarpous.   Having united carpels.

tepal.   Perianth parts undifferentiated into distinct sepals and petals.

testa.   The outer seed coat that is derived from the integuments of the ovule.

thallus.   A single plant body which lacks a differentiated root, stem, or leaf (e.g., algae and fungi).

tiller.   A shoot growing from the base of a grass stem.

tracheid.   An elongated, thick-walled, nonliving conducting and supporting cell found in the xylem of most vascular plants.

truncate.   Having the end square or even.

tuber.   A thickened, compressed, fleshy, usually underground stem.

turion.   A perennating winter bud that may separate from the parent and give rise to a new plant.

umbel.   A flat-topped or convex inflorescence in which the pedicels all arise from the apex of the peduncle.

unisexual.   Flowers that have either stamens or pistil(s) but not both in the same flower.

utricle.   A small, inflated, achene-like fruit; a small bladder.

vacuole.   A membrane-bound region within the cytoplasm; filled with watery liquid.

vernalization.   The natural or artificial induction of early flowering by exposure of seeds to low temperatures.

winter annual.   An annual that usually germinates in the late fall, may grow vegetatively during winter, and sets flowers and fruits in early spring.

xerophyte.   A plant that is adapted to dry or arid habitats.

xylem.   The principal water- and mineral-conducting tissue in vascular plants.

zygote.   The single diploid ($2n$) cell formed by the fusion of male and female gametes.

List of Crops

ABACA	*Musa textilis*
ALFALFA (LUCERNE)	*Medicago sativa*
ASPARAGUS	*Asparagus officinalis*
BAJRA (PEARL MILLET)	*Pennisetum americanum* or *typhoides*
BANANA	*Musa* spp.
BARLEY	*Hordeum vulgare*
BAY LAUREL	*Laurus nobilis*
BEAN	
BROAD BEAN	*Vicia faba*
CLUSTER BEAN (GUAR)	*Cyamopsis tetragonoloba*
FRENCH BEAN	*Phaseolus vulgaris*
LIMA BEAN	*Phaseolus lunatus*
MUNG BEAN (BLACK GRAM)	*Vigna radiata*
BEET, FODDER AND TABLE	*Beta vulgaris*
BERSEEM (CLOVER)	*Trifolium alexandrinum*
CABBAGE	*Brassica oleracea*
CACAO	*Theobroma cacao*
CARAWAY	*Carum ajowan*
CARROT	*Daucus carota*
CASSAVA (MANIOC)	*Manihot esculenta*
CAULIFLOWER	*Brassica oleracea*
CELERY	*Apium graveolens*
CINCHONA	*Cinchona calisaya*
CLOVER	
ALSIKE CLOVER	*Trifolium hybridum*
BERSEEM CLOVER	*Trifolium alexandrinum*

CRIMSON CLOVER	*Trifolium incarnatum*
HOP CLOVER	*Trifolium aureum*
RED CLOVER	*Trifolium pratense*
SUBTERRANEAN CLOVER	*Trifolium subterraneum*
WHITE CLOVER	*Trifolium repens*
COCONUT	*Cocos nucifera*
COFFEE	*Coffea arabica* and *canephora*
CORN (MAIZE)	*Zea mays*
COTTON	*Gossypium hirsutum*
COWPEA	*Vigna unguiculata*
CROWN VETCH	*Coronilla varia*
CUCUMBER	*Cucumis sativus*
DANDELION, RUSSIAN	*Taraxacum kok-saghyz*
DATE	*Phoenix dactylifera*
EGGPLANT	*Solanum melongena*
FIG	*Ficus carica*
FILBERT (SEE HAZELNUT).	
FLAX (LINSEED)	*Linum usitatissimum*
GARLIC	*Allium sativum*
GRAPE	*Vitis vinifera*
GUAR (CLUSTER BEAN)	*Cyamopsis tetragonoloba*
HAZELNUT (FILBERT)	
AMERICAN HAZELNUT	*Corylus americana*
EUROPEAN HAZELNUT	*Corylus avellana*
HEMP	*Cannabis sativa*
HOPS	*Humulus lupulus*
JUTE	*Corchorus capsularis* and *olitorius*
KAFIR CORN	*Sorghum bicolor*
KALE	*Brassica oleracea*
KENAF	*Hibiscus cannabinus*
LENTIL	*Lens culinaris*
LETTUCE	*Lactuca sativa*
LINSEED (FLAX)	*Linum usitatissimum*
LUCERNE (ALFALFA)	*Medicago sativa*
LUPINE	*Lupinus albus*
MAIZE (CORN)	*Zea mays*
MANGO	*Mangifera indica*
MANIHOT (CASSAVA)	*Manihot esculenta*
MANIOC (CASSAVA)	*Manihot esculenta*
MELON	*Cucumis melo*

MILLET	
RAGI	*Eleusine corcorana*
PEARL MILLET (BAJRA)	*Pennisetum americanum*
MULBERRY	*Morus* spp.
MUSTARD (India)	*Brassica juncea*
OATS	*Avena sativa*
OIL PALM	*Elaeis gunieensis*
OLIVE	*Olea europaea*
ONION	*Allium cepa*
PAPAYA	*Carica papaya*
PAPRIKA	*Capsicum annuum*
PARSNIP	*Pastinaca sativa*
PEA	
CHICKPEA	*Cicer arietinum*
COWPEA	*Vigna unguiculata*
GARDEN PEA	*Pisum sativum*
PIGEON PEA	*Cajanus cajun*
PEANUT	*Arachis hypogaea*
PEPPER	
GARDEN PEPPER	*Capsicum annuum*
CHILI PEPPER	*Capsicum annuum*
BLACK PEPPER	*Piper nigrum*
PINEAPPLE	*Ananas comosus*
POTATO	*Solanum tuberosum*
PYRETHRUM	*Chrysanthemum cinerariaefolium*
RADISH	*Raphanus sativus*
RAGI (MILLET)	*Eleusine corcorana*
RAMIE	*Boehmeria nivea*
RAPE (OIL SEED RAPE)	*Brassica napus*
RICE	*Oryza sativa*
ROSELLE	*Hibiscus sabdariffa*
RUBBER	*Hevea brasiliensis*
RYE	*Secale cereale*
SAFFLOWER	*Carthamus tinctorius*
SAL	*Shorea robusta*
SESAME	*Sesamum indicum* and *orientale*
SISAL	*Agave sisalana*
SORGHUM	*Sorghum bicolor*
SOYBEAN	*Glycine max*
STRAWBERRY	*Fragaria virginiana*

SUDAN GRASS	*Sorghum sudanense*
SUGAR BEET	*Beta vulgaris*
SUGARCANE	*Saccharum officinarum*
SUNFLOWER	*Helianthus annuus*
SWEET POTATO	*Ipomoea batatas*
TAPIOCA (CASSAVA)	*Manihot esculenta*
TARO	*Colocasia esculenta*
TEA	*Camellia sinensis*
TEAK	*Tectona grandis*
TEOSINTE	*Euchlaena mexicana*
TOBACCO	*Nicotiana tabacum*
TOMATO	*Lycopersicon esculentum*
TREFOIL, BIRDSFOOT	*Lotus corniculatus*
TURNIP	*Brassica rapa*
WHEAT	
BREAD WHEAT	*Triticum aestivum*
DURUM WHEAT	*Triticum durum*
EMMER	*Triticum dicoccum*

Herbicide, Growth Regulator, and Metabolite Nomenclature

ACROLEIN	2-propenal
ACRYLALDEHYDE	See acrolein
AMITROLE	1H-1,2,4-triazol-3-amine
ASULAM	methyl[(4-aminophenyl)sulfonyl]carbamate
ATRAZINE	6-chloro-N-ethyl-N'-(1-methylethyl)-1,3,5-triazine-2,4-diamine
CCC	(2-chloroethyl) trimethyl ammonium chloride
CHLOROTOLURON	See chlortoluron
CHLORSULFURON	2-chloro-N-[[(4-methoxy-6-methyl-1,3,5-triazin-2-yl)amino]carbonyl]benzenesulfonamide
CHLORTOLURON	N'-(3-chloro-4-methylphenyl)-N,N-dimethylurea
CLOPYRALID	3,6-dichloro-2-pyridinecarboxylic acid
CYANAZINE	2-[[4-chloro-6-(ethylamino)-1,3,5-triazin-2-yl]amino]-2-methylpropanenitrile
2,4-D	(2,4-dichlorophenoxy)acetic acid
DALAPON	2,2-dichloropropanoic acid
2,4-DB	4-(2,4-dichlorophenoxy)butanoic acid
DCMU	See diuron
DINOSEB	2-(1-methylpropyl)-4,6-dinitrophenol
DIURON	N'-(3,4-dichlorophenyl)-N,N-dimethylurea
2,4-DP	(±)-2-(2,4-dichlorophenoxy)propanoic acid
GLYPHOSATE	N-(phosphonomethyl)glycine
HEXAZINONE	3-cyclohexyl-6-(dimethylamino)-1-methyl-1,3,5-triazine-2,4(1H,3H)-dione
ISOPROTURON	N,N-dimethyl-N'-[4-(1-methylethyl)phenyl]urea

KINETIN	6-furfurylaminopurine
MALTOL	3-hydroxyl-2-methyl-4-pyrene
MCPA	(4-chloro-2-methylphenoxy)acetic acid
MCPB	4-(4-chloro-2-methylphenoxy)butanoic acid
METHAZOLE	2-(3,4-dichlorophenyl)-4-methyl-1,2,4-oxadiazolidine-3,5-dione
METHIBENZURON	*N*-(2-benzothiazolyl)-*N*,*N*'-dimethylurea
METOXURON	*N*'-(3-chloro-4-methoxyphenyl)-*N*,*N*-dimethyl urea
METRIBUZIN	4-amino-6-(1,1-dimethylethyl)-3-(methylthio)-1,2,4-triazin-5(4*H*)-one
MOLINATE	*S*-ethyl hexahydro-1*H*-azepine-1-carbothioate
NITROFEN	2,4-dichloro-1-(4-nitrophenoxy)benzene
PARAQUAT	1,1'-dimethyl-4,4'-bipyridinium ion
PICLORAM	4-amino-3,5,6-trichloro-2-pyridinecarboxylic acid
PRONAMIDE	3,5-dichloro (*N*-1,1-dimethyl-2-propynyl)benzamide
PROPACHLOR	2-chloro-*N*-(1-methylethyl)-*N*-phenylacetamide
PROPANIL	*N*-(3,4-dichlorophenyl)propanamide
PTEROLACTAM	5-methoxy-2-pyrridoline
SIMAZINE	6-chloro-*N*,*N*'-diethyl-1,3,5-triazine-2,4-diamine
TERBACIL	5-chloro-3-(1,1-dimethylethyl)-6-methyl-2,4(1*H*,3*H*)-pyrimidinedione
THIADIAZURON	*N*-phenyl-*N*-1,2,3-thidiazol-5-ylurea

AALDERS, A. and R. PIETERSE. 1986. Plant vigor as a misleading factor in the search for resistance in broad bean (Vicia faba) to *Orobanche crenata*. In: Biology and Control of *Orobanche*. Landbouwhogeschool, Wageningen, Netherlands, 140–149.

AAMODT, O. 1935. Germination of Russian pigweed upon ice and upon frozen soil. *Scientific Agric.* 15:507–508.

ABDULLAH, H. 1980. *Pseudomonas solanacearum* isolated from two new weed hosts. *FAO (Food & Agriculture Organization of United Nations) Plant Prot. Bull.* 28:79–81.

ABOU-RAYA, M. 1970. The uniform rhythm in absorption and release of labelled phosphate by host and parasite. *J. Bot.*, Egypt, 13:121–124.

ABRAMOV, N. 1969. Control of *Cirsium arvense* and *Sonchus arvensis*. *Lenikonoplya*, Moscow 14(8):34–35.

ABU-IRMAILEH, B. 1981. Response of hemp broomrape *Orobanche ramosa* infestation to some nitrogenous compounds. *Weed Sci.* 29:8–10.

ABU-SHAKRA, S., A. MIAH and A. SAGHIR. 1970. Germination of seed of branched broomrape *Orobanche ramosa*. *Hortic. Res.* 10:119–124.

———. 1971. Morphology and anatomy of branched broomrape seed *Orobanche ramosa*. *Proc. Intern. Seed Testing Assoc.* 36:252–257.

ACHESON, R., J. HARPER and H. MCNAUGHTON. 1956. Distribution of anthocyanin pigment in poppies. *Nature*, 1283–1284.

ADAMS, C. and H. BAKER. 1962. Weeds of cultivation and grazing lands. Chapter 22 in: *Agriculture and land use in Ghana.* Ed. by J. Wills, Oxford Press, London.

ADAMS, F., H. COLE and L. MASSIE. 1973. Element constitution of selected vascular plants from Pennsylvania: Submersed and floating-leaved species and rooted emergent species. *Environ. Pollution* 5:117–147.

ADAMS, M. and M. MCCRACKEN. 1974. Seasonal production of *Myriophyllum spicatum* component of the littoral of Lake Wingra, USA. *J. of Ecol.* 62:475–465.

ADAMS, M., J. TITUS and M. MCCRACKEN. 1974. Depth distribution of photosynthetic activity in *Myriophyllum spicatum* in Lake Wingra (USA). *Limnol. and Oceanog.* 19:377–389.

ADHIKARY, H. and S. CHATTERJEE. 1972. Vegetative and reproductive growth of eight commonly growing weeds in coal fields and in industrial areas of Burdwan, West Bengal: I. Effect of light. *Bull. Bot. Soc. Bengal* 26:99–103.

ADLAKHA, P. and K. CHIBBER. 1963. Studies on chicory: 1. Seed, germination, and effect of some plant hormones on germination and seedling growth. *Ind. J. Agric. Sci.* 33:205–214.

AELLEN, P. 1961. *Salsola* L. In: Hegi, G., *Illustrierte flora von Mitteleuropa*. Vol. 3:739–746. Carl Hanser, Munich.

———. 1964. *Salsola* L. In: *Flora Europaea* 1:104–107. Cambridge University Press.

AGAMALIAN, H. 1983. Competition of annual weeds in broccoli. *Proc. of 36th Western Soc. Weed Sci.* 36:192.

AGAMI, M. and Y. WAISEL. 1983. The effect of temperature and photoperiod on growth of *Najas marina*. *Proc. Intern. Symp. on Aquat. Macrophytes*, Nijmegen, Holland, pp. 16–20.

———. 1984. Germination of *Najas marina*. *Aquat. Bot.* 19:37–44.

———. 1988. The role of fish in distribution and germination of seeds of the submerged macrophytes *Najas marina* and *Ruppia maritima*. *Oecologia* 76:83–88.

AGAMI, M., S. BEER and Y. WAISEL. 1980. Growth and photosynthesis of *Najas marina* as affected by light intensity. *Aquat. Bot.* 9(3):285–289.

———. 1984. Seasonal variations in the growth capacity of

Najas marina as a function of various water depths at Yarkon springs, Israel. *Aquat. Bot.* 19:45–51.

AGGAG, M. and R. YOUSEF. 1972. Study of antimicrobial activity of chamomile oil *Matricaria chamomilla*. *Planta Medica* 22(2):140–144.

AGNEW, A. and J. FLUX. 1970. Plant dispersal by hares *Lepus capensis* in Kenya. *Ecol.* 51:735–737.

AGOGINO, G. and S. FEINHANDLER. 1957. Amaranth seeds from San Jose site in New Mexico. *Texas J. Sci.* 1957:154–156.

AHMED, S., A. MAMUN, M. ISLAM and S. HOSSAIN. 1986. Critical period of weed competition in transplanted Aus rice. *Bangladesh J. Agric.* 11:1–9.

AHRENS, W., L. WAX and E. STOLLER. 1981. Identification of triazine-resistant *Amaranthus* spp. *Weed Sci.* 29:345–348.

AHUJA, S., K. CHAUDHARY, K. SHARMA and I. BHATIA. 1974. Changes in the chemical composition of forages and its relationship with *in vitro* digestibility at different stages of maturity. *Ind. J. Animal Sci.* 44:725–736.

AIKEN, S. and J. MCNEILL. 1980. The discovery of *Myriophyllum exalbescens* Fernald in Europe and the typification of *M. spicatum* and *M. verticillatum*. *Bot. J. of Linn. Soc.* 80:213–222.

AIKEN, S., P. NEWROTH and I. WILE. 1979. The biology of Canadian weeds. 34. *Myriophyllum spicatum*. *Can. J. Plant Sci.* 59:201–215.

AKANBI, M. 1971. The biology, ecology and control of *Phalanta phalanta* **Lepidoptera : Nymphalidae** a defoliator of *Populus* spp. in Nigeria. *Bull. Entomol. Soc. Nigeria* 3:19–26.

AKOBUNDU, I. 1987. *A Handbook of West African Weeds.* The International Institute of Tropical Agriculture, Ibadan, Nigeria. p. 521.

ALAM, S. and R. KARIM. 1980. The black beetle: an efficient weed feeder in Bangladesh. *Intern. Rice Res. Newsl.* 5:23.

ALCORN, J. 1968. Occurrence and host range of *Ascochyta phaseolorum* in Queensland. *Aus. J. Biol. Sci.* 21:1143–1151.

ALDRICK, S., I. BUDDENHAGEN and A. REDDY. 1973. The occurrence of bacterial leaf blight in wild and cultivated rice in northern Australia. *Aus. J. Agric. Res.* 24:219–227.

ALDRIDGE, R. 1968. Throughfall under gorse at Taita, New Zealand. *New Zealand J. Sci.* 11(3):447–451.

ALEKOZAI, S. 1969. Control of *Orobanche* in Afghanistan. *PANS (Pest Articles and News Summaries)* 15:243.

ALEX, J. 1982. Canada (Weed Flora). In: W. Holzner and M. Numata, (Ed.), *Biology and Ecology of Weeds*. Dr. W. Junk, Publ., The Hague. pp. 309–331.

ALEX, J. and C. SWITZER. 1977. *Ontario Weeds.* University of Guelph Publication No. 505, Ontario, Canada.

ALI, A. and V. SOUZA MACHADO. 1984. A comparative analysis of leaf chlorophyll florescence, Hill reaction and

C^{14}–atrazine tracer studies to explain differential atrazine susceptibility in wild turnip rape *Brassica campestris* biotypes. *Can. J. Plant Sci.* 64:707–713.

ALI, B. and S. ADAM. 1978a. Toxicity of *Acanthospermum hispidum* to mice. *J. Comparative Pathol.* 88:443–448.

———. 1978b. Effects of *Acanthospermum hispidum* on goats. *J. Comparative Pathol.* 88:533–544.

ALI, M. and S. SANKARAN. 1981. Studies on weed control in direct seeded, puddled and non-puddled rice. *Proc. Ann. Conf. Ind. Soc. Weed Sci.*: 13.

ALIEV, S. 1971. Some factors influencing the form and depth of root penetration. *Izvestiya Sibirskogo Otdeleniya Akad. Nauk SSSR, Biologicheskikh Nauk* 5/6:28–32.

ALIKUNHI, K., V. RAMCHADRAN and H. CHAUDHURI. 1952. On the role of the duckweed, *Lemna minor*, in the preparation of carp nurseries. *Sci. and Culture* 17:436–437.

ALLAM, E., A. MORSY, M. ALI and A. ABO-EL-GHAR. 1978. Inhibition from some higher plants inhibiting TMV and CMV infection. *Egy. J. Phytopath.* 10:9–20.

ALLAN, R., R. CORRELL and R. WELLS. 1969. A new class of quinones from certain members of the family **Cyperaceae**. *Tetrahedron Letters* 53:4669–4672.

ALLARD, R. 1965. Genetic systems associated with colonizing ability in predominantly self-pollinated species. In: H. Baker and G. Stebbins, (Ed.). *The genetics of colonizing species*. Academic Press, New York.

ALLEN, O. and E. ALLEN. 1981. *The* **Leguminosae**: *Sourcebook of characteristics, uses and nodulation.* Univ. Wisconsin Press, Madison WI (USA).

ALLRED, K. 1966. Translocation of radioactive substances in the *Medicago-Cuscuta* complex after exposure to $C^{14}O_2$. *Advancing Frontiers of Plant Sci.* 16:1–9.

ALLRED, K. 1982. *Paspalum distichum* L. var. *indutum* Shinners **Poaceae**. *Great Basin Naturalist* 42:101–104.

ALLRED, K. and D. TINGEY. 1957. Dodder in alfalfa. *Farm and Home Sci.* 18:90–100.

———. 1964. Germination and spring emergence of dodder as influenced by temperature. *Weeds* 12:45–48.

ALLSOPP, A. 1951. *Marsilea* species: Materials for experimental study of morphogenesis. *Nature*, London, 168:301.

———. 1963. Morphogenesis in *Marsilea*. Linn. Society of London, *J. of Bot.* 58(373):417–427.

ALMEIDA, F., B. RODRIGUES and V. OLIVEIRA. 1984. Efeitos alelopaticos de plantas de culturas de inverno. *Abstr. 15th Congress Brazilian Herbicide and Weed Soc.*

ALSAADAWI, I. and E. RICE. 1982a. Allelopathic effects of *Polygonum aviculare* L. I. Vegetational patterning. *J. Chem. Ecol.* 8:993–1009.

———. 1982b. Allelopathic effects of *Polygonum aviculare* L.

II. Isolation, Characterization, and Biological Activity of Phytotoxins. *J. Chem. Ecol.* 8:1011–1023.

ALSTON, R. and H. IRWIN. 1961. The comparative extent of variation of free amino acids and certain "secondary" substances among *Cassia* species. *Am. J. Bot.* 48:35–39.

ALTONA, R. 1972. The influence of soil fertility on secondary succession. *Proc. Grassland Soc. S. Afr.* 7:20–22.

ALVAREZ, P. and M. DEL PILAR. 1971. Pharmacological action of medicinal plants on the nervous system. *Anales Inst. Farmacologia Espanola* 20:297–387. Cited *Biol. Abstr.* 1973, 56: No. 50978.

AMARATUNGA, K. 1973. *Spermacoce latifolia* Aublet, A new record for Sri Lanka. *Ceylon J. Sci., Biol. Sci.* 10:155–157.

AMBASHT, R. and K. RAM. 1976. Stratified primary productive structure of certain macrophyte weeds in a large Indian lake. *Proc. Aquatic Weeds of Southeast Asia*, 1973: 147–155. Ed. by C. Varshney, New Delhi, India.

AMEL'CHENKO, V. 1978. The under-development of the achenes of wormwood *Artemisia. Izvestiya Sibirskogo Otdeleniya Akad. Nauk SSSR, Seriya Biologicheskikh Nauk* 2:103–111.

AMOR, R. 1985. Seasonal emergence of weeds typically occurring in the Victorian wheat belt (Australia). *Plant Protec. Quart.* 1:18–20.

AMRITPHALE, D. and L. MALL. 1978. Allelopathic influence of *Saccharum spontaneum* L. on the growth of three varieties of wheat. *Sci. and Culture* 44:28–30.

ANANDALWAR, T. and R. VENKATESWARA. 1981. Weeds—a main source of ayurvedic formulations. *Proc. 8th Asian-Pacific Weed Sci. Soc. Conf.* 8(2):55–69.

ANANTHAKRISHNAN, T., R. VARATHARAJAN and K. GOPINATHAN. 1981. Pollination in *Wedelia chinensis* (Osbeck) Merr. and *Tridax procumbens* L. **Compositae** by thrips (**Thysanoptera:** insects). *Proc. Ind. National Sci. Acad., Part B Biological Sci.* 47:159–165.

ANAYA, A., L. RAMOS, R. CRUZ, J. HERNANDEZ and V. NAVA. 1987. Perspective on allelopathy in Mexican traditional Agro-ecosystems. *J. Chem. Ecol.* 13:2083–2101.

ANCIBOR, E. 1979. Systematic anatomy of vegetative organs of **Hydrocharitaceae**. *Bot. J. Linn. Soc.* 78:237–266.

ANDERSEN, J. and F. SALISBURY. 1977. Effect of daylight on flowering of redroot pigweed. *Proc. 30th Western Soc. Weed Sci. Conf.* 30:15–17.

ANDERSEN, R. 1968. *Germination and establishment of weeds for experimental purposes.* Weed Sci. Soc. Am.; Champaign, Illinois. p. 236.

ANDERSEN, R. and W. KOUKKARI. 1979. Rhythmic leaf movements of some common weeds. *Weed Sci.* 27:401–415.

ANDERSON, C. and K. BEST. 1965. Water use efficiency of barley and weeds grown in the greenhouse. *Soil Horizons* 6:15–16.

ANDERSON, E. 1956. What weeds cost us in Canada. *Proc. 15th Western Soc. Weed Sci. Conf.* 15:34–45.

ANDERSON, M. and J. KALFF. 1986. Nutrient limitation of *Myriophyllum spicatum* growth *in-situ. Freshwater Biol.* 16:735–744.

ANDERSON, M. and J. LOW. 1976. Use of sago pondweed by waterfowl on the delta marsh, Manitoba. *J. Wildlife Mgmt.* 40:233–234.

ANDERSON, R., R. BROWN and R. RAPPLEYE. 1965. Mineral composition of *Myriophyllum spicatum. Chesapeake Sci.* 6:68–72.

———. 1966. The mineral content of *Myriophyllum spicatum* in relation to its aquatic environment. *Ecol.* 47:844–846.

ANDREWS, F. 1956. *Flowering plants of the Sudan.* Vol. 3, **Compositae : Gramineae.** T. Buncle and Co. Ltd., Arbroath, Scotland.

ANGELL, G. 1950. Bracken fern control is another use for *Lotus major. Washington Farmer*, USA, 75:289, 296–297.

ANGERILLI, N. and B. BIERNE. 1974. Influences of some freshwater plants on the development and survival of mosquito larvae in British Columbia, Canada. *Can. J. Zool.* 52:813–815.

ANONYMOUS (Australia). 1891. Notes on weeds. *New South Wales Agric. Gaz.* 2:144.

——— (Denmark). 1960. The viability of weed seeds after storage in silage. *Meddelelse. Statens Forsogvirksomhed i Plantekultur* No. 633.

——— (India). 1960. Silage from weeds. *Ind. Farming* 10:15.

——— (Malaysia). 1964. Identification of plants on Malayan rubber estates: Plates 33–40, climbing and scrambling dicotyledons. *Planters Bull. Rubber Res. Inst. Malaya* 71:30–33.

——— (USA). 1970. Fresh manure can be a major source of weeds in cropland. *Crops and Soils Magazine* 22:26.

——— (Philippines). 1974. Autecology of *Scirpus maritimus. IRRI Ann. Rep 1973*, Los Banos, Philippines: 61–63.

——— (Australia). 1978. Plant research on secondary weeds. *Ann. Rep. Tasmanian Dept. Agric.* 1977–1978, No. 84.

——— (Canada). 1979a. Stink weed. *Res. Branch Rep., 1976–1978, Agric. Canada, Regina*, p. 328.

——— (Canada). 1979b. Growth and development of *Myriophyllum spicatum. Plant Sci. Dept. Rep., Lethbridge Res. Sta.; Alberta, Canada, 1979.* p. 338.

——— (China). 1979. China: *Azolla* propagation. *Soils Bull.* 41:68.

——— (United Kingdom). 1979. Development work 1978. *United Kingdom Agric. Development and Advisory Ser., 1978.* 125pp.

——— (Australia). 1982. Plant Quarantine Announcements—Australia. *FAO Plant Prot. Bull.* 29:31–37.

ANSARI, R. 1972. Effect of salinity on some *Brassica* oilseed varieties. *Pak. J. Bot.* 4:55–63.

ANT, H. 1970. Zur ausbreitung der Sumpfschraube, *Vallisne-*

ria spiralis **Hydrocharitaceae**, im Norden ihres areals. *Decheniana* 122:195–197.

APPALACHIAN REGIONAL COMMISSION. 1969. Acid mine drainage in Appalachia. Appendix F. The biological and ecological effects of acid mine drainage with particular emphasis to waters of the Appalachian region. *Appalachian Regional Comm.*, Washington D.C. p. 65.

AQUINO, M. and P. PAMPLONA. 1981. The influence of population density and some weeding practice on the yield of soybean. *Weed Sci. Soc. Philippines. Newsl.* 9:7.

ARAI, M. 1961. (Ecological studies on weeds in winter cropping on drained paddy fields). *J. Kanto-Tosan Agric. Exp. Sta.* 19:1–182.

ARAI, M. and H. CHISAKA. 1959. Changes of weed communities by methods of cultivation in winter cropping on drained paddy fields: II. Influence of harrowing and packing of soil on the quality of *Alopecurus aequalis*. *Proc. Crop Sci. Soc. Jap.* 27:385–386.

————. 1961a. Ecological studies on *Alopecurus aequalis* Sobol., a noxious weed in winter cropping: VII–VIII. On the primary dormancy of the seed. *Proc. Crop Sci. Soc. Jap.* 29:428–432.

————. 1961b. Ecological studies on *Alopecurus aequalis* Sobol., a noxious weed in winter cropping: IX. On the secondary dormancy of the seed. *Proc. Crop Sci. Soc. Jap.* 30:43–46.

ARAI, M. and T. KATAOKA. 1956a. Ecological studies on *Alopecurus aequalis* Sobol.: I. On the influence of soil moisture and of depth of soil layers over the seeds upon germination and emergence of them. II. On the temperature for germination and emergence, and seasonal variation in emerging capacity. *Proc. Crop Sci. Soc. Jap.* 24:275–278.

————. 1956b. Ecological studies on *Alopecurus aequalis* Sobol.: III. Influence of soil moisture on the dormancy and longevity of seeds. IV. Seasonal variation in the viable seed population and its vertical distribution within the soil. *Proc. Crop Sci. Soc. Jap.* 24:319–323.

————. 1960. Mechanism of competition between barley and weeds in winter cropping on drained paddy fields and a diagnosis method of the weed damage. *Proc. Crop Sci. Soc. Jap.* 29:133–136.

ARAI, M., T. KATAOKA and H. CHISAKA. 1958. Ecological studies on *Alopecurus aequalis* Sobol.: V. On the influence of light intensity upon the growth of the weed, viability of seeds at various stages of maturity and seed production. VI. On the compost and the methods of field management as agents in the seed dissemination. *Proc. Crop Sci. Soc. Jap.* 27:129–132.

ARANHA, C., H. LEITAO and R. PIO. 1980. Plantas invasoras de varzea no estado de Sao Paulo. *Planta Daninha* 3:85–95.

ARBER, A. 1920. *Water plants: A study of aquatic angiosperms.*

University Press, Cambridge. Reprinted 1963 by Cramer, Weinheim, West Germany, p. 436.

————. 1922. Studies on the intrafascicular cambium in monocotyledons. *Ann. Bot.* 36:251–256.

ARCHER, A. and B. AULD. 1982. A review of the ecology of sorrel *Rumex acetosella* in pastures. *Aus. Weeds* 1(3):15–19.

ARCHIBOLD, O. 1981. Buried viable propagules in native prairie and adjacent agricultural sites in central Saskatchewan. *Can. J. Bot.* 59:701–706.

ARCHIBOLD, O. and L. HUME. 1983. A preliminary survey of seed input into fallow fields in Saskatchewan. *Can. J. Bot.* 61:1216–1221.

ARISZ, W. 1963. Influx and efflux of electrolytes by leaves of *Vallisneria spiralis*: I. Active uptake and permeability. *Protoplasma* 57:5–26.

————. 1964. Influx and efflux of electrolytes: II. Leakage out of cells and tissues. *Acta Botan. Neerl.* 13:1–58.

ARMITT. J. 1968. The farm weed taint story. *Queensland Agric. J.* 94:2–7.

ARMSTRONG, K. 1968. Weed control on a Swaziland rice and sugar cane estate. *Proc. 9th Brit. Weed Control Conf.* 9:687–693.

ARNTZEN, C., K. PFISTER and K. STEINBACK. 1982. The mechanism of chloroplast triazine resistance: Alteration in the site of herbicide action. In: *Herbicide resistance in plants.* Ed. by H. LeBaron and J. Gressel; John Wiley & Sons, N.Y.

ARNY, A. 1932. *Variations in the organic reserves in underground parts of five perennial weeds from late April to November.* Univ. Minnesota Agric. Exp. Sta. Tech. Bull. No. 84.

ARTHUR, D. and S. SLINGER. 1979. Effect of dietary rape seed products on the selenium content of the meat and eggs. *Can. Inst. Food Sci. Technol. J.* 12:170–172.

ARTSCHWAGER, E. 1942. A comparative analysis of the vegetative characteristics of some variants of *Saccharum spontaneum*. *USDA Tech. Bull.* 811.

ARYA, V. 1979. Asclepin. *Drugs of the Future* 4:249–251.

ASHBY, E. 1948. Studies in the morphogenesis of leaves: Parts I and II. *New Phytologist* 47:177–195.

ASHBY, E. and T. OXLEY. 1935. The interaction of factors in the growth of *Lemna*: VI. Analysis of influence of light intensity and temperature on the assimilation rate and the rate of frond multiplication. *Ann. Bot.* 49:309–336.

ASHBY, E. and E. WANGERMANN. 1951. Studies in the morphogenesis of leaves: VII. Part II. Correlative effects of fronds in *Lemna minor*. *New Phytol.* 50:200–209.

ASHTON, F. and S. BISSELL. 1987. Influence of temperature and light on dwarf spikerush and slender spikerush growth. *J. Aquat. Plant Mgt.* 25:4–7.

ASHTON, F. and D. SANTANA. 1976. *Cuscuta* spp. (dodder): A literature review of its biology and control. *Div. Agric., Univ. Calif., Bull.* 1880. p. 24.

ASHTON, P. and R. WALMSLEY. 1976. The aquatic fern *Azolla* and its *Anabaena* symbiont. *Endeavor* 35:39–43.

ASHWORTH, L. 1976. Quantitative detection of seed of branched broomrape in California tomato soils. *Plant Dis. Rep.* 60:380–383.

ASPINALL, D. 1960. An analysis of competition between barley and white persicaria: II. The factors determining the course of competition. *Ann. Appl. Biol.* 48:637–654.

ASPINALL, D. and F. MILTHORPE. 1959. An analysis of competition between barley and white persicaria: I. The effects on growth. *Ann. Appl. Biol.* 47:156–172.

ASTON, H. 1973. *Aquatic plants of Australia.* Melbourne Univ. Press; Carlton, Victoria. p. 368.

ATTAWI, F. 1977. Morphological and anatomical studies of haustoria in *Orobanche. Berichte der Deutschen Botanischen Gesellschaft* 90:173–182.

ATTAWI, F. and H. WEBER. 1980. Parasitism and morphological anatomical structure of the secondary haustoria of *Orobanche* species. *Flora, Jena* 169:55–83.

ATWAL, B. and R. GOPAL. 1972. *Oxalis latifolia* and its control by chemical and mechanical methods in the hills. *Ind. J. Weed Sci.* 4:74–80.

AULAKH, M., N. PASRICHA and N. SAHOTA. 1980. Yield, nutrient concentration and quality of mustard crops as influenced by nitrogen and sulphur fertilizers. *J. Agric. Sci.* 94:545–549.

AULD, B., K. MENZ and R. MEDD. 1979. Bioeconomic model of weeds in pastures. *Agro-Ecosystems* 5:69–84.

AVDEEV, Y. and V. SHCHERBININ. 1976. A tomato specimen resistant to Egyptian broomrape *Orobanche aegyptiaca. Kartofel i Ovoshchi* 11:35–36.

AVERKIN, G. 1978a. The seed germination of some weed species in relation to temperature in the Novosibirsky province. *Byulleten Vsesoyuznogo Nauchno-Issledovatel'skogo Instituta Rastenievodstva* 78:67–68.

———. 1978b. The germination of weed seeds in different layers of the plowed horizon in relation to soil density. *Byulleten Vsesoyuznogo Nauchno-Issledovatel'skogo Instituta Rastenievodstva* 81:73–76.

AVERY, A., S. SATINA and J. RIETSMA. 1959. *Blakeslee: The genus Datura.* Ronald Press, N.Y. p. 289.

AYALA, S., O. QIUNTERO and P. BARRETO. 1975. Trypanosomes of lactiferous plants and their insect vectors in Colombia and Costa Rica. *Revista Biologia Tropical* 23:5–15.

AYENI, A., W. DUKE and I. AKOBUNDU. 1984. Weed interference in maize, cowpea and maize/cowpea intercrop in a sub-humid environment: III. Influence of land preparation. *Weed Res.* 24:439–448.

AZARIAN, K. 1954. Control measures against dodder poi-

soning in horses. *Izvestiya Akad. Nauk Armyanskoi SSR Biologicheskie Sel'skokhozyaistvennye Nauki* 7(11):37–44.

AZAROVA, E. and V. ARTEMENKO. 1979. Fruits of the pondweed *Potamogeton* of the European part of the USSR. *Byulleten Moskovskogo Obshchestva Ispytatelei Prirody Otdel Biologicheskii* 84:90–97.

BABA, K., S. ABE and D. MIZUNO. 1981. Antitumor activity of hot water extract of dandelion *Taraxacum officinale. Yakugaku Zasshi* 101:538–543.

BABATOLA, J. 1980. Studies on the weed hosts of the rice root nematode, *Hirschmanniella spinicaudata. Weed Res.* 20:59–61.

BABU, V. 1975. Ecological studies on *Borreria articularis*: III. Crop-weed competition. *Jap. J. Ecol.* 25:32–39.

BABU, V. and M. JOSHI. 1970. Studies on the physiological ecology of *Borreria articularis*: I. Seed production, germination, and seedling survival. *Trop. Ecol.* 11:126–139.

———. 1974. Ecological studies in *Borreria articularis*: II. Water relations. *Ann. Arid Zone* 13:94–102.

BACANOVIC, M. 1986. Setting the time when it is justified to apply herbicides in soya depending on dominant weed density. *Fragmenta Herbologica Jugoslavica* 15:5–27.

BADILA, P., M. LAUZAC and P. PAULET. 1985. Characteristics of light in floral induction in-vitro of *Cichorium intybus*, the possible role of phytochrome. *Physiol. Plantarum* 65:305–309.

BAILEY, C. 1884. Notes on the structure, the occurrence in Lancashire, and the source of origin, of *Naias graminea. J. of Bot.*, London. 22:305–333.

BAILOV, D. and M. SLAVKOV. 1974. A new albino form of the genus *Orobanche* on tobacco. *Comptes Rendus Acad. Agricole Georgi Dimitrov* 7:71–74.

BAIRD, W. and J. RIOPEL. 1980. Studies on the life history of *Conopholis americana* : **Orobanchaceae.** *Botan. Soc. Am.*, Misc. Series 159:9–16.

BAKER, H. 1965. Characteristics and modes of origin of weeds. pp. 147–172. In: *The genetics of colonizing species.* Ed. by H. Baker and G. Stebbins. Academic Press, N.Y.

———. 1972. Seed weight in relation to environmental conditions in California (USA). *Ecol.* 53:997–1010.

BAKER, J. and E. SONNIER. 1983. Red rice and its control. *Proc. Weed Control Rice Conf.*: 327–333. Ed. W. Smith, IRRI and Intern. Weed Sci. Soc.; Los Banos, Laguna, Philippines.

BAKSI, S. and A. CASE. 1971. Photo sensitization in guinea pigs due to ingestion of *Thlaspi arvense* seed. *Ind. Vet. J.* 48(10): 1001–1006.

BALBAA, C. 1973. Phytochemical and pharmaceutical investigations on *Cichorium intybus. Planta Medica* 24:133–144.

BALCIUNAS, J. and M. MINNO. 1985. Insects damaging *Hydrilla* in the USA. *J. Aquat. Plant Mgmt.* 23:77–83.

934   *Bibliography*

BALDEV, B. 1959. *In vitro* responses of growth and development in *Cuscuta reflexa*. *Phytomorphol.* 9:316–319.

———. 1962. *In vitro* studies of floral induction on stem apices of *Cuscuta reflexa*, a short day plant. *Ann. Bot.* 26:173–180.

BALDWIN, F. 1978. Red rice control in alternate crops. In: *Red rice research and control. Texas Agric. Exp. Sta. Bull.* No. 1270.

BALLARD, B., K. HAMEED, M. HALE and C. FOY. 1978. Germination of hemp broomrape, *Orobanche ramosa*, seeds in root exudates leached from rooting medium of susceptible and non-susceptible plants. *Plant Physiol.* 61 (4 Supplement) 16.

BALLARD, L. 1956. Flowering of skeleton weed. *J. Aus. Inst. Agric. Sci.* 22:191–238.

BALLING, S., and V. RESH. 1985. Seasonal patterns of pondweed standing crop and *Anopheles occidentalis* densities in Coyote Hills Marsh. In: *Proc. 52nd Ann. Conf. Calif. Mosquito and Vector Assn. (1984).* pp. 122–125.

BALOCH, G., I. DIN and M. GHANI. 1967. Biological control of *Cuscuta* spp. I. *Cuscuta* species and insects associated with these in West Pakistan. *Tech. Bull. Commonwealth Inst. Bio. Control* 8:149–158.

BALYAN, R. and V. BHAN. 1986a. Germination of horse purslane *Trianthema portulacastrum* in relation to temperature, storage conditions, seedling depth. *Weed Sci.* 34:513–515.

———. 1986b. Emergence growth and reproduction of horse purslane *Trianthema portulacastrum* as influenced by environmental conditions. *Weed Sci.* 34:516–519.

BANDEEN, J., G. STEPHENSON and E. COWETT. 1982. Discovery and distribution of herbicide-resistant weeds in North America. In: *Herbicide resistance in plants.* Ed. by H. LeBaron and J. Gressel; John Wiley & Sons, N.Y.

BANDOPADHYAY, M., N. PARDESHI, and T. SESHADRI. 1972. Components of *Silybum marianum*. *Ind. J. Chem.* 10(8):808–809.

BANERJI, A., G. CHINTALWAR, N. JOSHI and M. CHADHA. 1971. Isolation of ecdysterone from Indian plants. *Phytochem.* 10:2225–2226.

BANERJI, I. and S. PAL. 1959. A contribution to the life history of *Synedrella nodiflora*. *Bot. J. Linn. Soc.* 55:810–817.

BANKS, P., P. SANTELMANN and B. TUCKER. 1976. Influence of long-term soil fertility treatments on weed species in winter wheat. *Agron. J.* 68:825–827.

BANNON, J., J. BAKER and R. ROGERS. 1978. Germination of wild poinsettia *Euphorbia heterophylla*. *Weed Sci.* 26:221–225.

BAQAR, S., A. WARSI and S. ABID. 1966. Pharmacognostic studies on the stem and root of *Euphorbia helioscopia* L. *Pak. J. Scientific and Industrial Res.* 9:400–403.

BARBOSA, L., R. PITELLI and L. BENDIXEN. 1983. Annotated bibliography of weeds as reservoirs for organisms affecting crops in Brazil. *Ohio Agric. Res. Dev. Center, Res. Bull.* No. 1153; Wooster, Ohio USA.

BARCLAY, A. and R. CRAWFORD. 1982. Plant growth and survival under strict anaerobiosis. *J. Expt. Bot.* 33:541–549.

———. 1983. The effect of anaerobiosis on the carbohydrate levels in storage tissues of wetland plants. *Ann. Bot.* 51(2):255–259.

BARIUAN, F. 1985. Philippine medicinal weeds and their uses. *Weed Sci. Soc. Philippines Newsl.* 13(1):3–8.

BARKO, J. 1982. Influence of potassium source (sediment vs. open water) and sediment composition on the growth and nutrition of *Hydrilla verticillata*. *Aquat. Bot.* 12:157–172.

BARKO, J. and R. SMART. 1982. Comparative influences of light and temperature on growth and metabolism of selected submersed freshwater macrophytes. *Ecol. Monographs* 51:219–236.

———. 1985. Sediment composition: effects on growth of submersed aquatic vegetation. *1st Intern. Symp. Watermilfoil* (Myriophyllum spicatum) *and* **Haloragaceae** *Spp.*, Vancouver, Canada. pp. 72–78. Publ. by Aquat. Plant Mgmt. Soc., Vicksburg, Mississippi, (USA).

———. 1986. Sediment-related mechanisms of growth limitation in submersed macrophytes. *Ecol.* 67:1328–1340.

BARKO, J., D. HARDIN and M. MATTHEWS. 1982. Growth and morphology of submersed freshwater macrophytes in relation to light and temperature. *Can. J. Bot.* 60:877–887.

BARR, C. 1942. Reserve foods in the roots of whiteweed. *J. Agric. Res.* 64:275–280.

BARRALIS, G. 1968. Ecology of blackgrass *Alopecurus myosuroides* Huds. *Proc. 9th Brit. Weed Control Conf.* 9(1):6–8.

BARRALIS, G., J. GASQUEZ, P. JAN and S. SOFFIETTI. 1979. Comportment ecologique biologique des dicotyledones resistant a l'atrazine en France. (Physiological and ecological behavior of dicotyledons resistance to atrazine in France). *Proc. European Weed Res. Soc. Symp.: Influence of Different Factors on the Development and Control of Weeds.*

BARRALIS, G. and R. CHADOEUF-HANNEL. 1987. Potentiel Semencier des Terres Arables. *Weed Res.* 27:417–424.

BARRETT, S. 1983. Crop mimicry in weeds. *Econ. Bot.* 37:255–282.

BARRY, D. and A. JERMY. 1952. Observations on *Najas marina*. *Trans. Norfolk Norwich Nature Soc.* 17:294–297.

BARTINSKII, R. 1940. A new method of freeing the soil of broomrape. *Doklady Vsesoyuznoi Akad. Sel'skokhozyaistvennykh Nauk* 9:41–42.

BARTON, L. 1945. Respiration and germination studies of seeds in moist storage. *Ann. New York Acad. Sci.* 46:185–208.

BASIOUNY, F., W. HALLER and L. GARRARD. 1978a. Influence of growth regulators on sprouting of *Hydrilla* tubers and turions. *J. Exp. Bot.* 29:663–669.

———. 1978b. Survival of *Hydrilla verticillata* plants and propagules after removal from aquatic habitat. *Weed Sci.* 26(3):502–504.

BASKIN,C. and J. BASKIN. 1988. Germination ecophysiology of herbaceous plant species in a temperate region. *Am. J. Bot.* 75:286–305.

BASKIN, J. and C. BASKIN. 1977. Role of temperature in the germination ecology of 3 summer annual weeds. *Oecologia* 30:377–382.

———. 1981. Seasonal changes in the germination responses of buried *Lamium amplexicaule* seed. *Weed Res.* 21:299–306.

———. 1983. Germination and ecology of *Veronica arvensis*. *J. Ecol.* 71:57–68.

———. 1989. Role of temperature in regulating timing of germination in soil seed reserves of *Thlaspi arvense*. *Weed Res.* 29:317–326.

———. 1990. The role of light and alternating temperature on germination of *Polygonum aviculare* seed exhumed on various dates. *Weed Res.* 30:397–402.

BASSETT, I. and C. CROMPTON. 1982. The genus *Chenopodium* in Canada. *Can. J. Bot.* 60:586–610.

BASTARDO, H. 1979. Laboratory studies on the decomposition of littoral plants. *Polish Archives of Hydrobiology* 26(3):267–299.

BATES, A., E. BURNS and D. WEBB. 1985. Eurasian watermilfoil *Myriophyllum spicatum* in the Tennessee Valley: An update on biology and control. *Proc. First Intern. Symp. on Watermilfoil* (Myriophyllum spicatum) *and Related* Haloragaceae *Species*. Vancouver, Canada. Publ. by Aquat. Plant Mgmt. Soc., Vicksburg, Mississippi.

BATHO, G. 1939. Stinkweed and common mustard. *Manitoba Dept. Agric. Immigration Circ. 129*. p. 8.

BATTA, A. and S. RANGASWAMI. 1973. Chemical components of some vegetable drugs. *Phytochemistry.* 12:214–216.

BAUM, B. and L. BAILEY. 1984. Taxonomic studies in wall barley *Hordeum murinum* and sea barley *H. marinum*. 1. Character investigation assessment of new and traditional characters. *Can. J. Bot.* 62:753–762.

BAYER, D. 1958. Some factors affecting the germination of seeds and plant responses to herbicides of three species of smartweed, *Polygonum pennsylvanicum, P. persicaria* and *P. lapathifolium*. *Diss. Abstr.* 19:622–623.

BAYLEY, S. 1970. *The ecology and diseases of Eurasian water milfoil, Myriophyllum spicatum, in the Chesapeake Bay.* PhD Thesis, Johns Hopkins Univ., Maryland.

BAYLEY, S., H. RABIN and C. SOUTHWICK. 1968. Recent decline in the distribution and abundance of Eurasian milfoil in Chesapeake Bay. *Chesapeake Sci.* 9:171–183.

BEAL, E. 1977. A manual of marsh and aquatic plants of North Carolina with habitat data. *North Carolina Exp. Sta. Tech. Bull.* No. 247.

BEAL, W. 1898. *Seed dispersal.* Ginn and Company, Boston USA.

BEAN, G., M. FUSCO and W. KLARMAN. 1973. Lake venice disease of Eurasian milfoil in the Chesapeake Bay. *Chesapeake Sci.* 14:279–280.

BEARD, J. 1964. Effects of ice, snow and water covers on Kentucky bluegrass, annual bluegrass and creeping bentgrass. *Crop Sci.* 4:638–640.

———. 1970. An ecological study of annual bluegrass. *U.S. Golf Assoc. Green Sec. Rec.* 8:13–18.

———. 1973. *Turfgrass: Science and culture.* Prentice-Hall, Inc., Englewood Cliffs, New Jersey USA.

BEARE-ROGERS, J., E. NERA and H. HEGGTVEIT. 1974. Myocardial alteration in rats fed rapeseed oils containing high or low levels of erucic acid. *Nutrition and Metabolism* 17:213–222.

BEATLEY, J. 1973. Russian thistle *Salsola* species in western United States. *J. Range Mgt.* 26:225–226.

BECK-MANNAGETTA, G. 1890. Monographic der gattung *Orobanche*. *Bibliotheca Bot.* 19:1–275.

———. 1930. **Orobanchaceae**. In: *Das Pflanzenreich*. Ed. by A. Eengler; Wilhelm Engelmann, Ger. 96 (IV.261):1–348.

BECKING, J. 1976. Nitrogen fixation in some natural ecosystems in Indonesia. In *Symbiotic nitrogen fixation in plants*, ed. by P. Nutman. pp. 539–550. Cambridge Univ. Press, Cambridge.

BEGLEY, M., L. CROMBIE, P. HAM and D. WHITING. 1972. Terpenoid constituents of the insect repellent plant *Nicandra physalodes*: X-ray structure of a methyl steroid (Nic-3) acetate. *J. Chem. Soc., Chem. Commun.* (London). 19:1108.

BEILIN, I. 1967. *Bor'ba s povilikami i zarazikhami* (Control of dodder and broomrape). Kolos, Moscow, p. 88.

BEKECH, M. 1988. *Biology of horseweed, Conyza canadensis.* MSc Thesis, Dept. of Plant and Soil Sci., Univ. Massachusetts, USA.

BELALCAZAR, S., G. URIBE and H. THURSTON. 1968. Recognition of hosts of *Pseudomonas solancearum* (E. F. Sm.) in Colombia. *Revista Instituto Colombiano Agropecuario* 3:37–46.

BELL, A., J. NALEWAJA, A. SCHOOLER and S. ALAM. 1968. Variations in shape of perennial sowthistle. *North Dakota Farm Res.* 25(4):6–7.

BELL, P. and J. DUCKETT. 1976. Gametogensis and fertilization in *Pteridium*. *Bot. J. Linn. Soc.* 73:47–78.

BELL, P. and K. MUHLETHALER. 1962. The fine structure of the cells taking part in oogenesis in *Pteridium aquilinum*. *Ultrastructure Res.* 7:452–466.

BELL, V. and L. OLIVER. 1979. Germination, control and

competition of cut leaf groundcherry *Physalis angulata* in soybeans *Glycine max. Weed Sci.* 19:133–138.

BELLUE, M. 1933. New weeds confused with hoary cress. *Monthly Bull. Dept. Agric. Calif.* 22:288–293.

———. 1946. Weed seed handbook series VI. *Calif. Dept. Agric. Bull.* No. 135:159–166.

BENBROOK, C. 1991. Racing against the clock, pesticide-resistant biotypes gain ground. *Agrichemical Age* 35:30–33.

BENDALL, G. 1973. Control of slender thistle *Carduus pycnocephalus* and *C. tenuiflorus* in pasture by grazing management. *Aus. J. Agric. Res.* 24(6):831–837.

———. 1974. Slender thistle in pasture: Control by grazing management. *Tasmanian J. Agric.* 45(1):62–63.

———. 1975. Some aspects of the biology, ecology, and control of slender thistle *Carduus pycnocephalus* and *C. tenuiflorus* in Tasmania. *J. Aus. Inst. Agric. Sci.* 41:52–55.

BENDIXEN, L., D. REYNOLDS and R. RIEDEL. 1979. Annotated bibliography of weeds as reservoirs for organisms affecting crops: I. Nematodes. *Ohio Agric. Res. and Dev. Center (OARDC), Res. Bull.* No. 1109; Wooster, Ohio.

BENDIXEN, L., K. KIM, C. KOZAK and D. HORN. 1981. An annotated bibliography of weeds as reservoirs for organisms affecting crops: II. Arthropods. *Ohio Agric. Res. and Dev. Center, OARDC, Res. Bull.* No. 1125; Wooster, Ohio.

BENJAMIN, L. and M. WREN. 1978. Root development and source-sink relations in carrot, *Daucus carota. J. Experimental Bot.* 29:424–433.

BENNINK, G., R. VAN DEN BERG, H. KOOL and D. STEGWEE. 1970. Flowering in *Lemna minor. Acta Bot. Neerl.* 19:85–92.

BENYAMINI, Y., H. SOHIOKLER, M. SCHONFELD and B. RUBIN. 1989. Relationships between light intensity and growth parameters in triazine-resistant *Amaranthus hybridus* and *A. blitoides. 11th Long Ashton Symp. Herbicide Resistance in Weeds and Crops*, Univ. Bristol, England, 11:44–45.

BERES, I. 1983. Biology of *Datura stramonium. Novenyvedelem*, Hun. 19:535–540.

BERG, B. VAN DEN, J. BAKKER and D. PEGTEL. 1985. Phenotypic responses of *Ranunculus repens* populations in grassland subjected to different mowing regimes. *Acta Bot. Neerl.* 34:283–292.

BERGLUND, D. and J. NALEWAJA. 1969. Wild mustard competition in soybeans. *Proc. 24th North Central Weed Control Conf.* 24:83.

BERNASOR, P. and S. DE DATTA. 1981. Long term effects of reduced tillage on weed shifts in wetland rice. *Weed Sci. Soc. Philipp. Newsl.* 9(1):4.

BERNHARDT, E. and J. DUNIWAY. 1986. Decay of pondweed and *Hydrilla hibernacula* by fungi. *J. Aquat. Plant Mgmt.* 24:20–24.

BERNSTROM, P. 1952. Cytogenetic intraspecific studies in *Lamium*: I. *Hereditas* 38:163–220.

———. 1953. Cytogenetic intraspecific studies on *Lamium*: II. *Hereditas* 39:241–256.

———. 1955. Cytogenetic studies on relationships between annual species of *Lamium. Hereditas* 41:1–122.

BERRY, R. 1917. Bracken: Utilization and eradication. *Bull. West Scotland Agric. Coll.* No. 80:179–193.

BERTELS, A. 1957. Contribuicao ao conhecimento das *Ciperaceas* de Pelotas (RS). *Instituto Agronomico do Sol Boletin Tecnico No. 17*: 22–28; Pelotas, Brazil.

BERUBE, D. 1978. The basis for host plant specificity in *Tephritis dilacerata* and *T. formosa* (**Diptera : Tephritidae**). *Entomophaga* 23:331–337.

BEST, K. and G. MCINTYRE. 1972. Studies on the flowering of *Thlaspi arvense*: I. Influence of some environmental and genetic factors. *Bot. Gaz.* 133:454–459.

———. 1975. The biology of Canadian weeds. 9. *Thlaspi arvense. Can. J. Plant Sci.* 55:279–292.

BEST, M. and K. MANTAI. 1978. Growth of *Myriophyllum*: Sediment or lake water as the source of nitrogen and phosphorous. *Ecol.* 59:1075–1080.

BEST, P. 1977. Seasonal changes in mineral and organic components of *Ceratophyllum demersum* and *Elodea canadensis. Aquat. Bot.* 3:337–348.

BEVERSDORF, W., J. WEISS-LERMAN and L. ERICKSON. 1980. Registration of triazine-resistant *Brassica campestris* germplasm. *Crop Sci.* 20:289.

BEWICK, T., L. BINNING, W. STEVENSON and J. STEWART. 1987. A mycoherbicide for control of swamp dodder (*Cuscuta gronovii*). pp. 93–99. In: *Parasitic flowering plants*. Ed. by H. Weber and W. Forstreuter; Marburg, Germany.

BEWICK, T., L. BINNING, and B. YANDALL. 1988. A degreeday model for predicting the emergence of swamp dodder in cranberry. *J. Am. Soc. Hort. Sci.* 113:839–841.

BEZANCON, G., J. BOZZA, G. KOFFI and G. SECOND. 1978. Genetic diversity of indigenous rice in Africa. In: *Rice in Africa*. Ed. by I. Buddenhagen and G. Persley; Academic Press, N.Y.

BHALLA, I. and S. TANDON. 1967. Morphological diversity and chromosome number of *Trianthema portulacastrum* L. *Current Sci.* India 36:77–78.

BHAMBIE, S., M. JOSHI and M. GUPTA. 1977. Anatomical studies on certain members of **Aizoaceae**. *Proc. Ind. Acad. Sci., Section B* 85:399–406.

BHANDARI, D. and D. SEN. 1983. Allelopathy—an insight to Indian work. *Indian Rev. Life Sci.* 3:207–245.

BHARDWAJA, T. and J. BAIJAL. 1977. Vessels in the rhizome of *Marsilea. Phytomorphol.* 27(2):206–208.

BHARDWAJA, T. and A. MOHAMMAD. 1967. Light and the germination of *Marsilea quadrifolia* sporocarps. *American Fern Journal* 57(3):135–136.

BHARGAVA, L., D. HANDA and B. MATHUR. 1976. Occurrence of *Orobanche indica* on *Trigonella foenum-graecum* and *Physalis minima. Plant Dis. Rep.* 60:871–872.

BHATIA, R. and D. CHAWAN. 1976. Occurrence of phenolic substance in seed coats of *Cassia* species and their effect on early seedling growth. *Geobios* 3:214–216.

BHATTACHARYYA, G. and A. SHARMA. 1970. Cytological study of some members of **Compositae**. *Bull. Botan. Soc. Bengal* 24:31–36.

BHATTACHARYYA, J. and M. SARMA. 1970. Viability tests on jute seeds *Corchorus olitorius. Current Sci.* 39:378–379.

BHOWMIK, P. and J. DOLL. 1982. Corn and soybean response to allelopathic effects of weed and crop residues. *Agron. J.* 74:601–606.

———. 1983. Growth analysis of corn and soybean response to allelopathic effects of weed residues at various temperatures and photosynthetic photon flux densities. *J. Chem. Ecol.* 9:1263–1280.

———. 1984. Allelopathic effects of annual weed residues on growth and nutrient uptake of corn and soybeans. *Agron. J.* 76:383–388.

BIBBEY, R. 1935. Influence of environment upon the germination of weed seed. *Scientific Agric.* 16:141–150.

———. 1948. Physiological studies of weed seed germination. *Plant Physiol.* 23:467–484.

BIENIEK, M. and W. MILLINGTON. 1967. Differentiation of lateral shoots as thorns in *Ulex europaeus. Am. J. Bot.* 54:61–70.

———. 1968. Thorn formation in *Ulex europaeus* in relation to environmental and indigenous factors. *Bot. Gaz.* 129:145–150.

BIERZYCHUDEK, P. 1981. *Asclepias, Lantana*, and *Epidendrum*: A floral mimicry complex. *Biotropica* 13:54–58.

BIESBOER, D. 1984. Seasonal variation in nitrogen fixation, associated microbial populations, and carbohydrates in roots and rhizomes of *Typha latifolia. Can. J. Bot.* 62:1965–1967.

BIESBOER, D. and P. MAHLBERG. 1978. Accumulation of non-utilizable starch in laticifers of *Euphorbia heterophylla* and *E. myrsinites. Planta* 143:5–10.

BILL, S. 1969. Water weed problems of Australia. *Hyacinth Control J.* 8:1–6.

BINET, P. 1958. La morphogenes des feuilles; photoperiod, et developpement heteroblastique chez *Ulex europaeus. Rev. Generale Bot.* 65:365–389.

———. 1964. Action de la temperature et de la salinite sur la germination des graines de *Plantago maritima. Bull. Soc. Botanique France* III:407–411.

———. 1965. Action de la temperature et de la salinite sur germination des graines de *Cochlearia anglica. Revue Generale Botanique* 72:221–236.

BISCHOF, F. 1977. *Orobanche crenata.* In: *Diseases, pests and weeds in tropical crops.* pp. 605–607. Ed. by J. Kranz, H. Schmutterer and W. Koch. Publ. Paulparey, Hamburg.

———. 1984. Untersuchungen zur bestimmung der Keimfahigkeit von Samen einiger Orobanchearten. *Zeitschrift fur Pflanzenkrankheiten und Pflanzenschutz* 10:105–108.

BISCHOF, F. and M. FOROUGHI. 1971. Influence of pH of the soil on the attachment of *Orobanche aegyptiaca* to tomato and tobacco. *Iranian J. Plant Pathol.* 7:56–58.

BISCHOF, F. and W. KOCH. 1973. A contribution on the biology of *Orobanche aegyptiaca. Proc. 1st Symp. Parasitic Weeds, European Weed Res. Council*, Malta, 1:49–54.

BISTLINE, F. and H. RHOADES. 1984. Effect of *Meloidogyne incognita* on *Momordica charantia* seedling. *Nematropica* 14:90–92.

BISWAS, K. and C. CALDER. 1936. *Handbook of common water and marsh plants of India and Burma.* Health Bull. 24, Malaria Bull. II. Manager of Publications, Delhi.

BLACK, C., T. CHEN and R. BROWN. 1969. Biochemical basis for plant competition. *Weed Sci.* 17:338–344.

BLACKBURN, R. and L. WELDON. 1969. USDA technical report on controlling *Hydrilla verticillata. Weeds, Trees and Turf*, Oct. 1969:20–24.

BLACKBURN, R., L. WELDON, R. YEO and T. TAYLOR. 1969. Identification and distribution of certain similar-appearing submersed aquatic weeds in Florida. *Hyacinth Control J.* 8:17–22.

BLACKMAN, G. and W. TEMPLEMAN. 1938. The nature of the competition between cereal crops and annual weeds. *J. Agric. Sci.* 28:247–274.

BLACKSHAW, R. and J. DEKKER. 1988. Interference among *Sinapis arvensis, Chenopodium album* and *Brassica napus.* I. Yield response and interference for nutrients and water. *Phytoprotection* 69:105–120.

BLACKSHAW, R. and L. RODE. 1991. Effect of ensiling and rumen digestion by cattle on weed seed viability. *Weed Sci.* 39:104–108.

BLACKSHAW, R., G. ANDERSON and J. DEKKER. 1987. Interference of *Sinapis arvensis* and *Chenopodium album* in spring rapeseed *Brassica napus. Weed Res.* 27:207–213.

BLACKSHAW, R., G. WALKER and J. DEKKER. 1989. Interference among *Sinapis arvensis, Chenopodium album* and *Brassica napus.* II. Interference for light. *Phytoprotection* 70:7–14.

BLAKESLEE, A. 1921. Types of mutations and their possible significance in evolution. *Am. Nat.* 55:254–267.

BLAKLEY, N. and H. DINGLE. 1978. Competition: butterflies eliminate milkweed bugs from a Caribbean island. *Oecologia* 37:133–136.

BLANCHETTE, B. and G. LEE. 1981. The influence of environmental factors on infection of rush skeletonweed *Chondrilla juncea* by *Puccinia chondrillina. Weed Sci.* 29:364–367.

BLOOM, W. 1955. Comparative viability of sporocarps of

Marsilea quadrifolia in relation to age. *Illinois State Acad. Sci. Trans.* 47:72–76.

———. 1974. Spore viability in a fifty one year old sporocarp of *Marsilea quadrifolia. Proc. Indiana Acad. Sci.* 83:78.

BLOOMFIELD, J. and I. RUXTON. 1977. Effect of farmyard manure on weed introduction and crop establishment during land reclamation (Saudi Arabia). II. Weed increase and crop yields. *Joint Agric. Res. Dev. Project, Univ. N. Wales and Ministry Agric. Water, Saudi Arabia*, Publ. No. 87. 19 pg.

BOCHER, T. and K. LARSEN. 1957. Cytotaxonomical studies in the *Chrysanthemum leucanthemum* complex. *Watsonia* 4:11–16.

BOGART, J. and J. BEARD. 1973. Cutting height effects on the competitive ability of annual bluegrass *Poa annua. Crop Sci.* 65:513–514.

BOGDAN, A. 1965. Weeds of Kenya wheat. *Weed Res.* 5(4):351–352.

———. 1966. Weeds in herbage seeds in Kenya. *E. Afr. Agriculture and Forestry Journal* 32:63–66.

BOGIN, C. 1955. Revision of the genus *Sagittaria* : Alismataceae. *New York Bot. Garden Memoirs* 9:179–233.

BOGOMOLOVA, T. 1959. Fertilization and development of chicory seed. *Moskov Ordena Lenina Selskokhoz Akademia im K.A. Timiriazeva Doklady* 46:227–232.

———. 1960. Comparative embryological study of the fertilization in chicory. *Timiryazevskaya Selskokhoz Akad. Izvestiia* 35:196–199.

BOKX, J. 1970. Reactions of various plant species to inoculation with potato virus S. *Netherlands J. Plant Pathol.* 76:70–78.

BOLDT, P. and C. DE LOACH. 1985. Evaluating *Rhinocyllus conicus* on *Silybum marianum* in Texas. *Proc. 6th Intern. Symp. Bio. Control Weeds*, Agriculture Canada, Ottawa. 6:685–690.

BOLDT, P. and L. KOK. 1982. Bibliography of *Rhinocyllus conicus*, an introduced weevil for biological control of *Carduus* and *Silybum* thistles. *Bull. Entomol. Soc. Am.* 28(4)355–358.

BOLE, J. and J. ALLAN. 1978. Uptake of phosphorous from sediment by aquatic plants *Myriophyllum spicatum* and *Hydrilla verticillata. Water Res.* 12:353–358.

BOLURI, H. 1977. Survey of weeds in wheat fields in the Esfahan area, Iran. *Iranian J. Plant Pathol.* 13:19–20.

BONFIQ, G. and B. LINDNER. 1981. Interactions between weeds and spring wheat sown at various densities. *Mitteilungen aus der Biologischen Bundesanstalt fur Landund Forstwirtschaft*, Berlin, No. 203:101–102.

BONNEWELL, V., W. KOUKKARI and D. PRATT. 1983. Light, oxygen and temperature requirements for *Typha latifolia* seed germination. *Can. J. Bot.* 61:1330–1336.

BOODLE, L. 1914. On the trifoliate and other leaves of the gorse *Ulex europaeus. Ann. Bot.* 28:527–530.

BOOT, R., D. RAYNAL and J. GRIME. 1986. A comparative study of the influence of drought stress on flowering in *Urtica dioica* and *U. urens. J. Ecol.* 74:485–495.

BOOTH, V. 1964. Taraxien, the carotenoid ester in dandelion flowers. *Phytochemistry* 3:229–234.

BOOTH, W. 1941. Revegetation of abandoned fields in Kansas and Oklahoma. *Am. J. Bot.* 28:415–422.

BORG, P. 1964. On the relationship of arable weeds to some ecological factors of soil in the Helsinki district. *Ann. Botanici Fennici* 1:146–160.

BORNER, H. 1960. On the significance of plants on one another in agriculture and forestry. *Angew. Bot.* 34:192–211.

BORNKAMM, R. 1966. A seasonal rhythm of growth in *Lemna minor. Planta* (Berlin), 69:178–186.

———. 1986. Ruderal succession starting at different seasons. *Acta Soc. Bot. Pol.* 55:403–420.

BOROWIEC, S., U. GRINN and I. KUTYNA. 1972. The influence of soil conditions and kinds of crops on the constancy of occurrence of weeds. *Ekologia Polska* 20:199–217.

BOSE, T., T. BOSE, A. ROY and R. BASU. 1973. Studies on the photoperiodic responses in jute. *Proc. Ind. Sci. Congr.* 60:685–686.

BOSKOVIC, M. 1962. *Orobanche* on sunflower. *Matica Srpska*, Zbornik, Yug. 22:44–65.

BOSTOCK, S. 1978. Seed germination strategies of five perennial weeds. *Oecologia* 36:113–126.

BOSTOCK, S. and R. BENTON. 1979. The reproduction strategies of five perennial **Compositae**. *J. Ecol.* 67:91–107.

———. 1983. Dry weight costs and establishment of seeds and vegetative propagules. *Acta Oecologica, Oecologia Plantarum* 4(1):61–69.

BOSWORTH, S., C. HOVELAND, G. BUCHANAN and W. ANTHONY. 1980. Forage quality of selected warm-season weed species. *Agron. J.* 72:1050–1054.

BOULOS, L. 1961. Cytotaxonomy studies in the genus *Sonchus*: III. On distribution of *Sonchus arvensis* L. *Botaniska Notiser* 114:57–64.

BOURDODOT, G. and D. KELLY. 1986. Density and cover estimates of some non-palatable herbaceous pasture weeds. *Proc. 39th New Zealand Weed and Pest Control Conf.* 39:183–186.

BOURN, W. 1932. Ecological and physiological studies on certain aquatic angiosperms. *Contrib. Boyce Thompson Inst.* 4:425–429.

BOUTIN, C. and P. MORISSET. 1988. Etude de La Plasticite phenotypique chez le *Chrysanthemum leucanthemum*. I. Croissance, allocation de la biomasse et reproduction. *Can. J. Bot.* 66:2285–2298.

BOWES, G., A. HOLADAY, T. VAN and W. HALLER. 1977a. Photosynthetic and photorespiratory carbon metabolism in aquatic plants. *Proc. 4th Intern. Congr. Photosynthesis* (England), 4:289–298.

BOWES, G., T. VAN, L. GARRARD and W. HALLER. 1977b. Adaptation to low light levels by *Hydrilla. J. Aquatic Plant Mgt.* 15:32–35.

BOWMER, K., G. SAINTY, G. SMITH and K. SHAW. 1979. Management of *Elodea canadensis* in Australian irrigation systems: mechanical, cultural, biological and chemical control techniques. *J. Aquat. Plant Mgmt.* 17:4–12.

BOWMER, K., D. MITCHELL and D. SHORT. 1984. Biology of *Elodea canadensis* and its management in Australian irrigation systems. *Aquat. Bot.* 18:231–238.

BOYD, C. 1968. Freshwater plants: A potential source of protein. *Econ. Bot.* 22:359–368.

———. 1969a. The nutrient value of 3 species of water weeds. *Econ. Bot.* 23:123–127.

———. 1969b. Production, mineral absorption and biochemical assimilation by *Justicia americana* and *Alternanthera philoxeroides. Archiv fur Hydrobiologie* 66:139–160.

———. 1970a. Vascular aquatic plants for mineral nutrient removal from polluted waters. *Econ. Bot.* 24:95–103.

———. 1970b. Production, mineral accumulation and pigment concentration in *Typha latifolia* and *Scirpus americanus. Ecol.* 51:285–290.

———. 1971. Further studies on productivity, nutrient and pigment relationships in *Typha latifolia* populations. *Bull. Torrey Bot. Club* 98:144–150.

———. 1974. Utilization of aquatic plants. In: *Aquat. vegetation and its use and control.* pp. 107–115. Ed. by D. Mitchell. UNESCO, Paris.

BOYD, C. and R. BLACKBURN. 1970. Seasonal changes in the proximate composition of some aquatic weeds. *Hyacinth Control J.* 8:42–44.

BOYD, C. and E. SCARSBROOK. 1975. Chemical composition of aquatic weeds. pp. 144–150. *Proc. Symp. Water Quality and Mgmt. Through Biol. Control*, Gainesville, Florida USA.

BOYETTE, C., G. TEMPLETON and R. SMITH. 1979. Control of winged water primrose *Jussiaea decurrens* and northern joint vetch *Aeschynomene virginica* with fungal pathogens. *Weed Sci.* 27:497–501.

BOYLEN, C. and R. SHELDON. 1976. Submergent macrophytes: Growth under winter ice cover. *Sci.* 194:841–842.

BRANDLE, R. 1985. Carbohydrate content and vitality of isolated rhizomes of *Phragmites australis, Schoenoplectus lacustris* and *Typha latifolia* after an O_2 stress of several weeks. *Flora* 177:317–321.

BRAUN, M., W. KOCH and M. STIEFVATER. 1987. Solarization for soil sanitation, possibilities and limitations, demonstrated in trials in southern Germany and Sudan. *Gesunde Pflanzen* 39:301–309.

BRENAN, J. 1958. New noteworthy *Cassias* from tropical Africa. *Kew Bull.*: 231–252.

BRENCHLEY, W. 1918. Buried weed seeds. *J. Agric. Sci.* 9:1–31.

———. 1920. *Weeds of farm land.* Longmans, Green & Co., London.

———. 1940. The weed problem in non-rotation wheat-growing. *Empire J. Experimental Agric.* 8:126–139.

BRENCHLEY, W. and K. WARINGTON. 1930. The weed seed population of arable soil: I. Numerical estimation of viable seeds and observation on their natural dormancy. *J. Ecol.* 18:235–272.

———. 1933. The weed seed population of arable soil: II. Influence of crop, soil and methods of cultivation upon the relative abundance of viable seeds. *J. Ecol.* 21:103–127.

———. 1936. The weed seed populations of arable soil: III. The reestablishment of weed species after reduction by fallowing. *J. Ecol.* 24:479–501.

———. 1945. The influence of periodic fallowing on the prevalence of viable weed seeds in arable soil. *Ann. Appl. Biol.* 32(4):285–296.

BREZNY, O., I. MEHTA and R. SHARMA. 1973. Studies of evapotranspiration of some aquatic weeds. *Weed Sci.* 21:197–204.

BRIDGES D. and R. WALKER. 1985. Influence of weed management and cropping systems on sicklepod *Cassia obtussifolia* seed in the soil. *Weed Sci.* 33:800–804.

BRIESE, D. 1988. Weed status of 12 thistle species in New South Wales. *Plant Prot. Quart.* 3:135–141.

BRIGGS, D. 1976. Genecological studies of lead tolerance in groundsel, *Senecio vulgaris. New Phytol.* 77(1):173–186.

———. 1978. Genecological studies of salt tolerance in groundsel, *Senecio vulgaris*, with particular reference to roadside habitat. *New Phytol.* 81:381–390.

BRIGHT, O. 1928. The effects of exposure upon the structure of certain heath plants. *J. Ecol.* 16:323–365.

BRIONES, F., R. MENDOZA, and E. JAVIER. 1976. Seed production of Townsville stylo (*Stylosanthus humilis*). *Phil. J. Crop Science* 1:214–216.

BRITISH COLUMBIA MINISTRY OF ENVIRONMENT. 1981. A summary of biological research on Eurasian watermilfoil in British Columbia. *Information Bulletin IX.* British Columbia Ministry of Environment, Water Resource Branch, Victoria.

BRITISH GUIANA, DIRECTOR OF AGRICULTURE. 1959. *Report of the Director of British Guiana.*

BROOKS, D., E. KENNEDY and H. BEVINAKATTI. 1985. Strigol: Total synthesis and preparation of analogs. In: *The chemistry of allelopathy; biochemical interactions among plants.* Ed. by A. Thompson. Am. Chem. Soc., Washington D.C.

BROTONEGORO, S. and S. ABDULKADIR. 1976. Growth and nitrogen fixing activity of *Azolla pinnata. Ann. Bogorienses* 6:69–77.

BROWER, L. and S. GLAZIER. 1975. Localizations of heart poisons in the monarch butterfly. *Sci.* 188:19–25.

BROWN, A., J. DANIELS, B. LATTER and M. KRISHNANURTHI. 1969. Quantitative genetics of sugarcane: III. Potential for sucrose selection in *Saccharum spontaneum*. *Theoretical and Appl. Genetics* 39:79–87.

BROWN, E. and R. PORTER. 1942. The viability and germination of seeds of *Convolvulus arvensis* L. and other perennial weeds. *Iowa State Agric. Exp. Sta., Res. Bull. No. 294*:475–504.

BROWN, J. 1973. Vogtia malloi, *a newly introduced Pyralid* (**Lepidoptera**) *for the control of alligatorweed*. PhD Diss., Univ. Florida, Gainesville.

BROWN, J., F. DROMGOOLE, M. TOWSEY and J. BROWSE. 1974. Photosynthesis and photorespiration in aquatic macrophytes. *Royal Soc. New Zealand Bull.* 12:243–249.

BROWN, R. 1965. The germination of angiospermous parasite seeds. In: *Handbuch der pflanzenphysiologie*. Ed. by R. Ruhland. Germany. V. 15:925–932.

BROWN, S. and T. WHITWELL. 1988. Influence of tillage on horseweed, *Conyza canadensis. Weed Technol.* 2:269–270.

BROWN, W. 1913. The relation of the substratum to the growth of *Elodea. Philipp. J. Sci.* 8:1–20.

BROWNSEY, P. 1989. The taxonomy of bracken *Pteridium*, **Denstaedtiaceae**, in Australia. *Aus. Syst. Bot.* 2:113–128.

BRUNER, M. and T. BATTERSON. 1984. The effect of 3 sediment types on tuber production in *Hydrilla verticillata. J. Aquat. Plant Mgmt.* 22:95–97.

BRUNS, V. 1965. The effects of fresh water storage on the germination of certain weed seeds. *Weed Sci.* 13:38–41.

BRUNS, V. and R. COMES. 1965. Tuber population studies. *Annual Report of Weed Investigations Div., USDA, Prosser, Washington*, (Unpublished).

BRUNS, V. and L. RASMUSSEN. 1953, 1957. The effects of freshwater storage on the germination of certain weed seeds. I and II: White top, Russian knapweed, Canada thistle, morningglory and povertyweed. *Weeds* 2:138–147, 5:20–24.

———. 1958. The effects of fresh water storage on the germination of certain weed seeds. III. Quackgrass, green and yellow bristlegrass, watergrass, pigweed and halogeton. *Weeds* 6:42–48.

BRUST, G. and G. HOUSE. 1988. Weed seed destruction by arthropods and rodents in low-input soybean agroecosystems. *Am. J. Alternative Agric.* 3:19–25.

BRUTON, B. 1982. Horse purslane, *Trianthema portulacastrum*, as a host of *Macrophomina phaseolina. Phytopathology* 72:355.

BRZAC, T. 1957. Weeds as pig fodder. *Veterinarski Arkiv Zagreb* 27:210–218.

BUBAR, C. and I. MORRISON. 1984. Growth responses of green and yellow foxtail *Setaria viridis* and *S. lutescens* to shade. *Weed Sci.* 32:774–780.

BUCHANAN, G. and E. BURNS. 1971. Weed competition in cotton: I. Sicklepod and tall morningglory. *Weed Sci.* 19:576–579.

BUCHANAN, G., R. CROWLEY, J. STREET, and J. MCGUIRE. 1980. Competition of sicklepod (*Cassia obtusifolia*) and redroot pigweed (*Amaranthus retroflexus*) with cotton (*Gossypium hirsutum*). *Weed Sci.* 28:258–262.

BUCHANAN, G., C. HOVELAND and M. HARRIS. 1975. Response of weeds to soil *pH. Weed Sci.* 23:473–477.

BUCHANAN, G., E. HAUSER, W. ETHREDGE and S. CECIL. 1976. Competition of florida beggarweed and sicklepod with peanuts: II. Effects of cultivation, weeds and *SADH* (Dimethyl Hydrazide). *Weed Sci.* 24:29–39.

BUCHANAN, R., I. CULL, F. OTEY and C. RUSSELL. 1978. Hydrocarbon producing and rubber producing crops: Evaluation of United States plant species. *Econ. Bot.* 32:131–145.

BUCKMAN, A. 1855. On agricultural weeds. *J. Royal Agric. College*, Cirencester, 16:359–381.

BUDD, A., W. CHEPIL, and J. DOUGHTY. 1954. Germination of weed seeds: III. The influence of crops and fallow on the weed seed population of the soil. *Can. J. Agric. Sci.* 34:18–27.

BUDHIRAJA, R. and K. GARG. 1973. Anthelmintic activity of *Cassia occidentalis* L. *Ind. J. Pharmacy* 35:44–45.

BULCKE, R., M. VAN HIMME, and J. STRYCKERS. 1988. Tolerance to aminotriazole in weeds in long-term experiments in fruit plantations. *Proc. 8th Intern. Cong. Weed Biol. Ecol. Systematics* (Paris) 8(1):287–295.

BULL, L., A. DICK, J. KEAST and G. EDGAR. 1956. An experimental investigation of the hepatotoxic and other effects on sheep of consumption of *Heliotropium europaeum. Aus. J. Agric. Res.* 7:281–332.

BULL, L., C. CULVENOR and A. DICK. 1968. The pyrrolizidine alkaloids. In: *Frontiers of Biol.* Vol. 9, North-Holland Publ. Co., Amsterdam.

BULLOCK, S. and R. PRIMACK. 1977. Comparative experimental study of seed dispersal on animals. *Ecol.* 58:681–686.

BUNCE, J. 1981. Relationships between maximum photosynthetic rates and photosynthetic tolerance of low leaf water potentials. *Can. J. Bot.* 59:769–774.

BURDON, J., D. MARSHALL and R. GROVES. 1980. Isozyme variation in *Chondrilla juncea* in Australia. *Aus. J. Bot.* 28:193–198.

BURDON, J., R. GROVES and J. CULLEN. 1981. The impact of biological control on the distribution and abundance of *Chondrilla juncea* in southeastern Australia. *J. Appl. Ecol.* 18:957–966.

BURIAN, K. and C. WINTER. 1976. Die wirkung verschieden langer lichtperioden auf die photosynthese einiger graser. *Photosynthetica* 10:25–32.

BURK, C. 1977. A four year analysis of vegetation following an oil spill in a freshwater marsh. *J. Appl. Ecol.* 14:515–522.

BURKHALTER, A., L. CURTIS, R. LAZOR, M. BEACH and J. HUDSON. 1972. *Aquatic weed identification manual, and control.* pp. 41–42 Bur. Aquat. Plant Res. and Control, Florida Dept. Nat. Resources.

BURKILL, I. 1935. *A dictionary of the economic products of the Malay peninsula.* Vol. 1 and 2. Crown Agents for Colonies; 4 Millbank, London Eng. Reprinted 1966, Ministry Agric. and Cooperatives; Kuala Lumpur, Malaysia.

BURNSIDE, O., C. FENSTER, L. EVETTS and R. MUMM. 1981. Germination of exhumed weed seed in Nebraska. *Weed Sci.* 29:577–586.

BURNSIDE, O., G. WICKS and V. JOHNSON. 1984. Identification of competitive winter wheat *Triticum aestivum* selections to field pennycress *Thlaspi arvense* and downy brome *Bromus tectorum. Abstr. 24th Weed Sci. Soc. Am. Conf.* 24:55.

BURROWS, V. and P. OLSON. 1955. Reaction of small to various densities of wild mustard and their removal with 2,4–D or by hand. *Can. J. Agric. Sci.* 35:193–201.

BURTON, J., A. MUTAR, S. SLINGER and J. NIEL. 1977. The utilization of aquatic plants for animal feed. *Proc. 17th Ann. Meeting Aquat. Plant Mgmt. Soc.*, Minneapolis (USA).

BUSEY, P. and B. MYERS. 1979. Growth rates of turfgrasses propagated vegetatively. *Agron. J.* 71:817–821.

BUTCHER, R. 1933. Studies on the ecology of rivers: I. On the distribution of macrophytic vegetation in the rivers of Britain. *J. Ecol.* 21:58–91.

BUTTROSE, M., W. GRANT and U. LOTT. 1977. Reversible curvature of style branches of *Hibiscus trionum*, a pollination mechanism. *Aus. J. Bot.* 25(5):567–570.

BUVAT, R. 1960. L'infra-structure du cytoplasme vegeta'l d'apres cellules des ebauches foliaires d' *Elodea canadensis. Intern. Conf. Electron Microscopy, Trans.* 4(2):494–499.

BYERS, M. 1961. The extraction of protein from the leaves of some plants growing in Ghana. *J. Sci. Food Agric.* 12:20–30.

CALDWELL, O. 1899. On the life history of *Lemna minor.* Contribution from the Hull Botanical Laboratory. *Bot. Gaz.* 27:37–66.

CALVERT, H. and G. PETERS. 1981. The *Azolla-Anabaena Azollae* relationship: IX. Morphological analysis of leaf cavity hair populations. *New Phytol.* 89:327–335.

CAMILO, E. and G. JURGENS. 1975. Control de malezas en cafe y cacao. In: *Curso basico sobre control de malezas en la Republica Dominicana.* Sociedad Alemana Cooperaion Tecnica, Eschborn. pp. 147–158.

CAMPBELL, D. 1893. On the development of *Azolla filiculoides. Ann. Bot.* 7:155–187.

———. 1897. A morphological study of *Naias* and *Zanichellia. Proc. Calif. Acad. Sci. III. Bot.* 1:1–70.

CAMPBELL, E. 1924. Nitrogen content of weeds. *Bot. Gaz.* 78:103–115.

CAMPBELL, G. 1939. The anatomy of *Potamogeton pectinatus. Trans. and Proc. Bot. Soc. Edinburgh* 32:179–186.

CANDOLLE, M. DE. 1855. *Geographie botanique raisonnee.* Librairie de Victor Masson, Paris.

CANFIELD, D., K. LANGELAND, S. LINDA and W. HALLER. 1985. Relations between water transparency and maximum depth of macrophyte colonization in lakes. *J. Aquat. Plant Mgmt.* 23:25–28.

CAO, N. 1974. *Some aspects of the biology of* Scirpus maritimus. MSc Thesis, Dept. Agric. Bot., Univ. Philipp.; Los Banos.

CARESCHE, L. and A. WAPSHERE. 1974. Biology and host specificity of the chondrilla gall mite *Aceria chondrillae* (Ct.Can). *Bull. Entomol. Res.* 64:183–192.

———. 1975. The chondrilla gall midge *Cystiphora schmidti* **Diptera : Cecidomyiidae.** Part 2: Biology and host specificity. *Bull. Entomol. Res.* 65:55–64.

CARIGNAN, R. and J. KALFF. 1980. Phosphorus sources for aquatic weeds: Water or sediments. *Sci.* 207:987–988.

CARLQUIST, S. 1967. The biota of long distance dispersal: V. Dispersal to Pacific islands. *Bull. Torrey Bot. Club* 94:129–162.

CARLSON, G. 1965. Photoperiodic control of adventitious stem initiation on roots. *Crop Sci.* 5:248–250.

CARPENTER, S. 1980. Enrichment of Lake Wingra, Wisconsin, by submersed macrophyte decay. *Ecology.* 61:1145–1155.

CARPENTER, S. and M. ADAMS. 1979. Effects of nutrients and temperature on decomposition of *Myriophyllum spicatum* in a hard-water eutrophic lake. *Limnol. Oceanog.* 24:520–528.

CARPENTER, S. and A. GASITH. 1978. Mechanical cutting of submerged macrophytes: Immediate effects on littoral water chemistry and metabolism. *Water Res.* 12:55–57.

CARRERAS MATAS, L. 1976. Biochemical profile and discrimination of taxa from the genus *Silybum. Anales Inst. Bot. A. J. Cavinilles*, Madrid 32(2):363–380.

CARTER, E. 1950. *Acanthospermum hispidum* a noxious weed in Georgia. *Proc. 3rd Southern Weed Sci. Soc. Conf.* 3:23–25.

CARTER, V., N. RYBICKI and C. SCHULMAN. 1987. Effect of salinity and temperature on germination of monoecious *Hydrilla* propagules. *J. Aquat. Plant Mgmt.* 25:54–57.

CASE, A. 1957. Some aspects of nitrate intoxication in livestock. *J. Am. Vet. Medical Assoc.* 130:323–329.

CASE, A. 1969. Poison hemlock. *Missouri Vet.* 19:18–19.

CASELY, J., G. CUSSANS and R. ATKIN. 1991. *Herbicide resistance in weeds and crops.* Butterworth-Heinemann, London. pp. 24–37.

CASO, O. and N. KEFFORD. 1968. The bolting and flowering of *Chondrilla juncea* L. as influenced by temperature and photoperiod. *Aus. J. Biol. Sci.* 21:883–894.

———. 1973. Control of regeneration in roots of the deep-rooted weed *Chondrilla juncea* L. *Weed Res.* 13:148–157.

CASPARY, R. 1858. Die Hydrillen (Anacharideen Endl.). *Jahrbuch fur Wissenschaft Botanik* 1:377–513.

CASPER, S. 1979. Contributions to the taxonomy and chorology of European aquatic and marsh plants. 2. What is *Najas marina*. *Feddes Repertorium* 90(4):217–238.

CATLING, P., and I. DOBSON. 1985. The biology of Canadian weeds 69. *Potamogeton crispus*. *Can. J. Plant Sci.* 65:655–668.

CATLING, P. and W. WOJTAS. 1986. The water weeds *Elodea* and *Egeria* in Canada. *Can. J. Bot.* 64:1525–1541.

CAVERS, P. and M. STEEL. 1984. Patterns of change in seed weight over time in individual plants. *Am. Nat.* 124:324–335.

CELIS, A. 1984. Potential weed infestation of cultivated fields in the Valle Chancay-Lambayeque, Peru. *Abstr. 15th Cong. Brasileiro Herbicidas e Eravas Daninhas, and 7th Cong. Asoc. Lat. Amer. Malezas*; Belo Horizonte, Bra. 7:35–6.

CERDEIRA, A. and E. VOLL. 1980. Germination and emergence of *Euphorbia heterophylla* L. *13th Cong. Brasileiro de Herbicidas e Eravas Daninhas*; Bahia, Bra. 13:96–97.

CEZARD, R. 1973a. Some aspects peculiar to the biology of *Orobanches*. pp. 55–67. *Proc. 1st Symp. Parasitic Weeds, European Weed Res. Council*, Malta.

———. 1973b. *Orobanches*. II. Levee de la dormance de graines d'*Orobanches* par suppression d'une inhibition. *Bull., Acad. Soc. Lorraine des Sc.* 12:97–120.

CHABRECK, R. and A. PALMISANO, 1973. The effects of hurricane Camille on the marshes of the Mississippi River delta. *Ecology.* 54:1118–1123.

CHABROLIN, C. 1938. Contribution a l'etude de la germination des graines de l'*Orobanche* de la feve. *Ann. Service Bot. Agronom. Tunis* 14:91–145.

CHADOEUF-HANNEL, R. and G. BARRALIS. 1982. Germination behavior of seeds of *Amaranthus retroflexus* harvested under natural conditions. *Weed Res.* 22:361–369.

———. 1983. Development during storage of germinability of seeds of *Amaranthus retroflexus* harvested under different conditions. *Weed Res.* 23:109–117.

CHAGHTAI, S., S. KHAN and S. SULTAN. 1983. Germination response of some wild Papilionaceous seeds of various action spectra. *Biologia*, Lahore, 29:93–100.

CHAKRAVARTI, S. 1963. Weed control in India. *Ind. Agriculturalist* 7:23–58.

CHAKRAVARTY, A. and G. BHATI. 1971. Grazing studies in the arid and semi-arid zones of Rajasthan. V. Assessment of forage resources of forested and stabilized dunes

in the initial year of utilization. *Ann. Arid Zone* 10:176–179.

CHAKRAVARTY, A., R. RATAN and K. SINGH. 1970. Grazing studies in the arid and semi-arid zones of Rajasthan. VII. Utilization of vegetation cover, grazing behavior of sheep, and seasonal variation of crude protein content of plants in different pastures. *Ann. Arid Zone* 9:10–16.

CHALAM, G. 1942. An anatomical study of the shedding and non-shedding characters in the genus *Oryza*. *J. Ind. Bot. Soc.* 21:339–350.

CHALUKOV, K. 1973. A biological method of controlling *Orobanche ramosa* and *O. mutelii*. *Rastenii Zaschita* 2:20–24.

CHAMBERS, E. and L. HOLM. 1965. Phosphorus uptake as influenced by associated plants. *Weeds* 13:312–314.

CHAMBERS, P., D. SPENCE, and D. WEEKS. 1985. Photocontrol of turion formation by *Potamogeton crispus* in the laboratory and natural water. *New Phytologist* 99:183–194.

CHAMBERS, P., E. PREPAS, M. BOTHWELL and H. HAMILTON. 1989. Roots vs. shoots in nutrient uptake by aquatic macrophytes in flowing waters. *Can. J. Fisheries Aquat. Sci.* 46:435–439.

CHAMPNESS, S. and K. MORRIS. 1948. The population of buried viable seeds in relation to contrasting pasture and soil types. *J. Ecol.* 36:149–173.

CHAN, S. and C. HILLSON. 1968. Developmental morphology of the megasporangium and embryogeny in *Ipomoea reptans* and related species. *Bot. Gaz.* 129:150–156.

———. 1971. Developmental morphology of the microsporangium in *Ipomoea reptans*. *Bot. Gaz.* 132:224–229.

CHANCELLOR, R. 1964. Emergence of weed seedlings in the field and the effects of different frequencies of cultivation. *Proc. 7th Brit. Weed Control Conf.* 7:599–606.

———. 1976. Weed changes over 11 years in Wrenches, an arable fields. *Proc. 13th Brit. Weed Control Conf.* 13:681–686.

———. 1986. Decline of arable weed seeds during 20 years in soil under grass and the periodicity of seedling emergence after cultivation. *J. Appl. Ecol.* 23:631–637.

CHANCELLOR, R. and R. FROUD-WILLIAMS. 1986. Weed problems of the next decade in Britain. *Crop Prot.* 5:66–72.

CHAND, G. and P. SHUKLA. 1973. Use of unconventional feeds in broiler rations. *Ind. J. Animal Sci.* 43:1013–1017.

CHANDHOKE, N. and B. GHATAK. 1969. Studies on *Tagetes minuta*: Some pharmacological actions of the essential oil. *Ind. J. Med. Res.* 57:864–876.

CHANDLER, J. 1977. Competition of spurred anoda, velvetleaf, prickly sida, and Venice mallow in cotton. *Weed Sci.* 25(2):151–158.

CHANDRA, B. and R. SAHAI. 1979. Autecology of *Trianthema portulacastrum* L. *Ind. J. Ecol.* 6:17–21.

CHANDRA, N. 1976. The embryology of some species of *Eragrostis*. *Acta Bot. India* 4:36–43.

CHANDRASENA, P. 1936. *The chemistry and pharmacology of Ceylon and Indian medicinal plants*. H. & C. Press, Colombo.

CHANG, T. 1976. The origin, evolution, cultivation, dissemination, and diversification of Asian and African rices. *Euphytica* 25:425–441.

———. 1984. Conservation of rice genetic resources: luxury or necessity? *Sci.* 224:251–256.

CHANG, T., C. ADIR and T. JOHNSON. 1982. The conservation and use of rice genetic resources. *Advances Agron.* 35:38–91.

CHANG, W. 1970. The effect of weeds on rice in paddy field. I. Weed species and population density. *J. Taiwan Agric. Res.* 19:18–24.

———. 1973. Chemical weed control practice for rice in Taiwan. *PANS (Pest Articles and News Summaries)* 19:514–522.

CHAO, M. 1947. Growth of the dandelion scape. *Plant Physiol.* 22:393–406.

CHAPMAN, A., W. SHAW and S. RENAUD. 1981. Effects of temperature on the growth and acetylene reduction activity of *Azolla pinnata* from the Darwin region of northern Australia. *J. Aus. Inst. Agric. Sci.* 47:223–225.

CHARLES, D., M. SINGH and G. SANWAL. 1982. Biochemical changes during germination and seedling growth in *Cuscuta campestris*. *Physiol. Plantarum* 56:211–216.

CHARLES, O. and H. MULLER. 1975. Coffee weed *Cassia obtusifolia* toxicity response of laying hens. *Poultry Sci.* 54:1745.

CHARUDATTAN, R. and D. MCKINNEY. 1977. A fusarium disease of the aquatic weed *Hydrilla verticillata*. *Proc. Am. Phytopathol. Soc.* 4:222–232.

CHARUDATTAN, R. and H. WALKER. 1982. *Biological control of weeds with plant pathogens*. John Wiley & Sons, N.Y.

CHATER, A. and D. WEBB. 1972. *Orobanche*. In: *Flora Europaea*. Vol 3:286–293. (Ed.) T. Tutin, V. Haywood, N. Burgess, S. Walters and D. Webb. Univ. Press, Cambridge.

CHATURVEDI, S. and R. MURALIA. 1975. Germination inhibitors in some **Umbelliferae** seeds. *Ann. Bot.* 39:1125–1129.

CHAUDHURI, J. and A. SHARMA. 1978. Cytological studies on 3 aquatic weeds members of **Hydrocharitaceae** in relation to their morphological and ecological characteristics. *Cytologia* 43:1–20.

CHAUHAN, E. 1979. Pollination by ants in *Coronopus didymus*. *New Botanist*, New Delhi 6:39–40.

CHAUHAN, J., M. SULTAN and S. SRIVASTAVA. 1979. New glycoflavones from the root of *Phyllanthus niruri*. *Planta Medica* 32:217–222.

CHAURASIA, B., S. SIROHI and J. CHOHAN. 1972. Effect of harvesting period on the growth and yield of chicory. *Ind. J. Agric. Sci.* 42(12):1132–1134.

CHAUVIN, R. and P. LAVIE. 1956. Recherches sur la substance antibiotique du pollen. *Ann. Inst. Pasteur* 90:523–527.

CHAVAN, H. and P. TRIVEDI. 1962. Seed germination in some weeds. *Indian Forester* 88:436–439.

CHAWAN, D. 1971. Role of high temperature pretreatments on seed germination of desert species of *Sida* : **Malvaceae**. *Oecologia*, Berlin 6:343–349.

CHAWAN, D. and D. SEN. 1973. Chemical scarification for hard seed coat dormancy in arid zone species of *Sida*. *Broteria Ser Trimest Nat.* 42:25–30.

CHAWDHRY, M. 1974. Growth study of *Oxalis latifolia*. *E. African Agric. and Forestry J.* 39:402–406.

CHAWDHRY, M. and G. SAGAR. 1973. An autoradiographic study of the distribution of C^{14} labeled assimilates at different stages of development of *Oxalis latifolia* and *O. pes-caprae*. *Weed Res.* 13:430–437.

———. 1974a. Dormancy and sprouting of bulbs in *Oxalis latifolia* and *O. pes-caprae*. *Weed Res.* 14:349–354.

———. 1974b. Control of *Oxalis latifolia* and *O. pes-caprae* by defoliation. *Weed Res.* 14:293–299.

CHEADLE, V. 1942. The occurrence and types of vessels in the various organs of the plant in the **Monocotyledoneae**. *Am. J. Bot.* 29:441–450.

CHEAM, A. 1984. Coat-imposed dormancy controlling germination in wild radish and fiddle dock seeds. *Proc. 7th Aus. Weed Conf.* 7:184–190.

———. 1986. Seed production and seed dormancy in wild radish *Raphanus raphanistrum* and some possibilities for improving control. *Weed Res.* 26:405–413.

CHEMALE, V. and N. FLECK. 1982. Evaluation of soybean *Glycine max* (L.) Merrill cultivars in competition with *Euphorbia heterophylla* L. in three densities and two times after emergence. *Planta Daninha* 5:36–45.

CHEN, T., R. BROWN and C. BLACK. 1970. CO_2 compensation concentration, rate of photosynthesis, and carbonic anhydrase activity of plants. *Weed Sci.* 18:399–403.

CHEPIL, W. 1946a. Germination of weed seeds: I. Longevity, periodicity of germination and vitality of seeds in cultivated soil. *Scientific Agric.* 26:307–346.

———. 1946b. Germination of weed seeds: II. The influence of tillage treatments on germination. *Scientific Agric.* 26:347–357.

CHESNEY, R. 1956. "Staggers" in sheep. A review of some of the relevant information. *Brit. Vet. J.* 112(9):389–403.

CHI, K. 1948. *Weeds and lawn grasses*. Chung Hwa Book Co., Shanghai. p. 82.

CHIN, H. and S. ALI. 1981. Biology of *Euphorbia prunifolia* Jacq. seeds. *Proc. 8th Asian-Pacific Weed Sci. Soc. Conf.* 8:197–200.

CHIN, L. and F. FONG. 1978. Preliminary studies on the two most abundant macrophytes in Subang Lake. *Malaysian J. Agric.* 51:422–435.

CHIPPINDALE, H. and W. MILTON. 1934. On the viable seeds present in the soil beneath pastures. *J. Ecol.* 22:508–531.

CHISAKA, H. and K. NODA. 1983. Farmers' weed control technology in mechanized rice systems in East Asia. *Proc. Weed Control Rice Conf.*, IRRI, Los Banos, Philippines.

CHITAPONG, P. and R. ILNICKI. 1982. Effects of soybean row spacing, jimsonweed densities, and competition periods on soybean and jimsonweed competition. *Proc. 36th Northeastern Weed Sci Soc. Conf.* 36:9.

CHOKDER, A. 1958. Pond weeds of East Pakistan and their propagation. *Agric. Pakistan* 9(3):259–309.

CHOPRA, R. and R. CHATTERJEE. 1940. A comparative study of *Boerhavia diffusa* and the white and red flowered "varieties" of *Trianthema portulacastrum*. *Ind. J. Medical Res.* 28:475–480.

CHOUDHURI, G. 1966. Seed germination and flowering in *Vallisneria spiralis*. *Northwest Sci.* 40:31–35.

CHOUDHURY, A. and A. MUKHERJEE. 1971. Wild plants as alternate hosts of red spider mite, *Tetranychus telarius* L. **Tetranchidae : Acarina**. *Indian J. Entomol.* 33:108–110.

CHU, T., P. JUANG and K. SHANG. 1962. The wild cane *Saccharum spontaneum* in Taiwan. *Taiwan Sugar Exp. Sta. Rep.* 28:1–11.

CHUN, D., S. WILHELM and J. SAGEN. 1979. Components of record germination *in vitro* of *Orobanche ramosa*. *Proc. Suppl. 2nd Intern. Symp. Parasitic Weeds* 2:29–36. (Ed.) L. Musselman, A. Worsham, and E. Eplee. North Carolina State Univ., Raleigh, NC, USA.

CIFERRI, O. and G. POMA. 1963a. Fixation of CO_2 by *Cuscuta epithymum*. *Life Sci.* 3:152–162.

———. 1963b. CO_2 fixation by *Cuscuta epithymum*. *Giornale Botanica Italiano* 70:345–346.

CIVICO, R. and K. MOODY. 1979. The effect of the time and depth of submergence on the growth and development of some weed species. *Philipp. J. Weed Sci.* 6:41–49.

CLARK, G. and J. FLETCHER. 1909. *Farm weeds of Canada*, 2nd Ed., Dept. Agric. Dominion Can., Ottawa. p. 192.

CLARK, W. 1980. China's green manure revolution. *Sci.* 80(1):68–73.

CLAY, D. 1987. Results of a questionnaire on the worst weeds in vine and soft fruits. *Proc. Meeting EC Experts Group*: 157–160; Dublin, June 1985, published in Rotterdam. (Ed.) A. Balkema.

———. 1989. New developments in triazine and paraquat resistance and co-resistance in weed species in England. *Proc. Brighton Crop Prot. Conf. Weeds 1989* (1):317–324.

CLIFFORD, H. 1956. Seed dispersal on footwear. *Proc. Bot. Soc. Brit. Isles.*

———. 1959. Seed dispersal by motor vehicle. *J. Ecol.* 47:311–316.

COBLE, T. and B. VANCE. 1987. Seed germination in *Myriophyllum spicatum*. *J. Aquat. Plant Mgmt.* 25:8–10.

COBLEY, L. 1967. *Introduction to the botany of tropical crops.* Longmans, Green and Co. Ltd., London. 357pp.

COCK, M. and H. EVANS. 1984. Possibilities for biological control of *Cassia tora* and *C. obtusifolia*. *Trop. Pest Mgmt.* 30:339–350.

CODY, W. and C. CROMPTON. 1975. Biology of Canadian Weeds. 15. *Pteridium aquilinum* (L.) Kuhn. *Can. J. Plant Sci.* 55:1059–1072.

COHN, J. and R. RENLUND. 1953. Notes on *Azolla caroliniana*. *Am. Fern J.* 43:7–11.

COHN, M. and D. BUTERA. 1982. Seed dormancy in red rice *Oryza sativa*: II. Responses to cytokinins. *Weed Sci.* 30:200–205.

COHN, M. and J. HUGHES. 1981. Seed dormancy in red rice *Oryza sativa*: I. Effect of temperature on dry after-ripening. *Weed Sci.* 29:402–404.

COHN, M., D. BUTERA and J. HUGHES. 1983. Seed dormancy in red rice: III. Response to nitrite, nitrate, and ammonium ions. *Plant Physiol.* 73:381–384.

COLE, H. and A. HOLCH. 1941. The root habits of certain weeds of southeastern Nebraska. *Ecology.* 22:141–147.

COLER, R. and H. GUNNER. 1969. The rhizosphere of aquatic plant *Lemna minor*. *Can. J. Microbiol.* 15:964–966.

COLES, S. 1977. *Ranunculus repens* L. in Europe. *Watsonia* 11:353–366.

COLLINGE, W. 1913. Destruction and dispersal of weed seeds by wild birds. *J. Board Agric.* 20:15–26.

COLLINS, R. and D. WETHERELL. 1970. An analysis of free amino acids in wild carrot tissue cultures. *Phyton* 27:169–175.

COMES, R., V. BRUNS and A. KELLY. 1978. Longevity of certain weed and crop seeds in fresh water. *Weed Sci.* 26:336–344.

CONKLIN, A. and P. BISWAS. 1978. A survey of asymbiotic nitrogen fixation in the rhizosphere of weeds. *Weed Sci.* 26:148–150.

CONKLIN, M. 1976. *Genetic and biochemical aspects of the development of Datura.* Monographs in Development Biol. Vol. 12, S. Karger, Basel. 170pp.

CONOVER, J. 1964. The ecology, seasonal periodicity, and distribution of benthic plants in some Texas lagoons. *Bot. Marina* 7:4–41.

CONWAY, E. 1949. The autecology of bracken *Pteridium aquilinum*. The germination of the spore, the development of the prothallus and the young sporophyte. *Proc. Royal Soc. Edinburgh* 63:325–343.

———. 1952. Bracken the problem plant, a review of recent conclusions about its dominance and spread. *Scottish Agric.* 31:181–184.

———. 1957. Spore production in bracken. *J. Ecol.* 45:273–284.

CONWAY, E. and R. STEPHENS. 1957. Sporeling establishment in *Pteridium aquilinum*: effects of mineral nutrients. *J. Ecol.* 45:389–399.

CONWAY, G. and J. SLOCUMB. 1979. Plants used as abortifacients and emmenogogues by Spanish New Mexicans. *J. Ethnopharmacology* 1:241–261.

COOK, C. 1974. *Water plants of the world. A manual for identification of the genera of freshwater macrophytes.* Dr. W. Junk, The Hague, Netherlands. 561pp.

COOK, C. 1985. Worldwide distribution and taxonomy of *Myriophyllum* species. In: *1st Intern. Symp. Watermilfoil* Myriophyllum spicatum *and* **Haloragaceae** *spp.* 1:1–7.

COOK, C. and R. LUOND. 1982. A revision of the genus *Hydrilla*: **Hydrocharitaceae**. *Aquat. Bot.* 13:485–504.

COOK, G., L. WHICHARD, M. WALL, G. EGLEY, P. COGAN and P. LUHAN. 1972. Germination stimulants: II. The structure of strigol—a potent seed germination stimulant for witchweed *Striga asiatic*. *J. Am. Chem. Soc.* 94:6198–6199.

COOKE, D. and I. BLACK. 1987. *Biology and control of* Cuscuta campestris *and other* Cuscuta *spp.: A bibliographic review*. S. Australia Dept. Agric., Tech. Paper 18. 33pp.

COOPER-DRIVER, G. 1976. Chemotaxonomy and phytochemical ecology of bracken. *Botan. J. Linn. Soc.* 73:35–46.

COPPER, J., T. MAXWELL and A. OWENS. 1960. A study of the passage of weed seeds through the digestive tract of the chicken. *Poultry Sci.* 39:161–163.

CORDAS, D. 1954. Effect of branched broomrape *Orobanche ramosa* on tomatoes in California fields. *Plant Dis. Rep.* 38:926–927.

CORDUKES, W. 1977. Growth habit and heat tolerance of a collection of *Poa annua* plants in Canada. *Can. J. Plant Sci.* 57:1201–1203.

CORMACK, R. 1937. Development of root hairs by *Elodea canadensis*. *New Phytologist.* 36:19–25.

CORNER, E. 1952. *Wayside trees of Malaya.* Vol. 1. Gov. Printers, Singapore.

CORNS, W. 1960a. Combined effects of gibberellin and 2,4–D on dormant seeds of *Thlaspi arvense*. *Can. J. Bot.* 38:871–874.

———. 1960b. Effects of gibberellin treatments on germination of various species of weed seeds. *Can. J. Plant Sci.* 40:47–51.

CORNS, W. and C. FRANKTON. 1952. Hoary cresses in Canada with particular reference to their distribution and control in Alberta. *Scientific Agric.* 32:484.

CORRE, W. 1983a. Growth and morphogenesis of sun and shade plants. I. The influence of light intensity. *Acta Bot. Neerl.* 32:49–62.

———. 1983b. Growth and morphogenesis of sun and shade plants. II. The influence of light quantity. *Acta Bot. Neerl.* 32:183–202.

———. 1984. Growth and morphogenesis of sun and shade plants. IV. Competition between sun and shade plants in different light environments. *Acta Bot. Neerl.* 33:25–38.

CORRELL, D. and H. CORRELL. 1975. *Aquatic and wetland plants of southwestern United States.* Vol. 1 and 2. Stanford Univ. Press, Stanford, Calif. 1777pp.

CORSON, G. 1969. Cell division studies of the shoot apex of *Datura stramonium* during transition to flowering. *Am. J. Bot.* 56:1127–1134.

CORSON, G. and E. GIFFORD. 1969. Histochemical studies of the shoot apex of *Datura stramonium* during transition to flowering. *Phytomorphol.* 19:189–196.

COSTANZA, S., J. DEWET, and J. HARLAN. 1979. Literature review and numerical taxonomy of *Eragrostis tef* (T'ef). *Econ. Bot.* 33(4):413–424.

COUCH, H. 1979. Heat stress, not anthracnose is scourge of *Poa annua*. *Weeds, Trees and Turf* 18(6):47–56.

COUCH, R. and E. NELSON. 1985. *Myriophyllum spicatum* in North America. *1st Intern. Symp. Watermilfoil* Myriophyllum spicatum *and* **Haloragaceae** *spp.* 1:8–26.

COURTNEY, A. 1967. Germination ecology. In: *Rep. National Vegetable Res. Sta. (Great Britain) for 1966–1967.* pp. 76–77, 80–81.

———. 1968. Seed dormancy and field emergence in *Polygonum aviculare*. *J. Appl. Ecol.* 5:675–684.

COVARELLI, G. 1974. The influence of nitrogen fertilizer on the development of weeds in wheat. *Revista di Agronomia* 8:129–133.

COX, T. 1978. Effects of glyphosate on *Oxalis latifolia. Proc. 31st New Zealand Weed and Pest Control Conf.* 31:34–39.

COXWORTH, E., J. BELL and R. ASHFORD. 1969. Preliminary evaluation of Russian thistle, kochia, and garden atriplex as potential high protein content seed crops for semiarid areas. *Can. J. Plant Sci.* 49:427–434.

CRAIGMILES, J. 1978. Introduction to proceedings of symposium. *Red rice research and control.* pp. 5–6. Texas Agric. Exp. Sta. Bull. No. 1270.

CREEL, J., C. HOVELAND and G. BUCHANAN. 1968. Germination, growth, and ecology of sicklepod. *Weed Sci.* 16:396–400.

CRESCINI, F. and L. SPREAFICO. 1953. Piante coltivate contro erbe infestante. I. Ricerche intorno alla biologia dell germinazione degli acheni dell' *Artemisia vulgaris. Annali dell'Instituto Sperimentali por l'Agrumicoltura (NS)* 7:1597–1610.

CRESCINI, F., E. MARTINELLI and P. BELLINI. 1956. On the biology of weeds: II. Sensitivity to light and cold of achenes of *Artemisia vulgaris. Annali dell'Instituto Sperimentali por l'Agrumicoltura (NS)* 10:2157–2170.

CRESSWELL, E. and J. GRIME. 1981. Induction of a light requirement during seed development and its ecological consequences. *Nature* 291:583–585.

CRETE, P. 1959. Embryogenie du *Nicandra physalodes*. *Phytomorphol.* 9(2):163–167.

CROCKER, W. 1907. Germination of seeds of water plants. *Bot. Gaz.* 44:375–380.

CROCKER, W. and L. BARTON. 1953. *Physiology of seeds*. Chronica Botanica Co., Waltham, Mass.

CROCKETT, L. 1977. *Wildly successful plants*. Collier Books, N.Y.

CROSS, H. 1931. Laboratory germination of weed seeds. *Proc. Assoc. Official Seed Analysts* 24:125–128.

CUBERO, J. 1986. Breeding for resistance to *Orobanche* and *Striga*: A review. p. 127–138. *Proc. Workshop on Biology and Control of Orobanche*. (Ed.) S. ter Borg. Wageningen, Netherlands.

CULLEN, J. 1973. Seasonal and regional variation in the success of organisms imported to combat skeleton weed *Chondrilla juncea* L. in Australia. *Proc. 3rd Intern. Symp. Bio. Control Weeds* 3:111–117.

———. 1976. Evaluating the success of the program for biological control of *Chondrilla juncea* L. *Proc. 4th Intern. Symp. Bio. Control Weeds* 4:114–120.

———. 1980. Considerations in rearing *Bradyrrhoa gilveolella* for control of *Chondrilla juncea* in Australia. *Proc. 5th Intern. Symp. Bio. Control Weeds* 5:233–239.

CULLEN, J. and R. GROVES. 1977. The population biology of *Chondrilla juncea* L. in Australia. *Proc. Ecol. Soc. Aus.* 10:121–134.

CULVENOR, C. 1978. Prevention of pyrrolizidine alkaloid poisoning, animal adaptation, or plant control. pp. 189–200. In: *Effects of poisonous plants on livestock*. Ed. by R. Keeler, K. van Kampen and L. James. Academic Press, N.Y. 600pp.

CUNNELL, G. 1964. Further observations on aestivation in *Ranunculus repens* L. *New Phytol.* 63:1–11.

CUPERTINO, F., R. GROGAN, L. PETERSEN and K. KIMBLE. 1984. Tobacco streak virus infection of tomato and some natural weed hosts in California. *Plant Dis.* 68:331–333.

CURE, V., A. SNAIDER and A. CHIOSILO. 1970. Macrophytes from Frasinet pond and their influence on life of the ecosystem two years after the introduction of the grass carp (Romania). *Buletinul Inst. de Cercetari si Proiectari Piscicole* 29:5–27.

CURRIE, R. and T. PEEPER. 1986. Effect of harvest method on weed seed germination and the potential emergence of resistance. *Proc. Southern Weed Sci. Soc. Conf.* (USA). 39:395.

CURRIER, H. and C. SHIH. 1968. Sieve tubes and callose in *Elodea* leaves. *Am. J. Bot.* 55(2):145–152.

CUSHING, C. and P. OLSON. 1964. Effects of weed burning

on stream conditions. *Trans. Am. Fisheries Soc.* 92:303–305.

CUSSANS, G. 1966. The weed problem. *Proc. 8th Brit. Weed Control Conf.* 8:884–889.

CUTHBERTSON, E. 1965. Vernalization and flowering in skeleton weed *Chondrilla juncea*. *Aus. J. Exp. Agric. and Animal Husbandry* 5:324–332.

———. 1966. *Chondrilla juncea* L. in Australia: I. Some factors affecting flowering. *Aus. J. Agric. Res.* 17:457–464.

———. 1969. *Chondrilla juncea* L. in Australia: II. Preplanting weed control and wheat production. *Aus. J. Exp. Agric. and Animal Husbandry* 9:27–36.

———. 1970. *Chondrilla juncea* in Australia: III. Seed maturity and other factors affecting germination and establishment. *Aus. J. Exp. Agric. and Animal Husbandry* 10:63–66.

———. 1972. *Chondrilla juncea* in Australia: IV. Root morphology and regeneration from root fragments. *Aus. J. Exp. Agric. and Animal Husbandry* 12:528–534.

———. 1974. Seed development in *Chondrilla juncea* L. *Aus. J. Bot.* 22:13–14.

CUTTER, E. 1972. Regulation of branching in decussate species with unequal lateral buds. *Ann. Bot.* 36:207–220.

CZEKALSKI, M. 1981. *Nicandra physalodes*, a new fodder plant. *Kosmos Seria Biologica*, Warsaw 30(4):427–428.

CZOPEK, M. 1963. Studies on the external factors inducing the formation of turions in *Spirodela polyrhiza*. *Acta Societatis Botanicorum Poloniae* 32:199–211.

———. 1964. The action of kinetin, gibberellic acid and red light on the germination of turions of *Spirodela polyrhiza*. *Bull. Acad. Polonaise Sci. Ser. Biol.* 12:177–182.

DAAMS, J. 1975. Parasitic plants as weeds. *Acta Bot. Neerl.* 24:243–255.

DAFNI, A. and D. HELLER. 1980. The threat posed by alien weeds in Israel. *Weed Res.* 20:277–283.

DAFNI, A. and D. HELLER. 1982. Adventive flora of Israel, phytogeographical, ecological, and agricultural aspects. *Plant Systematics and Evol.* 140:1–18.

DAGHLIAN, C. 1981. A review of the fossil record of monocotyledons. *Bot. Rev.* 47:517–555.

DAILEY, O., A. PEPPERMAN and S. VAIL. 1987. Overview of synthetic approaches to strigol and its analogues. *Am. Chem. Soc. Symp. Series, ACS* 355:409–432.

DAIYA, K., H. SHARMA, D. CHAWAN and D. SEN. 1980. Effect of salt solutions of different osmotic potential on seed germination and seedling growth in some *Cassia* species. *Folia Geobotanica et Phytotaxonomica* 15:149–154.

DAIYA, K., H. SHARMA and D. CHAWAN. 1983. Effect of different moisture regimes on the growth of *Cassia* species. *Folia Geobotan. Phytotaxon.* 18:189–193.

DALE, H. 1956. Morphological effects of various temperatures, light intensities and photoperiods in experimental studies on morphological development of *Elodea canadensis*. PhD Diss., Univ. Toronto; Toronto, Canada.

————. 1957a. Developmental studies of *Elodea canadensis*. I. Morphological development at the shoot apex. *Can. J. Bot.* 35:13–24.

————. 1957b. Developmental studies of *Elodea canadensis*. II. Experimental studies on morphological effects in darkness. *Can. J. Bot.* 35:51–64.

————. 1970. Germination patterns in *Daucus carota* spp. *carota*. I. Variations in the 1967 collection. *Can. J. Bot.* 48:413–418.

————. 1974. The biology of Canadian weeds. 5. *Daucus carota*. *Can. J. Plant Sci.* 54:673–685.

DALE, H. and T. GILLESPIE. 1977. The influence of submersed aquatic plants on temperature gradients in shallow water bodies. *Can. J. Bot.* 55:2216–2225.

DALE, H. and P. HARRISON. 1966. Wild carrot seeds: Germination and dormancy. *Weeds* 14:201–204.

D'ALMEIDA, J. and G. RAMASWAMY. 1948. A contribution to the study of the ecological anatomy of the Indian **Cyperaceae**. *Univ. Bombay Bot. Memoirs* 1:1–63.

DALZIEL, J. 1937. *The useful plants of west tropical Africa.* Crown Agents, London. 88pp.

DANIEL, A., N. BAKTHAVATSALAM and N. KUMAR. 1984. Weed-crop interaction with reference to *Caliothrips indicus* on *Arachis hypogaea* and an alternate weed host *Achyranthes aspera*. *Entomol.* 9:47–51.

DANIEL, J., G. TEMPLETON, R. SMITH, JR. and W. FOX. 1973. Biological control of northern jointvetch in rice with an endemic fungal disease. *Weed Sci.* 21:303–307.

DANIELS, J. 1963. Experimental control of flowering in *Saccharum spontaneum* L. pp. 527–532. *Proc. 11th Intern. Soc. Sugar Cane Technologists.*

DANIELS, R. 1985. Studies in the growth of *Pteridium aquilinum* (L.) Kuhn (bracken). 1. Regeneration of rhizome segments. *Weed Res.* 25:381–388.

————. 1986. Studies in the growth of *Pteridium aquilinum* (L.) Kuhn (bracken). 2. Effects of shading and nutrient application. *Weed Res.* 26:121–126.

DANIELSON, R. 1962. Identification of water fern sporocarps in seed samples. *Proc. Assoc. Official Seed Analysts 1962,* 52:100–101.

DARLINGTON, C. and E. JANAKI-AMMAL. 1945. Adaptive iso-chromosomes in *Nicandra*. *Ann. Bot.* 9:267–281.

DARLINGTON, H. 1951. The seventy-year period for Dr. Beal's seed viability experiment. *Am. J. Bot.* 38:379–381.

DARLINGTON, H. and G. STEINBAUER. 1961. The eighty-year period for Dr. Beal's seed viability experiment. *Am. J. Bot.* 48:321–325.

DARMENCY, H. and C. AUJAS. 1988. A genetic approach of germination: An example in *Poa annua*. *Proc. Intern. Symp. Biol., Ecol., Systematics Weeds* 1:25–32.

DARMENCY, H. and J. GASQUEZ. 1981. Inheritance of tri-

azine resistance in *Poa annua*: Consequences for population dynamics. *New Phytol.* 89:487–493.

DARWENT, A. and C. ELLIOTT. 1979. Effect of grass species and row spacing on dandelion establishment and growth. *Can. J. Plant Sci.* 59:1031–1036.

DARWIN, C. 1839. *Journal of researches into geology and natural history of various countries visited by H.M.S. Beagle.* Published in London.

DAS, R. and B. GOPAL. 1969. Vegetative propagation in *Spirodela polyrhiza*. *Trop. Ecol.* 10:270–277.

DAS, T. and S. PAL. 1970. Effects of volatile substances of aromatic weeds on germination and subsequent growth of rice embryos. *Bull. Botan. Soc. Bengal* 24:101–103.

DAS, V. and K. RAO. 1975. Phytochemical phylogeny of the **Brassicaceae** (**Cruciferae**) from the **Capparidaceae**. *Die Naturwissenschaften* 62:577–578.

DAS, V. and M. SANTAKUMARI. 1977. Stomatal characteristics of some dicotyledonous plants in relation to the C_4 and C_3 pathways of photosynthesis. *Plant and Cell Physiol.* 18:935–938.

————. 1978. The incomplete evolution of C_4–photosynthesis within the pantropical taxon, *Boerhavia* : **Nyctaginaceae**. *Photosynthetica* 12:418–422.

DAS, V., K. VEERANJANEYULU and A. REDDY. 1981. Photosynthesis and bioproductivity in some crop and weed species. *Proc. Intern. Congr. Photosynthesis* Vol. 6:63–72. Ed. by G. Akoyunoglou. Photosynthesis and Productivity, Photosynthesis and Environment.

DASANAYAKE, M. 1960. Aspects of morphogenesis in a dorsiventral fern, *Pteridium aquilinum*. *Ann. Bot.*, London, 24:317–329.

DAS GUPTA, S. 1978. Weed seeds in marketed wheat and their identification. *Bull. Bot. Survey India* 20(1–4):69–71.

DASTGHEIB, F. 1989. Relative importance of crop seed, sheep manure, and irrigation water as sources of weed infestation. *Weed Res.* 29:113–116.

DATTA, N. and U. CHATTERJEE. 1969. Cytological studies on three species of *Alternanthera*. *Bull. Botan. Soc. Bengal* 23:27–29.

DATTA, R. 1958. Studies of the pollen tube in certain **Malvaceae**. *Madrono* 14:227–232.

DATTA, R. and P. CHAKRABORTY. 1975. Seed morphology of *Corchorus* species. *Broteria Serie Trimestral Ciencias Naturais*, Portugal, 44:147–153.

DATTA, R., B. PANDA, K. ROY, M. BOSE and T. DE. 1966. Cytotaxonomic studies of different *Corchorus* species. *Bot. Mag.* 79:467–473.

DATTA, S. 1959. Weeds and weed control. *Indian Agriculturalist* 3:26–36.

DATTA, S. and A. BANERJEE. 1973. Weight and number of weed seeds. *Proceedings of the 4th Asian-Pacific Weed Science Society Conference* Vol. 1:87–91.

————. 1976. The weight and number of seeds produced by

rice-field weeds. *PANS (Pest Articles and News Summaries)* 22(2):257–263.

DATTA, S. and K. BISWAS. 1968. Influence of temperature, light, stimulators, and their interaction on the germination and seedling growth of *Alternanthera sessilis*. *Oesterreichische Bot. Zeitschrift*, Vienna, 115:391–399.

———. 1970. Germination regulating mechanisms in aquatic angiosperms. I. *Ipomoea aquatica*. *Broteria, Serie Trimestral, Ciencias Naturais*, Lisbon, 37:175–185.

———. 1973. Autecological studies: Weeds of West Bengal. V. *Ipomoea aquatica*. *Bull. Botan. Soc. Bengal* 27:7–14.

———. 1979. Autecological studies on weeds of West Bengal. III. *Alternanthera sessilis*. *Bull. Bot. Soc. Bengal* 33(1/2):5–26.

DATTA, S. AND A. CHATTERJEE, 1980. Allelopathic potential of *Polygonum orientale* in relation to germination and seedling growth of weeds. *Flora (Jena)* 169:456–465.

DATTA, S. and K. GHOSH. 1982. Effects of pre-sowing treatment of mustard seeds with leaf and inflorescence extracts of *Chenopodium murale*. *Ind. J. Weed Sci.* 14:1–6.

———. 1987. Allelopathy in two species of *Chenopodium* inhibition of germination and seedling growth of certain weeds. *Acta Soc. Bot. Pol.* 56:257–270.

DAULTON, R. and R. CURTIS. 1964. The effects of *Tagetes* spp. on *Meloidogyne javanica* in southern Rhodesia. *Nematologica* 9:357–362.

DAUMAN, E. 1973. On the supposed significance of the central blossoms in the umbel of *Daucus carota* L. for pollination, ecology and as protection against grazing animals. *Preslia* 45:320–326.

DAUN, J. 1983. The composition of wild mustards and the effect of their admixture on the quality of rapeseed. *Abstr. 6th Intern. Rapeseed Conf.*, Paris, 6:70.

DAVIDSON, S. 1984–1985. Weeds: A legacy of drought. *Rural Res.* 125:4–6.

DAVIES, D. and G. WILLIAMS. 1987. Activity of Sulfonylurea herbicides on *Pteridium aquilinum* in south of Scotland. *Proc. Crop Protec. Northern Brit.* 1987:355–360.

DAVIS, D. and J. GRESSEL. 1981. Photosynthesis of leaves of triazine resistant variants to wild type *Brassica campestris*. *Israel J. Bot.* 30:49.

DAVIS, G. 1972. The effects of salinity on the photosynthetic respiratory ratio of *Myriophyllum spicatum*. *J. Elisha Mitchell Sci Soc.* 88:189.

DAVIS, G., M. JONES and D. DAVIS. 1973. Seed germination in *Myriophyllum spicatum*. *J. Elisha Mitchell Sci. Soc.* 89:246–247.

DAVIS, G., M. JONES, Z. LUNNEY and G. CLARK. 1974. Inhibition of sodium chloride toxicity in seedlings of *Myriophyllum spicatum* with calcium. *Plant and Cell Physiol.* 15:577–581.

DAVIS, G., E. VOLL, H. LORENZI and A. CHEHATA. 1977. Soybean yield response to control of *Brachiaria plan-*taginea and *Acanthospermum hispidum*. *Proc. 32nd Southern Weed Sci. Soc. Conf.* 32:333.

DAVIS, R., W. JOHNSON and F. WOODS. 1967. Weed root profiles. *Agron. J.* 59:555–556.

DAVIS, R., A. WIESE and J. PAFFORD. 1965. Root moisture extraction profiles of various weeds. *Weed Sci.* 13:98–100.

DAVISON, A. 1970. The ecology of *Hordeum murinum* L.: I. Analysis of the distribution in Britain. *J. Ecol.* 58:453–466.

———. 1971a. The ecology of *Hordeum murinum* L.: II. The ruderal habit. *J. Ecol.* 59:493–506.

———. 1971b. The effects of de-icing salt on roadside verges: I. Soil and plant analyses. *J. Appl. Ecol.* 8:555–560.

———. 1977. The ecology of *Hordeum murinum* L.: III. Some effects of adverse climate. *J. Ecol.* 65:523–530.

DAVISON, J. and H. ROBERTS. 1976. The influence of changing husbandry on weeds and weed control in horticulture. *Proc. 13th Brit. Weed Control Conf.* 13(3):1009–1017.

DAWSON, F. and U. KERN-HANSON. 1979. The effect of natural and artificial shade on the macrophytes of lowland streams and the use of shade as a management technique. *Intern. Rev. Gesamten Hydrobiologie* 64:437–455.

DAWSON, J. 1965. Prolonged emergence of field dodder. *Weeds* 13:373–374.

———. 1966. Response of field dodder to shade. *Weeds* 14:4–5.

———. 1984. A vegetative character that separates species of *Cuscuta*. *Proc. 3rd Intern. Symp. Parasitic Weeds* 3:184–187.

———. 1987. *Cuscuta* : **Convolvulaceae** and its control. *Proc. 4th Intern. Symp. Parasitic Flowering Plants* 4:137–149.

DAWSON, J. and V. BRUNS. 1975. Longevity of barnyardgrass, green foxtail, and yellow foxtail seeds in soil. *Weed Sci.* 23:437–440.

DAWSON, J., F. ASHTON, W. WELKER, J. FRANK and G. BUCHANAN. 1984. *Dodder and control*. USDA Farmers Bull. 2276. 24p.

DEAN, H. 1934. Host plants of *Cuscuta gronovii*. *Rhodora* 47:371–374.

———. 1935. Host plants of *Cuscuta glomerata*. *Proc. Iowa Acad. Sci.* 42:52–57.

———. 1937. Gall formation in host plants following haustorial invasion by *Cuscuta*. *Am. J. Bot.* 24:167–173.

———. 1942. Total length of stem developed from a single seedling of *Cuscuta*. *Proc. Iowa Acad. Sci.* 49:127–128.

———. 1954. Dodder overwintering as haustorial tissues within *Cuscuta* galls. *Proc. Iowa Acad. Sci.* 61:99–106.

DEARDEN, P. 1983. Anatomy of biological hazard: *Myriophyllum spicatum* L. in the Okanagan Basin. *J. Environ. Mgmt.* 17:47–61.

———. 1984. Public perception of a technological hazard: A case study of the use of 2,4–D to control Eurasian milfoil in the Okanagan Valley. *Can. Geographer* 28:324–340.

DEAT, M., G. SEMENT and P. FONTENAY. 1978. Role of

preceding crops on weed infestation of cotton in a crop rotation system. pp. 305–314. In: *Weeds and their control in the humid and subhumid tropics.* IITA; Ibadan, Nigeria.

DEBOURCIEU, L. 1977. Application of thin-layer electrofocusing to the chemotaxonomy of the genus *Datura. Plantes Medicinales Phytotherapie* 11(1):12–15.

DEBUSK, T. and J. RYTHER. 1981. Effects of seasonality and plant density on the productivity of some freshwater macrophytes. *Aquatic Bot.* 10:133–142.

DECELL, J. 1983. The Lake Conway, Florida, USA, white amur study. *Proc. 36th Southern Weed Sci. Soc. Conf.* 36:320–321.

DE DATTA, S. 1983. Perennial weeds and their control in rice in the tropics. *Proc. Weed Control Rice Conf.* pp. 255–272. Ed. W. Smith. IRRI and Intern. Weed Sci. Soc.; Los Banos, Philippines.

DE DATTA, S. and H. JEREZA. 1976. The use of cropping systems and land and water management to shift weed species. *Philipp. J. Crop Sci.* 1:173–178.

DE DATTA, S., F. BOLTON and W. LIN. 1979. Prospects for using minimum and zero tillage in tropical lowland rice. *Weed Res.* 19(1):9–16.

DEGROOTE, D. and R. KENNEDY. 1977. Photosynthesis in *Elodea canadensis,* four-carbon acid synthesis. *Plant Physiol.* 59:1133–1135.

DE JONG, T. and P. KLINKHAMER. 1985. The negative effects of litter of parent plants of *Cirsium vulgare* on their offspring: Autotoxicity immobilization? *Oecologia* 65:153–160.

DE JONG, T., G. KLINKHAMER, H. NELL and S. TROELSTRA. 1987. Growth and nutrient accumulation of the biennials *Cirsium vulgare* and *Cynoglossum officinale* under nutrient rich conditions. *Oikos* 48:62–72.

DELAHUNTY, E. 1962. Nodding thistle. *Proc. 15th New Zealand Weed and Pest Control Conf.* 15:24–28.

DELFOSSE, E. and J. CULLEN. 1980. New activities in biological control of weeds in Australia. I. Common heliotrope *Heliotropium europaeum. Proc. 5th Intern. Symp. Bio. Control Weeds,* Brisbane, 5:545–561.

———. 1982. Biological control of weeds of Mediterranean origin: A progress report. *Aus. Weeds* 1(3):25–30.

DELGADO, A. and M. SOUSA. 1977. Biologia floral del genero *Cassia* en la region de los Tuxtlas, Veracruz. *Boletin Soc. Botanica Mexicana* 37:5–52.

DELORIT, R. 1970. *Illustrated taxonomy manual of weed seed.* Agron. Publ., River Falls, Wisconsin. 175pp.

DEMAGGIO, A. 1977. Cytological aspects of reproduction in ferns. *Bot. Rev.* 43:427–448.

DEMALSY-FELLER, M. 1957. Etudes sur les hydropteridales. V. Gametophytes et gametogenese dans le genre *Marsilea. Cellule* 58(2):169–207.

DEMBINSKA, M. 1976. Wild corn plants gathered in the 9th to 13th centuries in light of paleobotanical materials. *Folia Quaternaria* 47:97–103.

DEMINT, R. and P. FRANK. 1974. Mode of nutrient uptake by submersed aquatic plants. *Abstr. 14th Weed Sci. Soc. Am. Conf.* 14: No. 30.

DENNY, P. 1972. Sites of nutrient absorption in aquatic macrophytes. *J. Ecol.* 60:819–829.

DEODIKAR, G., C. THAKAR, R. PHADKE and P. SHAH. 1958. Poisoning of honeybees foraging on *Euphoria geniculata. Bee World* 39:118–120.

DEOSTHALE, Y. and K. PANT. 1970. Nutrient composition of some red rice varieties. *Ind. J. Nutrition and Dietetics* 7:283–287.

DERSCHEID, L. and R. SCHULTZ. 1960. Achene development of Canada thistle and perennial sowthistle. *Weeds* 8:55–62.

DERSCHEID, L., R. NASH and G. WICKS. 1961. Thistle control with cultivation, cropping and chemicals. *Weeds* 9:90–102.

DESCHENES, J. and D. MOINEAU. 1972. Conditions de germination de quatre mauvaises herbes du Quebec. *Naturaliste Can.* 99:103–114.

DESHMUKH, P., S. CHAVAN and D. RENAPURKAR. 1982. A study of insecticidal activity of twenty indigenous plants (India). *Pesticides* 16:7–12.

DESHPANDE, A., K. VENKATASUBBAIAH, V. BANKAPUR and U. NALAWADI. 1979. Studies on floral biology of bitter gourd *Momordica charantia* L. *Mysore J. Agric. Sci.* 13:156–159.

DESROCHERS, A., J. BAIN and S. WARWICK. 1988. The biology of Canadian weeds. 89. *Carduus nutans* and *Carduus acanthoides. Can. J. Plant Sci.* 68:1053–1068.

DE VLAMING, V. and V. PROCTOR. 1968. Dispersal of aquatic organisms: Viability of seeds recovered from the droppings of captive kildeer and mallard ducks. *Am. J. Bot.* 55:20–26.

DEWET, J. and J. HARLAN. 1975. Weeds and domesticates: Evolution in the man-made habitat. *Econ. Bot.* 29:99–107.

DEWEY, L. 1894. The Russian thistle: its history as a weed. *USDA, Div. Bot. Bull.* No. 15:1–37.

DHARMARAJ, G., B. CHANDRA, N. NATARAJARTNAM and S. SUBRAMANIAM. 1988. Allelopathy of certain weed species. *Madras Agric. J.* 75:147–148.

DIARRA, A., R. SMITH, and R. TALBERT. 1985a. The interference of red rice *Oryza sativa* with rice *Oryza sativa. Weed Sci.* 33:644–649.

———. 1985b. Growth and morphological characteristics of red rice *Oryza sativa* biotypes. *Weed Sci.* 33:310–314.

DICKERMAN, J. and R. WETZEL. 1985. Clonal growth in *Typha latifolia:* Population dynamics and demography of the ramets. *J. Ecol.* 73:535–552.

DIETL, W. 1982. Pastures and meadows in the European Alps.

Chapter 32 in: *Biology and ecology of weeds*. Ed. by W. Holzner and M. Numata. Dr. W. Junk Publ., The Hague.

DIEZ, M., S. TALAVERA and P. GARCIA-MURILLO. 1988. Contribution to the palynology of hydrophytic non-entomophilous angiosperms. *Candollea* 43:147–158.

DIJK, G. VAN, D. THAYER and W. HALLER. 1986. Growth of *Hygrophila* and *Hydrilla* in flowing water. *J. Aquat. Plant Mgmt*. 24:85–87.

DILLMAN, A. 1931. The water requirements of certain crop plants and weeds in the northern Great Plains. *J. Agric. Res*. 42:187–238.

DIRAR, H. 1984. Kawal, meat substitute from fermented *Cassia obtusifolia* leaves. *Econ. Bot*. 38:342–349.

DIRVEN, J. 1970. Weed flora on fallow rice fields Surinam. *Surinaamse Landbouw* 18:47–63.

DNYANSAGAR, V. and S. MALKHERE. 1963. Development of the seed of *Trianthema portulacastrum* L. *Proc. Ind. Acad. Sci., Section B*, 57:343–355.

DOBZHANSKY, T. 1951. *Genetics and the origin of species*. Columbia Univ. Press, N.Y.

DODD, J. 1989. Phenology and seed production of variegated thistle *Silybum marianum* in Australia in relation to mechanical and biological control. *Weed Res*. 29:255–263.

DOING, H., E. BIDDISCOMBE and S. KNEDLHANS. 1969. Ecology and distribution of the *Carduus nutans* group nodding thistles in Australia. *Vegetatio* 17:313–351.

DOLL, J. 1984a. Are dandelions in forages important and can they be managed? *Proc. 8th Wisconsin Forage Council Symp*. 8:80–84.

———. 1984b. Effect of common dandelion on alfalfa drying time and yield. *Proc. 39th North Central Weed Control Conf*. 39:113–114.

DOLL, J. and W. PIEDRAHITA. 1976. Efectos de aplicaciones repitidas de paraquat y glifosato sobre las fluctuaciones de polaciones de malezas. *Revista COMALFI (Sociedad Colombiana de Malezas y Fisiologia Vegetal)* 3:291–295.

DOLL, J., W. PIEDRAHITA and P. ARGEL. 1976. Capacidad germinativa de semilla de 32 especies de malezas. *Revista COMALFI (Sociedad Colombiana de Malezas y Fisiologia Vegetal)* 3:82–93.

DOLL, J., P. ANDERSEN and R. DIAZ. 1977. An agro-economic survey of the weeds and weeding practices in cassava in Colombia. *Weed Res*. 17:153–160.

DOLL, R. 1981. Outline of evolution in the genus *Taraxacum* Zinn. *Biologische Rundschau* 19:103–104.

DOLLAHITE, I. and J. HENSON. 1965. Toxic plants as the etiologic agent of myopathies in animals. *Am. J. Vet. Res*. 26:749–752.

DOMINI, B. 1959. Germination of *Orobanche ramosa* independent of host presence. *Agricoltura Italiana* 59:219–222.

DONALD, W. and R. HOERAUF. 1985. Enhanced germina-

tion and emergence of dormant wild mustard *Sinapis arvensis* seed by two substituted phthalimides. *Weed Sci*. 33:894–902.

DOORENBOS, J. and P. RIEMANS. 1959. Effect of vernalization and daylength on number and shape of leaves in chicory and endive. *Acta Bot. Neerl*. 8:63–67.

DORNBERGER, K. and H. LICH. 1982. Screening nach antimikrobiell sowie potentiell cancerostatisch wirksamen pflanzeninhaltstoffen. *Pharmazie* 37(3):215–221.

DOROGOSTAYSKAYA, E. 1972. *Weeds of the far north of USSR*. Botanicheski Institut, Akad. Nauk SSSR, Leningrad. 172pp.

DORPH-PETERSEN, K. 1925. Examinations of the occurrence and vitality of various weed species under different conditions, made at the Danish State Seed Testing Station during the years 1896–1923. *Rep. 4th Intern. Seed Testing Congress*, Cambridge 4:124–138.

DORR, I. 1969. Feinstruktur intrezellular wachsender *Cucuta-Hyphae*. *Protoplasma* 67:123–137.

———. 1987. The haustorium of Cuscuta new structural results. *Proc. 4th Intern. Symp. Parasitic Flowering Plants* 4:163–170.

DORR, I. and R. KOLLMANN. 1974. Struktrelle grundlage des parasitismus bei *Orobanche*: I. Wachstum der Haustorialzellen im Wirtsgewebe. *Protoplasma* 80:245–259.

———. 1975. Structural features of parasitism of *Orobanche*: II. The differentiation of assimilate conducting elements within the haustorium. *Protoplasma* 83:185–201.

———. 1976. Structural features of parasitism of *Orobanche*: III. The differentiation of xylem connection to *O. crenata*. *Protoplasma* 89:235–249.

DOUGALL, D. and D. WETHERELL. 1974. Storage of wild carrot cultures in the frozen state. *Cryobiol*. 11:410–415.

DOUGLAS, D. 1880. Notes on water thyme *Anacharis alsinastrum* Bab. *Scientific Gossip* 16:227–229.

DOUST, J., L. DOUST, and A. GROTH. 1990. The biology of Canadian weeds. 95. *Ranunculus repens*. *Can. J. Plant Sci*. 70:1123–1141.

DOUST, L. 1981a. Population dynamics and local specialization in a clonal perennial *Ranunculus repens*. I. The dynamics of ramets in contrasting habitats. *J. Ecol*. 69:743–755.

———. 1981b. Population dynamics and local specialization in a clonal perennial *Ranunculus repens*. II. The dynamics of leaves and a reciprocal transplant-replant experiment. *J. Ecol*. 69:757–768.

———. 1981c. Intraclonal variation and competition in *Ranunculus repens*. *New Phytologist* 89:495–502.

———. 1987. Population dynamics and local specialization in a clonal perennial *Ranunculus repens*. III. Responses to light and nutrient supply. *J. Ecol*. 75:555–568.

DOUST, L. and J. DOUST. 1987. Leaf demography and clonal growth in female and male *Rumex acetosella. Ecol.* 68:2056–2058.

DRENNAN, P. and J. VAN STADEN. 1989. Enhancement of emergence in *Tagetes minuta* by light and temperature pretreatment. *Seed Sci. Technol.* 17:115–124.

DRURY, D. and L. WATSON. 1965. Anatomy and taxonomic significance of gross vegetative morphology in *Senecio. New Phytol.* 64:307–314.

D.S.I.R. 1958. *Water pollution research* 1957. Dept. Scientific and Industrial Res. His Majesty's Stationery Office, London.

DUBEY, N., N. KISHORE, O. SRIVASTAVA, A. DIKSHIT and S. SINGH. 1983. Fungi toxicity of some higher plants against *Rhizoctonia solani. Plant and Soil* 72:91–94.

DUBUY, H. and E. NEURNBERG. 1938. Growth, tropisms, and other movements. In: *Manual of Pteridology.* (Ed.) F. Verdoorn. M. Nijhoff, Publ., The Hague.

DUKE, J. 1961. Preliminary revision of the genus *Drymaria. Ann. Missouri Bot. Garden* 48:173–268.

———. 1979. Ecosystematic data on economic plants. *Quart. J. Crude Drug Res.* 17:91–110.

DUKE, J. and E. AYENSU. 1985. *Medicinal plants of China.* Reference Publications, Inc., Algonac, Michigan.

DUNBAR, A. 1973. Pollen development in the *Eleocharis palustris* group. 1. Ultrastructure and ontogeny. *Bot. Notiser* 126:197–254.

DUNN, C. 1977. A developmental study of oogenesis and embryogenesis in *Marsilea quadrifolia. Diss. Abstr. Intern. B* 37(8)3739–3740.

DUNN, P. 1976. Distribution of *Carduus nutans, C. acanthoides, C. pycnocephalus,* and *C. crispus* in the United States. *Weed Sci.* 24:518–524.

DURAN, J. and M. ESTRELLA. 1985. The effect of mechanical and chemical scarification on germination of charlock *Sinapis arvensis* seeds. *Seed Sci. Technol.* 13:155–163.

DURAN, J. and N. RETAMAL. 1985. Effect of gibberellic acid on germination of charlock *Sinapis arvensis* L. seeds. II. Origin of the mother plant. *Ann. Inst. Nacional Invest. Agrarias* 24:25–44.

DUTT, T., R. HARVEY and R. FAWCETT. 1982. Quality of hay containing perennial broadleaf weeds. *Agron. J.* 74:673–676.

———. 1983. Influence of herbicides on yield and botanical composition of alfalfa hay. *Agron. J.* 75:229–233.

DUVEL, J. 1905. *Vitality of buried seeds.* USDA, Bureau Plant Ind., Bull. No. 83.

DUVIGNEAUD, P., J. TIMPERMAN and J. MOMIQUET. 1975. Structure, biomass, mineral accumulation, productivity and lead content of some ruderal communities (*Artemisia vulgaris*). *Bull. Soc. Royale Bot. Belgique* 108:93–128.

DWYER, D. and H. DEGARMO. 1970. Greenhouse productivity and water use efficiency of selected desert shrubs and grasses under 4 soil moisture levels. *New Mexico Agric. Exp. Sta. Bull.* No. 570.

DWYER, D. and K. WOLDE-YOHANNIS. 1972. Germinations, emergence, water use, and production of Russian thistle. *Agron. J.* 64:52–55.

DYKYJOVA, D., P. ONDOK and D. HRADECKA. 1972. Growth rate and development of the root-shoot ratio of reedswamp macrophytes grown in winter hydroponic cultures. *Folia Geobotan. Phytotaxon.* 7:259–268.

EAGLESHAM, A. and A. SZALAY. 1983. Aerial stem nodules on *Aeschynomene* spp. *Plant Sci. Letters* 29:265–272.

EARLE, F. and Q. JONES. 1962. Analysis of seed samples from 113 plant families. *Econ. Bot.* 16:221–250.

EASLEY, J. and R. SHIRLEY. 1974. Nutrient elements for livestock in aquatic plants. *Hyacinth Control J.* 12:82–84.

EAST, J. 1955. The effect of certain plant preparations on the fertility of laboratory mammals: I. *Polygonum hydropiper. J. Endocrinol.* 12(4):252–260.

EASTIN, E. 1978. Additional red rice research in Texas. In: *Red rice research and control.* pp. 30–34. Texas Agric. Exp. Sta. Bull. No. 1270.

EATON, B., K. FELTNER and O. RUSS. 1973. Venice mallow competition in soybeans. *Weed Sci.* 21(2):89–94.

EDINBURGH SCHOOL OF AGRICULTURE. 1978. A survey of grasslands. *Edinburgh School of Agric., Ann. Rep 1977*: 93–94.

EDWARDS, M. 1968a. Dormancy in seeds of charlock: I. Developmental anatomy of the seed. *J. Exp. Bot.* 19:575–582.

———. 1968b. Dormancy in seeds of charlock: II. The influence of the seed coat. *J. Exp. Bot.* 19:583–600.

———. 1968c. Dormancy in seeds of charlock: III. Occurrence and mode of action of an inhibitor associated with dormancy. *J. Exp. Bot.* 19:601–610.

———. 1969. Dormancy in seeds of charlock: IV. Interrelationships of growth, oxygen supply and concentration of inhibitors. *J. Exp. Bot.* 20:876–894.

———. 1980. Aspects of the population ecology of charlock. *J. Appl. Ecol.* 17:151–171.

EDWARDS, W. 1972. Orobanche research at the Royal University of Malta. *PANS (Pest Articles and News Summaries)* 18:475–476.

EENINK, A. 1981. Compatibility and incompatibility in witloof-chicory *Cichorium intybus.* 1. The influence of temperature and plant age on pollen germination and production. *Euphytica* 30:71–76.

EGGINTON, G. and W. ROBBINS. 1920. Irrigation water as a factor in the dissemination of weed seeds. *Colorado Agric. College Exp. Sta. Bull.* No. 253.

EGLEY, G. 1983. Weed seed and seedling reductions by soil solarization with transparent polyethylene sheets. *Weed Sci.* 31:404–409.

———. 1984. Overwintering effects upon sensitivity of dor-

mant redroot pigweed seeds to germination stimulants. *Plant Physiol.* Suppl. 1, 75:70.

EGLEY, G. and J. CHANDLER. 1978. Germination and viability of weed seeds after 2.5 years in a 50 year buried seed study. *Weed Sci.* 26:230–239.

EGLEY, G. and J. DALE. 1970. Ethylene, 2–chloroethylphosphonic acid and witchweed germination. *Weed Sci.* 18:586–589.

EGUNJOBI, J. 1969a. *Some common weeds of western Nigeria.* Bull. Res. Div., Ministry Agric. and Natural Resources, Western State; Ibadan, Nig.

———. 1969b. Dry matter and nitrogen accumulation in secondary successions involving gorse *Ulex europaeus* and associated shrub trees. *New Zealand J. Sci.* 12:175–193.

———. 1971. Ecosystem processes in a stand of *Ulex europaeus.* 1. Dry matter production, litter fall, and efficiency of solar energy utilization. *J. Ecol.* 59:31–38.

EGUNJOBI, J. and A. KUPOLUYI. 1973. Studies on Nigerian weeds. 1. Biology and control of *Euphorbia heterophylla* L. *3rd Nigerian Weed Sci. Group Meeting* 3:42–46.

EHARA, K. and H. IKEDA. 1972. Studies on the ecological and growth characteristics of warm season native grasses. 4. *Paspalum distichum* L. *Scientific Bull. Faculty Agric., Kyushu Univ.* 26:435–439.

EHLERINGER, J. and I. FORSETH. 1980. Solar tracking by plants. *Sci.* 210:1094–1098.

EHRLE, E. 1960. *Eleocharis acicularis* in acid mine drainage. *Rhodora* 62(736):95–97.

EL-HADIDI, M. 1968. *Vallisneria spiralis* in Egypt. *Candollea* 23:51–58.

ELLIS, R. 1974. Comparative leaf anatomy of *Paspalum paspalodes* and *P. vaginatum.* *Bothalia* 11:235–241.

ELLIS, W. 1973. The breeding system and variations in populations in of *Poa annua* L. *Evolution* 27:656–662.

ELLISON, L. and C. ALDOUS. 1952. Influence of pocket gophers on vegetation of subalpine grassland in central Utah. *Ecology* 33:177–186.

ELMORE, C. and R. PAUL. 1983. Composite list of C_4 weeds. *Weed Sci.* 31:686–692.

ELMORE, H. and R. ADAMS. 1976. Scanning electron microscopic observations on the gametophyte and sperm of the bracken fern *Pteridium aquilinum.* *New Phytol.* 76:519–522.

ELSER, H. 1969. Observations on the decline of the water milfoil and other aquatic plants, Maryland, 1962–1967. *Hyacinth Control J.* 8:52–60.

EMMELIN, N. and W. FELDBERG. 1947. The mechanism of the sting of the common nettle *Urtica urens.* *J. Physiol.* 106:440–455.

EMON, J. VAN, and J. SEIBER. 1985. Chemical constituents and energy content of two milkweeds *Asclepias speciosa* and *A. curassavica.* *Econ. Bot.* 39:47–55.

ENGSTRAND, L. and M. GUSTAFSSON. 1973. Drawings of Scandinavian plants 89–90, *Chenopodium* L. *Botaniska Notiser* 126:273–276.

ENOMOTO, T. 1985. Plant succession and weeds in a new reclaimed polder in Japan. *Proc. 10th Asian-Pacific Weed Sci. Soc. Conf.* 10:61–66.

EPLEE, R. 1975. Ethylene: Witchweed seed germination stimulant. *Weed Sci.* 23:433–436.

ERICKSON, C. and W. DUKE. 1978. Release of phytotoxic residues from wild mustard *Brassica kaber.* *Proc. 32nd Northeastern Weed Sci. Soc. Conf.* 32:70.

ERICKSON, J. 1973. The utilization of various *Asclepias* species by monarch butterfly *Danaus plexippus.* *Psyche* 80:230–244.

ERNST-SCHWARZENBACH, M. 1945a. Zur blutenbiologie einiger *Hydrocharitaceen.* *Berichte der Schweizerischen Bot.Gesellschaft* 55:33–69.

———. 1945b. Kreuzungsversuche an *Hydrocharitaceen.* *Archiv Julius Klaus-Stiftung* 20:22–41.

ERVIO, L. 1981. The emergence of weeds in fields. *Ann. Agric. Fenniae* 20:292–303.

ESCARRE, J. and C. HOUSSARD. 1989. Differences in *Rumex acetosella* populations along a secondary succession: Biomass allocation. *Acta Oecologica* 10:3–19.

ESENBECK, E. 1914. Beitrage zur Biologie der Gattungen *Potamogeton* and *Scirpus.* *Flora, oder Allgemeine Bot. Zeit.,* N.S. 7:151–211.

ESLER, A. 1962. Some aspects of the autecology of *Oxalis latifolia* H.B.K. *Proc. 15th New Zealand Weed and Pest Control Conf.* 15:87–90.

ESTELITA-TEIXEIRA, M. 1978. Anatomical development of the underground system of *Oxalis latifolia.* II. Root system. *Bol. Botanica, Univ. S. Paulo.* 6:27–38 (in Portuguese).

———. 1982. Shoot anatomy of three bulbous species of *Oxalis.* *Ann. Bot.* 49:805–813.

———. 1984. Floral morphology of three *Oxalis* species. *Revista Brasileira Botanica* 7:41–48.

ETTEN, C. VAN, and H. TOOKEY. 1978. Glucosinolates in cruciferous plants. In *Effects of poisonous plants on livestock.* Ed. by R. Keeler, K. Van Kampen and L. James. Academic Press, NY USA.

ETTEN, C. VAN, R. MILLER, I. WOLFF, and Q. JONES. 1963. Amino acid composition of seeds from 200 angiospermous plant species. *Agriculture and Food Chemistry* 11:399–410.

EUW, J., L. FISHELSON, J. PARSONS, T. REICHSTEIN and M. ROTHSCHILD. 1967. Cardenolides (heart poisons) in a grasshopper feeding on milkweed. *Nature* 214:35–39.

EVANS, D. 1962. What about broomrape? *Agric. Gaz. New South Wales* 73:200–202.

EVANS, I. 1984. Bracken carcinogenicity. In: *Chemical carcinogens.* Ed. C. Searle. Am. Chem. Soc. Monograph No. 182:1171–1204.

————. 1986. The carcinogenic, mutagenic and teratogenetic toxicity of bracken. pp. 139–146. In: *Bracken, ecology, land use and control technology.* Ed. by R. Smith and J. Taylor. Parthenon Publ., Carnforth, Eng.

EVANS, R. and J. YOUNG. 1972. Germination and establishment of *Salsola* in relation to seedbed environment: II. Seed distribution, germination, seedling growth of *Salsola* and microenvironmental monitoring of the seedbed. *Agron. J.* 64:219–224.

EVANS, R., H. HOLBO, R. ECKERT and J. YOUNG. 1970. Influence of weed control and seeding methods on the functional environment of rangelands. *Weed Sci.* 18:154–162.

EVANS, R., J. YOUNG and R. HAWKES. 1978. Germination of Italian thistle *Carduus pycnocephalus* seeds. *Abstr. 18th Weed Sci. Soc. Am. Conf.* 18:63–64.

EVANS, W. 1964. Bracken poisoning of farm animals. *Vet. Rec.* 76:365–372.

EVANS, W. and E. EVANS. 1949. The effects of bracken *Pteris aquilina* in the diet of rats, and the problem of bracken poisoning in farm animals. *Brit. Vet. J.* 105:175–186.

EVENARI, M. 1949. Germination inhibitors. *Bot. Review* 15:153–194.

EVERIST, S. 1974. *Poisonous plants of Australia.* Angus and Robertson Publ., Sydney. 684pp.

EVERS, R. and R. LINK. 1972. *Poisonous plants of the midwest and their effects on livestock.* Special Publ. 24, College Agric., Univ. Illinois, Urbana. p. 165.

EVERSON, L. 1949. Preliminary studies to establish laboratory methods for germination of weed seeds. *Proc. Assoc. Official Seed Analysts* 39:84–89.

EWART, A. 1908. On the longevity of seeds. *Proc. Royal Soc. Victoria* 21:1–210.

EWUSIE, J. and E. QUAYE. 1977. Diurnal periodicity in some common flowers. *New Phytol.* 78:479–485.

EYLES, D. and J. ROBERTSON. 1963. *A guide and key to the aquatic plants of southeastern United States.* U.S. Public Health Service Bull. No. 286. 151pp.

FAGAN, T. and H. WATKINS. 1932. The chemical composition of the miscellaneous herbs of pastures. *Welsh J. Agric.* 8:144–151.

FAIRBAIRN, C. and B. THOMAS. 1959. The potential nutritive value of some weeds common to northeastern England. *J. Brit. Grassland Soc.* 14:36–46.

FAIZIEVA, S. 1978. Physiological characteristics of tomato varieties infected with Egyptian broomrape. *Uzbekskii Biologicheskii Zhurnal* 23:20–22.

FARRIS, M. 1984. Leaf size and shape variation associated with drought stress in *Rumex acetosella. Am. Midland Nat.* 111:358–363.

FEAST, P. and H. ROBERTS. 1973. Note on the estimation of viable weed seeds in soil samples. *Weed Res.* 13:110–113.

FEDORTSCHUK, W. VON. 1931. Embryologische unter-

suchung von *Cuscuta monogyna* and *C. epithymum. Planta Archiv fur Wissenschaftliche Bot.* 14:94–111.

FEDOTINA, V. 1973. Phytopathogenic mycoplasma-like organisms. *Zhurnal Obshchei Biologii* 34:758–768.

FEENY, P. 1977. Defensive ecology of the **Cruciferae.** *Ann. Missouri Bot. Garden* 64:221–234.

FEKETE, A. and D. RIEMER. 1973. Effects of varying phosphorous concentration on *Lemna minor* L. *Proc. 27th Northeastern Weed Sci Soc. Conf.* 27:109–114.

FEKETE, A., D. RIEMER and H. MOTTO. 1976. A bioassay using common duckweed to evaluate the release of available phosphorous from pond sediments. *J. Aquatic Plant Mgmt.* 14:19–25.

FELDMAN, I., M. MCCARTY and C. SCIFRES. 1968. Ecological and control studies on musk thistle. *Weed Sci.* 16:1–4.

FELTON, W. 1979. The competitive effect of *Datura* species on five irrigated summer crops. *Proc. 7th Asian-Pacific Weed Sci. Soc. Conf.* 7:98–104.

FENNER, M. 1980. Germination tests on thirty-two east African weed species. *Weed Res.* 20:135–138.

————. 1983. Relationships between seed weight, ash content and seedling growth in twenty-four species of **Compositae.** *New Phytol.* 95:697–706.

————. 1985. *Seed ecology.* Chapman and Hill, London. 151pp.

————. 1986. The allocation of minerals to seeds in *Senecio vulgaris* plants subjected to nutrient shortage. *J. Ecol.* 74:385–392.

FENWICK, G. 1989. Bracken *Pteridium aquilinum*—toxic effects and toxic constituents. *J. Sci. Food Agric.* 46:147–173.

FERNANDEZ-QUINTANILLA, C., L. NAVARETTE, V. SANCHEZ-GIRON and J. HERNANZ. 1984. The influence of direct drilling on the weed flora of cereal crops in central Spain. *Proc. 7th Intern. Colloquium on Weed Ecol., Biol., Systematics,* Paris, 7(1):431–436.

FERRARI, C. M. SPERANZA and P. CATIZONE. 1984. Weeds and crop management in north Italy. *Proc. 7th Intern. Colloquium on Weed Ecol., Biol., Systematics,* Paris, 7(1):411–420.

FERREN, W. 1973. Range extension of *Sagittaria montevidensis* in the Delaware River system. *Bartonia* 42:1–4.

FERREYA, R. 1970. *Flora invasora de los cultivos de Pucallpa y Tingo Maria.* National Major Univ. San Marcos. Lima, Peru. 265pp.

FIALA, K. 1971. Seasonal changes in the growth of clones of *Typha latifolia* in natural conditions. *Folia Geobotan. Phytotaxon.* 6:255–270.

————. 1978. Underground organs of *Typha angustifolia* and *T. latifolia,* their growth, propagation and production. *Acta Scientiarum Naturalium Acad. Scientarium Bohemoslovacae Brno* 12:3–46.

FIENNES, R. 1940. Grasses as weeds of pasture land in northern Uganda. *E. African Agric. J.* 5:255–258.

FILBIN, G. and R. HOUGH. 1985. Photosynthesis, photorespiration and productivity in *Lemna minor* L. *Limnol. Oceanogr.* 30:322–334.

FINLAYSON, C. 1980. *Aspects of the hydrobiology of the Leichhardt River–Lake Moondarra water supply system, Mount Isa* (Australia). PhD Diss., Mount Cook Univ. of North Queensland, Australia. p. 161.

FISCHER, M. 1987. On the origin of *Veronica persica*—a contribution to the history of a neophytic weed. *Plant Syst. and Evol.* 155:109–132.

FISCHER, R. 1963. A study of wheat crop physiology in relation to time of sowing, rate of sowing and fertilizer application. Master of Agricultral Science Thesis, University of Melbourne, Australia.

FISH, G. and G. WILL. 1966. Fluctuations in the chemical composition of the lake weeds from New Zealand. *Weed Res.* 6:346–349.

FISHER, D. 1982. Studies in the leaf of *Amaranthus retroflexus*. *Diss. Abstr. Intern. B* 42(7):2671.

FITTER, A. and C. ASHMORE. 1974. Response of two *Veronica* species to a simulated woodland light climate. *New Phytol.* 73:997–1001.

FLETCHER, R. and D. OSBORNE. 1966. Gibberellin, as a regulator of protein and ribonucleic acid synthesis during senescence in leaf cells of *Taraxacum officinale*. *Can. J. Bot.* 44:739–749.

FLETCHER, R., T. ODGEMA and R. HORTON. 1969. Endogenous gibberellin levels and senescence in *T. officinale*. *Planta* 86:98–102.

FLETCHER, W. and R. KIRKWOOD. 1979. The bracken fern *Pteridium aquilinum*; its biology and control. In: *Experimental biology of ferns*. Ed. by A. Dyer. Academic Press, N.Y.

FLUNKER, L., B. DAMRON and S. SUNDLOF. 1987. Jimsonweed seed contamination of broiler chick and white leghorn hen diets. *Nutrition Rep. Intern.* 36:551–556.

FOGELFORS, H. 1972. The development of some weed species under different light conditions and their competition ability in barley. *Proc. 13th Swedish Weed Conf.* 13(1):F4–5.

FOGG, G. 1950. Biological flora of the British Isles. *Sinapis arvensis* L. *J. of Ecol.* 38:415–429.

FORCELLA, F. 1985. Final distribution is related to rate of spread in alien weeds. *Weed Res.* 25:181–191.

FORCELLA, F. and S. HARVEY. 1988. Patterns of weed migration in northwestern United States. *Weed Sci.* 36:194–201.

FORCELLA, F. and H. WOOD. 1986a. Demography and control of *Cirsium vulgare* in relation to grazing. *Weed Res.* 26:199–206.

———. 1986b. Sequential flowering of thistles **Cynareae, Asteraceae** in southern Australia. *Aus. J. Bot.* 34:455–461.

FORD, H. 1981a. The demography of three populations of dandelion. *Biol. J. Linn. Soc.* 15:1–11.

———. 1981b. Competitive relationships amongst apomictic dandelion. *Biol. J. Linn. Soc.* 15:355–368.

FOREST, H. 1977. Study on submerged vascular plants in northern glacial lakes (New York State, United States). *Folia Geobot. Phytotaxon.*, Prague, 12:329–341.

FORSBERG, B. and C. FORSBERG. 1961. The freshwater environment for *Najas marina* in Scandinavia. *Svensk Botanisk Tidskrift* 55(4):604–612.

FORSBERG, C. 1965. Sterile germination of oospores of *Chara* and seeds of *Najas marina*. *Physiologia Plantarum* 18(1):128–137.

FORSYTH, C. and J. VAN STADEN. 1983. Germination of *Tagetes minuta* L. I. Temperature effects. *Ann. Bot.* 52:659–666.

FOTEDAR, J. and S. ROY. 1972. Cytotaxonomy of **Najadaceae**. *Plant Sci.*, (Lucknow) 4:21–24.

FOY, C., R. JAIN and R. JASCOBSOHN. 1989. Recent approaches for chemical control of broomrape *Orobanche* spp. In: *Reviews Weed Sci.* 4:123–152.

FRANCOIS, L. 1930. Recherches de geographie botanique sur le genre *Cuscuta*. *Ann. Sci. Agronomiques* 47:57–68.

FRANCOIS, M. 1951. *Decors exotiques et plants d' aquariums*. M. Francois, Argentuil, France.

FRANKLAND, B. 1976. Phytochrome control of seed germination in relation to the light environment. In: *Light and plant development*. pp. 477–491. Ed. by H. Smith. Butterworths, London.

FRANKLAND, J. 1976. Decomposition of bracken litter. *Bot. J. Linn. Soc.* 73:133–143.

FRATIANNE, D. 1965. The interrelationship between the flowering of dodder and the flowering of some long and short day plants. *Am. J. Bot.* 52:556–562.

FRAZEE, R. and E. STOLLER. 1974. Differential growth of corn, soybeans, and seven dicotyledonous weed seedlings. *Weed Sci.* 22:336–339.

FRAZIER, J. 1943. Nature and rate of development of the root system of *Lepidium draba*. *Bot. Gaz.* 105:244–248.

FREE, J. 1968. Dandelion *Taraxacum officinale* as a competitor to fruit trees for bee visits. *J. Appl. Ecol.* 5:169–178.

FREEMAN, J. and R. SIGAFUS. 1966. Life cycle study of red sorrel *Rumex acetosella*. *Abstr. 6th Weed Sci. Soc. Am. Conf.* 6: No. 60.

FREITAS-SACCHET, A., I. BOLDRINI and G. BORN. 1984. Cytogenetics and evolution of the native grasses of Rio Grande do Sul Brazil *Setaria* Beauv. *Revista Brasil Genetica* 7:535–548.

FRICK, H. 1985. Micronutrient tolerance and accumulation in the duckweed *Lemna*. *J. Plant Nutrition* 8:1131–1145.

FRICK, H. and H. MOHR. 1973. Phytochrome mediated

growth responses in green and etiolated *Lemna minor.* *Planta* 109:281–292.

FRIDRIKSSON, S. 1989. The volcanic island of Surtsey, Iceland, a quarter-century after it "rose from the sea." *Environ. Conserv.* 16:157–162.

FRIEND, D. 1968. Spectral requirements for flower initiation in two long-day plants, rape *Brassica campestris* cv. *ceres,* and spring wheat *Triticum aestivum. Physiologia Plantarum* 21:1185–1195.

———. 1969. *Brassica campestris* L. In: *The induction of flowering, some case histories.* pp. 364–375. Ed. by L. Evans. Cornell Univ. Press; Ithaca, N.Y.

FRIESEN, G. and L. SHEBESKI. 1960. Economic losses caused by weed competition in Manitoba grain fields. I. Weed species, their relative abundance and their effect on crop yields. *Can. J. Plant Sci.* 40:457–467.

FRIESEN, G., L. SHEBESKI and A. ROBINSON. 1960. Economic losses caused by weed competition in Manitoba grain fields. II. Effect of weed competition on protein content of cereal crops. *Can. J. Plant Sci.* 40:652–658.

FROHLICH, G. and W. RODEWALD. 1970. *Enfermedades y plagas de las plantas tropicales.* Offizin Andersen Nexo, Leipzig.

FROHNE, D. and H. PFANDER. 1984. *A colour atlas of poisonous plants.* Wolfe Publ. Ltd.; Stuttgart, Germany.

FROLISEK, M. 1987. Results of our studies on dodder *Cuscuta* spp. control in lucerne *Medicago sativa.* pp. 231–240. *Proc. 4th Intern. Symp. Parasitic Flowering Plants,* Marburg, Germany.

FROST, R. 1971. *Aspects of the comparative biology of the three weedy species of Amaranthus in southwestern Ontario.* Ph.D. Diss., Univ. Western Ontario; London, Ontario, Canada. 443pp.

FROUD-WILLIAMS, R. 1981. Germination behavior of *Bromus* species and *Alopecurus myosuroides. Proc. Grass Weeds in Cereals United Kingdom Conf.*: 31–40. Assoc. Appl. Biologists. Reading.

FROUD-WILLIAMS, R. and R. CHANCELLOR. 1982. A survey of grass weeds in cereals in central southern England. *Weed Res.* 22:163–171.

FROUD-WILLIAMS, R., R. CHANCELLOR and D. DRENNAN. 1984a. The effect of seed burial and soil disturbance on emergence and survival of arable weeds in relation to minimal cultivation. *J. Appl. Ecol.* 21:629–641.

FROUD-WILLIAMS, R., D. DRENNAN and R. CHANCELLOR. 1984b. The influence of burial and dry-storage upon cyclic change in dormancy, germination, and response to light in seeds of various arable weeds. *New Phytol.* 96:473–481.

FRYER, A. 1887. Notes on pondweeds. *J. Bot.,* London, 25:306–310.

FRYER, J. and R. CHANCELLOR. 1970. Herbicides and our changing weeds. *Bot. Soc. Brit. Isles Rep. No. 11*: 105–118.

FRYER, J. and K. KIRKLAND. 1970. Field experiments to investigate the long-term effects of repeated applications of MCPA, tri-allate, simazine and linuron: Report after 6 years. *Weed Res.* 10:133–158.

FUJII, T. 1962. Studies on the photoperiodic responses involved in the germination of *Eragrostis* seeds. *Bot. Mag.,* Tokyo, 75:56–62.

———. 1963a. Inhibitory effect of 5–bromouracil in photoperiodically induced germination of *Eragrostis* seed. *Plant and Cell Physiol.* 4:277–283.

———. 1963b. On the anaerobic process involved in the photoperiodically induced germination of *Eragrostis* seed. *Plant and Cell Physiol.* 6:357–359.

FUJII, T. and Y. YOKAHAMA. 1965. Physiology of light-requiring germination in *Eragrostis* seeds. *Plant and Cell Physiol.* 6:135–145.

FUNKE, G. 1937. Observations on the growth of water plants. *Biologisch Jaarboek* 4:316–344.

FURNKRANZ, D. 1966. Investigations of populations of the *Taraxacum officinale* complex in the contact area of diploid and polyploid biotypes. *Oesterreichische Botanische Zeitschrift* 113:427–447.

FYKSE, H. 1974. Research on *Sonchus arvensis* L.: I. Translocation of C^{14}–labeled assimilates. *Weed Res.* 14:305–312.

———. 1977. Research on *Sonchus arvensis* L., *Cirsium arvense* (L.) Scop. and *Tussilago farfara* L. Translocation of radioactive labeled carbohydrates and MCPA. *Meldinger fra Norgas Landburkshogskole* 56:1–22.

GACUTAN, A. 1979. Some factors affecting the germination of *Ipomoea triloba.* pp. 100–105. *Weed Sci. Rep., Dept. Agron., Univ. Philippines.* Los Banos.

GAERTNER, E. 1950. *Studies of seed germination, seed identification, and host relationships in dodders Cuscuta spp.* Cornell Agric. Exp. Sta. Memoir 294. 56pp.

GAFFER, M. 1981. Perennial weeds in the major crop fields of Bangladesh. *Proc. 8th Asian-Pacific Weed Sci. Soc. Conf.* 8:63–66.

GALE, W. and H. MOHR. 1976. Fish spawning in a large Pennsylvania river receiving mine effluents. *Proc. Pennsylvania Acad. Sci.* 50:160–162.

GALIL, J. and M. ZERONI. 1965. Nectar system of *Asclepias curassavica. Bot. Gaz.* 126:144–148.

GALLAHER, R., D. ASHLEY and R. BROWN. 1975. C^{14}–photosynthate translocation in C_3 and C_4 plants as related to leaf anatomy. *Crop Sci.* 15:55–59.

GALPIN, O. and R. SMITH. 1986. Bracken, stomach cancer and water supplies: is there a link. In: *Bracken, ecology, land use and control technology.* Ed. by R. Smith and J. Taylor. Parthenon Publ., Carnforth, Eng.

GALSTON, A. 1975. The water fern-rice connection. *Natural History Mag.* 84:10–11.

GAMOR, F. 1988. Dynamics of segetal vegetation of the

Ukranian Carpathians. *Ukrainskii Botanichii Zhurnal* 45:32–36.

GANGSTAD, E. and S. SOLYMOSY. 1973. *Control of alligatorweed in Louisiana and the Gulf Coast area.* United States Army Engineers Waterways Exp. Sta. Tech. Rep. No. 3, A3–A23.

GARBUTT, K. and J. WITCOMBE. 1986. The inheritance of seed dormancy in *Sinapis arvensis. Heredity* 56:25–31.

GARCIA-NOVO, F. and R. CRAWFORD. 1973. Soil aeration, nitrate reduction, and flooding tolerance in higher plants. *New Phytol.* 72:1031–1039.

GARDNER, W. 1921. Effect of light on germination of light sensitive seeds. *Bot. Gaz.* 71:249–288.

GARG, S., V. MATHU and R. CHAUDHURY. 1978. Screening of Indian plants for antifertility activity. *Ind. J. Exp. Bio.* 16:1077–1079.

GARMAN, H. 1903. The broomrapes. *Kentucky Agric. Exp. Sta. Bull.* 105:1–32.

GARVER, E., D. DUBBE and D. PRATT. 1988. Seasonal patterns in accumulation and partitioning of biomass and macronutrients in *Typha* spp. *Aquatic Bot.* 32:115–127.

GAST, M., F. GAUDIN-HARDING and M. OULD-AOUDIA. 1972. Cereals and pseudo-cereals harvested in central Sahara (Ahaggar): I. Uses and food values of some seeds from central Sahara. II. Analysis of some seeds from the Ahaggar region. *J. Agric. Trop. Bot. Appliquee* 19:50–58.

GAUR, Y. 1980. Nodulation studies in species of genus *Cassia. Zentralblatt Bakteriol Hyg. Abstr.* 135:201–204.

GAWLINSKI, S. 1963. Phosphorous uptake from fertilizers by weeds and culture plants. *Roczniki Gleboznawcze* 13:469–489.

GAYNOR, D. and L. MAC CARTER. 1981. Biology, ecology and control of gorse. *New Zealand J. Agric. Res.* 24:123–137.

GEORGE, J., K. HUTCHINSON and B. MOTTERSHEAD. 1970. Spear thistle *Cirsium vulgare* invasion of grazed pastures. *Proc. 11th Intern. Grassland Conf.*, Australia, 11:685–688.

GERLOFF, G. and P. KROMBHOLZ. 1966. Tissue analysis as a measure of nutrient availability for growth of angiosperm aquatic plants. *Limnol. and Oceanog.* 11:529–537.

GERRETSEN, F. and N. HAAGSMA. 1951. Occurrence of antifungal substances in *Brassica rapa, Brassica oleracea* and *Beta vulgaris. Nature* 168:659.

GHOBRIAL, G. 1981. Weed control in irrigated dry seeded rice. *Weed Res.* 21:201–204.

GHOSH, A., D. KIM and S. DE DATTA. 1971. Germination, growth rate, and control of the perennial sedge, *Scirpus maritimus,* in tropical rice. *Proc. 3rd Asian-Pacific Weed Sci. Soc. Conf.* 3, Volume 2:249–256.

GHOSH, C. and R. DATTA. 1975. Seed morphology of *Corchorus* species. *Seed res.* 3:119–122.

GHOSH, S. and P. BASU. 1983. Hormonal regulation of sex expression in *Momordica charantia. Physiologia Plantarum* 57:301–305.

GIDNAVAR, V. 1980. Portulace, a salt loving weed in salt-affected areas of Ghataprabha project. *Abstr. Ind. Weed Sci. Res.* 1982 No. 181.

GIER, L. and R. BURRESS. 1942. Anatomy of *Taraxacum officinale* Weber. *Trans. Kansas Acad. Sci.* 45:94–97.

GIFFORD, E. and P. RONDET. 1965. Cytohistological studies of the apical meristem of *Amaranthus retroflexus* under various photoperiodic regimes. *Bot. Gaz.* 126:248–298.

GILBERT, B. and F. PEMBER. 1935. Tolerance of certain weeds and grasses to toxic aluminum. *Soil Sci.* 39:425–429.

GILES, B. 1984. A comparison between quantitative and biochemical variation in the wild barley *Hordeum murinum. Evol.* 38:34–39.

GILES, B. and L. LEFKOVITCH. 1986. Taxonomic investigation of the *Hordeum murinum* complex. *Plant Systematics and Evol.* 153:181–197.

GILES, F., S. MIDDLETON and J. GRAU. 1973. Evidence for the accumulation of atmospheric lead by insects in areas of high traffic density. *Environ. Entomol.* 2:299–300.

GILL, L. 1969. A note on the cytomorphology of *Taraxacum officinale* complex. *Bull. Bot. Survey Ind.* 11:204–205.

GILL, N. 1938. The viability of weed seeds at various stages of maturity. *Ann. Appl. Biol.* 25(1):447–456.

GILLILAND, H. 1971. *Flora of Malaya.* Vol. 3, *Grasses.* Government Printing Office, Singapore.

GILLY, C. 1941. The status of *Eleocharis parvula* var. *anachaeta* (Torr.) Svenson. *Am. Midland Naturalist* 26:65–68.

GINZO, H. and P. LOVELL. 1973a. Aspects of the comparative physiology of *Ranunculus bulbosus* L. and *R. repens* L. I. Response to nitrogen. *Ann. Bot.* 37:753–764.

———. 1973b. Aspects of the comparative physiology of *Ranunculus bulbosus* L. and *R. repens* L. II. Carbon dioxide assimilation and distribution of photosynthesis. *Ann. Bot.* 37:765–776.

GLANDON, R. and C. MCNABB. 1978. The uptake of boron by *Lemna minor. Aquatic Bot.* 4:53–64.

GLASS, E. 1971. *Plant protection problems in Southeast Asia.* pp. 66–76. Cornell Univ. Rep. of E. Asian Pest Mgmt. Study Team, on contract AID/csd-3296, United States Dept. of Agriculture, Washington, D.C.

GLICK, P. 1939. *Distribution of insects, spiders and mites in the air.* USDA Tech. Bull. 673. 132pp.

GLIESSMAN, S. 1976. Allelopathy in a broad spectrum of environments as illustrated by bracken. *Bot. J. Linn. Soc.* 73:95–104.

GLIESSMAN, S. and C. MULLER. 1978. The allelopathic mechanisms of dominance in bracken in southern California. *J. Chem. Ecol.* 4:337–362.

GLUCK, H. 1906. Die Turionen von *Potamogeton crispus.* pp.

151–158. In: *Biologische und morphologische Unter-suchungen uber Wasser und Sumpfgewachse.* Gustav Fish-er Verlag, Jena.

GLUE, D. and L. MATTHEWS. 1957. Weed identification, *Silybum marianum. New Zealand J. Agric.* 95:547.

GODFREY, G. 1935. Hitherto unreported hosts of the root-knot nematode. *Plant Dis. Rep.* 19:29–31.

GODFREY, R. and J. WOOTEN. 1979. *Aquatic and wetland plants of southeastern United States: Monocotyledons.* Univ. Georgia Press; Athens, Georgia. 712pp.

GODSHALK, G. and R. WETZEL. 1976. Decomposition of macrophytes and the metabolism of organic matter in sediments and freshwater. In: *Interactions between sedi-ments and freshwater.* pp. 284–264. Dr. W. Junk Publ., The Hague.

GOEDON, R. and D. RICKER. 1980. Mortality of *Rhinocyllus conicus* in milk thistle flowerheads in southern California, United States. *Prot. Ecol.* 2:47–56.

GOFF, L. and A. COLEMAN. 1984. A new regulatory mecha-nism of parasitism. *Proc. Nat. Acad. Sci.* 81:5420. (USA).

GOLD, A., J. SAGEN and S. WILHELM. 1979. California soils suppressive to branched broomrape. *Proc. Suppl. 2nd In-tern. Symp. Parasitic Weeds* 2:1. Ed. by L. Musselman, A. Worsham and R. Eplee. North Carolina State Univ.; Raleigh, USA.

GOLOVA, T. 1967. Determination of dodders by their seeds. *Byulleten Moskovskogo Obshchestva Ispytatelei Pirody Otdel Biologicheskii* 72:67–80.

GOLUBIC, S. 1961. "Seeballe"-ein seltsamer standort der blaualgen ("Seaballs" a rare location for blue-green algae). *Hydrobiologia* 18:109–120.

———. 1963. Hydrostatischer druck light und submerse veg-etation im Vranasee. *Intern. Rev. Gesamten Hydrobiol* 48:1–7.

GOMEZ, A. and H. RIVERA. 1987. Descripcion de malezas en plantaciones de cafe. Cenicafe, Chinchina, Colombia.

GOMEZ, M. 1981. Carotene content of some green leafy veg-etables of Kenya and effects of dehydration and storage on carotene retention. *J. Plant Foods* 3:231–244.

GONZALEZ, A. and A. RODRIGUEZ. 1981. Life cycle of *Orobanche ramosa* in 2 soils and at different dates. *Jor-nado Cientifico Tecnico Sunidad Vegetal*: 21. Villa Clara, Cuba.

GOOD, J., N. MINTON and C. JAWORSKI. 1965. Relative susceptibility of selected cover crops and coastal bermu-da grass to plant nematodes. *Phytopathology.* 55:1026–1030.

GOOD, R. 1964. *The geography of flowering plants.* Longmans, Green & Co., London. 518pp.

GOODWIN, M., I. MORRISON and A. THOMAS. 1986. A weed survey of pedigreed alfalfa seed fields in Manitoba. *Can. J. Plant Sci.* 66:413–416.

GOPAL, B. 1967. Contribution of *Azolla pinnata* R.Br. to the

productivity of temporary ponds at Varanashi. *Trop. Ecol.* 8:126–130.

———. 1968. Ecological studies on the genus *Marsilea.* I. Water relations. *Trop. Ecol.* 9:153–170.

———. 1969a. Ecological studies on the genus *Marsilea.* II. Edaphic factors. *Trop. Ecol.* 10:278–291.

———. 1969b. Responses of some Indian species of *Marsilea* to different temperature treatments. *Am. Fern J.* 59:150–152.

GORINI, F. 1982. Vegetable schedules. 2. Leafy vegetables 2.46. Dandelions. *Informator di Ortoflorofrutticoltura* 23:7–9.

GORSKI, T. 1975. Germination of seeds in the shadow of plants. *Physiologia Plantarum* 34:342–346.

GORTNER, R. 1934. Lake vegetation as a possible source of forage. *Sci.* 80:531–533.

GOSS, W. and E. BROWN. 1939. Buried red rice seed. *J. Am. Soc. Agron.* 31:633–637.

GOSWAMI, N. and J. SAHA. 1969. Radiophosphorus tracing of the rooting pattern of jute. *J. Ind. Soc. Soil Sci.* 17:507–514.

GOTTLIEB, J. 1958. Development of bracken fern *Pteridium aquilinum.* I. General morphology of the sporeling. *Phy-tomorphol.* 8:184–194.

GOTTLIEB, J. and T. STEEVES. 1961. Development of the bracken fern. III. Ontogenetic changes in the shoot apex and in the pattern of differentiation. *Phytomorphology* 11:230–242.

GOUDEY, J., H. SAINI and M. SPENCER. 1988. Role of ni-trate in regulating germination of *Sinapis arvensis* L. wild mustard. *Plant Cell Environ.* 11:9–12.

GOVINDARAJALU, E. 1974. The systematic anatomy of south Indian **Cyperaceae**, *Eleocharis rynchospora* and *scleria. Adansonia* 14(4):581–632.

———. 1976. The systematic anatomy of south Indian **Cyper-aceae**, *Scirpus. Adansonia* Series 2, 16(1):13–38.

GRACE, J. 1983. Autotoxic inhibition of seed germination by *Typha latifolia*: An evaluation. *Oecologia* 59:366–369.

GRACE, J. and R. WETZEL. 1978. The production biology of Eurasian milfoil *Myriophyllum spicatum*: A review. *J. Aquat. Plant Mgmt.* 16:1–11.

———. 1981a. Habitat partitioning and competitive dis-placement in cattails *Typha*: Experimental field studies. *Am. Naturalist* 118:463–474.

———. 1981b. Effects of size and growth rate on vegetative re-production in *Typha. Oecologia,* Berlin, 50:158–161.

———. 1982. Niche differentiation between two rhizoma-tous plant species: *Typha latifolia* and *T. angustifolia. Can. J. Bot.* 60:46–57.

GRAHAM, M., and J. SCHOOLEY. 1985. Toxicity of *Myrio-phyllum* and *Potamogeton* to mosquito larvae. p. 141. In: *Proc. 52nd Ann. Conf. Calif. Mosquito and Vector Control Assn.* (1984).

GRANSTROM, B. 1959. Studies on the competition between weeds and cultivated plants. *Vaxtodling, Plant Husbandry* 10:11–21.

GRANT-LIPP, A. 1966. Some properties of the seeds of skeleton weeds *Chondrilla juncea* L. *CSIRO Field Sta. Rec.* 5:17–24.

GRAW, D. 1979. The influence of soil *pH* on the efficiency of vesicular-arbuscular mycorrhiza. *New Phytol.* 82:687–695.

GRAY, D. 1979. The germination response to temperature of carrot seeds from different umbels and times of harvest of the seed crop. *Seed Sci. Technol.* 7:169–178.

GRAY, E., E. MCGEHEE and D. CARLISLE. 1973. Seasonal variation in flowering of common dandelion. *Weed Sci.* 21:230–232.

GRECHKANEV, O. and V. RODIONOV. 1971. *Heliotropium europaeum* in allelopathy. In: *Biochemical and physiological bases for plant interactions in phytocenosis*. Ed. by A. Grozinsky. Naukova Dunka Press, Kiev. 2:94–100.

GREEN, D. 1963. Further simple experiments on the greenhouse germination of some east African weed species. *PANS (Pest Articles and News Summaries)* 9:43–46.

GREEN, D. and B. KALOGERIS. 1967. A screening trial of herbicides in cotton, 1965. *PANS (Pest Articles and News Summaries)* 13:133–138.

GREENHAM, C., V. HULL and M. WARD. 1972. Electrical characteristics as discriminant criteria for three forms of skeleton weed *Chondrilla juncea*. *J. Exp. Bot.* 23:210–215.

GREGG, W. 1973. Ecology of the annual grass *Setaria lutescens* on old fields of the Pennsylvania Piedmont. *Proc. Nat. Acad. Natural Sci. Philadelphia* 124:135–196.

GREIG-SMITH, P. 1948. Biological flora of the British Isles. *J. Ecol.* 36:339–355.

GRESSEL, J. 1979. Genetic herbicide resistance; projections on appearance in weeds and breeding for it in crops. In: *Plant regulation and world agriculture*. Ed. by T. Scot. Plenum Press.

———. 1989. Prevention and management of herbicide resistance: Theoretical aspects. In: Herbicide resistance symp., *Abstr. 37th Weed Sci. Soc. Am. Conf.* 37: No. 302.

GRESSEL, J. and L. HOLM. 1964. Chemical inhibition of crop germination by weed seeds and the nature of inhibition by *Abutilon theophrasti*. *Weed Res.* 4:44–53.

GRIGNAC, P. 1978. The evolution of resistance to herbicides in weedy species. *Agro-Ecosystems* 4:377–385.

GRIME, J. and R. HUNT. 1975. Relative growth rate: Its range and adaptive significance in local flora. *J. Ecol.* 63:393–422.

GRIST, D. 1975. *Rice*. Longmans, Green and Co. Ltd., London.

GROH, H. and C. FRANKTON. 1949. *Canadian weed survey, 7th Report 1948*. Dominion of Canada, Dept. of Agriculture, Ottawa.

GROSS, K. 1981. Predictions of fate from rosette size in four "biennial" plant species: *Verbascum thapus, Oenothera biennis, Daucus carota,* and *Tragopogon dubius. Oecologia* 48:209–213.

———. 1984. Effects of seed size and growth form on seedling establishment of six monocarpic perennial plants. *J. Ecol.* 72:369–387.

GROSS, K. and P. WERNER. 1982. Colonizing abilities of "biennial" plant species in relationship to ground cover: Implications for their distributions in a successional sere. *Ecol.* 63:921–931.

GROVES, R. and V. HULL. 1970. Variation in density and cover of *Chondrilla juncea* L. in southeastern Australia. *CSIRO Field Station Record* 9:57–71.

GROVES, R. and P. KAYE. 1989. Germination and phenology of seven introduced thistle species in southern Australia. *Aus. J. Bot.* 37:351–359.

GROVES, R. and J. WILLIAMS. 1975. Growth of skeleton weed *Chondrilla juncea* L. as affected by growth of subterranean clover *Trifolium subterraneum* L. and infection by *Puccinia chondrillina* Bubak & Syd. *Aus. J. Agric. Res.* 26:257–263.

GRUZDEV, G., and N. PRISHCHEPO. 1984. Seed viability of *Cuscuta campestris* under natural and laboratory conditions. *Izvestiia Timiriazevskaia Sel'skokhoziaistvennaia Akad.* 4:174–176.

GRUZDEV, G. and A. TULIKOV. 1966. Peculiarities of vegetative reproduction of yellow sowthistle *Sonchus arvensis* and creeping thistle *Cirsium setosum* M.B. *Izvestiia Timiriazevskaia Sel'skokhoziaistvennaia Akad.* 1966(6):83–95.

GUANTES, M. and B. MERCADO. 1975. Competition of *Cyperus rotundus, Echinochloa colonum* and *Trianthema portulacastrum* with cotton. *Philipp. Agric.* 59:167–177.

GUETTARD, J. 1744. Memoire sur l'adherence de la *Cuscute* aux autres plantes. pp. 170–190. *Histoire Acad. Royale Sci.* Paris. Seen in Kuijt, J. 1969.

GUGNANI, D., S. BANENJEE and D. SINGH. 1975. Germination capacity in relation to seed coat color in cabbage and mustard. *Seed Sci. Technol.* 3:575–579.

GUILLARMOD, A. 1979. *Myriophyllum* in southern Africa. *Proc. 3rd National Weeds Conf. South Africa* 3:141–149.

GUILLEMENT, R. 1972. Studies on the competition between blackgrass and soft winter wheat. *Phytoma* 24:9–12.

GUILLERM, J. and J. MAILLET. 1982. Western Mediterranean countries of Europe. Chapter 20 in: *Biology and ecology of weeds*. Ed. by W. Holzner and M. Numata. Dr. W. Junk Publ., The Hague.

GUMMESSON, G. 1979. Changes in weed species composition in 1952–1977. In: Weeds and weed control, *Proc. 20th Swedish Weed Conf.* 20:173–178.

GUNASEKERA, S., G. CORDELLAND and N. FANSWORTH.

1981. Plant anti-cancer agents. 20 Constituents of *Nicandra physalodes*. *Planta Medica* 43(4):389–391.

GUNCAN, A. 1982. Artemisia vulgaris: *Its biology and control in tea and hazelnut plantations in Turkey.* Ataturk Univ. Proj. No. TOAG-276. 45pp.

GUNN, C. and C. RITCHIE. 1988. *Identification of disseminules listed in the Federal Noxious Weed Law.* USDA Tech. Bull. 1719. Washington, D.C.

GUNNING. B. 1966. Grazing management for control of barley grass. *Proc. 19th New Zealand Weed and Pest Control Conf.* 19:127–130.

GUNSTONE, F., S. STEWARD, J. CORNELIUS and T. HAMMONDS. 1972. New tropical seed oils. *J. Sci. Food Agric.* 23:53–60.

GUPPY, H. 1893. The river Thames as an agent in plant dispersal. *Bot. J. Linn. Soc.* 29:333–346.

———. 1894. On the habits of *Lemna minor, L. gibba* and *L. polyrhiza*. *Bot. J. Linn. Soc.* 30:323–330.

———. 1894–1897. *Germination of seeds of aquatic plants.* Proc. Royal Physical Soc., Edinburgh. 13:344–360.

———. 1897. On the postponement of the germination of seeds of aquatic plants. *Proc. Royal Physical Soc. Edinburgh* 13:344–360.

———. 1906. Observations of a naturalist in the Pacific between 1896 and 1899. *Plant Dispersal*, Vol. 2. Macmillan, London.

GUPTA, B., K. NANDRA, I. THIND and A. CHOPRA. 1982. Chemical composition and *in vitro* dry matter digestibility of *Poa annua* L. at five stages of growth. *J. Res. Punjab Agric. Univ.* 19:270–272.

GUPTA, D. and S. MUKHERJEE. 1973. Seed polysaccharide of *Cassia occidentalis* L. *Ind. J. Chem.* 11:505–506.

GUPTA, K. 1962. *Marsilea.* Council Scientific and Industrial Res., Bot. Monograph No. 2; New Delhi. 113pp.

GUPTA, R., Y. GAUR, S. MALHORCA and B. DUTTA. 1966. Medicinal plants of the Indian arid zone. *J. Agric. Trop. Bot. Appl.* 13:247–288.

GUPTA, S. and K. DARGAN. 1970. Water requirements of white jute *Corchorus capsularis* and tossa jute *C. olitorius*. *Ind. J. Agric. Sci.* 40:505–511.

GUPTA, S., A. BHAGWAT and A. RAM. 1972. Cardiac stimulant activity of the saponin of *Achyranthes aspera* L. *Ind. J. Medical Res.* 60:462–471.

GUSEV, Y. 1972. Review of the genus *Amaranthus* in the USSR. *Botanicheskii Zhurnal* 57:457–464.

GUSTAVSSON, A. 1989. Growth of annual dicotyledonous weeds. *Crop Produc. Sci.* 5:1–106.

GUTHRIE, R. and D. CHERRY. 1979. The uptake of chemical elements from coal ash and settling basin effluent by primary producers: Relative concentrations in predominant plants. pp. 217–222. In: *The science of total environment.* Elsevier Sci. Publ., Amsterdam.

GUTTERMAN, Y. 1972. *Seed ecology.* Butterworths, London.

HAAG, R. 1979. The ecological significance of dormancy in some rooted aquatic plants. *J. Ecol.* 67:727–738.

HAAG, R. and P. GORHAM. 1977. Effects of thermal effluent on standing crop and net production of *Elodea canadensis* and other submerged macrophytes in Lake Wabamun, Alberta, Canada. *J. Appl. Ecol.* 14:835–852.

HABIB, S. and A. RAHAN. 1988. Evaluation of some weed extracts against field dodder on alfalfa *Medicago sativa*. *J. Chem. Ecol.* 14:443–452.

HABOVSTIAK, J. and A. JAVORKOVA. 1977. The rate of development of some species with increasing altitude. *Vedecke Prace Vyskumneho Ustavu Luk a Pasienkov v Banskej Bystrici* 12:73–82.

HADERLIE, L. and M. MCCARTY. 1980. Musk thistle flower induction. *Proc. 34th North Central Weed Control Conf.* 34:100–101.

HAEGI, L. 1976. A taxonomic account of *Datura* L.: **Solanaceae** in Australia with a note on *Brugmansia* Pers. *Aus. J. Bot.* 24:415–435.

HAFLIGER, E. 1982. *Monocotyledonous weeds.* Vol. 3 of Monocotyledonous weeds excluding grasses. Ed. by E. Hafliger. Documenta, Ciba Geigy, Basel.

HAGOOD, E., T. BAUMAN, J. WILLIAMS and M. SCHREIBER. 1981. Growth analysis of soybean competition with jimsonweed *Datura stramonium*. *Weed Sci.* 29:500–504.

HAIZEL, K. 1972. The productivity of mixtures of two and three species. *J. Appl. Ecol.* 9:601–608.

HAKANSSON, A. 1954. Meiosis and pollen mitosis in x-rayed and untreated spikelets of *Eleocharis palustris*. *Hereditas* 40:325–345.

HAKANSSON, S. 1969. Experiments with *Sonchus arvensis* L.: I. Development and growth, and the response to burial and defoliation in different developmental stages. *Lantbrukshogskolans Annaler* 35:989–1030.

———. 1982. Multiplication, growth, and persistence of perennial weeds. pp. 123–135. Chap. 11 in: *Biology and ecology of weeds.* Ed. by W. Holzner and M. Numata. Dr. W. Junk Publ., The Hague.

———. 1983. Seasonal variation in the emergence of annual weeds, an introductory investigation in Sweden. *Weed Res.* 23(5):313–324.

HAKANSSON, S. and B. WALLGREN. 1972a. Experiments with *Sonchus arvensis* L.: II. Reproduction, plant development and response to mechanical disturbance. *Swedish J. Agric. Res.* 2:3–14.

———. 1972b. Experiments with *Sonchus arvensis* L.: III. The development from reproductive roots cut into different lengths and planted at different depths, with and without competition from barley. *Swedish J. Agric. Res.* 2:15–26.

HALE, M. 1982. Allelopathic potential of *Artemisia vulgaris* rhizomes. *Plant Physiol.* 69:4. (Supplement 23).

HALLER, W. 1974. *Photosynthetic characteristics of the sub-*

mersed aquatic plants Hydrilla, Southern Naiad, and Vallisneria. Ph.D. Diss., Univ. of Florida, Gainesville (USA). 87pp.

————. 1977. *Hydrilla, a new and rapidly spreading aquatic weed problem.* Inst. Food and Agricultural Sci., Circular S-245; Univ. of Florida, Gainesville.

————. 1989. Personal communication regarding use of insects and pathogens for biological control of *Hydrilla.* Univ. of Florida, Gainesville (USA).

HALLER, W., J. MILLER and L. GARRARD. 1976. Seasonal production and germination of *Hydrilla* vegetative propagules. *J. Aquat. Plant Mgmt.* 14:26–29.

HALLER, W. and D. SUTTON. 1975. Community structure and competition between *Hydrilla* and *Vallisneria.* *Hyacinth Control J.* 13:48–50.

HALLER, W., D. SUTTON and W. BARLOWE. 1974. Effects of salinity on growth of several aquatic macrophytes. *Ecology* 55:891–894.

HAMEL, A. and P. DANSEREAU. 1949. L'aspect ecologique du probléme des mauvaises herbes. *Bull. Service Biogeographie, Univ. Montreal* 5:1–41.

HAMMERTON, J. 1962. A preliminary study of the competition between kale and three weed species of the genus *Polygonum.* *Weed Res.* 2:274–282.

————. 1964. Variations in the after-ripening requirement of *Polygonum aviculare* L. seeds. *Proc. 7th Brit. Weed Control Conf.* 7:628–634.

————. 1965. Studies on weed species of the genus *Polygonum* L.: I. Physiological variation within *P. persicaria* L. *Weed Res.* 5:13–26.

————. 1966. Studies on weed species of the genus *Polygonum* L.: III. Variations in susceptibility to 2–(2,4–dichlorophenoxy) propionic acid within *P. lapathifolium.* *Weed Res.* 6:132–141.

————. 1967a. Studies on weed species of the genus *Polygonum* L.: IV. Variations in seed weight and germination behavior in *P. lapathifolium.* *Weed Res.* 7:1–21.

————. 1967b. Studies on weed species of the genus *Polygonum* L.: V. Variations in seed weight, germination behavior and seed polymorphism in *P. persicaria* L. *Weed Res.* 7:331–348.

————. 1969. Intraspecific variations in spray retention. *Weed Res.* 9:154–157.

————. 1989. Personal communication.

HAMMERTON, J. and M. JALLOQ. 1970. Studies on weed species of genus *Polygonum* L.: VI. Environmental effects on seed weight, seed polymorphism and germination behavior in *P. lapathifolium* and *P. persicaria.* *Weed Res.* 10:204–217.

HAMMERTON, J. and M. NUTTALL. 1971. Studies on weed species of the genus *Polygonum* L.: VII. Effects of nutrition and other factors on seed characteristics and germination behavior of *P. lapathifolium.* *Weed Res.* 11:94–98.

HAMOR, F. 1978. Seed productivity of *Setaria glauca* (L.) Beauv. *Ukrains'kii Botanichnii Zhurnal* 35: 489–493.

HAMRICK, J. and J. LEE. 1987. Effect of soil surface topography and litter cover on germination growth and survival of musk thistle *Carduus nutans.* *Am. J. Bot.* 74:451–457.

HANCOCK, J. 1977. Relationship of genetic polymorphism and ecological amplitude in a successional species of *Erigeron.* *Bull. Torrey Bot. Club* 104(3):279–281.

HANF, M. 1983. *The arable weeds of Europe with their seedlings and seeds.* BASF Aktiengesellschaft; Ludwigshafen, Ger. 494pp.

HANNAM, D. 1985. Poisoning in the pig. *Vet. Record* 116:322.

HANSEN, K. 1911. Weeds and their vitality. *Ugeskrift Forlandmaend* 56:149.

HARA, H. 1953. *Ludwigia* versus *Jussiaea.* *J. Jap. Bot.* 28:1–6.

HARADA, H. 1966. Effects of photoperiod on the formation of flower buds by flower stalk sections of *Cichorium intybus* in tissue culture. *Bot. Mag.,* Tokyo, 79:119–123.

HARADA, J. and M. YANO. 1983. Plant growth inhibiting substances contained in **Polygonaceae.** *Proc. 9th Asian-Pacific Weed Sci. Soc. Conf.* 9:71–75.

HARAZTI, E., F. KOVACS and J. BOKORI. 1956. Lovak kiserleti etetese a kompaktban leggyakrebban eloforduló' gyuommagvakkal (I) (Experimental feeding to horses of weed seeds occurring in fodder "kompakt" *Datura stramonium*). *Magyar Allatorvosok Lapja,* Budapest 11:236–241.

HARDCASTLE, W. 1958. A rapid laboratory method of screening herbicides against aquatic plants. *Weeds* 6:64–65.

HARGROVE, T. and T. CHANG. 1978. History of rice offers clues for rewarding germ plasm preservation. *IRRI Reporter* No. 1/78, pp.1–2.

HARLAN, J., J. DEWET and E. PRICE. 1973. Comparative evolution of cereals. *Evolution* 27:311–325.

HARMS, L. 1968. Cytotaxonomic studies in *Eleocharis* subspecies *palustris*: central United States taxa. *Am. J. Bot.* 55:966–974.

HAROLD, R. and J. NALEWAJA. 1977. Proximate mineral and amino acid composition of 15 weed seeds. *J. Animal Sci.* 44:389–394.

HARPER, J. 1957. Flora of the British Isles. *Ranunculus acris* L., *R. repens* L. and *R. bulbosus* L. *J. Ecol.* 45:289–342.

————. 1958. Famous plants 8: The buttercups. *New Biol.* 26:3–19.

————. 1960. Factors controlling plant numbers. In: *The biology of weeds.* Symp. Brit. Ecol. Soc.; Blackwell Scientific Publ., Oxford. pp. 119–132.

————. 1964. The individual in the population. In: *Brit. Ecological Soc. Jubilee Symp.* Ed. by A. MacFayden and P. Newbould.

————. 1966. The reproductive biology of the British poppies.

Reproductive biology and taxonomy of vascular plants. Bot. Soc. Brit. Isles, Rep. No. 9:26–39.

———. 1977. *The population biology of plants.* Academic Press, London.

HARPER, J. and I. MCNAUGHTON. 1960. The inheritance of dormancy in inter- and intraspecific hybrids of *Papaver. Heredity* 15:315–320.

———. 1962. The comparative biology of closely related species living in the same area: VII. Interference between individuals in pure and mixed populations of *Papaver* species. *New Phytol.* 61:175–188.

HARPER, J. and J. OGDEN. 1970. The reproductive strategy of higher plants. I. The concept of strategy with special reference to *Senecio vulgaris. J. Ecol.* 58:681–698.

HARPER, J. and J. WHITE. 1974. The demography of plants. *Ann. Rev. Ecol. Syst.* 5:419–463.

HARPER, R. 1959. Heliotropism in *Sida rhombifolia. J. Alabama Acad. Sci.* 31:179–181.

HARRADINE, A. 1985. Dispersal and establishment of slender thistle *Carduus pycnocephalus* as affected by ground cover. *Aus. J. Agric.* Res. 36:791–797.

HARRINGTON, K., A. POPAY, A. ROBERTSON and H. MCPHERSON. 1988. Resistance of nodding thistle to MCPA in Hawkes Bay. *Proc. 41st New Zealand Weed and Pest Control Conf.* 41:219–222.

HARRIS, G. 1959. The significance of buried weed seeds in agriculture. *Proc. 12th New Zealand Weed and Pest Control Conf.* 12:85–92.

HARRIS, G. 1961. The periodicity of germination in some grass species. *New Zealand J. of Agric. Res.* 4:253–260.

HARRIS, G. and P. LOVELL. 1980a. Growth and reproduction strategies in *Veronica* spp. *Ann. Bot.* 45:447–458.

———. 1980b. Adventitious root formation in *Veronica* spp. *Ann. Bot.* 45:549–568.

———. 1980c. Localized spread of *Veronica filiformis, V. agrestis* and *V. persica. J. Appl. Ecol.* 17:815–826.

HARRIS, P. and A. WILKINSON. 1981. *Cirsium vulgare,* bull thistle **Compositae**. pp. 147–153. In: *Biological control programs against insects and weeds in Canada, 1969–1980.* Ed. by J. Kelleher.

HARRIS, S. 1957. Ecological effects of drawdown operations for the purpose of improving waterfowl habitat. *Diss. Abstr.* 17(9):1857.

HARRIS, W. 1968. *A Study of the variation and ecology of* Rumex acetosella. Ph.D. Diss., Canterbury Univ.; Christchurch, N.Z.

———. 1969a. Environmental effects on the sex ratio of *Rumex acetosella. Proc. New Zealand Ecological Soc.* 15:51–54.

———. 1969b. Seed characters and organ size in the cytotaxonomy of *Rumex acetosella. New Zealand J. Bot.* 7:125–141.

———. 1970a. Genecological aspects of flowering and vege-

tative reproduction in *Rumex acetosella. New Zealand J. Bot.* 8:99–113.

———. 1970b. Yield and habit of New Zealand populations of *Rumex acetosella* at three altitudes in Canterbury. *New Zealand J. Bot.* 8:114–131.

———. 1971. The effects of fertilizer and lime on the competitive interactions of *Rumex acetosella* with *Trifolium repens* and *Lolium* spp. *New Zealand J. Agric. Res.* 14:185–207.

———. 1972. Shading, defoliation, temperature, growth stage and fertility, on competition between *Rumex, Trifolium* and *Lolium. New Zealand J. Agric. Res.* 15:687–705.

HARRISON, R. and H. DALE. 1966. The effect of grazing and clipping on the control of wild carrot. *Weeds* 14:285–288.

HARROLD, R. and J. NALEWAJA. 1977. Proximate, mineral and amino acid composition of 15 weed seeds. *J. Animal Sci.* 44:389–394.

HART, R. 1980. The coexistence of weeds and restricted native plants on serpentine barrens in southeastern Pennsylvania. *Ecol.* 61:688–701.

HARTLEY, J. and I. POPAY. 1982. Lime helps to halt gorse seedling establishment. *New Zealand J. Agric.* 145:19–20.

HARTLEY, M. 1976. The barley grass problem in New Zealand. *Proc. 13th Brit. Weed Control Conf.* 13:575–581.

———. 1983. Effect of Scotch thistle on sheep growth rates. *Proc. 36th New Zealand Weed and Pest Control Soc.* 36:86–88.

HARTLEY, M. and C. ATKINSON. 1972. Effects of chemical removal of barley grass on lamb growth rates. *Proc. 25th New Zealand Weed and Pest Control Conf.* 25:23–28.

HARTLEY, M. and P. THAI. 1979. Effect of pasture species and grazing by sheep on survival of seedling gorse *Ulex europaeus. Proc. 32nd New Zealand Weed and Pest Control Conf.* 32:297–302.

———. 1982. Effects of pasture species, fertilizers, and grazing management on the survival of gorse seedlings. *New Zealand J. Exp. Agric.* 10:193–196.

HARTLEY, M., D. EDMONDS, P. THAI, A. POPAY and P. SANDERS. 1980. Survival of gorse seedlings under grazing, treading and mowing. *Proc. 33th New Zealand Weed and Pest Control Conf.* 33:161–164.

HARTOG, C. DEN and G. VAN DER VELDE. 1986. Invasions of plants and animals into coastal, brackish, and fresh water of the Netherlands. *Proc. Koninklijke Nederlands Akademie van Wetenschappen, Series C: Biological and Medical Sci.* 90:31–37.

HARVEY, B. and D. HARPER. 1982. Tolerance to bipyridylium herbicides. pp. 215–234. In: *Herbicide resistance in plants.* Ed. by H. LeBaron and J. Gressel. John Wiley & Sons, New York.

HARVEY, R. 1930. Tracing the transportation stream with dyes. *Am. J. Bot.* 17:657–661.

HARVEY, R. and J. FOX. 1973. Nutrient removal using *Lemna minor*. *J. Pollution Control Federation* 45:1928–1938.

HASAN, S. 1972. Specificity and host specialization of *Puccinia chondrillina*. *Ann. Appl. Biol.* 72:257–263.

HASAN, S. and A. WAPSHERE. 1973. The biology of *Puccinia chondrillina*, a potential biological control agent of skeleton weed. *Ann. Appl. Biol.* 74:325–332.

HASEEB, A., B. SINGH, A. KAHN and S. SAXENA. 1978. Evaluation of nematicidal property in certain alkaloid-bearing plants. *Geobios* 5:116–118.

HASKOVA, B. and F. SLAVONOVSKY. 1968. Hibernation and vegetative multiplication of *Potamogeton crispus*. *Spisy Prirodovedecke Fakulty Univ. J. Purkyne v Brne* 497:361–367.

HASLAM, S. 1978. *River plants, the macrophytic vegetation of water courses*. Cambridge Univ. Press, Cambridge.

HASSAN, Y., S. EL-HINDAWY, S. BASSIONY and M. ALLA. 1974. *Cassia occidentalis* as coffee substitute in Egypt. *Egy. J. Hortic.* 1:137–143.

HAUSER, W., E. LEGNER, R. MEDVED and S. PLATT. 1976. *Tilapia*: A management tool. *Fisheries*, Calif. USA 1:24.

HAUSER, W., E. LEGNER and F. ROBINSON. 1977. Biological control of aquatic weeds by fish in irrigated channels. pp. 139–145. *Proc. of Conf. on Water Mgmt. for Irrig. and Drainage, ASCE.* Reno, Nevada.

HAWK, W. 1956. Hematuria in dairy heifers probably due to a plant toxin. *J. Am. Vet. Med. Assoc.* 28:261.

HAWTON, D., T. QUINLAN and K. SHAW. 1975. Control of chickweed *Drymaria cordata* in declining tropical pastures. *Trop. Grasslands* 9:229–233.

HAY, J. 1970. Weed control in wheat, oats and barley. In: *FAO Intern. Weed Control Conf.* pp. 38–48. Ed. by J. Holstun, Weed Sci. Soc. Am.; Champaign, Illinois (USA). Held June 1990, Davis, California.

HAYASHI, I. 1984. Secondary succession of herbaceous communities in Japan: seed production of successional dominants. *Jap. J. Ecol.* 34:375–382.

HAYNES, R. 1977. The **Najadaceae** in southeastern United States. *J. Arnold Arboretum* 58:161–170.

HAYWARD, H. 1956. Plant growth under saline conditions. In: *Arid Zone Research. Utilization of Saline Water.* 41–42.

HEARD, A. 1963. Weed populations on arable land after four-course rotations and after short leys. *Ann. Appl. Biol.* 52:177–184.

HEATHER, J., R. MITTAL and C. SIH. 1974. The total synthesis of dl-strigol. *J. Am. Chem. Soc.* 96:1976–1977.

HEFFRON, C., J. REID and W. HASCHEK. 1977. Chemical composition and acceptability of aquatic plants in diets of sheep and pregnant goats. *J. Animal Sci.* 45:1166–1172.

HEGELMAIER, F. 1868. *Die Lemnaceen. Eine monographische untersuchung*. Engelmann, Leipzig.

———. 1871. Ueber die fruktifikationstheile von *Spirodela*. *Botanische Zeitung Jahrgang* 29:621–629, 645–66.

HEIDE-JORGENSEN, H. 1987. Changes in the cuticle structure during development and attachment of the upper haustorium of *Cuscuta*, *Cassytha* and *Viscum*. *4th Intern. Symp. Parasitic Flowering Plants* 4:319–334.

HEILMAN, A. 1960. *Developmental floral and pollen morphology of* Hibiscus trionum L. Ph.D. Diss., Ohio State Univ., Columbus. 80pp.

HEINER, T. 1970. *Competitive ability of 5 populations of* Amaranthus retroflexus. Ph.D. Diss., Iowa State Univ.; Ames, Iowa.

HELDER, R. and M. VAN HARMELEN. 1982. The carbon assimilation pattern in the submerged leaves of the aquatic angiosperm *Vallisneria spiralis*. *Acta Bot. Neerl.* 31(4):281–296.

HELLQUIST, C. 1980. Correlation of alkalinity and the distribution of *Potamogeton* in New England (United States). *Rhodora* 82:331–344.

HELLUM, A. 1964. *Factors influencing frond size of bracken on sandy soils in northern Michigan (United States)*. Univ. Microfilms Inc.; Ann Arbor, Michigan.

HELPERT, C. and E. EASTIN. 1978. Basic red rice research in Texas. pp. 27–29. In: *Red rice: research and control.* Texas Agric. Exp. Sta., Bull. 1270.

HELSEL, D. and A. BAKER. 1989. Biology and control of watermilfoil: An annotated bibliography. *Coll. Agric., Univ. New Hampshire*, Durham, USA.

HENDERSON, J. and S. WELLER. 1985. Biology and control of *Artemisia vulgaris*. *Proc. 40th North Central Weed Control Conf.* 40:100–101.

HENRARD, J. 1950. *Monograph of the genus* Digitaria. Universitaire Pers Leiden, Leiden, Netherlands.

HENRY, W. and T. BAUMAN. 1985. Zone of competitive influence of two large seeded annual broadleaf weeds in soybean. *Proc. 40th North Central Weed Control Conf.* 40:6–7.

HENSON, I. 1969. Studies on the regeneration of perennial weeds in the glasshouse. I. Temperate species. *Temporary Rep., Weed Res. Organization No. 12*; Yarnton, Eng. 23pp.

HENTGES, J., R. SHIRLEY and G. COMBS. 1971. Processed plants for animal nutrition. *Inst. Food and Agric. Sci. Ann. Rep.*; Univ. Florida.

HENTY, B. 1969. A manual of grasses of New Guinea. *Dept. Forestry New Guinea, Bot. Bull.* 1:167–168.

HEPP, F. 1974. Effect of soil loosening of different depths on weediness. *Kerteszeti Egyetem Kozlemenyei* 38:383–392 (Hungary).

HEPPER, F. 1973. Problems in naming *Orobanche* and *Striga*. *Proc. 1st Symp. Parasitic Weeds, European Weed Res. Council*, Malta 1:9–17.

HERNANDEZ, S. 1978. Weeds and their control in Senegal. In: *Weeds and their control in the humid and subhumid tropics.* Ed. by O. Akobundu. Ibadan, Nig.

HERRON, J. 1953. *Study of seed production identification and seed germination of* Chenopodium *spp.* Cornell Univ. Agric. Exp. Sta., Memoir 320.

HETTIARACHCHI, P., and L. TRIEST. 1986. Isozyme polymorphism of *Potamogeton pectinatus.* pp. 163–168. In: *Proc. 7th Int. Symp. Aquat. Weeds* (1986).

HEWSON, R. 1969. Weed competition studies. Page 99 in: *Rep. National Vegetable Res. Sta.*; Wellesbourne, England.

HEWSON, R., H. ROBERTS and W. BOND. 1973. Weed competition in spring-sown broad beans. *Hortic. Res.* 13:25–32.

HEYWOOD, V. 1978. *Flowering plants of the world.* Mayflower Books (Elsevier), N.Y.

HICKS, L. 1932. Flower production in **Lemnaceae**. *Ohio J. of Sci.* 32:115–131.

HIGGINS, J., R. WALKER and T. WHITWELL. 1985. Coffee sena *Cassia obtusifolia* competition with cotton *Gossypium hirsutum. Weed Sci.* 34:52–56.

HILBIG, W. 1982. Mongolia. In: *Biology and ecology of weeds.* pp. 277–279. Ed. by W. Holzner and M. Numata. Dr. W. Junk Publ., The Hague.

———. 1987. Changes in the weed flora in southern part of the German Democratic Republic. *Hercynia* 24:371–384.

HILL, B. 1979. Uptake and release of nutrients by aquatic macrophytes. *Aquat. Bot.* 7:87–93.

———. 1987. *Typha* productivity in a Texas pond: Implications for energy and nutrient dynamics in freshwater wetlands. *Aquatic Bot.* 27:385–394.

HILL, D. 1977. The role of *Anabaena* in the *Azolla-Anabaena* symbiosis. *New Phytol.* 78:611–616.

HILL, J. and E. LORD. 1986. Dynamics of pollen tube growth in wild radish *Raphanus raphanistrum*: I. Order of fertilization. *Evolution* 40:1328–1333.

———. 1987. Dynamics of pollen tube growth in wild radish *Raphanus raphanistrum*: II. Morphology, cytochemistry and ultra structure of transmitting tissues, and path of pollen tube growth. *Am. J. Bot.* 74:988–997.

HILLER, L. and W. KELLY. 1979. The effect of post-vernalization temperature on seedstalk elongation and flowering in carrots. *J. Am. Soc. Hort. Sci.* 104:253–257.

HILLMAN, F. 1897. Nevada weeds: III. Nevada and other weed seeds. *Nevada State Univ. Agric. Exp. Sta., Bull.* No. 38.

HILLMAN, W. 1961. The **Lemnaceae**, or duckweeds. A review of the descriptive and experimental literature. *Bot. Rev.* 27:221–287.

HILLMAN, W. and D. CULLEY. 1978. The uses of duckweed. *Am. Scientist* 66:442–451.

HILTON, J. 1983. Influence of light on the germination of *Senecio vulgaris. New Phytol.* 94:29–37.

HILTON, J. and OWEN, P. 1985. Light and dry storage influences on the respiration of germinating seeds of five species. *New Phytol.* 99:523–531.

HINES, D. 1971. New cytological conditions in *Eleocharis acicularis. Am. J. Bot.* 58:458–460.

HINNERI, S. 1976. On the ecology and phenotypic plasticity of vascular hydrophytes in a sulfate rich, acidotrophic freshwater reservoir, Finland. *Ann. Botanici Fennici* 13:97–105.

HINTIKKA, V. 1988. Induction of secondary dormancy in seeds of *Barbarea stricta* and *B. vulgaris* by chlormequat and daminozide, and its termination by gibberellic acid. *Weed Res.* 28:7–11.

HIRON, R. 1973. An investigation into the processes involved in germination of *Orobanche crenata*, using a new bioassay technique. *Proc. 1st Symp. Parasitic Weeds, European Weed Res. Council,* Malta 1:76–88.

HIRONO, I. 1981. Natural carcinogenic products of plant origin. *Critical Rev. Toxicol.* 8:235–277.

HITROVO, V. 1912. Sur la voilure des organes de propagation des plantes messicoles de niveaux differents. *Angewandte Botanik* 5:103–108. Seen in *Weeds of the world*, by L. King.

HOAGLAND, R. 1978. Isolation and some properties of an aryl acylamidase from red rice, *Oryza sativa* L., that metabolizes 3,4–dichloropropionanilide. *Plant and Cell Physiol.* 19:1019–1027.

HOAGLAND, R. and R. PAUL. 1978. A comparative scanning electron microscope study of red rice and several commercial rice *Oryza sativa* varieties. *Weed Sci.* 26:619–625.

HOCKLEY, J. 1974. And alligator weed spreads in Australia. *Nature,* London, 250:704.

HOCOMBE, S. 1961. Simple experiments on the greenhouse germination of some east African weed species. *Colonial Pesticides Research Unit.* (Arusha, Tanganyika). Miscellaneous Report #285. 8pp.

HODD, T. and P. HODD. 1982. *Grasses of western India.* Bombay Natural History Soc.

HODGE, W. 1956. Chinese water chestnut or matai: A paddy crop of China. *Econ. Bot.* 10:49–65.

HODGE, W. and D. BISSET. 1955. *The Chinese water chestnut.* United States Dept. of Agric. Circular No. 956. 16pp.

HODGSON, A. 1978. Rapeseed adaptation in northern New South Wales, Australia. I. Phenological responses to vernalization temperatures and photoperiod by annual and biennial cultivars of *Brassica campestris, Brassica napus* and wheat. *Aus. J. Agric. Res.* 29:693–710.

HODGSON, G. 1970. Effects of temperature on the growth and development of *Lemna minor*, under conditions of natural daylight. *Ann. Bot.* 34:365–381.

HODGSON, J. 1952. Control of white top *Cardaria draba* by combined chemical, cropping, and tillage methods. *Res. Rep. 13th Western Weed Control Conf.* 13:11.

———. 1955. Whitetop and its control. *Idaho Agric. Exp. Sta. Bull.* No. 243. 18pp.

HODGSON, R. 1966. Growth and carbohydrate status of sago pondweed. *Weed Sci.* 14:263–268.

HODOSY, S. 1981. Biological control of broomrapes, *Orobanche ramosa*, a tomato parasite. I. Occurrence and adaptability of *Fusarium* spp. to control broomrape in Hungary. *Zoldsegtermesztesi Kutato Intezet Bulletinje* 14:21–29.

HOEFERT, L. 1979. Ultrastructure of developing sieve elements in *Thlaspi arvense*: I. The immature state. *Am. J. Bot.* 66:925–932.

———. 1980. Ultrastructure of developing sieve elements in *Thlaspi arvense*: II. Maturation. *Am. J. Bot.* 67:194–201.

HOEFERT, L. and S. MARTIN. 1984. Developmental changes in germinating *Thlaspi arvense* seeds. *Am. J. Bot.* 71:14–15.

HOFFMAN, B. 1980. Inimigos naturais de plantas daninhas. In: *Informe Anual 1979–1982 Empresa Brasileira de Pesquisa Agropecuaria*; Londrina, Parana. pp. 251–253.

HOFFMAN, G., M. HOGAN and L. STANLEY. 1980. Germination of plant species common to reservoir shores in the northern Great Plains. *Bull. Torrey Bot. Club* 107:506–513.

HOFFMANN, C., E. VOLL and A. CERDEIRA. 1979. Effect of *Euphorbia heterophylla* L. competition on soybeans. *EMBRAPA (Empresa Brasilera de Pesquisa Agropecuaria) Ann. Rep.* Londrina, Bra. pp. 248–250.

HOFSTEN, C. VON. 1947. Investigations of germination biology in some weed species. *Vaxtodling* 2:91–107.

HOHN, K. 1952. Nachreifestudien an *Datura* seeds. *Planta* 40:407–418.

HOLADAY, A. 1979. Regulation of photosynthesis, photorespiration, and biomass in the submersed aquatic angiosperm *Hydrilla verticillata*. *Diss. Abstr. Intern. B* 39:5731 (USA).

HOLADAY, A. and G. BOWES 1980. C_4 acid metabolism and dark CO_2 fixation in a submersed aquatic macrophyte, *Hydrilla verticillata*. *Plant Physiol.* 65:331–335.

HOLDSWORTH, D. 1980. Tradition medicinal plants of the North Solomons Province, Papau New Guinea. *Quart. J. Crude Drug Res.* 18:33–44.

HOLDSWORTH, M. and P. NUTMAN. 1947. Flowering responses in a strain of *Orobanche minor*. *Nature* 160:223–224.

HOLLIDAY, R., P. PUTWAIN, and A. DAFNI. 1976. The evolution of herbicide resistance in weeds and its implications for the farmer. *Proc. Brit. Crop Prot. Conf.—Weeds* 3:937–946.

HOLLIS, J. 1972. Nematicide-weeds interaction in rice fields. *Plant Dis. Rep.* 56:420–424.

HOLM, L., D. PLUCKNETT, J. PANCHO and J. HERBERGER. 1977. *The world's worst weeds: Distribution and biology.* Univ. Hawaii Press, Honolulu; reprinted 1991, Krieger Publ. Co., Malabar, FL USA. 610pp.

HOLM, L., J. PANCHO, J. HERBERGER and D. PLUCKNETT. 1979. *A geographical atlas of world weeds.* John Wiley & Sons, N.Y.; reprinted 1991, Krieger Publ. Co., Malabar, FL USA. 390pp.

HOLM, R. 1972. Volatile metabolites controlling germination in buried weed seeds. *Plant Physiol.* 50:293–297.

HOLM, R. and M. MILLER. 1972. Weed seed germination responses to chemical and physical treatments. *Weed Sci.* 20:150–153.

HOLMBERG, D., F. RYAN, and K. STEWARD. 1993. Structure and biochemical characteristics of seeds of Hydrilla (*Hydrilla verticillata*). *Abstr. 33rd Weed Sci. Soc. Am. Conf.* 33:97.

HOLMES, N. and B. WHITTON. 1977. Macrophytes of the river Wear. 1966–1976. *Naturalist,* Leeds 102:53–73.

HOLM-NIELSEN, L. 1979. Comments on the distribution and evolution of the genus *Phyllanthus*: **Euphorbiaceae**. In: *Tropical botany.* pp. 277–290. Ed. by K. Larsen and L. Holm-Nielsen. Academic Press.

HOLMQUIST, C. 1971. Northerly localities for 3 aquatic plants, *L. trisulea, Ceratophyllum demersum* and *Myriophyllum spicatum*. *Botaniska Notiser* 124:335–342.

HOLT, B. 1972. Effect of arrival time on recruitment, mortality, and reproduction in successional plant populations. *Ecol.* 53:668–673.

HOLT, J. 1988. Reduced growth competitiveness, and photosynthetic efficiency of triazine-resistant *Senecio vulgaris* from California. *J. Appl. Ecol.* 25:307–318.

HONDELMANN, W. and W. RADATZ. 1984. Variation in some plant and oil seed characteristics of pennycress *Thlaspi arvense*. *Zeitschrift fur Pflanzenzuechtung* 92(4):328–343.

HOOGERS, B. and H. VAN DER WEIJ. 1971. The development cycle of some aquatic plants in the Netherlands. *Proc. 3rd Intern. Symp. Aquat. Weeds*, European Weed Res. Council, Oxford, 3:3–18.

HOPE, A. 1927. The dissemination of weed seeds by irrigation water in Alberta, Canada. *Scientific Agric.* 7:268–276.

HORNE, F. 1953. The significance of weed seeds in relation to crop production. *Proc. 1st Brit. Weed Control Conf.* 1:372–398.

HORNG, L. 1980. Interference of pale smartweed *Polygonum lapathifolium* with cabbage *Brassica oleracea*. *Weed Res.* 28:381–384.

HORNG, L. and L. LEU. 1978. The effects of depth and duration of burial on the germination of ten annual weed seeds. *Weed Sci.* 26:4–10.

HOROWITZ, M., A. GEVELBERG and H. BUCSBAUM. 1983a. Dodder seeds: Characteristics and implications for the dissemination and control of the parasite. *Hassadeh* 63:1776–1779.

HOROWITZ, M., Y. REGEV and G. HERZLINGER. 1983b. Solarization for weed control. *Weed Sci.* 31:170–179.

HORVATH, Z. 1983. Data on the biology of *Smicronyx junger-manniae* living on dodder plants. *Novenyvedelem* 19:501–508.

HOSAMANI, M., B. SHIVARAJ and C. KURDIKERI. 1971. Seed production potentialities of common weeds of Dharwar. *PANS (Pest Articles and News Summaries)* 17:237–239.

HOTCHKISS, N. 1967. *Underwater and floating-leaved plants of the United States and Canada*. U.S. Bur. Sport Fisheries and Wild Life, Resource Publ. 44, Washington, D.C. 123pp.

HOUGH, R. 1974. Photorespiration and productivity in submersed aquatic vascular plants. *Limnol. Oceanog.* 19:912–927.

———. 1979. Photosynthesis, respiration, and organic carbon release in *Elodea canadensis*. *Aquat. Bot.* 7(1):1–11.

HOVELAND, C. and G. BUCHANAN. 1973. Weed seed germination under simulated drought. *Weed Sci.* 21:322–324.

HOVELAND, C., G. BUCHANAN and M. HARRIS. 1976. Response of weeds to soil phosphorus and potassium. *Weed Sci.* 24:194–201.

HOVELAND, C., G. BUCHANAN, R. CROWLEY, D. TEEM and J. MCGUIRE. 1978. Response of weed and crop species to shade. *Abstr. 18th Weed Sci. Soc. Am. Conf.* 18:1–2.

HOVIN, A. 1957. Bulk emasculation by high temperatures in annual bluegrass *Poa annua* L. *Agron. J.* 49:463.

HOWARD-WILLIAMS, C. 1981. Studies on the ability of a *Potamogeton pectinatus* community to remove dissolved nitrogen and phosphorous compounds from lake water. *J. Appl. Ecol.* 18:619–637.

HOWARD-WILLIAMS, C. and B. ALLANSON. 1981. Phosphorus cycling in a dense *Potamogeton pectinatus* bed. *Oecologia* 49:56–66.

HOWARD-WILLIAMS, C. and B. DAVIES. 1978. The influence of periphyton on leaf surface structure of a *Potamogeton pectinatus* leaf. *Aquat. Bot.* 5:87–91.

———. 1979. The rates of dry matter and nutrient loss from decomposing *Potamogeton pectinatus* in a brackish south temperate coastal lake (Africa). *Freshwater Biol.* 9:13–21.

HOWARD-WILLIAMS, C. and B. WALKER. 1974. Vegetation of a tropical African lake: Classification and ordination of the vegetation of lake Chilwa (Malawi). *J. Ecol.* 62:831–853.

HOWARTH, S. and J. WILLIAMS. 1968. Biological flora of the British Isles, *Chrysanthemum leucanthemum* L. *J. Ecol.* 56:585–595.

HOWELL, J. 1959. Distribution data on weedy thistles in western north America. *Leaflets of Western Bot.* 9:17–32.

HOWELL, W. and G. MINK. 1981. Viruses isolated from wild carrot and poison hemlock. *Plant Dis.* 65:277–279.

HOWITT, J. 1908. The perennial sow thistle and some other weed pests of 1908. *Ontario Dept. Agric., Bull.* 168. 24pp.

HOWLAND, G. and M. EDWARDS. 1979. Photomorphogenesis of fern gametophytes. In: *The experimental biology of ferns*. Ed. by A. Dyer. Academic Press, N.Y.

HROUDOVA, Z. 1980. Occurrence of *Sagittaria sagittifolia* at different depths of water. *Folia Geobotan. et Phytotaxon.*, Prague 15(4):415–419.

HROUDOVA, Z., L. HROUDA, P. ZAKRAVSKY and I. OSTRY. 1988. Ecobiology and distribution of *Sagittaria sagittifolia* L. in Czechoslovakia. *Folia Geobotan. et Phytotaxon.* 23:337–373.

HSIAO, A. 1980. The effect of sodium hypochlorite, gibberellic acid, and light on seed dormancy and germination of stinkweed *Thlaspi arvense* and wild mustard *Brassica kaber*. *Can. J. Plant Sci.* 60:643–650.

HSIAO, A., and W. HUANG. 1989a. Apical dominance in the shoot and its possible role in the survival of *Paspalum distichum* L. *Weed Res.* 29:327–334.

HSIAO, A., and W. HUANG. 1989b. Effects of flooding on rooting and sprouting of isolated stem segments and on plant growth of *Paspalum distichum* L. *Weed Res.* 29:335–344.

HSIEH, T., A. SCHOOLER, A. BELL and J. NALEWAJA. 1972. Cytotaxonomy of three *Sonchus* species. *Am. J. Bot.* 59:789–796.

HUA, H., H. KEAN and H. TEO. 1973. Preliminary studies on picloram in mixture for general weed control. *Proc. 4th Asian-Pacific Weed Sci. Soc. Conf.* 4:151–161.

HUANG, W. and A. HSIAO. 1987. Factors affecting seed dormancy and germination of *Paspalum distichum*. *Weed Res.* 27:405–415.

HUANG, W., A. HSIAO and L. JORDAN. 1987. Effects of temperature, light, and certain growth regulating substances on sprouting, rooting and growth of single-node rhizome and shoot segments of *Paspalum distichum* L. *Weed Res.* 27:57–67.

HUBBARD, C. 1926. *East African pasture plants. I. East African grasses*. The Crown Agents for the Colonies, London.

HUDSON, W. 1918. *Far away and long ago. A history of my early life*. J. W. Dent, London. 332pp.

HUEY, B. and F. BALDWIN. 1978. Red rice control. In: *Red rice: Research and control*. pp. 19–25. Texas Agric. Exp. Sta., Bull. 1270.

HUGHES, H. 1971. Control of the water weed problem in the Rewa river. *Fiji Agric. J.* 33:67–72.

HUGHES, J. and A. RICHARDS. 1989. Isozymes and the status of *Taraxacum* **Asteraceae** agamospecies. *Bot. J. Linn. Soc.* 99:365–376.

HUGHES, W. 1938. *Studies into the biology of some* Rumex *species*. M.Sc. Thesis, Univ. Wales.

HULINA, N. 1987. Weeds in the drainage system in the Gornja

Posavina Region. *Fragmenta Herbologica Jugoslavica* 16:73–83.

HULL, A. and J. EVANS. 1973. Musk thistle *Carduus nutans*: An undesirable range plant. *J. Range Mgt.* 26:383–385.

HULL, V. and R. GROVES. 1973. Variation in *Chondrilla juncea* L. in southeastern Australia. *Aus. J. Bot.* 21:113–135.

HULTEN, E. 1964. *The circumpolar plants.* Vol. 1. Vascular cryptograms, conifers, monocotyledons. Almqvist and Wiksell, Stockholm.

HUME, L. 1982. The long-term effects of fertilizer application and three rotations on weed communities in wheat. *Can. J. Plant Sci.* 62:741–750.

———. 1984. The effect of seed maturity, storage on the soil surface, and buried on seeds of *Thlaspi arvense. Can. J. Plant Sci.* 64(4):961–970.

———. 1987. Long term effects of 2,4–D application on plants. I. Effects on the weed community in weed crop. *Can. J. Bot.* 65:2530–2536.

———. 1988. Long term effects of 2,4–D application on plants. II. Herbicide avoidance by *Chenopodium album* and *Thlaspi arvense. Can. J. Bot.* 66:230–235.

HUME, L. and O. ARCHIBOLD. 1986. The influence of a weedy habitat on the seed bank of an adjacent cultivated field. *Can. J. Bot.* 64:1879–1883.

HUNDT, R. 1978. Studies on development of new forest lands on former strip mining sites in the Duebener Heide, East Germany. *Vegetatio.* 38:1–12.

HUNT, G. and R. LUTZ. 1959. Seed production of curly-leaved pondweed and its significance to waterfowl. *J. Wildlife Mgt.* 23:405–408.

HUNTER, J. 1953. The composition of bracken: some major and trace element constituents. *J. Sci. Food Agric.* 4:10–20.

HUNTER, J. and A. LINDEN. 1958. The *Oxalis* problem: Growth characteristic and control of two species. *New Zealand Gardener* 15:23–32.

HUNYADI, K. 1973. Weed problems in the southwest arable lands of Hungary. *Proc. Yugoslav. Symp. Weed Control in Hilly and Mountainous Areas, Sarajevo:* 61–66.

HURLE, K. 1974. Effect of long-term weed control measures on viable weed seeds in the soil. *Proc. 12th Brit. Weed Control Conf.* 12:1145–1152.

HURST, E. 1942. *The poison plants of New South Wales.* Shelling Printing Works, Ltd., Sydney. 241pp.

HURTT, W. and R. TAYLORSON. 1979. Field studies on chemical promotion of weed emergence. *Abstr. 19th Weed Sci. Soc. Am. Conf.* 19: No. 83.

HUSAK, S. 1978. Control of reed and reed mace stands. Chap. 7.2 in: *Pond littoral ecosystems.* Ed. by D. Dykyjova and J. Kvet. Springer-Verlag, N.Y.

HUSAK, S. and H. OTAHELOVA. 1986. Contribution to the ecology of *Marsilea quadrifolia* L. *Folia Geobotan. et Phytotaxon.* 21:85–89.

HUTCHINSON, C. and G. SEYMOUR. 1982. Biological flora of the British Isles. No. 153 *Poa annua* L. *J. Ecol.* 70:887–901.

HUTCHINSON, G. 1970. The chemical ecology of 3 species of *Myriophyllum. Limnol. Oceanog.* 15:1–5.

HUTCHINSON, I., J. COLOSI and R. LEWIN. 1984. The biology of Canadian weeds. 63. *Sonchus asper* (L.) Hill and *S. oleraceus* L. *Can. J. Plant Sci.* 64:731–744.

HUTCHINSON, J. and J. DALZIEL. 1936. *Flora of west tropical Africa.* Vol. 3, Part 2. Crown Agents for the Colonies, London.

———. 1968. *Flora of west tropical Africa.* Vol. 3, Part 1. 2nd Edition, F. Hepper. Crown Agents for Overseas Gov. and Admin., London.

HUTCHISON, J. and F. ASHTON. 1979. Effect of desiccation and scarification on the permeability and structure of the seed coat of *Cuscuta campestris. Am. J. Bot.* 66:40–46.

———. 1980. Germination of field dodder *Cuscuta campestris. Weed Sci.* 28:330–333.

HUXLEY, P. and A. TURK. 1966. Factors which affect the germination of seeds of six common east African weeds. *Exp. Agric.* 2(1):17–25.

HWANG, W., S. CHA and S. LEE. 1981. Extraction of anti-cancer components from Korean medicinal plants and the determination of their cytotoxic activities on cancer cells. *Korean Biochemical J.* 13:25–40.

IBRAHIM, N., A. BABIKER, W. EDWARDS and C. PARKER. 1985. Activity of extracts from *Euphorbia* species on the germination of *Striga* species. *Weed Res.* 25:135–140.

ICKES, G., H. FONG, P. SCHIFF, R. PERDUE and N. FARNSWORTH. 1973. Antitumor activity and preliminary phytochemical examination of *Tagetes minuta* **Compositae.** *J. Pharmocological Sci.* 62:1009–1011.

IDRIS, H. and F. MILTHORPE. 1966. Light and nutrient supplies in the competition between barley and charlock. *Oecologia Plantarum* 1:143–164.

IDRIS, M. and M. BESHIR. 1979. On the distribution and dynamics of weed populations in the Sudan Gezira. Berichte aus dem Fachgebiet Herbologie der Univ. Hohenheim, No. 18, *Weed Res.*19:15–23.

IGNACIUK, R. and J. LEE. 1980. The germination of 4 annual strand-line species. *New Phytol.* 84(4):581–591.

IITA (Intern. Inst. Trop. Agric.). 1977. Pest management. *IITA Ann. Rep.*: 66; Ibadan, Nig.

IKEDA, H. and T. EMOTO. 1973. Effect of temperature on vegetative growth in four ecotypes of *Paspalum distichum* L. *Proc. Crop Sci. Soc. Jap.* 42:131–134.

IKEDA, H. and M. OYAMADA. 1980. Studies on the growth and development in knotgrass *Paspalum distichum* L. 3. On the underground growth. *Bull. Faculty Agric. Miyazaki Univ.* 27:93–97.

———. 1982. Variation of the glumaceous flowers in knotgrass *Paspalum distichum* L. *Bull. Faculty of Agric. Miyazaki Univ.* 29:307–310.

IKEDA, H., M. OYAMADA and T. TAKAHASHI. 1988. Studies on growth and development in knotgrass *Paspalum distichum*: V. Growth and morphological characteristics of stolons. *Bull. Faculty Agric., Miyazaki Univ.* 35:129–132.

IKEDA, H., M. OYAMADA and N. YAMADA. 1983. Control of knotgrass *Paspalum distichum* L. in the paddy field. *Bull. Faculty Agric. Miyazaki Univ.* 30:51–55.

ILANGOVAN, M., K. MUTHUCHELIAN and K. PALIWAL. 1990. Nitrate reductase in weeds as a function of leaf age, extra nitrate application and photosynthetic photon flux density. *Geobios* 17:22–26.

IMBAMBA, S., M. NDAWULA-SENYIMBA and G. PAPA. 1977. The effect of soil moisture stress on photosynthesis, transpiration and leaf enlargement in some Kenyan vegetable plants. *E. Afr. Agric. and Forestry J.* 42:309–315.

IMBAMBA, S. and L. TIESZEN. 1977. Influence of light and temperature in some C_3 and C_4 vegetable plants from Kenya. *Physiologia Plantarum* 39:311–316.

INAMDAR, J. and M. GANGADHARA. 1975. Structure and ontogeny, classification and organographic distribution of trichomes in some **Cucurbitaceae**. *Feddes Rep.* 86:307–320.

———. 1978. Structure and ontogeny of stomata in some **Euphorbiaceae**. *Phyton* 19:37–60.

INAMDAR, J., R. PATEL and D. BHATT. 1971. Structure and development of stomata in some leptosporangiate ferns. *Ann. Bot.* 35:643–651.

INAMDAR, J., K. PATEL and R. PATEL. 1973. Plasmodesmata in the trichomes and leaf epidermis of some **Asclepiadaceae**. *Ann. Bot.* 37:657–660.

IRRI (Intern. Rice Res. Inst.). 1976. Zero and minimum tillage. *IRRI. Ann. Rep.*: 192–194. Los Banos, Philippines.

———. 1977. Weed control. *IRRI Ann. Rep.*: 192–194. Los Banos, Philippines.

———. 1981. *Azolla* growth and temperature. *Res. Highlights* 1980: 68–69. Los Banos, Philippines.

———. 1987. *Azolla* utilization. *Proc. Workshop Azolla Use*: 296. Los Banos, Philippines.

IRWIN, H. and B. TURNER. 1960. Chromosomal relationship and taxonomic consideration in the genus *Cassia. Am. J. Bot.* 47:309–318.

ISELY, D. 1944. *A study of the conditions that affect germination of* Scirpus *seeds*. Cornell Univ. Agric. Exp. Sta. Memoirs No. 257. 28pp.

ISIKAWA, S., T. FUJII and Y. YOKAHAMA. 1961. Photoperiodic control of germination of *Eragrostis* seeds. *Botan. Mag.*, Tokyo, 74:14–18.

ISMAIL, A. and M. OBEID. 1976. A study of assimilation and translocation in *Cuscuta hyalina, Orobanche ramosa* and *Striga hermonthica. Weed Res* 16:87–92.

ISRAEL, S., I. DORR and R. KOLLMAN. 1980. Das phloem der haustorien *Cuscuta. Protoplasma* 103:309–321.

ISWARAN, V., A. SEN and R. APTE. 1980. A nitrogen fixing bacterium associated with *Azolla pinnata. Science and Culture* 46:224–225.

ITO, O. and I. WATANABE. 1985. Availability to rice plants of nitrogen fixed by *Azolla. Soil Sci. Plant Nutri.* 31:91–104.

IVANOVA, I. 1970. Certain characteristic features of flowering and pollination in duckweeds. *Botanicheskii Zhurnal SSSR* 55:649–658.

IVENS, G. 1967. *East African weeds and their control*. Oxford Univ. Press, Nairobi. 244 pp.

———. 1979. Effects of pasture species and sheep grazing on establishment of sown *Ulex europaeus. Proc. 7th Asian-Pacific Weed Sci. Soc. Conf.* 7:355–365.

———. 1982. Seasonal germination and establishment of gorse. *Proc. 35th New Zealand Weed Pest Control Conf.* 35:152–156.

———. 1983. The influence of temperature on germination of gorse. *Weed Res.* 23:207–216.

IVENS, G. and F. MLOWE. 1980. A study of competition between seedlings of gorse *Ulex europaeus* and perennial rye *Lolium perenne* by means of a replacement series experiment. *Weed Res.* 20:183–191.

IZARD , C. and H. HITIER. 1953. Obtention de la germination *in vitro* des graines de l'*Orobanche* du Tabac. *Comptes Rendus Hebomadaires Seances Acad. Agric. France* 39:567–569.

IZARD, C. and H. HITIER. 1958. The effect of 1,3–dichloro-propane, 1,2–dichloropene, Rindite and gibberellin on the germination of seeds of *Orobanche*, a parasite of tobacco. *Comptes Rendus Hebomadaires Seances Acad. Sci. France* 246:2659–2661.

JACKSON, D. 1960. A growth study of *Oxalis latifolia* H.B.K. *New Zealand J. Sci.* 3:600–609.

JACOB, F. 1966. The release of the flowering process in the short day plant *Cuscuta reflexa. Flora Allgemeine Botanische Zeitung* 156:558–572.

JACOBS, D. 1947. An ecological life-history of *Spirodela polyrhiza*, greater duckweed, with emphasis on the turion phase. *Ecological Monographs* 17:437–469.

JACOBSOHN, R. 1986. Broomrape avoidance and control: Agronomic problems and available methods. pp. 18–24. *Proc. Workshop on Biology and Control of Orobanche*. Ed. by S. ter Borg. Wageningen, Netherlands.

JACOBSOHN, R., A. GREENBERGER, J. KATAN, M. LEVI and H. ALON. 1980. Control of Egyptian broomrape *Orobanche aegyptiaca* and other weeds by means of solar heating of soil by polyethylene mulching. *Weed Sci.* 28:312–316.

JACOBSON, M., R. REDFERN and G. MILLS Jr. 1975. Naturally occurring insect growth regulators. II. Screening of insect and plant extracts as insect juvenile hormone mimics. *Lloydia* 38:455–472.

JAHN-DEESBACH, W. and M. VOGT. 1960. Investigation on the weed flora in nutrient deficiency experiments carried out over several years at Thyrow near Berlin. *Z. Acker Pflanzenbau* 110:216–229.

JAIN, B. 1987. Development of the staminate flower of *Najas marina*. *Beitraege zur Biologie Pflanzen* 61:401–410.

JAIN, N. and J. SAHA. 1971. Effect of storage length on seed germination in jute (*Corchorus* spp.). *Agron. J.* 63:636–638.

JAITLY, S. and G. SRIVASTAVA. 1970. Development and structure of seed of *Coronopus didymus* (L.) Smith. *Agra Univ. J. Res. Sci.* 19(1):1–8.

JANA, S. and M. CHOUDHURI. 1979. Photosynthetic, photorespiratory and respiratory behavior of three submersed aquatic angiosperms. *Aquat. Bot.* 7:13–19.

———. 1980. Senescence in submerged aquatic angiosperms: Changes in intact and isolated leaves during aging. *New Phytol.* 86:191–198.

———. 1982a. Ethylene production and senescence in submerged aquatic angiosperms. *Aquat. Bot.* 13:359–365.

———. 1982b. Characterization of chilling sensitivity of three submerged aquatic angiosperms. *J. Aquat. Plant Mgmt.* 20:33–36.

———. 1984. Synergistic effects of heavy metal pollutants on senescence in submerged aquatic angiosperms. *Water Air Soil Pollution* 21:351–357.

JANAUER, G. 1981. *Elodea canadensis* and its dormant apices: An investigation of organic and mineral constituents. *Aquat. Bot.* 11:231–243.

JANIYA, J. and K. MOODY. 1981. Suppression of weeds in transplanted rice *Oryza sativa* L. with *Azolla pinnata* R.Br. *Proc. 12th Ann. Conf. Pest Control Council Philipp.*, Univ. Philipp., Los Banos, Laguna, 12:13–15.

———. 1984. Use of *Azolla* to suppress weeds in transplanted rice. *Trop. Pest Mgmt.* 30:1–6.

JANSSEN, J. 1973. Effects of light, temperature and seed age on the germination of the winter annuals *Veronica arvensis* L. and *Myosotis ramosissima* Rochel ex. Schult. *Oecologia* 12:141–146.

JASH, M. and A. SHARMA. 1970. Cytotaxonomy of some Indian **Onagraceae**. *Plant Sci.*, Lucknow, 2:17–33.

JEFFERY, L. and J. NALEWAJA. 1970. Studies of the achene dormancy in fumitory. *Weed Sci.* 18:345–348.

———. 1973. Changes in fumitory achenes during low temperature after-ripening. *Weed Sci.* 21:310–313.

JENKINS, L. and E. JACKMAN. 1938. White top. *Oregon State College Ext. Bull.* No. 522. 3pp.

JENSEN, H. 1969. Content of buried seeds in arable soil in Denmark and its relation to the weed population. *Dansk Botanisk Arkiv* 27:7–56.

———. 1979. Key to and description of the fruits of some *Rumex* species. *Seed Sci. Technol.* 7:525–528.

JESSUP, D., H. BOERMANS and N. KOCK. 1986. Toxicosis in tule elk caused by ingestion of poison hemlock. *J. Am. Vet. Med. Assoc.* 189:1173–1175.

JOBSON, H. and B. THOMAS. 1964. The composition of gorse. *J. Sci. Food Agric.* 15:652–656.

JOEL, A. 1929. Weed distribution and crop character in relation to soil type in Saskatchewan. *Scientific Agric.* 9:675–688.

JOEL, D. 1987. Identification of *Orobanche* seeds. pp. 434–443. *Proc. 4th Intern. Symp. Parasitic Flowering Plants.* Ed. by H. Weber and W. Forstreuter. Marburg, Germany.

———. 1988. A key for the identification of *Orobanche* seeds. *Phytoparasitica* 16:376.

JOHANNES, H. 1974. Ist *Eleocharis acicularis* in der lage den aufwuchs submerser Pflanzen wirksam zu verhindern. (*E. acicularis* may prevent the growth of submerged plants). pp. 114–121. *4th Intern. Symp. Aquatic Weeds*, Vienna.

JOHNSON, A., G. ROSEBERY and C. PARKER. 1976. A novel approach to *Striga* and *Orobanche* control using synthetic germination stimulants. *Weed Res.* 16:223–227.

JOHNSON, B. and J. MANNING. 1974. *Hydrilla*—the most serious threat to Louisiana water resources. *Louisiana Conservationist* 26:26–29.

JOHNSON, D. 1898. On the development of the leaf and sporocarp in *Marsilea quadrifolia*. *Ann. Bot.* 12:119–145.

JOHNSON, H. and M. HATCH. 1968. Distribution of the C_4 dicarboxylic acid pathway of photosynthesis and its occurrence in dicotyledonous plants. *Phytochemistry.* 7:374–380.

JOHNSON, L. and B. BRIGGS. 1962. Taxonomic and cytological notes on *Acetosa* and *Acetosella* in Australia. *Contributions New South Wales National Herbarium* 3:165–169.

JOHNSON, T. and R. HENSMAN. 1910. Agricultural seeds and their weed impurities: A source of Ireland's aging flora. *Scientific Proc., N.S. series.* 12:446–462. Royal Dublin Soc. (Ireland).

JOHNSTON, M. 1962. Commonly occurring impurities in pasture seed. *New Zealand J. Agric.* 105:122–131.

JOHNSTONE, I., B. COFFEY, and C. HOWARD-WILLIAMS. 1985. The role of recreational boat traffic in interlake dispersal of macrophytes: A New Zealand case study. *J. Environmental Mgt.* 20:263–279.

JOHONSON, E. 1969. Archeological evidence for utilization of wild rice. *Rice Science* 163:276–277.

JOHRI, B. 1987. Embryology of *Cuscuta*. pp. 445–452. *Proc. 4th Intern. Symp. Parasitic Flowering Plants.* Ed. by H. Weber and W. Forstreuter. Marburg, Germany.

JOHRI, B. and B. TIAGI. 1952. Floral morphology and seed formation in *Cuscuta reflexa*. *Phytomorphology* 2:162–180.

JONES, C. and R. FIRN. 1978. The role of photoecolysteroids in bracken fern *Pteridium aquilinum* as a defense against phytophagos insect attack. *J. Chem. Ecol.* 4:117–138.

JONES, D. 1987. *Encyclopedia of ferns.* Timber Press; Portland, Oregon, USA.

JONES, D., K. CHRISTIAN and R. SNAYDON. 1971. Chemical composition and *in vitro* digestibility of some weed species during summer. *Aus. J. Exp. Agric. and Animal Husbandry* 11:403–406.

JONES, M. and L. BAILEY. 1956. Light effects on the germination of seeds of henbit *Lamium amplexicaule. Plant Physiol.* 31:347–349.

JONES, M., J. PONTI, A. TAVASSOLI and P. DIXON. 1978. Relationships of the Ethiopian cereal t'ef, *Eragrostis tef* (Zucc.) Trotter: Evidence from morphology and chromosome number. *Ann. Bot.* 42:1369–1373.

JONES, R., G. DRUMMOND and R. CHATHAM. 1981. *Heliotropium europaeum* poisoning of pigs. *Aus. Vet. J.* 57:396.

JORDAN, J. 1981. Pre-chilling to −196° C on weed seed germination. *Proc. 36th North Central Weed Control Conf.* 36:150–151.

JORDAN, L. 1983. Weeds affect citrus growth, yield, physiology, fruit quality. Vol. 2:481–483. *Proc. Intern. Soc. of Citriculture,* 1981.

JORDAN, T. and D. WHIGHAM. 1988. The importance of standing dead shoots of the narrow leaved cattail *Typha angustifolia* L. *Aquatic Bot.* 29:319–328.

JORGENSEN, P. 1970. The genus *Chenopodium* in Norway. *Norwegian J. Bot.* 20:303–319.

JOS, J. 1963. The structure and development of seeds in **Convolvulaceae:** *Ipomoea* species. *Agra Univ. J. Res. Sci.* 12:247–260.

JOSHI, M. and B. NIGAM. 1970. Autecological studies on Rajasthan desert plants. 3. Seed output and germination in *Trianthema portulacastrum* L. *Trop. Ecol.* 11:140–147.

JOVET, P. 1966. Notes (taxonomy) on *Erigeron crispus, E. naudini,* and their interspecific hybrids, and with *E. canadensis. Ann. Bot.* 28:53–58.

JOVET, P. and M. GUEDES. 1972. *Paspalum distichum* L. and *P. paspalodes* (Michx.) Scribn. *Taxon* 21:546.

JOY, K. 1969. Nitrogen metabolism of *Lemna minor:* I. Growth nitrogen sources and amino acid inhibition. *Plant Physiol.* 44:845–848.

JOYCE, J. and W. HALLER and D. COLLE. 1980. Investigation of the presence and survivability of *Hydrilla* propagules in waterfowl. *Aquatics* 2(3):10–14.

JUDD, W. 1969. The insects associated with flowering wild carrot *Daucus carota* in southern Ontario. *Proc. Entomol. Soc. Ontario* 100:176–181.

JULIANO, J. 1940. Viability of some Philippine weed seeds. *Philipp. Agriculturist* 29:313–326.

JULIEN, M. 1973. Physiology of flowering in *Saccharum:* I.

Daylength control of floral initiation and development in *S. spontaneum* L. *J. Exp. Bot.* 24:549–557.

———. 1982. The biological control of weeds: A world catalog of agents and their target weeds. *Commonwealth Agric. Bureaux, U.K.* p. 168.

JULIEN, M. and A. BOURNE. 1988. Alligator weed is spreading in Australia. *Plant Prot. Quart.* 3:91–98.

JULIEN, M. and J. BROADBENT. 1980. Biology of Australian weeds 3. *Alternanthera philoxeroides* (Mart.) Grisb. *J. Aus. Inst. Agric. Sci.* 46:150–155.

JUNG, Y., K. PARK, J. LEE and U. KANG. 1987. Research and development of new forage-green manure crops. 1. Ecological characteristics and value of *Aeschynomene indica. Res. Dept. Rural Develop. Admin., Crops, Korea Republic* 29:294–298.

JUPP, B. and D. SPENCE. 1977. Limitations of macrophytes in a eutrophic lake, Loch Leven: II. Wave action, sediments, and waterfowl grazing. *J. Ecol.* 65:431–446.

JUQUET, M. 1966. Embryogenesis of **Cyperaceae,** development of the embryo in *Scirpus maritimus. Comptes Rendus des Seances de l'Academie des Sciences, Ser. D* 236(22):1710–1713.

JURGENS, G. 1977. Lista de las malezas que afectan cultivos agricolas en la Republica Dominicana. (Liste der unkrauter landwirtschaftlicher kulturen in der Dominikanischen Republik). *Berichte aus dem Fachgebiet Herbologie der Univ. Hohenheim;* Stuttgart, Germany.

JUSTICE, O. 1941. A study of dormancy in seeds of *Polygonum. Cornell Univ. Agric. Exp. Sta., Memoir* 235. 43pp.

KABEN, H. 1963. The role of soil in allelopathic manifestations. *Naturwissenschaften* 50(18):601.

KABULOV, D. 1966. Broomrape a dangerous weed. *Sel'skokhozyaistvennaya Uzbek* 8:46–48.

KACHELREISS, S. 1988. Methode zur Bestimmung von Orobanchesamen. *Zeitschrift fur Pflanzenkrankheiten und Pflanzenschutz.* Stuttgart-Hohenheim. XI:55–56.

KADMAN-ZAHAVI, A. 1957. Effects of red and far red radiation on seed germination. *Nature* 180 (4593):996–997.

———. 1960. Effects of short and continuous illuminations on the germination of *Amaranthus retroflexus* seeds. *Israel Res. Council Bull. D* 9:1–20.

KADONO, Y. 1980. Photosynthetic carbon sources in some *Potamogeton* species. *Bot. Magazine* (Tokyo) 93:185–194.

KADRY, A. and H. TEWFIC. 1956a. Seed germination in *Orobanche crenata. Svensk Botanisk Tidskrift* 50:270–286.

———. 1956b. A contribution to the morphology and anatomy of seed germination in *Orobanche crenata. Bot. Notiser* 109:385–399.

KAINTH, N. and A. TARIQ. 1969. Preliminary studies on anthesis and pollination in the genus *Saccharum. West Pak. J. Agric. Res.* 7:147–151.

KALIWAL, B. and R. APPASWAMY. 1979. Dose and durational effect of carrot seed extract *Daucus carota* implantation in albino rats. *Comparative Physiological Ecol.* 4:92–97.

KAMEL, S. 1956. Chemistry and toxicology of the Egyptian plant *Orobanche minor*. *Revue d'Elevage et de Medecine Veterinaire des Pays Tropicaux*, Paris 9:43–48.

KANIEWSKI, K. 1965. Fruit histogenesis in *Nicandra physalodes*. *Bull. Acad. Polonaise Sci. Serie Sci. Biologique* 13(9):553–556.

KANODIA, K. and R. GUPTA. 1972. Common weeds of karif crops in western Rajasthan. *Ind. J. Weed Sci.* 4:41–56.

KAPIL, R., D. LAMBA and H. BRAR. 1971. Integration of bee behavior with aphid control for seed production of *Brassica campestris* var. *toria*. *Ind. J. Entomol.* 33:221–223.

KAPLAN, D. and G. PETERS. 1981. The *Azolla-Anabaena Azollae* relationship: X. $^{15}N_2$ fixation and transport in main stem axes. *New Phytol.* 89:337–346.

KAPLANIS, J., M. THOMPSON, W. ROBBINS and B. BRYCE. 1967. Insect hormones: Alpha-ecdysone and 20–hydroxyecdysone in bracken fern. *Sci.* 157:1436–1438.

KAPOOR, L., K. HANDA, I. CHOPRA, B. ABROL and I. CHANDRA. 1956. Cultivation of *Chenopodium ambrosioides* in Jammu and Kashmis. *J. Scientific Industrial Res.* 15A:35–38.

KAPUSTA, G. 1979. Seedbed tillage and herbicide influence on soybean *Glycine max* weed control and yield. *Weed Sci.* 27:520–526.

KARAPETYAN, N. 1972. Effects of depth and duration of burial on dodder on germination in soil (Armenia). *Sel'skokhozyaistvennykh Nauk*, Armyanskoi, SSR. 5:49–54.

KARAWYA, M., K. AWAAD, J. SVABAND and T. FAHMY. 1968. A historical study of *Matricaria chamomilla*. *Planta Medica* 16:166–173.

KARPISCAK, M. and O. GROSZ. 1979. Dissemination trails of Russian thistle *Salsola kali* in recently fallowed fields. *Arizona-Nevada Acad. Sci.* 14(2):50–52.

KARSSEN, C. 1980/1981. Patterns of change in dormancy during burial of seeds in soil. *Israel J. Bot.* 29:65–73.

KARVE, A. 1962. Regulation of photomorphogenic processes in *Cassia tora* L. by circadian rhythms. *Planta* 58:257–260.

KASAHARA, Y. 1953. Studies on the weeds of arable land in Japan. *Berichte des Ohara Inst. Landwirtschaftliche Forschungen*, Baud X, Heft 1. p. 72–109.

———. 1982. Weeds of Japan. Chap. 26 in: *Biology and ecology of weeds*. Ed. by W. Holzner and M. Numata. Dr. Junk Publ., The Hague.

KASASIAN, L. 1971a. *Orobanche* spp. *PANS (Pest Articles and News Summaries)* 17:35–41.

———. 1971b. *Weed control in the tropics*. Leonard Hill Books, London. 307pp.

———. 1973. Miscellaneous observations on the biology of *Orobanche crenata* and *O. aegyptiaca*. *Proc. 1st Symp.*

Parasitic Weeds, European Weed Res. Council, Malta 1:68–75.

KASMYOVA, K. 1966. Histochemical investigation of seeds and pollen of certain species of *Erigeron*. *Glasnik Botanischeskago SADA Byulleten* 62:99–102.

KASPER, J. 1980. Development of the common dandelion *Taraxacum officinale* Web. in permanent grass stands as dependent on level of fertilization and site conditions. *Vedecke Prace Vyskumneho Ustavu Luk a Pasienkov v Banskej Bystrici* 15:53–66.

KASTING, R., U. PITTMAN, J. HORRICKS, R. DOWNEY and S. DUBETZ. 1974. Toxin from the straw residue of rape. *Can. J. Plant Sci.* 54:447–448.

KASTURE, A. and S. WADODKAR. 1971. Preliminary phytochemical study of *Tridax procumbens* L. *Ind. J. Pharmacy* 33:96.

KATAN, J. 1981. Solar heating (solarization) of soil for control of soilborne pests. *Ann. Rev. Phytopath.* 19:211–236.

KATAYAMA T. 1969a. Botanical studies in the genus *Oryza*. Part I. Morphological and anatomical investigations of glume and leaf surface with SUMP and histological method. *Memoirs Faculty Agric., Kagoshima Univ.* 7:89–118.

———. 1969b. Botanical studies in the genus *Oryza*. Part II. Germination behavior. *Memoirs Faculty Agric., Kagoshima Univ.* 7:89–119.

———. 1970a. Botanical studies in the genus *Oryza*. Part IV. Flowering order in a panicle. *Memoirs Faculty Agric., Kagoshima Univ.* 7:219–241.

———. 1970b. Botanical studies in the genus *Oryza*. Part V. Flowering time. *Memoirs Faculty Agric., Kagoshima Univ.* 7:243–256.

———. 1974. Photoperiodism in the genus *Oryza*. IV. Combinations of plant age, day length and number of treatments. *Proc. Crop Sci. Soc. Jap.* 43:224–236.

KATAYAMA, T. and H. IKEDA. 1975. Cytogenetical studies on *Paspalum distichum* L. *Cytologia* 40:759–764.

KAUL, A. 1972. Effect of light, salt and naturally occurring substances on seed germination of *Alternanthera sessilis*. *Trop. Ecol.* 13:96–103.

KAUL, V., P. ZUTSHI and K. VASS. 1973. Aquatic weeds in Kashmir. pp. 79–83. *Proc. Aquat. Weeds in Southeast Asia*, New Delhi. Ed. by C. Varshney and J. Rzoska.

KAUL, V., S. NIGAM and K. DHAR. 1976. Antimicrobial activities of the essential oils of *Artemisia vulgaris, A. vestita* and *A. absinthium*. *Ind. J. Pharmacy* 38:21–22.

KAUSHIK, D. 1963. *The influences of salinity on the growth and reproduction of marsh plants*. Ph.D. Diss., Utah State Univ.; Logan, Utah.

KAWABATA, Z., R. TATSUKAWA and K. SATO. 1986. Growth of duckweed and nutrient removal in a paddy field irrigated with sewage effluent. *Intern. J. Environ. Studies* 27:277–285.

KAWANO, S. and S. MIYAKE. 1983. The productive and reproductive biology of flowering plants. X. Reproductive energy and propagule output of five congeners of the genus *Setaria*: **Gramineae**. *Oecologia* 57:6–13.

KAWASHIMA, C., M. NAKAJIMA, K. CHIBA and T. HIRANO. 1977. Studies on the control of the perennial weed, sea clubrush. I. The development of the weed and key points to control it. *Bull. Akita Prefectural Coll. Agric.* 52(3):1–10.

KAWASHIMA, C., K. CHIBA and T. HIRANO. 1981. Studies on the control of perennial weed, sea club-brush. II. Emergence and sprouting of buds on the tubers. *Weed Res. J., Weed Sci. Soc. Jap.* 26(2):123–128.

KAY, S. and W. HALLER. 1984. Evidence for the existence of distinct alligatorweed *Alternanthera philoxeroides* biotypes. *J. Aquat. Plant Mgmt.* 20:37–41.

KAZMI, S. 1963–1964. Revision der gattung *Carduus*. *Mitteilungen der Botanischen Staatssammlung*, Muenchen. Teil I. 5:139–198. Teil II. 5:279–550.

KEAST, A. 1984. The introduced aquatic macrophyte *Myriophyllum spicatum*, as a habitat for fish and their invertebrate prey. *Can. J. Zool.* 62:1289–1303.

KEDDY, P. 1976. Lakes as islands: The distributional ecology of two aquatic plants, *Lemna minor* L. and *L. trisulca* L. *Ecology* 57:353–359.

KEDDY, P. and P. CONSTABEL. 1986. Germination of ten shoreline plants in relation to seed size, soil particle size and water level: An experimental study. *J. Ecol.* 74:133–141.

KEDDY, P. and T. ELLIS. 1985. Seedling recruitment of 11 wetland plant species along a water level gradient: Shared or distinct responses? *Can. J. Bot.* 63:1876–1879.

KEEVER, C. 1950 Causes of succession on old fields of the piedmont, North Carolina. *Ecological Monographs* 20:229–250.

KEFFORD, N. and O. CASO. 1972. Organ regeneration on excised roots of *Chondrilla juncea* and its chemical regulation. *Aus. J. Biological Sci.* 25:691–706.

KEHAR, N. 1949. Investigations on famine rations, kans *Saccharum spontaneum* L., a reorientation in its use as cattle feed. *Ind. J. Vet. Sci. Animal Husbandry* 17:211–221.

KEIL, G. 1940. Das wurzelwerk von *Taraxacum officinale* Weber. Eine untersuchung uber den bewurzelungstyp und seine beeinflussung durch den boden. *Botanisches Zentralblatt* 60:57–96.

KEISERS, J. 1985. Control of red rice *Oryza rufipogon* in rice *O. sativa*. *Surinaamse Landbouw* 33:35–43.

KELDIBEKOV, S. 1972. *Hydrilla verticillata* in Uzbekistan. *Kultivirovanie Vodoroslei i Vysshikh Vodnykh Rastenii v Uzbekistane*. pp. 132–135.

KELLEY, A. and V. BRUNS. 1975. Dissemination of weed seeds by irrigation water. *Weed Sci.* 23:486–493.

KELLMAN, M. 1978. Microdistribution of viable weed seed in two tropical soils. *J. Biogeography* 5:291–300.

KELLY, D., H. CAMERON and J. ALEX. 1988. Wind dispersal of nodding thistle seeds and pappi. *Proc. 41st New Zealand Weed and Pest Control Conf.* 41:207–209.

KEMP, P., G. WILLIAMS and D. MAY. 1977. Temperature relations of gas exchange in altitudinal populations of *Taraxacum officinale*. *Can. J. Bot.* 55:2496–2502.

KEMPEN, H. and J. GRAF. 1981. Weed seed production. *Proc. 34th Western Soc. Weed Sci. Conf.* 34:78–81.

KENDRICK, J., J. TUCKER and S. PEOPLES. 1955. Nitrate poisoning in cattle due to ingestion of variegated thistle *Silybum marianum*. *J. Am. Vet. Med. Assoc.* 126:53–56.

KESKITALO, J. and L. HEITTO. 1987. Over wintering of benthic vegetation outside the Olkiluoto nuclear power station, west coast of Finland. *Ann. Bot. Fennici* 24:231–243.

KESKITALO, J. and E. ILUS. 1987. Aquatic macrophytes outside the Olkiluoto nuclear power station, west coast of Finland. *Ann. Bot. Fennici* 24:121–123.

KHAN, A. and I. CHAUDHRI. 1957. Studies on the seed dormancy of *Asphodelus tenuifolius*. *Proc. Pak. Sci. Conf.*, Lahore, 9:25–26.

KHAN, A. and T. ZAFAR. 1981. *Smicronyx* spp. attacking *Cuscuta* spp. in Pakistan. *Biologia* 27:265–273.

KHAN, D., S. SHAUKAT and M. FAHEEMUDDIN. 1984. Germination studies of certain desert plants. *Pak. J. Bot.* 16:231–235.

KHAN, M. 1969. Regeneration in relation to root size in *Taraxacum officinale*. *Pak. J. Scientific Industrial Res.* 12:310–311.

———. 1972. Distribution of peroxidase in regenerating root segments of *Taraxacum officinale*. *Pak. J. Bot.* 4:99–110.

———. 1973. Anatomy of regenerating root segments of *Taraxacum officinale* Web. *Pak. J. Sci.* 5:71–77.

———. 1975. Regeneration of *Taraxacum* roots in relation to carbon and nitrogen supply. *Pak. J. Bot.* 7:161–167.

KHAN, R. 1942. A contribution to embryology of *Jussiaea repens*. *J. Ind. Bot. Soc.* 21:267–282.

KHANNA, P. 1965. A contribution to the embryology of *Cyperus rotundus* L., *Scirpus mucronatus* L., and *Kyllinga melanospora* Nees. *Can. J. Bot.* 43:1539–1547.

KHANNA, P., S. JAIN, A. PANAGARIYA and V. DIXIT. 1981. Hypoglycemic activity of polypeptide-p from a plant source. *J. Natural Products* 6:648–655.

KHANNA, S. 1968. Biochemical aspects of parasitism by angiosperm parasites: Phenolics in parasites and hosts. *Physiologia Plantarum* 21:949–959.

KHOSHOO, T. and S. SOBTI. 1958. Cytology of Indian species of *Artemisia*. *Nature* 181:853–854.

KHURANA, S. 1970. *Trianthema monogyna* and *Boerhavia diffusa* unrecorded hosts of brinjal mosaic disease. *Plant Dis. Rep.* 54:437–438.

KIGEL, J., M. OFIR and D. KOLLER. 1977. Control of the germination responses of *Amaranthus retroflexus* seeds by their parental photothermal environment. *J. Exp. Bot.* 28:1125–1136.

KIGEL, J., A. GIBLY and M. NEGBI. 1979. Seed germination in *Amaranthus retroflexus* as affected by the photoperiod and age during flower induction of the parent plants. *J. Exp. Bot.* 30:997–1002.

KILTZ, B. 1930. Perennial weeds which spread vegetatively. *J. Am. Soc. Agron.* 22:216–234.

KIM, S. and T. KATAOKA. 1978. Oxygen requirement for germination of weed seeds. *J. Korean Soc. Crop Sci.* 23:145–149.

KIM, S. and K. MOODY. 1980. Types of weed community in transplanted lowland rice and relationship between yield and weed weight in weed communities. *J. Korean Soc. Crop Sci.* 25(3):1–8.

KIMBEL, J. 1982. Factors influencing potential intralake colonization by *Myriophyllum spicatum*. *Aquatic Bot.* 14:295–307.

KIMMELL, A. 1936. Anatomical study of the seedling of *Hibiscus trionum*. *Bot. Gaz.* 98:178–189.

KINCH, R. and D. TERMUNDE. 1957. Germination of perennial sow thistle and Canada thistle at various stages of maturity. *Proc. Assoc. Official Seed Analysts North Am.* 47:165–166.

KING, L. 1966. *Weeds of the world: biology and control.* Interscience Publ., New York. pp. 526.

KINGSBURY, J. 1964. *Poisonous plants of the United States and Canada.* Prentice-Hall Inc., New Jersey. pp. 626.

KIRK, L., T. PAVLYCHENKO, T. KOSSAR and D. ANDERSON. 1941. Report of investigations 1939. *Res. Lab. Plant Ecol., Univ. Saskatchewan*; Regina, Canada. 75pp.

KIRK, L., T. PAVLYCHENKO, and W. KOSSAR. 1943. Report of investigations. *Res. Lab. Plant Ecol., Univ. Saskatchewan*; Regina, Canada. 7pp.

KIRKPATRICK, B. and F. BAZZAZ. 1979. Influence of certain fungi on seed germination and seedling survival of four colonizing annuals. *J. Appl. Ecol.* 16:515–527.

KIRKPATRICK, B., L. WAX and E. STOLLER. 1983. Competition of jimsonweed with soybean. *Agron. J.* 75:833–836.

KISELEV, A. 1971. Biological control of weeds. In: *Sornye Rasteniya i Mery Borba s-Nimi*, Moscow: 159–161.

KIVILAAN, A. and R. BANDURSKI. 1973. The ninety year period for Dr. Beal's seed viability experiment. *Am. J. Bot.* 60:140–145.

KJAER, A. 1940. Germination of buried and dry stored seeds. *Proc. Intern. Seed Testing Assoc.* 12:167–190.

———. 1948. Germination of buried and dry stored seed. II. 1934–1944. *Proc. Intern. Seed Testing Assoc.* 14:19–26.

KJAER, A., J. CONTI and I. LARSEN. 1953. Iso-thiocyanates: IV. A systematic investigation of the occurrence and chemical nature of volatile iso-thiocyanates in seeds in various plants. *Acta Chemica Scaninavica* 7:1276.

KLAINE, S. 1986. Influence of thiadiazuron on propagule formation in *Hydrilla verticillata*. *J. Aquat. Plant Mgmt.* 24:80–82.

KLAINE, S. and C. WARD. 1984. Environmental and chemical control of vegetative dormant bud production in *Hydrilla verticillata*. *Ann. Bot.* 53:503–514.

KLEBESADEL, L. 1969. Life cycles of field pennycress in the subarctic as influenced by time of seed germination. *Weed Sci.* 17:563–566.

KLEIN, W. 1956. Investigation of the minimum temperature for germination of agriculture weeds. *Zeitschrift fur Acker und Pflanzenbau* 101:395–430.

KLEY, F. VAN DER. 1956. On the variations in contents and in interrelations of minerals in dandelion *Taraxacum officinale* Weber and pasture grasses. *Netherlands J. Agric. Sci.* 4:314–332.

KLINGMAN, G., F. ASHTON and L. NOORDHOFF. 1982. *Weed science: Principles and practices.* John Wiley & Sons, N.Y. 376pp.

KLINKHAMER, P. and T. DE JONG. 1988. The importance of small-scale disturbance for seedling establishment in *Cirsium vulgare* and *Cynoglossum officinale*. *J. Ecol.* 76:383–392.

KLINKHAMER, P., T. DE JONG and E. MEELIS. 1987. Delay of flowering in the biennial *Cirsium vulgare*, size effects and devernalization. *Oikos* 49:303–308.

KLINKHAMER, P., T. DE JONG and E. VAN DER MEIJDEN. 1988. Production, dispersal and predation of seeds of biennial *Cirsium vulgare*. *J. Ecol.* 76:403–414.

KLOOT, P., and K. BOYCE. 1982. Allelopathic effects of wireweed *Polygonum aviculare*. *Aus. Weeds* 1:11–14.

KLOPATEK, J. 1978. Nutrient dynamics of fresh water riverine marshes and the role of emergent macrophytes. pp. 195–216. In: *Freshwater wetlands: Ecological processes and management potential.* Academic Press, N.Y.

KLOSTERBOER, A. 1978. Red rice control in Texas. In: *Red rice: Research and control.* pp. 35–37. Texas Agric. Exp. Sta., Bull. 1270.

KLYUEVA, M. and G. PAMUKCHI. 1978. Broomrape midge—natural enemy of broomrape in Moldavia. *Izvestiya Akad. Nauk Moldavskoi SSR, Seriya Biologicheskikh Khimicheskikh Nauk* 4:21–25.

KLYUEVA, M. and G. PAMUKCHI. 1982. Technology of the use of *Phytomyza*. *Zaschita Rastenii* (Moscow) 1:33–34.

KNAAP, W. VAN DER. 1985. Human influence on the natural Arctic vegetation in the 17th century and climatic change since 1600 A.D. in Spitzbergen; a paleobotanical study. *Arctic Alpine Res.* 17:371–388.

KNOBLOCH, I. 1954. Developmental anatomy of chicory: The root. *Phytomorphology* 4:47–54.

———. 1955. Developmental anatomy of *Cichorium intybus*: The stem. *Phytomorphology* 5:146–154.

KNUTH, P. 1908. *Handbook of flower pollination. Vol. II. The fertilization of flowers by insects.* Oxford Clarendon Press, London. 703pp.

KOBAYASHI, A., S. MORIMOTO, Y. SHIBATA, K. YA-MASHITA and M. NUMATA. 1980. 10–carbon polyacetylenes as allelopathic substances in dominants in early stages of secondary succession. *J. Chem. Ecol.* 6(1):119–132.

KOBLOVA, M. 1962. The effect of ecological and geographic factors on seed germination in *Amaranthus retroflexus*. *Uchenye Zapiski Kabardino-Balkarsk Univ.* 12:91–102.

KOCH, S. 1974. The *Eragrostis pectinacea-pilosa* complex in North and Central America (**Gramineae : Eragrostoideae**). *Illinois Biological Monograph No. 48.* 74pp.

KOCH, W. 1964. Some observations on changes in weed populations under continuous cereal cropping and with different methods of weed control. *Weed Res.* 4:351–356.

———. 1967. Germination of weed seeds. *Wissenschaftliche Zeitschrift Martin Luther Univ. Halle-Wittenberg, Phytopathologische Vortragsreihe* 16:1005–1015.

———. 1968. Environmental factors affecting the germination of some annual grasses. *Proc. 9th Brit. Weed Control Conf.* 9:14–19.

———. 1969. Einfluss von umweltfaktoren auf die samenphase annueller Unkrauter insbesondere unter dem Gesichtspunkt der unkrautbekampfung. *Arbeit der Univ. Hohenheim, Band 50*, Eugen Ulmer, Stuttgart.

———. 1970. Temperaturanspruche von unkrautern bei der keimung. (Temperature requirements of weeds for germination). *Saatgut Wirtschaft* 22:85–86.

KOCH, W. and H. KOCHER. 1968. The significance of the nutrient factors on the competition between crop plants and weeds. *Zeitschrift fur Pflanzenkrankheiten und Pflanzenschutz* 4:79–87.

KOCH, W. and B. RADEMACHER. 1966. Competition between crop plants and weeds: I. Absolute and relative development of cereals and some weed species. *Weed Res.* 6:243–253.

KOHJI, J., H. HAGIMOTO and Y. MASUDA. 1979. Georeaction and elongation of the flower stalk in a poppy, *Papaver rhoeas* L. *Plant and Cell Physiol.* 20:375–386.

KOHJI, J., K. NISHITANI and Y. MASUDA. 1981. A study on the mechanism of nodding initiation of the flower stalk in a poppy, *Papaver rhoeas* L. *Plant and Cell Physiol.* 22:413–422.

KOHN, G. and E. CUTHBERTSON. 1975. Response of skeleton weed *Chondrilla juncea* to applied superphosphate and grazing management. *Aus. J. Exp. Agric. and Animal Husbandry* 15:102–104.

KOHUT, R. and S. KRUPA. 1977. Sensitivity of selected species of native vegetation to ozone. *Proc. Am. Phytopathological Soc.* 4:88.

KOK, L., T. MCAVOY and W. MAYS. 1986. Impact of tall fescue grass and *Carduus* thistle weevils on growth and development of musk thistle *Carduus nutans*. *Weed Sci.* 34:966–971.

KOLK, H. 1947. Studies in germination biology in weeds. *Vaxtodling, Plant Husbandry* 2:108–164.

———. 1962. Viability and dormancy of dry stored weed seeds. *Vaxtodling, Plant Husbandry* 18:1–192.

KOLLER, D., J. KIGEL and S. OVADIA. 1977a. A kinetic analysis of the facultative photoperiodic response in *Amaranthus retroflexus*. *Planta* 136:13–19.

———. 1977b. The facultative photoperiodic response in reproductive development of *Amaranthus retroflexus*: Changes in the dose response during ontogeny. *Planta* 137:133–138.

KOLLMAN, A. and M. WALI. 1976. Intraseasonal variations in environmental and productivity relations of *Potamogeton pectinatus* communities. *Archiv fur Hydrobiologie, Supplementband* 50(4):439–472.

KOLLMAN, G. and D. STANIFORTH. 1969. Influence of soil compaction on weed seedling emergence. *Abstr. 9th Weed Sci. Soc. Am. Conf.* 9: No. 147.

———. 1972. Hormonal aspects of seed dormancy in yellow foxtail. *Weed Sci.* 20:472–477.

KOLYADKO, I. 1972. The harm caused by branched broomrape. *Zaschita Rastenii* 17:37.

KOMAROV, V., (Ed.) 1968. *Flora of the U.S.S.R.* Vol. 1. Translated from Russian by Israel Program for Scientific Translation, Jerusalem.

KOMMEDAHL, T., and A. LINCK. 1957. The ecological effects of different preceding crop plants on *Setaria glauca* in flax. *Minn. Acad. Sci. Proc.* 25:90–94.

KOMOLAFE, D. 1976. Weed problems in tree crops in Nigeria. *PANS (Pest Articles and News Summaries)* 22:250–256.

KONAR, R. and R. KAPOOR. 1974. Embryology of *Azolla pinnata*. *Phytomorphol.* 24:228–261.

KONDRA, Z., D. CAMPBELL and J. KING. 1983. Temperature effects on germination of rapeseed *Brassica napus* L. and *B. campestris* L. *Can. J. Plant Sci.* 63:1063–1065.

KONDRATEVA-MELVIL, E. 1986. Correlation between the development of root and shoot systems in annual dicotyledonous plants. *Botanicheskii Zhurnal SSSR* 71:1321–1330.

KOR, B. 1944. The vernalization of jute. *Current Sci.* 13:130–131.

KORSMO, E. 1930. *Unkrauter im Akerbau der Neuzeit.* Springer Verlag, Berlin.

———. 1935. Ugressfro (Weed seeds). Gyldendal Norsk Forlag, Oslo. 175pp.

———. 1954. *Anatomy of Weeds.* Grondahl & Sons Forlag, Oslo.

KORSMO, E., T. VIDME and H. FYKSE. 1981. *Korsmos' Ograsplanscher.* Lts Forlag AB, Stockholm.

KOSHY, J. and P. MATHEW. 1985. Cytology of the genus *Cleome* L. *Cytologia* 50:283–287.

KOSINA, R. 1978. The cultivated wild plants from the XI century granaries on the Cathedral-Island in Wroclaw. *Berichte der Deutschen Botanischen Gesellschaft.* 91:121–127.

KOSINOVA, J. 1974. Studies on the weed flora of cultivated land in Egypt: III. Distribution types. *Botanische Jahrbuecher fur Systematik Pflanzengeschichte und Pflanzengeographie* 94(4):449–458.

KOTALAWALA, J. 1976. Noxious water vegetation in Sri Lanka. *Proc. Regional Seminar Noxious Aquatic Vegetation 1973,* New Delhi.

KOTHARI, M. and G. SHAR. 1975. Epidermal structures and ontogeny of stomata in the **Papilionaceae** tribe **Hedysareae.** *Bot. Gaz.* 136:372–379.

KOTHEKAR, V., Gen. Ed. 1970. *A Handbook of Pests, Diseases, and Weeds of Quarantine Significance* (USSR). Kolos Publishers, Moscow. Translated and published for the Agric. Res. Serv.-U.S. Dept. Agric. by Amerind Publishing Co. Pvt. Ltd. New Delhi. pp. 206–224.

KOUL, M. 1964. Cytogenetics of polyploids: I. Cytology of polyploid *Artemisia vulgaris. Cytologia* 29(4):407–414.

———. 1964–1965. Genecological studies in *Artemisia vulgaris. J. Scientific Res. Banaras Univ.* 15(1):104–119.

KOVACS, M. 1982. Chemical composition of the lesser reedmace *Typha angustifolia* in Lake Balaton Hungary. *Acta Bot. Acad. Sci. Hun.* 28:297–308.

KOVACS, M., I. NYARY and L. TOTH. 1984. The microelement content of some submerged and floating aquatic plants. *Acta Bot. Hungarica* 30:173–186.

KOYAMA, T. 1958. Taxonomic study of the genus *Scirpus. Journal of the Faculty of Science, Tokyo Univ., Section 3.* 7(6):271–366.

KOZHOVA, O., V. PANTOVA, and S. TIMOFEEVA. 1985. *Elodea canadensis* in Lake Baikal. *Gidrobiologia Zhurnal.* 21(1):82–84.

KRAATZ, G. and R. ANDERSEN. 1980. Leaf movements in sicklepod *Cassia obtusifolia* in relation to herbicide response. *Weed Sci.* 28:551–556.

KRACK, K. 1959. Investigations on the excretion of undigested clover, grass, and weed seeds by birds and the effect of passage through the stomach and intestines on their germinability. *Zeitschrift fur Acker und Pflanzenbau* 107:405–434.

KRAJNCIC, B. 1974. Photoperiodic responses of **Lemnaceae** from northeastern Slovenia, Yugoslavia. *Acta Bot. Croatica* 33:81–88.

KRATTINGER, K. 1975. Genetic mobility in *Typha. Aquatic Bot.* 1:57–70.

———. 1983. Estimation of size and number of individual plants within populations of *Typha latifolia* L. using isoelectrofocusing. *Aquat. Bot.* 15:241–247.

KREIG, M. 1964. *Green medicine.* Rand McNally, N.Y. 462pp.

KRENNER, J. 1958. The natural history of the sunflower broomrape *Orobanche cumana. Acta Bot., Acad. Scientiarum Hungaricae* 4:113–144.

KRIBBEN, F. 1951. Die bluten bildung von *Orobanche* in abhangigkeit von der entwicklungs-phase des wirtes. *Deutsche Bot. Gesellschaft Berichte* 64:353–355.

KROCHMAL, A., R. WALTERS and R. DOUGHTY. 1971. *A guide to medicinal plants of Appalachia.* USDA handbook No. 400.

KROLIKOWSKA, J. 1978. The transpiration of helophytes. *Ekologia Polska* 26:193–212.

KROPAC, Z. 1966. Estimation of weed seeds in arable soil. *Pedobiologia* 6:105–128.

———. 1973. Weedy *Orobanche* species of Czechoslovakia and the range of their parasitism. pp. 35–43. *Proc. 1st Symp. Parasitic Weeds, European Weed Res. Council,* Malta.

KUIJT, J. 1969. *The biology of parasitic flowering plants.* Univ. California Press, Berkeley, Calif. 246pp.

———. 1977. Haustoria of phanerogamic parasites. *Ann. Rev. Phytopathology* 17:91–118.

KUIJT, J. and R. TOTH. 1976. Ultra structure of angiosperm haustoria: A review. *Ann. Bot.* 40:1121–1130.

KULASOORIYA, S., W. HIRIMBUREGAMA and R. DE SILVA. 1980. Effect of light, temperature and phosphorous on the growth and nitrogen fixation in *Azolla pinnata* native to Sri Lanka. *Oecologia Plantarum* 1(4):355–365.

KULKARNI, D., M. HOSAMANI and P. HUGAR. 1973. Fungal diseases harbored by common weeds in and around Dharwar. *Ind. J. Weed Sci.* 5:6–10.

KUMAR, S. 1983. Biomass and productivity of maize cropland ecosystem. *Acta Bot. Indica* 11:210–213.

KUMAR, U. 1977. Morphogenetic regulation of seed germination in *Orobanche aegyptiaca. Can. J. Bot.* 55:2613–2621.

KUMARI, A. and R. KOHLI. 1984. Studies on the dormancy and macromolecular drifts during germination in *Cassia occidentalis* L. seed. *J. Tree Sci.* 3:111–125.

KUMARI, V. and L. NARAYANA. 1980. A contribution to the embryology of **Oxalidaceae.** *J. Jap. Bot.* 55:171–179.

KUMMER, A. 1951. *Weed seedlings.* Univ. Chicago Press, Chicago. 435pp.

KUNII, H. 1982. Life cycle and growth of *Potamogeton crispus* in a shallow pond Ojaga-Ike, Japan. *Bot. Magazine* 95:109–124.

KUPCHAN, S., J. KNOX, J. KELSEY and J. SAENZ. 1964. Calotropin, a cytotoxic principle isolated from *Asclepias curassavica* L. *Sci.* 146:1685–1686.

KURAUCHI, I. 1956. The resistance of the rice-field ecosystem to the temporary invasion of salt water with special reference to the weed communities. *Jap. J. Ecol.* 5:167–171.

KURTH, H. 1967. The germinative behavior of weeds. *SYS Reporter* 3:6–11.

KUTSCHERA, L. 1960. *Wurzelatlas of mitteleuropaischer ackerunkrauter und kulturpflanzen*. DLG Verlags GMBH, Frankfurt, Germany.

KUTUZOV, G. and G. STEPANENKO. 1969. The interrelationships of plants in a field community. *Doklady Vsesoyuznoi Akad. Sel'skokozyaistvennykh Nauk imeni V. I. Lenina* 8:17–19.

KUUSI, T. and K. AUTIO. 1985. The bitterness properties of dandelion. I. Sensory investigations. *Lebensm-Wiss Technol* 18:339–346.

KVET, J. 1975. Transpiration in seven plant species colonizing a fishpond shore. *Biol. Plantarum (Praha)* 17:434–442.

KVET, J., J. SVOBODA and K. FIALA. 1969. Canopy development in stands of *Typha latifolia* and *Phragmites communis* Trin. in South Moravia. *Hydrobiologia Bucuresti* 10:63–75.

KWON, S., R. SMITH, and R. TALBERT. 1991. Interference of red rice *Oryza sativa* densities in rice (*O. sativa*). *Weed Science* 39:169–174.

LACEFIELD, D. and E. GRAY. 1970. The life cycle of nodding thistle in Kentucky. *Proc. 25th North Central Weed Control Conf.* 25:105–107.

LACEY, E. 1980. Influence of hygroscopic movement on seed dispersal in *Daucus carota*. *Oecologia* (Berl.) 47:110–114.

———. 1981. Seed dispersal in wild carrot *Daucus carota*. *Michigan Botanist* 20:15–20.

———. 1982. Timing of seed dispersal in *Daucus carota*. *Oikos*. 39:83–91.

———. 1984. Seed mortality in *Daucus carota* populations: Latitudinal effects. *Am. J. Bot.* 71:1175–1182.

———. 1986. The genetic and environmental control of reproductive timing in a short-lived monocarpic species *Daucus carota*. *J. Ecol.* 74:73–86.

———. 1988. Latitudinal variation in reproductive timing of a short-lived monocarp, *Daucus carota*. *Ecol.* 69:220–232.

LACEY, E. and R. PACE. 1983. Effect of parental flowering and dispersal times on offspring fate in *Daucus carota*. *Oecologia* 60:274–278.

LACOR, M. 1968. Flowering of *Spirodela polyrhiza*. *Acta Bot. Neerl.* 17(5):357–359.

———. 1969. On the influence of gibberellic acid and kinetin on the germination of turions of *Spirodela polyrhiza*. *Acta Bot. Neerl.* 18(4):550–557.

———. 1970. Some physiologic and morphogenetic aspects of flowering of *Spirodela polyrhiza*. *Acta Bot. Neerl.* 19:53–60.

LAHSER, C. 1967. *Tilapia mossambica* as a fish for aquatic weed control. *Progressive Fish Culturist* 29(1):48–50 (USA).

LAKSHMANAN, C. 1951. A note on the occurrence of turions in *Hydrilla*. *J. Bombay Natural History Soc.* 49:802–804.

LAKSHMANAN, K. 1965. Embryological studies in the **Hydrocharitaceae**: IV. Post fertilization development in *Hydrilla verticillata*. Phyton. (Argentina) 22:45–50.

LAMBERS, H. 1976. Respiration and NADH oxidation of the roots of flood tolerant and flood intolerant *Senecio* spp. as affected by anaerobiosis. *Physiologia Plantarum* 37:117–122.

LAMBERS, H., E. STEINGROVER and G. SMAKMAN. 1979. The significance of oxygen transport and of metabolic adaptation in the flood-tolerance of *Senecio* species. *Physiol. Plantarum* 43:277–281.

LANDOLT, E. 1957. Physiologische and okologische Untersuchungen an **Lemnaceen**. *Berichte der Schweizerischen Botanischen Gesellschaft* 67:271–410.

———. 1975. Morphological differentiation and geographical distribution of the *Lemna gibba–Lemna minor* group. *Aquatic Bot.* 1:345–363.

LANE, D. 1979. The significance of noxious weeds on the roadsides in agricultural areas of Victoria, Australia. *Weed Res.* 19:151–156.

LANE, H. and M. KASPERBAUER. 1965. Photomorphogenic responses of dodder seedlings. *Plant Physiol.* 40:109–116.

LANGELAND, K. 1989. Karyotypes of *Hydrilla* populations in the United States. *J. Aquat. Plant Mgmt.* 27:111–115.

LANGELAND, K., and D. SUTTON. 1980. Regrowth of *Hydrilla verticillata* from axillary buds. *J. Aquat. Plant. Mgmt.* 18:27–29.

LANGHAMMER, L. 1969. Anatomie und histochemie der fruchte von *Silybum*. *Planta Medica* 17:268–275.

LANGSTON, V. and T. HARGER. 1983. Potential for late season infestation by wild poinsettia. *Proc. 38th Southern Weed Sci. Soc. Conf.* 38:77.

LANGSTON, V., T. HARGER and P. JOHNSEY. 1984. Potential for adventitious regeneration of selected weed species. *Weed Sci.* 32:360–363.

LANIGAN, G. 1970–1972. Metabolism of pyrrolizidine alkaloids in the ovine rumen: 2. Some factors affecting rate of alkaloid breakdown by rumen fluid *in vitro*. 3. Competitive relationship between heliotrine and methanogenesis in rumen fluid *in vitro*. 4. Effects of chloralhydrate and halogenated methanes on methanogenesis and alkaloid metabolism in fistulated sheep. *Aus. J. Agric. Res.* 21:633–639 (1970); 22:123–130 (1971); 23:1085–1091 (1972).

LANIGAN, G. and L. SMITH. 1970. Metabolism of the pyrrolizidine alkaloids in the ovine rumen. 1. Formation of 7-α-hydroxy-1-α-methyl-8-α-pyrrolizidine from heliotrine and lasiocarpine. *Aus. J. Agric. Res.* 21:493–500.

LANIGAN, G., A. PAYNE and J. PETERSON. 1978. Antimethanogenic drugs and *Heliotropium europaeum* poisoning in penned sheep. Aus. J. Agric. Res. 29:1281–1292.

LAPIROV, A. 1985. Morphology and development of the terminal bud in the tuber of *Potamogeton pectinatus*. Bi-

ologiya Vnutrennykh Vod Informatsionii Byulleten 68:15–19.

LARSON, M. and E. SCHWARZ. 1980. Allelopathic inhibition of black locust, red clover and black alder by six common herbaceous species. *Forest Sci.* 26:511–520.

LAUER, E. 1953. Uber die Keimtemperatur von Ackerunkrautern und deren einfluss auf die zusammensetzung von Unkrautgesellschaften. *Flora Oder Allgemeine Botanische Zeitung* 140:551–595.

LAUNERT, E. 1968. A monographic survey of the genus *Marsilea* L.: I. The species of Africa and Madagascar. *Senckenbergiana Biologica* 49:273–315.

LAW, R. 1981. The dynamics of a colonizing population of *Poa annua. Ecol.* 62:1267–1277.

LAWRENCE, D. 1976. Morphological variation of *Elodea* in western Massachusetts: Field and laboratory. *Rhodora* 78:739–749.

LAWRENCE, J. and W. MIXON. 1970. Comparative nutrient content of aquatic plants from different habitats. *Proc. 23rd Southern Weed Sci. Soc. Conf.* 23:306–310.

LAWRENCE, M. 1981. *Relationships of southeast Australian species of* Senecio *deduced from studies of morphology, reproductive biology, and cytogenetics.* Ph.D. Diss., Univ. Adelaide, Australia.

LAWRENCE, M., M. AFZAL and J. KENRICK. 1978. The genetical control of self-incompatibility in *Papaver rhoeas. Heredity* 40:239–253.

LAWSON, H. and J. WISEMAN. 1974. Weed competition. *Rep. Scottish Hortic. Res. Sta. 1974,* Dundee: 1–24.

LAWTON, J. 1988. Biological control of bracken in Britain: Constraints and opportunities. *Philosophical Trans. Royal Soc. London* B318:335–355.

LAZARIDES, M. 1980. *The tropical grasses of Southeast Asia.* J. Cramer, Vaduz. 225pp.

LEATHER, G. 1983. Sunflowers *Helianthus annuus* are allelopathic to weeds. *Weed Sci.* 31:37–42.

LEBARON, H. and J. GRESSEL. 1982. *Herbicide resistance in plants.* John Wiley & Sons, N.Y. 400pp.

LECK, M. and K. GRAVELINE. 1979. The seed bank of a freshwater tidal marsh. *Am. J. Bot.* 66:1006–1015.

LECRENIER, A., V. TILKIN and J. RONCHAINE. 1955. Contribution a l'etude morphologique de la chicoree witloof. *Rep. 14th Intern. Hortic. Congr.* Vol. 1. pp. 581–588.

LEE, C. and H. CHANG. 1958. Morphological studies of *Sagittaria sinensis* (*S. sagittifolia*): I. The anatomy of roots. *Acta Botanica Sinica* 7(2):71–86.

LEE, C. and Y. OH. 1987. A morphological taxonomic study of Korean **Pteridaceae**. *Kor. J. Plant Taxonomy* 17:155–166.

LEE, J. and J. HAMRICK. 1983. Demography of two natural populations of musk thistle *Carduus nutans. J. Ecol.* 71:923–936.

LEE, S. and P. CAVERS. 1981. The effects of shade on growth, development and resource allocation patterns of three species of foxtail *Setaria. Can. J. Bot.* 59:1776–1786.

LEE, S. and I. ENOCH. 1977. Weed succession in the peat swamp forest cleared for pineapple cultivation. *Proc. 6th Asian-Pacific Weed Sci. Soc. Conf.* pp. 375–380.

LEE, W., R. ALLEN and P. JOHNSON. 1986. Succession and dynamics of gorse *Ulex europaeus* communities in the Dunedin Ecological District, New Zealand. *New Zealand J. Bot.* 24:279–292.

LEELA, D. 1985. Allelopathy in *Acanthospermum hispidum. Proc. 10th Asian-Pacific Weed Science Society Conf.* 10:19–22.

LEEUWEN, B. VAN. 1981a. Influence of micro-organisms on the germination of the monocarpic *Cirsium vulgare* in relation to disturbance. *Oecologia* 48:112–115.

———. 1981b. The role of pollination in the population biology of the monocarpic species *Cirsium palastre* and *Cirsium vulgare. Oecologia* 51:28–32.

———. 1983. The consequences of predation in the population biology of *Cirsium palastre* and *Cirsium vulgare. Oecologia* 58:178–187.

LEEUWEN, B. VAN, and A. VAN BREEMAN. 1980. Similarities and differences in some biennials. *Acta Bot. Neerl.* 29:209–210.

LEFEVRE, C. and W. CHAPPELL. 1962. A growth inhibitor from *Artemisia vulgaris. Proc. Am. Soc. Plant Physiol.* Abstr. 37: No. 906.

LEFEVRE, P. 1956. Influence du milieu et des conditions d'exploration sur le developpement des plantes adventices. Effet particulier du *pH* et l'etat calcique. *Ann. Agronomiques,* Paris, 7:299–347.

LEGERE, A. and M. SCHREIBER. 1989. Competition and canopy architecture as affected by soybean *Glycine max* row width and density of redroot pigweed *Amaranthus retroflexus. Weed Sci.* 37:84–92.

LEGNER, E. 1979. Update of biological aquatic weed control with fish in irrigation canals in California's lower desert. *Abstr. 19th Weed Sci. Soc. Am. Conf.* 19:62–63.

LEGNER, E. and C. MURRAY. 1981. Feeding rates and growth of the fish *Tilapia zillii* on *Hydrilla verticillata, Potamogeton pectinatus,* and *Myriophyllum spicatum* and interactions in irrigation canals of southern California. *Mosquito News* 41:241–250.

LEGUIZAMON, E. and H. ROBERTS. 1982. Seed production by an arable weed community. *Weed Res.* 22:35–39.

LEIPOLD, H., F. OEHME and J. COOK. 1973. Congenital arthrogryposis associated with ingestion of jimsonweed by pregnant sows. *Am. Vet. Med. Assoc. J.* 162:1059–1060.

LEITAO, F., C. ARANHA and O. BACCHI. 1972. *Plantas invasoras de culturas no estado de Sao Paulo.* Empresa Grafica da Revista dos Tribunais; Sao Paulo, Brazil.

LEITAO, H., N. BANZATO and L. AZZINI. 1972. Estudios de competicao entre o arroz vermelho e o arroz cultivado. *Bragantia* 31:249–258.

LEKIC, M. 1970a. Phytophagus insects observed on parasitic phanerogams of the genera *Orobache* and *Cuscuta. Proc. 1st Intern. Symp. Bio. Control Weeds.* pp. 21–24.

———. 1970b. The role of the dipteron *Phytomyza orobanchia* in reducing phanerogam populations of the genus *Orobanche vojvodina. Savremena Poljoprivreda* 18:627–637. (Yugoslavia)

LESSARD, P., W. WILSON, H. OLANDER, Q. ROGERS and V. MENDEL. 1986. Clinicopathologic study of horses surviving pyrrolizidine alkaloid (*Senecio vulgaris*) toxicosis. *Am. J. Veterinary Res.* 47:1776–1780.

LEVITT, J., J. LOVETT and P. GARLICK. 1984. *Datura stramonium* allelochemicals, longevity in soil, and ultrastructural effects on root tip cells of *Helianthus annuus. New Phytol.* 97:213–218.

LEVY, E. 1940. Pasture weeds. 1. Their ecological relationship to the pasture sward (New Zealand). *Bull. Commonwealth Bureau of Pastures and Forage Crops* 27:144–152.

LEWIN, R. 1948. Biological flora of the British Isles: *Sonchus oleraceus* and *Sonchus asper. J. Ecol.* 36:203–233.

LEWIS, J. 1961. The influence of water level, soil depth and type on the survival of crop and weed seeds. *Proc. Intern. Seed Testing Assoc.* 26:68–85.

———. 1963. Longevity of seed. In: *Republic of Welsch Plant Breeding Station, 1962.*

———. 1973. Longevity of crop and weed seeds: Survival after 20 years in soil. *Weed Res.* 13:179–191.

LEWIS, K. and B. JOHN. 1961. Hybridization in a wild population of *Eleocharis palustris. Chromosoma* 12(4):433–448.

LEWIS, W. and M. LEWIS. 1977. *Medical botany: Plants affecting man's health.* John Wiley & Sons, N.Y. 514pp.

LI, YANG-HAN. 1987. Parasitism and integrated control of dodder on soybean. pp. 497–499. *Proc. 4th Intern. Symp. Parasitic Flowering Plants.*

LIEFFERS, V. and J. SHAY. 1981. The effects of water level on the growth and reproduction of *Scirpus maritimus* var. *paludosus. Can. J. Bot.* 59:118–121.

———. 1982a. Seasonal growth and standing crop of *Scirpus maritimus* var. *paludosus* in Saskatchewan. *Can. J. Bot.* 60:117–125.

———. 1982b. Distribution and variation in growth of *Scirpus maritimus* var. *paludosus* on the Canadian prairies. *Can. J. Bot.* 60:1938–1949.

LIEM, A. 1980. Effects of light and temperature on anthesis of *Holcus lanatus, Festuca rubra* and *Poa annua. Grana* 19:21–29.

LILLIE, R. 1986. The spread of Eurasian watermilfoil *Myriophyllum spicatum* in Davis Lake, Sauk County, Wisconsin (USA). *Lake and Reservoir Mgmt.* 2:64–68.

LIN, Y. and T. YANG. 1974. Studies on anti-leukemic substance, cordacin. I. Isolation and characterization. *Chinese J. Microbiol.* 7:47–56.

LINCOLN, W. 1981. Laboratory germination of *Cirsium vulgare*—bull or spear thistle. *Newsl. Assoc. Official Seed Analysts* 55:67–68.

LINHART, Y. 1976. Density dependent seed germination strategies in colonizing versus non-colonizing plant species. *J. Ecol.* 64:375–380.

LINKE, K. 1987. Research on the seeds and developing seedlings of *Striga* and *Orobanche. PLITS (Institut fur Pflanzenproduktion in den Tropen und Subtropen)* 5:1–93.

LINKE, K. and W. VOGT. 1987. A method and its application for observing germination and early development of *Striga* and *Orobanche. Proc. 4th Intern. Symp. Parasitic Flowering Plants* 4:501–509. Ed. by H. Weber and W. Forstreuter. Marburg, Germany.

LINN, J., R. GOODRICH, D. OTTERBY, J. MEISKE and E. STABA. 1975. Nutritive value of dried or ensiled aquatic plants. 1. Chemical composition, 2. Digestibility by sheep. *J. Animal Sci.* 41:601–615.

LIOR, E., J. KIGEL and B. RUBIN. 1985. Reproductive biology and eradication of *Euphorbia geniculata. Phytoparasitica* 13:230–231.

LISTOWSKI, A. and I. JACKOWSKA. 1965. Observations on plant development: XI. On the rhythm of flowering of *Taraxacum officinale. Acta Societatis Botanicorum Poloniae* 34:549–561.

LISTOWSKI, A. and A. JASMANOWICZ. 1969. Observations on the development of plants: XVI. Developmental rhythm and flowering of *Setaria glauca. Acta Societatis Botanicorum Poloniae* 38:641–651.

LITTLE, E. 1979. *Handbook of utilization of aquatic plants: A review of world literature.* Fisheries Technical Paper #187, 176pp. Food and Agriculture Organization of the UN, Rome.

LITTLEFIELD, N., H. PATTEE and K. ALLRED. 1966. Movement of sugar in the alfalfa dodder association. *Weeds* 14:52–54.

LITYNSKI, M. and M. PEPLINSKA. 1970. Studies on the growth and fructification of vegetable seed plants: I. Observations of the biology of growth and the fructification of carrot *Daucus carota. Hodowla Roslin Aklimatyzacja I Nasiennictwo* 14:191–211.

LLOYD, D. 1956. Remarks on the possible biocontrol program with the weed *Acanthospermum hispidum* DC. *Can. Entomologist* 88:613–622.

LOCZY, S., R. CARIGNAN and D. PLANAS. 1983. The role of roots in carbon uptake by the submersed macrophytes, *Myriophyllum spicatum, Vallisneria americana* and *Heteranthera dubia. Hydrobiologia* 98:3–7.

LODHI, M. 1979. Allelopathic potentials of *Salsola kali* and its possible role in rapid disappearance of weedy stage during revegetation. *J. Chem. Ecol.* 5:429–437.

LODKINA, M. 1977. Specific aspects of pollen sac development in some species of **Najadaceae** and **Lemnaceae**. *Botanicheskii Zhurnal*, Leningrad 61(11):1536–1545.

LOHAMMAR, G. 1938. Wasserchemie und höhere vegetation Schwedische seen. *Symbolae Bot. Upsaliensis* 111:1–250.

LOKTEV, N. 1958. Spreading of the seeds of various weed plants by seeds of *Bromus secalinus*. *Botanicheskii Zhurnal SSSR* 43:1314–1316.

LONG, H. 1911. Weeds and their destruction. *Transactions Highland Agric. Soc. Scotland* 1–2:45–83.

LONGSTRETH, D. and C. MASON. 1984. The effect of light on the growth and dry matter allocation patterns of *Alternanthera philoxeroides*. *Bot. Gaz.* 145:105–109.

LONGSTRETH, D., J. BOLANOS and J. SMITH. 1984. Salinity effects on photosynthesis and growth in *Alternanthera philoxeroides*. *Plant Physiol.* 75:1044–1047.

LONGSTRETH, D., J. BOLANOS and R. GODDARD. 1985. Photosynthetic rate and mesophyll surface area in expanding leaves of *Alternanthera philoxeroides* grown at 2 light levels. *Am. J. Bot.* 72:14–19.

LOPEZ, J. and M. MATTIACCI. 1983. Dano de "sanguiaria" *Polygonum aviculare* L. durante la implantacion de una pastura cultivad. *Proc. 19th Argentine Weeds and Their Control Meeting* 19:246–251.

LOPEZ, L. and A. OLIVERA. 1970. Determinacion del contenido en vitaminas "C" de diversos vegetales alimenticios de Trujillo y zonas proximas. *Boletin Sociedad Quimica Peru* 36:23–30.

LORD, E. 1979. Development of cleistogamous and chasmogamous flowers in *Lamium amplexicaule*, an example of heteroblastic inflorescence development. *Bot. Gaz.* 140:39–50.

———. 1980a. Physiological controls on the production of cleistogamous and chasmogamous flowers in *Lamium amplexicaule* L. *Ann. Bot.* 44:757–766.

———. 1980b. An anatomical basis for the divergent floral forms in the cleistogamous species *Lamium amplexicaule*. *Am. J. Bot.* 67:1430–1441.

———. 1981. Cleistogamy: A tool for the study of floral morphogenesis function, and evolution. *Bot. Rev.* 47(4):421–449.

———. 1982a. Effect of daylight on open flower production in the cleistogamous species *Lamium amplexicaule* L. *Ann. Bot.* 49:261–263.

———. 1982b. Floral morphogenesis in *Lamium amplexicaule* L. **Labiatae** with a model for the evolution of the cleistogamous flower. *Bot. Gaz.* 143(1):63–72.

LORENZI, H. 1982. *Plantas daninhas do Brasil*. Editora Franciscana; Piracicaba, Brazil. 425pp.

LOSCH, R. and E. KRUG. 1979. Studies on the stomatal behavior of *Veronica persica* and *V. hederifolia*. pp. 89–96. *Proc. EWRS Symp. Influence of Different Factors on the Development and Control of Weeds*.

LOTTI, C. and C. PARDOSSI. 1977. Composizione minerale ospiteparassita in plante infestate da **Orobanchaceae**. *Agricoltura Italiana* 106:155–165.

LOUSLEY, J. 1968. A glabrous perennial *Sonchus* in Britain. *Proc. Botan. Soc. Brit. Isles* 7(2):151–157.

LOVATO, A. and P. VIGGNIANI. 1974. Laboratory germination and field emergence of some weed species. *Revista Agronomia* 8:108–112. Cited in *Weed Abstr.* 1975, 24: No. 2301.

LOVE, A. 1961. Some notes on *Myriophyllum spicatum*. *Rhodora* 63:139–145.

LOVETT, J. 1986. Allelopathy: The Australian experience. pp. 75–99. In: *The science of allelopathy*. Ed. by A. Putnam and C. Tang. John Wiley & Sons, N.Y.

LOVETT, J., J. LEVITT, A. DUFFIELD AND N. SMITH. 1981. Allelopathic potential of *Datura stramonium*. *Weed Res.* 21:165–170.

LOW, K. and C. LEE. 1979. Effect of car exhausts on lead contamination in vegetables grown adjacent to Kuala Lumpur highway in Malaysia. *Pertanika* 2:149–151.

LOWDAY, J. 1987. The effects of cutting and asulam on numbers of frond buds and biomass of fronds and rhizomes of bracken *Pteridium aquilinum*. *Ann. Appl. Biol.* 110:175–184.

LOYAL, D. and H. SINGH. 1978. A further investigation of the morphology of vessels in *Marsilea*. *Proc. Ind. Acad. Sci., Section B* 87:335–346.

LUBIGAN, R. and B. MERCADO. 1974. Effect of different densities of *Scirpus maritimus* on yield of lowland rice. *Philipp. Weed Sci. Bull.* 1(2):60–63.

———. 1976–1977. Chemical control of *Scirpus maritimus* and mixed *S. maritimus-Echinochloa crusgalli* populations in lowland transplanted rice. *Philippine Agriculturist* 60:280–284.

LUCIANI-GRESTA, F. 1975. The photoperiodic behavior of *Tagetes minuta* of Sicily. *Bull. Soc. Botanique France* 122:363–366.

LUKOVIN, S. and V. KITENKO. 1974. An important method of dodder control. *Selskoe Khozyaistvo Kirozyizii* 4:20–23.

LUKOVIN, S. and A. RUDENKO. 1975. Dodder destruction by flaming. *Zaschita Rastenii* 20:47–49.

LUMIS, G., G. HOFSTRA and R. LUMIS. 1973. Sensitivity of roadside trees and shrubs to aerial drift of de-icing salt. *Hortscience* 8:475–479.

LUMPKIN, T. and D. PLUCKNETT. 1980. *Azolla*: Botany, physiology, and use as a green manure. *Econ. Bot.* 34:111–153.

LUNDBERG, F. 1957. New facts on *Cuscuta australis*. *Bot. Notiser* 110:123–124.

LUSH, W. 1988. Biology of *Poa annua* in a temperate zone putting green. II. The seed bank. *J. Appl. Ecol.* 25:989–997.

———. 1989. Adaptation and differentiation of golf course

populations of annual bluegrass *Poa annua. Weed Sci.* 37:54–59.

———. 1951. Verbreitung und Okologie der hoheren Wasserpflanzen im Brackwasser der Ekenas-gegend in Sud Finnland. *Acta Bot. Fennica* 49:1–231; 50:1–370.

LYMAN, J. and N. ELLSTRAND. 1984. Clonal diversity in *Taraxacum officinale* **Compositae**, an apomict. *Heredity* 53:1–10.

LYSHEDE, O. 1982. Diagnostic differences in the seed coat structure in *Raphanus sativus* and *R. raphanistrum. Seed Sci. Technol.* 10:167–178.

———. 1984. Seed structure and germination in *Cuscuta pedicellata* with some notes on *C. campestris. Nordic J. Bot.* 4:669–674.

———. 1985. Morphological and anatomical features of *Cuscuta pedicellata* and *C. campestris. Nordic J. Bot.* 5:65–77.

MABERLY, S. and D. SPENCE. 1983. Photosynthetic inorganic carbon use by freshwater plants. *J. Ecol.* 71:705–724.

MCATEE, W. 1917. Propagation of wild duck foods. *USDA Bull.* No. 465. 40pp.

MCAVOY, T. and L. KOK. 1981. Biological studies of *Ceutorhynchus punctiger* Gyll. **Coleoptera : Curculionidae**, a dandelion seed-feeding weevil. *Virginia J. Sci.* 32:77.

MCBARRON, E. 1983. *Poisonous plants: A handbook for farmers and graziers (Australia).* Inkata Press, Sydney. 150pp.

MCCANN, C. 1942. Observations on Indian duckweeds, **Lemnaceae.** *J. Bombay Nat. History Soc.* 43:148–162.

MCCARTY, M. 1964. New and problem weeds: musk thistle. *Proc. 20th North Central Weed Control Conf.* 20:62–63.

———. 1982. Musk thistle *Carduus thoermeri* seed production. *Weed Sci.* 30:441–445.

———. 1985. A nursery study of large-flowered taxa of *Carduus. Weed Sci.* 33:664–668.

———. 1986. A 15 year phenological record of pasture plants near Lincoln, Nebraska. *Weed Sci.* 34(2):218–224.

MCCARTY, M. and C. SCIFRES. 1969. Life cycle studies with musk thistle *Carduus nutans. Univ. Nebraska Agric. Exp. Sta., Res. Bull.* No. 230. 15pp.

MCCARTY, M., C. SCIFRES, A. SMITH and G. HORST. 1969. Germination and early seedling development of musk and plumeless thistle. *Univ. Nebraska Agric. Exp. Sta., Res. Bull.* No. 229 (USA).

MCCARTY, M., C. SCIFRES, and L. ROBISON. 1984. The descriptive guide for major Nebraska thistles. *Univ. Nebraska Agric. Exp. Sta. Bull.* SB493. 24pp.

MCCARTY, M., D. KLINGMAN and L. MARROW. 1974. Interrelations of weed-control and pasture-management methods at Lincoln, Nebraska, 1949–1969. *USDA Tech. Bull.* No. 1473.

MCCOMBIE, A. and I. WILE. 1971. Ecology of aquatic vascular plants in southern Ontario (Canada) impoundments. *Weed Sci.* 19:225–228.

MCCORD, C. and H. LOYACANO. 1978. Removal and utilization of nutrients by Chinese water chestnut in catfish ponds. *Aquaculture* 13:143–155.

MCCREA, C. and K. HEAD. 1981. Sheep tumors in northeast Yorkshire. II. Experimental production of tumors. *Brit. Vet. J.* 137:21–30.

MCELGUNN, J., D. HEINRICHS and R. ASHFORD. 1972. Effects of initial harvest date on productivity and persistence of alfalfa and bromegrass. *Can. J. Plant Sci.* 52:801–804.

MCFARLAND, D. and J. BARKO. 1990. Temperature and daylight effects on growth and tuber formation in *Hydrilla. J. Aquat. Plant Mgmt.* 28:15–19.

MCILRAITH, A., G. ROBINSON and J. SHAY. 1989. A field study of competition and interaction between *Lemna minor* and *Lemna trisulca. Can J. Bot.* 67:2904–2911.

MCINTOSH, A., B. SHEPARD, R. MAYES, G. ATCHISON and D. NELSON. 1978. Some aspects of sediment distribution and macrophyte cycling of heavy metals in a contaminated lake. *J. Environ. Quality* 7(3):301–305.

MCINTYRE, G. and K. BEST. 1975. Studies on the flowering of *Thlaspi arvense*: A competitive study of early and late-flowering strains. *Bot. Gaz.* 136:151–158.

———. 1978. Studies on the flowering of *Thlaspi arvense*: Genetic and ecological differences between early and late-flowering strains. *Bot. Gaz.* 139:190–195.

MCLAY, C. 1976. The effect of *pH* on the population growth of three species of duckweed: *Spirodela oligorhiza, Lemna minor* and *Wolffia arrhiza. Freshwater Biol.* 6:125–136.

MAC LEOD, D. 1961a. Photosynthesis in *Cuscuta. Experientia* 17:542–547.

———. 1961b. Some anatomical and physiological observations on two species of *Cuscuta. Transactions Bot. Soc. Edinburgh* 39:302–315.

———. 1963. The parasitism of *Cuscuta. New Phytol.* 62:257–263.

MCMILLAN, C. 1959. Salt tolerance within a *Typha* population. *Am. J. Bot.* 46:521–526.

MACNAEIDHE, F. and P. CURRAN. 1980. Weed ecology of agricultural peatlands. *Res. Rep. Faculty General Agric., Univ. College*; Dublin, Ireland.

———. 1982. Weed colonization of bogs taken into cultivation and seed dormancy of *Polygonum* invaders. *Irish J. Agric. Res.* 21:199–209.

MCNAUGHTON, I. 1976. Turnip and relatives *Brassica campestris* **Cruciferae.** In: *Evolution of crop plants.* Ed. by N. Simmonds. Longman, N.Y.

MCNAUGHTON, I. and J. HARPER. 1960. The comparative biology of closely related species living in the same area: I. External breeding-barriers between *Papaver* species. *New Phytol.* 59:15–26.

———. 1964. Biological flora of the British Isles, No. 99 *Papaver rhoeas* L. *J. Ecol.* 52:767–793.

MCNAUGHTON, J. 1966. Ecotype function in the *Typha* community-type. *Ecol. Monographs* 36:297–325.

MCNAUGHTON, S. 1968. Autotoxic feedback in relation to germination and seedling growth in *Typha latifolia*. *Ecol.* 49:367–369.

———. 1973. Comparative photosynthesis of Quebec and California ecotypes of *Typha latifolia*. *Ecol.* 54:1260–1270.

———. 1975. R- and k- selection in *Typha*. *Am. Naturalist* 109:251–261.

MCNAUGHTON, S., R. CAMPBEU, R. FREYER, J. MYLROIE and K. RODLAND. 1974. Photosynthetic properties and root chilling responses of altitudinal ecotypes of *Typha latifolia* L. *Ecol.* 55:168–172.

MCNEIL, J. 1981. Taxonomy and distribution in eastern Canada of *Polygonum arenastrum* (4X = 40) and *P. monspeliense* (6X = 60), introduced members of the *P. aviculare* complex. *Can. J. Bot.* 59:2744–2751.

MCNEILLY, T. 1981. Ecotypic differentiation in *Poa annua*: Interpopulation differences in response to competition and cutting. *New Phytol.* 88:539–547.

MCVEAN, D. 1966. Ecology of *Chondrilla juncea* L. in southeastern Australia. *J. Ecol.* 54:345–365.

MCWILLIAMS, E. 1966. *Ecotypic differentiation within* Amaranthus retroflexus, A. hybridus *and* A. powelli. Ph.D. thesis, Iowa State Univ.; Ames, Iowa, USA. 174pp.

MCWILLIAMS, E., R. LANDERS and J. MAHLSTEDE. 1966. Ecotypic differentiation in response to photoperiodism in several species of *Amaranthus*. *Proc. Iowa Acad. Sci.* 73:44–51.

———. 1968. Variation in seed weight and germination in populations of *Amaranthus retroflexus*. *Ecol.* 49:290–296.

MADHUSOODANAN, K. and M. PAL. 1981. Cytology of vegetable *Amaranths*. *Bot. J. Linn. Soc.* 82(1):61–68.

MADSEN, J. and C. BOYLEN. 1989. Eurasian watermilfoil seed ecology from an oligotrophic and a eutrophic lake. *J. Aquat. Plant Mgmt.* 27:119–121.

MADSEN, S. 1962. Germination of buried and dry stored seeds III, 1934–1960. *Proc. 27th Intern. Seed Testing Assoc.* 27:920–928.

MAGERS, A. 1970. Honey plants of the Missouri valley. *Am. Bee J.* 110:94.

MAGUIRE, B. 1934. Report in a personal letter to W. Muenscher, May, 1934. See Muenscher (1936).

MAGUIRE, J. and A. OVERLAND. 1959. *Laboratory germination of seeds of weedy and native plants*. Washington Agric. Exp. Sta., Circ. 349; Pullman, Washington. 15pp.

MAHAJAN, S. 1980. Autecology and floral biology of *Trianthema portulacastrum*. *Geobios* 7:161–163.

———. 1982. Seed germination of *Trianthema portulacastrum* L. *Vijnana Parishad Anusandhan Patrika* 25:125–129.

MAHESHWARI, P. and B. JOHRI. 1950. The occurrence of persistent pollen tubes in *Hydrilla*, *Ottelia*, and *Boer-*

havia, together with discussion of possible significance in the life-history of angiosperms. *J. Ind. Bot. Soc.* 29:48–51.

MAHESHWARI, S. and N. MAHESHWARI. 1963. The female gametophyte, endosperm, and embryo of *Spirodela polyrhiza*. *Beitrage zur Biologie der Pflanzen* (Berlin) 39(2):179–188.

MAHTO, R., M. PRASAD and S. HUSSAIN. 1970. Effect of seed treatment and different levels of phosphate manuring on kashni weed *Cichorium intybus* in berseem *Trifolium alexandrinum*. *Allahabad Farmer* 44(3):143–148.

MAIDEN, J. 1894. Lucerne or Queensland hemp *Sida rhombifolia*. An Australian weed with great possibilities of usefulness. *Agric. Gaz. New South Wales* 5:537–544.

MAJISU, B. 1970. A potentially dangerous weed of rice in east Africa. *E. African Agric. and Forestry Res. Organization*, Newsl. 60; Nairobi.

MAJOR, D. 1975. Stomatal frequency and distribution in rape. *Can. J. Plant Sci.* 55:1077–1078.

———. 1977. Influence of seed size on yield and yield components of rape. *Agron. J.* 69:541–543.

MAJUMDER, R., K. TIWARI, S. BHATTACHARJEE and A. NAIR. 1978. Some folklore medicine from Assam and Meghalaya. *Quart. J. Crude Drug Res.* 16:185–189.

MALEK, L. 1981. The effect of drying on *Spirodela polyrhiza* turion germination. *Can. J. Bot.* 59:104–105.

MALEK, L. and Y. ODA. 1979. The effect of red and blue light on turion production. *Plant Physiol.* 63(5): suppl. 156.

MALHOTRA, S. 1976. Remedy for aquatic weeds in Bhakra canals. *Proc. Regional Seminar, Noxious Aquatic Vegetation* 1973; New Delhi.

MALICK, K. and N. MAJUMDAR. 1974. Observations and critical notes on Indian *Drymaria*. *Bull. Botan. Survey Ind.* 16:151–153.

MALICKI, L. amd C. BERECIOWA. 1986. Uptake of more important mineral components by common field weeds on loess soils. *Acta Agrobotanica* 39:129–141.

MALL, L. 1957. Contribution to the autecology of *Cassia tora* L. and *C. obtusifolia* L. *J. Univ. Saugar*, 6 (Sec.B): 35–54.

MALL, L. and S. SHARMA. 1967. Ecological study of a few soil heaps of Ujjain. *J. of Vikram University* 11:15–26.

MALL, L., S. BILLORE and C. MISRA. 1973. A study on the community chlorophyll content with reference to height and dry weight. *Trop. Ecol.* 14:81–83.

MALONE, C. and V. PROCTOR. 1965. The dispersal of *Marsilea mucronata* by water birds. *Am. Fern J.* 55:167–170.

MANI, M. 1979. *Ecology and phytogeography of high altitude plants of the northwest Himalaya*. Oxford and IBH Publ. Co., New Delhi.

MANI, V., K. GAUTAM and G. KULSHRESTHA. 1976. Progress of aquatic weed control in India and suggestions for further research. *Proc. Regional Seminar, Noxious Aquatic Vegetation 1973*; New Delhi.

MANN, H. 1981. Common dandelion *Taraxacum officinale*

control with 2,4–D and mechanical treatments. *Weed Sci.* 29:704–708.

MANN, H. and P. CAVERS. 1979. The regenative capacity of root cuttings of *Taraxacum officinale* under natural conditions. *Can. J. Bot.* 57:1783–1791.

MANTAI, K. and M. NEWTON. 1982. Root growth in *Myriophyllum spicatum* a specific response to nutrient availability? *Aquat. Bot.* 13:45–56.

MANTHEY, D. and J. NALEWAJA. 1987. Germination of two foxtail (*Setaria*) species. *Weed Tech.* 1:302–304.

MANTLE, P. and S. SHAW. 1977. Role of weed grasses in the etiology of ergot disease in wheat. *Ann. Appl. Biol.* 86:339–351.

MANUEL, J. and B. MERCADO. 1977. Biology of *Paspalum*: I. Pattern of growth and asexual reproduction. *Philipp. Agriculturist* 61:192–198.

MANUEL, J., B. MERCADO and R. LUBIGAN. 1979. Approaches to the control of *Paspalum distichum* L. in lowland rice. *Philipp. Agriculturist* 62:255–261.

MAPPLEBECK, L., V. SOUZA MACHADO, and B. GRODZINSKI. 1982. Seed germination and seedling growth characteristics of atrazine-susceptible and resistant biotypes of *Brassica campestris*. *Can. J. Plant Sci.* 62:733–739.

MARADUFU, A., R. LUBEGA, and F. DORN. 1978. Isolation of 5E ocimenone, a mosquito larvacide from *Tagetes minuta*. *Lloydia* 41:181–183.

MARCHAND, P. 1985. Oxygen evolution by *Elodea canadensis* under ice and snow: A case for winter photosynthesis in subnivean vascular plants. *Aquilo Ser Bot.* 23:57–61.

MARGARA, J. 1974. On the condition of vegetative development and that of inflorescences of newly formed buds starting from fragments of flower stalks of *Cichorium intybus*. *Comptes Rendus Hebdomadaires des Seances Academie des Sci., Series D* 278:1195–1198.

MARIAPPAN, V. and P. NARAYANASAMY. 1972. *Acanthospermum hispidum* DC., A new host of tomato leaf curl virus. *Madras Agric. J.* 59:355–357.

———. 1977. Characterization of viruses affecting weeds: I. Mosaic diseases. *Madras Agric. J.* 64:106–112.

MARIAPPAN, V., C. GOVINDASWAMI and K. RAMAKRISHNAN. 1973. A note on the *Achyranthes aspera* L., mosaic virus occurring around Coimbatore, Tamil Nadu. *Ind. J. Weed Sci.* 5:48–49.

MARIMUTHU, R., B. SUBRAMANIAN, I. KOTHARI and J. INAMDAR. 1989. Lactiferous taxa as a source of energy and hydrocarbon. *Econ. Bot.* 43:255–261.

MARKS, M. 1983. Timing of emergence and reproduction in some tropical dicotyledonous weeds. *Weed Res.* 23:325–332.

MARKS, M. and C. AKOSIM. 1984. Achene dimorphism and germination in three composite weeds. *Trop. Agric.*, Trinidad, 61:69–73.

MARKS, M. and A. NWACHUKU. 1986. Seed-bank characteristics in a group of tropical weeds. *Weed Res.* 26:151–157.

MARSCHALL, C. 1925. Differentiation of sporangia in *Marsilea quadrifolia*. *Bot. Gaz.* 79:85–94.

MARSHAL, E. 1984. The ecology of a land drainage channel: II. Biology, chemistry and submerged weed control. *Water Res.*, 18:817–825.

MARSHALL, E. 1987. Hanford's radioactive tumbleweed. *Sci.* 236:1616–1620.

MARSHALL, G. 1987. A review of the biology and control of selected weed species in the genus *Oxalis*: *O. stricta* L., *O. latifolia* H.B.K., and *O. pes-caprae* L. *Crop Protection* 6:355–364.

MARSHALL, G., and J. GITARI. 1988. Studies on the growth and development of *Oxalis latifolia*. *Ann. Appl. Biol.* 112:143–150.

MARSICO, O. 1978. *Chondrilla juncea* L.: A new weed in Argentina. *Revista Asociacion Argentina de Malezas* 6:41–45.

MARSTON, M. and W. HEYDECKER. 1966. Rapid clonal multiplication of chicory from shoots, roots, and leaves. *Royal Hortic. Soc. J.* 91(12):510–512.

MARTEN, G. and R. ANDERSEN. 1975. Forage nutritive value and palatability of 12 common annual weeds. *Crop Sci.* 15:821–827.

MARTEN, G., C. SHEAFFER and D. WYSE. 1987. Forage nutritive value and palatability of perennial weeds. *Agron. J.* 79:980–986.

MARTIN, E. and G. LARBALESTIER. 1977. A membrane-bound plastid inclusion in the epidermis of leaves of *Taraxacum officinale*. *Can. J. Bot.* 55:222–225.

MARTIN, F. and R. RUBERTE. 1978. *Survival and subsistence in the tropics*. Antillan College Press, Mayaguez, Puerto Rico. 243pp.

MARTIN, J. 1943. Germination studies of the seeds of some common weeds. *Proc. Iowa Acad. Sci.* 50:221–228.

MARTINOLI, G. and P. OGLIOTTI. 1970. Cytotaxonomical studies in *Artemisia vulgaris* and *A. verlotorum*. *Giornale Bot. Italiano* 104(5):373–387.

MARTINS, C. and D. DECARVALHO. 1982. A successional stage community dominated by *Pteridium aquilinum* in Lavras, Brazil. *Planta Daninha* 5:35–39.

MARTINSSON, K. 1984. The flowering of *Lemna minor*. *Svensk Bot. Tidskr.* 78:9–15.

MARX, J. 1977. Nitrogen fixation: prospects for genetic manipulation. *Sci.* 196:638–641.

MARY, T. and C. MALIK. 1971. Cytological studies in some *Digitaria* species. *Genetica Iberia* 23:1167–1181.

MASCAZZINI, F. 1939. Commercial quality of alfalfa seed for export during the years 1932–38 weed seeds found. *Revista Argentina Agronomia* 6:212–229.

MASEFIELD, G. 1939. Weeds of high altitude districts in Uganda. *E. African Agric. J.* 5:157–158.

MASON, R. 1960. Three waterweeds of the family **Hy-drocharitaceae** in New Zealand. *New Zealand J. Sci.* 3:382–395.

MASSEY, J. and G. SOWELL. 1969. Effects of spring arrangement and anthracnose on *Cassia occidentalis* L. *Agron. J.* 61:749–750.

MATAI, S. 1976. Protein from water weeds. pp. 369–373. In: *Aquatic weeds in South East Asia.* Ed. by C. Varshney and J. Rzoska. Dr. Junk Publ., The Hague.

MATHON, C. 1980. Photoperiodic reactions in the Congo Zaire ruderal plants. *Bull. Societe Botanique France Letters Botaniques* 127:355–364.

MATHUR, P. 1965. Weed control in sugarcane in north India. *Ind. Inst. Sugarcane Res. Tech. Bull.* 2. 23pp.

MATTHEWS, D. 1963. Laboratory identification of seeds of some thistles: *Cirsium arvense, C. vulgare, Carduus nutans. Proc. Intern. Seed Testing Assoc.* 28:19–26.

MATTHEWS, L. 1975. *Weed control by chemical methods.* New Zealand Ministry of Agric. and Fisheries; Gov. Printer, Bull. No. 329; Wellington.

MATTOCKS, A. 1972. Toxicity and metabolism of *Senecio* alkaloids. In: *Phytochemical ecology,* Chapter 11. Ed. by J. Harborne. Academic Press, NY.

MATUMURA, M. 1967. Genecological studies on foxtail grass, *Alopecurus aequalis,* in Japan. *Res. Bull. Faculty Agric., Gifu-ken Prefect Univ.* 25:129–208.

MAURYA, D., H. BAGHA and B. SONI. 1973. Preliminary pharmacological studies in *Erigeron canadensis. Ind. J. Pharmacy* 35(2):62–63.

MAXNUK, M. 1985. Bottom tillage treatments for Eurasian watermilfoil control. *1st Intern. Symp. on watermilfoil* Myriophyllum spicatum, *and related* **Haloragaceae** *spp.* 1:163–172.

MAYR, F. 1915. Hydropoten an Wasser und Sumpfpflanzen. *Botanisches Zentralblatt, Beihefte* (Leipzig) 32:278.

MAZER, S. 1987. The quantitative genetics of the life history and fitness components in *Raphanus raphanistrum*: Ecological and evolutionary consequences of seed weight variation. *Am. Naturalist* 130:891–914.

MAZER, S., A. SNOW and M. STANTON. 1986. Fertilization dynamics and parental effects upon fruit development in *Raphanus raphanistrum*: Consequences for seed size variation. *Am. J. Bot.* 73:500–511.

MEADLY, G. 1965. *Weeds of western Australia.* Dept. Agric., W. Australia. 173pp.

MEDD, R. 1979. Control of *Carduus nutans* in permanent pasture. *Proc. 7th Asian-Pacific Weed Sci. Soc. Conf.* 7:177–179.

———. 1981. Distribution of some *Carduus, Cirsium, Onopordum* and *Silybum* species in New South Wales. *Proc. 8th Asian-Pacific Weed Sci. Soc. Conf.* 8:161–165.

MEDD, R. and J. LOVETT. 1978. Biological studies of *Carduus nutans* (L.) spp. *nutans*: I. Germination and light re-

quirement of seedlings. II. Vernalization and phenological development. *Weed Res.* 18:363–372.

MEDD, R. and R. SMITH. 1978. Prediction of the potential distribution of *Carduus nutans* (nodding thistle) in Australia. *J. Appl. Ecol.* 15:603–612.

MEERTS, P. and C. LEFEBVRE. 1988. Population variation and adaptation in the specific complex *Polygonum aviculare* L. *Acta Oecol./Oecol. Plantarum* 9:105–107.

MEHRA, P. and S. CHODA. 1978. Cyto-taxonomical studies in the genus *Euphorbia. Cytologia* 43:217–236.

MEHTA, I. and R. SHARMA. 1972. Control of aquatic weeds by the white amur (fish) in Rajasthan, India. *Hyacinth Control J.* 10:16–19.

———. 1976. Effects of weeds on the capacity of the Chambal irrigation system in Kota, Rajasthan. *Proc. Regional Seminar Noxious Aquat. Vegetation 1973*; New Delhi.

MEHTA, K. 1934. The root system of *Asphodelus tenuifolius. J. Ind. Bot. Soc.* 13:271–276.

MEIJER, L. and D. SUTTON. 1987. Influence of plant position on growth of duckweed. *J. Aquat. Plant Mgmt.* 25:28–30.

MEISSNER, R. and C. MULDER. 1974. Herbicidal control of volunteer *Silybum marianum* in wheat. *Agroplantae* 6(4):87–88.

MEISSNER, R., P. NEL, and E. BEYERS. 1986. Allelopathic influence of *Tagetes* and *Bidens* infested soils on seedling growth of certain crop species. *S. African J. Plant and Soil* 3:176–180.

MEKENIAN, M. and R. WILLEMSEN. 1975. Germination characteristics of *Raphanus raphanistrum*: I. Laboratory studies. *Bull. Torrey Bot. Club* 102:243–252.

MELIKYAN, A. and N. KHANDZHYAN. 1968. The stem anatomy of certain species of *Cuscuta* in relation to their taxonomy. *Biologicheskii Zhurnal Armenii* 21:79–86.

MELKANIA, N., J. SINGH and K. BISHT. 1982. Allelopathic potential of *Artemisia vulgaris* and *Pinus roxburghii. Proc. Ind. Nat. Sci. Acad.* B 48:685–688.

MELNIKOVA, T. 1983. Morphological-biological characteristics of *Silybum marianum* seeds as sowing material (Soviet Union). *Khimiko-farmat Sevticheskii Zhurnal* 17:958–963.

MENDIETA, R. and S. AMO. 1981. *Plantas medicinales del estado de Yucatan.* Compania Editorial Continental, Mexico City.

MERCADO, B., C. MALABAYABAS and S. GUMASING. 1971. Responses of some lowland weed species to salinity. I. *Scirpus maritimus* to sodium chloride. *Philipp. Agriculturist* 55:253–259.

MERCER, H., F. NEAL, J. HIMES and G. EDDS. 1967. *Cassia occidentalis* toxicosis in cattle. *J. Am. Vet. Med. Assoc.* 151:735–741.

MESTON, A., W. SAUNDERS and J. NOTT. 1971. Some chemical properties of soils from areas of barley grass

Hordeum murinum L. infestation. *New Zealand J. Agric. Res.* 14:334–351.

MESTRE, J. 1957. Composées-cynarées; development de l'embryon chez le *Carduus nutans. Acad. Sci., Comptes Rendus, Paris, Series D* 245:355–358.

METCALFE, C. 1971. *Anatomy of the monocotyledons.* V. **Cyperaceae**. Clarendon Press, Oxford. 595pp.

METZGER, J. 1983. Promotion of germination of dormant weed seeds by substituted phthalimides and gibberellic acid. *Weed Sci.* 31:285–289.

———. 1988. Localization of the site of perception of thermoinductive temperatures in *Thlaspi arvense. Plant Physiol.* 88:424–428.

MEZYNSKI, P. and D. COLE. 1974. Germination of dandelion seed on a thermogradient plate. *Weed Sci.* 22:506–507.

MICHAEL, P. 1968a. Perennial and annual pasture species in the control of *Silybum marianum. Aus. J. Exp. Agric. and Animal Husbandry* 8:101–105.

———. 1968b. Thistles in southeastern Australia, some ecological and economic considerations. *Proc. 1st Victorian Weed Conf.* (Melbourne) 1:12–16.

———. 1970. Biology and ecology of thistles. *Proc. Weed Soc. New South Wales* 3:3–6.

———. 1972. The weeds themselves, early history and identification. *Proc. Weed Soc. New South Wales* 5:3–18.

———. 1977. Some weedy species of *Amaranthus* and *Conyza/Erigeron* naturalized in the Asian-Pacific region. *Proc. 6th Asian-Pacific Weed Sci. Soc. Conf.* (Indonesia) 6(1):87–95.

MICHAUX, B. 1989. Reproductive and vegetative biology of *Cirsium vulgare. New Zealand J. Bot.* 27:401–414.

MICKEL, J. and F. VOTAVA. 1971. Leaf epidermal studies in *Marsilea. Am. Fern J.* 61:101–109.

MIEJERS, T. 1963. The anatomy of *Senecio vulgaris. Pharmaceutisch Weekblad* 98:153–174.

MIJATOVIC, K. and D. STOJANOVIC. 1973. Distribution of *Orobanche* species on agricultural crops in Yugoslavia. pp. 28–33. *Proc. 1st Symp. Parasitic Weeds, European Weed Res. Council*, Malta.

MILEY, W., J. DYKE, J. LESLIE and G. KOBYLINSKI. 1980. Final report on weed control in 4 Florida lakes using grass carp. *Proc. 33rd Southern Weed Sci. Soc. Conf.* 33:211–212.

MILKOWSKA, J., T. KRZACZEK and A. PRZYCHODZEN. 1975. Anatomical and histochemical investigations on some species of the genus *Rumex. Ann. Univ. Mariae Curie-Sklodowska*, Sect. D. Med., 30:225–232.

MILLAR, J. 1973. Vegetation changes in shallow marshlands under improving moisture regime. *Can. J. Bot.* 51:1443–1457.

MILLENER, L. 1961. Daylength as related to vegetative development in *Ulex europaeus*: I. The experimental approach. *New Phytologist* 60:339–354.

———. 1962. Daylength as related to vegetative development in *Ulex europaeus*. II. Ecotypic variation with latitude. *New Phytologist* 61(2):119–127.

MILLER, C. and J. DUCKETT. 1979. A study of stelar ultrastructure in the heterosporous water fern *Marsilea quadrifolia. Ann. Bot.* 44:231–238.

MILLER, J. 1968. Fern gametophtes as experimental material. *Bot. Rev.* 34:361–440.

MILLER, J., L. GARRARD and W. HALLER. 1976. Some characteristics of *Hydrilla* tubers from Lake Ocklawaha (Florida USA) during drawdown. *J. Aquat. Plant Mgmt.* 14:29–31.

MILLER, P. 1980. Reproduction and survival of *Xiphinema americanum* on selected woody plants, crops, and weeds. *Plant Dis.* 64:174–175.

MILLER, R., J. STOUT and K. LEE. 1956. Biological and chemical changes following scrub-burning on a New Zealand hill soil. *New Zealand J. Sci. Technol.* 37:290–314.

MILLER, T., A. RAINS and R. THORPE. 1963. The nutritive value and agronomic aspects of some fodders in northern Nigeria: II. Silages. *J. Brit. Grassland Soc.* 18:223–229.

MILLSPAUGH, C. 1892. *Your weeds and your neighbors*. West Virginia Agric. Exp. Sta., Bull. No. 33; Morgantown, West Virginia.

MILTON, W. 1943. The buried viable seed content of a midland calcareous soil. *Empire J. Exp. Agric.* 11:155–171.

———. 1948. The buried viable seed content of upland soils in Montgomershire. *Empire J. Exp. Agric.* 16:163–177.

MIRANDE, M. 1901. Researches physiologique et anatomique sur le Cuscutacees. *Bull. Sci. France et Belgique* 34:1–281.

MIRASHI, M. and P. BHOGAONKAR. 1974. Anatomy of *Acanthospermum hispidum* DC. *Proc. Ind. Acad. Sci.* 79:154–159.

MISHRA, R. and R. KAMAL. 1972. Rhizosphere fungal flora of certain Euphorbiaceous plants. *Mycopathologia and Mycologia Applicata* 46:73–79.

MISRA, G. and N. DAS. 1969. Studies on the control of the aquatic weeds of India. *Hyacinth Control J.* 8:40–41.

MISRA, L. and D. SHARMA. 1980. Nutrient depletion capability of wood sorrel. *Proc. Ind. Soc. Weed Sci./OUAT Weed Sci. Conf.*, Bhubaneswar.

MISRA, M. 1972. Cytological studies in some Indian *Potamogeton* and *Aponogeton* species. *Bull. Bot. Soc. Bengal* 26:47–52.

MISRA, R. 1969. Ecological studies of noxious weeds, common to India and America, which are becoming an increasing problem in the upper Gangetic plains. *Final Tech. Rep., Agric. Res. Program, Public Law No. 480, Grant No. FG-In-213, Project No. A7–CR-106.* U.S.D.A. II:372–408.

MISRA, R., K. SINGH and J. SINGH. 1968. Role of provenance trials in the study of population differentiation. *Bull. Bot. Survey Ind.* 10:312–318.

MITCHELL, D. 1978. *Aquatic weeds in Australian inland waters.* Aus. Gov. Publ. Service, Canberra.

MITCHELL, D. and P. ORR. 1985. *Myriophyllum* in Australia. *1st Intern. Symp. on watermilfoil* Myriophyllum spicatum *and Related* Haloragaceae *spp.* 1:27–34.

MITCHELL, E. 1926. Germination of seeds of plants native to Dutchess County, New York, United States. *Bot. Gaz.* 81:108–112.

MITICH, L. 1989. Common dandelion—the lion's tooth. *Weed Tech.* 3:537–539.

MITRA, E. 1955. Contribution to our knowledge of freshwater plants: I. On some aspects of the structure and life history of *Hydrilla verticillata* with notes on its autecology. *J. Asiatic Soc.* 21:1–17.

———. 1956. Notes on germination of turions in *Hydrilla verticillata. Current Sci.* 25:25–26.

———. 1960. Contribution to our knowledge of Indian freshwater plants: III. Behavior of *Hydrilla verticillata* in nature and under experimental conditions. *Bull. Bot. Soc. Bengal.* 14:73–75.

———. 1964. Contribution to our knowledge of Indian freshwater plants: IV. On some aspects of the morphological and anatomical studies of turions of *Hydrilla verticillata. J. Asiatic Soc.* 6:17–27.

MITRA, G. and N. BOSE. 1957. Rooting and histological responses of detached leaves to indolbutyric acid with special reference to *Boerhavia diffusa* L. *Phytomorphology* 7:370–381.

MITRA, R. and S. JAIN. 1985. Concept of *Phyllanthus niruri* in Indian flora. *Bull. Bot. Surv. Ind.* 27:151–176.

MITRA, R., S. MEHROTRA, B. MEHROTRA and L. KAPOOR. 1974. Pharmacognostic study of *Asclepias curassavica* L. *Bull. Bot. Survey Ind.* 16:82–88.

MITZNER, L. 1976. Biological control of nuisance aquatic macrophytes by white amur (fish). *Proc. 31st N. Central Weed Control Conf.* 31:105–106.

MIURA, H. and M. IWATA. 1979. Effect of nitrogen, phosphorous and potassium on anthocyanin content of the seedlings of *Polygonum hydropiper* L. *J. Jap. Soc. Hortic. Sci.* 48:91–98.

———. 1981. Effect of light on anthocyanin content of seedlings of benitade *Polygonum hydropiper* L. *J. Jap. Soc. Hortic. Sci.* 50:44–52.

MIZUSHIMA, M. 1957. A revision of *Drymaria cordata* Willd. *J. Jap. Bot.* 32:61–81.

MODIWALA, Q. and P. DUBEY. 1976. Dormancy, germination and seedling emergence in weeds of kharif season. *Geobios* 3:42–44.

MOHAMED-SALEEM, M. and M. FAWUSI. 1983. A note on the effects of tropical weed decomposition on seed germination and seedling growth of some agricultural crops. *Agric., Ecosystems, and Environ.* 10:347–352.

MOHAMMAD, H., S. HUSAIN and J. AL-ZARARI. 1981. Effect of plant extracts of some poisonous plants of Iraq on mortality of citrus nematode. *Acta Bot. Indica* 9:198–200.

MOHINDER, P. and T. KHOSHOO. 1974. Grain *Amaranths.* In: *Evolutionary studies in world crops.* Ed. by J. Hutchinson. Cambridge Univ. Press, Cambridge.

MOISEY, F. 1974. *The effects of weeds on sugar beet crop.* Ph.D. Diss., Univ. of Nottingham, United Kingdom. 402pp.

MOJA, A. 1958. A means of weed control: Lucerne in relation to mugwort *Artemisia vulgaris. Ann. Istituto Sperimentali Agrumicoltura* (N.S.) 12(4):1115–1126.

MOKSHIN, V. 1978. Characteristics of growth of thistle root systems with minimum tillage. *Sibirskii Vestnik Sel'skokhozyaistvennoi Nauki* No. 6.

MOLGAARD, P. 1977. Competitive effect of grass on establishment and performance of *Taraxacum officinale. Oikos* 29:376–382.

MOLLOY, L. and A. WILSON. 1969. Initial biochemical reaction in germination of pollen grains. *J. Exp. Bot.* 64:457–464.

MOLNAR, V. 1971. A summary of research work on skeleton weed control and eradication. *Keith Turnbull Res. Sta., Pamphlet No. 31*; Victoria, Australia.

MONAGHAN, N. and W. FELTON. 1979. The effect of seed coat treatment on the germination of *Datura ferox* and *D. stramonium. Proc. 7th Asian-Pacific Weed Sci. Soc. Conf.* 7:311–312.

MONDAL, S. and S. ROY. 1984. Pollen production in weeds associated with some rice cultivars in Burdwan district, West Bengal, India. *Geophytology* 14:74–81.

MONDRAGON, G., A. FISCHER and A. TASISTRO. 1981. Estudio del periodo critico de competencia con las malezas en dos variedades de cebada *Hordeum vulgare* yen dos fechas de siembra. pp. 96–126. *Proc. 2nd National Weed Sci. Soc. Mex. Congr.*

MONTEGUT, J. 1965. The ecophysiology of weed seeds in crops. *2ᵉ Colloque sur la Biologie des Mauvaises Herbs*, Grignon.

MONTGOMERY, F. and S. YANG. 1960. Cytological studies in the genus *Erigeron. Can. J. Bot.* 38:381–386.

MOORE, A. 1969. *Azolla:* Biology and agronomic significance. *Bot. Rev.* 35:35–57.

MOORE, B., H. GIBBONS, W. FUNK, T. MCKARNS, J. NYZNYK and M. GIBBONS. 1983. Enhancement of internal cycling P by aquatic macrophytes, with implications for lake management. pp. 113–118. *Proc. 3rd Conf. N. Am. Lake Mgmt.*

MOORE, C. 1956. Observations on autecology of *Heliotropium europaeum* in New South Wales and Victoria. pp. 1–12. In: *Division of Plant Industry, Commonwealth Scientific and Industrial Res. Organization, Tech. Paper No. 7*; Melbourne, Australia.

MOORE, L. 1950. Mat plants of the genus *Raoulia* as weeds in pastural land. *Proc. 7th Intern. Bot. Congr.* 7(1):677–678.

MOORE, R. 1964. *Chondrilla juncea* L. skeleton weed in Australia. *Proc. 7th Brit. Weed Control Conf.* 7(2):563–568.

MOORE, R. and G. MULLIGAN. 1958. A study of the natural hybridization between *Carduus acanthoides* and *C. nutans. Proc. Intern. Congr. Genetics* 10:193.

MOORE, R. and J. ROBERTSON. 1964. Studies on skeleton weed competition from pasture plants. *CSIRO Field Sta. Record* 3:69–72.

MOREIRA, I. and M. VASCONCELOS. 1979. Establecimento de plantas de graminhao *Paspalum paspalodes* (Michx.) Scribn. *Anais do Inst. Superior Agronomia* 38:71–83.

MORELLI, I. 1978. Constituents of *Silybum marianum* and their use in therapy. *Bull. Chimico Farmaceutico* 117:258–267.

MORENO, M., J. CUBERO and A. MARTIN. 1979. Meiotic behavior in *Orobanche crenata*. pp. 73–78. *Proc. 2nd Intern. Symp. Parasitic Weeds*. Ed. by L. Musselman, A. Worsham and R. Eplee. N. Carolina State Univ., Raleigh, N. Carolina, USA.

MORGAN, D. and H. SMITH. 1979. A systematic relationship between phytochrome-controlled development and species habitat in simulated natural radiation. *Planta* 145:253–258.

MORINAGA, T. 1926a. Effect of alternating temperatures upon the germination of seeds. *Am. J. Bot.* 13:141–158.

———. 1926b. The favorable effect of reduced oxygen supply upon the germination of certain weeds. *Am. J. Bot.* 159–166.

MORISHIMA, H. and H. OKA. 1980. The impact of copper pollution on water foxtail *Alopecurus aequalis* Sobol. Populations and winter weed communities in rice fields. *Agro-Ecosystems* 6:33–49.

MORRISON, I. and D. MURICE. 1980. Competitive ability of green and yellow foxtail in wheat. Cited *Weed Sci. Soc. Am.*, Abstr. No. 164.

MORRISON, J. 1958. *Hordeum murinum* in Holland. *Acta Botanica Neerl.* 7:654–664.

MORTON, J. 1967. The balsam pear an edible medicinal and toxic plant. *Econ. Bot.* 21:57–68.

———. 1975. Cattails *Typha* spp. weed problem or potential crop? *Econ. Bot.* 29:7–29.

MOSS, G. 1959. The gorse seed problem. *Proc. 12th New Zealand Weed and Pest Control Conf.* 12:59–64.

MOSS, S. 1979. Influence of tillage and method of straw disposal on the survival and growth of blackgrass *Alopecurus myosuroides*, and its control by chlortoluron and isoproturon. *Ann. Appl. Biol.* 91:91–100.

———. 1980a. A study of populations of blackgrass *Alopecurus myosuroides* in winter wheat, as influenced seed shed in the previous crop cultivation system and straw disposal method. *Ann. Appl. Biol.* 94:121–126.

———. 1980b. Some effects of burning cereal straw on seed vi-

ability, seedling establishment and control of *Alopecurus myosuroides* Huds. *Weed Res.* 20:271–276.

———. 1980c. The agro-ecology of blackgrass *Alopecurus myosuroides* Huds. in modern cereal growing systems. *Agric. Dev. Advis. Ser. Quart. Rev.* 38:170–191.

———. 1981a. The response of *Alopecurus myosuroides* during a four year period to different cultivation and straw disposal systems. pp. 15–21. *Proc. Conf. Grass Weeds in Cereals in United Kingdom*. Reading Assoc. Appl. Biologists.

———. 1981b. Techniques for the assessment of *Alopecurus myosuroides. Proc. Conf. Grass Weeds in Cereals in United Kingdom*: 101–107. Reading. Assoc. Appl. Biologists.

———. 1983. The production and shedding of *Alopecurus myosuroides* Huds. seeds in winter cereal crops. *Weed Res.* 23:45–51.

———. 1985. The survival of *Alopecurus myosuroides* Huds. seeds in soil. *Weed Res.* 25:201–211.

———. 1987a. Influence of tillage, straw disposal system and seed return on the population dynamics of *Alopecurus myosuroides* Huds. in winter wheat. *Weed Res.* 27:313–320.

———. 1987b. Herbicide resistance in black-grass *Alopecurus myosuroides. Proc. 1987 Brit. Crop. Protec. Conf., Weeds* 3:879–886.

MOURSI, M., T. RIZK, and H. EL-DEEPAH. 1979. Weed seed germination to freezing and leaching treatments. *Egy. J. Agron.* 2:211–220.

MOVSESIAN, T. and K. AZARIAN. 1971. Pathological changes in cattle poisoned by dodder *Cuscuta campestris. Biologicheskii Zhurnal Armenii* 24:67–70.

MOYER, J. 1984. Yield and nutrient composition of orchardgrass hay as affected by dandelion control. *Can. J. Plant Sci.* 64:295–302.

MOYLE, J. 1945. Some chemical factors influencing the distribution of aquatic plants in Minnesota. *Am. Midland Naturalist* 34:402–420.

MUDGAL, V. 1975. Studies on medicinal properties of *Convolvulus pluricaulis* and *Boerhavia diffusa. Planta Medica* 28:62–68.

MUENSCHER, W. 1930. *Perennial sowthistle and related weeds*. Cornell Univ. Ext. Bull. 195. New York. 12pp.

———. 1933. Aquatic vegetation of the upper Hudson (river) watershed. *New York State Conservation Dept., Ann. Rep. Supplement* 22:216–238.

———. 1936a. *Storage and germination of seeds of aquatic plants*. Cornell Univ. Exp. Sta. Bull. 652. pp. 3–16.

———. 1936b. The germination of seeds of *Potamogeton. Ann. Bot.* 50:805–821.

———. 1955. *Weeds*. 2nd Ed. The Macmillan Co., New York. 580pp.

MUHONEN, M., J. SHOWMAN and R. COUCH. 1983. Nutrient absorption by *Spirodela polyrhiza. J. Aquat. Plant Mgmt.* 21:107–109.

MUKHERJEE, P. 1978. Studies on the karyotype of *Eragrostis pilosa. Bull. Bot. Soc. Bengal* 32:63–65.

MUKHERJEE, S. 1957. Origin and distribution of *Saccharum. Bot. Gaz.* 119:55–61.

MUKUMOV, K. 1974. Transpiration intensity of some varieties of melon crops in relation to infection by broomrape. *Nauchnye, Trudy, Samarkandskii Gosudarstvennyi Universitet imeni A. Navoi,* USSR, 207:127–133.

MULLAN, D. 1941. The biology and anatomy of *Scirpus grossus. J. Bombay Natural History Soc.* 45:402–407.

MULLER, D. 1936. On the anatomy of *Ipomoea aquatica* with special reference to development of aerenchyma upon injury. *J. Ind. Bot. Soc.* 15:39–50.

MULLER, S., A. VAN DER MERWE, H. SCHILDKNECHT, and J. VISSER. 1993. An automated system for large-scale recovery of germination stimulants and other root exudates. *Weed Sci.* 41:138–143.

MULLIGAN, G. 1965. Recent colonization by herbaceous plants in Canada. pp. 127–146. In: *The genetics of colonizing species.* Ed. by H. Baker and G. Stebbins. Academic Press, N.Y.

———. 1972. Autogamy, allogamy and pollination in some Canadian weeds. *Can. J. Bot.* 50:1767–1771.

MULLIGAN, G. and L. BAILEY. 1975. The biology of Canadian weeds. No. 8. *Sinapis arvensis* L. *Can. J. Plant Sci.* 55:171–183.

MULLIGAN, G. and J. FINDLAY. 1974. The biology of Canadian weeds. No. 3. *Cardaria draba, C. chalepensis* and *C. pubescens. Can. J. Plant Sci.* 54:149–160.

MULLIGAN, G. and C. FRANKTON. 1962. Taxonomy of the genus *Cardaria* with particular reference to the species introduced into North America. *Can. J. Bot.* 40(11):1411–1425.

MULLIGAN, G. and R. MOORE. 1961. Natural selection among hybrids between *Carduus acanthoides* and *C. nutans* in Ontario. *Can. J. Bot.* 39:269–279.

MULLIGAN, H., A. BARANOWSKI and R. JOHNSON. 1976. Nitrogen and phosphorus fertilization of aquatic vascular plants and algae in replicated ponds: I. Initial response to fertilization. *Hydrobiologia* 48:109–116.

MULLVERSTEDT, R. 1963a. Investigations on the germination of weed seeds as influenced by oxygen partial pressure. *Weed Res.* 3:154–163.

———. 1963b. Investigations on the causes of increased emergence of weeds following mechanical weed control measures, post-emergence. *Weed Res.* 3:298–303.

MUNIYAPPA, T., T. RAMACHANDRA and K. KRISHNAMURTHY. 1983. Biology and chemical control of *Oxalis latifolia. Ind. J. Weed Sci.* 15:182–187.

MUNN, M. 1919. Spraying lawns with iron sulfate to eradicate

dandelion. *New York Agric. Exp. Sta. Bull. 466,* Geneva, NY USA.

MURRAY, D., D. THURLOW and G. BUCHANAN. 1976. Sicklepod in the southeast. *Weeds Today* 7(2):12–14.

MURRAY, M. 1940. The genetics of sex determination in the family **Amaranthaceae.** *Genetics* 25:409–431.

MURTHY, S. and J. RAO. 1978. Ecological studies and chemical control of some terrestrial weeds. *Comparative Physiol. Ecol.* 3:61–64.

MURTY, V. 1962. *Cassia tora* L. leaf meal as a component of poultry rations. *Poultry Sci.* 41:1026–1028.

MUSSELMAN, L. 1980. The biology of *Striga, Orobanche,* and other root-parasitic weeds. *Ann. Rev. Phytopathology.* 18:463–489.

———. 1982. Parasitic weeds in arable land. Chapter 16 in: *Biology and ecology of weeds.* Ed. by W. Holzner and M. Numata. Dr. W. Junk Publ., The Hague.

———. 1986. Taxonomy of *Orobanche.* pp. 2–10. *Proc. Workshop on Biology and Control of Orobanche.* Ed. by S. ter Borg. Wageningen, Netherlands.

MUSSELMAN, L. and W. MANN. 1976. A survey of surface characteristics of seeds of **Scrophulariaceae** and **Orobanchaceae** using scanning electron microscopy. *Phytomorphology* 26:370–378.

MUZTAR, A. 1976. *Chemical composition and nutritive value of fresh water macrophytes.* M.Sc. Thesis, Univ. Guelph, Ontario. 113pp.

MUZTAR, A., S. SLINGER and J. BURTON. 1976. Nutritive value of aquatic plants for chicks. *Poultry Sci.* 55:1917–1922.

———. 1978. Chemical composition of aquatic macrophytes: 1. Investigation of organic constituents and nutritional potential. 2. Amino acid composition and protein and non-protein fractions. 3. Mineral composition and the potential for nutrient removal from lake water. *Can. J. Plant Sci.* 58:829–862.

MYATT, O. 1971. Vine weeds in the Herbert River District. *Cane Growers Quarterly Bull.* 34:121–123.

MYERS, L. and J. LIPSETT. 1958. Competition between skeleton weed *Chondrilla juncea* L. and cereals in relation to nitrogen supply. *Aus. J. Agric. Res.* 9:1–12.

NADEAU, L. and I. MORRISON. 1983. Root development of two *Setaria* species under different soil moisture regimes. *Aspects Appl. Biol.* 4:125–134.

NAGAHISA, M. and A. HATTORI. 1964. Studies on oxalic acid oxidase in green leaves. *Plant and Cell Physiol.* 5:205–215.

NAGAI, T., Y. WATANABE and F. HAGIWARA. 1979. The relationship between copper content of orchard soils and the weed composition in Japanese pear orchards. *Bull. Faculty Agric., Tottori Univ.* 31:29–36.

NAGY, A., G. PALESS, and G. VIDA. 1978. Differential protein synthesis after red light illumination in germinating fern spores. *Biol. Plantarum* (Praha) 20:193–200.

NAIDU, K., G. RAJENDRUDU and V. DAS. 1980. Dark respiration of leaves in selected C₄ and C₃ tropical weed species. *Zeitschrift fur Pflanzenphysiologie* 99:85–88.

NAKAGAWA, K., M. MIYAHARA and K. HATTORI. 1973. Biology and control of perennial **Cyperaceae** in Japan. pp. 203–208. *Proc. 4th Asian-Pacific Weed Sci. Soc. Conf.*

NAKAMURA, S. 1970. Germination of *Polygonum hydropiper* L. seeds. *Yamaguti Univ. Faculty Agric. Bull.* 21:73–83.

NAKONESHNY, W. and G. FRIESEN. 1961. The influence of a commercial fertilizer treatment on weed competition in spring wheat. *Can. J. Plant Sci.* 41:231–238.

NALEWAJA, J., D. COLLINS and C. SWALLERS. 1972. Weeds in sunflowers. *N. Dakota Farm Res.* 29(6):3–6.

NANDA, K. 1961. Some observations on the emergence, growth and flowering of branches in *Papaver rhoeas*. *Phyton*, (Buenos Aires) 16:27–43.

NANDAKUMAR, S. and P. KRISHNAN. 1976. The resting metabolism of dodder seeds. *Phytochemistry*. 15(11):1639–1641.

NANDI, S. 1982. Bovine haematuria of Indian hills: A haemorrhagic syndrome due to development of transition cell carcinomas of the urinary bladder, associated with consumption of Himalayan weeds. *Deutsche Tierarztliche Wochenschrift* 89:479–482.

NARWAL, R. 1972. Population differentiation in *Amaranthus viridis*. *Current Sci.* 41:299–300.

NASH, S. and S. WILHELM. 1960. Stimulation of broomrape seed germination. *Phytopathology* 50:772–774.

NATIONAL ACADEMY OF SCIENCE. 1976a. Harvesting and using aquatic weeds. pp. 65–108. In: *Making aquatic plants useful: Some perspectives for developing countries.* National Acad. Sci., Washington D.C.

———. 1976b. The use of herbivorous animals for aquatic plant control. pp. 1–64. In: *Making aquatic plants useful: Some perspectives for developing countries.* National Acad. Sci., Washington D.C.

NAYLOR, R. 1970. The prediction of blackgrass infestation. *Weed Res.* 10:296–299.

———. 1972a. The nature and consequence of interference by *Alopecurus myosuroides* Huds. on the growth of winter wheat. *Weed Res.* 12:137–143.

———. 1972b. Biological flora of the British Isles: *Alopecurus myosuroides* Huds. *J. Ecol.* 60:611–622.

———. 1972c. Aspects of the population dynamics of the weed *Alopecurus myosuroides* Huds. in winter cereal crops. *J. Appl. Ecol.* 9:127–139.

NAYLOR, R. and A. ABDALLA. 1982. Variation in germination behavior. *Seed Sci. Technol.* 10:67–76.

NEGI, O. 1962. Studies in wild *Saccharum spontaneum*, *S. robustum* and *Erianthus arundinaceus*. *Ind. J. Sugarcane Res.* 6:201–207.

NEHER, R. 1968. Ethnobotany of *Tagetes. Econ. Bot.* 22:317–325.

NEL, P. 1955. Dodder, a menace to agriculture. *Farming S. Afr.* 30:511–517.

NELSON, D. and R. NYLUND. 1962. Competition between peas grown for processing and weeds. *Weeds* 10:224–229.

NEMOTO, M. 1982. Weeds of pastures and meadows in Japan. Chapter 34. In: *Biology and ecology of weeds.* Ed. by W. Holzner and M. Numata. Dr. W. Junk Publ., The Hague.

NEMOTO, M. and V. PONGSKUL. 1985. Secondary succession at the shifting cultivation site in northeast Thailand. *Proc. 10th Asian-Pacific Weed Sci. Soc. Conf.* 10:67–74.

NEMOTO, M., M. NUMATA and M. KANDA. 1977. The role of weeds in sown meadows in Japan. pp. 614–622. *Proc. 6th Asian-Pacific Weed Sci. Soc. Conf.*

NEOGI, B., M. PRASAD and R. RAO. 1989. Ethnobotany of some weeds of Khasi and Garo Hills, Meghalaya, northeastern India. *Econ. Bot.* 43:473–479.

NESTER, P., T. HARGER and L. MCCORMICK. 1979 Weed watch: Wild poinsettia. *Weeds Today* 10:24–25.

NETLAND, J. 1984. Growth habit, longevity and capacity for vegetative propagation in different populations of *Poa annua* L. *Nordisk Jordbrugsforskning* 66:169.

NEWSOM, I. 1952. *Sheep disease.* Williams and Wilkins, Baltimore.

NEWTON, R. 1977. Abscisic acid effects on fronds and roots of *Lemna minor* L. *Am. J. Bot.* 64:45–49.

NEWTON, R., D. SHELTON, S. DISHAROON and J. DUFFEY. 1978. Turion formation and germination in *Spirodela polyrhiza*. *Am. J. Bot.* 65:421–428.

NEWTON, S., J. MARTIN, J. FERGUSON, and D. GRAY. 1979. Grass carp aid in removal of weeds in irrigation canals and reservoirs. *Arkansas Farm Res.* 28:12.

NICHOLLS, D. 1973. Weed movement and distribution in a grazed tropical pasture. pp. 92–104. *Proc. 4th Asian-Pacific Weed Sci. Soc. Conf.*

NICHOLS, S. 1975. Identification and management of Eurasian watermilfoil in Wisconsin. *Transactions Wisconsin Acad. Sci., Arts, and Letters* 63:116–128.

———. 1976. The nitrogen nutrition of *Myriophyllum spicatum*: Variation of plant tissue nitrogen concentration with season and site in Lake Wingra (USA). *Freshwater Biol.* 6:137–144.

NICHOLS, S. and S. MORI. 1971. The littoral macrophyte vegetation of Lake Wingra. *Transactions Wisconsin Acad. Sci., Arts and Letters* 59:107–119.

NICKELL, L. 1960. Antimicrobial activity of vascular plants. *Econ. Bot.* 13:281–318.

NIELSEN, H. and S. PINNERUP. 1982. Reduced cultivation and weeds. *Proc. 23rd Swedish Weed Conf.* 23(2):370–384.

NIEMAN, P. 1979. Effect of weeds on cereal yield. In: *Biologische Bundesanstalt fur Land- und Forstwirtschaft in*

Berlin and Braunschweig, German Federal Republic, 1978 Annual Report. pp. 52–53.

NIJS, J. DEN, K. SORGDRAGER and J. STOOP. 1985. Biosystematic studies of the *Rumex acetosella* complex: IX. Cytogeography of the complex in the Iberian Peninsula and taxonomic discussion. *Bot. Helvetica* 95:141–156.

NIKLAS, K. 1987. Pollen capture and wind-induced movement of compact and diffuse grass panicles: Implications for pollination efficiency. *Am. J. Bot.* 74:74–89.

NIKOLAEV, K. 1964. Research into the toxicity of wild radish *R. raphanistrum. Veterinarno Meditsinski Nauki* 1:31–35.

NIKOLAEVA, V. 1981. Anatomical structure of the vegetative organs of chicory. *Rastitel nye Resursy* 17(4):550–553.

NODA, K. 1969. Specific hazardous weeds and their control on paddy rice fields. pp. 97–111. *2nd Asian-Pacific Weed Sci. Soc. Conf.*

———. 1970. Problems of weed control in Japan. *Bull. Kyushu Agric. Exp. Sta.* 15:125–140.

———. 1977. Integrated weed control in rice. pp. 17–46. In: *Integrated control of weeds.* Ed. by J. Fryer and S. Matsunaka. Univ. Tokyo Press.

NODA, K. and S. EGUCHI. 1973. Some anatomical characteristics in the leaf blades of principal weeds. *Weed Res. Japan* 15:59–65.

NODA, K., K. IBARAKI, S. EGUCHI and K. OZAWA. 1965. Studies on the ecological characteristics of the annual weed, cleaver, and its chemical control on drained winter paddy fields for wheat plants in temperate Japan. *Bull. Kyushu Agric. Exp. Sta.* 11:345–374.

NODA, K., C. PRAKONGVONGS, M. TEERAWATSAKUL and L. CHAIWIRATNUKUL. 1983. Biological characteristics of tropical weed species in Thailand and their significance in weed control. *Proc. 9th Asian-Pacific Weed Sci. Soc. Conf.* 9:108–119.

NORLINDH, T. 1972. Notes on the variation and taxonomy in the *Scirpus maritimus* complex. *Bot. Notiser* 125:397–405.

NORRIS, R. 1981. Weed competition in seedling alfalfa. *Abstr. 31st Weed Sci. Soc. Am. Conf.* 31:86.

NORRIS, R. and C. SCHONER. 1980. Yellow foxtail *Setaria lutescens* biotype studies: Dormancy and germination. *Weed Sci.* 28:159–163.

NORTH, J. and D. LIVINGSTON. 1970. Chemical control of *Alopecurus myosuroides* in winter wheat. *Proc. 10th Brit. Weed Control Conf.* 10:84–90.

NOUGAREDE, A., E. GIFFORD and P. RONDET. 1965. Cytohistological studies of the apical meristem of *Amaranthus retroflexus* under various photoperiods. *Bot. Gaz.* 126:281–298.

NUMATA, M. and N. YOSHIZAWA. 1975. *Weed flora of Japan, illustrated in color.* Kyokai Publ. Co. 109a.

NUTTALL, W. 1982. The effect of seedling depth, soil mois-

ture regime, and crust strength on emergence of rape cultivars. *Agron. J.* 74:1018–1022.

NUWANYAKPA, M., K. BOLSEN, G. POSLER, M. DIAZ and F. RIVERA. 1983. Nutritive value of seven tropical weed species during the dry season. *Agron. J.* 75:566–569.

NWANKITI, O., E. ANOSIKE and E. AGBAKWURU. 1976. A quick selection method for hybrids of *Emilia* **Senecioneae: Compositae.** *Zeitschrift fur Pflanzenzuechtung* 77:170–173.

O'BRIEN, T. 1963. The morphology and growth of *Pteridium aquilinum* var. *esculentum. Ann. Bot.* 27:253–267.

———. 1964. Problems in the control of bracken fern of Victoria. *J. Aus. Inst. Agric. Sci.* 4:119–127.

O'BRYAN, K. and T. PEEPER. 1986. Development and competition of musk thistle *Carduus nutans* with winter wheat. *Abstr. 26th Weed Sci. Soc. Am. Conf.* 26:57–58.

O'DONOVAN, J. 1985. Influence of temperature on growth of hempnettle *Galeopsis tetrahit* L. and smartweed *Polygonum lapathifolium* L. *Proc. 40th North Cent. Weed Control Conf.* 40:100.

ODUM, S. 1965. Germination of ancient seeds: Floristical observations and experiments with archeologically dated soil samples. *Dansk Botanisk Arkiv* 24(2):1–70.

———. 1974. Seeds in ruderal soils, their longevity and contribution to the flora of disturbed ground in Denmark. *Proc. 12th Brit. Weed Control Conf.* 12:1131–1144.

OEZTUERK, M., H. REHDER and H. ZIEGLER. 1981. Biomass production of 3 and 4 carbon pathway plant species in pure and mixed culture with different water supply. *Oecologia* 50:73–81.

OGAWA, K. 1978. Germination pattern of a native dandelion *Taraxacum platycarpum* as compared with introduced dandelions. *Jap. J. Ecol.* 28:9–15.

OGBE, F. and J. WILLIAMS. 1978. Evolution in indigenous west African rices. *Econ. Bot.* 32:59–64.

OGBONNAYA, C. 1988. Aspects of the autecology of *Tridax procumbens. Nigerian J. Weed Sci.* 1:83–89.

OGDEN, E. 1943. The broad-leaved species of *Potamogeton* of North America north of Mexico. *Rhodora* 45:57–105, 119–163, 171–214.

OGG, A. and J. DAWSON. 1984. Time of emergence of eight weed species. *Weed Sci.* 32:327–335.

O'HARA, P., K. PIERCE and W. READ. 1969. Degenerative myopathy associated with ingestion of *Cassia occidentalis* L.: Clinical and pathological features of the experimentally induced disease. *Am. J. Vet. Res.* 30:2173–2180.

———. 1970. Effects of vitamin E and selenium on *Cassia occidentalis* intoxication in cattle. *Am. J. Vet. Res.* 31:2151–2156.

OHASHI, H. and I. ICHIKAWA. 1960. A study of vernalization on American wormseed. I. The influence of various temperatures on development and yield. *Bot. Mag. Tokyo* 73:239–244.

OHSAWA, M. 1982. Weeds of tea plantations. Chapter 37 in: *Biology and ecology of weeds*. Ed. by W. Holzner and M. Numata. Dr. Junk Publ., The Hague.

OINONEN, E. 1967a. Spore regeneration of bracken in Finland in the light of the dimensions and age of its clones. *Acta Forestalia Fennica* 83(1) 96pp.

———. 1967b. The correlation between the size of Finnish bracken *Pteridium aquilinum* clones and certain periods of site history. *Acta Forestalia Fennica* 83(2) 51pp.

———. 1968. The size of *Lycopodium clavatum* and *L. annotinum* stands as compared to that of *L. complatum* and *Pteridium aquilinum* stands, the age of the tree stand, and the dates of fire on the site. *Acta Forestalia Fennica* No. 87. 53pp.

OKA, H. and W. CHANG. 1959. The impact of cultivation on populations of wild rice *Oryza sativa* f. *spontanea*. *Phyton* 13:105–117.

OKA, H. and H. MORISHIMA. 1971. The dynamics of plant domestication: Cultivation experiments with *Oryza perennis* and its hybrid with *O. sativa*. *Evol.* 25:356–364.

OKADA, K., S. ALONSO and R. RODRIGUEZ. 1985. A hexaploid cytotype of *Alternanthera philoxeroides* as a new weed of agricultural land near Balcarce, in the province of Buenos Aires. *Revista de Investigaciones Agropecuarias* 20:37–53.

OKI, Y., K. IMANISHI, and K. NAKAGAWA. 1989. Studies on the habitats and morphological variation of three submerged aquatic weeds (in Japan), *Egeria*, *Hydrilla*, and *Elodea*. *Nogaku Kenkyu* 62:31–48.

OKLAND, J. 1962. A find of *Sagittaria sagittifolia* in Pasvik (Northern Norway), with remarks on investigations in water courses before regulation of water levels. *Blyttia* 20(4):168–171.

OKONKWO, S. 1966. Studies on *Striga senegalensis*: III. *In vitro* culture of seedlings. Establishment and cultures. *Am. J. Bot.* 53:687–697.

OKOTH, J. 1973. *Tagetes minuta* L. as a repellent and insecticide against adult mosquitoes. *E. African Medical J.* 50:317–322.

OKUMA, M. and S. CHIKURA. 1984. Ecology and control of a subspecies of *Paspalum distichum* L.: IV. Possibility of reproduction by seeds. *Weed Res.*, Japan, 29:45–50.

OKUMA, M., S. CHIKURA and J. YOSHIDOME. 1983a. Ecology and control of a subspecies of *Paspalum distichum* L.: II. Morphological characters and growth habit. *Weed Res.*, Japan, 28:25–30.

OKUMA, M., S. CHIKURA and Y. MORIYAMA. 1983b. Ecology and control of a subspecies of *Paspalum distichum* L.: III. Ecological investigations on sprouting stems. *Weed Res.*, Japan, 28:31–34.

OKUSANYA, O. 1979. Quantitative analysis of the effects of photoperiod, temperature, salinity, and soil types on the germination and growth of *Corchorus olitorius*. *Oikos* 33:444–450.

OLADIRAN, J. and P. MUMFORD. 1985. The stimulation of seed germination by temperature and light on agronomic *Amaranthus* species. *Biochemie und Physiol. der Pflanzen* 180:45–54.

OLADOKUN, M. 1978. Nigerian weed species: Intraspecific competition. *Weed Sci.* 26:713–718.

OLIFIRENKO, V. 1959. Some observations on dodder. *Botanicheskii Zhurnal* (Leningrad) 44:1664–1665.

OLIVER, L. and M. SCHREIBER. 1974. Competition for CO_2 in a heteroculture. *Weed Sci.* 22:125–130.

OLIVER-BEVER, B. 1986. *Medicinal plants in tropical West Africa*. Cambridge Univ. Press, Cambridge.

OLIVIERI, I. 1984. Effects of *Puccinia cardui-pycnocephali* on slender thistle *Carduus pycnocephalus* and *C. tenuiflorus*. *Weed Sci.* 32(4):508–510.

OLIVIERI, I., M. SWAN, and P. GOUYON. 1983. Reproductive system and colonizing strategy of two species of *Carduus* (**Compositae**). *Oecologia* (*Berlin*) 60:114–117.

OLORODE, O. and A. OLORUNFEMI. 1973. The hybrid origin of *Emilia praetermissa* **Senecioneae : Compositae**. *Ann. Bot.*, London, 37:185–191.

OLSON, H., R. BEACHBOARD, R. ANDERSON and L. EDMONSON. 1953. Skunkweed flavor in cream and butter. *Oklahoma Agric. Exp. Sta. Bull.* No. 401. 22pp.

O'NEILL, E. 1972. Alkali bulrush seed germination and culture. *J. Wildlife Mgmt.* 36(2):649–652.

ONG, C. and C. MARSHALL. 1975. Assimilate distribution in *Poa annua* L. *Ann. Bot.* 39:413–421.

ONG, C., C. MARSHALL and G. SAGAR. 1978. The effects of nutrient supply on flowering and seed production in *Poa annua* L. *J. Brit. Grassland Soc.* 33:117–121.

OOMES, M. and W. ELBERSE. 1976. Germination of six grassland herbs in microsites with different water contents. *J. Ecol.* 64:745–755.

OORSCHOT, J. and H. STRAATHOF. 1988. On the occurrence and distribution of chloroplastic resistance of weeds to triazines in the Netherlands. *Proc. 8th Intern. Symp. Weed Ecol., Biol., Systematics* 8(1):267–275.

OOSTING, H. 1942. An ecological analysis of the plant communities of the Piedmont, North Carolina. *Am. Midland Naturalist* 28:1–128.

ORCHARD, H. 1956. Weeds of South Australia: Spear thistle. *J. Agric.* South Aus., p. 491.

ORDTEX, G. 1949. The aquinaldos: Major bee plants of Cuba. *Am. Bee J.* 89:72–73.

ORMOND, N. 1973. Contribuicao ao estudo biosistematico e ecologica de *Ludwigia octovalvis*. *Revista Brasiliera de Biol.* 33:87–107.

ORR, A. 1978. Inflorescence development in *Brassica campestris* L. *Am. J. Bot.* 65:466–470.

OSMAN, H. and B. FADALLA. 1974. The effect of level of

water intake on some aspects of digestion and nitrogen metabolism of the desert sheep of the Sudan. *J. Agric.*, Cambridge, 82:61–69.

OSOTSAPAR, Y. and B. MERCADO. 1976. Morphology and anatomy of *Eleocharis dulcis. Kalikasan* 5(3):332–340.

OSTROW-SCHWEBEL, J. 1979. An abscisic acid-induced separation layer in *Lemna minor* L. *Florida Sci.* 42:172–176.

OSWEILER, G., W. BUCK and E. BICKNELL. 1969. Production of perirenal oedema in swine with *Amaranthus retroflexus. Am. J. Vet. Res.* 30:557–566.

OTTO, H. and W. HILBIG. 1987. Changes in the segetal flora of Oberlausitz by soil improvement measures in agriculture. *Abhandlungen und Berichte des Naturkundemuseums* 60:43–47.

OUREN, T. 1959. Om skipsfartens betydning for Norges flora. (The influence of shipping on Norwegian flora). *Blyttia* 17:97–118.

OVESNOV, A. and A. SHCHEKINA. 1959. The effect of subterranean parts of couchgrass and sowthistle on germination of the seeds of meadow herbs. Translation of Doklady Akademii Nauk SSSR 127:224–226. *Doklady Botan. Sci. Sections* 127:220–222.

OYER, E. 1976. Lesser known vegetables with apparent ability to withstand stress conditions. *Proc. Crop tolerance to suboptimal land conditions.* 343pp. Ed. by G. Jung. Special Publ. No. 32, Am. Soc. Agron.; Madison, Wisconsin, USA.

OZER, Z. 1982. *The influence of passage through the gastrointestinal tract of sheep on meadow plant seeds, and effect of duration in a dung heap.* Ataturk Univ. Yayinlari No. 597. 57pp.

PAATELA, J. and L. ERVIO. 1971. Weed seeds in cultivated soils in Finland. *Ann. Agric. Fenniae* 10:144–152.

PABLICO, P. and K. MOODY. 1985. A survey of lowland rice field weeds in central and southern Luzon, Philippines. pp. 1–21. *Proc. 16th Annual Conf. Pest Control Council* (Philippines).

———. 1986. Lowland rice field weeds in Nueva Ecija, Philippines. *Intern. Rice Res. Newsl.* 11(2):29.

PADHYE, M. 1963. Two types of embryo development in *Passiflora foetida. Current Sci.* 32:373–374.

PADHYE, M. and B. DESHPANDE. 1960. The male and female gametophytes of *Passiflora foetida. Proc. Ind. Acad. Sci., Sect. B.* 52(4):124–130.

PADMANABHAN, D. 1968. Development from zygote to seedling in *Tridax procumbens* L. *Ind. Bot. Soc. J.* 47:94–112.

PAGE, C. 1976. The taxonomy and phytogeography of bracken: A review. *Bot. J. Linn. Soc.* 73:1–34.

———. 1986. The strategies of bracken as a permanent ecological opportunist. In: *Ecology, land use and control technology.* Ed. by R. Smith and J. Taylor. Parthenon Publ. Co., Carnforth, Eng.

PAGE, R., S. VEZEY, O. CHARLES and T. HOLLIFIELD. 1977. Effects on feed consumption and egg production of coffee bean seed *Cassia obtusifolia* feed to white leghorn hens. *Avian Dis.* 21:90–96.

PAINTER, D. 1988. Long term effects of mechanical harvesting on Eurasian watermilfoil. *J. Aquat. Plant Mgmt.* 26:25–29.

PAINTER, D. and J. WALTHO. 1985. Short term impact of harvesting of Eurasian watermilfoil. pp. 187–201. *Proc. 1st Intern. Symp. Watermilfoil* Myriophyllum spicatum *and Related* **Haloragaceae** *spp.*

PAL, A. 1979. Cytological races in *Nicandra physalodes. Cell and Chromosome Newsl.* 2(2):23–25.

PALMBLAD, I. 1968. Competition in experimental populations of weeds with emphasis on the regulation of population size. *Ecol.* 49(1):26–34.

———. 1969. Population variation in germination of weedy species. *Ecol.* 50:746–748.

PALOMINO, G., R. VIVEROS and R. BYE. 1988. Cytology of five Mexican species of *Datura* **Solanaceae**. *Southwestern Naturalist* 33:85–90.

PAMMEL, L. 1894. Botany of the Russian thistle. *Iowa Agric. Exp. Sta. Bull.* No. 26. 33pp.

———. 1898. The Russian thistle. *Iowa Agric. Exp. Sta. Bull.* No. 38. 24pp.

———. 1911. *Manual of poisonous plants.* Torch Press, Cedar Rapids, Iowa (USA).

———. 1913. The weed flora of Iowa. *Geological Survey Bull.* No. 4, Des Moines, Iowa (USA).

PAMPLONA, P. and M. MADRID. 1979. Weed control in corn and sorghum in the Philippines. pp. 101–111. *Proc. Weed Sci. Soc. Philipp. Symp. Weed Control in Trop. Crops.*

PAMPLONA, P., J. IMLAN, J. HEFERVEZ, R. ACASIO and A. MERCADO. 1976. Approaches in controlling *Rottboellia exaltata* and *Boerhavia diffusa* in corn fields. *Mindanao Inst. Technol. Res. J.* 6:16–23.

PANCHO, J. 1964. Seed sizes and production capacities in common weed species of the rice fields of the Philippines. *Philipp. Agric.* 48:307–316.

PANCHO, J. and J. KIM. 1985. Reproductive biology of weeds in vegetables in the highlands of Benguet, Luzon, Philippines. *Philipp. J. Weed Sci.* 12:75–98.

PANCHO, J. and S. OBIEN. 1983. *Manual of weeds of tobacco farms in the Philippines.* New Mercury Printing Press; Quezon City, Philippines.

PANDEY, H., K. MISRA and K. MUKERJEE. 1971. Phosphate uptake and its incorporation in some crop plants and their associated weeds. *Ann. Bot.* 35:367–372.

PANDEY, Y. 1971. *Cassias* commonly occurring or cultivated in India. *Bombay Natural History Soc.* 68:311–317.

PANDEYA, S. 1953. Variations in leaf form in *Marsilea quadrifolia. Proc. Ind. Sci. Congress* 40:84–85.

PANDYA, R., M. KHAN, S. GUPTA and K. DHINDSA. 1973. Effect of seed size upon germination, moisture uptake, seedling growth, dry weight changes and soluble sugars under polyethylene glycol induced stress. *Biochemie und Physiol. der Pflanzen* 164:80–87.

PANDYA, S. and V. PATHAK. 1980. Seed dormancy imposed by covering structures in *Achyranthes aspera. Geobios* 7:74–76.

PANDYA, S. and B. PUROHIT. 1976 Ecological studies of crop weed association of jowar *Sorghum vulgare* Pers. crop fields at Rajkot. *J. Ind. Bot. Soc.* 55:14–24.

PANETSOS, C. 1963. *Sources of variation in wild populations of* Raphanus. Ph.D. Diss., Univ. Calif. (USA).

PANETTA, F. and J. DODD. 1987. The biology of Australian weeds. 16. *Chondrilla juncea* L. *J. Aus. Inst. Agric. Sci.* 53:83–95.

PANJE, R. 1970. The evolution of a weed. *PANS (Pest Articles and News Summaries)* 16:590–595.

———. 1972. In what way has *Saccharum spontaneum* contributed to the agronomic behavior of commercial sugarcanes? *Ind. J. Agron.* 17:216–220.

PANJE, R. and K. SRINIVASAN. 1959. Studies in *Saccharum spontaneum.* The flowering behavior of latitudinally displaced populations. *Bot. Gaz.* 120:193–202.

PANT, D. 1943. On the morphology and anatomy of the root system in *Asphodelus tenuifolius. J. Ind. Botan. Soc.* 22:1–26.

PANT, D. and B. MEHRA. 1961. Nodal anatomy of *Boerhavia diffusa* L. *Phytomorphology* 11:384–405.

PANTER, K., R. KEELER and D. BAKER. 1988. Toxicoses in livestock from the hemlocks (*Conium* and *Cicuta* spp.). *J. Animal Sci.* 66:2407–2413.

PARHAM, J. 1958. Weeds of Fiji. *Dept. Agric. Bull.* No. 35; Suva, Fiji.

PARK, R. 1965. Benzyl thiocyanate taint in the milk of dairy cattle ingesting *Coronopus didymus. Nature* 207:640.

PARK, R. and J. ARNETT. 1969. Weed taints in dairy produce: 2. *Coronopus* or land cress taint in milk. *J. Dairy Res.* 36:37–46.

PARKER, C. 1978. Parasitic weeds and their control in the tropics. *Proc. Nigeria Weed Sci. Soc.,* Series No. 3:22–49.

———. 1986. Scope of the agronomic problems caused by *Orobanche* species. pp. 11–17. *Proc. Workshop on Biology and Control of Orobanche.* Ed. by S. ter Borg. Wageningen, Netherlands.

PARKER, C. and M. DEAN. 1976. Control of wild rice in rice. *Pesticide Sci.* 7:403–416.

PARKER, C. and A. WILSON. 1986. Parasitic weeds and their control in the Near East. *FAO Plant Protec. Bull.* 34:83–98.

PARMELEE, R., M. BEARE and J. BLAIR. 1989. Decomposition and nitrogen dynamics of surface weed residues in no-till agroecosystems under drought conditions: Influence of resource quality and the decomposer community. *Soil Biol. Biochem.* 21:97–103.

PARRISH, J. and F. BAZZAZ. 1982. Responses of plants from three successional communities to a nutrient gradient. *J. Ecol.* 70:233–248.

PARSONS, W. 1973. *Noxious weeds of Victoria, Australia.* Inkata Press, Melbourne, Australia. 300pp.

———. 1977. *The ecology and physiology of two species of* Carduus *as weeds of pastures in Victoria.* Ph.D. Diss., Univ. Melbourne, Melbourne, Australia.

———. 1979. Taxonomy of two species of *Carduus* in Australia. pp. 305–310. *Proc. 7th Asian-Pacific Weed Sci. Soc. Conf.*

PARSONS, W. and E. CUTHBERTSON. 1992. *Noxious weeds of Australia.* Inkata Press, Sidney, Australia. 692pp.

PASS, D., G. HOGG, R. RUSSELL, J. EDGAR, I. TENCE and L. RIKARD-BELL. 1979. Poisoning of chickens and ducks by pyrrolizidine alkaloids of *Heliotropium europaeum. Aus. Vet. J.* 55(6):284–288.

PATE, D. 1979. A study of the germination requirements of bristly starbur *Acanthospermum hispidum* DC. *Proc. 32nd Southern Weed Sci. Soc. Conf.* p. 330.

PATEL, B. and C. PATEL. 1972. Study on the partial replacement of concentrate mixture by byproducts mixture from the ration of bullocks. *Ind. J. Nutrition Dietetics* 9:157–160.

PATEL, B., N. PATEL and Y. DAVE. 1976. Pericarpial study in the developing fruit of *Cassia occidentalis* L. *Flora* (Jena) 65:215–222.

PATNAIK, S. 1976. Autecology of *Ipomoea aquatica. J. Inland Fisheries Soc.,* India, 8:77–82.

PATTEE, H., K. ALLRED and H. WIEBE. 1965. Photosynthesis in dodder. *Weed Sci.* 13:193–194.

PATTEN, B. 1954. Status of some American species of *Myriophyllum* as revealed by the discovery of intergrade material between *M. exalbescens* and *M. spicatum* in New Jersey. *Rhodora* 56:213–225.

———. 1955. Germination of the seed of *Myriophyllum spicatum. Bull. Torrey Bot. Club* 82:50–56.

———. 1956. Notes on the biology of *Myriophyllum spicatum* in a New Jersey lake. *Bull. Torrey Bot. Club:* 83:5–18.

PATTERSON, C. 1956. Effects of chemical weed control on beekeeping. *New Zealand Journal of Agriculture* 92:530–532.

PATTERSON, D. 1976. C_4 photosynthesis in smooth pigweed. *Weed Sci.* 24:127–130.

———. 1985. Comparative ecophysiology of weeds and crops. pp. 101–129. In: *Weed physiology,* Vol. I, *Reproduction and ecophysiology.* Ed. by S. Duke. CRC Press, Boca Raton, FL USA.

PATTERSON, D. and E. FLINT. 1983. Comparative water relations, photosynthesis, and growth of soybean *Glycine max* and seven associated weeds. *Weed Res.* 31:318–323.

PAUL, V. 1984. Preliminary results of field trials on the effect of weeds and grasses on the yield of winter rye with particular regard to variety, sowing rate, and value of control. *Zeitschrift fur Pflanzenkrankheiten und Pflanzenschutz* 10:169–174.

PAVLYCHENKO, T. 1937. Quantitative study of the entire root system of weed and crop plants under field conditions. *Ecol.* 18:62–79.

PAVLYCHENKO, T. and J. HARRINGTON. 1934. Competitive efficiency of weeds and cereal crops. *Can. J. Res.* 10:77–94.

———. 1935. Root development of weeds and crops in competition under dry farming. *Scientific Agric.* 16:151–160.

PAWLAK, J., D. MURRAY and B. SMITH. 1990. Influence of capsule age on germination of nondormant jimsonweed seed *Datura stramonium. Weed Tech.* 4:31–34.

PAWLOWSKI, F., T. KAPELUSZNY, A. KOLASA and Z. LECYK. 1967–1968. Fertility of some species of ruderal weeds. *Ann. Univ. Mariae Curie-Slodowska (Poland). Section E, Agric.* 22:221–231.

PAZOUREK, J. 1977. The volumes of anatomical components in leaves of *Typha angustifolia* L. and *T. latifolia* L. *Biol. Plant.* 19:129–135.

PEARSALL, W. 1920. The aquatic vegetation of the English lakes. *J. Ecol.* 8:163–201.

PEARSALL, W. and E. GORHAM. 1956. Production ecology. 1. Standing crops of natural vegetation. *Oikos* 7:193–201.

PEEL, A. 1974. *Transport of nutrients in plants.* Butterworths, London.

PEGTEL, D. 1972. Effects of temperature and moisture on the germination of two ecotypes of *Sonchus arvensis* L. *Acta Bot. Neerl.* 21:48–53.

———. 1973. Aspects of ecotypic differentiation in the perennial sowthistle. *Acta Horticulturae* 32:55–71.

———. 1974. Effect of crop rotation on the distribution of two ecotypes of *Sonchus arvensis* L. in the Netherlands. *Acta Bot. Neerl.* 23:349–350.

PELTIER, W. and E. WELCH. 1969. Factors affecting growth of rooted aquatics in a river. *Weed Sci.* 17:412–416.

———. 1970. Factors affecting growth of rooted aquatic plants in a reservoir. *Weed Sci.* 18:7–9.

PELTON, J. 1956. A study of seed dormancy in eighteen species of high altitude Colorado plants. *Butler Univ. Bot. Studies* (Indiana, USA) 13:74–84.

PEMADASA, M. 1976. Interference in populations of three weed species. *J. Appl. Ecol.* 13:899–913.

———. 1979. Movements of abaxial and adaxial stomata. *New Phytol.* 82:69–80.

PEMADASA, M. and N. KANGATHARALINGAM. 1977. Factors affecting germination of some **Compositaes.** *Ceylon J. Sci., Biological Sci.* 12:157–168.

PEMADASA, M. and M. WICKRAMASINGHE. 1979. Effects of some soil factors on seed germination. *Cey. J. Sci.* 13:1–18.

PENDLAND, J. 1979. Ultrastructural characteristics of *Hydrilla* leaf tissue. *Tissue and Cell* 11:79–88.

PENFOUND, W. 1940. The biology of *Achyranthes philoxeroides* (Mart.) Grisb. *Midland Naturalist* 24:248–252.

PENFOUND, W. and E. RICE. 1957. Plant population changes in a native prairie plot plowed annually over a five year period. *Ecol.* 38:148–150.

PENG, S. 1984. *The biology and control of weeds in sugarcane.* Elsevier, N.Y.

PENKAUSKENE, E. and E. SHIMIKUNAITE. 1973. Experience of cultivating knotweed in the Lithuanian SSR. *Rastit. Resur.* 9:588–595.

PENNYPACKER, B., P. WILSON and S. WILHELM. 1979. Anatomic changes resulting from the parasitism of tomato by *Orobanche ramosa. Phytopathology* 69:741–748.

PENUELAS, J. and A. VERDAGUER. 1987. *Elodea canadensis* a l'embassament de la Torrassa: Record de fondaria per a una fanerogama d'aigua dolca. *Bulleti Inst. Catalana d'Historia Natural* 54(6):79–81.

PEREZ, E. 1956. *Plantas utiles de Colombia.* 3rd Edition. Sucesores de Riva Deneyra, Madrid, Spain.

PERKINS, M. and M. SYTSMA. 1987. Harvesting and carbohydrate accumulation in Eurasian watermilfoil. *J. Aquat. Weed Mgmt.* 25:57–62.

PERRY, T. 1968. Dormancy, turion formation, and germination by different clones of *Spirodela polyrhiza. Plant Physiol.* 43:1866–1869.

PERSECA, T., M. DORDEA, I. POP and B. DARIE. 1976. Researches on the interspecific amino acid content in *Polygonum.* In: *Contributii Botanice, Gradina Botanica Univ. Babes-Bolyai' din Cluj-Napoca.* pp. 215–220.

PESCHKEN, D. 1982. Host specificity and biology of *Cystiphora sonchi*, a candidate for the biological control of *Sonchus* species. *Entomophaga* 27:405–416.

PESCHKEN, D., A. THOMAS and R. WISE. 1983. Loss in yield of rapeseed *Brassica napus* and *Brassica campestris* caused by perennial sowthistle *Sonchus arvensis* in Saskatchewan and Manitoba. *Weed Sci.* 31:740–744.

PETERS, G. 1975. The *Azolla-Anabaena* relationship: III. Studies on metabolic capabilities and a further characterization of the symbiont. *Archives Microbiol.* 103:113–122.

PETERS, G., H. CALVERT, D. KAPLAN and M. PENCE. 1981a. Morphological and physiological aspects of leaf development in the *Azolla-Anabaena* symbiosis. In: *Current perspectives in nitrogen fixation,* p. 456. Eds. A. Gibson and W. Newton. Elsevier, North Holland.

PETERS, G., O. ITO, V. TYAGI, B. MAYNE, D. KAPLAN and H. CALVERT. 1981b. Photosynthesis and N_2 fixation in the *Azolla-Anabaena* symbiosis. In: *Current perspectives in nitrogen fixation,* pp. 121–130. Eds. A. Gibson and W. Newton; Elsevier, North Holland.

PETERS, G., H. CALVERT, D. KAPLAN, O. ITO and R. TOIA. 1982. The *Azolla-Anabaena* symbiosis: Morphology, physiology and use. *Isr. J. Bot.* 31:305–323.

PETERS, R., J. MEADE and P. SANTELMANN. 1963. Life history studies as related to weed control in the Northeast (USA): II. Yellow foxtail and giant foxtail. *Univ. Rhode Isl. Exp. Sta. Bull.* No. 369. 18pp.

PETROV, D. 1970. A new physiological race of sunflower broomrape *Orobanche cumana* Wallrath in Bulgaria. In: *Plant protection in the service of agriculture*, pp. 37–48. Ed. by I. Kovachevski et al. Bulgaria Acad. Sci. Press.

PETTERSON, B. 1940. A case of long distance dispersal of plants through the import of timber. *Acta Phytogeographica Suecica* 13:96–100.

PETUNOVA, ANGELA 1995. Controlling Weeds Resistant to 2,4-D in Russian cereal crops. *Resistant Pest Management* 7(2):23.

PETZOLD, K. 1959. Effect of combine harvesting on weediness. *Zeitung fur Acker und Pflanzenbau* 109:49–78.

———. 1979. Combine harvesting and weeds. pp. 287–292. *Proc. European Weed Res. Soc. Symp.*; Mainz, Germany.

PEVERLY, J. 1985. Element accumulation and release by macrophytes in a wetland stream. *J. Environ. Quality* 14:137–142.

PEVERLY, J. and J. BRITTAIN. 1978. Effect of *Myriophyllum spicatum* on phosphorus movement between sediment and water. *J. Great Lakes Res.* 4:62–68.

PFISTER, K., K. STEINBACK, G. GARDNER and C. ARNTZEN. 1981. Photoaffinity labeling of an herbicide receptor protein in chloroplast membranes. *Proc. Nat. Acad. Sci.* 78:981–985.

PHEANG, C. and I. MUCHSIN. 1975. Aquatic weed control using grass carp *Ctenopharyngodon idella*. pp. 406–419. *Proc. 3rd Indonesian Weed Sci. Conf.*

PIETERS, A. and V. CHARLES. 1901. The seed coats of certain species of the genus *Brassica. USDA, Division of Bot. Bull.* No. 29, Washington, D.C.

PIETERSE, A. 1977. Biological control of aquatic weeds: Perspectives for the tropics. *Aquat. Bot.* 3:133–141.

———. 1979. The broomrapes **Orobanchaceae**—a review. *Abstr. Trop. Agric.* 5(3):9–35.

———. 1981. *Hydrilla verticillata*—a review. *Abstr. Trop. Agric* 7:9–34.

PIETERSE, A., A. EBBERS, and J. VERKLEIJ. 1984a. A comparative study on isoenzyme patterns in *Hydrilla verticillata* from Ireland and Poland. *Aquat. Bot.* 18:299–303.

PIETERSE, A., H. STAPHORST, and J. VERKLEIJ. 1984b. Some effects of nitrogen and phosphorus concentration on the phenology of *Hydrilla verticillata. J. of Aquat. Plant Mgmt.* 22:62–63.

PIETERSE, A., J. VERKLEIJ, and H. STAPHORT. 1985. A comparative study on isoenzyme patterns, morphology, and chromosome number of in *Hydrilla verticillata* in Africa. *J. Aquat. Plant Mgmt.* 23:72–76.

PIETSCH, W. 1981. Zur bioindikation *Najas marina* und *Hydrilla verticillata* in Reicher Gewsser mitteleuropas. *Feddes Repertorium* 92:125–174.

PIGGIN, C., T. REEVES, H. BROOKE and G. CODE. 1978. Germination of wild radish *Raphanus raphanistrum* L. pp. 233–240. *Proc. 1st Conf. Council Aus. Weed Societies.*

PIJL, L. VAN DER. 1969. *Principles of dispersal in higher plants.* Springer-Verlag, Heidelberg. 154pp.

———. 1982. *Principles of dispersal in higher plants.* 3rd Revision. Publ. Springer-Verlag.

PINOWSKI, J. and Z. WOJCIK. 1968. Production of weeds in fields and the degree to which their seeds are consumed by the tree sparrow *Passer montanus. Ekologia Polska* (B) 14:297–302.

PIP, E. and K. SIMMONS. 1986. Aquatic angiosperms at unusual depths in Shoal Lake, Manitoba, Canada. *Can. Field Nat.* 100:354–358.

PIPER, G. 1983. Rush skeletonweed. *Weeds Today* 14(1):5–7.

PIROFSKY, B., R. BEAULIEU, and G. DAVIES. 1981. Inhibition of lymphocyte growth by *Ulex europaeus* seed extracts. *Immunology* 43(4):653–662.

PISTRICK, K. 1987. Taxonomical investigations in the genus *Raphanus* L. *Kulturpflanze* 0(35):225–332.

PITMAN, J. and R. PITMAN. 1986. Transpiration and evaporation from bracken *Pteridium aquilinum* in open habitats. In: *Bracken, ecology, land use, and control technology*, pp. 259–272. Ed. by R. Smith and J. Taylor. Parthenon Publ. Co., Carnforth, Eng.

PIZZOLONGO, P. 1966. On the behavior of plantlets of *Cuscuta pentagona* in monochromatic light and in darkness. *Annali Facolta Sci. Agraria, Univ. Napoli*, Portici, 1:116–125.

PLACE, I. 1953. Influence of bracken *Pteridium aquilinum* on establishment of spruce and fir seedlings. *Pulp Paper Mag. Can.* 54:169–172.

PLAS, F. 1971. **Lemnaceae**—M. Flora Malesiana Ser. 1. *Spermatophyta* 7:219–237.

PLAVSIC-GOJKOVIC, N., K. DUBRAVEC, M. BRITVEC and B. PALCIC. 1988. Transpiration of leaves of maize and some weeds. *Fragmenta herbologica* 17:25–35.

POEL, L. 1951. Soil aeration in relation to *Pteridium aquilinum. J. Ecol.* 39:182–191.

———. 1960. The estimation of oxygen diffusion rates in soils. *J. Ecol.* 48:733–736.

———. 1961. Soil aeration as a limiting factor in the growth of *Pteridium aquilinum. J. Ecol.* 49:107–111.

POGGIALI, R. 1967. Some observations on the germination of *Chenopodium album* and *ambrosioides. Webbia* 22:67–73.

POLITIS, D., A. WATSON and W. BRUCKART. 1984. Susceptibility of musk thistle and related Composites to *Puccinia carduorum. Phytopathology* 74(6):687–691.

POLLARD, F. and G. CUSSANS. 1976. The influence of tillage on the weed flora of four sites sown to successive crops of spring barley. pp. 1019–1028. *Proc. 13th Brit. Weed Control Conf.*

———. 1981. The influence of tillage on the weed flora in a succession of winter cereal crops on a sandy loam soil. *Weed Res.* 21:185–190.

POLLARD, F., S. MOSS, G. CUSSANS and R. FROUD-WILLIAMS. 1982. The influence of tillage on the weed flora in a succession of winter wheat crops on a clay loam soil and a silt loam soil. *Weed Res.* 22:129–136.

POLUNIN, N. 1951. Seeking airborne botanical particles about the North Pole. *Svensk Botanisk Tidskrift* 45:320–354.

———. 1959. *Circumpolar arctic flora.* Oxford Univ. Press, London.

POND, W. 1905. The biological relation of aquatic plants to the substratum. *Rep. United States Comm. Fish and Fisheries* 19:483.

POOK, E. 1983. The effect of shade on the growth of variegated thistle (*Silybum marianum*) and cotton thistle (*Onopordum* sp.). *Weed Res.* 23:11–17.

POPAY, A. 1973. Germination and dormancy in the seeds of certain East African weed species. pp. 77–81. *Proc. 4th Asian-Pacific Weed Sci. Soc. Conf.*

———. 1980. Nodding thistle *Carduus nutans*, a plant noxious to grazing livestock in crops and pastures: Biology, significance, and control. *Farm Production and Practice*, New Zealand Ministry Agric. and Fisheries, Issue 359.

———. 1981. Germination of seeds of five annual species of barley grass. *J. Appl. Ecol.* 18:547–558.

POPAY, A. and G. IVENS. 1982. East Africa. Chapter 31 in: *Biology and ecology of weeds.* Ed. by W. Holzner and M. Numata. Dr. Junk Publ., The Hague.

POPAY, A. and E. ROBERTS. 1970a. Factors involved in the dormancy and germination of *Capsella bursa-pastoris* and *Senecio vulgaris. J. Ecol.* 58:103–122.

———. 1970b. Ecology of *Capsella bursa-pastoris* and *Senecio vulgaris* in relation to germination behavior. *J. Ecol.* 58:123–139.

POPAY, A. and P. SANDERS. 1975. Effect of depth of burial on seed germination and seedling emergence of barley grass *Hordeum murinum* L. *New Zealand J. Exp. Agric.* 3:77–80.

———. 1982. Seasonal variation in salinity of soils supporting different levels of barley grass *Hordeum murinum* L. *New Zealand J. Agric. Res.* 25:223–227.

POPAY, A. and A. THOMPSON. 1979. Some aspects of the biology of *Carduus nutans* in New Zealand. pp. 343–346. *Proc. 7th Asian-Pacific Weed Sci. Soc. Conf.*

PORTER, R. 1936. *Noxious and other bad weeds of Iowa.* Iowa State College Agric. and Mechanic Arts, Ext. Circ. No. 201.

POTTS, G. 1970. Studies on the changing role of weeds of the genus *Polygonum* in the diet of the partridge *Perdix perdix* L. *J. Appl. Ecol.* 7:567–576.

POVILAITIS, B. 1956. Dormancy studies with seeds of various weeds. *Comptes Rendus de l' Assoc. Intern. d'Essais de Semences*, Copenhagen, 21:88–111.

POWELL, R. and E. SMITH. 1978. Tumble weed dermatitis. *Archives Dermatology* 114:751–754.

POWERS, K., R. NOBLE and R. CHABRECK. 1978. Seed distribution by waterfowl in southwestern Louisiana. *J. Wildlife Mgt.* 42:598–605.

PRAKASH, S. 1981. Cruciferous oilseeds in India. In: *Brassica crops and wild allies*, pp. 151–164. Ed. by S. Tsunoda, K. Hinata and C. Gomez-Campo. Japanese Scientific Societies Press, Tokyo.

PRAKASH, S. and K. HINATA. 1980. Taxonomy, cytogenetics, and origin of crop *Brassicas*, a review. *Opera Botanica* 55:1–57.

PRAMANIK, T. and S. DATTA. 1986. Plant regeneration and ploidy variation in culture derived plants of *Asclepias curassavica* L. *Plant Cell Rep.* 3:219–222.

PRASAD, K. 1977. The development and structure of the basal body in the ovule and seed of some species of **Cruciferae**. *Botanische Jahrbuecher fur Systematik Pflanzengeschichte und Pflanzengeographie* 98(2):266–272.

PRASAD, T. and D. SINGH. 1978. Gametophytes and seed development in *Nicandra physalodes. J. Ind. Bot. Soc.* 57:76–83.

PRENTKI, R., T. GUSTAFSON and M. ADAMS. 1978. Nutrient movement in lake shore marshes. pp. 169–194. In: *Freshwater wetlands: Ecological processes and management potential.* Academic Press, N.Y.

PRENTKI, R., M. ADAMS, S. CARPENTER, A. GASITH, L. SMITH and P. WEILER. 1979. The role of submersed weedbeds in internal loading and interception of allochthonous materials in Lake Wingra, Wisconsin. *Archiv fur Hydrobiologie Supplementband* 57:221–250.

PRESS, M., N. SHAH and G. STEWART. 1986. The parasitic habit: trends in metabolic reductionism. pp. 96–106. In: *Biology and Control of Orobanche.* Ed. by S. ter Borg. Landbouwhogeschool, Wageningen, Netherlands.

PRIETO, M. and S. LEON. 1975. *Weeds of sesame in the state of Portuguesa.* Ministry Agric., Caracas, Venezuela.

PRISZTER, S. 1950. Examens d' *Amaranthus*: II. Caracteristique generale de la famille des **Amaranthaceae** et ses members. *Hungary Univ. Sci. Agraires, Ann. Faculte Horti Viticult.* Vol. 1:79–82.

PRIVAT, G. 1960. Researches sur les phanerogames parasites. *Ann. Sci. Naturelles*, Series 12, 1:721–871.

PROBATOVA, N., and T. BUCH. 1981. *Hydrilla verticillata* in the Soviet Far East. *Botanicheskii Zhurnal.* 66:208–214.

PROTOSENKO, N. 1981. Prospects of using the method of biological control against dodder in the Chu lowlands of

Kirghizia. *Entomologicheski Issledovaniya V Kirgizii* 14:104–109.

PUENTES, M., J. PERCIRAS and M. CASAL. 1988. Study of seedbank of *Ulex europaeus* shrublands in Galicia, Spain. *Revue D'Ecologie et de Biologie du Sol* 25:251–224.

PUNT, W. and J. RENTROP. 1973. Pollen morphology of the *Phyllanthus* species occurring in the continental United States. *Rev. Paleobot. Palynol.* 16:243–260.

PURI, H. 1971. Macro- and micromorphology leaf and seed of *Gynandropsis pentaphylla. Quart. J. Crude Drug Res.* 11:1805–1811.

PURIVETH, P. 1980. Decomposition of emergent macrophytes in a Wisconsin marsh. *Hydrobiologia* 72:231–242.

PURSEGLOVE, J. 1965. Contributions to the discussion of a paper given by J. Harper, "Establishment, aggression, and cohabitation in weedy species." In: *The genetics of colonizing species.* Eds. H. Baker and G. Stebbins. Academic Press, New York. p. 266.

———. 1968. *Tropical crops, dicotyledons 1.* Longmans, Green & Co., London.

———. 1972. *Tropical crops, monocotyledons.* John Wiley & Sons, N.Y.

PURVIS, C., R. JESSOP and J. LOVETT. 1985. Selective regulation of germination and growth of annual weeds by crop residues. *Weed Res.* 25:415–421.

PUTNAM, A. and C. TANG. 1986. *The science of allelopathy.* Wiley-Interscience, N.Y. 317pp.

PUTNAM, M., T. BOOSINGER, J. SPANO, J. WRIGHT, A. WIGGANS, and G. D'ANDREA. 1988. Evaluation of *Cassia obtusifolia* (sicklepod) seed consumption in Holstein calves. *Vet. Hum. Toxicol.* 30:316–318.

PUTWAIN, P. and J. HARPER. 1972. Studies in the dynamics of plant populations. V. Mechanisms governing the sex ratio in *Rumex acetosella* and *R. acetosa. J. Ecol.* 60:113–129.

PUTWAIN, P., D. MACHIN and J. HARPER. 1968. Studies in the dynamics of plant populations. II. Components and regulation of natural population of *Rumex acetosella. J. Ecol.* 56:421–431.

PUTWAIN, P., A. MORTIMER, P. ULF-HANSEN and D. WATSON. 1989. Population ecology and selection for herbicide resistance. *Abstr. 29th Weed Sci. Soc. Am. Conf.* 25:134–135.

QUALLS, C. 1980. *Senecio vulgaris* toxicity in the horse. *Diss. Abstr. Intern.* 41B:2080–2081.

QUIMBY, P. 1974. Environmental effect on budbreak of alligator weed *Alternanthera philoxeroides. Abstr. 14th Weed Sci. Soc. Am. Conf.* 14:32–33.

QUIMBY, P. and S. KAY. 1977. Hypoxic quiescence in alligatorweed. *Physiol. Plantarum* 40:163–168.

QUIMBY, P., J. POTTER and S. DUKE. 1978. Photosystem II and hypoxic quiescence in alligatorweed. *Physiol. Plantarum* 44:246–250.

RAATIKAINEN, M. and T. RAATIKAINEN. 1972. Weed colonization of cultivated fields in Finland. *Ann. Agric. Fenn.* 11:100–110.

RAATIKAINEN, M., T. RAATIKAINEN, and J. MUKULA. 1985. The biomass of weeds in winter cereal fields in Finland. *Ann. Agric. Fenn.* 24:1–30.

RABINOWITZ, D. 1978. Abundance and diaspore weight in rare and common prairie grasses. *Oecologia* 37:213–219.

RABINOWITZ, D. and J. RAPP. 1980. Seed rain in a North American tall grass prairie. *J. Appl. Ecol.* 17:793–802.

———. 1981. Dispersal abilities of seven sparse and common grasses from a Missouri prairie. *Am. J. Bot.* 68:616–624.

RABINOWITZ, D., J. RAPP and P. DIXON. 1984. Competitive abilities of sparse grass species: Means of persistence or cause of abundance. *Ecol.* 65:1144–1154.

RACOVITZA, A. 1959. New observations on the germination of the seeds of *Orobanche ramosa. J. Agric. Tropicale et Botanique Appliquee* 6:111–114.

———. 1960. Contribution to the knowledge of host and stimulating plants on *Orobanche ramosa. Studii Cercetari Agronomice Acad., Filiala Cluj* 11:139–143.

RADCLIFFE, J. 1985. Grazing management of goats and sheep for gorse *Ulex europaeus* control. *New Zealand J. Exp. Agric.* 13(2):181–190.

RADEMACHER, B. and J. OZOLINS. 1952. Einfluss der getreide Konkurrez und des nahrstoffgehalts um keimsubstrat. *Angewandte Botanik* 24:69–93.

RADEMACHER, B., F. KOLB and H. BORNER. 1961. Experiments on the interaction between cultivated plants and weeds in water culture. *Weed Res.* 1:44–58.

RADEMACHER, B., W. KOCH and K. HURLE. 1970. Changes in weed flora as the result of continuous cropping of cereals and the annual use of the same weed control measures since 1956. pp. 1–6. *Proc. 10th Brit. Weed Control Conf.*

RADOSEVICH, S. and A. APPLEBY. 1973a. Relative susceptibility of two common groundsel *Senecio vulgaris* biotypes to six *s*-triazines. *Agron. J.* 65:553–558.

———. 1973b. Studies on the mechanism of resistance to simazine in common groundsel. *Weed Sci.* 21:497–500.

RADOSEVICH, S. and J. HOLT. 1982. Physiological responses and fitness of susceptible and resistant weed biotypes to triazine herbicides. In: *Herbicide resistance in plants.* Ed. by H. Lebaron and J. Gressel. John Wiley & Sons, N.Y.

RADOSEVICH, S., K. STEINBACK and C. ARNTZEN. 1979. Effect of photosystem II inhibitors on the thylakoid membranes of two common groundsel *Senecio vulgaris* biotypes. *Weed Sci.* 27:216–218.

RAGHAVAN, R. and S. KAMBLE. 1979. Cytology of some angiosperms from western Ghats India. *Maharashtra Vidnyan Mandir Patrika* 14:52–54.

RAGHAVENDRA, A. and V. DAS. 1976. Diversity in the biochemical and biophysical characteristics of C_4 dicotyledonous plants. *Ind. J. Plant Physiol.* 19:101–112.

RAHAN, M., Z. LAMID and D. SJAHBUDDIN. 1975. Weeds in inundated rice field in West Sumatra. *Proc. 3rd Indonesian Weed Sci. Conf.* 3:269–278.

RAHMAN, A. 1982. New Zealand (weeds). Chapter 27 in: *Biology and ecology of weeds.* Ed. by W. Holzner and M. Numata. Dr. Junk Publ., The Hague.

RAI, B. 1973. The red rice problem in Guyana. *PANS (Pest Articles and News Summaries)* 19:557–559.

RAJAN, A. and S. SANKARAN. 1974. Studies on crop-weed competition for nutrient and its effect on grain yield of maize (var. Ganga-5). *Madras Agric. J.* 61:413–416.

RAJU, M. 1954. Pollination mechanism in *Passiflora foetida. Proc. National Inst. Sci. Ind.* 20:431–436.

RAKHIMOV, U. 1967. Transpiration and diffusion pressure deficit of broomrape and the plant host. *Soviet Plant Physiol.* 14:631–632.

RAKOV, N. 1971. Blossoming of *Elodea. Priroda,* Moscow 1:90.

RAMACHANDRAN, V., T. RAMAPRABHU and S. SINGH. 1976. A survey of aquatic weed infestations in Andhra Pradesh. *Proc. Regional Seminar, Noxious Aquatic Vegetation,* New Delhi, 1973.

RAMAIAH, K. 1987. Control of *Striga* and *Orobanche* species—a review. pp. 637–647. *Proc. 4th Intern. Symp. Parasitic Flowering Plants.* Ed. by H. Weber and W. Forstreuter. Marburg, Germany.

RAMAKRISHNAN, P. 1963. Contributions to the ecological life history of *Setaria glauca* Beauv. *J. Ind. Bot. Soc.* 42:118–129.

RAMAKRISHNAN, P. and R. JAIN. 1965a. Mineral uptake by the edaphic ecotypes in *Tridax procumbens* L. *Proc. National Inst. Sci. Ind., Part B: Biological Sci.* 31:219–228.

———. 1965b. Germinability of the seeds of the edaphic ecotypes in *Tridax procumbens* L. *Trop. Ecol.* 6:47–55.

RAMAKRISHNAN, P. and S. LEKHI. 1972. Germination behavior of *Trianthema* species related to solute concentration of the medium. *Current Sci.* 41:713–714.

RAMIREZ, G. and A. ROMERO. 1978. El Pacifico como agente diseminante en el littoral Chileno. (The Pacific Ocean as a transporting agent on the Chilian coast). *Ecologia* (Argentina) 3:19–30.

RAMSON, A., K. ARLT, P. ERFURTH and M. HANSEL. 1982. The occurrence of the most important pests in plant production in the German Democratic Republic 1982. *Nachrichtenblatt fur den Deutschen Pflanzenschutzdienst in der DDR* 36(4):65–85.

RANSOM, E. 1935. The interrelations of catalase, respiration, after-ripening and germination in some dormant seeds of the Polygonaceae. *Am. J. Bot.* 22:815–825.

RANTZIEN, H. 1952. Notes on some tropical African species of *Najas* in Kew herbarium. *Kew Bull.* 1952:29–40.

RAO, A. and S. CHIN. 1972. Branched and separate root hairs in *Melastoma malabathricum. Cytologia* 37:111–118.

RAO, A. and K. MOODY. 1990. Weed seed contamination in rice seed. *Seed Sci. Technol.* 18:139–146.

RAO, H. 1935. The structure and life history of *Azolla pinnata* R.Br. with remarks on the fossil history of the Hydropterideae. *Proc. Ind. Acad. Sci.* 2:175–200.

RAO, J., K. RAO and S. MURTHY. 1979. Allelopathic effect of some weeds of vegetable crops on the germination and early growth of bajra. *Trop. Ecol.* 20:5–8.

RAO, P. and B. REDDY. 1982. Comparative germination profiles of the seeds in the biotypes of *Trianthema portulacastrum. Ind. Bot. Reporter* 1:23–26.

RAO, R. 1968. *Ultrastructure of* Spirodela polyrhiza (L.) Schleiden with special reference to chloroplast development during turion germination. Ph.D. Diss., North Carolina State Univ., Raleigh, NC USA.

RAO, V., and N. RAO. 1974. Factors responsible for non-nodulating nature of some legumes. *Proc. Indian Nat. Acad. Sci.* 40:613–617.

RASMUSSEN, L. 1947. The physiological action of 2,4–dichlorophenoxyacetic acid on dandelion *Taraxacum officinale. Plant Physiol.* 22:377–392.

RATCLIFFE, R. and A. OAKES. 1982. Yellow sugarcane aphid resistance in selected *Digitaria* germ plasm. *J. Econ. Entomol.* 75:308–314.

RATRA, P. and K. MISRA. 1970. Seasonal variation in chemical composition of *Achyranthes aspera* L. and *A. bidentata* BL. *Ind. Forester* 96:372–375.

RAUSCHERT, S. 1974. Nomenklatorische probleme in der gattung *Matricaria* L. *Folia Geobotan. Phytotaxon.* 9:249–260.

RAVEL, P. and U. CHATTERJI. 1968. Effect of heat treatment on germination of the seeds of the arid-zone plant, *Trianthema portulacastrum* L. *Proc. 56th Ind. Sci. Congr., Part III, Abstr., Section VI, Bot.* 56:399–400.

RAVEN, P. 1963. The Old World species of *Ludwigia,* including *Jussiaea,* with a synopsis of the genus, **Onagraceae**. *Reinwardtia,* Jakarta, 6:327–347 (Indonesia).

RAVN, K. 1964. Couchgrass control in the autumn. *Tolvmandsbladet* 36:457–459.

RAWLENCE, D. and J. WHITTON. 1977. Elements in aquatic macrophytes, water, plankton and sediments, in 3 North Island lakes of New Zealand. *New Zealand J. Marine and Freshwater Res.* 11:73–94.

REDDI, E. and C. REDDI. 1984. Pollination ecology of *Euphorbia geniculata. J. Bombay Nat. Hist. Soc.* 81:571–582.

REDDY, B. and P. RAO. 1985. Relative competitive abilities in pot cultures of two biotypes of *Trianthema portulacastrum. Ind. J. Ecol.* 12:209–215.

REDDY, K. and W. DEBUSK. 1985. Growth characteristics of aquatic macrophytes cultured in nutrient-enriched water: II. *Azolla,* duckweed, *Salvinia. Econ. Bot.* 39:200–208.

REDDY, K. and K. PORTIER. 1987. Nitrogen utilization by *Typha latifolia* L. as affected by temperature and rate of nitrogen application. *Aquatic Bot.* 27:127–138.

REDFERN, M. and R. CAMERON. 1985. Density and survival of *Urophora stylata* on *Cirsium vulgare* **Compositae** in relation to flower head and gall size. *Proc. 11th Intern. Symp. Bio. Control Weeds* 11:553–577.

REECE, P. and R. WILSON. 1983. Effects of Canada thistle *Cirsium arvense* and musk thistle *Carduus nutans* control on grass herbage. *Weed Sci.* 31:488–492.

REED, L. 1976. The long-range transport of air pollutants. *Ambio* 5:202.

REED, W. and H. KAYUMBO. 1965. Detailed studies of pests. *Tanzania Western Cotton Growing Area, Progress Rep. Exp. Sta.*: 13–16.

REEDERS, H., M. VAN SCHOUBROECK, W. VAN VIERSSEN, B. GOPAL and A. PIETERSE. 1986. Aquatic weeds and their implications for agriculture in the Chambal irrigated area, Kota, India. pp. 251–255. *Proc. 7th Intern. Symp. Aquatic Weeds.*

REES, W. 1978. The ecology of the Kafue Lechwe: The food supply. *J. Appl. Ecol.* 15:177–191.

REEVES, T., G. CODE and C. PIGGIN. 1981. Seed production and longevity, seasonal emergence, and phenology of wild radish *Raphanus raphanistrum. Aus. J. Exp. Agric. and Animal Husbandry* 21:524–530.

REGAN, J. and R. BELL. 1964. Preliminary studies on the effects of photoperiod, temperature and light intensity on the growth of *Polygonum pennsylvanicum, P. persicaria* and *P. scabrum. Proc. 18th Northeast Weed Sci. Soc.* 18:148–152.

REGEHR, D. and F. BAZZAZ. 1976. Low temperature photosynthesis in successional winter annuals. *Ecol.* 57:1297–1303.

REGEHR, D. and F. BAZZAZ. 1979. The population dynamics of *Erigeron canadensis,* a successional winter annual. *Journal of Ecology* 67(3)923–934.

REGNIER, E., M. SALVUCCI and M. STOLLER. 1985. Photosynthetic acclimation to irradiance in soybean and associated weeds. *Proc. North Central Weed Control Conf.* 40:78–79.

REINGANUM, C. 1986. New method for identifying forms of skeleton weed *Chondrilla juncea* L. *Plant Protec. Quart.* 1:109–110.

REINHARDT, E., G. BURGER and G. WEISE. 1980. Zur erkundung der phytotoxischen wirkung von zink, kadmium und kupfer auf *Elodea canadensis* durch erfassen der deplasmolyszeit. *Acta Hydrochimica et Hydrobiologica* 8(2):149–160.

REISMAN-BERMAN, O., J. KIGEL and B. RUBIN. 1988. Factors involved in the germination of *Datura ferox* and *D. stramonium. Phytoparasitica* 16(4):371–372.

RENFREW, J. 1973. *Paleoethnobotany: The prehistory of food plants of the Near East and Europe.* Columbia Univ. Press, N.Y. 248pp.

REPP, G. 1961. The salt tolerance of plants, basic research and tests. *Proc. Teheran Symp. Arid Zone Res. (UNESCO), Salinity Problems Arid Zones* 14:153–161.

RETIG, B. and L. HOLM. 1971. Influence of four weeds on enzyme components of cabbage, tomato and lettuce seedlings. *Weed Sci.* 19:735–739.

RETIG, B., L. HOLM and B. STRUCKMEYER. 1972. Effects of weeds on the anatomy of roots of cabbage and tomato. *Weed Sci.* 20:33–36.

RETZINGER, E. 1984. Growth and development of sicklepod *Cassia obtusifolia* selections. *Weed Sci.* 32:608–611.

REUSS, H. and G. BACHTHALER. 1988. Studies on the influence of production technology and ecological factors on quantitative and qualitative changes of regional weed flora on arable land. *Bayerisches Landwirtschaftliches Jahrbuch* 65:167–220.

RHOADS, W., E. FROLICH and A. WALLACE. 1967. Germination of Russian thistle *Salsola kali* seeds. *Calif. Agric.* 21(7):2.

RICE, H. and W. LAETSCH. 1967. Observations on the morphology and physiology of *Marsilea* sperm. *Am. J. Bot.* 54(7):856–866.

RICHARDS, A. 1973. The origin of *Taraxacum* agamospecies. *Bot. J. Linn.* Soc. 66:189–211.

RICHARDS, R. and N. THURLING. 1978a. Variation between and within species of rapeseed *Brassica campestris* and *B. napus* in response to drought stress: I. Sensitivity at different stages of development. *Aus. J. Agric. Res.* 29:469–477.

———. 1978b. Variation between and within species of rapeseed *Brassica campestris* and *B. napus* in response to drought stress: II. Growth and development under natural drought stress. *Aus. J. Agric. Res.* 29:479–490.

RICHARDSON, M. 1980. Yield loss in barley associated with *Sinapis arvensis* L. (charlock) after continuous routine use of herbicides. *Weed Res.* 20:295–298.

RIDLEY, H. 1930. *The dispersal of plants throughout the world.* Reeve and Ashford, Kent.

RIEMER, D. and S. TOTH. 1969. A survey of the chemical composition of *Potamogeton* and *Myriophyllum* in New Jersey. *Weed Sci.* 17:219–223.

RIEPMA, P. 1963. Herbicide effect and plant succession when using paraquat and amitrole against *Paspalum conjugatum* and *Melastoma malabathricum. J. Rubber Res. Inst. Malaya* 18:15–27.

———. 1964. Weed control with pre-emergence herbicides in tropical plantations crops. *World Review of Pest Control* (Fisons) 4(2):64–74.

———. 1965. *The reaction of weeds to herbicides. Experiments in 1965.* Rubber Res. Inst. Malaya, Document 48, Res. Archives.

RIETSMA, J., B. BLONDEL, S. SATINA and A. BLAKESLEE. 1955. Studies on ovule and embryo growth in *Datura*: I. A growth analysis. *Am. J. Bot.* 42:449–455.

RIJN, P. VAN. 1968. Ecological aspects of weed control in cotton in the Ord River Valley, Australia: I. Conditions affecting germination of weeds. *Aus. J. Exp. Agric. and Animal Husbandry* 8:620–624.

RIMON, D. and E. GALUN. 1968. Morphogenesis of *Spirodela oligorhiza*. *Bot. Gaz.* 129:138–144.

RIOPEL, J. 1979. Experimental studies on induction of haustoria in *Agalinis purpurea*. *Proc. 2nd Symp. Parasitic Weeds*. Ed. by L. Musselman, A. Worsham and R. Eplee. N. Carolina State Univ., Raleigh, USA.

———. 1983. The biology of parasitic flowering plants: Physiological aspects. pp. 13–34. In: *Vegetative compatibility in plants*. Ed. by R. Moore. Baylor Univ. Press, Waco, USA.

RIVALS, P. 1960. On the life history and problems of control of *Oxalis latifolia*. *J. Agric. Tropicale et Botanique Appliquee* 7:397–405.

RIVARD, P. and P. WOODARD. 1989. Light, ash, and *p*H effects on the germination and seedling growth of *Typha latifolia*. *Can. J. Bot.* 67:2783–2787.

RIZK, A., G. WASSEL and F. HAMMOUDA. 1970. A phytochemical study of the seeds of *Silybum marianum* growing in Egypt. *United Arab Republic J. Chem.* 13:49–54.

RIZK, T., W. NORMAND and L. SLOANE. 1969. Studies of *Sida* species in Louisiana. p. 340. *Proc. 22nd Southern Weed Sci. Soc.*

ROBB, S. 1963. *Oxalis latifolia* Kunth. *New Phytol.* 62:75–79.

ROBERTS, E. and S. BENJAMIN. 1979. The interaction of light, nitrate and alternating temperatures on the germination of *Chenopodium album*, *Capsella bursa-pastoris* and *Poa annua* before and after chilling. *Seed Sci. Technol.* 7:379–392.

ROBERTS, H. 1936. Seed production in the dandelion. *Scientific Agric.* 17:235–242.

———. 1958. Studies on the weeds of vegetable crops: I. Initial effects of cropping on the weed seed in the soil. *J. Ecol.* 46:759–768.

———. 1962. Studies on the weeds of vegetable crops: II. Effect of six years of cropping on the weed seeds in the soil. *J. Ecol.* 50:803–813.

———. 1963. Studies on the weeds of vegetable crops: III. Effects of different primary cultivations on the weed seeds in the soil. *J. Ecol.* 51:83–95.

———. 1979. Periodicity of seedling emergence and seed survival in some **Umbelliferae**. *J. Appl. Ecol.* 16:195–201.

———. 1986. Seed persistence in soil and seasonal emergence in plant species from different habitats. *J. Appl. Ecol.* 23:639–656.

ROBERTS, H. and J. BODDRELL. 1983. Seed survival and periodicity of seedling emergence in eight species of **Cruciferae**. *Ann. Appl. Biol.* 103:301–309.

———. 1984. Seed survival and periodicity of seedling emergence in four weedy species of *Papaver*. *Weed Res.* 24:195–200.

———. 1985. Seed survival and seasonal emergence in some species of *Geranium*, *Ranunculus* and *Rumex*. *Ann. Appl. Biol.* 107:231–238.

ROBERTS, H. and R. CHANCELLOR. 1979. Periodicity of seedling emergence and achene survival in some species of *Carduus*, *Cirsium* and *Onopordum*. *J. Appl. Ecol.* 16:641–647.

———. 1986. Seed banks of some arable soils in the English midlands. *Weed Res.* 26:251–257.

ROBERTS, H. and P. DAWKINS. 1967. Effect of cultivation on the number of viable weed seeds in soil. *Weed Res.* 7:290–301.

ROBERTS, H. and P. FEAST. 1970. Seasonal distribution of emergence in some annual weeds. *Exp. Hortic.* 21:36–41.

———. 1972. Fate of seeds of some annual weeds in different depths of cultivated undisturbed soil. *Weed Res.* 12:316–324.

———. 1973. Emergence and longevity of seeds of annual weeds in cultivated and undisturbed soil. *J. Appl. Ecol.* 10:133–143.

———. 1974. Observations on the time of flowering in mayweeds. *J. Appl. Ecol.* 11:223–229.

ROBERTS, H. and J. NEILSON. 1980. Seed survival and periodicity of seedling emergence in some *Atriplex*, *Chenopodium*, *Polygonum* and *Rumex*. *Ann. Appl. Biol.* 94:111–120.

———. 1981a. Changes in the soil seed bank of four long-term crop-herbicides experiments. *J. Appl. Ecol.* 18:661–668.

———. 1981b. Seed survival and periodicity of seedling emergence in twelve weedy species of **Compositae**. *Ann. Appl. Biology* 97:325–334.

———. 1982. Seed banks of soils under vegetable cropping in England. *Weed Res.* 22:13–16.

ROBERTS, H. and M. POTTER. 1980. Emergence patterns of weed seedlings in relation to cultivation and rainfall. *Weed Res.* 20:377–386.

ROBERTS, H. and M. RICKETTS. 1979. Quantitative relationship between the weed flora after cultivation and the seed population in the soil. *Weed Res.* 19:269–275.

ROBERTS, H. and F. STOKES. 1965. Studies on the weeds of vegetable crops: V. Final observation on an experiment with different primary tillages. *J. Appl. Ecol.* 2:307–315.

———. 1966. Studies on the weeds of vegetable crops: VI. Seed populations of soil under commercial cropping. *J. Appl. Ecol.* 3:181–190.

ROBERTS, J. 1986. Stomatal conductance and transpiration from a bracken understorey in a pine plantation. pp. 249–258. In: *Bracken, ecology, land use and control tech-*

nology. Ed. by R. Smith and J. Taylor. Parthenon Publ. Co., Carnforth, Eng.

ROBERTSON, W. 1906. Cirrhosis of the liver in stock in Cape Colony, produced by two species of *Senecio, S. burchellii* and *S. latifolius. J. Comparative Pathol. and Therapeutics* 19:97–111.

ROBERTUS-KOSTER, E. 1969. Differentiatie van *Scirpus maritimus* in Nederland. *Gorteria* 4(11):193–200.

ROBSON, T. 1976. A review of the distribution of aquatic weeds in the tropics and sub-tropics. *Proc. Regional Seminar, Noxious Aquatic Vegetation,* New Delhi, 1973.

ROCHECOUSTE, E. 1959. *Weeds of Mauritius: Cassia occidentalis* L. Mauritius Sugar Industry Res. Inst. Leaflet No. 2. Reduit, Mauritius.

————. 1967. *Weed control in sugar cane.* Mauritius Sugar Industry Res. Inst. Reduit, Mauritius.

RODRIGUEZ, D., T. LEE and C. CHICHESTER. 1975. Comparative study of the carotenoid composition of the seeds of ripening *Momordica charantia* and tomatoes. *Plant Physiol.* 56:526–529.

RODRIGUEZ, P., O. PAZ and G. VERDICIA. 1983. A study of possible agents in the dissemination of weed seeds. *Centro Agricola* (Cuba) 10:55–65.

RODRIGUEZ, S. and S. CEPERO. 1984. Cantidad de semillas producidas por algunas especies de malas hierbas. *Centro Agricola* 11:45–50.

ROEBUCK, J. 1972. Long term control of *Alopecurus myosuroides* in winter wheat. pp. 726–730. *Proc. 11th Brit. Weed Control Conf.*

ROGACHEV, I. 1969. Our experience in the control of dodder. *Zaschita Rastenii* 14(10):50–51.

ROGER, P. and P. REYNAUD. 1979. First results on the ecology of *Azolla africana* in Senegal. *Oecologia Plantarum* 14:75–84.

ROGERS, B. and F. STEARNS. 1958. Preliminary studies on the germination of weed seeds. pp. 7–10. *Proc. 12th Northeastern Weed Sci. Soc.*

ROGERS, K. and C. BREEN. 1980. Growth and reproduction of *Potamogeton crispus* in a South African lake. *J. Ecol.* 68:561–571.

ROGERS, R., J. GIBSON and K. REICHMANN. 1979. The toxicity of *Cassia occidentalis* for cattle. *Aus. Vet. J.* 55:408–412.

ROGERS, S. 1969. Studies on British poppies. I. Some observations on the reproductive biology of the British species of *Papaver. Watsonia* 7:55–63.

————. 1971. Studies on British poppies. IV. Some aspects of variability in the British species *Papaver* and their relation to breeding mechanisms and ecology. *Watsonia* 8:263–276.

ROGERSON, A. and S. BINGHAM. 1964. A growth study and seasonal characteristics of *Artemisia vulgaris.* pp. 360–363. *Proc. 17th South. Weed Sci. Soc.*

ROJAS, L. and M. DE CASTRO. 1985. Drought and foliar histology. I. Species *Saccharum* **Poaceae.** *Cienc. Agric.* 23:42–46.

ROLA, H. and J. ROLA. 1984. Competition of **Anthemideae** in winter wheat, Poland. pp. 331–337. *Proc. 7th Intern. Symp. Weed Ecol., Biol., Systematics.*

ROLA, J. 1979. The combined effect of crop plants and herbicides on the weed population. pp. 281–285. *Proc. European Weed Res. Soc. Symp.*; Mainz, Germany.

ROLSTON, M. and F. SINEIRO-GARCIA. 1974. Response of gorse seedlings to defoliation and shading. pp. 2–5. *Proc. 27th New Zealand Weed and Pest Control Conf.*

ROMBACH, J. 1976. Effects of light and phytochrome in heterotrophic growth of *Lemna minor* L. *Meded. Landbouwhogeschool Wageningen* 76:1–114.

ROMEIKE, A. 1965. Hygrine, the chief alkaloid in *Nicandra physalodes* roots. *Naturwissenschaften* 52(22):619.

————. 1966. Occurrence of tropinone in *Nicandra physalodes* roots. *Naturwissenschaften* 53(3):82.

ROODEN, J. VAN, M. AKKERMANS and R. VAN DER VEEN. 1970. A study on photoblastism in seeds of some tropical weeds. *Acta Bot. Neerl.* 19:257–264.

ROOT, R. and S. CHAPLIN. 1976. The life-styles of tropical milkweed bugs *Oncopeltus* (**Hemiptera: Lygaeidae**) utilizing the same host. *Ecol.* 57:132–140.

RORSLETT, B. and D. BERGE. 1986. *Elodea canadensis* in Norway in the 1980s. *Blyttia* 44:119–125.

ROSCOE, M. 1927. Cytological studies in the genus *Typha. Bot. Gaz.* 84:392–408.

ROSENBERGER, G. and W. HEESCHEN. 1960. Adlerfarn (*Pteris aquilina*) die Ursache des sog. Stallrotes der Rinder (Haematuria vesicalis bovis chronica). *Deutsche Tierarztliche Wochenschrift* 67:201.

ROSENTHAL, R., R. SCHIRMAN and W. ROBOCKER. 1968. Root development of rush skeleton weed. *Weed Sci.* 16:213–217.

ROSNITSCHEK-SCHIMMEL, I. 1983. Biomass and nitrogen partitioning in a perennial and an annual nitrophilic species of *Urtica. Zeitschrift Pflanzenphysiologie* 109:215–225.

ROST, T. 1975. The morphology of germination in *Setaria lutescens*: Effects of covering structures and chemical inhibitors on dormant and non-dormant florets. *Annals of Bot.* 39:21–30.

ROTHAMSTED EXPERIMENTAL STATION. 1963. *Alopecurus myosuroides. Rep. Rothamsted Exp. Sta. 1962.* p. 94.

ROTHMALER, W. 1941. Revision der Genisteen: I. Monographien der Gattungen um *Ulex. Botanische Jahrbuecher Fur Systematik Pflanzengeschichte und Pflanzengeographie* 72:69–116.

ROTHROCK, P. and R. WAGNER. 1975. *Eleocharis acicularis*: The autecology of an acid tolerant sedge. *Castanea* 40(4):279–289.

ROW, L., C. SRINIVASULU, M. SMITH and G. RAO. 1966. Crystalline constituents of **Euphorbiaceae**: V. New lignans from *Phyllanthus niruri* L. The constitution of phyllanthin. *Tetrahedron* 22:2899–2908.

ROW, L., N. SARMA, T. MATUURA and R. NAKASHIMA. 1978. Physalins E and H, new physalins from *Physalis angulata* and *P. lancifolia*. *Phytochemistry* 17:1641–1645.

ROY, A. 1973. Natural occurrence of *Corticium sasakii* on some weeds. *Current Sci.* 42:842–843.

ROY, S. 1921. A preliminary classification of the wild rices of the Central Provinces and Berar. *Agric. J. Ind.* 16:365–380.

ROZEMA, J., F. BIJL, T. DUECK and H. WESSELMAN. 1982. Salt spray stimulated growth in strand line species. *Physiol. Plantarum* 56:204–210.

RUBIN, B. and A. BENJAMIN. 1983. Solar heating of soil: Effect on weed control and on soil-incorporated herbicides. *Weed Sci.* 31:819–825.

———. 1984. Solar heating of the soil: Involvement of environmental factors in the weed control process. *Weed Sci.* 32:138–142.

RUDESCU, L., C. NICULESCU and I. CHIRV. 1965. *Monografia stufului den Delta Dunarii*. Editura Acad. Republicii Romania, Bucharest. 205pp.

RUSCH, R. 1965a. Zur morphologischen differenzierung von kamille-arten gattungen *Anthemis* and *Matricaria* im rosettenstadium. *Weed Res.* 5:68–74.

———. 1965b. To identify our chamomile *Anthemis* and *Matricaria* in the early stages. *Zeitschrift fur Pflanzenkrankheiten und Pflanzenschutz* 3:103–106.

RUSOFF, L., S. ZERINGUE, A. ACHACOSO, and D. CULLEY. 1978. Feeding value of duckweed, an aquatic plant, family **Lemnaceae**, for ruminants. *J. Dairy Sci.*, Supplement 61. p. 186.

RUSSWURM, W. and B. MARTIN. 1977a. Studies on the occurrence of dandelion *Taraxacum officinale* Web. in lucerne. *Archiv fur Acker- und Pflanzenbau und Bodenkunde* 21:513–519.

———. 1977b. Studies on the germination behavior of dandelion *Taraxacum officinale* Web. under specific conditions. *Nachrichtenblatt fur den Deutschen Pflanzenschutzdienst in der DDR* 31:223–227.

RUTHERFORD, P. and P. THODAY. 1976. Clonal production of tap-rooted plants of chicory. *J. Hortic. Sci.* 51:167–168.

RUTHERFORD, P. and E. WESTON. 1968. Carbohydrate changes during cold storage of some inulin-containing roots and tubers. *Phytochemistry* 7:175–180.

RYAN, F. 1988. Partial characterization of a major family of proteins in the turions of *Hydrilla verticillata*. *Physiologia Plantarum* 73:486–493.

———. 1989. Isozymic variability in monoecious *Hydrilla* in the United States. *J. Aquat. Plant Mgmt.* 27:10–15.

RYAN, G. 1970. Resistance of common groundsel to simazine and atrazine. *Weed Sci.* 18:614–616.

RYAN, J., D. RIEMER and S. TOTH. 1972. Effects of fertilization on aquatic plants, water and bottom sediments. *Weed Sci.* 20:482–486.

RYANG, H., J. CHUN and Y. MOON. 1978. Control of the perennial weed *Scirpus maritimus* in reclaimed paddy fields of west seashore. II. Physiological and ecological characteristics of *S. maritimus*. *J. Korean Soc. Crop Sci.* 23(1):64–73.

RYBERG, M. 1960. A morphological study of the **Fumariaceae** and the taxonomic significance of the characters examined. *Acta Horti Bergiani* 19:121–248.

RYMER, L. 1976. The history and ethnobotany of bracken. *Bot. J. Linn. Soc.* 73:151–176.

———. 1979. Ethnobotany and native distribution of gorse in Britain. *Environ. Conserv.* 6:211–213.

SABET, K., F. ISHAG and O. KHALIL. 1969. Studies on the bacterial disease of Sudan crops. VII. New records. *Ann. Appl. Biol.* 63:357–369.

SABNIS, T. 1921. The physiological anatomy of the plants of the Indian desert. *J. Ind. Bot. Soc.* 2:157–173, 217–235.

SACHAN, S. and M. SHARMA. 1980. Two new hosts of *Oidiopsis taurica*, powdery mildew, on *Asclepias curassavica* and *Reinwardtia trigyna*. *Ind. J. Mycol. Plant Pathol.* 9:92.

SADYKOV, B. and M. UMAROV. 1980. Detection of nitrogen-fixing activity in the plant phyllosphere. *Microbiol.* 49:125–128.

SAEED, M. and M. MALIK. 1961. Amino acid composition of the proteins of *Asphodelus tenuifolius*. *Pak. J. Scientific Res.* 13:144–148.

SAEED, S., M. SADIQ and A. AHMAD. 1977. *Biology of fern weeds*. Dept. Bot., Agric. Univ. Faisalabad, Pakistan. PL-480 Rep. Project No. A17–CR–2.

SAEGER, A. 1929. Flowering of **Lemnaceae**. *Bull. Torrey Botan. Club* 56:351–358.

SAGAR, G. and A. MORTIMER. 1976. An approach to the study of the population dynamics of plants with special reference to weeds. pp. 1–47. In *Applied biology*, Vol. 1. Ed. by T. Coaker. Academic Press, NY, USA.

SAGE, R. and R. PEARCY. 1987. Nitrogen use efficiency of C_3 and C_4 plants. I. Leaf nitrogen, growth and biomass partitioning in *Chenopodium album* and *Amaranthus retroflexus*. II. Leaf nitrogen effects on gas exchange characteristics of above species. *Plant Physiol.* 84:954–963.

SAGE, R., R. PEARCY, and J. SEEMAN. 1987. The nitrogen use efficiency of C_3 and C_4 plants. III. Leaf nitrogen effects on the activity of carboxylating enzymes of *Chenopodium album* and *Amaranthus retroflexus*. *Plant Physiol.* 85:355–359.

SAGHIR, A., C. FOY, K. HAMEED, C. DRAKE and S. TOLIN. 1973. Studies on biology and control of *Orobanche*. pp.

106–116. *Proc. 1st Symp. Parasitic Weeds, European Weed Res. Council*, Malta.

SAHAI, A. and K. SHIVANNA. 1982. Seed germination and seedling morphogenesis in parasitic angiosperms of the Families **Scrophulariaceae** and **Orobanchaceae**. *Seed Sci. Tech.* 10:565–583.

SAHAI, R. and N. AGRAWAL. 1975. Effect of growth substances on the sprouting behavior of subterranean turions of *Hydrilla verticillata. Geobios* (Jodhpur) 2:22–23.

SAHAI, R. and A. SINHA. 1969. The sprouting behavior of the dormant apices of *Potamogeton crispus. Experientia* 25:653.

———. 1976. Productivity of submerged macrophytes in polluted and non-polluted regions of the eutrophic lake, Ramgarh. *Proc. Aquatic Weeds Southeast Asia* (1973), New Delhi. pp. 131–140.

SAHAY, S. 1974. Pollen morphology of *Heliotropium. J. Palynol.* 9:167–176.

SAINI, H., P. BASSI, J. GOUDEY and M. SPENCER. 1987. Breakage of seed dormancy of field pennycress *Thlaspi arvense* by growth regulators, nitrate, and environmental factors. *Weed Sci.* 35:802–806.

SAITOH, M., K. NARITA, and S. ISIKAWA. 1970. Photosynthetic nature of some aquatic plants in relation to temperature. *Bot. Mag.* (Tokyo) 83:10–12.

SALAGEANU, N. and G. FABIAN-GALAN. 1968. Studies on the nutrition of *Cuscuta* species. *Revue Roumaine Biologie Serie Botanique* 13:321–324.

SALE, P. and R. WETZEL. 1983. Growth and metabolism of *Typha* species in relation to cutting treatments. *Aquatic Bot.* 15:321–334.

SALISBURY, E. 1929. The biological equipment of species in relation to competition. *J. Ecol.* 17:197–222.

———. 1942. *The reproductive capacity of plants.* G. Bell and Sons Ltd., London. 227pp.

———. 1962. The biology of garden weeds. *J. Royal Hort. Soc.* 87:458–470.

———. 1964. *Weeds and aliens.* 2nd Ed. Collins, London. 384pp.

SALLE, G. 1987. Origin of conducting tissues in flowering parasitic plants. *Bulletin de la Societe Botanique de France* 134:81–95.

SALVUCCI, M. 1979. Enzymes associated with C_4 acid metabolism in submersed aquatic macrophyte species. *Plant Physiol.* Suppl. 63:2.

SALVUCCI, M. and G. BOWES. 1981. Induction of reduced photorespiratory activity in submersed and amphibious aquatic macrophytes. *Plant Physiol.* 67:335–340.

———. 1983. Two photosynthetic mechanisms mediating the low photorespiratory state in submersed aquatic angiosperms *Myriophyllum spicatum, Hydrilla verticillata. Plant Physiol.* 73:488–496.

SALZMANN, R. 1954. Untersuchungen uber die Lebensdauer von Unkrautsamen im Boden. *Mitteilungen der Schweizerischen Landwirtschaftliche* 10(2):170–176.

SAMILOVA, R. and T. LAGODICH. 1977. The glycoside olitoriside from *C. olitorius* (Literature review). *Vrachebnoe Delo* 1:27–31.

SAMPATH, S. 1973. Origins of cultivated rice. *Ind. J. Genetics Plant Breeding* 33:157–161.

SAMPATH, S. and R. MISHRA. 1971. Occurrence of symbiosis in species of *Amaranthus. Current Sci.* 40:111–112.

SAMSON, J. 1972. Weed control in wetlands: *Ipomoea. Surinaamse Landbouw* 20:15–21.

SANCHEZ, P. and H. URANGA. 1990. Weeds of tobacco nurseries with sandy soil. *Proc. of ALAM (Asociacion Latino Americana de Malezas) Conference,* Cuba. Abstract B-19. p. 82.

SANCHEZ, R. 1967. Some observations about the effect of light on the leaf shape in *Taraxacum officinale* L. *Meded. Landbouwhogeschool Wageningen* 67:1–11.

———. 1971. Phytochrome involvement in the control of leaf shape of *Taraxacum officinale* L. *Experientia* 27:1234–1237.

SANDERS, M. 1948. Embryo development in four species of *Datura* following self and hybrid pollination. *Am. J. Bot.* 35:525–532.

SANKARAN, T., T. NAG RAJ and K. PONNAPPA. 1974. *Evaluation of natural enemies associated with witchweed, nutsedge and several other aquatic weeds occurring in India.* Commonwealth Inst. Bio. Control, Tech. Rep., 1968–1974, Ind. Sta., Bangalore Ind. 65pp.

SANT, H., R. SINGH and D. PANDEY. 1979. Productivity of *Asphodelus tenuifolius,* common weed of cultivated fields in India. pp. 445–446. *Proc. 7th Asian-Pacific Weed Sci. Soc. Conf.* (Australia).

SANTELMANN, P. and J. MEADE. 1961. Variation in morphological characteristics and dalapon susceptibility within the species *Setaria lutescens* and *S. faberii. Weeds* 9:406–410.

SANTELMANN, P., J. MEADE and R. PETERS. 1963. Growth and development of yellow foxtail and giant foxtail. *Weed Sci.* 11:139–142.

SANTOS, F. and STUBBLEBINE. 1987. Aspects of the determination of the number of flowers and sex allocation in *Acanthospermum hispidum* DC. *Rev. Brasilera Bot.* 10:99–104.

SAPEK, A., B. SAPEK and J. LAMBERT. 1980. Nickel content in the grassland vegetation. pp. 215–220. *Proc. 3rd Trace Element Symp. on Nickel.*

SARASWAT, V. 1980. Ecology of weeds in jute fields in India. *Trop. Pest Mgt.* 26:45–50.

SARMA, M. 1969. Jute. Review article. *Field Crops Abstr.* 22:323–336.

SARPE, N. and C. TORGE. 1980. The effect of a weed association of *Sinapis, Setaria, Erigeron, Amaranthus, Cirsium,* and *Convolvulus* on root production of sugar beets. pp. 105–112. In: *Neue Ergebnisse aus der Herbologishen Forschung von Okologischen und Technologischen Aspekte der Herbizidanwendung.* Vortrage eines Symp., Inst. fur Pflanzenschutz Forschung Kleinmachnow, Leipzig, Tagungsbericht No. 182.

SARUKHAN, J. 1974. Studies on plant demography: *Ranunculus repens* L., *R. bulbosus* L. and *R. acris* L. II. Reproductive strategies and population dynamics. *J. Ecol.* 62:151–177.

———. 1976. On relative pressures and energy allocation in populations of *Ranunculus repens, R. bulbosus* and *R. acris. Ann. Missouri Bot. Garden* 63:290–308.

SARUKHAN, J. and J. HARPER. 1973. Studies on plant demography: *Ranunculus repens* L., *R. bulbosus* L., and *R. acris* L. I. Population flux and survivorship. *J. Ecol.* 61:675–716.

SASAKAWA, H., B. TRUNG and S. YOSHIDA. 1986. Stem nodulation on *Aeschynomene indica* plants by isolated rhizobia. *Soil Sci. Plant Nutri.* 32:145–150.

SASTROUTOMO, S. 1980a. Dormancy and germination in axillary turions of *Hydrilla verticillata. Bot. Mag.* (Japan) 93:265–273.

———. 1980b. Environmental control of turion formation in curly pondweed (*Potamogeton crispus*). *Physiologia Plantarum* 49:261–264.

———. 1981. Turion formation, dormancy, and germination of curly pondweed, *Potamogeton crispus. Aquatic Bot.* 10:161–173.

SASTROUTOMO, S. and A. YUSRON. 1987. Buried weed seed population in arable soils. pp. 45–55. *Proc. 11th Asian-Pacific Weed Sci. Soc. Conf.*

SASTRY, K. 1957. *Common weeds of cultivated and grasslands of Mysore.* India Gov. Press, Singapore.

SASTRY, M. and R. SEETHARAMAN. 1978. Inheritance of grain shattering and lay habit and their interrelationship in rice. *Ind. J. Genetics Plant Breeding* 38:318–321.

SATENDRA, K. 1980. Seed germination in *Trianthema portulacastrum* L.: Effect of pretreatments on germination. *Ind. J. Ecol.* 7:229–236.

SAUER, J. 1950. Grain *Amaranthus*: Survey of their history and classification. *Ann. Missouri Bot. Garden.* 37:561–632.

———. 1967. The grain *Amaranths* and their relatives: A revised taxonomic and geographic survey. *Ann. Missouri Bot. Garden* 54:103–137.

SAUER, J. and G. STRUIK. 1964. A possible ecological relation between soil disturbance, light-flash, and seed germination. *Ecol.* 45:884–886.

SAUERBORN, J. 1990. Zur Wirt-Parasit Interaktion hoherer Pflanzen in Ackerkulteren. *PLITS (Institut fur Pflanzenproduktion in den Tropen und Subtropen)* 8:281–293.

———. 1991. The economic importance of the phytoparasites

Orobanche and *Striga. Proc. 5th Symp. on Parasitic Weeds,* Nairobi, Kenya. pp. 137–143.

SAUERBORN, J., and M. SAXENA. 1987. Effect of soil solarization on *Orobanche* spp. infestation and other pests in faba bean and lentil. pp. 733–744. *Proc. 4th Intern. Symp. Parasitic Flowering Plants.* Ed. by H. Weber and W. Forstreuter. Marburg, Germany.

SAUERBORN, J., W. KOCH and J. WRAGE. 1988. On the influence of light, temperature, depth of burial and water stress on the germination of selected weed species. *Zeitschrift fur Pflanzenkrankheiten und Pflanzenschutz* 11:47–53.

SAUVAGEAU, C. 1889. Sur la racine du *Najas. J. Bot.* (Paris) 3:3–11.

———. 1894. Notes biologiques sur les *Potamogetons. J. Bot.* (Paris) 8:1–9, 21–43, 45–58, 98–106, 112–123, 140–148, 165–172.

SAWADA, S., M. TAKAHASHI and Y. KASAISHI. 1982. Population dynamics and production processes of indigenous and naturalized dandelions subjected to artificial disturbance by mowings. *Jap. J. Ecol.* 32:143–150.

SAXENA, B. and J. SRIVASTAVA. 1973. *Tagetes minuta* L. oil—a new source of juvenile hormone mimicking substance. *Ind. J. Exp. Biol.* 11:56–58.

SAXENA, T. 1973. Gametophyte and seed development in *Nicandra physalodes. Proc. Ind. Sci. Congr. Assoc.* 60:333–334.

SCANNELL, M. and D. WEBB. 1976. The identity of Renvyle *Hydrilla. Irish Naturalists J.* 18:327–331.

SCHAAD, N. and J. DIANESE. 1981. Cruciferous weeds as sources of inoculum of *Xanthomonas campestris* in black rot of crucifers. *Phytopathology* 71:1215–1220.

SCHAFER, H. 1969. Structure of the gynoecium of *Nicandra physalodes. Kulturpflanze* 17:187–189.

SCHARDT, J. 1987. *1987 Florida aquatic flora survey report.* Florida Dept. of Natural Resources, Tallahassee, Florida. p. 49.

SCHENK, H. 1885. Die biolgie der wassergewachse. *Verhandlungen Naturhistorische Vereines Preussischen Rheinlande* 42:217–380.

SCHIMMING, W. and C. MESSERSMITH. 1988. Freezing resistance of overwintering buds of four perennial weeds. *Weed Sci.* 36:568–573.

SCHIMPF, D. 1977. Seed weight of *Amaranthus retroflexus* in relation to moisture and length of growing season. *Ecol.* 58:450–453.

SCHIRMAN, R. and W. ROBOCKER. 1967. Rush skeleton weed—threat to dryland agriculture. *Weed Sci.* 15:310–312.

SCHMIDT, D. 1971. Comparative yield and composition of eight tropical leafy vegetables grown at two soil fertility levels. *Agron. J.* 63:546–550.

SCHMIDT, D., D. THONG and T. TAM. 1964. Annual weed as a forage crop. *World Crops* 16:46–49.

SCHMIDT, K. 1978. A Contribution to the understanding of the morphology and anatomy of the **Marsileaceae**. *Beitraege zur Biologie der Pflanzen* 54:41–92.

SCHMIDT, R. and F. EVANS. 1980. Skin irritants of the sun spurge, *Euphorbia helioscopia*. *Contact Dermatitis* 6:204–210.

SCHNEIDER, B. 1947. *Feeds of the world*. Jarrett Printing Co., Charlestown, WV USA.

SCHOKKER, A. 1988. Survival of weed seeds and tubers in cattle manure and maize silage. *Verslagan, Centrum voor Agrobiologisch Onderzoek* No. 90. 34pp.

SCHONBECK, M. and G. EGLEY. 1979. Ethylene stimulation of pigweed seed germination. *Plant Physiol.* Suppl. 69, 63:5.

SCHONER, C., R. NORRIS and W. CHILCOTE. 1978. Yellow foxtail *Setaria lutescens* biotype studies: Growth and morphological characteristics. *Weed Sci.* 26:632–636.

SCHREIBER, M. 1977. Longevity of foxtail taxa in undisturbed sites. *Weed Sci.* 25:66–72.

SCHREIBER, M. and L. OLIVER. 1969. Micro-environment of weed competition in alfalfa establishment. *Abstr. 9th Weed Sci. Soc. Am. Conf.* 9: No. 156.

SCHREIBER, M. and P. ORWICK. 1978. Influence of nitrogen fertility on growth of foxtail *Setaria* taxa. *Weed Sci.* 26:547–550.

SCHROEDER, D. 1973. The phytophagous insects attacking *Sonchus* spp. (**Compositae**) in Europe. pp. 92–96. *Proc. 3rd Intern. Symp. Bio. Control Weed.*

SCHROEDER, M., J. DELI, E. SCHALL and G. WARREN. 1974. Seed composition of 66 weed and crop species. *Weed Sci.* 22:345–348.

SCHUESSLER, R. 1960. The captivating cattail. *Crops and Soils* 13(20):13.

SCHULTES, R. 1970. The botanical and chemical distribution of hallucinogens. *Ann. Rev. Plant Physiol.* 21:571–598.

SCHULTZ, G., Y. HWANG and M. MULLA. 1983. Toxicity and attractancy of *Myriophyllum* against mosquitoes. *Proc. 38th Am. Mosquito Control Assoc. Meeting* 38:68–69.

SCHUMAN, G. and G. HOWARD. 1978. *Artemisia vulgaris*: an ornamental plant for disturbed land reclamation. *J. Range Mgt.* 31:392–396.

SCHUTT, P., H. SCHUCK, A. SYDOW and H. HATZEL-MANN. 1975. Allelopathic effect of forest weeds: I. Influence of weed extracts on the development of root hairs of *Picea abies* seedlings. *Forstwissenschaftliches, Centralblatt* 94:43–53.

SCHWEIZER, E. and R. ZIMDAHL. 1984. Weed seed decline in irrigated soil after six years of corn and herbicides. *Weed Sci.* 32:76–93.

SCHWERZEL, P. 1967. Seed production of some common Rhodesian weeds. *PANS (Pest Articles and News Summaries)* 13(3):215–217.

———. 1970a. Weed phenology and life-span observations. *PANS (Pest Articles and News Summaries)* 16:511–515.

———. 1970b. Weed seed production study. *PANS (Pest Articles and News Summaries)* 16:357.

———. 1983. Effect of clipping on the survival of some common weeds in Zimbabwe. *Zimbabwe Agric. J.* 80(1):37–39.

SCHWERZEL, P. and P. THOMAS. 1979. Effects of cultivation frequency on the survival of seeds of six weeds commonly found in Rhodesia. *Rhodesia Zimbabwe Agric. J.* 76(5):195–199.

SCHWERZEL, P., P. THOMAS and H. OOSTERMAN. 1980/81. Weed biology. *Ann. Rep. Weed Res. Team 1979–1980, Dept. of Res. and Special Services*, Henderson Res. Sta., Zimbabwe.

SCOLYMOSI, P. 1988. Occurrence and conditions of development of *Conyza canadensis* populations co-resistant to atrazine and paraquat along the Szentendre (Hungary) local railway line. *Novenyvedelem* 24:120–122.

SCOTT, K. and P. PUTWAIN. 1981. Maternal inheritance of simazine resistance in a population of *Senecio vulgaris*. *Weed Res.* 21:137–140.

SCULTHORPE, C. 1967. *The biology of aquatic vascular plants*. Edward Arnold Ltd., London, England. 610pp.

SCURFIELD, G. 1962. *Cardaria draba*. *J. Ecol.* 50(2):489–499.

SEAMAN, J. 1987. Pyrrolizidine alkaloid poisoning of sheep in New South Wales. *Aus. Vet. J.* 64:164–167.

SEEHAUS, C. 1860. *Hydrilla verticillata* (L.f. L.) Casp. var. *pomeranica* (Rchb) Casp. *Verhandlugen des botanisches verins fur Deutsche Provinz Brandenburg*, No. 2:95–102. Seen in: Arber, A. 1920.

SEGALL, H., D. WILSON, J. DALLAS and W. HADDON. 1985. Trans-4–hydroxy-2–hexenal: A metabolite from the macrocyclic pyrrolizidine alkaloid, senecionine. *Sci.* 229:472–475.

SEIBER, J., C. NELSON and S. LEE. 1982. Cardenolides in the latex and leaves of seven *Asclepias* species and *Calotropis procera*. *Phytochemistry* 21:2343–2348.

SELLECK, G. 1961. An ecological study of *Cardaria* spp. in Saskatchewan. *Proc. 11th Western Can. Weed Control Conf.* 11:61–63.

———. 1965. An Ecological study of lens- and globe-podded hoary cresses in Saskatchewan. *Weeds* 12:19–22.

SEMENIKHINA, K. and K. BALASHEV. 1978. Flowering of *Elodea canadensis* in water bodies of the Ukraine. *Ukrainskyi Botanichnyi Zhurnal* 35:524–525.

SEN, A. and N. PAUL. 1959. Changes in nitrogen and organic matter contents of soil associated with growth of some summer wild legumes. *Ind. J. Agric. Sci.* 29:140–146.

SEN, D. 1981. Ecological approaches to Indian weeds. *Geobios Intern.*, Jodhpur, India.

SEN, D. and L. HARSHA. 1974. Ecophysiological studies on stomatal regulation in *Allium cepa* and *Asphodelus tenuifolius*. *Flora* (Jena) 163:14–25.

SEN, U. 1983. Stomatal structure and stomatogenesis in *Azolla pinnata*. *Ann. Bot.* 52:201–204.

SEN GUPTA, J. and N. SEN. 1944. On photoperiod effect of jute. *Ind. J. Agric. Sci.* 14:196–202.

———. 1952. Further investigation on photoperiod effect on jute. *Ind. J. Agric. Sci.* 22:1–32.

SERBANESCU-JITARIU, G. 1973. Investigations on the gynoecium, the fruit, and the germination of the seeds of *Sagittaria sagittifolia*. *Analele Univ. Bucuresti Biol. Vegetala* 22:17–24.

———. 1986. Observations on the gynoecium of *Najas marina*. *Revue Roumaine de Biologie, Serie Biologie Vegetale* 31:23–26.

SETTY, P. and P. KRISHNAN. 1970. Influence of shading on the gross composition of *Cuscuta* species on *Medicago sativa*. *Physiol. Plantarum* 23:1017–1023.

SEXSMITH, J. 1964. Morphological and herbicide susceptibility differences among strains of hoary cress. *Weeds* 12:19–22.

SGAMBATTI-ARAUJO, L. 1978. *Germination and dormancy studies in* Poa annua *L.* Ph.D. Diss., Univ. Calif., Riverside, CA, USA.

SHAH, C. 1964. Embryo development in *Eleocharis palustris*. *Nature Canada* 35(2):41–49.

SHAH, J. and Y. DAVE. 1970. Tendrils of *Passiflora foetida*: histogenesis and morphology. *Am. J. Bot.* 57:786–793.

SHALOM, N., R. JACOBSOHN and Y. COHEN. 1988. Resistance to *Orobanche* spp. in sunflower *Helianthus annuus*. *Phytoparasitica* 16:378–379.

SHAMSHER, V. 1979. Mosaic virus disease of *Tridax procumbens* L. *Ghana J. Sci.* 17:89–90.

SHANTZ, H., R. PIEMEISEL and L. PIEMEISEL. 1927. The water requirement of plants at Akron, Colorado. *J. Agric. Res.* 34:1093–1190.

SHARAF, A. and S. NEGM. 1969. Pharmacological study of *Corchorus olitorius* seeds with special reference to its cardio-vascular activity. *Qualitas Plantarum et Materiae Vegetabiles* 17:305–312.

SHARITZ, R., S. WINERITER, M. SMITH and E. LIU. 1980. Comparison of isozymes among *Typha* species in the eastern United States. *Am. J. Bot.* 67:1297–1303.

SHARMA, A. and N. BHATTACHARYYA. 1957. Cytology of *Asphodelus tenuifolius*. *Caryologia* 10:330–339.

SHARMA, B. 1981. A phytosociological study of a weed community in fallow land in the semi-arid zone of India. *Weed Sci.* 29:287–291.

SHARMA, B. and P. SINGH. 1974. Pharmacognostic study of seeds of *Silybum marianum*. *Plant Sci.* (Lucknow) 6:34–37.

SHARMA, B., K. VIVEKANANTHAN and N. RATHAKR-
ISHNAN. 1974. *Cassia intermedia* **Caesalpiniaceae**—a new species from south India. *Ind. Acad. Sci. Proc., Section B* 80:301–306.

SHARMA, D. and A. SINGH. 1980. The evaluation of leaf protein quality in three aquatic plants. *Aquat. Bot.* 8:279–284.

SHARMA, K., R. UPADHYAYA and J. SAXENA. 1973. Studies on the utility of a weed, taratej *Coronopus didymus* in dietary of sheep. *Ind. Vet. J.* 50(3):272–274.

SHARMA, M. 1972. Studies in the flower of *Datura stramonium* in relation to bee-botany. *J. Palynol.* 8:17–21.

———. 1977. The role of the common sparrow in the control of weeds of the major crops in the Meerut district. *Ind. J. Agric. Sci.* 47:224.

———. 1978. Aquatic and marshy angiosperms of Punjab. *Bull. Botan. Soc. Bengal* 31:52–60.

SHARMA, S., Y. SHUKLA and J. TANDON. 1972. Constituents of *Colocasia formicata*, *Sagittaria sagittifolia*, *Ipomoea paniculata*, *Paspalum scrobiculatum*, and *Duabanga sonneratiodes*. *Phytochemistry* 11:2621–2623.

SHARMA, V. and O. SINGH. 1972. Root galls in chicory, *Cichorium intybus*. *Current Sci.* 41:194–196.

SHARMA, V. and A. SRIVASTAVA. 1973. Anatomical studies on root gall of chicory, *Cichorium intybus*. *Acta Agronomica Acad. Scientiarum Hungaricae* 22:131–136.

SHASHKOV, V., P. KOLMAKOV, E. VOLKOV and L. TRIFONOVA. 1977. The influence of rhizomatous weeds in spring wheat crops on the utilization of nitrogen, phosphorous and potassium. *Agrokhimiya* 14:57–59.

SHASTRY, S. and S. SHARMA. 1974. Rice. In: *Evolutionary studies in world crops*. Ed. by J. Hutchinson. Cambridge Univ. Press, Cambridge, England.

SHAY, J. and C. SHAY. 1986. Prairie marshes in western Canada with specific reference to the ecology of five emergent macrophytes. *Can. J. Bot.* 64:443–454.

SHEAFFER, C. and D. WYSE. 1982. Common dandelion (*Taraxacum officinale*) control in alfalfa (*Medicago sativa*). *Weed Abstr.* 30:216–220.

SHEFFIELD, E. 1984. Apospory in the fern *Pteridium aquilinum*. I. Low-temperature scanning electron microscopy. *Cytobios* 39:171–176.

SHEFFIELD, E. and P. BELL. 1979. Ultrastructural aspects of sporogenesis in a fern, *Pteridium aquilinum*. *Ann. Bot.* 44:393–405.

———. 1981a. Experimental studies of apospory in ferns. *Ann. Bot.* 47:187–195.

———. 1981b. Cessation of vascular activity correlated with aposporous development in *Pteridium aquilinum*. *New Phytol.* 88:533–538.

SHEFFIELD, E., P. WOLF and C. HAUFLER. 1989. How big is a bracken plant? *Weed Res.* 29:455–460.

SHEIKH, K. 1969. Studies of root distribution and root anatomy of *Paspalum distichum* L. *Pak. J. Bot.* 1:107–117.

SHELDON, J. 1974. The behavior of seeds in soil. *J. Ecol.* 62:47–66.

SHELDON, J. and F. BURROWS. 1973. The dispersal effectiveness of the achene-pappus units of selected **Compositae** in steady winds with convection. *New Phytol.* 72:665–675.

SHELDON, R. and C. BOYLEN. 1977. Maximum depth inhabited by aquatic vascular plants. *Am. Midland Naturalist* 97:248–254.

SHEPHERD, J. 1969. The distribution of nematodes in Rhodesian soil. *Tobacco Forum Rhodesia* 32:10–12.

SHEPHERD, U. and D. BOWLING. 1973. Active accumulation of sodium by roots of five aquatic species. *New Phytol.* 72:1075–1080.

SHERIFF, A. and N. MAHALAKSHMI. 1969. The karyotype of *Jussiaea suffruticosa. Current Sci.* 38:23–24.

SHETLER, S. and L. SKOG. 1978. A provisional checklist of species for the flora of North America. Missouri Bot. Garden, St. Louis.

SHETTY, S. and R. MAITI. 1978. Some observations on the root system of some tropical dicotyledonous weeds. *Ind. J. Weed Sci.* 10:41–48.

SHETTY, S., M. SIVAKUMAR and S. RAM. 1982. Effect of shading on the growth of some common weeds of the semi-arid tropics. *Agron. J.* 74:1023–1029.

SHIBATA, O. 1981. Physiological and ecological studies in environmental adaptation of plants. I. Germination behavior of weed seeds collected from different altitudes. *J. Fac. Sci. Shinshu Univ.* 16:97–106.

SHIBAYAMA, H. and M. MIYAHARA. 1977. Seasonal changes of growth of aquatic weeds and their control. pp. 258–262. *Proc. 6th Asian-Pacific Weed Sci. Soc. Conf.*

SHIMOJIMA, H. 1967. Physiological and ecological studies on the control of slender spikerush *Eleocharis acicularis. Shiga Agric. Exp. Sta., Special Bull.*, Kusatsu, Japan. 52pp.

SHIMWELL, D. 1973. Ecology and phenology of annual communities on intertidal muds. *Watsonia* 9:270–271.

SHIN, Y. 1963. Influence of certain properties of paddy soils such as *pH* value, and contents of available phosphate, on the growth of *Alopecurus aequalis. Korean Min. Agric., Forestry Official Rural Development Res. Dept.* 6:23–26.

SHODIEV, P. 1980. Weed seeds in cotton field top soils. *Uzbekskii Biologicheskii Zhurnal* 0(2):35–38.

SHORTHOUSE, J. 1980. Modification of the flower heads of *Sonchus arvensis* family **Compositae** by the gall former *Tephritis dilacerata* (order **Diptera**, family **Tephritidae**). *Can. J. Bot.* 58:1534–1540.

SHRIVASTAVA, G. 1960. A contribution to the study of **Amaranthaceae**. *Achyranthes asper* var. *prophyristachya* Hook. *f. Ind. Bot. Soc. J.* 39:309–313.

SHUGG, A. and G. VIVIAN. 1973. Barley grass seed: Its effect on the value of sheep products. pp. 82–86. *Proc. 26th New Zealand Weed and Pest Control Conf.*

SHULL, G. 1914. The longevity of submerged seeds. *Plant World* 17:329–337.

SHUMOVICH, W. and F. MONTGOMERY. 1955. The perennial sowthistle in northeastern North America. *Can. J. Agric. Sci.* 35:601–605.

SHURTLEFF, J. and H. COBLE. 1985. Interference of certain broadleaf weed species in soybeans *Glycine max. Weed Sci.* 33:654–657.

SIBASAKI, T., and Y. ODA. 1979. Heterogeneity of dormancy in the turions of *Spirodela polyrhiza. Plant and Cell Physiol.* 20:563–571.

SIDHU, M., and M. BALJINDER. 1983. Reproductive biology of some important weeds of wheat in Punjab, India. *9th Proc. Asian Pacific Weed Sci. Soc.*, Manila, pp. 96–103.

SIEBER, V. and B. MURRAY. 1979. The cytology of the genus *Alopecurus Gramineae. Bot. J. Linn. Soc.* 79:343–355.

SIEBERT, S. 1987. Land use intensification in tropical uplands: Effects on vegetation, soil fertility, and erosion. *Forest Ecology and Management* 21:37–96.

SILBERSCHMIDT, K. 1955. *Asclepias curassavica*, a natural host of cucumber mosaic virus in Brazil. *Plant Dis. Rep.* 39:555–557.

SILVA, G. and H. TOKESHI. 1979. Reaction of some weeds to *Verticillium albo-atrum. Summa Phytopathologica* 5:85–89.

SILVER, W., A. JUMPAND and A. PUKATSKI. 1974. Nitrogen fixation associated with fresh water and marine angiosperms. *Abstr. Ann. Meeting Soc. Microbiologists*: 199.

SILVERTOWN, J. and B. SMITH. 1989. Germination and population structure of spear thistle (*Cirsium vulgare*) in relation to experimentally controlled sheep grazing. *Oecologia* 81:369–373.

SILVERTOWN, J. and M. TREMLETT. 1989. Interactive effects of disturbance and shade upon colonization of grassland. *Functional Ecol.* 3:229–235.

SIMMONDS, N. 1945. Biological flora of the British Isles: *Polygonum. J. Ecol.* 33:117–139.

———. 1976. *Evolution of crop plants.* Ed. by N. Simmonds. Longman, Inc., New York. 340pp.

SIMON, B. 1984. Studies in Australian grasses. *Austrobaeleya* 2:21–24.

SIMONDS, A. 1938. The anatomical development of *Lepidium draba. J. Agric. Res.* 57:911–928.

SIMPSON, C., B. DAMRON and R. HARMS. 1971. Toxic myopathy of chicks fed *Cassia occidentalis* seed. *Avian Dis.* 15:284–290.

SINGH, B. and R. RASTOGI. 1969. Chemical investigation of *Asclepias curassavica* L. *Ind. J. Chem.* 7:1105–1110.

SINGH, B. and L. SINGH. 1939. Relative absorption of nutrients by weeds of arable land. *Soil Sci.* 47:227–235.

SINGH, D. 1976. Jute, *Corchorus* spp. In: *Evolution of crop plants.* Ed. by N. Simmonds. Longman, Inc., New York. 339pp.

SINGH, D. and B. GANGWAR. 1987. Rice fields in south Andaman, India. *Intern. Rice Res. Newsl.* 12:47.

SINGH, G. and S. SAINI. 1960. Three new purple-leaved rice strains to help you wipe out wild rice from your rice fields. *Ind. Farming* 10:6–7.

SINGH, G., B. GUPTA and H. SINGH. 1982. Composition, nutritive value and nutrient utilization of *Trianthema portulacastrum*. *Asian J. Dairy Res.* 1:118–122.

SINGH, H. and M. SAROHA. 1975. Effect on viability and germination percentage of weed seeds treated with 2,4–D at different stages of seed development. *PANS (Pest Articles and News Summaries)* 21:289–294.

SINGH, J. 1968. Comparison of growth performance and germination behavior of seeds of *Cassia tora* L. and *C. obtusifolia*. *Trop. Ecol.* 9:64–71.

———. 1969. Growth performance and dry matter yield of *Cassia tora* L. as influenced by population density. *J. Indian Bot. Soc.* 48:141–148.

SINGH, J. and N. SINGH. 1971. Studies on the physiology of host parasite relationship in *Orobanche*: I. Respiratory metabolism of host parasite. *Physiol. Plantarum* 24:380–386.

SINGH, M., W. OGREN and J. WIDHOLM. 1974. Photosynthetic characteristics of several C_3 and C_4 plant species grown under different light intensities. *Crop Sci.* 14:563–566.

SINGH, O. 1979. Sulphur deficiency and alkaloid content in mustard (*Brassica campestris* L. var. *sarson*) Prain plants. *Ind. J. Plant Physiol.* 22:78–80.

SINGH, P. 1977. The use of *Azolla pinnata* as a green manure for rice. *Intern. Rice Newsl.* 2:7.

———. 1981. Potentiality of blue-green algae and *Azolla* biofertilizers in rice cultivation in India. In: *Current perspectives in nitrogen fixation.* Eds. A. Gibson and W. Newton. Elsevier, North Holland.

SINGH, P. and P. KRISHNAN. 1971a. Effect of root parasitism by *Orobanche* on the respiration and chlorophyll content of *Petunia*. *Phytochemistry* 10:315–318.

———. 1971b. Biochemical changes observed in the metabolism of *Petunia* during infection singly and in combination by *Cuscuta* and *Orobanche*. II. Nucleic acid metabolism. *Ind. J. Biochem. Biophysics* 8:187–190.

———. 1977a. Isolation of mitochondria from *Orobanche*, a "total" root angiospermic parasite. *Physiologia Plantarum* 39:179–184.

———. 1977b. Enzymatic activity in mitochondria from *Orobanche*. *Physiologia Plantarum* 40:145–152.

SINGH, P. and S. SAXENA. 1972. Effect of maturity on the oxalate and cation contents of six leafy vegetables. *Ind. J. Nutrition Diet* 9:269–276.

SINGH, R. 1956. Development of endosperm and embryo in *Phyllanthus niruri* L. *Agra Univ. J. Res.* 5:163–167.

SINGH, R. and K. PANDEY. 1984. Development and structure of seeds and fruits in **Compositae-Cynareae**. *Phytomorphology* 34:1–10.

SINGH, R., P. SARKAR and A. GHOSH. 1983. Tolerance of rice weeds for natural flood water submergence. *Intern. Rice Res. Newsl.* 8(5):19–20.

SINGH, S. 1981. Physicochemical characteristics and macrophytes of Naukuchiya Tal, a mid altitude lake of Kumaun, Himalaya, India. *Trop. Ecol.* 22:40–53.

SINGH, S. and M. PAVGI. 1975. Observations on seed germination in *Orobanche*. *Science and Culture* 41:296–298.

SINGH, S., T. RAMAPRABHU and K. JANARDHAN. 1967. Observations on the phenology and reproductive capacity of some freshwater weeds in Orissa with suggestions on their control. *Proc. National Acad. Sci. India* (B) 37:148–160.

SINGH, V. 1964. Morphological and anatomical studies in Helobiae: I. Vegetative anatomy of some members of **Potamogetonaceae**. *Proc. Ind. Acad. Sci., Series B* 60:214–231.

———. 1965a. Morphological and anatomical studies in Helobiae: II. Vascular anatomy of the flower of **Potamogetonaceae**. *Bot. Gaz.* 126:137–144.

———. 1965b. Morphological and anatomical studies in Helobiae: III. Vascular anatomy of the node and flower of **Najadaceae**. *Proc. Ind. Acad. Sci., Series B* 61:98–108.

———. 1978. Critical taxonomic notes on some of the species *Cassia* L. found in India. *J. Bombay Natural History Soc.* 75:434–443.

SINGH, V., D. JAIN and M. SHARMA. 1974. Epidermal studies in *Ipomoea* **Convolvulaceae**. *Bangladesh J. Bot.* 3:31–36.

SINGHAL, B. and D. SEN. 1981. Structural modifications in capitulum and dispersal strategies in some weeds of **Compositae**. *Abstr. Ind. Weed Sci. Soc. Conf.*

SINGY, D. 1962. Structure and development of the ovule and seed of *Passiflora foetida*. *Agra Univ. J. Res. Sci.* 11(3):99–110.

SINHA, A. and R. SAHAI. 1973. Contribution to the ecology of Indian aquatics: V. Seasonal changes in the biomass and rate of production of two perennial submerged macrophytes *Hydrilla verticillata* and *Najas graminea* in Gorakhpur, India. *Trop. Ecol.* 17:19–28.

SIRIWARDANA, T. and R. ZIMDAHL. 1983. Competition between barnyard grass (*Echinochloa crusgalli*) and redroot pigweed (*Amaranthus retroflexus*). *Abstr. 23rd Weed Sci. Soc. Am. Conf.* 23:61.

SIROHI, S. and D. SURYANARAYANA. 1970. Studies on the effect of different dates of sowing and seed rate on the growth and yield of chicory. *Punjab Agric. Univ. J. Res.* 7:42–44.

SITKIN, R. 1976. *Parasite-host interactions of field dodder* (*Cuscuta campestris*). M.Sc. Thesis, Cornell Univ., Ithaca, New York, USA. 64pp.

SKIPPER, E. 1922. The ecology of gorse *Ulex* with special reference to the growth forms on Hindhead Common. *J. Ecol.* 10:24–52.

SLACK, E. 1981. *The phenological development of redroot pigweed* (Amaranthus retroflexus). M.Sc. Thesis, Utah State Univ., Logan, UT, USA.

SMALL, E. 1977. Numerical taxonomic analysis of the *Daucus carota* complex. *Can. J. Bot.* 56:248–276.

SMALL, E. and R. DESJARDINS. 1978. Comparative gas exchange physiology in the *Daucus carota* complex. *Can. J. Bot.* 56:1739–1743.

SMALL, J. 1918. Origin and development of the **Compositae**: IX. Fruit dispersal in the **Compositae**. *New Phytologist.* 17:200–230.

SMITH, A. and A. AGIZA. 1951. The amino acids of several grassland species, cereals and bracken. *J. Sci. Food Agric.* 2:503–520.

SMITH, B. 1934. A taxonomic and morphological study of the genus *Cuscuta* (dodders) in North Carolina. *J. Elisha Mitchell Sci. Soc.* 50:283–302.

SMITH, B., P. EMBLING, M. AGNEW, D. LAUREN and P. HOLLAND. 1988. Carcinogenicity of bracken fern (*Pteridium esculentum*) in New Zealand. *New Zealand Vet. J.* 36:56–58.

SMITH, C., and J. BARKO. 1990. Ecology of Eurasian milfoil. *J. Aquat. Plant Mgmt.* 28:55–64.

SMITH, C., D. SHAW, and L. NEWSON. 1992. Arrowleaf sida (*Sida rhombifolia*) and prickly sida (*S. spinosa*): germination and emergence. *Weed Res.* 32:103–109.

SMITH, D. 1978. Effects of cardiac glycoside storage on growth rate and adult size in the butterfly *Danaus chrysippus* L. *Experientia* 34:845–846.

SMITH, G. 1938. *Cryptogamic botany.* Vol. 2. *Bryophytes and pteridophytes.* McGraw-Hill Book Co., New York. 380pp.

———. 1971. Resumé of studies and control of Eurasian watermilfoil in the Tennessee Valley (USA) from 1960 through 1969. *Hyacinth Control J.* 9:23–5.

SMITH, J. 1917. *Weeds of Alberta, Canada.* Alberta Dept. Agric., Bull. No. 2.

SMITH, L. 1977. Growth and control of *Sida rhombifolia* L. pp. 193–198. *Proc. 6th Asian-Pacific Weed Sci. Soc. Conf.*

SMITH, L. and J. KADLEC. 1985. Fire and herbivory in a Great Salt Lake marsh. *Ecol.* 66:259–265.

SMITH, L. and L. KOK. 1984. Dispersal of musk thistle *Carduus nutans* seed. *Weed Sci.* 32:120–125.

SMITH, R. 1981. Control of red rice (*Oryza sativa*) in water-seeded rice *O. sativa. Weed Sci.* 29:663–666.

———. 1983. Weeds of major importance in rice and yield losses due to weed competition. *Proc. Weed Control Rice Conf. 1981,* IRRI, Philippines.

———. 1989. Cropping and herbicide systems for red rice (*Oryza sativa*) control. *Weed Tech.* 3:414–419.

SMITH, R. and S. CROWE. 1987. Fanweed toxicosis in cattle:

Case history, analytical method, suggested treatment for fanweed detoxification. *Vet. and Human Toxicol.* 29:155–156.

SMITH R. and J. TAYLOR. 1986. *Bracken, ecology, land use and control technology.* Ed. by R. Smith and J. Taylor. Parthenon Publ. Co., Carnforth, Lancashire, UK.

SMITH, T. 1972. *Jimsonweed (*Datura stramonium*) growth, development, and control.* M.Sc. Thesis, Univ. of Delaware, USA.

SOANE, I. and A. WATKINSON. 1979. Clonal variation in populations of *Ranunculus repens. New Phytol.* 82:557–573.

SOEDARSAN, A., N. SOEDARSAN, and H. SANTIKA. 1976. Effects of some weed species on the growth of young tea. pp. 87–91. *Proc. 5th Asian-Pacific Weed Sci. Soc. Conf.* (Tokyo, 1975).

SOEDER, 1985. Fern constituents: Including occurrence, chemotaxonomy and physiological activity. *Bot. Rev.* 51:442–536.

SOERJANI, M. 1986. Environmental considerations in the novel approach of aquatic vegetation management. pp. 33–49. In: Weeds and the environment in the tropics. *Proc. 10th Asian-Pacific Weed Sci. Soc. Conf.*

SOLBRIG, O. and B. SIMPSON. 1974. Components of regulation of a population of dandelions in Michigan. *J. Ecol.* 62:473–486.

———. 1977. A garden experiment on competition between biotypes of the common dandelion (*Taraxacum officinale*). *J. Ecol.* 65:427–430.

SOLEREDER, H. 1913. Systematisch-anatomische Untersuchung des Blattes der Hydrocharitaceen. *Beihefte Botanische Zentralblatt* 30:24–104.

SONNIER, E. 1978. Cultural control of red rice. In: *Red rice: Research and control,* pp. 10–15. Texas Agric. Exp. Sta. Bull. No. 1270.

SONNIER, E. and J. BAKER. 1980. Red rice studies: Water management experiment. *Ann. Progress Rep. Louisiana Rice Exp. Sta.* 72:186–192.

SORIANO, A., B. DE EILBERG, and A. SUERO. 1963a. Effect of vertical movements of weed seeds buried in the soil on dormancy and germination. *3rd. Reunion Nacional Sobre Malezas Y Su Control,* Buenos Aires, Argentina. 1963.

SORIANO, A., B. DE EILBERG and E. SLABNIK. 1963b. Seed germination behavior of annual weeds. *Revistade Investigacion Agricola* 17:447–464.

SOTELO, A., B. LUCAS, A. UVALLE and F. GIRAL. 1980. Chemical composition and toxic factors content of 16 leguminous seeds. II. *Quart. J. Crude Drug Res.* 18:9–16.

SOUZA MACHADO, V. and J. BANDEEN. 1982. Genetic analysis of chloroplast atrazine resistance in *Brassica campestris* cytoplasmic inheritance. *Weed Sci.* 30:281–285.

SPARKE, C. 1979. Seed populations in the soil in hill land infested with bracken *Pteridium aquilinum.* pp. 265–272.

Proc. European Weed Res. Soc.: Influence of different factors in the development and control of weeds. Blackwell Publ., Oxford, England.

SPEARMAN, G. and K. JOHNSON. 1989. Redroot pigweed toxicosis in animals. *Can. Vet. J.* 30:255–256.

SPENCE, D. 1964. The macrophyte vegetation of freshwater lakes, swamps, and associated fens. In: *Vegetation of Scotland.* pp. 306–425. Ed. by J. Burett. Oliver and Boyd, Edinburgh.

———. 1967. Factors controlling the distribution of freshwater macrophytes with particular reference to Lochs of Scotland. *J. Ecol.* 55:147–170.

———. 1982. The zonation of plants in freshwater lakes. *Advances in Ecol. Res.* 12:37–124.

SPENCER, D. and L. ANDERSON. 1986. Photoperiod responses in monoecious and dioecious *Hydrilla verticillata. Weed Sci.* 34:551–557.

SPENCER, D., L. ANDERSON, M. AMES and F. RYAN. 1987. Variation in *Hydrilla verticillata* propagule weight. *J. Aquat. Plant Mgmt.* 25:11–14.

SPENCER, E. 1940. *Just weeds.* Charles Scribner's Sons, NY, USA. 317pp.

SPICER, K. and P. CATLING. 1988. The biology of Canadian weeds. 88. *Elodea canadensis. Can. J. Plant Sci.* 68:1035–1051.

SPIRA, T. and L. WAGNER. 1983. Viability of seeds up to 211 years old extracted from adobe brick buildings of California and northern Mexico. *Am. J. Bot.* 70:303–307.

SREERAMULU, N. and A. CHANDE. 1983. Chemical composition of some fodder grasses of the Dar es Salaam region, Tanzania. *Trop. Agric.* 60:228–229.

SRINIVASAN, K. and M. BATCHA. 1963a. Notes on induction of flowering in trailing shoots of clones of *Saccharum spontaneum. Current Sci.* 32:36–38.

———. 1963b. Performance of clones of *Saccharum* species and allied genera under conditions of water-logging. pp. 571–578. *Proc. 11th Congr. Intern. Sugarcane Technologists.*

SRINIVASAN, S. 1980. *Azolla* manuring and grain yields of rice. *IRRI Newsl.* 5:25.

SRIVASTAVA, A. 1978. Study of leaf epidermis in the genus *Digitaria* Rich. **Gramineae.** *J. Ind. Bot. Soc.* 57:155–160.

SRIVASTAVA, A. and K. MISRA. 1968. Ecotypic differentiation in *Boerhavia diffusa* L. *Trop. Ecol.* 9:52–63.

ST. JOHN, H. 1976. Additions to the higher flora of Wake Island Pacific plant studies 30. *Phytologia* 34:284.

STAHLER, L. and E. WHITEHEAD. 1950. The effect of 2,4–D on potassium nitrate levels in leaves of sugar beets. *Sci.* 112:749–750.

STANDIFER, L. 1980. A technique for estimating weed seed populations in cultivated soil. *Weed Sci.* 28:134–138.

———. 1983. Some effects of soil temperatures on dormancy of annual bluegrass *Poa annua* L. seeds. *Abstr. 23rd Weed Sci. Soc. Am. Conf.* 23: No. 149.

STANDIFER, L. and P. WILSON. 1988. Dormancy studies in three populations of *Poa annua* L. seeds. *Weed Res.* 28:359–363.

STANDIFER, L., P. WILSON and R. PORCHE-SORBET. 1984. Effects of solarization on soil weed seed populations. *Weed Sci.* 32:569–573.

STANIFORTH, D. 1957. Effects of annual grass weeds on the yield of corn. *Agron. J.* 49:551–555.

———. 1961. Responses of corn hybrids to yellow foxtail competition. *Weeds* 9:132–136.

———. 1965. Competitive effects of three foxtail species on soybeans. *Weeds* 13:191–193.

STANIFORTH, R. and P. CAVERS. 1976. An experimental study of water dispersal in *Polygonum* spp. *Can. J. Bot.* 54:2587–2596.

———. 1977. The importance of cottontail rabbit in the dispersal of *Polygonum* spp. *J. Appl. Ecol.* 14:261–267.

———. 1979a. Distribution and habitats of four annual smartweeds in Ontario. *Can. Field Naturalist* 93:378–385.

———. 1979b. Field and laboratory germination responses of achenes of *Polygonum lapathifolium, P. pennsylvanicum* and *P. persicaria. Can. J. Bot.* 57:877–885.

STANLEY, R. 1976. Response of Eurasian watermilfoil to subfreezing temperatures. *J. Aquat. Plant Mgmt.* 14:36–39.

STANLEY, R. and A. NAYLOR. 1972. Photosynthesis in Eurasian watermilfoil *Myriophyllum spicatum. Plant Physiol.* 50:149–151.

STANT, M. 1964. The anatomy of the **Alismataceae.** *J. Linn. Soc.* 23:336–373.

STANTON, M. 1984a. Seed variation in wild radish; effect of seed size on components of seedling and adult fitness. *Ecol.* 1105–1112.

———. 1984b. Developmental and genetic sources of seed weight variation in *Raphanus raphanistrum. Am. J. Bot.* 71:1090–1098.

———. 1985. Seed size and emergence time within a stand of wild radish *Raphanus raphanistrum:* The establishment of a fitness hierarchy. *Oecologia* 67:524–531.

STANTON, M. and S. MAZER. 1986. Some consequences and causes of seed size variation in wild radish *Raphanus raphanistrum. Am. J. Bot.* 73:659.

STANTON, M., A. SNOW and S. HANDEL. 1986. Floral evolution: Attractiveness to pollinators increases male fitness. *Sci.* 232:1625–1626.

STANTON, M., J. BERECZKY and H. HASBROUCK. 1987. Pollination thoroughness and maternal yield regulation in wild radish *Raphanus raphanistrum. Oecologia* 74:68–76.

STANTON, M., A. SNOW, S. HANDEL and J. BERECZKY. 1989. The impact of a flower-color polymorphism on mating patterns in experimental populations of wild radish *Raphanus raphanistrum. Evolution* 43:335–346.

STEBBINS, G. 1957. Self-fertilization and variability in the higher plants. *Am. Nat.* 91:337–354.

STEEL, M., P. CAVERS and S. LEE. 1983. Biology of Canadian weeds. No. 59. *Setaria glauca* (L.) Beauv. and *S. verticillata* (L.) Beauv. *Can. J. Plant Sci.* 63:711–725.

STEEMAN-NIELSEN, E. 1947. Photosynthesis of aquatic plants with special reference to the carbon sources. *Dansk Botanisk Arkiv* 12(8):77pp.

———. 1954. On the preference of some freshwater plants in Finland for brackish waters. *Botanisk Tidsskrift* 51:242–247.

STEFUREAC, T. and T. FRATILESCU. 1979. Contribution to the study of the reciprocal action on the seeds of a plant during germination. *Studii Cercetari Biologie Vegetal* 31:55–61.

STEINBAUER, G. and P. FRANK. 1954. Primary dormancy and germination requirements of seeds of certain **Cruciferae**. pp. 176–181. *Proc. 44th Ann. Meeting Assoc. Official Seed Analysts.*

STEINBAUER, G. and B. GRIGSBY. 1958. Dormancy and germination characteristics of the seeds of sheep sorrel *Rumex acetosella.* pp. 118–120. *Proc. 48th Ann. Meeting Assoc. Official Seed Analysts.*

———. 1960. Dormancy and germination of the docks. pp. 112–117. *Proc. 50th Ann. Meeting Assoc. Official Seed Analysts.*

STEINBAUER, G., B. GRIGSBY, L. CORREA, and P. FRANK. 1955. A study of methods for obtaining laboratory germination of certain weed seeds. pp. 48–52. *Proc. 45th Ann. Meeting Assoc. Official Seed Analysts.*

STEINER, E. 1983. The Blue Sailor: weed of many uses. *Michigan Botanist* 22:63–67.

STEPHANS, E., J. EASLEY, R. SHIRLEY, and J. HENTGES. 1973. Availability of nutrient mineral elements and potential toxicants in aquatic plant diets fed to steers. *Proc. 32nd Soil Crop Sci. Soc. Florida Conf.* 32:30–32.

STEVENS, A. 1932. The number and weight of seeds produced by weeds. *Am. J. Bot.* 19:784–794.

STEVENS, O. 1924. Perennial sow thistle. *North Dakota Agric. Exp. Sta. Bull.* No. 181. 44pp.

———. 1943. *Russian thistle life history and growth.* North Dakota Agric. Exp. Sta. Bull. No. 326.

———. 1957. Weights of seeds and numbers per plant. *Weeds* 5:46–55.

———. 1960. Weed development notes. *Res. Rep., North Dakota Agric. Exp. Sta.* No. 1:10.

STEWARD, K. 1969. Effects of growth regulators and herbicides on germination of *Hydrilla* turions. *Weed Sci.* 17:299–301.

———. 1970. Nutrient removal potentials of various aquatic plants. *Hyacinth Control J.* 8:34–35.

———. 1973. The phosphorous nutrition of *Hydrilla. Abstr. 13th Weed Sci. Soc. Am. Meeting* 13: No. 35.

———. 1984. Growth of *Hydrilla verticillata* in hydrosoils of different composition. *Weed Sci.* 32:371–375.

STEWARD, K. and R. ELLISTON. 1973. Growth of *Hydrilla* in solution culture at various nutrient levels. *Florida Scientist* 36:228–233.

STEWARD, K. and T. VAN. 1987. Comparative studies of monoecious and dioecious *Hydrilla verticillata* biotypes. *Weed Sci.* 35:204–210.

STEWART, G. 1926. Effect of color, scarification and dry heat on germination of alfalfa seed and its impurities. *J. Am. Soc. Agronomy* 18:743–760.

STEYN, D. 1933. Poisoning of human beings by weeds contained in wheat (bread poisoning). *Farming South Africa* 9:45–46.

———. 1934. *The toxicology of plants in South Africa.* Central News Agency Ltd., Johannesburg. p. 631.

STOJANOVIC, D. 1959. A contribution to the biology of *Cuscuta epithymum*, vegetative hibernation. *Zastita Bilja* 51:47–49.

STOJANOVIC, D. and K. MIJATOVIC. 1973. Distribution, biology and control of Cuscuta species in Yugoslavia. *Proc. 1st Symp. Parasitic Weeds, European Weed Res. Council*, Malta.

STOLLER, E. and L. WAX. 1973. Periodicity of germination and emergence of some annual weeds. *Weed Sci.* 21:574–580.

———. 1974. Dormancy changes and fate of some annual weeds in the soil. *Weed Sci.* 22:151–155.

STOLLER, E. and E. WEBER. 1970. Lipid constituents of some common weed seeds. *J. Agric. Food Chem.* 18:361–364.

STRANDHEDE, S. 1965. Problems within the *Eleocharis palustris* complex. *Botaniska Notiser* 118(4):446–447.

———. 1966. Morphologic variation and taxonomy in European *Eleocharis*, subspecies *palustris. Opera Botanica* 10(I). 187pp.

———. 1967. *Eleocharis*, subseries *Eleocharis* in North America. *Botaniska Notiser* 120:355–368.

———. 1973. Pollen development in the *Eleocharis palustris* group: II. Cytokinesis and microspore degeneration. *Botaniska Notiser* 126:255–265.

STREET, J., G. BUCHANAN, R. CROWLEY and J. MCGUIRE. 1981. Influence of cotton (*Gossypium hirsutum*) densities on competitiveness of pigweed (*Amaranthus* spp.) and sicklepod (*Cassia obtusifolia*). *Weed Sci.* 29:253–256.

STRELYAEVA, N. 1978. The germination of broomrape seeds under artificial conditions. *Sel'skokhozyaistvennaya Biologiya* 70:691–694.

STRUIK, G. 1967. Growth habits of dandelion, daisy, catsear and hawbit in New Zealand grasslands. *New Zealand J. Agric. Res.* 10:331–344.

STRYCKERS, J. 1958. Onderz ekinaen naar de toepassinusmogelijkheden van synthetische groeistoffen als selektieve herbiciden im grasland en akkerbouwgewassen. Gent Rijkslandbouwhogsch Rep.: 100. Cited: *Herbicide resistance in plants* 1982. pp. 49. Eds. H. LaBaron and J. Gressel. John Wiley & Sons, NY.

STRYCKERS, J. and P. DELPUTTE. 1965. The biological spread of blackgrass, *Alopecurus myosuroides* Huds. *Revue L'Agric.*, Brussels 18:813–836.

STRYCKERS, J. and M. VAN HIMME. 1972. Review of the results obtained for the cropping year 1970–71 by the Centrum Voor Onkruidonderzoek. pp. 35–37. In: *Biological and phenological study of* Alopecurus myosuroides. Rijksuniversiteit, Gent, Belgium.

STRYCKERS, J., M. VAN HIMME, and R. BULCKE. 1979. Review of results obtained for the cropping period 1976–1977–1978 by the Centrum voor Onkruidonderzoek, Belgium. *Fakulti von de Landouwwetenschappen, Rijksuniversiteit, Gent. Mededling* 30:177–178.

STUANES, A. 1972. Long-term changes in weed flora. *Norsk Landbruk (Oslo)* 4:3–8.

STUCKEY, L. and J. FORSYTH. 1971. Distribution of naturalized *Carduus nutans* mapped in relation to geology in northwestern Ohio. *Ohio J. Sci.* 71:1–15.

STUCKEY, R. 1985. Distributional history of *Najas marina* (spiny naiad) in North America. *Bartonia* 51:2–16.

STUCKEY, R., J. WEHRMEISTER AND R. BARTOLOTTA. 1978. Submersed aquatic vascular plants in ice-covered ponds of central Ohio. *Rhodora* 80:575–579.

SUAGHARA, S. 1981. Studies on the shift in weed vegetation in the maturation process of farms. II. A weed shift by the alteration of the soil acidity. *Weed Res. Japan.* 26:233–238.

SUBBIAH, E., S. SANKARAN and Y. MORACHAN. 1974. Chemical weed control in ragi. *Agriculture Agro-Industries J.*, India, 7:31–33.

SUBRAMAINAN, S., P. SETHI and G. ADAM. 1973. Structure of nicandrenone from *Nicandra physalodes*. *Ind. J. Pharmacy* 35(4):123–124.

SUBUDHI, B. and P. SINGH. 1978. Nutritive value of the water fern *Azolla pinnata* for chicks. *Poultry Sci.* 57:378–380.

———. 1979a. Effect of macronutrients and pH on the growth, nitrogen fixation and soluble sugar content of the water fern *Azolla pinnata*. *Biologica Plantarum* 21:66–70.

———. 1979b. Effect of phosphorous and nitrogen on growth, chlorophyll, amino nitrogen, soluble sugar contents and algal heterocysts of water fern *Azolla pinnata*. *Biologica Plantarum* 21(6):401–406.

SUBUDHI, B. and I. WATANABE. 1981. Differential phosphorous requirements of *Azolla* species and strains in phosphorous-limited continuous culture. *Soil Sci. Plant Nutrition* 27:237–247.

SUCKCHAROEN, S. 1978. Mercury accumulation in *Ipomoea aquatica* near a caustic soda factory in Thailand. *Water, Air, Soil Pollution* 10:451–455.

SUD, S. 1934. A preliminary note on the study of *Azolla pinnata* R.Br. *J. Ind. Bot. Soc.* 13:189–197.

SUDARMIYATI, S. 1975. Preliminary study on the autecology of *Hydrilla verticillata*. *Proc. 3rd Indonesian Weed Sci. Conf.* 3:392–405.

SUDARMIYATI, S. and I. IKUSHIMA. 1978. Ecological observations on the *Hydrilla* stand in Rawa Pening lake, central Java. *Biotrop Newsl., (Indonesia)* 25:3.

SUGHA, S. 1979. Effects of weed extracts on wheat germination. *Science and Culture* 45:65–66.

SULLIA, B. 1973. Effect of root exudates and extracts on rhizosphere fungi. *Plant and Soil* 39:197–200.

SUMARYONO and BASUKI, 1986. Growth and reproduction of *Cyperus Kyllingia* and *C. brevifolius*. *Biotrop Special Publ. No. 24*: 137–143.

SUNDERLAND, N. 1960. Germination of the seeds of angiospermous root parasites. *British Ecological Soc. Symp. (1959)* 1:83–89.

SURANGE, S. and G. PENDSE. 1972. Pharmacognostical studies of *Boerhavia erecta* Gaert. and its comparison with *Boerhavia diffusa* L. *Quart. J. Crude Drug Res.* 12:1937–1950.

SURI, O., R. KANT, R. JAMWAL, K. SURI and C. ATAL. 1982. *Boerhavia diffusa*, a new source of phytoecdysones. *Planta Medica* 44:180–181.

SUTTON, D. 1974. Utilization of *Hydrilla* by the white amur. *Hyacinth Control J.* 12:66–70.

———. 1977. Onsight inspection of the grass carp in the USSR and other European countries, 1977. *Florida Dept. Natural Resources Rep.*, Tallahassee. 47pp.

———. 1986. Influence of allelopathic chemicals on sprouting of *Hydrilla* tubers. *J. Aquat. Plant Mgmt.* 24:88–90.

SUTTON, D. and W. BARLOW. 1981. Growth competition between *Hydrilla* and *Vallisneria*. *Proc. 25th Southern Weed Sci. Soc.* 25:391.

SUTTON, D. and W. ORNES. 1975. Phosphorous removal from static sewage effluent using duckweed. *J. Environmental Quality* 4:367–370.

SUTTON, D., V. VANDIVER, R. HESTAND and W. MILEY. 1978. Use of the grass carp for control of *Hydrilla* in small ponds. pp. 91–102. *Proc. 1st Grass Carp Conf.*; Gainesville, Florida, USA.

SUTTON, D., R. LITTELL and K. LANGELAND. 1980. Intraspecific competition of *Hydrilla verticillata*. *Weed Sci.* 28:425–428.

SUZUKI, E. 1984. Ecesic pattern of *Saccharum spontaneum* on Anak Krakatau Island, Indonesia. *Jap. J. Ecol.* 34:383–388.

SUZUKI, E. and M. NUMATA. 1982. Succession on a sandy coast following the construction of banks planted with *Elymus mollis*. *Jap. J. Ecol.* 32:129–142.

SUZUKI, M. and T. SUTO. 1975. Emergence of weeds in paddy rice fields. I. Relation between temperature and emergence. *Weed Res.*, Japan, 20(3):105–109.

SVEDELIUS, N. 1932. On the different types of pollination in *Vallisneria spiralis* and *V. americana* Michx. *Svensk Bot. Tidskrift* 26:1–12.

SVENSON, H. 1944. The New World species of *Azolla. Am. Fern J.* 34:69–85.

SWAMINATHAN, M. 1961. Morphology, cytology, and breeding behavior of hybrids between *Corchorus olitorius* and *C. capsularis. Current Sci.* 30:67–68.

SWAMY, B. and K. LAKSHMANAN. 1962. Contributions to the embryology of the **Najadaceae**. *J. Ind. Botan. Soc.* 41:247–267.

SWARBRICK, J. 1984. Weeds of Australia, 4. **Verbenaceae**: The lantanas, fog fruit, verbenas, and the snakeweeds (*Stachytarpheta*). *Aus. Weeds* 3:20–21.

SWARBRICK, J., C. FINLAYSON and A. CAULDER. 1982. The biology and control of *Hydrilla verticillata*. In: *Biotrop Special Publ. No. 16*. SEAMO Regional Center Tropical Biol.; Bogor, Idonesia.

SWIETOCHOWSKI, B. and W. SONTA. 1962. The influence of soil humidity on growth and development of some segetal weeds. *Roczniki Nauk Rolniczych* 85(Ser. A):1–28.

SZABO, T. 1984. Nectar secretion in dandelion. *J. Apicultural Res.* 23:204–208.

SZCZEPANSKA, W. 1971. Allelopathy among the aquatic plants. *Polskie Archiwum Hydrobiologii* 18:17–30.

TADULINGAM, C. and G. VENKATANARAYANA. 1955. *A handbook of some south Indian weeds*. Madras Gov. Press, Serial No. 38/1954. 488pp.

TAKABAYASHI, and K. NAKAYAMA. 1979. Emergence depth of main weed seeds. *Weed Res. Jap.* 24:281–285.

TAKAHASHI, N. 1961. Studies on the dormancy of wild rice seed. II. Role of seed coat, embryo and endosperm in dormant seed. *Bull. Inst. Agric. Res., Tohoku Univ.* 13:1–12.

TAKAHATA, Y. and K. HINATA. 1980. A variation study of subtribe Brassicinae by principal component analysis. In: *Brassica crops and wild allies*. Eds. S. Tsunoda, K. Hinata and C. Gomez-Campo. Japanese Scientific Societies Press, Tokyo.

TAKASO, T., and F. BOUMAN. 1984. Ovule ontogeny and seed development in *Potamogeton natans* with a note on the campylotropous ovule. *Acta Bot. Neerlandica* 33:519–533.

TAKAYANAGI, K. 1981. Seed storage and viability tests. pp. 308–321. In: *Brassica crops and wild allies*. Eds. S. Tsunoda, K. Hinata and C. Gomez-Campo. Japanese Scientific Societies Press, Tokyo.

TAKEMATSU, T., M. KONNAI and Y. TAKEUCHI. 1976. Weeds of cultivated fields, and herbicides, in China. *Bull. College Agric., Utsunomiya Univ.* 9(3):91–107.

TAKEMOTO, D., C. DUNFORD and M. MCMURRAY. 1982. Auto toxic and cytostatic effects of the bitter melon *Momordica charantia* on human lymphocytes. *Toxicon* 20:593–600.

TAKEUCHI, Y. 1985. Characteristics of arable land weed flora in Japan. *Abstr. 25th Weed Sci. Soc. Am. Conf.* 25: No. 275.

TAN, B., P. PAYAWAL, I. WATANABE, N. LACDAN, and C. RAMIREZ. 1986. Modern taxonomy of *Azolla*: A review. *Philippine Agric.* 69:491–512.

TAN, Y. 1970. Composition and nutritive value of some grasses, plants and aquatic weeds tested as diets. *J. Fish Bio.* 2:253–257.

TANAKA, O., H. WADA, T. YOKOYAMA and H. MURAKAMI. 1987. Environmental factors controlling capitulum opening and closing of dandelion. *Plant Cell Physiol.* 28:727–730.

TANAKA, T. 1976. *Tanaka's cyclopedia of edible plants of the world*. Keigaku Publ., Tokyo. 924pp. (In English).

TANDON, S. and I. BHALLA. 1967–1968. Cytological studies of morphological variants of some **Compositae**. *Portugaliae Acta Biologica*, Ser. A 10:95–98.

TAPARIA, A., T. TALMALE and V. SHARMA. 1978. Utilization of *Cassia tora* seeds in growth rations of buffalo calves. *Ind. J. Animal Sci.* 48:804–810.

TARVER, D., J. RODGERS, M. MAHLER and R. LAZOR. 1979. *Aquatic and wetland plants of Florida*. 2nd Ed. Bureau Aquatic Plant Res. and Control, Florida Dept. Natural Resources, Tallahassee FL USA.

TATEDA, M. and S. ISIKAWA. 1968. On the weight of seeds of wild 450 species. *Memoirs Faculty Education, Hirosaki Univ.* 19:9–21.

TATEOKA, T. 1964. Taxonomic studies of the genus *Oryza*. pp. 15–21. In: *Rice genetics and cytogenetics*. Elsevier Publishing Co., N.Y.

TATEOKA, T. and J. PANCHO. 1963. A cytotaxonomic study of *Oryza minuta* and *O. officinalis. Botan. Mag.*, Tokyo, 76:366–373.

TAWADA, S. 1972. A yellow flowered form of *Asclepias. Jap. J. Bot.* 77:203.

TAYLOR, J. 1986. The bracken problem, a local hazard and global issue. pp. 21–42. In: *Bracken, ecology, land use and control technology*. Ed. by R. Smith and J. Taylor. Parthenon Publ., Carnforth, England.

———. 1988. Bracken in the environment. *Aspects Appl. Biol.* 17:75–86.

TAYLOR, R. 1987. Populational variation and biosystematics interpretations in weedy dandelion. *Bull. Torrey Bot. Club* 114:109–120.

TAYLORSON, R. 1972. Phytochrome control of dormancy and germination in buried weed seeds. *Abstr. 12th Weed Sci. Soc. Am. Conf.* 12: No. 23.

———. 1979. Response of weed seeds to ethylene and related hydrocarbons. *Weed Sci.* 27:7–10.

TAYLORSON, R. and M. BROWN. 1977. Accelerated after-ripening for overcoming seed dormancy in grass weeds. *Weed Sci.* 25:473–476.

TAYLORSON, R. and S. HENDRICKS. 1969. Action of phytochrome during prechilling of *Amaranthus retroflexus*. *Plant Physiol.* 44:821–825.

———. 1971. Changes in the phytochrome expressed by germination of *Amaranthus retroflexus* seeds. *Plant Physiol.* 47:619–622.

———. 1972. Rehydration of phytochrome in imbibing seeds of *Amaranthus retroflexus* seeds. *Plant Physiol.* 49:663–665.

———. 1976. Interactions of phytochrome and exogenous gibberellic acid on germination of *Lamium amplexicaule* seeds. *Planta* (Berlin) 132:65–70.

TAZAKI, T. and T. USHIJIMA. 1977. Vegetation in the neighborhood of smelting factories and the amount of heavy metals absorbed and accumulated by various species. In: *Vegetation science and environmental protection*. Eds. A. Miyawaki and R. Tuxen.

TEEM, D., C. HOVELAND and G. BUCHANAN. 1980. Sicklepod (*Cassia obtusifolia*) and coffee senna (*Cassia occidentalis*): Geographic distribution, germination and emergence. *Weed Sci.* 28:68–71.

TEERAWATSAKUL, M., Y. MURATA and T. KUSANAGI. 1987. Photosynthesis and transpiration of *Euphorbia geniculata* and *E. hirta*. *Weed Res. Japan* 32:97–103.

TEETER, W. 1965. The effect of sodium chloride on the sago pondweed. *J. Wildlife Mgt.* 29:838–845.

TELTSCHEROVA, L. and S. HEJNY. 1973. The germination of some *Potamogeton* species from south Bohemian fish ponds. *Folia Geobotan. Phytotaxon.*, Praha, 8:231–239.

TER BORG, S. 1986. Effects of environmental factors on *Orobanche* host relationships; review and some recent results. *Proc. Workshop on the Biology and Control of Orobanche*. Ed. by S. ter Borg. Wageningen, Netherlands.

TERPSTRA, R. 1986. Behavior of weed seed in soil clods. *Weed Sci.* 34:889–895.

TERRELL, E. 1976. The correct names for pearl millet and yellow foxtail. *Taxon* 25:297–304.

TERRY, P. 1970. A herbicide trial to evaluate the control of *Cyperus rotundus*, annual grasses and annual broadleaved weeds in coffee. pp. 157–173. *Proc. 4th E. African Herbicide Conf.*

THESIGER, W. 1980. *The last nomad*. E. P. Dutton, Publ.

THIERET, J. 1971. Observations on some aquatic plants in northwestern Minnesota. *Michigan Botanist* 10:117–124.

THODAY, M. 1911. On the histological relations between *Cuscuta* and its host. *Ann. Bot.* 25:655–682.

THOMAS, A. 1985. Weed survey system used in Saskatchewan for cereal and oilseed crops. *Weed Sci.* 33:34–43.

THOMAS, A. and R. WISE. 1983. Weed surveys of Saskatchewan cereal and oilseed crops from 1976 to 1979. *Agric. Can., Weed Survey Series*, Publ. 83–86.

———. 1984. Manitoba weed surveys: Cereal and oilseed crops from 1978 to 1981. *Agric. Can., Weed Survey Series*, Publ. 84–81.

———. 1986. Weed surveys of Saskatchewan sunflower fields, 1985. *Agric. Can., Weed Survey Series*, Publ. 86–81.

THOMAS, A., A. MOORE and H. FORCELLA. 1984. Drought feeding and the dispersal of weeds. *J. Aus. Inst. Agric. Sci.* 50:103–107.

THOMAS, G., J. RAWSON and J. LADEWIG. 1980. Effect of weed competition and inter-row cultivation on yield of grain sorghum. *Queensland J. Agric. and Animal Sci.* 37:47–51.

THOMAS, P. 1970. A survey of the weeds of arable lands in Rhodesia. *Rhodesia Agric. J.* 67:34–37.

———. 1975. *Annual Report 1973–1974*. Dept. Res. and Special Services, Henderson Res. Sta., Salisbury, Rhodesia.

———. 1976. *Annual Report 1974–1975*. Dept. Res. and Special Services, Henderson Res. Sta., Salisbury, Rhodesia.

———. 1979. *Annual Report 1977–1978*. Dept. Res. and Special Services, Henderson Res. Sta., Salisbury, Rhodesia.

———. 1980. *Annual Report 1978–1979*. Dept. Res. and Special Services, Henderson Res. Sta., Salisbury, Rhodesia.

———. 1982. *Annual Report 1979–1980*. Dept. Res. and Special Services, Henderson Res. Sta., Salisbury, Rhodesia.

THOMAS, P. and P. SCHWERZEL. 1968. A cotton weed competition experiment. pp. 737–743. *Proc. 9th Brit. Weed Control Conf.*

———. 1982. The facts about weeds and their effects on crops. *Proc. 4th National Weed Conf. S. Africa*, 1981. Ed. by H. van deVenter and M. Mason.

THOMPSON, A. 1974. Effect of fertilizer and pasture competition on gorse growth and establishment. *Proc. 27th New Zealand Weed and Pest Control Conf.* 27:6–10.

THOMPSON, C. and W. WITT. 1987. Germination of cutleaf groundcherry (*Physalis angulata*), smooth groundcherry (*P. virginica*) and eastern black nightshade (*Solanum ptycanthum*). *Weed Sci.* 35:58–62.

THOMPSON, J. 1925. Studies in irregular nutrition. No. 1. The parasitism of *Cuscuta reflexa*. *Trans. Royal Soc. Edinburgh* 54:343–364.

THOMPSON, K. and J. GRIME. 1983. Comparative study of germination responses to diurnally fluctuating temperatures. *J. Appl. Ecol.* 20:141–156.

THOMPSON, K. and J. WHATLEY. 1984. A thermogradient bar apparatus for the study of the germination requirements of buried seeds *in situ*. *New Phytologist* 96:459–471.

THOMPSON, S. 1988. Range expansion by alien weeds in the coastal farmlands of Guyana. *J. Biogeography* 15:109–118.

THURLOW, D. and G. BUCHANAN. 1972. Competition of sicklepod with soybeans. *Weed Sci.* 20:379–384.

THURSTON, E. and N. LERSTEN. 1969. The morphology and toxicology of plant stinging hairs. *Bot. Rev.* 35:393–412.

THURSTON, J. 1960. Dormancy in weed seeds. In: The biology of weeds. Ed. J. Harper. Blackwell Scientific Publ., Oxford, England.

———. 1964. Germination of *Alopecurus myosuroides* Huds. blackgrass. pp. 349–51. *Proc. 7th Brit. Weed Control Conf.*

———. 1972a. *Alopecurus myosuroides* and its control. pp. 977–987. *Proc. 11th Brit. Weed Control Conf.*

———. 1972b. Biology of weed species: Blackgrass (*Alopecurus myosuroides*). *Rothamsted Exp. Sta. Rep. 1971:* 115–117.

TIAGI, B. and S. TAIMNI. 1963. Floral morphology and embryology of *Vernonia cinerascens* Schult. and V. *cinerea* Less. *Agra Univ. J. Res.* 12(2):123–137.

TIAGI, Y. and N. AERY. 1981. Biogeochemical studies in zinc deposit areas Zawar Mines, Rajasthan, India. *Proc. Ind. National Sci. Acad.,* (B) 47:867–887.

TILEY, G. 1970. Weeds (of Uganda). pp. 297–317. In: *Agriculture in Uganda*. Ed. by J. Jameson. Publ. for Ministry of Agriculture and Forestry of Uganda by Oxford University Press, Oxford, England.

TIMSON, J. 1965a. Fruit variation in *Polygonum persicaria* L. *Watsonia* 6:106–108.

———. 1965b. A study of the hybridization in *Polygonum* section *persicaria*. *J. Linn. Soc., Bot.* 59:155–161.

———. 1965c. Germination in *Polygonum*. *New Phytologist* 64:179–186.

———. 1966. *Polygonum hydropiper* L. *J. Ecol.* 54:815–821.

TINKLIN, R. and D. BOWLING. 1969. The water relations of bracken: A preliminary study. *J. Ecol.* 57:669–671.

TITUS, J. 1977. *The comparative ecology of three submerged macrophytes*. Ph.D. Diss., Univ. Wisconsin, Madison WI USA. 195pp.

TITUS, J. and M. ADAMS. 1979. Coexistence and comparative light relations of the submersed macrophytes *Myriophyllum spicatum* and *Vallisneria americana*. *Oecologia* 40:273–286.

TITUS, J., R. GOLDSTEIN, M. ADAMS, J. MANKIN, P. WEILER, H. SHUGART and R. BOOTH. 1975. A production model for *Myriophyllum spicatum*. *Ecol.* 56:1129.

TIWARI, S., S. BHADAURIA, M. VADDORIA and D. DAYAL. 1985. Allelopathic effects of weeds in soybean, groundnut, and greengram. *Current Sci.* 54:434–435.

TJEPKEMA, T. and H. EVANS. 1976. Nitrogen fixation associated with *Juncus balticus* and other plants of Oregon wetlands. *Soil Biol. Biochem.* 8:505–509.

TKACHUK, R. and V. MELLISH. 1977. Amino acid and proximate analyses of weed seeds. *Can. J. Plant Sci.* 57:243–249.

TOIDA, Y. 1972. Nematicidal effect of Mexican marigold *Tagetes minuta*, against nematodes associated with mulberry. *Jap. J. Nematol.* 1:18–21.

TOKARNIA, C., J. DOBEREINER and C. CANELLA. 1972. Experimental poisoning of cattle by *Asclepias curassavi-* ca. *Pesquisa Agropecuaria Brasileira, Serie Veterinaria* 7:31–39.

TOKELA, M. 1971. Occurrence of weed seeds in Finnish timothy and red clover seed. *Finland Maataloushallituksen Tiedonantoja* 370:41–47.

TOLBERT, N. and C. OSMOND. 1976. Photorespiration in marine plants. *Aus. J. Plant Physiol.* 3:1–139.

TOMAN, J. and F. STARY. 1965. *Matricaria chamomilla* oder *Matricaria recutita*. *Taxon* 14:224–228.

TOMLINSON, J. 1970. Weed plants as sources of cucumber mosaic virus. *Ann. Appl. Biol.* 66:11–16.

TOMSON, H. 1918. *Seed production in 1918*. Massachusetts Agric. College, Ext. Bull. No. 20.

TONKIN, J. 1968a. The occurrence of broad-leaved weed seeds in samples of cereals tested by the official seed testing station, Cambridge. pp. 1199–1204. *Proc. 9th Brit. Weed Control Conf.*

———. 1968b. The occurrence of some annual grass weed seeds in samples tested by the official seed testing station, Cambridge. pp. 1–5. *Proc. 9th Brit. Weed Control Conf.*

TONKIN, J. and A. PHILLIPSON. 1973. The presence of weed seeds in cereal seed drills in England and Wales during spring 1970. *J. National Inst. Agric. Bot.* 13:1–8.

TOOLE, E. and E. BROWN. 1946. Final results of the Duvel buried seed experiment. *J. Agric. Res.* 72:201–210.

TOPHAM, P. and H. LAWSON. 1981. Measurement of weed species diversity in crop/weed competition studies. *Weed Res.* 22:285–293.

TORRES, R. 1986. *Orobanche ramosa*, phanerogamous parasite, host plant species. *Ciencia y Tecnica en la Agric., Tabaco* 9:7–17.

TORRES, W., M. NAKANO, D. NOBRE and N. MOMOSE. 1971. Poisoning of chickens caused by *Cassia occidentalis* L. *O Biologico* 37:204–208.

TOURTE, Y. 1975a. The ultrastructural study of oogenesis of a fern, *Pteridium aquilinum*: 1. Evolution of nuclear structures. *J. Microscopie et de Biologie Cellulaire* 22:87–108.

———. 1975b. The ultrastructural study of oogenesis of a fern, *Pteridium aquilinum*: 2. Development of mitochondria and plastids. *J. Microscopie et de Biologie Cellulaire* 23:301–316.

TOWNSEND, C. 1973. I. Notes on **Amaranthaceae**. *Kew Bull.* 28:141–146.

———. 1974. II. Notes on **Amaranthaceae**. *Kew Bull.* 29:461–475.

TRENT, L., R. HESTAND and C. CARTER. 1978. Toxicity of sulphuric acid to aquatic plants and organisms. *J. Aquat. Mgmt.* 16:40–43.

TRIPATHI, R. 1968. Certain autecological observations on *Asphodelus tenuifolius*, a troublesome weed of Indian agriculture. *Trop. Ecol.* 9(2):208–219.

———. 1977. Weed problems: An ecological perspective. *Trop. Ecol.* 18:138–148.

TROST, W. and G. HALBACH. 1978. Anti-phalloidin and anti-alpha aminitin action of silybin in comparison with compounds similar to structural parts of silybin. *Experientia* 34(8):1051–1052.

TRUSCOTT, F. 1958. On the regeneration of new shoots from isolated dodder haustoria. *Am. J. Bot.* 45:169–176.

TRYON, A. 1941. A revision of the genus *Pteridium*. *Rhodora* 43:1–31, 37–67.

TSENOVA, M. 1975. ^{35}S translocation and reduction in *Sinapis arvensis* L. depending upon the light regime. *Comptes Rendus de l'Academie Agricole Georgi Dimitrov* 8:7–10.

TSIVION, Y. 1978a. Host tissue determination of xylem formation in the haustorium of *Cuscuta*. *Israel J. Bot.* 27:122–130.

———. 1978b. Physiological concepts of the association between parasitic angiosperms and their hosts: A review. *Israel J. Bot.* 27:103–121.

TSUKAMOTO, Y., S. MATSUBARA and F. HATORI. 1971. Vernalization of the ox-eye daisy *Chrysanthemum leucanthemum*. *J. Jap. Hortic. Soc.* 40:69–73.

TSUNODA, S. 1981. Eco-physiology of wild and cultivated forms in *Brassica* and allied genera. pp. 109–120. In: *Brassica crops and wild allies*. Eds. S. Tsunoda, K. Hinata and C. Gomez-Campo. Japanese Scientific Societies Press, Tokyo.

TUAN, D. and T. THUYER. 1967. Introducing *Azolla* into the crop rotation of rice growing areas as a major crop. *Joint Publ. Res. Ser. Translation*, North Vietnam, 119:45–53.

TUCAKOV, J. 1957. The areas and the exploitation of the *Matricaria chamomilla* in Yugoslavia. *Materiae Vegetabilis* 2:161–173.

TUCKER, C. 1981. Relationships between culture density and the composition of the three floating aquatic macrophytes. *Hydrobiologia* 85:73–76.

TUCKER, J. and J. SAUER. 1958. Aberrant *Amaranthus* populations of the Sacramento–San Joaquin Delta, California. *Madrono* 14:252–261.

TULIKOV, A. 1971. The biological action of field crops on corn sowthistle (*Sonchus arvensis* L.). *Doklady TSKHA (Timiryazevskaya Selsko'khozyaistvennaya Akademiya)* 168:184–189.

TURNER, B. and E. KARLANDER. 1975. Photoperiodic control of floral initiation in sicklepod (*Cassia obtusifolia*) L. *Bot. Gaz.* 136:1–4.

TURNER, N. 1984. Counter irritant and other medicinal uses of plants in **Ranunculaceae** by native peoples in British Columbia, Canada, and neighboring areas. *J. Ethnopharmacology* 11:181–202.

TURNER, T., D. WADDINGTON and T. WATSCHKE. 1979. The effect of soil fertility levels on dandelion and crabgrass encroachment of Merion Kentucky bluegrass. pp. 280–286. *Proc. 33rd Northeastern Weed Sci. Soc. Conf.*

TUTIN, T. 1952. Origin of *Poa annua* L. *Nature* 169:160.

———. 1957. A contribution to the experimental taxonomy of *Poa annua*. *Watsonia* 4:1–10.

TYUREBAEV, S. 1977. The use of dodder gall beetle for the biological control of field dodder. *Vestnik Sel'skokhozyaistvennoi Nauki Kazakhstana* 20:116–117.

UBRIZSY, G. 1968. Long term experiments on the flora-changing effect of chemical weedkillers in plant communities. *Acta Agronomica Academiae Scientiarum Hungaricae* 17:171–193.

UDEL'NOVA, T., S. YUFEROVA and E. BIOCHENKA. 1971. Iron, copper and manganese compounds in the leaves of higher plants. *Izvestiya Akad. Nauk SSSR, Seriya Biologicheskaya* 199(1):100–105.

UENO, O., M. SAMEJIMA and T. KOYAMA. 1989. Distribution and evolution of C_4 syndrome in *Eleocharis*, a sedge group inhabiting wet and aquatic environments, based on culm anatomy and carbon isotope ratios. *Ann. Bot.* 64:425–438.

UGBOROGHO, R. 1980. Floral mechanism as an aid to the classification of the *Sida rhombifolia* complex (**Malvaceae**) in Nigeria. *Bull. Inst. Fondam Afr. Noire. Ser. A Sci. Nat.* 42:107–121.

———. 1982. Cytogenetic studies on the *Sida rhombifolia* complex of Nigeria. *Cytologia* 47: 11–20.

ULJANOVA, T. 1985. Specific composition of weed plants of the Soviet far eastern flora. *Botanicheskii Zhurnal* 70:482–490.

UMEMOTO, K. 1974. Pattern of calcium oxalate crystals in the leaves of *Polygonum longisetum* and *P. persicaria* grown from 4000 year-old seed. *Chem. Pharm. Bull.* (Tokyo) 22:1429–1430.

UNGAR, I. 1978. Halophyte seed germination. *Bot. Rev.* 44:233–264.

UNGUREAN, L. 1973. Some aspects of organogenesis in the species *Orobanche ramosa* and *O. brassicae*. *Lucrari Stiintifice Institutul Agronomic -Nicolae Balcescu- Horticultura* 16:15–18.

UNITED STATES DEPARTMENT OF AGRICULTURE. 1970. *Selected weeds of the United States*, Agric. Handbook No. 366.

UNTERLADSTATTER, R. 1977. *Guia para la identificaion y control de malezas*. Commite Obras Publicas de Santa Cruz, Bolivia.

UPADHYAY, K., R. DWIVEDI and G. SINGH. 1977. Additional hosts of the root-knot nematode, *Meloidogyne javanica*. *Indian J. Mycol. Plant Pathol.* 7:103.

UPHOF, J. 1968. *Dictionary of economic plants*. 2nd Ed. J. Cramer, N.Y.

URTON, N. 1945. Dodders and lucerne in South Africa. *South African J. Sci.* 41:231–237.

VAIL, S., O. DAILEY, W. CONNICK AND A. PEPPERMAN. 1985. Strigol synthesis and related structure-bioactivity studies. pp. 445–446. *Chemistry of allelopathy; Biochem-*

ical interactions among plants. Am. Chem. Soc., Washington, D.C.

VALDEZ, R. 1968. Survey, identification and host parasite relationships of root-knot nematodes occurring in some parts of the Philippines. *Philipp. Agriculturist* 51:802–824.

VALENTINE, D. and A. RICHARDS. 1967. Sexuality and apomixis in *Taraxacum. Nature* 214:114.

VALLETE, R. 1978. Influence de la temperature sur la germination des semences de chicoree de Bruxelles. *Bull. Recherches Agronomiques de Gembloux* 13:183–196.

VAN, T. 1989. Differential responses to photoperiods in monoecious and dioecious *Hydrilla verticillata. Weed Sci.* 37:552–556.

VAN, T. and W. HALLER. 1979. Growth of *Hydrilla* in various soil types. pp. 292–294. *Proc. 32nd Southern Weed Sci. Soc.*

VAN, T., W. HALLER, and G. BOWES. 1976. Comparison of the photosynthetic characteristics of three submersed aquatic plants. *Plant Physiol.* 58:761–768.

VAN, T., W. HALLER, G. BOWES, and L. GARRAD. 1977. Effects of light quality on growth and chlorophyll composition in *Hydrilla. J. Aquat. Plant Mgmt.* 15:29–31.

VAN, T., W. HALLER, and G. BOWES. 1978. Some aspects of competitive biology of *Hydrilla. Proc. European Weed Res. Soc. Intern. Symp. Aquatic Weeds*, Amsterdam, 5:117–126.

VANDIVER, V. and D. SUTTON. 1988. The introduction of grass carp to small agricultural ditches in Florida. *Abstr. 28th Weed Sci. Soc. of Am. Conf.* 28:40.

VARSHNEY, C. and J. RZOSKA. Eds. 1976. Aquatic weeds in South East Asia. *Proc. Regional Seminar Noxious Aquatic Vegetation*, New Dehli, 1973. 396pp.

VASCONCELOS, M., I. MOREIRA and M. ROSA. 1979. Effect of high temperature on rhizome bud sprouting of weeds. *Anais do Inst. Superior Agronomia* 38:85–90.

VASCONCELOS, T., G. SA and I. MODESTO. 1984. Effect of temperature, light, depth and duration of burial on the germination of certain weeds. In: *Comptes Rendus du 7 eme Calloque Intern. Ecologie, Biologie, Systematiquedes Mauvaises Herbes* 7:13–20.

VASILEVSKAYA, V. and L. PROKOPENKO. 1982. Anatomical structure of the rhizome in *Marsilea quadrifolia. Botanicheskii Zhurnal* 67(11):1513–1517.

VASYURA, V. 1975. Dynamics of broomrape seed germination at different depths in the soil. *Tabak* (USSR) 36(4):54–55.

VATS, O. 1984. Ecology of some aquatic weeds of north India. *J. Res. Punjab Agric. Univ.* 21:343–348.

VEERANJANEYULU, K. and V. DAS. 1984. Stomatal frequency and resistance in leaves of some tropical members of **Asteraceae**. *Proc. Ind. Nat. Sci. Acad. Series B,* 50:317–320.

VEGA, M., E. PALLER and R. LUBIGAN. 1971. The effect of continuous herbicide treatments on weed populations and yield of lowland rice. *Philipp. Agriculturist* 55:204–209.

VEKHOV, N. 1988. New data on the distribution of *Potamogeton pectinatus* and *Utricularia vulgaris* in the Arctic (Yakutsk). *Botanicheskii Zhurnal* (Leningrad) 73:1027–1028.

VELEZ, I. and J. VAN OVERBECK. 1950. *Plantas indeseables en los cultivos tropicales.* Editorial Universitaria, Rio Pierdras, Puerto Rico.

VENGRIS, J. 1963. The effect of time of seedling growth and development of rough pigweed and yellow foxtail. *Weeds* 11:48–50.

VENGRIS, J., M. DRAKE, W. COLBY and J. BART. 1953. Chemical composition of weeds and accompanying crop plants. *Agron. J.* 45:213–218.

VENGRIS, J., W. COLBY and M. DRAKE. 1955. Plant nutrient competition between weeds and corn. *Agron. J.* 47:213–216.

VENKATESH, B. and P. SHETTY. 1978. Studies on the growth rate of the grass carp fed on 2 aquatic weeds and a terrestrial grass. *Aquaculture* 13:45–54.

VENKATESH, C. 1956. Structure and dehiscence of the anther in *Najas. Botaniska Notiser* 109:75–82.

VERGARA, B., K. MOODY and R. VISPERAS. 1977. Autecology of *Scirpus maritimus*, IV. Suggested control under field conditions. *Philipp. Weed Sci. Bull.* 4:7–12.

VERKLEIJ, J., and A. PIETERSE. 1986. Identification of *Hydrilla verticillata* strains by means of isozyme patterns. pp. 381–388. *Proc. 7th European Weed Res. Soc. Intern. Symp. Aquatic Weeds.*

VERKLEIJ, J., A. PIETERSE, G. HORNEMAN and M. TORENBEEK. 1983. A comparative study of the morphology and isoenzyme pattern of *Hydrilla verticillata. Aquat. Bot.* 17:43–59.

VERMA, H., L. AWASTHI and K. MUKERJEE. 1979a. Prevention of virus infection and multiplication by extracts from medicinal plants. *Phytopathologische Zeitschrift* 96:70–76.

VERMA, H., L. AWASTHI and K. SAXENA. 1979b. Isolation of the virus inhibitor from the root extract of *Boerhavia diffusa* inducing systemic resistance in plants. *Can. J. Bot.* 57:1214–1217.

VERNON, R. 1979. Weed Control in Zambia's maize. pp. 72–84. *Proc. 7th Weed Science Conference.*

VERNON, R. 1983. *Field guide to important arable weeds in Zambia.* Balding and Mansell Ltd., London. 151 pp.

VIERSSEN, W. VAN. 1982. Some notes on the germination of seeds of *Najas marina. Aquatic Bot.* 12(2):201–203.

———. 1986. A comparison of some morphological characteristics of four *Hydrilla* strains under different environmental conditions. pp. 369–374. *Proc. 7th European Weed Res. Soc. Intern. Symp. Aquatic Weeds.*

VIGFUSSON, E. 1970. On polyspermy in charlock (*Sinapis arvensis* L.). *Hereditas* 70:23–38.

VIINIKKA, Y. 1975. Allocyclic regions and banding patterns in the chromosomes of *Najas marina*. *Hereditas* 81(1):47–54.

———. 1978. Spontaneous chromosome breakage in natural populations of *Najas marina*. *Hereditas* 88(2):279–283.

VILLIERS, D., C. GARBERS and R. LAURIE. 1971. Synthesis of tagetenones and their occurrence in oil of *Tagetes minuta*. *Phytochemistry* 10:1359–1361.

VINCENT, E. and E. ROBERTS. 1977. The interaction of light, nitrate and alternating temperature in promoting the germination of dormant seeds of common weed species. *Seed Sci. Technol.* 5:659–670.

———. 1979. The influence of chilling, light and nitrate on the germination of dormant seeds of common weed species. *Seed Sci. Technol.* 7:3–14.

VISPERAS, R. and B. VERGARA. 1976. Autecology of *Scirpus maritimus*. I. Growth characteristics and competition with rice. II. Effect of light, temperature, and moisture. III. Effect of shoot cutting on flowering. *Philipp. Weed Sci. Bull.* 3:1–32.

VISSER, J. 1981. *South African parasitic flowering plants*. Juta Co., Capetown.

———. 1989. Germination requirements of some root-parasitic flowering plants. *Naturwissenschaften* 76:253–261.

VLADIMIROVA, Z. 1968. The flora of Lake Kenon. *Uchenye Zapiski Chelyabinskogo Gosudarstvennoggo Pedagogicheskogo Instituta* 19:116–122. (Translated from *Zhurnal Biol.*, 1969, No. 10V412).

VOEMEL A., J. HOELZL, A. CEYLAN and R. MARQUARD. 1977. The lipid and flavanoid contents in the seeds of *Silybum marianum* under extremely varied ecological conditions. *Zeitschrift fur Acker und Pflanzenbau* 144:90–102.

VOGEL, F. 1926. Beitrage zur Kenntnis der Standortsanspruche von Ackerrettich (*Raphanus raphanistrum*) und Ackersenf (*Sinapis arvensis*). *Bayerisches Landwirt Shaftliches Jahrbuch* 16(4/5)149–230.

VOGEL, G., W. TROST, R. BRAATZ, K. ODENTHAL, K. BRUESEWITZ, H. ANTWEILER and R. SEEGER. 1975. Pharmacodynamics, site, and mechanisms of action of silymarin, the antihepatoxic principle from *Silybum marianum*. 1. Acute toxicology, tolerance, general and special pharmacology. 2. Special studies on site and mechanism of action (also in organs other than liver). *Arzneimittel Forschung* 25:82–89, 179–188.

VOHORA, S., S. SHAH, S. NAQVI, S. AHMAD and M. KHAN. 1983. Studies on *Trianthema portulacastrum*. *Planta Medica* 47:106–108.

VOROB'EV, N. 1968. Competition between maize and weeds. *Vestnik Sel'skokhozyaistvennoi Nauki*, Moscow, 13:30–35.

VRANCEANU, A., N. PIRVU, F. STOENESCU, and F. PACUREANU. 1986. Some aspects of the interaction of *Helianthus annuus* with *Orobanche cumana* and its influence in sunflower breeding. pp. 181–189. In: *Biology and Control of Orobanche*. Landbouwhogeschool, Wageningen, Netherlands.

WACHNIK, Z. 1962. Leaves of chicory *Cichorium intybus* as a cause of poisoning of pigs. *Medycyna Weterynaryjna* (Poland) 18:493–495.

WADDINGTON, J. 1980. Chemical control of dandelion (*Taraxacum officinale*) and perennial sowthistle (*Sonchus arvensis*) in alfalfa (*Medicago sativa*) grown for seed. *Weed Sci.* 28:164–167.

WADDINGTON, J. and K. BOWREN. 1978. Effects of crop residues on production of barley, bromegrass and alfalfa in the greenhouse and of barley in the field. *Can. J. Plant Sci.* 58:249–255.

WAGENVOORT, W. and N. OPSTAL. 1979. Effect of constant and alternating temperatures, rinsing, stratification and fertilizer on germination of weed species. *Scientia Horticulturae* 10:15–20.

WAGNER, H., P. DIESEL, and M. SEITZ. 1974. Chemistry and analysis of silymarin from *Silybum marianum*. *Arzneimittel Forschung* 24:466–471.

WAHL, S. 1988. Changes in the species composition of the weed flora under differential cropping systems for several years: Results of Lautenbach project. *Mitteilungen aus der Biologischen Bundesanstalt fur Land- und Forstwirtschaft Berlin-Dahlem* No. 245:132–147.

WAHLQUIST, A. 1969. Floral induction in some members of the **Umbelliferae** in response to cold treatment, photoperiod, gibberellic acid and kinetin. *Diss. Abstr. (B)* 29:3229–3230.

WAIN, R., W. HALLER and D. MARTIN. 1984. Genetic relationship among two forms of alligatorweed. *J. Aquat. Plant Mgmt.* 22:104–105.

———. 1985. Isozymes in studies of aquatic plants. *J. Aquat. Plant Mgmt.* 23:42–45.

WAISEL, Y. 1970. Phenology and vegetative reproduction of some submerged water weeds. *Proc. 4th Israeli Weed Control Conf.* 4:32–35.

WAISEL, Y. and M. AGAMI. 1983. Are roots essential for the growth of *Najas marina*? pp. 287–291. *Proc. Intern. Symp. Aquatic Macrophytes*. Nijmegen, Netherlands.

WAISEL, Y. and Z. SHAPIRO. 1971. Functions performed by roots of some submerged hydrophytes. *Israel J. Bot.* 20:69–77.

WAISEL, Y., M. AGAMI and Z. SHAPIRO. 1982. Uptake and transport of ^{86}Rb, ^{32}P, ^{36}Cl, and ^{22}Na by four submerged hydrophytes. *Aquat. Bot.* 13(2):179–186.

WALDRON, L. 1904. Vitality and growth of buried weed seeds. *North Dakota Agric. Exp. Sta. Bull.* No. 26:439–457.

WALI, M. and P. FREEMAN. 1973. Ecology of some mined areas in North Dakota. In: *Some environmental aspects of strip-mining in North Dakota*. North Dakota Geological Survey, Educational Series, No. 5: 25–47; Grand Forks, North Dakota.

WALKER, H. 1966. Review of literature on *Orobanche* with suggestions for its control. *Food and Agriculture Organization, United Nations* No. 61–B/1288. 6pp.

WALKER, N. and I. GRAY. 1970. The glucosinate of land cress *Coronopus didymus* and its enzymic degradation products as precursors of off-flavor in milk—A review. *J. Agric. Food Chem.* 18:346–352.

WALKER, R., L. WELLS, and J. MCGUIRE. 1989. Bristly starbur (*Acanthospermum hispidum*) interference in peanuts (*Arachis hypogaea*). *Weed Sci.* 37:196–200.

WALTER, H. and W. KOCH. 1984. Nature and importance of weeds, pests and diseases in smallholder vegetable production in Khartoum. *Acta Horticulturae* 143:67–83.

WALTERS, S. 1949. Biological flora of the British Isles: *Eleocharis* R. Br. *J. Ecol.* 37:192–206.

WALTERS, T. and D. DECKER-WALTERS. 1988. Balsampear *Momordica charantia*, **Cucurbitaceae**. *Econ. Bot.* 42:286–288.

WALTON, D. 1975. European weeds and other alien species in the sub-antarctic. *Weed Res.* 15:271–282.

WANGERMANN, E. and E. ASHBY. 1951. Studies in the morphogenesis of leaves: VII, Part I. Effects of light intensity and temperature on the cycle of aging and rejuvenation in the vegetative life history of *Lemna minor*. *New Phytologist* 51:186–199.

WANGERMANN, E. and H. LACEY. 1955. Studies in the morphogenesis of leaves: X. Preliminary experiments on the relation between nitrogen nutrition, rate of respiration and rate of aging of fronds of *Lemna minor*. *New Phytologist* 54:182–198.

WAPAKALA, W. 1966. A note on the persistence of mulch grasses. *Kenya Coffee* 31:111–112.

WAPSHERE, A. 1970. The effect of human intervention on the distribution and abundance of *Chondrilla juncea* L. *Proc. Advanced Study Inst. Dynamics Numbers Population* (Oosterbeek): 469–477.

WAPSHERE, A., S. HASAN, W. WAHBA and L. CARESCHE. 1974. The ecology of *Chondrilla juncea* in the western Mediterranean. *J. Appl. Ecol.* 11:783–799.

WARNES, D. and R. ANDERSEN. 1984. Decline of wild mustard (*Brassica kaber*) seeds in soil under various cultural and chemical practices. *Weed Sci.* 32:214–217.

WARWICK, M. 1984. Buried seeds in arable soils in Scotland. *Weed Res.* 24:261–268.

WARWICK, S. 1979. The biology of Canadian weeds. 37. *Poa annua* L. *Can. J. Plant Sci.* 59:1053–1066.

———. 1980a. Geneology of lawn weeds: VII. The response of different growth forms of *Plantago major* L. and *Poa annua* L. to simulated trampling. *New Phytologist* 85:461–469.

———. 1980b. Differential growth between and within triazine-resistant biotypes of *Senecio vulgaris*. *Weed Res.* 20:299–303.

WARWICK, S. and D. BRIGGS. 1978. The genecology of lawn weeds. I. Population differentiation in *Poa annua* L. in a mosaic environment of bowling green lawns and flower beds. *New Phytologist* 81:711–723.

WATANABE, I., N. BERJA and D. DEL ROSARIO. 1980. Growth of *Azolla* in paddy fields as affected by phosphorous fertilizer. *Soil Sci. Plant Nutrition* 26:301–307.

WATANABE, Y. and F. HIROKAWA. 1975a. Requirement of temperature conditions in germination of annual weed seeds and its relation to seasonal distribution of emergence in the field. pp. 38–41. *Proc. 5th Asian-Pacific Weed Sci. Soc. Conf.*

———. 1975b. Ecological studies on the germination and emergence of annual weeds. 3. Changes in emergence and viable seeds in cultivated and uncultivated soil. *Weed Res. Jap.* 19:14–19.

WATSON, D., A. MORTIMER and P. PUTWAIN. 1987. The seed bank dynamics of triazine-resistant and susceptible biotypes of *Senecio vulgaris* implications for control strategies. In: *Proc. of the British Crop Protection Conference, Weeds.* 3:917.

WATSON, G. 1963. Cover plants in Malayan rubber plantations. *World Crops* 15:48–52.

WATSON, W., R. BARLOW and K. BARNETT. 1965. Bright Blindness, a condition prevalent in Yorkshire hill sheep. *Vet. Rec.* 1060–1069.

WATSON, W., S. TERLECKI, D. PATTERSON, D. SWEASY, C. HEBERT and J. DONE. 1972. Experimentally-produced retinal degeneration (bright blindness) in sheep. *Brit. Vet. J.* 128:457–469.

WATT, A. 1940. Contributions to the ecology of bracken *Pteridium aquilinum*. I. The rhizome. *New Phytol.* 39:401–422.

———. 1942. Contributions to the ecology of bracken *Pteridium aquilinum*. II. The frond and the plant. *New Phytol.* 42:103–126.

———. 1945. Contributions to the ecology of bracken *Pteridium aquilinum*. III. Frond types and the make up of the population. *New Phytol.* 44:156–178.

———. 1947. Contributions to the ecology of bracken *Pteridium aquilinum*. IV. The structure of the community. *New Phytol.* 46:97–121.

———. 1950. Contributions to the ecology of bracken *Pteridium aquilinum*. V. Bracken and frost. *New Phytol.* 49:308–327.

———. 1954. Contributions to the ecology of bracken *Pteridium aquilinum*. VI. Frost and the advance and retreat of bracken. *New Phytol.* 53:117–130.

———. 1955. Contributions to the ecology of bracken *Pterid-*

ium aquilinum. VII. Bracken and litter. 1. Origin of the rings. *New Phytol.* 55:369–381.

———. 1964. Some factors affecting bracken in Breckland. *J. Ecol.* 52:63–77.

———. 1967. The differentiation and fate of the bracken *Pteridium aquilinum* fronds and their relation to the age structure of the shoot and frond population. *New Phytol.* 66:75–84.

———. 1969. Contributions to the ecology of bracken *Pteridium aquilinum.* VII. Bracken and litter. 2. Crown form. *New Phytol.* 68:841–859.

———. 1970. Contributions to the ecology of bracken *Pteridium aquilinum.* VII. Bracken and litter. 3. The cycle of change. *New Phytol.* 69:431–449.

———. 1971. Contributions to the ecology of bracken *Pteridium aquilinum.* VIII. The marginal and hinterland plant. *New Phytol.* 70:967–986.

———. 1976. The ecological status of bracken. *Bot. J. Linn. Soc.* 73:217–239.

WATT, J. and M. BREYER-BRANDWIJK. 1962. *The medicinal and poisonous plants of southern and eastern Africa.* (English). E. S. Livingstone Ltd., Edinburgh.

WAY, J. and N. MOORE. 1969. Aquatic herbicide trials at Oxton Lakes, Nottinghamshire. *Rep. Monks Woods Exp. Sta., National Environ. Res. Council,* 1966–68: 15–16.

WEAVER, J. 1926. *Root development of field crops.* McGraw-Hill, N.Y. 291pp.

WEAVER, J. and T. FITZPATRICK. 1934. The prairie. *Ecological Monographs* 4:109–295.

WEAVER, S. 1985. Geographic spread of *Datura stramonium* in association with soybeans and maize in Ontario, Canada. *Proc. Brighton Crop Protec. Conf.—Weeds,* pp. 403–410.

———. 1986. Factors affecting threshold levels and seed production of jimsonweed *Datura stramonium* in soybeans *Glycine max. Weed Res.* 26:215–223.

WEAVER, S. and E. MCWILLIAMS. 1980. Biology of Canadian weeds. 44. *Amaranthus retroflexus, A. powellii* and *A. hybridus. Can. J. Plant Sci.* 60:1215–1234.

WEAVER, S. and S. WARWICK. 1984. The biology of Canadian weeds. 64. *Datura stramonium. Can. J. Plant Sci.* 64:979–991.

WEAVER, S., V. DIRKS and S. WARWICK. 1985. Variation and climatic adaptation in northern populations of *Datura stramonium. Can. J. Bot.* 63:1303–1308.

WEBB, W. 1975. *Borreria*-trends in control. *Cane Growers Quart. Bull.* 39(2):62–63.

WEBSTER, B. and T. STEEVES. 1958. Morphogenesis in *Pteridium aquilinum*: General morphology and growth habit. *Phytomorphology and Growth Habit* 8:30–41.

WEBSTER, G. 1957. A monographic study of the West Indian species of *Phyllanthus. J. Arnold Arboretum* 38:295–373.

———. 1970. A revision of *Phyllanthus* (**Euphorbiaceae**) in the continental United States. *Brittonia* 22:44–76.

WEDGE, R. and J. BURRIS. 1982. Effects of light and temperature on duckweed photosynthesis. *Aquatic Bot.* 12:133–140.

WEE, Y. 1970. Weed succession observations on arable peat land. *Malayan Forester* 33:63–69.

WEED RESEARCH ORGANIZATION (WRO) (England). 1923–1982. *Annotated Bibliographies on the* Cuscutas. WRO, Long Ashton Research Station, Long Ashton, Bristol BS18-19AF, England. No. 32 covers 1923–1970; No. 146 covers 1979–1982.

———. 1940 onward. *Annotated Bibliographies on the* Orobanches. WRO, Long Ashton Research Station, Long Ashton, Bristol BS18-19AF, England.

WEHMEYER, A. and E. ROSE. 1983. Important indigenous plants used in the transkei as food supplements. *Bothalia* 14:613–615.

WEHNER, D. and T. WATSCHKE. 1981. Heat tolerance of Kentucky bluegrass, perennial ryegrass and annual bluegrass. *Agron. J.* 73:79–84.

WEHRMEISTER, J. 1978. An ecological life history of the pondweed *Potamogeton crispus* in North America. In: M.S. Thesis, Ohio State Univ., Columbus, Ohio. p. 157.

WEHSARG, O. 1918. Die verbreitung und Bekmpfung der Ackerunkrauter in Deutschland. *Arbeitsgemeinschaft der Deutsche Landwirt Gesellschaft* 1:294.

WEIN, K. 1932. Die alteste Einfurungs- und Einburgerungsgeschichte des *Erigeron canadensis. Botanisches Archiv* 34:394–418.

WEINBERGER, P. 1963. On reciprocal influences between barley, rape and various weed species. *Flora Jena* 153:242–281.

WELBANK, P. 1963. A comparison of competitive effects of some common weed species. *Ann. Appl. Biol.* 51:107–125.

WELCH, D. 1984. Studies in the grazing of heather moorland in northeast Scotland: 3. Floristics. *J Appl. Ecol.* 21:209–226.

WELIHINDA, J., G. ARVIDSON, E. GYLFE, B. HELLMAN and E. KARLSSON. 1982. Insulin-releasing activity of the tropical plant *Momordica charantia. Acta Biologica Medica Germanica* 41:1229–1240.

WELKIE, G. and M. CALDWELL. 1970. Leaf anatomy of species in some dicotyledon families as related to the C_3 and C_4 pathways of carbon fixation. *Can. J. Bot.* 48:2135–2146.

WELLER, M. 1975. Studies of cattails in relation to management for marsh wildlife. *Iowa State J. Res.* 49(4):383–412.

WELLER, S. and M. DENTON. 1976. Cytogeographic evidence for the evolution of distyly from tristyly in North America species of *Oxalis,* section. *Ionoxalis. Am. J. Bot.* 63:120–125.

WELLINGTON, P. 1957. Assessment and control of the dissemination of weeds by crop seeds. In: *The biology of weeds*. Ed. J. Harper. Blackwell Scientific Publ., Oxford, England.

WELLINGTON, P. and S. HITCHINGS. 1965. Germination and seedling establishment of blackgrass *Alopecurus myosuroides* Huds. *J. National Inst. Agric. Bot.* 10:262–273.

———. 1966. Seed dormancy and the winter annual habit in blackgrass *Alopecurus myosuroides* Huds. *J. National Inst. Agric. Bot.* 10:628–643.

WELLS, G. 1969. Skeleton weed (*Chondrilla juncea*) in Victorian Mallee: I. Competition with legumes. *Aus. J. Exp. Agric. and Animal Husbandry* 9:521–527.

———. 1970 Skeleton weed (*Chondrilla juncea*) in the Victorian Mallee: II. Effect of legumes on soil fertility, subsequent wheat crop and weed population. *Aus. J. Exp. Agric. and Animal Husbandry* 10:622–629.

———. 1971a. Skeleton weed (*Chondrilla juncea*) in the Victorian Mallee: IV. Effects of fallowing on wheat yield and weed populations. *Aus. J. Exp. Agric. and Animal Husbandry* 11:313–319.

———. 1971b. The ecology and control of skeleton weed (*Chondrilla juncea*) in Australia. *J. Aus. Inst. Agric. Sci.* 37:122–137.

———. 1974. The biology of *Poa annua* and its significance in grasslands. *Herbage Abstr.* 44:385–391.

———. 1979. Annual weed competition in wheat crops: The effect of weed density and applied nitrogen. *Weed Res.* 19:185–191.

WELLS, G. and R. HAGGAR. 1974. Herbage yields of ryegrass swards invaded by *Poa* species. *J. Brit. Grassland Soc.* 29:109–111.

———. 1984. The ingress of *Poa annua* into perennial ryegrass swards. *Grass and Forage Sci.* 39:297–303.

WELTON, F. and J. CARROLL. 1941. *Control of lawn weeds and the renovation of lawns*. Ohio Agric. Exp. Sta., Bull. 619.

WELTY, R. 1977. *Lamium amplexicaule* (henbit): A new host for *Sclerotinia sclerotiorum. Plant Dis. Rep.* 61(6):508–510.

WESSON, G. and P. WAREING. 1967. Light requirements of buried seed. *Nature* 232:600–601.

———. 1969a. The role of light in the germination of naturally occurring populations of buried weed seeds. *J. Exp. Bot.* 20:402–413.

———. 1969b. The induction of light sensitivity in weed seed by burial. *J. Exp. Bot.* 20:414–425.

WESTING, A. 1969. Plants and salt in roadside environments. *Phytopathology* 59:1174–1179.

WESTLAKE, D. 1967. Some effects of low-velocity currents on the metabolism of aquatic macrophytes. *J. Exp. Bot.* 18:187–205.

WETALA, M. 1978. Weed problems and control practices in Uganda. pp. 213–220. *Proc. Weeds and their control in the humid and subhumid tropics.* Conf. Ser. No. IITA, Ibadan.

WETALA, M. and L. SAMBI. 1977. Effect of cutting and burying bulbs on sprouting and early development of *Oxalis latifolia* under two moisture regimes. pp. 233–238. *Proc. 6th Asian-Pacific Weed Sci. Soc. Conf.*

WETHERELL, D. 1969. Phytochrome in cultured wild carrot tissue. I. Synthesis. *Plant Physiol.* 44:1734–1737.

WHATLEY, J. and B. GUNNING. 1981. Chloroplast development in *Azolla* roots. *New Phytologist* 89:129–138.

WHEATLEY, W. 1971. Thistles—prickly problem of pasture improvement. *Agric Gaz. New South Wales* 82:258–261.

WHITE, G., B. WILLINGHAM, W. SKROLA, J. MASSEY, J. HIGGINS, W. CALHOUN, A. DAVIS, D. DOLAN and F. EARLE. 1971. Agronomic evaluation of prospective new crop species. *Econ. Bot.* 25:22–43.

WHITE, J. and J. STRANDBERG. 1978. Early root growth of carrots in organic soil. *J. Am. Soc. Hort. Sci.* 103:344–347.

———. 1979. Physical factors affecting carrot root growth: Water saturation of soil. *J. Am. Soc. Hort. Sci.* 104:414–416.

WHITE, R. 1961. Vessels in roots of *Marsilea quadrifolia*. *Sci.* 133(3458):1073–1074.

———. 1963. Tracheary elements of ferns. II. Morphology of tracheary elements; conclusions. *Am. J. Bot.* 50:514–522.

———. 1979. Experimental investigations of fern sporophyte development. p. 657. In: *Experimental biology of ferns.* Ed. by A. Dyer. Academic Press, N.Y.

WHITEHEAD, C. and C. SWITZER. 1963. The differential response of strains of wild carrot to 2,4–D and related herbicides. *Can. J. Plant Sci.* 43:255–262.

WHITEMAN, P., T. BULL, and J. GLASZIOU. 1963. The physiology of sugar cane. VI Effects of temperature, light, and water on set germination and early growth of *Saccharum* spp. *Australian J. Biol. Sciences* 16:416–428.

WHITING, F., D. YOUNG, A. PHILLIPS, W. MURRO and H. STEVES. 1958. The effects on the odor and flavor of meat from feeding refuse screenings with a high *Thlaspi arvense* content fattening cattle. *Can. J. Animal Sci.* 38:48–52.

WHITNEY, P. 1986. Factors affecting Orobanche seed germination. pp. 42–49. *Proc. Workshop on Biology and Control of Orobanche.* Ed. by S. ter Borg. Wageningen, Netherlands.

WHITNEY, P. and C. CARSTEN. 1981. Chemotropic response of broomrape radicles to host root exudates. *Ann. Bot.* 48:919–921.

WHITTET, J. 1968. *Weeds.* 2nd Ed. New South Wales Dept. Agric., Gov. Printer, Sidney. 487pp.

WHITTIER, D. 1964. The influence of cultural conditions on the induction of apogamy in *Pteridium* gametophytes. *Am. J. Bot.* 51:730–737.

————. 1966. Natural apospory in *Pteridium? Am. Fern J.* 56:61–64.

————. 1971. The value of ferns in an understanding of the alternation of generations. *Bio. Sci.* 21:225–227.

WHITTIER, D. and T. STEEVES. 1960. The induction of apogamy in the bracken fern. *Can. J. Bot.* 38:925–930.

WIDDOWSON, F., A. JOHNSON and A. PENNY. 1980. Multifactorial experimentation on continuous winter wheat grown in sandy clay soil at Saxmundham, Suffolk. *J. Agric. Sci.* 94:155–170.

WIESE, A. and L. BINNING. 1984. Calculating the threshold temperature of development for weeds. *Proc. 39th North Central Weed Control Conf.* 39:106–107.

WIESE, A. and R. DAVIS. 1967. Weed emergence from two soils at various moistures, temperatures and depths. *Weeds* 15:118–121.

WIJK, R. VAN. 1986. Life cycle characteristics of *Potamogeton pectinatus* in relation to control. pp. 375–380. In: *Proc. 7th Int. Symp. Aquatic Weeds* (1986).

————. 1988. Ecological studies on *Potamogeton pectinatus*. I. General characteristics, biomass production, and life cycles under field conditions. *Aquatic Botany* 31:211–258.

WIJNHEIJMER, E., W. BRANDENBURG and S. TER BORG. 1989. Interaction between wild and cultivated carrots (*Daucus carota*) L. in the Netherlands. *Euphytica* 40:147–154.

WILD, H. 1946. Upright star-bur (*Acanthospermum hispidum*) DC. A new method of control. *Rhodesia Agric. J.* 43:585–589.

————. 1961. Harmful aquatic plants in Africa and Madagascar. *Kirkia* 2:1–68.

WILE, I., J. NEIL, G. LUMIS and J. POS. 1978. Production and utilization of aquatic plant compost. *J. Aquat. Plant Mgmt.* 16:24–27.

WILES, T. and D. HAYWARD. 1981. The principles and practice of weed control for no-tillage soybean in southern Brazil using the bipyridyl herbicides. *Trop. Pest Mgt.* 27:388–400.

WILHELM, S. 1954. Deleterious effect of drying on survival of broomrape *Orobanche ramosa* seed in soil. *Plant Dis. Rep.* 38:890–892.

WILHELM, S. and L. BENSON. 1954. Vertical distribution of broomrape seed in tomato field soil. *Plant Dis. Rep.* 38:553–554.

WILKINSON, R. 1963. Effects of light intensity and temperature on the growth of waterstargrass, coontail, and duckweed. *Weed Sci.* 11:287–290.

————. 1964. Effects of red-light intensity on the growth of water star grass, coontail and duckweed. *Weeds* 12:312–313.

————. 1970a. Sicklepod fatty acid response to photoperiod. *Plant Physiol.* 46:463–465.

————. 1970b. Sicklepod leaflet, petiole, stem, and seed total hydrocarbon content. *Bot. Gaz.* 131:281–284.

WILLERDING, U. 1981. Ur und Fruhgeschichtliche sowie mittelalterliche Unkrautfunde in mitteleuropa. *Zeitschrift fur Pflanzenkrankheiten und Pflanzenschutz* 9:65–74.

WILLIAMS, E. 1983. Germinability and enforced dormancy in seeds of species of indigenous grassland. *Ann. Appl. Biol.* 102:557–566.

————. 1985. Long-term effects of fertilizer on the botanical composition and soil seed populations of a permanent grass sward. *Grass and Forage Sci.* 40:479–483.

WILLIAMS, G. 1987. The control of bracken in pastures. *Fourrages* 112:383–397.

WILLIAMS, G. and A. FOLEY. 1976. Seasonal variations in the carbohydrate content of bracken. *Bot. J. Linn. Soc.* 73:87–93.

WILLIAMS, J. 1966. Variation in germination of several *Cirsium* species. *Trop. Ecol.* 7:1–7.

WILLIAMS, W., G. KENNEDY, R. YAMAMOTO, J. THACKER and J. BORDNER. 1980. 2–Tridecanone: A naturally occurring insecticide from tomato, *Lycopersicon hirsutum* f. *glabratum. Sci.* 207:888–889.

WILSON, A. 1981. *Euphorbia heterophylla*: A review of distribution, importance and control. *Trop. Pest Mgt.* 27:32–38.

WILSON, B. 1979. The effect of controlling *Alopecurus myosuroides* Huds. and *Avena fatua* L. individually and together, in mixed infestations on the yield of wheat. *Weed Res.* 19:193–199.

WILSON, B. and G. CUSSANS. 1983. The effect of weeds on yield and quality of winter cereals in the U.K. pp. 121–129. *Proc. 10th Intern. Congr. Plant Protec.*, Brighton, England.

WILSON, B. and K. WRIGHT. 1990. Predicting the growth and competitive effects of annual weeds in wheat. *Weed Res.* 30:201–211.

WILSON, D. 1968. Gorse control at a profit. *Tasmanian J. Agric.* 39:89–92.

WILSON, K. 1957. Extension growth in primary cell walls with special reference to *Elodea canadensis. Ann. Bot.* (N.S.) 21(81):1–11.

WILSON, R. 1980. Dissemination of weed seeds by surface irrigation water in western Nebraska. *Weed Sci.* 28:87–92.

WILSON-JONES, K. 1958. Studies on the weed population of the Sudan Gezira scheme. *Proc. African Weed Control Conf.*: 220–229. Victoria falls, Rhodesia.

WINDHOLZ, M. 1983. *The Merck Index, an encyclopedia of chemicals, drugs, and biologicals.* 10th Ed. Merck and Co. Inc., Rahway, New Jersey.

WIRJAHARDJA, S. and E. NURFILMARASA. 1975. Some autecological aspects of wild rice. pp. 18–32. *Proc. 3rd Indonesia Weed Sci. Conf.*

WIRJAHARDJA, S. and C. PARKER. 1977. Chemical control

of wild and red rice. pp. 316–322. *Proc. 6th Asian-Pacific Weed Sci. Soc. Conf.*

WIRJAHARDJA, S., E. GUHARDJA and J. WIROATMODJO. 1983. Wild rice and its control. *Proc. Weed Control Rice Conf.*, IRRI, Philippines.

WITCOMBE, J. and W. WHITTINGTON. 1972. The effects of selection for reduced dormancy in charlock (*Sinapis arvensis*). *Heredity* 29:37–49.

WITTS, K. 1960. The germination of *Polygonum* species in the field and in the glass-house. *J. Ecol.* 48:215–217.

WOHLGEMUTH, K., G. SCHAMBER, A. MISEK and J. CRENSHAW. 1987. Pigweed is toxic to pigs. *North Dakota Farm Res.* 44:21–22.

WOLEK, J. 1974. Experimental control of flowering in *Spirodela polyrhiza* strain 7401. *Berichte des Geobotanischen Instituts der Eidgenoessischen Technischen Hochschule Stiftung Ruebel Zuerich* 42:163–170.

———. 1979. Competition and allelopathy between *Spirodela polyrhiza* and *Wolffia arrhiza*. *Fragmenta Floristica Geobotan.* (Cracow) 25:281–350.

WOLF, F. 1943. The microbiology of the upper air. *Bull. Torrey Bot. Club* 70:1–14.

WOLF, P., C. HAUFLER, and E. SHEFFIELD. 1988. Maintenance of genetic variation in the clonal weed *Pteridium aquilinum*. *Saas Bull. Biochem. Biotechnol.* 1:46–50.

WOLF, S., C. DEOM, R. BEACHY and W. LUCAS. 1989. Movement protein of tobacco mosaic virus modifies plasmodesmatal size exclusion limit. *Sci.* 246:377–378.

WOLFF, P. 1980. Die Hydrilleae (**Hydrocharitaceae**) in Europa. *Goettinger Floristische Rundbriefe* 14:33–56.

WOLSWINKEL, P. 1974a. Complete inhibition of setting and growth of fruits of *Vicia faba*, resulting from the draining of the phloem system by *Cuscuta* species. *Acta Botanica Neerl.* 23:48–60.

———. 1974b. Enhanced rate of C^{14} solute release to the free space by the phloem of *Vicia faba* stems parasitized by *Cuscuta*. *Acta Botanica Neerl.* 23:177–188.

———. 1975. The active role of the host *Vicia faba* in the transfer of nutrient elements from the phloem to the parasite *Cuscuta*: Metabolically controlled K and Mg release from the free space. *Acta Botanica Neerl.* 24:211–224.

———. 1977. *Physiological aspects of a parasitic relationship. The effect of* Cuscuta *on its host.* Ph.D. Diss., Univ. Utrecht, Netherlands.

WONG, M., W. LAU, S. LI and C. TANG. 1983. Root growth of two grass species on iron ore tailings at elevated levels of manganese, iron and copper. *Environ. Res.* 30:26–33.

WONG, P. 1966. Weed control under partial shade with weedazol, sodium chlorate, and 2,4–D. *Planters Bull., Rubber Res. Inst. Malaya* 87:191–196.

WOO, Y. and E. PUSHPARAJAH. 1971. Weed control in groundnuts, soya beans and maize. pp. 291–296. *Proc. 3rd Asian-Pacific Weed Sci. Soc. Conf.*

WOOD, A., M. ROBERTSON and W. KITTS. 1958. Studies on nutritive value of refuse screening. I. The essential amino acid content of certain weed seeds. *Can. J. Animal Sci.* 38:97–102.

WOODLAND, D., I. BASSETT and C. CROMPTON. 1976. The annual species of stinging nettle in North America. *Can. J. Bot.* 54:374–383.

WOODWELL, G. 1963. The ecological effects of radiation. *Scientific Am.* 208:40–49.

WORSHAM, A., G. KLINGMAN and D. MORELAND. 1962. Promotion of germination of *Striga asiatica* seed cumarin derivatives and effects on seedling development. *Nature* 195:199–201.

WOZAKOWSKA-NATKANIEC, H. 1977. Ecological differentiation of *Lemna minor* and *Spirodela polyrhiza* populations. *Acta Soc. Bot. Pol.* 46:201–230.

WRUCKE, M. and W. ARNOLD. 1982. The long-term influence of reduced tillage on weed and soil factors. pp. 50–51. *Proc. 37th North Central Weed Control Conf.* USA.

WU, L., I. TILL-BOTTRAUD and A. TORRES. 1987. Genetic differentiation in temperature-enforced seed dormancy among golf course populations of *Poa annua* L. *New Phytologist* 107:623–631.

WULFF, R. and M. BRICENO. 1976. Light and temperature interaction in the photocontrol of germination of seeds of *Ludwigia octovalvis*. *Planta* 128:195–199.

WULFF, R. and E. MEDINA. 1969. Germination of seeds in *Jussiaea suffruticosa*. *Plant and Cell Physiol.* 10:503–511.

WULFF, R., I. ARIAS, M. PONCE, and V. MUNOZ. 1972. A bimodal temperature response and effect of light intensity in the photocontrol of germination of seeds in *Jussiaea suffruticosa*. *Planta* (Berlin) 107:369–373.

WYLIE, R. 1904. The morphology of *Elodea canadensis*. *Bot. Gaz.* 37:1–22.

———. 1917. The pollination of *Vallisneria spiralis*. *Bot. Gaz.* 63:135–145.

———. 1921. Some aspects of fertilization of *Vallisneria*. *Am. J. Bot.* 28:169–174.

YAMAMOTO, H. and T. OHBA. 1977. Studies on ecological changes and control of weeds in upland irrigation culture. 3. Effect of soil moisture on dormancy breaking of seeds of principal annual weeds on upland fields. 4. Effect of soil moisture on emergence patterns of principal weeds. *Weed Res. Jap.* 22:29–38.

YAMASUE, Y., Y. FUKUMOTO and K. UEKI. 1983. C_3 and C_4 weeds at three different crop habitats of an experimental farm. pp. 50–59. *Proc. 9th Asian-Pacific Weed Sci. Soc. Conf.*

YASSIN, M. and L. BENDIXEN. 1982. Weeds as hosts of the cotton whitefly *Bemisia tabaci*. *Abstr. 22nd Weed Sci. Soc. of Am. Conf.* No. 211.

YATAZAWA, M. and H. SUSILO. 1980. Development of upper stem nodules in *Aeschynomene indica* under experimental conditions. *Soil Sci. Plant Nutrition* 26:317–319.

YATAZAWA, M. and S. YOSHIDA. 1979. Stems and nodules in *Aeschynomene indica* and their capacity for nitrogen fixation. *Physiol. Plantarum* 45:293–295.

YEO, R. 1964. Life history of common cattail. *Weeds* 12:284–288.

———. 1965. Life history of sago pond weed. *Weeds* 13:314–321.

———. 1966. Yields of propagules of certain aquatic plants. *Weeds* 14:110–113.

———. 1979. Morphological development and germination of dwarf spikerush *Eleocharis coloradoensis*. *Weed Sci.* 27(4):380–385.

———. 1980a. Life history and ecology of dwarf spikerush *Eleocharis coloradoensis*. *Weed Sci.* 28(3):263–272.

———. 1980b. Spikerush may help control weeds. *Calif. Agric.* 34(4):12–13.

———. 1986. Dormancy in slender spikerush seed *Eleocharis acicularis*. *J. Aquat. Plant Mgmt.* 24:11–16.

YEO, R. and R. DOW. 1978. Germination of seed of dwarf spikerush *Eleocharis coloradoensis*. *Weed Sci.* 26(5):425–431.

YEO, R. and W. MCHENRY. 1977. *Hydrilla*, a new noxious aquatic weed in California. *California Agric.* 3(10):4–5.

YEO, R. and J. THURSTON. 1979. Survival of seed and tubers of dwarf spikerush *Eleocharis coloradoensis* after exposure to extreme temperatures. *Weed Sci.* 27(4):434–436.

YEO, R., R. FALK and J. THURSTON. 1984. The morphology of *Hydrilla* (*Hydrilla verticillata* (L.f.) Royle). *J. Aquat. Plant Mgmt.* 22:1–17.

———. 1985. Morphology of slender spikerush seed *Eleocharis acicularis*. *J. Aquat. Plant Mgmt.* 23:83–87.

YEPES, J. 1978. Study of the weed *Cleome gynandra* L. *Revista COMALFI* 5:49–53.

YODA, K., T. KIRA, H. OGAWA and K. HOZUMA. 1963. Intraspecific competition among higher plants. XI. Self thinning in overcrowded pure stands under cultivated and natural conditions. *J. Biol. Osaka City Univ.* 14:107–129.

YOSHIDA, J., Y. KONDO, and R. NAKAMURA. 1979. Ensilage of *Paspalum distichum* and its feeding value. *Scientific Rep. Faculty Agric., Ibaraki Univ.* 27:47–52.

YOSHII, K. and F. VARON DE AGUDELO. 1977. Effects of *Tagetes minuta* y *Crotalaria spectabilis* on the nematode population and subsequent soybean yield. *Fitopatologia* 12:15–19.

YOUNG, D. 1958. *Oxalis* in the British Isles. *Watsonia* 4:51–69.

YOUNG, F. 1986. Russian thistle *Salsola iberica* growth and development in wheat *Triticum aestivum*. *Weed Sci.* 34:901–905.

YOUNG, F. and L. MORROW. 1984. Effect of small grains and crop canopy removal on Russian thistle growth and development. *Proc. 37th Western Soc. Weed Sci. Conf.* 37:164–165.

YOUNG, J. and R. EVANS. 1972. Germination and establishment of *Salsola* in relation to seed bed environment. 1. Temperature, after-ripening, and moisture relations of *Salsola* seeds as determined by laboratory studies. *Agron. J.* 64:214–218.

———. 1973. Mucilaginous seed coats. *Weed Sci.* 21:52–54.

———. 1979. Germination ecology of barbwire Russian thistle. *Abstr. 19th Weed Sci. Soc. Am. Conf.* p. 84.

———. 1985. Russian thistle: The weed that won the west. *Weeds Today* 16:4–7.

YOUNG, J., R. EVANS and R. ECKERT. 1969. Population dynamics of downy brome. *Weed Sci.* 17:20–26.

YOUNG, J., R. EVANS, R. GIFFORD and R. ECKERT. 1970. Germination characteristics of three species of **Cruciferae**. *Weed Sci.* 18:41–48.

YOUNG, J., R. EVANS and R. HAWKES. 1978. Milk thistle *Silybum marianum* seed germination. *Weed Sci.* 26(4):395–398.

YUNCKER, T. 1932. The genus *Cuscuta*. *Torrey Bot. Club Memoirs* 18:113–331.

———. 1935. Insect galls on species of *Cuscuta*. *Proc. Ind. Acad. Sci.* 43:70–71.

ZABKIEWICZ, J. and R. GASKIN. 1978a. Effect of fire on gorse seeds. pp. 47–52. *Proc. 31st New Zealand Weed and Pest Control Conf.*

———. 1978b. Seasonal variation of gorse *Ulex europaeus* surface wax and trichomes. *New Phytol.* 81:367–373.

ZAHNLEY, J. and J. FITCH. 1941. Effect of ensiling on the viability of weed seeds. *Agron. J.* 33:816–822.

ZAHRAN, K. 1982. *Control of parasitic plants (broomrape and dodder) in different crops in Egypt*. Final Tech. Rep., Agric. Res Prog., Public law 480 (USA). Project No. Eg-ARS-15. 53pp.

ZAKI, M. and M. TEWFIK. 1974. Trials on the germination of *Orobanche* seeds (*in vitro*). *Egy. J. Bot.* 17:179–181.

ZANARDI, D. 1962. Possibilities of chemical weed killing in vineyards. *Agric. Vet. Chem.* 3(1):29–30.

ZANDONELLA, P. and M. LECOCQ. 1977. Pollen morphology and mode of pollination among the **Amaranthaceae**. *Pollen et Spores* 19:119–142.

ZAPRZALKA, J. and R. PETERS. 1982. Growth of dandelion as influenced by time and fertility levels. *Proc. 36th Northeastern Weed Sci. Soc. Conf.* 36:29–32.

ZH ELEV, N. 1987. The biological role of exogenic factors in broomrape germination. *Rasteniev'd Nauki* 24:36–43.

ZHOU, B., G. BLASKO and G. CORDELL. 1988. Alternanthin, a glycosylated flavanoid from *Alternanthera philoxeroides*. *Phytochemistry* 27:3633–3636.

ZIMDAHL, R. 1980. *Weed-crop competition: A review*. Intern.

Plant Protection Center, Oregon State Univ., USA. 197pp.

———. 1989. *Weeds and words: The etymology of scientific names of weeds and crops.* Iowa State Univ. Press, Ames, Iowa, USA.

ZIMMERMAN, C. 1962. Autotrophic development of dodder *Cuscuta pentagona* in vitro. *Crop Sci.* 2:449–450.

ZIMMERMAN, J. and M. LECHOWICZ. 1982. Responses to moisture stress in male and female plants of *Rumex acetosella. Oecologia* 53:305–309.

ZOLLINGER, R. and J. KELLS. 1987. Edaphic and environmental factors affecting the growth and development of perennial sowthistle (*Sonchus arvensis*). In: *Proc. North Central Weed Control Conf.* (U.S.) 42:1.

———. 1988. Perennial sowthistle (*Sonchus arvensis* L.) interference in soybean and dry edible beans. In: *Proc. North Central Weed Control Conf.* (U.S.) 43:90.

ZON, J. VAN. 1973. Studies on the biological control of aquatic weeds in the Netherlands. pp. 31–38. *Proc. 3rd Intern. Symp. Bio. Control Weeds.* Montpellier, France.

ZUBERER, R. 1984. Microbial colonization of some duckweeds **Lemnaceae**: Examination by scanning and transmission electron and light microscopy. *Aquatic Bot.* 18:275–285.

ZUTSHI, D. and K. VASS. 1976. Ecology of macrophyte vegetation in Kashmir lakes. *Proc. Regional Seminar Aquatic Weeds Southeast Asia* 1:396. Dr. Junk Publ., The Hague.

ZWANENBURG, B., G. MHEHE, G. LAM, F. DOMMERHOLT and M. KISHIMBA. 1986. The search for new germination stimulants of *Striga. Proc. Workshop on Biology and Control of Orobanche.* Ed. by S. ter Borg. Wageningen, Netherlands.

ZWERGER, P. and K. HURLE. 1986. Changes in viability and germination capacity of weed seeds in soil. *Mededelingen van de Faculteit Landbouwwetenschappen, Rijksuniversiteit, Gent* 51:325–332.

List of Common Weed Names

a-aka-ukikusa	Azolla pinnata: Japan
aarvederkruid	Myriophyllum spicatum: Belgium
abou vel bou-quir	Raphanus raphanistrum: Algeria
abou vel bou-toum	Raphanus raphanistrum: Tunisia
abrazantes	Lamium amplexicaule: Spain
abu efein	Chenopodium murale: Egypt
abu eloffein	Momordica charantia: Sudan
abu qarn	Cleome gynandra: Egypt
abu'oqeila	Paspalum distichum: Egypt
abu-stirt	Hordeum murinum: Lebanon
acacia-acasiahan	Cassia tora: Philippines
acedera	Oxalis latifolia: Colombia, Mexico
	Rumex acetosella: Peru, Venezuela
acedera menor	Rumex acetosella: Spain
acederilla	Oxalis latifolia: Mexico
	Rumex acetosella: Argentina, Mexico, Spain
acetosa minore	Rumex acetosella: Italy
achicoria	Cichorium intybus: Argentina, Chile, Peru, Venezuela
achicoria amarga	Cichorium intybus: Spain
achicoria dulce	Chondrilla juncea: Spain
achicoria juncal	Chondrilla juncea: Spain
achicoria silvestre	Cichorium intybus: Spain, Uruguay
	Taraxacum officinale: Spain
achochilla	Momordica charantia: Ecuador
achyranthes	Achyranthes aspera: Hawaii
Acker Gasedistel	Sonchus arvensis: Germany
Acker-Ehrenpreis	Veronica persica: Germany

Acker-Fuchsschwanzgras	Alopecurus myosuroides: Germany
Acker-Senf	Brassica kaber: Germany
Ackerhellerkraut	Thlaspi arvense: Germany
Ackerrettich	Raphanus raphanistrum: Germany
Ackersaudistel	Sonchus arvensis: Germany
Ackertaschelkraut	Thlaspi arvense: Germany
adaluzia	Veronica persica: Bolivia
adas el-moya	Spirodela polyrhiza: Egypt
adelaarsvaren	Pteridium aquilinum: Belgium
adeus brasil	Euphorbia heterophylla: Brazil
Adlerfarn	Pteridium aquilinum: Germany
ads el-maia	Spirodela polyrhiza: Egypt
aeia morningglory	Ipomoea triloba: Hawaii
afata	Sida rhombifolia: Argentina, Bolivia
afayn	Heliotropium europaeum: Lebanon
afeen	Heliotropium europaeum: Egypt
afein	Heliotropium europaeum: Egypt
aftab parast	Heliotropium europaeum: Iran
agas-moro	Vernonia cinerea: Philippines
ager-raevehale	Alopecurus myosuroides: Denmark
ager-svinemaelk	Sonchus arvensis: Denmark
agerkal	Brassica campestris: Denmark
agersennep	Brassica kaber: Denmark
agosto	Tagetes minuta: Paraguay
ahipody	Setaria glauca: Madagascar
ahitrakely	Polygonum aviculare: Madagascar
ahosuolaheina	Rumex acetosella: Finland
aigret	Marsilea quadrifolia: Spain
ajenjo	Artemisia vulgaris: Venezuela
ajonc	Ulex europaeus: France
ajonc d'Europe	Ulex europaeus: Canada
ak hindiba	Chondrilla juncea: Turkey
akban ndene	Momordica charantia: Nigeria
akendronyaza	Cleome gynandra: Madagascar
akerdylle	Sonchus arvensis: Norway
akerkal	Brassica campestris: Norway, Sweden
akerknaa	Polygonum persicaria: Sweden
akerpilot	Polygonum persicaria: Sweden
akerrattika	Raphanus raphanistrum: Sweden
akerreddik	Raphanus raphanistrum: Norway

akerreverumpe	Alopecurus myosuroides: Norway
akersenap	Brassica kaber: Sweden
akersennep	Brassica kaber: Norway
akersineblom	Senecio vulgaris: Norway
akervortemjolk	Euphorbia helioscopia: Norway
akeyo	Cleome gynandra: Kenya
akkermelkdistel	Sonchus arvensis: Belgium, Netherlands
akreer	Heliotropium europaeum: Iran
akrep otu	Heliotropium europaeum: Turkey
al-dhorbaih	Chenopodium ambrosioides: Saudi Arabia
al-zorbaih	Chenopodium ambrosioides: Saudi Arabia
`alaaq	Potamogeton pectinatus: Egypt
alambrillo	Polygonum aviculare: Mexico
alavangu pillu	Vernonia cinerea: Sri Lanka
albaka	Stachytarpheta jamaicensis: Philippines
alcanache	Paspalum distichum: Portugal
alena	Boerhavia diffusa: Hawaii
aleponoura	Alopecurus myosuroides: Greece
alga di chiana	Vallisneria spiralis: Italy
Algen Farn	Azolla pinnata: Germany
algodaozinho do campo	Asclepias curassavica: Brazil
algodon de seda	Asclepias curassavica: Dominican Republic
algodoncillo	Asclepias curassavica: Colombia, Puerto Rico
aliaga	Ulex europaeus: Argentina
aliaga tojo	Ulex europaeus: Chile
alkekenje	Physalis angulata: Argentina
alligator grass	Alternanthera philoxeroides: United States
alligatorweed	Alternanthera philoxeroides: Australia, New Zealand, United States
almeirao	Cichorium intybus: Portugal
almindelig brandbaeger	Senecio vulgaris: Denmark
almindelig pengeurt	Thlaspi arvense: Denmark
almindelig sumpstra	Eleocharis palustris: Denmark
almorejo glauco	Setaria glauca: Spain
alopecuro	Alopecurus myosuroides: Spain
alotxa	Chondrilla juncea: Spain
alpasotis	Chenopodium ambrosioides: Philippines
alpiste	Brassica campestris: Colombia
altabaca	Conyza canadensis: Spain
amapola	Papaver rhoeas: Colombia, Spain
amapola roja	Papaver rhoeas: Chile

amapola silvestre	Papaver rhoeas: Argentina
amarante a racine rouge	Amaranthus retroflexus: Canada
amarante recourbee	Amaranthus retroflexus: France
amarante reflechie	Amaranthus retroflexus: France
amaranthe reflechie	Amaranthus retroflexus: Tanzania, Tunisia
amaranthe verte	Amaranthus viridis: France
amaranto	Alopecurus myosuroides: Italy
	Amaranthus retroflexus: Italy, Spain
amarella	Artemisia vulgaris: Italy
amargon	Taraxacum officinale: Argentina, Bolivia, Spain
amargosa	Taraxacum officinale: Brazil
amarra-pinto	Boerhavia diffusa: Brazil
amatarika	Amaranthus retroflexus: Madagascar
ambatimadu	Trianthema portulacastrum: India
ambrosia	Chenopodium ambrosioides: Brazil
amendoim bravo	Euphorbia heterophylla: Brazil
	Euphorbia prunifolia: Brazil
American elodea	Elodea canadensis: United States
amerika-oni-azami	Cirsium vulgare: Japan
amor de negro	Acanthospermum hispidum: Brazil
ampalaya	Momordica charantia: Philippines
ampalia	Momordica charantia: Philippines
ampeon prxy	Saccharum spontaneum: Cambodia
Ampfer-knoterich	Polygonum lapathifolium: Germany
Ampferblattriger Knoterich	Polygonum lapathifolium: Germany
ampferblattriger knoterich	Polygonum lapathifolium: Switzerland
anadraisoa	Senecio vulgaris: Madagascar
anakalsotsy	Phyllanthus niruri: Madagascar
anangeaika	Heliotropium europaeum: Madagascar
anasoria	Cleome gynandra: India
anatarika	Drymaria cordata: Madagascar
anatsiriny	Marsilea quadrifolia: Madagascar
anatsonga	Brassica campestris: Madagascar
andadasi	Cassia occidentalis: Philippines
	Cassia tora: Philippines
andhajhara	Achyranthes aspera: India
andi mi	Momordica charantia: Paraguay
andmat	Lemna minor: Norway, Sweden
anganiay	Tridax procumbens: Madagascar
angel's hair	Cuscuta campestris: United States

List of Common Weed Names 1029

anggereman   Ludwigia hyssopifolia: Indonesia
angosacha   Sida rhombifolia: Peru
angud   Achyranthes aspera: Philippines
ankari   Vernonia cinerea: India
ankta   Vernonia cinerea: India
annual bluegrass   Poa annua: Alaska, Canada, Hawaii, Malaysia,
                                  South Africa, United States
annual groundcherry   Physalis angulata: Australia
annual meadowgrass   Poa annua: England, Sri Lanka
annual nettle   Urtica urens: Australia, England
annual poa   Poa annua: Australia, England
ansarina-malhada   Conium maculatum: Portugal
anserine murale   Chenopodium murale: Morocco
antibala   Sida rhombifolia: India
aobiyu   Amaranthus viridis: Japan
aogeito   Amaranthus retroflexus: Japan
apamaranga   Achyranthes aspera: India
apang   Achyranthes aspera: India
apanga   Pteridium aquilinum: Madagascar
apilanvieras   Cuscuta epithymum: Finland
apoi-apoian   Cleome gynandra: Philippines
apple of Peru   Nicandra physalodes: Australia, Hawaii, Kenya,
                                  New Zealand, South Africa, Thailand, United States,
                                  Zimbabwe
apulid   Eleocharis dulcis: Philippines
                               Scirpus maritimus: Philippines
aqrabana   Heliotropium europaeum: Egypt
aquiline   Pteridium aquilinum: France
aquinaldo marrullero   Ipomoea triloba: Cuba
aragan   Najas graminea: Philippines
arai keerai   Marsilea quadrifolia: India
araich   Cassia tora: Bangladesh
arakilioun   Polygonum lapathifolium: Algeria
araktiooun   Polygonum persicaria: Algeria
arareng   Cleome gynandra: Egypt
archucha   Momordica charantia: Colombia
arge   Hordeum murinum: Madagascar
arkuvit hacktamim   Polygonum lapathifolium: Israel
armoedskruid   Conyza canadensis: South Africa
armoise   Artemisia vulgaris: Reunion
armoise vulgaire   Artemisia vulgaris: Canada, France

`arous el-bahr	Ludwigia adscendens: Egypt
arpa	Hordeum murinum: Turkey
arrow-head	Sagittaria sagittifolia: Australia
arrowhead	Sagittaria sagittifolia: England
arrowleaf sida	Sida rhombifolia: United States
arroz colorado	Oryza sativa: Argentina
arroz macho	Oryza sativa: Argentina
arroz preto	Oryza sativa: Brazil
arroz rojo	Oryza sativa: Bolivia, Colombia, Costa Rica, Cuba, Ecuador, Honduras, Mexico, Nicaragua, Panama, Paraguay, Peru, Puerto Rico, Venezuela
arroz vermelho	Oryza sativa: Brazil
artemisa	Artemisia vulgaris: Spain
artemisia	Artemisia vulgaris: Italy
artemisia vulgare	Artemisia vulgaris: Italy
arttorne	Ulex europaeus: Sweden
asb vash	Setaria glauca: Iran
ashnaan	Salsola kali: Egypt
asinan	Paspalum distichum: Indonesia
asphodelus	Asphodelus tenuifolius: United States
assa-er-rai	Polygonum aviculare: Lebanon
assenzio selvatico	Artemisia vulgaris: Italy
Astige Sommerwurz	Orobanche ramosa: Germany
at-hagg	Boerhavia diffusa: Egypt
atac	Amaranthus retroflexus: Argentina
ataco	Amaranthus retroflexus: Argentina
ataco coman	Amaranthus retroflexus: Bolivia
atacu	Amaranthus retroflexus: Spain
atafaris	Datura stramonium: Ethiopia
atik	Boerhavia diffusa: India
aurora	Ipomoea triloba: Philippines
avoadinha	Conyza canadensis: Portugal
aworo ona	Synedrella nodiflora: Nigeria
aya-porotillo	Cassia occidentalis: Colombia
aya-poroto	Cassia occidentalis: Colombia
	Cassia tora: Bolivia
ayam	Trianthema portulacastrum: Philippines
ayapana sauvage	Vernonia cinerea: Mauritius
aysh wa gubn	Raphanus raphanistrum: Lebanon, Saudi Arabia
azdinhas	Rumex acetosella: Portugal
azeda	Rumex acetosella: Brazil

b-aka-ukikusa	Azolla pinnata: Japan	
babadotan	Synedrella nodiflora: Indonesia	
babol	Cardaria draba: Spain	
baboon	Matricaria chamomilla: Iraq	
baboonij	Matricaria chamomilla: Iraq	
babouning	Matricaria chamomilla: Egypt	
babowan	Cleome gynandra: Indonesia	
bachelors buttons	Cichorium intybus: United States	
badisnla	Phyllanthus niruri: India	
bagat-bagat guela	Achyranthes aspera: Philippines	
bagem kremah	Alternanthera sessilis: Indonesia	
bagra	Cleome gynandra: India	
bahamon	Raphanus raphanistrum: Morocco	
baho-baho	Cassia tora: Philippines	
bai hua cai	Cleome gynandra: China	
bajam	Amaranthus viridis: Indonesia	
bajem ajam	Amaranthus viridis: Indonesia	
bajem dempo	Amaranthus viridis: Indonesia	
bakalanga	Drymaria cordata: Philippines	
bakbaka	Paspalum distichum: Philippines	
bakkestjerne	Conyza canadensis: Denmark	
bakkeveronika	Veronica arvensis: Norway	
balabalangutan	Cyperus haspan: Philippines	
balabalanoyan	Cleome gynandra: Philippines	
balakbak	Ludwigia octovalvis: Philippines	
balangot	Typha angustifolia: Philippines	
balao	Nicandra physalodes: Brazil	
balaozinho	Physalis angulata: Brazil	
balatong-aso	Cassia occidentalis: Philippines	
	Cassia tora: Philippines	
balsam apple	Momordica charantia: Hawaii, United States	
balsam pear	Momordica charantia: Australia, Fiji	
balsamina	Momordica charantia: Bolivia, Colombia, Peru	
balsamino	Momordica charantia: Panama	
balsamito	Momordica charantia: El Salvador	
balsamo	Momordica charantia: El Salvador	
bambul otu	Heliotropium europaeum: Turkey	
banar	Cassia occidentalis: India	
banara	Setaria glauca: India	
banari	Setaria glauca: India	

B

banat	Typha angustifolia: Malaysia
banchathail	Passiflora foetida: India
bandera espanola	Asclepias curassavica: Argentina
Banks melastoma	Melastoma malabathricum: United States
banpat	Corchorus olitorius: India
baracklevelu keserufu	Polygonum persicaria: Hungary
barbasco	Polygonum persicaria: Colombia
barbatana	Synedrella nodiflora: Brazil
barbicha-de-alemao	Eragrostis pilosa: Brazil
barbouf	Momordica charantia: Senegal
barda	Typha latifolia: Saudia Arabia
barigaua	Ludwigia hyssopifolia: Philippines
barley grass	Hordeum murinum: New Zealand, United States
barok	Asphodelus tenuifolius: Saudi Arabia
barooga weed	Heliotropium europaeum: Australia
barrilla pinchosa	Salsola kali: Spain
baru china	Artemisia vulgaris: Indonesia
basal-esh sheitan	Asphodelus tenuifolius: Saudi Arabia
basbasot	Sida rhombifolia: Philippines
baseng-baseng	Sida rhombifolia: Philippines
bastardcress	Thlaspi arvense: Canada
basterapplliepie	Nicandra physalodes: South Africa
bataban	Cassia occidentalis: Mexico
batatilla	Ipomoea triloba: Colombia
batbat	Polygonum aviculare: Lebanon, Saudi Arabia
bawang-bawang	Scirpus maritimus: Philippines
bee nettle	Lamium amplexicaule: Lebanon, United States
beguu	Eleocharis dulcis: Indonesia
Beifuss	Artemisia vulgaris: Germany
bejuco	Ipomoea triloba: Argentina
belladona del pobre	Datura stramonium: Dominican Republic, Puerto Rico
benba de negro	Euphorbia heterophylla: Venezuela
bencenuco	Asclepias curassavica: Colombia
bendukasa	Aeschynomene indica: India
beo tam	Spirodela polyrhiza: Vietnam
beo-daw	Azolla pinnata: Vietnam
beo-hoa dan	Azolla pinnata: Vietnam
beo-iau	Azolla pinnata: Vietnam
bereda	Nicandra physalodes: Madagascar
berela	Sida rhombifolia: India

bergsyra	Rumex acetosella: Sweden
beroberoka	Sonchus asper: Madagascar
berro	Cardaria draba: Spain
Berufkraut	Conyza canadensis: Germany
bet-bet	Polygonum lapathifolium: Morocco
beurhoh	Momordica charantia: Senegal
bexiga	Nicandra physalodes: Brazil
bhaji	Alternanthera sessilis: India
	Amaranthus viridis: Trinidad
bhoomyamalaki	Phyllanthus niruri: India
bhukat	Asphodelus tenuifolius: India
bibi-inok	Cyperus brevifolius: Philippines
bicho	Cassia tora: Colombia
bichomacho	Cassia tora: Colombia
bidende pileurt	Polygonum hydropiper: Denmark
biedone	Amaranthus retroflexus: Italy
bielun dziedzierzawa	Datura stramonium: Poland
bijvoet	Artemisia vulgaris: Belgium, Netherlands
bilanamanut	Alternanthera sessilis: Philippines
bilu-bilu	Stachytarpheta jamaicensis: Philippines
bimpolu	Scirpus mucronatus: Indonesia
Binsen Knorpelsata	Chondrilla juncea: Germany
bird rape	Brassica campestris: Australia, Canada
bird's eye speedwell	Veronica persica: Canada
birhni	Oryza sativa: India
bisalyakarmi	Tridax procumbens: India
bishkapra	Trianthema portulacastrum: India
bishkatal	Polygonum hydropiper: India
bishkatali	Polygonum hydropiper: Bangladesh
bishkhopra	Boerhavia diffusa: India
bishop's beard	Heliotropium europaeum: Australia
bitter gourd	Momordica charantia: Fiji
bitter weed	Chenopodium ambrosioides: Jamaica
bittercress	Coronopus didymus: Australia
bitterpilort	Polygonum hydropiper: Sweden
bla busthirse	Setaria glauca: Norway
black pigweed	Trianthema portulacastrum: Australia
black thistle	Cirsium vulgare: Australia
blackgrass	Alopecurus myosuroides: England, New Zealand
blackweed	Elodea canadensis: New Zealand

bladder hibiscus	Hibiscus trionum: Lebanon, South Africa
bladder ketmia	Hibiscus trionum: Australia, United States
blagron skaermaks	Setaria glauca: Denmark
bledo	Amaranthus retroflexus: Argentina, Chile, Spain, Venezuela
	Amaranthus viridis: Dominican Republic, Honduras
bledo manso	Amaranthus viridis: Cuba
bleg pileurt	Polygonum lapathifolium: Denmark
blessed milk-thistle	Silybum marianum: South Africa
blessed thistle	Silybum marianum: Canada, United States
blind nettle	Lamium amplexicaule: United States
blooarfi	Polygonum aviculare: Iceland
blood flower	Asclepias curassavica: Hawaii, Jamaica
blood-stanch	Conyza canadensis: Canada
blookunykra	Potamogeton natans: Iceland
blue daisy	Cichorium intybus: Canada, United States
blue dandelion	Cichorium intybus: United States
blue sailors	Cichorium intybus: Canada, United States
bluinanvolah	Phyllanthus niruri: India
Blutkraut Wegetritt	Polygonum aviculare: Germany
bo xit	Synedrella nodiflora: Vietnam
boanga	Cleome gynandra: Zaire
bobang	Saccharum spontaneum: Philippines
boboan	Cleome gynandra: Indonesia
boejoeng-boejoeng	Vernonia cinerea: Indonesia
boerekers	Thlaspi arvense: Belgium
boerhavia	Boerhavia diffusa: Hawaii, Tanzania
bojure	Vernonia cinerea: Nigeria
bokat	Asphodelus tenuifolius: India
bokti	Daucus carota: Indonesia
bolomaros	Stachytarpheta jamaicensis: Philippines
bolsa mullaca	Physalis angulata: Peru
bolsilla	Phyllanthus niruri: Colombia
bomba	Physalis angulata: El Salvador
bonga-bonga	Alternanthera sessilis: Philippines
boos	Saccharum spontaneum: Egypt
boos el-gezzair	Saccharum spontaneum: Egypt
boos giddawi	Saccharum spontaneum: Egypt
borlitas	Emilia sonchifolia: Colombia
borroneillo	Veronica persica: Spain

borstebladet vandaks	Potamogeton pectinatus: Denmark
borstnate	Potamogeton pectinatus: Sweden
borsus keserufu	Polygonum hydropiper: Hungary
bosbrandnetel	Urtica urens: South Africa
botao de ouro	Ranunculus repens: Brazil
	Synedrella nodiflora: Brazil
boton de oro	Ranunculus repens: Argentina, Chile, Spain
boton de oro rastrero	Ranunculus repens: Spain
botrice	Chenopodium ambrosioides: Mauritius
bouton d'or	Ranunculus repens: France
bracken	Pteridium aquilinum: Australia, Canada, England, New Zealand, United States
bracken fern	Pteridium aquilinum: Hawaii
braende naelde	Urtica urens: Denmark
branched broomrape	Orobanche ramosa: Lebanon, South Africa, United States
brannassala	Urtica urens: Sweden
Brazil tea	Stachytarpheta jamaicensis: Philippines
bred-kaveldun	Typha latifolia: Sweden
bredbladet dunhammer	Typha latifolia: Denmark
brede caya	Cleome gynandra: Mauritius
brede chinois	Artemisia vulgaris: Mauritius
brede emballages	Alternanthera sessilis: Mauritius
brede malabar	Amaranthus viridis: Mauritius
brede waterpest	Elodea canadensis: Netherlands
bredo	Amaranthus retroflexus: Brazil
	Amaranthus viridis: Brazil
bredo blanco	Amaranthus viridis: Mexico
Breitblattriger Rohrkolben	Typha latifolia: Germany
Breitblattriges Schilf	Typha latifolia: Germany
breitt dunkjevle	Typha latifolia: Norway
brenninetla	Urtica urens: Iceland
breskova dresen	Polygonum persicaria: Yugoslavia
bristlegrass	Setaria geniculata: Barbados, New Zealand, Trinidad
	Setaria glauca: Lebanon
bristly starbur	Acanthospermum hispidum: United States
broad-leaved pondweed	Potamogeton natans: England
brocha	Emilia sonchifolia: Brazil
broom weed	Sida rhombifolia: Trinidad
brosse melkdistel	Sonchus asper: Netherlands
brumstik	Sida rhombifolia: New Guinea

brusca	Cassia occidentalis: Venezuela
brusca cimarrona	Cassia tora: Dominican Republic
brusca hembra	Cassia tora: Dominican Republic
brusca macho	Cassia occidentalis: Dominican Republic
bucho-de-ra'	Physalis angulata: Brazil
buckbush	Salsola kali: Australia
buenvaron	Senecio vulgaris: Spain
bugang	Saccharum spontaneum: Philippines
bujung-bujung	Vernonia cinerea: Indonesia
bulabod	Vernonia cinerea: Philippines
bulka	Papaver rhoeas: Yugoslavia
bull thistle	Cirsium vulgare: Australia, Canada, England, Hawaii, United States
	Silybum marianum: Australia
bulrush	Typha angustifolia: Australia, Fiji
	Typha latifolia: Australia
bulunakuta	Stachytarpheta jamaicensis: Sri Lanka
burning nettle	Urtica urens: United States
burot	Artemisia vulgaris: Norway
bush stinging nettle	Urtica urens: South Africa
bushy pondweed	Najas marina: United States
	Potamogeton pectinatus: United States
buslig	Scirpus maritimus: Philippines
bust-tjonnaks	Potamogeton pectinatus: Norway
butter weed	Conyza canadensis: United States
butterfly weed	Asclepias curassavica: Hawaii
butterweed	Conyza canadensis: Canada
buy	Poa annua: Turkey
buyangsamalam	Ludwigia octovalvis: Malaysia
bylica pospolita	Artemisia vulgaris: Poland
caa-ruru	Amaranthus retroflexus: Argentina
caatai	Polygonum hydropiper: Paraguay
cabelo de cao	Poa annua: Portugal
cabelos	Cuscuta epithymum: Portugal
cabeza de arricra	Phyllanthus niruri: Mexico
cacadean	Ludwigia hyssopifolia: Indonesia
cadillo chichoborugo	Achyranthes aspera: Colombia
cadillo chisaca	Tridax procumbens: Colombia
cadillo de mazorca	Achyranthes aspera: Colombia
cadillo lagana	Boerhavia erecta: Colombia
cafe cimarron	Cassia occidentalis: Argentina

C

cafe de bonpland	Cassia occidentalis: Argentina, Colombia
cafe do diablo	Euphorbia heterophylla: Brazil
cafe do Paraquay	Cassia occidentalis: Brazil
cafe negro	Cassia occidentalis: Brazil
cafecillo	Cassia occidentalis: Argentina, Bolivia, Colombia, Paraguay
caguazo	Passiflora foetida: Dominican Republic
cajon del diablo	Datura stramonium: Bolivia
calabacita	Momordica charantia: Paraguay
calachin	Coronopus didymus: Argentina
calaica	Momordica charantia: Honduras
calavo cimarron	Ludwigia octovalvis: Peru
calderugia	Senecio vulgaris: Italy
caledonia	Chenopodium murale: Dominican Republic
calerona	Asclepias curassavica: Mexico
camalote	Alternanthera philoxeroides: Argentina
camapu	Physalis angulata: Brazil
camaru	Physalis angulata: Brazil
caminadora	Polygonum aviculare: Colombia
camomila	Matricaria chamomilla: Spain
camomila dos alemaes	Matricaria chamomilla: Brazil
camomila vulgar	Matricaria chamomilla: Brazil
camomilla	Matricaria chamomilla: Italy
camomille	Matricaria chamomilla: Tunisia
camomille echte kamille	Matricaria chamomilla: Belgium
camomille ordinaire	Matricaria chamomilla: France
campainha	Ipomoea triloba: Brazil
campanilla	Ipomoea triloba: Colombia, El Salvador, Honduras, Panama
cana uba	Saccharum spontaneum: Venezuela
Canada fleabane	Conyza canadensis: Austria, Canada, Hawaii, India, Iraq, Trinidad
Canada waterweed	Elodea canadensis: Canada
Canadian fleabane	Conyza canadensis: England, Jamaica, New Zealand
Canadian pondweed	Elodea canadensis: Australia, England, New Zealand
canchaagua	Veronica persica: Argentina
canem bord	Conyza canadensis: Spain
canne sauvage	Saccharum spontaneum: Mauritania
capa de reina	Fumaria officinalis: Spain
capa rosa	Lemna minor: Brazil
capellanes	Cardaria draba: Spain

capim da praia	Paspalum distichum: Brazil
capim de uma so cabeca	Cyperus brevifolius: Brazil
capim pe de galinah	Poa annua: Brazil
capim-barbicha-de-alemao	Eragrostis pilosa: Brazil
capin atana	Eragrostis pilosa: Brazil
capin panasco	Eragrostis pilosa: Brazil
capitao de sala	Asclepias curassavica: Brazil
capomille	Matricaria chamomilla: Italy
capuli cimarron	Nicandra physalodes: Bolivia, Peru
	Physalis angulata: Peru
capuli de la costa	Nicandra physalodes: Peru
carcho	Carduus pycnocephalus: Chile
cardaria	Cardaria draba: Chile
cardilla	Carduus pycnocephalus: Chile
cardimuelle	Sonchus asper: Spain
cardinche	Sonchus asper: Spain
cardito	Carduus pycnocephalus: Argentina
cardo	Carduus nutans: Argentina
	Cirsium vulgare: Chile
	Sonchus asper: Uruguay
cardo almizclero	Carduus nutans: Spain
cardo asinino	Cirsium vulgare: Italy
cardo asnal	Silybum marianum: Argentina, Uruguay
cardo blanco	Silybum marianum: Argentina, Chile, Colombia
cardo borriquero	Silybum marianum: Spain
cardo burro	Silybum marianum: Uruguay
cardo crespo	Carduus pycnocephalus: Argentina, Uruguay
cardo de banado	Carduus nutans: Argentina
cardo de clavero	Carduus pycnocephalus: Spain
cardo de Santa Maria	Silybum marianum: Portugal
cardo del caballo	Carduus nutans: Argentina
cardo del diablo	Salsola kali: Argentina
cardo della Madonna	Silybum marianum: Italy
cardo gallofer	Silybum marianum: Spain
cardo lanceolado	Cirsium vulgare: Spain
cardo lechero	Silybum marianum: Argentina
cardo leiteiro	Silybum marianum: Portugal
cardo mariano	Silybum marianum: Argentina
cardo Mariano	Silybum marianum: Italy, Spain
cardo menchado	Silybum marianum: Chile
cardo morto	Senecio vulgaris: Portugal

cardo negro	Carduus nutans: Argentina
	Cirsium vulgare: Argentina, Uruguay
cardo pendiente	Cardaria draba: Argentina
	Carduus nutans: Argentina
cardo rojo	Carduus nutans: Spain
cardo rosso	Carduus nutans: Italy
cardo ruso	Carduus nutans: Uruguay
	Salsola kali: Argentina, Chile
cardo russo	Chenopodium murale: Mexico
cardo santo	Silybum marianum: Chile
carilla	Momordica charantia: Barbados, Trinidad
carot	Daucus carota: Cambodia
carota	Daucus carota: Italy
carota salvatica	Daucus carota: Italy
carotte sauvage	Daucus carota: Belgium, Canada, France, Mauritius, Tunisia
carrapichno	Acanthospermum hispidum: Colombia
carrapicho de brejo	Alternanthera philoxeroides: Brazil
carrapicho de carneiro	Acanthospermum hispidum: Brazil
carraspique	Thlaspi arvense: Argentina, Spain
carrot	Daucus carota: Australia
carrot weed	Coronopus didymus: Australia
carry me seed	Phyllanthus niruri: Jamaica
carura aspero	Amaranthus retroflexus: Brazil
caruru	Amaranthus retroflexus: Brazil
caruru bredo verde	Amaranthus viridis: Brazil
caruru comun	Amaranthus viridis: Brazil
caruru gigante	Amaranthus retroflexus: Brazil
caruru verde	Amaranthus viridis: Brazil
carvalhas	Potamogeton crispus: Portugal
casse-puante	Cassia occidentalis: Mauritius
cassepuante	Cassia tora: Mauritius
castanho	Scirpus mucronatus: Portugal
cat's tail grass	Setaria pallide-fusca: Fiji
catapanza	Passiflora foetida: Nicaragua
caterpillar weed	Heliotropium europaeum: Australia
cattail	Typha latifolia: Canada
cay-nan	Eleocharis dulcis: Indonesia
cebada ratonera	Hordeum murinum: Spain
cebadilla	Hordeum murinum: Chile, Spain
	Poa annua: Spain

cecendet	Physalis angulata: Indonesia
cemtinodia	Polygonum aviculare: Portugal
cenizo	Chenopodium murale: Spain, Venezuela
cenoura	Daucus carota: Portugal
cenoura brava	Daucus carota: Portugal
cenoura selvagem	Daucus carota: Brazil
centinoda	Polygonum aviculare: Italy
centinode	Polygonum aviculare: France
ceplukan	Physalis angulata: Indonesia
ceplukan blunsun	Passiflora foetida: Indonesia
cerasea	Momordica charantia: Jamaica
cerasee bush	Momordica charantia: Trinidad
cerassea	Momordica charantia: Barbados
cerbatana	Synedrella nodiflora: Colombia, Cuba, Puerto Rico
cerraja	Sonchus arvensis: Spain
	Sonchus asper: Spain
cerraja arvense	Sonchus arvensis: Spain
cerraja aspera	Sonchus asper: Colombia
cerraja brava	Sonchus asper: Argentina
cerraja comun	Sonchus asper: Spain
cerraja macho	Sonchus asper: Peru
cetim	Emilia sonchifolia: Philippines
cevada dos ratos	Hordeum murinum: Portugal
chaff-flow	Achyranthes aspera: Australia
chak krahan	Azolla pinnata: Cambodia
chak pos kra bey	Azolla pinnata: Cambodia
chakavat	Cassia tora: India
chakramarda	Cassia tora: India
chakunda panevartakla	Cassia tora: India
chali thuga	Cyperus haspan: India
chamico	Datura stramonium: Bolivia, Colombia, Cuba, Peru, Puerto Rico
chamico azul	Datura stramonium: Chile
chamico grande	Datura stramonium: Argentina
chamizo	Salsola kali: Mexico
champang michel	Achyranthes aspera: India
chanal	Corchorus olitorius: India
chanchi	Alternanthera philoxeroides: India
	Alternanthera sessilis: India
chantol phnom	Marsilea quadrifolia: Cambodia
chao-soo-ho	Poa annua: Taiwan

chardal hasadeh	Brassica kaber: Israel
chardon a tetes denses	Carduus pycnocephalus: Morocco
chardon a trochets	Carduus pycnocephalus: France
chardon lanceole	Cirsium vulgare: France
chardon Marie	Silybum marianum: France
chardon nu	Carduus nutans: France
chardon penche	Carduus nutans: Canada, France
chardon vulgaire	Cirsium vulgare: Canada
charlock	Brassica campestris: Kenya
	Brassica kaber: Australia, England, Greece, Iraq, Lebanon, New Zealand
	Raphanus raphanistrum: Canada, England
chaulai	Amaranthus viridis: India
chavel chino	Emilia sonchifolia: Cuba
chechra	Scirpus mucronatus: Bangladesh
chenopode des murs	Chenopodium murale: France
chenopode ambroisine	Chenopodium ambrosioides: France
chepica	Paspalum distichum: Chile
chicharillo	Drymaria cordata: Venezuela
chichitoun	Achyranthes aspera: Micronesia
chickweed	Drymaria cordata: Trinidad
chicoree	Cichorium intybus: France
chicoree amere	Cichorium intybus: France, Morocco
chicoree sauvage	Cichorium intybus: Canada, France
chicoria	Cichorium intybus: Spain
	Taraxacum officinale: Argentina, Colombia
chicoria do cafe	Cichorium intybus: Portugal
chicory	Cichorium intybus: Australia, Canada, England, Greece, Iraq, Lebanon, New Zealand, South Africa, United States
chil chil	Tagetes minuta: Argentina
chilaka	Amaranthus viridis: India
chilena	Setaria geniculata: Peru
chileperro	Polygonum persicaria: Guatemala
chilicua	Setaria geniculata: Peru
chilillo	Polygonum aviculare: Argentina
chilinchil	Cassia tora: Colombia
chillo	Polygonum hydropiper: Mexico
	Polygonum persicaria: Mexico
chin-se-gou-wei-ysao	Setaria glauca: Taiwan
chinchila	Tagetes minuta: Brazil

chinchilla	Tagetes minuta: Argentina
chinese arrowhead	Sagittaria sagittifolia: United States
Chinese lantern	Nicandra physalodes: Kenya, Tanzania
Chinese waterchestnut	Eleocharis dulcis: United States
chinytngsat	Cassia occidentalis: Indonesia
chiori	Amaranthus retroflexus: Bolivia
chiquichique	Cassia tora: Venezuela
chirchra	Achyranthes aspera: India
chiria-ka-dana	Setaria glauca: Pakistan
chischina	Drymaria cordata: El Salvador
chnamat	Amaranthus viridis: India
choeug bangkong	Alternanthera sessilis: Cambodia
chohwa	Datura stramonium: Rhodesia
chondrilla	Chondrilla juncea: Argentina, Lebanon
chondrille a tige de Jone	Chondrilla juncea: France
chondrille effilee	Chondrilla juncea: France
chotopana	Lemna minor: India
chow roi bhajee	Amaranthus viridis: Trinidad
chrysantheme des moissons	Chrysanthemum leucanthemum: France
chual	Chenopodium murale: Mexico
chuchapitos	Lamium amplexicaule: Portugal
chum bao	Passiflora foetida: Vietnam
chum het tet	Cassia occidentalis: Thailand
chumhetthai	Cassia tora: Thailand
chung-nin	Eleocharis palustris: China
churristate	Ipomoea triloba: Costa Rica
chut mu	Scirpus mucronatus: Thailand
cichorei	Cichorium intybus: Belgium
Cichorienwegwarte	Cichorium intybus: Germany
Cichorienwurzel	Cichorium intybus: Germany
cicoria	Cichorium intybus: Italy
cicoria selvatica	Cichorium intybus: Italy
cicuta	Conium maculatum: Argentina, Brazil, Chile, Colombia, Venezuela
cicuta da europa	Conium maculatum: Brazil
cicuta maggiore	Conium maculatum: Italy
cicuta negra	Conium maculatum: Uruguay
cien nudos	Polygonum aviculare: Argentina, Belgium, Colombia, Spain
cienta	Conium maculatum: Argentina
cigue	Conium maculatum: Brazil

cigue maculee	Conium maculatum: Canada
cikorie	Cichorium intybus: Denmark
cinco-cinco	Cleome gynandra: Philippines
cineraria	Senecio vulgaris: Colombia
citaco	Amaranthus viridis: Argentina
cizana	Rumex acetosella: Venezuela
clavellinas	Ludwigia octovalvis: Cuba
clavito	Ludwigia adscendens: Colombia
clavo de agua	Ludwigia adscendens: Colombia
clavo silvestre	Ludwigia octovalvis: Peru
clover broomrape	Orobanche minor: South Africa, United States
clover dodder	Cuscuta epithymum: Canada, New Zealand, United States
co chua le	Emilia sonchifolia: Vietnam
co nen	Typha angustifolia: Vietnam
co-nan	Eleocharis dulcis: Indonesia
coat bottoms	Tridax procumbens: Malaysia
coban degnegi	Polygonum aviculare: Turkey
cocola	Cardaria draba: Italy
coffee senna	Cassia occidentalis: Australia, Hawaii, New Caledonia, United States
coffee weed	Cichorium intybus: Canada
coffee-weed	Cichorium intybus: Iraq, Lebanon, United States
cok senelik yabani tere	Cardaria draba: Turkey
cola de rata	Alopecurus myosuroides: Spain
cola de zorra	Alopecurus myosuroides: Spain
	Conyza canadensis: Mexico
cola de zorra amarilla	Setaria glauca: Mexico
cola de zorro	Setaria geniculata: Argentina, Bolivia, Paraguay, Uruguay
	Setaria glauca: Colombia
cola de zorro amarilla	Setaria glauca: Argentina
cola de zorro patagonica	Hordeum murinum: Argentina
colher de folha larga	Potamogeton natans: Portugal
colombiana	Boerhavia erecta: Colombia
colomina	Fumaria officinalis: Spain
coloradilla	Polygonum aviculare: Ecuador
colt's tail	Conyza canadensis: Canada
colza	Brassica campestris: Brazil, Mexico, Uruguay
comida de murcielago	Cassia tora: El Salvador
common amaranth	Amaranthus retroflexus: England

common broomrape	Orobanche minor: England
common cattail	Typha latifolia: United States
common dandelion	Taraxacum officinale: South Africa, United States
common dodder	Cuscuta campestris: United States
common duckweed	Lemna minor: Australia, Canada, England, United States
common field speedwell	Veronica persica: England
common fumitory	Fumaria officinalis: Australia
common gorse	Ulex europaeus: England
common groundsel	Senecio vulgaris: Canada, Lebanon, United States
common poppy	Papaver rhoeas: England
common sida	Sida rhombifolia: Australia
common spike-rush	Eleocharis palustris: England
common thorn apple	Datura stramonium: South Africa
common vernonia	Vernonia cinerea: Malaysia
conejitos	Fumaria officinalis: Spain
	Lamium amplexicaule: Spain
consumption weed	Emilia sonchifolia: Trinidad
coora	Tagetes minuta: Brazil
copal	Euphorbia heterophylla: Guatemala
coquelicot	Papaver rhoeas: Belgium, France, Morocco, Tunisia
corazon de Maria	Euphorbia heterophylla: Cuba
corda-de-viola	Ipomoea triloba: Brazil
coreggiola	Polygonum aviculare: Italy
corena	Ulex europaeus: Chile
corn poppy	Papaver rhoeas: Lebanon, United States
corn sowthistle	Sonchus arvensis: England
corn speedwell	Veronica arvensis: Canada, United States
coronope pinnatifide	Coronopus didymus: France
corralera	Chenopodium murale: Dominican Republic
corredora	Polygonum aviculare: Guatemala
correguela	Polygonum aviculare: Paraguay
correguela de los caminos	Polygonum aviculare: Spain
corriola	Ipomoea triloba: Brazil
Corsican thistle	Carduus pycnocephalus: England, South Africa
cortadera	Cyperus brevifolius: Cuba
coryla vine	Momordica charantia: British Guiana
cosy pilla	Digitaria longiflora: Sri Lanka
cota-buona	Chrysanthemum leucanthemum: Italy
couch paspalum	Paspalum distichum: South Africa
cranson dravier	Cardaria draba: Canada, France

cravo de defunto	Tagetes minuta: Brazil
creeping buttercup	Ranunculus repens: Australia, Canada, England, Ireland, New Zealand, United States
creeping spiderling	Boerhavia diffusa: United States
creeping spikerush	Eleocharis palustris: United States
creeping swamp	Ipomoea aquatica: Hawaii
creeping waterprimrose	Ludwigia adscendens: United States
cresione selvatico	Ranunculus repens: Italy
crespigno spinoso	Sonchus asper: Italy
crespillo	Pteridium aquilinum: El Salvador
crespione comune	Sonchus arvensis: Italy
crespione dei campi	Sonchus arvensis: Italy
cristas	Polygonum persicaria: Spain
cruz de malta	Ludwigia octovalvis: Brazil
cuajrilla	Acanthospermum hispidum: Argentina, Colombia
Cuba jute	Sida rhombifolia: Hawaii
culantrillo	Ludwigia octovalvis: Dominican Republic
cumbungi	Typha angustifolia: Australia
cunde amor	Momordica charantia: Mexico
cunde amor grande	Momordica charantia: Mexico
cundeamor	Momordica charantia: Cuba, Dominican Republic, Puerto Rico, Venezuela
cupid's paintbrush	Emilia sonchifolia: Jamaica, Trinidad
cupid's shaving brush	Emilia sonchifolia: Malaysia, Trinidad
cuquta maior	Conium maculatum: Brazil
curled pondweed	Potamogeton crispus: England, New Zealand
curly pondweed	Potamogeton crispus: Australia
curly-leaved pondweed	Potamogeton crispus: Canada
curlyleaf pondweed	Potamogeton crispus: United States
cuscuta	Cuscuta epithymum: Argentina
cuscuta del trifoglio	Cuscuta epithymum: Italy
cuscuta du thym	Cuscuta epithymum: Canada
cuscute de champs	Cuscuta campestris: Canada, France, Morocco
cuscute du trefle	Cuscuta epithymum: France
cutleaf groundcherry	Physalis angulata: United States
cykoria podroznik	Cichorium intybus: Poland
daddagu	Momordica charantia: Nigeria
dafira	Digitaria velutina: Egypt
dagat	Paspalum distichum: Philippines
daisy	Conyza canadensis: Jamaica
dalbattu	Passiflora foetida: Sri Lanka

D

dan-gywe	Cassia tora: Burma
dandelion	Taraxacum officinale: Australia, Canada, Fiji, Hawaii, New Zealand
danghet	Cassia tora: Cambodia
dao koa cao	Achyranthes aspera: China
daon tolod	Alternanthera sessilis: Indonesia
datoura	Datura stramonium: Egypt
datura	Datura stramonium: Fiji, Puerto Rico, Saudi Arabia
datura stramoine	Datura stramonium: France
daturah	Datura stramonium: Lebanon
dauco marino	Daucus carota: Italy
daucus carotte	Daucus carota: France
dead nettle	Lamium amplexicaule: Australia, Iran, Lebanon
dead weed	Conyza canadensis: Jamaica
deil el-faar	Setaria glauca: Egypt
delgiyu	Sonchus asper: Indonesia
demo	Ipomoea aquatica: Nigeria
deniruve	Typha angustifolia: Fiji
denisoqe	Typha angustifolia: Fiji
denjiso	Marsilea quadrifolia: Japan
dent-de-lion	Taraxacum officinale: France
dente de leao	Taraxacum officinale: Brazil
dente di leone	Taraxacum officinale: Italy
dente-de-leao	Taraxacum officinale: Portugal
deshollinador	Setaria geniculata: Puerto Rico
devil's gut	Cuscuta epithymum: New Zealand
devil's horsewhip	Achyranthes aspera: Kenya, Uganda, Zimbabwe
devil's trumpet	Datura stramonium: Jamaica
deydahaan	Papaver rhoeas: Egypt
dhatura	Datura stramonium: India
dhimdo	Amaranthus viridis: India
dhutura	Datura stramonium: Bangladesh
diente de leon	Taraxacum officinale: Argentina, Chile, Colombia, Ecuador, Mexico, Peru, Spain, Uruguay
dijotang kuda	Synedrella nodiflora: Indonesia
dikenli soda otu	Salsola kali: Turkey
dimmjaca	Fumaria officinalis: Yugoslavia
djampang piit	Digitaria longiflora: Indonesia
djawi rowo	Emilia sonchifolia: Indonesia
djombang	Emilia sonchifolia: Indonesia

dodder	Cuscuta campestris: Australia
	Cuscuta epithymum: England
dognettle	Urtica urens: Canada
dokot-dokot	Achyranthes aspera: Philippines
doku-ninjin	Conium maculatum: Japan
dolle kervel	Conium maculatum: Belgium
dombo	Achyranthes aspera: Zimbabwe
door weed	Polygonum aviculare: Lebanon
doornappel	Datura stramonium: Belgium, Netherlands
dormidera	Cassia tora: Puerto Rico
Dornige Gansedistel	Sonchus asper: Germany
Dornige Saudistel	Sonchus asper: Germany
drijfblad	Marsilea quadrifolia: Netherlands
drijvend fonteinkruid	Potamogeton natans: Belgium
drimaria	Drymaria cordata: Puerto Rico
drug fumitory	Fumaria officinalis: South Africa
drymaria	Drymaria cordata: Hawaii
dubbay	Cuscuta campestris: Saudi Arabia
duckweed	Lemna minor: Hawaii, New Zealand, South Africa
duda	Cassia occidentalis: Philippines
duist	Alopecurus myosuroides: Belgium, Netherlands
duivekerval	Fumaria officinalis: Netherlands
duivekervel	Fumaria officinalis: Belgium
duivelsnaaigaren	Cuscuta epithymum: Netherlands
dukhain	Setaria glauca: Iraq
dungurachirombo	Chenopodium ambrosioides: Rhodesia
duraznillo	Polygonum lapathifolium: Argentina, Chile, Spain
	Polygonum persicaria: Chile, Spain
duraznillo de agua	Ludwigia adscendens: Argentina
duskamarant	Amaranthus retroflexus: Norway
duvar arpasi	Hordeum murinum: Turkey
dvornik oputina	Polygonum aviculare: Yugoslavia
dvornik papreni	Polygonum hydropiper: Yugoslavia
dvornik pticji	Polygonum aviculare: Yugoslavia
dvornik tankoklasni	Polygonum hydropiper: Yugoslavia
dvornik veliki	Polygonum lapathifolium: Yugoslavia
	Polygonum persicaria: Yugoslavia
eagle fern	Pteridium aquilinum: Canada
eastern bracken	Pteridium aquilinum: Canada
ebimo	Potamogeton crispus: Japan

E

ebisu-gusa	Cassia tora: Taiwan
ebisugusa	Cassia tora: Japan
Echte Kamille	Matricaria chamomilla: Germany
echte kamille	Matricaria chamomilla: Netherlands
Echter Beifuss	Artemisia vulgaris: Germany
Echter Erdrauch	Fumaria officinalis: Germany
ederella	Veronica arvensis: Italy
eelgrass	Vallisneria spiralis: New Zealand, United States
eelweed	Vallisneria spiralis: Australia, England
eendekroos	Lemna minor: South Africa
eenjarige blougras	Poa annua: South Africa
egela	Euphorbia heterophylla: Nigeria
eilaab	Digitaria velutina: Egypt
Einjahrige Rispe	Poa annua: Germany
Einjahriges Rispengras	Poa annua: Germany, Switzerland
einstape	Pteridium aquilinum: Norway
ejirin	Momordica charantia: Nigeria
ejote de inviero	Cassia tora: Guatemala
ejotil	Cassia tora: Guatemala
ekiabulo	Tagetes minuta: Angola
ekor andjing	Setaria glauca: Indonesia
eliotropio	Heliotropium europaeum: Italy
elodea	Elodea canadensis: Argentina, Australia, Puerto Rico
elodee du Canada	Elodea canadensis: Canada, France
emilia	Emilia sonchifolia: Australia
enaarig rapgraes	Poa annua: Denmark
enceng-enceng	Cleome gynandra: Indonesia
enea	Typha angustifolia: Chile, Colombia, Dominican Republic, Honduras, Venezuela
	Typha latifolia: Colombia, Spain, Venezuela
eneas	Typha angustifolia: Puerto Rico
enigi	Alternanthera sessilis: Nigeria
enoletna latovka	Poa annua: Yugoslavia
enredadera	Ipomoea triloba: Argentina
ensalada de ranas	Ranunculus repens: Argentina
epasote	Chenopodium ambrosioides: Dominican Republic
epazote	Chenopodium ambrosioides: Mexico
epitimo	Cuscuta epithymum: Spain
erba calderina	Senecio vulgaris: Italy
erba calenzola	Euphorbia helioscopia: Italy
erba codina	Alopecurus myosuroides: Italy

erba kali	Salsola kali: Italy
erba nocca	Scirpus maritimus: Italy
erba pepe	Polygonum hydropiper: Italy
erba ruota	Lamium amplexicaule: Italy
erba saetta	Sagittaria sagittifolia: Italy
erba storna	Thlaspi arvense: Italy
erbe di San Giovanni	Artemisia vulgaris: Italy
erbe nocca	Scirpus maritimus: Spain
erect boerhavia	Boerhavia erecta: South Africa
erect spiderling	Boerhavia erecta: United States
erigeron du Canada	Conyza canadensis: Tunisia
erispela	Boerhavia diffusa: Guatemala
erva belida	Ranunculus repens: Portugal
erva das verrugas	Heliotropium europaeum: Portugal
erva de bicho	Polygonum persicaria: Brazil
erva de jacare	Alternanthera philoxeroides: Brazil
erva de lavaderia	Momordica charantia: Brazil
erva de paina	Asclepias curassavica: Brazil
erva de pato	Spirodela polyrhiza: Brazil
erva de Santa Maria	Chenopodium ambrosioides: Brazil
erva de touro	Tridax procumbens: Brazil
erva do espeto	Scirpus mucronatus: Portugal
erva fome	Cardaria draba: Portugal
erva formigueira	Chenopodium ambrosioides: Portugal
erva muda	Polygonum aviculare: Portugal
erva pessegueira	Polygonum persicaria: Portugal
erva pomba rola	Chenopodium ambrosioides: Brazil
erva pombinha	Phyllanthus niruri: Brazil
erva tosto	Boerhavia diffusa: Brazil
erva-azeda	Rumex acetosella: Portugal
erva-de-fogo	Artemisia vulgaris: Portugal
erva-pessegueira-bastarda	Polygonum lapathifolium: Portugal
erva-toira-menor	Orobanche minor: Portugal
erva-toira-ramosa	Orobanche ramosa: Portugal
escoba	Sida rhombifolia: Argentina, Colombia, Honduras
escoba babosa	Sida rhombifolia: Venezuela
escoba blanca	Sida rhombifolia: Venezuela
escoba dura	Sida rhombifolia: Argentina, Uruguay
escoba lechosa	Euphorbia heterophylla: Bolivia, Colombia
escoba negra	Sida rhombifolia: Colombia

escobilla	Sida rhombifolia: Colombia, Honduras, Mexico
esek turpu	Raphanus raphanistrum: Turkey
eshnaan	Salsola kali: Egypt
eskobang-haba	Sida rhombifolia: Philippines
espadana	Typha angustifolia: Colombia
	Typha latifolia: Spain
espeto	Scirpus mucronatus: Portugal
espiga de agua	Potamogeton natans: Spain
	Potamogeton pectinatus: Argentina
espiguilla	Poa annua: Spain
espinho de carneiro	Acanthospermum hispidum: Brazil
espinho de cigano	Acanthospermum hispidum: Colombia
espinillo	Synedrella nodiflora: Cuba
espino amarillo	Ulex europaeus: Chile
espinoso	Acanthospermum hispidum: Bolivia
estramonino	Datura stramonium: Brazil
estramonio	Datura stramonium: Argentina, Dominican Republic, Portugal, Puerto Rico, Spain
estrelinha	Drymaria cordata: Brazil
estrella	Acanthospermum hispidum: Bolivia
estrume novo	Elodea canadensis: Portugal
etternassla	Urtica urens: Sweden
etupaela	Boerhavia diffusa: Nigeria
euphorbe reveil matin	Euphorbia helioscopia: France
euphorbe reveil-matin	Euphorbia helioscopia: Belgium
euphorbe revelle-matin	Euphorbia helioscopia: Canada
Eurasian watermilfoil	Myriophyllum spicatum: Canada, Europe, United States
Europaischer Stechginster	Ulex europaeus: Germany
European dodder	Cuscuta epithymum: Australia
European heliotrope	Heliotropium europaeum: Iraq, Lebanon, United States
European pepperwort	Marsilea quadrifolia: United States
European turnsole	Heliotropium europaeum: Iraq
europese heliotroop	Heliotropium europaeum: Netherlands
ewo	Ludwigia octovalvis: New Guinea
faar	Setaria glauca: Egypt
fako muhar	Setaria glauca: Hungary
falsa	Emilia sonchifolia: Brazil
falsa coclearia	Cardaria draba: Spain
false ipecacuanha	Asclepias curassavica: Fiji, Trinidad

F

false primrose	Ludwigia octovalvis: Fiji
falso joa de capote	Nicandra physalodes: Brazil
faltarenpris	Veronica arvensis: Sweden
faltveronika	Veronica arvensis: Sweden
fandrolakana	Paspalum distichum: Madagascar
fanorimena	Asclepias curassavica: Madagascar
fantakuen	Synedrella nodiflora: Philippines
fantrotrar amleazaha	Brassica kaber: Madagascar
fanweed	Thlaspi arvense: Canada
farolita	Nicandra physalodes: Bolivia
farolito	Nicandra physalodes: Argentina
fary	Saccharum spontaneum: Madagascar
fatten barrow	Synedrella nodiflora: Trinidad
fausse camomille	Matricaria chamomilla: France
feccia	Fumaria officinalis: Italy
fedegoso	Cassia occidentalis: Argentina, Brazil
	Cassia tora: Brazil
fedegoso verdadeiro	Cassia occidentalis: Brazil
fedegoso-branco	Cassia tora: Brazil
federacao	Acanthospermum hispidum: Brazil
feio	Pteridium aquilinum: Brazil
Feld Gasedistel	Sonchus arvensis: Germany
Feld-Ehrenpreis	Veronica arvensis: Germany
Feldkamille	Matricaria chamomilla: Germany
Feldmohn	Papaver rhoeas: Germany
felfel el ma	Polygonum hydropiper: Algeria
felpa	Pteridium aquilinum: Puerto Rico
felse aquilina	Pteridium aquilinum: Italy
fennel pondweed	Potamogeton pectinatus: Australia
fennel-leaved pondweed	Potamogeton pectinatus: England
ferny azolla	Azolla pinnata: Australia
fersken pileurt	Polygonum persicaria: Denmark
ferskenbladet pileurt	Polygonum persicaria: Denmark
feto	Pteridium aquilinum: Brazil
feto-ordinario	Pteridium aquilinum: Portugal
fettistel akermolke	Sonchus arvensis: Sweden
Feuermohn	Papaver rhoeas: Germany
field dodder	Cuscuta campestris: Canada, England, United States
field kale	Brassica kaber: Iraq
field milk thistle	Sonchus arvensis: England

field pennycress	Thlaspi arvense: Canada, United States
field poppy	Papaver rhoeas: Australia, England, Lebanon, New Zealand
field speedwell	Veronica arvensis: New Zealand
fienarola annua	Poa annua: Italy
figl	Raphanus raphanistrum: Egypt
figueira do inferno	Datura stramonium: Brazil
figueire do inferno	Datura stramonium: Portugal
fihaniya	Chenopodium ambrosioides: Egypt
fijaila	Raphanus raphanistrum: Iraq
fijjaylah	Raphanus raphanistrum: Lebanon
fire plant	Euphorbia heterophylla: Hawaii
fireweed	Conyza canadensis: Canada
firyas	Carduus pycnocephalus: Lebanon
fiss el-kalb	Chenopodium ambrosioides: Egypt
fiss-el-kilaab	Chenopodium murale: Saudi Arabia
fisseih	Chenopodium murale: Egypt
flea wort	Conyza canadensis: United States
fleabane	Conyza canadensis: Fiji, Iraq
fleche-d'eau	Sagittaria sagittifolia: France
fleur de jalousie	Amaranthus viridis: France
fleur terre	Fumaria officinalis: France
floajurt	Polygonum persicaria: Iceland
floating Malayan willow herb	Ludwigia adscendens: Malaysia
floatingleaf pondweed	Potamogeton natans: United States
Floh-Knoterich	Polygonum persicaria: Germany
flor amarilla	Synedrella nodiflora: Colombia, Honduras
	Tridax procumbens: Mexico
flor anaranjada	Asclepias curassavica: Mexico
flor azul	Lamium amplexicaule: Argentina
flor de clavo	Ludwigia octovalvis: Peru
flor de la reina	Asclepias curassavica: Peru
flor de muerte	Asclepias curassavica: Colombia, Peru
flor de nabo	Raphanus raphanistrum: Mexico
flor de pasion silvestre	Passiflora foetida: Puerto Rico
flor de pelota	Euphorbia heterophylla: Brazil
flor de seda	Asclepias curassavica: Bolivia, Peru
flor de un pajarito	Fumaria officinalis: Uruguay
flor escondida	Phyllanthus niruri: Venezuela
flor rubi	Lamium amplexicaule: Argentina
flora de pajarito	Fumaria officinalis: Argentina

floras paint-brush	Emilia sonchifolia: Hawaii
florcilla	Brassica kaber: Colombia
flores paint brush	Emilia sonchifolia: Thailand
floreta	Cardaria draba: Spain
flower of an hour	Hibiscus trionum: Canada, Lebanon, Rhodesia, United States
flower stinking passion	Passiflora foetida: Philippines
foetid cassia	Cassia tora: Australia, Malaysia
fomm el-samakah	Lamium amplexicaule: Egypt
forasacco	Hordeum murinum: Italy
forga'a	Ludwigia adscendens: Egypt
fosseish	Chenopodium murale: Egypt
fougere aigle	Pteridium aquilinum: France
fougere d'aigle	Pteridium aquilinum: Canada
fougere d'eau	Marsilea quadrifolia: France
freikaal	Ludwigia adscendens: Egypt
frijolillo	Cassia occidentalis: Guatemala, Honduras, Panama
	Cassia tora: El Salvador
fu ping	Lemna minor: China
Fuchshirse	Setaria glauca: Germany
fuchsschwanz	Alopecurus myosuroides: Switzerland
Fuchsschwanz	Amaranthus retroflexus: Germany
fugl barri	Raphanus raphanistrum: Lebanon, Saudi Arabia
fujul	Raphanus raphanistrum: Iraq
fulful el ma	Polygonum hydropiper: Saudi Arabia
fumaria	Fumaria officinalis: Italy
fumaria ou erva moleirinha	Fumaria officinalis: Portugal
fumeterre	Fumaria officinalis: France, Mauritius
fumeterre officinale	Fumaria officinalis: Belgium, Canada, France
fumitory	Fumaria officinalis: Canada, England, Lebanon, New Zealand, United States
fumosterno	Fumaria officinalis: Italy
funcho selvagem	Conium maculatum: Brazil
furansugiku	Chrysanthemum leucanthemum: Japan
furze	Ulex europaeus: Australia
fushizaki-so	Synedrella nodiflora: Taiwan
fushizakiso	Synedrella nodiflora: Japan
ga ge su lu	Momordica charantia: Liberia
gabi-gabi	Ludwigia adscendens: Philippines
gaddnate	Potamogeton natans: Sweden
gaga busan	Ludwigia octovalvis: Indonesia

G

galatgat	Ipomoea aquatica: Philippines
galiroa	Najas marina: Portugal
galjeru	Trianthema portulacastrum: India
gallitos	Lamium amplexicaule: Spain
gallocreste	Fumaria officinalis: Spain
gama	Typha latifolia: Japan
gamba rusa	Alternanthera philoxeroides: Argentina, Paraguay
gambarrosa	Alternanthera philoxeroides: Uruguay
gana barri	Cardaria draba: Saudi Arabia
gandia narron	Ludwigia octovalvis: Mauritius
ganggeng	Hydrilla verticillata: Indonesia
ganthian	Ipomoea aquatica: India
garafuni	Momordica charantia: Nigeria
garden calalu	Amaranthus viridis: Trinidad
garjri	Coronopus didymus: India
gaspeldoorn	Ulex europaeus: Netherlands
gatemelde	Chenopodium murale: Norway
gatmalla	Chenopodium murale: Sweden
gauai-gauai	Sagittaria sagittifolia: Philippines
gayanggang runti	Hydrilla verticillata: Indonesia
gazel lokmasi	Alternanthera sessilis: Turkey
Gebrauchlicher Erdrauch	Fumaria officinalis: Germany, Germany
gedangan	Corchorus olitorius: Indonesia
Gefleckter Schierling	Conium maculatum: Germany
gekleurde de euporbia	Euphorbia prunifolia: South Africa
gekroesd fonteinkruid	Potamogeton crispus: Netherlands
gekruld fonteinkruid	Potamogeton crispus: Belgium
Gelbe Borstenhirse	Setaria glauca: Austria, Germany
Gelber Fuchsschwanz	Setaria glauca: Germany
gele peen	Daucus carota: Netherlands
gele wortel	Daucus carota: Netherlands
gelenggang ketchil	Cassia tora: Malaysia
gelenggang padang	Cassia tora: Malaysia
gelincik	Papaver rhoeas: Turkey
Gemeine Kratzdistel	Cirsium vulgare: Germany
Gemeine Pfeilkresse	Cardaria draba: Germany
Gemeine Wasserschraube	Vallisneria spiralis: Germany
Gemeine Wegwarte	Cichorium intybus: Germany
Gemeine Wucherblume	Chrysanthemum leucanthemum: Germany
Gemeiner Beifuss	Artemisia vulgaris: Germany

Gemeiner Erdrauch	Fumaria officinalis: Germany
Gemeiner Knoterich	Polygonum persicaria: Germany
Gemeiner Lowenzahn	Taraxacum officinale: Germany
Gemeines Greiskraut	Senecio vulgaris: Germany
Gemeines Kreuzkraut	Senecio vulgaris: Germany
Gemeines Sumpfried	Eleocharis palustris: Germany
Gemeinestrandbinse	Scirpus maritimus: Germany
gendjoran	Digitaria longiflora: Indonesia
genje jawa	Artemisia vulgaris: Indonesia
gerda	Polygonum aviculare: Algeria
gevlekte scheerling	Conium maculatum: Belgium
gevlekte silybum	Silybum marianum: South Africa
Gewohnlicher Beifuss	Artemisia vulgaris: Germany
Gewohnliches Greiskraut	Senecio vulgaris: Germany
gewone duivekerval	Fumaria officinalis: Netherlands
gewone duiwekerwel	Fumaria officinalis: South Africa
gewone stinkblaar	Datura stramonium: South Africa
gewongan	Stachytarpheta jamaicensis: Indonesia
gewoon kruiskruid	Senecio vulgaris: Netherlands
ghadar	Polygonum lapathifolium: Lebanon, Saudi Arabia
ghas	Poa annua: India
ghazar	Saccharum spontaneum: Egypt
ghazl	Potamogeton crispus: Egypt
giant duckweed	Spirodela polyrhiza: United States
giant pigweed	Trianthema portulacastrum: Australia
giftkjeks	Conium maculatum: Norway
Gilb-fennich	Setaria glauca: Germany
ginestra spinosa	Ulex europaeus: Italy
ginga	Hydrilla verticillata: Philippines
girilla	Brassica kaber: Egypt
gitanillas	Fumaria officinalis: Spain
giunco tondo	Eleocharis palustris: Italy
glagah	Saccharum spontaneum: Indonesia
gletang	Tridax procumbens: Indonesia
gletangan	Synedrella nodiflora: Indonesia
	Tridax procumbens: Indonesia
go'ded	Chondrilla juncea: Lebanon
goathead	Acanthospermum hispidum: United States
gogoat	Alternanthera sessilis: Philippines
golandrina	Boerhavia diffusa: El Salvador

gold-byg	Hordeum murinum: Dahomey
gole jeez	Orobanche ramosa: Iran
golondrina	Boerhavia erecta: Colombia
	Drymaria cordata: Colombia, Venezuela
	Stachytarpheta jamaicensis: Colombia
	Veronica persica: Colombia
golondrina erecta	Euphorbia heterophylla: Mexico
gonorrea	Polygonum aviculare: Colombia
goose grass	Poa annua: Australia
gooseberry	Physalis angulata: Jamaica
gorczyca polna	Brassica kaber: Poland
gorse	Ulex europaeus: Australia, Canada, Hawaii, New Zealand, United States
gorusica	Brassica kaber: Yugoslavia
gota de sangre	Euphorbia heterophylla: Bolivia, Colombia
gra bynke	Artemisia vulgaris: Denmark
gra kolvhirs	Setaria glauca: Sweden
grahirs	Setaria glauca: Sweden
gram d'algua	Paspalum distichum: Spain
grama	Paspalum distichum: Venezuela
	Setaria geniculata: Peru
grama colorado	Paspalum distichum: El Salvador, Mexico
grama de fidoeos	Eragrostis pilosa: Venezuela
grama de forquilha	Paspalum distichum: Brazil
grama doce	Paspalum distichum: Brazil
gramigna delle vie	Poa annua: Italy
gramilla	Paspalum distichum: Argentina
gramilla blanca	Paspalum distichum: Argentina
gramilla brava	Paspalum distichum: Uruguay
gramilla del tiempo	Paspalum distichum: Argentina
gramilla dulce	Paspalum distichum: Argentina
graminhao	Paspalum distichum: Portugal
granadilla	Passiflora foetida: Honduras, Jamaica
granadilla cimarrona	Passiflora foetida: Peru
granadilla colorado	Passiflora foetida: El Salvador
granadilla montes	Passiflora foetida: El Salvador
grande cique	Conium maculatum: France
grande fougere	Pteridium aquilinum: Canada, France
grande Margherita	Chrysanthemum leucanthemum: Italy
grande Marguerita	Chrysanthemum leucanthemum: France
grande massette	Typha latifolia: Belgium

Graugrune Borstenhirse	Setaria glauca: Germany, Switzerland
great reedmace	Typha latifolia: England
green amaranth	Amaranthus viridis: Australia
green ginger	Artemisia vulgaris: United States
green kyllinga	Cyperus brevifolius: Hawaii
green pigweed	Amaranthus viridis: Sri Lanka
grobo	Artemisia vulgaris: Sweden
gront honsegras	Polygonum lapathifolium: Norway
groot nimfkruid	Najas marina: Netherlands
Grosse Wasserlinse	Spirodela polyrhiza: Germany
Grosser Ehrenpreis	Veronica persica: Germany
Grosses Nixenkraut	Najas marina: Germany
grote ereprijs	Veronica persica: Belgium, Netherlands
grote lisdodde	Typha latifolia: Belgium, Netherlands
ground chestnut	Eleocharis dulcis: United States
groundsel	Senecio vulgaris: Australia, England, New Zealand
Gruner Fuchsschwanz	Amaranthus viridis: Germany
Grunfeste	Chondrilla juncea: Germany
guacara	Synedrella nodiflora: Honduras
guanina	Cassia occidentalis: Cuba
	Cassia tora: Cuba
guanxuma	Sida rhombifolia: Brazil
guaxima	Sida rhombifolia: Brazil
gulltorn	Ulex europaeus: Norway
gum succory	Chondrilla juncea: Lebanon
gunbainazuna	Thlaspi arvense: Japan
gunda buti	Euphorbia helioscopia: Pakistan
gusanillo	Setaria geniculata: Colombia, Cuba
	Setaria glauca: Colombia
gusanito	Setaria geniculata: El Salvador
gusano	Setaria geniculata: El Salvador
hachijona	Sonchus arvensis: Japan
hae-chao	Hydrilla verticillata: China
haew soeng kratien	Eleocharis dulcis: Thailand
hageng	Brassica kaber: Argentina
hai-kinpoge	Ranunculus repens: Japan
hai-or ingi	Stachytarpheta jamaicensis: Sri Lanka
halook	Orobanche ramosa: Saudi Arabia
halouk	Orobanche ramosa: Egypt
halud shiallja	Setaria glauca: Bangladesh

H

haluk-rihi	Orobanche ramosa: Lebanon
hamadaikon	Raphanus raphanistrum: Japan
hamel	Alternanthera sessilis: Egypt
hammonida	Rumex acetosella: Morocco
hamnkrassing	Coronopus didymus: Sweden
hamool	Alternanthera sessilis: Egypt
	Cuscuta campestris: Saudi Arabia
handab	Cichorium intybus: Lebanon
handabah	Cichorium intybus: Lebanon
hang ping	Azolla pinnata: China
hangod	Achyranthes aspera: Philippines
hanhentatar	Polygonum persicaria: Finland
hapsivita	Potamogeton pectinatus: Finland
harawa	Corchorus olitorius: India
hardon Marie	Silybum marianum: Canada
harendong	Melastoma malabathricum: Indonesia
harf mashrigi	Cardaria draba: Saudi Arabia
harutade	Polygonum persicaria: Japan
havijk	Daucus carota: Iran
havsevaks	Scirpus maritimus: Norway
havssav	Scirpus maritimus: Sweden
havuc	Daucus carota: Turkey
hazardana	Phyllanthus niruri: India
heart-podded hoary cress	Cardaria draba: Canada
heartleaf drymary	Drymaria cordata: United States
Hederich	Raphanus raphanistrum: Germany
hederik	Brassica kaber: Belgium
hedge fumitory	Fumaria officinalis: United States
hedionda	Cassia occidentalis: Colombia, Puerto Rico
heelaagoog	Eragrostis pilosa: Saudi Arabia
helecho	Pteridium aquilinum: Colombia, Ecuador
helecho alambre	Pteridium aquilinum: Puerto Rico
helecho comun	Pteridium aquilinum: Spain
helecho marrano	Pteridium aquilinum: Puerto Rico
heliotrope	Heliotropium europaeum: Australia, England, France, Iran
heliotrope d'erope	Heliotropium europaeum: Morocco
hemlock	Conium maculatum: Australia, England, New Zealand
hemp broomrape	Orobanche ramosa: England
henbit	Lamium amplexicaule: Canada, England, Lebanon, New Zealand, United States

henbit dead-nettle	Lamium amplexicaule: England
hennepvreter	Orobanche ramosa: Netherlands
herana	Cyperus haspan: Madagascar
herba a balais	Sida rhombifolia: New Caledonia
herba aux charpentiers	Senecio vulgaris: France
herbe aux cochons	Polygonum aviculare: France
herbe bleue	Stachytarpheta jamaicensis: New Caledonia
herbe caille	Tridax procumbens: Mauritius
herbe de las calenturas	Polygonum aviculare: Spain
herbe de Saint Jean	Artemisia vulgaris: France
herbe gandia	Conyza canadensis: Mauritius
herbe la mare	Ludwigia octovalvis: Mauritius
herbe pintade	Boerhavia diffusa: Mauritius
herbe sergent	Achyranthes aspera: Mauritius
herbe tricorne	Acanthospermum hispidum: Mauritius
herhe pistache	Cassia tora: Mauritius
herik	Brassica kaber: Belgium, Netherlands
Herzschotchen	Thlaspi arvense: Germany
hestehamp	Conyza canadensis: Norway
hharsha	Brassica kaber: Lebanon
hhash el agrab	Heliotropium europaeum: Lebanon
hhummad saghir	Rumex acetosella: Saudi Arabia
hibiscus trionum	Hibiscus trionum: New Zealand
hierba alligator	Alternanthera philoxeroides: Paraguay
hierba blanca	Boerhavia erecta: Colombia, Mexico
hierba cana	Senecio vulgaris: Argentina, Chile, Spain
hierba de cabro	Boerhavia diffusa: Guatemala
hierba de chivo	Polygonum aviculare: Guatemala
hierba de cristo	Rumex acetosella: Mexico
hierba de la culebra	Fumaria officinalis: Chile
hierba de la perdiz	Poa annua: Chile
hierba de la vibora	Asclepias curassavica: Mexico
hierba de puerco	Boerhavia diffusa: Mexico
hierba de punta	Poa annua: Spain
hierba de San Juan	Artemisia vulgaris: Spain
hierba del caballo	Conyza canadensis: Mexico
hierba del duende	Euphorbia heterophylla: El Salvador
hierba del gallinazo	Chenopodium murale: Peru
hierba del salitre	Fumaria officinalis: Chile
hierba del toro	Tridax procumbens: El Salvador, Honduras
hierba hedionda	Cassia occidentalis: Cuba

hierba lechosa	Euphorbia heterophylla: Cuba
hierba mala de pascua	Euphorbia heterophylla: Guatemala
hierba roja	Rumex acetosella: Mexico
hierba tora	Orobanche ramosa: Spain
hiiren ohra	Hordeum murinum: Finland
hillis	Potamogeton crispus: Egypt
hime-gama	Typha angustifolia: Japan
himekugu	Cyperus brevifolius: Japan
himemukashiyomogi	Conyza canadensis: Japan
himesuiba	Rumex acetosella: Japan
hin-nu-nwe	Amaranthus viridis: Burma
hindiba	Cichorium intybus: Iraq
hindiba barri	Chondrilla juncea: Lebanon
hjerteskulpet karse	Cardaria draba: Denmark
hlaoarfi	Polygonum aviculare: Iceland
ho ping	Azolla pinnata: China
hoary cardaria	Cardaria draba: South Africa
hoary cress	Cardaria draba: Australia, England, Greece, Iraq, Lebanon, New Zealand, United States
hoary pepperwort	Cardaria draba: England
hoenderbeet	Lamium amplexicaule: Belgium, Netherlands
hog weed	Boerhavia diffusa: Ghana, Trinidad
hog's cress	Coronopus didymus: Australia
hogweed	Conyza canadensis: Canada
	Physalis angulata: Jamaica, Trinidad
	Polygonum aviculare: Australia, England
hoja morada	Boerhavia erecta: Mexico
hollyleaf naiad	Najas marina: England, United States
holy thistle	Silybum marianum: Jordan, United States
honaga-inubiyu	Amaranthus viridis: Japan
honningkarse	Cardaria draba: Norway
honsegraes	Polygonum aviculare: Denmark
honsegress	Polygonum persicaria: Norway
horoz ibigi	Amaranthus viridis: Turkey
horoz kuyruga	Amaranthus retroflexus: Turkey
horreig	Urtica urens: Egypt
horse purslane	Trianthema portulacastrum: United States
horsetidsel	Cirsium vulgare: Denmark
horseweed	Conyza canadensis: Canada, England, Fiji, Philippines, United States
hoshi-asagao	Ipomoea triloba: Japan

hossumo	Najas graminea: Japan
hotokenza	Lamium amplexicaule: Japan
hozakinofusamo	Myriophyllum spicatum: Japan
hrapavi stir	Amaranthus retroflexus: Yugoslavia
hsio-li-gou-wei-tsao	Setaria geniculata: Taiwan
hu-plachow	Emilia sonchifolia: Thailand
huacatay	Chenopodium ambrosioides: Peru
huachapurga	Euphorbia heterophylla: Peru
huamicara	Coronopus didymus: Peru
huang hua mu	Sida rhombifolia: China
hudasura	Rumex acetosella: Iceland
huevillo	Physalis angulata: El Salvador
huevo de gato	Physalis angulata: Cuba
huevo de sapo	Physalis angulata: Venezuela
huevo de tortuga	Physalis angulata: El Salvador
huichun	Polygonum aviculare: Argentina, Chile
huichuri	Polygonum aviculare: Mexico
huinar	Sida rhombifolia: Mexico
huiro	Potamogeton pectinatus: Chile
hulaya	Cleome gynandra: Philippines
hulhul	Cleome gynandra: India
hulluruoho	Datura stramonium: Finland
hummaydah	Polygonum lapathifolium: Lebanon
hurrayk	Urtica urens: Lebanon
hutan	Cassia occidentalis: Malaysia
huye que te cojo	Emilia sonchifolia: Puerto Rico
hvid okseodje	Chrysanthemum leucanthemum: Denmark
hydrilla	Hydrilla verticillata: Australia, New Zealand, United States

I

i'jairbeh	Heliotropium europaeum: Iraq
ibaramo	Najas marina: Japan
ibigicana	Chenopodium ambrosioides: Rhodesia
idem	Sida rhombifolia: Indonesia
idropepe	Polygonum hydropiper: Italy
ilimaaseeb	Boerhavia diffusa: Egypt
impia	Conyza canadensis: Italy
inai pasir	Ludwigia hyssopifolia: Malaysia
inata	Hydrilla verticillata: Philippines
India lovegrass	Eragrostis pilosa: United States
Indian goosefoot	Chenopodium ambrosioides: England
Indian jointvetch	Aeschynomene indica: United States

indian lovegrass	Eragrostis pilosa: Fiji
indigo	Cassia occidentalis: Reunion
indishe waterpest	Hydrilla verticillata: Netherlands
injeh-injehan	Ipomoea triloba: Indonesia
ironweed	Polygonum aviculare: England
	Vernonia cinerea: Fiji, Trinidad
iscorian	Boerhavia diffusa: El Salvador
	Boerhavia erecta: Colombia, El Salvador
isigan otu	Urtica urens: Turkey
isogi	Cleome gynandra: Zaire
it-sit	Boerhavia diffusa: Pakistan
Italian thistle	Carduus pycnocephalus: Lebanon, United States
itsit	Trianthema portulacastrum: India
jaboticaa	Drymaria cordata: Brazil
Jahrige Rispe	Poa annua: Germany
jala	Hydrilla verticillata: India
Jamaica vervain	Stachytarpheta jamaicensis: Hawaii
Jamaican snakeweed	Stachytarpheta jamaicensis: Australia
Jamestown weed	Datura stramonium: Lebanon
jangli chaulai	Amaranthus viridis: India
jaramado	Raphanus raphanistrum: Mexico
jaramago	Brassica kaber: Spain
jaramago blanco	Raphanus raphanistrum: Spain
jaramla	Phyllanthus niruri: India
jarayupriya	Conyza canadensis: India
jarilla	Conyza canadensis: Mexico
jasmin del rio	Cleome gynandra: Puerto Rico
Java bean	Cassia tora: Australia
jazar barri	Daucus carota: Iraq
Jean Robert	Euphorbia prunifolia: Madagascar
jednogodisnja livadarka	Poa annua: Yugoslavia
Jew's mallow	Corchorus olitorius: Egypt
jhanji	Hydrilla verticillata: Bangladesh
jhaojhanji	Najas graminea: Bangladesh
jimsonweed	Datura stramonium: Canada, Hawaii, Lebanon, Rhodesia, United States, Zambia
jina la kawaida	Acanthospermum hispidum: East Africa
jinaleh	Ludwigia hyssopifolia: Malaysia
jinnaibrah	Cardaria draba: Iraq
joa de capote	Nicandra physalodes: Brazil
John crow pea	Cassia occidentalis: Jamaica

J

jointed charlock	Raphanus raphanistrum: Australia
jointed radish	Raphanus raphanistrum: Canada
jombang	Sonchus arvensis: Indonesia
	Sonchus asper: Indonesia
	Taraxacum officinale: Indonesia
Jonca	Scirpus maritimus: Spain
jordrok	Fumaria officinalis: Norway, Sweden
jow piyazee	Hordeum murinum: Iran
juhsoska	Rumex acetosella: Hungary
jukutibun	Drymaria cordata: Indonesia
junco	Typha angustifolia: Colombia
	Typha latifolia: Colombia
junco de espiga	Eleocharis palustris: Spain
junco-marreco	Eleocharis palustris: Portugal
Jung Fernkraut Wider	Artemisia vulgaris: Germany
ka'a ruru	Amaranthus viridis: Paraguay
ka'a ruru pe	Boerhavia diffusa: Paraguay
ka'are	Chenopodium ambrosioides: Paraguay
ka-thok-rok	Passiflora foetida: Thailand
kabal-kabalan	Cassia occidentalis: Philippines
kabar	Brassica kaber: Saudi Arabia
kabar afrit	Brassica kaber: Lebanon
kabshoo-lignah	Amaranthus viridis: Egypt
kadaladi	Achyranthes aspera: India
kadkadot	Cyperus brevifolius: Philippines
kadu-du	Melastoma malabathricum: Thailand
kahi	Saccharum spontaneum: Pakistan
kaka tundi	Asclepias curassavica: India
kakara	Momordica charantia: India
kakarewoan	Spirodela polyrhiza: Indonesia
kakle	Momordica charantia: Ghana
kalami sag	Ipomoea aquatica: India
kali	Salsola kali: Lebanon
Kali-Salzkraut	Salsola kali: Germany
kallaghan	Silybum marianum: Iraq
kalmi-sak	Ipomoea aquatica: Bangladesh
kalmisak	Ipomoea aquatica: India
kalurai	Amaranthus viridis: Thailand
kambang pendjit	Ludwigia adscendens: Indonesia
kamfonteinkruid	Potamogeton pectinatus: Belgium

K

kamilica	Matricaria chamomilla: Yugoslavia
Kamille	Matricaria chamomilla: Germany
kamilleblom	Matricaria chamomilla: Norway
kamitsure	Matricaria chamomilla: Japan
kamkamote	Ipomoea triloba: Philippines
Kammformiges	Potamogeton pectinatus: Germany
kamokamotihan	Ipomoea triloba: Philippines
kamole	Ludwigia octovalvis: Hawaii
kamomill	Matricaria chamomilla: Sweden
kamomillasaunio	Matricaria chamomilla: Finland
kamping pauy	Ludwigia adscendens: Cambodia
kamra-kamra	Drymaria cordata: Philippines
kan-mai-nion	Alopecurus myosuroides: China
kanada-binka	Conyza canadensis: Sweden
kanadamo	Elodea canadensis: Japan
Kanadan koiransilma	Conyza canadensis: Finland
Kanadese fijnstraal	Conyza canadensis: Netherlands
Kanadese fijnstrall	Conyza canadensis: Belgium
Kanadese skraalhans	Conyza canadensis: South Africa
Kanadisches	Conyza canadensis: Germany
Kanadischy Wasserpest	Elodea canadensis: Germany
kanadisk	Conyza canadensis: Denmark
kanaka	Euphorbia heterophylla: Philippines
kanalli dari	Paspalum distichum: Turkey
kanarya otu	Senecio vulgaris: Turkey
kanching baju	Tridax procumbens: Malaysia
kandi-kandilaan	Stachytarpheta jamaicensis: Philippines
kangkong	Ipomoea aquatica: Philippines
kangkong ayer	Ipomoea aquatica: Malaysia
kangkong dapa	Ludwigia adscendens: Philippines
kangni	Setaria glauca: Pakistan
kanjata	Acanthospermum hispidum: Zambia
kans ghas	Saccharum spontaneum: India
kanta jhanji	Najas graminea: Bangladesh
kantataba	Trianthema portulacastrum: Philippines
kanubsuban	Scirpus mucronatus: Philippines
kapii	Eragrostis pilosa: Paraguay
kappai-kirai	Amaranthus viridis: Sri Lanka
karafuto-irakusa	Urtica urens: Japan
karakusa-nazuna	Coronopus didymus: Japan

karee	Heliotropium europaeum: Saudi Arabia
karela	Momordica charantia: India
karga	Oryza sativa: India
kariyartharani	Stachytarpheta jamaicensis: India
kasandi	Cassia occidentalis: India
kash	Saccharum spontaneum: Bangladesh, India
kasingsat	Cassia occidentalis: Indonesia
kasinyawo	Acanthospermum hispidum: Nigeria
kasivinda	Cassia occidentalis: India
kasni	Cichorium intybus: India
kassaradam	Ludwigia adscendens: Bangladesh
katanpuni	Oxalis latifolia: Uganda
katapunuttu	Stachytarpheta jamaicensis: India
kathshola	Aeschynomene indica: India
katisan	Aeschynomene indica: Indonesia
katjeprek	Passiflora foetida: Indonesia
katkatud	Boerhavia diffusa: Philippines
katkeratatar	Polygonum hydropiper: Finland
kattu nerinji	Acanthospermum hispidum: India
kaumoce	Cassia tora: Fiji
kaunisiga	Melastoma malabathricum: Fiji
kavalu	Setaria geniculata: Sri Lanka
kavmoce	Cassia occidentalis: Fiji
kawalu	Setaria glauca: Sri Lanka
kayu ragi	Ludwigia hyssopifolia: Celebes Islands
kayu-apu dadak	Azolla pinnata: Indonesia
ke-aritaso	Chenopodium ambrosioides: Japan
kecubung lutik	Datura stramonium: Indonesia
kecubung wulung	Datura stramonium: Indonesia
keela nelli	Phyllanthus niruri: India
keerai	Ipomoea aquatica: India
keremak	Alternanthera sessilis: Malaysia
kerla	Momordica charantia: Fiji
kesra	Ludwigia adscendens: Bangladesh
kete pung	Cassia occidentalis: Malaysia
ketepeng cilik	Cassia tora: Indonesia
ketepeng kecil	Cassia tora: Indonesia
ketepeng leutik	Cassia tora: Indonesia
ketmia	Hibiscus trionum: United States
ketmie trilobee	Hibiscus trionum: Canada

ketotadyke	Veronica arvensis: Finland
khaki	Tagetes minuta: Malawi
khali weed	Tagetes minuta: Natal
khar bathua	Chenopodium murale: India
kharaawa	Ludwigia adscendens: Egypt
khardal	Brassica kaber: Egypt
khardal barri	Brassica kaber: Iran, Iraq, Lebanon
khardal-barri	Brassica kaber: Saudi Arabia
khass zelf	Potamogeton crispus: Egypt
khat-mon	Sida rhombifolia: Thailand
khati-buti	Oxalis latifolia: India
khatta palak	Rumex acetosella: India
khenza	Chenopodium murale: Saudi Arabia
khi-lekthet	Cassia occidentalis: Thailand
khlong-khleng-khi-nok	Melastoma malabathricum: Thailand
khmuoch	Cassia occidentalis: Cambodia
	Cassia tora: Cambodia
khomhin pak	Boerhavia diffusa: Thailand
khorfe	Polygonum aviculare: Iran
khudan	Carduus pycnocephalus: Lebanon
khudipana	Lemna minor: Bangladesh, Pakistan
khudra	Corchorus olitorius: Sudan
khutora	Amaranthus viridis: India
ki ler pi	Cassia occidentalis: Thailand
ki papesan	Ipomoea triloba: Indonesia
kidachikinbai	Ludwigia octovalvis: Japan
kiddike	Raphanus raphanistrum: Denmark
kierana	Scirpus maritimus: Madagascar
kikania haola	Datura stramonium: Hawaii
kikitoun	Achyranthes aspera: Micronesia
kiku-nigana	Cichorium intybus: Japan
kilitis	Amaranthus viridis: Thailand
kilitis pak-kham-tia	Amaranthus viridis: Thailand
kin-enokoro	Setaria glauca: Japan
kingojika	Sida rhombifolia: Japan
kingyomo	Myriophyllum spicatum: Japan
kipot-kipot	Emilia sonchifolia: Philippines
kir teresi	Cardaria draba: Turkey
kirmizi koklu tilki kuyrugu	Amaranthus retroflexus: Turkey
kiselica mala	Rumex acetosella: Yugoslavia
kishu-suzumenohie	Paspalum distichum: Japan

klao	Oryza sativa: Thailand
Klapperrose	Papaver rhoeas: Germany
klaproes	Papaver rhoeas: Belgium
klaproos	Papaver rhoeas: Netherlands
Klatsch-mohn	Papaver rhoeas: Germany
Klatschrose	Papaver rhoeas: Germany
klavervreter	Orobanche minor: Belgium
klaverwarkruid	Cuscuta epithymum: Belgium
klawerbesmrapp	Orobanche minor: South Africa
Kleeseide	Cuscuta epithymum: Germany
Kleeteufel	Orobanche minor: Germany
klein dodder	Cuscuta epithymum: South Africa
klein kroos	Lemna minor: Belgium, Netherlands
klein kruiskruid	Senecio vulgaris: Belgium, Netherlands
kleine brandnetel	Urtica urens: Belgium, Netherlands
Kleine Brennessel	Urtica urens: Germany
kleine lisdodde	Typha angustifolia: Belgium
Kleine Nessel	Urtica urens: Germany
Kleine Sommerwurz	Orobanche minor: Germany
Kleine Wasserlinse	Lemna minor: Germany
Kleiner Ampfer	Rumex acetosella: Germany
Kleiner Sauerampfer	Rumex acetosella: Germany
kloeroek	Melastoma malabathricum: Indonesia
klover-gyvelkvaeler	Orobanche minor: Denmark
klover-silke	Cuscuta epithymum: Denmark
knappsav	Eleocharis palustris: Sweden
Knauelkopfige Distel	Carduus pycnocephalus: Germany
knikbloem	Chondrilla juncea: Netherlands
knikkende distel	Carduus nutans: Netherlands
knopherik	Raphanus raphanistrum: Belgium, Netherlands
knopige duizendknoop	Polygonum lapathifolium: Netherlands
knotgrass	Paspalum distichum: Fiji, Sri Lanka, United States
	Polygonum aviculare: England
knotroot	Setaria geniculata: New Zealand, Trinidad
knotroot foxtail	Setaria geniculata: United States
knotweed	Polygonum aviculare: Alaska, Australia, England, Lebanon
	Polygonum lapathifolium: Lebanon
knudet pileurt	Polygonum lapathifolium: Denmark
knutig pilort	Polygonum lapathifolium: Sweden
ko-azegayatsuri	Cyperus haspan: Japan

ko-ukilusa	Lemna minor: Japan
ko-ukiyagara	Scirpus maritimus: Japan
kodidimborona	Oxalis latifolia: Madagascar
kodimathulai	Passiflora foetida: Sri Lanka
kok chaang	Typha angustifolia: Thailand
kok ta krap	Scirpus maritimus: Thailand
kollebloem	Papaver rhoeas: Belgium
kolong-kulong	Vernonia cinerea: Philippines
kombwe	Hibiscus trionum: Zambia
kong kong bulu	Ipomoea triloba: Malaysia
koota	Corchorus olitorius: India
koperdraadgras	Polygonum aviculare: South Africa
korn valmue	Papaver rhoeas: Denmark
kornvallmo	Papaver rhoeas: Sweden
kornvalmue	Papaver rhoeas: Norway
korolla	Momordica charantia: Bangladesh
koropo	Physalis angulata: Nigeria
korsbo	Senecio vulgaris: Sweden
korsikaanse dissel	Carduus pycnocephalus: South Africa
kotobuki-giku	Tridax procumbens: Taiwan
kotobukigiku	Tridax procumbens: Japan
kotochu lalampah	Artemisia vulgaris: Thailand
kottiram	Aeschynomene indica: India
koyun otu	Artemisia vulgaris: Turkey
krangkong	Ludwigia adscendens: Indonesia
kraping puoy	Ludwigia adscendens: Cambodia
Krauses Laichkraut	Potamogeton crispus: Germany
krema	Alternanthera sessilis: Indonesia
krenkre	Corchorus olitorius: Sierra Leone
Kreuzkraut	Senecio vulgaris: Germany
Kriechender Hahnenfuss	Ranunculus repens: Germany
krodde	Brassica kaber: Netherlands
krokot	Trianthema portulacastrum: Indonesia
kroontjeskruid	Euphorbia helioscopia: Belgium, Netherlands
kruiehondebossie	Chenopodium ambrosioides: South Africa
kruipende boterbloem	Ranunculus repens: Belgium, Netherlands
kruipertje	Hordeum murinum: Netherlands
kruset vandaks	Potamogeton crispus: Denmark
krusnate	Potamogeton crispus: Sweden
krustjonnaks	Potamogeton crispus: Norway

krvavac	Lamium amplexicaule: Yugoslavia
krypsoleie	Ranunculus repens: Norway
ku gua	Momordica charantia: China
kucuk labada	Rumex acetosella: Turkey
kuk-chao	Vallisneria spiralis: China
kunaybrah	Cardaria draba: Lebanon
kuppai keerai	Amaranthus viridis: India
kuradakorigaddi	Setaria pallide-fusca: India
kuraila	Momordica charantia: India
kurelei	Hydrilla verticillata: India
kureli	Hydrilla verticillata: Bangladesh
kuromo	Hydrilla verticillata: Japan
kurrays-uj-jaji	Lamium amplexicaule: Lebanon
kurukalunggai	Phyllanthus niruri: Philippines
kurunggut	Passiflora foetida: Philippines
kusa-tokeiso	Passiflora foetida: Japan
kusanemu	Aeschynomene indica: Japan
kusfarat el hhimar	Fumaria officinalis: Lebanon
kut kin	Pteridium aquilinum: Thailand
kuti pana	Spirodela polyrhiza: Bangladesh
kutipana	Azolla pinnata: Bangladesh, Pakistan
kuvadio	Cassia tora: India
kweek paspalum	Paspalum distichum: South Africa
kyet-hin-ga	Momordica charantia: Malaysia
kylanurmikka	Poa annua: Finland
kyllinga	Cyperus brevifolius: Hawaii
kynsimokrassi	Cardaria draba: Finland
laban el-homa	Euphorbia prunifolia: Egypt
labresto	Cichorium intybus: Portugal
	Raphanus raphanistrum: Portugal
lady's thistle	Silybum marianum: Canada
lady's thumb	Polygonum persicaria: Canada
lady's thumb smartweed	Polygonum persicaria: United States
laege-jordrog	Fumaria officinalis: Denmark
lagarto	Alternanthera philoxeroides: Mexico
lagoom spurge	Phyllanthus niruri: Australia
lagunilla	Alternanthera philoxeroides: Argentina, Uruguay
Laichkraut	Potamogeton pectinatus: Germany
laijabori	Drymaria cordata: India
laiteron apre	Sonchus asper: Belgium, France

L

laiteron des champs	Sonchus arvensis: Belgium, Canada, France
laiteron epineux	Sonchus asper: France
laiteron rude	Sonchus asper: Canada
lalandy	Ipomoea aquatica: Madagascar
lamier	Lamium amplexicaule: Tunisia
lamier amplexicaule	Lamium amplexicaule: Belgium, Canada, France
lamiera feuilles embrassantes	Lamium amplexicaule: Morocco
lamio	Lamium amplexicaule: Spain
lamium	Lamium amplexicaule: Argentina, Chile
lamlampaka	Emilia sonchifolia: Philippines
lampong	Datura stramonium: Thailand
land cress	Coronopus didymus: Australia
lang kakiebos	Tagetes minuta: South Africa
langklits-kafblom	Achyranthes aspera: South Africa
langsana merah	Cleome gynandra: Indonesia
lanni	Trianthema portulacastrum: Saudi Arabia
lapsaua	Cichorium intybus: Portugal
lapulevelu keserufu	Polygonum lapathifolium: Hungary
large duckweed	Spirodela polyrhiza: Australia
lastron piquant	Sonchus asper: Mauritius
latjira	Achyranthes aspera: India
lattuga ranina	Potamogeton crispus: Italy
	Potamogeton natans: Italy
lattugaccio	Chondrilla juncea: Italy
lav ranunkel	Ranunculus repens: Denmark
lava-pratos	Cassia occidentalis: Brazil
lavaravina	Rumex acetosella: Madagascar
leap-the-field	Salsola kali: Soviet Union
lebsan	Raphanus raphanistrum: Algeria
leche de la virgin	Euphorbia heterophylla: Bolivia
leche de sapo	Euphorbia heterophylla: Mexico
leche vana	Euphorbia heterophylla: Dominican Republic
lechecilla	Euphorbia heterophylla: Colombia
lechera	Euphorbia heterophylla: Peru
lecherina	Euphorbia helioscopia: Spain
lecheron	Euphorbia heterophylla: Argentina
lecheruela	Euphorbia helioscopia: Spain
lechetrenza	Euphorbia helioscopia: Chile
lechetrenza comun	Euphorbia helioscopia: Spain
lechetrenza medicinal	Euphorbia helioscopia: Argentina

lechetres	Euphorbia heterophylla: Paraguay
lechilla	Euphorbia heterophylla: Mexico
lechillo	Euphorbia heterophylla: Mexico
lechocinos	Senecio vulgaris: Spain
lechosa	Euphorbia heterophylla: Ecuador
lechosilla	Asclepias curassavica: Mexico
lechosito	Euphorbia heterophylla: Venezuela
lechugilla	Sonchus asper: Dominican Republic
	Taraxacum officinale: Chile
lechuguilla	Sonchus arvensis: Spain
	Taraxacum officinale: Colombia
leiteira	Euphorbia heterophylla: Brazil
leituga-branca	Chondrilla juncea: Portugal
lele duji	Momordica charantia: Nigeria
lemanas	Passiflora foetida: Indonesia
lengua de vaca	Achyranthes aspera: Venezuela
	Rumex acetosella: Colombia
lengua de pajaros	Polygonum aviculare: Belgium
lengue de pajaro	Polygonum aviculare: Spain
lenteja de agua	Lemna minor: Argentina, Colombia
lentejilla	Lemna minor: Colombia
lentejuela de agua	Lemna minor: Spain
lenticchia d'acqua	Lemna minor: Italy
lenticule mineure	Lemna minor: Canada
lentiha d'agua	Spirodela polyrhiza: Brazil
lentiha da agua	Lemna minor: Brazil
lentihas de agua menores	Lemna minor: Portugal
lepidier	Cardaria draba: France
lepidium	Cardaria draba: United States
lerotho	Cleome gynandra: South Africa
lerotu	Cleome gynandra: South Africa
lesser crabgrass	Digitaria longiflora: Malaysia
lesser dodder	Cuscuta epithymum: South Africa
lesser duckweed	Lemna minor: United States
lesser swinecress	Coronopus didymus: Australia, England
leuchantheme vulgaire	Chrysanthemum leucanthemum: France
leuleuntjann	Vernonia cinerea: Indonesia
leveaosmankaami	Typha latifolia: Finland
li chun hua	Papaver rhoeas: China
lian sheng gui zi hua	Asclepias curassavica: China

liane merveille	Momordica charantia: Senegal
libd	Carduus pycnocephalus: Egypt
lidah ular	Sida rhombifolia: Malaysia
liden andemad	Lemna minor: Denmark
liden naelde	Urtica urens: Denmark
lidentvetand	Lamium amplexicaule: Denmark
lifaytah	Brassica kaber: Lebanon
liftah	Brassica kaber: Saudi Arabia
light blue snakeweed	Stachytarpheta jamaicensis: Australia
likhlaakh	Silybum marianum: Egypt
likulu	Hibiscus trionum: Zambia
limbagat	Stachytarpheta jamaicensis: Philippines
limo-mesto	Potamogeton pectinatus: Portugal
limpia botella	Setaria geniculata: Venezuela
	Setaria glauca: Venezuela
limpia frascos	Setaria glauca: Colombia
lisaan el kelb	Carduus pycnocephalus: Egypt
lisan el tair	Amaranthus viridis: Sudan
lisan-ul-kalb	Carduus pycnocephalus: Lebanon
lislis	Cardaria draba: Egypt, Saudi Arabia
lissan al teir	Chenopodium murale: Saudi Arabia
little bell	Ipomoea triloba: Hawaii
little ironweed	Vernonia cinerea: Hawaii, United States
liyang pula	Spirodela polyrhiza: Philippines
llengua d'oca	Potamogeton natans: Spain
loblaoka	Polygonum lapathifolium: Iceland
login ajaui	Scirpus mucronatus: Indonesia
lombokan	Ludwigia hyssopifolia: Indonesia
loogkruid	Salsola kali: Netherlands
lopo-lopo	Achyranthes aspera: Philippines
lopucha poina	Raphanus raphanistrum: Poland
lorq	Ludwigia adscendens: Egypt
love in a mist	Passiflora foetida: Australia, Hawaii, Jamaica, Malaysia
lovetann	Taraxacum officinale: Norway
lu ping	Azolla pinnata: China
lua ma	Oryza sativa: Vietnam
lubanga	Cleome gynandra: Zaire, Zambia
luchecillo	Potamogeton pectinatus: Chile
lumanda	Hibiscus trionum: Zambia
lumba-lumba	Momordica charantia: Mali

lumot-lumotan	Hydrilla verticillata: Philippines
lundi	Setaria glauca: Pakistan
lupok-lupok	Passiflora foetida: Philippines
luputu	Pteridium aquilinum: Zambia
luqmet el-hamal	Alternanthera sessilis: Egypt
lusai	Hydrilla verticillata: Philippines
lusakasaka	Corchorus olitorius: Zambia
luya luyang	Paspalum distichum: Philippines
machadita	Vernonia cinerea: Cuba
madahalu	Passiflora foetida: Sri Lanka
madar keserufu	Polygonum aviculare: Hungary
maelkebotte	Taraxacum officinale: Denmark
magarza	Matricaria chamomilla: Spain
magmansi	Vernonia cinerea: Philippines
mahabanky	Paspalum distichum: Madagascar
Maiblume	Taraxacum officinale: Germany
maioba	Cassia occidentalis: Brazil
majina ya kawaida	Digitaria velutina: Kenya
makahiyang lalaki	Aeschynomene indica: Philippines
makikipapatya	Matricaria chamomilla: Turkey
mal cascada	Asclepias curassavica: Colombia
mal-casada	Polygonum lapathifolium: Portugal
mala kislica	Rumex acetosella: Yugoslavia
mala mujer	Acanthospermum hispidum: Dominican Republic
malapako	Ludwigia octovalvis: Philippines
malatungau	Melastoma malabathricum: Philippines
malcha	Ludwigia adscendens: Bangladesh
maleiterir	Euphorbia helioscopia: Portugal
malingan	Ipomoea triloba: Indonesia
malitkalabaw	Paspalum distichum: Philippines
malukhia	Corchorus olitorius: Saudi Arabia
malva	Sida rhombifolia: Brazil, Dominican Republic, Honduras, Mexico
malva de cochino	Sida rhombifolia: Cuba
malva-preta	Sida rhombifolia: Brazil
malvavisco	Sida rhombifolia: Uruguay
mamam	Cleome gynandra: Indonesia
maman pasi	Ludwigia adscendens: Malaysia
mamang	Cleome gynandra: Indonesia
mamanga	Cassia occidentalis: Brazil
mamona	Euphorbia helioscopia: Spain

M

mamuri	Cassia tora: Bolivia
man chiang hung shu	Azolla pinnata: China
manakatud	Ludwigia hyssopifolia: Philippines
manamat	Momordica charantia: Mali
mang kre	Melastoma malabathricum: Thailand
mangayamangaya	Cleome gynandra: Zaire
manzana espinosa	Datura stramonium: Spain
manzanilla	Matricaria chamomilla: Argentina, Chile, Spain, Uruguay, Venezuela
manzanilla bastarda	Matricaria chamomilla: Spain
manzanilla comun	Matricaria chamomilla: Peru
manzanilla de aragon	Matricaria chamomilla: Spain
manzanilla loca	Matricaria chamomilla: Spain
mara pah	Momordica charantia: Thailand
marabawang	Scirpus maritimus: Philippines
maracuja-da-pedra	Passiflora foetida: Brazil
maravilla	Momordica charantia: Venezuela
marchew zwyczajna	Daucus carota: Poland
mare's tail	Conyza canadensis: Canada, Iraq, United States
margaca das boticas	Matricaria chamomilla: Portugal
Margarita	Chrysanthemum leucanthemum: Argentina, Chile, Colombia
	Nicandra physalodes: Angola, Argentina
	Tagetes minuta: Argentina
Margarita mayor	Chrysanthemum leucanthemum: Spain
Margariton	Chrysanthemum leucanthemum: Spain
margose	Momordica charantia: Mauritius
Margriet	Chrysanthemum leucanthemum: Belgium, Netherlands
Margrit	Chrysanthemum leucanthemum: Indonesia
Marguerite	Chrysanthemum leucanthemum: France
Marguerite blanche	Chrysanthemum leucanthemum: Canada
marhi-ki-bam	Alternanthera sessilis: India
mariadistel	Silybum marianum: Netherlands
mariam anna dikeni	Silybum marianum: Turkey
Marian thistle	Silybum marianum: Canada
marianilla	Asclepias curassavica: Mexico
mariballa	Passiflora foetida: Dominican Republic
marie therese	Artemisia vulgaris: Reunion
marie-goujeat	Passiflora foetida: Netherlands
Mariendistel	Silybum marianum: Germany

marietidsel	Silybum marianum: Denmark
marine naiad	Najas marina: United States
marite	Najas marina: Venezuela
maritistel	Silybum marianum: Norway
mark-aerenpris	Veronica arvensis: Denmark
marshpepper smartweed	Polygonum hydropiper: Canada, England, United States
marticorena	Ulex europaeus: Chile
maruna	Artemisia vulgaris: Finland
maruriayh	Chondrilla juncea: Lebanon
marxant	Amaranthus retroflexus: Spain
masaflora	Passiflora foetida: Philippines
maskros	Taraxacum officinale: Sweden
maslacak	Taraxacum officinale: Yugoslavia
massalah	Polygonum aviculare: Iraq
massette	Typha latifolia: France
mastec	Chondrilla juncea: Spain
masteguera borda	Cichorium intybus: Spain
mastruco	Chenopodium ambrosioides: Brazil
	Coronopus didymus: Brazil
mastruco do brejo	Drymaria cordata: Brazil
mastuerzo	Cardaria draba: Spain
	Coronopus didymus: Argentina, Paraguay
mastuerzo hembra	Coronopus didymus: Uruguay
mastuerzo oriental	Cardaria draba: Spain
mastuerzo silvestre	Coronopus didymus: Spain
mata	Pteridium aquilinum: Fiji
mata alfalfa	Sida rhombifolia: Argentina
mata caballo	Asclepias curassavica: Bolivia, Mexico
mata ganado	Euphorbia heterophylla: Ecuador
mata lele	Spirodela polyrhiza: Indonesia
mata pasto	Cassia tora: Brazil
mata pavo	Boerhavia diffusa: Cuba
mata-pasto	Cassia occidentalis: Brazil
matacabra cha do Mexico	Chenopodium ambrosioides: Brazil
matai	Eleocharis dulcis: China
matapasto liso	Cassia tora: Brazil
matricaire	Matricaria chamomilla: Tunisia
matricaire camomille	Matricaria chamomilla: Canada, France
matricaria	Matricaria chamomilla: Portugal
matsubai	Eleocharis acicularis: Japan

Mauer-Gansefuss	Chenopodium murale: Germany
Mause-Gerste	Hordeum murinum: Germany
mausegerste	Hordeum murinum: Netherlands
mauseschwanz-ahnlicher	Alopecurus myosuroides: Switzerland
mavi cicekli canavarotu	Orobanche ramosa: Turkey
mavoadala	Tagetes minuta: Madagascar
mazotillo	Achyranthes aspera: Colombia
mazzasorda	Typha latifolia: Italy
mbanda	Tagetes minuta: Rhodesia
mecanachil	Drymaria cordata: India
mecanilha	Matricaria chamomilla: Brazil
Meer Binse	Scirpus maritimus: Germany
Meer-Sime	Scirpus maritimus: Germany
melao de Sao Tana	Momordica charantia: Brazil
melaozinho	Momordica charantia: Brazil
melastome	Melastoma malabathricum: Hawaii
meligai	Ludwigia hyssopifolia: Indonesia
melon melonan	Passiflora foetida: Philippines
meloykhia	Corchorus olitorius: Egypt
meltonate	Physalis angulata: Guatemala
mendongan	Scirpus mucronatus: Indonesia
meniran	Phyllanthus niruri: Indonesia
menta selvagem	Lamium amplexicaule: Brazil
menta silvestre	Veronica arvensis: Argentina
menting	Cassia occidentalis: Indonesia
mentinha	Veronica arvensis: Brazil
	Veronica persica: Brazil
mentruz	Coronopus didymus: Brazil
mercer grass	Paspalum distichum: New Zealand
meri-nakinruoho	Najas marina: Finland
merikaisla	Scirpus maritimus: Finland
Mexican marigold	Tagetes minuta: New Zealand, Rhodesia, Zambia
Mexican tea	Chenopodium ambrosioides: Australia, Fiji, Hawaii, Jamaica, New Zealand, United States
mezquitillo	Cassia occidentalis: Mexico
michi-yanagi	Polygonum aviculare: Japan
miki palaoa	Cassia occidentalis: Hawaii
Milchdistel	Sonchus arvensis: Germany
milha amarela	Setaria glauca: Portugal
milha glauca	Setaria glauca: Portugal

milk thistle	Silybum marianum: Australia, Canada, Iran, United States
millet sauvage	Setaria pallide-fusca: Mauritius
mimbra	Ludwigia adscendens: Colombia
	Ludwigia hyssopifolia: Cambodia, Colombia
mimbuzu	Momordica charantia: Angola
mintina	Chenopodium ambrosioides: Egypt
miona	Silybum marianum: Colombia
miraculous bush	Momordica charantia: Barbados
mirim	Emilia sonchifolia: Brazil
misbredie	Amaranthus viridis: South Africa
misji repak	Alopecurus myosuroides: Yugoslavia
misk otu	Artemisia vulgaris: Turkey
mitikanduri	Alternanthera sessilis: India
mive sok ne-gya	Tridax procumbens: Burma
mizukinbai	Ludwigia adscendens: Japan
mjukplister	Lamium amplexicaule: Sweden
mjuktvitann	Lamium amplexicaule: Norway
moddad	Ludwigia adscendens: Egypt
moddeid	Boerhavia diffusa: Egypt, Saudi Arabia
	Paspalum distichum: Egypt
Mohrrube	Daucus carota: Germany
mol okhta	Corchorus olitorius: Sudan
monara kudumbiya	Vernonia cinerea: Sri Lanka
monggo-monggohan	Cassia tora: Philippines
mongoose tail	Setaria glauca: Fiji
monte espinoso	Salsola kali: Chile
moquillo	Cassia occidentalis: Guatemala
moraar	Senecio vulgaris: Lebanon, Saudia Arabia
moradilla	Boerhavia diffusa: Guatemala
moreas	Momordica charantia: Cambodia
morningglory	Ipomoea aquatica: Hawaii
morogozy	Momordica charantia: Madagascar
morot	Daucus carota: Sweden
morrar	Senecio vulgaris: Egypt
morrones dobles	Lamium amplexicaule: Spain
mosquito fern	Azolla pinnata: United States
mossy passion flower	Passiflora foetida: Australia
mostacilla	Brassica campestris: Argentina, Mexico
	Raphanus raphanistrum: Uruguay

mostarda	Brassica campestris: Brazil
	Brassica kaber: Brazil
mostarda dos campos	Brassica kaber: Portugal
mostaza	Brassica campestris: Chile, Mexico, Paraguay
	Brassica kaber: Dominican Republic, Mexico
mostaza arvense	Brassica kaber: Spain
mostaza silvestre	Brassica campestris: Colombia
	Brassica kaber: Spain, Uruguay
motha	Cyperus haspan: India
motherwort	Artemisia vulgaris: England, United States
motojobobo embolsado	Physalis angulata: Bolivia
mouiswildegars	Hordeum murinum: South Africa
mouse barley	Hordeum murinum: South Africa, United States
mousetail grass	Alopecurus myosuroides: Lebanon
moutarde des champs	Brassica kaber: Canada, France, Morocco, Tunisia
moutarde des oiseaux	Brassica campestris: Canada
moutarde sauvage	Brassica kaber: France
mrkva	Daucus carota: Yugoslavia
mubumacembere	Nicandra physalodes: Zimbabwe
mugikusa	Hordeum murinum: Japan
mugweed	Artemisia vulgaris: United States
mugwort	Artemisia vulgaris: Canada, England, United States
Mugwurz Wermut	Artemisia vulgaris: Germany
muhole	Cleome gynandra: Zaire
mukkopeera	Passiflora foetida: India
mukkurattai	Boerhavia diffusa: India
mukkuthipoo	Tridax procumbens: India
mukochi	Pteridium aquilinum: Zambia
mukukwa	Hibiscus trionum: Zambia
mukunu-venna	Alternanthera sessilis: Sri Lanka
mule tail	Conyza canadensis: United States
mullaca	Physalis angulata: Colombia
mullum bimby couch	Cyperus brevifolius: Australia
munchira	Setaria geniculata: Colombia
muntinab	Chenopodium murale: Lebanon
muong hor	Cassia tora: Vietnam
muop dang hoan	Momordica charantia: Vietnam
muop dong	Momordica charantia: Vietnam
mur-gasefod	Chenopodium murale: Denmark
mura-saki-mukashi-yomogi	Vernonia cinerea: Japan

musebygg	Hordeum murinum: Norway
mushilu	Pteridium aquilinum: Zambia
musk thistle	Carduus nutans: England, United States
mutanda zyeelo	Tagetes minuta: Zambia
muti-muti	Ipomoea triloba: Philippines
Mutterkraut	Matricaria chamomilla: Germany
muurganzevoet	Chenopodium murale: Netherlands
muurhondebossie	Chenopodium murale: South Africa
mwaisilah	Polygonum lapathifolium: Iraq
myriophylle en epi	Myriophyllum spicatum: Belgium, Canada
myrkkykatko	Conium maculatum: Finland
na'eem	Achyranthes aspera: Saudi Arabia
nabica	Raphanus raphanistrum: Brazil
nabillo	Raphanus raphanistrum: Mexico
nabo	Brassica campestris: Argentina, Brazil, Colombia, Paraguay, Puerto Rico, Spain
	Raphanus raphanistrum: Brazil
nabo blanco	Brassica campestris: Argentina
nabo branco	Brassica campestris: Brazil
nabo salvaje	Brassica campestris: Argentina, Paraguay
nabo silvestre	Brassica campestris: Argentina, Bolivia, Mexico, Paraguay, Uruguay
nadel-simse	Eleocharis acicularis: Germany
nae harng hern	Azolla pinnata: Laos
nae pawng han	Hydrilla verticillata: Laos
nae yai	Spirodela polyrhiza: Thailand
naedaeng	Azolla pinnata: Thailand
nafal	Cardaria draba: Egypt, Saudi Arabia
nafir	Datura stramonium: Lebanon
naide marine	Najas marina: France
naivelai	Cleome gynandra: India
nana kamby	Euphorbia heterophylla: Paraguay
nandukkal pillu	Digitaria longiflora: Sri Lanka
nang kim	Eleocharis dulcis: Vietnam
nang ngat	Eleocharis dulcis: Vietnam
narrow-leaved cattail	Typha angustifolia: Cambodia, Canada
narrowleaf cattail	Typha angustifolia: United States
naru	Paspalum distichum: Pakistan
natesarv	Najas marina: Sweden
navette sauvage	Brassica campestris: France
nayuruvi	Achyranthes aspera: India

N

nchesa	Acanthospermum hispidum: Zambia
nea kan to sarng	Alternanthera sessilis: Laos
nebo cimarron	Raphanus raphanistrum: Mexico
nebo silvestre	Raphanus raphanistrum: Mexico
needle spikerush	Eleocharis acicularis: United States
nefer	Datura stramonium: Egypt
negro	Cirsium vulgare: Chile
negro coffe	Cassia occidentalis: Malaysia
nela usiti	Phyllanthus niruri: India
nellittali	Aeschynomene indica: India
nenang belanguh	Ludwigia adscendens: Indonesia
nerkka-kora	Setaria pallide-fusca: India
nervillo	Drymaria cordata: Colombia
nettle	Urtica urens: New Zealand
nettle goosefoot	Chenopodium murale: Hawaii
nettle-leaved fathen	Chenopodium murale: New Zealand
nettle-leaved goosefoot	Chenopodium murale: England, Lebanon, South Africa
nettleleaf goosefoot	Chenopodium murale: Australia, United States, Zimbabwe
nettleleaf vervain	Stachytarpheta jamaicensis: New Caledonia
neu-mao-chaon	Eleocharis acicularis: China
ngoni	Pteridium aquilinum: Zambia
nicktistel	Carduus nutans: Sweden
nih-chain	Myriophyllum spicatum: China
Nikende Distel	Carduus nutans: Germany
nikkende tidsel	Carduus nutans: Denmark
nikketistel	Carduus nutans: Norway
niknikitan	Achyranthes aspera: Philippines
nilhue	Sonchus asper: Chile
nilhue caballuno	Sonchus asper: Chile
nino muerto	Asclepias curassavica: Panama
niruri	Phyllanthus niruri: Hawaii
nitna	Chenopodium ambrosioides: Egypt
niwayanagi	Polygonum aviculare: Japan
njivni lisicjirep	Alopecurus myosuroides: Yugoslavia
no'oeim	Achyranthes aspera: Saudi Arabia
noborogiku	Senecio vulgaris: Japan
noce spinosa	Datura stramonium: Italy
noche buena	Euphorbia heterophylla: Mexico

nodding thistle	Carduus nutans: Australia, Canada, New Zealand, Tasmania, United States
nodeweed	Synedrella nodiflora: Hawaii
nohara-hijiki	Salsola kali: Japan
nongue morado	Datura stramonium: Venezuela
nora-ninjin	Daucus carota: Japan
Nordamerikanishe Seide	Cuscuta campestris: Germany
Noterheinich	Amaranthus viridis: Germany
nsangani	Digitaria longiflora: Zambia
nseeto	Acanthospermum hispidum: Zambia
nuokkukarhiainen	Carduus nutans: Finland
nya nya	Momordica charantia: Ghana
nyeve	Cleome gynandra: Zimbabwe
nyinya	Momordica charantia: Ghana
o-aka-ukikusa	Azolla pinnata: Japan
o-inu-tade	Polygonum lapathifolium: Japan
o-inunofuguri	Veronica persica: Japan
occhietta della madonna	Veronica persica: Italy
odort	Conium maculatum: Sweden
oficial de sala	Asclepias curassavica: Brazil, Colombia
ognicha	Brassica kaber: Poland
olivarda	Conyza canadensis: Spain
olowonjeja	Trianthema portulacastrum: Nigeria
ombimboalareo	Stachytarpheta jamaicensis: Madagascar
ong tsoi	Ipomoea aquatica: China
oni-hire-azami	Carduus pycnocephalus: Japan
oni-nogeshi	Sonchus asper: Japan
onigahongula	Nicandra physalodes: Angola
opret anarant	Amaranthus retroflexus: Denmark
Orakelblume	Chrysanthemum leucanthemum: Germany
orange foxtail	Alopecurus aequalis: England, New Zealand
orge des rats	Hordeum murinum: France, Morocco, Tunisia
orge queue de rat	Hordeum murinum: France
orientveronika	Veronica persica: Norway
ornebregne	Pteridium aquilinum: Denmark
orobanche	Orobanche minor: Chile
orobanche du chanvre	Orobanche ramosa: France
orobanche du trefle	Orobanche minor: France
orobanche mineure	Orobanche minor: France
orobanche rameuse	Orobanche ramosa: France

O

orozuz	Conyza canadensis: Puerto Rico
ortica piccola	Urtica urens: Italy
ortie	Urtica urens: France
ortie brulante	Urtica urens: Canada, France
ortie rouge aux feuilles rondes	Lamium amplexicaule: France
ortiga	Urtica urens: Argentina, Colombia, Uruguay
ortiga blanca	Urtica urens: Colombia
ortiga brava	Urtica urens: Argentina
ortiga chica	Urtica urens: Argentina
ortiga comun	Urtica urens: Chile, Spain
ortiga de hojas	Lamium amplexicaule: Spain
ortiga mansa	Lamium amplexicaule: Argentina
ortiga menor	Urtica urens: Spain
ortiga muerta	Lamium amplexicaule: Spain
ortiga negra	Urtica urens: Argentina, Chile
oruga silvestre	Raphanus raphanistrum: Spain
orzo selvatico	Hordeum murinum: Italy
oseille	Oxalis latifolia: Mauritius
ota karisi	Ipomoea aquatica: Fiji
otavalvati	Sonchus asper: Finland
oxeye daisy	Chrysanthemum leucanthemum: Australia, Canada, England, Hawaii, New Zealand, United States
oxygenweed	Elodea canadensis: New Zealand
oyo	Corchorus olitorius: Nigeria
ozmak	Cardaria draba: Iran
paabilis	Boerhavia erecta: Philippines
paanbalibis	Boerhavia diffusa: Philippines
paardebloem	Taraxacum officinale: Belgium, Netherlands
pabio	Setaria glauca: Italy
pacha	Lemna minor: India
pachar	Ludwigia octovalvis: Philippines
pacific meadow foxtail	Alopecurus myosuroides: United States
packurmul	Polygonum hydropiper: India
pactilla	Rumex acetosella: Ecuador
paddy lucerne	Sida rhombifolia: New Zealand
paddy's lucerne	Sida rhombifolia: Australia, Fiji
padi ketek	Oryza sativa: Indonesia
paeng puey	Ludwigia adscendens: Thailand
pagel	Momordica charantia: India
pahal-kai	Momordica charantia: Sri Lanka
pahk pai	Polygonum hydropiper: Thailand

P

paico	Chenopodium ambrosioides: Argentina, Chile, Colombia, Panama, Paraguay, Peru, Spain, Venezuela
paico macho	Chenopodium ambrosioides: Argentina, Uruguay
pain blanc	Cardaria draba: France
painted euphorbia	Euphorbia prunifolia: South Africa
painted spurge	Euphorbia heterophylla: Australia, United States
paiten	Setaria geniculata: Argentina
paivankakkara	Chrysanthemum leucanthemum: Finland
paja amarga	Paspalum distichum: Colombia
paja de estera	Typha angustifolia: Chile
pajamarioba	Cassia occidentalis: Brazil
pajarera	Drymaria cordata: Colombia
pajon blanco	Setaria geniculata: Dominican Republic
pak pawd	Ludwigia adscendens: Laos
pak ped dam	Alternanthera sessilis: Thailand
pak ped nam	Alternanthera philoxeroides: Thailand
pakis gemblung	Pteridium aquilinum: Indonesia
pakong buwaya	Pteridium aquilinum: Philippines
paku gila	Pteridium aquilinum: Indonesia
paku rincang	Pteridium aquilinum: Indonesia
pakurmal	Polygonum hydropiper: Bangladesh
pale knotweed	Polygonum lapathifolium: Australia
pale persicaria	Polygonum lapathifolium: England, Lebanon
pale pigeon grass	Setaria glauca: Australia
pale smartweed	Polygonum lapathifolium: Canada, United States
pale willow weed	Polygonum lapathifolium: New Zealand
palia	Momordica charantia: Philippines
palitaria	Drymaria cordata: Honduras
palma	Pteridium aquilinum: El Salvador
palo de leche	Boerhavia erecta: El Salvador
pana	Azolla pinnata: India
panee marich	Polygonum persicaria: Bangladesh, India
pangeor	Ludwigia adscendens: Indonesia
panicastrella	Setaria glauca: Italy
panicastrella scura	Setaria glauca: Italy
panico glauco	Setaria glauca: Italy
panimarich	Polygonum hydropiper: Bangladesh
panluilui	Paspalum distichum: Philippines
pannankani	Alternanthera sessilis: Sri Lanka
panquica	Tridax procumbens: Mexico

paparean	Oryza sativa: Indonesia
papavero salvatico	Papaver rhoeas: Italy
papayilla	Momordica charantia: Peru
papegaaienkruid	Amaranthus retroflexus: Netherlands
papoila-das-searas	Papaver rhoeas: Portugal
papolas	Cardaria draba: Spain
papoula ordinaria	Papaver rhoeas: Portugal
para-para'i	Phyllanthus niruri: Paraguay
parchita de culebra	Passiflora foetida: Venezuela
parchita de montana	Passiflora foetida: Venezuela
pare	Momordica charantia: Indonesia
parece-mas-nao-e	Euphorbia heterophylla: Brazil
parhar	Cleome gynandra: India
paria	Momordica charantia: Indonesia, Philippines
paroka	Momordica charantia: Guatemala
parrots-feather	Myriophyllum spicatum: South Africa
partasana	Typha angustifolia: Brazil
pasau na haba	Corchorus olitorius: Philippines
pasau-hupai	Ludwigia hyssopifolia: Philippines
pascua	Euphorbia heterophylla: Peru
pascueta	Conyza canadensis: Puerto Rico
pascuita	Euphorbia heterophylla: El Salvador, Venezuela
pasionariang-mabaho	Passiflora foetida: Philippines
pasote	Chenopodium ambrosioides: Puerto Rico, Venezuela
paspalo distico	Paspalum distichum: Italy
paspalon du-turi	Paspalum distichum: Israel
paspalum a deux epis	Paspalum distichum: Morocco
passerage	Cardaria draba: France
passerage drave	Cardaria draba: France
pasta miuda	Lemna minor: Brazil
pastenade	Daucus carota: France
pastillo de invierno	Poa annua: Argentina
pastinaca selvatica	Daucus carota: Italy
pastito de invierno	Poa annua: Uruguay
pasto azul anual	Poa annua: Colombia
pasto chanchero	Polygonum aviculare: Argentina
pasto de invierno	Poa annua: Argentina
pasto de las liendres	Poa annua: Chile
pasto del pollo	Polygonum aviculare: Chile
pasto setaria	Setaria geniculata: Paraguay

pata de gallina	Lamium amplexicaule: Argentina
	Poa annua: Colombia
pata de perdiz	Poa annua: Chile
pata jhanji	Potamogeton crispus: Bangladesh
	Vallisneria spiralis: Bangladesh
pata parinta	Corchorus olitorius: India
pata showla	Vallisneria spiralis: Bangladesh
patasewla	Vallisneria spiralis: India
patharchata	Trianthema portulacastrum: India
paturin annuel	Poa annua: Belgium, Canada, France, Morocco, Switzerland
pava kai	Momordica charantia: India
pavot coquelicot	Papaver rhoeas: France
pazote	Chenopodium ambrosioides: Puerto Rico
pazun-sa	Alternanthera sessilis: Burma
pe-de-ganso	Chenopodium murale: Portugal
pega-pega	Setaria geniculata: Chile
pega-pinto	Boerhavia diffusa: Brazil
pego pinto	Drymaria cordata: Brazil
pel de ca	Poa annua: Spain
pelillo	Eleocharis acicularis: Mexico
	Poa annua: Argentina
pelo de chancho	Poa annua: Brazil
pelo de rata	Poa annua: Uruguay
pelosa	Poa annua: Spain
pelovillakko	Senecio vulgaris: Finland
peltoemakki	Fumaria officinalis: Finland
peltokaali	Brassica campestris: Finland
peltoretikka	Raphanus raphanistrum: Finland
peltotaskuruoho	Thlaspi arvense: Finland
peltovalvatti	Sonchus arvensis: Finland
penasco	Eragrostis pilosa: Brazil
pendientitos	Fumaria officinalis: Spain
pengeurt	Thlaspi arvense: Norway
penningort	Thlaspi arvense: Sweden
pennycress	Thlaspi arvense: England, New Zealand
peo de fraile	Datura stramonium: Colombia, Puerto Rico
pepe b'acqua	Polygonum hydropiper: Italy
peperbos cardaria	Cardaria draba: South Africa
peperetan	Eleocharis dulcis: Indonesia
pepino	Momordica charantia: Mexico

pepperwort	Marsilea quadrifolia: India, Iran
perdeblom	Taraxacum officinale: South Africa
perejillon cicuta	Conium maculatum: Spain
perennial peppergrass	Cardaria draba: Canada, Lebanon, United States
perennial sowthistle	Sonchus arvensis: Australia, Canada, England, New Zealand, United States
peria	Momordica charantia: Hawaii, Indonesia, Malaysia
peria laut	Momordica charantia: Malaysia
permot	Passiflora foetida: Indonesia
Persian speedwell	Veronica persica: Australia, United States
Persian tadyke	Veronica persica: Finland
persicaire acre	Polygonum hydropiper: France
persicaire douce	Polygonum persicaria: France
persicaire pale	Polygonum lapathifolium: Canada
persicaria	Polygonum persicaria: Argentina, Australia, England, Italy, Portugal, Scotland, Spain
persicaria de pe vermelho	Polygonum persicaria: Brazil
persicaria maggiore	Polygonum lapathifolium: Italy
persicaria mayor	Polygonum lapathifolium: Spain
persicaria mordaz	Polygonum hydropiper: Portugal
persicaria picante	Polygonum hydropiper: Spain
persicaria salcerella	Polygonum lapathifolium: Italy
Persischer Ehrenpreis	Veronica persica: Germany
Peru apple	Nicandra physalodes: Natal
perumpunnhu	Corchorus olitorius: India
perumpunnkku poondu	Corchorus olitorius: India
perzikkruid	Polygonum persicaria: Belgium, Netherlands
pesca miuda	Lemna minor: Brazil
peste d'acqua	Elodea canadensis: Italy
peste d'eau	Elodea canadensis: Belgium
petite grenadille	Passiflora foetida: Reunion
petite lentille-deau	Lemna minor: France
petite ortie	Urtica urens: Belgium, France
petite oseille	Rumex acetosella: Belgium, Canada, France
peupeuteyan	Aeschynomene indica: Indonesia
peyavarai	Cassia occidentalis: India
Pfeffer-Knoterich	Polygonum hydropiper: Germany
Pfeilkraut	Sagittaria sagittifolia: Germany
Pfeilkresse	Cardaria draba: Germany
Pfennigkraut	Thlaspi arvense: Germany

Pfirsch-Knoterich	Polygonum persicaria: Germany
Pfirsichblattriger Knoterich	Polygonum persicaria: Germany
phak bung	Ipomoea aquatica: Laos
phak buong	Ipomoea aquatica: Thailand
phak phai nam	Polygonum hydropiper: Thailand
phak sian	Cleome gynandra: Thailand
phak sian khaao	Cleome gynandra: Thailand
phak som sian	Cleome gynandra: Thailand
phak-bia-hin	Trianthema portulacastrum: Thailand
phak-khom-lin	Boerhavia diffusa: Thailand
phak-khral	Synedrella nodiflora: Thailand
phak-krom	Amaranthus viridis: Thailand
phak-pet-thai	Alternanthera sessilis: Thailand
phakchi-daeng	Daucus carota: Thailand
phan nguu	Achyranthes aspera: Thailand
phanafuli	Tridax procumbens: India
phiphru	Oxalis latifolia: India
phong	Saccharum spontaneum: Thailand
phong phot	Polygonum lapathifolium: Thailand
phti thmar	Trianthema portulacastrum: Cambodia
phutuka	Melastoma malabathricum: India
phyllanthus	Phyllanthus niruri: Argentina
pi-tsi	Eleocharis dulcis: China
piagillo	Poa annua: Chile
pica pica	Ulex europaeus: Chile
pichicara	Coronopus didymus: Peru
pie danserino	Chenopodium murale: Italy
pie di nibbio	Ranunculus repens: Italy
pied rouge	Polygonum persicaria: France
pigaeble	Datura stramonium: Denmark
piggeple	Datura stramonium: Norway
pihatatar	Polygonum aviculare: Finland
piikkiohdakke	Cirsium vulgare: Finland
pijlkruid	Sagittaria sagittifolia: Belgium, Netherlands
pijlkruidkers	Cardaria draba: Belgium, Netherlands
pikkulimaska	Lemna minor: Finland
pilblad	Sagittaria sagittifolia: Denmark, Norway, Sweden
pilose eragrostis	Eragrostis pilosa: United States
pimenta de agua	Polygonum hydropiper: Portugal
pimentilla	Polygonum persicaria: Spain

pimienta de agua	Polygonum hydropiper: Spain
	Polygonum lapathifolium: Argentina
pincel	Emilia sonchifolia: Brazil
pincel de amor	Emilia sonchifolia: Dominican Republic
pincelillo de poeta	Emilia sonchifolia: Dominican Republic
ping	Marsilea quadrifolia: China
pink convolvulus	Ipomoea aquatica: Australia
	Ipomoea triloba: Australia
pinyin	Achyranthes aspera: China
	Cleome gynandra: China
	Polygonum hydropiper: China
piojillo	Poa annua: Chile, Colombia
piquant jambe	Tridax procumbens: Dominican Republic
pira	Amaranthus retroflexus: Venezuela
pira blanca	Amaranthus viridis: Venezuela
pirinac	Oryza sativa: Turkey, Yugoslavia
pissat des chiens	Cleome gynandra: Mauritius
pissenlit	Taraxacum officinale: Belgium, Canada, France
pit-pit	Saccharum spontaneum: New Guinea
pixaca	Hordeum murinum: Spain
platanillo	Asclepias curassavica: Colombia, Puerto Rico
	Cassia occidentalis: Cuba
platanillo lechoso	Asclepias curassavica: Bolivia
platanito	Cleome gynandra: Colombia
pluma grande	Pteridium aquilinum: Brazil
poa	Poa annua: Ecuador, Greece, Spain
poa annua	Poa annua: New Zealand
poc poc	Passiflora foetida: Reunion
poc-poc sauvage	Passiflora foetida: Mauritius
poimuvita	Potamogeton crispus: Finland
poison hemlock	Conium maculatum: Canada, Lebanon, United States
poison Joanna	Asclepias curassavica: Trinidad
poisonous cape	Physalis angulata: Jamaica
poivre d'eau	Polygonum hydropiper: Belgium, France
pokasungo	Vernonia cinerea: India
pokok lang bulu	Passiflora foetida: Malaysia
poligono a foglia di romice	Polygonum lapathifolium: Italy
poligono pata de perdiz	Polygonum lapathifolium: Spain
poligono pejiguera	Polygonum persicaria: Spain
poma	Silybum marianum: Colombia

pomme epineuse	Datura stramonium: France, Morocco
pondweed	Potamogeton pectinatus: New Zealand
pong pode	Polygonum lapathifolium: Thailand
popoja	Physalis angulata: Ecuador
porkkana	Daucus carota: Finland
porter bush	Synedrella nodiflora: Barbados, Trinidad
potamot	Potamogeton natans: France
potamot crepu	Potamogeton crispus: Belgium, Canada, France
potamot negeant	Potamogeton natans: Belgium
potamot pectine	Potamogeton pectinatus: Belgium, Canada, France
potato weed	Heliotropium europaeum: Australia
potato-vine	Ipomoea aquatica: Australia
	Ipomoea triloba: Australia
pottakanchi	Rumex acetosella: India
prastkrage	Chrysanthemum leucanthemum: Sweden
presseguera	Polygonum persicaria: Spain
prestekrage	Chrysanthemum leucanthemum: Norway
Pretoria sida	Sida rhombifolia: South Africa
prickly saltwort	Salsola kali: Australia, England, United States
prickly sowthistle	Sonchus asper: England, New Zealand
pride weed	Conyza canadensis: Canada
primrose willow	Ludwigia octovalvis: Hawaii
prince of wales feather	Amaranthus viridis: Australia
prostrate knotweed	Polygonum aviculare: Canada, South Africa, United States
prutas taungan	Passiflora foetida: Philippines
przymiotno Kanadyjskie	Conyza canadensis: Poland
pteris aigle	Pteridium aquilinum: France
pticja dresen	Polygonum aviculare: Yugoslavia
pugo-pugo	Cyperus brevifolius: Philippines
puliyarai	Oxalis latifolia: Sri Lanka
punarnava	Boerhavia diffusa: India
punxo	Scirpus mucronatus: Spain
purple sow thistle	Emilia sonchifolia: Australia
purple thorn apple	Datura stramonium: New Zealand
purple-flowered oxalis	Oxalis latifolia: Australia
purua grass	Scirpus maritimus: New Zealand
purun	Typha angustifolia: Indonesia
putok-putokan	Physalis angulata: Philippines
puyui	Ipomoea triloba: Mexico

Q

pyazi	Asphodelus tenuifolius: India, Pakistan
pystykeiholehti	Sagittaria sagittifolia: Finland
qalye	Salsola kali: Egypt
qanderoonak	Chondrilla juncea: Iran
qardaab	Polygonum lapathifolium: Egypt
qato cuva	Pteridium aquilinum: Fiji
qeddaab	Polygonum hydropiper: Egypt
	Polygonum lapathifolium: Egypt
	Polygonum persicaria: Egypt
qirilla	Brassica kaber: Saudi Arabia
qoddaad	Polygonum aviculare: Egypt
	Polygonum lapathifolium: Egypt
qooddaaby	Polygonum lapathifolium: Egypt
qordaab	Polygonum aviculare: Egypt
	Polygonum hydropiper: Egypt
	Polygonum lapathifolium: Egypt
	Polygonum persicaria: Egypt
qordeyb	Polygonum hydropiper: Egypt
	Polygonum lapathifolium: Egypt
	Polygonum persicaria: Egypt
quato	Pteridium aquilinum: Fiji
quebra pedra	Phyllanthus niruri: Brazil
Queen Ann's lace	Daucus carota: Canada, United States
Queensland pigeon grass	Setaria pallide-fusca: Australia
quelite	Amaranthus retroflexus: Mexico
quelite cenizo	Chenopodium murale: Mexico
quelite de coyote	Chenopodium murale: Mexico
Quendel-Seide	Cuscuta epithymum: Germany
quenouille a feuilles etroites	Typha angustifolia: Cambodia, Canada
quenouille a feuilles larges	Typha latifolia: Canada
queue derat	Stachytarpheta jamaicensis: Mauritius
quiebra arado	Asclepias curassavica: Argentina
quimpe	Coronopus didymus: Argentina
quinchihue	Tagetes minuta: Chile
quinguilla	Chenopodium murale: Chile
quinine weed	Phyllanthus niruri: Jamaica
quininito	Phyllanthus niruri: Dominican Republic
quinino del pobre	Phyllanthus niruri: Puerto Rico
quinoa negra	Chenopodium murale: Argentina, Uruguay
quinquilho	Datura stramonium: Brazil

quintilho	Nicandra physalodes: Brazil
quita soliman	Asclepias curassavica: Peru
raapzaad	Brassica campestris: Netherlands
rabanillo	Raphanus raphanistrum: Spain
rabanito salvaje	Raphanus raphanistrum: Paraguay
rabaniza comun	Raphanus raphanistrum: Spain
rabano	Raphanus raphanistrum: Argentina, Chile, Ecuador
rabano cimarron	Raphanus raphanistrum: Peru
rabano morado	Raphanus raphanistrum: Colombia
rabano mostaza	Raphanus raphanistrum: Colombia
rabano silvestre	Raphanus raphanistrum: Peru, Spain, Uruguay
rabito	Setaria glauca: Mexico
rabito peludo	Setaria glauca: Cuba
rabizon	Raphanus raphanistrum: Argentina
rabo de buey	Vernonia cinerea: Puerto Rico
rabo de chancho	Achyranthes aspera: Colombia
rabo de gato	Achyranthes aspera: Cuba
rabo de lobo	Orobanche minor: Spain
rabo de rajao	Tagetes minuta: Brazil
rabo de raposa	Alopecurus myosuroides: Portugal
	Setaria geniculata: Brazil
rabo de raton	Achyranthes aspera: Colombia, Puerto Rico
rabo de zorra	Setaria glauca: Dominican Republic
rabo de zorro	Setaria geniculata: Peru, Puerto Rico
	Setaria glauca: Venezuela
radia	Raphanus raphanistrum: Madagascar
radicchio	Cichorium intybus: Italy
radice bravio	Taraxacum officinale: Brazil
radicha	Taraxacum officinale: Argentina
radicheta	Cichorium intybus: Argentina
	Taraxacum officinale: Argentina
radis ravenelle	Raphanus raphanistrum: France
radis sauvage	Raphanus raphanistrum: Canada, France
rafanistro	Raphanus raphanistrum: Italy
ragradi	Achyranthes aspera: Philippines
rague	Eragrostis pilosa: Paraguay
railway weed	Tridax procumbens: Trinidad
rain	Chenopodium murale: Saudi Arabia
raiz colorada	Alternanthera philoxeroides: Argentina, Paraguay, Uruguay

R

rajasthan	Boerhavia diffusa: India
rajkot	Boerhavia diffusa: India
rambaton blunsun	Passiflora foetida: Indonesia
ramenas	Raphanus raphanistrum: South Africa
rami cina	Corchorus olitorius: Indonesia
ramiary	Datura stramonium: Madagascar
ramilamina	Azolla pinnata: Madagascar
ramkarse	Coronopus didymus: Norway
ramolaccio selvatico	Raphanus raphanistrum: Italy
ramput tahi babi	Stachytarpheta jamaicensis: Malaysia
ran bo	Marsilea quadrifolia: Vietnam
rapa	Brassica campestris: Italy
rapastrello	Raphanus raphanistrum: Italy
rapiente	Paspalum distichum: Cuba
rashad el-barr	Coronopus didymus: Egypt
rau deu	Alternanthera sessilis: Vietnam
rau dua trau	Ludwigia adscendens: Vietnam
raudt honsegras	Polygonum lapathifolium: Norway
Rauhe Gansedistel	Sonchus asper: Germany
Rauhe Saudiste	Sonchus asper: Germany
Rauhhaariger Amarant	Amaranthus retroflexus: Germany
rautanokkonen	Urtica urens: Finland
ravastrello	Raphanus raphanistrum: Italy
ravelle	Raphanus raphanistrum: Tunisia
ravenelle	Raphanus raphanistrum: Algeria, Belgium, France, Morocco
rdest kolankowaty	Polygonum lapathifolium: Poland
rdest ostrogorzki	Polygonum hydropiper: Poland
rdest plamisty	Polygonum persicaria: Poland
rdest ptasi	Polygonum aviculare: Poland
rdest szczawiolistny	Polygonum lapathifolium: Poland
red flowering fumitory	Fumaria officinalis: Australia
red garden sorrel	Oxalis latifolia: South Africa
red groundsel	Emilia sonchifolia: Barbados
red head cottonbush	Asclepias curassavica: Australia
red ludwigia	Ludwigia adscendens: United States
red pualele	Emilia sonchifolia: Hawaii
red rice	Oryza sativa: Guyana, United States
red shank	Polygonum hydropiper: Ireland
red sorrel	Rumex acetosella: England, Hawaii, United States
red tassel-flower	Emilia sonchifolia: United States

red top	Asclepias curassavica: Trinidad
redhead	Asclepias curassavica: Jamaica, Trinidad
	Euphorbia heterophylla: British Honduras
redroot	Amaranthus retroflexus: Australia, New Zealand
redroot pigweed	Amaranthus retroflexus: Canada, Lebanon, United States
redshank	Polygonum persicaria: England, Scotland
reesa	Oryza sativa: India
regop boerhavia	Boerhavia erecta: South Africa
regop sterklits	Acanthospermum hispidum: South Africa
relogio	Sida rhombifolia: Brazil
renkavle	Alopecurus myosuroides: Sweden
renkli ballibaba	Lamium amplexicaule: Turkey
renoncule rampante	Ranunculus repens: Canada, France
renouee a feuilles de patience	Polygonum lapathifolium: France, Switzerland
renouee des oiseaux	Polygonum aviculare: Canada, France, Switzerland, Tunisia
renouee noueuse	Polygonum lapathifolium: France
renouee persicaire	Polygonum persicaria: Canada, France
renouee poivre d'eau	Polygonum hydropiper: Canada, France
repcsenyretek	Raphanus raphanistrum: Hungary
repusnjaca	Conyza canadensis: Yugoslavia
rere	Cassia occidentalis: Nigeria
resquemona	Polygonum hydropiper: Spain
retirante	Acanthospermum hispidum: Brazil
reveille-matin	Euphorbia helioscopia: Morocco
revormstorel	Euphorbia helioscopia: Sweden
revsmorblomma	Ranunculus repens: Sweden
rhombiod ilima	Sida rhombifolia: Hawaii
ribbon weed	Vallisneria spiralis: Australia, United States
rikkapuntarpaa	Alopecurus myosuroides: Finland
rikkasinappi	Brassica kaber: Finland
rikkavoikukka	Taraxacum officinale: Finland
riverweed	Elodea canadensis: New Zealand
rodadora	Salsola kali: Mexico
rodilla de pollo	Boerhavia diffusa: Colombia
rodkhaa	Polygonum lapathifolium: Sweden
rodknae	Rumex acetosella: Denmark
romacilla	Rumex acetosella: Chile
romerillo de loma	Tridax procumbens: Cuba
rond nu-nut	Drymaria cordata: Indonesia

rong la ha	Hydrilla verticillata: Vietnam
rong toc tien	Myriophyllum spicatum: Vietnam
ronsyleinikki	Ranunculus repens: Finland
rooituinsuring	Oxalis latifolia: South Africa
rosilla	Tridax procumbens: Mexico
rosolaccio	Papaver rhoeas: Italy
Rote Borstenhirse	Setaria glauca: Germany
Rotgelber Fuchschwanz	Alopecurus aequalis: Germany
rough sowthistle	Sonchus asper: Australia
rough-chaff flower	Achyranthes aspera: South Africa
roughseed bulrush	Scirpus mucronatus: United States
roughseed club-rush	Scirpus mucronatus: England
ru svinemaelk	Sonchus asper: Denmark
rubah sila	Ludwigia adscendens: Indonesia
Rubsen	Brassica campestris: Germany
rukd	Chenopodium murale: Saudi Arabia
rummadah	Euphorbia helioscopia: Lebanon
rumpt kerechut	Scirpus mucronatus: Malaysia
rumput babi	Synedrella nodiflora: Malaysia
rumput kumbah	Scirpus mucronatus: Malaysia
rumput tahi babi	Vernonia cinerea: Malaysia
runch	Raphanus raphanistrum: England
Rundblatterige Taubnessel	Lamium amplexicaule: Germany
rupa chico	Urtica urens: Argentina
rush skeletonweed	Chondrilla juncea: United States
Russian cactus	Salsola kali: United States
Russian thistle	Salsola kali: Canada, Hungary, Lebanon, United States
Russian tumbleweed	Salsola kali: Canada, South Africa, United States
Russiese rolbossie	Salsola kali: South Africa
ruwe melkdistel	Sonchus asper: Netherlands
ryunohigemo	Potamogeton pectinatus: Japan
rzodkiew swirzepa	Raphanus raphanistrum: Poland
sa'dah	Euphorbia helioscopia: Lebanon
saa'da	Euphorbia helioscopia: Egypt
saca-rolhas	Vallisneria spiralis: Portugal
sacabyche	Physalis angulata: Puerto Rico
saeppola	Conyza canadensis: Italy
saeta de aqua	Sagittaria sagittifolia: Spain
safeea	Setaria glauca: Egypt
sagikat	Ipomoea triloba: Philippines

S

sagit	Vernonia cinerea: Philippines
sago pondweed	Potamogeton pectinatus: Australia, Canada, United States
sahaderi	Vernonia cinerea: India
sahadevibari	Sonchus arvensis: India
sahtere	Fumaria officinalis: Turkey
sailor's tobacco	Artemisia vulgaris: United States
Saint Mary's thistle	Silybum marianum: Australia, England, United States
sakaran	Datura stramonium: Sudan
sakit	Alternanthera sessilis: Philippines
sakomteet	Boerhavia diffusa: Egypt
sakran	Heliotropium europaeum: Lebanon
saladillo	Paspalum distichum: Puerto Rico
salaillo	Paspalum distichum: Puerto Rico
salcerella	Polygonum lapathifolium: Italy
salebyeo	Oryza sativa: Korea
salkim otu	Poa annua: Turkey
salsabuni	Trianthema portulacastrum: India
salsola kali	Salsola kali: France
saltmarsh bulrush	Scirpus maritimus: United States
saltwort	Salsola kali: New Zealand
saluyot	Corchorus olitorius: Philippines
sam	Trianthema portulacastrum: Vietnam
samambaia	Pteridium aquilinum: Brazil
sameeha	Poa annua: Saudi Arabia
samiryuma	Heliotropium europaeum: Lebanon
sampasampalukan	Phyllanthus niruri: Philippines
san pedro	Phyllanthus niruri: Philippines
sanaetade	Polygonum lapathifolium: Japan
sananjalka	Pteridium aquilinum: Finland
sandia de culebra	Passiflora foetida: El Salvador
sandk	Cassia occidentalis: Cambodia
sandri	Vernonia cinerea: India
sangre de toro	Rumex acetosella: Colombia
sangria	Asclepias curassavica: El Salvador
sangrina	Polygonum aviculare: Chile, Mexico
sanguinaria	Alternanthera sessilis: Dominican Republic, Puerto Rico
	Polygonum aviculare: Argentina, Chile, Mexico, Paraguay, Uruguay
sanguinaria mayor	Polygonum aviculare: Spain

sanguinha	Polygonum aviculare: Portugal
sano haag kai	Aeschynomene indica: Thailand
sansamwa	Hibiscus trionum: Zambia
santh	Boerhavia diffusa: India
santhi	Trianthema portulacastrum: India
santi	Boerhavia diffusa: India
santoma cimarrona	Alternanthera sessilis: Dominican Republic
sanve	Brassica kaber: France
sarai hankarok	Hydrilla verticillata: Thailand
saramago	Raphanus raphanistrum: Brazil, Portugal
saramo	Achyranthes aspera: Philippines
sarani	Trianthema portulacastrum: India
saray	Hydrilla verticillata: Indonesia
sarbatana	Synedrella nodiflora: Puerto Rico
sari tuylu dari	Setaria glauca: Turkey
sarijamala	Conyza canadensis: Madagascar
saroto	Acanthospermum hispidum: India
sarrac	Conium maculatum: Chile
saru-sonborial	Sida rhombifolia: India
sasamon	Digitaria longiflora: Philippines
sasawi langit	Vernonia cinerea: Indonesia
sat	Setaria glauca: Burma
sataraq	Fumaria officinalis: Lebanon
Saudistel	Sonchus arvensis: Germany
saulcette	Polygonum lapathifolium: France
sav mao prey	Passiflora foetida: Cambodia
saxifraga	Phyllanthus niruri: Brazil
scarlet fruited passion flower	Passiflora foetida: Hawaii
scavjelistna dresen	Polygonum lapathifolium: Yugoslavia
scented mayweed	Matricaria chamomilla: England
schapezuring	Rumex acetosella: Belgium, Netherlands
schedefonteinkruid	Potamogeton pectinatus: Netherlands
Schmalblattriges Schild	Typha angustifolia: Germany
Schwimmendes Laichkraut	Potamogeton natans: Germany
scirpe des marais	Eleocharis palustris: Belgium
scirpe maritime	Scirpus maritimus: France
scirpe mucronee	Scirpus mucronatus: France
scotch thistle	Cirsium vulgare: Australia, New Zealand, South Africa
scrambling speedwell	Veronica persica: New Zealand
scripe maritime	Scirpus maritimus: Morocco

sea club-rush	Scirpus maritimus: England
sea clubrush	Scirpus maritimus: Japan
sea scirpus	Scirpus mucronatus: Soviet Union
seaside purslane	Trianthema portulacastrum: Ghana
seda seda	Asclepias curassavica: Bolivia
seed underleaf	Phyllanthus niruri: Jamaica, Trinidad
seiyo-tanpopo	Taraxacum officinale: Japan
sekran	Chenopodium murale: Saudi Arabia
selaseh dandi	Stachytarpheta jamaicensis: Malaysia
selepat tungau	Ipomoea triloba: Malaysia
selvatana	Synedrella nodiflora: Dominican Republic
semainyuruvi	Stachytarpheta jamaicensis: India
semi-contra	Chenopodium ambrosioides: Jamaica
semm el-faar	Datura stramonium: Egypt
sempre noiva	Polygonum aviculare: Portugal
sempre noiva dos passarinhos	Polygonum aviculare: Brazil
senape	Brassica kaber: Italy
senape selvatica	Brassica kaber: Italy
senape vera	Brassica kaber: Italy
senavu	Cassia tora: India
sendudok	Melastoma malabathricum: Malaysia
senecio comun	Senecio vulgaris: Argentina
senecon commun	Senecio vulgaris: Belgium, France
senecon vulgaire	Senecio vulgaris: Canada, France
seneve	Brassica kaber: France
senggani	Melastoma malabathricum: Indonesia
senill	Potamogeton pectinatus: Spain
sennari-houzuki	Physalis angulata: Japan
senorita	Asclepias curassavica: El Salvador
sensitive vetch	Aeschynomene indica: Fiji
sentemiento	Stachytarpheta jamaicensis: Philippines
senting	Cassia occidentalis: Indonesia
sepivapeippi	Lamium amplexicaule: Finland
serenti	Alternanthera sessilis: Mauritius
serio grass	Saccharum spontaneum: Australia
serrada mayor	Scirpus maritimus: Spain
serralha	Emilia sonchifolia: Brazil
	Sonchus asper: Brazil
serralha aspera	Sonchus asper: Portugal
serralha espinhosa	Sonchus asper: Portugal

sessile joyweed	Alternanthera sessilis: Hawaii, United States
sessile-flowered globe amaranth	Alternanthera sessilis: Egypt
seta	Sagittaria sagittifolia: Portugal
setaire glauque	Setaria glauca: Canada, France, Switzerland
setaria	Setaria glauca: Italy
seytan elmasi	Datura stramonium: Turkey
seytan keneviri	Hibiscus trionum: Turkey
sha'ar el bint	Potamogeton pectinatus: Egypt
sha'er el hosaan	Potamogeton pectinatus: Egypt
sha-ir-ud-dib	Hordeum murinum: Lebanon
shabat al ghul	Polygonum aviculare: Lebanon, Saudi Arabia
shaka'ik-un-naman	Papaver rhoeas: Lebanon
shaknatey	Amaranthus viridis: Bangladesh
shalhaw	Paspalum distichum: Iraq
shamrock	Oxalis latifolia: Australia
shar el-far	Setaria glauca: Egypt
shar-choa	Potamogeton crispus: China
shar-el-aguz	Urtica urens: Lebanon
sharba	Euphorbia prunifolia: Egypt
shatareh	Fumaria officinalis: Iran
shawkaran	Conium maculatum: Lebanon
sheathed cyperus	Cyperus haspan: Malaysia
shebbet	Hibiscus trionum: Egypt, Saudi Arabia
sheep sorrel	Rumex acetosella: Canada
sheep's sorrel	Rumex acetosella: England, New Zealand
shikuriyyah	Cichorium intybus: Lebanon
shinaan	Salsola kali: Egypt
shirobana-chosen-assgao	Datura stramonium: Japan
shoak sinnaari	Silybum marianum: Egypt
shok el-gamal	Silybum marianum: Egypt
shola takkai	Aeschynomene indica: India
shooreh	Salsola kali: Iran
shore thistle	Carduus pycnocephalus: Australia
short awn foxtail	Alopecurus aequalis: England, United States
short leaved kyllinga	Cyperus brevifolius: Malaysia
short-awned foxtail	Alopecurus aequalis: Canada
shrun-sue-chio-bye	Paspalum distichum: China
shuang-suei-tsue-bai	Paspalum distichum: Taiwan
shui-liao	Polygonum hydropiper: China
shungwa	Cleome gynandra: Zambia

shwaired	Hordeum murinum: Iraq
shyojoso	Euphorbia heterophylla: Japan
sibama yauli	Acanthospermum hispidum: Zimbabwe
sican saci	Setaria glauca: Turkey
sicklepod	Cassia tora: United States
sida	Sida rhombifolia: Argentina, New Zealand
sidagoeri	Sida rhombifolia: Indonesia
sidda	Saccharum spontaneum: Philippines
sidowolo	Tridax procumbens: Indonesia
sifa otu	Conyza canadensis: Turkey
sigli	Corchorus olitorius: Ghana
sigorei	Cichorium intybus: South Africa
siitan	Amaranthus viridis: Thailand
sikori	Cichorium intybus: Norway
sikuri	Cichorium intybus: Finland
silkkiunikko	Papaver rhoeas: Finland
sinaguri	Sida rhombifolia: Philippines
sinapis	Brassica kaber: Argentina
sinertavapantaheina	Setaria glauca: Finland
singa ng-dagat	Ludwigia adscendens: Philippines
Singapore rhododendron	Melastoma malabathricum: Malaysia
sinjo proso	Setaria glauca: Yugoslavia
sinna-kirai	Amaranthus viridis: Sri Lanka
sinutan	Sida rhombifolia: Philippines
siri-kirai-	Amaranthus viridis: Sri Lanka
sitna kopriva	Urtica urens: Yugoslavia
sitronmelde	Chenopodium ambrosioides: Norway
sivi muhar	Setaria glauca: Yugoslavia
skaerm-vortemaelk	Euphorbia helioscopia: Denmark
skarntyde	Conium maculatum: Denmark
skeleton weed	Chondrilla juncea: Australia
skotse dissel	Cirsium vulgare: South Africa
slender amaranth	Amaranthus viridis: Hawaii, United States
slender foxtail	Alopecurus myosuroides: Australia, England, Lebanon, United States
slender pigeon grass	Setaria geniculata: Australia
slender spikerush	Eleocharis acicularis: United States
slender thistle	Carduus pycnocephalus: Australia
slender winged thistle	Carduus pycnocephalus: New Zealand
slender-flowered thistle	Carduus pycnocephalus: Australia
small nettle	Urtica urens: Australia, England, Lebanon

small sorrel	Rumex acetosella: England
small tufted lovegrass	Eragrostis pilosa: United States
small-leaf horseweed	Conyza canadensis: Hawaii
smanesle	Urtica urens: Norway
smasyre	Rumex acetosella: Norway
snotterbelletjie	Cleome gynandra: South Africa
soda	Salsola kali: Portugal
sodaort	Salsola kali: Sweden
sodaurt	Salsola kali: Denmark, Norway
soetulgel	Eleocharis acicularis: Korea
sofeira	Senecio vulgaris: Turkey
soffione	Taraxacum officinale: Italy
soft lovegrass	Eragrostis pilosa: Australia
soft roly-poly	Salsola kali: Australia
sohbyrthit	Achyranthes aspera: India
Sonnen Wolfsmilch	Euphorbia helioscopia: Germany
Sonnenwende	Heliotropium europaeum: Germany
Sonnenwendige Wolfsmilch	Euphorbia helioscopia: Germany
sorosi	Momordica charantia: Costa Rica, Dominican Republic, Guatemala
sorrel	Rumex acetosella: Australia
sotblomster	Matricaria chamomilla: Sweden
sotkamomill	Matricaria chamomilla: Sweden
souchet des marais	Eleocharis palustris: France
soude	Salsola kali: France
soude kali	Salsola kali: Morocco
soude roulante	Salsola kali: Canada
southern reedmace	Typha angustifolia: England
sow weed	Boerhavia diffusa: Trinidad
sowthistle	Sonchus asper: Fiji
spear grass	Eragrostis pilosa: United States
spear thistle	Cirsium vulgare: Australia, England, Hawaii, Tasmania
speedwell	Veronica arvensis: England
speerdistel	Cirsium vulgare: Netherlands
spider flower	Cleome gynandra: Australia, South Africa, Zimbabwe
spiked watermilfoil	Myriophyllum spicatum: England
spikerush	Eleocharis palustris: United States
spikklubba	Datura stramonium: Sweden
spindlepod	Boerhavia erecta: Kenya
spini da ranocchi	Najas marina: Italy

spiny annual sowthistle	Sonchus asper: Canada
spiny naiad	Najas marina: United States
spiny sowthistle	Sonchus asper: United States
Spitzgras	Poa annua: Germany
spotted lady's thumb	Polygonum persicaria: England
spotted persicaria	Polygonum persicaria: Ireland
spotted thistle	Silybum marianum: Australia
spreading hog weed	Boerhavia diffusa: Thailand
spreading hogweed	Boerhavia diffusa: Malaysia
spurge	Euphorbia prunifolia: Australia
sragne	Oryza sativa: Cambodia
srunen	Synedrella nodiflora: Indonesia
Stachel-Teichsimse	Scirpus mucronatus: Germany
staggerwort	Senecio vulgaris: Canada
star burr	Acanthospermum hispidum: Australia, Hawaii
starzec zwyczajny	Senecio vulgaris: Poland
stavelj mali	Rumex acetosella: Yugoslavia
Stechapfel	Datura stramonium: Germany
Stengelumfassende	Cardaria draba: Germany
Stengelumfassende Taubnessel	Lamium amplexicaule: Germany
stink blaar	Datura stramonium: Natal
stinkbaar	Datura stramonium: Rhodesia
stinking passion flower	Passiflora foetida: Australia
stinking Roger	Tagetes minuta: Australia, Rhodesia
stinking weed	Cassia occidentalis: Jamaica, Trinidad
stinking Willie	Senecio vulgaris: Canada
stinkweed	Tagetes minuta: Hawaii
	Thlaspi arvense: Canada
stivdylle	Sonchus asper: Norway
stivt havfrugras	Najas marina: Norway
stor najade	Najas marina: Denmark
storkronet aerenpris	Veronica persica: Denmark
stornesle	Urtica urens: Norway
straatgras	Poa annua: Belgium, Netherlands
straites rhododendron	Melastoma malabathricum: Malaysia
stramoine commune	Datura stramonium: Canada
stramonio	Datura stramonium: Italy
stramonium	Datura stramonium: Rhodesia
strand-kogleaks	Scirpus maritimus: Denmark
strangle vine	Cuscuta campestris: United States

succiamiele della carota	Orobanche minor: Italy
succiamiele ramoso	Orobanche ramosa: Italy
succory	Cichorium intybus: Iraq, Lebanon, Poland, United States
Sudlicher Rohrkolben	Typha angustifolia: Germany
suea-saan-kha	Vernonia cinerea: Thailand
sugam pilla	Digitaria longiflora: Sri Lanka
sui-mien	Marsilea quadrifolia: China
suico	Tagetes minuta: Paraguay
suique	Tagetes minuta: Argentina
suket ganjahan	Artemisia vulgaris: Indonesia
Sumpf-simse	Eleocharis palustris: Germany
sumpsevaks	Eleocharis palustris: Norway
sumting	Cassia occidentalis: Philippines
sun euphorbia	Euphorbia helioscopia: South Africa
sun spurge	Euphorbia helioscopia: Australia, Canada, England, Lebanon, United States
suncanac	Heliotropium europaeum: Yugoslavia
suntha	Cleome gynandra: Zambia
suoluikka	Eleocharis palustris: Finland
surajvarta	Cleome gynandra: India
surib	Phyllanthus niruri: Sudan
sush uni	Marsilea quadrifolia: India
sushavi	Momordica charantia: India
susni-sak	Marsilea quadrifolia: Bangladesh
suzumeno-katabira	Poa annua: Japan
suzumeno-teppo	Alopecurus aequalis: Japan
svinamarant	Amaranthus retroflexus: Sweden
svintistel	Sonchus asper: Sweden
svommende vandaks	Potamogeton natans: Denmark
swamp morningglory	Ipomoea aquatica: United States
swarnalata	Cuscuta campestris: India
swet	Trianthema portulacastrum: India
swine watercress	Coronopus didymus: Hawaii
swinecress	Coronopus didymus: Hawaii, United States
synedrella	Synedrella nodiflora: Hawaii, United States
szczaw poiny	Rumex acetosella: Poland
ta-suei-khan-mai-tsao	Alopecurus myosuroides: Taiwan
taboa	Typha angustifolia: Brazil
	Typha latifolia: Brazil
tabouret des champs	Thlaspi arvense: Belgium, France

T

tabouret perfolie	Thlaspi arvense: Canada
tabtabokol	Boerhavia diffusa: Philippines
tabtabukol	Trianthema portulacastrum: Philippines
tabua larga	Typha latifolia: Portugal
tabua-estreita	Typha angustifolia: Portugal
tachi-inunofuguri	Veronica arvensis: Japan
taching-baka	Sida rhombifolia: Philippines
tagabang	Corchorus olitorius: Philippines
tagalog	Aeschynomene indica: Philippines
tagtago	Alternanthera sessilis: Philippines
tagua tagua	Passiflora foetida: Puerto Rico
taguilinau	Emilia sonchifolia: Philippines
tagulinau	Vernonia cinerea: Philippines
taimboritsiloz	Chenopodium ambrosioides: Madagascar
taindalitra	Setaria glauca: Madagascar
taindambo	Setaria glauca: Madagascar
taiwan tsunaso	Corchorus olitorius: Japan
taiwan-hachijona	Sonchus arvensis: Japan
taj khoroos	Amaranthus retroflexus: Iran
takala	Cassia tora: India
taklang-duron	Ludwigia hyssopifolia: Philippines
talahib	Saccharum spontaneum: Philippines
talangkau	Ludwigia octovalvis: Philippines
talikod	Phyllanthus niruri: Philippines
tall fleabane	Conyza canadensis: South Africa
tall khaki weed	Tagetes minuta: South Africa
tamalaika	Cleome gynandra: Sudan
tamaleekah	Cleome gynandra: Egypt
tambak-tambak merait	Emilia sonchifolia: Malaysia
tambalisa	Cassia occidentalis: Philippines
tamlang	Trianthema portulacastrum: Vietnam
tanduliya	Amaranthus viridis: India
tanenanashi	Spirodela polyrhiza: Japan
tangara	Boerhavia diffusa: Brazil
Tannli	Orobanche minor: Germany
tantandok	Cleome gynandra: Philippines
tantipu	Cassia tora: India
tape grass	Vallisneria spiralis: Canada
tape weed	Vallisneria spiralis: United States
taperiba	Cassia occidentalis: Argentina

taperva	Cassia occidentalis: Paraguay
	Cassia tora: Paraguay
taperva moroti	Cassia tora: Paraguay
taperva sayju	Cassia tora: Paraguay
tapete	Datura stramonium: Colombia
taporita	Sida rhombifolia: Bolivia
taqiyit el-ghoraab	Lamium amplexicaule: Egypt
tar sentaran	Tridax procumbens: Indonesia
tar vine	Boerhavia diffusa: Kenya
tar-vine	Boerhavia diffusa: Australia
taramao	Raphanus raphanistrum: Mexico
tararues	Cassia occidentalis: Brazil
tarassaco	Taraxacum officinale: Italy
taraxaco	Taraxacum officinale: Brazil
taraxacon	Taraxacum officinale: Spain
tartor thistle	Salsola kali: United States
taru-taru	Oxalis latifolia: Bolivia
tarweed	Boerhavia diffusa: Zimbabwe
tasneirinha	Senecio vulgaris: Portugal
tatoora	Datura stramonium: Saudi Arabia
tatoorah	Datura stramonium: Iran
tatoore	Datura stramonium: Iran
tatoura	Datura stramonium: Egypt
tatula	Datura stramonium: Yugoslavia
tayilaktan	Ludwigia octovalvis: Philippines
te espanol	Chenopodium ambrosioides: Spain
teel sheitaani	Hibiscus trionum: Egypt
teel-sheitani	Hibiscus trionum: Saudi Arabia
teen tuk kae	Tridax procumbens: Thailand
Teichlinse	Spirodela polyrhiza: Germany
telaspio	Thlaspi arvense: Spain
telekan	Trianthema portulacastrum: Indonesia
telorirana	Hibiscus trionum: Madagascar
tembang	Eleocharis dulcis: Indonesia
tempuyung	Sonchus arvensis: Indonesia
terblansbossie	Hibiscus trionum: South Africa
tete	Amaranthus viridis: Nigeria
Texas cockspur	Acanthospermum hispidum: United States
thagarai	Cassia occidentalis: India
thail el-faras	Conyza canadensis: Iraq

thanet cress	Cardaria draba: England
thannoum	Chenopodium murale: Saudi Arabia
thei phelwangi	Drymaria cordata: India
thikri	Boerhavia diffusa: India
thorn apple	Datura stramonium: Australia, England, Fiji, Jamaica, Lebanon, Rhodesia, Zambia
thoup susi	Typha angustifolia: Thailand
three-lobe morningglory	Ipomoea triloba: United States
thuy huong	Typha angustifolia: Vietnam
thuy kieu hoa ban	Najas graminea: Vietnam
thuy thao	Hydrilla verticillata: Vietnam
tian na	Ludwigia hyssopifolia: Thailand
tiga jiluga	Aeschynomene indica: India
tigbau	Saccharum spontaneum: Philippines
tilbagebjet anarant	Amaranthus retroflexus: Denmark
tilki kuyrugu	Alopecurus myosuroides: Turkey
timiansnikjetrad	Cuscuta epithymum: Norway
timun dendang	Passiflora foetida: Malaysia
tingir bangau	Ludwigia adscendens: Malaysia
tingkil	Ipomoea triloba: Indonesia
tino-tino	Physalis angulata: Philippines
tipatia weed	Oxalis latifolia: India
tipicha guazu	Sida rhombifolia: Argentina
tiririca roxa	Cyperus haspan: Brazil
titapat	Corchorus olitorius: India
tithymale	Euphorbia helioscopia: France
titimalo dos vales	Euphorbia helioscopia: Portugal
tjalintjing gede	Oxalis latifolia: Indonesia
tjebungan	Drymaria cordata: Indonesia
tjeploekan	Nicandra physalodes: Indonesia
tjeplukan	Physalis angulata: Indonesia
tobchangeih	Cleome gynandra: Egypt
tobioe	Saccharum spontaneum: Indonesia
toccoro	Nicandra physalodes: Peru
todaigusa	Euphorbia helioscopia: Japan
tojo	Ulex europaeus: Argentina, Brazil, Spain
tojo-arnal	Ulex europaeus: Portugal
toloache	Datura stramonium: Mexico
toltolaya	Physalis angulata: Philippines
tomatillo	Physalis angulata: Honduras, Mexico
tomillo de agua	Elodea canadensis: Puerto Rico

tope-tope	Physalis angulata: Dominican Republic
topotopo	Physalis angulata: Venezuela
torito	Acanthospermum hispidum: Argentina, Bolivia
tornassol	Heliotropium europaeum: Portugal
tornblad	Ulex europaeus: Denmark
toro rati	Acanthospermum hispidum: Paraguay
tossa jute	Corchorus olitorius: England, India
toston	Boerhavia diffusa: Dominican Republic, Puerto Rico, Venezuela
	Boerhavia erecta: Cuba, Dominican Republic, Venezuela
	Trianthema portulacastrum: Philippines, Venezuela
totora	Typha angustifolia: Argentina, Chile, Uruguay
	Typha latifolia: Argentina, Chile
tradgardsveronika	Veronica persica: Sweden
trainasse	Polygonum aviculare: Belgium, France, Switzerland
trakoun kantek	Ipomoea aquatica: Cambodia
trakuon	Ipomoea aquatica: Indonesia
tramport	Polygonum aviculare: Sweden
tranpgras	Polygonum aviculare: Sweden
trebol	Oxalis latifolia: Mexico
trebol de huerta	Oxalis latifolia: Spain
trebol de jardin	Oxalis latifolia: Colombia
trebol falso	Oxalis latifolia: Colombia
trefle	Oxalis latifolia: Mauritius
trevo	Oxalis latifolia: Brazil
trevo de quatro folhas	Marsilea quadrifolia: Portugal
tri baldiran	Conium maculatum: Turkey
triangulo	Scirpus maritimus: Portugal
tridax	Cassia tora: Philippines
	Tridax procumbens: Hawaii, Puerto Rico
tridax daisy	Tridax procumbens: Australia, United States
trimona	Datura stramonium: Jamaica
tripa de sapa	Alternanthera philoxeroides: Brazil
tro skot	Polygonum aviculare: Yugoslavia
tropical chickweed	Drymaria cordata: Australia
tsanaso	Corchorus olitorius: Taiwan
tsihitafotora	Corchorus olitorius: Madagascar
tsihitafototra	Cuscuta campestris: Madagascar
tsindahoro	Sida rhombifolia: Madagascar
tsiontsiona	Emilia sonchifolia: Madagascar

tsipopoka	Passiflora foetida: Madagascar
tsuma	Cleome gynandra: Zimbabwe
tsuru-nogeito	Alternanthera sessilis: Japan
tuhod-manok	Synedrella nodiflora: Philippines
tuintjeagras	Poa annua: Belgium
tule	Typha latifolia: Mexico
tungao-tungao	Melastoma malabathricum: Philippines
tungras	Polygonum aviculare: Norway
tunki	Tridax procumbens: India
tunrapp	Poa annua: Norway
turnah	Polygonum aviculare: Saudi Arabia
turnepo-amarelo	Brassica campestris: Portugal
turnsole	Heliotropium europaeum: Lebanon
turota	Cassia tora: India
turujero	Euphorbia heterophylla: Bolivia
tutahuira	Veronica persica: Peru
tutuvaco	Typha angustifolia: Chile
twin cress	Coronopus didymus: Australia, New Zealand
tyabo-mehisiba	Digitaria longiflora: Taiwan
typxa guasu	Sida rhombifolia: Paraguay
tznon matzui	Raphanus raphanistrum: Israel
ualisualison	Sida rhombifolia: Philippines
udahalu	Passiflora foetida: Sri Lanka
ugrasheliotrop	Heliotropium europaeum: Norway
ukikusa	Spirodela polyrhiza: Japan
ukontatar	Polygonum lapathifolium: Finland
uler-uleran	Setaria glauca: Indonesia
ulisiman	Trianthema portulacastrum: Philippines
ulude	Cleome gynandra: Zimbabwe
undakanta	Achyranthes aspera: India
updoli	Rumex acetosella: India
upright starbur	Acanthospermum hispidum: South Africa, Zambia, Zimbabwe
urang aring	Ludwigia octovalvis: Indonesia
urtiga	Urtica urens: Brazil
urtiga menor	Urtica urens: Portugal
usubeni-nigana	Emilia sonchifolia: Japan
uzlati dvornik	Polygonum lapathifolium: Yugoslavia
vadrepce	Brassica kaber: Hungary
vagri	Cleome gynandra: India
vagtistel	Cirsium vulgare: Sweden

U

V

vagvarda	Cichorium intybus: Sweden
valatendro	Potamogeton natans: Madagascar
vallisneria	Vallisneria spiralis: Netherlands
vallisnerie en spirale	Vallisneria spiralis: France
valsk krasse	Cardaria draba: Sweden
vaminta	Cleome gynandra: India
vandpest	Elodea canadensis: Denmark
vanleg honsegras	Polygonum persicaria: Norway
vanleg tjonnaks	Potamogeton natans: Norway
vanlig korsort	Senecio vulgaris: Sweden
vanlig pilort	Polygonum lapathifolium: Sweden
	Polygonum persicaria: Sweden
variegated thistle	Silybum marianum: Australia, New Zealand, Tasmania
various-leaved euphorbia	Euphorbia heterophylla: Hawaii
varkensgras	Polygonum aviculare: Belgium, Netherlands
varpasveifgras	Poa annua: Iceland
vary	Oryza sativa: Madagascar
vassourinha	Sida rhombifolia: Brazil
	Synedrella nodiflora: Brazil
vasspepar	Polygonum hydropiper: Norway
vasspest	Elodea canadensis: Norway
vato	Typha angustifolia: Chile
vatofotsy	Achyranthes aspera: Madagascar
vattenpest	Elodea canadensis: Sweden
veelwortelig kroos	Spirodela polyrhiza: Belgium
vegtistel	Cirsium vulgare: Norway
vej-pileurt	Polygonum aviculare: Denmark
vejigon	Physalis angulata: Colombia
veldereprijs	Veronica arvensis: Netherlands
veldwarkruid	Cuscuta campestris: Netherlands
veldzuring	Rumex acetosella: Belgium
vellai	Ipomoea aquatica: India
vellugtende kamille	Matricaria chamomilla: Denmark
velvet finger grass	Digitaria velutina: Kenya
venadillo	Conyza canadensis: Colombia
venice mallow	Hibiscus trionum: United States
venturosa	Synedrella nodiflora: Colombia
verbena	Setaria geniculata: Malaysia
	Stachytarpheta jamaicensis: Puerto Rico
verbena azul	Stachytarpheta jamaicensis: Colombia

verbena cimarona	Stachytarpheta jamaicensis: Cuba
verbena de las Antilles	Stachytarpheta jamaicensis: Philippines
verbena morada	Stachytarpheta jamaicensis: Dominican Republic
verdolaga	Polygonum aviculare: Mexico
	Trianthema portulacastrum: Peru
verdolaga blanca	Trianthema portulacastrum: Colombia
verdolaga de cochi	Trianthema portulacastrum: Mexico
verdolaga de hoja ancha	Trianthema portulacastrum: El Salvador, Guatemala, Mexico, Nicaragua, Puerto Rico
verdolaga rastrera	Trianthema portulacastrum: Argentina
verdolagilla	Trianthema portulacastrum: Dominican Republic
verdolegon	Trianthema portulacastrum: Venezuela
vergerette du Canada	Conyza canadensis: Canada, France
vernonia	Vernonia cinerea: Australia, Puerto Rico
veronica	Veronica arvensis: Argentina, Chile
	Veronica persica: Chile, Ecuador
veronica arvense	Veronica arvensis: Spain
veronica querciola	Veronica persica: Italy
veronique de Perse	Veronica persica: Belgium, Canada
veronique de perse	Veronica persica: France
veronique des champs	Veronica arvensis: Canada, France
verrucaria	Heliotropium europaeum: Spain
verruguera	Heliotropium europaeum: Spain
vertakte besmraap	Orobanche ramosa: South Africa
vervain	Stachytarpheta jamaicensis: Barbados, Jamaica, Trinidad
vesirutto	Elodea canadensis: Finland
viborano	Asclepias curassavica: Honduras
Vierblattriger Kleefarn	Marsilea quadrifolia: Germany
viernes santo	Phyllanthus niruri: Colombia
vihrea revonhanta	Amaranthus retroflexus: Finland
viisisateinen	Euphorbia helioscopia: Finland
vild gulerod	Daucus carota: Dahomey
vildkorn; bolmort	Hordeum murinum: Sweden
vill gulrot	Daucus carota: Norway
villbygg	Hordeum murinum: Norway
viltige duizend knoop	Polygonum lapathifolium: Belgium
vinagrerita	Rumex acetosella: Spain
vinagrillo	Orobanche minor: Turkey
	Oxalis latifolia: Cuba, Venezuela
	Rumex acetosella: Argentina, Chile

vingerblaatee	Cleome gynandra: South Africa
vinorama	Asclepias curassavica: Honduras
viola	Marsilea quadrifolia: Spain
violettilla	Veronica persica: Colombia
vishakapara	Trianthema portulacastrum: India
vitige duizendknoop	Polygonum lapathifolium: Netherlands
vitroe	Poa annua: Sweden
vlasnjaca	Poa annua: Yugoslavia
voamahatsara	Cassia tora: Madagascar
voeduisendknoop	Polygonum aviculare: South Africa
Vogelknoterich	Polygonum aviculare: Germany
vogelknoterich	Polygonum aviculare: Switzerland
volantin	Cleome gynandra: Cuba
volantines de cinco hojas	Cleome gynandra: Puerto Rico
volondrana	Ludwigia adscendens: Madagascar
volondrano	Ludwigia octovalvis: Madagascar
votasef	Eleocharis palustris: Iceland
vulpin a courtes aretes	Alopecurus aequalis: Canada
vulpin des champs	Alopecurus myosuroides: Belgium, France, Switzerland
vulpin fauve	Alopecurus aequalis: France

W

walini	Scirpus mucronatus: Indonesia
wall barley	Hordeum murinum: England, United States
wall goosefoot	Chenopodium murale: Iraq
wall speedwell	Veronica arvensis: England, Lebanon
warabi	Pteridium aquilinum: Japan
wart cress	Coronopus didymus: United States
wase-abana	Saccharum spontaneum: Japan
Wasserpest	Elodea canadensis: Germany
Wasserpfeffer	Polygonum hydropiper: Germany
Wasserpfeffer-Knoterich	Polygonum hydropiper: Germany, Switzerland
water chestnut	Eleocharis dulcis: Hawaii
water couch	Paspalum distichum: Australia, England, Sri Lanka
water lentil	Lemna minor: United States
water nymph	Najas marina: United States
water pepper	Polygonum hydropiper: Australia, New Zealand, Pakistan
water primrose	Ludwigia adscendens: Australia
	Ludwigia octovalvis: United States
water thyme	Hydrilla verticillata: Australia

water velvet	Azolla pinnata: United States
water weed	Hydrilla verticillata: Fiji
water willow	Ludwigia octovalvis: Philippines
water-pepper	Polygonum hydropiper: England
waterbies	Eleocharis palustris: Belgium
waterduisendblarr	Myriophyllum spicatum: South Africa
waternut	Eleocharis dulcis: United States
waterpepper	Polygonum hydropiper: Belgium, Netherlands
waterpest	Elodea canadensis: Belgium
watra adroe	Paspalum distichum: Surinam
welriekende ganzevoet	Chenopodium ambrosioides: Netherlands
West Indian chickweed	Drymaria cordata: United States
whin	Ulex europaeus: Australia
white charlock	Raphanus raphanistrum: Kenya, Lebanon
white-dirty cream	Tridax procumbens: Ghana
whitetop	Cardaria draba: Canada, Lebanon, United States
whiteweed	Cardaria draba: Canada, Lebanon, Tasmania
Wider Mohn	Papaver rhoeas: Germany
wiechlina roczna	Poa annua: Poland
Wiesen Wucherblume	Chrysanthemum leucanthemum: Germany
wild barley	Hordeum murinum: England, Hawaii, Lebanon
wild cape gooseberry	Physalis angulata: Fiji
wild carrot	Conium maculatum: Australia
	Daucus carota: Canada, England, New Zealand, United States
wild chamomile	Matricaria chamomilla: Canada, England, United States
wild chamomille	Matricaria chamomilla: New Zealand
wild cherry	Physalis angulata: Jamaica
wild coffee	Cassia occidentalis: Trinidad
wild daisy	Tridax procumbens: Fiji
wild gooseberry	Nicandra physalodes: Zambia
	Physalis angulata: Ghana, South Africa, Zambia, Zimbabwe
wild gulerod	Daucus carota: Denmark
wild ipecacuanha	Asclepias curassavica: Jamaica
wild jute	Corchorus olitorius: Zambia
wild marigold	Tagetes minuta: Hawaii, United States
wild mustard	Brassica kaber: Australia, Canada, England, Lebanon, United States

wild parsnip	Conium maculatum: Australia
wild passion fruit	Passiflora foetida: Fiji
wild physalis	Physalis angulata: South Africa
wild poinsettia	Euphorbia heterophylla: Fiji, United States
wild radish	Raphanus raphanistrum: Australia, Canada, England, Lebanon, New Zealand, South Africa, United States
wild rice	Oryza sativa: Australia, Zimbabwe
wild senna	Cassia occidentalis: Jamaica
wild spider flower	Cleome gynandra: Hawaii
wild spurge	Euphorbia prunifolia: Hawaii
wild succory	Cichorium intybus: Canada
wild tomato	Physalis angulata: Jamaica
wild turnip	Brassica campestris: Australia, Canada, England, Hawaii, New Zealand, United States
	Raphanus raphanistrum: Canada
wild water lemon	Passiflora foetida: Malaysia
wilde appelliefie	Physalis angulata: South Africa
wilde cichorei	Cichorium intybus: Netherlands
Wilde Mohre	Daucus carota: Germany
wilde peen	Daucus carota: Belgium, Netherlands
wilde sopropo	Momordica charantia: Surinam
wilde wortel	Daucus carota: Belgium
wildemostert	Raphanus raphanistrum: South Africa
Wilder Ackersenf	Brassica kaber: Germany
Wilder Rettich	Raphanus raphanistrum: Germany
willow primrose	Ludwigia octovalvis: Australia
willow weed	Polygonum hydropiper: New Zealand
	Polygonum lapathifolium: England
	Polygonum persicaria: England, New Zealand
wind witch	Salsola kali: Soviet Union
winter grass	Poa annua: Australia, Tasmania
wiregrass	Eleocharis palustris: United States
wireweed	Polygonum aviculare: Australia, England, New Zealand
witte krodde	Thlaspi arvense: Belgium, Netherlands
wlosnica sina	Setaria glauca: Poland
Wohlriechender Gansefuss	Chenopodium ambrosioides: Germany
wormseed	Chenopodium ambrosioides: Jamaica, Rhodesia, Zambia
wormseed goosefoot	Chenopodium ambrosioides: South Africa
wortel	Daucus carota: Indonesia

X,Y

wu-yu	Eleocharis dulcis: China
wyczyniec polny	Alopecurus myosuroides: Poland
xian pu	Typha latifolia: China
ya'did	Chondrilla juncea: Lebanon
ya-chongkatiam	Eleocharis dulcis: Thailand
ya-la-ong	Vernonia cinerea: Thailand
yaa haangmaa noi	Setaria glauca: Thailand
yaa khat	Sida rhombifolia: Thailand
yabani	Hordeum murinum: Turkey
yabani hardal	Brassica kaber: Turkey
yabani hindiba	Cichorium intybus: Turkey
yagod-no-kang kang	Emilia sonchifolia: Philippines
yagomyum	Melastoma malabathricum: Philippines
yaguil	Ulex europaeus: Chile
yambaru-higotai	Vernonia cinerea: Japan
yanagitabe	Polygonum hydropiper: Japan
yankeeweed	Elodea canadensis: New Zealand
yellow bristle grass	Setaria glauca: England, Fiji, Hawaii, New Zealand
yellow foxtail	Setaria glauca: Canada, Hawaii, Lebanon, United States
yellow willow herb	Ludwigia octovalvis: Fiji
yerba de clavo acuatica	Ludwigia adscendens: Puerto Rico
yerba de enea	Typha angustifolia: Puerto Rico
yerba de estrella	Drymaria cordata: Puerto Rico
yerba de la calentura	Asclepias curassavica: Cuba
yerba de la vibora	Asclepias curassavica: Argentina
yerba de nicotea	Ludwigia octovalvis: Dominican Republic
yerba de puerco	Boerhavia diffusa: Dominican Republic, Puerto Rico
	Boerhavia erecta: Dominican Republic
yerba de Santa Maria	Artemisia vulgaris: Philippines
	Chenopodium ambrosioides: Uruguay
yerba de sosa	Orobanche ramosa: Cuba
yerba del campo	Sonchus arvensis: Argentina
yerba del ciervo	Coronopus didymus: Argentina
yerba del susto	Chenopodium murale: Bolivia
yerba lechera	Euphorbia heterophylla: Dominican Republic
yerba morada	Vernonia cinerea: Dominican Republic
yerba socialista	Emilia sonchifolia: Puerto Rico
	Vernonia cinerea: Puerto Rico
yerkugoligery	Trianthema portulacastrum: India
yomogi	Artemisia vulgaris: Japan

yosai	Ipomoea aquatica: Japan, Taiwan
yuquillo	Asclepias curassavica: Venezuela
yuyito	Senecio vulgaris: Colombia
yuyo	Amaranthus retroflexus: Peru
	Brassica campestris: Chile, Colombia
yuyo colorado	Amaranthus retroflexus: Argentina
yuyo de san vicente	Artemisia vulgaris: Argentina
yuyo esqueleto	Chondrilla juncea: Argentina
yuyo negro	Chenopodium murale: Argentina, Uruguay
yuyo paloma	Fumaria officinalis: Argentina
zacate azul	Poa annua: Mexico
zacate poa	Poa annua: Mexico
zaghil	Urtica urens: Lebanon
zaghleel	Papaver rhoeas: Egypt
zamarraga	Conyza canadensis: Spain
zanahoria	Daucus carota: Puerto Rico
zanahoria silvestre	Daucus carota: Chile, Dominican Republic, Peru, Spain, Venezuela
zangabil et kilab	Polygonum hydropiper: Saudi Arabia
Zapfen	Orobanche minor: Germany
zara	Momordica charantia: Senegal
ze qi	Euphorbia helioscopia: China
zeebies	Scirpus maritimus: Netherlands
zeegroene naaldaar	Setaria glauca: Netherlands
zenetrga	Cichorium intybus: Yugoslavia
Zichorie	Cichorium intybus: Germany
ziphan khalhal	Setaria glauca: Israel
Zuruckgekrummter	Amaranthus retroflexus: Germany
zutenica	Chondrilla juncea: Yugoslavia
Zweiknotiger Krahenfuss	Coronopus didymus: Germany

Index